A-Z STAFFORDSHIRE

CONTENTS

REFERENCE

Motorway	**M6**	Car Park (Selected)	P
Primary Route	**A34**	Church or Chapel	†
Under Construction		Cycleway (Selected)	
A Road	A5013	Fire Station	■
Proposed		Hospital	H
B Road	B5066	House Numbers (A & B Roads only)	13 8
Dual Carriageway		Information Centre	i
One-way Street		Junction Name (M6 Toll only)	BURNTWOOD JUNCTION
Traffic flow on A Roads is indicated by a heavy line on the driver's left. Large Scale Pages only		National Grid Reference	498
Restricted Access		Park & Ride	Science Park P+R
Pedestrianized Road		Police Station	▲
Track / Footpath		Post Office	★
Residential Walkway		Toilet:	
		without facilities for the Disabled	▽
		with facilities for the Disabled	▽
Railway	Station Heritage Station Level Crossing Tunnel	Viewpoint	☀
Local Authority Boundary		Educational Establishment	
National Park Boundary		Hospital or Hospice	
Posttown Boundary		Industrial Building	
Postcode Boundary (within Posttown)		Leisure or Recreational Facility	
Built-up Area	SASH ST	Place of Interest	
		Public Building	
		Shopping Centre or Market	
Map Continuation	32 Large Scale Centres 152 Road Map Pages 160	Other Selected Buildings	

SCALE

Map Pages 6-149	Map Pages 150-153
1:16,896 3¾ inches (9.52 cm) to 1 mile 5.9cm to 1km	1:8,448 7½ inches (19.05 cm) to 1 mile 11.8cm to 1km
0 ¼ ½ Mile	0 ⅛ ¼ Mile
0 250 500 Metres	0 100 200 300 400 Metres

Copyright of Geographers' A-Z Map Company Ltd.

Fairfield Road, Borough Green, Sevenoaks, Kent TN15 8PP
Telephone: 01732 781000 (Enquiries & Trade Sales)
01732 783422 (Retail Sales)
www.a-zmaps.co.uk

Ordnance Survey This product includes mapping data licensed from Ordnance Survey® with the permission of the Controller of Her Majesty's Stationery Office.

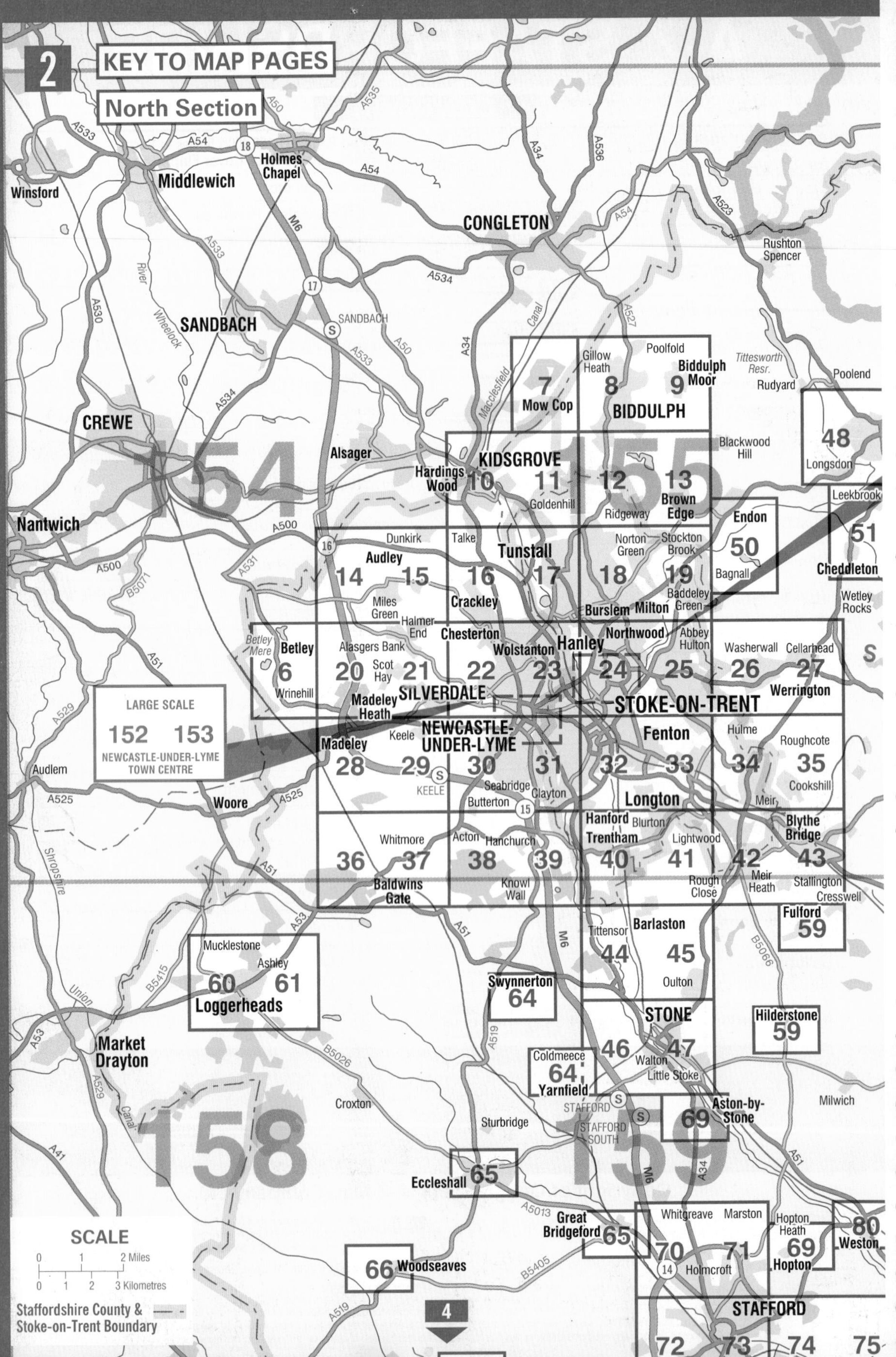

Winsford

Middlewich

Holmes Chapel

CONGLETON

Rushton Spencer

SANDBACH

Tittesworth Resr.

Rudyard

Poolend

Poolfold

Gillow Heath

Biddulph Moor

CREWE

Alsager

7 Mow Cop

8

9

BIDDULPH

Blackwood Hill

Longsdon

48

Nantwich

Hardings Wood

KIDSGROVE

10

11

Goldenhill

12 Ridgeway

13 Brown Edge

Endon

50 Bagnall

Leekbrook

Cheddleton

51

Dunkirk

Talke

Tunstall

Norton Green

Stockton Brook

Wetley Rocks

Audley

14

15

16

17

18

19 Baddeley Green

Miles Green

Crackley

Burslem

Milton

Halmer End

Chesterton

Wolstanton

Hanley

Northwood

Abbey Hulton

Washerwall

Cellarhead

Betley Mere

Betley

6 Wrinehill

Alsagers Bank

Scot Hay

20

21

22

23

24

25

26

27 Werrington

SILVERDALE

Madeley Heath

STOKE-ON-TRENT

LARGE SCALE

152   153

NEWCASTLE-UNDER-LYME TOWN CENTRE

Madeley

Keele

NEWCASTLE-UNDER-LYME

Fenton

Hulme

Roughcote

28

29 KEELE

30

31

32

33

34

35 Cookshill

Woore

Seabridge

Butterton

Clayton

15

Longton

Meir

Blythe Bridge

Hanford

Blurton

Lightwood

Meir Heath

43

Whitmore

Acton

Hanchurch

Trentham

40

41

42

Stallington

Cresswell

Audlem

36

37

38

39

Baldwins Gate

Knowl Wall

Rough Close

Fulford

59

Mucklestone

Ashley

Tittensor

Barlaston

60

61

Loggerheads

Market Drayton

44

45 Oulton

Hilderstone

59

Milwich

Swynnerton

64

STONE

Croxton

Coldmeece

64 Yarnfield

46

Walton

Little Stoke

47

Aston-by-Stone

69

158

Sturbridge

STAFFORD

STAFFORD SOUTH

Eccleshall

65

159

Great Bridgeford

65

Whitgreave

Marston

Hopton Heath

69

Hopton

80 Weston

66 Woodseaves

Holmcroft

70

71

STAFFORD

72

73

74

75

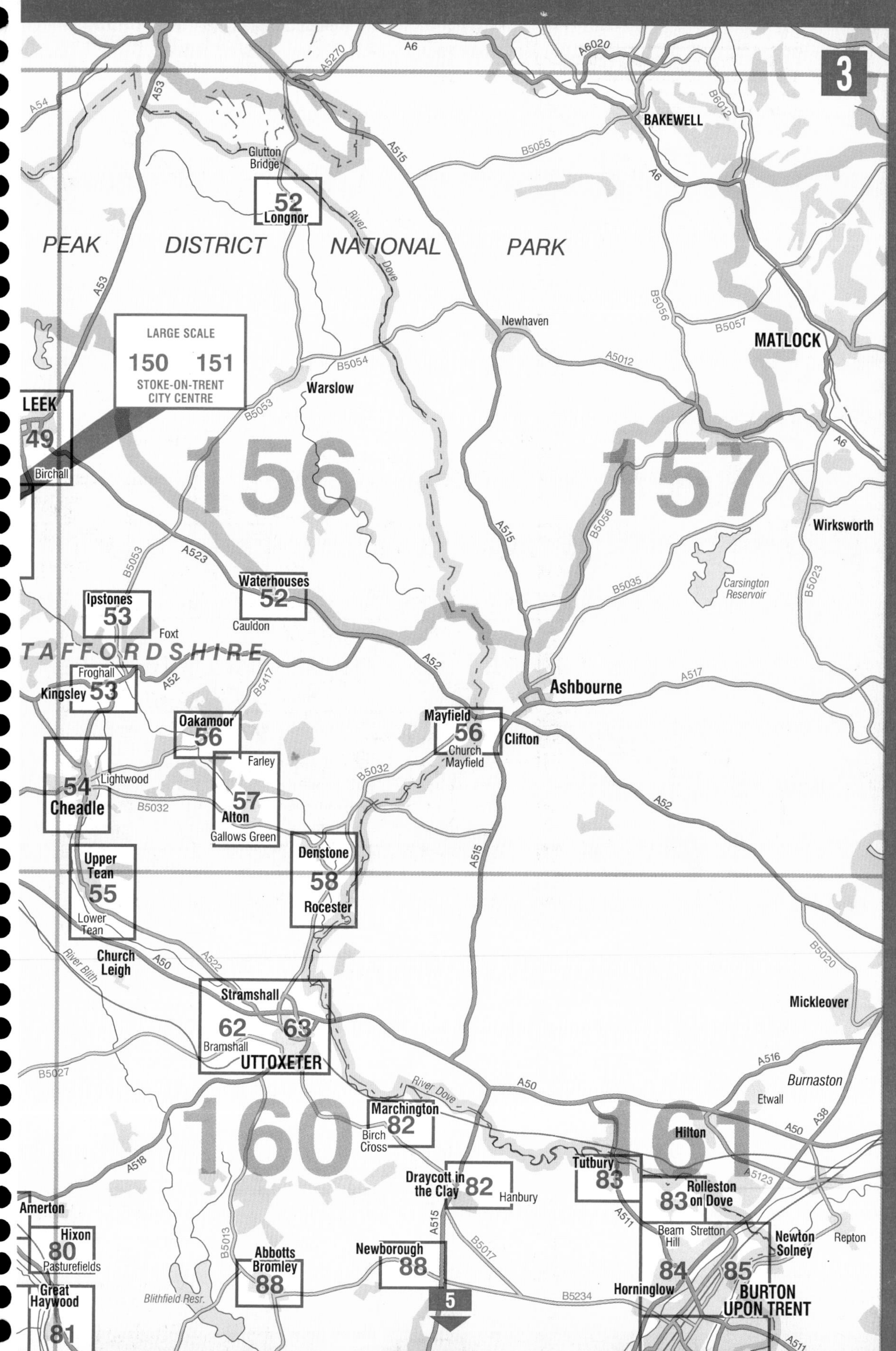

3

BAKEWELL

MATLOCK

PEAK DISTRICT NATIONAL PARK

Glutton Bridge

52 Longnor

Newhaven

Wirksworth

LARGE SCALE
150 151
STOKE-ON-TRENT
CITY CENTRE

Warslow

156

157

LEEK

49

Birchall

Carsington Reservoir

Ipstones
53

Foxt

Waterhouses
52

Cauldon

TAFFORDSHIRE

Froghall

Kingsley 53

Oakamoor
56

Farley

Mayfield
56

Clifton

Ashbourne

Church Mayfield

54
Cheadle

Lightwood

B5032

57
Alton

Gallows Green

Denstone

58
Rocester

Upper Tean
55

Lower Tean

Church Leigh

Stramshall

62   63

Bramshall

UTTOXETER

Mickleover

Burnaston

Etwall

160

161

Marchington
82

Birch Cross

Hilton

Draycott in the Clay 82

Hanbury

Tutbury
83

83 Rolleston on Dove

Amerton

Hixon
80

Pasturefields

Abbotts Bromley
88

Newborough
88

Beam Hill

Stretton

Newton Solney

Repton

84   85

Horninglow

BURTON UPON TRENT

Great Haywood
81

Blithfield Resr.

5

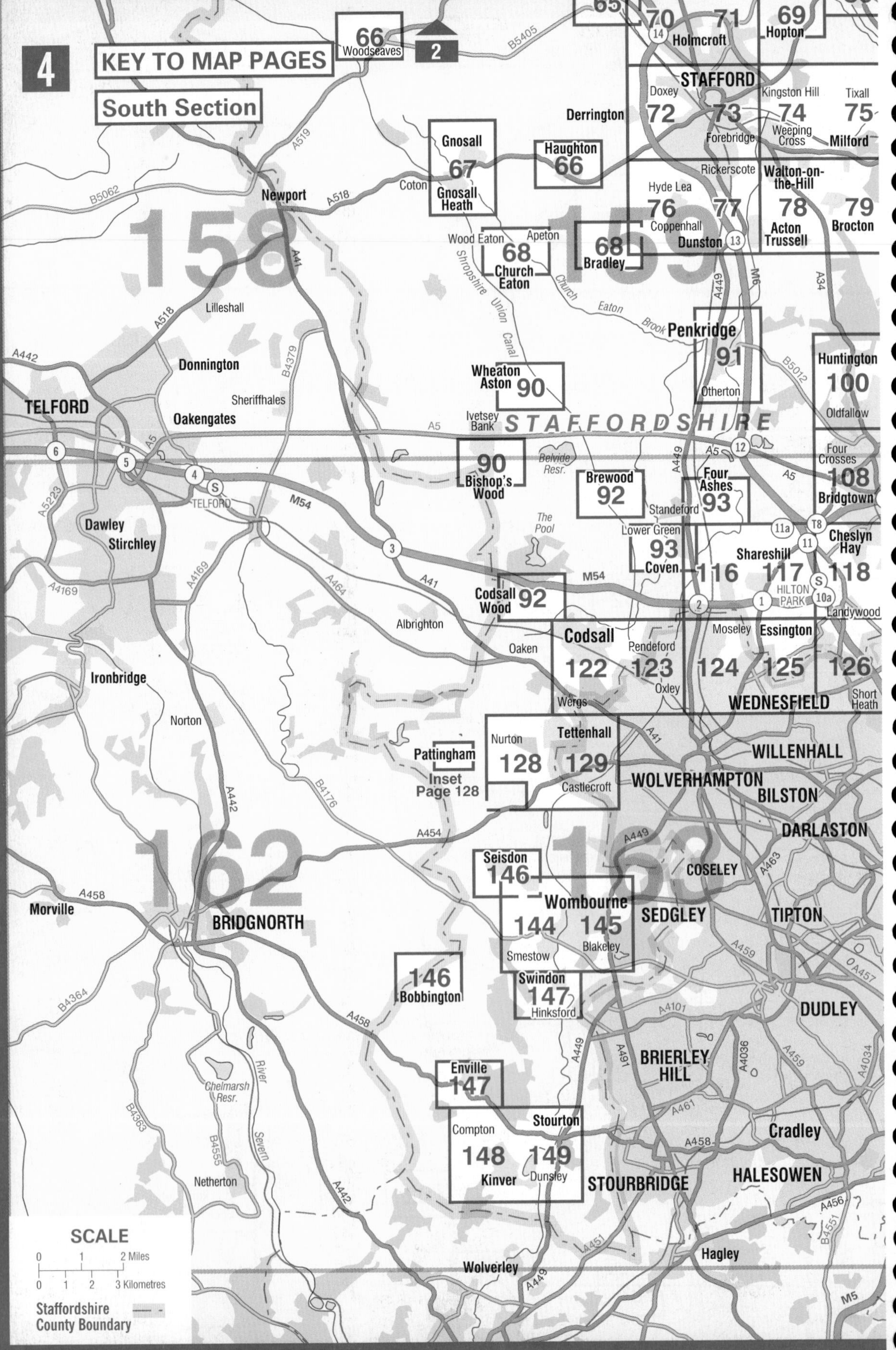

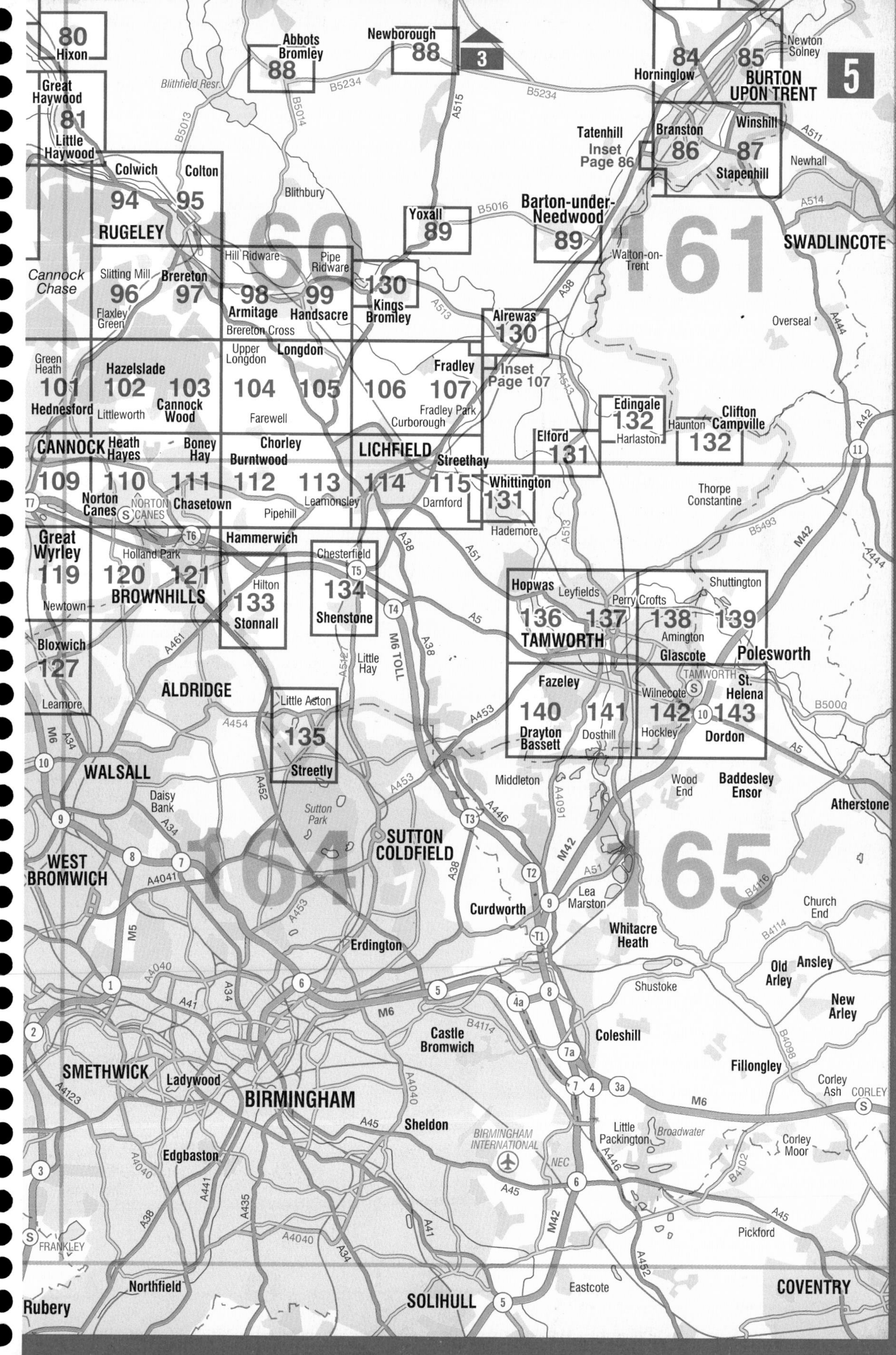

80 Hixon
Abbots Bromley 88
Newborough 88
3
84 Horninglow
85 BURTON UPON TRENT
Newton Solney
Great Haywood 81 Little Haywood
Blithfield Resr.
B5234
B5014
A515
B5013
Tatenhill
Inset Page 86
Branston 86
Winshill 87 Stapenhill
A511
Newhall
Colwich 94
Colton 95
RUGELEY
Blithbury
Yoxall 89
B5016
Barton-under-Needwood 89
A514
SWADLINCOTE
160
161
Walton-on-Trent
Cannock Chase
Slitting Mill 96 Flaxley Green
Brereton 97
Hill Ridware 98 Armitage
Pipe Ridware 99 Handsacre
Brereton Cross
130 Kings Bromley
A513
Alrewas 130
A38
Overseal
A444
Green Heath 101 Hednesford
Hazelslade 102 Littleworth
103 Cannock Wood
Upper Longdon 104 Farewell
Longdon 105
106
Fradley 107 Fradley Park Curborough
Inset Page 107
Edingale 132 Harlaston
Haunton
Clifton Campville 132
CANNOCK
Heath Hayes 110
Boney Hay 111
Chorley Burntwood 112
113 Leamonsley
LICHFIELD 114
Streethay 115 Darnford
Whittington 131
Elford 131
A42
11
109
T7
Norton Canes
NORTON CANES
Chasetown
Pipehill
Hademore
Thorpe Constantine
B5493
M42
A444
Hammerwich
T6
A38
A51
Great Wyrley 119
Holland Park 120 121 BROWNHILLS
Hilton 133 Stonnall
Chesterfield T5 134 Shenstone
T4
A5
Hopwas
Leyfields
Perry Crofts
Shuttington
136 137 TAMWORTH
138 Amington Glascote
139 Polesworth
Newtown
Bloxwich 127 Leamore
A461
ALDRIDGE
A5127
M6 TOLL
Little Hay
A38
Fazeley
TAMWORTH
Wilnecote
St. Helena
B5000
A454
Little Aston 135 Streetly
A453
140 Drayton Bassett
141 Dosthill
142 Hockley
10
143 Dordon
A5
M6
A34
10
WALSALL
A452
A453
Middleton
Wood End
Baddesley Ensor
Atherstone
Daisy Bank
Sutton Park
SUTTON COLDFIELD
T3
A446
A4091
9
A34
WEST BROMWICH
8
7
A4041
164
165
M42
T2
A51
A38
Lea Marston
B4116
Curdworth
9
Church End
M5
A453
Erdington
T1
Whitacre Heath
B4114
1
A4040
A41
A34
6
5
M6
4a
8
Shustoke
Old Arley
Ansley
New Arley
2
B4114
Castle Bromwich
Coleshill
B4098
7a
A4040
Fillongley
SMETHWICK
Ladywood
A4123
BIRMINGHAM
7
4
3a
M6
Corley Ash
CORLEY
A45
Sheldon
BIRMINGHAM INTERNATIONAL
Little Packington
Broadwater
Corley Moor
3
Edgbaston
A4040
NEC
A446
B4102
A441
A435
A38
A45
6
M42
A45
A41
A4040
A34
A452
Pickford
FRANKLEY
Northfield
Eastcote
COVENTRY
Rubery
SOLIHULL
5

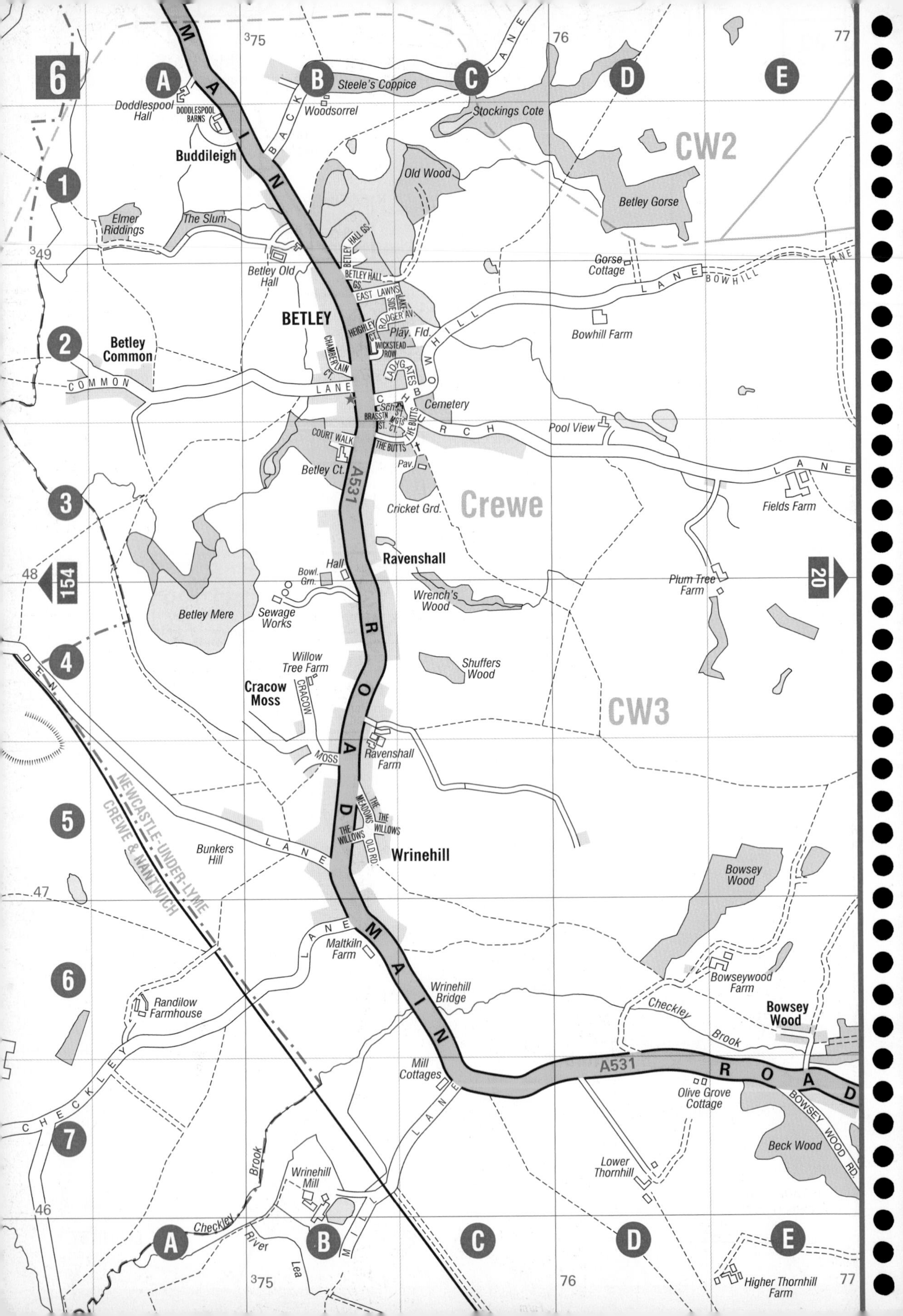

A
B
C
D
E
375
76
77
1
2
3
4
5
6
7
349
48
47
46
Doddlespool Hall
DODDLESPOOL BARNS
Buddileigh
Steele's Coppice
Woodsorrel
Stockings Cote
CW2
Old Wood
Betley Gorse
Elmer Riddings
The Slum
BACK LANE
MAIN ROAD
BETLEY HALL GS.
Betley Old Hall
Gorse Cottage
BOWHILL LANE
Bowhill Farm
BETLEY
EAST LAWNS
LAKE SIDE
RODGER AV.
HEIGHLEY CT.
Play. Fld.
WICKSTEAD ROW
CHAMBERLAIN CT.
LADYGATES
Betley Common
COMMON LANE
CHURCH LANE
Cemetery
Sch.
ST. MGTS CT.
BRASSTN ST.
THE BUTTS
COURT WALK
Pool View
Pav.
Betley Ct.
A531
Crewe
Cricket Grd.
Fields Farm
Ravenshall
Hall
Bowl. Grn.
Plum Tree Farm
Wrench's Wood
Betley Mere
Sewage Works
Willow Tree Farm
Shuffers Wood
Cracow Moss
CRACOW MOSS
CW3
DEN LANE
Ravenshall Farm
NEWCASTLE-UNDER-LYME
CREWE & NANTWICH
THE MEADOWS
THE WILLOWS
OLD RD.
Wrinehill
Bunkers Hill
Bowsey Wood
Maltkiln Farm
Bowseywood Farm
Wrinehill Bridge
Randilow Farmhouse
Checkley Brook
Bowsey Wood
CHECKLEY LANE
Mill Cottages
Olive Grove Cottage
BOWSEY WOOD RD.
Beck Wood
Lower Thornhill
Wrinehill Mill
Brook
Checkley
River
Lea
MILL LANE
Higher Thornhill Farm

154
20

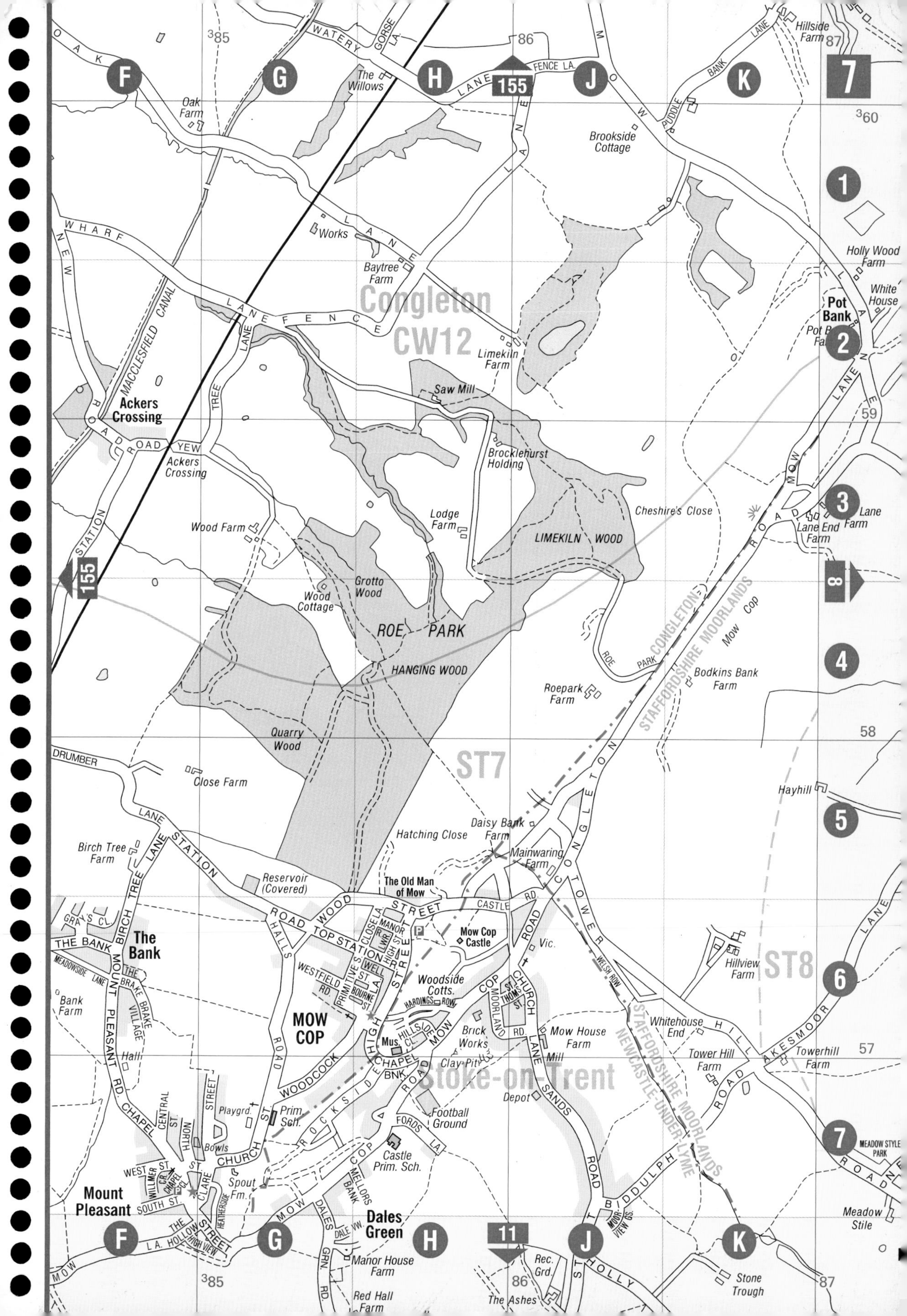
7
Congleton
CW12
ST7
ST8
Stoke-on-Trent
MOW COP
ROE PARK
LIMEKILN WOOD
HANGING WOOD
Grotto Wood
Quarry Wood
Ackers Crossing
Pot Bank
The Bank
Mount Pleasant
Dales Green
The Old Man of Mow
Mow Cop Castle
Oak Farm
The Willows
Works
Baytree Farm
Limekiln Farm
Saw Mill
Brocklehurst Holding
Lodge Farm
Wood Farm
Wood Cottage
Cheshire's Close
Lane End Farm
Lane Farm
Bodkins Bank Farm
Roepark Farm
Close Farm
Birch Tree Farm
Reservoir (Covered)
Hatching Close
Daisy Bank Farm
Mainwaring Farm
Hayhill
Hillview Farm
Whitehouse End
Tower Hill Farm
Towerhill Farm
Mow House Farm
Mill
Depot
Brick Works
Clay Pit
Football Ground
Castle Prim. Sch.
Prim. Sch.
Playgrd.
Bowls
Spout Fm.
Hall
Bank Farm
Woodside Cotts.
Mus.
Vic.
Brookside Cottage
Hillside Farm
Holly Wood Farm
White House
Meadow Stile
MEADOW STYLE PARK
Stone Trough
Manor House Farm
Red Hall Farm
Rec. Grd.
The Ashes
OAK
WATERY GORSE LA.
FENCE LA.
LANE
MOW LANE
PUDDLE BANK LANE
WHARF
NEW ROAD
LANE FENCE
MACCLESFIELD CANAL
TREE LANE
YEW ROAD
STATION
ROE PARK
CONGLETON
STAFFORDSHIRE MOORLANDS
Mow Cop
MOW ROAD
DRUMBER
LANE STATION ROAD
BIRCH TREE LANE
WOOD STREET
CASTLE RD.
TOP STATION RD.
HALLS ROAD
WESTFIELD RD.
PRIMITIVE ST.
CLOSE LA.
MANOR RD.
LWR. HIGH ST.
HIGH STREET
WELL ST.
BOURNE ST.
HARDINGS ROW
HILLSIDE CL.
COP MOORLAND RD.
ST. THOMAS ST.
CHURCH LANE
CONGLETON ROAD
TOWER
WELSH ROW
STAFFORDSHIRE MOORLANDS
NEWCASTLE-UNDER-LYME
HILL
AKESMOOR LANE
ROAD
WOODCOCK ROAD
CHAPEL BNK.
ROCKSIDE
MOW ROAD
FORDS LA.
COP
MELLORS BANK
MOW COP
DALES GRN. RD.
DALE VW.
SANDS ROAD
BIDDULPH ROAD
MOOR VIEW GS.
HOLLY
THE BANK
GRAYS CL.
MEADOWSIDE LANE
MOUNT PLEASANT RD.
THE BRAKE
BRAKE VILLAGE
CHAPEL
CENTRAL ST.
NORTH ST.
STREET
CHURCH ST.
CLARE ST.
WEST ST.
WILLMER ST.
CR. CHAPEL
SOUTH ST.
HEATHERSIDE
THE HOLLOW
HIGH VIEW
MOW LA.
F G H J K
155
11
8
1 2 3 4 5 6 7
385 86 87 360 59 58 57

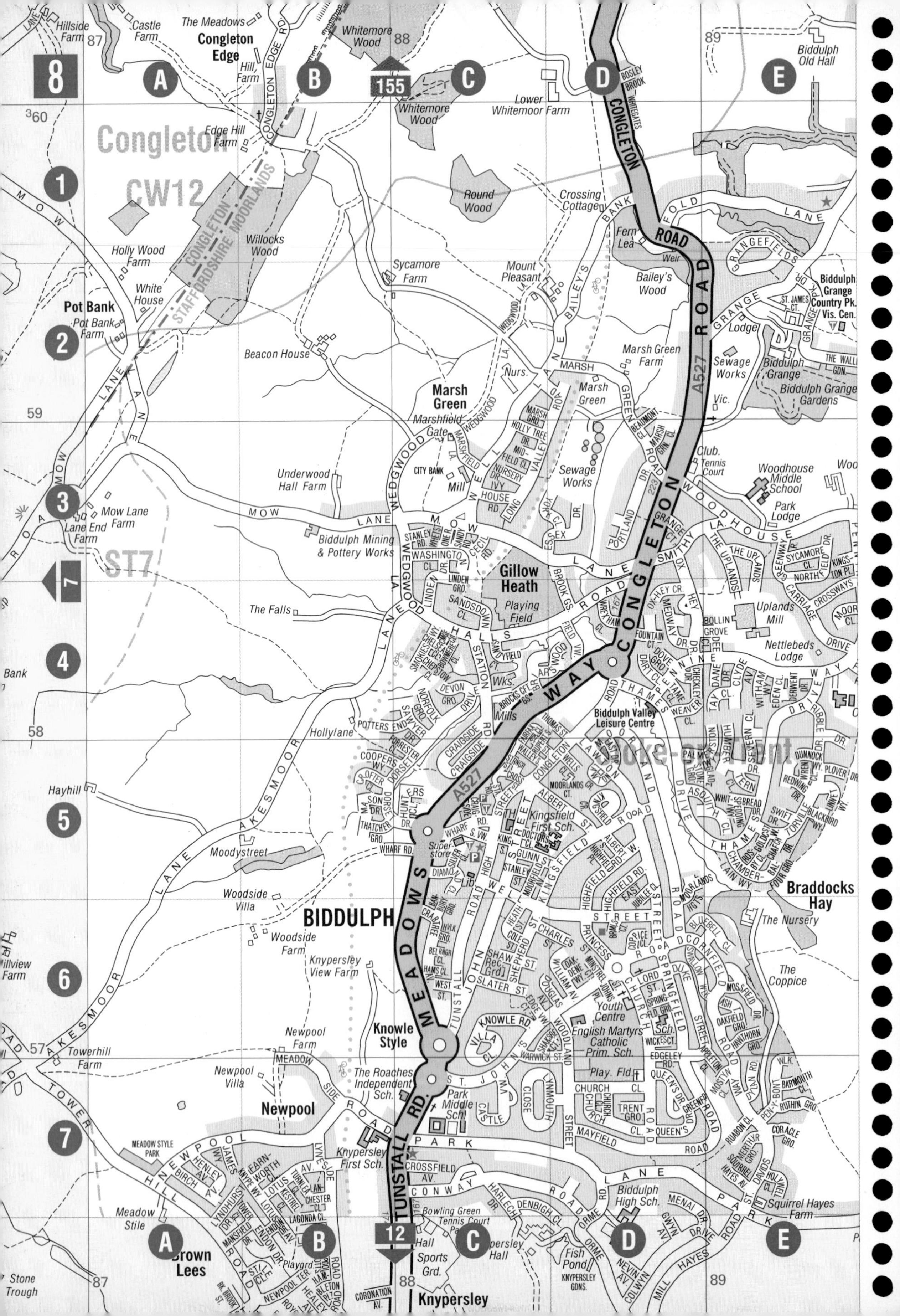
8
Congleton
CW12
ST7
Congleton Edge
Whitemore Wood
155
Biddulph Old Hall
Pot Bank
Marsh Green
Gillow Heath
BIDDULPH
Knowle Style
Newpool
Brown Lees
Knypersley
Braddocks Hay
Biddulph Grange Country Pk. Vis. Cen.
Biddulph Grange Gardens
Biddulph Valley Leisure Centre
Woodhouse Middle School
English Martyrs Catholic Prim. Sch.
Biddulph High Sch.
The Roaches Independent Sch.
Knypersley First Sch.
Park Middle Sch.
Kingsfield First Sch.
Biddulph Mining & Pottery Works
A527
CONGLETON ROAD
CONGLETON WAY
MEADOWS
TUNSTALL RD.
MOW LANE
AKESMOOR LANE
PARK LANE
12
7

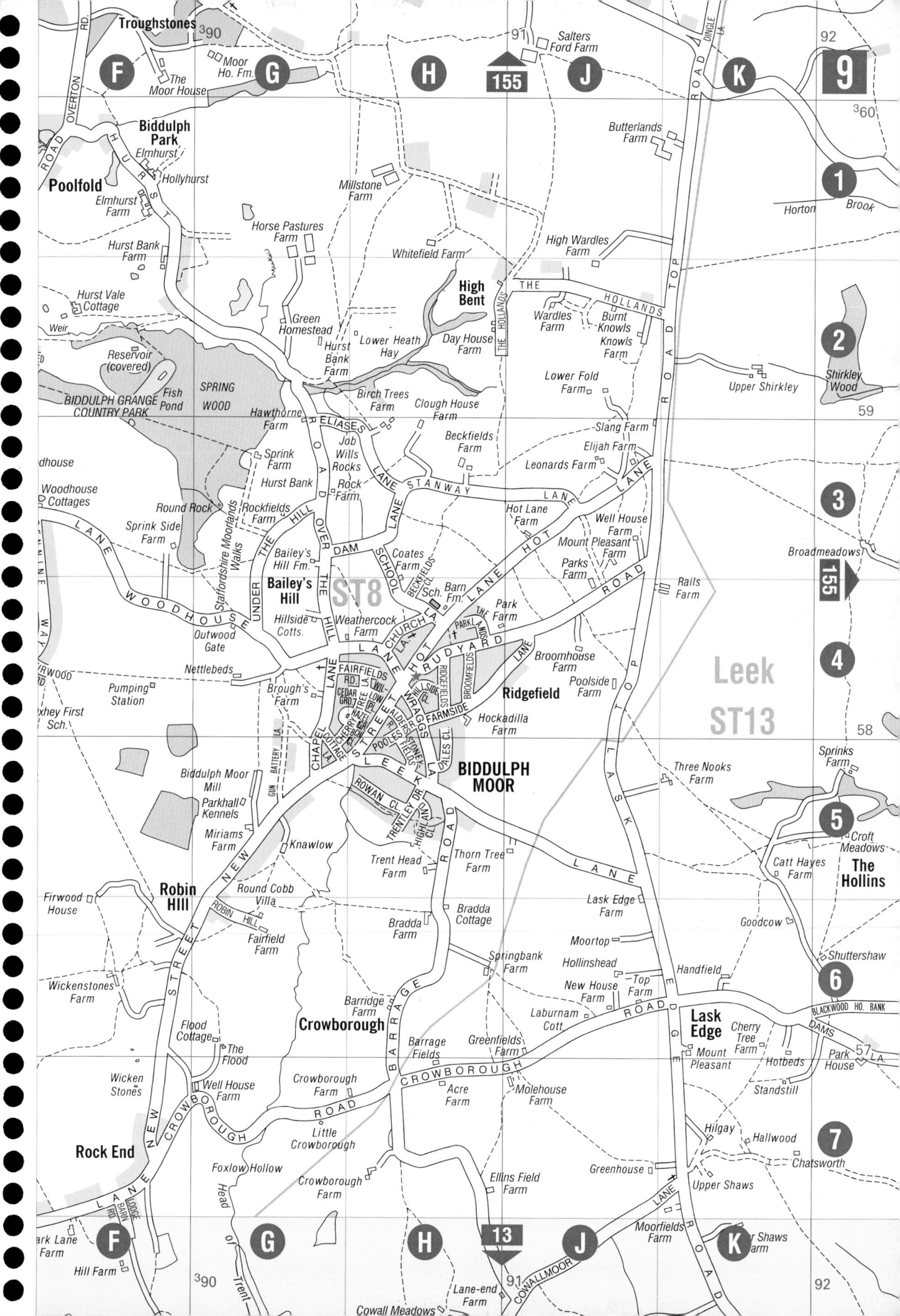
9
155
13
Troughstones
The Moor House
Moor Ho. Fm.
Salters Ford Farm
Biddulph Park
Elmhurst
Hollyhurst
Poolfold
Elmhurst Farm
Millstone Farm
Butterlands Farm
Horton
Brook
Horse Pastures Farm
Hurst Bank Farm
Whitefield Farm
High Wardles Farm
High Bent
Hurst Vale Cottage
Weir
Green Homestead
Lower Heath Hay
Day House Farm
Wardles Farm
Burnt Knowls
Knowls Farm
Reservoir (covered)
Hurst Bank Farm
Fish Pond
SPRING WOOD
BIDDULPH GRANGE COUNTRY PARK
Birch Trees Farm
Clough House Farm
Lower Fold Farm
Upper Shirkley
Shirkley Wood
Hawthorne Farm
Job Wills Rocks
Beckfields Farm
Slang Farm
Elijah Farm
Leonards Farm
Sprink Farm
Hurst Bank
Rock Farm
Woodhouse Cottages
Round Rock
Rockfields Farm
Hot Lane Farm
Well House Farm
Mount Pleasant Farm
Broadmeadows
Sprink Side Farm
Staffordshire Moorlands Walks
Bailey's Hill Fm.
Coates Farm
Parks Farm
Rails Farm
Bailey's Hill
ST8
Sch.
Barn Fm.
Park Farm
Hillside Cotts.
Weathercock Farm
Outwood Gate
Nettlebeds
Broomhouse Farm
Leek
ST13
Pumping Station
Brough's Farm
Poolside Farm
Ridgefield
Hockadilla Farm
BIDDULPH MOOR
Sprinks Farm
Three Nooks Farm
Biddulph Moor Mill
Parkhall Kennels
Miriams Farm
Knawlow
Croft Meadows
Catt Hayes Farm
The Hollins
Trent Head Farm
Thorn Tree Farm
Round Cobb Villa
Robin Hill
Firwood House
Lask Edge Farm
Bradda Cottage
Bradda Farm
Fairfield Farm
Goodcow
Moortop
Springbank Farm
Hollinshead
Shuttershaw
Wickenstones Farm
Handfield
New House Farm
Top Farm
Barridge Farm
Laburnam Cott.
Lask Edge
Cherry Tree Farm
Crowborough
Flood Cottage
The Flood
Barrage Fields
Greenfields Farm
Mount Pleasant
Hotbeds
Park House
Wicken Stones
Well House Farm
Crowborough Farm
Acre Farm
Molehouse Farm
Standstill
Little Crowborough
Hilgay
Hallwood
Rock End
Foxlow Hollow
Chatsworth
Crowborough Farm
Ellins Field Farm
Greenhouse
Upper Shaws
Hill Farm
Moorfields Farm
Lane-end Farm
Cowall Meadows
Head of Trent
OVERTON ROAD
HURST ROAD
DINGLE LA.
ROAD TOP
THE HOLLANDS
ELIASES LANE
STANWAY LANE
HOT LANE
HILL OVER THE HILL
UNDER THE HILL
DAM LANE
SCHOOL LANE
BECKFIELDS CL.
WOODHOUSE LANE
CHURCH LA.
RUDYARD ROAD
PARKLANDS
FAIRFIELDS RD.
CEDAR GRO.
HAZEL GR.
CHERRY TREE LA.
COTTAGE CL.
CHAPEL LA.
WILLOW PL.
ALDERS
STONEY FIELDS
WRAGGS LA.
RIDGEFIELDS
BROOMFIELDS
FARMSIDE
DALES CL.
POOLES RD.
LEEK STREET
GUN BATTERY LA.
ROWAN CL.
TRENTLEY DR.
HIGHLAND CL.
LASK EDGE ROAD
NEW STREET
ROBIN HILL
BARRAGE ROAD
CROWBOROUGH ROAD
BLACKWOOD HO. BANK
DAMS LA.
LANE ROAD
BARN LODGE RD.
COWALLMOOR LANE
F G H J K
1 2 3 4 5 6 7
390 91 92 360 59 58 57

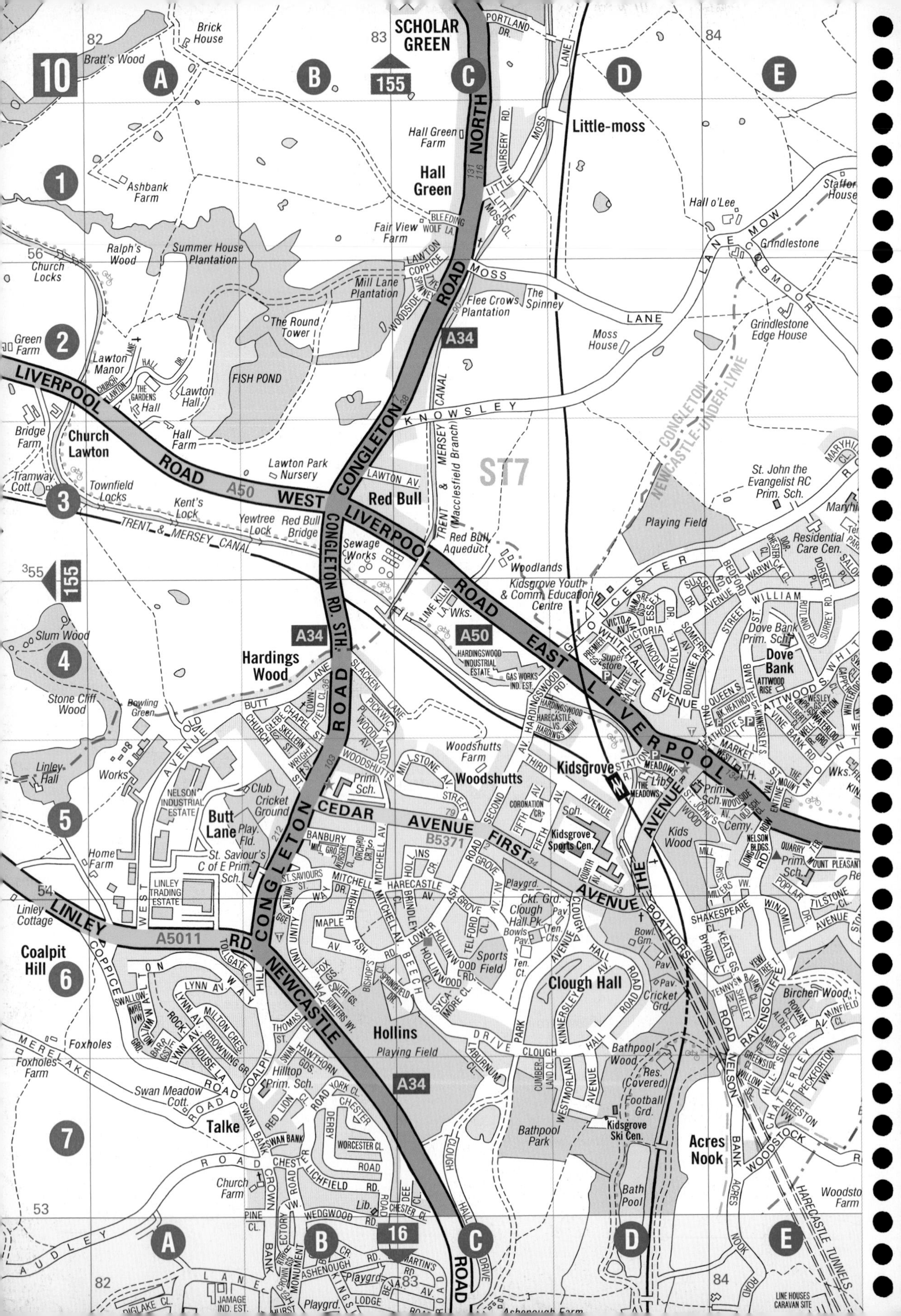
SCHOLAR GREEN
155
Brick House
Bratt's Wood
Hall Green Farm
Hall Green
Little-moss
Ashbank Farm
Hall o'Lee
Stafford House
Grindlestone
Ralph's Wood
Summer House Plantation
Church Locks
Fair View Farm
Mill Lane Plantation
Flee Crows Plantation
The Spinney
The Round Tower
Grindlestone Edge House
Green Farm
Lawton Manor
Lawton Hall
FISH POND
Moss House
MOSS LANE
KNOWSLEY
Bridge Farm
Church Lawton
Hall Farm
Lawton Park Nursery
LIVERPOOL ROAD WEST
A50
A34
Red Bull
ST7
Tramway Cott.
Townfield Locks
Kent's Lock
Yewtree Lock
Red Bull Bridge
TRENT & MERSEY CANAL
CONGLETON ROAD
CONGLETON RD. STH.
Sewage Works
Red Bull Aqueduct
Woodlands
Playing Field
St. John the Evangelist RC Prim. Sch.
Residential Care Cen.
Kidsgrove Youth & Comm. Education Centre
LIVERPOOL ROAD EAST
Slum Wood
Hardings Wood
HARDINGSWOOD INDUSTRIAL ESTATE
GAS WORKS IND. EST.
Dove Bank Prim. Sch.
Dove Bank
Stone Cliff Wood
Bowling Green
Linley Hall
Works
Woodshutts Farm
Woodshutts
Kidsgrove
NELSON INDUSTRIAL ESTATE
Club Cricket Ground
Butt Lane
Play. Fld.
Prim. Sch.
CEDAR AVENUE
B5371
FIRST AVENUE
Kidsgrove Sports Cen.
Kids Wood
St. Saviour's C of E Prim. Sch.
Home Farm
LINLEY TRADING ESTATE
Linley Cottage
LINLEY RD.
A5011
Coalpit Hill
NEWCASTLE ROAD
Clough Hall Pk.
Sports Field
Clough Hall
Cricket Grd.
Birchen Wood
Foxholes
Foxholes Farm
Swan Meadow Cott.
Hollins Playing Field
Hilltop Prim. Sch.
Bathpool Wood
Res. (Covered)
Football Grd.
Kidsgrove Ski Cen.
Talke
Bathpool Park
Acres Nook
Church Farm
Bath Pool
Woodstock Farm
HARECASTLE TUNNELS
16
LINE HOUSES CARAVAN SITE
JAMAGE IND. EST.
AUDLEY LANE

Mount Pleasant
Dales Green
Castle Prim. Sch.
Spout Fm.
Manor House Farm
Red Hall Farm
Holly Farm
Rec. Grd.
The Ashes
Stone Trough
Harriseahead
Red Lion Farm
Hollin House Farm
Wain Lea Farm
Wain Lea
Brieryhurst
Dukes Farm
Blue Pot Farm
Stoke-on-Trent
Cobmoor Cottage Fm.
The Rookery
Comm. Cen.
Thursfield Prim. Sch.
Playing Field
Maytree
Chestnut Farm
Trubshaw Edge Farm
Trubshaw Farm
Trubshaw
Bullocks Ho.
Stadmorslow
Maryhill Prim. Sch.
Whitehill
Thursfield Lodge
Rec. Grd.
Newchapel Observatory
Works
Red Row
Bowling Green
Pav.
BIRCHENWOOD COUNTRYSIDE PARK
Football Pitches
Newchapel
Lane Ends
Club
Packmoor Prim. Sch.
Comm. Cen.
Packmoor
Reservoirs
NEWCASTLE-UNDER-LYME
STOKE-ON-TRENT
Vic.
KIDSGROVE
Oldcott Farm
A50
GOLDENHILL (PUBLIC) GOLF COURSE
Petersfields
Playground
Pumping Station
Reservoir (covered)
Gill Bank
Lower Gill Bank Farm
Res. (covered)
Woodstock
Goldenhill
Club House
Depot
Colclough Fm.
Prim. Sch.
ST6
Turnhurst
Middlehurst Special Sch.
Claybourne Home
WESTCLIFFE HOSP.
Cricket Ground
Westcliffe
Play. Fld.
Goldenhill Prim Sch.
Quarry Cottage
Latebrook
Latebrook House
Ferney Lea Farm
Brindley Sch.
Play. Fld
Meadow Stile
Stadmor Farm
7
12
17
F G H J K
1 2 3 4 5 6 7
85 86 87
56 55 54 53

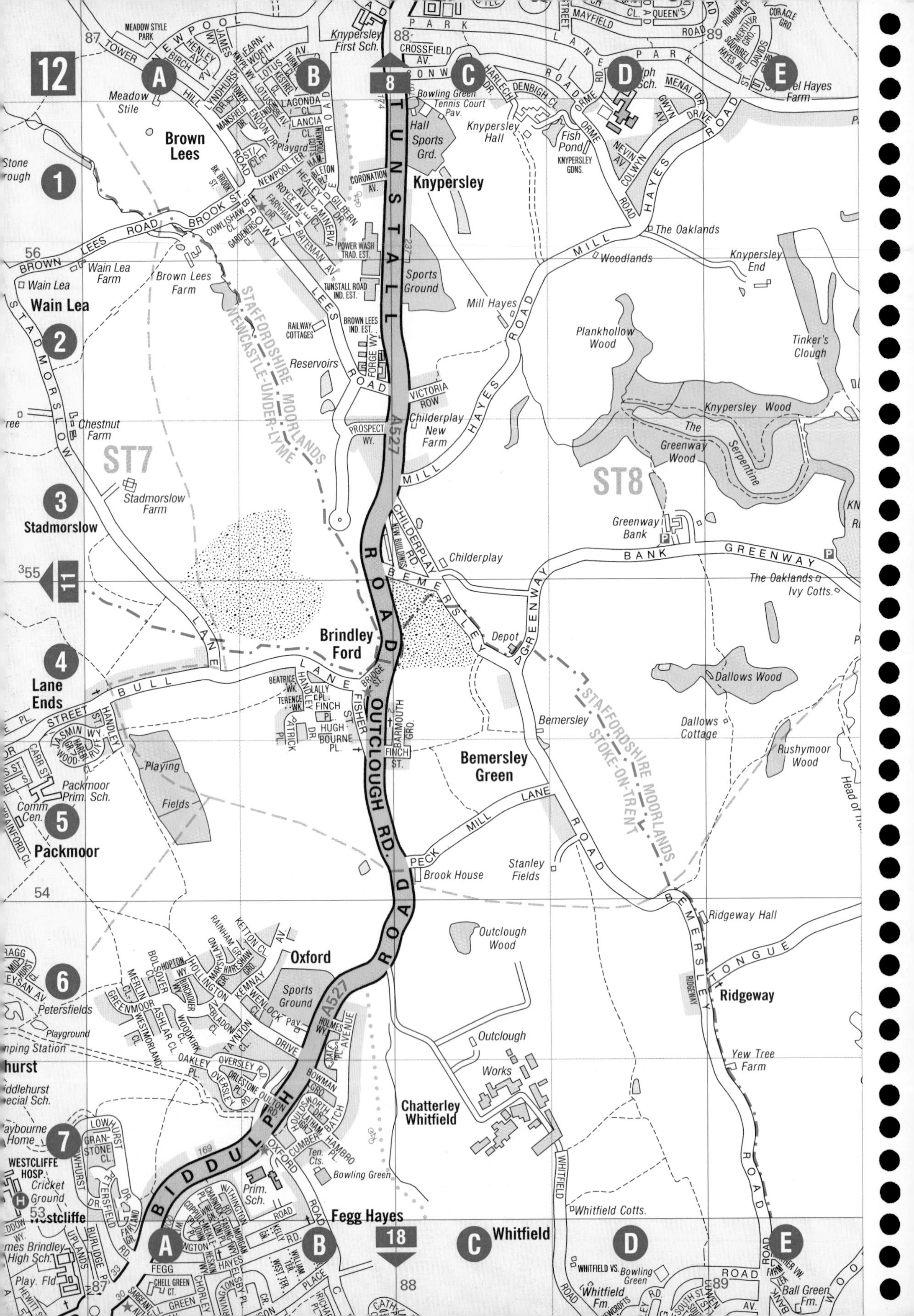
12
8
11
18
Brown Lees
Knypersley
Wain Lea
Stadmorslow
Lane Ends
Packmoor
Brindley Ford
Bemersley Green
Oxford
Chatterley Whitfield
Fegg Hayes
Whitfield
Ridgeway
Westcliffe
ST7
ST8
TUNSTALL ROAD
A527
OUTCLOUGH RD.
BIDDULPH ROAD
STAFFORDSHIRE MOORLANDS
NEWCASTLE-UNDER-LYME
STOKE-ON-TRENT
Knypersley Wood
Plankhollow Wood
Dallows Wood
Rushymoor Wood
Greenway Wood
Outclough Wood
Tinker's Clough
Knypersley Hall
Fish Pond
Sports Ground
Playing Fields
Reservoirs
Meadow Stile
Wain Lea Farm
Brown Lees Farm
Chestnut Farm
Stadmorslow Farm
Childerplay New Farm
Mill Hayes
The Oaklands
Woodlands
Knypersley End
Greenway Bank
Bemersley
Depot
Dallows Cottage
Stanley Fields
Brook House
Ridgeway Hall
Yew Tree Farm
Outclough
Works
Whitfield Cotts.
Whitfield Fm.
Ball Green Fm.
Bowling Green
Packmoor Prim. Sch.
Knypersley First Sch.
Ivy Cotts.
WESTCLIFFE HOSP.
Cricket Ground

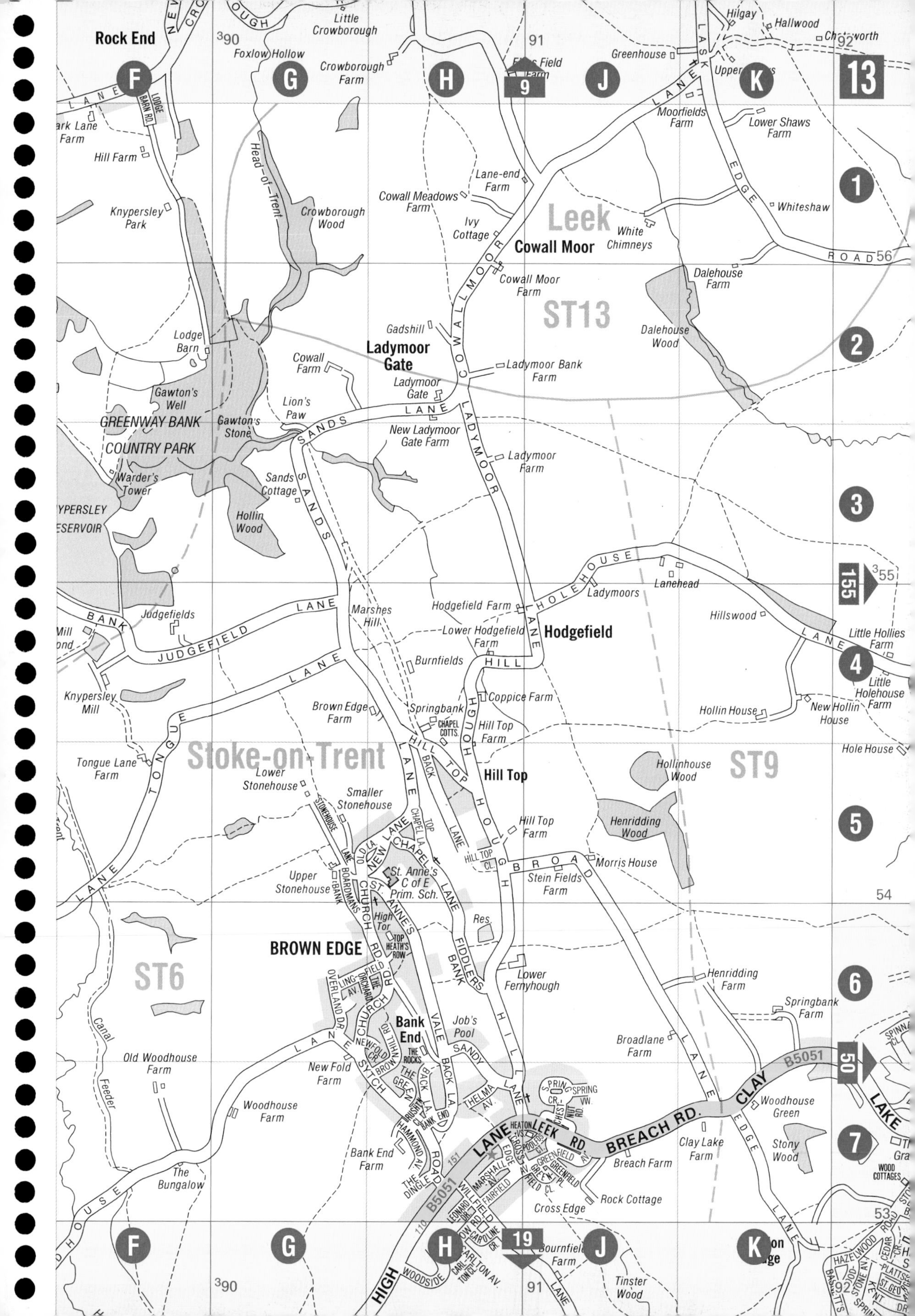
13
Rock End
Foxlow Hollow
Little Crowborough
Crowborough Farm
Hilgay
Hallwood
Chatsworth
Greenhouse
Moorfields Farm
Lower Shaws Farm
Lane-end Farm
Cowall Meadows Farm
Ivy Cottage
Leek
White Chimneys
Cowall Moor
Whiteshaw
Knypersley Park
Hill Farm
Crowborough Wood
Head-of-Trent
Dalehouse Farm
Cowall Moor Farm
ST13
Gadshill
Ladymoor Gate
Dalehouse Wood
Lodge Barn
Cowall Farm
Ladymoor Bank Farm
Gawton's Well
Lion's Paw
GREENWAY BANK COUNTRY PARK
Gawton's Stone
New Ladymoor Gate Farm
Warder's Tower
Ladymoor Farm
Sands Cottage
Hollin Wood
Lanehead
Ladymoors
Hodgefield Farm
Hodgefield
Lower Hodgefield Farm
Judgefields
Marshes Hill
Hillswood
Little Hollies Farm
Burnfields
Coppice Farm
Knypersley Mill
Brown Edge Farm
Springbank
Hill Top Farm
Hollin House
New Hollin House
Little Holehouse Farm
Hole House
Tongue Lane Farm
Stoke-on-Trent
Lower Stonehouse
Smaller Stonehouse
Hill Top
Hollinhouse Wood
ST9
Henridding Wood
Hill Top Farm
Morris House
Upper Stonehouse
St. Anne's C of E Prim. Sch.
Stein Fields Farm
High Tor
Res.
BROWN EDGE
Lower Fernyhough
Henridding Farm
ST6
Bank End
Job's Pool
Springbank Farm
Broadlane Farm
Old Woodhouse Farm
New Fold Farm
Woodhouse Farm
Woodhouse Green
Clay Lake Farm
Breach Farm
Stony Wood
Bank End Farm
The Bungalow
Rock Cottage
Cross Edge
Bournfield Farm
Tinster Wood
JUDGEFIELD LANE
TONGUE LANE
SANDS LANE
COWALL MOOR
LADYMOOR
HOLEHOUSE LANE
HILL TOP
HOUGH HILL
BROAD LANE
BREACH RD.
CLAY LAKE
LEEK RD.
HIGH LANE
B5051
FIDDLERS BANK
CHAPEL LANE
CHURCH RD
SANDY LANE
LASK EDGE
ROAD

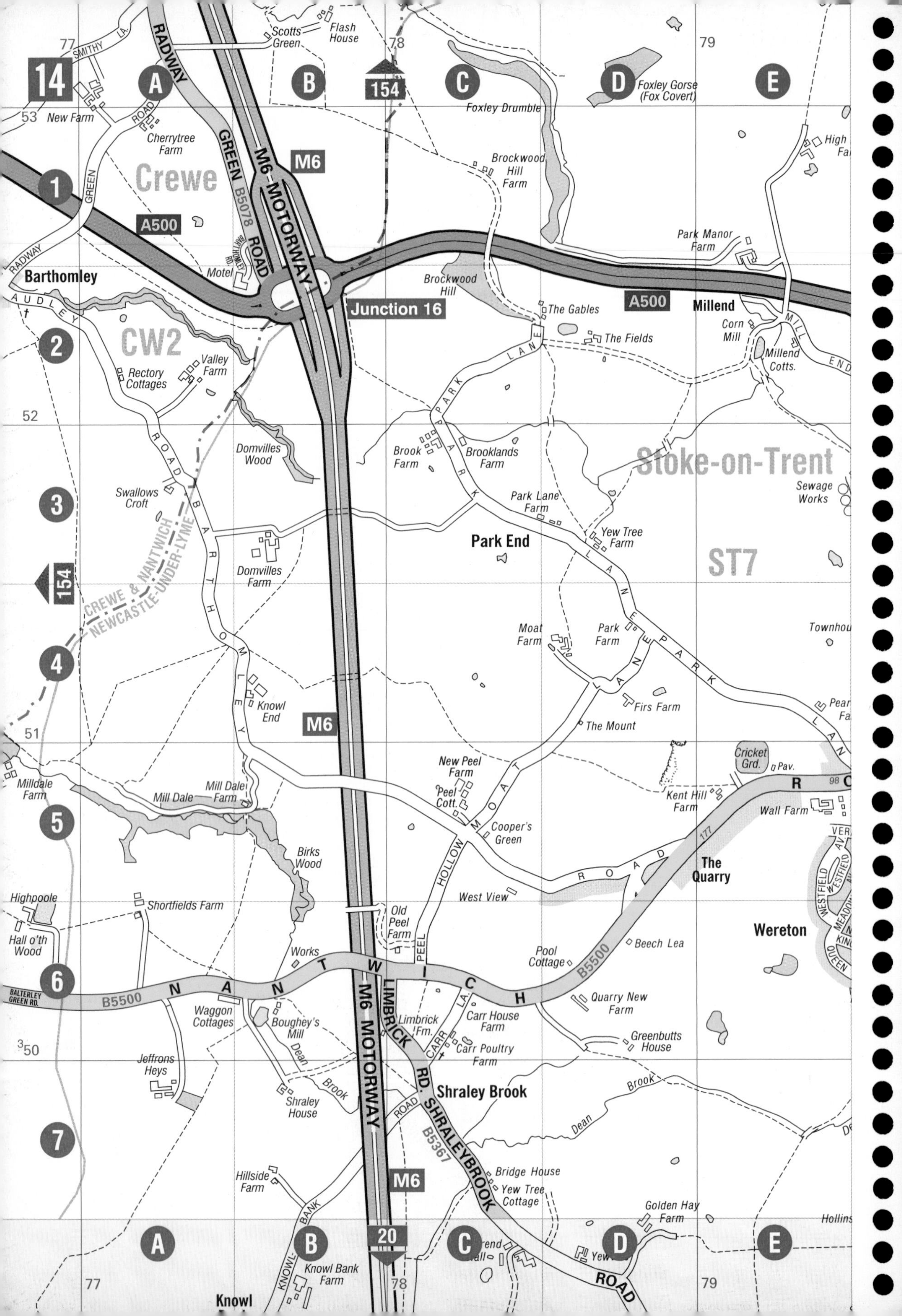
14
Crewe
CW2
Stoke-on-Trent
ST7
Barthomley
Park End
Millend
Shraley Brook
Wereton
The Quarry
Knowl
Junction 16
M6 MOTORWAY
M6
A500
B5078
B5500
B5367
154
20
RADWAY GREEN ROAD
SMITHY LA.
AUDLEY ROAD
BARTHOMLEY ROAD
PARK LANE
MOAT LANE
HOLLOW LANE
PEEL LANE
NANTWICH ROAD
LIMBRICK RD.
SHRALEYBROOK ROAD
KNOWL BANK
CARR LA.
BALTERLEY GREEN RD.
CREWE & NANTWICH
NEWCASTLE-UNDER-LYME
Scotts Green
Flash House
New Farm
Cherrytree Farm
Foxley Gorse (Fox Covert)
Foxley Drumble
Brockwood Hill Farm
Brockwood Hill
Park Manor Farm
High Fa
Motel
The Gables
The Fields
Corn Mill
Millend Cotts.
Rectory Cottages
Valley Farm
Domvilles Wood
Domvilles Farm
Brook Farm
Brooklands Farm
Swallows Croft
Park Lane Farm
Yew Tree Farm
Sewage Works
Moat Farm
Park Farm
Townhou
Firs Farm
The Mount
Knowl End
Pear Fa
Cricket Grd.
Pav.
New Peel Farm
Peel Cott.
Kent Hill Farm
Wall Farm
Milldale Farm
Mill Dale
Mill Dale Farm
Cooper's Green
Birks Wood
West View
Highpoole
Shortfields Farm
Hall o'th Wood
Old Peel Farm
Works
Pool Cottage
Beech Lea
Waggon Cottages
Boughey's Mill
Limbrick Fm.
Carr House Farm
Quarry New Farm
Carr Poultry Farm
Greenbutts House
Jeffrons Heys
Shraley House
Dean Brook
Hillside Farm
Bridge House
Yew Tree Cottage
Golden Hay Farm
Hollins
Knowl Bank Farm
WESTFIELD AV.
MEADOW
QUEEN
VER
A B C D E
1 2 3 4 5 6 7
77 78 79
53 52 51 50

15
Foxley
Foxley Farm
F
G
H
J
K
155
21
16
380
81
82
New Springs
Eardleyend
The White Cottage
Wrench's Coppice
Eardleyend Cottages
Dunkirk Farm
Eardley Hall
Meadowside
Dunkirk
Eardley Hall Cottage
Meadow View
Parrot's Drumble Nature Reserve
Warehouse
Diglake Cl.
A500
Oaklea Ct.
Hullock's Pool Road
Cross Farm
Workhouse Cottages
Hullock's Pool
Bonnie Braes Farm
Woodlands Farm
Pool Ho.
New Farm
Great Oak Farm
Oakdene Farm
Great Oak Road
Bignall End Road
Football Ground
Park Farm
Brierly Brook
Diglake
Diglake Farm
Wedgwood's Monument
Bignall Hill Reservoir (Covered)
Ravensmead Prim. Sch.
Bignall End
Playing Field
Butters Green
Castle Hill
Comm. Cen.
Old Road
Chapel St.
New Rd.
B5500
Raven's La.
Bignall
Butters Green Farm
Bignall Hill
Hill
Boyles Hall
Audley
Audley Theatre
Bowl. Grn.
Four Winds
Megacre
Crofton Farm
Cricket Grd.
Boon Hill
Wood Lane
Wood Lane Prim. Sch.
Hougher Wall
Bungalow Farm
Ryehill Farm
Grange Farm
White House Farm
Rye Hills
Miles Green
Miles Green Farm
Peggy's Bank
Apedale Road
Woodhouse Farm
Robin Hood Farm
Springwood
Newcastle ST5
Wynbank Farm
Halmer End
Play. Field
Sir Thomas Boughey
Miry Wood
Apedale House
Hilltop Bungalow
1
2
3
4
5
6
7
53
52
51
50

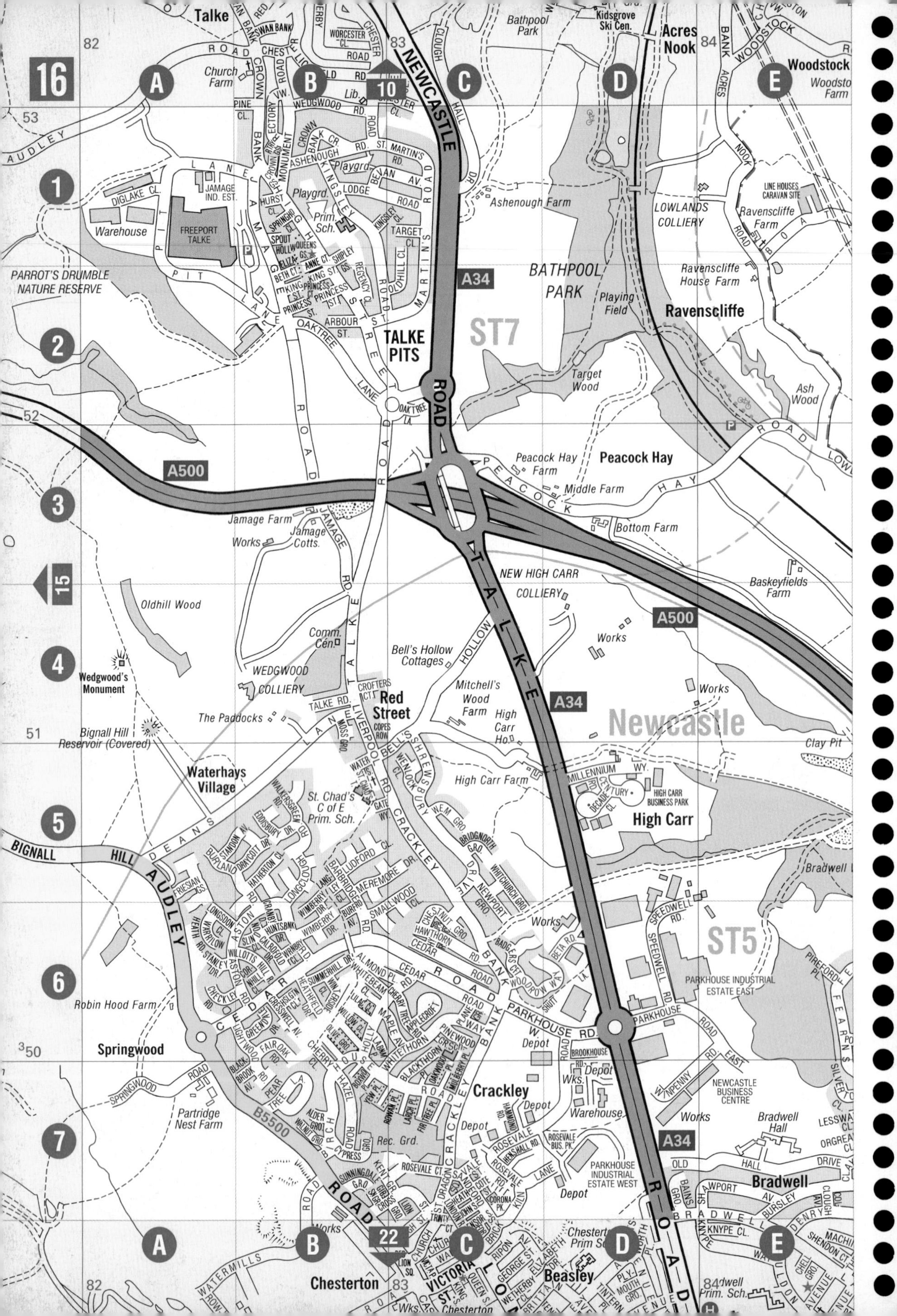
Talke
Church Farm
Bathpool Park
Kidsgrove Ski Cen.
Acres Nook
Woodstock
Woodstock Farm
10
NEWCASTLE
AUDLEY
JAMAGE IND. EST.
FREEPORT TALKE
Warehouse
PARROT'S DRUMBLE NATURE RESERVE
Ashenough Farm
LOWLANDS COLLIERY
LINE HOUSES CARAVAN SITE
Ravenscliffe Farm
Ravenscliffe House Farm
Ravenscliffe
BATHPOOL PARK
Playing Field
A34
ST7
TALKE PITS
Target Wood
Ash Wood
A500
Peacock Hay Farm
Peacock Hay
Middle Farm
Bottom Farm
Jamage Farm
Jamage Cotts.
Works
15
NEW HIGH CARR COLLIERY
Baskeyfields Farm
Oldhill Wood
Comm. Cen.
Bell's Hollow Cottages
Wedgwood's Monument
WEDGWOOD COLLIERY
Mitchell's Wood Farm
High Carr Ho.
Red Street
The Paddocks
Bignall Hill Reservoir (Covered)
Newcastle
Clay Pit
Waterhays Village
St. Chad's C of E Prim. Sch.
High Carr Farm
HIGH CARR BUSINESS PARK
High Carr
BIGNALL HILL
Bradwell
ST5
PARKHOUSE INDUSTRIAL ESTATE EAST
Robin Hood Farm
Springwood
Depot
Crackley
NEWCASTLE BUSINESS CENTRE
Partridge Nest Farm
Rec. Grd.
Warehouse
Bradwell Hall
B5500
PARKHOUSE INDUSTRIAL ESTATE WEST
Bradwell
22
Chesterton
Beasley
Chesterton Prim Sch.
Bradwell Prim. Sch.

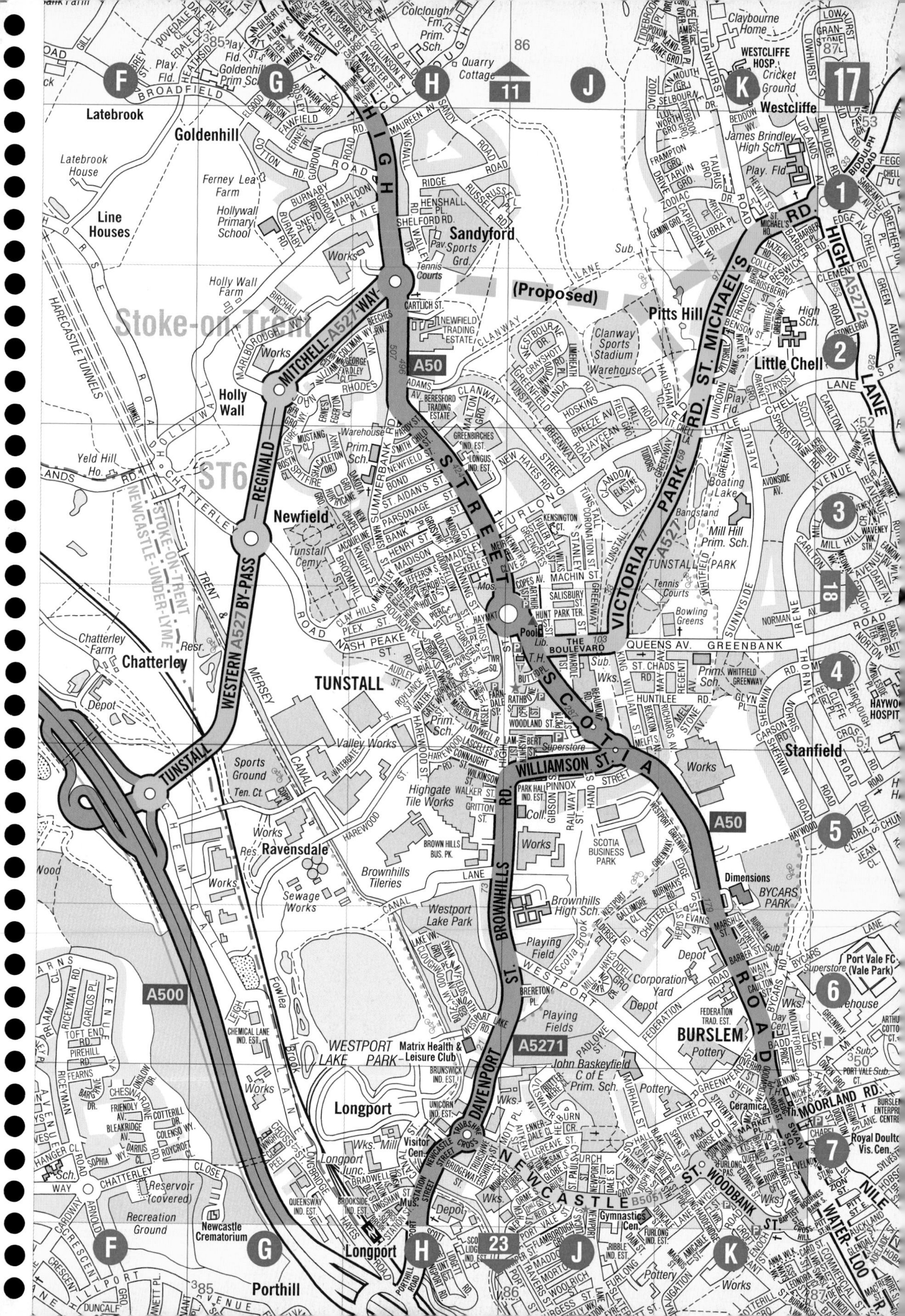
F
G
H
J
K
11
86
85
87
Latebrook
Goldenhill
Latebrook House
Ferney Lea Farm
Hollywall Primary School
Line Houses
Holly Wall Farm
Stoke-on-Trent
Holly Wall
Yeld Hill Ho.
ST6
Chatterley Farm
Chatterley
Depot
Sandyford
Sports Grd.
Tennis Courts
(Proposed)
NEWFIELD TRADING ESTATE
A50
BERESFORD TRADING ESTATE
Newfield
Tunstall Cemy.
TUNSTALL
Westcliffe
WESTCLIFFE HOSP.
Cricket Ground
James Brindley High Sch.
Claybourne Home
Pitts Hill
Little Chell
High Sch.
Clanway Sports Stadium
Warehouse
Boating Lake
Bandstand
Mill Hill Prim. Sch.
TUNSTALL PARK
Tennis Courts
Bowling Greens
VICTORIA PARK RD.
ST. MICHAEL'S RD.
A527
A5272
HIGH STREET
SCOTIA
WESTERN A527 BY-PASS
REGINALD
MITCHELL A527 WAY
TUNSTALL
THE BOULEVARD
QUEENS AV.
GREENBANK
Superstore
WILLIAMSON ST.
Valley Works
Highgate Tile Works
Sports Ground
Ravensdale
Sewage Works
Brownhills Tileries
BROWN HILLS BUS. PK.
SCOTIA BUSINESS PARK
Brownhills High Sch.
Westport Lake Park
WESTPORT LAKE PARK
Matrix Health & Leisure Club
Playing Field
Playing Fields
Corporation Yard
Depot
A5271
BROWNHILLS RD.
DAVENPORT ST.
Longport
Visitor Cen.
Longport Junc.
Newcastle Crematorium
Recreation Ground
Reservoir (covered)
Porthill
A500
John Baskeyfield C of E Prim. Sch.
Pottery
BURSLEM
Ceramica
Gymnastics Cen.
Dimensions
BYCARS PARK
Port Vale FC (Vale Park)
Superstore
Stanfield
Royal Doulton Vis. Cen.
MOORLAND RD.
NEWCASTLE ST.
ST. WOODBANK ST.
WATERLOO RD.
NILE ST.
Works
Pottery
Stoke-on-Trent
Newcastle-under-Lyme
1
2
3
4
5
6
7
18
23

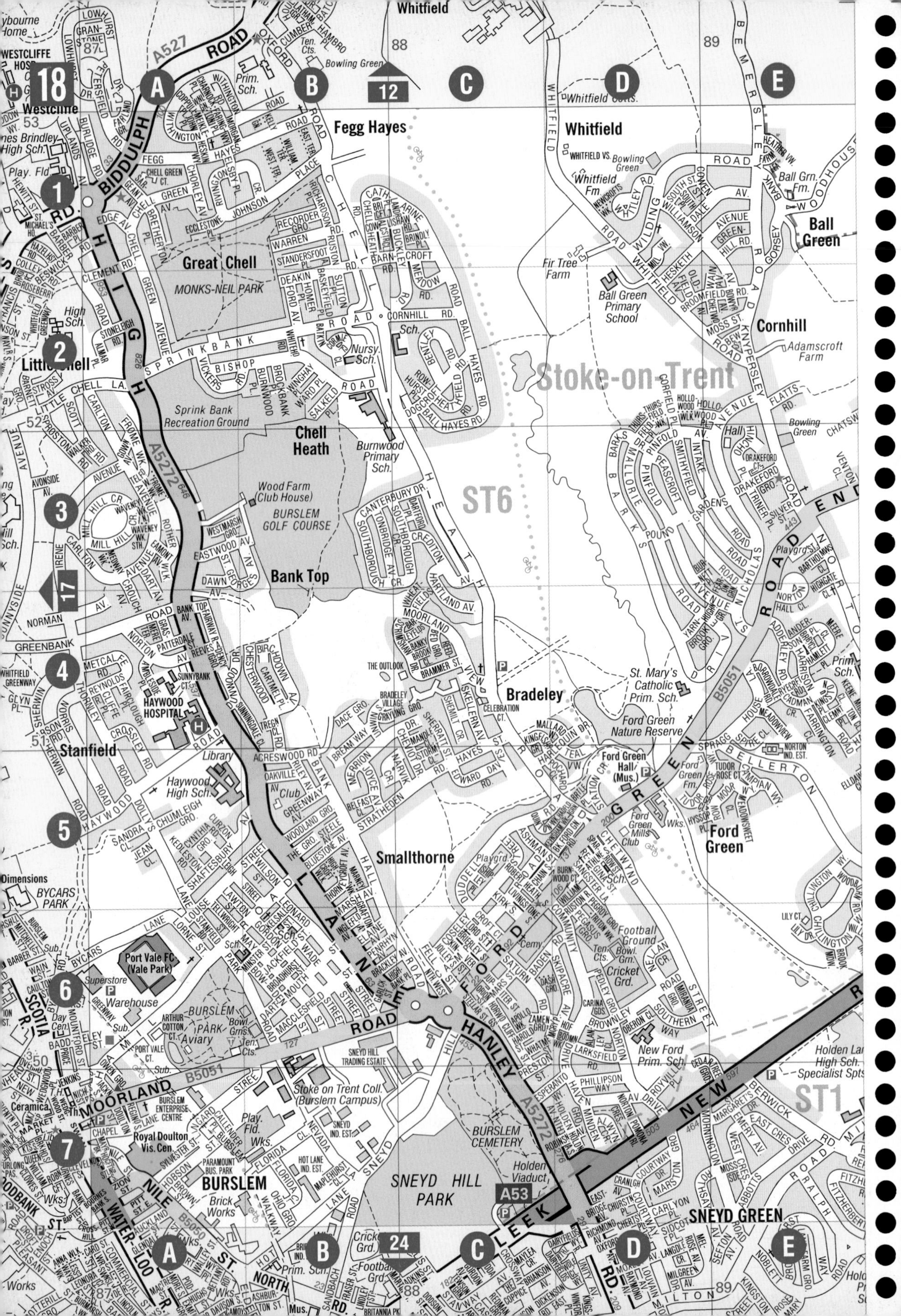

18
Whitfield
Fegg Hayes
Great Chell
MONKS-NEIL PARK
Little Chell
Sprink Bank Recreation Ground
Chell Heath
Burnwood Primary Sch.
Wood Farm (Club House)
BURSLEM GOLF COURSE
Bank Top
Stoke-on-Trent
ST6
Ball Green Primary School
Ball Green
Cornhill
Adamscroft Farm
Fir Tree Farm
Whitfield Fm.
Bradeley
St. Mary's Catholic Prim. Sch.
Ford Green Nature Reserve
Ford Green Hall (Mus.)
Ford Green
Smallthorne
HAYWOOD HOSPITAL
Stanfield
Haywood High Sch.
Library
Port Vale FC (Vale Park)
BYCARS PARK
Superstore
Warehouse
BURSLEM PARK
Royal Doulton Vis. Cen.
BURSLEM
Brick Works
Stoke on Trent Coll. (Burslem Campus)
SNEYD HILL TRADING ESTATE
SNEYD HILL PARK
BURSLEM CEMETERY
Holden Viaduct
New Ford Prim. Sch.
Cricket Grd.
Football Ground
SNEYD GREEN
ST1
Holden Lane High Sch. Specialist Spts
Ceramica
A527
BIDDULPH ROAD
HIGH LANE
A5272
B5051
MOORLAND ROAD
HANLEY ROAD
FORD GREEN ROAD
NORTON ROAD
LEEK NEW ROAD
A53
B5050
WATERLOO ROAD
NILE ST.
12
17
24
88
89

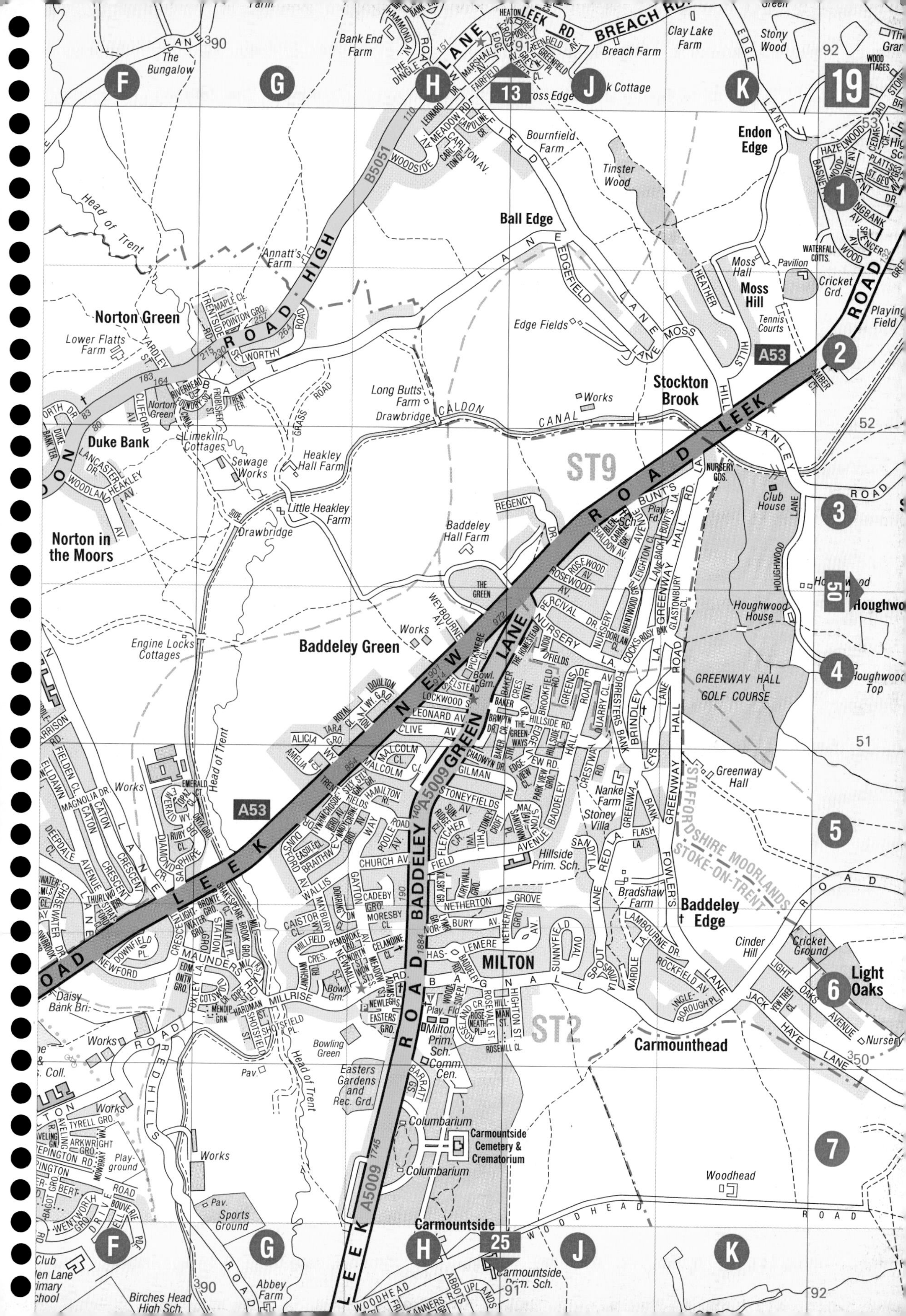

19
13
25
50
F
G
H
J
K
1
2
3
4
5
6
7
The Bungalow
Bank End Farm
Breach Farm
Clay Lake Farm
Stony Wood
Endon Edge
Bournfield Farm
Tinster Wood
Ball Edge
Annatt's Farm
Norton Green
Lower Flatts Farm
Edge Fields
Moss Hall
Moss Hill
Pavilion
Cricket Grd.
Playing Field
Tennis Courts
Stockton Brook
Long Butts Farm
Drawbridge
CALDON CANAL
Works
Duke Bank
Limekiln Cottages
Sewage Works
Heakley Hall Farm
Little Heakley Farm
Norton in the Moors
Head of Trent
Baddeley Hall Farm
ST9
Club House
Houghwood House
Houghwood Top
GREENWAY HALL GOLF COURSE
Greenway Hall
Engine Locks Cottages
Baddeley Green
The Green
Nanke Farm
Stoney Villa
Hillside Prim. Sch.
Bradshaw Farm
Baddeley Edge
STAFFORDSHIRE MOORLANDS
STOKE-ON-TRENT
Cinder Hill
Cricket Ground
Light Oaks
MILTON
ST2
Carmounthead
Daisy Bank Bri.
Bowling Green
Easters Gardens and Rec. Grd.
Milton Prim. Sch.
Comm. Cen.
Columbarium
Carmountside Cemetery & Crematorium
Woodhead
Sports Ground
Carmountside
Carmountside Prim. Sch.
Abbey Farm
Birches Head High Sch.
LEEK ROAD
NEW LEEK ROAD
BADDELEY GREEN LANE
HIGH LANE
BREACH RD.
LEEK RD.
A53
A5009
B5051
WOODHEAD ROAD
JACK HAYE LANE
STANLEY ROAD
BAGNALL ROAD
EDGEFIELD LANE
MOSS LANE
HOUGHWOOD LANE
GREENWAY HALL ROAD
FOWLER'S LANE
MILLRISE
REDHILLS ROAD

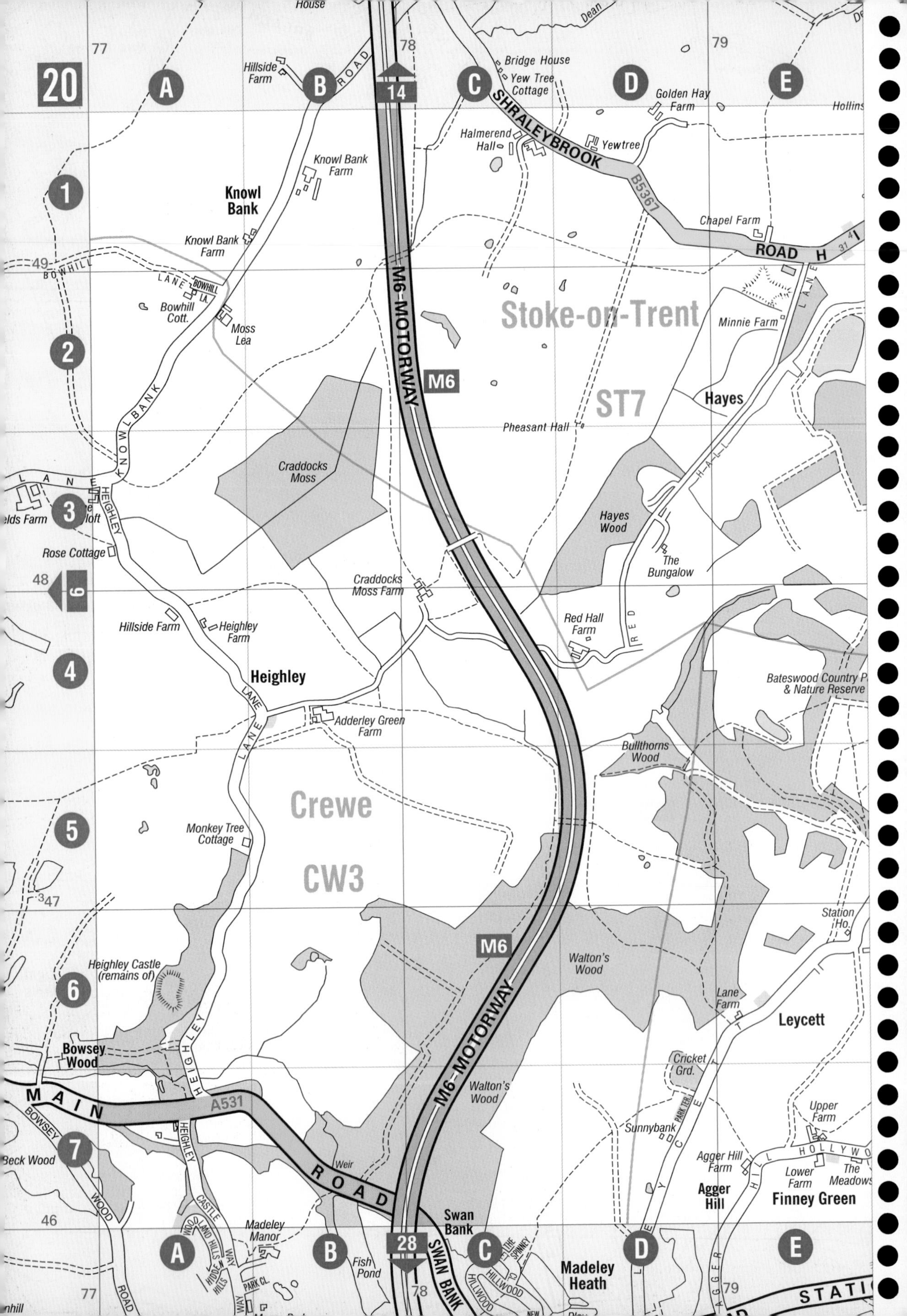
20
A
B
C
D
E
1
2
3
4
5
6
7
Hillside Farm
Bridge House
Yew Tree Cottage
Golden Hay Farm
Hollins
SHRALEYBROOK
Halmerend Hall
Yewtree
B5367
Knowl Bank Farm
Knowl Bank
Chapel Farm
ROAD
Knowl Bank Farm
BOWHILL
BOWHILL LANE
Bowhill Cott.
Moss Lea
Stoke-on-Trent
Minnie Farm
M6-MOTORWAY
M6
ST7
Hayes
KNOWLBANK
Pheasant Hall
LANE
Craddocks Moss
HALL
HEIGHLEY
Rose Cottage
Hayes Wood
The Bungalow
Craddocks Moss Farm
Red Hall Farm
RED
Hillside Farm
Heighley Farm
Heighley
Bateswood Country Park & Nature Reserve
Adderley Green Farm
Bullthorns Wood
Crewe
Monkey Tree Cottage
CW3
Station Ho.
M6
Walton's Wood
Heighley Castle (remains of)
Lane Farm
Leycett
Bowsey Wood
Cricket Grd.
MAIN
A531
Walton's Wood
Upper Farm
BOWSEY
Sunnybank
PARK TER.
HOLLYWOOD
Beck Wood
Agger Hill Farm
Lower Farm
The Meadows
Weir
ROAD
Agger Hill
Finney Green
WOOD
Swan Bank
Madeley Manor
SWAN BANK
Fish Pond
Madeley Heath
THE SPINNEY
HILLWOOD
PARK CL.
AGGER
STATI
14
28
6
77
78
79
49
48
47
46

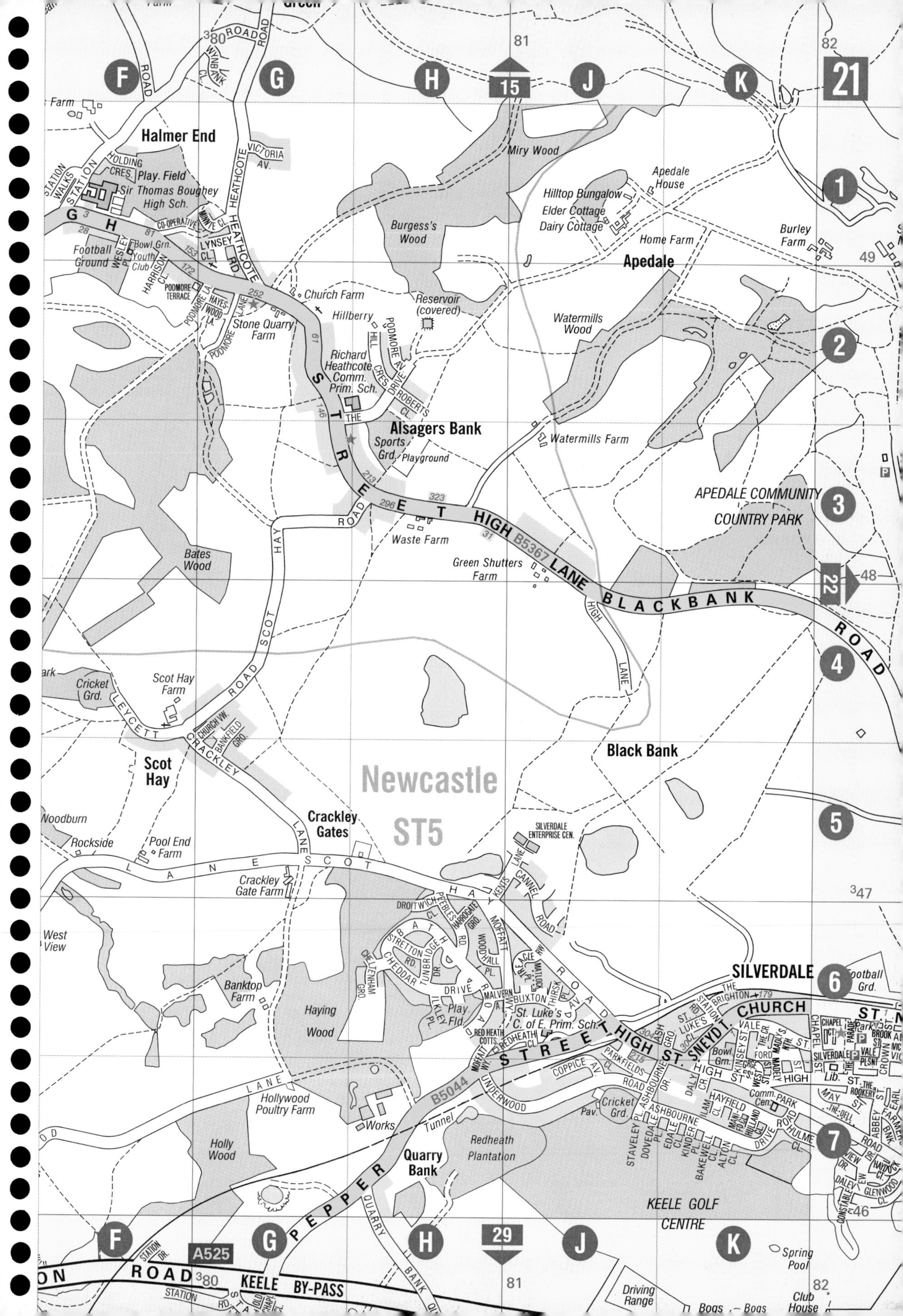

21
15
29
22
F
G
H
J
K
1
2
3
4
5
6
7
81
82
380
49
48
347
46
Halmer End
Play. Field
Sir Thomas Boughey High Sch.
Football Ground
Bowl.Grn.
Youth Club
Church Farm
Stone Quarry Farm
Hillberry
Reservoir (covered)
Richard Heathcote Comm. Prim. Sch.
Alsagers Bank
Sports Grd.
Playground
Waste Farm
Green Shutters Farm
Miry Wood
Burgess's Wood
Hilltop Bungalow
Elder Cottage
Dairy Cottage
Apedale House
Home Farm
Burley Farm
Apedale
Watermills Wood
Watermills Farm
APEDALE COMMUNITY COUNTRY PARK
HIGH STREET
B5367
HIGH LANE
BLACKBANK ROAD
Bates Wood
Scot Hay Farm
Cricket Grd.
Scot Hay
SCOT HAY ROAD
LEYCETT
CRACKLEY
Black Bank
Newcastle ST5
Crackley Gates
Woodburn
Rockside
Pool End Farm
SCOT LANE
Crackley Gate Farm
SILVERDALE ENTERPRISE CEN.
KEYS LANE
CANNEL ROAD
West View
Banktop Farm
Haying Wood
Play. Fld.
St. Luke's C. of E. Prim. Sch.
SILVERDALE
Football Grd.
CHURCH ST.
HIGH STREET
HIGH ST.
B5044
Hollywood Poultry Farm
Works
Tunnel
Holly Wood
Quarry Bank
Redheath Plantation
Cricket Grd.
Pav.
Comm. Cen.
Lib.
KEELE GOLF CENTRE
PEPPER
QUARRY BANK
Spring Pool
A525
ROAD
KEELE BY-PASS
STATION RD.
STATION DR.
Driving Range
Club House
Bogs

22
A
B
C
D
E
1
2
3
4
5
6
7
16
21
30
152
Nest Farm
AUDLEY
B5500
RD.
Works
Rec. Grd.
ROSEVALE
ROSEVALE BUS. PK.
PARKHOUSE INDUSTRIAL ESTATE
Depot
T-A-L-K-E
A34
Bradwell
Bradwell Prim. Sch.
BRADWELL HOSPITAL
Chesterton Prim Sch.
Beasley
VICTORIA ST.
LONDON
Chesterton Pk.
WATERMILLS
ROWHURST
Works
Saw Mill
Burley Farm
ROWHURST CLOSE IND. ESTATE
APEDALE
Chesterton Community Sports Centre
Ten. Cts.
CHESTERTON
Chesterton High Sch.
Playing Field
WOLSTANTON RD.
DIMSDALE
B5369
Church Fields
Playing Field
Broad Meadow
B5500
ROAD
Spts. Grd.
Depot
Offices
Dimsdale Hall Farm
Club House
WOLSTANTON GOLF COURSE
Apedale Heritage Centre
LOOMER ROAD IND. EST.
LYMEDALE COURT ENTERPRISE CEN.
HOLDITCH IND. EST.
Stoke Speedway
LYMEDALE BUSINESS PARK
APEDALE COMMUNITY COUNTRY PARK
BRYMBO
BRINDLEY CT.
COALDALE
Depot
Ashfield
Bakery
BLACKBACK
Hooters Hall Farm
Newcastle
ST5
Sports Ground
RISTS IND. EST.
Works
LIVERPOOL ROAD
Whitebarn
Lyme Brook
COTSWOLD
B5367
Cemetery
MILEHOUSE
LANE
B5368
Superstore
Cross Heath
Gorsty Bank
ROAD HIGH STREET
Football Ground
Works
Knutton
Knutton Rec. Cen.
Enterprise Cen.
LOWER
KNUTTON
LANE
SILVERDALE
Football Grd.
CHURCH
B5044
ST.
NEWCASTLE ST.
SILVERDALE
STONEWALL IND. EST.
Lib.
Jun. Sch.
Depot
St. John Fisher RC High Sch.
Newcastle-under-Lyme College
Sports Ground
Cemetery
Silverdale Prim. Sch.
SILVERDALE BUSINESS PARK
NEWCASTLE-UNDER-LYME
Comm. Cen.
Lyme Brook
Playing Fields
Nursery
Playing Fields
Spring Pool
Poolfields
Job's Wood
Club House
Field House
Caravan Park
CEMETERY

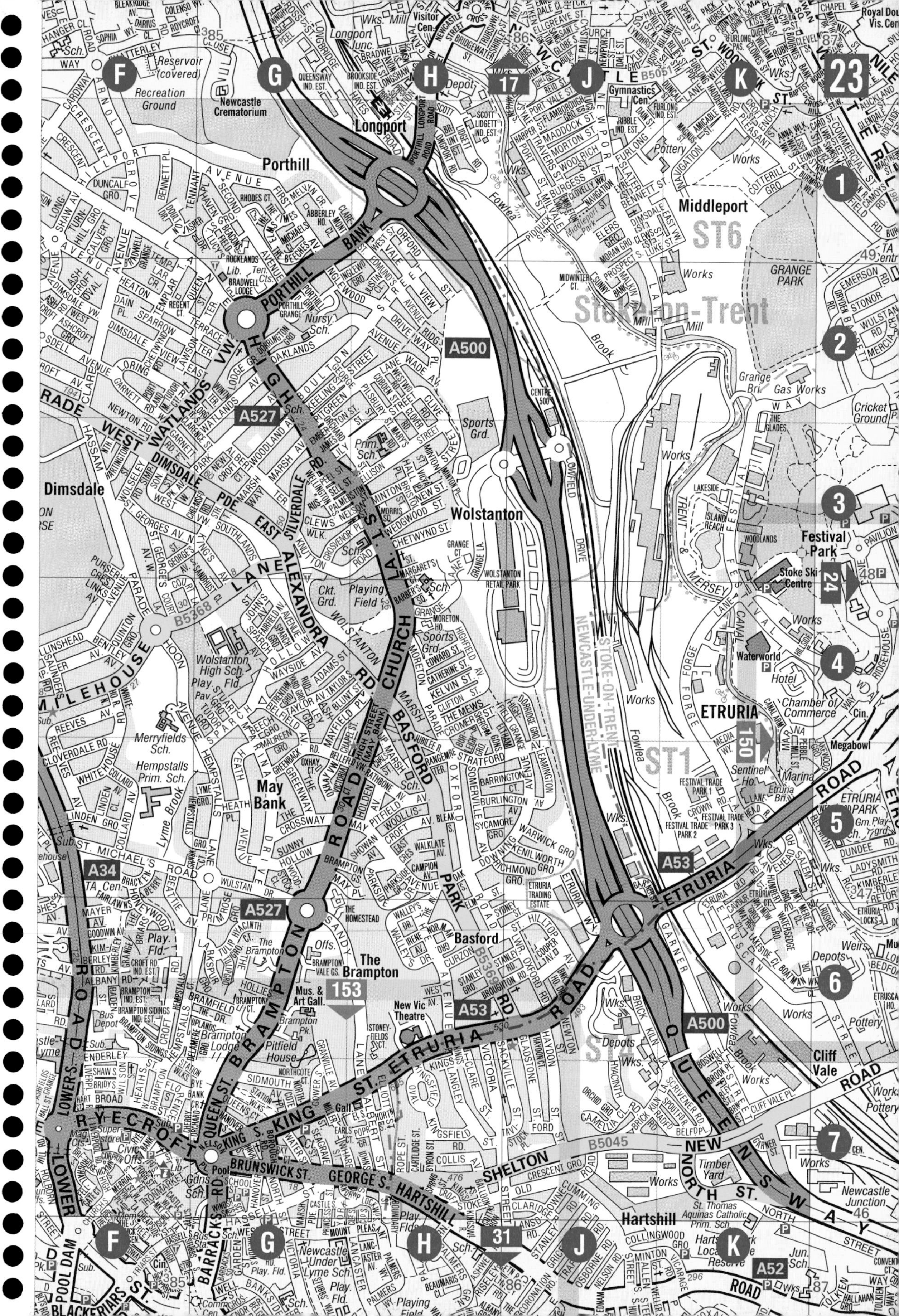
F
G
H
J
K
17
Longport
Porthill
Middleport
ST6
Stoke-on-Trent
Newcastle Crematorium
Recreation Ground
Reservoir (covered)
Visitor Cen.
Longport Junc.
Queensway Ind. Est.
Brookside Ind. Est.
Scott Lidgett Ind. Est.
Gymnastics Cen.
Ribble Ind. Est.
Pottery
Works
Grange Park
Grange Bri.
Gas Works
Cricket Ground
The Glades
Lakeside
Island Reach
Woodlands
Festival Park
Stoke Ski Centre
24
48
Waterworld
Hotel
Chamber of Commerce
Cin.
Megabowl
Etruria
150
Sentinel Ho.
Marina
Festival Trade Park 1
Festival Trade Park 2
Festival Trade Park 3
Etruria Park
Wolstanton
Wolstanton Retail Park
Sports Grd.
Centre 500
A500
A527
A53
A34
A52
B5051
B5368
B5369
B5045
Dimsdale
Watlands Vw.
West Dimsdale Pde.
East
High St.
Church La.
Alexandra Rd.
Porthill Bank
Porthill Grange
Bradwell Lodge
Nursy. Sch.
Prim. Sch.
Ckt. Grd.
Playing Field
Wolstanton High Sch. Play. Fld.
Merryfields Sch.
Hempstalls Prim. Sch.
Lyme Brook
May Bank
Basford
The Brampton
The Homestead
Mus. & Art Gall.
153
New Vic Theatre
Brampton Pk.
Pitfield House
Brampton Ind. Est.
Brampton Sidings Ind. Est.
Croft Rd. Ind. Est.
Bus Depot
Play. Fld.
Etruria Trading Estate
Brampton Road
Etruria Road
Queen St.
King St.
Ryecroft
Lower St.
Brunswick St.
George St.
Hartshill Rd.
Shelton
New
North St.
Queensway
Milehouse
Hoon
Lane
Stoke-on-Trent
Newcastle-under-Lyme
Fowlea Brook
ST1
ST4
Depots
Timber Yard
Hartshill
St. Thomas Aquinas Catholic Prim. Sch.
Hartshill Local Nature Reserve
Newcastle Under Lyme Sch.
Play. Fld.
Playing Fields
Civic Offs.
Pool Dam
Blackfriars
31
Cliff Vale
Newcastle Junction
Etruria Locks
Depots
1
2
3
4
5
6
7

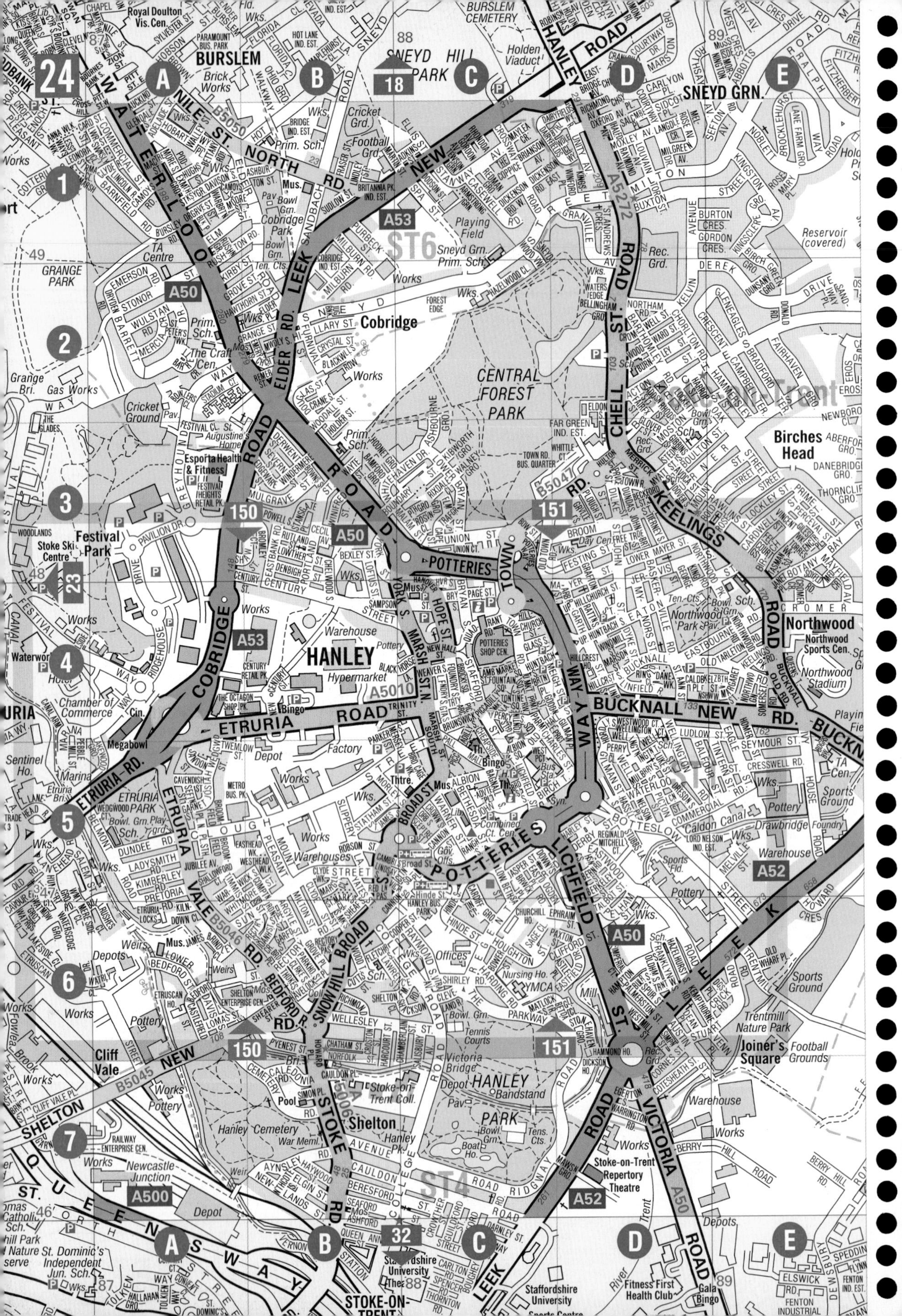

24
A
B
C
D
E
1
2
3
4
5
6
7
18
23
32
150
151
BURSLEM
Royal Doulton Vis. Cen.
Brick Works
BURSLEM CEMETERY
SNEYD HILL PARK
Holden Viaduct
SNEYD GRN.
NORTH RD.
NEW
HANLEY ROAD
WATERLOO ROAD
NILE ST.
B5050
A53
ST6
LEEK RD.
ELDER RD.
Cobridge Park
Cricket Grd.
Football Grd.
Playing Field
Sneyd Grn. Prim. Sch.
MILTON STREET
A5272
CHELL ST.
ROAD
Rec. Grd.
Reservoir (covered)
GRANGE PARK
TA Centre
A50
Cobridge
The Craft Cen.
Grange Bri.
Gas Works
Cricket Ground
CENTRAL FOREST PARK
FAR GREEN IND. EST.
TOWN RD. BUS. QUARTER
B5047
Stoke-on-Trent
Birches Head
Esporta Health & Fitness
FESTIVAL HEIGHTS RETAIL PK.
Festival Park
Stoke Ski Centre
CANAL
POTTERIES
TOWN
KEELINGS ROAD
HANLEY
Hypermarket
Warehouse
A5010
POTTERIES SHOP CEN.
Northwood
Northwood Sports Cen.
Northwood Stadium
Northwood Park
Chamber of Commerce
Megabowl
Bingo
ETRURIA ROAD
ETRURIA RD.
BUCKNALL NEW RD.
Sentinel Ho.
Marina
ETRURIA PARK
ETRURIA VALE
MARSH ST. S.
Depot
Factory
Works
Thtre.
POTTERIES WAY
LICHFIELD ST.
Caldon Canal
Drawbridge
Sports Ground
Pottery
A52
LEEK
Warehouses
Offices
Nursing Ho.
YMCA
Mill
Trentmill Nature Park
Joiner's Square
Football Grounds
Sports Ground
Weirs
B5046
BEDFORD RD.
SNOW HILL
BROAD ST.
Cliff Vale
NEW
B5045
SHELTON
Hanley Cemetery
War Meml.
Stoke-on-Trent Coll.
Shelton
Hanley Pk.
HANLEY PARK
Bandstand
Victoria Bridge
Tennis Courts
ST4
STOKE RD.
RIDGWAY
ROAD
VICTORIA ROAD
A50
Stoke-on-Trent Repertory Theatre
RAILWAY ENTERPRISE CEN.
Newcastle Junction
A500
QUEENSWAY
Staffordshire University
Fitness First Health Club
Gala Bingo
STOKE-ON-TRENT
FENTON INDUSTRIAL
Warehouse
Depots
River Trent
St. Dominic's Independent Jun. Sch.

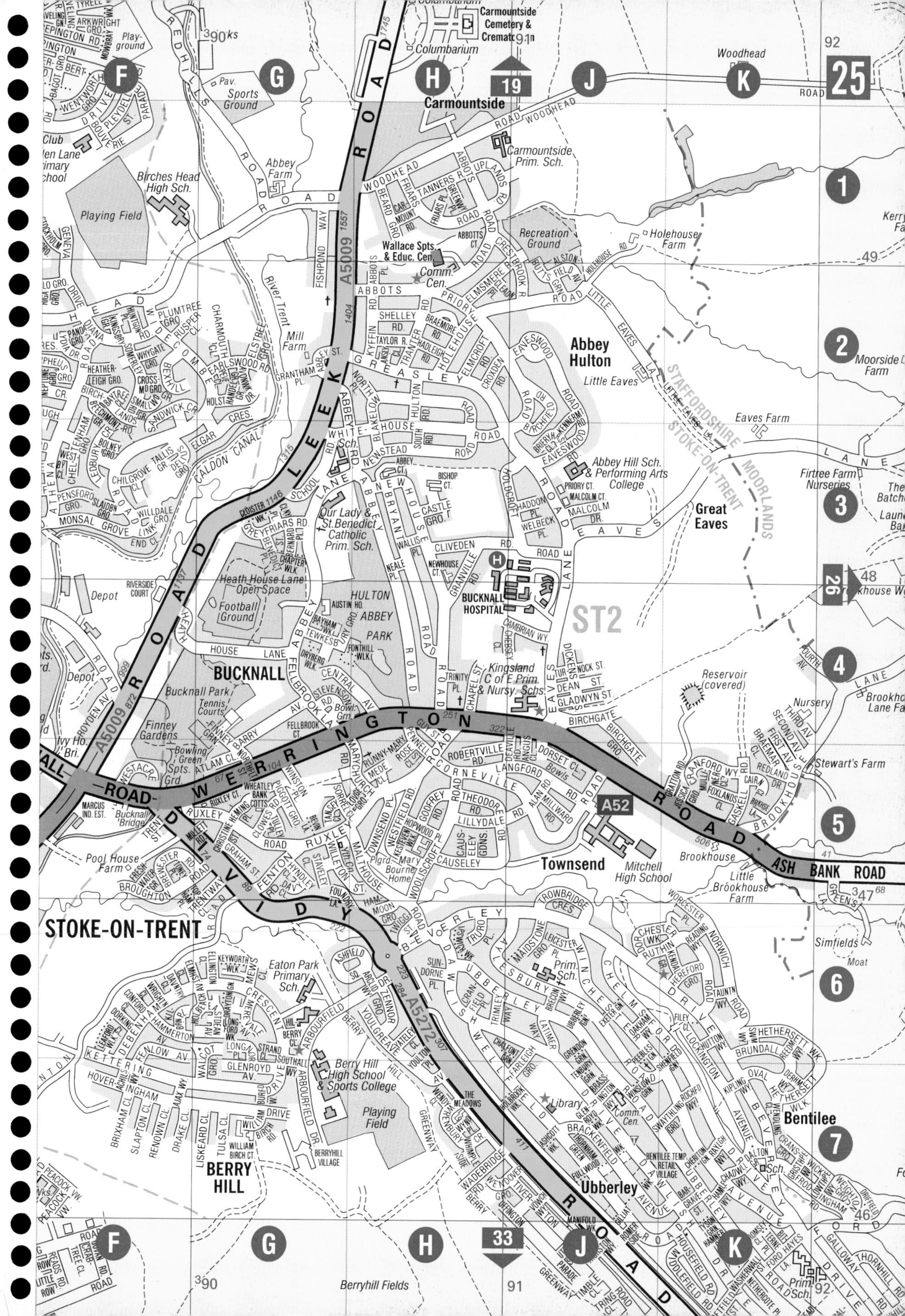
25
19
26
33
F
G
H
J
K
1
2
3
4
5
6
7
390
91
92
49
48
47
46
Carmountside Cemetery & Crematorium
Columbarium
Woodhead
WOODHEAD ROAD
Carmountside
Carmountside Prim. Sch.
Playground
Sports Ground
Pav.
Birches Head High Sch.
Playing Field
Abbey Farm
Recreation Ground
Holehouse Farm
Wallace Spts. & Educ. Cen.
Comm. Cen.
River Trent
Mill Farm
LEEK ROAD
A5009
Abbey Hulton
Little Eaves
Eaves Farm
Firtree Farm Nurseries
Moorside Farm
STAFFORDSHIRE MOORLANDS
STOKE-ON-TRENT
Great Eaves
Abbey Hill Sch. & Performing Arts College
Our Lady & St.Benedict Catholic Prim. Sch.
CALDON CANAL
Heath House Lane Open Space
Football Ground
Depot
RIVERSIDE COURT
HULTON ABBEY PARK
BUCKNALL HOSPITAL
ST2
BUCKNALL
Bucknall Park
Tennis Courts
Finney Gardens
Bowling Green
Spts. Grd.
Ivy Ho. Bri.
Kingsland C of E Prim. & Nursy. Schs.
Reservoir (covered)
Nursery
Brookhouse Lane Farm
Stewart's Farm
WERRINGTON ROAD
A52
ASH BANK ROAD
MARCUS IND. EST.
Bucknall Bridge
Pool House Farm
DAVIDSON ROAD
Townsend
Mitchell High School
Brookhouse
Little Brookhouse Farm
Simfields
Moat
Mary Bourne Home
Plgrd.
STOKE-ON-TRENT
Eaton Park Primary Sch.
Prim. Sch.
A5272
Berry Hill High School & Sports College
Playing Field
Library
Comm. Cen.
BENTILEE TEMP. RETAIL VILLAGE
Bentilee
BERRY HILL
BERRYHILL VILLAGE
Ubberley
Berryhill Fields
Prim. Sch.
ROAD

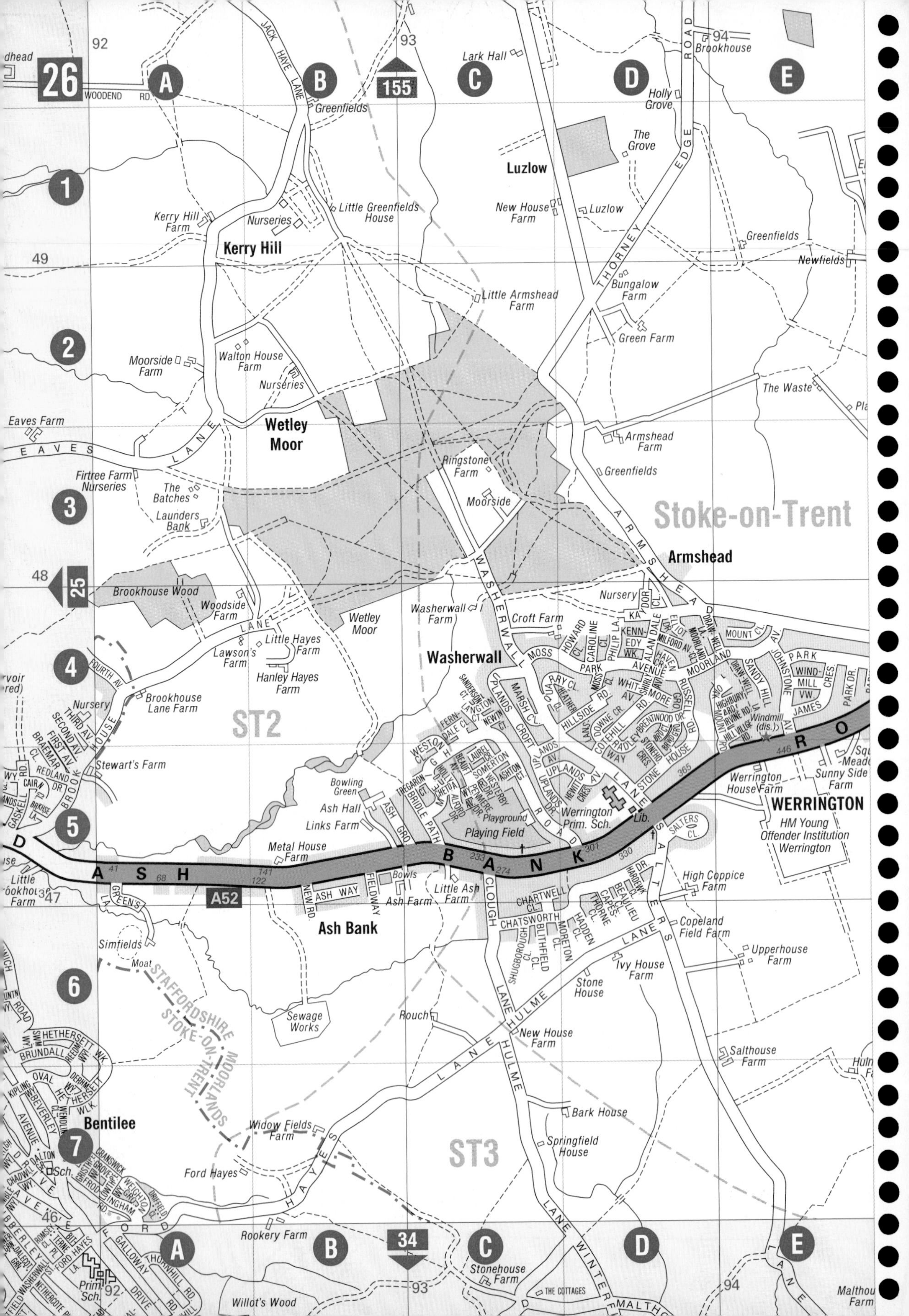
26
155
25
34
Kerry Hill
Wetley Moor
Luzlow
Armshead
Washerwall
Stoke-on-Trent
WERRINGTON
Ash Bank
Bentilee
ST2
ST3
ASH BANK RD
A52
Brookhouse Wood
Little Greenfields House
Little Armshead Farm
Walton House Farm
Kerry Hill Farm
Moorside Farm
Eaves Farm
Firtree Farm Nurseries
The Batches
Launders Bank
Woodside Farm
Little Hayes Farm
Lawson's Farm
Hanley Hayes Farm
Brookhouse Lane Farm
Stewart's Farm
Ringstone Farm
Moorside
Washerwall Farm
Croft Farm
Bungalow Farm
Green Farm
Armshead Farm
Greenfields
New House Farm
Holly Grove
The Grove
Brookhouse
Newfields
The Waste
Werrington Prim. Sch.
Playing Field
Werrington House Farm
HM Young Offender Institution Werrington
Sunny Side Farm
High Coppice Farm
Copeland Field Farm
Upperhouse Farm
Ivy House Farm
Stone House
New House Farm
Salthouse Farm
Bark House
Springfield House
Widow Fields Farm
Ford Hayes
Rookery Farm
Stonehouse Farm
Willot's Wood
Sewage Works
Simfields
Metal House Farm
Links Farm
Ash Hall
Ash Farm
Little Ash Farm
STAFFORDSHIRE MOORLANDS
STOKE-ON-TRENT

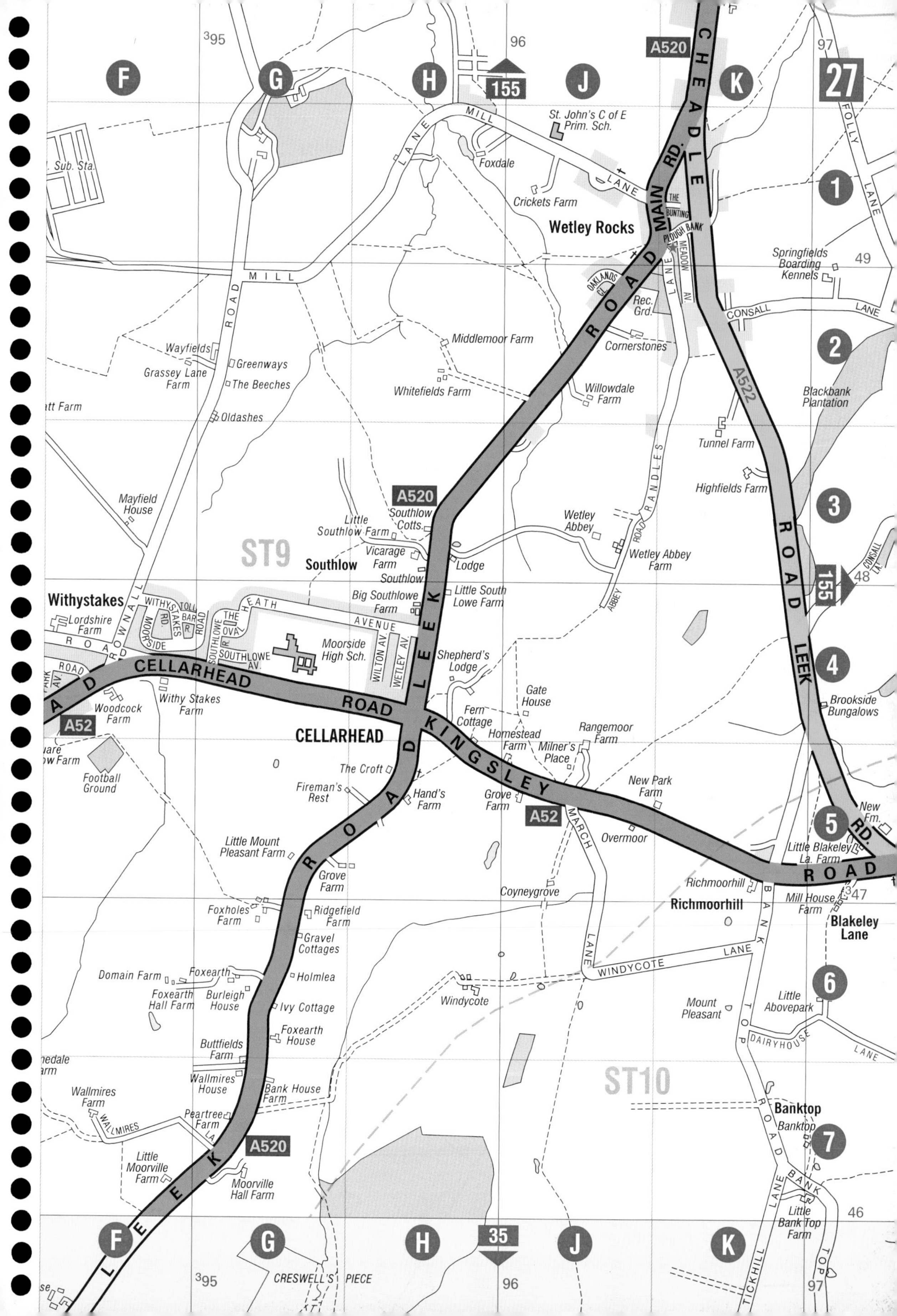

27
155
35
Wetley Rocks
Cellarhead
Withystakes
Southlow
Richmoorhill
Blakeley Lane
Banktop
ST9
ST10
A520
A52
A522
Cheadle Road
Main Rd.
Leek Road
Cellarhead Road
Kingsley Road
Mill Lane
Consall Lane
Folly Lane
Windycote Lane
Dairyhouse Lane
Randles Road
Abbey
St. John's C of E Prim. Sch.
Moorside High Sch.
Foxdale
Crickets Farm
Middlemoor Farm
Whitefields Farm
Willowdale Farm
Cornerstones
Tunnel Farm
Highfields Farm
Springfields Boarding Kennels
Blackbank Plantation
Wetley Abbey
Wetley Abbey Farm
Wayfields
Greenways
The Beeches
Grassey Lane Farm
Oldashes
Mayfield House
Little Southlow Farm
Southlow Cotts.
Vicarage Farm
Lodge
Big Southlowe Farm
Little South Lowe Farm
Lordshire Farm
Woodcock Farm
Withy Stakes Farm
Football Ground
Shepherd's Lodge
Gate House
Fern Cottage
Homestead Farm
Milner's Place
Rangemoor Farm
Brookside Bungalows
The Croft
Fireman's Rest
Hand's Farm
Grove Farm
New Park Farm
Overmoor
Little Mount Pleasant Farm
Coyneygrove
Little Blakeley La. Farm
Mill House Farm
Foxholes Farm
Ridgefield Farm
Gravel Cottages
Holmlea
Domain Farm
Foxearth
Foxearth Hall Farm
Burleigh House
Ivy Cottage
Windycote
Mount Pleasant
Little Abovepark
Foxearth House
Buttfields Farm
Wallmires House
Wallmires Farm
Bank House Farm
Peartree Farm
Little Moorville Farm
Moorville Hall Farm
Little Bank Top Farm
Creswell's Piece
Rec. Grd.
Sub. Sta.

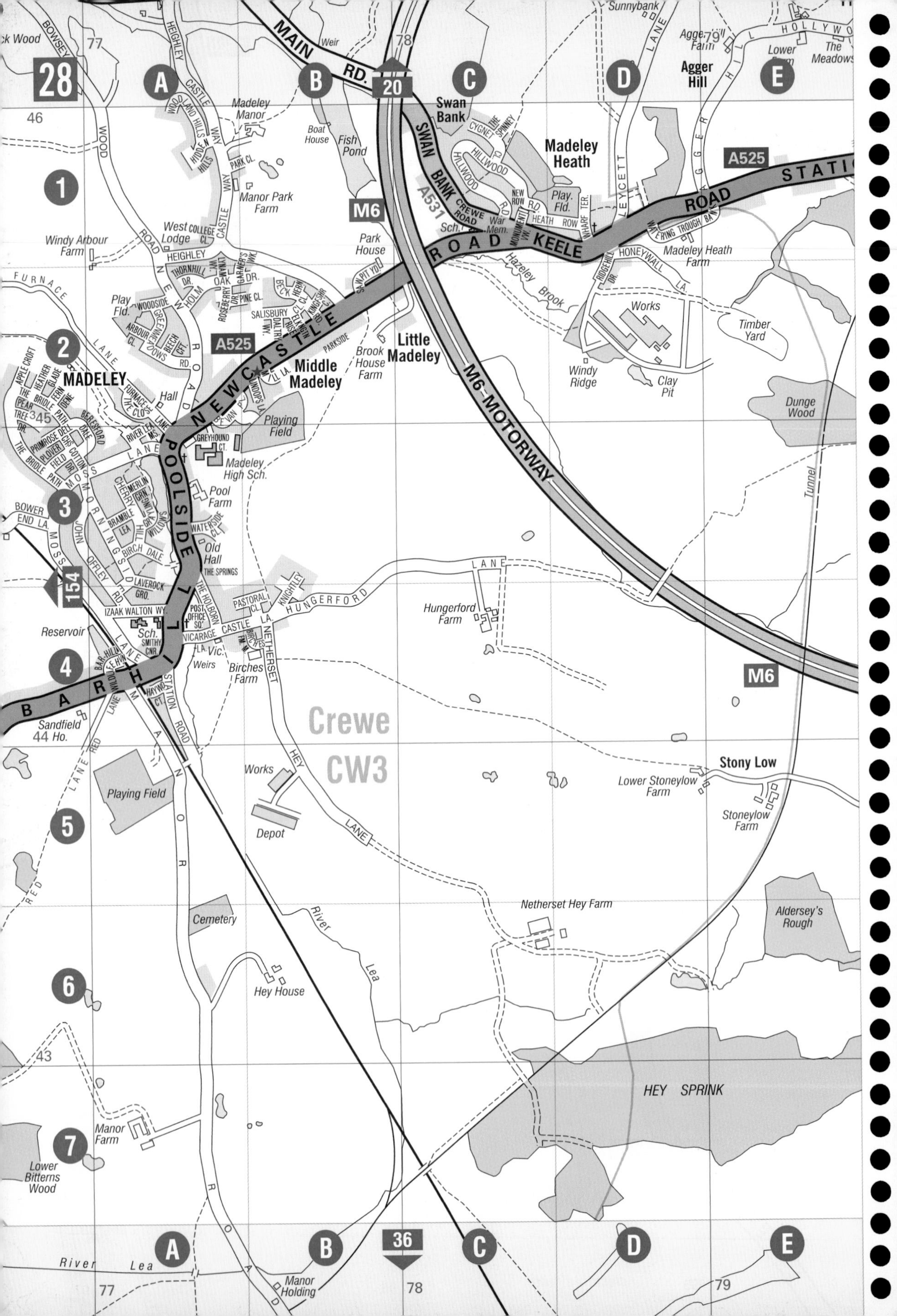
MADELEY
Middle Madeley
Little Madeley
Madeley Heath
Swan Bank
Agger Hill
Madeley Manor
Manor Park Farm
West Lodge
Windy Arbour Farm
Park House
Brook House Farm
Madeley Heath Farm
Works
Timber Yard
Windy Ridge
Clay Pit
Dunge Wood
Madeley High Sch.
Pool Farm
Old Hall
Hungerford Farm
Reservoir
Birches Farm
Sandfield Ho.
Playing Field
Depot
Stony Low
Lower Stoneylow Farm
Stoneylow Farm
Netherset Hey Farm
Aldersey's Rough
Cemetery
Hey House
HEY SPRINK
Manor Farm
Lower Bitterns Wood
Manor Holding
Crewe CW3
M6 MOTORWAY
A525
A531
NEWCASTLE ROAD
KEELE ROAD
STATION ROAD
POOLSIDE
BAR HILL
MANOR ROAD
HUNGERFORD LANE
NETHERSET HEY LANE
MOSS LANE
FURNACE LANE
River Lea
Tunnel
Boat House
Fish Pond
Sunnybank
Lower Farm
The Meadows
20
36
154

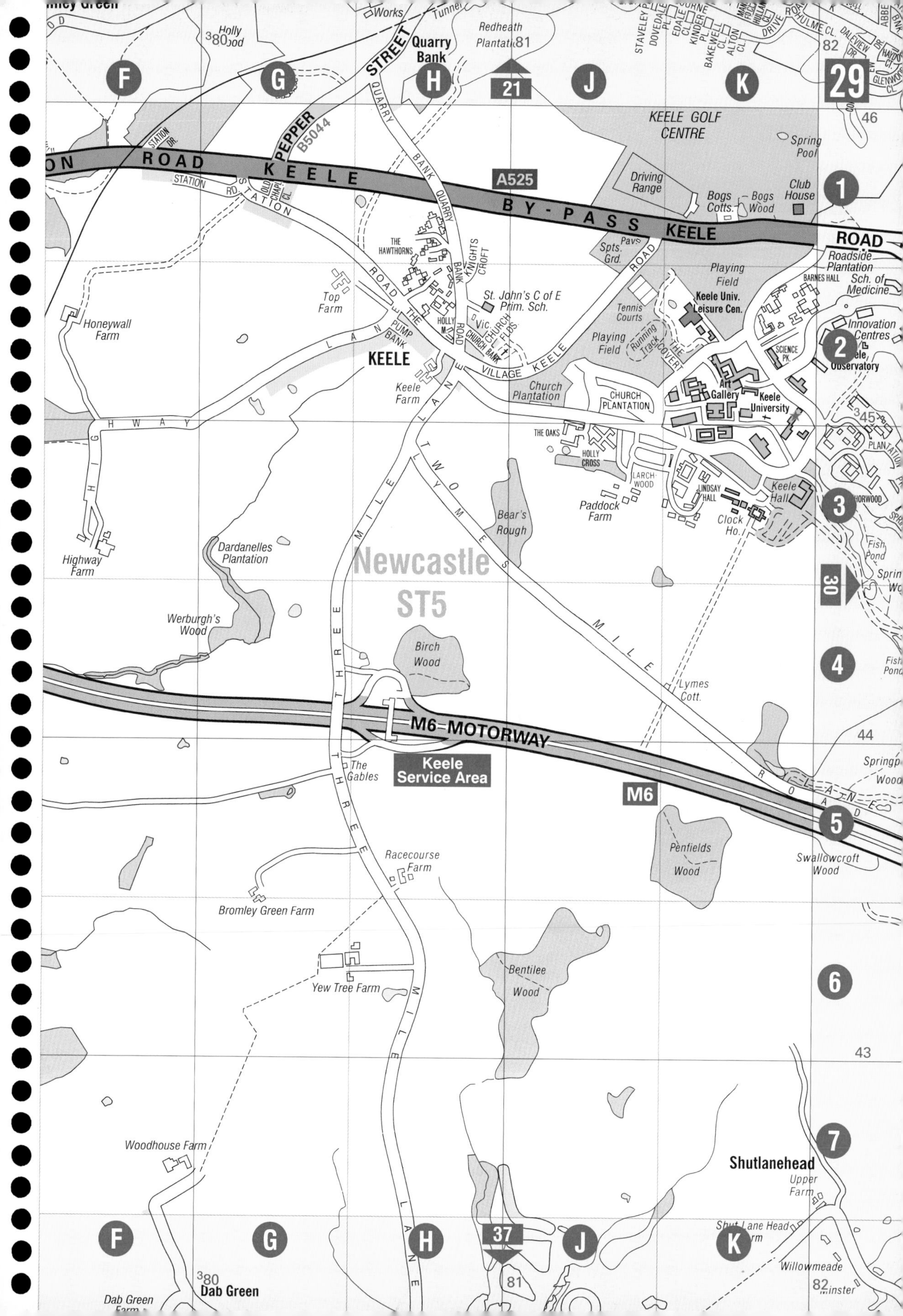
Quarry Bank
Redheath Plantation
21
KEELE GOLF CENTRE
Spring Pool
PEPPER STREET
B5044
QUARRY BANK
STATION RD
KEELE BY-PASS
A525
Driving Range
Bogs Cotts.
Bogs Wood
Club House
KEELE ROAD
Roadside Plantation
Sch. of Medicine
Innovation Centres
Playing Field
Keele Univ. Leisure Cen.
Tennis Courts
Running Track
THE COVERT
Spts. Grd.
Pavs
THE HAWTHORNS
KNIGHTS CROFT
Top Farm
St. John's C of E Prim. Sch.
Vic.
CHURCH BANK
Honeywall Farm
PUMP BANK
KEELE
VILLAGE
Keele Farm
Church Plantation
CHURCH PLANTATION
Art Gallery
Keele University
SCIENCE PK.
BARNES HALL
THE OAKS
HOLLY CROSS
LARCH-WOOD
LINDSAY HALL
Paddock Farm
Keele Hall
Clock Ho.
HIGHWAY
Highway Farm
Dardanelles Plantation
Bear's Rough
Newcastle ST5
TWO MILE LANE
LYMES ROAD
THREE MILE LANE
Werburgh's Wood
Birch Wood
Lymes Cott.
Fish Pond
M6 MOTORWAY
M6
The Gables
Keele Service Area
Penfields Wood
Swallowcroft Wood
Racecourse Farm
Bromley Green Farm
Yew Tree Farm
Bentilee Wood
Woodhouse Farm
Shutlanehead
Upper Farm
Willowmeade
Dab Green
Dab Green Farm
37
30
F G H J K
1 2 3 4 5 6 7
46 45 44 43
380 81 82

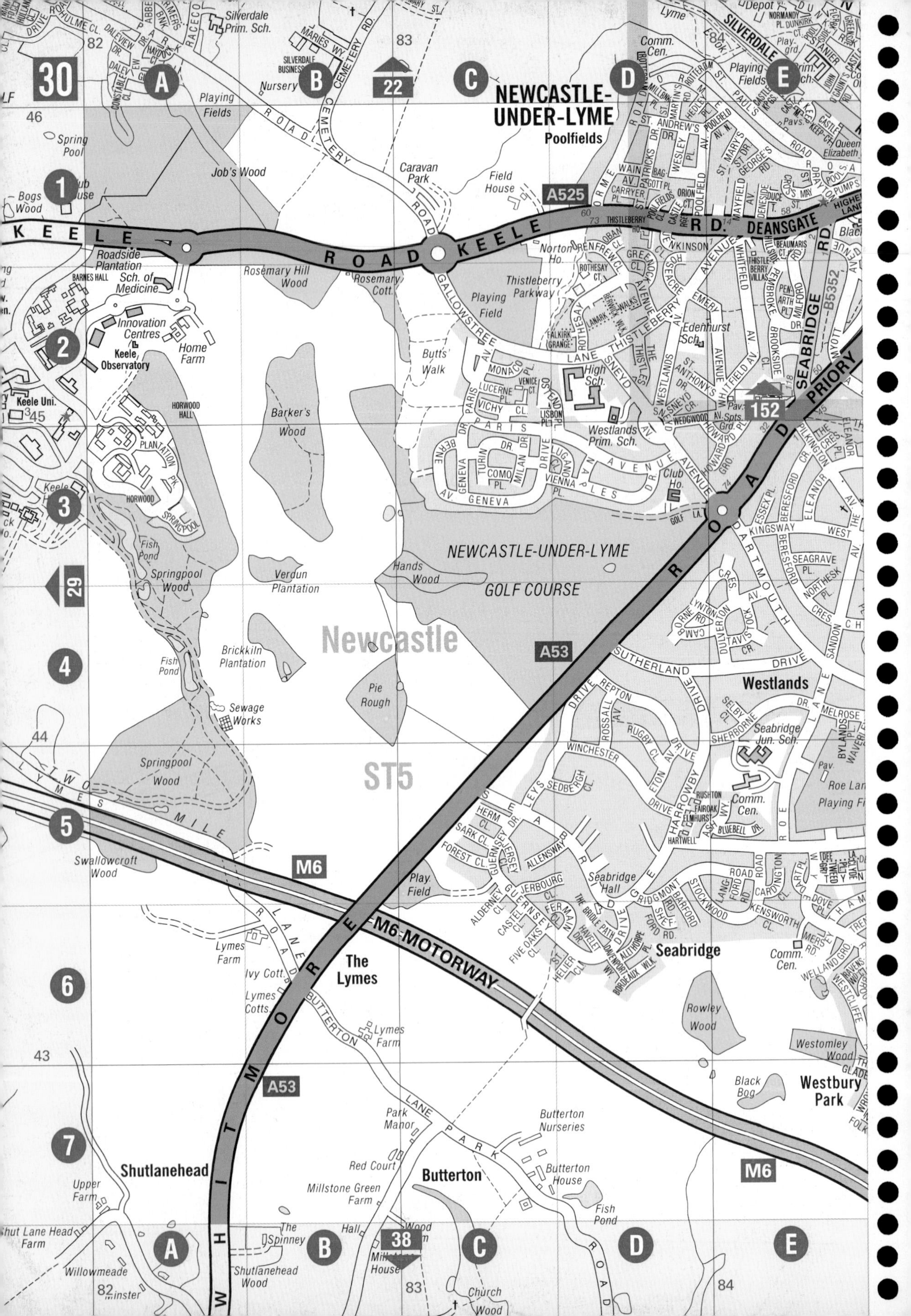
30
22
29
38
152
NEWCASTLE-UNDER-LYME
Poolfields
Keele Road
A525
A53
M6
M6 MOTORWAY
Deansgate
Seabridge
Priory Road
Whitmore Road
Newcastle
ST5
NEWCASTLE-UNDER-LYME GOLF COURSE
Westlands
Seabridge
The Lymes
Butterton
Shutlanehead
Westbury Park
Job's Wood
Barker's Wood
Springpool Wood
Verdun Plantation
Brickkiln Plantation
Pie Rough
Hands Wood
Rowley Wood
Keele Observatory
Keele Uni.
Sch. of Medicine
Innovation Centres
Home Farm
Sewage Works
Silverdale Prim. Sch.
Caravan Park
Rosemary Hill Wood
Swallowcroft Wood
Lymes Farm
Butterton Nurseries
Butterton House
Westlands Prim. Sch.
Seabridge Jun. Sch.
Seabridge Hall
Black Bog
Westomley Wood
Shutlanehead Wood
Church Wood

31
23
153
32
39
F
G
H
J
K
1
2
3
4
5
6
7
Hartshill
HARTSHILL ROAD
QUEENSWAY
A52
A34
A53
A519
A500
B5045
B5041
BLACKFRIARS RD.
LONDON ROAD
NEWCASTLE ROAD
CLAYTON ROAD
STONE ROAD
LONDON ROAD
LYME VALLEY PARKWAY
BRUNSWICK ST.
GEORGE S.
NORTH
Timber Yard
Works
St. Thomas Aquinas Catholic Prim. Sch.
Hartshill Park Local Nature Reserve
St. Dominic's Independent Jun. Sch.
OUTPATIENTS DEPT.
NORTH STAFFORDSHIRE ROYAL INFIRMARY
Stoke Cemetery
The Willows Prim. Sch.
St. Peter's C of E High Sch. & International Language Coll.
CITY GENERAL HOSPITAL
Maternity Unit
Nurses Res.
Clinical Educ. Cen.
HARPLANDS HOSPITAL
Newcastle Under Lyme Sch.
Playing Field
Superstore
Cemetery
Friarswood Prim. Sch.
The Coppice School
Tennis Courts
Football Grd.
Total Fitness
Springfields
Stoke-on-Trent
Football Ground
Clayton Sports Cen.
Bakery
Superstore
Thistley Hough High Sch.
Playing Fields
Langdale Inf. Sch.
Nursy. Sch.
Clayton
Lib.
Our Lady & St. Werburghs RC Prim. Sch.
HOSP.
Clayton High Sch.
Clayton Fm.
Dark Wood
Fox Covert
Leas Wood
Claytonwood Farm
Athletic Track
Sports Club
Playing Flds
Hanford Bridge
Trent Vale Pumping Sta.
St. Joseph's Playing Fields
Oak Hill
Oakhill Primary School
Trent Vale
St. Joseph's Prep. Sch.
Warehouse
Factory
NEWCASTLE-UNDER-LYME
STOKE-ON-TRENT
Lyme Brook
RIVER TRENT
Northwood
ST4
Penkhull

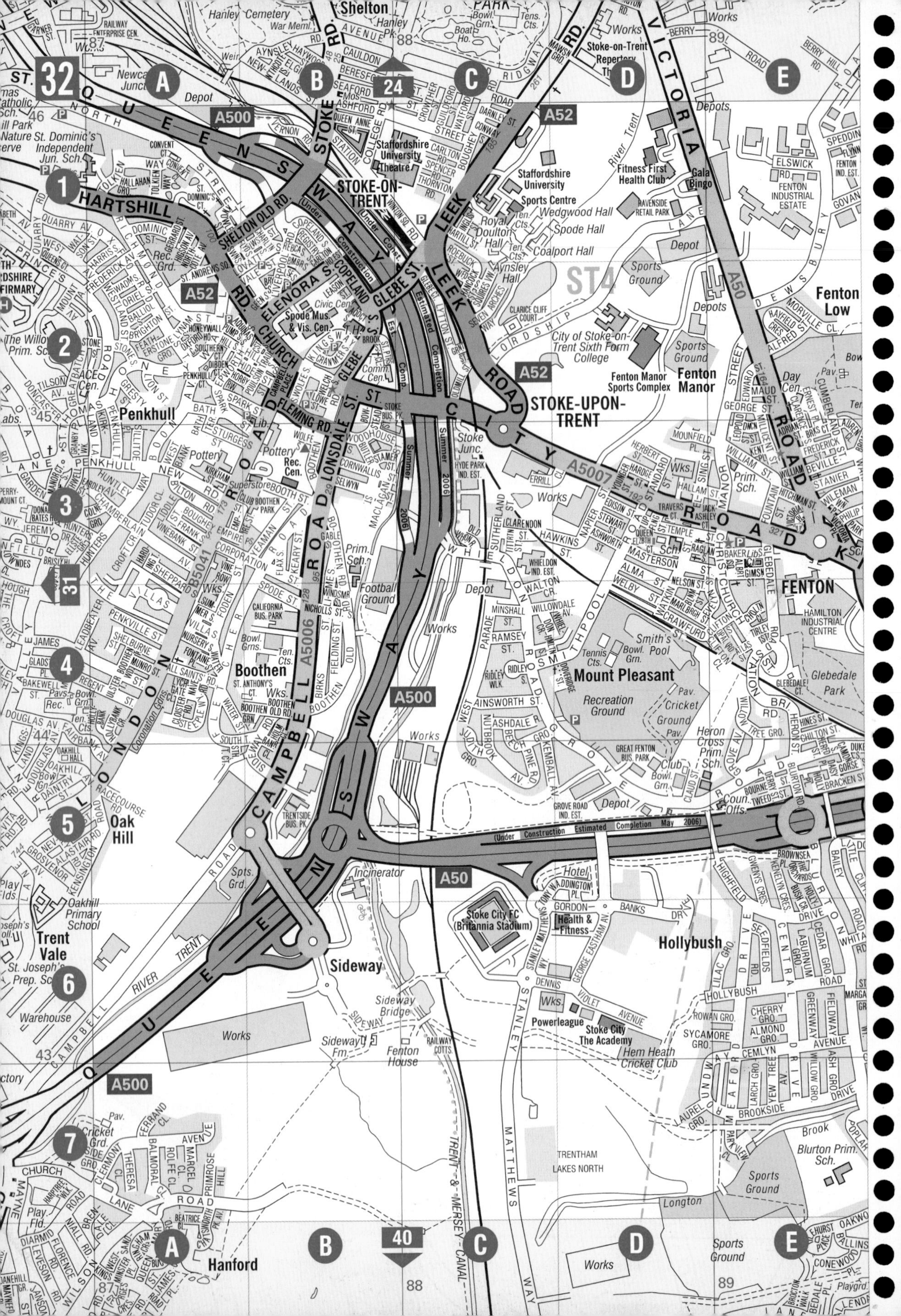
32
A
B
C
D
E
1
2
3
4
5
6
7
24
31
40
87
88
89
Shelton
Hanley Cemetery
War Meml.
Hanley Pk.
Works
Stoke-on-Trent Repertory Th.
Depot
A500
A52
A50
A5007
A5006
B5041
QUEENSWAY
HARTSHILL RD.
STOKE RD.
LEEK RD.
VICTORIA RD.
ST. DOMINIC'S Independent Jun. Sch.
Staffordshire University Theatre
STOKE-ON-TRENT
Staffordshire University
Sports Centre
Royal Doulton Hall
Wedgwood Hall
Spode Hall
Coalport Hall
Aynsley Hall
Fitness First Health Club
RAVENSIDE RETAIL PARK
Gala Bingo
Depots
FENTON INDUSTRIAL ESTATE
ST4
Sports Ground
City of Stoke-on-Trent Sixth Form College
Fenton Manor Sports Complex
Fenton Manor
Fenton Low
STOKE-UPON-TRENT
CITY ROAD
Spode Mus. & Vis. Cen.
Civic Cen.
Penkhull
Pottery
Rec. Cen.
Superstore
Stoke Junc.
HYDE PARK IND. EST.
The Willows Prim. Sch.
Football Ground
WHIELDON IND. EST.
Boothen
CALIFORNIA BUS. PARK
Mount Pleasant
Smith's Pool
Recreation Ground
Cricket Ground
Heron Cross Prim. Sch.
FENTON
HAMILTON INDUSTRIAL CENTRE
Glebedale Park
GREAT FENTON BUS. PARK
GROVE ROAD IND. EST.
Coun. Offs.
(Under Construction Estimated Completion May 2006)
Incinerator
Oak Hill
Oakhill Primary School
Trent Vale
St. Joseph's Prep. Sch.
Warehouse
Spts. Grd.
Sideway
Stoke City FC (Britannia Stadium)
Health & Fitness
Hotel
Hollybush
Powerleague
Stoke City The Academy
Hem Heath Cricket Club
Sideway Bridge
Sideway Fm.
Fenton House
RAILWAY COTTS.
TRENT & MERSEY CANAL
STANLEY MATTHEWS WAY
TRENTHAM LAKES NORTH
Blurton Prim. Sch.
Sports Ground
Longton
Brook
Cricket Grd.
Hanford
Works

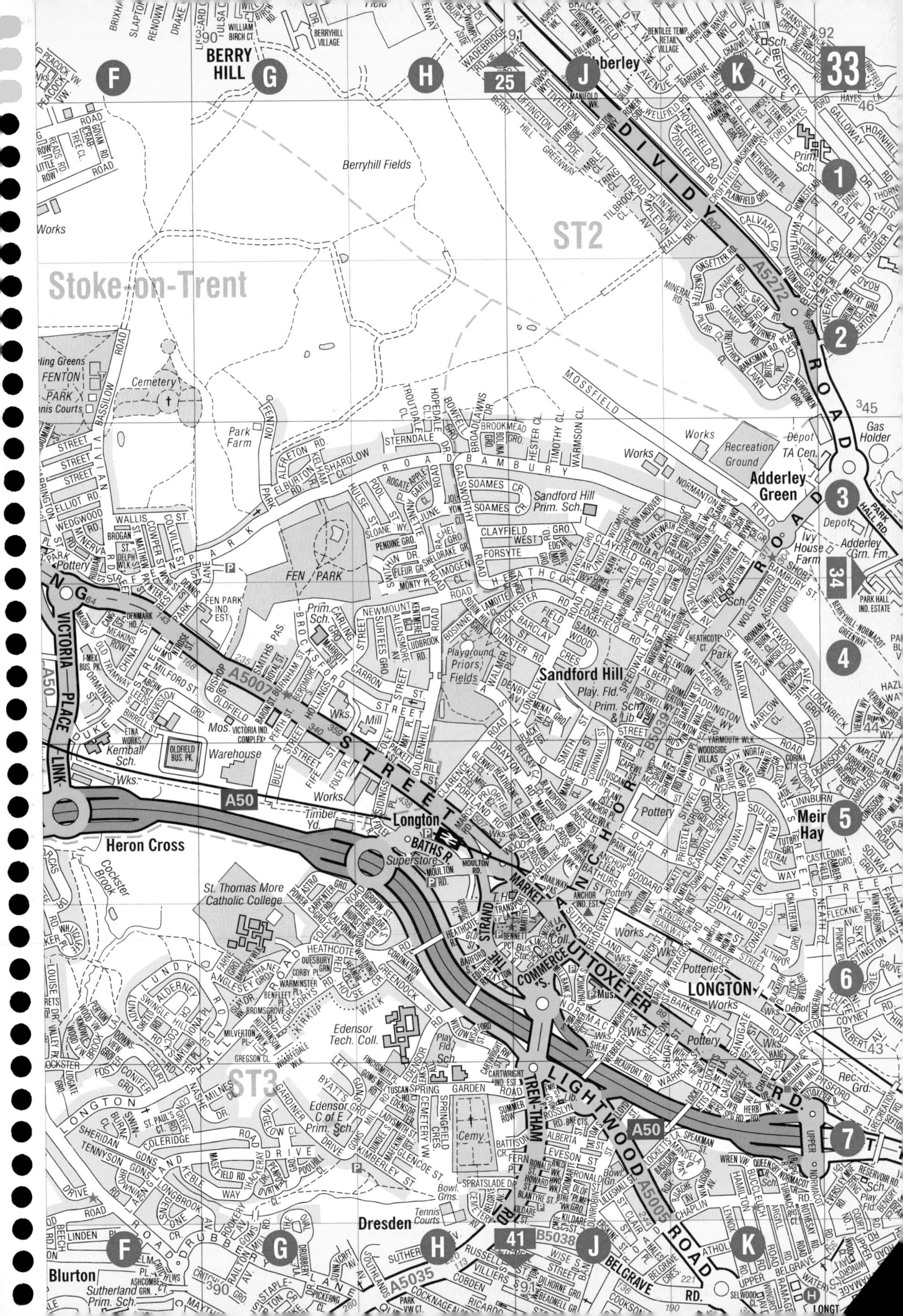
33
Berryhill Fields
Stoke-on-Trent
ST2
ST3
BERRY HILL
Sandford Hill
Adderley Green
Meir Hay
Heron Cross
LONGTON
Longton
Dresden
Blurton
DIVIDY ROAD
A5272
A5007
A50
A5005
A5035
B5039
B5038
25
34
41

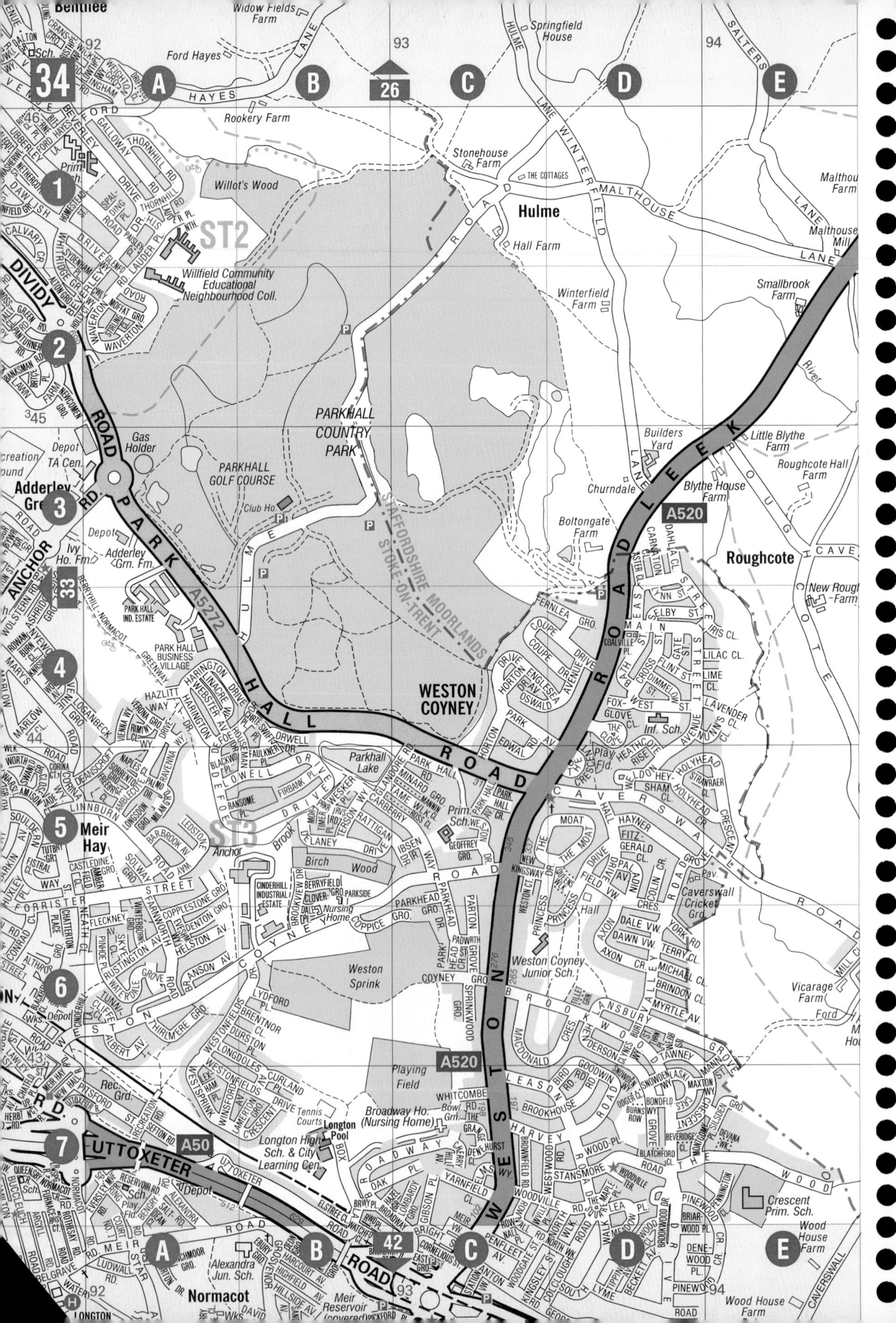
Widow Fields Farm
Springfield House
Ford Hayes
HAYES LANE
26
Rookery Farm
Stonehouse Farm
THE COTTAGES
Hulme
MALTHOUSE LANE
Malthouse Farm
Malthouse Mill
Willot's Wood
ST2
Hall Farm
WINTERFIELD LANE
Willfield Community Educational Neighbourhood Coll.
Winterfield Farm
Smallbrook Farm
DIVIDY
PARKHALL COUNTRY PARK
Gas Holder
PARKHALL GOLF COURSE
Builders Yard
Little Blythe Farm
Roughcote Hall Farm
Blythe House Farm
Churndale
Club Ho.
Adderley Grn. Fm.
Adderley Green
ANCHOR RD.
Ivy Ho. Fm.
STAFFORDSHIRE MOORLANDS
STOKE-ON-TRENT
Boltongate Farm
A520
LEEK ROAD
Roughcote
New Roughcote Farm
33
PARK HALL IND. ESTATE
PARK HALL BUSINESS VILLAGE
A5272
PARK HALL ROAD
WESTON COYNEY
Inf. Sch.
Parkhall Lake
Meir Hay
ST3
Anchor
Birch Wood
Prim. Sch.
CINDERHILL INDUSTRIAL ESTATE
Nursing Home
Caverswall Cricket Grd.
Weston Coyney Junior Sch.
Weston Sprink
CAVERSWALL ROAD
Vicarage Farm
Playing Field
WESTON ROAD
Rec. Grd.
Tennis Courts
Longton Pool
Broadway Ho. (Nursing Home)
Longton High Sch. & City Learning Cen.
UTTOXETER ROAD
A50
Crescent Prim. Sch.
Wood House Farm
42
Alexandra Jun. Sch.
Normacot
Meir Reservoir (covered)
92
93
94
A
B
C
D
E
1
2
3
4
5
6
7

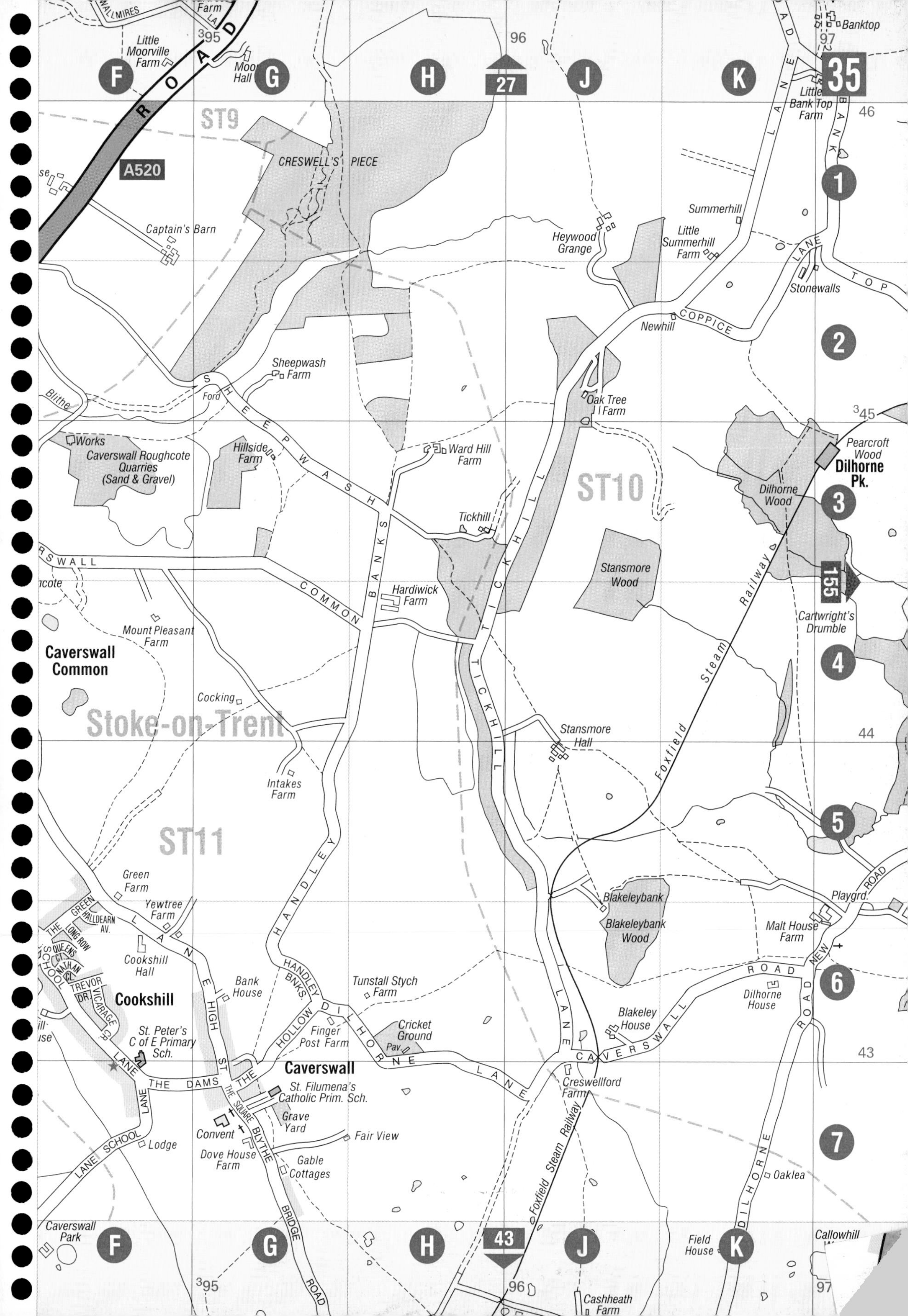

Dilhorne Pk.

ST9
ST10
ST11

A520

Stoke-on-Trent

Caverswall Common

Cookshill

Caverswall

Caverswall Park

Grid labels (top): F G H 27 J K 35
Grid labels (bottom): F G 43 H J K
Numbers (right side): 1 2 3 155 4 5 6 7

Little Moorville Farm
Moor Hall
Creswell's Piece
Captain's Barn
Heywood Grange
Little Summerhill Farm
Summerhill
Stonewalls
Newhill
COPPICE LANE
BANK TOP LANE
Banktop
Little Bank Top Farm
46
96
97
45
44
43

Sheepwash Farm
Ford
Blithe
Works
Caverswall Roughcote Quarries (Sand & Gravel)
Hillside Farm
Ward Hill Farm
Oak Tree Farm
Tickhill
Hardiwick Farm
SHEEPWASH BANKS
COMMON
TICKHILL
Stansmore Wood
Dilhorne Wood
Pearcroft Wood
Cartwright's Drumble
Foxfield Steam Railway

Mount Pleasant Farm
Cocking
Intakes Farm
Green Farm
Yewtree Farm
Cookshill Hall
Bank House
Handley BNKS
HANDLEY LANE
HIGH ST
HOLLOW
DILHORNE LANE
Tunstall Stych Farm
Finger Post Farm
Cricket Ground
Pav
Stansmore Hall
Blakeleybank
Blakeleybank Wood
Blakeley House
Malt House Farm
Dilhorne House
Playgrd.
NEW ROAD
CAVERSWALL LANE
Creswellford Farm
Dove House Farm
Convent
St. Filumena's Catholic Prim. Sch.
St. Peter's C of E Primary Sch.
Grave Yard
Gable Cottages
Fair View
THE SQUARE
THE DAMS
SCHOOL LANE
LANE
HIGH ST
BRIDGE ROAD
BLYTHE
Lodge
Field House
Oaklea
Callowhill
Cashheath Farm
DILHORNE ROAD
395
96
97

395

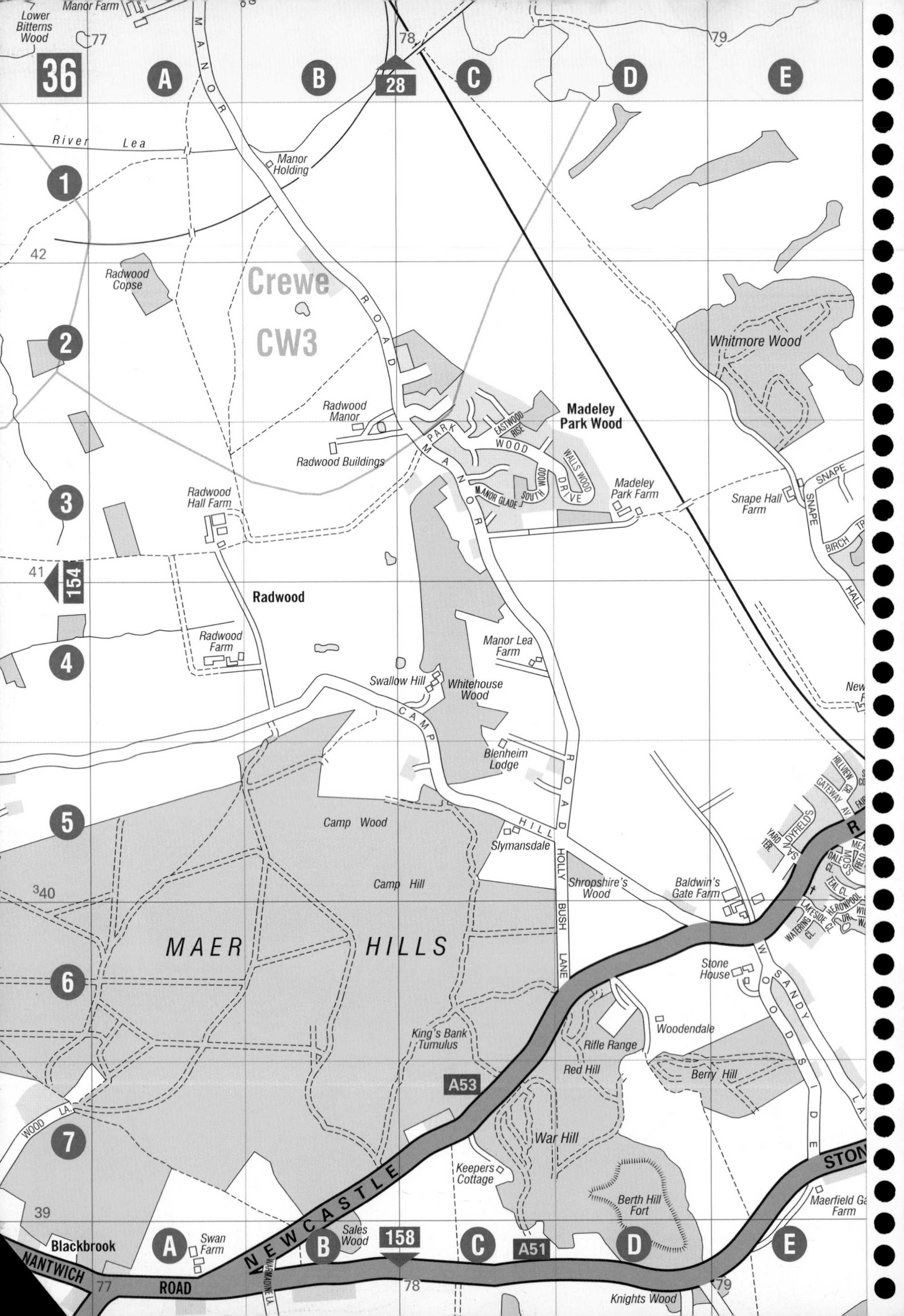
Lower Bitterns Wood
Manor Farm
77
78
79
A
B
C
D
E
28
River Lea
Manor Holding
MANOR ROAD
1
42
Radwood Copse
Crewe
CW3
2
Whitmore Wood
Radwood Manor
Radwood Buildings
PARK
EASTWOOD RISE
WOOD
Madeley Park Wood
WALLS WOOD DRIVE
SOUTH WOOD
MANOR GLADE
MANOR
Madeley Park Farm
SNAPE
Snape Hall Farm
BIRCH
HALL
3
Radwood Hall Farm
41
154
Radwood
Radwood Farm
4
Manor Lea Farm
Swallow Hill
Whitehouse Wood
CAMP
Blenheim Lodge
ROAD
5
Camp Wood
HILL
Slymansdale
HOLLY BUSH LANE
Shropshire's Wood
Baldwin's Gate Farm
340
Camp Hill
MAER HILLS
6
Stone House
WOODSIDE
SANDY
Woodendale
King's Bank Tumulus
Rifle Range
Red Hill
Berry Hill
A53
WOOD LA.
7
War Hill
Keepers Cottage
NEWCASTLE
Berth Hill Fort
STONE
Maerfield Ga Farm
39
Blackbrook
Swan Farm
Sales Wood
158
A51
NANTWICH ROAD
WARMADINE LA.
Knights Wood

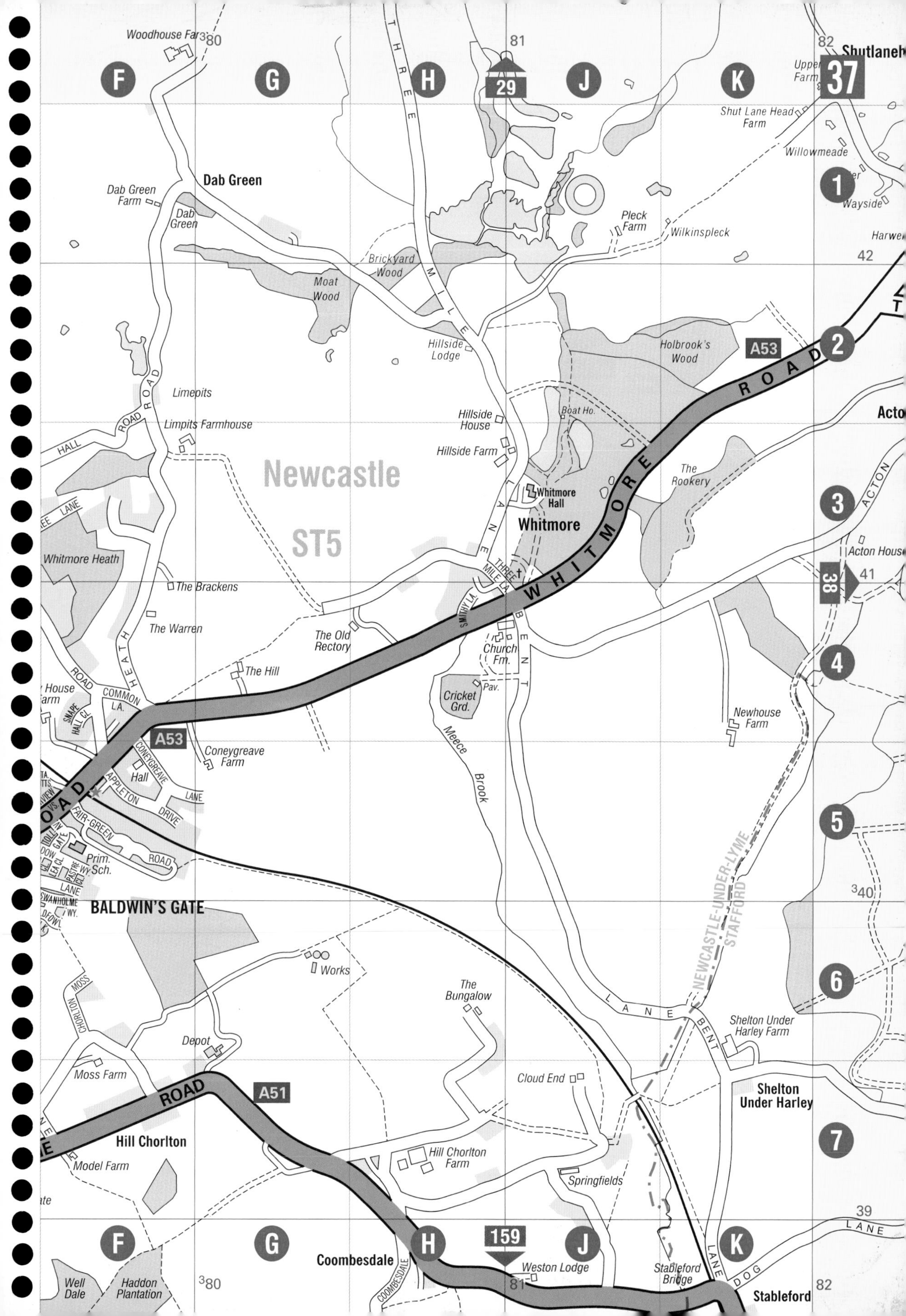

37
F
G
H
J
K
29
159
38
Shutlaneh
Woodhouse Farm
Upper Farm
Shut Lane Head Farm
Willowmeade
Wayside
Harwe
Dab Green
Dab Green Farm
Pleck Farm
Wilkinspleck
Brickyard Wood
Moat Wood
Hillside Lodge
Holbrook's Wood
A53
WHITMORE ROAD
THREE MILE LANE
Limepits
Limpits Farmhouse
HALL ROAD
Boat Ho.
Hillside House
Hillside Farm
Acto
Newcastle
ST5
The Rookery
Whitmore Hall
Whitmore
ACTON
Acton House
Whitmore Heath
The Brackens
The Warren
SMITHY LA.
The Old Rectory
BENT LANE
Church Fm.
The Hill
HEATH ROAD
COMMON LA.
SNAPE HALL CL.
Cricket Grd.
Pav.
Newhouse Farm
Meece Brook
Coneygreave Farm
CONEYGREAVE LANE
APPLETON DRIVE
Hall
FAIR-GREEN ROAD
Prim. Sch.
BALDWIN'S GATE
SWANHOLME WY.
NEWCASTLE-UNDER-LYME
STAFFORD
Works
The Bungalow
CHORLTON MOSS
Depot
Moss Farm
Shelton Under Harley Farm
Cloud End
Shelton Under Harley
A51
ROAD
Hill Chorlton
Model Farm
Hill Chorlton Farm
Springfields
DOG LANE
Coombesdale
COOMBESDALE
Weston Lodge
Stableford Bridge
Stableford
Well Dale
Haddon Plantation
80
81
82
42
41
40
39
1
2
3
4
5
6
7

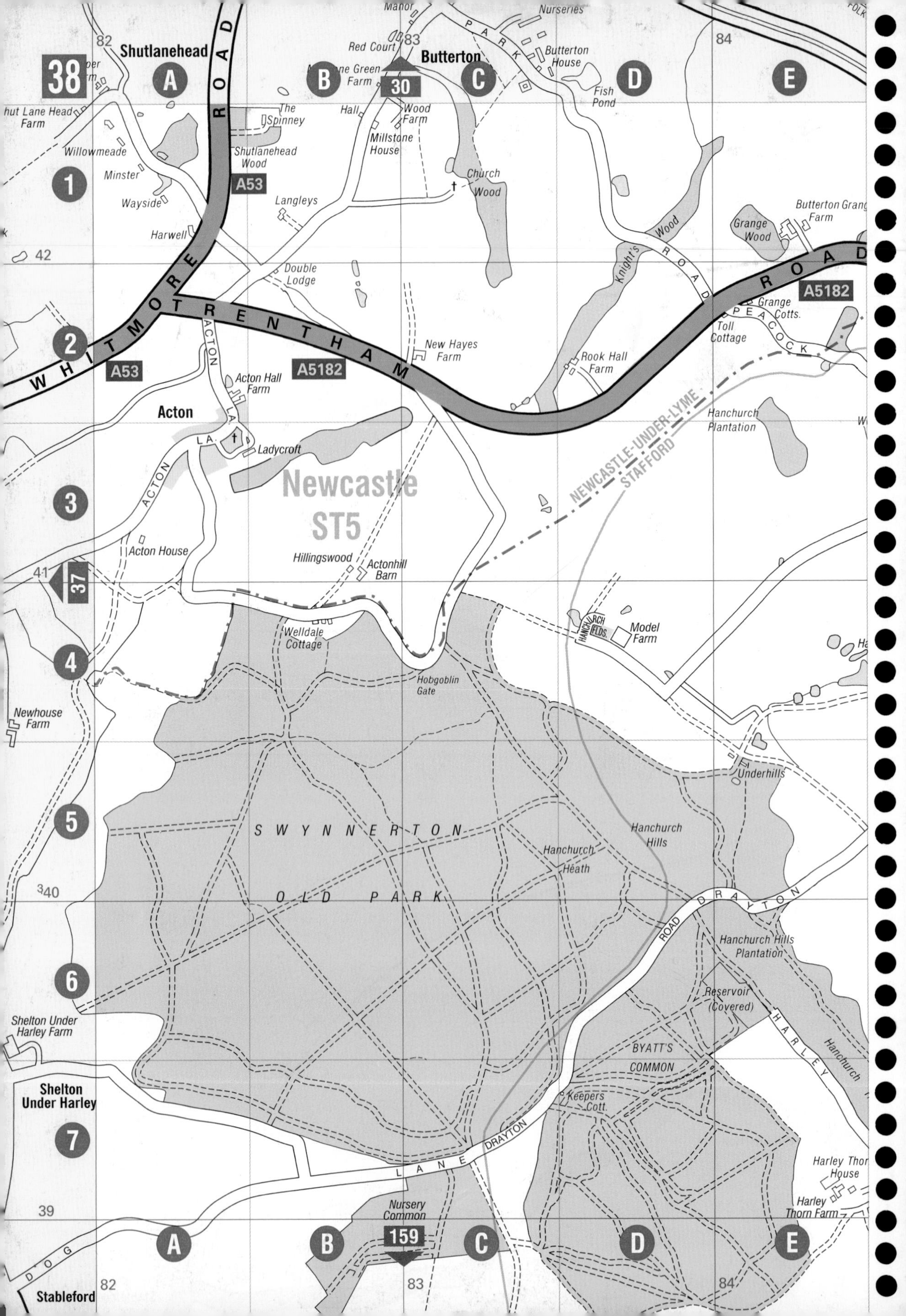
Shutlanehead
Butterton
Nurseries
Manor
Red Court
Butterton House
Fish Pond
Shut Lane Head Farm
The Spinney
Hall
Wood Farm
Millstone House
Willowmeade
Minster
Shutlanehead Wood
Church Wood
Wayside
Langleys
Harwell
Double Lodge
Knight's Wood
Butterton Grange Farm
Grange Wood
WHITMORE ROAD
TRENTHAM ROAD
A53
A5182
PARK
Grange Cotts.
Toll Cottage
PEACOCK
New Hayes Farm
Rook Hall Farm
ACTON LANE
Acton Hall Farm
Acton
Ladycroft
Hanchurch Plantation
Newcastle
ST5
NEWCASTLE-UNDER-LYME
STAFFORD
Acton House
Hillingswood
Actonhill Barn
HANCHURCH FLDS.
Model Farm
Welldale Cottage
Hobgoblin Gate
Newhouse Farm
Underhills
SWYNNERTON
OLD PARK
Hanchurch Hills
Hanchurch Heath
DRAYTON ROAD
Hanchurch Hills Plantation
Reservoir (Covered)
HARLEY
Hanchurch
Shelton Under Harley Farm
BYATT'S COMMON
Keepers Cott.
Shelton Under Harley
DRAYTON LANE
Harley Thorn House
Harley Thorn Farm
Nursery Common
DOG
Stableford
A B C D E
1 2 3 4 5 6 7
82 83 84
42 41 340 39
30 37 159

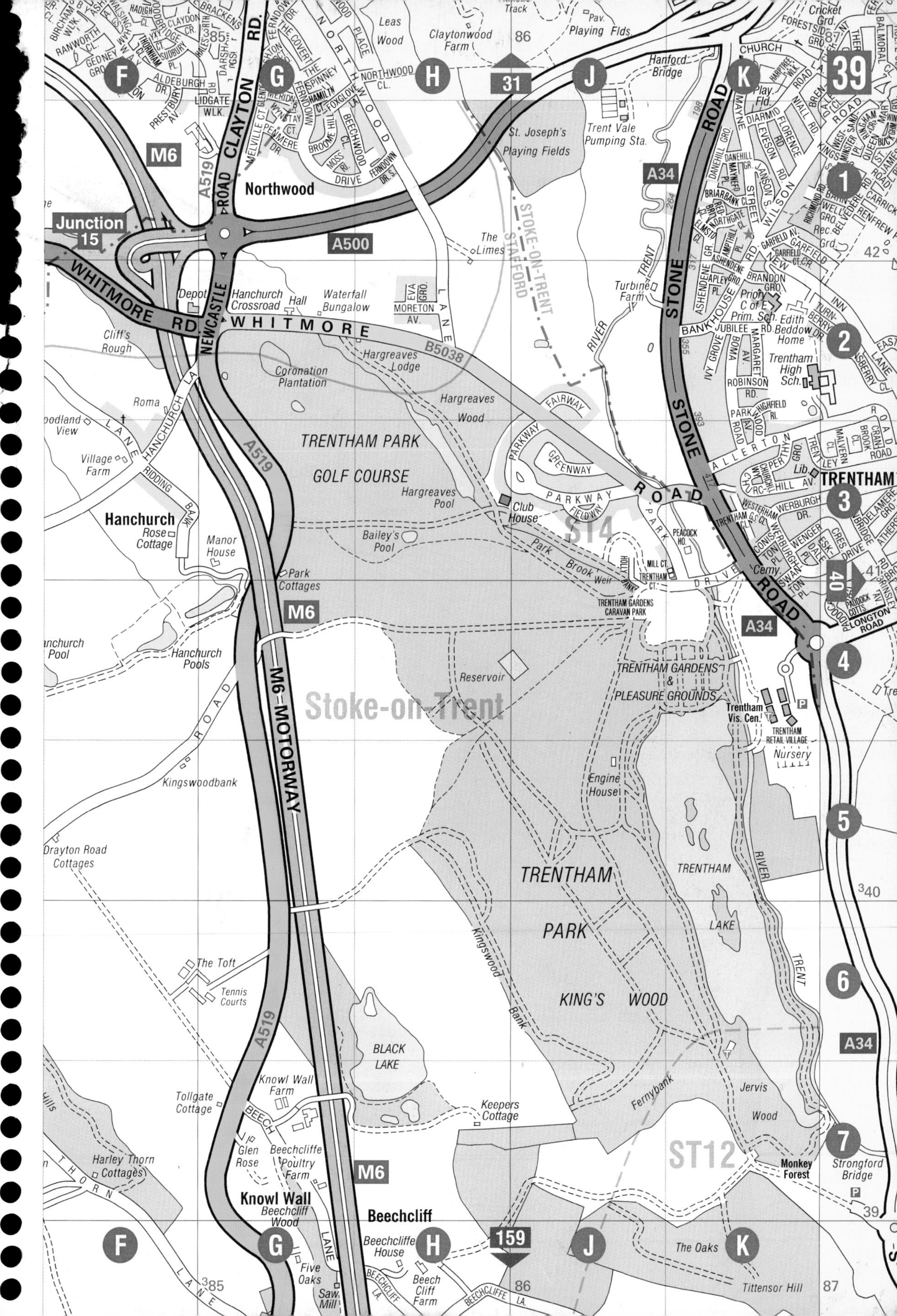

39
Northwood
Junction 15
WHITMORE RD.
NEWCASTLE ROAD
CLAYTON RD.
A500
A519
M6
M6 MOTORWAY
B5038
Hanchurch
Hanchurch Crossroad
TRENTHAM PARK GOLF COURSE
Coronation Plantation
Hargreaves Wood
Hargreaves Pool
Bailey's Pool
Club House
ST4
St. Joseph's Playing Fields
Trent Vale Pumping Sta.
Hanford Bridge
Claytonwood Farm
Leas Wood
STOKE-ON-TRENT STAFFORD
A34
STONE ROAD
TRENTHAM
Trentham High Sch.
Edith Beddow Home
Priory C of E Prim. Sch.
Turbine Farm
TRENTHAM GARDENS CARAVAN PARK
TRENTHAM GARDENS & PLEASURE GROUNDS
Trentham Vis. Cen.
TRENTHAM RETAIL VILLAGE
Nursery
Reservoir
Stoke-on-Trent
Engine House
TRENTHAM PARK
KING'S WOOD
TRENTHAM LAKE
RIVER TRENT
Kingswood Bank
Fernybank
Jervis Wood
ST12
Monkey Forest
Strongford Bridge
BLACK LAKE
Keepers Cottage
Knowl Wall Farm
Knowl Wall
Beechcliff
Beechcliff Wood
Beechcliffe House
Beech Cliff Farm
Five Oaks
Saw Mill
The Oaks
Tittensor Hill
Tollgate Cottage
Glen Rose
Beechcliffe Poultry Farm
Harley Thorn Cottages
The Toft
Tennis Courts
Drayton Road Cottages
Kingswoodbank
Hanchurch Pools
Manor House
Rose Cottage
Village Farm
Roma
Cliff's Rough
Park Cottages
31
40
159
F G H J K
1 2 3 4 5 6 7
385 86 87

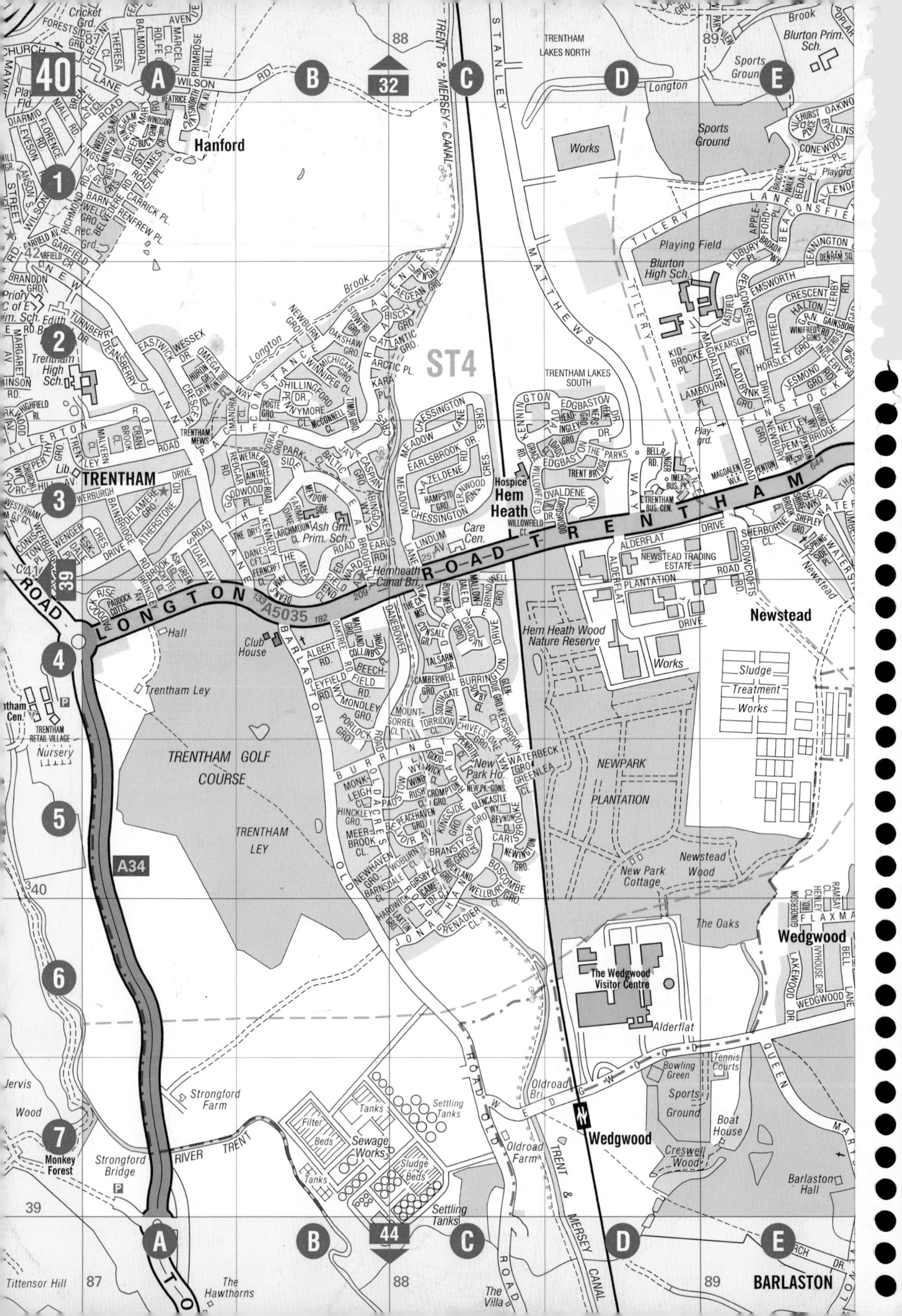

32
44
39
A
B
C
D
E
1
2
3
4
5
6
7
87
88
89
Hanford
TRENTHAM
Hem Heath
Newstead
Wedgwood
BARLASTON
ST4
TRENTHAM LAKES NORTH
TRENTHAM LAKES SOUTH
Works
Sports Ground
Playing Field
Blurton High Sch.
Blurton Prim. Sch.
Trentham High Sch.
Ash Grn. Prim. Sch.
LONGTON ROAD
TRENTHAM ROAD
A5035
A34
STANLEY MATTHEWS WAY
TRENT & MERSEY CANAL
TILERY LANE
NEWSTEAD TRADING ESTATE
PLANTATION DRIVE
ALDERFLAT DRIVE
Hem Heath Wood Nature Reserve
Sludge Treatment Works
NEWPARK PLANTATION
Newstead Wood
New Park Cottage
The Oaks
The Wedgwood Visitor Centre
Alderflat
TRENTHAM GOLF COURSE
TRENTHAM LEY
Trentham Ley
Club House
Hall
Nursery
TRENTHAM RETAIL VILLAGE
Hemheath Canal Bri.
Hospice
Care Cen.
New Park Ho.
BARLASTON OLD ROAD
Strongford Farm
Strongford Bridge
RIVER TRENT
Sewage Works
Filter Beds
Tanks
Settling Tanks
Sludge Beds
Oldroad Bri.
Oldroad Farm
Bowling Green
Tennis Courts
Boat House
Creswell Wood
Barlaston Hall
Jervis Wood
Monkey Forest
Tittensor Hill
The Hawthorns
The Villa

41
33
45
42
Dresden
Blurton
Florence
Cocknage
Hartwell
Barlaston Common
Rough Close Common
Stoke-on-Trent
Stone
ST3
ST12
ST15
STOKE-ON-TRENT
STAFFORD
QUEEN'S PARK
DOUGLAS MACMILLAN HOSPICE
LONGTON COTTAGE HOSP.
Lightwood Driving Range
BELGRAVE ROAD
LIGHTWOOD ROAD
A5035
A5005
B5038
BARLASTON ROAD
COCKNAGE ROAD
WOODPARK LANE
BLURTON ROAD
HARTWELL LANE
Penfold Farm
Blurton Grange Farm
Blurton Poultry Farm
Clark's Wood
Reservoir (Covered)
Cocknage Farm
Ivy Cottage
Coldriding Farm
Cocknage Wood
South Cocknage Farm
Lodge Farm
Crowcrofts
The Woodlands
Glazleyfield
Copper Beech
The Cedars
The Hollies
Heather Lodge
Rose Cottage
Woodend Farm
Woodeaves
Hall Farm
Top Farm
Beech House
The Beeches
Hurden Hall
Hartwell Cottage
Glazeley Fields
Hartwell Farm
Great Hartwell Farm
Beech Cottage
Little Hartwell
Rugby Football Ground
Barlaston Park
Market Garden
Sports Grd.
Residential Home
Blurton Park
Cricket Grd.
Sutherland Prim. Sch.
F G H J K
1 2 3 4 5 6 7

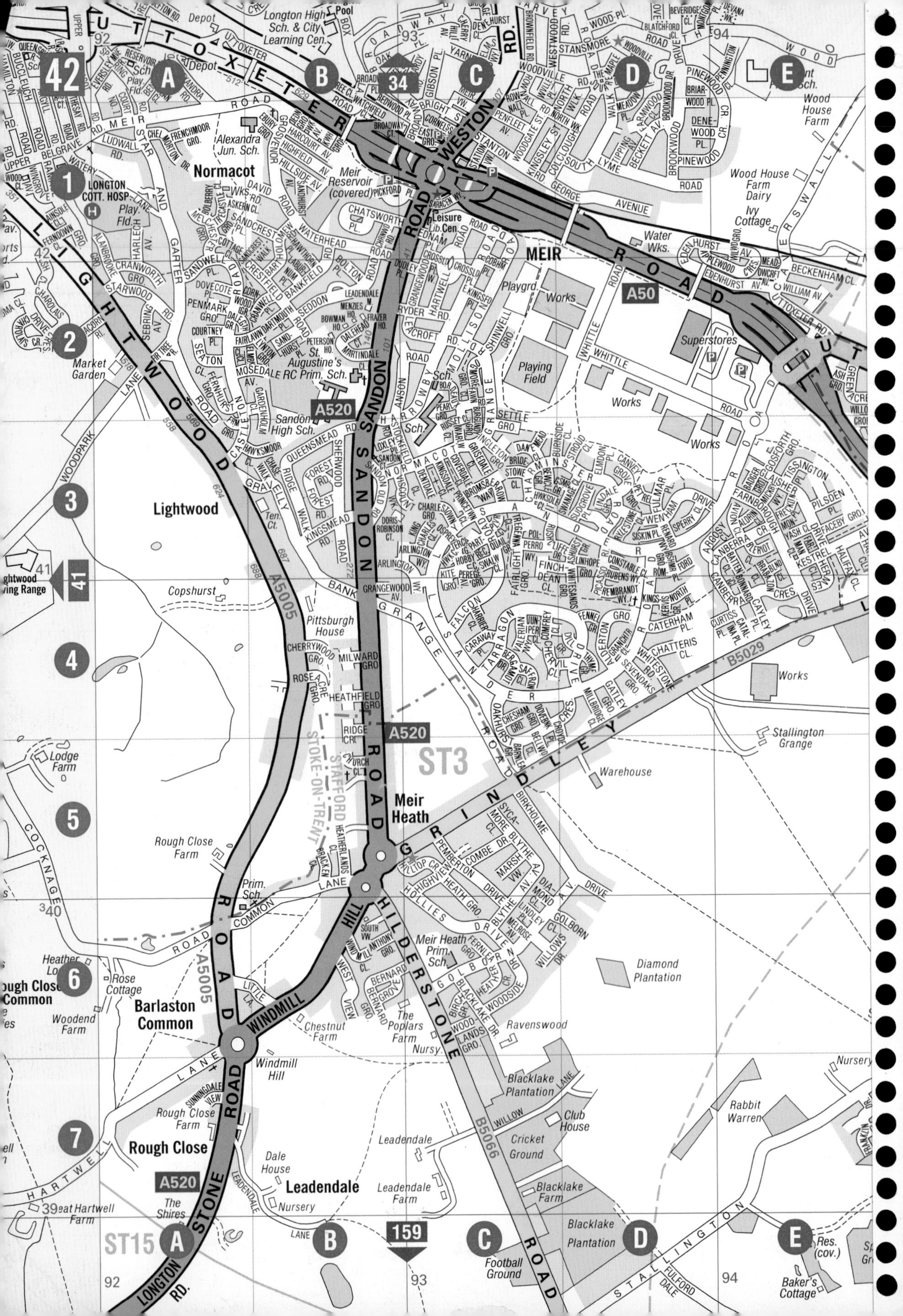
42
A
B
C
D
E
1
2
3
4
5
6
7
34
41
159
Normacot
Meir
Lightwood
Meir Heath
Barlaston Common
Rough Close
Leadendale
ST3
ST15
UTTOXETER RD.
WESTON ROAD
SANDON ROAD
LIGHTWOOD ROAD
STONE ROAD
GRINDLEY LANE
HILDERSTONE ROAD
WINDMILL HILL
A50
A520
A5005
B5029
B5066
Longton High Sch. & City Learning Cen.
Alexandra Jun. Sch.
LONGTON COTT. HOSP.
Meir Reservoir (covered)
Leisure Cen.
Water Wks.
Works
Superstores
Playing Field
Wood House Farm
Wood House Farm Dairy
Ivy Cottage
St. Augustine's RC Prim. Sch.
Sandon High Sch.
Copshurst
Pittsburgh House
Lodge Farm
Rough Close Farm
Warehouse
Stallington Grange
Diamond Plantation
Meir Heath Prim. Sch.
Ravenswood
Chestnut Farm
The Poplars Farm
Windmill Hill
Blacklake Plantation
Club House
Cricket Ground
Blacklake Farm
Rabbit Warren
Leadendale Farm
Dale House
Woodend Farm
Rose Cottage
Football Ground
Baker's Cottage
92
93
94

43
35
155
159
59
F
G
H
J
K
1
2
3
4
5
6
7
Stoke-on-Trent
ST11
Blythe Bridge
(Caverswall Rd.)
BLYTHE
BRIDGE
Moor
Green
Forsbrook
Blythe Marsh
Draycott in
the Moors
Stonehouses
Gorstybirch
Stallington
Saverley
Green
Caverswall
Park
Callowhill
Wood
Field
House
Cashheath
Farm
Cashheath
Farm Cottages
Foxfield
Railway
Mus.
Moor Green
Farm
Heath
House
Exhibition
Farm
Forsbrook
Cemetery
Holly Hedge
Farm
Calverhay
Farm
Aynsley
Sch.
Springcroft
Prim. Sch.
Forsbrook
C of E
Prim. Sch.
Blythe Bridge
High Sch.
Wood Grove
Farm
Myrtle
Grove
New Park
Cairneycroft
Rec.
Grd.
Hall
The
Farm
Mill
Pond
Mill
Prim.
Sch.
Coach
Depot
Playing
Field
Works
A50
A521
Marsh
House
Marsh House
Farm
Woodlands
Higher Gorsty
Birch
The
Uplands
Lower
Gorsty Birch
STAFFORDSHIRE MOORLANDS
STAFFORD
Stallington
Farm
Stallington Hall
Farm
Little Leacroft
Farm
Stallington
Sprink
Leacroft
Hall
Saverley Green
Farm
Saverley House
Farm
The
Hollows
Farm
Rookery
Cottage
UTTOXETER
CHEADLE ROAD
GRINDLEY LANE
CAVERSWALL ROAD
STALLINGTON ROAD
FULFORD ROAD
UTTOXETER RD.
Foxfield Steam Railway
River Blithe
Roman Road
Convent
Lodge
House Farm
Gable
Cottages
Fair View
Oaklea
Stables
Hall
395
96
97
42
41
340
39

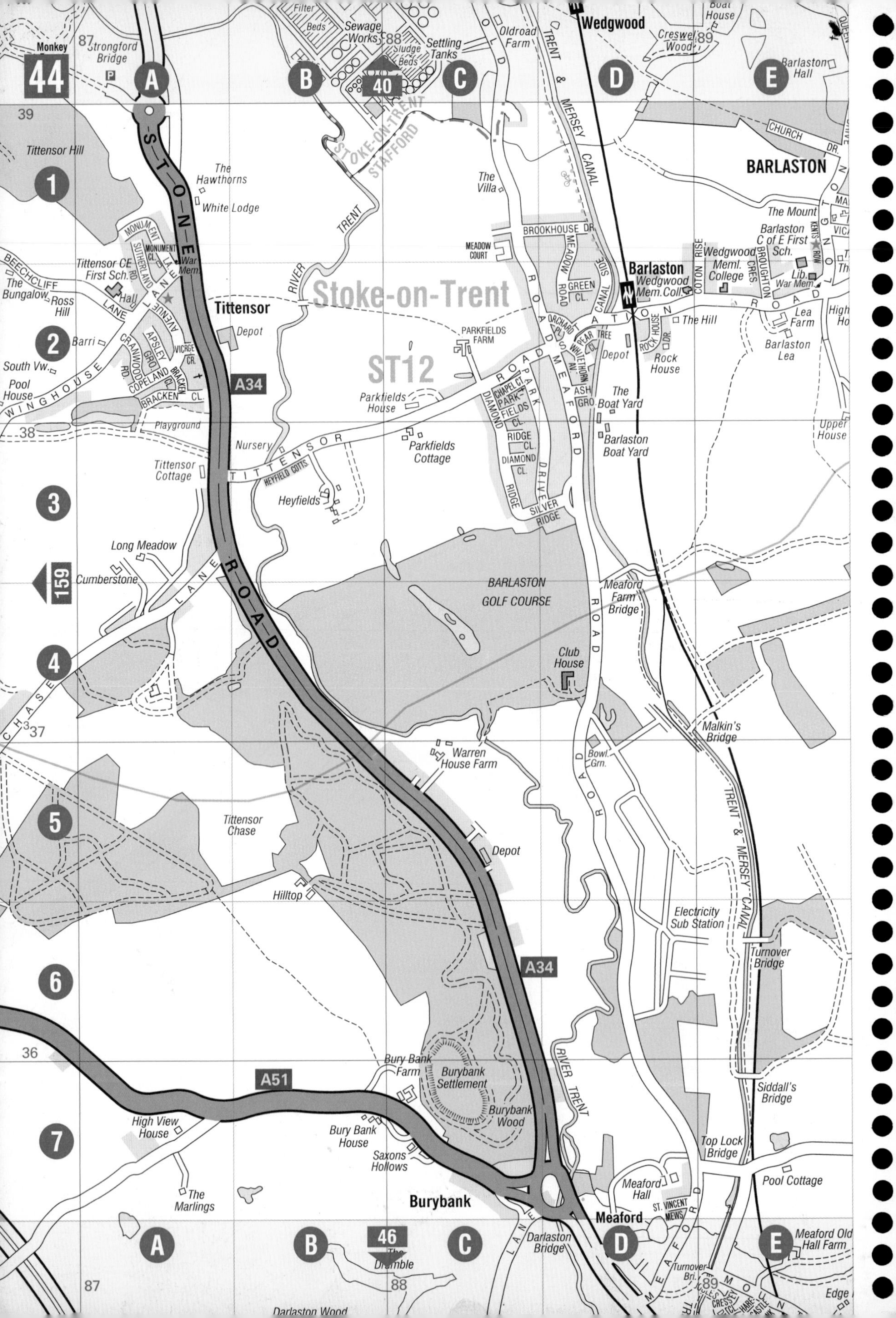

44
Monkey
Strongford Bridge
Filter Beds
Sewage Works
Sludge Beds
Settling Tanks
40
Oldroad Farm
Wedgwood
Creswell Wood
Boat House
Barlaston Hall
Tittensor Hill
STOKE-ON-TRENT
STAFFORD
The Hawthorns
White Lodge
The Villa
CHURCH DR.
BARLASTON
The Mount
Barlaston C of E First Sch.
Wedgwood Meml. College
Lib.
War Mem.
BROOKHOUSE DR.
MEADOW COURT
MEADOW ROAD
GREEN CL.
Barlaston
Wedgwood Mem. Coll.
TRENT & MERSEY CANAL
RIVER TRENT
Stoke-on-Trent
Tittensor CE First Sch.
Hall
BEECHCLIFF
The Bungalow
Ross Hill
LANE
MONUMENT LA.
SUTHERLAND RD.
AVENUE
War Mem.
Tittensor
Depot
STATION ROAD
The Hill
Lea Farm
Barlaston Lea
Rock House
PARKFIELDS FARM
ST12
Barri
South Vw.
Pool House
WINGHOUSE LANE
CRANWOOD RD.
APSLEY GRO.
COPELAND
BRACKEN CL.
A34
Parkfields House
PARK FIELDS
DIAMOND CL.
RIDGE CL.
ASH GRO.
The Boat Yard
Barlaston Boat Yard
Playground
Nursery
TITTENSOR ROAD
HEYFIELD COTTS.
Parkfields Cottage
Tittensor Cottage
Heyfields
SILVER RIDGE
Upper House
Long Meadow
Cumberstone
159
STONE ROAD
BARLASTON GOLF COURSE
Meaford Farm Bridge
Club House
MEAFORD ROAD
CHASE LANE
Malkin's Bridge
Warren House Farm
Bowl. Grn.
Tittensor Chase
Depot
Hilltop
Electricity Sub Station
Turnover Bridge
Siddall's Bridge
Bury Bank Farm
Burybank Settlement
Burybank Wood
A51
High View House
Bury Bank House
Saxons Hollows
Top Lock Bridge
Pool Cottage
The Marlings
Burybank
Meaford Hall
ST. VINCENT MEWS
Meaford
Darlaston Bridge
46
The Dramble
Meaford Old Hall Farm
Turnover Bri.
Edge
Darlaston Wood
MOLL

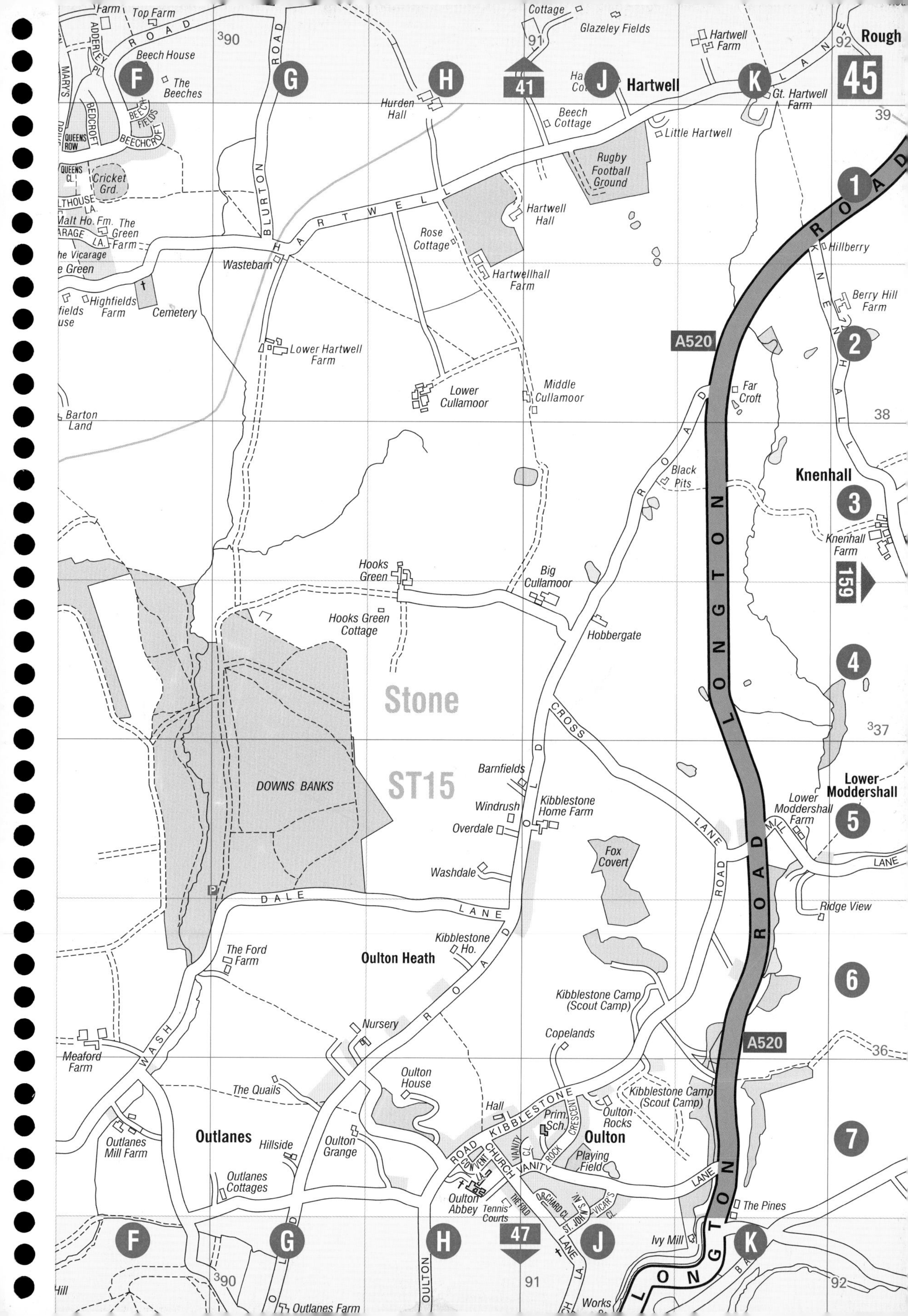
Top Farm
Beech House
The Beeches
Hurden Hall
Glazeley Fields
Hartwell Farm
Hartwell
Rough
Gt. Hartwell Farm
Beech Cottage
Little Hartwell
Rugby Football Ground
Cricket Grd.
Malt Ho. Fm.
The Green Farm
Hartwell Hall
Rose Cottage
Wastebarn
Hartwellhall Farm
Hillberry
Berry Hill Farm
Highfields Farm
Cemetery
Lower Hartwell Farm
A520
Lower Cullamoor
Middle Cullamoor
Far Croft
Barton Land
Black Pits
Knenhall
Knenhall Farm
Hooks Green
Big Cullamoor
Hooks Green Cottage
Hobbergate
Stone
ST15
Barnfields
DOWNS BANKS
Windrush
Kibblestone Home Farm
Overdale
Lower Moddershall
Lower Moddershall Farm
Fox Covert
Washdale
Ridge View
Kibblestone Ho.
The Ford Farm
Oulton Heath
Kibblestone Camp (Scout Camp)
Nursery
Copelands
Meaford Farm
Oulton House
The Quails
Hall
Oulton Rocks
Outlanes
Outlanes Mill Farm
Hillside
Oulton Grange
Prim. Sch.
Oulton
Playing Field
Outlanes Cottages
Oulton Abbey
Tennis Courts
The Pines
Ivy Mill
Outlanes Farm
Works
HARTWELL ROAD
BLURTON ROAD
ADDERLEY PL.
BEECHCROFT
BEECH FIELDS
QUEENS ROW
QUEENS CL.
KNENHALL LANE
LONGTON ROAD
CROSS LANE
DALE LANE
OLD ROAD
WASH DALE
MILL LANE
KIBBLESTONE ROAD
CHURCH LA.
VANITY LANE
VANITY CL.
ROCK CRESCENT
ORCHARD CL.
ST. JOHN'S AV.
VICAR'S CL.
CONVENT LA.
THE FOLD
OULTON ROAD
41
47
159

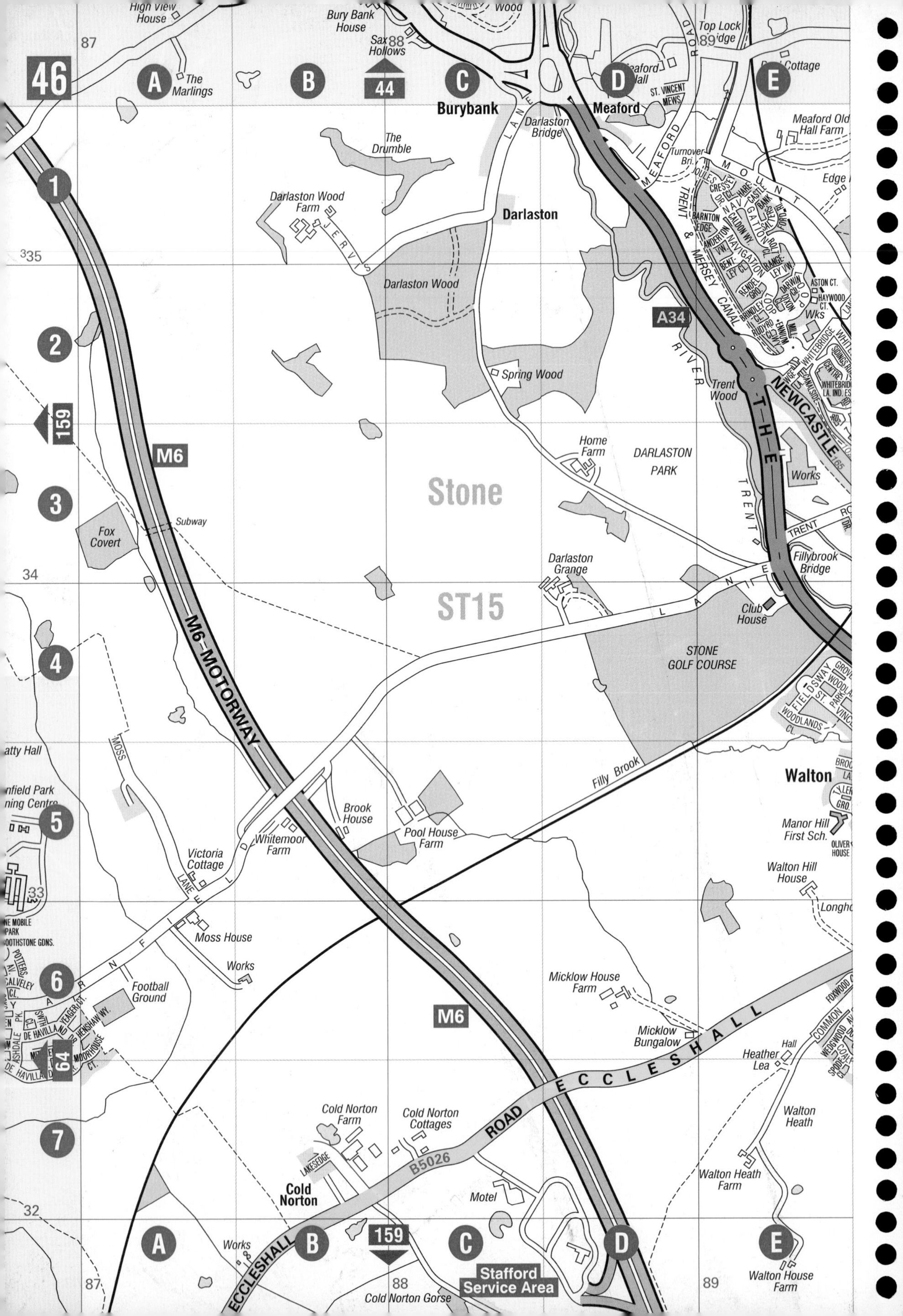
High View House
Bury Bank House
Sax Hollows
The Marlings
44
Burybank
Meaford
Meaford Hall
ST. VINCENT MEWS
Top Lock Bridge
Poel Cottage
Meaford Old Hall Farm
Darlaston Bridge
The Drumble
Turnover Bri.
MEAFORD ROAD
MOUNT
Edge
Darlaston Wood Farm
JERVIS
Darlaston
TRENT & MERSEY CANAL
Darlaston Wood
A34
RIVER TRENT
Spring Wood
Trent Wood
NEWCASTLE
THE
159
M6
Home Farm
DARLASTON PARK
Works
Stone
Subway
Fox Covert
TRENT
Fillybrook Bridge
Darlaston Grange
ST15
LANE
Club House
STONE GOLF COURSE
M6 MOTORWAY
WOODLANDS CL.
MOSS
Filly Brook
Walton
Brook House
Whitemoor Farm
Pool House Farm
Manor Hill First Sch.
OLIVER HOUSE
Victoria Cottage
Walton Hill House
Moss House
Works
Micklow House Farm
Football Ground
M6
Micklow Bungalow
ECCLESHALL
Heather Lea
Hall
64
ROAD
Cold Norton Farm
Cold Norton Cottages
Walton Heath
B5026
LAKESEDGE
Walton Heath Farm
Cold Norton
Motel
Works
159
Stafford Service Area
Walton House Farm
Cold Norton Gorse
87
88
89
335
34
33
32
A
B
C
D
E
1
2
3
4
5
6
7

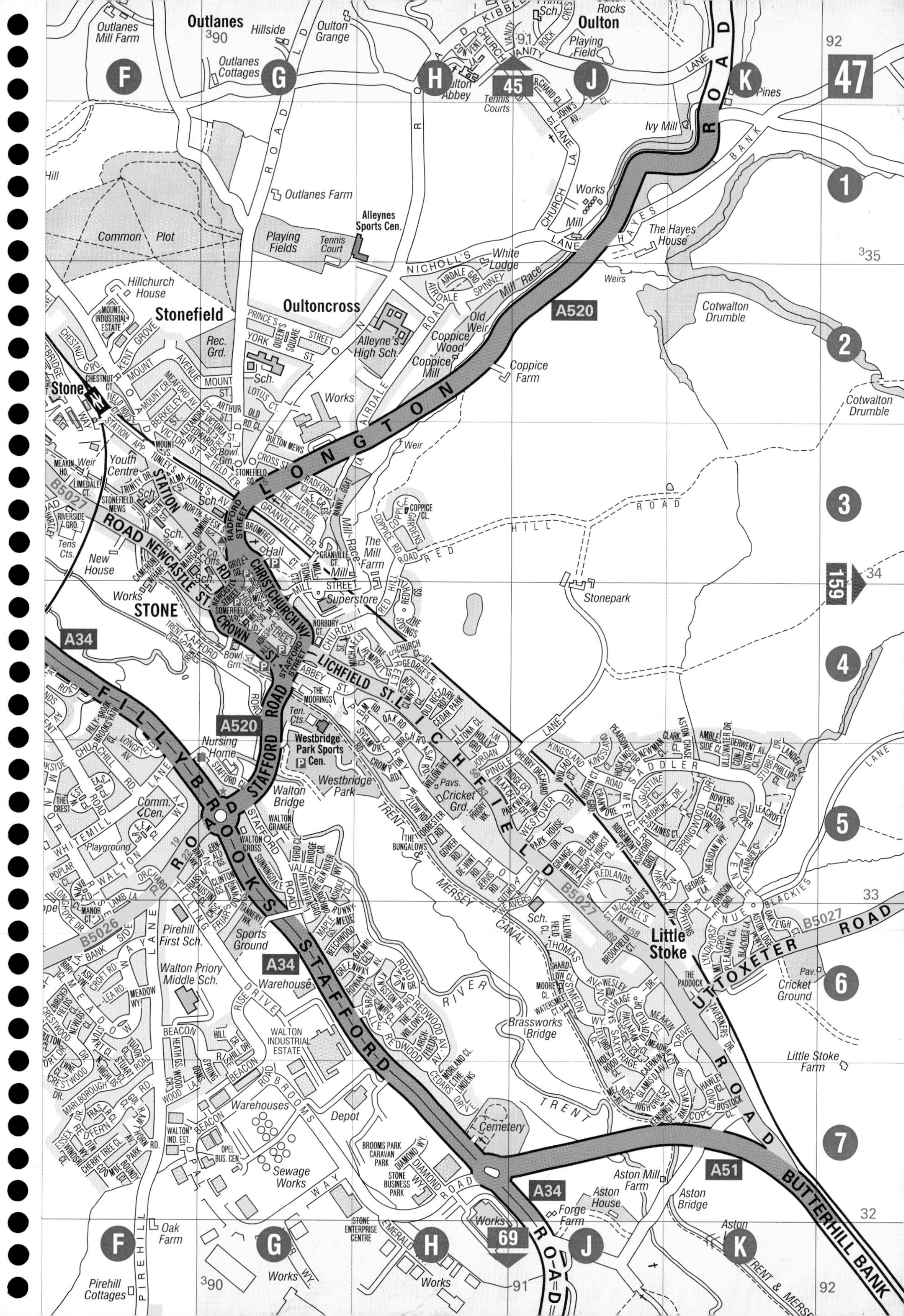

47
45
159
69
Outlanes
Outlanes Mill Farm
Hillside
Oulton Grange
Outlanes Cottages
Oulton
Oulton Abbey
Playing Field
Tennis Courts
Ivy Mill
Pines
Outlanes Farm
Common Plot
Playing Fields
Tennis Court
Alleynes Sports Cen.
Works
Mill
The Hayes House
Nicholl's Lane
White Lodge
Weirs
Hillchurch House
Stonefield
Oultoncross
Mill Race
Old Weir
A520
Cotwalton Drumble
Mount Industrial Estate
Rec. Grd.
Alleyne's High Sch.
Coppice Wood
Coppice Mill
Coppice Farm
Stone
Longton Road
Weir
Youth Centre
Station Road
B5027
Newcastle Road
Red Hill Road
New House
The Mill Farm
Hall
Superstore
Stonepark
Works
STONE
A34
Lichfield St.
Christchurch Wy.
Stafford Street
Westbridge Park Sports Cen.
Westbridge Park
Nursing Home
Walton Bridge
Filly Brook
Comm. Cen.
Playground
Saddler Avenue
Cricket Grd.
Pavs.
The Bungalows
Mersey Canal
Trent
Little Stoke
Uttoxeter Road
Cricket Ground
B5026
Pirehill First Sch.
Sports Ground
Walton Priory Middle Sch.
Warehouse
Walton Industrial Estate
River
Brassworks Bridge
Little Stoke Farm
Warehouses
Depot
Cemetery
Walton Ind. Est.
Opel Bus. Cen.
Sewage Works
Brooms Park Caravan Park
Stone Business Park
Aston Mill Farm
Aston House
Aston Bridge
A51
Butterhill Bank
Forge Farm
Oak Farm
Stone Enterprise Centre
Works
Aston
Pirehill Cottages
Stafford Road
F
G
H
J
K
1
2
3
4
5
6
7

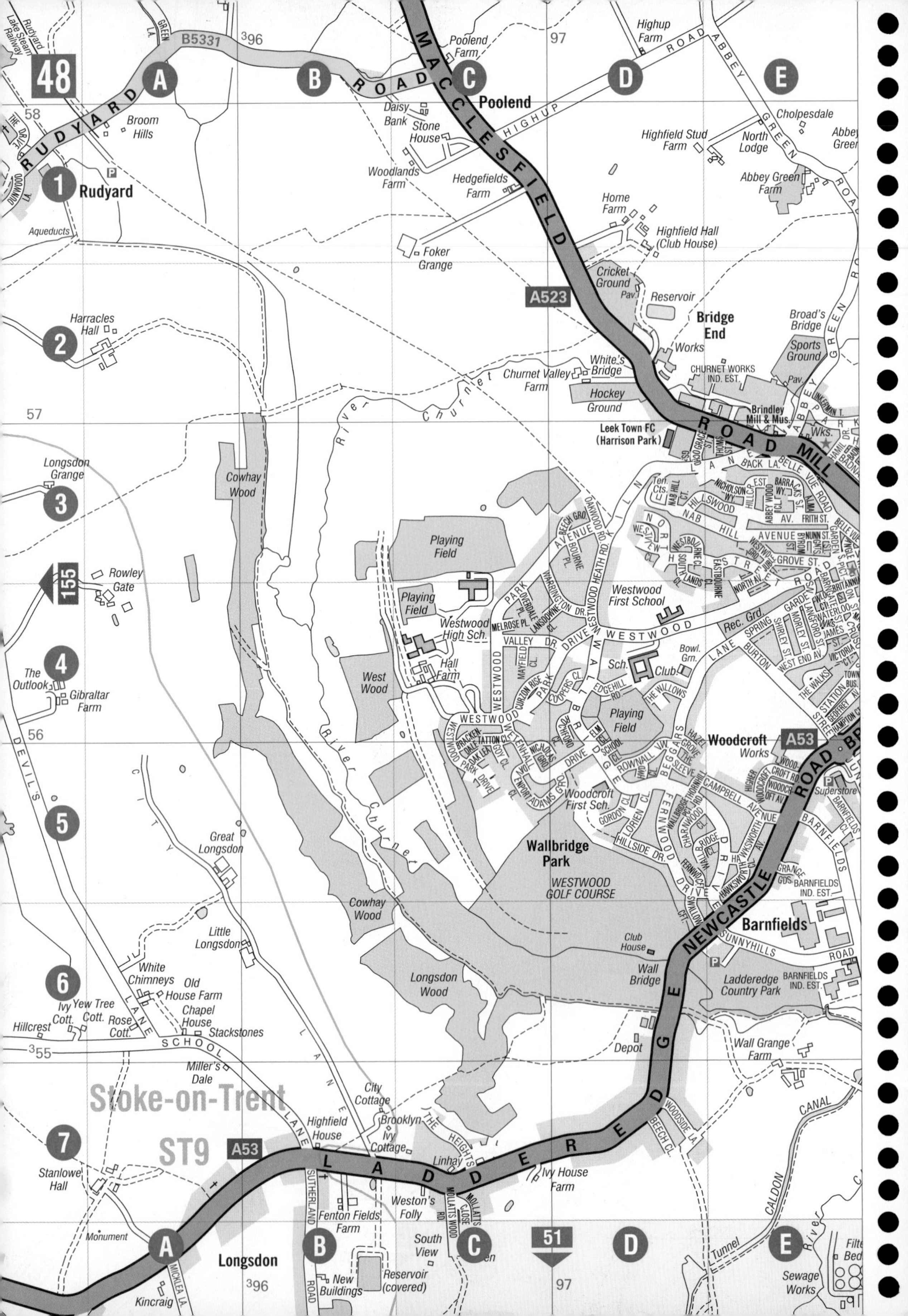
48
Rudyard Lake Steam Railway
B5331
RUDYARD ROAD
Broom Hills
Rudyard
Aqueducts
Poolend Farm
MACCLESFIELD
Poolend
Daisy Bank
Stone House
HIGHUP
Woodlands Farm
Hedgefields Farm
Foker Grange
Highup Farm
ROAD
ABBEY GREEN ROAD
Cholpesdale
Highfield Stud Farm
North Lodge
Abbey Green
Abbey Green Farm
Home Farm
Highfield Hall (Club House)
Cricket Ground
Pav.
Reservoir
A523
Bridge End
Broad's Bridge
Sports Ground
Works
CHURNET WORKS IND. EST.
Harracles Hall
White's Bridge
Churnet Valley Farm
Hockey Ground
River Churnet
Leek Town FC (Harrison Park)
Brindley Mill & Mus.
Wks.
MILL ROAD
Longsdon Grange
Cowhay Wood
BACK LA.
BELLE VUE ROAD
NICHOLSON WY.
NAB HILL AV.
FRITH ST.
GROVE ST.
Playing Field
Rowley Gate
155
Westwood First School
Westwood High Sch.
WESTWOOD
Rec. Grd.
West Wood
Hall Farm
The Outlook
Gibraltar Farm
Sch.
Club
Bowl. Grn.
WESTWOOD PARK DRIVE
Playing Field
Woodcroft
Works
A53
DEVIL'S LANE
WEST END AV.
Woodcroft First Sch.
Superstore
Great Longsdon
Wallbridge Park
WESTWOOD GOLF COURSE
CAMPBELL AVENUE
BARNFIELDS
BARNFIELDS IND. EST.
Barnfields
Cowhay Wood
Little Longsdon
Club House
NEWCASTLE ROAD
SUNNYHILLS ROAD
White Chimneys
Old House Farm
Wall Bridge
Ladderedge Country Park
Longsdon Wood
Chapel House
Ivy Cott.
Yew Tree Cott.
Rose Cott.
Hillcrest
Stackstones
SCHOOL LANE
Depot
Wall Grange Farm
Miller's Dale
City Cottage
Stoke-on-Trent
ST9
Highfield House
Brooklyn
Ivy Cottage
THE HEIGHTS
LADDEREDGE
WOODSIDE LA.
BEECH CL.
CANAL
Stanlowe Hall
A53
Linhay
Ivy House Farm
SUTHERLAND ROAD
Fenton Fields Farm
Weston's Folly
MOLLATTS WOOD RD.
MOLLATTS CLOSE
CALDON
South View
51
Tunnel
River
Monument
Longsdon
New Buildings
Reservoir (covered)
Sewage Works
MICKLEA LA.
Kincraig
396
97
58
57
56
355
A
B
C
D
E
1
2
3
4
5
6
7

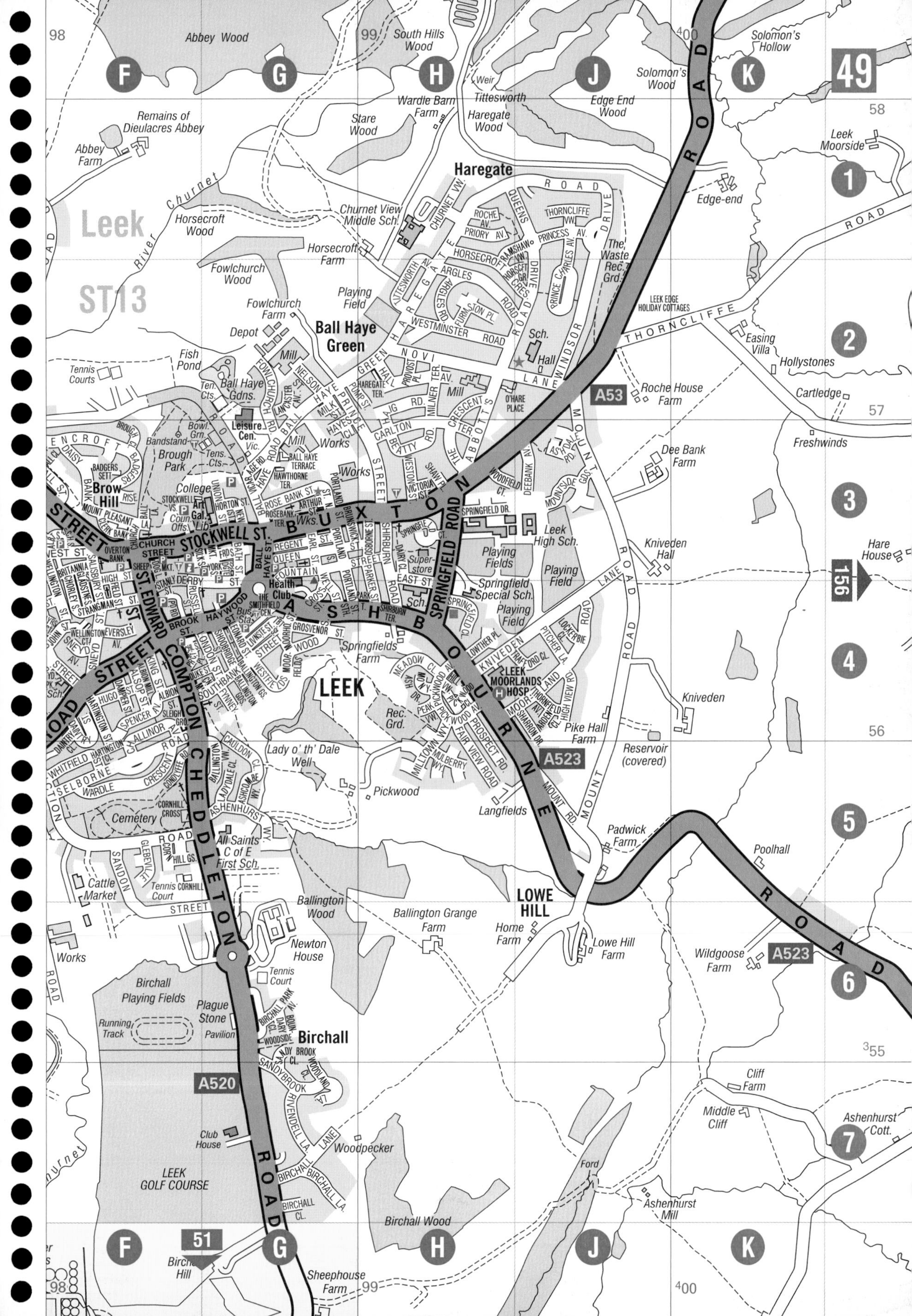

49
Abbey Wood
South Hills Wood
Solomon's Hollow
Solomon's Wood
Weir
Wardle Barn Farm
Tittesworth
Haregate Wood
Edge End Wood
Remains of Dieulacres Abbey
Abbey Farm
Stare Wood
Leek Moorside
Haregate
Edge-end
Leek
ST13
River Churnet
Horsecroft Wood
Churnet View Middle Sch.
Horsecroft Farm
Fowlchurch Wood
The Waste Rec. Grd.
Playing Field
Fowlchurch Farm
LEEK EDGE HOLIDAY COTTAGES
Depot
Ball Haye Green
Easing Villa
Hollystones
Fish Pond
Tennis Courts
Ball Haye Gdns.
Sch.
Hall
A53
Roche House Farm
Cartledge
Leisure Cen.
Bandstand
Brough Park
Mill
Works
Freshwinds
Dee Bank Farm
Brow Hill
College
Art Gal.
Lib.
Coun. Offs.
Wks.
Leek High Sch.
Playing Fields
Kniveden Hall
Hare House
156
Health Club
Super-store
Springfield Special Sch.
Playing Field
Springfields Farm
LEEK
LEEK MOORLANDS HOSP.
Kniveden
Rec. Grd.
Lady o' th' Dale Well
Pike Hall Farm
Reservoir (covered)
A523
Pickwood
Langfields
Cemetery
All Saints C of E First Sch.
Padwick Farm
Poolhall
Cattle Market
Tennis Court
Ballington Wood
LOWE HILL
Ballington Grange Farm
Home Farm
Lowe Hill Farm
Works
Newton House
Wildgoose Farm
Birchall Playing Fields
Plague Stone
Running Track
Pavilion
Birchall
A520
Cliff Farm
Middle Cliff
Ashenhurst Cott.
Club House
Woodpecker
LEEK GOLF COURSE
Ford
Ashenhurst Mill
Birchall Wood
51
Birchall Hill
Sheephouse Farm
BUXTON ROAD
ASHBOURNE ROAD
STOCKWELL ST.
CHURCH STREET
ST. EDWARD STREET
COMPTON
CHEDDLETON ROAD
SPRINGFIELD ROAD
MOUNT ROAD
THORNCLIFFE ROAD
WINDSOR DRIVE
WESTMINSTER ROAD
HAREGATE ROAD
NOVI LANE
MILNER TER.
CARLTON
SHIRBURN ROAD
KNIVEDEN
BROOK ST.
HAYWOOD ST.
DERBY ST.
REGENT ST.
QUEEN ST.
EAST ST.
SOUTHBANK
ASHENHURST WY.
CORNHILL CROSS
SANDON ROAD
BIRCHALL LANE
SANDYBROOK
A
B
F
G
H
J
K
1
2
3
4
5
6
7
98
99
400
58
57
56
55

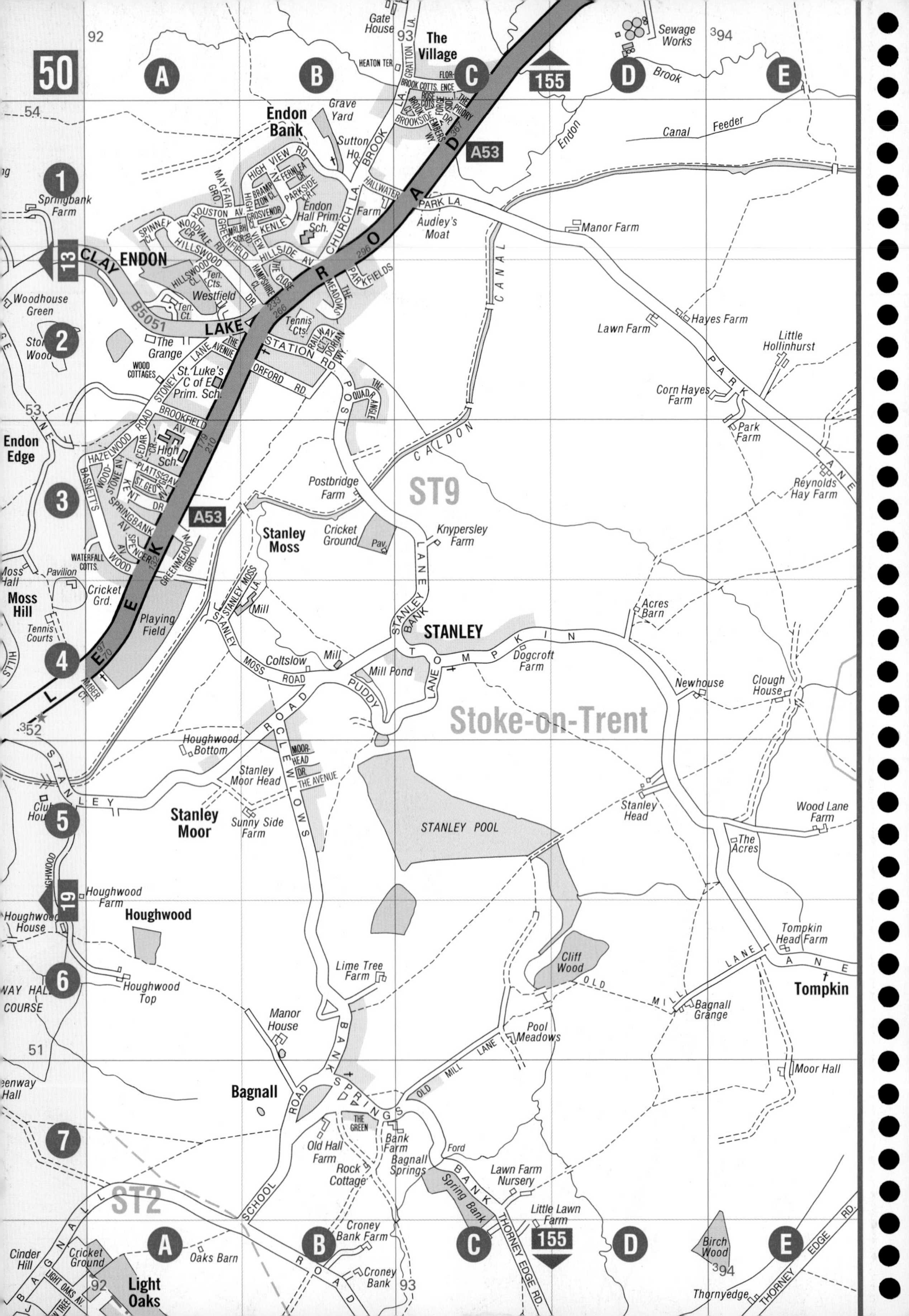
ENDON
Endon Bank
The Village
Endon Edge
Moss Hill
STANLEY
Stanley Moss
Stanley Moor
Houghwood
Bagnall
Tompkin
Light Oaks
Stoke-on-Trent
ST9
ST2
LEEK ROAD
A53
B5051
STANLEY POOL
Canal Feeder
CALDON CANAL
PARK LANE
TOMPKIN LANE
STANLEY MOSS LANE
SCHOOL ROAD
CLEWLOWS BANK
SPRINGS BANK
OLD MILL LANE
THORNEY EDGE RD.
BAGNALL ROAD
Postbridge Farm
Knypersley Farm
Dogcroft Farm
Lawn Farm
Hayes Farm
Manor Farm
Corn Hayes Farm
Park Farm
Reynolds Hay Farm
Little Hollinhurst
Acres Barn
Newhouse
Clough House
Stanley Head
Wood Lane Farm
The Acres
Tompkin Head Farm
Bagnall Grange
Moor Hall
Pool Meadows
Cliff Wood
Lime Tree Farm
Manor House
Old Hall Farm
Rock Cottage
Bank Farm
Bagnall Springs
Lawn Farm Nursery
Little Lawn Farm
Croney Bank Farm
Croney Bank
Oaks Barn
Birch Wood
Thornyedge
Houghwood Farm
Houghwood House
Houghwood Top
Houghwood Bottom
Stanley Moor Head
Sunny Side Farm
Sewage Works
Gate House
Audley's Moat
Springbank Farm
Woodhouse Green
The Grange
Coltslow
Mill Pond
Cricket Ground
Playing Field
13
19
155

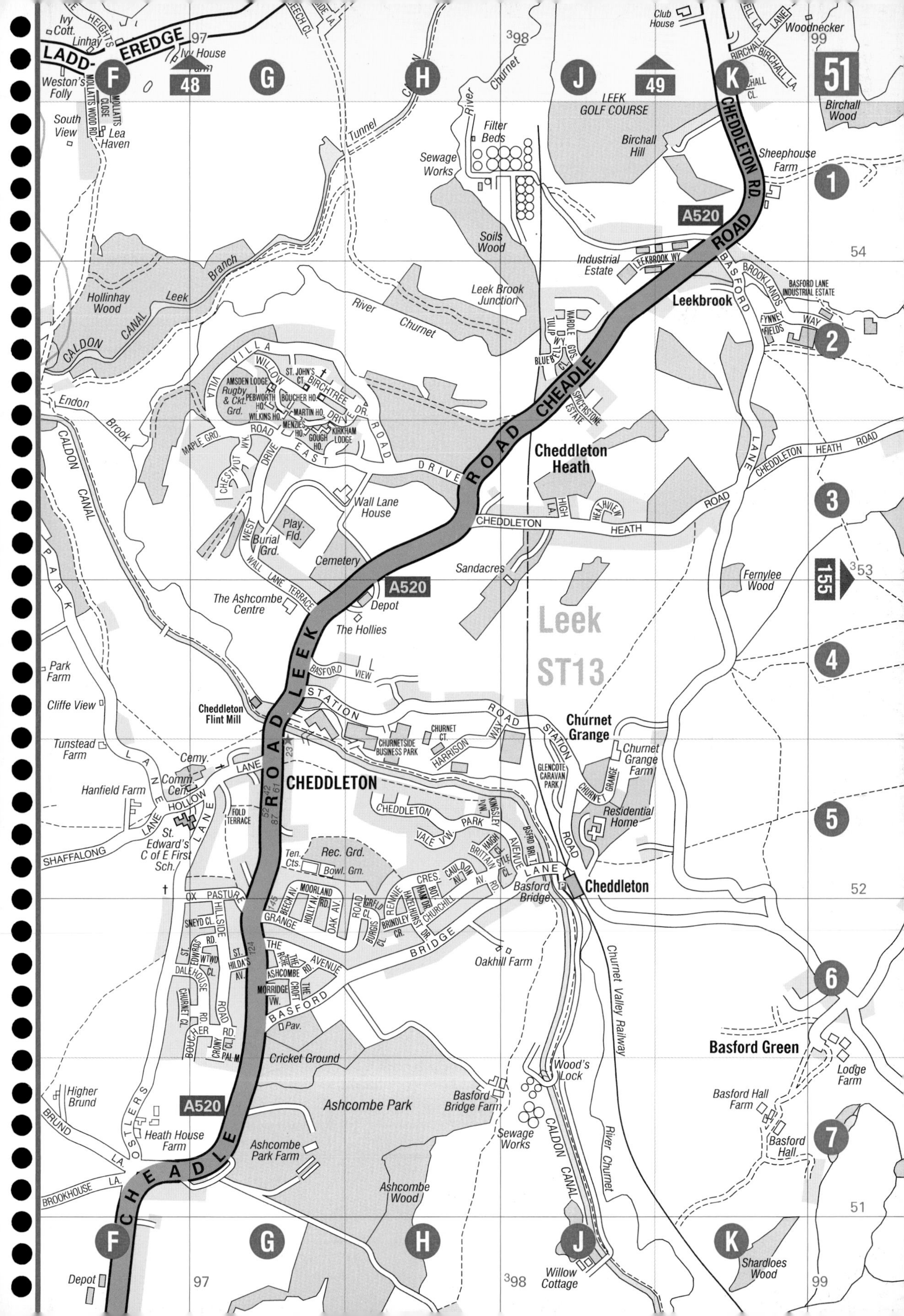
LADD-EREDGE
Ivy Cott.
Linhay
Ivy House Farm
Weston's Folly
MOLLATTS CLOSE
MOLLATTS WOOD RD.
South View
Lea Haven
48
49
Leek Golf Course
Birchall Hill
Sheephouse Farm
Birchall Wood
Woodnecker
Club House
Filter Beds
Sewage Works
Soils Wood
River Churnet
Tunnel
CHEDDLETON RD.
A520
Industrial Estate
LEEKBROOK WY.
Leek Brook Junction
Leekbrook
BASFORD LANE INDUSTRIAL ESTATE
BROOKLANDS
FYNNEY FIELDS WAY
Hollinhay Wood
Leek Branch
CALDON CANAL
River Churnet
Endon Brook
VILLA ROAD
WILLOW DR.
ST. JOHN'S CT.
BIRCHTREE DR.
AMSDEN LODGE
Rugby & Ckt. Grd.
PEBWORTH HO.
BOUCHER HO.
MARTIN HO.
WILKINS HO.
MENZIES HO.
GOUGH HO.
KIRKHAM LODGE
MAPLE GRO.
CHESTNUT WK.
DRIVE EAST
WARDLE GDS.
TULIP WY.
BLUEBELL CL.
SPICERSTONE ESTATE
CHEADLE ROAD
Cheddleton Heath
HIGH LA.
HEATHVIEW
CHEDDLETON HEATH ROAD
Wall Lane House
Play. Fld.
Burial Grd.
WEST WALL LANE TERRACE
Cemetery
Sandacres
Fernylee Wood
155
The Ashcombe Centre
Depot
The Hollies
LEEK ROAD
Leek
ST13
Park Farm
Cliffe View
BASFORD VIEW
STATION ROAD
Cheddleton Flint Mill
CHURNET CT.
CHURNETSIDE BUSINESS PARK
HARRISON WAY
Churnet Grange
Churnet Grange Farm
GLENCOTE CARAVAN PARK
CHURNET GRANGE
Residential Home
Tunstead Farm
Cemy.
Comm. Cen.
Hanfield Farm
HOLLOW LANE
SHAFFALONG LANE
St. Edward's C of E First Sch.
FOLD TERRACE
CHEDDLETON
CHEDDLETON PARK
VALE VW.
KINGSLEY VW.
HAIGH CL.
BRITAIN
STILE CL.
AVENUE
BSFRD BRI. TER.
Rec. Grd.
Ten. Cts.
Bowl. Grn.
OX PASTURE
HILLSIDE
MOORLAND RD.
BEECH AV.
HOLLY AV.
OAK AV.
GRANGE
RENNIE
HAM DR.
BOTT CRES.
CAULDON AV.
CHURCHILL AV.
GRFLD CL.
BURGIS CL.
BRINDLEY CR.
HAZELHURST DR.
Basford Bridge
Cheddleton
BASFORD BRIDGE LANE
SNEYD CL.
ST. EDWARDS RD.
WTWD CL.
ST. HILDA'S AV.
THE ROCHE
THE RD.
AVENUE
ASHCOMBE
MORRIDGE VW.
THE CROFT
DALEHOUSE
CHURNET CL.
BOUCHER RD.
CRONY CL.
PAL M
Pav.
Oakhill Farm
Churnet Valley Railway
Basford Green
Lodge Farm
Cricket Ground
Wood's Lock
Higher Brund
OSTLERS LA.
BRUND LA.
Heath House Farm
Ashcombe Park
Basford Bridge Farm
Sewage Works
CALDON CANAL
River Churnet
Basford Hall Farm
Basford Hall
Ashcombe Park Farm
BROOKHOUSE LA.
Ashcombe Wood
Depot
Willow Cottage
Shardloes Wood
F G H J K
1 2 3 4 5 6 7
97 398 99
54 353 52 51

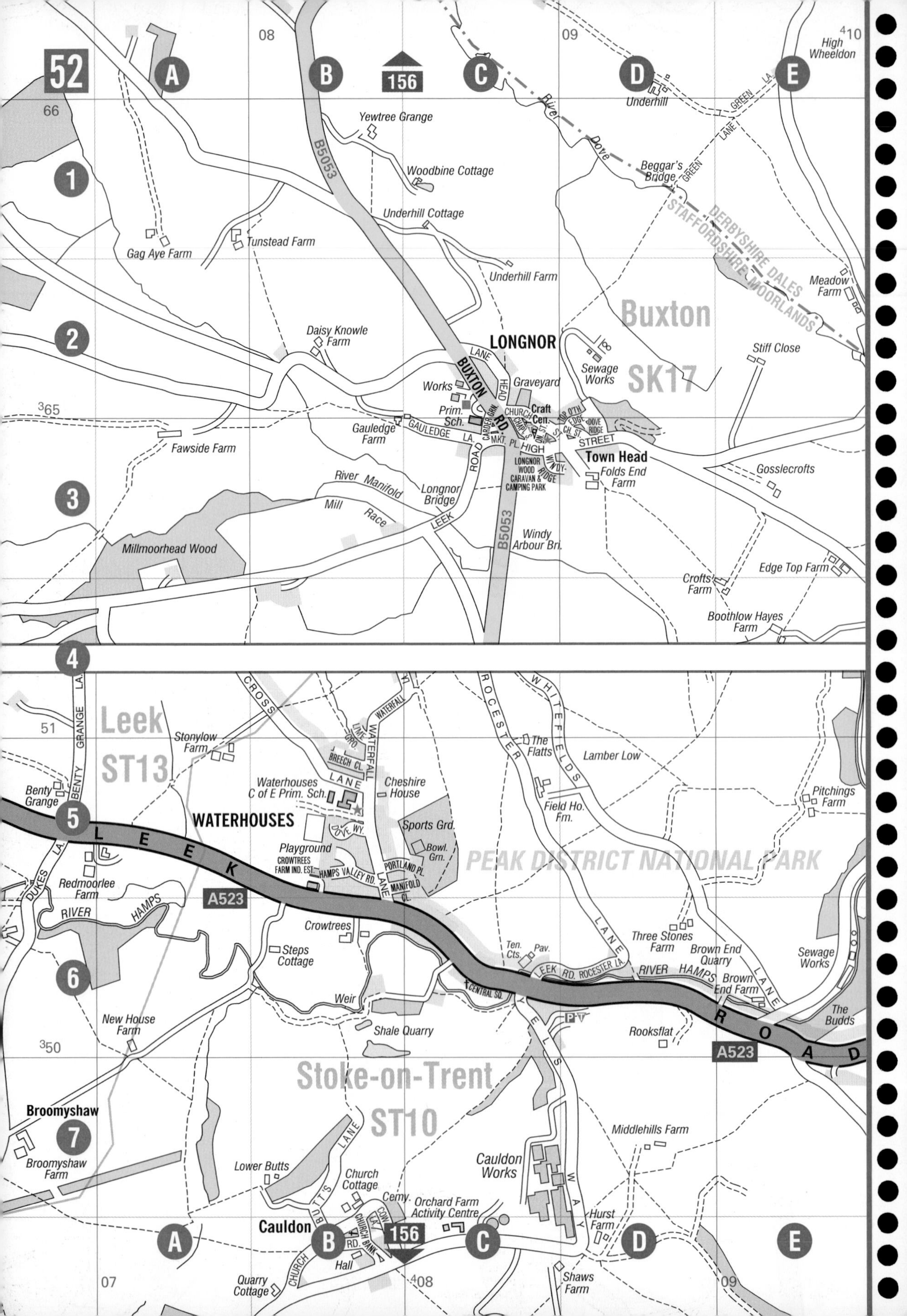
156
LONGNOR
Buxton
SK17
Yewtree Grange
Woodbine Cottage
Underhill Cottage
Tunstead Farm
Gag Aye Farm
Underhill Farm
Underhill
High Wheeldon
Beggar's Bridge
River Dove
DERBYSHIRE DALES
STAFFORDSHIRE MOORLANDS
Meadow Farm
Stiff Close
Daisy Knowle Farm
Sewage Works
Graveyard
Works
Craft Cen.
Prim. Sch.
Gauledge Farm
GAULEDGE LA.
Fawside Farm
Town Head
Folds End Farm
Gosslecrofts
River Manifold
Longnor Bridge
Mill Race
Millmoorhead Wood
Windy Arbour Bri.
LONGNOR WOOD CARAVAN & CAMPING PARK
Edge Top Farm
Crofts Farm
Boothlow Hayes Farm
B5053
Leek
ST13
Stonylow Farm
Benty Grange
BENTY GRANGE LA.
WATERHOUSES
Waterhouses C of E Prim. Sch.
Cheshire House
Sports Grd.
Bowl. Grn.
Playground
CROWTREES FARM IND. EST.
HAMPS VALLEY RD.
PORTLAND PL.
The Flatts
Lamber Low
Field Ho. Fm.
PEAK DISTRICT NATIONAL PARK
Pitchings Farm
Redmoorlee Farm
RIVER HAMPS
A523
LEEK ROAD
Crowtrees
Steps Cottage
Weir
Shale Quarry
Ten. Cts.
Pav.
Three Stones Farm
Brown End Quarry
Brown End Farm
Sewage Works
The Budds
Rooksflat
New House Farm
Stoke-on-Trent
ST10
Broomyshaw
Broomyshaw Farm
Middlehills Farm
Cauldon Works
Lower Butts
Church Cottage
Orchard Farm Activity Centre
Cemy.
Cauldon
Hurst Farm
Hall
Quarry Cottage
Shaws Farm
CHURCH BANK

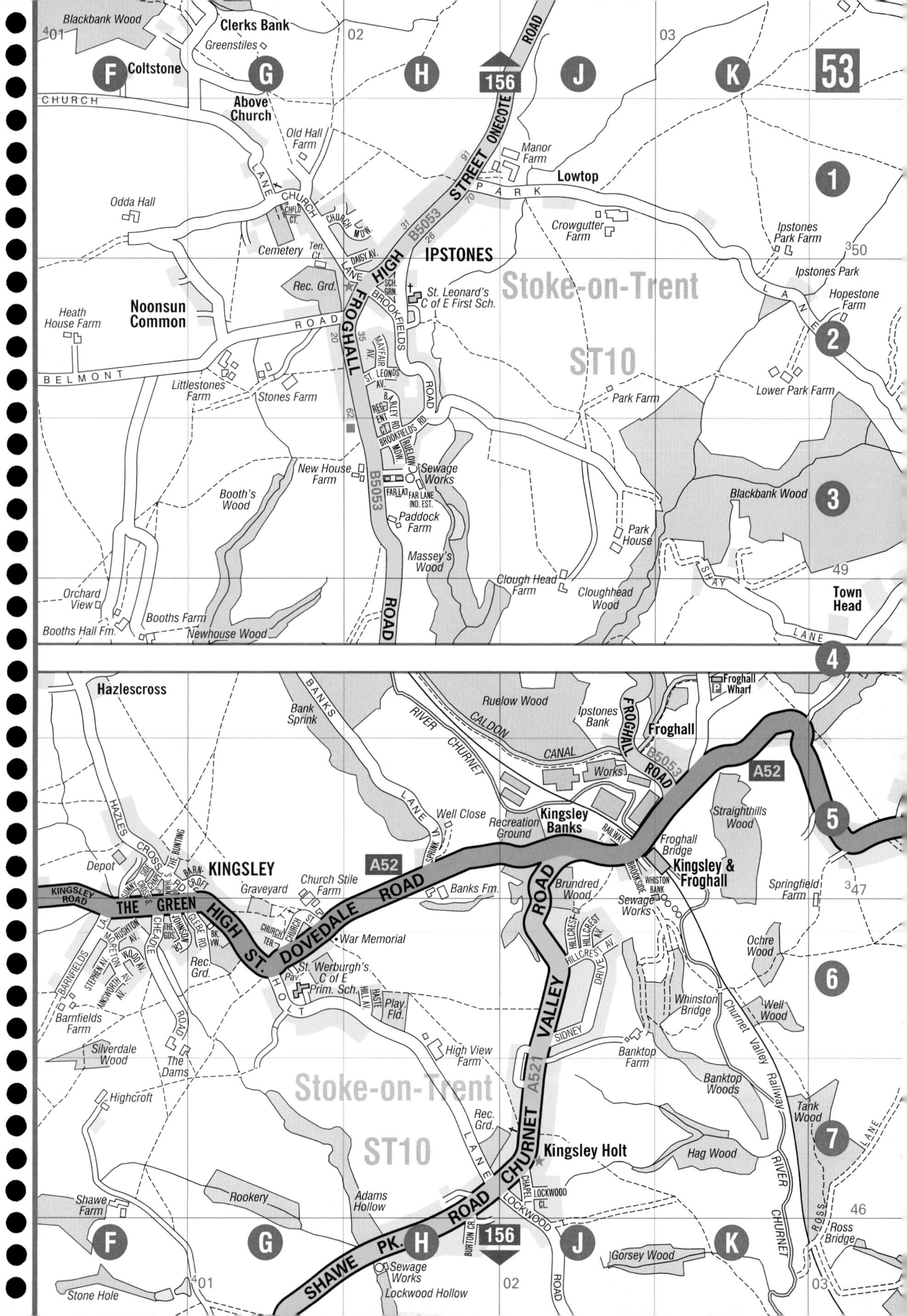

Blackbank Wood
Clerks Bank
Greenstiles
Coltstone
Above Church
Old Hall Farm
Manor Farm
Lowtop
Odda Hall
Crowgutter Farm
Ipstones Park Farm
Ipstones Park
Hopestone Farm
Cemetery
Rec. Grd.
IPSTONES
St. Leonard's C of E First Sch.
Stoke-on-Trent
Noonsun Common
Heath House Farm
ST10
Littlestones Farm
Stones Farm
Park Farm
Lower Park Farm
New House Farm
Sewage Works
Paddock Farm
Booth's Wood
Massey's Wood
Park House
Clough Head Farm
Cloughhead Wood
Town Head
Orchard View
Booths Farm
Booths Hall Fm.
Newhouse Wood
Hazlescross
Bank Sprink
Ruelow Wood
Ipstones Bank
Froghall
Froghall Wharf
Works
Well Close
Recreation Ground
Kingsley Banks
Straighthills Wood
Froghall Bridge
Kingsley & Froghall
Depot
KINGSLEY
Church Stile Farm
Graveyard
Banks Fm.
Brundred Wood
Sewage Works
Springfield Farm
Ochre Wood
War Memorial
St. Werburgh's C of E Prim. Sch.
Rec. Grd.
Play. Fld.
Whinston Bridge
Well Wood
Barnfields Farm
Silverdale Wood
The Dams
High View Farm
Banktop Farm
Banktop Woods
Highcroft
Stoke-on-Trent
Tank Wood
ST10
Rec. Grd.
Kingsley Holt
Hag Wood
Rookery
Adams Hollow
Shawe Farm
Ross Bridge
Gorsey Wood
Sewage Works
Lockwood Hollow
Stone Hole
Churnet Valley Railway
A52
A521
B5053
156

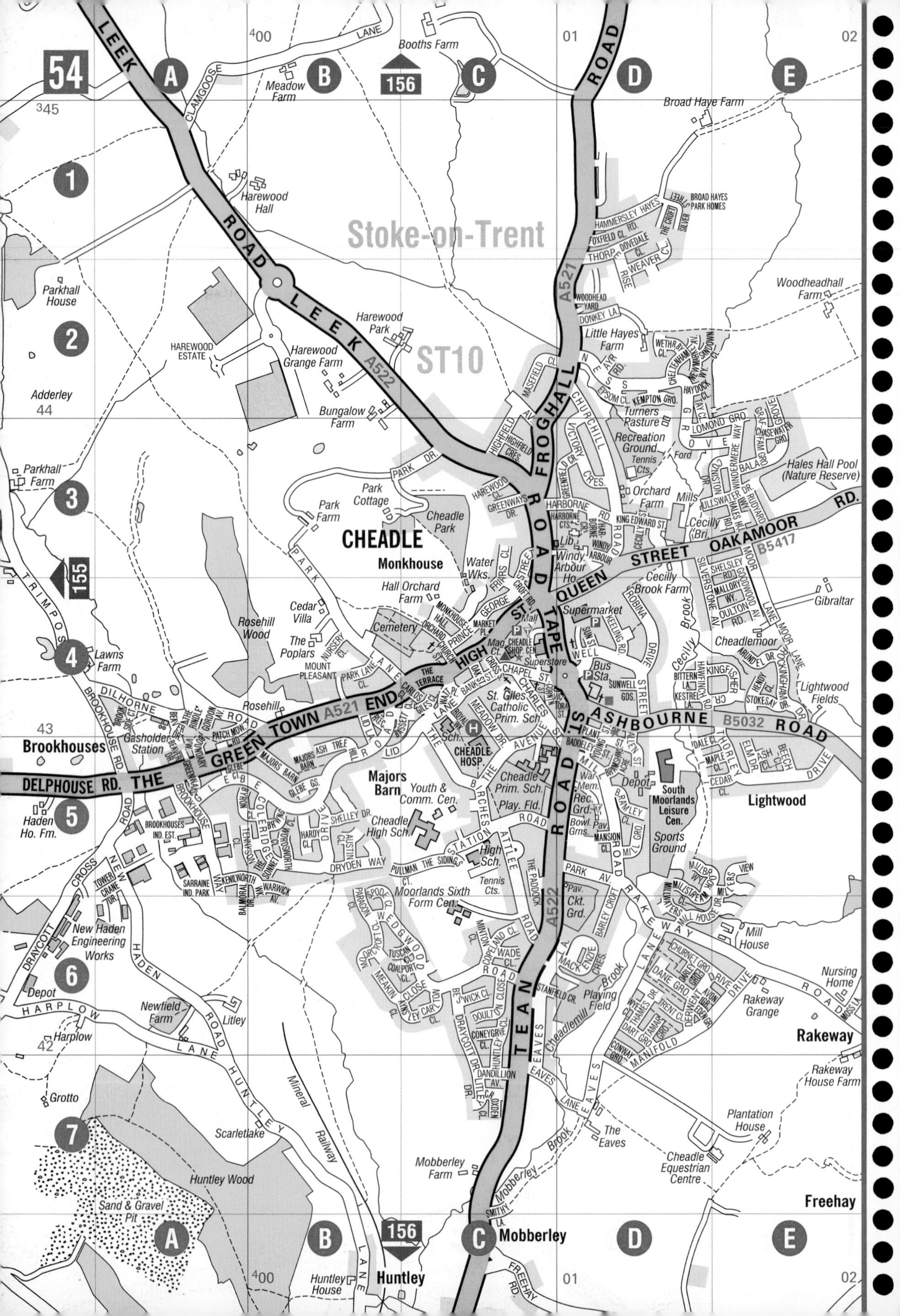
156
Booths Farm
Meadow Farm
Clamgoose Lane
Leek Road
Froghall Road
Broad Haye Farm
Broad Hayes Park Homes
Harewood Hall
Stoke-on-Trent
Parkhall House
Harewood Estate
Harewood Park
Harewood Grange Farm
ST10
A522
A521
Woodheadhall Farm
Little Hayes Farm
Adderley
Bungalow Farm
Turners Pasture
Recreation Ground
Parkhall Farm
Park Cottage
Park Farm
Cheadle Park
Hales Hall Pool (Nature Reserve)
Orchard Farm
Mills
CHEADLE
Monkhouse
Water Wks.
Oakamoor Rd.
Queen Street
B5417
155
Trimpos
Hall Orchard Farm
Cecilly Brook Farm
Gibraltar
Cedar Villa
Rosehill Wood
Supermarket
Cemetery
Cheadle Shop. Cen.
Superstore
Cheadlemoor
The Poplars
Mount Pleasant
Lawns Farm
High St.
Tape St.
Bus Sta.
Lightwood Fields
Dilhorne Road
Rosehill
Green Town End
St. Giles Catholic Prim. Sch.
Ashbourne Road
B5032
Gasholder Station
Brookhouses
Cheadle Hosp.
Delphouse Rd.
The Green
Majors Barn
Cheadle Prim. Sch.
Play. Fld.
South Moorlands Leisure Cen.
Sports Ground
Lightwood
Haden Ho. Fm.
Youth & Comm. Cen.
Cheadle High Sch.
War Mem.
Rec. Grd.
Bowl. Grns.
Brookhouses Ind. Est.
High Sch.
Tennis Cts.
Sarraine Ind. Park
Moorlands Sixth Form Cen.
Pav.
Ckt. Grd.
Park Av.
Rakeway
Mill House
New Haden Engineering Works
Nursing Home
Rakeway Grange
Depot
Newfield Farm
Litley
Harplow Lane
Playing Field
Cheadlemill
Brook
Rakeway
Harplow
Grotto
Tean Road
Eaves Lane
Rakeway House Farm
Scarletlake
Huntley Lane
Mineral Railway
The Eaves
Plantation House
Huntley Wood
Mobberley Farm
Cheadle Equestrian Centre
Sand & Gravel Pit
Freehay
Mobberley
Huntley House
Huntley
Freehay Rd.
A
B
C
D
E
1
2
3
4
5
6
7
345
44
43
42
400
01
02

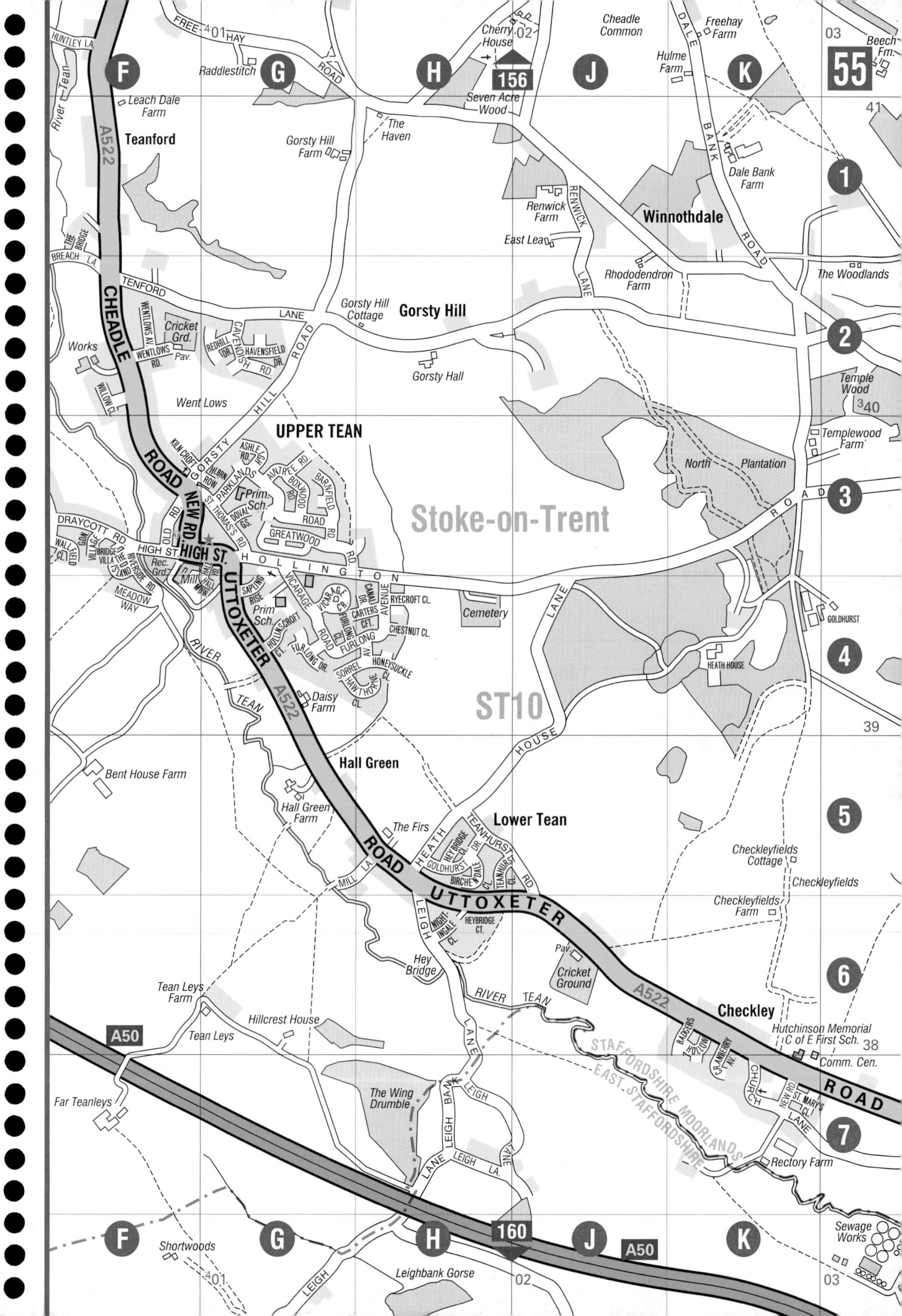
55
156
160
F
G
H
J
K
1
2
3
4
5
6
7
03
41
40
39
38
401
02
Teanford
Gorsty Hill
UPPER TEAN
Stoke-on-Trent
ST10
Hall Green
Lower Tean
Checkley
Winnothdale
Cheadle Common
Freehay Farm
Beech Fm.
Cherry House
Raddlestitch
Leach Dale Farm
Seven Acre Wood
The Haven
Gorsty Hill Farm
Hulme Farm
Dale Bank Farm
Renwick Farm
East Lea
Rhododendron Farm
The Woodlands
Gorsty Hill Cottage
Gorsty Hall
Temple Wood
Templewood Farm
North Plantation
Works
Cricket Grd.
Pav.
Went Lows
Prim. Sch.
Rec. Grd.
Mill
Cemetery
GOLDHURST
HEATH HOUSE
Daisy Farm
Bent House Farm
Hall Green Farm
The Firs
Checkleyfields Cottage
Checkleyfields
Checkleyfields Farm
Hey Bridge
Cricket Ground
Tean Leys Farm
Tean Leys
Hillcrest House
Far Teanleys
The Wing Drumble
Hutchinson Memorial C of E First Sch.
Comm. Cen.
Rectory Farm
Sewage Works
Shortwoods
Leighbank Gorse
A522
A50
CHEADLE ROAD
UTTOXETER ROAD
HIGH ST.
NEW RD.
HOLLINGTON ROAD
TENFORD LANE
GORSTY HILL ROAD
FREEHAY ROAD
DALE BANK ROAD
RENWICK LANE
HEATH HOUSE LANE
LEIGH LANE
LEIGH BANK
LEIGH LA.
MILL LA.
HUNTLEY LA.
BREACH LA.
THE BRIDGE
DRAYCOTT RD.
OLD RD.
MEADOW WAY
RIVERSIDE RD.
THE ISLAND
BRIDGE VILLA
VILLAGE GDN.
WALL FIELD CL.
WILLOW CL.
WENTLOWS AV.
WENTLOWS RD.
REDHILL DR.
CAVENDISH RD.
HAVENSFIELD DR.
KILN CROFT
HLBRN ROW
PARKLANDS
ASHLEY RD.
AINTREE RD.
BOXWOOD RD.
BARNFIELD RD.
GREATWOOD RD.
DOVAL GS.
ST. THOMAS'S RD.
SAPLING RISE
VICARAGE ROAD
VICARAGE CR.
CANAL DR.
AVENUE
CARTERS CFT.
FURLONG CL.
FURLONG
FURLONG DR.
HOLLINSCROFT CT.
RYECROFT CL.
CHESTNUT CL.
HONEYSUCKLE AV.
SORREL CL.
HAWTHORNE CL.
TEANHURST RD.
TEANHURST CL.
HEYBRIDGE CL.
GOLDHURST DR.
BIRCHDALE CL.
NIGHTINGALE CL.
HEYBRIDGE CT.
BADGERS HOLLOW
CRANBERRY AV.
CHURCH LANE
NEW RD.
ST. MARY'S CL.
River Tean
RIVER TEAN
STAFFORDSHIRE MOORLANDS
EAST STAFFORDSHIRE

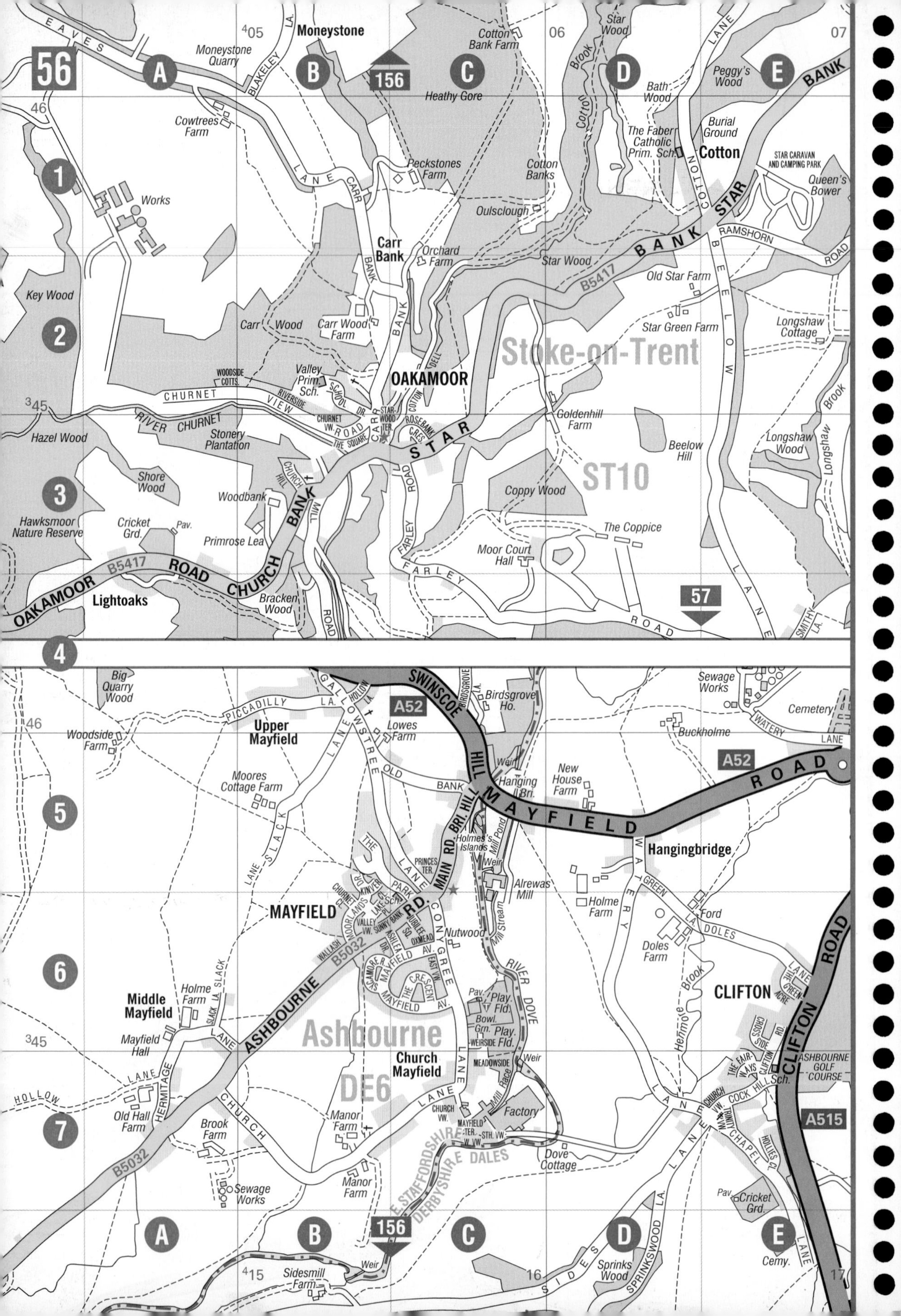
EAVES
Moneystone Quarry
BLAKELEY LA.
Moneystone
156
Cotton Bank Farm
Star Wood
Cotton Brook
LANE
Peggy's Wood
BANK
Heathy Gore
Bath Wood
Cowtrees Farm
The Faber Catholic Prim. Sch.
Burial Ground
Cotton
STAR CARAVAN AND CAMPING PARK
Queen's Bower
Peckstones Farm
CARR LANE
Cotton Banks
Works
Oulsclough
COTTON
STAR
RAMSHORN ROAD
Carr Bank
Orchard Farm
BANK
Star Wood
B5417
Old Star Farm
Key Wood
Carr Wood
Carr Wood Farm
Star Green Farm
Longshaw Cottage
Stoke-on-Trent
BEELOW LANE
WOODSIDE COTTS.
Valley Prim. Sch.
SCHOOL DR.
OAKAMOOR
DELL
CHURNET
RIVERSIDE
CHURNET VIEW
ROAD
STARWOOD TER.
COTTON
ROSEBANK CRES.
Goldenhill Farm
Brook
Longshaw
RIVER CHURNET
Hazel Wood
Stoney Plantation
THE SQUARE
CARR
STAR
Beelow Hill
Longshaw Wood
Shore Wood
CHURCH HILL
MILL
FARLEY ROAD
Coppy Wood
ST10
Woodbank
Hawksmoor Nature Reserve
Cricket Grd.
Pav.
Primrose Lea
BANK
The Coppice
Moor Court Hall
OAKAMOOR ROAD
B5417
CHURCH
FARLEY
Lightoaks
Bracken Wood
ROAD
ROAD
57
SMITHY LA.
Big Quarry Wood
GALLOWSTREE LANE
HOLLOW LA.
SWINSCOE HILL
BIRDSGROVE LA.
Birdsgrove Ho.
Sewage Works
Cemetery
PICCADILLY LA.
A52
Upper Mayfield
Lowes Farm
Buckholme
WATERY LANE
Woodside Farm
OLD BANK
Weir
Hanging Bri.
New House Farm
A52
MAYFIELD ROAD
Moores Cottage Farm
BRI. HILL
MAIN RD.
Holmes's Islands
Mill Pond
SLACK LANE
THE LANE
PRINCES TER.
Weir
Hangingbridge
WATERY
GREEN
Alrewas Mill
PARK
Holme Farm
CHURNET CL.
KINVER DR.
LANE CL.
Sch.
MOORLANDS
VALLEY VW.
SUNNY BANK
RD.
JUBILEE SQ.
Ford
MAYFIELD
CONYGREE
Nutwood
LA. DOLES
OXMEAD
WALLASH
B5032
ASHLEA
Mill Stream
Doles Farm
SLACK
SYCAMORE DR.
MAYFIELD AV.
EAST VW.
RIVER DOVE
CLIFTON ROAD
THE CRESCENT
Hollow Brook
THE GREEN
ACRE
Middle Mayfield
Holme Farm
SLACK LA.
MAYFIELD AV.
Pav.
Play. Fld.
CLIFTON
Bowl. Grn.
Play. Fld.
Hemmore Brook
CROSS SIDE
ASHBOURNE
Ashbourne
WEIRSIDE
Mayfield Hall
LANE
Church Mayfield
MEADOWSIDE
Weir
ASHBOURNE GOLF COURSE
HERMITAGE
LANE
THE FAIRWAYS
CLIFTON
Sch.
DE6
Mill Race
HOLLOW
CHURCH VW.
Factory
CHURCH
COCK HILL
TRINITY
CHAPEL
A515
Old Hall Farm
Brook Farm
CHURCH
Manor Farm
MAYFIELD TER.
MAYFIELD W. VW.
STH. VW.
Dove Cottage
HOLLIES CL.
B5032
STAFFORDSHIRE
E. STAFFORDSHIRE DALES
DERBYSHIRE DALES
DERBYSHIRE
LANE
Manor Farm
Sewage Works
Pav.
Cricket Grd.
SPRINKSWOOD LA.
156
SIDES
Sprinks Wood
LANE
Weir
Sidesmill Farm
Cemy.
A
B
C
D
E
1
2
3
4
5
6
7
405
06
07
46
345
415
16
17

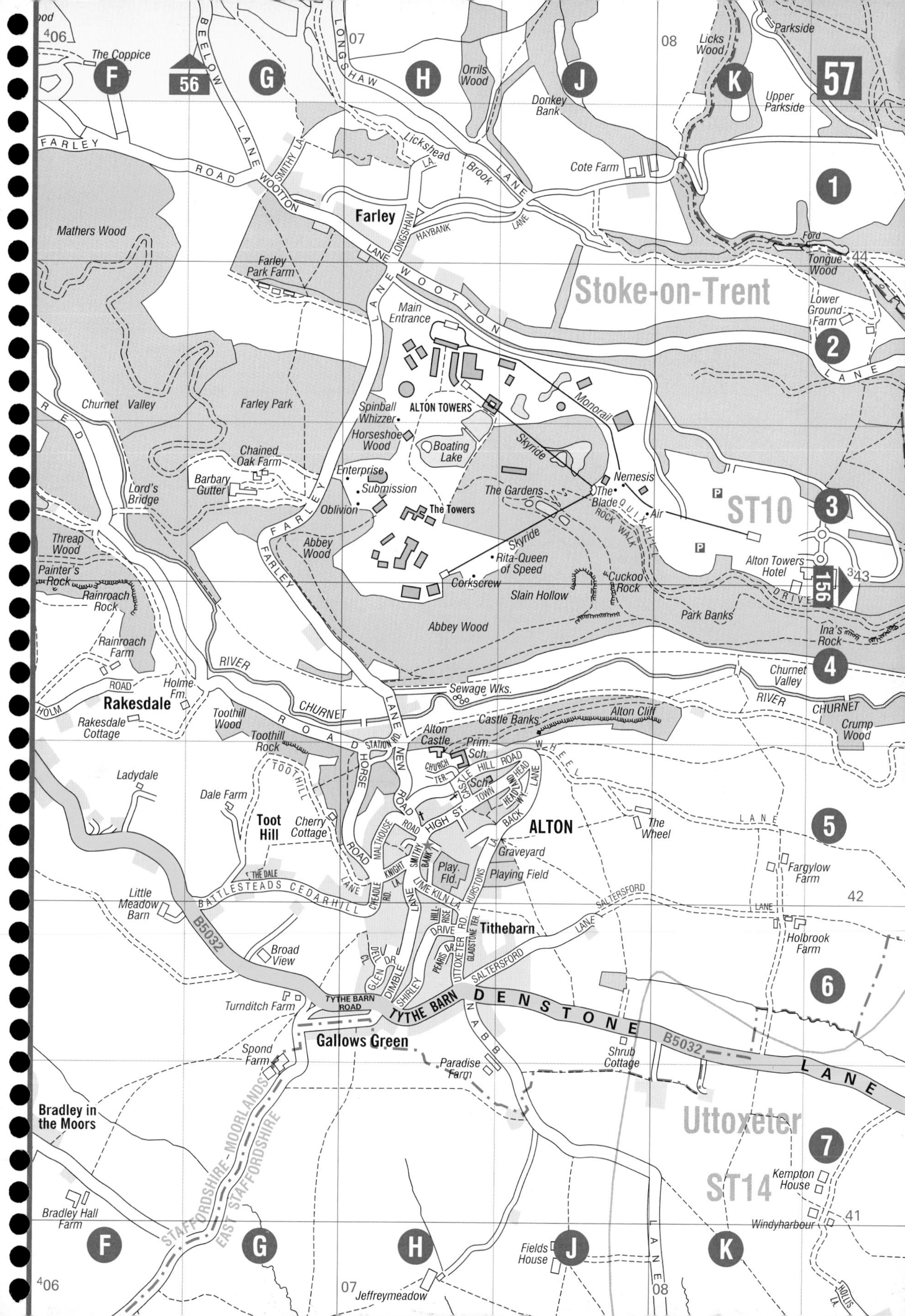

57
56
156
F
G
H
J
K
1
2
3
4
5
6
7
406
07
08
44
43
42
41
The Coppice
Parkside
Licks Wood
Orrils Wood
Donkey Bank
Upper Parkside
Cote Farm
Farley Road
Beelow Lane
Longshaw Lane
Smithy La.
Lickshead La.
Lickshead Brook
Farley
Wootton Lane
Haybank
Mathers Wood
Ford
Tongue Wood
Farley Park Farm
Stoke-on-Trent
Lower Ground Farm
Main Entrance
Lane
Churnet Valley
Farley Park
Spinball Whizzer
ALTON TOWERS
Monorail
Horseshoe Wood
Boating Lake
Skyride
Chained Oak Farm
Barbary Gutter
Lord's Bridge
Enterprise
Submission
Oblivion
The Towers
The Gardens
Nemesis
The Blade
Quixhill
Rock Walk
Air
ST10
Threap Wood
Painter's Rock
Rainroach Rock
Abbey Wood
Rita-Queen of Speed
Corkscrew
Slain Hollow
Cuckoo Rock
Alton Towers Hotel
Drive
Park Banks
Ina's Rock
Rainroach Farm
River Churnet
Road
Holm Road
Holme Fm.
Rakesdale
Rakesdale Cottage
Toothill Wood
Toothill Rock
Sewage Wks.
Castle Banks
Alton Cliff
Churnet Valley
Crump Wood
Alton Castle
Prim. Sch.
Station Rd.
Horse Road
New Road
Church Ter.
Castle Hill Road
Sch.
Town Head
Back Lane
Wheel Lane
Toothill
Ladydale
Dale Farm
Toot Hill
Cherry Cottage
High St.
Malthouse Road
ALTON
The Wheel
Smithy Bank
Graveyard
Play. Fld.
Playing Field
Fargylow Farm
The Dale
Battlesteads
Cedarhill
Cheadle Rd.
Knight La.
Lime Kiln La.
Hurstons
Little Meadow Barn
Saltersford Lane
Holbrook Farm
B5032
Hill Rise
Drive
Gladstone Ter.
Uttoxeter Rd.
Pearis Dr.
Tithebarn
Broad View
Dell Cl.
Glen Dr.
Dimble
Shirley
Turnditch Farm
Tythe Barn Road
Tythe Barn
Denstone Lane
Nabb
Gallows Green
Spond Farm
Paradise Farm
Shrub Cottage
Bradley in the Moors
Staffordshire Moorlands
East Staffordshire
Uttoxeter
ST14
Kempton House
Windyharbour
Bradley Hall Farm
Fields House
Jeffreymeadow
Hollis La.

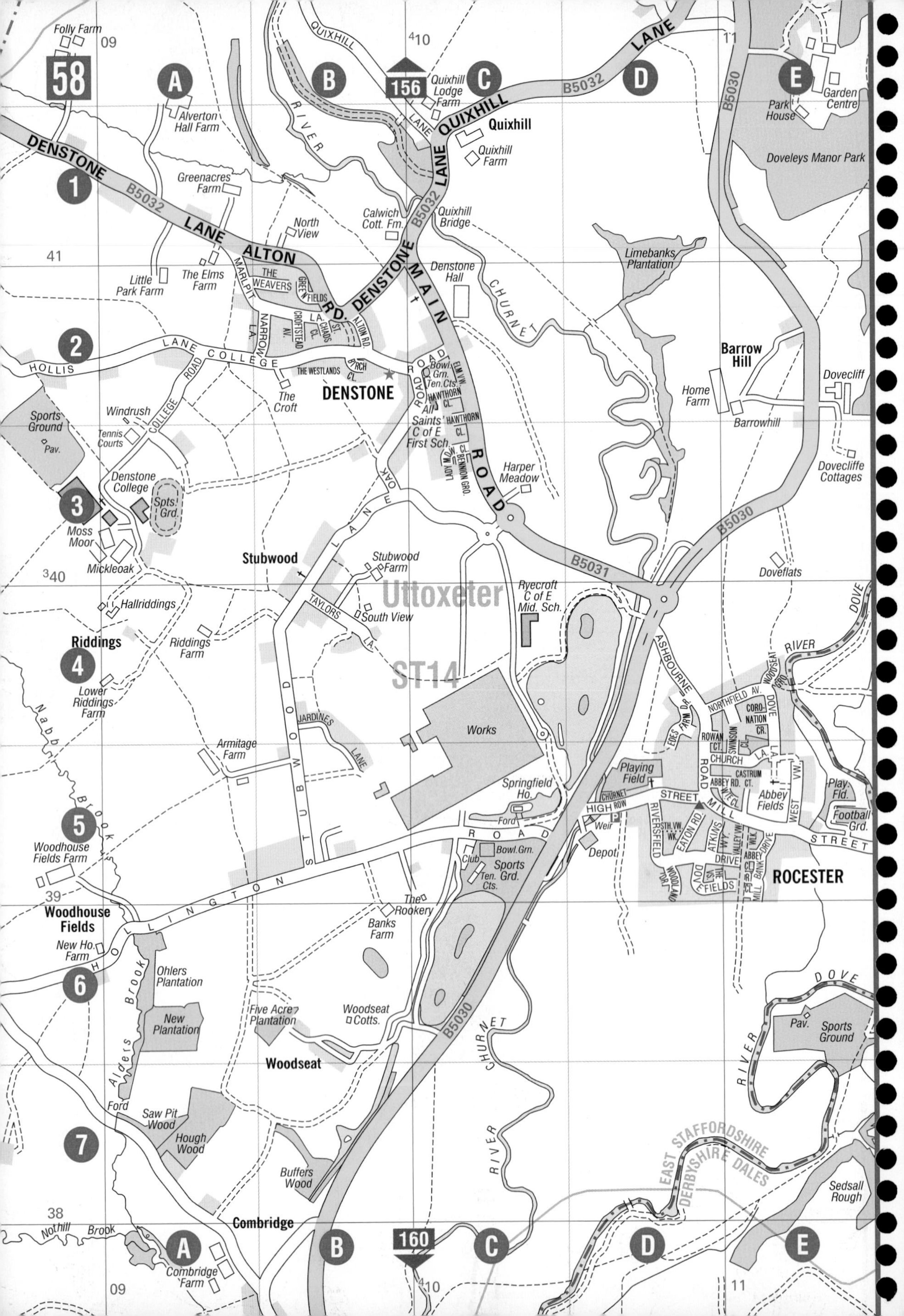

Folly Farm
Alverton Hall Farm
DENSTONE LANE
B5032
ALTON LANE
Greenacres Farm
Little Park Farm
The Elms Farm
North View
Calwich Cott. Fm.
QUIXHILL
RIVER
Quixhill Lodge Farm
QUIXHILL LANE
Quixhill
Quixhill Farm
Quixhill Bridge
B5032
Denstone Hall
CHURNET
Limebanks Plantation
B5030
Park House
Garden Centre
Doveleys Manor Park
Barrow Hill
Home Farm
Barrowhill
Dovecliff
Dovecliffe Cottages
DENSTONE RD.
MAIN ROAD
THE WEAVERS
HOLLIS LANE
COLLEGE ROAD
THE WESTLANDS
DENSTONE
The Croft
Windrush
Sports Ground
Pav.
Tennis Courts
Denstone College
Spts. Grd.
Moss Moor
Mickleoak
Hallriddings
Riddings
Riddings Farm
Lower Riddings Farm
Stubwood
Stubwood Farm
OAK LANE
TAYLORS LA.
South View
Uttoxeter
ST14
Ryecroft C of E Mid. Sch.
B5031
Harper Meadow
All Saints' C of E First Sch.
Doveflats
ASHBOURNE ROAD
RIVER DOVE
Works
JARDINES LANE
Armitage Farm
STUBWOOD
Springfield Ho.
Playing Field
HIGH STREET
CHURCH LA.
MILL STREET
WEST VW.
ABBEY RD.
Abbey Fields
Play. Fld.
Football Grd.
ROCESTER
Weir
Depot
Club
Bowl. Grn.
Sports Grd.
Ten. Cts.
The Rookery
Banks Farm
HOLLINGTON ROAD
Nabb Brook
Woodhouse Fields Farm
Woodhouse Fields
New Ho. Farm
Ohlers Plantation
New Plantation
Alders Brook
Five Acre Plantation
Woodseat Cotts.
Woodseat
Ford
Saw Pit Wood
Hough Wood
Buffers Wood
RIVER CHURNET
Pav.
Sports Ground
RIVER DOVE
EAST STAFFORDSHIRE
DERBYSHIRE DALES
Sedsall Rough
Nothill Brook
Combridge
Combridge Farm
156
160

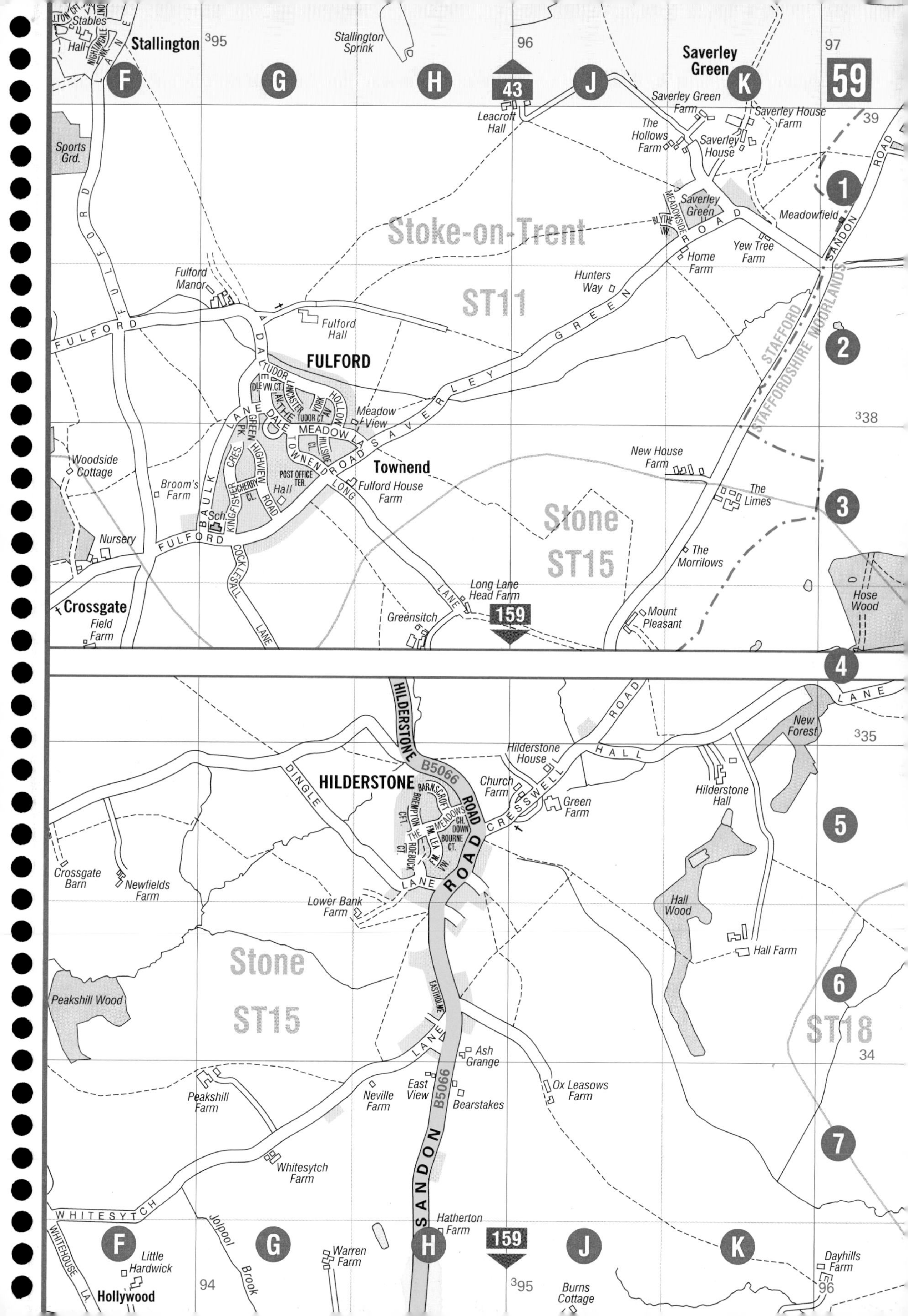
Stallington
Stables
Hall
Stallington Sprink
Saverley Green
43
Leacroft Hall
Saverley Green Farm
Saverley House Farm
The Hollows Farm
Saverley House
Sports Grd.
Saverley Green
Meadowfield
Stoke-on-Trent
Yew Tree Farm
Home Farm
Hunters Way
Fulford Manor
ST11
Fulford Hall
FULFORD
Meadow View
Townend
Fulford House Farm
New House Farm
The Limes
Woodside Cottage
Broom's Farm
Hall
Sch
Stone
ST15
The Morrilows
Nursery
Long Lane Head Farm
Crossgate
Field Farm
Greensitch
159
Mount Pleasant
Hose Wood
STAFFORD
STAFFORDSHIRE MOORLANDS
HILDERSTONE
Hilderstone House
Church Farm
Green Farm
New Forest
Hilderstone Hall
Crossgate Barn
Newfields Farm
Lower Bank Farm
Hall Wood
Hall Farm
Stone
ST15
Peakshill Wood
ST18
Ash Grange
Peakshill Farm
Neville Farm
East View
Bearstakes
Ox Leasows Farm
Whitesytch Farm
Hatherton Farm
Warren Farm
Little Hardwick
Hollywood
Burns Cottage
Dayhills Farm
Jolpool Brook
159

60
Napley Heath
Winnington
Napley House
Napley Rd.
The Haven
Napley
B5415
B5026
Cowleasow Drumble
Buckley's Drumble
Cowleasow
Bedded Plantation
St. Mary's C of E Prim. School
Mucklestone
Rock
Studley Farm
Beasley Bank
Woodlake
The Forty Acres
Eccleshall Road
Eccleshall Road Farm
Market Drayton TF9
White House Farm
Loggerheads
158
West View
Lane
Tadgdale Farm
Tadgedale
Mucklestone Road
Leighton's Drumble
Sewage Works
The Folly
A53
Wickey Tree Farm
Rowney Farm
Market Drayton Rd.
Newcastle
Eccleshall
Hugo Meynell C of E Prim. Sch.
Kestrel
Sewage Works
Sports Ground
Burnt Wood
Oaklands Farm
Parkhill Farm
Blore Heath Farm
Park
Blore
Blore Farm
Lane
Flash
72
73
74
38
37
36
35

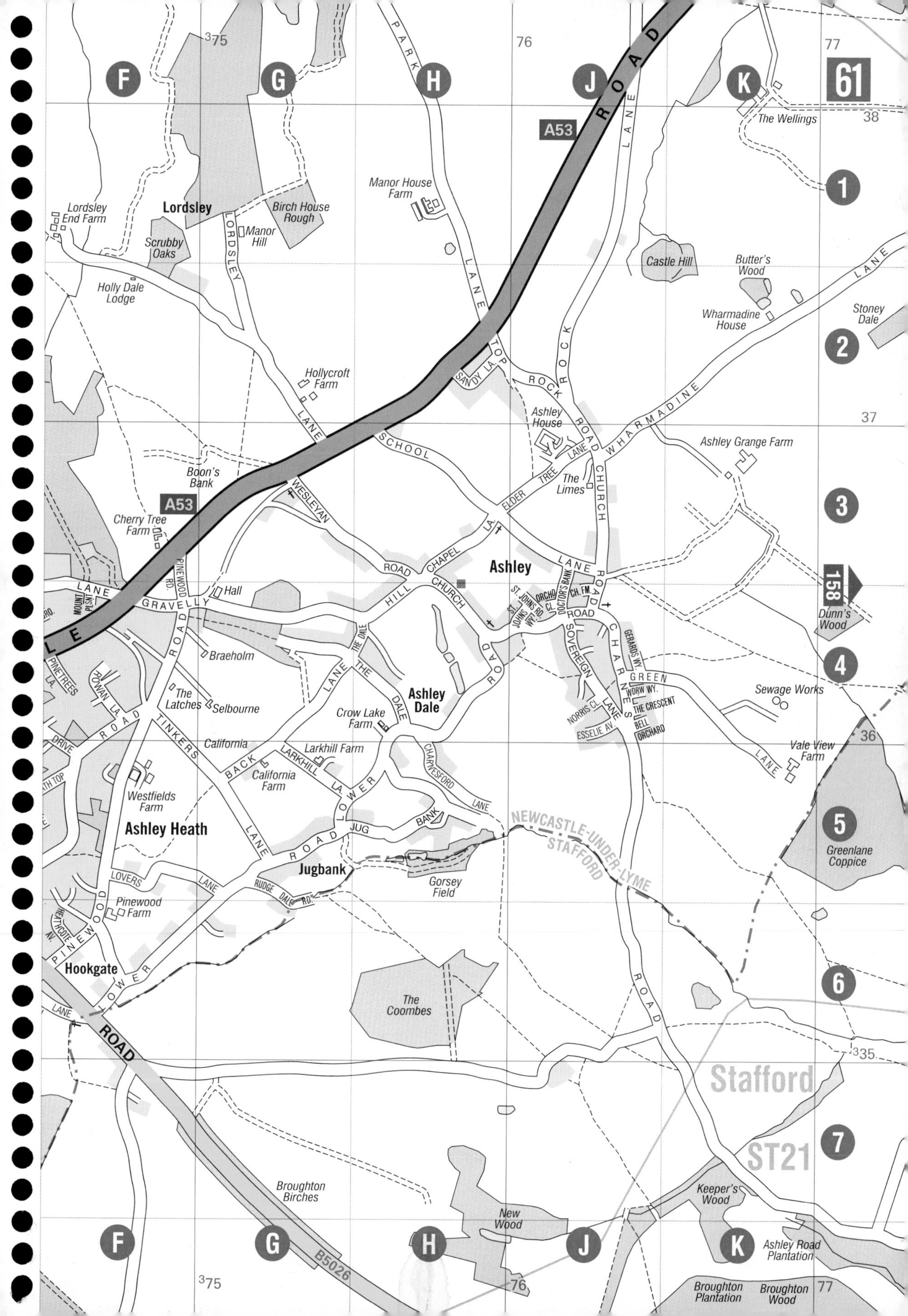
Lordsley
Lordsley End Farm
Scrubby Oaks
Birch House Rough
Manor Hill
Manor House Farm
Holly Dale Lodge
Castle Hill
Butter's Wood
Wharmadine House
Stoney Dale
The Wellings
Hollycroft Farm
Ashley House
Ashley Grange Farm
The Limes
Boon's Bank
Cherry Tree Farm
A53
Ashley
Hall
Braeholm
Dunn's Wood
Sewage Works
The Latches
Selbourne
Ashley Dale
Crow Lake Farm
California
Larkhill Farm
California Farm
Westfields Farm
Ashley Heath
Vale View Farm
Greenlane Coppice
Jugbank
Gorsey Field
Pinewood Farm
Hookgate
NEWCASTLE-UNDER-LYME
STAFFORD
The Coombes
Stafford
ST21
Broughton Birches
New Wood
Keeper's Wood
Ashley Road Plantation
Broughton Plantation
Broughton Wood
B5026
158

Overfole
School Ho. Fm.
Strines Farm
Pingle Cottage
HOLLINGTON
Flashes Farm
Beamhurst Bri.
Mount Pleasant
Mill Farm
Tennis Cts.
Springfields
Chapel Farm
Weir
Mill Pond
Hill House Farm
ST. MICHAEL'S RD.
VICARAGE
POPPIT'S LA.
A50
A522
Beamhurst
Waterloo Farm
LANE
RIVER
WATERLOO PARK
Warehouse
Deggs Leasow
View Farm
Broad View
LEIGH
Lightwood Fields
Park's Farm
The Parks
Uttoxeter
Banktop Farm
PIGEONHAY
Dagdale Farm
160
ST14
Dagdale
Yew Tree Farm
Small Farm
Springfield Farm
Alba Lodge
Park Fields
Hurst Farm
Dagdale Brook
Strawberry Farm
B5027
Park Grange
Roycroft Lodge
Reservoir (covered)
Pav.
Ckt. Grd.
BRAMSHALL
Stock's Farm
STOCKS LANE
The Elms Farm
Park Place
Grange Farm
Ford
Bramshall
Brooklyn
Crossings Farm
ORCHARD
BENNETTS
Brook
Picknal
Bakers Pit Plantation
Wellbank Plantation
Green Farm
The Dearndales
Gendall's Coppice
The Cottages
LOXLEY LANE
Sewage Works
Wellbank Plantation
Eastfield Plantation
Lower Eastfield Plantation
Lower Leasow
A518
STAFFORD
B5013
Highfields Hall

63
Creighton
Crakemarsh
Crakemarsh Farm
Creighton Farm
Stramshall
Stramshall Farm
Depot
Spath Farm
Spath
Spath Cottage Farm
Cottonmill Farm
Leasows Farm
Works
RIVER TEAN
A50
A518
B5030
THE DOVE WAY
Ashbourne
DE6
EAST STAFFORDSHIRE
DERBYSHIRE DALES
RIVER DOVE
Sidford Wood
Eaton Hall Farm
Playing Fields
Sewage Works
Noah's Ark
Dove Bri.
160
NEW ROAD
A522
CHEADLE ROAD
ASHBOURNE RD.
The Heath
The Wharf
Depot
Sports Field
Tennis Cts.
High Sch.
UTTOXETER
DERBY ROAD
DOVEFIELDS IND. EST.
The Willows
Superstore
BROOKSIDE BUS. PK.
STONE ROAD
B5027
SMITHFIELD RD.
HIGH ST.
TOWN MEADOWS WY.
Livestock Market
Heritage Cen.
Youth Cen.
Oldfields Hall Middle School
Picknalls First Sch.
Mount Pleasant
Uttoxeter Leisure Cen.
Hockley Bri.
Works
BRIDGE ST. IND. EST.
Uttoxeter
Paddock
Stands
UTTOXETER RACECOURSE CARAVAN CLUB SITE
UTTOXETER RACECOURSE
Picknal Brook
Cemetery
Balance Hill
OLD KNOTTY WAY
ROAD
Stables
Spring Bank
Woodside
Greenhills
Moorhouse Farm
HIGH WOOD ROAD
B5017
Hazelwalls
Blount's Green
The Cottage
Field Head Farm
Woodgate
UTTOXETER GOLF CLUB
Club House
WOOD LANE
TIMBER LANE

Clifford's Wood
Eastwood
159
Calloway Pit
Long Compton Farm
A51
White House
Stabhill Plantation
Closepit Plantation
Sandyford Farm
Reservoir (covered)
Stone
ST15
Glebe House
Queenswood Lodge
Kennels Cottages
Lodge Covert
SWYNNERTON
Graveyd.
MOORFIELDS INDUSTRIAL ESTATE
NEWCASTLE ROAD
A519
Stafford
ST21
Rectory Gds.
Swynnerton Hall
Sports Grd.
Playing Field
Primary Sch.
Cricket Ground
Pav.
SWYNNERTON PARK
The Dixons
The Crossash
Playing Field
Cotes Heath
Cotes
Upper Pool Plantation
Pilstones Wood
Tennis Courts
Beatty Hall
M6
Yarnfield Park Training Centre
Stone
Howard Hall
BOOTHSTONE MOBILE HOME PARK
BOOTHSTONE GDNS.
First Sch.
Victoria Cottage
Moss House
Works
Coldmeece
ST15
YARNFIELD
Football Ground
46
Gorse Cottage
Greengorse Cottage
Works
COLD MEECE ESTATE
Walnut Tree Farm
Depot
Mere Brook
Kennels
159

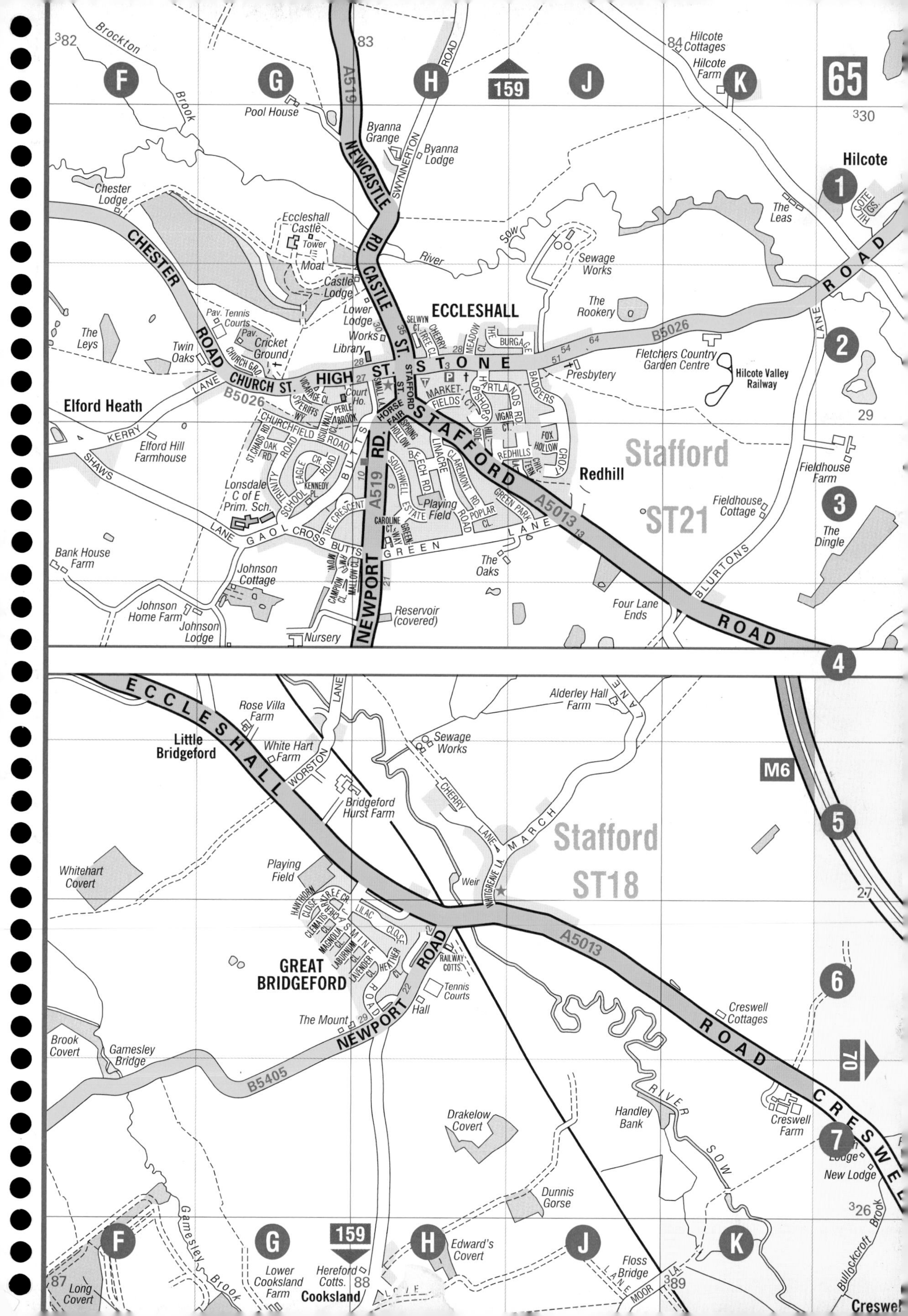

ECCLESHALL
Elford Heath
Redhill
Hilcote
Little Bridgeford
GREAT BRIDGEFORD
Cooksland
Creswell
Stafford ST21
Stafford ST18
Chester Lodge
Eccleshall Castle
Tower
Moat
Castle Lodge
Lower Lodge
Works
Library
Court Ho.
Pool House
Byanna Grange
Byanna Lodge
Hilcote Cottages
Hilcote Farm
The Leas
Sewage Works
The Rookery
Fletchers Country Garden Centre
Hilcote Valley Railway
Presbytery
The Leys
Twin Oaks
Pav. Tennis Courts
Cricket Ground
Elford Hill Farmhouse
Lonsdale C of E Prim. Sch.
Playing Field
Fieldhouse Farm
Fieldhouse Cottage
The Dingle
The Oaks
Four Lane Ends
Bank House Farm
Johnson Cottage
Johnson Home Farm
Johnson Lodge
Reservoir (covered)
Nursery
Rose Villa Farm
White Hart Farm
Bridgeford Hurst Farm
Alderley Hall Farm
Sewage Works
Whitehart Covert
Playing Field
Weir
Railway Cotts.
Tennis Courts
Hall
The Mount
Creswell Cottages
Creswell Farm
New Lodge
Brook Covert
Gamesley Bridge
Drakelow Covert
Handley Bank
Dunnis Gorse
Edward's Covert
Lower Cooksland Farm
Hereford Cotts.
Floss Bridge
Long Covert
NEWCASTLE RD.
CASTLE ST.
HIGH ST.
STONE ROAD
CHESTER ROAD
CHURCH ST.
STAFFORD ROAD
NEWPORT RD.
ECCLESHALL ROAD
NEWPORT ROAD
CRESWELL
A519
A5013
B5026
B5405
M6
SWYNNERTON ROAD
KERRY LANE
SHAWS LANE
GAOL BUTTS
GREEN LANE
BLURTONS LANE
WORSTON LANE
CHERRY LANE
MARCH LANE
WHITGREAVE LA.
MOOR LA.
River Sow
Brockton Brook
Gamesley Brook
Bullockcroft Brook
F G H J K
1 2 3 4 5 6 7
159
70

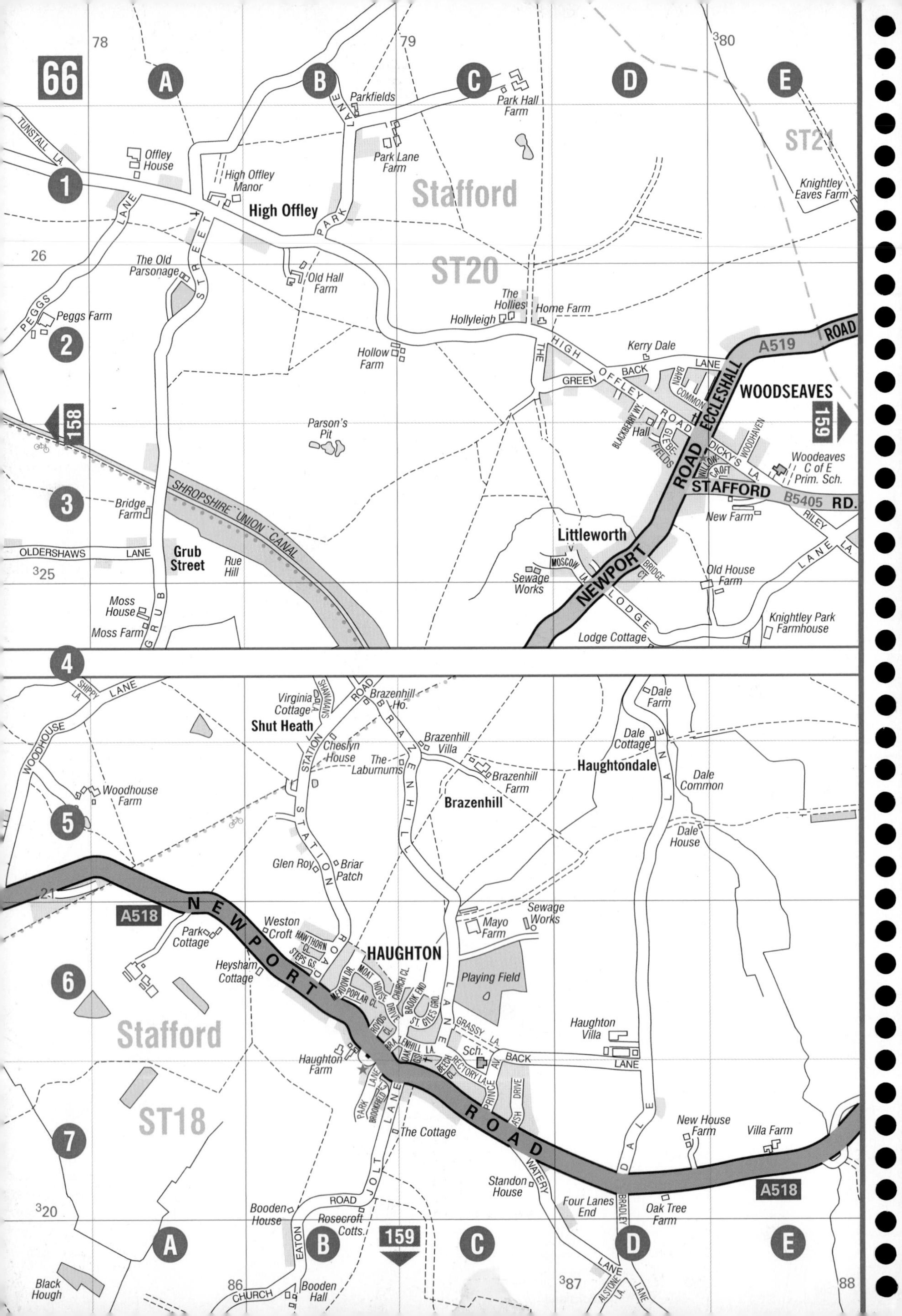

High Offley
Stafford
ST20
ST21
Offley House
High Offley Manor
Parkfields
Park Hall Farm
Park Lane Farm
The Old Parsonage
Old Hall Farm
Peggs Farm
The Hollies
Home Farm
Hollyleigh
Hollow Farm
Kerry Dale
WOODSEAVES
Knightley Eaves Farm
Parson's Pit
Bridge Farm
SHROPSHIRE UNION CANAL
Grub Street
Rue Hill
Littleworth
Sewage Works
Moss House
Moss Farm
Woodeaves C of E Prim. Sch.
New Farm
Old House Farm
Knightley Park Farmhouse
Lodge Cottage
TUNSTALL LA.
PEGGS LANE
STREET
PARK LANE
HIGH OFFLEY ROAD
THE GREEN
BACK LANE
ECCLESHALL ROAD
A519
NEWPORT ROAD
STAFFORD RD.
B5405
RILEY LA.
LANE
OLDERSHAWS LANE
GRUB
MOSCOW LA.
BRIDGE CT.
LODGE
Shut Heath
Virginia Cottage
Brazenhill Ho.
Cheslyn House
The Laburnums
Brazenhill Villa
Brazenhill Farm
Brazenhill
Dale Farm
Dale Cottage
Haughtondale
Dale Common
Dale House
Woodhouse Farm
Glen Roy
Briar Patch
Weston Croft
Park Cottage
Heysham Cottage
HAUGHTON
Mayo Farm
Sewage Works
Playing Field
Haughton Villa
Sch.
Haughton Farm
The Cottage
Standon House
Four Lanes End
New House Farm
Villa Farm
Oak Tree Farm
Booden House
Rosecroft Cotts.
Booden Hall
Black Hough
Stafford
ST18
A518
NEWPORT ROAD
SHIPPY LA.
LANE
WOODHOUSE
STATION ROAD
SHAWMANS LA.
BRAZENHILL LANE
GRASSY LA.
BACK LANE
RECTORY LA.
PRINCE AV.
ASH DRIVE
JOLT LANE
PARK LANE
WATERY LANE
DALE LANE
BRADLEY LANE
ALSTONE LA.
CHURCH
EATON
ROAD

158
159
159

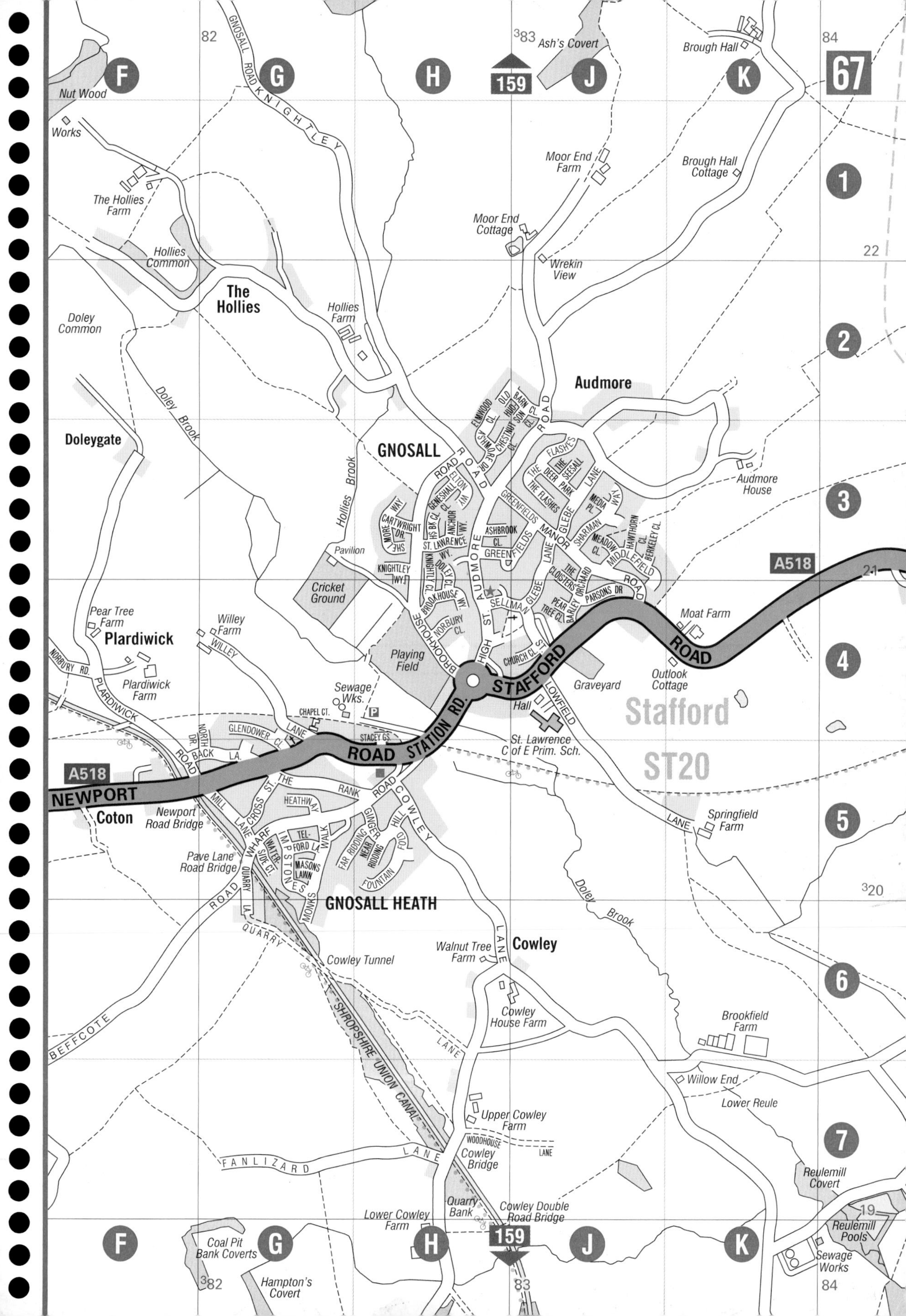

Nut Wood
Works
The Hollies Farm
Hollies Common
The Hollies
Hollies Farm
Doley Common
Doley Brook
Doleygate
GNOSALL
Hollies Brook
Audmore
Audmore House
Moor End Farm
Moor End Cottage
Wrekin View
Brough Hall
Brough Hall Cottage
Ash's Covert
Cricket Ground
Pavilion
Playing Field
Pear Tree Farm
Plardiwick
Plardiwick Farm
Willey Farm
Sewage Wks.
Moat Farm
Outlook Cottage
Graveyard
Hall
St. Lawrence C of E Prim. Sch.
Stafford
ST20
STAFFORD ROAD
STATION RD.
NEWPORT ROAD
A518
Coton
Newport Road Bridge
Pave Lane Road Bridge
GNOSALL HEATH
Springfield Farm
Doley Brook
Cowley
Walnut Tree Farm
Cowley Tunnel
Cowley House Farm
SHROPSHIRE UNION CANAL
Brookfield Farm
Willow End
Lower Reule
Upper Cowley Farm
Cowley Bridge
FANLIZARD LANE
BEFFCOTE
Reulemill Covert
Reulemill Pools
Sewage Works
Quarry Bank
Cowley Double Road Bridge
Lower Cowley Farm
Coal Pit Bank Coverts
Hampton's Covert
159

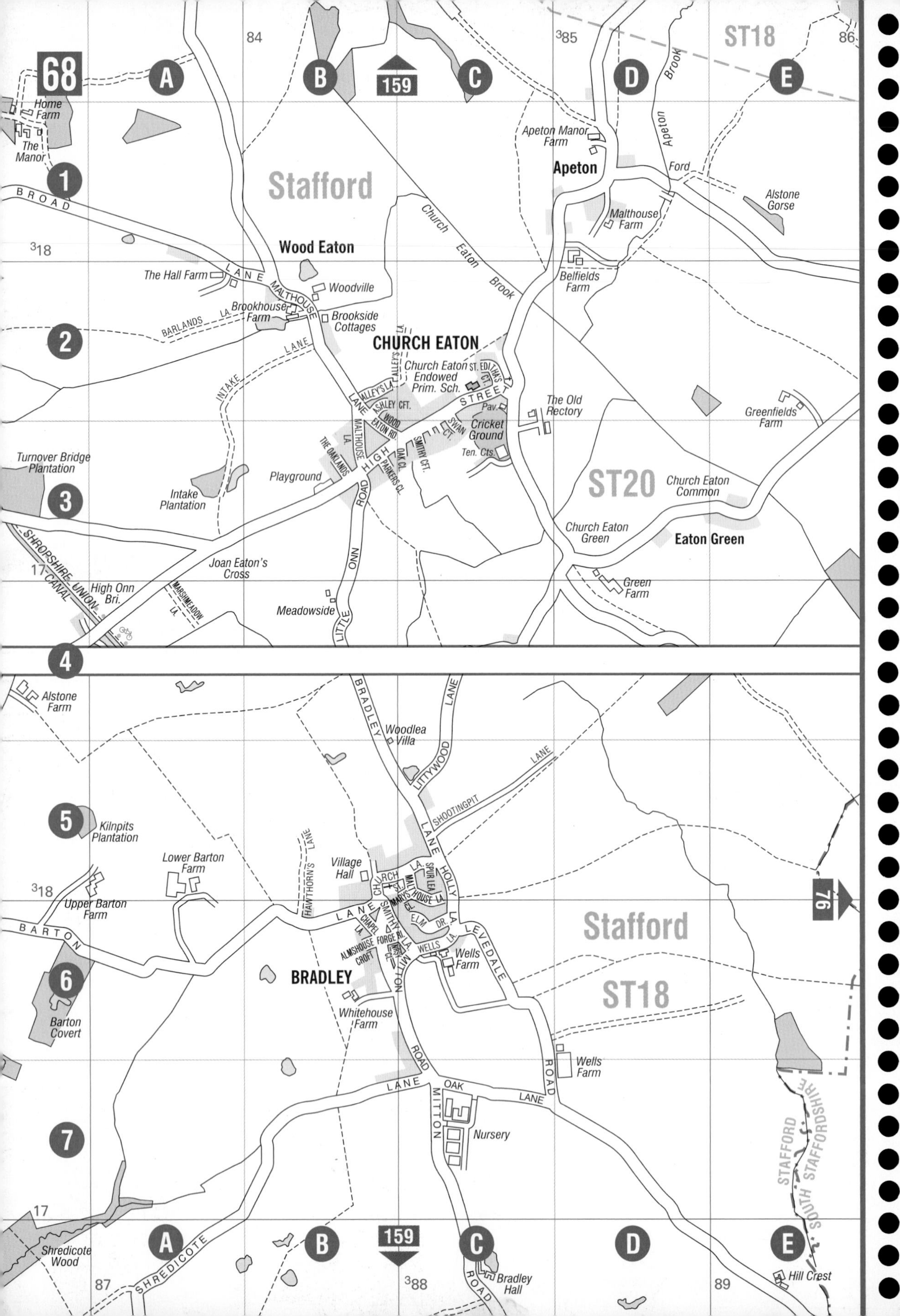

68

A B **159** C D E

84 385 86 **ST18**

Stafford

Home Farm
The Manor

1

B R O A D

³18

Apeton Manor Farm

Apeton Ford

Alstone Gorse

Wood Eaton

Church Eaton Brook

Malthouse Farm

The Hall Farm Woodville

Belfields Farm

MALTHOUSE LANE

BARLANDS LA. Brookhouse Farm Brookside Cottages

2

CHURCH EATON

Church Eaton Endowed Prim. Sch.

ST. EDWARD'S

ALLEY'S LA.

INTAKE LANE

WOOD EATON RD.

STREET

SWAN

Pav.

The Old Rectory

Greenfields Farm

Turnover Bridge Plantation

Intake Plantation

THE OAKLANDS

MALTHOUSE

HIGH

Playground

OAK CL.

PARKERS CL.

SMITHY CFT.

SWAN CFT.

Cricket Ground

Ten. Cts.

ST20

Church Eaton Common

3

ROAD

LITTLE ONN

Church Eaton Green

Church Eaton Green

Eaton Green

SHROPSHIRE UNION CANAL

High Onn Bri.

MARSHMEADOW LA.

Joan Eaton's Cross

Meadowside

Green Farm

17

4

Alstone Farm

BRADLEY LANE

Woodlea Villa

LITTYWOOD LANE

LANE

76

5

Kilnpits Plantation

Lower Barton Farm

HAWTHORN'S LANE

Village Hall

SHOOTINGPIT LANE

HOLLY LANE

SPUR LA.

MALTHOUSE LA.

Stafford

³18

Upper Barton Farm

BARTON

CHURCH LANE

CHAPEL LA.

SMITHY LA.

MILL

ELM DR.

WELLS

LEVEDALE LA.

ST18

6

Barton Covert

BRADLEY

ALMSHOUSE CROFT

FORGE LA.

Wells Farm

Whitehouse Farm

Wells Farm

ROAD

ROAD

7

LANE

OAK

MITTON

OAK LANE

Nursery

STAFFORD

SOUTH STAFFORDSHIRE

17

Shredicote Wood

A SHREDICOTE **B** **159** **C** **D** **E** Hill Crest

87 ³88 Bradley Hall 89 ROAD

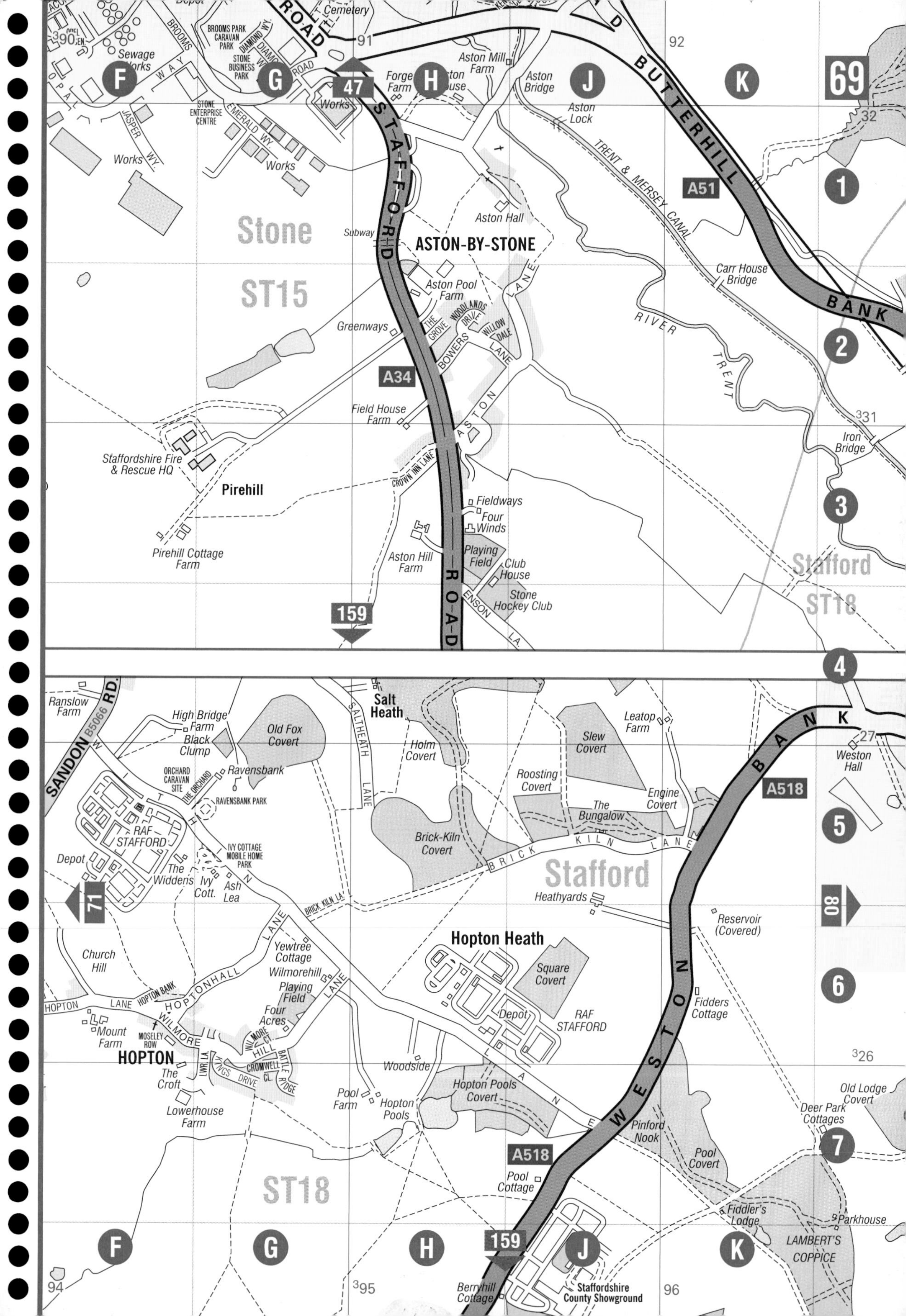
Cemetery
ROAD
Sewage Works
BROOMS PARK CARAVAN PARK
DIAMOND WY.
STONE BUSINESS PARK
BROOMS WAY
STONE ENTERPRISE CENTRE
EMERALD WY.
JASPER WY.
Works
47
Forge Farm
Aston Mill Farm
Aston Bridge
Aston Lock
TRENT & MERSEY CANAL
BUTTERHILL BANK
A51
Stone
ST15
Subway
STAFFORD ROAD
ASTON-BY-STONE
Aston Hall
Aston Pool Farm
Greenways
THE GROVE
WOODLANDS DRIVE
WILLOW DALE
BOWERS LANE
Carr House Bridge
RIVER TRENT
A34
Field House Farm
ASTON LANE
Iron Bridge
Staffordshire Fire & Rescue HQ
Pirehill
CROWN INN LANE
Fieldways
Four Winds
Pirehill Cottage Farm
Aston Hill Farm
Playing Field
Club House
Stone Hockey Club
ENSON LA.
Stafford
ST18
159
F
G
H
J
K
1
2
3
4
5
6
7
91
92
90
32
331
Ranslow Farm
SANDON RD. B5066
High Bridge Farm
Black Clump
Old Fox Covert
Salt Heath
SALTHEATH LANE
Holm Covert
Leatop Farm
Slew Covert
Weston Hall
27
ORCHARD CARAVAN SITE
THE ORCHARD
Ravensbank
RAVENSBANK PARK
Roosting Covert
Engine Covert
WESTON BANK
A518
RAF STAFFORD
Depot
The Widdens
Ivy Cott.
Ash Lea
IVY COTTAGE MOBILE HOME PARK
The Bungalow
Brick-Kiln Covert
BRICK KILN LANE
BRICK KILN LA.
Stafford
Heathyards
71
80
Reservoir (Covered)
Church Hill
Yewtree Cottage
Wilmorehill
Hopton Heath
Square Covert
Playing Field
Four Acres
HOPTON LANE
HOPTON BANK
HOPTONHALL LANE
WILMORE HILL
WILMORE CT.
Mount Farm
MOSELEY ROW
HOPTON
The Croft
LWR. LA.
KINGS DRIVE
CROMWELL CL.
BATTLE RIDGE
Lowerhouse Farm
Depot
RAF STAFFORD
Fidders Cottage
326
Woodside
Hopton Pools Covert
Pool Farm
Hopton Pools
Pinford Nook
Old Lodge Covert
Deer Park Cottages
Pool Covert
Pool Cottage
ST18
Fiddler's Lodge
Parkhouse
LAMBERT'S COPPICE
Berryhill Cottage
Staffordshire County Showground
94
395
96

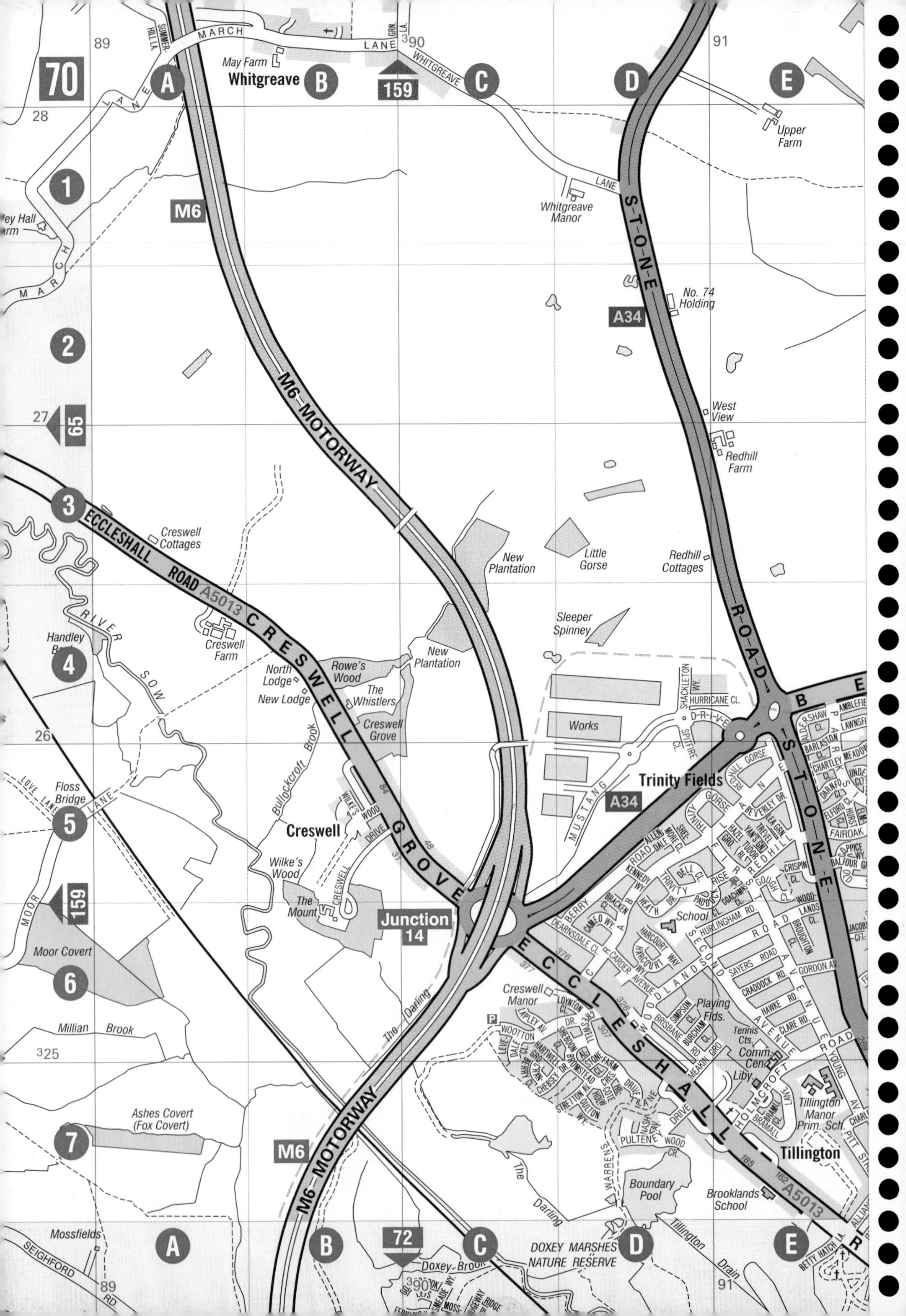

70
Whitgreave
May Farm
MARCH LANE
SUMMERHILL LA.
GRN. LA.
WHITGREAVE
159
Upper Farm
LANE
Whitgreave Manor
M6
STONE ROAD
No. 74 Holding
A34
M6–MOTORWAY
West View
Redhill Farm
65
ECCLESHALL ROAD
A5013
Creswell Cottages
New Plantation
Little Gorse
Redhill Cottages
RIVER SOW
Creswell Farm
Handley
Sleeper Spinney
Rowe's Wood
New Plantation
North Lodge
New Lodge
The Whistlers
Creswell Grove
Works
SHACKLETON WY.
HURRICANE CL.
DRIVE
SPITFIRE CL.
Bullockcroft Brook
Floss Bridge
LOVE LANE
Trinity Fields
MUSTANG
CRESWELL GROVE
Creswell
WILKE'S WOOD DRIVE
Wilke's Wood
The Mount
Junction 14
MOOR LANE
Moor Covert
School
Creswell Manor
The Darling
Playing Flds.
Millian Brook
Tennis Cts.
Comm. Cen.
Liby.
Tillington Manor Prim. Sch.
Ashes Covert (Fox Covert)
Tillington
Boundary Pool
Brooklands School
Mossfields
SEIGHFORD RD
72
Doxey Brook
DOXEY MARSHES NATURE RESERVE
Tillington Drain
BETTY HATCH LA.
1
2
3
4
5
6
7
A
B
C
D
E
89
90
91
28
27
26
325

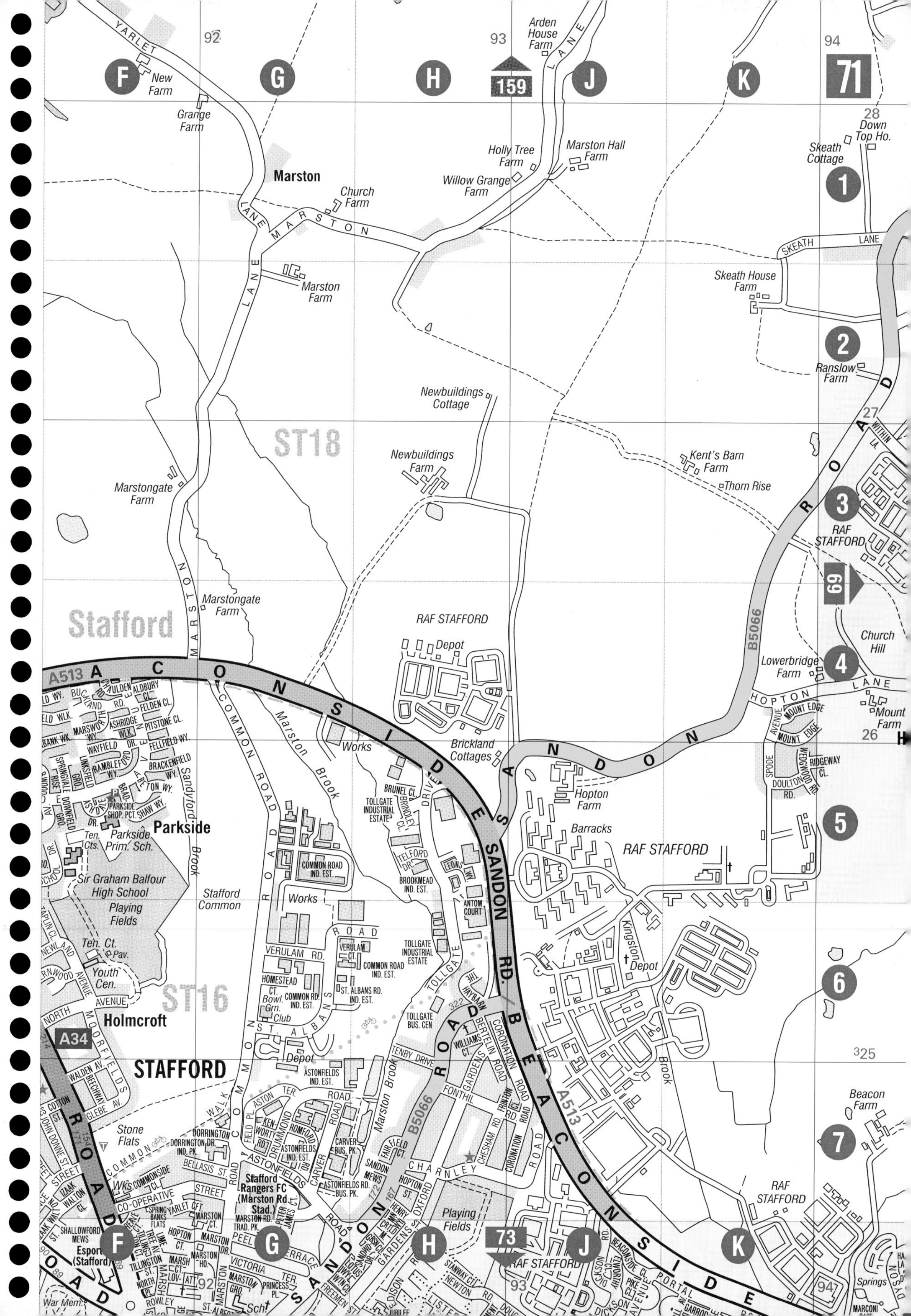
92
93
94
F
G
H
J
K
159
69
73
1
2
3
4
5
6
7
28
27
26
325
YARLET
New Farm
Grange Farm
Arden House Farm
LANE
Holly Tree Farm
Marston Hall Farm
Skeath Cottage
Down Top Ho.
Marston
Church Farm
Willow Grange Farm
MARSTON
LANE
SKEATH LANE
Marston Farm
Skeath House Farm
Ranslow Farm
Newbuildings Cottage
ST18
Newbuildings Farm
Kent's Barn Farm
Thorn Rise
WITHIN LA.
Marstongate Farm
RAF STAFFORD
Marstongate Farm
Stafford
RAF STAFFORD
Depot
Church Hill
B5066
Lowerbridge Farm
HOPTON LANE
Mount Farm
MOUNT EDGE
AVENUE
A513
ACONSIDE
Works
Marston Brook
Brickland Cottages
SANDON
SPODE
WEDGWOOD RD.
RIDGEWAY CL.
DOULTON RD.
COMMON ROAD
TOLLGATE INDUSTRIAL ESTATE
BRUNEL CL.
BRINDLEY CL.
DRIVE
Hopton Farm
Barracks
RAF STAFFORD
Parkside
PARKSIDE SHOP. PCT.
Parkside Prim. Sch.
Sandyford Brook
TELFORD DR.
BROOKMEAD IND. EST.
COMMON ROAD IND. EST.
LEONS WY.
ANTOM COURT
Sir Graham Balfour High School
Playing Fields
Stafford Common
Works
SANDON RD.
ROAD
Kingston Depot
Brook
VERULAM RD.
VERULAM CT.
COMMON ROAD IND. EST.
TOLLGATE INDUSTRIAL ESTATE
Teh. Ct.
Pav.
Youth Cen.
HOMESTEAD CT.
Bowl. Grn. Club
COMMON RD. IND. EST.
ST. ALBANS RD. IND. EST.
ST16
TOLLGATE
THE HAYBARN
AVENUE
Holmcroft
A34
ST. ALBANS
TOLLGATE BUS. CEN
322
ROAD
WILLIAMS CT.
BERTELIN ROAD
CORONATION ROAD
BEACONSIDE
A513
Depot
TENBY DRIVE
STAFFORD
ASTONFIELDS IND. EST.
Marston Brook
FONTHILL
Beacon Farm
B5066
ASTON TER
ROAD
Stone Flats
DORRINGTON CL.
DORRINGTON DR. IND. PK.
COMMON
ASTONFIELDS IND. EST.
CARVER BUS. PK.
FAIRFIELD CT.
CHESHAM RD.
CORONATION
ROAD
Wks. COMMONSIDE
CO-OPERATIVE
STREET
BELLASIS ST.
ASTONFIELDS
Stafford Rangers FC (Marston Rd. Stad.)
SANDON MEWS
ASTONFIELDS RD. BUS. PK.
HOPTON ST.
CHARNLEY
OXFORD
Playing Fields
RAF STAFFORD
YARLET CFT.
MARSTON CT.
MARSTON RD. TRAD. PK.
PETER JAMES CT.
SHALLOWFORD MEWS
Esport (Stafford)
HOPTON CT.
PEEL
TERRACE
MARSTON DR.
SANDON
GARDENS
RAF STAFFORD
PORTAL
Springs
MARSH CT.
VICTORIA
TER
PRINCESS PL.
MARSTON GRO.
ROWLEY
War Mem.
Sch.
STANWAY CT.
NEWTON
RD.
DICKSON
AVENUE
MARCONI
ROAD

(Fox Covert)
Mossfields
West Point
Burley
Aston Hill Farm
Depot
Aston
Thorny Croft
Aston Farm
Aston Hall Farm
Holly Bush Farm
Glen Farm
ST18
Sewage Works
Playing Field
Derrington
Castle View Estate
Boons Industrial Estate
The Pingotts
Home Farm
Berry Ring Farm
Berry Ring Fort
Berry Ring
Billington Farm
Highfield House
Whitehouse
Thorneyfields Farm
Doxey Brook
Doxey Fields
Doxey Bridge
Doxey
Castle Grange
Doxey House
Vicarage
Aston Bank Farm
Doxey Marshes Nature Reserve
Tillington
Brooklands School
Tennis Courts
Club
Cricket Grd.
Bowling Greens
Pavs.
Football Ground
Works
Castletown
Burleyfields
Hill Farm
Barn Cottages
Stafford Castle Golf Course
Club House
Sports Fld.
Stafford Castle
Castle Wood
Visitor Centre
Western Downs
King Edward VI High School
Playing Fld.
Play Area
Highfields
M6 Motorway
A518
A5013
Newport Road
Castle Bank
Doxey Road
Aston Bank
Seighford Road
Derrington Lane
Thorneyfields Lane
Kingsway
Redgrave Drive
Martin Drive
Crescent
The Drive
Bagot St
Somerset Road
Barnes Road

70
159
76

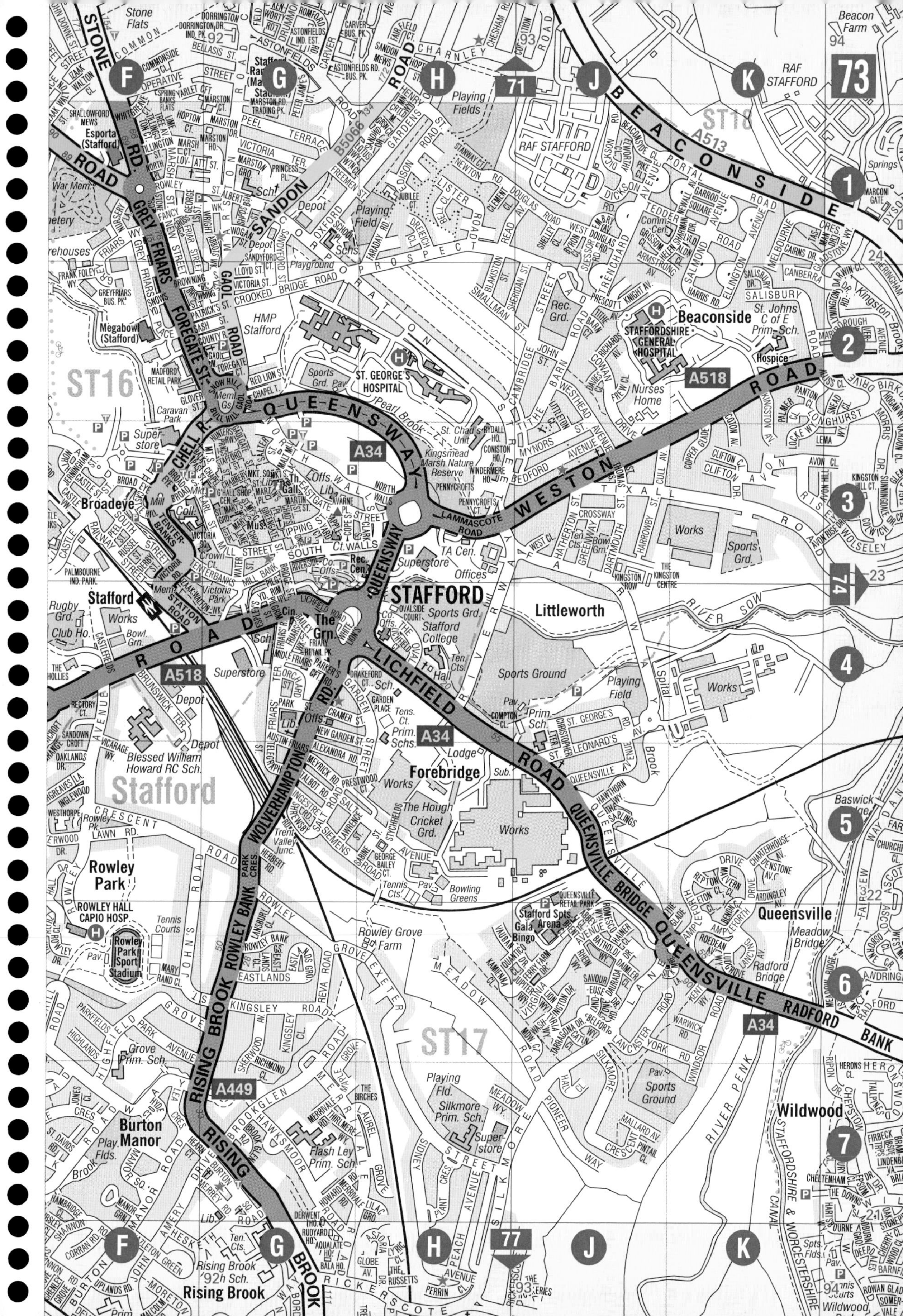

73
71
74
77
F
G
H
J
K
1
2
3
4
5
6
7
ST16
ST17
ST18
STAFFORD
Stafford
Beaconside
Broadeye
Littleworth
Forebridge
Rowley Park
Burton Manor
Rising Brook
Queensville
Wildwood
Baswick
RAF STAFFORD
Beacon Farm
HMP Stafford
ST. GEORGE'S HOSPITAL
STAFFORDSHIRE GENERAL HOSPITAL
Hospice
Nurses Home
Stafford College
ROWLEY HALL CAPIO HOSP.
Rowley Park Sport Stadium
Blessed William Howard RC Sch.
St. Johns C of E Prim. Sch.
Silkmore Prim. Sch.
Flash Ley Prim. Sch.
Grove Prim. Sch.
Rising Brook Sch.
The Hough Cricket Grd.
Sports Ground
Playing Fields
Playing Field
Rec. Grd.
Works
Superstore
Stafford Spts. Arena
Gala Bingo
Megabowl (Stafford)
Esporta (Stafford)
Kingsmead Marsh Nature Reserve
Victoria Park
The Grn.
Trent Valley Junc.
Rowley Grove Farm
Radford Bridge
Meadow Bridge
Springs
STONE RD.
GREY FRIARS
FOREGATE ST.
SANDON ROAD
GAOL ROAD
QUEENSWAY
WESTON ROAD
BEACONSIDE
PORTAL ROAD
LICHFIELD ROAD
QUEENSVILLE BRIDGE
QUEENSVILLE
RADFORD BANK
WOLVERHAMPTON RD.
ROWLEY BANK
RISING BROOK
CROOKED BRIDGE ROAD
PROSPECT ROAD
TIXALL ROAD
SILKMORE LANE
RIVER SOW
RIVER PENK
STAFFORDSHIRE & WORCESTERSHIRE CANAL
A34
A449
A513
A518
B5066

74
A
B
C
D
E
1
2
3
4
5
6
7
159
73
78
Beacon Farm
RAF STAFFORD
Brickhouse Farm
Stafford Lodge
A518
BEACON BUSINESS PARK
STAFFORDSHIRE TECHNOLOGY PARK
Staffordshire University (Stafford Campus)
BEACONSIDE
WESTON ROAD
A513
Blackheath Covert
Staffordshire University (Stafford Campus)
Lower Hanyards
Queen's Low
Hanyards Spinney
King's Low
Crab Covert
Weston Rd. High Sch.
Beaconside Sports Centre
Rec. Grd.
Stafford Crematorium
Tixall Rd. Cemetery
BLACKHEATH LANE
HANYARDS
Kingston Hill
Kingston Pool Covert
ST16
Hanyards
Tixall Heath Farm
Brancote Row New Cottages
New Cottages
TIXALL ROAD
Stone Cottage
ST. THOMAS LANE
St. Thomas Priory Farm
RIVER SOW
St. Thomas Mill Farm
Mill Stream
St. Thomas Bridge
Froghall Cottage
Little Brancote
Reservoir
Hartley Park Homes
Brancotegorse Covert
Brancote Farm
Sewage Works
Lodgefield Bridge
Baswick Bridge
Baswich
Weeping Cross
Queensville
Meadow Bridge
Radford Bridge
Stoneford Bridge
Brancote
STAFFORDSHIRE & WORCESTERSHIRE CANAL
RIVER
Walton Bridge
ST17
Leasowes Jun. & Inf. Schs.
St. Annes RC Prim Sch.
RADFORD BANK
A34
WEEPING CROSS
A513
MILFORD ROAD
MAIN ROAD
Wildwood
Police H.Q.
Hillcroft Park
CANNOCK ROAD
Walton High Sch.
Walton Farm
Milford Lodge
Tennis Courts
Wildwood

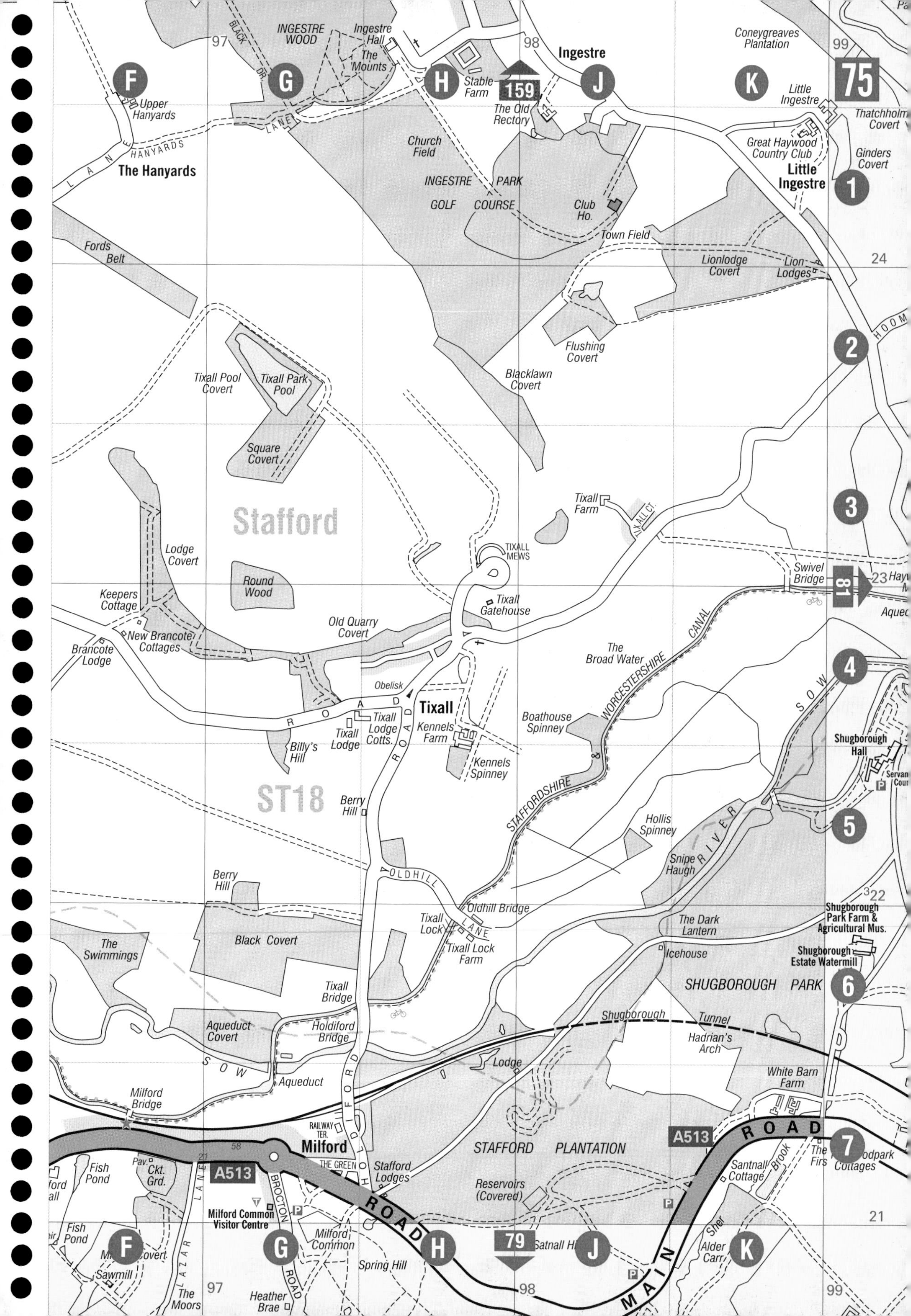

75
Ingestre
INGESTRE WOOD
Ingestre Hall
The Mounts
Stable Farm
159
The Old Rectory
Coneygreaves Plantation
Little Ingestre
Thatchholm Covert
Great Haywood Country Club
Ginders Covert
Upper Hanyards
HANYARDS LANE
The Hanyards
Church Field
INGESTRE PARK GOLF COURSE
Club Ho.
Town Field
Fords Belt
Lionlodge Covert
Lion Lodges
Flushing Covert
Blacklawn Covert
Tixall Pool Covert
Tixall Park Pool
Square Covert
Stafford
Lodge Covert
Round Wood
Tixall Farm
TIXALL MEWS
Swivel Bridge
81
Tixall Gatehouse
Keepers Cottage
New Brancote Cottages
Brancote Lodge
Old Quarry Covert
The Broad Water
Obelisk
Tixall
Tixall Lodge Cotts.
Tixall Lodge
Kennels Farm
Kennels Spinney
Boathouse Spinney
Billy's Hill
ST18
STAFFORDSHIRE & WORCESTERSHIRE CANAL
Berry Hill
Shugborough Hall
Hollis Spinney
Snipe Haugh
RIVER SOW
OLDHILL LANE
Oldhill Bridge
Tixall Lock
Tixall Lock Farm
Black Covert
The Swimmings
The Dark Lantern
Icehouse
Shugborough Park Farm & Agricultural Mus.
Shugborough Estate Watermill
SHUGBOROUGH PARK
Tixall Bridge
Holdiford Bridge
Aqueduct Covert
Shugborough Tunnel
Hadrian's Arch
Lodge
Aqueduct
White Barn Farm
Milford Bridge
RAILWAY TER.
Milford
THE GREEN
HOLDIFORD ROAD
Stafford Lodges
STAFFORD PLANTATION
A513
ROAD
Santnall Cottage
Brook
The Firs
Fish Pond
Pav.
Ckt. Grd.
Milford Common Visitor Centre
BROCTON ROAD
Reservoirs (Covered)
Milford Common
Spring Hill
79
LAZAR LANE
Sawmill
The Moors
Heather Brae
MAIN ROAD
Alder Carr
97
98
99
24
23
22
21
1
2
3
4
5
6
7
F
G
H
J
K

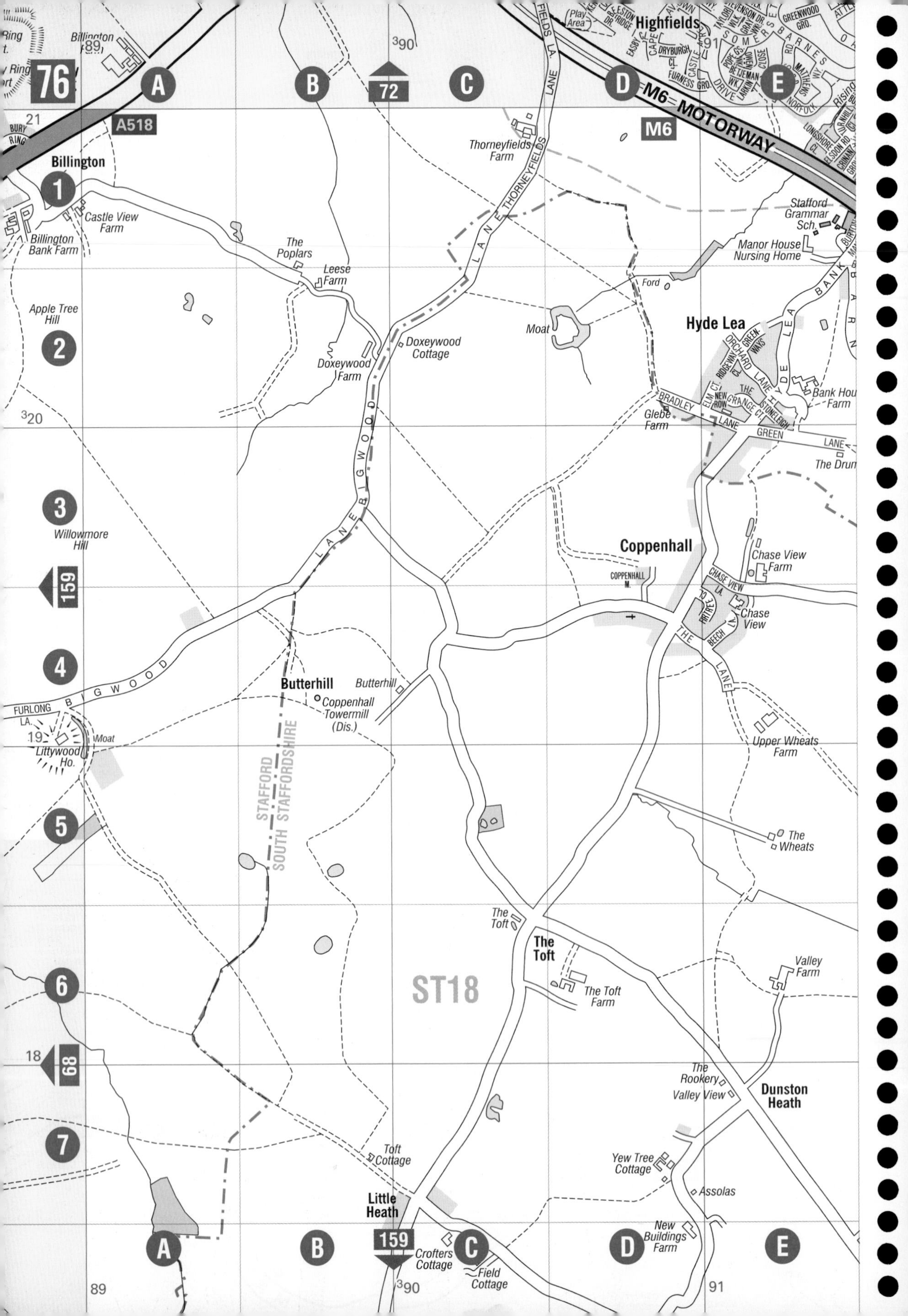

A518

Billington

Billington
Bank Farm

Castle View
Farm

The
Poplars

Leese
Farm

Apple Tree
Hill

Doxeywood
Farm

Doxeywood
Cottage

Moat

Thorneyfields
Farm

M6

M6 MOTORWAY

Highfields

Play
Area

Stafford
Grammar
Sch.

Manor House
Nursing Home

Hyde Lea

Bank House
Farm

Willowmore
Hill

159

BRADLEY

Glebe
Farm

GREEN

LANE

The Drum

Coppenhall

COPPENHALL
M

Chase View
Farm

Chase
View

CHASE VIEW LA.

THE BEECH LANE

FURLONG LA.

BIGWOOD

Butterhill

Butterhill

Coppenhall
Towermill
(Dis.)

Littywood
Ho.

19

Moat

STAFFORD
SOUTH STAFFORDSHIRE

Upper Wheats
Farm

The
Wheats

ST18

The
Toft

The
Toft

The Toft
Farm

Valley
Farm

18

68

The
Rookery

Valley View

Dunston
Heath

Toft
Cottage

Yew Tree
Cottage

Assolas

Little
Heath

159

Crofters
Cottage

Field
Cottage

New
Buildings
Farm

89

91

390

320

390

21

72

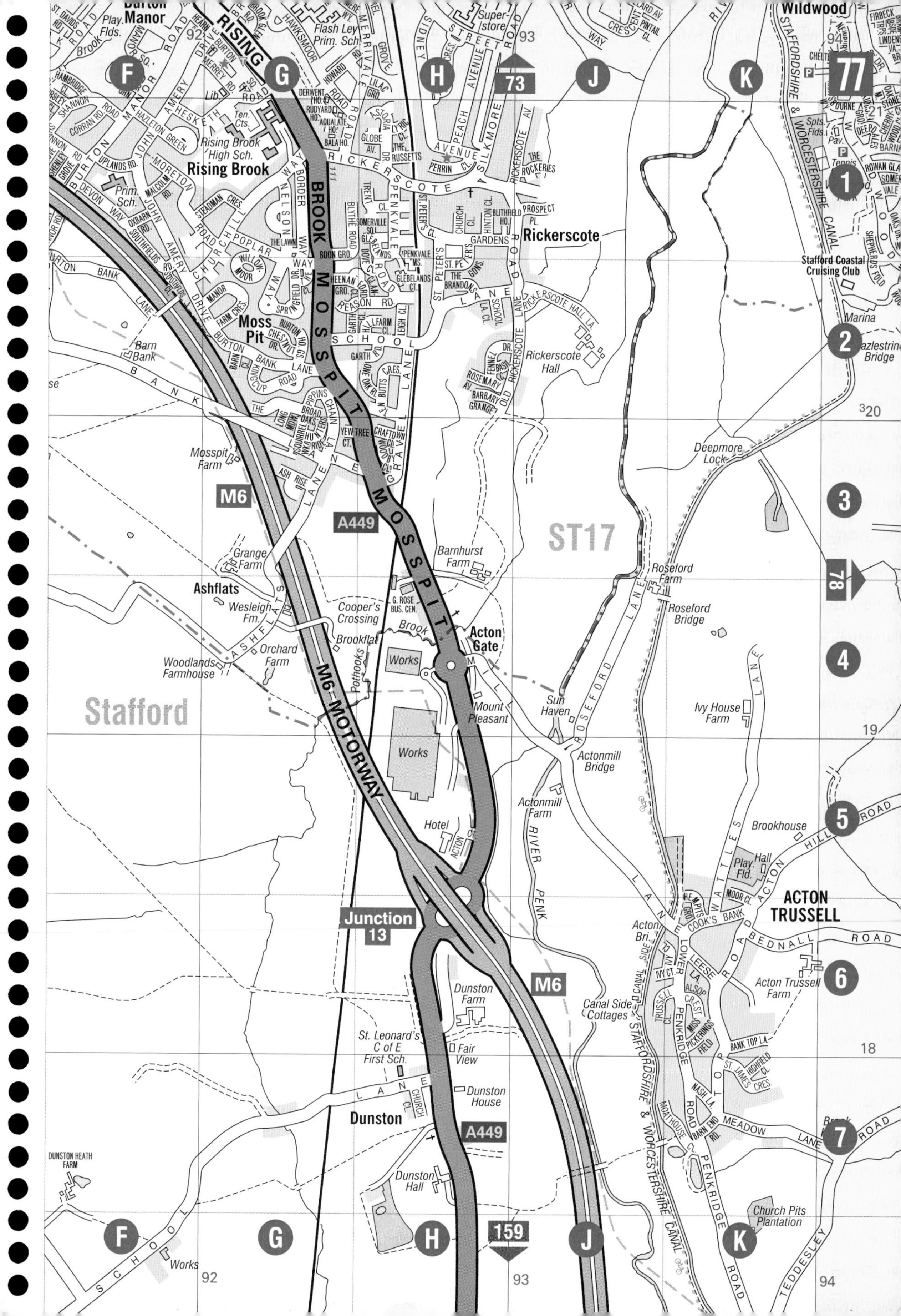

77
73
78
159
Burton Manor
Rising Brook
Rising Brook High Sch.
Moss Pit
Rickerscote
Wildwood
Stafford Coastal Cruising Club
Marina
Hazlestrine Bridge
Rickerscote Hall
Deepmore Lock
ST17
Barnhurst Farm
Roseford Farm
Roseford Bridge
Grange Farm
Ashflats
Wesleigh Fm.
Cooper's Crossing
Brookflat
Acton Gate
Mosspit Farm
Orchard Farm
Woodlands Farmhouse
Stafford
Works
Mount Pleasant
Sun Haven
Ivy House Farm
Actonmill Bridge
Actonmill Farm
Hotel
Brookhouse
Hall
ACTON TRUSSELL
Junction 13
M6
A449
M6 MOTORWAY
MOSSPIT
BROOK
RISING
Dunston Farm
St. Leonard's C of E First Sch.
Fair View
Dunston House
Dunston
Dunston Hall
Canal Side Cottages
Acton Trussell Farm
Church Pits Plantation
DUNSTON HEATH FARM
Barn Bank
STAFFORDSHIRE & WORCESTERSHIRE CANAL
RIVER PENK
92
93
94
320
19
18

78
Wildwood
Wildwood Park
Tennis Courts
Schools
Stafford Coastal Cruising Club
Marina
Hazlestrine Bridge
Hazlestrine
STAFFORDSHIRE & WORCESTERSHIRE CANAL
CANNOCK ROAD
A34
Police H.Q.
Hillcroft Park
74
MILFORD ROAD
A513
Walton High Sch.
Walton Farm
Walton-on-the-Hill
Moor Covert
Cressel Wood
Oakridge Prim. Sch.
Brocton Park Farm
Acton Hill
Acton Hill Farm
Acton Hill Cottages
The Villa
The Shepherds
The Larchery
Stafford
ST17
77
Club House
Derwick Ind. Est.
Newtown
Cottage Farm
Manor Farm
Brocton Cross Roads
Brocton Football Grd.
SOUTH STAFFORDSHIRE
STAFFORD
The Acorns
ACTON HILL ROAD
TEDDESLEY ROAD
BEDNALL ROAD
ACTON TRUSSELL
Acton Trussell Farm
Bednall Villa
Rowley Moor
Lower Farm
Bednall
Mount Pleasant
All Saints C of E Primary School
Bednall Head
Torwood
Belt View Farm
Brook House
Plashes Farm
Church Pits Plantation
The Barn
Hill House
Moors Covert Farm
Moors Covert
Brook Cottage
159
A B C D E
1 2 3 4 5 6 7
94 395 96

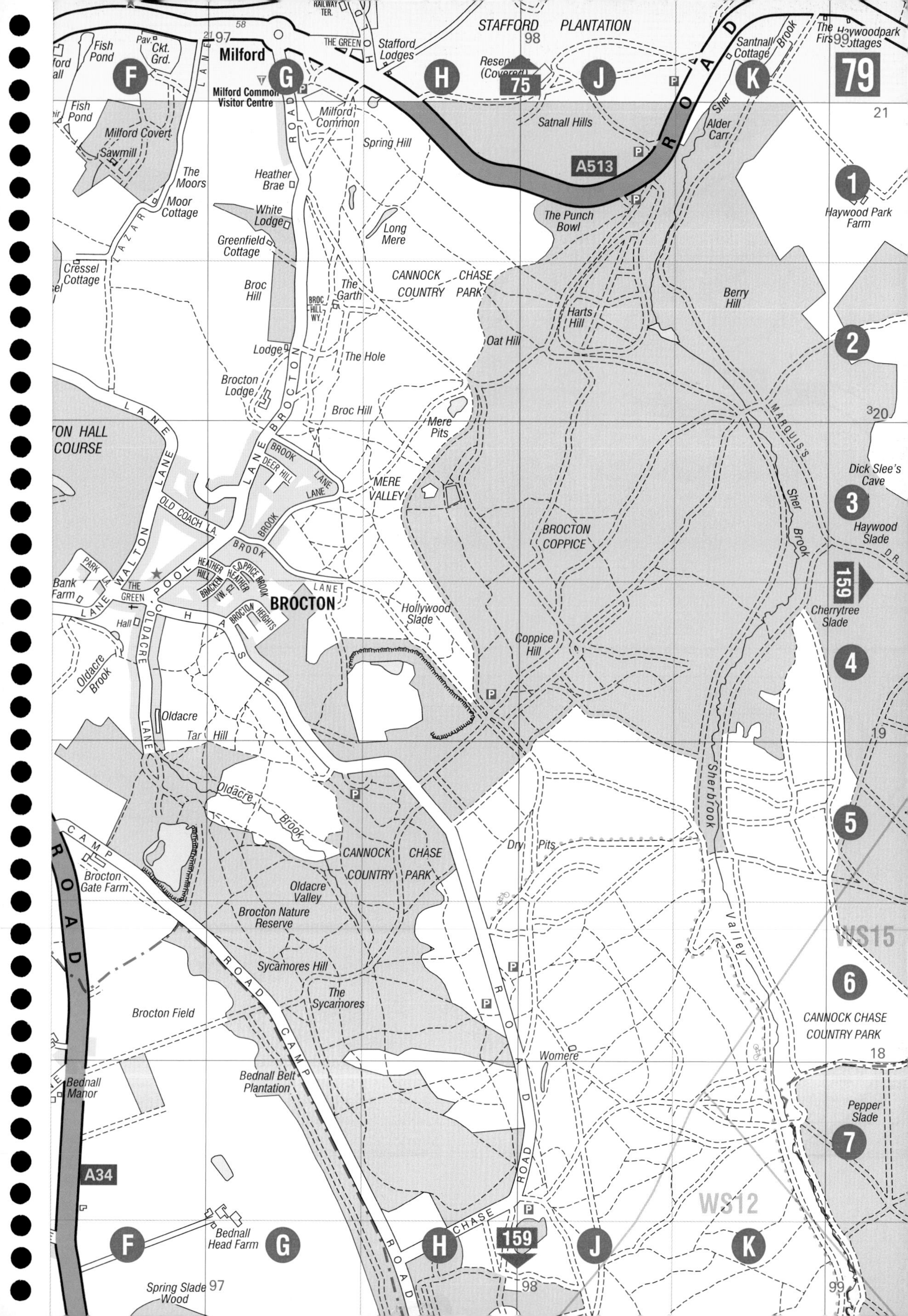

Grid references (top): F, G, H, J, K — **79**
Grid numbers (right edge): 1, 2, 3, 4, 5, 6, 7
Grid references (bottom): F, G, H, J, K

Top area:
- STAFFORD PLANTATION — 98
- 21, 97, 58
- Milford
- Milford Common Visitor Centre
- THE GREEN
- Stafford Lodges
- Reservoir (Covered) — **75**
- RAILWAY TER.
- Santnall Cottage — 99
- Sher Brook
- The Haywoodpark Cottages / Firs
- Alder Carr
- 21

Milford/Brocton area (left):
- Fish Pond
- Pav. Ckt. Grd.
- ...ford Hall
- Fish Pond
- Milford Covert
- Sawmill
- The Moors
- Moor Cottage
- Cressel Cottage
- Heather Brae
- White Lodge
- Greenfield Cottage
- Broc Hill
- The Garth
- BROC HILL WY.
- Long Mere
- Spring Hill
- Milford Common

Central:
- CANNOCK COUNTRY CHASE PARK
- Harts Hill
- Oat Hill
- The Punch Bowl
- Satnall Hills
- A513
- Berry Hill
- Haywood Park Farm
- MARQUIS'S
- 3 20

Middle-left (Brocton):
- Lodge
- Brocton Lodge
- Broc Hill
- Mere Pits
- The Hole
- MERE VALLEY
- ...TON HALL COURSE
- OLD COACH LA.
- DEER HILL LANE
- BROCTON LANE
- BROOK
- LANE
- WALTON LANE
- POOL
- HEATHER HILL
- BRACKEN
- COPPICE BROOK
- BROCTON HEIGHTS
- CHASE
- BROCTON
- Bank Farm
- PARK
- THE GREEN
- Hall
- Oldacre Brook
- BROCTON COPPICE
- Coppice Hill
- Hollywood Slade
- Sherbrook
- Dick Slee's Cave
- Haywood Slade
- D.R.
- **159** Cherrytree Slade

Lower-central:
- Oldacre
- Tar Hill
- Oldacre Brook
- CANNOCK CHASE COUNTRY PARK
- Brocton Gate Farm
- Oldacre Valley
- Brocton Nature Reserve
- Sycamores Hill
- The Sycamores
- Brocton Field
- Dry Pits
- Valley
- Sherbrook
- WS15
- CANNOCK CHASE COUNTRY PARK
- 18

Bottom:
- CAMP ROAD
- A34
- Bednall Manor
- Bednall Belt Plantation
- Womere
- CHASE ROAD
- **159**
- Pepper Slade
- WS12
- Bednall Head Farm
- Spring Slade Wood — 97
- 98
- 99

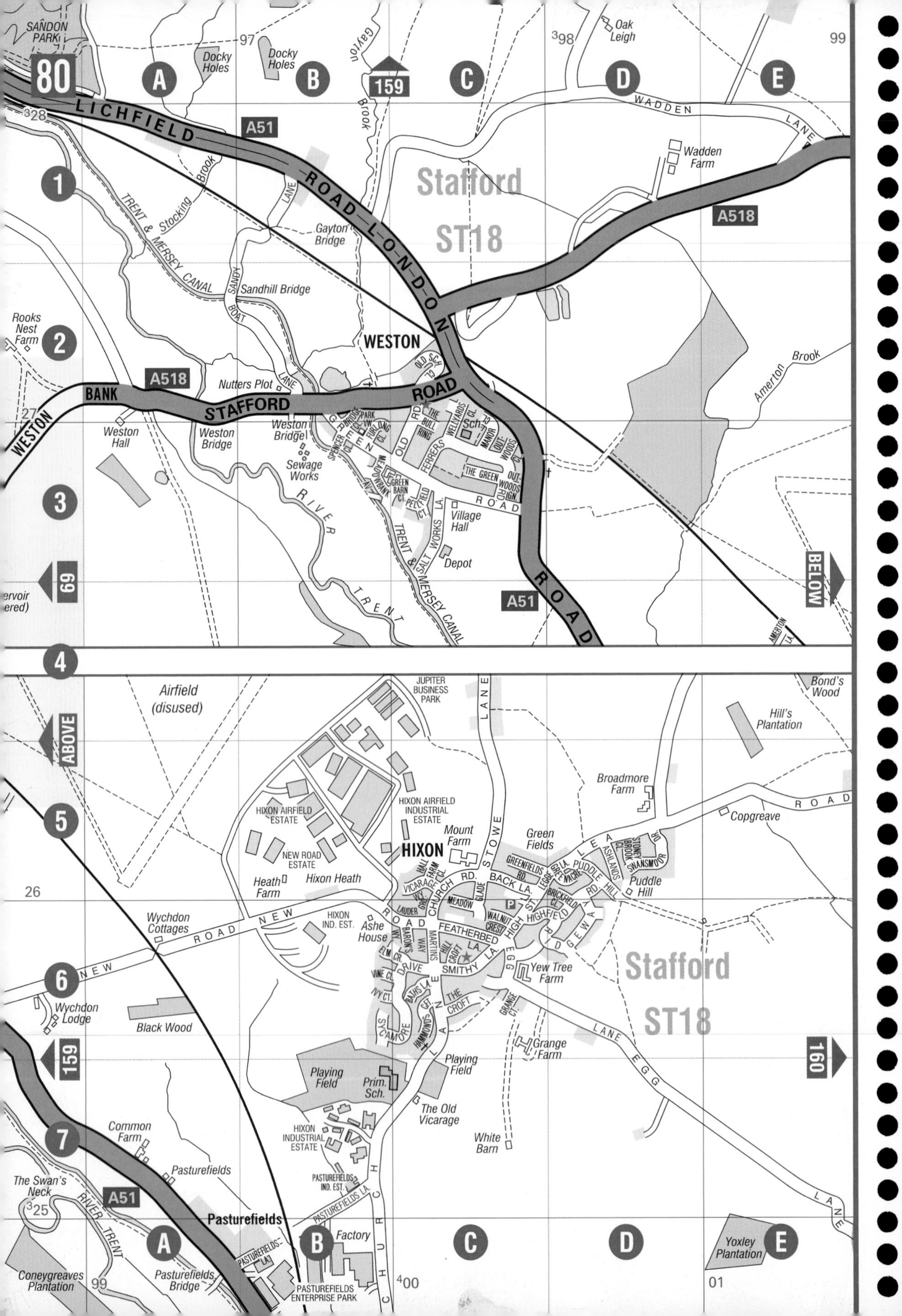
80
SANDON PARK
Docky Holes
Docky Holes
Gayton Brook
159
Oak Leigh
WADDEN LANE
Wadden Farm
LICHFIELD ROAD
LONDON ROAD
A51
A518
Stafford
ST18
Stocking Brook
TRENT & MERSEY CANAL
Gayton Bridge
SANDY BOAT LANE
Sandhill Bridge
Rooks Nest Farm
WESTON
Amerton Brook
Nutters Plot
WESTON BANK
STAFFORD ROAD
Weston Hall
Weston Bridge
Weston Bridge
Sewage Works
RIVER TRENT
OLD RD.
FERRERS
THE GREEN
Village Hall
Depot
SALT WORKS LA.
BELOW
69
ABOVE
Airfield (disused)
JUPITER BUSINESS PARK
STOWE LANE
Bond's Wood
Hill's Plantation
Broadmore Farm
Copgreave
HIXON AIRFIELD ESTATE
HIXON AIRFIELD INDUSTRIAL ESTATE
Mount Farm
HIXON
Green Fields
NEW ROAD ESTATE
Heath Farm
Hixon Heath
CHURCH RD.
BACK LA.
Puddle Hill
Wychdon Cottages
NEW ROAD
HIXON IND. EST.
Ashe House
FEATHERBED LA.
SMITHY LA.
Yew Tree Farm
EGG LANE
Wychdon Lodge
Black Wood
Grange Farm
159
160
Playing Field
Prim. Sch.
Playing Field
The Old Vicarage
White Barn
Common Farm
HIXON INDUSTRIAL ESTATE
Pasturefields
PASTUREFIELDS IND. EST.
The Swan's Neck
PASTUREFIELDS LA.
Pasturefields
Factory
CHURCH LANE
Yoxley Plantation
Coneygreaves Plantation
Pasturefields Bridge
PASTUREFIELDS ENTERPRISE PARK

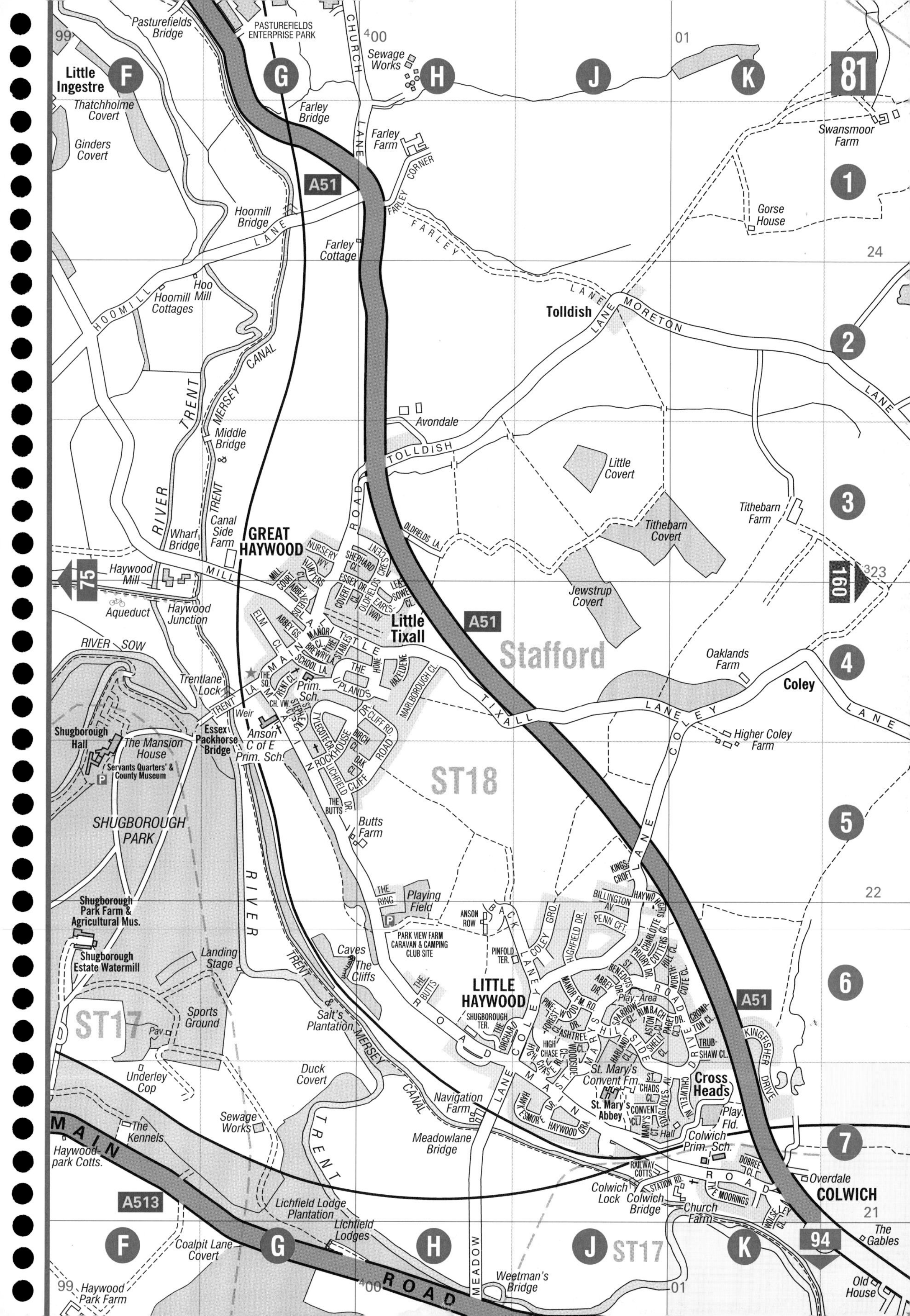
Pasturefields Bridge
PASTUREFIELDS ENTERPRISE PARK
Little Ingestre
Thatchholme Covert
Ginders Covert
Sewage Works
Farley Bridge
Farley Farm
FARLEY CORNER
A51
Hoomill Bridge
Farley Cottage
Swansmoor Farm
Gorse House
Hoo Mill
Hoomill Cottages
HOOMILL LANE
Tolldish
MORETON LANE
TRENT & MERSEY CANAL
RIVER TRENT
Middle Bridge
Avondale
TOLLDISH
Little Covert
Tithebarn Farm
Tithebarn Covert
Wharf Bridge
Canal Side Farm
GREAT HAYWOOD
Jewstrup Covert
Haywood Mill
Aqueduct
Haywood Junction
Little Tixall
Stafford
RIVER SOW
Trentlane Lock
Oaklands Farm
Coley
Shugborough Hall
The Mansion House
Servants Quarters' & County Museum
Essex Packhorse Bridge
Weir
Anson C of E Prim. Sch.
Prim. Sch.
TIXALL LANE
COLEY LANE
Higher Coley Farm
ST18
SHUGBOROUGH PARK
Butts Farm
Shugborough Park Farm & Agricultural Mus.
Playing Field
PARK VIEW FARM CARAVAN & CAMPING CLUB SITE
ANSON ROW
Shugborough Estate Watermill
Landing Stage
Caves
The Cliffs
LITTLE HAYWOOD
ST17
Sports Ground
Pav.
Salt's Plantation
Underley Cop
Duck Covert
St. Mary's Convent Fm.
St. Mary's Abbey
Cross Heads
KINGFISHER DRIVE
Navigation Farm
The Kennels
Sewage Works
Meadowlane Bridge
Haywood-park Cotts.
Colwich Prim. Sch.
Overdale
COLWICH
A513
Lichfield Lodge Plantation
Lichfield Lodges
Colwich Lock
Colwich Bridge
Church Farm
Coalpit Lane Covert
MAIN ROAD
MEADOW LANE
Weetman's Bridge
Haywood Park Farm
The Gables
Old House
75
160
94

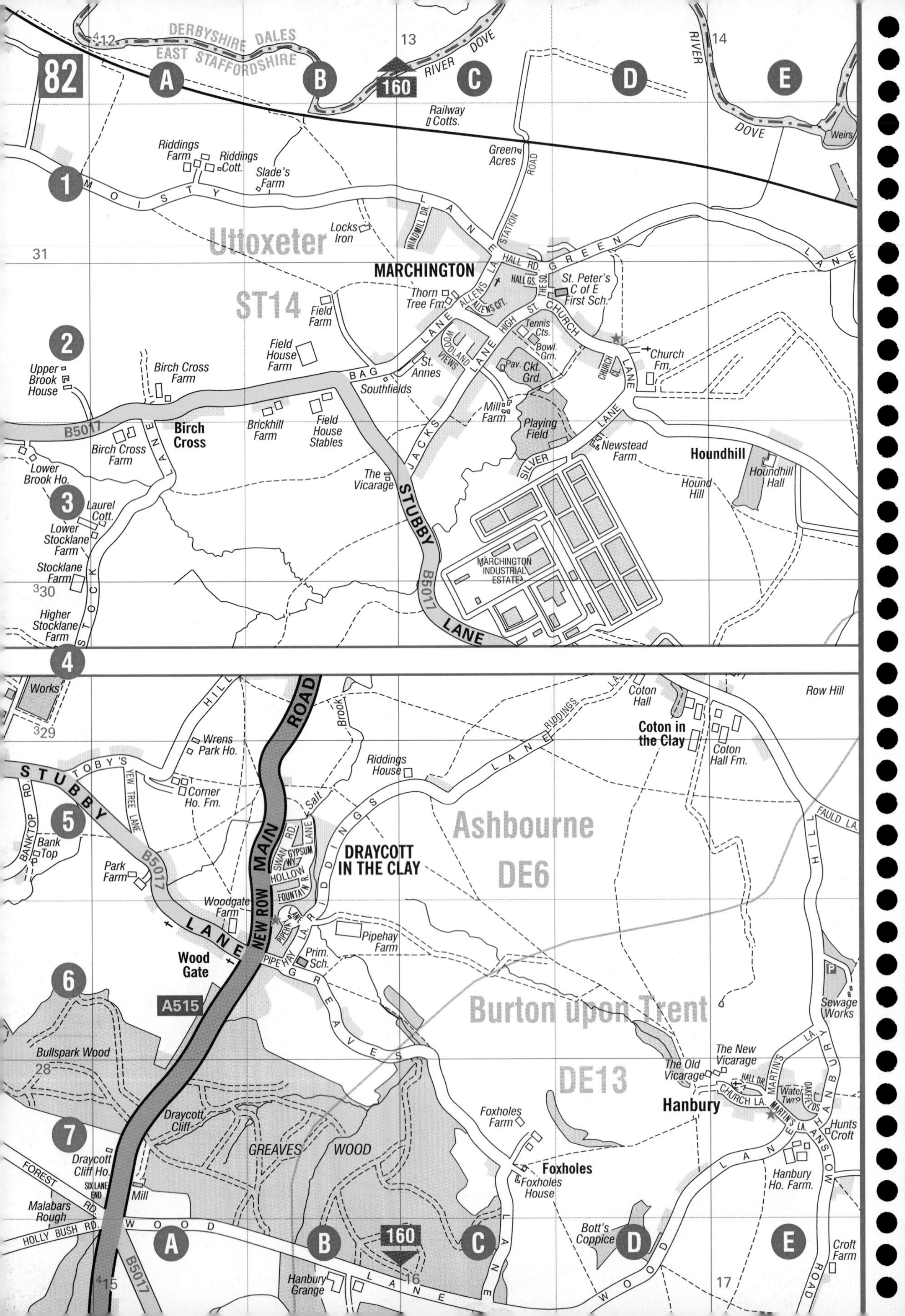
DERBYSHIRE DALES
EAST STAFFORDSHIRE
160
RIVER DOVE
Railway Cotts.
Riddings Farm
Riddings Cott.
Slade's Farm
MOISTY LANE
Green Acres
STATION ROAD
Uttoxeter
Locks Iron
WINDMILL DR.
MARCHINGTON
HALL RD.
GREEN LANE
HALL GS.
THE SQ.
St. Peter's C of E First Sch.
ST14
Field Farm
Thorn Tree Fm.
ALLENS LA.
ALLENS CFT.
HIGH ST.
CHURCH LANE
Tennis Cts.
Bowl. Grn.
Church Fm.
CHURCH CL.
Field House Farm
Upper Brook House
Birch Cross Farm
BAG LANE
St. Annes
WOODLAND VIEWS
Pav.
Ckt. Grd.
Southfields
Mill Farm
Playing Field
B5017
Birch Cross
Brickhill Farm
Field House Stables
JACKS LANE
SILVER LANE
Newstead Farm
Houndhill
Houndhill Hall
Hound Hill
Lower Brook Ho.
The Vicarage
STUBBY LANE
Laurel Cott.
Lower Stocklane Farm
Stocklane Farm
STOCK LANE
MARCHINGTON INDUSTRIAL ESTATE
Higher Stocklane Farm
Works
HILL
NEW ROW MAIN ROAD
Brook
Coton Hall
Row Hill
RIDDINGS LANE
Coton in the Clay
Coton Hall Fm.
Wrens Park Ho.
TOBY'S
YEW TREE LANE
Riddings House
BANKTOP RD.
Corner Ho. Fm.
Salt
Ashbourne
FAULD LA.
Bank Top
SWAN RD.
GYPSUM WY.
HOLLOW
FOUNTAIN R.
DRAYCOTT IN THE CLAY
DE6
HILL
Park Farm
Woodgate Farm
PIPEHAY LANE
Pipehay Farm
Wood Gate
Prim. Sch.
GREAVES
A515
Burton upon Trent
Sewage Works
Bullspark Wood
The New Vicarage
The Old Vicarage
HALL DR.
MARTIN'S LA.
DE13
CHURCH LA.
Water Twr.
OAKFIELDS
HANBURY HILL
Hanbury
Foxholes Farm
Draycott Cliff
Hunts Croft
GREAVES WOOD
Foxholes
Foxholes House
Draycott Cliff Ho.
ANSLOW LANE
Hanbury Ho. Farm.
FOREST RD.
SIX LANE END
Mill
Malabars Rough
HOLLY BUSH RD.
WOOD LANE
Bott's Coppice
Croft Farm
Hanbury Grange
ROAD

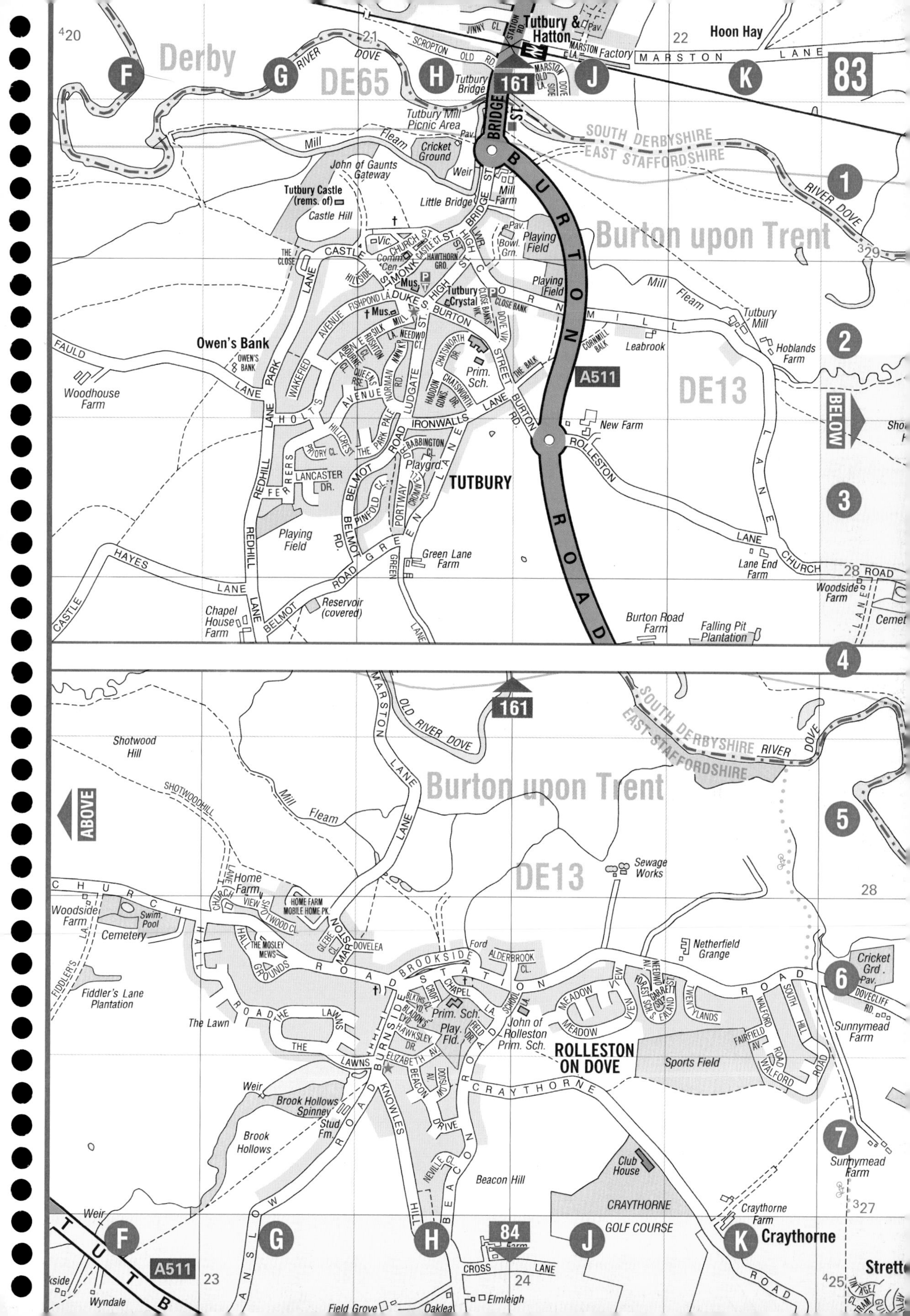
Tutbury & Hatton
Hoon Hay
Derby
DE65
Marston Lane
South Derbyshire
East Staffordshire
River Dove
Tutbury Mill Picnic Area
Cricket Ground
John of Gaunts Gateway
Tutbury Castle (rems. of)
Castle Hill
Little Bridge
Mill Farm
Burton upon Trent
Owen's Bank
Woodhouse Farm
Tutbury Crystal
Prim. Sch.
DE13
A511
New Farm
Tutbury Mill
Hoblands Farm
Leabrook
TUTBURY
Playing Field
Green Lane Farm
Chapel House Farm
Reservoir (covered)
Burton Road Farm
Falling Pit Plantation
Lane End Farm
Woodside Farm
Shotwood Hill
Sewage Works
Home Farm
Home Farm Mobile Home Pk.
Woodside Farm
Swim. Pool
Cemetery
Fiddler's Lane Plantation
The Lawn
Netherfield Grange
Cricket Grd.
Sunnymead Farm
John of Rolleston Prim. Sch.
ROLLESTON ON DOVE
Sports Field
Brook Hollows Spinney
Brook Hollows
Stud Fm.
Beacon Hill
Club House
CRAYTHORNE GOLF COURSE
Craythorne Farm
Craythorne
Elmleigh
Field Grove
Oaklea
Wyndale
Cross Lane
Craythorne Road
161
84
ABOVE
BELOW

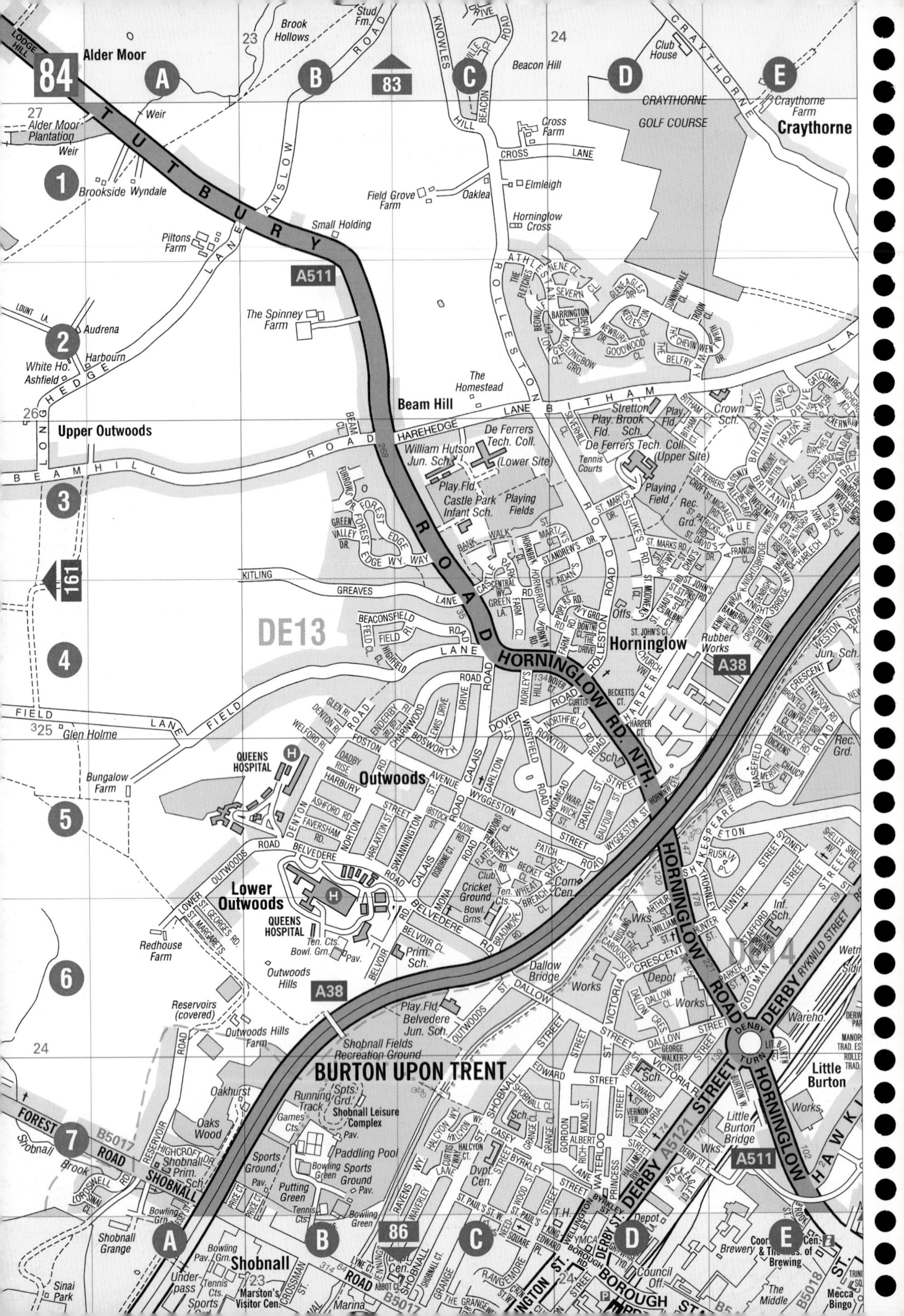

84
83
86
161
Alder Moor
Brook Hollows
Stud Fm.
Beacon Hill
Club House
Craythorne
Craythorne Farm
CRAYTHORNE GOLF COURSE
Alder Moor Plantation
Weir
Brookside
Wyndale
TUTBURY
ANSLOW LANE
Small Holding
Piltons Farm
Field Grove Farm
Oaklea
Elmleigh
Horninglow Cross
Cross Farm
CROSS LANE
A511
The Spinney Farm
Audrena
Harbourn
White Ho.
Ashfield
LOUNT LA.
LONG HEDGE
Upper Outwoods
BEAM HILL
Beam Hill
The Homestead
HAREHEDGE LANE
BITHAM
ROLLESTON
ROAD
William Hutson Jun. Sch.
De Ferrers Tech. Coll. (Lower Site)
De Ferrers Tech. Coll. (Upper Site)
Stretton Brook Sch.
Play. Fld.
Crown Sch.
Tennis Courts
Playing Field
Castle Park Infant Sch.
Playing Fields
FOREST EDGE
GREEN VALLEY DR.
KITLING GREAVES LANE
DE13
BEACONSFIELD
HIGHFIELD
Horninglow
HORNINGLOW RD. NTH.
Rubber Works
A38
Offs.
FIELD LANE
Glen Holme
Bungalow Farm
QUEENS HOSPITAL
Outwoods
Lower Outwoods
Redhouse Farm
Outwoods Hills
Reservoirs (covered)
Outwoods Hills Farm
Prim. Sch.
Cricket Ground
Dallow Bridge
Works
Depot
HORNINGLOW ROAD
DERBY TURN
DE14
Little Burton
Wareho.
Play. Fld.
Belvedere Jun. Sch.
Shobnall Fields Recreation Ground
BURTON UPON TRENT
Oakhurst
Oaks Wood
FOREST ROAD
B5017
Shobnall Prim. Sch.
Running Track
Shobnall Leisure Complex
Paddling Pool
Sports Ground
Putting Green
Bowling Green
Shobnall Grange
Shobnall
Under-pass
Marston's Visitor Cen.
Sinai Park
DERBY ST.
A5121
Little Burton Bridge
A511
Council Off.
YMCA
Brewery
Coors Visitor Cen. & The Mus. of Brewing
The Middle
Mecca Bingo
B5018
BOROUGH
Dvpt. Cen.

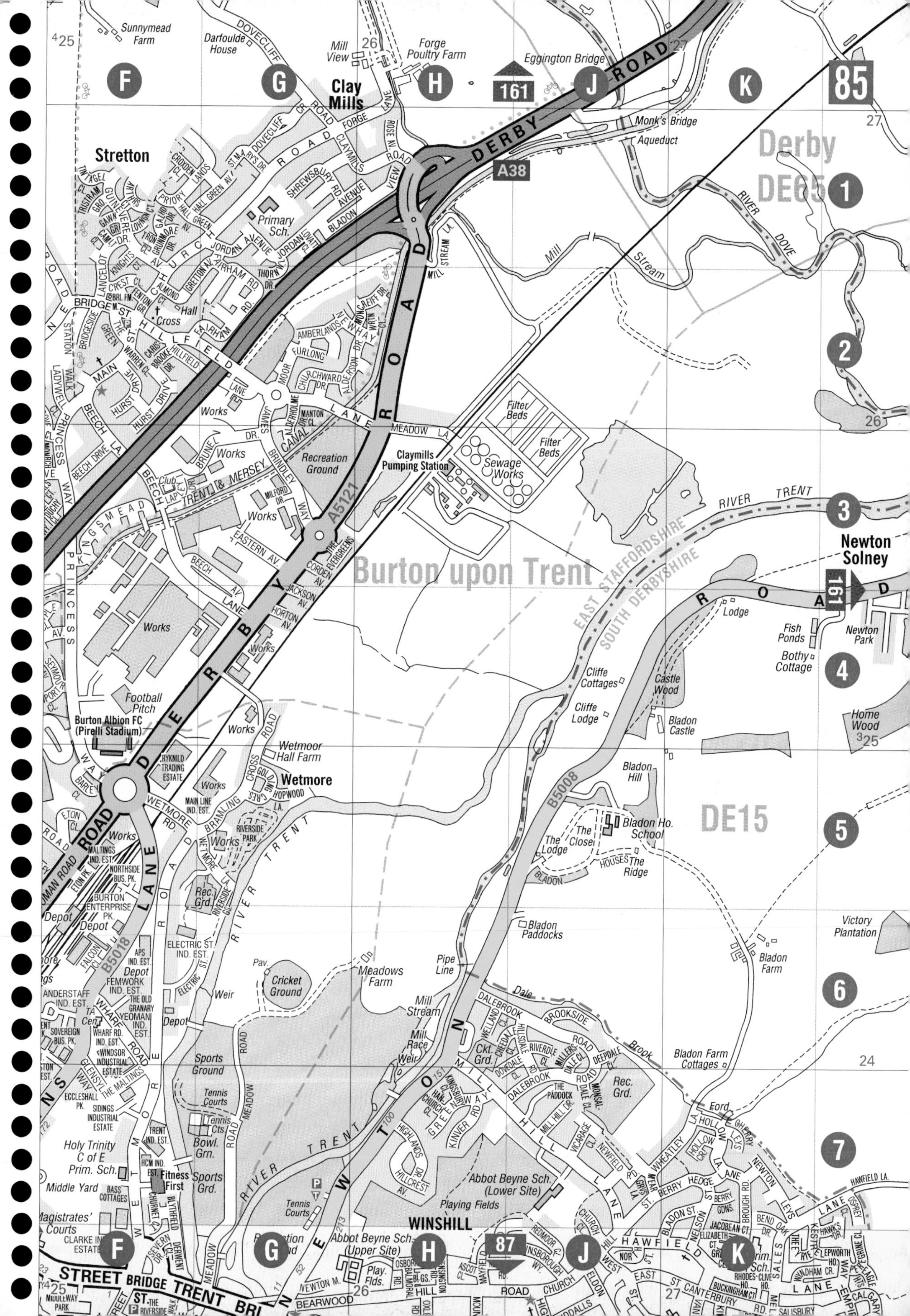
85
Clay Mills
Stretton
Derby DE65
Burton upon Trent
Newton Solney
Wetmore
WINSHILL
DE15
DERBY ROAD
A38
A5121
B5008
B5018
RIVER TRENT
RIVER DOVE
EAST STAFFORDSHIRE
SOUTH DERBYSHIRE
Claymills Pumping Station
Sewage Works
Filter Beds
Burton Albion FC (Pirelli Stadium)
Football Pitch
Recreation Ground
Monk's Bridge
Aqueduct
Eggington Bridge
Forge Poultry Farm
Mill View
Darfoulde House
Sunnymead Farm
Primary Sch.
Wetmoor Hall Farm
Bladon Castle
Bladon Hill
Bladon Ho. School
Bladon Paddocks
Bladon Farm
Bladon Farm Cottages
Cliffe Cottages
Cliffe Lodge
Castle Wood
Home Wood
Victory Plantation
Newton Park
Fish Ponds
Bothy Cottage
Lodge
Meadows Farm
Cricket Ground
Sports Ground
Abbot Beyne Sch. (Lower Site)
Abbot Beyne Sch. (Upper Site)
Playing Fields
Holy Trinity C of E Prim. Sch.
Magistrates' Courts
Middle Yard
161
87

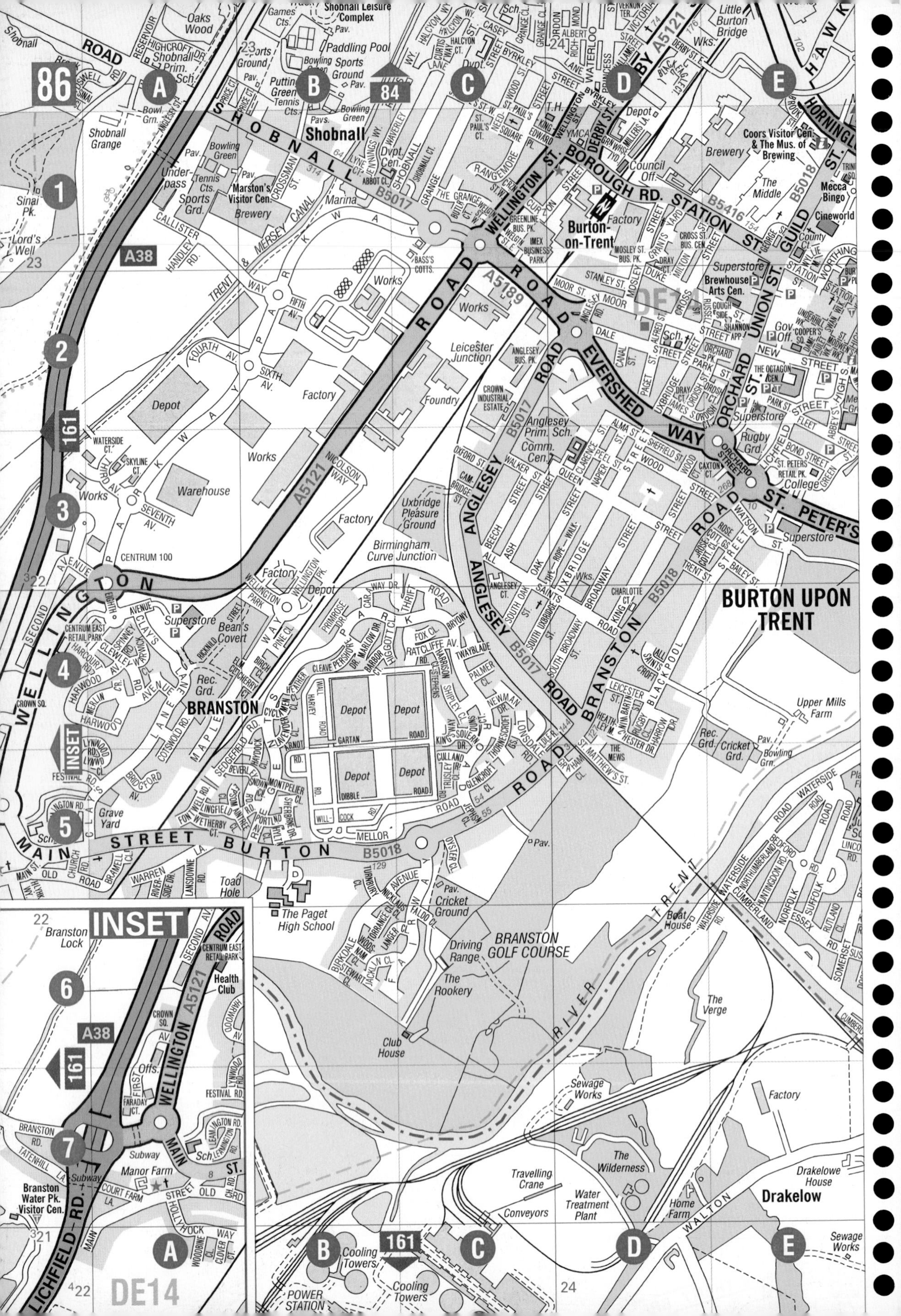
BURTON UPON TRENT
BRANSTON
Shobnall
Burton-on-Trent
Drakelow
INSET
BRANSTON GOLF COURSE
RIVER TRENT
DE14

WINSHILL
STAPENHILL
Burton upon Trent
Stanton
Bond End
DE15
EAST STAFFORDSHIRE
SOUTH DERBYSHIRE
ASHBY ROAD
A511
A444
A5189
B5008
B5353
STAPENHILL ROAD
STANTON ROAD
WOODLAND ROAD
NEWTON ROAD
TRENT BRI. STREET
BRIDGE
PARK ROAD
Trent Washlands
Recreation Ground
Cemetery
Scalpcliff Hill
Tower Woods
Waterloo Clump
Brizlincote Hall Farm
Forest Dell
Model Dairy Farm
Paulet High School
Robert Sutton RC High School
Edge Hill Jun. Sch.
Violet La. Inf. Sch.
Stanton Primary School
Newhall Park Farm
The Shrubbery
Heath Farm
Stanton Manor
Manor Farm
Hill Farm
Stanton House Cotts.
Stanton House
Meadowside Leisure Centre
Burton College
Ox Hay Pleasure Ground
Horse Holme
Stapenhill Viaduct
St. Peter's Bridge
Ferry Bridge
Burton Bridge
SuperBowl 2000
Magistrates' Courts
Holy Trinity C of E Prim. Sch.
Abbot Beyne Sch. (Upper Site)
Tower View Prim. Sch.
85
161

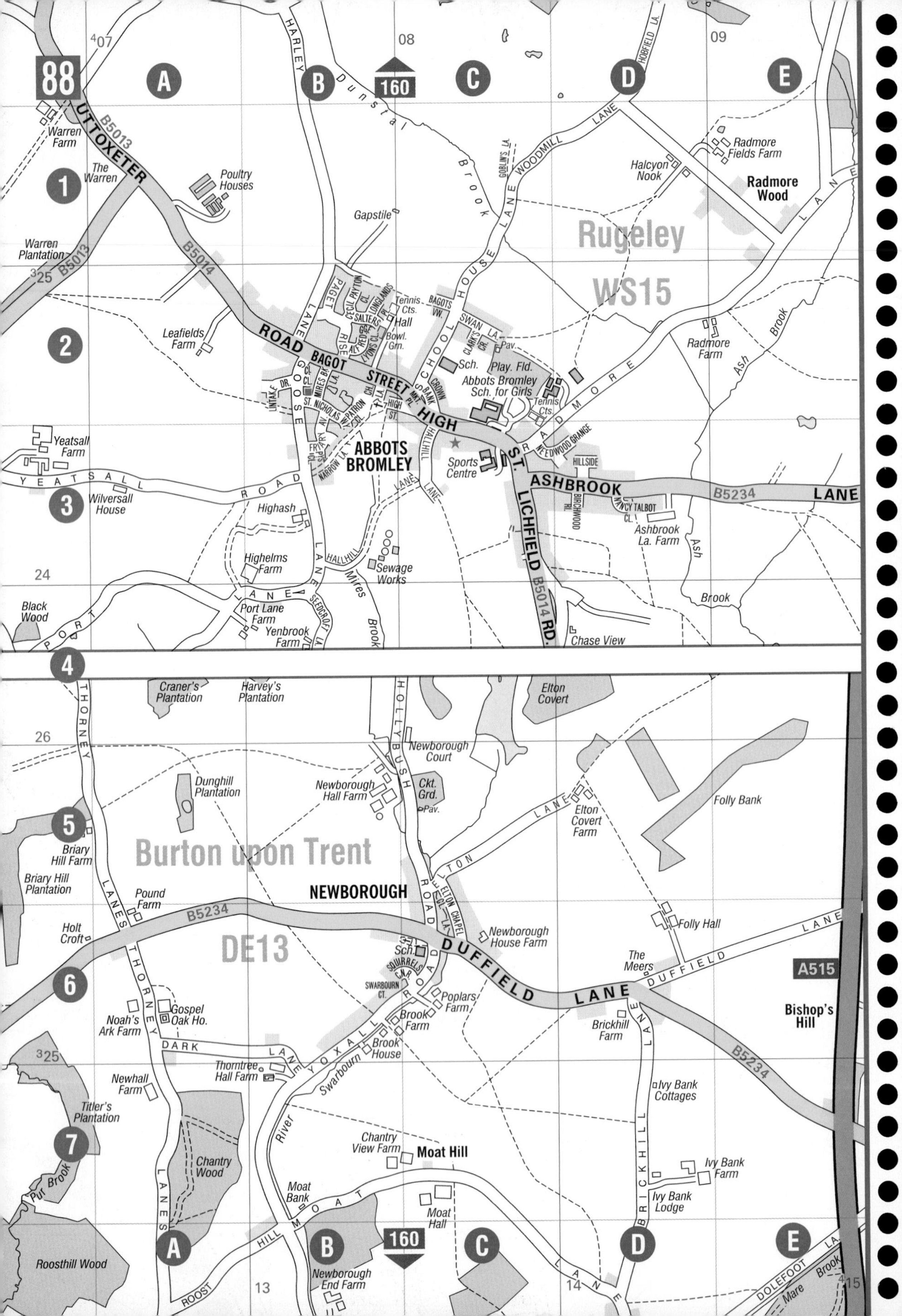
160
Abbots Bromley
Rugeley
WS15
Burton upon Trent
DE13
NEWBOROUGH
Uttoxeter Road
B5013
B5014
B5234
A515
Bagot Street
High Street
St. Lichfield Rd.
Ashbrook Lane
Radmore Lane
Woodmill Lane
School House Lane
Goose Lane
Yeatsall Road
Port Lane
Hallhill Lane
Harley Lane
Hobfield La.
Goblin's La.
Dunstal Brook
Mires Brook
Ash Brook
Warren Farm
The Warren
Warren Plantation
Poultry Houses
Gapstile
Leafields Farm
Yeatsall Farm
Wilversall House
Highash
Highelms Farm
Port Lane Farm
Yenbrook Farm
Black Wood
Sewage Works
Sports Centre
Sch.
Play. Fld.
Abbots Bromley Sch. for Girls
Tennis Cts.
Hall
Bowl. Grn.
Pav.
Halcyon Nook
Radmore Fields Farm
Radmore Wood
Radmore Farm
Ashbrook La. Farm
Chase View
Needwood Grange
Hillside
Nancy Talbot Cl.
Birchwood
Craner's Plantation
Harvey's Plantation
Elton Covert
Thorney Lanes
Hollybush Road
Newborough Court
Dunghill Plantation
Newborough Hall Farm
Ckt. Grd.
Elton Lane
Elton Covert Farm
Folly Bank
Briary Hill Farm
Briary Hill Plantation
Pound Farm
Holt Croft
Elton Chapel
Newborough House Farm
Folly Hall
The Meers
Duffield Lane
Bishop's Hill
Squirrels Cnr.
Swarbourn Ct.
Poplars Farm
Brook Farm
Brook House
Noah's Ark Farm
Gospel Oak Ho.
Dark Lane
Yoxall Road
Thorntree Hall Farm
Newhall Farm
Titler's Plantation
Brickhill Farm
Brickhill Lane
Ivy Bank Cottages
Ivy Bank Farm
Ivy Bank Lodge
Swarbourn
River
Chantry View Farm
Moat Hill
Chantry Wood
Moat Bank
Moat Lane
Moat Hall
Hill
Roost
Roosthill Wood
Newborough End Farm
Pur Brook
Dolefoot La.
Mare Brook

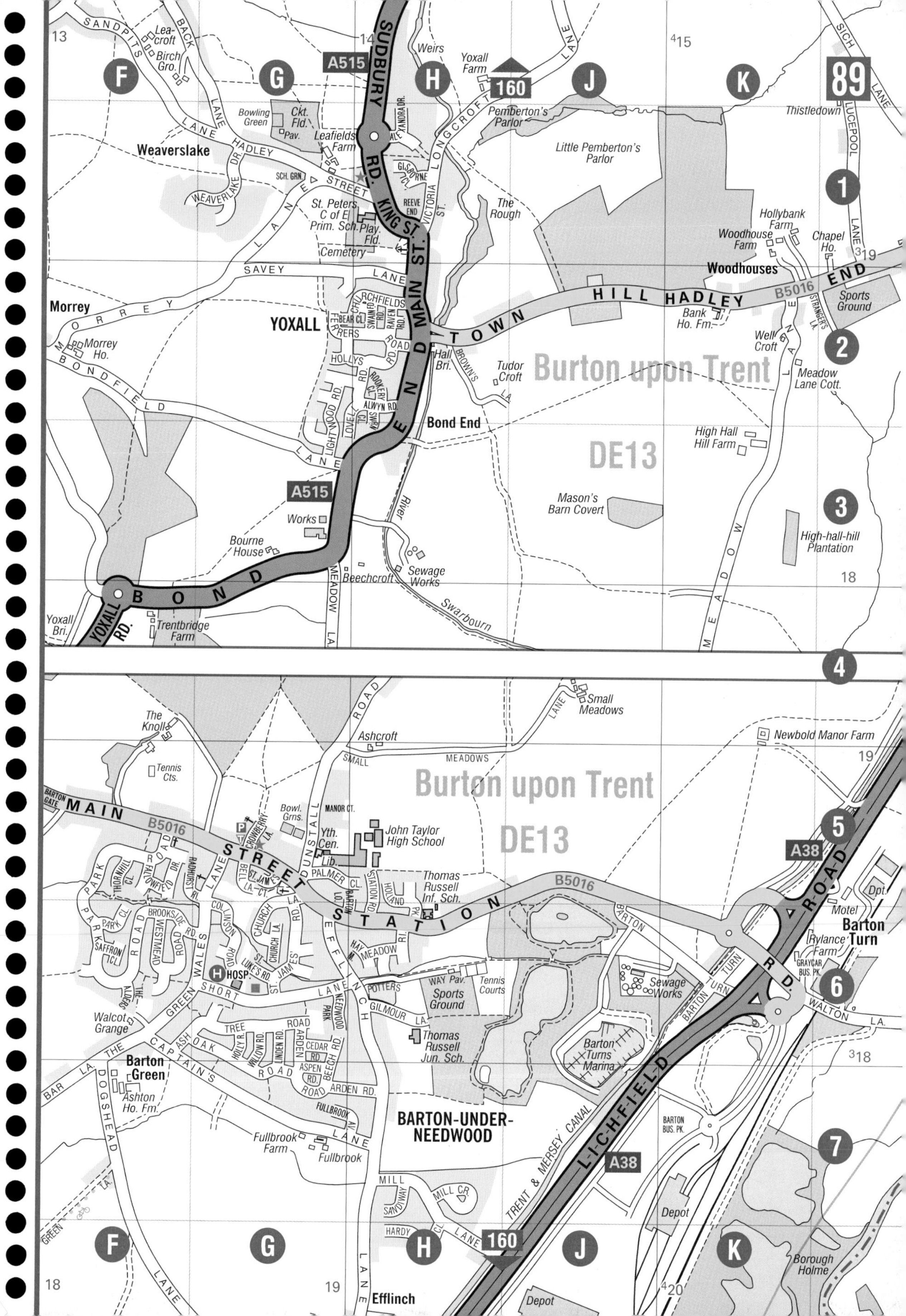

Grid references across top and bottom: **F**, **G**, **H**, **J**, **K**; side grid: **1**, **2**, **3**, **4**, **5**, **6**, **7**

Page number: **89**

- 13   14   15
- SANDPITS LA
- BACK LANE
- Lea-croft, Birch Gro.
- A515
- SUDBURY RD
- Weirs
- Yoxall Farm
- 160
- Pemberton's Parlor
- Little Pemberton's Parlor
- Thistledown
- SICH LANE
- LUCEPOOL LANE
- Bowling Green
- Ckt. Fld. Pav.
- Leafields Farm
- HADLEY LANE
- ALEXANDRA DR.
- LONGCROFT
- VICTORIA ST.
- GLADSTONE
- REEVE END
- The Rough
- Hollybank Farm
- Woodhouse Farm
- Chapel Ho.
- Weaverslake
- SCH. GRN.
- STREET
- KING ST.
- St. Peters C of E Prim. Sch. Play. Fld.
- Cemetery
- SAVEY LANE
- END
- TOWN
- HILL HADLEY END
- Woodhouses
- B5016
- STRINGERS LA.
- Sports Ground
- Morrey
- MORREY
- Morrey Ho.
- BONDFIELD
- YOXALL
- RCHFIELDS
- SWAN RD.
- BEAR CL.
- RAVEN
- HOLLYS
- RD.
- LOVELL
- HOOKER RD.
- ALWYN RD.
- SWAN
- Hall Bri.
- BROWNS
- Tudor Croft
- LA.
- Bank Ho. Fm.
- Well Croft
- Meadow Lane Cott.
- Burton upon Trent
- DE13
- High Hall Hill Farm
- Bond End
- A515
- Works
- River
- Mason's Barn Covert
- High-hall-hill Plantation
- 18
- Bourne House
- BOND
- Beechcroft
- Sewage Works
- MEADOW LANE
- Swarbourn
- MEADOW
- Yoxall Bri.
- YOXALL RD.
- Trentbridge Farm
- 4

- The Knoll
- Tennis Cts.
- Ashcroft
- SMALL MEADOWS
- Small Meadows
- Newbold Manor Farm
- 19
- BARTON GATE
- MAIN STREET
- B5016
- CRANBERRY LA.
- Bowl. Grns.
- MANOR CT.
- Yth. Cen.
- Lib.
- John Taylor High School
- Thomas Russell Inf. Sch.
- B5016
- A38
- LICHFIELD ROAD
- Motel
- Barton Turn
- Rylance Farm
- GRAYCAR BUS. PK.
- Dpt.
- Burton upon Trent
- DE13
- PARK ROAD
- THORNHILL
- RADNOR
- HADWIN LA.
- BELL LA.
- ST. JAM. CT.
- DUNSTALL
- PALMER CL.
- STATION ROAD
- HOLLAND
- BARTON TURN RD.
- WALTON LA.
- PARK CL.
- WESTMEAD
- SAFFRON CL.
- BROOKSIDE
- COLINSON ROAD
- CHURCH WALES
- CHURCH LA.
- ST LUKE'S RD.
- ST JAMES
- CHURCH RD.
- HAY MEADOW
- Thomas Russell Jun. Sch.
- WAY
- Pav. Sports Ground
- Tennis Courts
- Sewage Works
- Barton Turns Marina
- H HOSP
- SHORT
- GREEN
- THE CAPTAIN'S
- TREE
- OAK
- HOLLY RD.
- WILLOW RD.
- LINDEN RD.
- CEDAR RD.
- ASPEN
- BEECH RD.
- ARDEN RD.
- NEEDWOOD PARK
- EFFLINCH LANE
- GILMOUR LA.
- POTTERS
- Walcot Grange
- Barton Green
- Ashton Ho. Fm.
- BAR LA.
- DOGSHEAD LA.
- ASH
- MOLLY RD.
- ARDEN ROAD
- FULLBROOK ROAD
- Fullbrook Farm
- Fullbrook
- BARTON-UNDER-NEEDWOOD
- MILL LANE
- MILL CR.
- SAVDWAY
- HARDY CL.
- 160
- TRENT & MERSEY CANAL
- A38
- BARTON BUS. PK.
- Depot
- GREEN LA.
- Efflinch
- 18   19   20
- Borough Holme
- Depot
- BARTON TURN (roundabout)

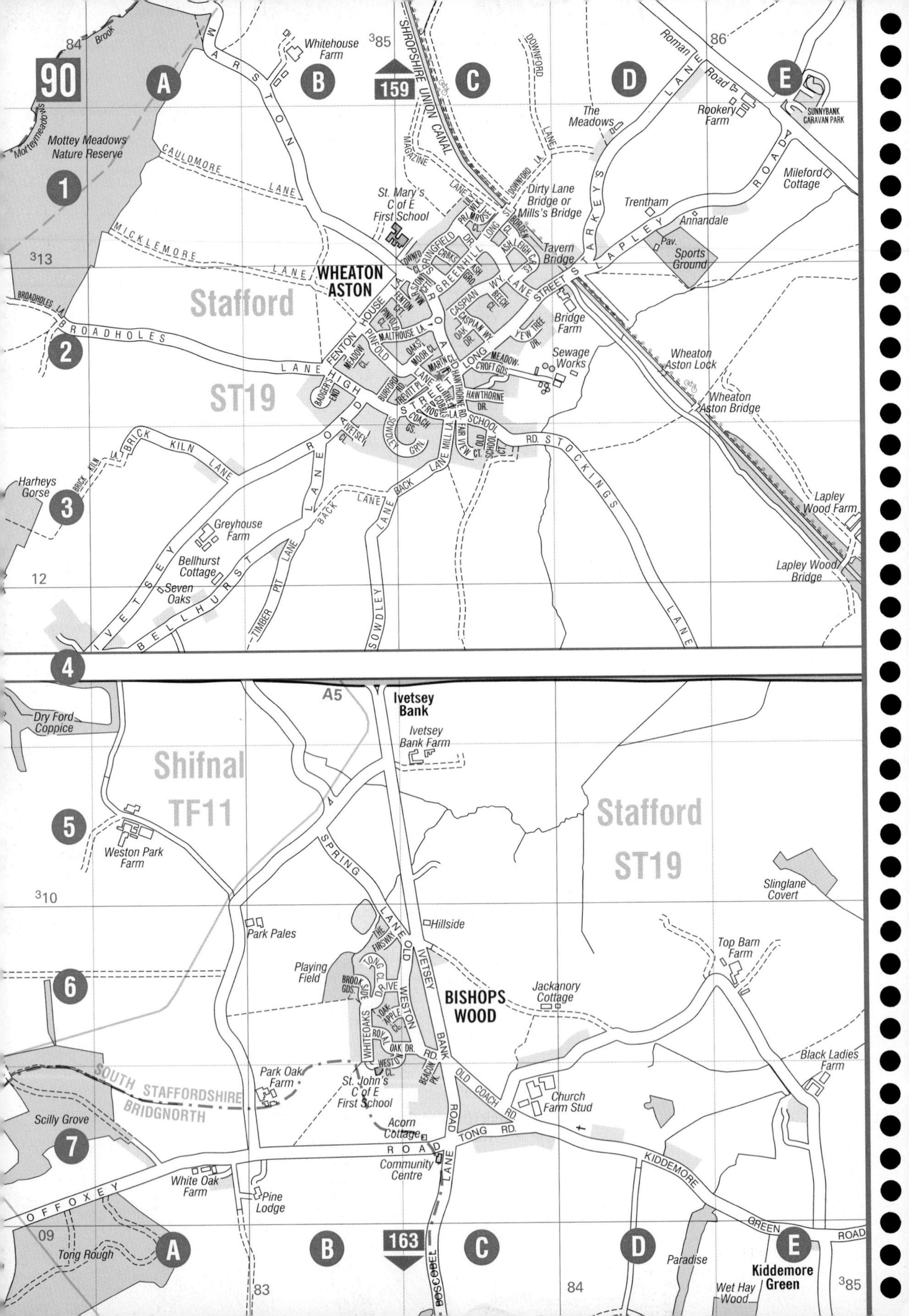

90
159
163
Wheaton Aston
Stafford
ST19
Shifnal
TF11
Bishops Wood
Ivetsey Bank
Kiddemore Green
Mottey Meadows Nature Reserve
Whitehouse Farm
Shropshire Union Canal
St. Mary's C of E First School
Dirty Lane Bridge or Mills's Bridge
Tavern Bridge
The Meadows
Rookery Farm
Sunnybank Caravan Park
Mileford Cottage
Trentham
Annandale
Sports Ground
Bridge Farm
Sewage Works
Wheaton Aston Lock
Wheaton Aston Bridge
Harheys Gorse
Greyhouse Farm
Bellhurst Cottage
Seven Oaks
Lapley Wood Farm
Lapley Wood Bridge
Dry Ford Coppice
Ivetsey Bank Farm
Weston Park Farm
Slinglane Covert
Park Pales
Hillside
Top Barn Farm
Playing Field
Jackanory Cottage
Black Ladies Farm
Park Oak Farm
St. John's C of E First School
Church Farm Stud
Scilly Grove
South Staffordshire
Bridgnorth
Acorn Cottage
Community Centre
White Oak Farm
Pine Lodge
Tong Rough
Paradise
Wet Hay Wood
A5

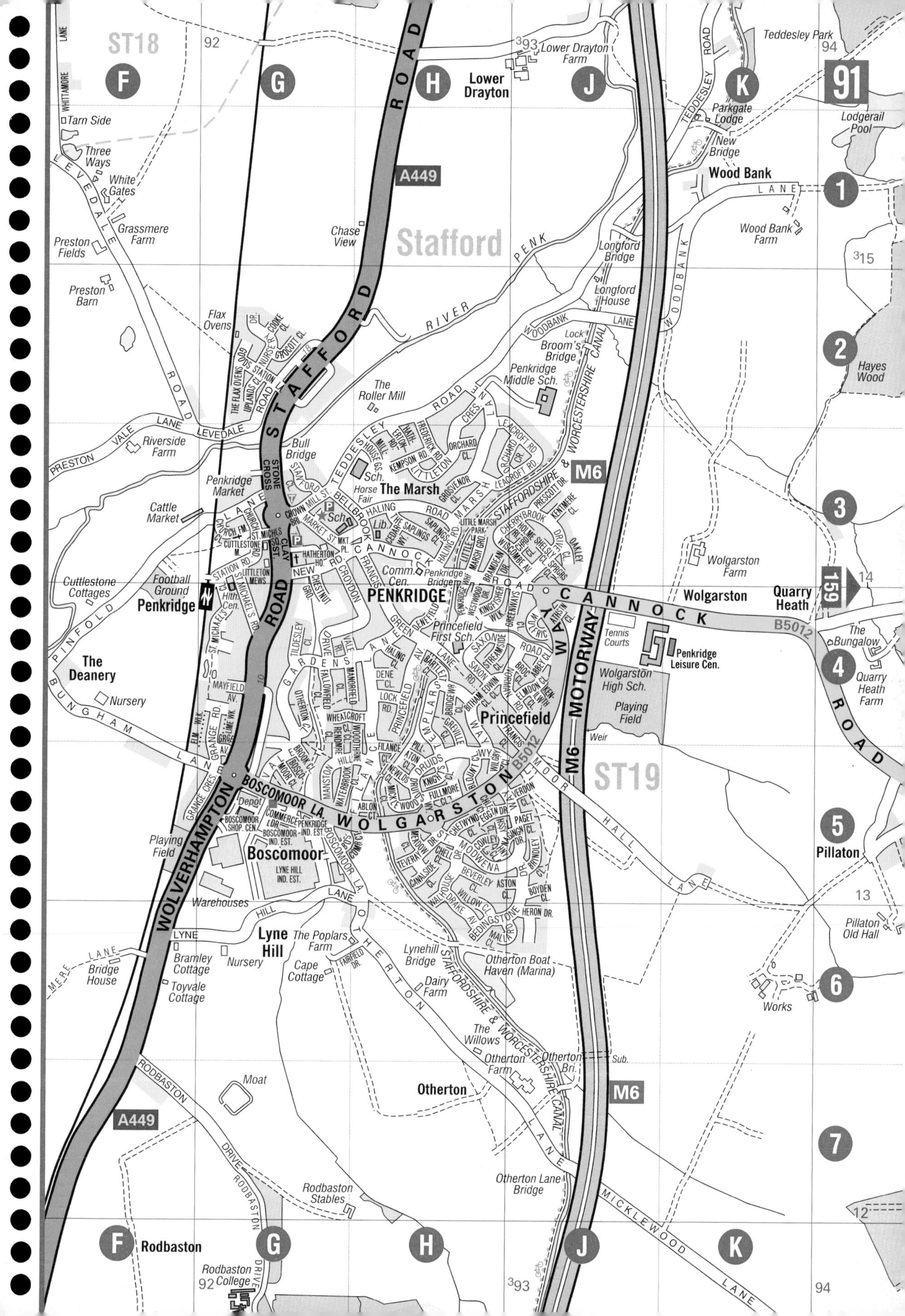
ST18
92
93
94
F
G
H
J
K
Lower Drayton Farm
Lower Drayton
Teddesley Park
Tarn Side
Three Ways
White Gates
Parkgate Lodge
Lodgerail Pool
New Bridge
Wood Bank
Wood Bank Farm
A449
Grassmere Farm
Preston Fields
Preston Barn
Chase View
Stafford
Longford Bridge
Longford House
15
Flax Ovens
River Penk
Woodbank Lane
Lock
Broom's Bridge
Penkridge Middle Sch.
Hayes Wood
The Roller Mill
Riverside Farm
Bull Bridge
Penkridge Market
Cattle Market
The Marsh
Horse Fair
M6
Wolgarston Farm
Cuttlestone Cottages
Football Ground
Penkridge
PENKRIDGE
Comm. Cen.
Penkridge Bridge
Wolgarston
Quarry Heath
159
14
Tennis Courts
Penkridge Leisure Cen.
B5012
The Bungalow
The Deanery
Nursery
Princefield First Sch.
Wolgarston High Sch.
Playing Field
Quarry Heath Farm
Weir
Princefield
ST19
Boscomoor
Depot
Boscomoor Shop. Cen.
Boscomoor Ind. Est.
Penkridge Ind. Est.
Lyne Hill Ind. Est.
Playing Field
Pillaton
Warehouses
13
Lyne Hill
The Poplars Farm
Pillaton Old Hall
Bramley Cottage
Nursery
Cape Cottage
Lynehill Bridge
Otherton Boat Haven (Marina)
Bridge House
Toyvale Cottage
Dairy Farm
Works
The Willows
Otherton Farm
Otherton Bri.
Sub.
Moat
Otherton
A449
Rodbaston Stables
Otherton Lane Bridge
12
Rodbaston
Rodbaston College
Stafford Road
Wolverhampton Road
Cannock Road
M6 Motorway
Staffordshire & Worcestershire Canal
Wolgarston Way
Boscomoor La.
Levedale Road
Preston Vale Lane
Pinfold Lane
Bungham Lane
Teddesley Road
Woodbank Lane
Micklewood Lane
Otherton Lane
Rodbaston Drive
Pillaton Hall Lane
Mere Lane
Lyne Hill Lane
1
2
3
4
5
6
7

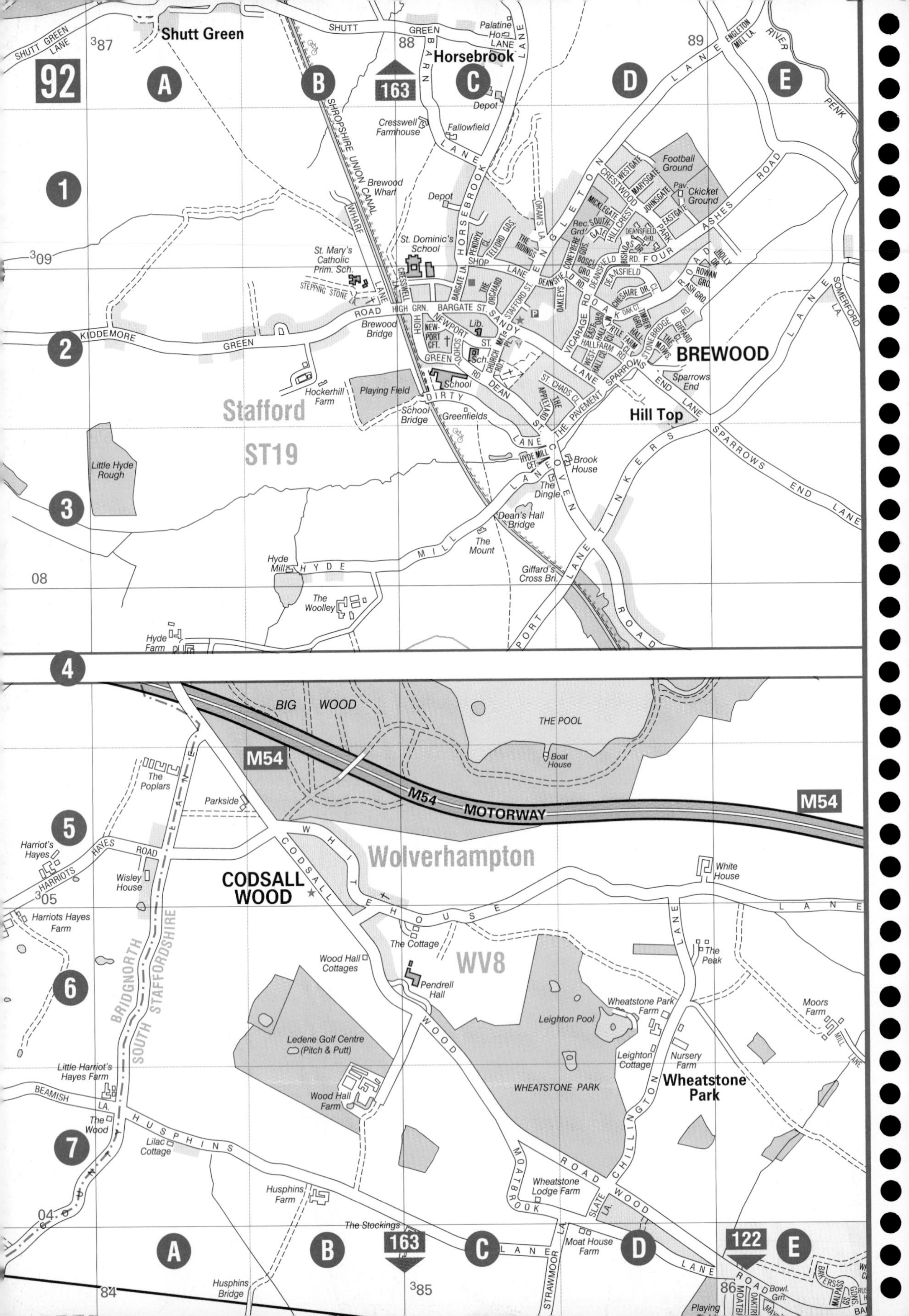
Shutt Green
SHUTT GREEN LANE
SHUTT GREEN LANE
387
88
89
163
163
122
A
B
C
D
E
1
2
3
4
5
6
7
Horsebrook
Palatine Ho.
BARN LANE
ENGLETON MILL LA.
RIVER PENK
Depot
Cresswell Farmhouse
Fallowfield
SHROPSHIRE UNION CANAL
HORSEBROOK LANE
Brewood Wharf
WHARF LANE
Depot
Football Ground
Ckicket Ground
Pav.
WESTGATE
MARYSGATE
CRESTWOOD
JOHNSGATE
EASTGATE
MICKLEGATE
HILLCREST
SOUTH GATE
PARK
Rec. Grd.
DEANSFIELD
ENGLETON LANE
FOUR ASHES ROAD
St. Dominic's School
St. Mary's Catholic Prim. Sch.
STEPPING STONE LA.
309
PENDRYL CL.
TELFORD GDS.
THE RIDINGS
ORAM'S LA.
CONEYBERE GDS.
BOSCL GRO.
HOLLY GRO.
ROWAN GRO.
ASH GRO.
SHOP LANE
BARGATE LA.
THE ORCHARD
CRESSWELL LA.
DEANSFIELD RD.
OAKLEYS
CHESHIRE DR.
OAK CT.
TIMBER GRO.
GIFFARD CL.
THE MDWS.
HIGH GRN.
BARGATE ST.
SANDY LANE
STAFFORD ST.
VICARAGE RD.
OAK RD.
KIDDEMORE GREEN ROAD
Brewood Bridge
NEWPORT CFT.
NEWPORT ST.
Lib.
MKT. PL.
HIGH GREEN
SCHOOL RD.
CHURCH RD.
Sch.
EAST HALL CL.
WEST HALL CL.
HALLFARM RD.
MYRTLE FARM
STONEBRIDGE RD.
BREWOOD
Sparrows End
SPARROWS END LANE
School
Hockerhill Farm
Playing Field
DIRTY LANE
DEAN ST.
ST. CHADS CL.
THE APPLEYARD
THE PAVEMENT
Hill Top
Stafford
ST19
School Bridge
Greenfields
Little Hyde Rough
HYDE MILL CFT.
Brook House
HYDE MILL LANE
The Dingle
COVEN ROAD
TINKERS LANE
SOMERFORD LA.
SPARROWS END LANE
Dean's Hall Bridge
The Mount
Hyde Mill
HYDE
Giffard's Cross Bri.
PORT LANE
08
The Woolley
Hyde Farm
BIG WOOD
THE POOL
M54
Boat House
M54 MOTORWAY
M54
The Poplars
LANE
Parkside
Harriot's Hayes
HAYES ROAD
HARRIOTS
Wisley House
Wolverhampton
CODSALL WOOD
WHITEHOUSE LANE
CODSALL
White House
305
Harriots Hayes Farm
The Cottage
WV8
The Peak
CHILLINGTON LANE
Wood Hall Cottages
Pendrell Hall
BRIDGNORTH
SOUTH STAFFORDSHIRE
Wheatstone Park Farm
Leighton Pool
Moors Farm
MILL LANE
Ledene Golf Centre (Pitch & Putt)
Leighton Cottage
Nursery Farm
Little Harriot's Hayes Farm
WOOD ROAD
WHEATSTONE PARK
Wheatstone Park
BEAMISH LA.
Wood Hall Farm
The Wood
HUSPHINS LANE
Lilac Cottage
Wheatstone Lodge Farm
MOATBROOK LA.
SLATE LA.
Husphins Farm
04
The Stockings
Moat House Farm
STRAWMOOR LA.
Husphins Bridge
384
385
86
MOATBROOK
OAKTREE
BAKERS GDNS.
MALPASS
Bowl. Grn.
Playing

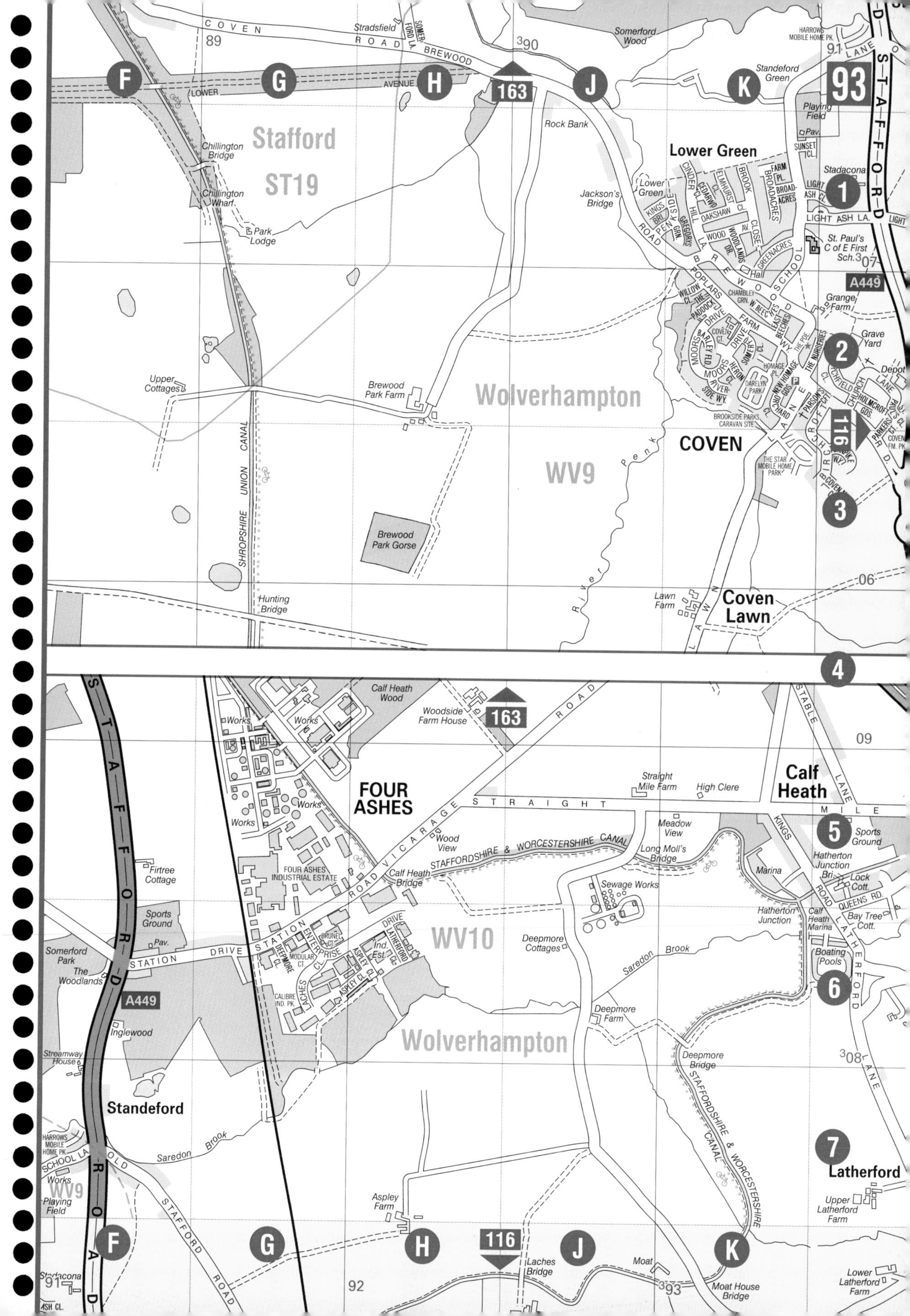
Stafford
ST19
Wolverhampton
WV9
Lower Green
COVEN
Coven Lawn
Rock Bank
Jackson's Bridge
Chillington Bridge
Chillington Wharf
Park Lodge
Upper Cottages
Brewood Park Farm
Brewood Park Gorse
Hunting Bridge
SHROPSHIRE UNION CANAL
River Penk
Somerford Wood
Standeford Green
Stradsfield
COVEN ROAD
BREWOOD
LOWER AVENUE
Playing Field
St. Paul's C of E First Sch.
Grange Farm
Grave Yard
Depot
Lawn Farm
BROOKSIDE PARKS CARAVAN SITE
THE STAR MOBILE HOME PARK
HARROWS MOBILE HOME PK.
Stadacona
A449
STAFFORD ROAD
FOUR ASHES
Calf Heath Wood
Woodside Farm House
Calf Heath
Straight Mile Farm
High Clere
STRAIGHT MILE
VICARAGE ROAD
STAFFORDSHIRE & WORCESTERSHIRE CANAL
Calf Heath Bridge
Long Moll's Bridge
Meadow View
Wood View
FOUR ASHES INDUSTRIAL ESTATE
Sewage Works
Marina
Hatherton Junction
Hatherton Junction Bri.
Lock Cott.
QUEENS RD.
Bay Tree Cott.
Calf Heath Marina
Boating Pools
Sports Ground
WV10
Deepmore Cottages
Saredon Brook
Deepmore Farm
Deepmore Bridge
Wolverhampton
Firtree Cottage
Sports Ground
Somerford Park
The Woodlands
STATION DRIVE
Inglewood
Streamway House
Standeford
Works
WV9
Playing Field
SCHOOL LA.
OLD STAFFORD ROAD
Aspley Farm
Laches Bridge
Moat
Moat House Bridge
Latherford
Upper Latherford Farm
Lower Latherford Farm
LATHERFORD LANE
KINGS ROAD
STABLE LANE
Works
CALIBRE IND. PK.
163
116
F G H J K
1 2 3 4 5 6 7
89 390 91 92 393 06 307 09 308

94
81
160
96
ST18
ST17
Stafford
Cross Heads
St. Mary's Convent Fm.
St. Mary's Abbey
Colwich Prim. Sch.
Play. Fld.
Railway Cotts.
Colwich Lock
Colwich Bridge
Church Farm
COLWICH
Overdale
The Gables
Old House
Wolseley Cottages
Wolseley Bridge
Bishton
Bishton Farm
Bishton Lane Farm
Bishton Hall Farm
St. Bede's School (Bishton Hall)
Sports Grd.
Pav.
Taft Old House
The Wolseley Centre
River Trent
Bellamour Lane
Orchard La.
A51
A513
Kingfisher Dr.
Main Road
Station Rd.
The Moorings
Dobree Cl.
Oak Edge
Oakedge Park
Sow Street
South Street
Buller's Wood
Cuckoo's Field
Round Hill
Long Covert
Stafford Brook
Chapel Hill
Sewage Works
WOLSELEY PARK
Little Birches
Jubilee Plantation
Lion's Den
Gorse Covert
Wolseley Park House
STAFFORD CANNOCK CHASE
Wolseley Road
Stafford Road
Stafford Brook Rd.
Stafford Brook Farm
Burnt Plantation
Middle Lodge Farm
Scarborough
Westring
Rest Harrow
Windycot
Birchbrae
Dorfield
Brook Road
Chase Road
Bower Lane
Etchinghill
Recreation Ground
Playing Field
Prim. Sch.
Sch.
Bower Farm
Shooting Butts Rd.
Stonehouse Road
Heathfield Farm
Cricket Ground
Tennis Courts
Penkridge Bank
Bevin's Birches
Seven Springs
Brook
Etching Hill Road
Mount Road
West Butts Rd.
East Butts Rd.
Peakes Road
Church La.
Woodcock
Pump La.
Finches Hill
Antler Dr.
Crestwood Rise
Oakwood
Chaseley Cl.
Brinkburn Cl.
Larkholme Cl.
Henley Grange
Oakfield Cl.
Sheringham Dr.
Kelvedon Wy.
Lawns
Cheveley
Foxglove
Bilberry
Moorland
Woodhey
The Oaklands
Fairmount Wy.
Charnwood
Woodthorne Cl.
Arden Cl.
Upfield Wy.
Moss Green
Bracken
Catkin
Gorseburn
Roseway
Highland
Cambrian La.
Daywell Rise
Shugborough
A B C D E
1 2 3 4 5 6 7
01 02 03
18 19 20 21

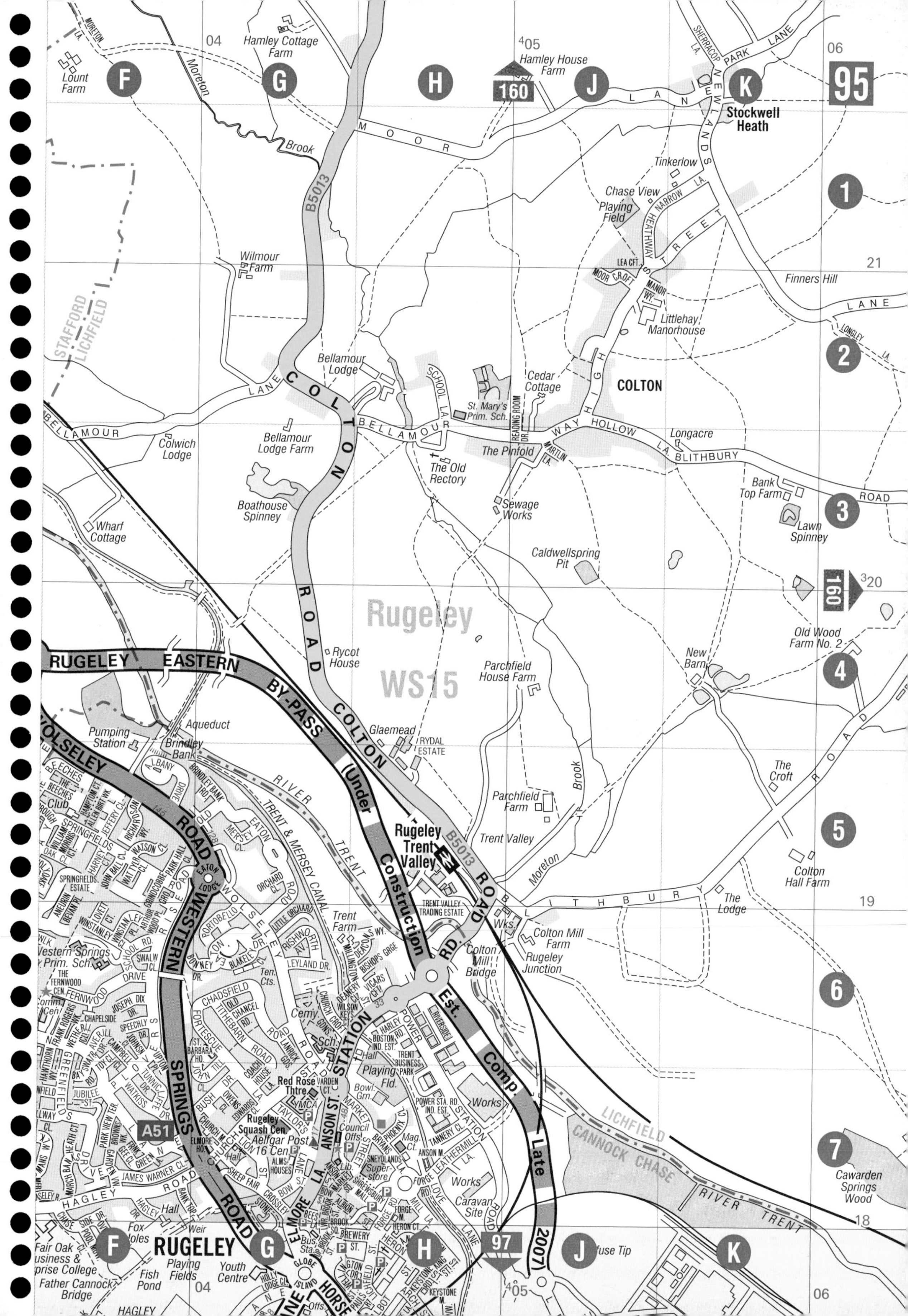

Lount Farm
Hamley Cottage Farm
Hamley House Farm
Moreton Brook
MOOR LANE
Stockwell Heath
NEWLANDS
SHERRACOP LA.
PARK LANE
Tinkerlow
Chase View Playing Field
NARROW LA.
HEATHWAY
STREET
LEA CFT.
MOOR CROFT
MANOR WY.
Littlehay Manorhouse
Finners Hill
LANE
LONGLEY LA.
Wilmour Farm
STAFFORD
LICHFIELD
B5013
COLTON ROAD
Bellamour Lodge
SCHOOL LA.
Cedar Cottage
COLTON
St. Mary's Prim. Sch.
READING ROOM DR.
HIGH
HOLLOW WAY
BELLAMOUR LANE
Colwich Lodge
Bellamour Lodge Farm
The Pinfold
MARTLIN LA.
Longacre
BLITHBURY ROAD
The Old Rectory
Boathouse Spinney
Sewage Works
Bank Top Farm
Lawn Spinney
Wharf Cottage
Caldwellspring Pit
Rugeley
WS15
Rycot House
Parchfield House Farm
Old Wood Farm No. 2
New Barn
RUGELEY EASTERN BY-PASS (Under Construction)
Aqueduct
Pumping Station
Brindley Bank
Glaemead
RYDAL ESTATE
WOLSELEY ROAD
RIVER TRENT
TRENT & MERSEY CANAL
Parchfield Farm
Brook
The Croft
Rugeley Trent Valley
Trent Valley
Moreton
Colton Hall Farm
The Lodge
TRENT VALLEY TRADING ESTATE
Trent Farm
Wks.
Colton Mill Farm
Rugeley Junction
Colton Mill Bridge
Western Springs Prim. Sch.
WESTERN SPRINGS ROAD
Est. Comp. Late 2007
STATION ROAD
Cemy.
Sch.
Playing Fld.
Bowl. Grn.
BOSTON IND. EST.
TRENT BUSINESS PARK
POWER STA. RD. IND. EST.
Works
Red Rose Thtre
YMCA
Rugeley Squash Cen.
Aelfgar Post 16 Cen.
Council Offs.
Mag. Ct.
LICHFIELD
CANNOCK CHASE
RIVER TRENT
Cawarden Springs Wood
A51
JAMES WARNER CL.
HAGLEY ROAD
Hall
Super-store
Works
Caravan Site
Fox Holes
Weir
RUGELEY
Playing Fields
Youth Centre
Fish Pond
Fair Oak Business & Enterprise College
Father Cannock Bridge
Bus Sta.
BREWERY ST.
Refuse Tip
97
160
04
05
06
21
20
19
18
F G H J K
1 2 3 4 5 6 7

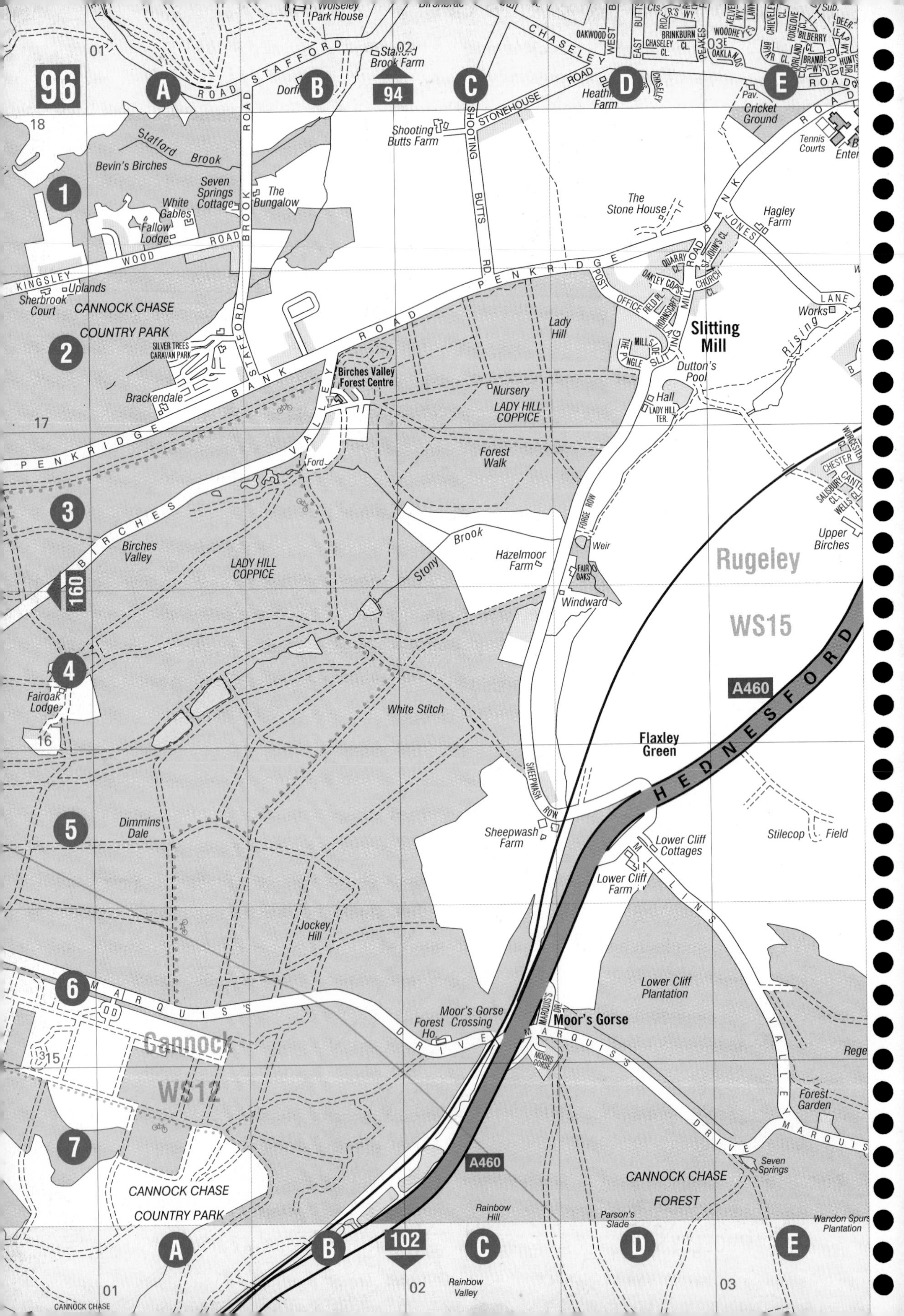

Wolseley Park House
Stafford Brook Farm
94
STAFFORD ROAD
CHASELEY ROAD
OAKWOOD
WEST BUTTS
EAST BUTTS
CHASELEY CL.
BRINKBURN CL.
WOODHEYS
OAKLANDS
PEAKES
CHIEVELEY CL.
FOXGLOVE CL.
BILBERRY
BRAMBLE WY.
BRIAR CL.
STONEHOUSE ROAD
Heath Farm
CHASELEY
Pav.
Cricket Ground
Tennis Courts
Shooting Butts Farm
SHOOTING BUTTS RD.
Stafford Brook
Bevin's Birches
Seven Springs Cottage
The Bungalow
White Gables
Fallow Lodge
WOOD ROAD
KINGSLEY
Uplands
Sherbrook Court
CANNOCK CHASE COUNTRY PARK
SILVER TREES CARAVAN PARK
Brackendale
STAFFORD BROOK ROAD
PENKRIDGE BANK ROAD
The Stone House
Hagley Farm
JONES
QUARRY CL.
OAKLEY COPSE
ST. JOHN'S CL.
CHURCH CL.
POST OFFICE
FIELD PL.
HORNSCROFT
MILL ROAD
LANE
Works
Rising
Lady Hill
Slitting Mill
MILLS
THE PINGLE
SLITTING MILL
Dutton's Pool
Birches Valley Forest Centre
Nursery
LADY HILL COPPICE
Hall
LADY HILL TER.
Forest Walk
Ford
VALLEY
BIRCHES
WORCESTER
CHESTER
SALISBURY CL.
CANTERBURY
WELLS CL.
Upper Birches
Birches Valley
LADY HILL COPPICE
Stony Brook
Hazelmoor Farm
FORGE ROW
Weir
FAIR OAKS
Windward
160
Rugeley
WS15
A460
HEDNESFORD ROAD
Fairoak Lodge
White Stitch
Flaxley Green
SHEEPWASH ROW
Sheepwash Farm
Dimmins Dale
Lower Cliff Cottages
MIFFLINS VALLEY
Lower Cliff Farm
Stilecop Field
Jockey Hill
Lower Cliff Plantation
MARQUIS'S DRIVE
Moor's Gorse Crossing
Forest Ho.
MARQUIS'S DR.
Moor's Gorse
MOORS GORSE
Cannock
WS12
Forest Garden
Seven Springs
A460
CANNOCK CHASE FOREST
CANNOCK CHASE COUNTRY PARK
Rainbow Hill
Parson's Slade
Wandon Spurs Plantation
102
Rainbow Valley
CANNOCK CHASE

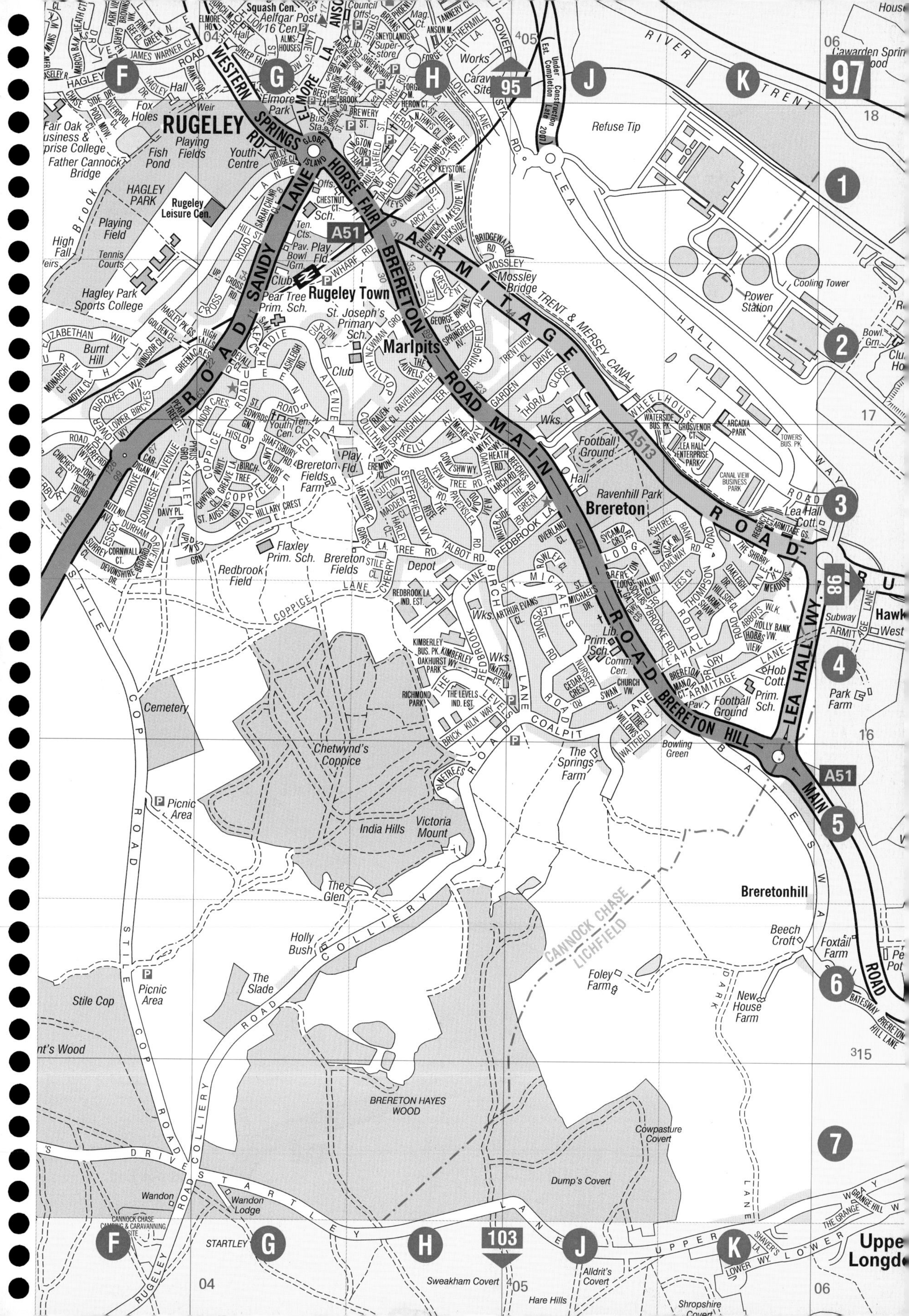

97
95
103
86
RUGELEY
Rugeley Town
Marlpits
Brereton
Brereton Hill
Brereton Hill
Brereton Fields
Brereton Fields Farm
Brereton Hayes Wood
Chetwynd's Coppice
India Hills
Victoria Mount
The Glen
Holly Bush
The Slade
Stile Cop
Cemetery
Picnic Area
Wandon
Wandon Lodge
Startley
Cannock Chase Camping & Caravanning Site
Cowpasture Covert
Dump's Covert
Sweakham Covert
Hare Hills
Alldrit's Covert
Shropshire Covert
Foley Farm
Beech Croft
Foxtail Farm
New House Farm
Park Farm
The Springs Farm
Bowling Green
Football Ground
Ravenhill Park
Power Station
Cooling Tower
Refuse Tip
River Trent
Trent & Mersey Canal
Mossley Bridge
Cawarden Springs Wood
Hagley Park
Hagley Park Sports College
Rugeley Leisure Cen.
Playing Fields
Playing Field
Youth Centre
Fish Pond
Fox Holes
Weir
Father Cannock Bridge
High Fall
Burnt Hill
Redbrook Field
Flaxley Prim. Sch.
St. Joseph's Primary Sch.
Pear Tree Prim. Sch.
Elmore Park
Squash Cen.
Aelfgar Post 16 Cen.
Works
Depot
Wks.
Hall
Lea Hall Cott.
Hob Cott.
Prim. Sch.
Comm. Cen.
Lib.
Towers Bus. Pk.
Waterside Bus. Pk.
Arcadia Park
Lea Hall Enterprise Park
Canal View Business Park
Redbrook La. Ind. Est.
Kimberley Bus. Pk.
Oakhurst Park
Richmond Park
The Levels Ind. Est.
Cannock Chase
Lichfield
A51
A513
Armitage Road
Main Road
Sandy Lane
Horse Fair
Western Springs Rd.
Lea Hall Wy.
Coalpit Lane
Colliery Road
Stile Cop Road
Startley Lane
Upper Lower Way
Batesway
Under Construction Est. Completion Late 2007
Upper Longdon
F
G
H
J
K
1
2
3
4
5
6
7
04
05
06
18
17
16
15

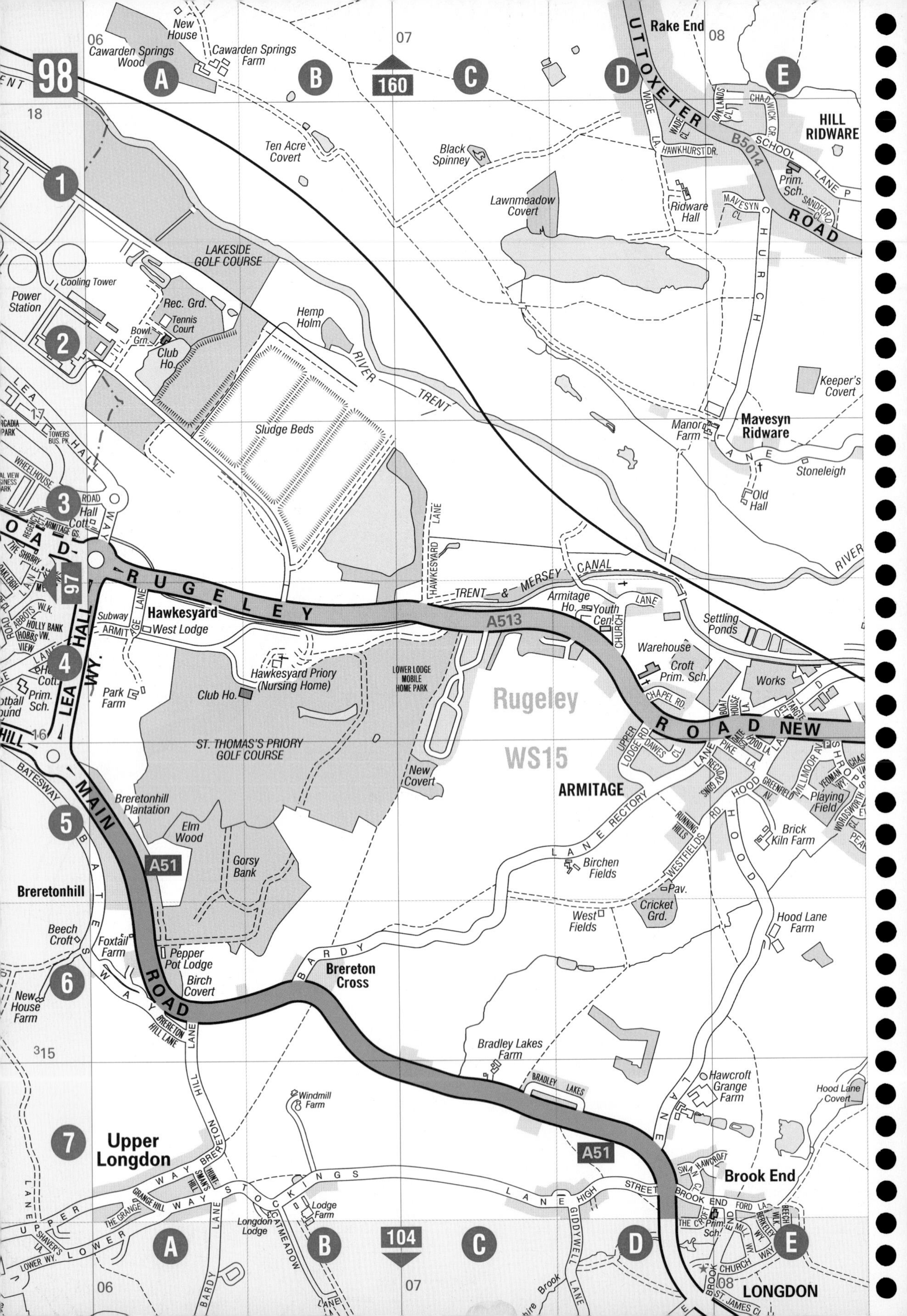
Rake End
Cawarden Springs Wood
New House
Cawarden Springs Farm
160
Ten Acre Covert
Black Spinney
Lawnmeadow Covert
UTTOXETER ROAD
B5014
HILL RIDWARE
Ridware Hall
Prim. Sch.
LAKESIDE GOLF COURSE
Cooling Tower
Power Station
Rec. Grd.
Tennis Court
Club Ho.
Hemp Holm
RIVER TRENT
Sludge Beds
Keeper's Covert
Manor Farm
Mavesyn Ridware
Stoneleigh
Old Hall
RUGELEY ROAD
TRENT & MERSEY CANAL
Armitage Ho.
Youth Cen.
Settling Ponds
Hawkesyard
West Lodge
A513
Warehouse
Croft Prim. Sch.
Works
Hawkesyard Priory (Nursing Home)
Club Ho.
LOWER LODGE MOBILE HOME PARK
Rugeley
WS15
ROAD NEW
Park Farm
ST. THOMAS'S PRIORY GOLF COURSE
New Covert
ARMITAGE
Playing Field
Breretonhill Plantation
Elm Wood
Gorsy Bank
MAIN ROAD
A51
Birchen Fields
Brick Kiln Farm
Breretonhill
Cricket Grd.
West Fields
Hood Lane Farm
Beech Croft
Foxtail Farm
Pepper Pot Lodge
Birch Covert
Brereton Cross
New House Farm
Bradley Lakes Farm
Windmill Farm
Hawcroft Grange Farm
Hood Lane Covert
Upper Longdon
Brook End
Lodge Farm
Longdon Lodge
104
LONGDON
97

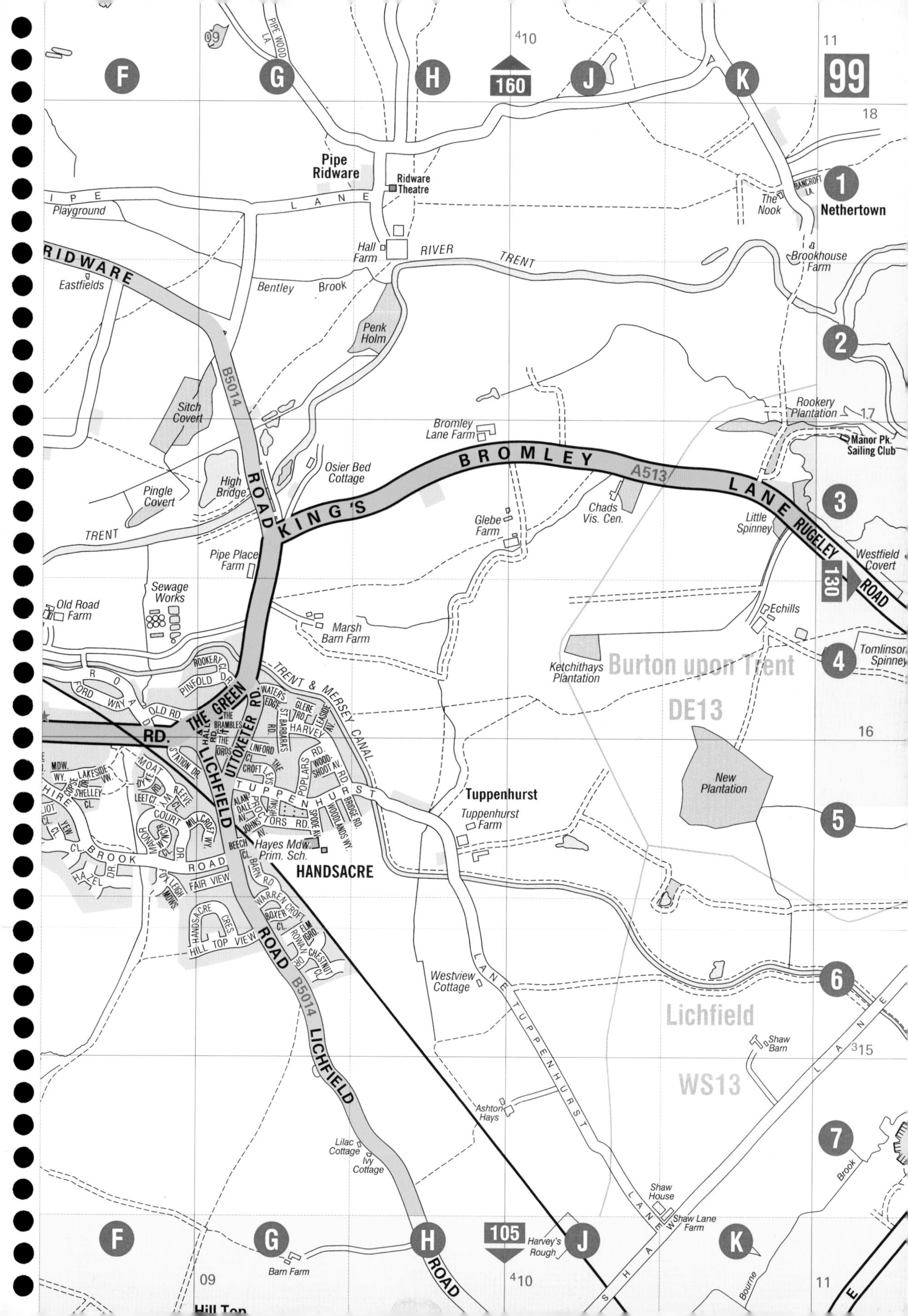
Pipe Ridware
Ridware Theatre
PIPE LANE
Playground
Hall Farm
RIVER TRENT
Bentley Brook
RIDWARE
Eastfields
Penk Holm
B5014
Sitch Covert
High Bridge
Pingle Covert
Osier Bed Cottage
Bromley Lane Farm
KING'S BROMLEY LANE
A513
Chads Vis. Cen.
Glebe Farm
Little Spinney
RUGELEY ROAD
Westfield Covert
Nethertown
The Nook
BANCROFT LA.
Brookhouse Farm
Rookery Plantation
Manor Pk. Sailing Club
TRENT
Pipe Place Farm
Sewage Works
Old Road Farm
Marsh Barn Farm
Echills
Tomlinson Spinney
Ketchithays Plantation
Burton upon Trent
DE13
New Plantation
TRENT & MERSEY CANAL
ROOKERY CL.
PINFOLD DR.
OLD RD.
THE GREEN
UTTOXETER RD.
LICHFIELD ROAD
STATION DR.
TUPPENHURST LA.
Tuppenhurst
Tuppenhurst Farm
Hayes Mdw. Prim. Sch.
HANDSACRE
BROOK ROAD
FAIR VIEW
HILL TOP VIEW
HANDSACRE CRES.
WARREN CROFT
Westview Cottage
LANE TUPPENHURST
Lichfield
WS13
Shaw Barn
Ashton Hays
Lilac Cottage
Ivy Cottage
Shaw House
SHAW LANE
Shaw Lane Farm
Harvey's Rough
Barn Farm
Brook
Bourne
Hill Top
160
130
105
F G H J K
1 2 3 4 5 6 7
09
410
11
18
17
16
315

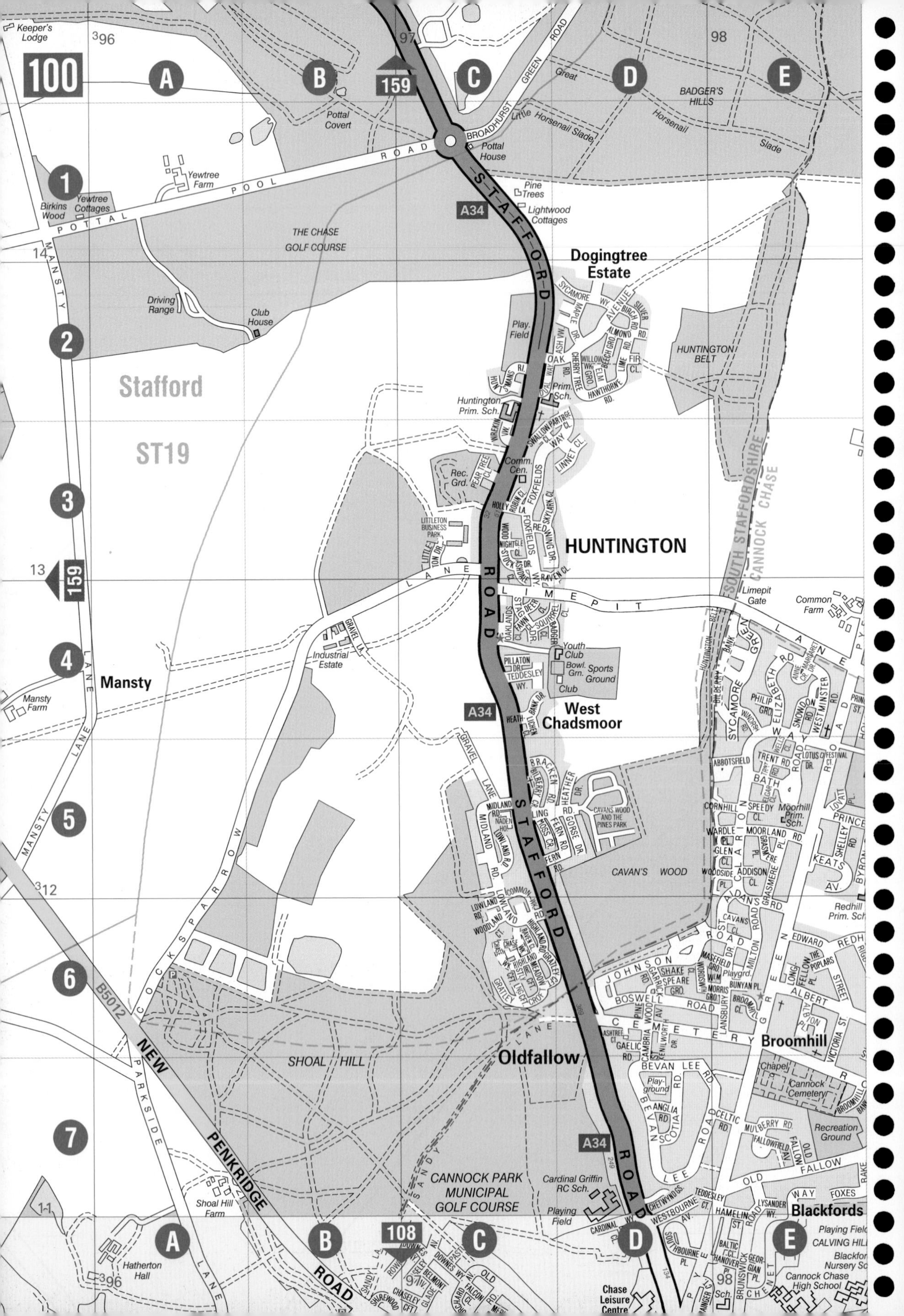
100
159
108
Keeper's Lodge
Pottal Covert
Pottal House
Yewtree Farm
Birkins Wood
Yewtree Cottages
POTTAL POOL ROAD
BROADHURST GREEN ROAD
Great Horsenail Slade
Little Horsenail Slade
BADGER'S HILLS
Pine Trees
Lightwood Cottages
THE CHASE GOLF COURSE
Dogingtree Estate
Driving Range
Club House
Stafford
ST19
HUNTINGTON BELT
Huntington Prim. Sch.
Rec. Grd.
Comm. Cen.
LITTLETON BUSINESS PARK
HUNTINGTON
SOUTH STAFFORDSHIRE
CANNOCK CHASE
LIMEPIT LANE
Limepit Gate
Common Farm
Industrial Estate
Mansty
Mansty Farm
MANSTY LANE
Youth Club
Bowl. Grn.
Sports Ground
Club
West Chadsmoor
A34
STAFFORD ROAD
GRAVEL LANE
COCKSPARROW LANE
CAVANS WOOD AND THE PINES PARK
CAVAN'S WOOD
Moorhill Prim. Sch.
Redhill Prim. Sch.
B5012
NEW PENKRIDGE ROAD
PARKSIDE LANE
SHOAL HILL
Oldfallow
Broomhill
Chapel
Cannock Cemetery
Play-ground
Recreation Ground
CANNOCK PARK MUNICIPAL GOLF COURSE
Cardinal Griffin RC Sch.
Playing Field
Shoal Hill Farm
Hatherton Hall
Blackfords
Playing Field
Cannock Chase High School
Chase Leisure Centre
Calving Hill
A B C D E
1 2 3 4 5 6 7

101
159
160
102
109
F
G
H
J
K
1
2
3
4
5
6
7
13
12
11
BRINDLEY HEATH
CANNOCK CHASE ENTERPRISE CENTRE
CANNOCK
COUNTRY
West Cannock Farm
Playing Field
BRINDLEY VALLEY
Pye Green
Green Heath
WS12
Cannock
Pye Green Valley Primary School
Blake High School
Pyegreen Valley
William Baxter Sch.
Cannock Sports Stadium
Recreation Ground
West Hill
High Town
Chadsmoor
WS11
Hednesford
HEDNESFORD
HEDNESFORD HILLS
Landfill Site
Sandy Slade
Hednesford Hills Common
Stringers Corner
Museum of Cannock Chase
Hednesford Hills Nature Reserve
Hednesford Park
Cockpit Hill
Church Hill
Hill Top
Kingsmead High Sch.
Duncan's Hill
Hednesford Town FC (Keys Park)
Distribution Centre
Wimble
Spoil Heap
Public Open Space
Chadsmoor C of E Jun. Sch.
Health Club
STATION ROAD
RUGELEY ROAD
CANNOCK ROAD
EAST CANNOCK RD.
UXBRIDGE ST.
RUGELEY ST.
VICTORIA ST
MARKET ST.
HEDNESFORD ROAD
EASTERN WAY
KEYS PARK
LITTLEWORTH ROAD
RAWNSLEY ROAD
A460
A4601
B5013
B4154

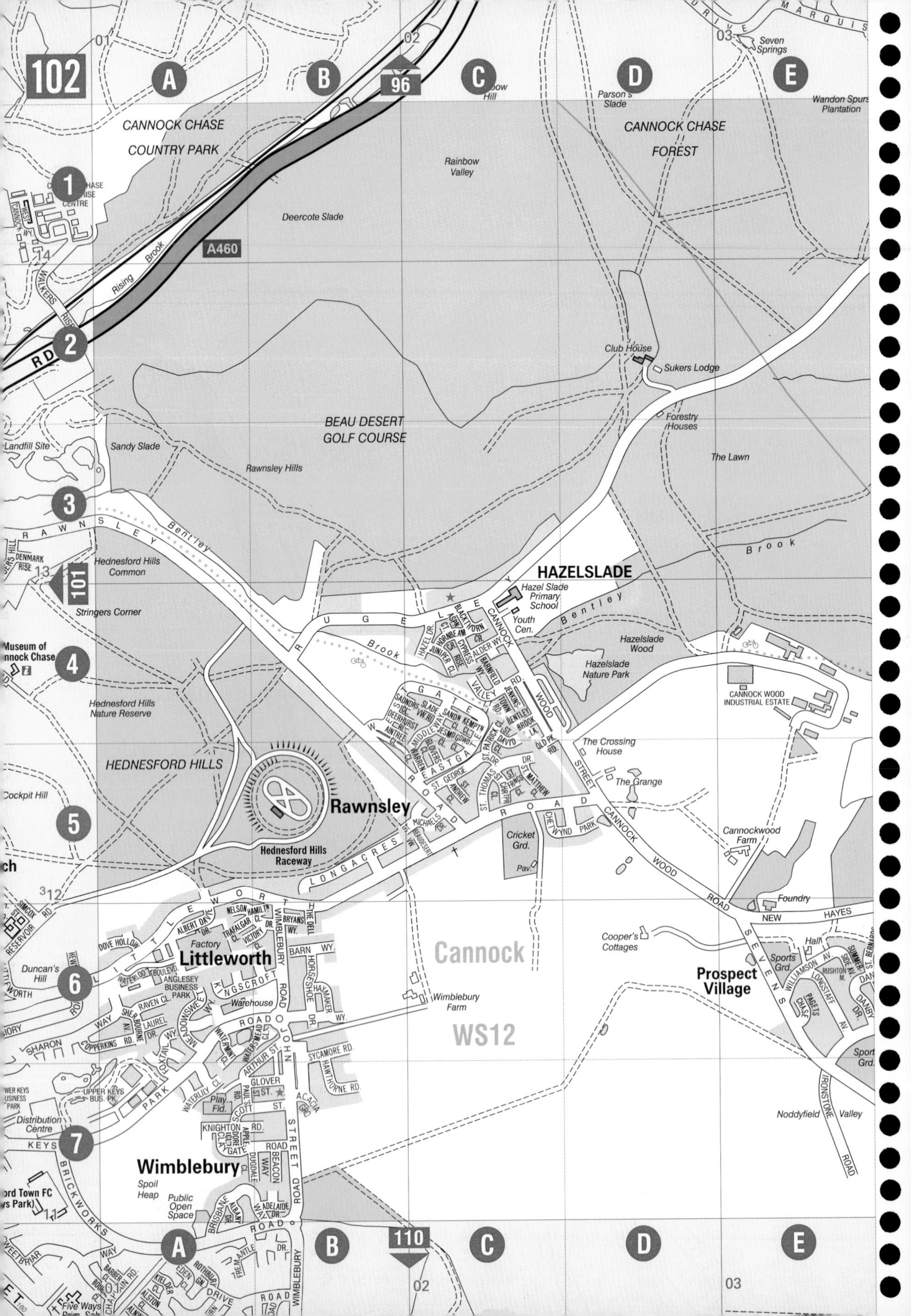
CANNOCK CHASE
COUNTRY PARK
CANNOCK CHASE
FOREST
Rainbow
Valley
Deercote Slade
A460
Rising Brook
Parson's
Slade
Seven
Springs
Wandon Spurs
Plantation
Club House
Sukers Lodge
Forestry
Houses
The Lawn
BEAU DESERT
GOLF COURSE
Sandy Slade
Landfill Site
Rawnsley Hills
RAWNSLEY
Bentley
Brook
HAZELSLADE
Hazel Slade
Primary
School
Youth
Cen.
Hazelslade
Wood
Hazelslade
Nature Park
Hednesford Hills
Common
Stringers Corner
Museum of
Cannock Chase
Hednesford Hills
Nature Reserve
HEDNESFORD HILLS
Cockpit Hill
Rawnsley
Hednesford Hills
Raceway
CANNOCK WOOD
INDUSTRIAL ESTATE
The Crossing
House
The Grange
Cannockwood
Farm
Foundry
Cricket
Grd.
Pav.
CANNOCK WOOD ROAD
NEW HAYES
LONGACRES
LITTLEWORTH
Littleworth
Factory
ANGLESEY
BUSINESS
PARK
Warehouse
Cannock
Cooper's
Cottages
Prospect
Village
Sports
Grd.
Wimblebury
Farm
WS12
Duncan's
Hill
UPPER KEYS
BUS. PK.
Distribution
Centre
Play
Fld.
Wimblebury
Spoil
Heap
Public
Open
Space
Noddyfield Valley
IRONSTONE ROAD
BRICKWORKS
WIMBLEBURY ROAD
JOHN STREET
SYCAMORE RD.
HAWTHORNE RD
Five Ways

96
101
110

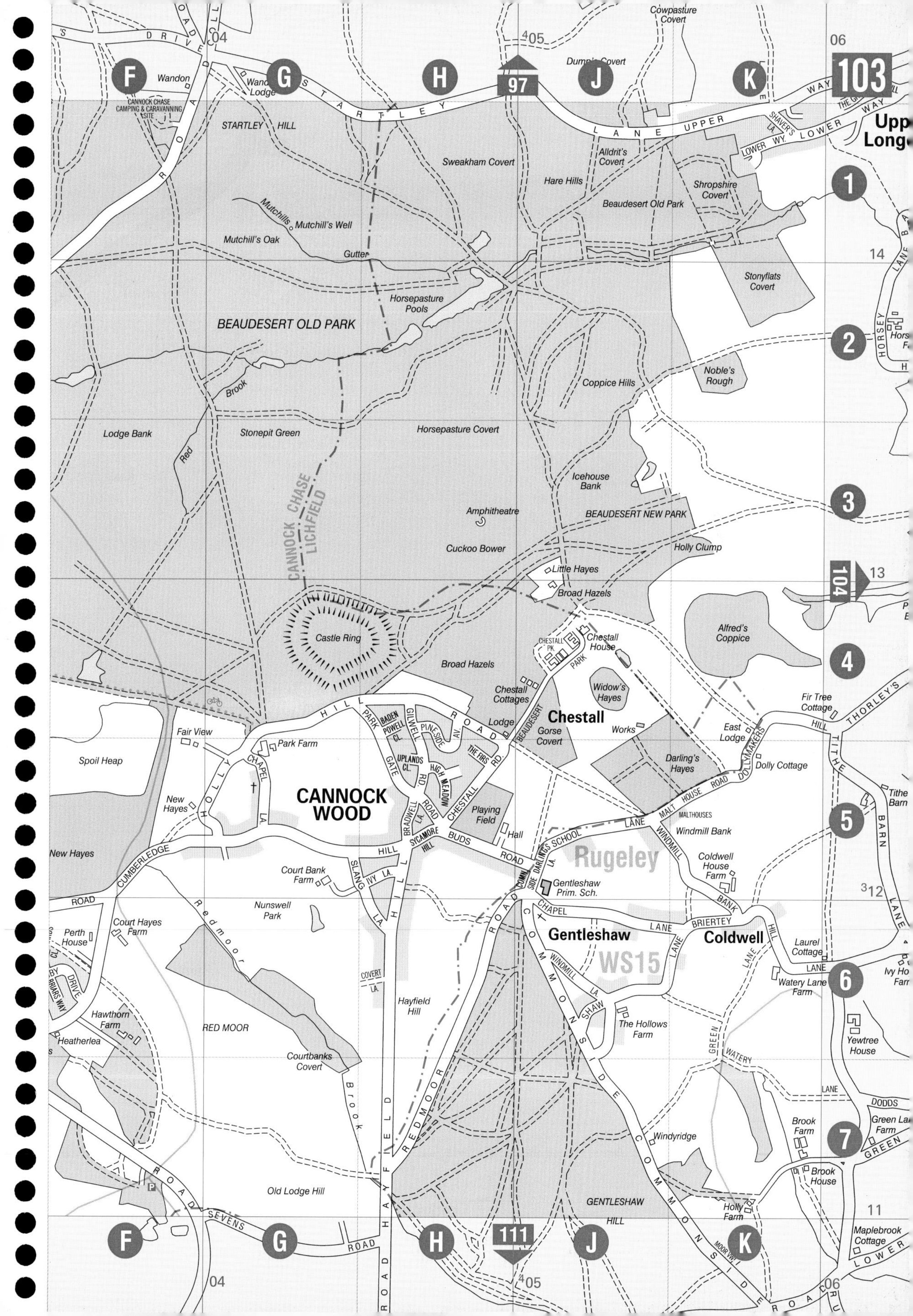
103
97
111
104
F
G
H
J
K
1
2
3
4
5
6
7
04
405
06
14
13
12
11
Cowpasture Covert
Dumpit Covert
Wandon
Wandon Lodge
CANNOCK CHASE CAMPING & CARAVANNING SITE
STARTLEY HILL
STARTLEY LANE
UPPER LONGDON
LOWER WAY
LOWER WY.
SHAVER'S LA.
THE GREEN
Sweakham Covert
Alldrit's Covert
Hare Hills
Shropshire Covert
Beaudesert Old Park
Mutchills
Mutchill's Well
Mutchill's Oak
Gutter
Stonyflats Covert
Horsepasture Pools
BEAUDESERT OLD PARK
Brook
Red
Noble's Rough
Coppice Hills
HORSEY LANE
Lodge Bank
Stonepit Green
Horsepasture Covert
Icehouse Bank
CANNOCK CHASE
LICHFIELD
Amphitheatre
BEAUDESERT NEW PARK
Cuckoo Bower
Holly Clump
Little Hayes
Broad Hazels
Alfred's Coppice
Castle Ring
Chestall House
CHESTALL PK.
PARK
Broad Hazels
Chestall Cottages
Widow's Hayes
Fir Tree Cottage
THORLEY'S
Fair View
Park Farm
HILL ROAD
BADEN POWELL CL.
GILWELL
PINESIDE AV.
PARK GATE
Lodge
BEAUDESERT
Chestall
Gorse Covert
Works
East Lodge
THE FIRS RD.
TITHE BARN
Spoil Heap
HOLLY
CHAPEL LA.
UPLANDS CL.
HIGH MEADOW
CHESTALL ROAD
Darling's Hayes
DOLLYMAKERS
Dolly Cottage
CANNOCK WOOD
Playing Field
MALT HOUSE ROAD
MALTHOUSES
Tithe Barn
New Hayes
BRADWELL LA.
Hall
LANE
Windmill Bank
SYCAMORE HILL
BUDS ROAD
SCHOOL LA.
DARLINGS
Rugeley
WINDMILL
New Hayes
CUMBERLEDGE HILL
Court Bank Farm
SLANG LA.
IVY LA.
Gentleshaw Prim. Sch.
Coldwell House Farm
BANK
ROAD
Nunswell Park
COMMON SIDE
CHAPEL LANE
BRIERTEY
Perth House
Court Hayes Farm
Redmoor
Gentleshaw
Coldwell
HILL
Laurel Cottage
WS15
WINDMILL LA.
Ivy House Farm
DRIVE
BRIARS WAY
COVERT LA.
LANE
Watery Lane Farm
Hayfield Hill
SHAW
Hawthorn Farm
RED MOOR
The Hollows Farm
Heatherlea
GREEN
WATERY
Yewtree House
Courtbanks Covert
LANE
DODDS
Green Lane Farm
Windyridge
Brook Farm
GREEN
REDMOOR
HAYFIELD ROAD
Brook
Brook House
ROAD
Old Lodge Hill
GENTLESHAW HILL
Holly Farm
SEVENS ROAD
Maplebrook Cottage
LOWER
MOOR VW.
ROAD

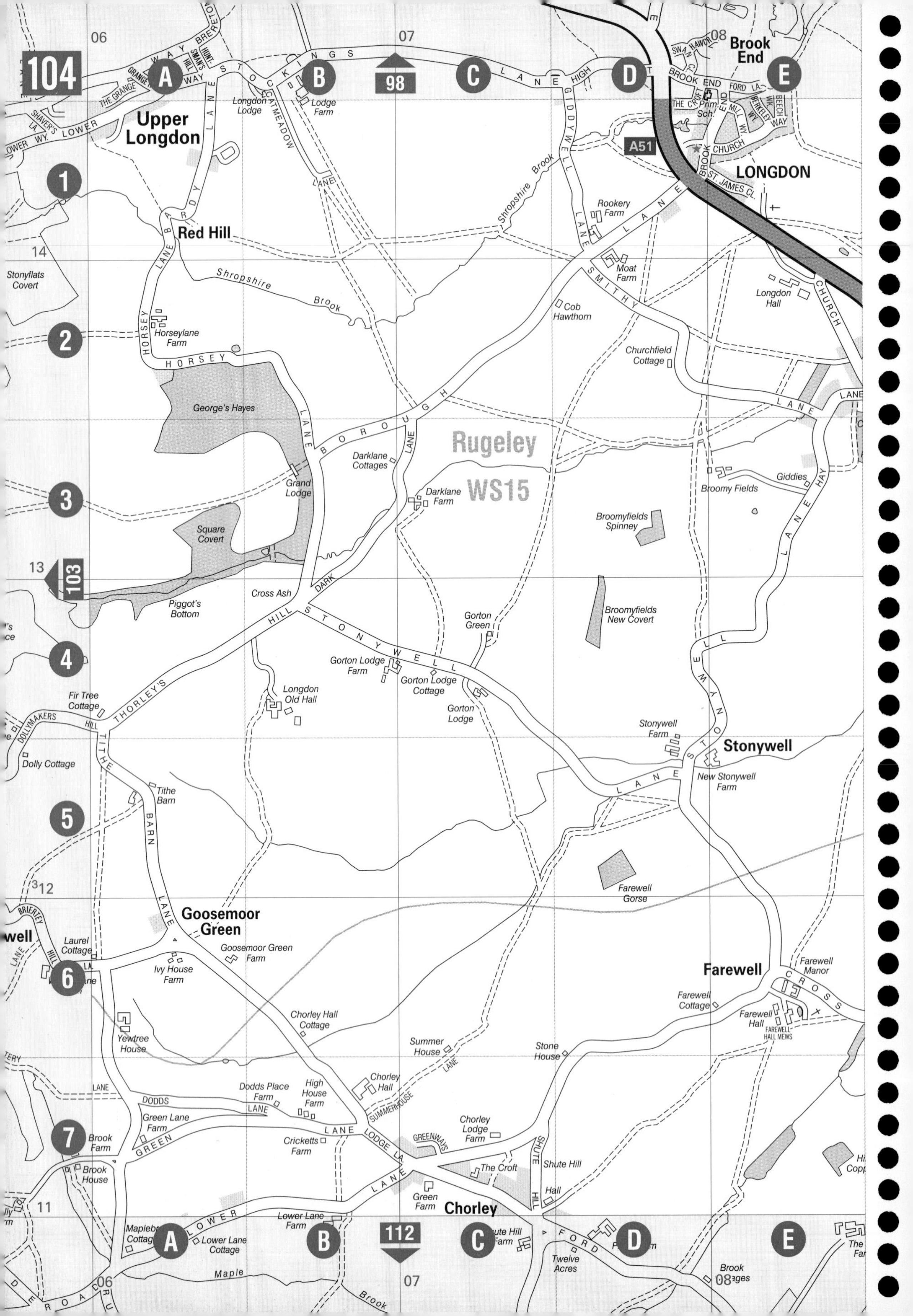

Upper Longdon
Red Hill
Longdon Lodge
Lodge Farm
Brook End
LONGDON
Rookery Farm
Moat Farm
Longdon Hall
Cob Hawthorn
Churchfield Cottage
Horseylane Farm
George's Hayes
Rugeley
WS15
Darklane Cottages
Darklane Farm
Grand Lodge
Square Covert
Broomy Fields
Giddies
Broomyfields Spinney
Broomyfields New Covert
Stonyflats Covert
Cross Ash
Piggot's Bottom
Gorton Green
Gorton Lodge Farm
Gorton Lodge Cottage
Gorton Lodge
Longdon Old Hall
Fir Tree Cottage
Dolly Cottage
Stonywell Farm
Stonywell
New Stonywell Farm
Tithe Barn
Farewell Gorse
Goosemoor Green
Goosemoor Green Farm
Laurel Cottage
Ivy House Farm
Farewell
Farewell Manor
Farewell Cottage
Farewell Hall
FAREWELL HALL MEWS
Chorley Hall Cottage
Yewtree House
Summer House
Stone House
Chorley Hall
Dodds Place Farm
High House Farm
Green Lane Farm
Brook Farm
Brook House
Cricketts Farm
Chorley Lodge Farm
The Croft
Shute Hill
Hall
Green Farm
Chorley
Lower Lane Farm
Lower Lane Cottage
Twelve Acres
A51
98
103
112

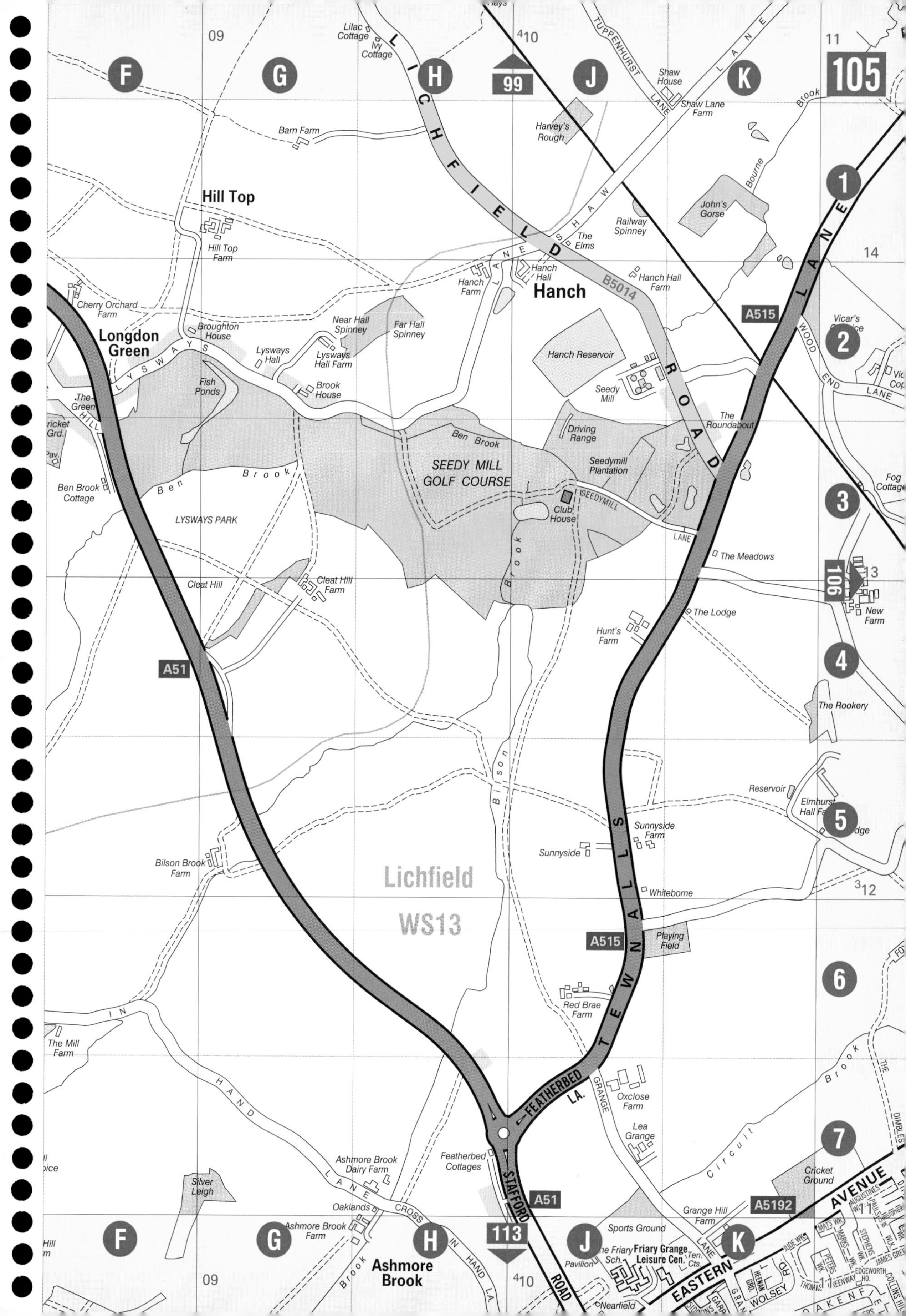
Hill Top
Hill Top Farm
Longdon Green
Cherry Orchard Farm
Broughton House
Lysways Hall
Lysways Hall Farm
Near Hall Spinney
Far Hall Spinney
Brook House
Fish Ponds
Barn Farm
Lilac Cottage
Ivy Cottage
LICHFIELD ROAD
B5014
Hanch
Hanch Hall
Hanch Farm
Hanch Reservoir
Hanch Hall Farm
Harvey's Rough
TUPPENHURST LANE
Shaw House
Shaw Lane Farm
SHAW LANE
The Elms
Railway Spinney
John's Gorse
Bourne Brook
A515
LANE
WOOD END LANE
Seedy Mill
The Roundabout
Driving Range
Seedymill Plantation
SEEDY MILL GOLF COURSE
Ben Brook
Club House
SEEDYMILL LANE
The Meadows
LYSWAYS PARK
Ben Brook Cottage
The Green
Cleat Hill
Cleat Hill Farm
A51
The Lodge
Hunt's Farm
New Farm
The Rookery
Fog Cottage
Bilson Brook
Reservoir
Sunnyside Farm
Sunnyside
Bilson Brook Farm
Whiteborne
Lichfield
WS13
A515
Playing Field
TEWNALLS
Red Brae Farm
The Mill Farm
HAND IN HAND LANE
FEATHERBED LA.
GRANGE
Oxclose Farm
Lea Grange
Circuit Brook
Cricket Ground
Silver Leigh
Ashmore Brook Dairy Farm
Featherbed Cottages
STAFFORD ROAD
A51
A5192
EASTERN AVENUE
Oaklands
CROSS IN HAND LA.
Ashmore Brook Farm
Ashmore Brook
Sports Ground
Grange Hill Farm
Friary Grange Leisure Cen.
Pavilion
Nearfield
WOLSEY RD.
99
106
113
09
410
11
14
13
312
F G H J K
1 2 3 4 5 6 7

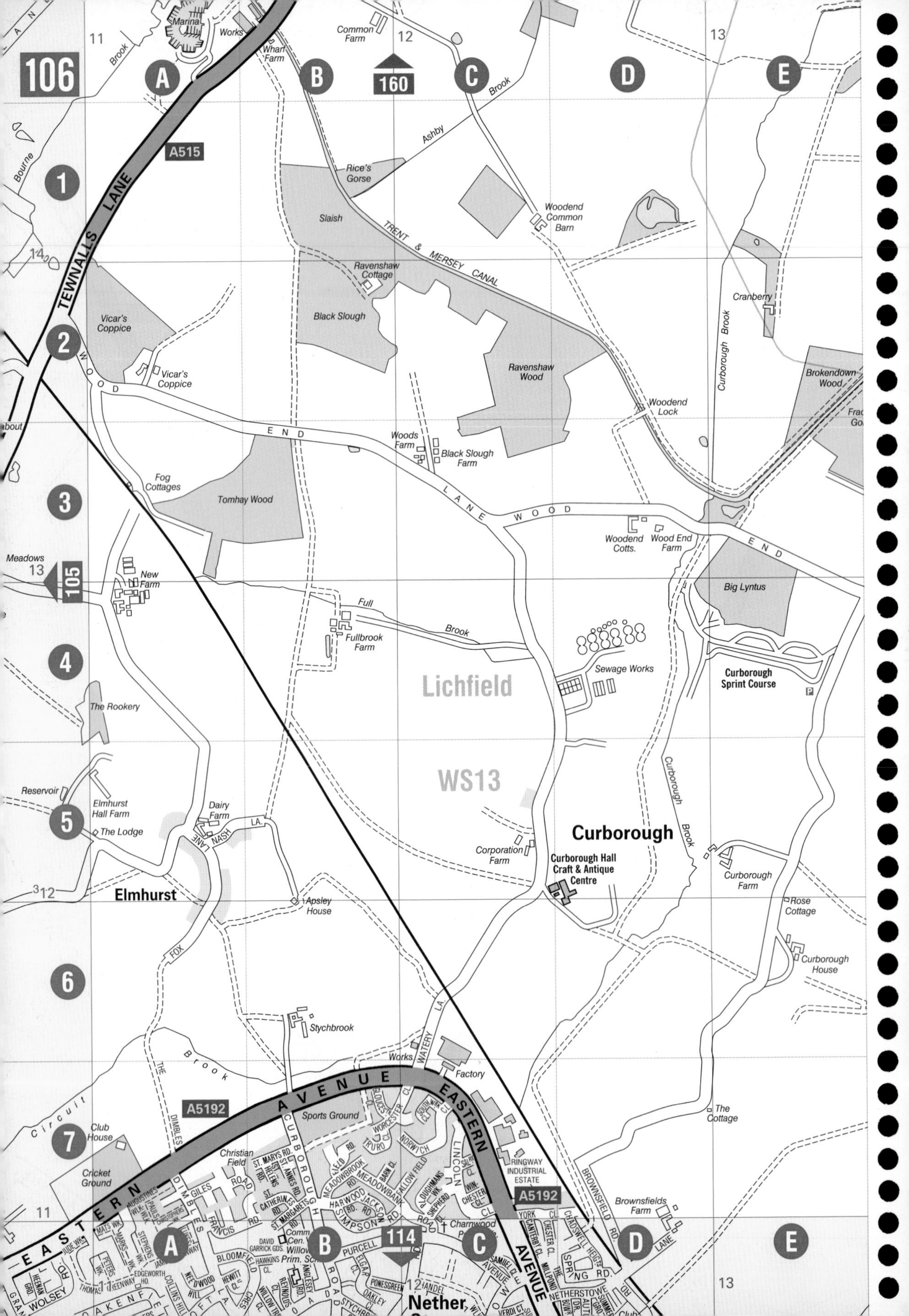
A
B
C
D
E
1
2
3
4
5
6
7
11
12
13
160
105
114
A515
A5192
TEWNALLS LANE
Marina
Works
Wharf Farm
Common Farm
Brook
Ashby
Bourne
Rice's Gorse
Slaish
TRENT & MERSEY CANAL
Woodend Common Barn
Ravenshaw Cottage
Black Slough
Cranberry
Curborough Brook
Vicar's Coppice
Ravenshaw Wood
Brokendown Wood
WOOD END LANE
Woodend Lock
Woods Farm
Black Slough Farm
Fog Cottages
Tomhay Wood
Woodend Cotts.
Wood End Farm
Meadows
New Farm
Full Brook
Fullbrook Farm
Big Lyntus
Sewage Works
Lichfield
Curborough Sprint Course
The Rookery
WS13
Reservoir
Elmhurst Hall Farm
The Lodge
Dairy Farm
NASH LA.
Curborough
Corporation Farm
Curborough Hall Craft & Antique Centre
Curborough Farm
Elmhurst
Apsley House
Rose Cottage
Curborough House
FOX LANE
Stychbrook
WATERY LA.
Works
Factory
THE DIMBLES
Circuit
AVENUE
EASTERN
Sports Ground
The Cottage
Club House
Christian Field
Cricket Ground
RINGWAY INDUSTRIAL ESTATE
BROWNSFIELD RD.
Brownsfields Farm
Charnwood
Nether
Willow Prim. Sch.

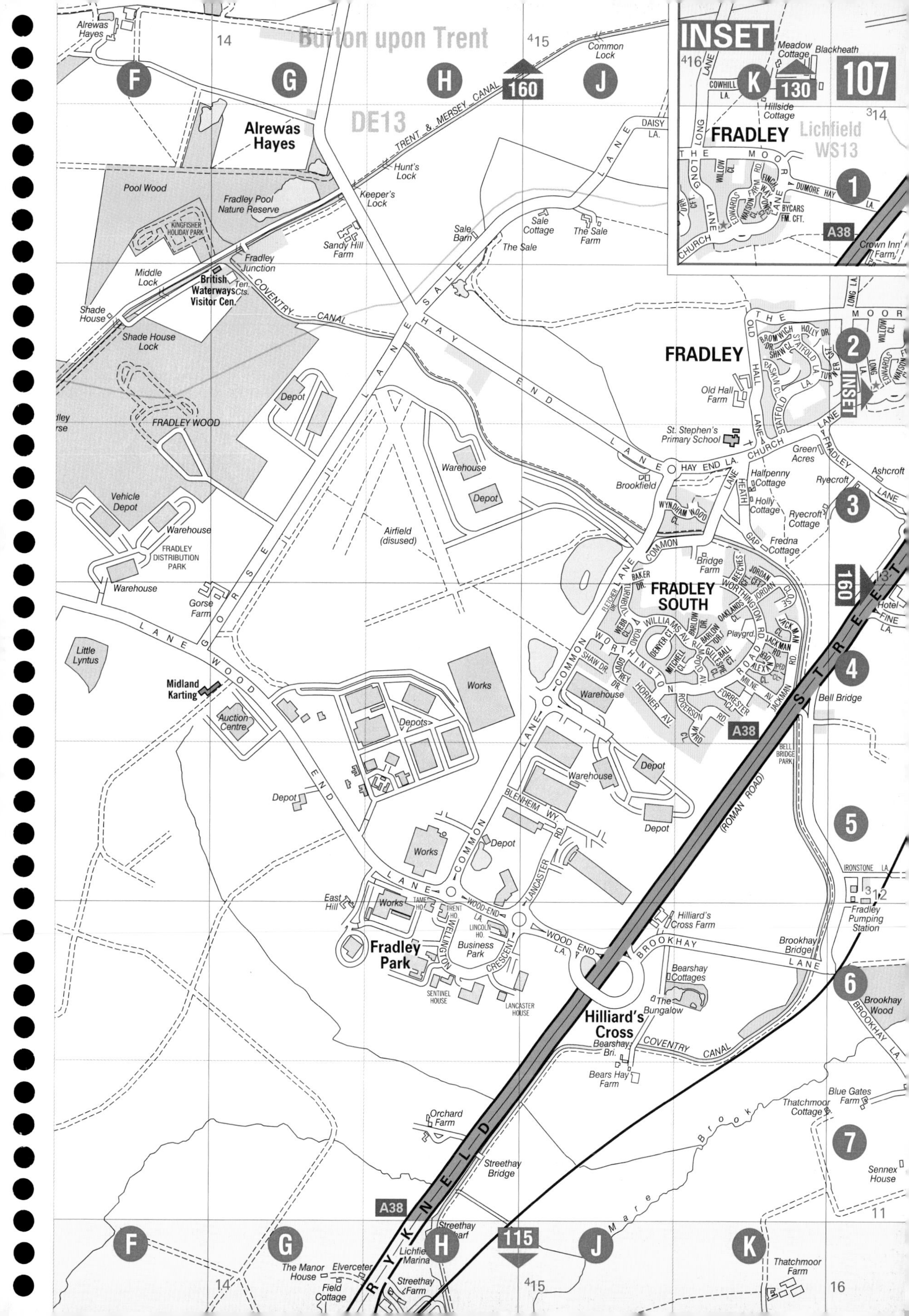

107
INSET
Burton upon Trent
DE13
Lichfield
WS13
160
130
115
Alrewas Hayes
Fradley Pool Nature Reserve
Pool Wood
Kingfisher Holiday Park
Trent & Mersey Canal
Hunt's Lock
Keeper's Lock
Common Lock
Sandy Hill Farm
Fradley Junction
Middle Lock
British Waterways Visitor Cen.
Shade House
Shade House Lock
Coventry Canal
Fradley Wood
Vehicle Depot
Warehouse
Fradley Distribution Park
Gorse Farm
Gorse Lane
Wood End Lane
Little Lyntus
Midland Karting
Auction Centre
Hay End Lane
Daisy La.
Sale Barn
Sale Cottage
The Sale
The Sale Farm
Airfield (disused)
Depot
Works
Depots
FRADLEY
FRADLEY SOUTH
Old Hall Farm
St. Stephen's Primary School
Brookfield
Church Lane
Common Lane
Halfpenny Cottage
Holly Cottage
Ryecroft
Ryecroft Cottage
Green Acres
Fredna Cottage
Ashcroft
Bridge Farm
Hotel
Playgrd.
Bell Bridge
Bell Bridge Park
Ryknield Street
(Roman Road)
A38
Blenheim Wy.
Lancaster Rd.
Fradley Park
Business Park
Wellington Crescent
East Hill
Sentinel House
Lancaster House
Hilliard's Cross Farm
Hilliard's Cross
Brookhay Lane
Brookhay Bridge
Bearshay Cottages
The Bungalow
Bearshay Bri.
Bears Hay Farm
Ironstone La.
Fradley Pumping Station
Brookhay Wood
Blue Gates Farm
Thatchmoor Cottage
Sennex House
Orchard Farm
Streethay Bridge
Streethay Wharf
Lichfield Marina
Streethay Farm
The Manor House
Elvercetor
Field Cottage
Thatchmoor Farm
Mare Brook
Meadow Cottage
Blackheath
Hillside Cottage
Cowhill La.
Long Lane
The Moor
Dumore Hay La.
Bycars Fm. Cft.
Crown Inn Farm
Church

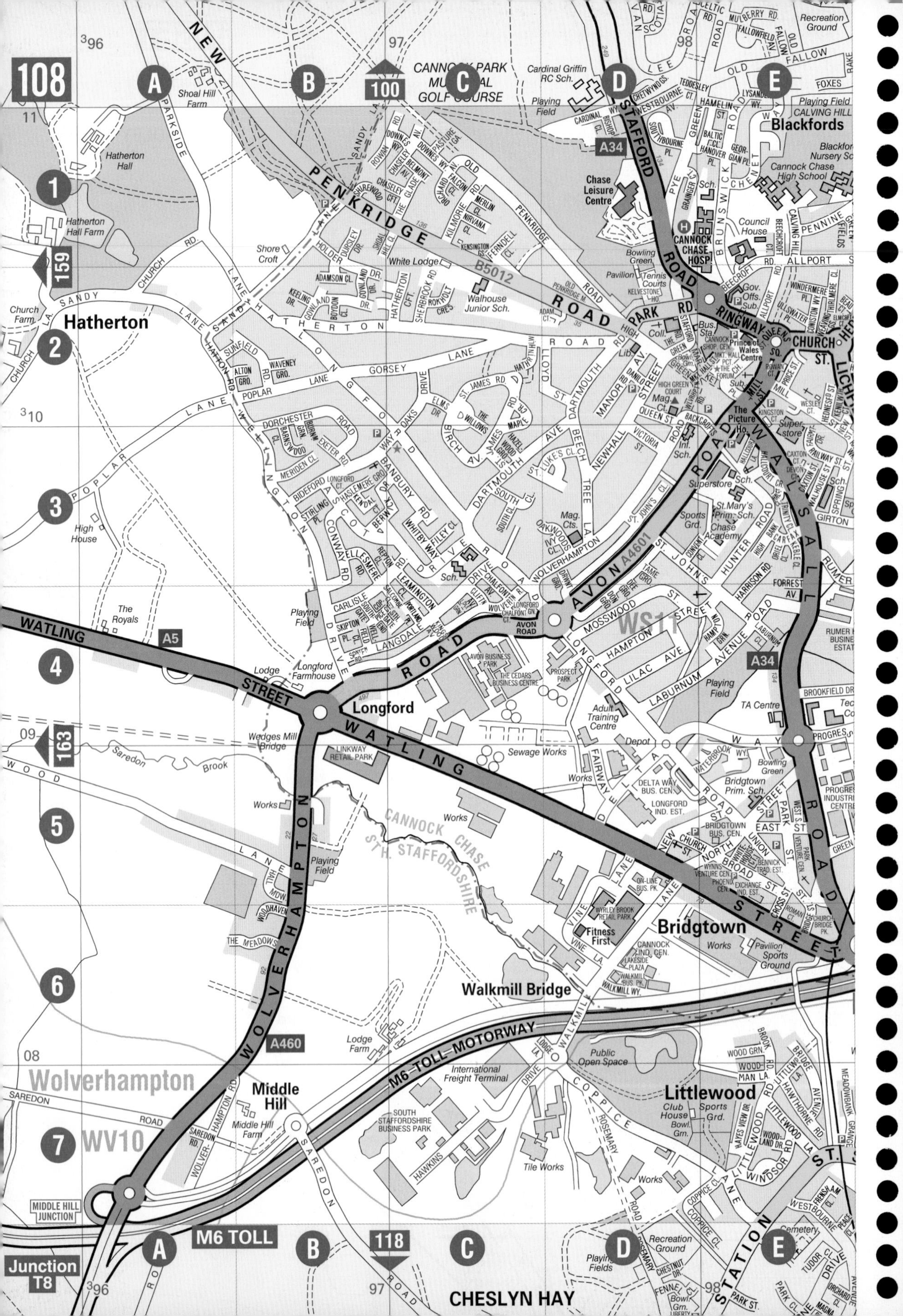
108
100
159
163
118
Hatherton
Hatherton Hall
Hatherton Hall Farm
Shoal Hill Farm
Church Farm
CANNOCK PARK MUNICIPAL GOLF COURSE
Cardinal Griffin RC Sch.
Playing Field
Blackfords
Cannock Chase High School
Recreation Ground
Chase Leisure Centre
CANNOCK CHASE HOSP.
Council House
Walhouse Junior Sch.
White Lodge
Shore Croft
PENKRIDGE ROAD
B5012
A34
STAFFORD ROAD
RINGWAY
CHURCH ST.
HATHERTON ROAD
GORSEY LANE
POPLAR LANE
SANDY LANE
LONGFORD ROAD
WELLINGTON DRIVE
A4601
AVON ROAD
WOLVERHAMPTON ROAD
WALSALL ROAD
WS11
High House
The Royals
WATLING STREET
A5
Longford
Longford Farmhouse
Lodge
Wedges Mill Bridge
Saredon Brook
WOOD LANE
LINKWAY RETAIL PARK
AVON BUSINESS PARK
THE CEDARS BUSINESS CENTRE
PROSPECT PARK
Sewage Works
Adult Training Centre
DELTA WAY
LONGFORD IND. EST.
Bridgtown Prim. Sch.
Bridgtown
Works
Playing Field
CANNOCK CHASE
STH. STAFFORDSHIRE
WYRLEY BROOK RETAIL PARK
Fitness First
Walkmill Bridge
Pavilion Sports Ground
A460
M6 TOLL MOTORWAY
Lodge Farm
International Freight Terminal
Public Open Space
Littlewood
Wolverhampton
WV10
Middle Hill
Middle Hill Farm
MIDDLE HILL JUNCTION
SOUTH STAFFORDSHIRE BUSINESS PARK
Tile Works
Junction T8
M6 TOLL
CHESLYN HAY
Recreation Ground
Playing Fields
STATION ST.
Cemetery
SAREDON ROAD

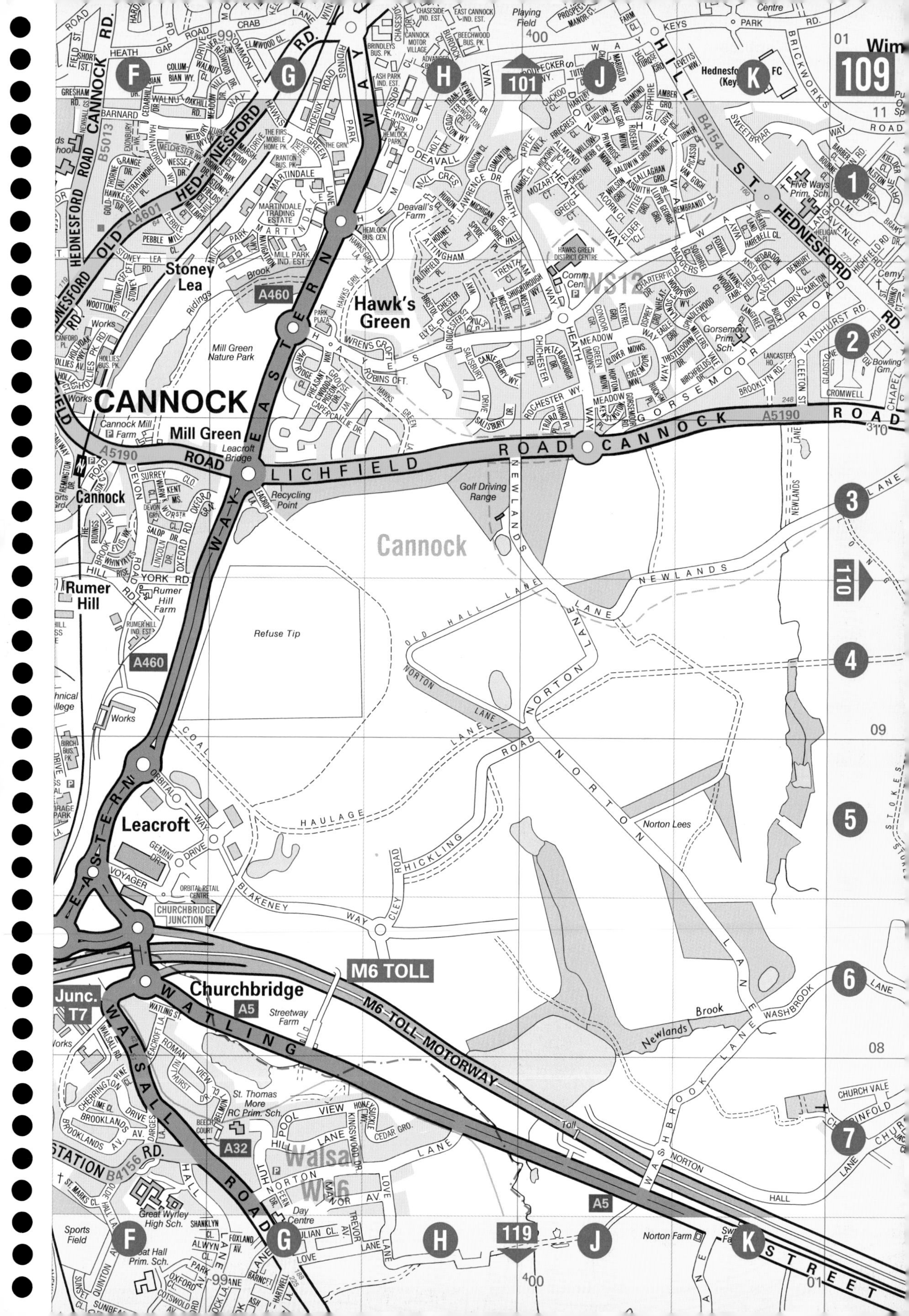

109
101
110
119
CANNOCK
Cannock
Hawk's Green
Stoney Lea
Mill Green
Rumer Hill
Leacroft
Churchbridge
Mill Green Nature Park
Refuse Tip
Golf Driving Range
Norton Lees
Norton Farm
Newlands Brook
WS12
LICHFIELD ROAD
CANNOCK ROAD
EASTERN WAY
WATLING STREET
WALSALL ROAD
M6 TOLL
M6 TOLL MOTORWAY
A5190
A460
A5
A32
B4154
B5013
A4601
B4156
CHURCHBRIDGE JUNCTION
Junc. T7

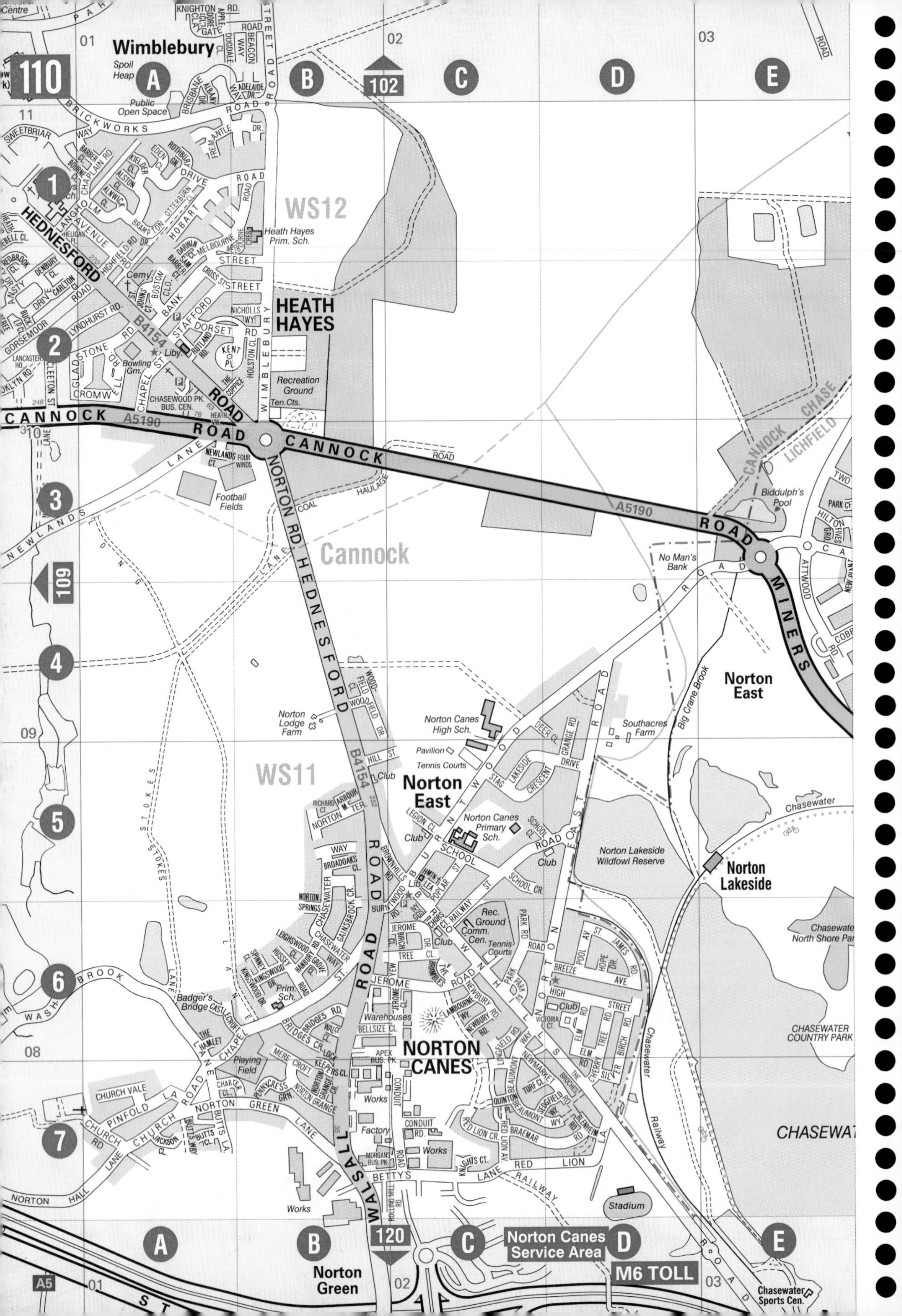
Wimblebury
HEATH HAYES
Cannock
WS12
WS11
Norton East
NORTON CANES
Norton Lakeside
Norton Green
Chasewater North Shore Park
CHASEWATER COUNTRY PARK
Norton Lakeside Wildfowl Reserve
Norton Canes Service Area
M6 TOLL
CANNOCK ROAD
HEDNESFORD ROAD
NORTON RD
WALSALL ROAD
MINERS ROAD
A5190
B4154
102
109
120
Heath Hayes Prim. Sch.
Norton Canes High Sch.
Norton Canes Primary Sch.
Recreation Ground
Football Fields
Playing Field
Stadium
Chasewater Sports Cen.
Biddulph's Pool
No Man's Bank
Southacres Farm
Norton Lodge Farm
Big Crane Brook

103
Rugeley WS15
GENTLESHAW HILL
Windyridge
Brook Farm
Holly Farm
Malthbrook Cottage
SEVENS ROAD
HAYFIELD HILL
COMMONSIDE
PADBURY LA.
OGLEY HAY LANE
Redmoor Brook
The Hawthornes
Bleak House Farm
Coney Lodge Farm
Boney Hay Prim. Sch.
Nag's Farm
Mosty Lea
SPRINGLE STYCHE LA.
Castle Farm
Gorstey Ley
Boney Hay
Comm. Cen.
Redwood Park
RYECROFT SHOPPING CENTRE
Holly Grove Prim. Sch.
BIDDULPH MOBILE HOME PARK
IRONSTONE ROAD
HIGH STREET
SPINNEY STREET
Ten.Ct.
Chase Terrace Park
Bowl.Grn.
Chase Terrace
Chase Terrace Prim. Sch.
BURNTWOOD TOWN SHOP. CEN.
Depot
Open Space
Playing Field
Tennis Courts
Chase Terrace High Sch.
Sankey's Corner
Liby.
CHASEWATER CT. BUSINESS PK
CHASE PARK INDUSTRIAL ESTATE
ACORN STARTER UNITS
CHASETOWN IND. EST.
Works
Depots
112
Highfields Prim. Sch.
MORLEY ROAD SHOPPING CEN.
Burntwood Park
BRIDGE CROSS ROAD
CANNOCK ROAD
A5190
Burntwood
WS7
MILESTONE WAY
Youth Centre
Sports Ground
Burntwood Leisure Cen.
Football Ground
Playgrd.
Warehouses
CHASEWATER IND. EST.
Springhill Prim. Sch.
Warehouse
Ball's Mount
MOUNT ROAD IND. EST.
Railway
Chasewater Heaths
CHASETOWN
St. Joseph & St. Theresa RC Prim. Sch.
HIGH STREET
B5011
CHASE ROAD
NORTON LA.
Coppy Nook
COPPY NOOK LANE
HAMMERWICH HOSP.
Chasetown
Playing Field
Recreation Ground
Chasetown Sch.
Cemetery
Leisure Cen.
Coun. Offs.
Mem. Pk.
Club Ho.
Sports Ground
QUEEN ST. IND. EST.
Ridgeway Prim. Sch.
Chasewater Outdoor Education Cen.
Chase Sailing Club
Tennis Courts
Chasetown High Sch.
Highfields
HIGHFIELDS ROAD
Play. Fld.
POOL COTTAGES
Brooklyn Farm
Triangle
Crane Brook
OGLEY HAY RD.
HANNEY HAY RD.
WHARF LANE
121
BURNTWOOD JUNCTION
Junction T6
Anglesey Wharf
WYRLEY & ESSINGTON CANAL
Anglesey Branch
The Forest
Brook Farm
F
G
H
J
K
1
2
3
4
5
6
7
04
405
06
08
09
310

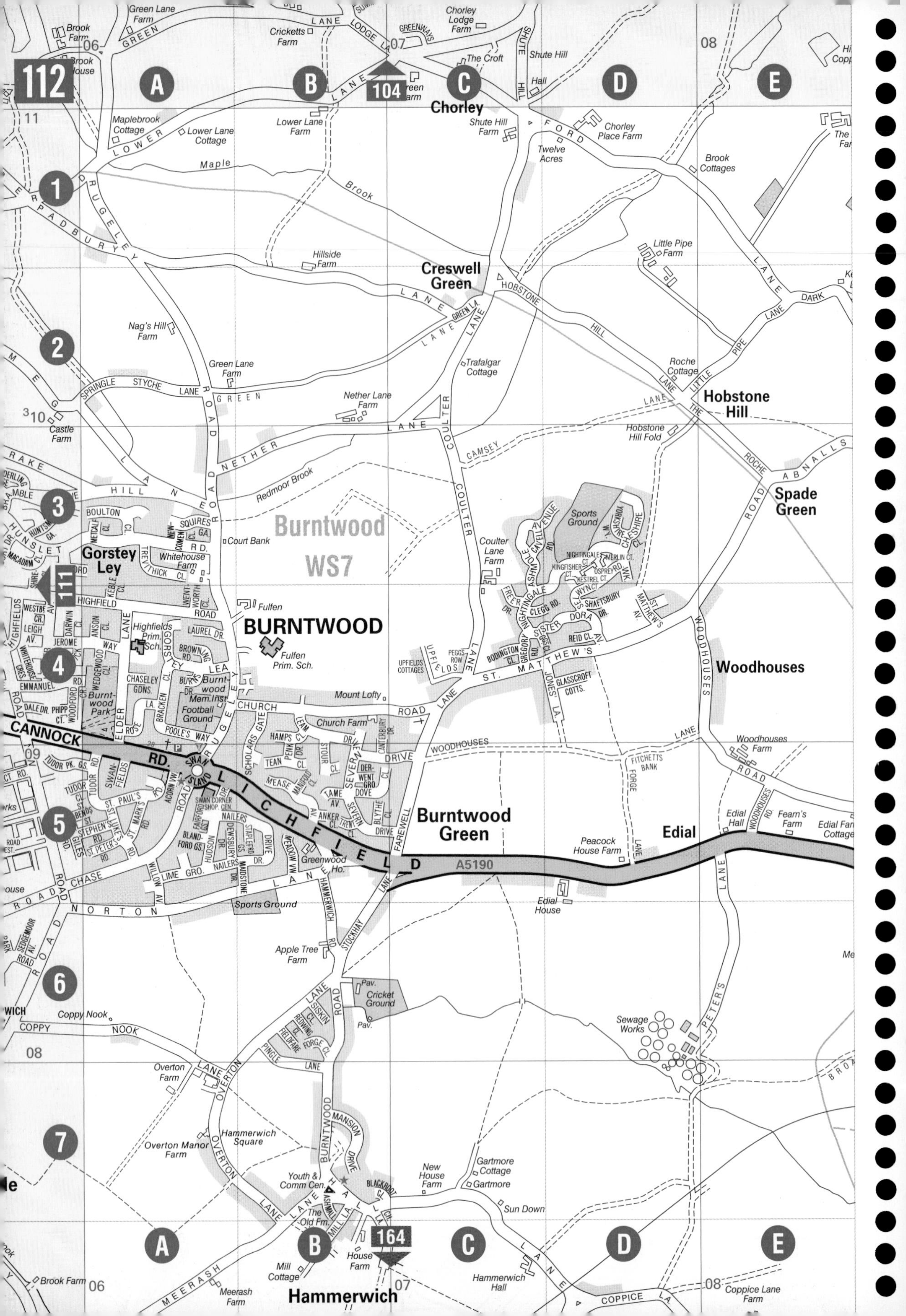

112
104
111
164
Chorley
Creswell Green
Hobstone Hill
Spade Green
Burntwood WS7
BURNTWOOD
Gorstey Ley
Woodhouses
Burntwood Green
Edial
Hammerwich
Fulfen Prim. Sch.
Highfields Prim. Sch.
Burntwood Park
Burntwood Mem. Inst.
Football Ground
Sports Ground
Cricket Ground
Sewage Works
Chorley Lodge Farm
Green Lane Farm
Cricketts Farm
Brook Farm
Brook House
The Croft
Shute Hill
Hall
Maplebrook Cottage
Lower Lane Cottage
Lower Lane Farm
Shute Hill Farm
Chorley Place Farm
Twelve Acres
Brook Cottages
Little Pipe Farm
Hillside Farm
Nag's Hill Farm
Green Lane Farm
Trafalgar Cottage
Nether Lane Farm
Roche Cottage
Hobstone Hill Fold
Castle Farm
Court Bank
Whitehouse Farm
Coulter Lane Farm
Fulfen
Mount Lofty
Upfields Cottages
Church Farm
Woodhouses Farm
Edial Hall
Fearn's Farm
Edial Farm Cottage
Peacock House Farm
Greenwood Ho.
Edial House
Apple Tree Farm
Coppy Nook
Overton Farm
Overton Manor Farm
Hammerwich Square
Youth & Comm Cen.
The Old Fm.
New House Farm
Gartmore Cottage
Gartmore
Sun Down
Mill Cottage
House Farm
Hammerwich Hall
Meerash Farm
Brook Farm
Coppice Lane Farm
A5190
CANNOCK RD.
LICHFIELD RD.
SWAN ISLAND
Swan Corner Shop. Cen.
Maple Brook
Redmoor Brook

113
105
114
F
G
H
J
K
1
2
3
4
5
6
7
09
410
11
08
A5192
A51
A5190
A461
WS13
WS14
Lichfield
LICHFIELD
Ashmore Brook
Pipehill
Leamonsley
Silver Leigh
Ashmore Brook Dairy Farm
Featherbed Cottages
Lea Grange
Club House
Oaklands
Ashmore Brook Farm
Sports Ground
Grange Hill Farm
The Friary Sch.
Friary Grange Leisure Cen.
Ten. Cts.
Pavilion
Nearfield Ho.
The Hedgehog
Abnalls Farm
Robin Wood
Pipe Coppice
Abnalls
Darwin's Bath
Victoria Osiers
Pipe Hall
Fitzherbert Firs
The Dell
The Slang
Lady Muriel's Belt
Pipe Green
THE PARK
Maple Hayes Hall Sch.
Parker's Plantin
Peace Plantation
Maple Hayes
Leamansley House
Fish Ponds
Jubilee Wood
Leamonsley Mill Farm
Sloppy Wood
The Roundabouts
Herbert's Spinney
Leamonsley Wood
Upper Hilltop Farm
Lower Hilltop Farm
Edial Farm
Edial House
Pipe Grange
Sandyway Farm
Pipe Grange Farm
Mickle Hills Farm
Heathcote Cottage
Pipe Marsh
Tollgate Cottage
Fosseway Farm
Pipehill Farm
Fosseway Court
Barn Cottage
Pipe Hill Manor
Sandfields Cottage
Sandfields Lodge
Deans Slade Farm
Water Works
Pipe Place Farm
Pipe Place
Aldershawe Hall
Aldershawe
Chestnut Lodge
Harehurst Hill
Superstore
Wks. Depot
Pitch & Putt Course
Football Ground
BEACON PARK
Leamonsley Brook
Playing Fields
Bowling Grn.
Rec.
Christ Church C of E Prim. Sch.
Hall
STAFFORD ROAD
WESTERN BY-PASS
EASTERN AVENUE
ASHMORE BROOK
CROSS IN HAND LANE
ABNALLS LANE
GRANGE LANE
WALSALL ROAD
FOSSEWAY
FOSSEWAY LANE
GREEN LANE
CLAYPIT LANE
SAINTE FOY AV.
BEACON STREET
WOLSEY RD.
WESTON RD.
CHRISTCHURCH LA.

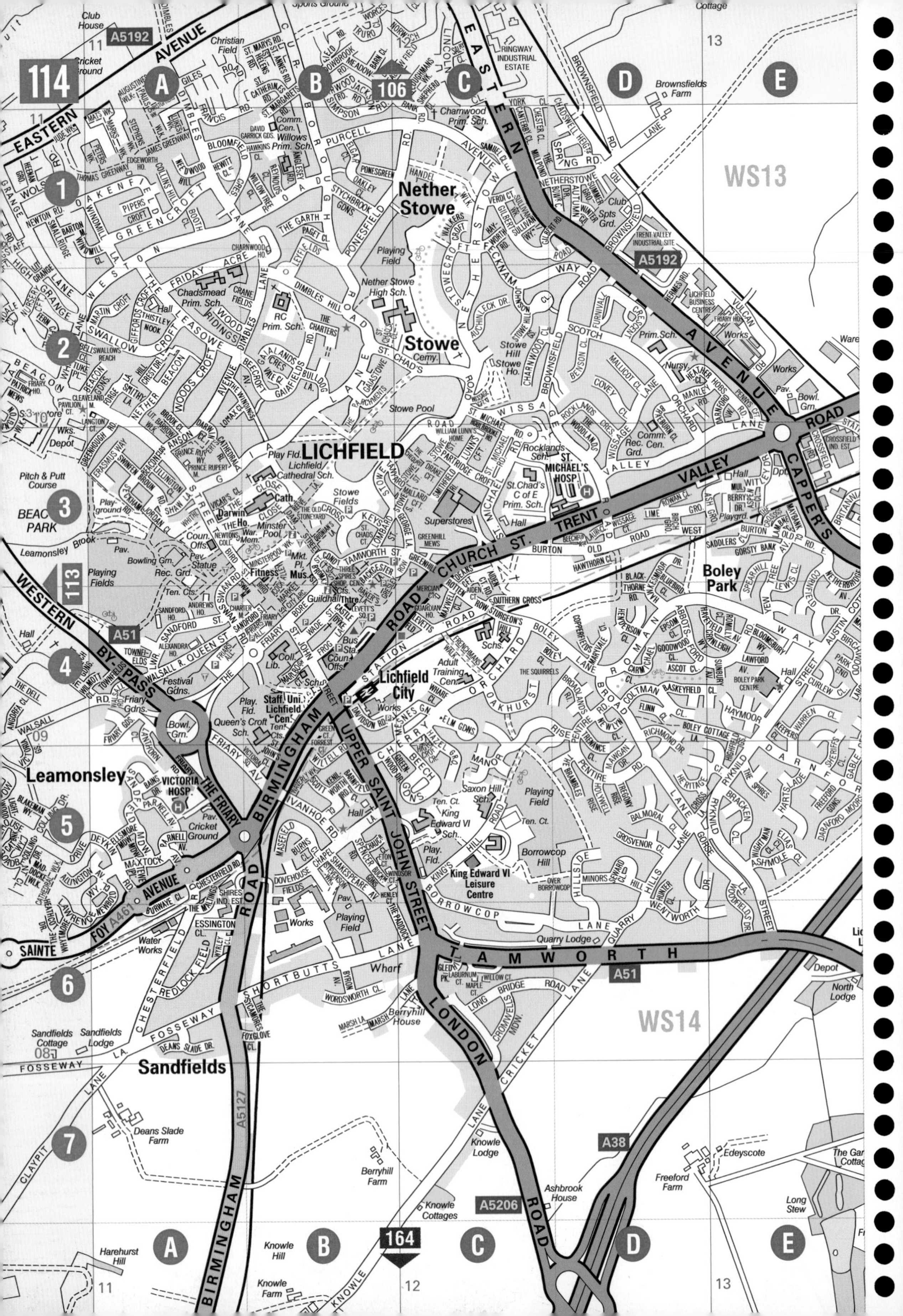
A5192
EASTERN AVENUE
106
113
164
A B C D E
1 2 3 4 5 6 7
11 12 13
Club House
Cricket Ground
Christian Field
RINGWAY INDUSTRIAL ESTATE
Brownsfields Farm
WS13
Nether Stowe
Charnwood Prim. Sch.
Willows Prim. Sch.
Comm. Cen.
Playing Field
Nether Stowe High Sch.
Chadsmead Prim. Sch.
RC Prim. Sch.
Stowe
Cemy.
Stowe Hill
Stowe Ho.
Stowe Pool
LICHFIELD
Lichfield Cathedral Sch.
Cath.
Darwin Ho.
Minster Pool
Stowe Fields
Superstores
Rocklands Sch.
ST. MICHAEL'S HOSP.
St. Chad's C of E Prim. Sch.
TRENT VALLEY INDUSTRIAL SITE
LICHFIELD BUSINESS CENTRE
Works
Prim. Sch.
Nursy.
Comm. Rec. Cen. Grd.
Bowl. Grn.
CAPPER'S LANE
ROAD
CHURCH ST.
TRENT VALLEY
Hall
Boley Park
Pitch & Putt Course
BEACON PARK
Leamonsley Brook
Playing Fields
Bowling Grn.
Rec. Grd.
Mkt. Pl.
Mus.
Guildhall
Thtre.
Bus Sta.
Coun. Offs.
Coll. Lib.
Festival Gdns.
Friary Gdns.
WESTERN BY-PASS
A51
Lichfield City
Staff. Uni. Lichfield Cen.
Queen's Croft Sch.
Adult Training Cen.
THE SQUIRRELS
BOLEY PARK CENTRE
Leamonsley
VICTORIA HOSP.
Cricket Ground
Saxon Hill Sch.
King Edward VI Sch.
Playing Field
Borrowcop Hill
King Edward VI Leisure Centre
UPPER SAINT JOHN STREET
BIRMINGHAM ROAD
THE FRIARY
AVENUE
Water Works
Works
Playing Field
SAINTE
TAMWORTH
Quarry Lodge
Wharf
Berryhill House
LONDON ROAD
WS14
Depot
North Lodge
Sandfields Cottage
Sandfields Lodge
Sandfields
FOSSEWAY
A5127
Deans Slade Farm
Knowle Lodge
Berryhill Farm
A38
Edeyscote
Freeford Farm
Long Stew
Ashbrook House
A5206
Knowle Cottages
Harehurst Hill
Knowle Hill
Knowle Farm
CLAYPIT LANE
CRICKET LANE
KNOWLE LANE

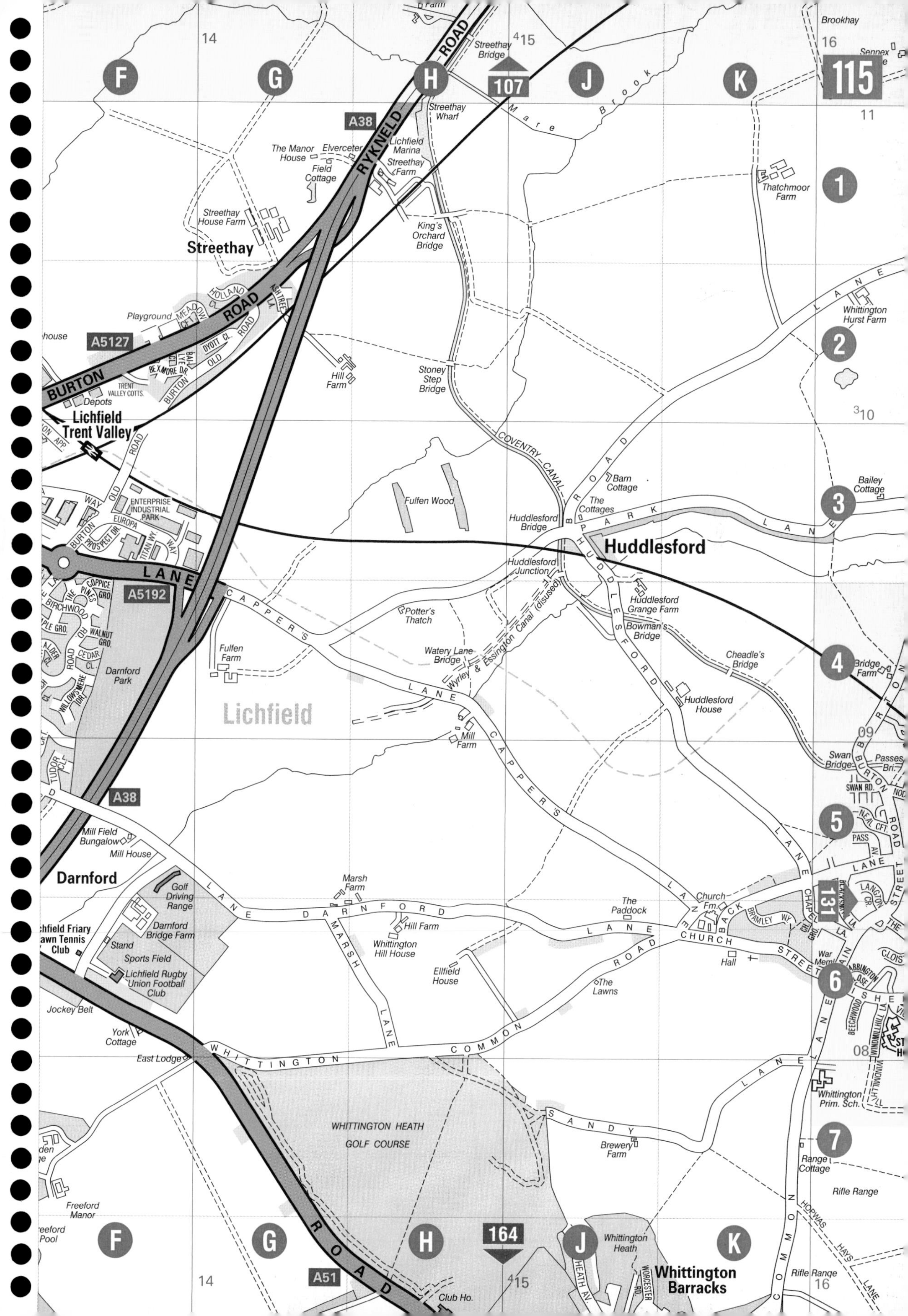

Streethay Bridge
107
Streethay Wharf
Mare Brook
Brookhay
A38
RYKNELD ROAD
The Manor House
Elverceter
Field Cottage
Lichfield Marina
Streethay Farm
Thatchmoor Farm
Streethay House Farm
Streethay
King's Orchard Bridge
Whittington Hurst Farm
Playground
A5127
BURTON ROAD
Hill Farm
Stoney Step Bridge
Depots
TRENT VALLEY COTTS.
Lichfield Trent Valley
COVENTRY CANAL
Barn Cottage
Bailey Cottage
Fulfen Wood
ENTERPRISE INDUSTRIAL PARK
The Cottages
Huddlesford Bridge
PARK LANE
Huddlesford
Huddlesford Junction
A5192
Potter's Thatch
Huddlesford Grange Farm
Bowman's Bridge
Cheadle's Bridge
Fulfen Farm
Watery Lane Bridge
Wyrley & Essington Canal (disused)
Bridge Farm
Darnford Park
Lichfield
Huddlesford House
Mill Farm
CAPPERS LANE
Swan Bridge
Passes Bri.
A38
Mill Field Bungalow
Mill House
Darnford
Golf Driving Range
Marsh Farm
DARNFORD LANE
Church Fm.
The Paddock
131
Hill Farm
Whittington Hill House
Darnford Bridge Farm
Lichfield Friary Lawn Tennis Club
Stand
Sports Field
Lichfield Rugby Union Football Club
CHURCH STREET
Hall
War Meml
Ellfield House
The Lawns
Jockey Belt
York Cottage
East Lodge
WHITTINGTON COMMON ROAD
Whittington Prim. Sch.
WHITTINGTON HEATH GOLF COURSE
SANDY LANE
Brewery Farm
Range Cottage
Rifle Range
Freeford Manor
164
Whittington Heath
Whittington Barracks
A51
Club Ho.
Rifle Range
HOPWAS HAYS LANE

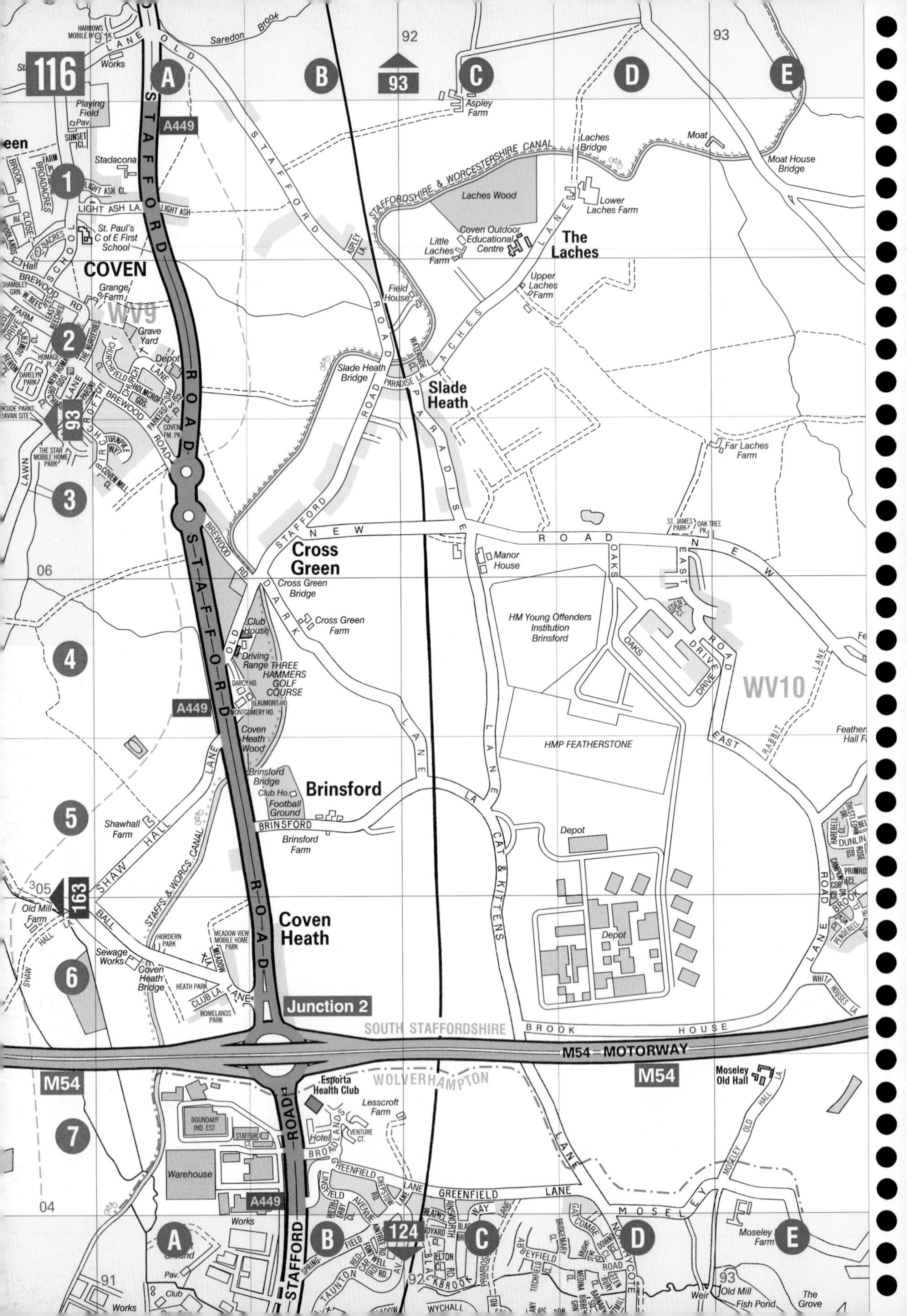
116
A
B
C
D
E
92
93
COVEN
WV9
The Laches
Slade Heath
Cross Green
Brinsford
Coven Heath
WV10
STAFFORD ROAD
A449
STAFFORDSHIRE & WORCESTERSHIRE CANAL
Laches Wood
Lower Laches Farm
Aspley Farm
Moat
Moat House Bridge
Laches Bridge
Coven Outdoor Educational Centre
Little Laches Farm
Upper Laches Farm
Field House
Slade Heath Bridge
PARADISE LA.
Far Laches Farm
NEW ROAD
Manor House
Cross Green Bridge
Cross Green Farm
HM Young Offenders Institution Brinsford
HMP FEATHERSTONE
Driving Range
THREE HAMMERS GOLF COURSE
Coven Heath Wood
Brinsford Bridge
Football Ground
Brinsford Farm
Shawhall Farm
Depot
CAT & KITTENS LANE
Old Mill Farm
Sewage Works
Coven Heath Bridge
Junction 2
SOUTH STAFFORDSHIRE
WOLVERHAMPTON
M54 MOTORWAY
M54
BROOK HOUSE
Esporta Health Club
Lesscroft Farm
BOUNDARY IND. EST.
Warehouse
Hotel
Works
GREENFIELD LANE
MOSELEY
Moseley Old Hall
Moseley Farm
Old Mill
Fish Pond
The Grove
Weir
Playing Field
Stadacona
St. Paul's C of E First School
Grange Farm
Grave Yard
Saredon Brook
93
163
124
1
2
3
4
5
6
7
06
05
04
91

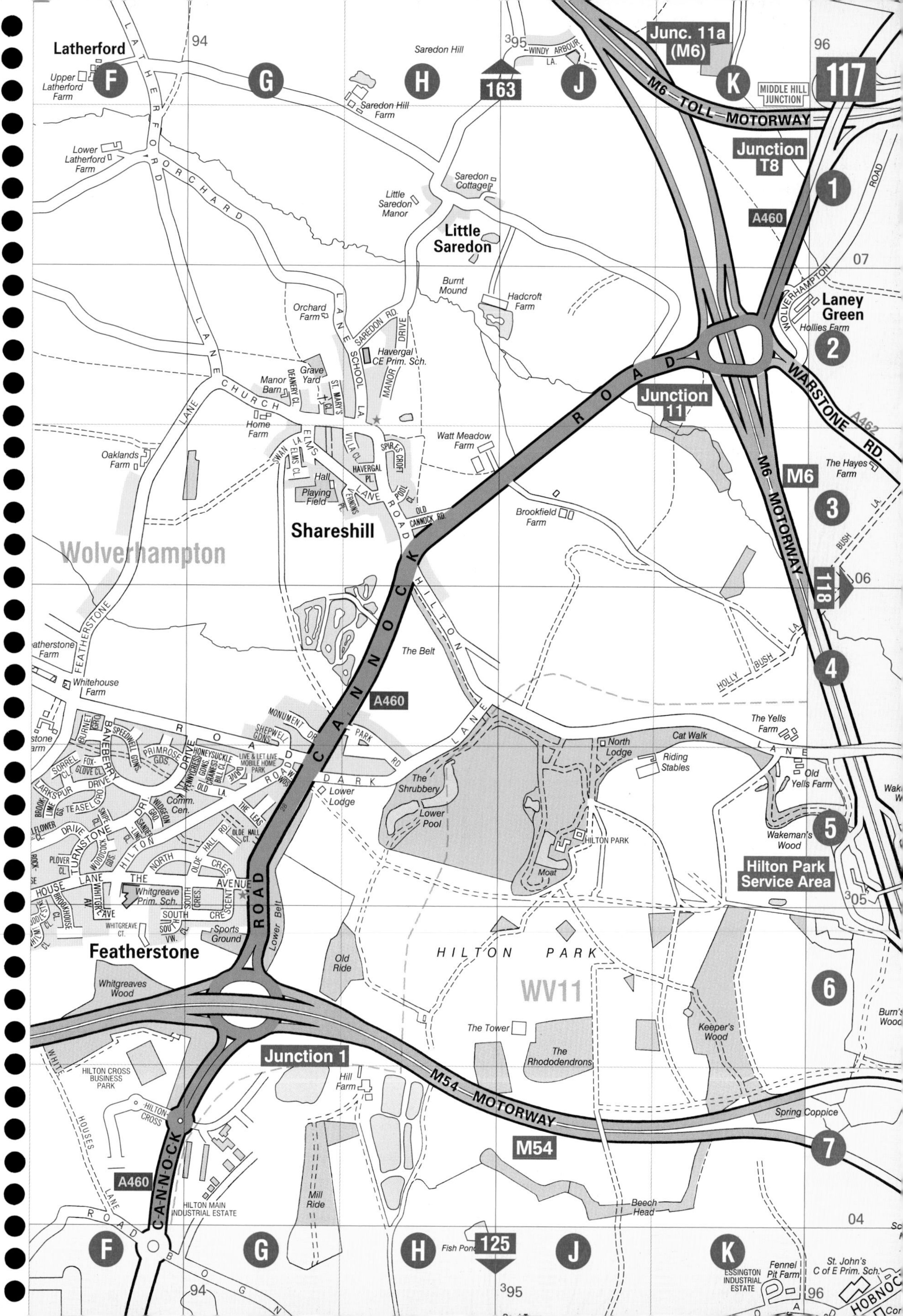

Latherford
Upper Latherford Farm
Lower Latherford Farm
Saredon Hill
Saredon Hill Farm
Junc. 11a (M6)
117
163
MIDDLE HILL JUNCTION
M6 TOLL MOTORWAY
Junction T8
A460
Saredon Cottage
Little Saredon Manor
Little Saredon
Burnt Mound
Hadcroft Farm
Orchard Farm
Havergal CE Prim. Sch.
Laney Green
Hollies Farm
WARSTONE RD.
A462
Junction 11
Grave Yard
Manor Barn
Home Farm
Oaklands Farm
Watt Meadow Farm
The Hayes Farm
M6
M6 MOTORWAY
Hall
Playing Field
Brookfield Farm
Shareshill
Wolverhampton
118
The Belt
Featherstone Farm
Whitehouse Farm
A460
CANNOCK ROAD
HILTON LANE
The Yells Farm
Cat Walk
North Lodge
Riding Stables
Old Yells Farm
The Shrubbery
Lower Pool
Lower Lodge
Comm. Cen.
Moat
HILTON PARK
Wakeman's Wood
Hilton Park Service Area
Whitgreave Prim. Sch.
Sports Ground
Lower Belt
Featherstone
Old Ride
HILTON PARK
WV11
Whitgreaves Wood
The Tower
Keeper's Wood
The Rhododendrons
Junction 1
HILTON CROSS BUSINESS PARK
Hill Farm
M54 MOTORWAY
Spring Coppice
M54
HILTON MAIN INDUSTRIAL ESTATE
Mill Ride
Beech Head
125
Fish Pond
ESSINGTON INDUSTRIAL ESTATE
Fennel Pit Farm
St. John's C of E Prim. Sch.

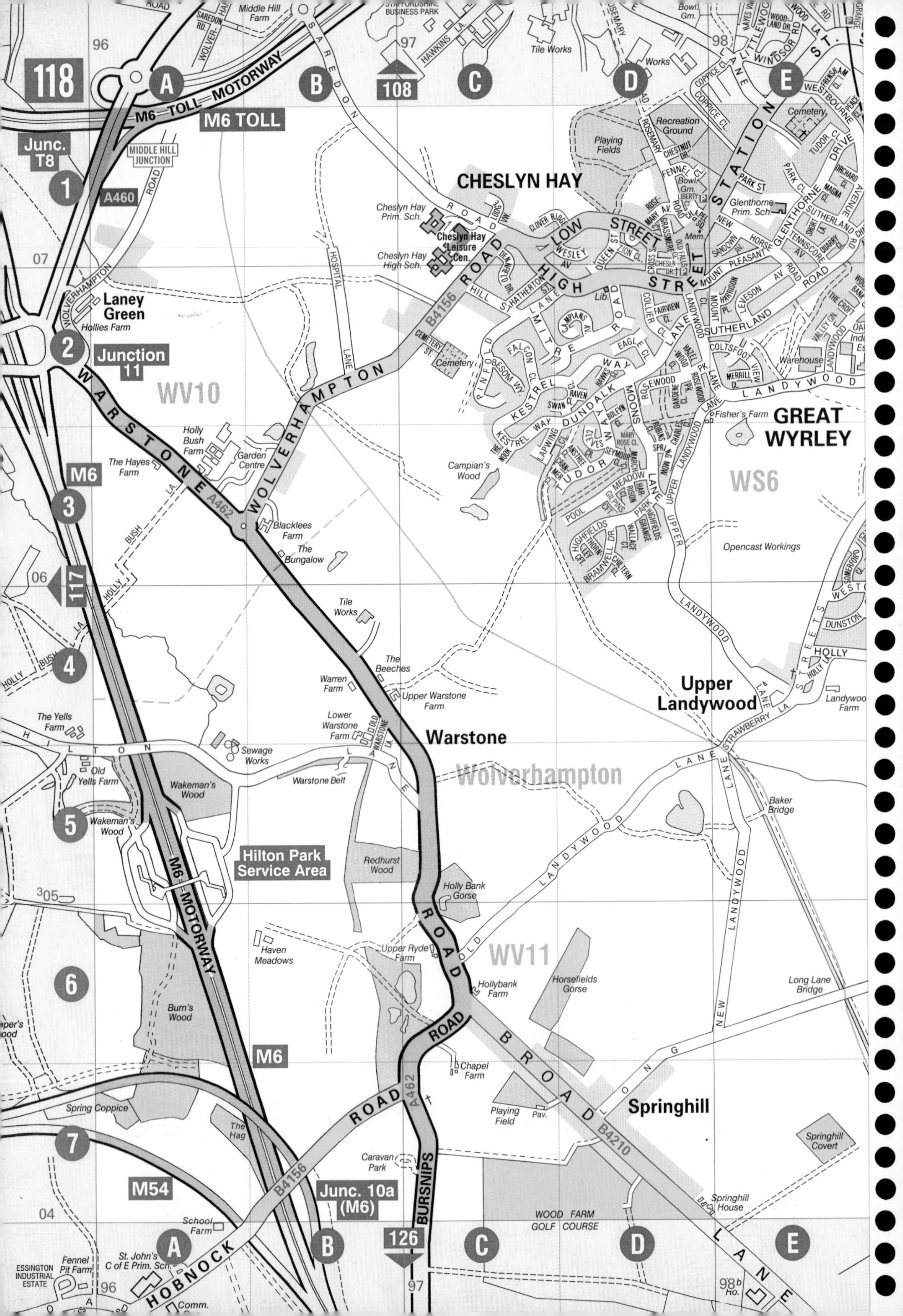

118
Junc. T8
Junction 11
Junc. 10a (M6)
108
117
126
M6 TOLL
M6 TOLL MOTORWAY
MIDDLE HILL JUNCTION
Middle Hill Farm
A460
M6
M6 MOTORWAY
M54
A462
B4156
B4210
CHESLYN HAY
GREAT WYRLEY
Laney Green
Hollies Farm
WV10
WV11
WS6
Wolverhampton
Warstone
Upper Landywood
Springhill
Cheslyn Hay Prim. Sch.
Cheslyn Hay Leisure Cen.
Cheslyn Hay High Sch.
Cemetery
Recreation Ground
Playing Fields
Glenthorne Prim. Sch.
Tile Works
Works
Holly Bush Farm
Garden Centre
The Hayes Farm
Blacklees Farm
The Bungalow
Campian's Wood
Opencast Workings
Fisher's Farm
Warehouse
The Beeches
Warren Farm
Upper Warstone Farm
Lower Warstone Farm
Sewage Works
Warstone Belt
The Yells Farm
Old Yells Farm
Wakeman's Wood
Hilton Park Service Area
Redhurst Wood
Holly Bank Gorse
Haven Meadows
Upper Ryde Farm
Hollybank Farm
Horsefields Gorse
Burn's Wood
Chapel Farm
Playing Field
Pav.
Spring Coppice
The Hag
Caravan Park
School Farm
St. John's C of E Prim. Sch.
Fennel Pit Farm
ESSINGTON INDUSTRIAL ESTATE
WOOD FARM GOLF COURSE
Springhill House
Springhill Covert
Landywood Farm
Baker Bridge
Long Lane Bridge
WOLVERHAMPTON ROAD
WARSTONE ROAD
HIGH STREET
LOW STREET
STATION STREET
LANDYWOOD LANE
UPPER LANDYWOOD LANE
NEW LANDYWOOD LANE
STRAWBERRY LANE
BROAD LANE
BURSNIPS ROAD
HOBNOCK ROAD
HILTON LANE
LONG LANE
OLD ROAD
HOLLY BUSH LANE
SAREDON ROAD
HOSPITAL LANE
MITRE ROAD
KESTREL WAY
DUNDALK LANE
TUDOR WAY
MOONS LANE
MOUNT PLEASANT
SUTHERLAND ROAD
GLENTHORNE DRIVE
ROSEMARY ROAD
96
97
98
07
06
05
04
A
B
C
D
E
1
2
3
4
5
6
7

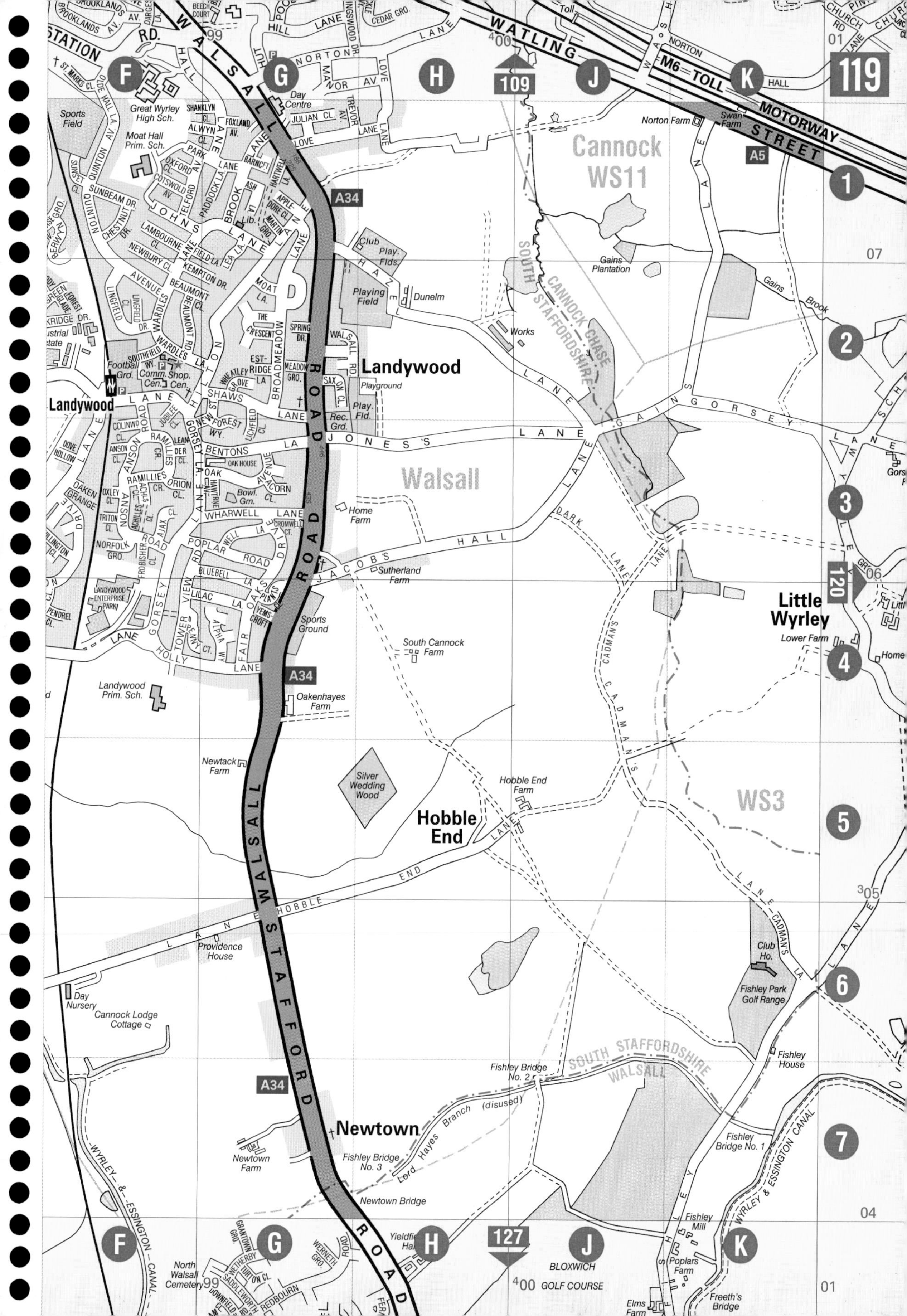
Cannock
WS11
Landywood
Walsall
Little Wyrley
Hobble End
WS3
Newtown
WALSALL ROAD
STAFFORD ROAD
WATLING STREET
M6 TOLL MOTORWAY
A34
A5
Great Wyrley High Sch.
Moat Hall Prim. Sch.
Landywood Prim. Sch.
Sports Field
Playing Field
Sports Ground
Gains Plantation
Norton Farm
Swan Farm
Home Farm
Sutherland Farm
South Cannock Farm
Oakenhayes Farm
Newtack Farm
Silver Wedding Wood
Hobble End Farm
Lower Farm
Providence House
Cannock Lodge Cottage
Day Nursery
Fishley Park Golf Range
Fishley House
Fishley Bridge No. 1
Fishley Bridge No. 2
Fishley Bridge No. 3
Newtown Bridge
Newtown Farm
Fishley Mill
Poplars Farm
Elms Farm
Freeth's Bridge
North Walsall Cemetery
BLOXWICH GOLF COURSE
WYRLEY & ESSINGTON CANAL
Lord Hayes Branch (disused)
SOUTH STAFFORDSHIRE
CANNOCK CHASE
JONES'S LANE
GAINS LANE
GORSEY LANE
JACOBS HALL LANE
DARK LANE
CADMAN'S LANE
HOBBLE END LANE
HOLLY LANE
WHARWELL LANE
SHAWS LANE
NORTON LANE
LOVE LANE
STATION RD.
109
127
120

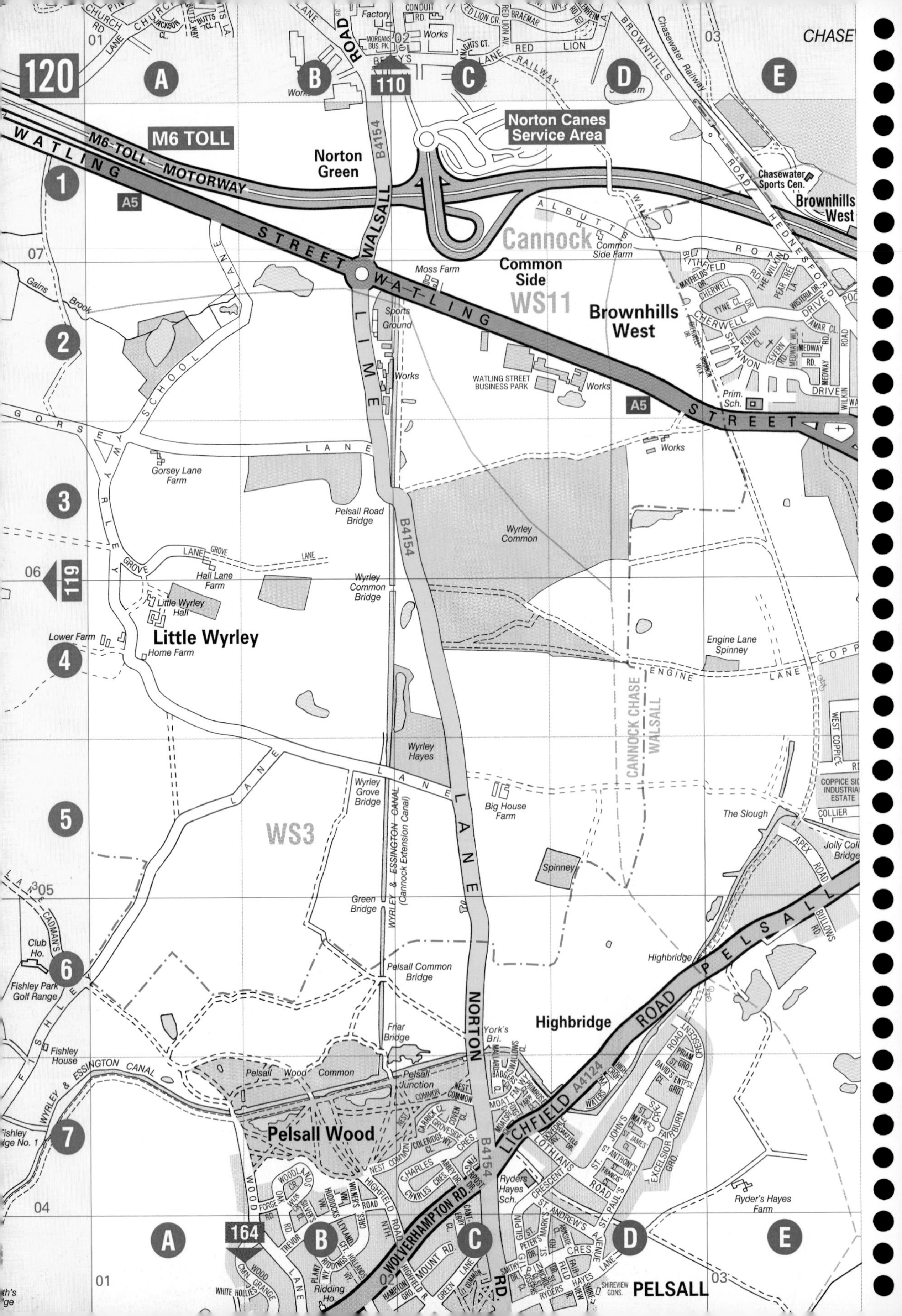
M6 TOLL
M6 TOLL MOTORWAY
WATLING STREET
A5
Norton Green
Norton Canes Service Area
110
Cannock
Common Side
WS11
Brownhills West
Chasewater Sports Cen.
Brownhills West
Moss Farm
Sports Ground
Works
WATLING STREET BUSINESS PARK
Gorsey Lane Farm
Pelsall Road Bridge
Wyrley Common
Hall Lane Farm
Wyrley Common Bridge
Little Wyrley Hall
Little Wyrley
Lower Farm
Home Farm
Engine Lane Spinney
CANNOCK CHASE
WALSALL
Wyrley Hayes
Wyrley Grove Bridge
Big House Farm
WS3
The Slough
COPPICE SIDE INDUSTRIAL ESTATE
Jolly Collier Bridge
Spinney
Green Bridge
WYRLEY & ESSINGTON CANAL (Cannock Extension Canal)
Highbridge
Club Ho.
Fishley Park Golf Range
Pelsall Common Bridge
Fishley House
Friar Bridge
York's Bri.
Highbridge
Pelsall Wood Common
Pelsall Junction
Pelsall Wood
LICHFIELD ROAD A4124
PELSALL ROAD
NORTON LANE
B4154
LIME LANE
WALSALL ROAD
Ryders Hayes Sch.
Ryder's Hayes Farm
164
Ridding Ho.
PELSALL
119
A B C D E
1 2 3 4 5 6 7

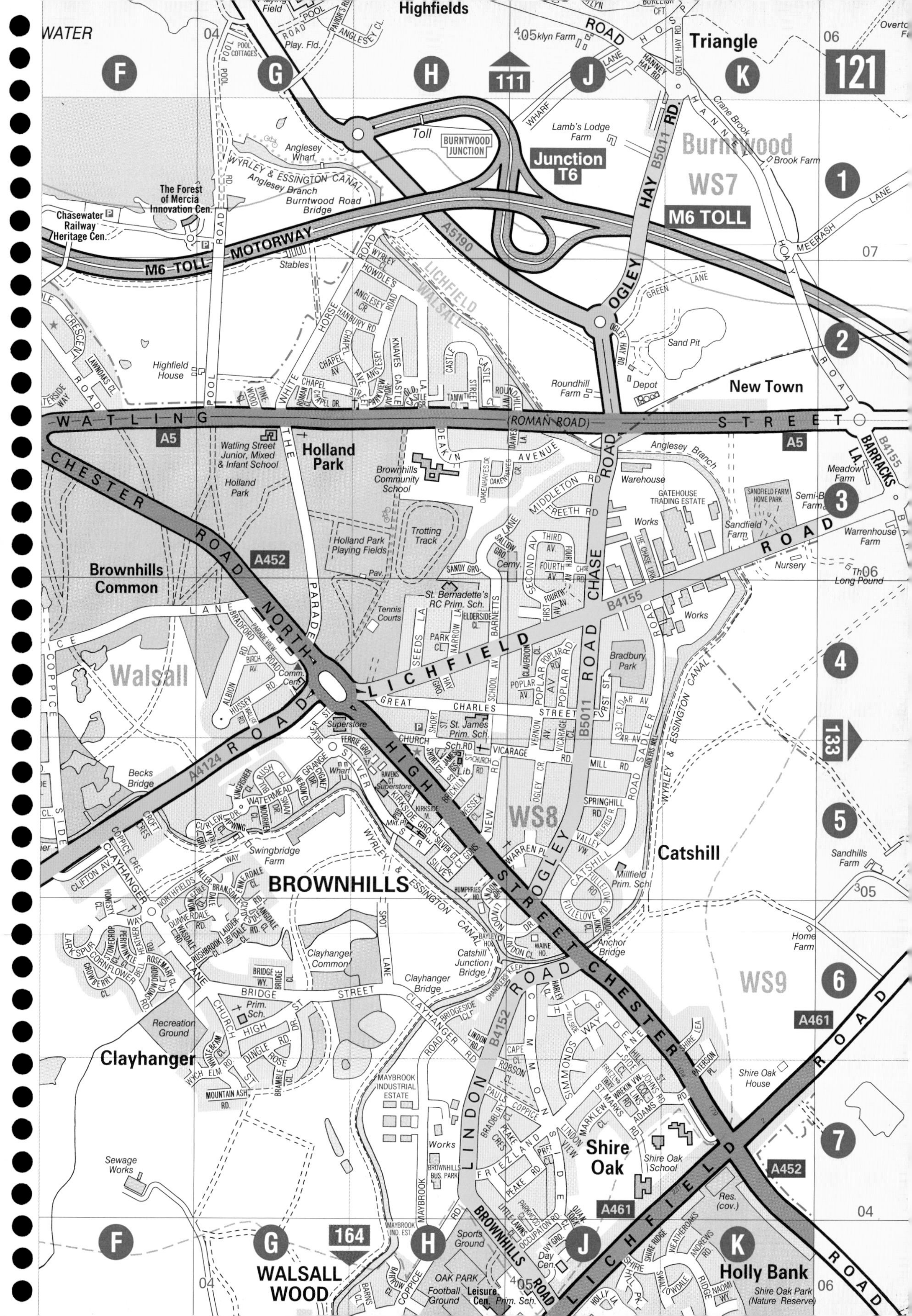
Highfields
Triangle
Burntwood
WS7
Junction T6
BURNTWOOD JUNCTION
Toll
M6 TOLL
M6 TOLL MOTORWAY
WYRLEY & ESSINGTON CANAL Anglesey Branch
Burntwood Road Bridge
Anglesey Wharf
The Forest of Mercia Innovation Cen.
Chasewater Railway Heritage Cen.
Lamb's Lodge Farm
Brook Farm
Sand Pit
New Town
Roundhill Farm
Depot
Highfield House
WATLING STREET (ROMAN ROAD)
A5
Holland Park
Brownhills Community School
Watling Street Junior, Mixed & Infant School
Holland Park Playing Fields
Trotting Track
Brownhills Common
Walsall
St. Bernadette's RC Prim. Sch.
Tennis Courts
Gatehouse Trading Estate
Sandfield Farm
Meadow Farm
Warrenhouse Farm
Long Pound
Nursery
Works
Bradbury Park
CHESTER ROAD NORTH
A452
LICHFIELD ROAD
B4155
CHASE ROAD
B5011
Superstore
St. James Prim. Sch.
Lib.
Wharf
Becks Bridge
WS8
Catshill
Millfield Prim. Sch.
BROWNHILLS
Swingbridge Farm
Clayhanger Common
Clayhanger Bridge
Catshill Junction Bridge
Anchor Bridge
Sandhills Farm
Home Farm
WS9
A461
Recreation Ground
Clayhanger
Maybrook Industrial Estate
Brownhills Bus. Park
Shire Oak
Shire Oak School
Shire Oak House
Sewage Works
Sports Ground
Oak Park Football Ground
Leisure Cen.
Prim. Sch.
Day Cen.
Walsall Wood
Holly Bank
Shire Oak Park (Nature Reserve)
Res. (cov.)
BROWNHILLS ROAD
LICHFIELD ROAD
A452
F G H J K
1 2 3 4 5 6 7

111
133
164

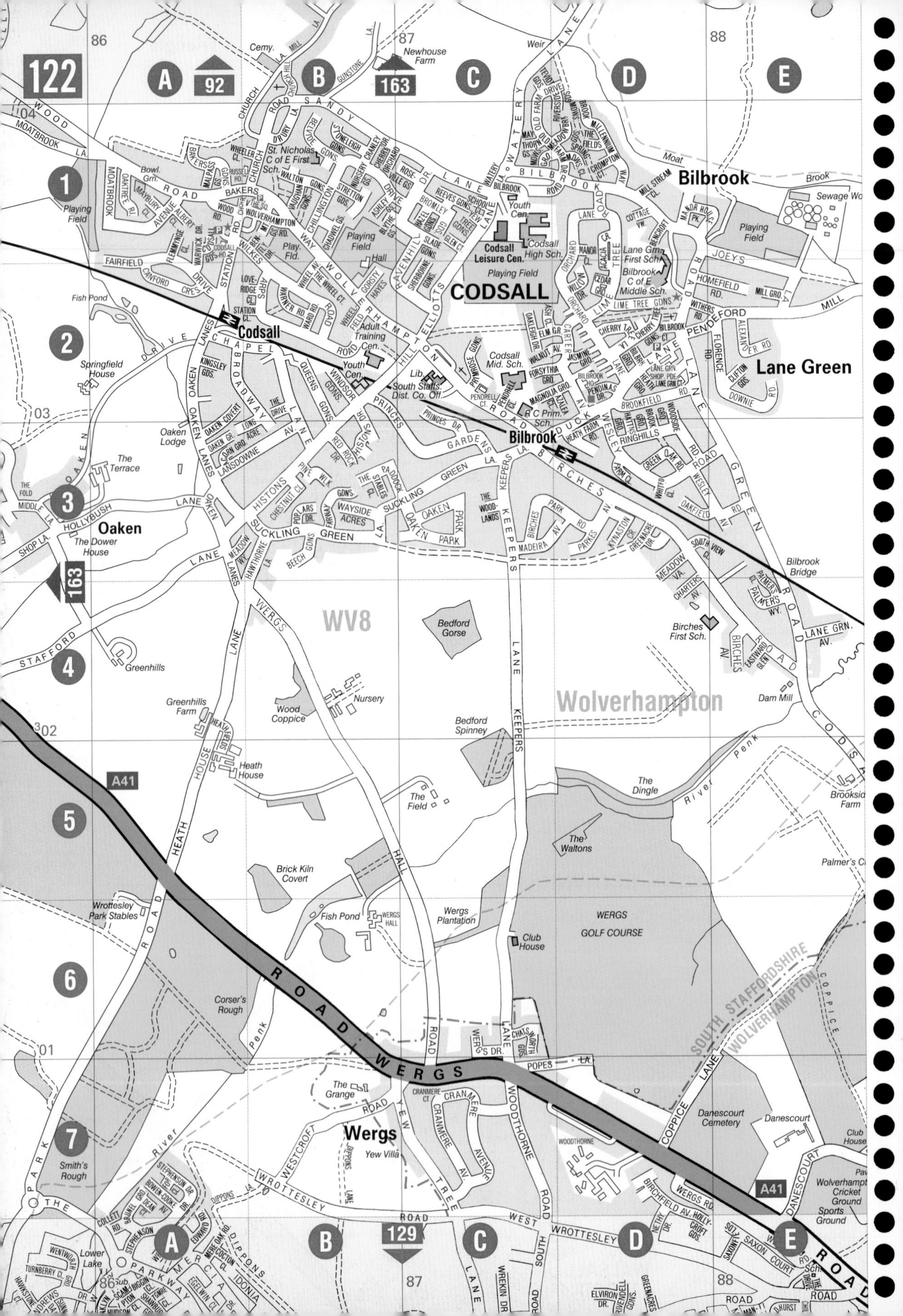
92
163
129
A
B
C
D
E
1
2
3
4
5
6
7
86
87
88
04
03
02
01
CODSALL
Bilbrook
Lane Green
Oaken
Wergs
WV8
Wolverhampton
Codsall
Bilbrook
Codsall Leisure Cen.
Codsall High Sch.
Playing Field
Codsall Mid. Sch.
St. Nicholas C of E First Sch.
Lane Grn. First Sch.
Bilbrook C of E Middle Sch.
Birches First Sch.
R C Prim. Sch.
Adult Training Cen.
Youth Cen.
Lib.
South Staffs. Dist. Co. Off.
Hall
Play. Fld.
Bowl. Grn.
Cemy.
Newhouse Farm
Weir
Sewage Wo
Fish Pond
Springfield House
Oaken Lodge
The Terrace
The Dower House
Greenhills
Greenhills Farm
Heath House
Wood Coppice
Nursery
Bedford Gorse
Bedford Spinney
The Field
Brick Kiln Covert
Fish Pond
Wergs Hall
Wergs Plantation
Club House
WERGS GOLF COURSE
The Waltons
The Dingle
River Penk
Dam Mill
Bilbrook Bridge
Brooksid Farm
Palmer's C
Wrottesley Park Stables
Corser's Rough
Smith's Rough
The Grange
Yew Villa
Lower Lake
Danescourt Cemetery
Danescourt
Club House
Wolverhampt Cricket Ground
Sports Ground
SOUTH STAFFORDSHIRE
WOLVERHAMPTON
A41
WERGS ROAD
WOOD LA.
MOATBROOK LA.
BAKERS WAY
WOLVERHAMPTON ROAD
SANDY LANE
CHURCH ROAD
BILBROOK ROAD
WATERY LANE
HILTON ROAD
ELLIOTTS LA.
CHAPEL LANE
OAKEN LANES
OAKEN DRIVE
OAKEN LANE
SUCKLING GREEN LANE
KEEPERS LANE
BIRCHES ROAD
DUCK LA.
PENDEFORD MILL LA.
LANE GREEN ROAD
CODSALL ROAD
WERGS HALL ROAD
HEATH HOUSE LANE
STAFFORD ROAD
HOLLYBUSH LANE
PARK ROAD
THE PARKWAY
WROTTESLEY ROAD
WEST WROTTESLEY ROAD
YEW TREE LANE
WOODTHORNE ROAD
COPPICE LANE
DANESCOURT
POPES LA.
WERGS DR.
SOUTH LANE
WREKIN DR.
COPPICE

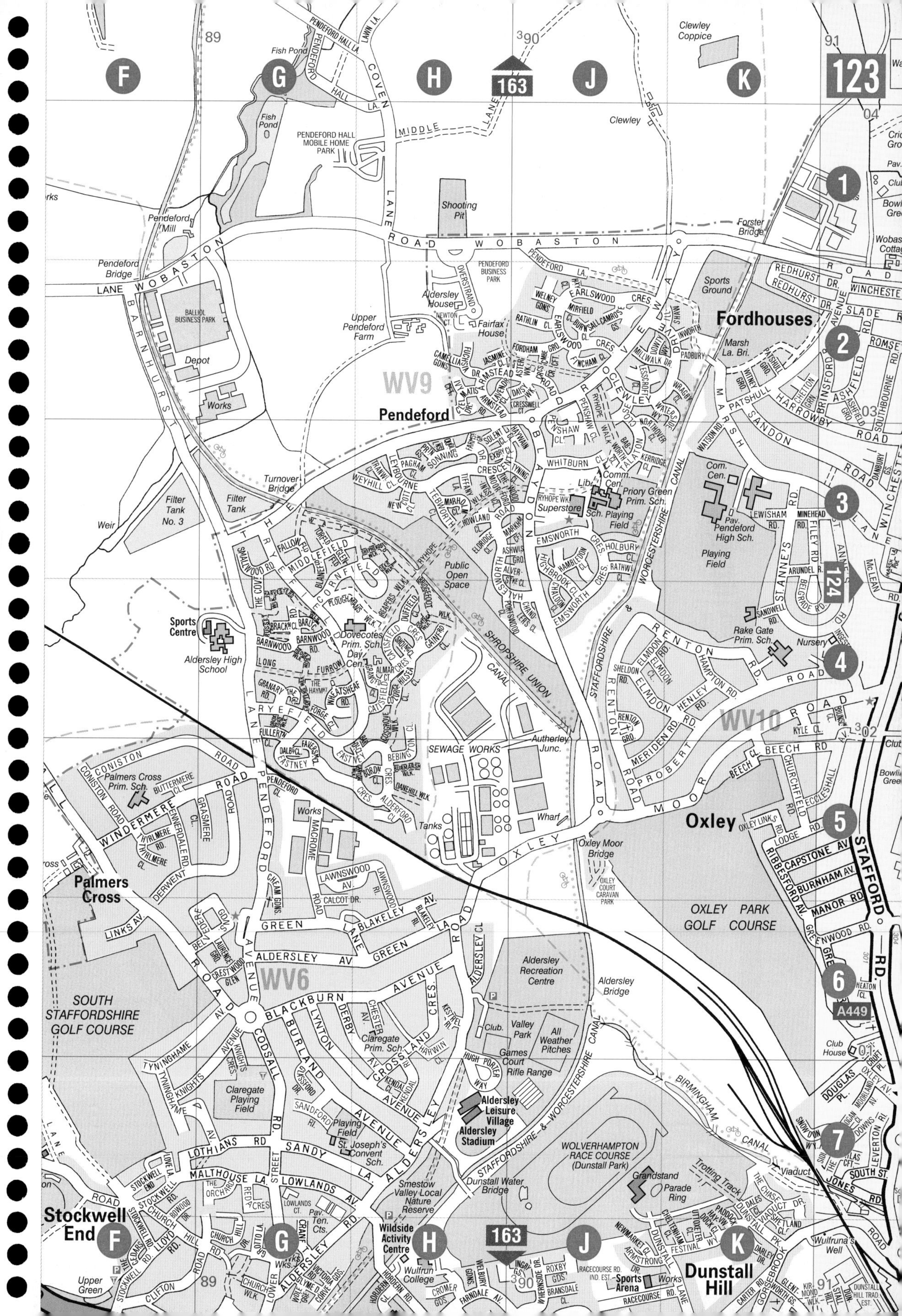
123
163
124
F
G
H
J
K
1
2
3
4
5
6
7
89
390
91
04
03
02
01
Fish Pond
Pendeford Hall La.
Lawn La.
Coven Lane
Pendeford Hall Mobile Home Park
Middle Lane
Clewley Coppice
Clewley
Shooting Pit
Pendeford Mill
Wobaston Road
Forster Bridge
Pendeford Bridge
Lane Wobaston
Balliol Business Park
Depot
Works
Barnhurst Lane
Pendeford Business Park
Aldersley House
Upper Pendeford Farm
Fairfax House
Sports Ground
Fordhouses
Marsh La. Bri.
Redhurst Dr.
Winchester Rd.
Slade Rd.
Romsey
Patshull Av.
Harrowby Rd.
Southbourne
Sandon Road
WV9
Pendeford
Earlswood Cres.
Blaydon Road
Cleveley Rd.
Whitburn Cl.
Com. Cen.
Pendeford High Sch.
Playing Field
Lewisham Rd.
Minehead Rd.
St. Anne's Rd.
Arundel Rd.
Belgrade Rd.
Rake Gate Prim. Sch.
Nursery
Turnover Bridge
Filter Tank No. 3
Filter Tank
Weir
Lib.
Comm. Cen.
Priory Green Prim. Sch.
Superstore
Sch. Playing Field
Public Open Space
Shropshire Union Canal
Staffordshire & Worcestershire Canal
Sports Centre
Aldersley High School
The Ryefield
Cornfield
Dovecotes Prim. Sch.
Day Cen.
Sewage Works
Autherley Junc.
Tanks
Wharf
Renton Road
Hampton Rd.
Henley Rd.
WV10
Probert Rd.
Beech Rd.
Kyle Cl.
Churchfield
Eccleshall
Moor
Oxley
Oxley Links
Lodge
Capstone Av.
Burnham Av.
Manor Rd.
Ribbesford Av.
Stafford Rd.
Oxley Moor Bridge
Oxley Court Caravan Park
Oxley Park Golf Course
Coniston Road
Palmers Cross Prim. Sch.
Windermere Road
Pendeford Avenue
Works
Macrome Road
Lawnswood Av.
Calcot Dr.
Blakeley Av.
Green Lane
Palmers Cross
Links Av.
Aldersley Av.
Aldersley Road
Aldersley Recreation Centre
Aldersley Bridge
WV6
Blackburn Avenue
South Staffordshire Golf Course
Codsall Rd.
Claregate Prim. Sch.
Crossland Cres.
Club.
Valley Park
Games Court
All Weather Pitches
Rifle Range
Hugh Porter Way
Aldersley Leisure Village
Aldersley Stadium
Claregate Playing Field
Playing Field
St. Joseph's Convent Sch.
Sandy Lane
Lothians Rd.
Malthouse La.
Lowlands Av.
Stockwell Rd.
Birmingham Canal
Wolverhampton Race Course (Dunstall Park)
Grandstand
Parade Ring
Trotting Track
Viaduct
Dunstall Water Bridge
Smestow Valley Local Nature Reserve
Wildside Activity Centre
Wulfrun College
Stockwell End
Upper Green
Racecourse Rd. Ind. Est.
Sports Arena
Works
Dunstall Hill
Dunstall Lane
Wulfruna's Well
Club House
A449
Jones Rd.
South St.
Heaton Cl.
Douglas Pl.

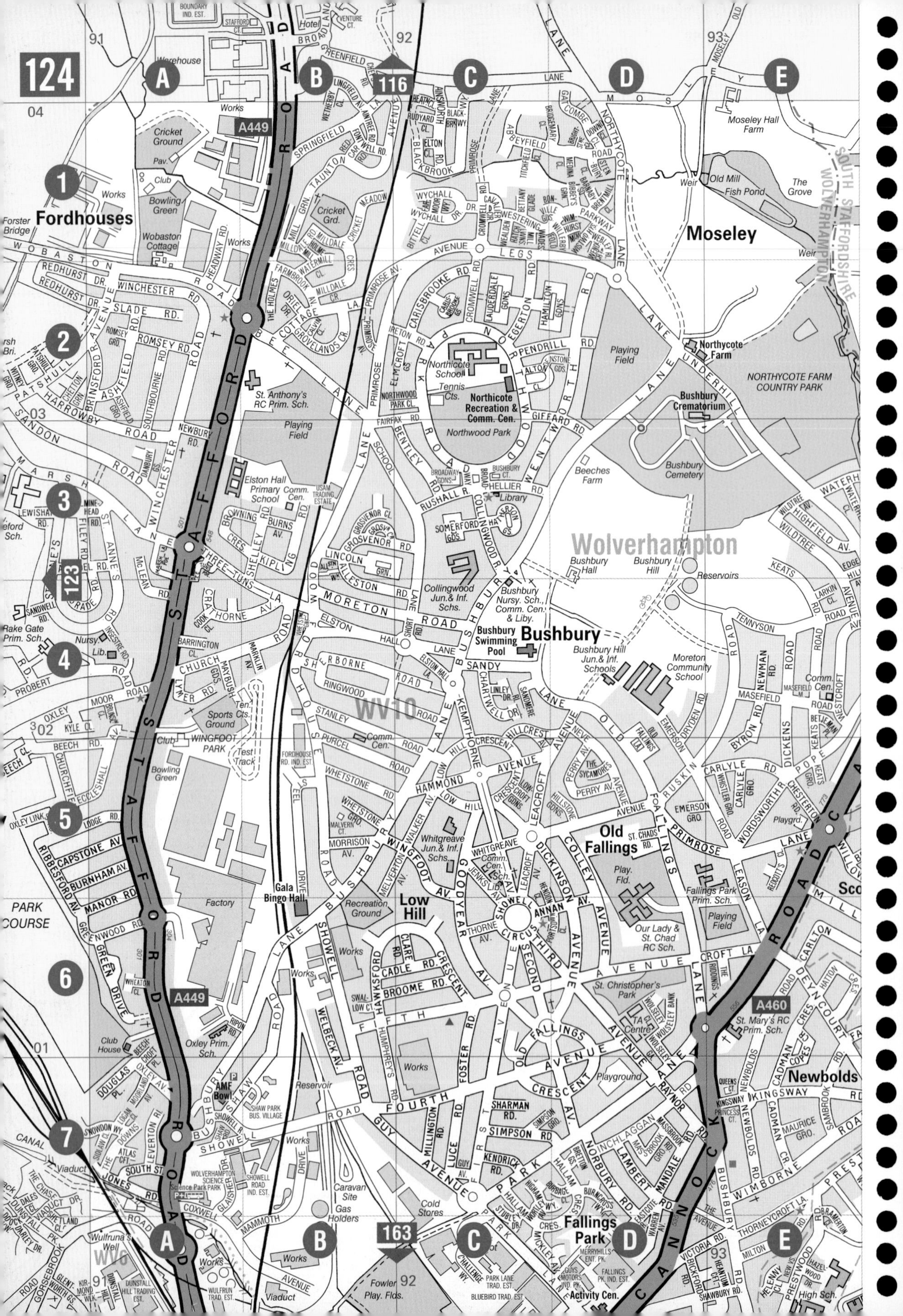

116
123
163
A B C D E
1 2 3 4 5 6 7
91 92 93
04 03 02 01
Fordhouses
Moseley
Wolverhampton
Bushbury
Old Fallings
Low Hill
Fallings Park
Newbolds
WV10
WV6
A449
A460
STAFFORD ROAD
MOSELEY LANE
NORTHYCOTE LANE
UNDERHILL LANE
WOBASTON ROAD
WINCHESTER RD.
REDHURST DR.
SLADE RD.
ROMSEY RD.
HARROWBY ROAD
SANDON ROAD
MARSH LANE
PRIMROSE LANE
LEGS AVENUE
CARISBROOKE RD.
CROMWELL RD.
EGERTON RD.
PENDRILL RD.
GIFFARD RD.
WENTWORTH RD.
COLLINGWOOD RD.
BUSHBURY LANE
MORETON ROAD
ELSTON HALL LANE
SANDY LANE
OLD FALLINGS LANE
THREE TUNS LA.
CHURCH ROAD
MOOR ROAD
PROBERT ROAD
FORDHOUSE ROAD
STANLEY ROAD
PURCEL ROAD
WHETSTONE ROAD
HAMMOND AVENUE
LOW HILL CRESCENT
KEMPTHORNE AVENUE
WINGFOOT AV.
GOODYEAR AV.
SHOWELL CIRCUS
FIFTH AVENUE
FOURTH AVENUE
GUY AVENUE
PARK LANE
CANNOCK ROAD
PRIMROSE LANE
RUSKIN ROAD
CARLYLE RD.
TENNYSON ROAD
MASEFIELD ROAD
KEATS ROAD
WILDTREE AV.
HIGHFIELD AV.
KINGSWAY
WIMBORNE RD.
THORNEYCROFT LA.
COXWELL AV.
MAMMOTH DR.
Moseley Hall Farm
Old Mill Fish Pond
The Grove
Weir
Northycote Farm
NORTHYCOTE FARM COUNTRY PARK
Bushbury Crematorium
Bushbury Cemetery
Beeches Farm
Playing Field
Northicote School
Northicote Recreation & Comm. Cen.
Northwood Park
Library
Collingwood Jun.& Inf. Schs.
Bushbury Nursy. Sch., Comm. Cen. & Liby.
Bushbury Swimming Pool
Bushbury Hall
Bushbury Hill
Reservoirs
Bushbury Hill Jun.& Inf. Schools
Moreton Community School
St. Anthony's RC Prim. Sch.
Elston Hall Primary School
USAM TRADING ESTATE
Cricket Ground
Bowling Green
Wobaston Cottage
Works
Sports Ground
WINGFOOT PARK
Test Track
Factory
Gala Bingo Hall
Recreation Ground
Whitgreave Jun.& Inf. Schs.
Our Lady & St. Chad RC Sch.
Fallings Park Prim. Sch.
St. Christopher's Park
TA Centre
St. Mary's RC Prim. Sch.
Playground
Oxley Prim. Sch.
AMF Bowl
SHAW PARK BUS. VILLAGE
Reservoir
Caravan Site
Gas Holders
Cold Stores
WOLVERHAMPTON SCIENCE PARK
SHOWELL ROAD IND. EST.
Wulfruna's Well
DUNSTALL HILL TRADING EST.
WULFRUN TRAD. EST.
Fowler Play. Flds.
PARK LANE TRAD. EST.
BLUEBIRD TRAD. EST.
MERRYHILLS ENT. PK.
FALLINGS PK. IND. EST.
Activity Cen.
High Sch.
Rake Gate Prim. Sch.
Canal
Viaduct
SOUTH STAFFORDSHIRE
WOLVERHAMPTON

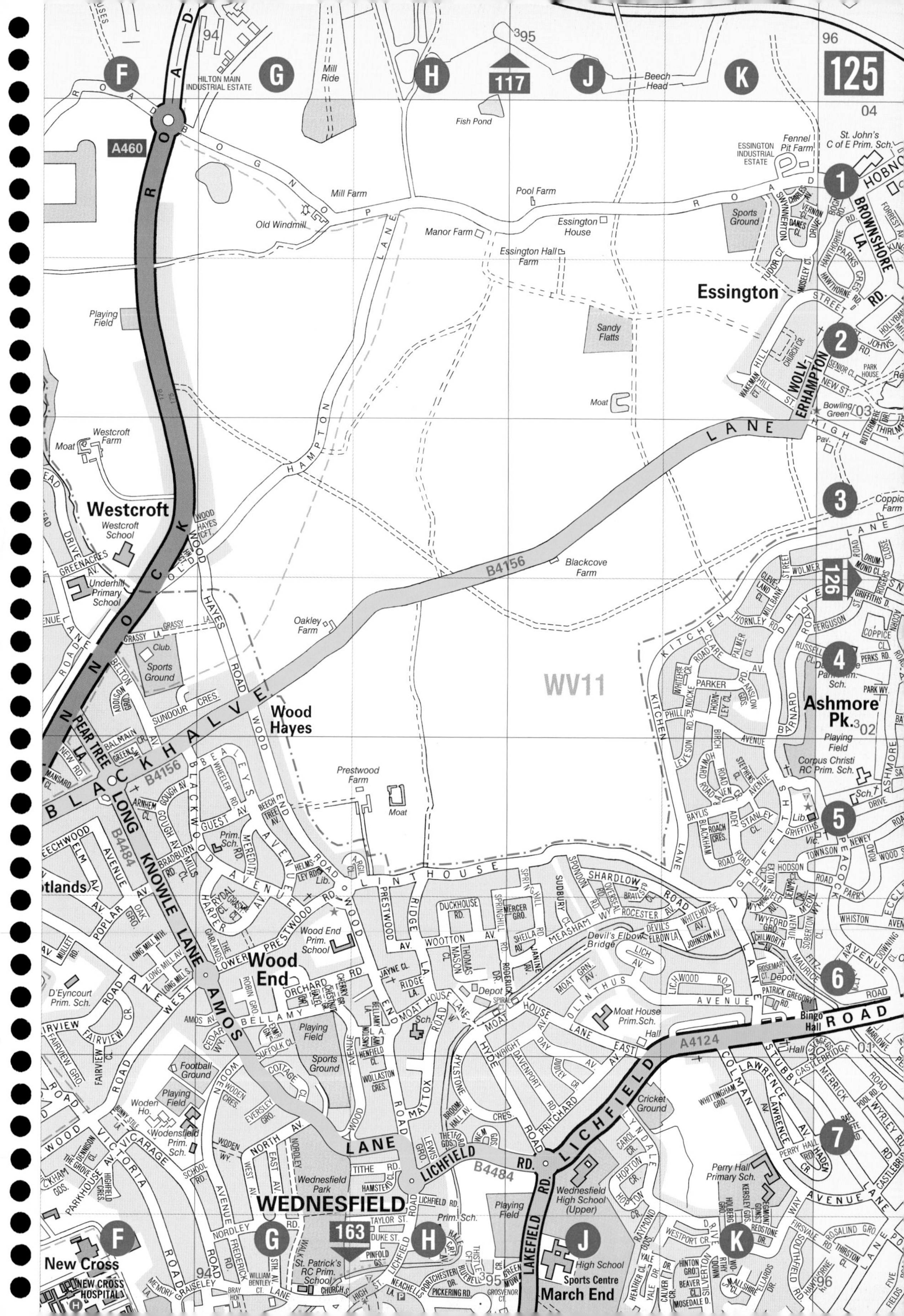
117
126
163
Essington
Westcroft
Wood Hayes
Ashmore Pk.
Wood End
WEDNESFIELD
New Cross
March End
WV11
A460
B4156
B4484
A4124
CANNOCK ROAD
BLACKHALVE LANE
LONG KNOWLE LANE
AMOS LANE
LICHFIELD RD.
LINTHOUSE LANE
KITCHEN LANE
HAMPTON LANE
HILTON MAIN INDUSTRIAL ESTATE
ESSINGTON INDUSTRIAL ESTATE
Mill Farm
Old Windmill
Pool Farm
Manor Farm
Essington House
Essington Hall Farm
Sandy Flatts
Fish Pond
Beech Head
Westcroft Farm
Westcroft School
Underhill Primary School
Oakley Farm
Blackcove Farm
Prestwood Farm
Wood End Prim. School
Moat House Prim.Sch.
Wednesfield High School (Upper)
Wednesfield Park
St. Patrick's RC Prim. School
Perry Hall Primary Sch.
Corpus Christi RC Prim. Sch.
D'Eyncourt Prim. Sch.
Wodensfield Prim. Sch.
NEW CROSS HOSPITAL
Cricket Ground
Sports Ground
Playing Field
Bingo Hall
Devil's Elbow Bridge

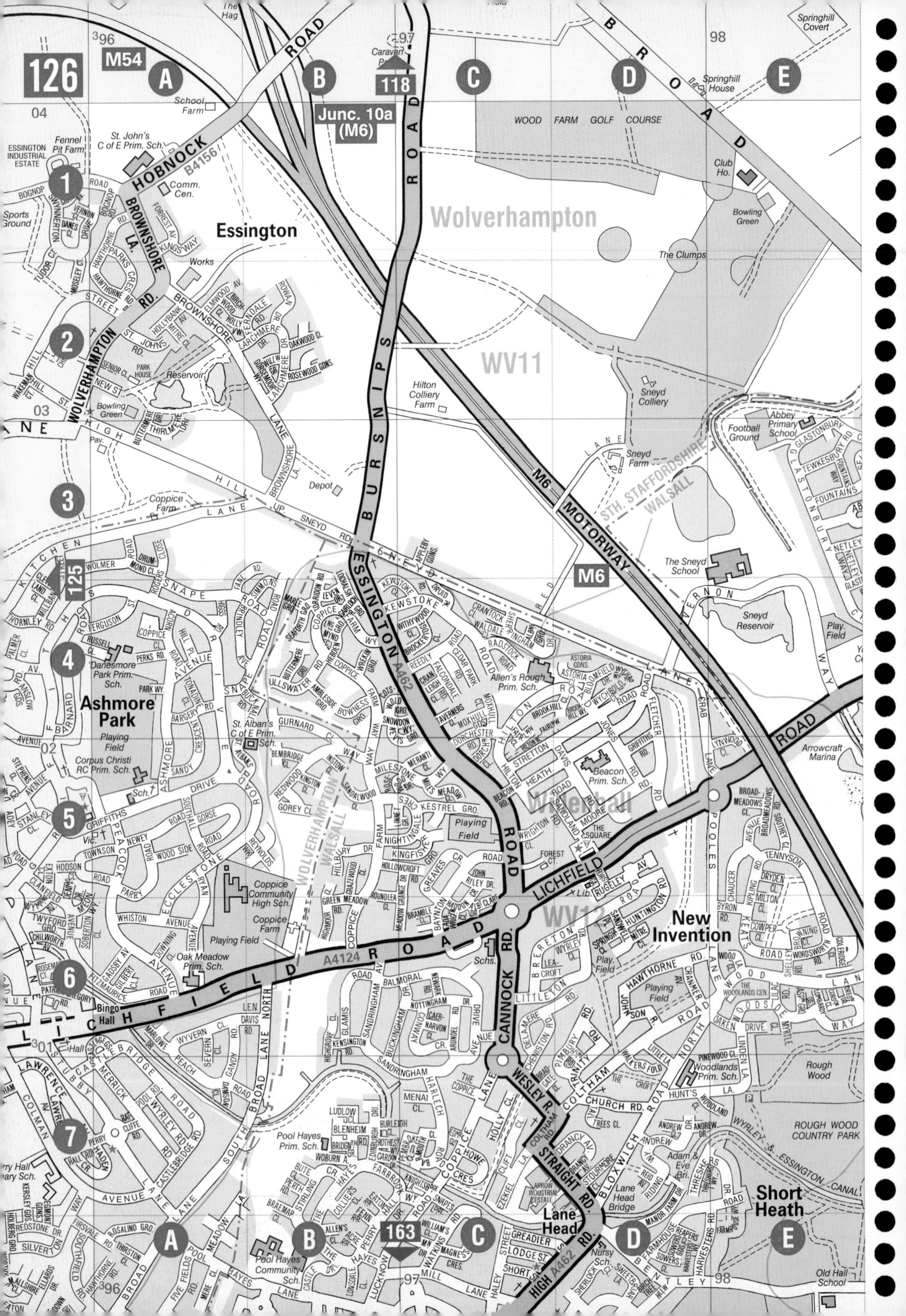
Essington
Wolverhampton
WV11
WV12
Ashmore Park
Wednesfield
New Invention
Short Heath
Lane Head
WOOD FARM GOLF COURSE
ROUGH WOOD COUNTRY PARK
Junc. 10a (M6)
M54
M6
MOTORWAY
BURSNIPS ROAD
ESSINGTON ROAD
LICHFIELD ROAD
CANNOCK RD.
HOBNOCK ROAD
BROAD ROAD
118
125
163

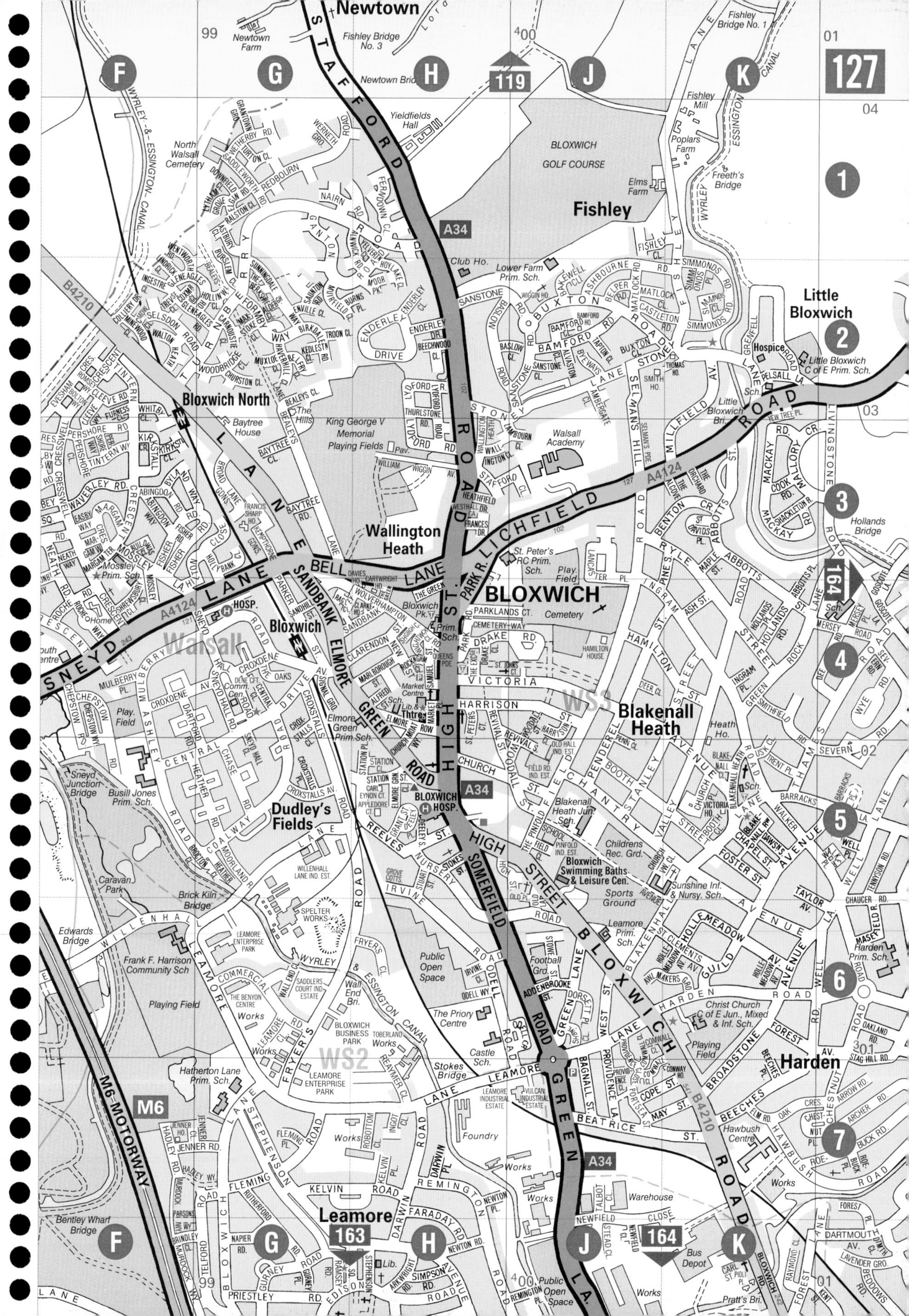
127
Newtown
Newtown Farm
Fishley Bridge No. 3
Newtown Bridge
Fishley Bridge No. 1
119
F
G
H
J
K
Yieldfields Hall
North Walsall Cemetery
WYRLEY & ESSINGTON CANAL
BLOXWICH GOLF COURSE
Fishley Mill
Poplars Farm
Elms Farm
Freeth's Bridge
Fishley
STAFFORD ROAD
A34
Club Ho.
Lower Farm Prim. Sch.
Little Bloxwich
Hospice
Little Bloxwich C of E Prim. Sch.
Little Bloxwich Bri.
B4210
Bloxwich North
Baytree House
The Hills
King George V Memorial Playing Fields
Walsall Academy
LICHFIELD ROAD
A4124
Wallington Heath
Mossley Prim. Sch.
St. Peter's RC Prim. Sch.
Play. Field
BLOXWICH
Cemetery
Hollands Bridge
164
SNEYD LANE
BELL LANE
HOSP.
Bloxwich
Walsall
Bloxwich Pk.
Prim. Sch.
Market Centre
Lib. & Thtre.
HIGH ST.
HAMILTON HOUSE
WS3
Blakenall Heath
Heath Ho.
Play. Field
Elmore Green Prim. Sch.
BLOXWICH HOSP.
Sneyd Junction Bridge
Busill Jones Prim. Sch.
Dudley's Fields
Blakenall Heath Jun. Sch.
Childrens Rec. Grd.
Bloxwich Swimming Baths & Leisure Cen.
Sports Ground
Sunshine Inf. & Nursy. Sch.
Caravan Park
Brick Kiln Bridge
WILLENHALL LANE IND. EST.
SPELTER WORKS
LEAMORE ENTERPRISE PARK
Public Open Space
Leamore Prim. Sch.
Football Grd.
Harden Prim. Sch.
Edwards Bridge
Frank F. Harrison Community Sch
Playing Field
SADDLERS COURT IND. ESTATE
Wall End Bri.
The Priory Centre
Christ Church C of E Jun., Mixed & Inf. Sch.
Playing Field
BLOXWICH BUSINESS PARK
WS2
Castle Sch.
Hatherton Lane Prim. Sch.
M6
M6 MOTORWAY
Stokes Bridge
LEAMORE INDUSTRIAL ESTATE
VULCAN INDUSTRIAL ESTATE
Harden
Hawbush Centre
Foundry
Works
Warehouse
Bentley Wharf Bridge
Leamore
163
Lib.
Bus Depot
Public Open Space
Pratt's Bri.
1
2
3
4
5
6
7
99
400
01
04
03
02
301

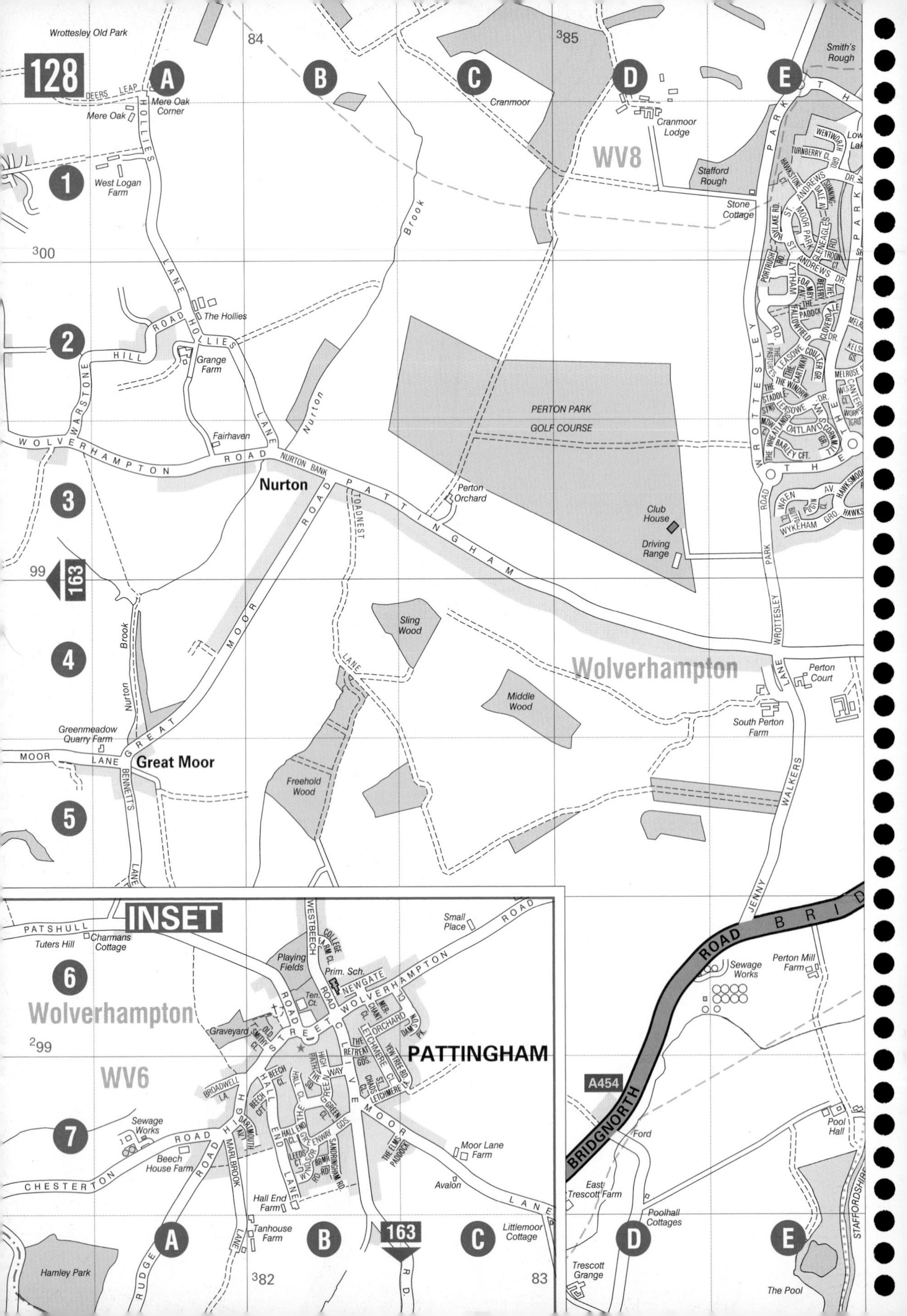

A   **B**   **C**   **D**   **E**

1

2

3

4

5

6

7

Wrottesley Old Park

84   ³85

Smith's Rough

DEERS LEAP LA

Mere Oak Corner

Mere Oak

Cranmoor

Cranmoor Lodge

Stafford Rough

WV8

Stone Cottage

West Logan Farm

300

The Hollies

Grange Farm

Fairhaven

WOLVERHAMPTON ROAD

WARSTONE HILL

HOLLIES LANE

Nurton

Nurton

NURTON BANK

Nurton

ROAD

PATTINGHAM

TOADNEST

Perton Orchard

PERTON PARK
GOLF COURSE

Club House

Driving Range

WROTTESLEY ROAD

THE PARK

WENTWORTH

TURNBERRY CL

ST. ANDREWS

MOOR PARK

THE PADDOCK

THE WINDROW

THE LEASOWE

COTLER RD

CARTWAY

THE STADDLE

OATLANDS

THE WHEATLANDS

BARLEY CFT

WYKEHAM GRO

WREN AV

HAWKSMOOR

HAWKS

WROTTESLEY

99 ◄ **163**

Brook

Nurton

GREAT MOOR LANE

Sling Wood

Wolverhampton

Perton Court

Greenmeadow Quarry Farm

MOOR LANE

Great Moor

Middle Wood

South Perton Farm

BENNETTS LANE

Freehold Wood

WALKERS LANE

JENNY LANE

INSET

PATSHULL

Tuters Hill

Charmans Cottage

COLLEGE LANE CL

WESTBEECH

Playing Fields

Prim. Sch.

Small Place

ROAD

Sewage Works

Perton Mill Farm

BRIDGNORTH ROAD

Wolverhampton

²99

WV6

Graveyard

BROADWELL LA

NEWGATE

WOLVERHAMPTON

Ten. Ct.

ORCHARD

THE RETREAT

DAM PL

LETCHMERE

YEW TREE RD

STREET

HIGH

SWIFT CL

BEECH CFT

HALL CL

PATTS

CL

GREEN

KENWAY

HALL END

LEEDS CL

SANDINGHAM RD

BIRMINGHAM RD

PATTINGHAM

CHAUS

LETCHMERE

CLIVE

MOOR LANE

A454

BRIDGNORTH

Ford

East Trescott Farm

Pool Hall

STAFFORDSHIRE

Sewage Works

Beech House Farm

ROAD

MARLBROOK

CHESTERTON ROAD

DARMOUTH

BEECH CFT

HALL END LANE

THE ELMS PADDOCK

Moor Lane Farm

Avalon

Poolhall Cottages

Hall End Farm

Tanhouse Farm

RUDGE LANE

A   **B**   **163**   **C**   **D**   **E**

Hamley Park

³382   83

Littlemoor Cottage

Trescott Grange

The Pool

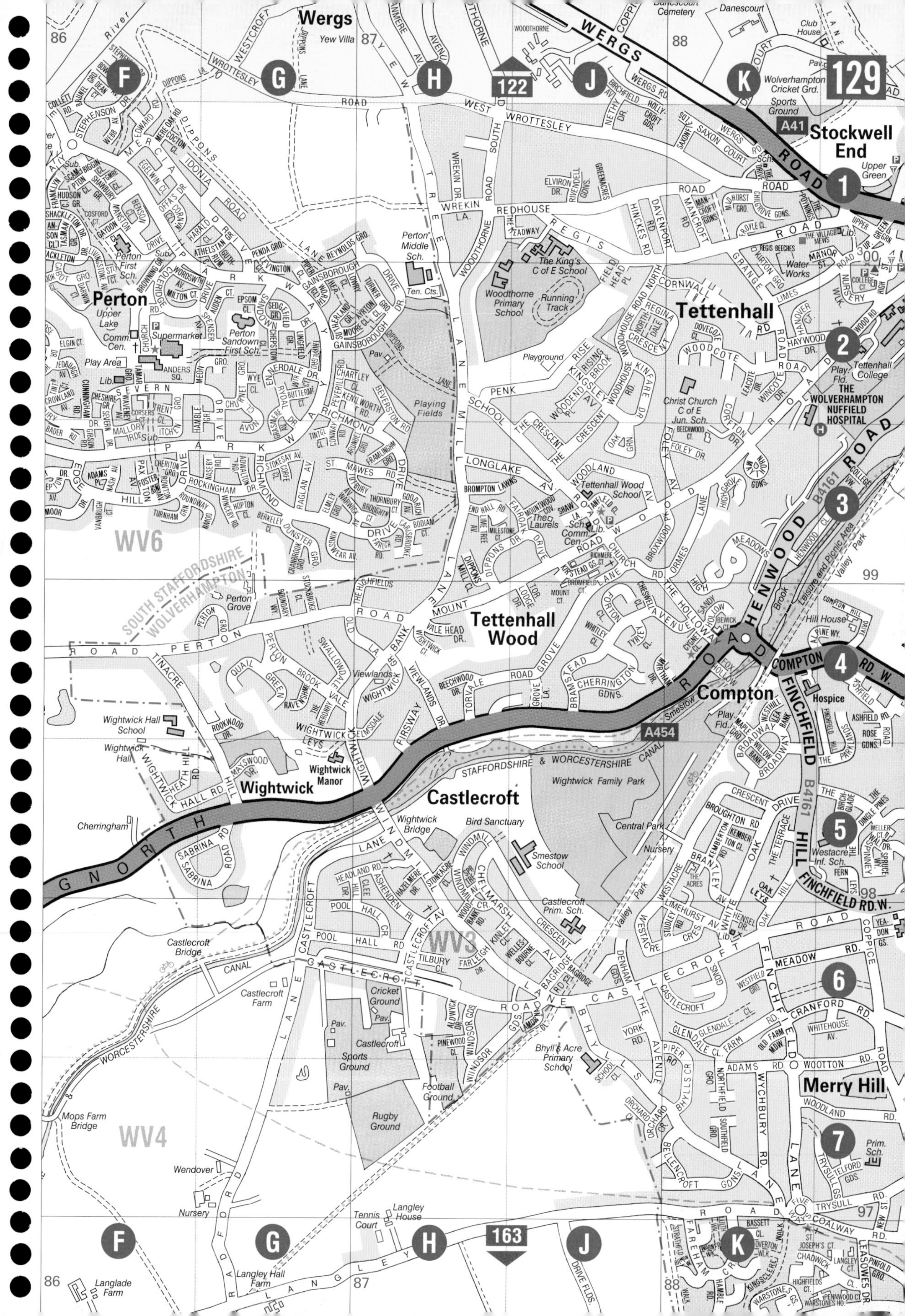
129
122
163
Wergs
Stockwell End
Perton
Tettenhall
Tettenhall Wood
Compton
Wightwick
Castlecroft
Merry Hill
WV6
WV3
WV4
SOUTH STAFFORDSHIRE
WOLVERHAMPTON
A41
A454
B4161
WERGS ROAD
WEST WROTTESLEY ROAD
WROTTESLEY ROAD
REGIS ROAD
PERTON ROAD
MOUNT ROAD
WOODTHORNE ROAD
FINCHFIELD HILL
FINCHFIELD RD. W.
COMPTON RD. W.
HENWOOD ROAD
CASTLECROFT ROAD
CASTLECROFT LANE
WINDMILL LANE
LANGLEY ROAD
TRESCOTT ROAD
STAFFORDSHIRE & WORCESTERSHIRE CANAL
Yew Villa
Danescourt Cemetery
Danescourt
Club House
Wolverhampton Cricket Grd.
Sports Ground
Upper Green
Perton Middle Sch.
Woodthorne Primary School
The King's C of E School
Running Track
Perton First Sch.
Perton Sandown First Sch.
Supermarket
Upper Lake
Play Area
Playing Fields
Playground
Christ Church C of E Jun. Sch.
Tettenhall College
THE WOLVERHAMPTON NUFFIELD HOSPITAL
Water Works
Tettenhall Wood School
The Laurels
Perton Grove
Wightwick Hall School
Wightwick Hall
Wightwick Manor
Viewlands
Wightwick Bridge
Bird Sanctuary
Wightwick Family Park
Smestow School
Central Park
Castlecroft Prim. Sch.
Hospice
Westacre Inf. Sch.
Leisure and Picnic Area
Valley Park
Hill House
Cherringham
Castlecroft Bridge
Castlecroft Farm
Cricket Ground
Castlecroft Sports Ground
Football Ground
Rugby Ground
Bhyll's Acre Primary School
Mops Farm Bridge
Wendover
Nursery
Tennis Court
Langley House
Langley Hall Farm
Langlade Farm
Prim. Sch.
FIVE WAYS
86
87
88
97
98
99
00
F
G
H
J
K
1
2
3
4
5
6
7

Rugeley
Nethertown
The Nook
Brookhouse Farm
WS15
River Blithe
River Trent
160
E. Staffs. Lichfield
A515
Yoxall Road
Saddlesall
New Trent
Mill House
Weir
Bromley Hall
Rookery Plantation
Manor Pk. Sailing Club
Church Farm Mews
Church La.
Leofric Cl.
The Grange
The Croft
Myatt's Lane
New Buildings Farm
Eastfields Farm
Alrewas Road
A513
War Meml.
Lanes Cl.
Manor Rd.
Park
Bowl. Grn.
Fox Ct.
Beech Av.
Manor Wlk.
Lewis's La.
Bradbury La.
Broome Cl.
Kings Wlk.
Sch.
Ckt. Grd.
Pav.
Football Grd.
King's Bromley
Gilliards Croft
Vicarage La.
Vicarage Croft
Victoria Mdw.
Lant Cl.
Chamberlain Cl.
Cockshut Lane
Woodshoot
The Lant
Victory Farm
Little Spinney
Rugeley Road
99
Westfield Covert
White Oaks
The Belt
Lichfield Road
Echills
Tomlinson's Spinney
Shaw Lane
Far End
Shawlane Farm
Crawley Lane
Crawley Lodge
Burton upon Trent
DE13
The Old Farmhouse
Crawley Brook
Bourne Brook
Overley
Pyford Brook Cottage
Pyford Brook
River Trent
Weir
Trent & Mersey Canal
Willowbrook Farm (Camping & Caravan Site)
Stafford La.
Mill Stream
Mill End La.
Coton Cl.
Church Road
Essington House Farm
Alrewas
Park Road
Gaskell's Bridge
Post Office Rd.
The Moorings
Essington Cl.
Audley Cl.
William IV Rd.
Exchange Rd.
Dark Lane
Selwyn Cl.
Micklehome Dr.
Micklehome Drive
Salters Gn. Wy.
Park Rd.
Mays Wlk.
Butts Cl.
Manor Fields
Mill End
Main Street
Works
The Homestead
Sewage Works
Kings Bromley Rd.
Kent's Bridge
Bagnall Lock
Swallow Cl.
Heron Ct.
Walkfield
Furlong Lane
Deepmore Cl.
Lock Rd.
Chaseview
Churchill Cres.
All Saints' C of E Prim. Sch.
Furlong Cl.
Inge Dr.
Oakfield Road
Burway Mdw.
Poppy Gdns.
Cricket Ground
Pav.
Daisy La.
The Crofts
Noon Cft.
Anson Rd.
Wellfield Rd.
Station Yard
Croxall Road
Somerville Rd.
Wilkins Cft.
Mellor Dr.
Foxton Cl.
Turton Cl.
Fox Lane
Burton Road
National Memorial Arboretum
Visitor Centre
Underpass
Bagnall
Daisy Lane
Long Lane
Lichfield
WS13
Meadow Cott.
Blackheath
Cowhill Lane
Moo Moo Cottage
Hillside Cottage
Ryknild Street
(Roman Road)
A38
Ryknild House
Ridge Lane
Barley Grn. La.
Barley Green La.
107
160
The Moor
Bromwich Dr.
Holly Dr.
Shaw Cl.
Stafford
Willow Cl.
Farm Way
Finch
Dumore Hay La.
A
B
C
D
E
1
2
3
4
5
6
7
11
12
13
16
14
15
17
18

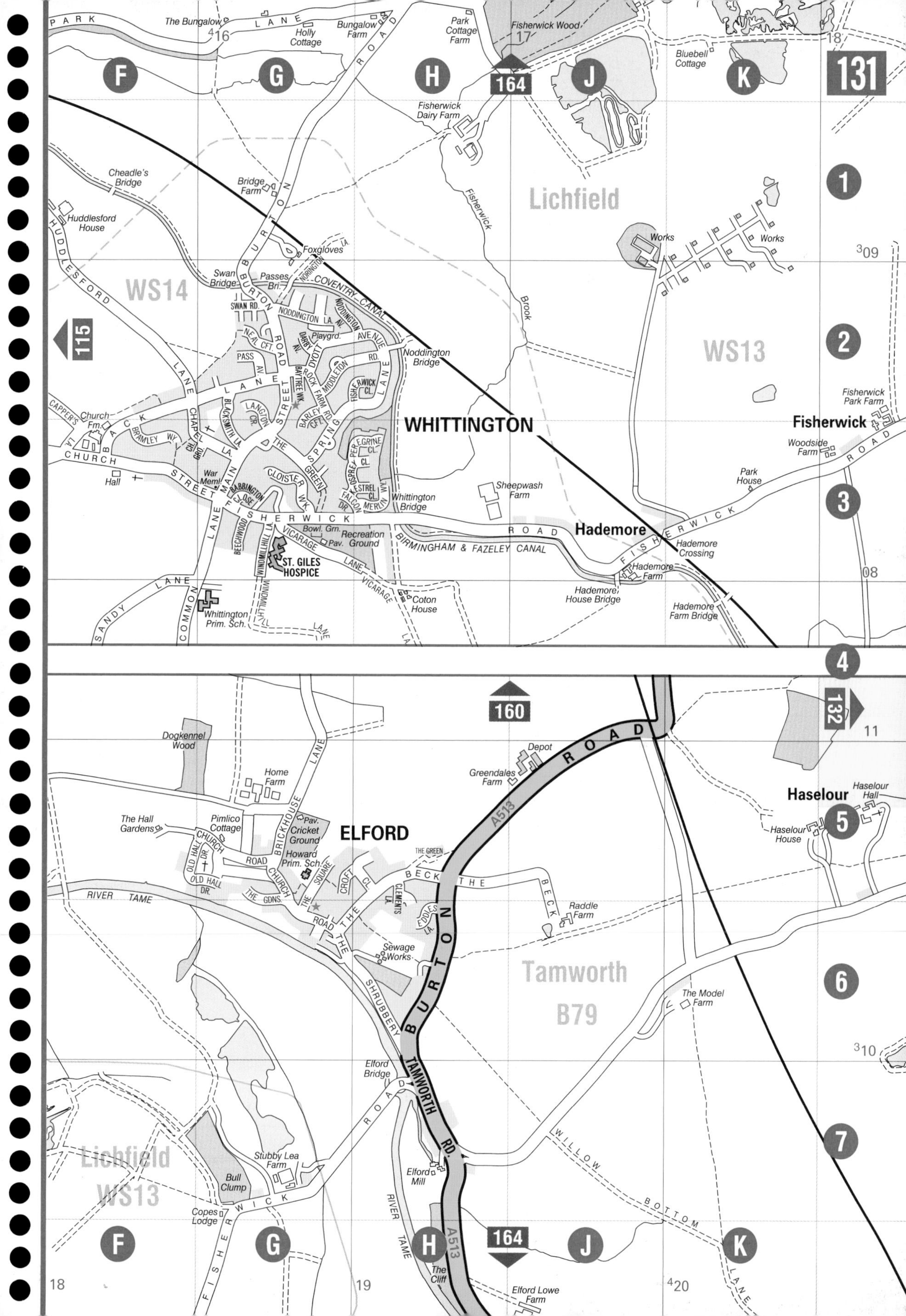

F G H J K

1

2

3

4

5

6

7

The Bungalow
416

The
Holly
Cottage

Bungalow
Farm

Park
Cottage
Farm

Fisherwick Wood

18

164

Bluebell
Cottage

Fisherwick
Dairy Farm

Cheadle's
Bridge

Bridge
Farm

Huddlesford
House

Foxgloves

309

Works

Works

Lichfield

WS14

115

Swan
Bridge

Passes
Bri.

SWAN RD.

NEAL CFT.
PASS AV.

CHAPEL LA.

Playgrd.

Noddington
Bridge

NODDINGTON LA. N.
NODDINGTON LA.

DARBY CFT.
DYOTT AV.
AVENUE

Noddington
Bridge

WS13

Fisherwick
Park Farm

Church
Fm.

Bramley
Way

LANGTON
CR.

BLACKSMITH LA.

MIDDLETON RD.

BARLEY CFT.
FISH FLD.

R.WICK
CL.

SPRING LA.

Fisherwick

Woodside
Farm

Park
House

CAPPER'S LA.
BACK LANE

CLOISTER WK.

THE GREEN

PERGRINE CL.
GOSPREY CL.

SP. CL.

STREL CL.
FALCON
MERLIN

War
Meml.
Hall

ABBINGTON
CLOSE

BEECHWOOD

FISHERWICK LANE MAIN

VICARAGE

Bowl. Grn.
Pav.

Recreation
Ground

Whittington
Bridge

WHITTINGTON

Sheepwash
Farm

Brook

ROAD

Hademore

FISHERWICK ROAD

Hademore
Crossing

08

ST. GILES
HOSPICE

COMMON LANE
SANDY LANE

WINDMILL HILL LA.
WHITTINWOOD

Whittington
Prim. Sch.

VICARAGE LANE

Coton
House

BIRMINGHAM & FAZELEY CANAL

Hademore
House Bridge

Hademore
Farm

Hademore
Farm Bridge

160

132

11

Dogkennel
Wood

Depot

Greendales
Farm

BURTON

ROAD

A513

Haselour

Haselour
Hall

Home
Farm

Pimlico
Cottage

The Hall
Gardens

BRICKHOUSE LANE

Pav.
Cricket
Ground

Howard
Prim. Sch.

ELFORD

THE GREEN

Haselour
House

CHURCH DR.
OLD HAL

CHURCH
ROAD

THE GDNS.

THE SQUARE

THE CROFT

CLEMENTS LA.
FIDDLERS LA.

BECK THE

Raddle
Farm

Tamworth
B79

RIVER TAME

OLD HALL DR.

THE ROAD

Sewage
Works

BURTON

BECK

The Model
Farm

310

SHRUBBERY ROAD

Elford
Bridge

TAMWORTH RD.

WILLOW BOTTOM LANE

Lichfield
WS13

FISHERWICK LANE

Stubby Lea
Farm

Bull
Clump

Copes
Lodge

Elford
Mill

RIVER TAME

A513

The
Cliff

164

Elford Lowe
Farm

F G H J K

18 19 420

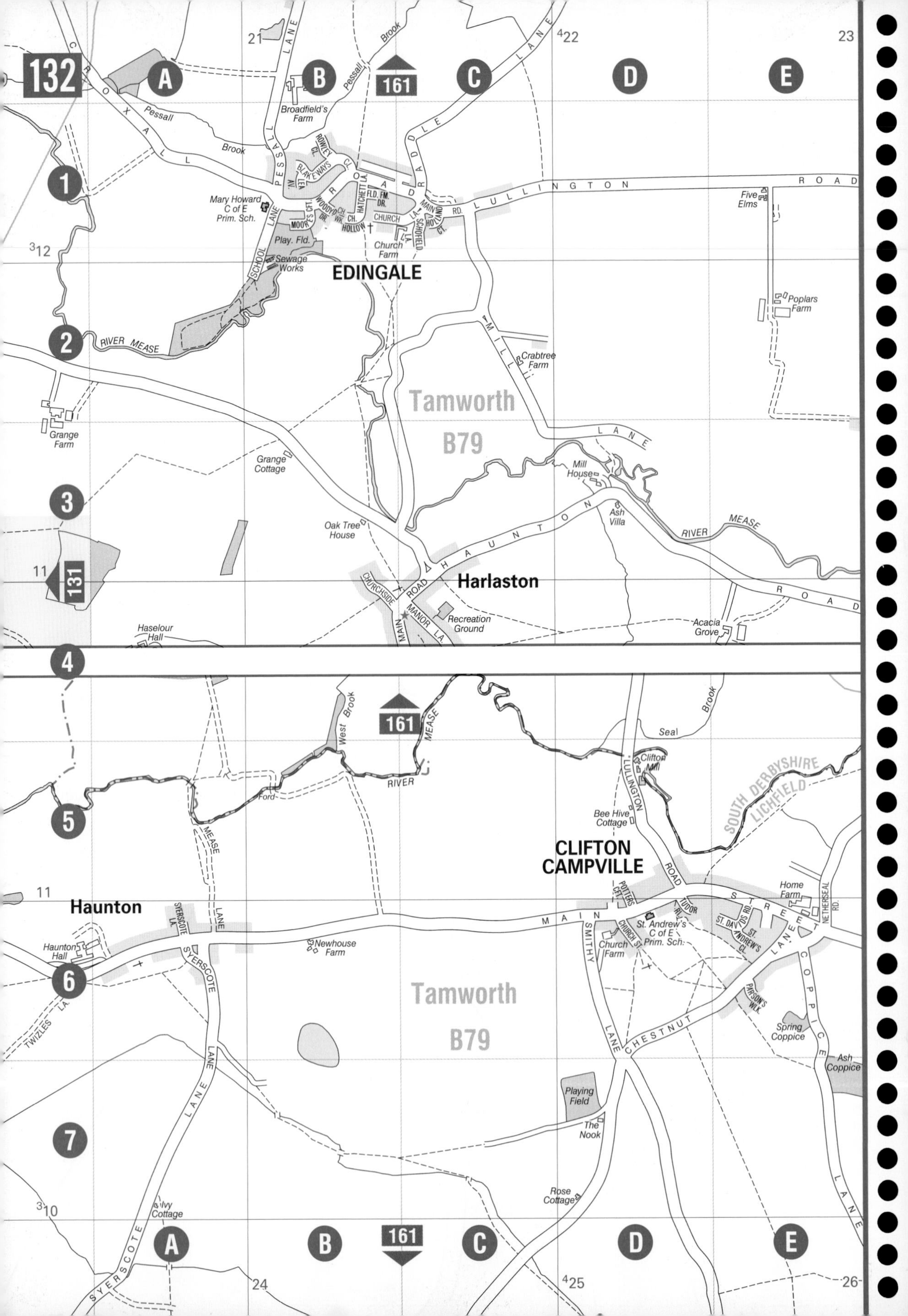

A
B
C
D
E
161
21
422
23
Broadfield's Farm
Pessall Brook
EDINGALE
Mary Howard C of E Prim. Sch.
Play. Fld.
Sewage Works
Church Farm
LULLINGTON ROAD
Five Elms
Poplars Farm
RIVER MEASE
Crabtree Farm
Tamworth
B79
Grange Farm
Grange Cottage
Mill House
Ash Villa
Oak Tree House
Harlaston
Recreation Ground
Haselour Hall
Acacia Grove
131
312
11
West Brook
Seal Brook
Clifton Mill
Bee Hive Cottage
Ford
CLIFTON CAMPVILLE
SOUTH DERBYSHIRE
LICHFIELD
Home Farm
St. Andrew's C of E Prim. Sch.
Church Farm
Haunton
Haunton Hall
Newhouse Farm
Spring Coppice
Ash Coppice
Playing Field
The Nook
Rose Cottage
Ivy Cottage
310
24
425
26
1
2
3
4
5
6
7

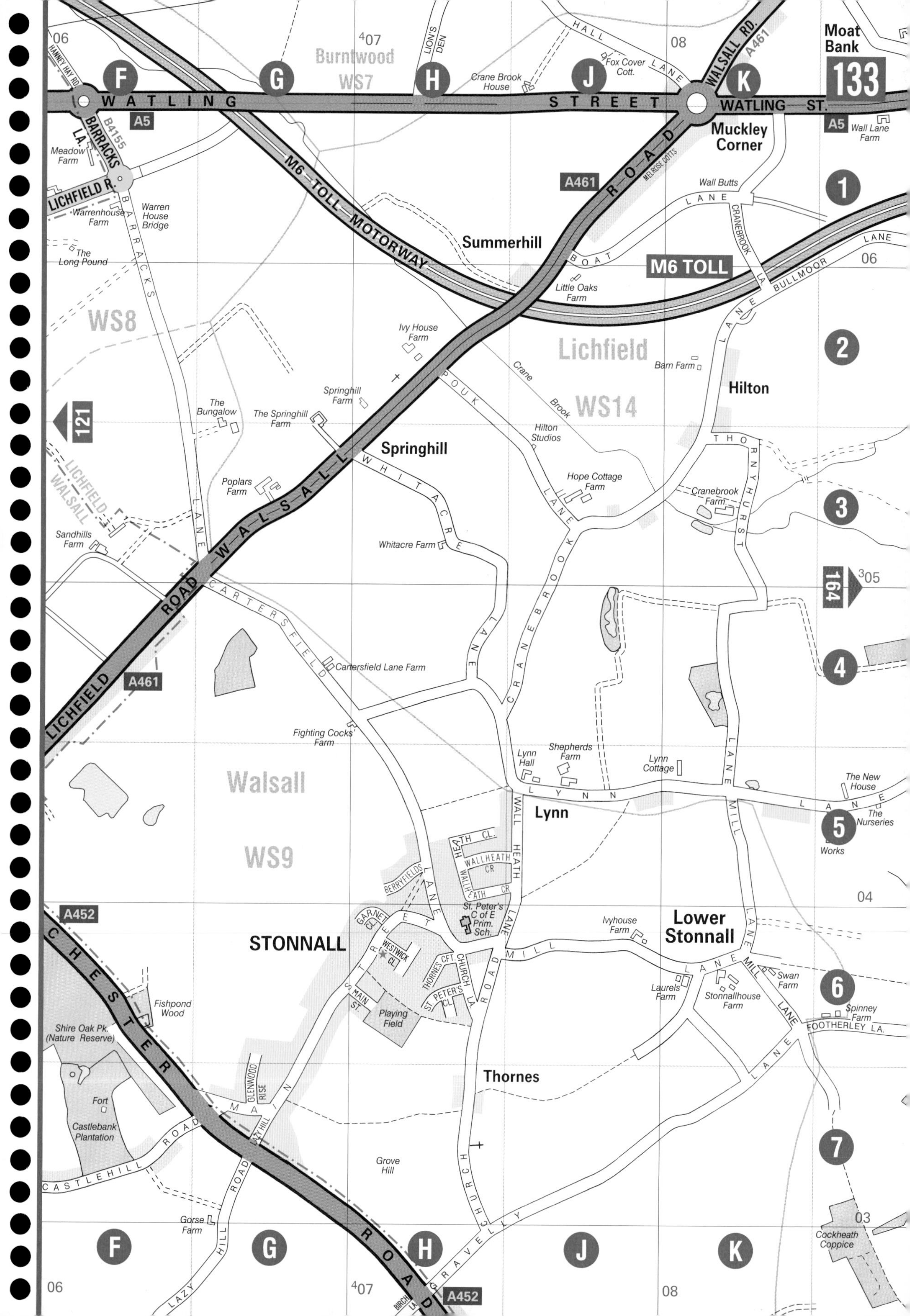

Burntwood
WS7

F
G
H
J
K

W A T L I N G   S T R E E T
WATLING ST.

A5
A5   Wall Lane Farm

Muckley Corner

Fox Cover Cott.

Crane Brook House

Hall Lane

Lions Den

Walsall Rd.
A461

Meadow Farm

Barracks La.
B4155

Lichfield Rd.

Warrenhouse Farm

Warren House Bridge

A461   ROAD

Melrose Cotts

Wall Butts

Cranebrook La.

Wall Lane

Bullmoor La.

Lane

1

The Long Pound

M6 TOLL MOTORWAY

Summerhill

Little Oaks Farm

M6 TOLL

06

2

WS8

Ivy House Farm

Lichfield

WS14

Barn Farm

Hilton

121

Springhill Farm

The Bungalow

The Springhill Farm

Crane Brook

Hilton Studios

Thornyhurst

Cranebrook Farm

3

Lichfield
Walsall

Poplars Farm

Springhill

WHITACRE LANE

Hope Cottage Farm

164   305

Sandhills Farm

ROAD WALSALL

POUK LANE

Whitacre Farm

CRANEBROOK LANE

4

CARTERSFIELD

Cartersfield Lane Farm

LICHFIELD

A461

Fighting Cocks Farm

Lynn Hall

Shepherds Farm

Lynn Cottage

The New House

The Nurseries

Walsall

Lynn

LYNN

LANE

5

WS9

WALLHEATH CR

Works

BERRYFIELDS

WALL HEATH

MILL LANE

A452

GARNET

WESTWICK CL

THORNES CFT

St. Peter's C of E Prim. Sch.

Ivyhouse Farm

Lower Stonnall

Swan Farm

6

STONNALL

MAIN ST.

ST. PETER'S CL

CHURCH LA.

ROAD

Laurels Farm

Stonnallhouse Farm

Spinney Farm

FOOTHERLEY LA.

Fishpond Wood

Shire Oak Pk. (Nature Reserve)

GLENWOOD RISE

MAIN

Playing Field

Thornes

CHURCH

GRAVELLY

MILL LANE

Fort

Castlebank Plantation

CHESTER

LAZY HILL

ROAD

Grove Hill

7

03

Gorse Farm

CASTLEHILL ROAD

HILL

LAZY

BIRCH LA.

A452   ROAD

Cockheath Coppice

F
G
H
J
K

06
407
08

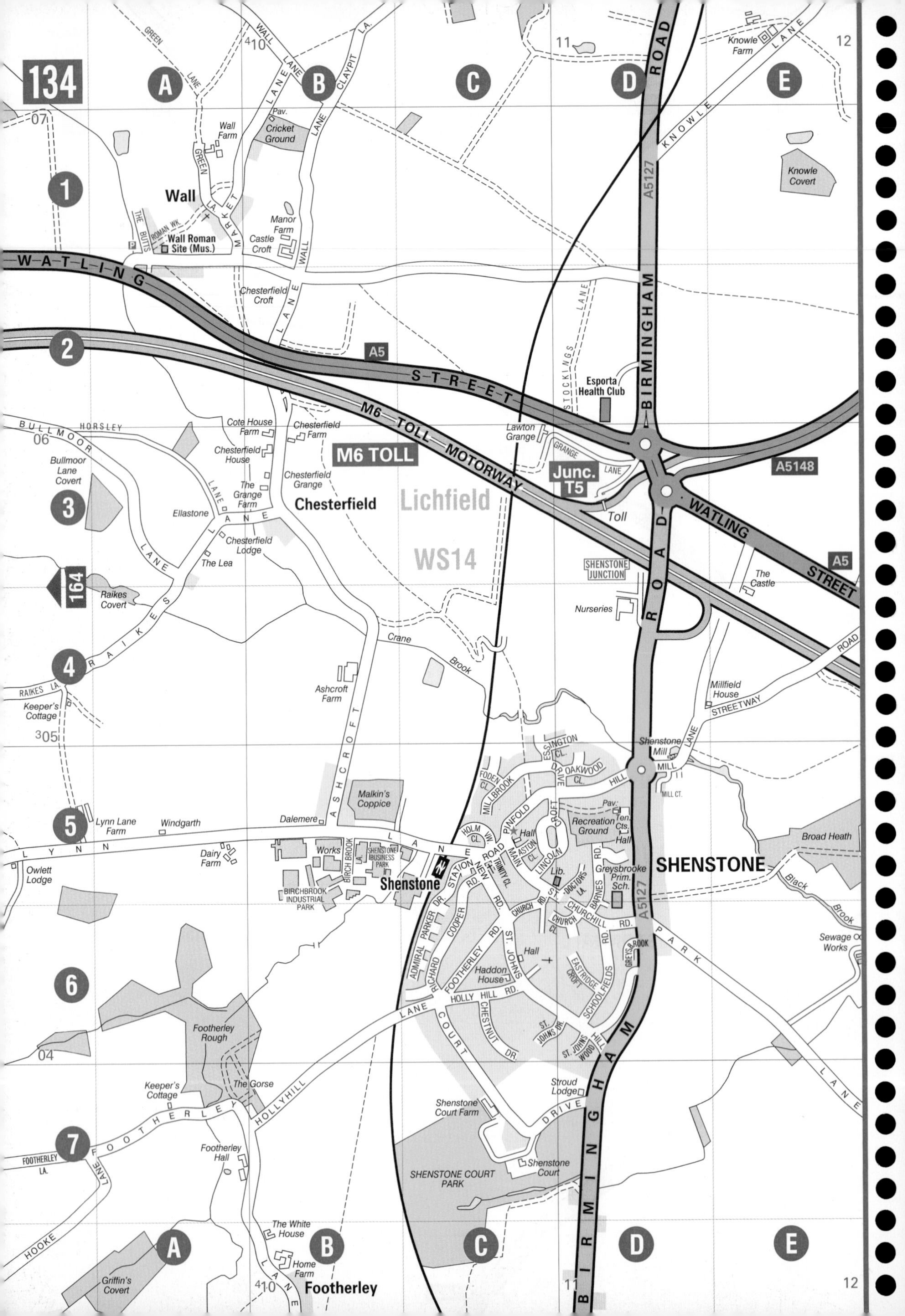

Wall
Wall Farm
Cricket Ground
Pav.
Manor Farm
Castle Croft
Wall Roman Site (Mus.)
THE BUTTS
ROMAN WK.
GREEN LANE
WALL LANE
MARKET LA.
CLAYPIT LA.
WATLING STREET
A5
Chesterfield Croft
M6 TOLL MOTORWAY
M6 TOLL
Esporta Health Club
STOCKINGS LANE
BIRMINGHAM ROAD
A5127
Knowle Farm
KNOWLE LANE
Knowle Covert
Lawton Grange
GRANGE LANE
Junc. T5
Toll
A5148
BULLMOOR LANE
HORSLEY
Bullmoor Lane Covert
Cote House Farm
Chesterfield Farm
Chesterfield House
Chesterfield Grange
The Grange Farm
Chesterfield
Lichfield
WS14
Ellastone
Chesterfield Lodge
The Lea
Raikes Covert
RAIKES LANE
RAIKES LA.
Keeper's Cottage
SHENSTONE JUNCTION
The Castle
Nurseries
Crane Brook
Ashcroft Farm
ASHCROFT LANE
Millfield House
STREETWAY ROAD
Shenstone Mill
MILL LANE
MILL CT.
ESSINGTON CL.
OAKWOOD CL.
FODEN CL.
MILLBROOK DRIVE
Malkin's Coppice
Lynn Lane Farm
Windgarth
Dalemere
LYNN LANE
Dairy Farm
Owlett Lodge
Works
SHENSTONE BUSINESS PARK
BIRCH BROOK LA.
BIRCHBROOK INDUSTRIAL PARK
Shenstone
STATION ROAD
HOLM VW.
HOLM CL.
PINFOLD HILL
CROFT
Hall
Recreation Ground
Ten. Cts.
MAIN ST.
ASTON CL.
LINCOLN CROFT
Lib.
DOCTORS LA.
Greysbrooke Prim. Sch.
BARNES RD.
SHENSTONE
Broad Heath
Black Brook
TRINITY CL.
NEW RD.
PARKER DR.
COOPER
CHURCH RD.
CHURCHILL RD.
CHURCH CL.
ADMIRAL RICHARD
FOOTHERLEY RD.
ST. JOHNS RD.
EASTRIDGE CROFT
SCHOOLFIELDS
GREYSBROOK
PARK LANE
Sewage Works
Haddon House
HOLLY HILL RD.
CHESTNUT DR.
ST. JOHNS DR.
ST. JOHNS WOOD
HILL
COURT DRIVE
Footherley Rough
The Gorse
Keeper's Cottage
HOLLYHILL LANE
FOOTHERLEY LANE
FOOTHERLEY LA.
Footherley Hall
Stroud Lodge
Shenstone Court Farm
Shenstone Court
SHENSTONE COURT PARK
HOOKE
The White House
Home Farm
Footherley
Griffin's Covert
164
A B C D E
1 2 3 4 5 6 7
410 11 12
07 06 305 04

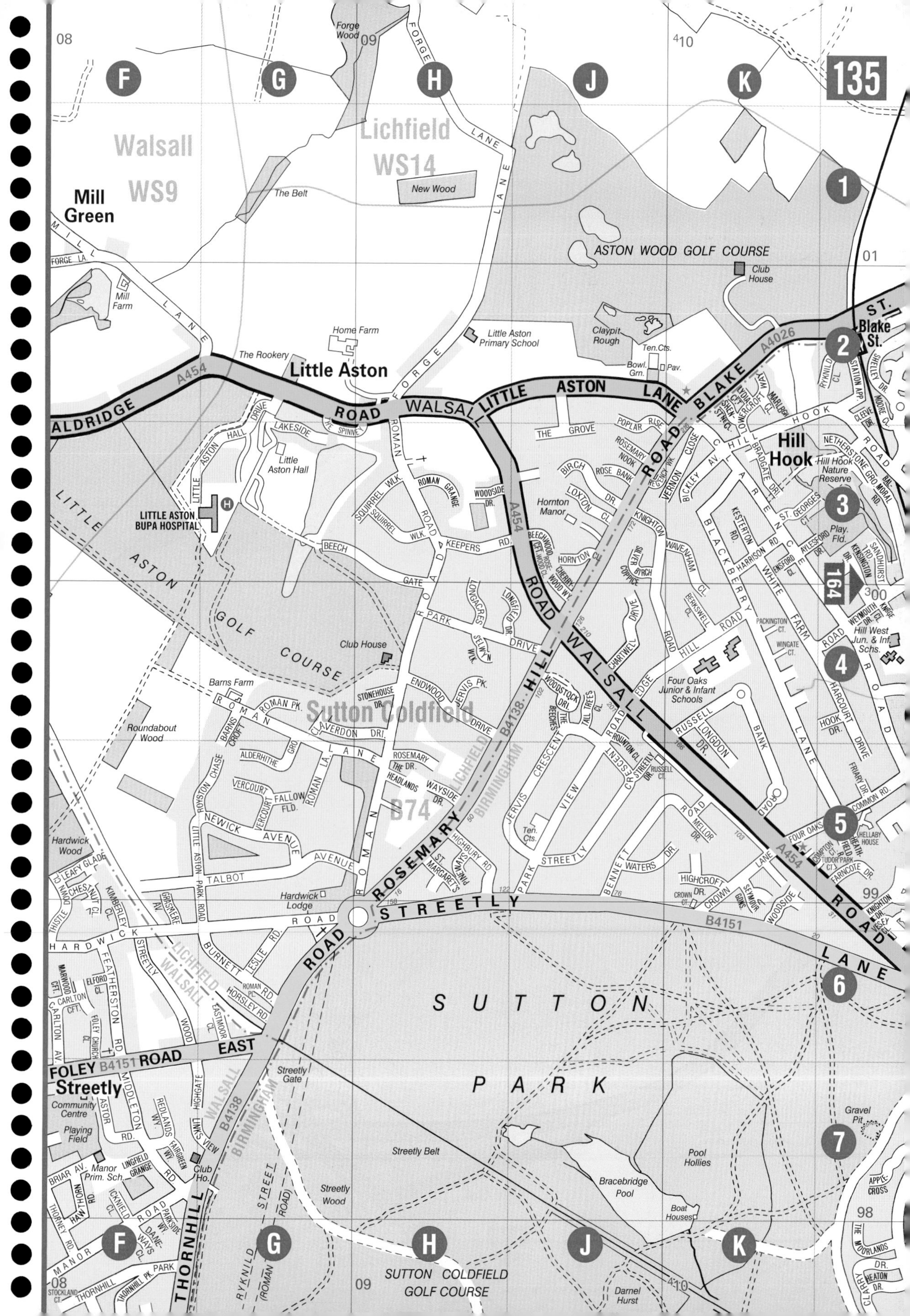

Walsall
WS9
Lichfield
WS14
Mill Green
Forge Wood
The Belt
New Wood
ASTON WOOD GOLF COURSE
Club House
Mill Farm
Home Farm
Little Aston Primary School
Claypit Rough
Ten.Cts.
Bowl. Grn.
Pav.
The Rookery
Little Aston
ALDRIDGE ROAD
WALSALL ROAD
LITTLE ASTON LANE
BLAKE ST.
Blake St.
Hill Hook
Hill Hook Nature Reserve
Play. Fld.
Little Aston Hall
LITTLE ASTON BUPA HOSPITAL
LITTLE ASTON GOLF COURSE
Club House
Hornton Manor
Barns Farm
Roundabout Wood
Sutton Coldfield
B74
Four Oaks Junior & Infant Schools
Hill West Jun. & Inf. Schs.
Ten. Cts.
Hardwick Wood
Hardwick Lodge
Streetly
Community Centre
Playing Field
Manor Prim. Sch.
Club Ho.
Streetly Gate
SUTTON PARK
Streetly Belt
Streetly Wood
Bracebridge Pool
Pool Hollies
Boat Houses
Gravel Pit
SUTTON COLDFIELD GOLF COURSE
Darnel Hurst
STREETLY LANE
FOLEY ROAD EAST
THORNHILL ROAD
RYKNILD STREET (ROMAN ROAD)
LICHFIELD ROAD
BIRMINGHAM ROAD
ROSEMARY HILL ROAD
164

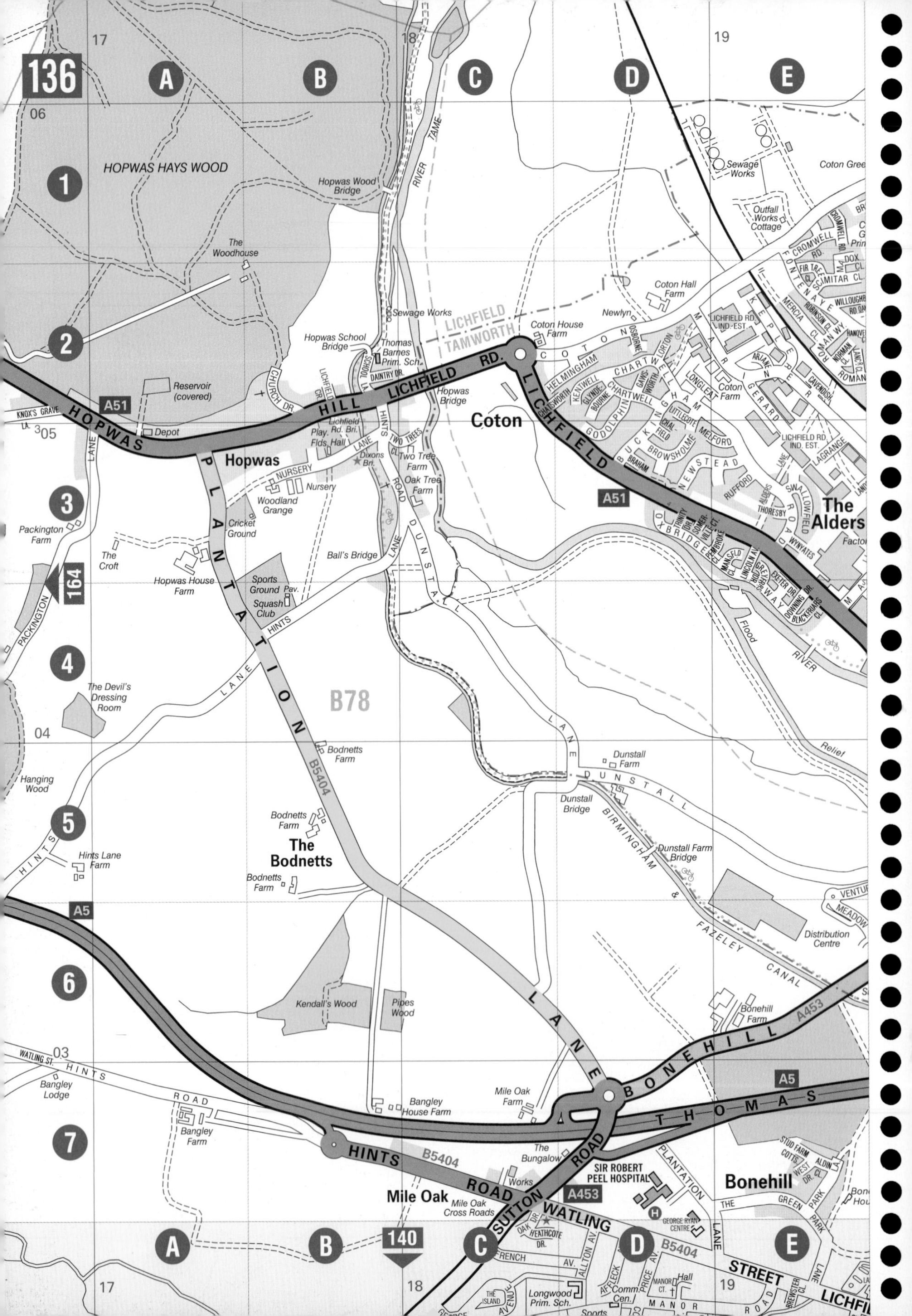

HOPWAS HAYS WOOD
Hopwas Wood Bridge
The Woodhouse
Reservoir (covered)
Depot
KNOX'S GRAVE LA.
HOPWAS HILL
LICHFIELD RD.
A51
Hopwas
PLANTATION
B5404
NURSERY
Nursery
Woodland Grange
Cricket Ground
Packington Farm
The Croft
Hopwas House Farm
Sports Ground
Pav.
Squash Club
HINTS
LANE
PACKINGTON
164
The Devil's Dressing Room
B78
Hanging Wood
Bodnetts Farm
The Bodnetts
Hints Lane Farm
A5
Kendall's Wood
Pipes Wood
WATLING ST.
HINTS ROAD
Bangley Lodge
Bangley Farm
Bangley House Farm
Mile Oak Farm
Mile Oak
Mile Oak Cross Roads
B5404
140
Sewage Works
Hopwas School Bridge
Thomas Barnes Prim. Sch.
DAINTRY DR.
SCHOOL LA.
CHURCH DR.
LICHFIELD CR.
Lichfield Rd. Bri.
Play. Flds. Hall
Dixons Br.
TWO TREES CL.
Two Tree Farm
Oak Tree Farm
Ball's Bridge
DUNSTALL LANE
RIVER TAME
Hopwas Bridge
LICHFIELD
TAMWORTH
Coton
Coton House Farm
Newlyn
Coton Hall Farm
Sewage Works
Outfall Works Cottage
Coton Green
COTON
HELMINGHAM
CHATSWORTH
KENTWELL
GLYNDEBOURNE
CHARTWELL
GODOLPHIN
GAWSWORTH
LORTON
OSBORNE
BUCKINGHAM
LITTLECOTE
CHALFIELD
BROWSHOLME
MELFORD
BRAHAM
NEWSTEAD
LONGLEAT
Coton Farm
MARIGOLD
GERARD
ARJANE
LICHFIELD RD. IND. EST.
KEPLER
CROMWELL RD.
FIR TREE CL.
DOX CL.
SCIMITAR CL.
FONTENAYE
MERCIA CL.
ROBINSON CL.
ROMAN WY.
NORMAN
WILLOUGHBY RD.
HANOVER
CAVENDISH
ROMAN
LICHFIELD RD. IND. EST.
LAGRANGE
RUFFORD
THORESBY
ALDERS LANE
SWALLOWFIELD ROAD
WYNYATES
The Alders
Factory
TRINITY DR.
SOMERVILLE CT.
OXBRIDGE
PEMBROKE CL.
MANSFIELD CL.
LINCOLN AV.
GREYFRIARS
EXETER DR.
DOWNING DR.
BLACKFRIARS CL.
WAY
Flood
RIVER
Relief
Dunstall Farm
Dunstall Bridge
DUNSTALL
BIRMINGHAM & FAZELEY CANAL
Dunstall Farm Bridge
Distribution Centre
VENTURE
MEADOW
Bonehill Farm
A453
BONEHILL
A5
THOMAS
LANE
SUTTON ROAD
The Bungalow
Works
SIR ROBERT PEEL HOSPITAL
PLANTATION LANE
A453
WATLING STREET
GEORGE RYAN CENTRE
OAK DR.
HEATHCOTE DR.
FRENCH AV.
ALLTON AV.
AFFLECK AV.
PRICE AV.
MANOR CT.
Hall
Comm. Cen.
MANOR
Longwood Prim. Sch.
THE ISLAND
AVENUE
Sports
Bonehill
STUD FARM COTTS.
WEST DR.
ALDIN CL.
THE GREEN
PARK
B5404
BREWSTER CL.
LANE
ROAD
LICHFIELD
17
18
19
06
05
04
03
A B C D E
1 2 3 4 5 6 7

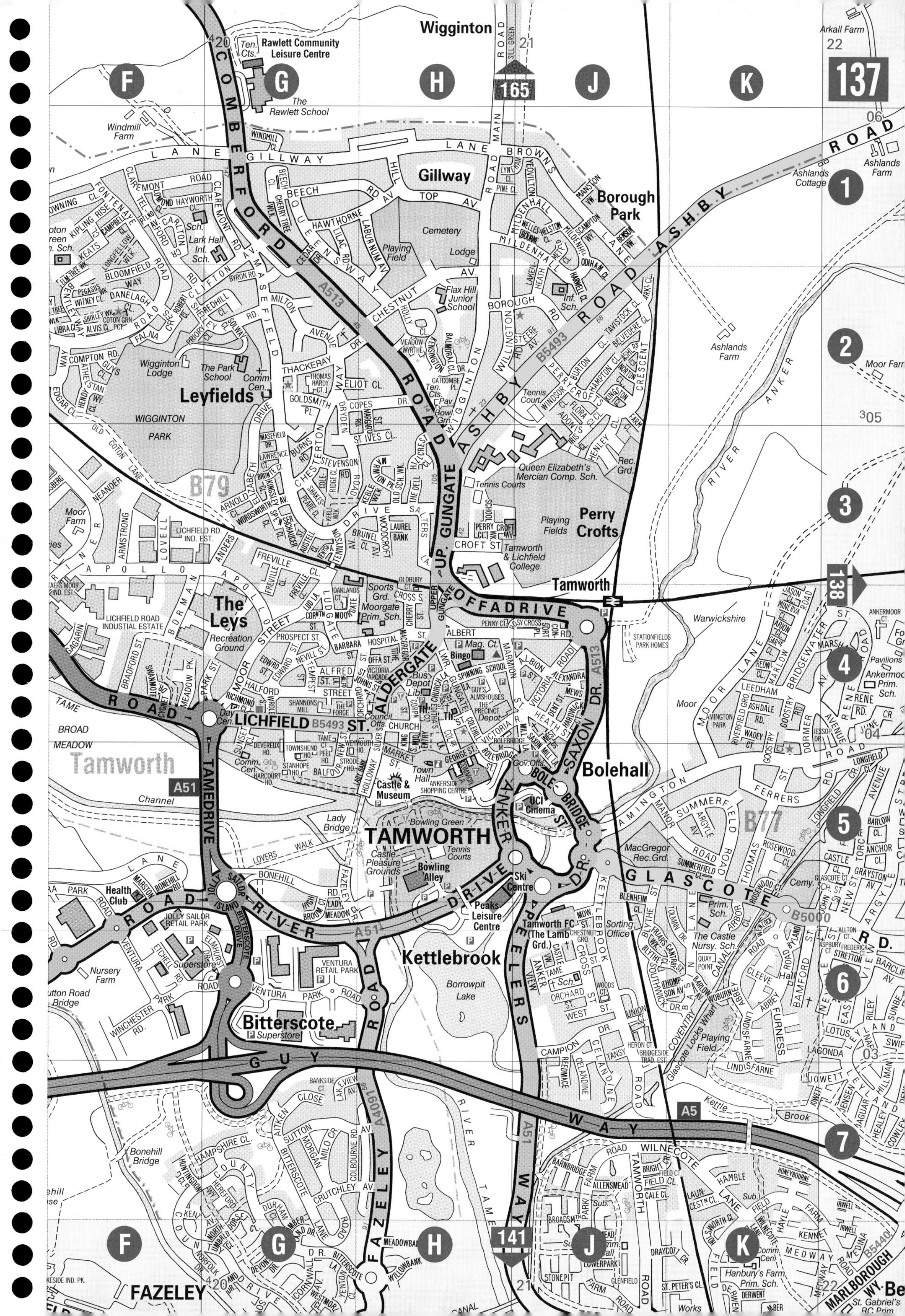
Wigginton
Rawlett Community Leisure Centre
The Rawlett School
F
G
H
J
K
165
22
Arkall Farm
Windmill Farm
Ashlands Farm
Ashlands Cottage
1
2
3
4
5
6
7
Gillway
Borough Park
Cemetery
Playing Field
Lodge
Flax Hill Junior School
Inf. Sch.
Lark Hall Inf. Sch.
Ashlands Farm
Moor Farm
RIVER ANKER
Leyfields
Wigginton Lodge
The Park School
Comm. Cen.
WIGGINTON PARK
Tennis Court
Queen Elizabeth's Mercian Comp. Sch.
Rec. Grd.
Tennis Courts
Playing Fields
Perry Crofts
Tamworth & Lichfield College
B79
LICHFIELD RD. IND. EST.
LICHFIELD ROAD INDUSTRIAL ESTATE
Tamworth
138
Warwickshire
STATIONFIELDS PARK HOMES
The Leys
Recreation Ground
Sports Grd.
Moorgate Prim. Sch.
Bingo
Mag. Ct.
Bus Depot
Lib.
Council Offs.
Depot
LICHFIELD ST.
B5493
BROAD MEADOW
Tamworth
A51
Channel
Day Cen.
Comm. Cen.
Castle & Museum
Town Hall
ANKERSIDE SHOPPING CENTRE
Gov. Offs.
Bolehall
UCI Cinema
TAMWORTH
Bowling Green
Lady Bridge
Castle Pleasure Grounds
Tennis Courts
Bowling Alley
Health Club
JOLLY SAILOR RETAIL PARK
Superstore
Nursery Farm
VENTURA RETAIL PARK
Bitterscote
Superstore
Kettlebrook
Ski Centre
Peaks Leisure Centre
Tamworth FC (The Lamb Grd.)
Borrowpit Lake
Sorting Office
MacGregor Rec. Grd.
B77
GLASCOTE
B5000
Prim. Sch.
The Castle Nursy. Sch.
Glascote Locks Wharf
Playing Field
Coventry Canal
Cemy.
A5
WAY
GUY
Kettle Brook
Bonehill Bridge
A4091
FAZELEY
RIVER TAME
141
F
G
H
J
K
Comm. Cen.
Hanbury's Farm Prim. Sch.
St. Gabriel's RC Prim.
MARLBOROUGH
420
21
22
FAZELEY

Arkall Farm
22
23
24
A
B
C
D
E
165
06
LICHFIELD
B5493
TAMWORTH
ASHBY
ROAD
Amington Hall Cottages
Amington Old Hall Cotts.
Ashlands Cottage
Ashlands Farm
Amington Hall
Ling Cottage
Decoy Barn
The Decoy
Cow Barn
Amington Old Hall
Moor Farm
Royals Farm
Warren Farm
Alvecote Pools Nature Reserve
RIVER ANKER
ANKER
05
MOOR
LANE
AMINGTON PARK
SHUTTINGTON
ROAD
137
BRINDLEY
DRIVE
Tamworth
Greenacres Primary Sch.
TAMWORTH MUNICIPAL GOLF COURSE
Football Ground
Pavilions
Ankermoor Prim. Sch.
COVENTRY
CANAL
TAMWORTH
ROAD
Prim. Sch.
Rec. Grd.
WOODHOUSE
MERCIAN
WAY
Cemy.
Sports Cen.
Tennis Courts
Woodhouse High Sch.
Playing Field
WOODLAND
AMINGTON
FERRERS
04
GLASCOTE
ROAD
B5000
The Woodlands Prim. Sch.
Playing Field
Glascote Meeting Room
Bowling Green
B77
Amington
Reservoir (covered)
Amington Heath Prim. Sch.
Quince Tree Sch.
Playing Field
Works
AMINGTON IND. EST.
MERCIAN PARK
Tamworth & District Indoor Bowls Cen.
Bowling Green
TAMWORTH BUS. PK.
AMBER BUSINESS VILLAGE
Lodge Farm
TAMWORTH MUNICIPAL GOLF COURSE
Club House
03
MARLBOROUGH
WAY
Lakeside Prim. Sch.
Glascote
Glascote Heath Prim. Sch.
Oakhill Prim. Sch.
Play. Fld.
Kettle Brook
A5
THOMAS
GUY
WAY
DARWELL PARK
Priory Park Karting Circuit
TAMWORTH
NTH. WARWICKSHIRE
GLASCOTE RD.
B5080
142
Belgrave
B5440
Stoneydelph Prim. Sch.
Comm. Cen.
1
2
3
4
5
6
7

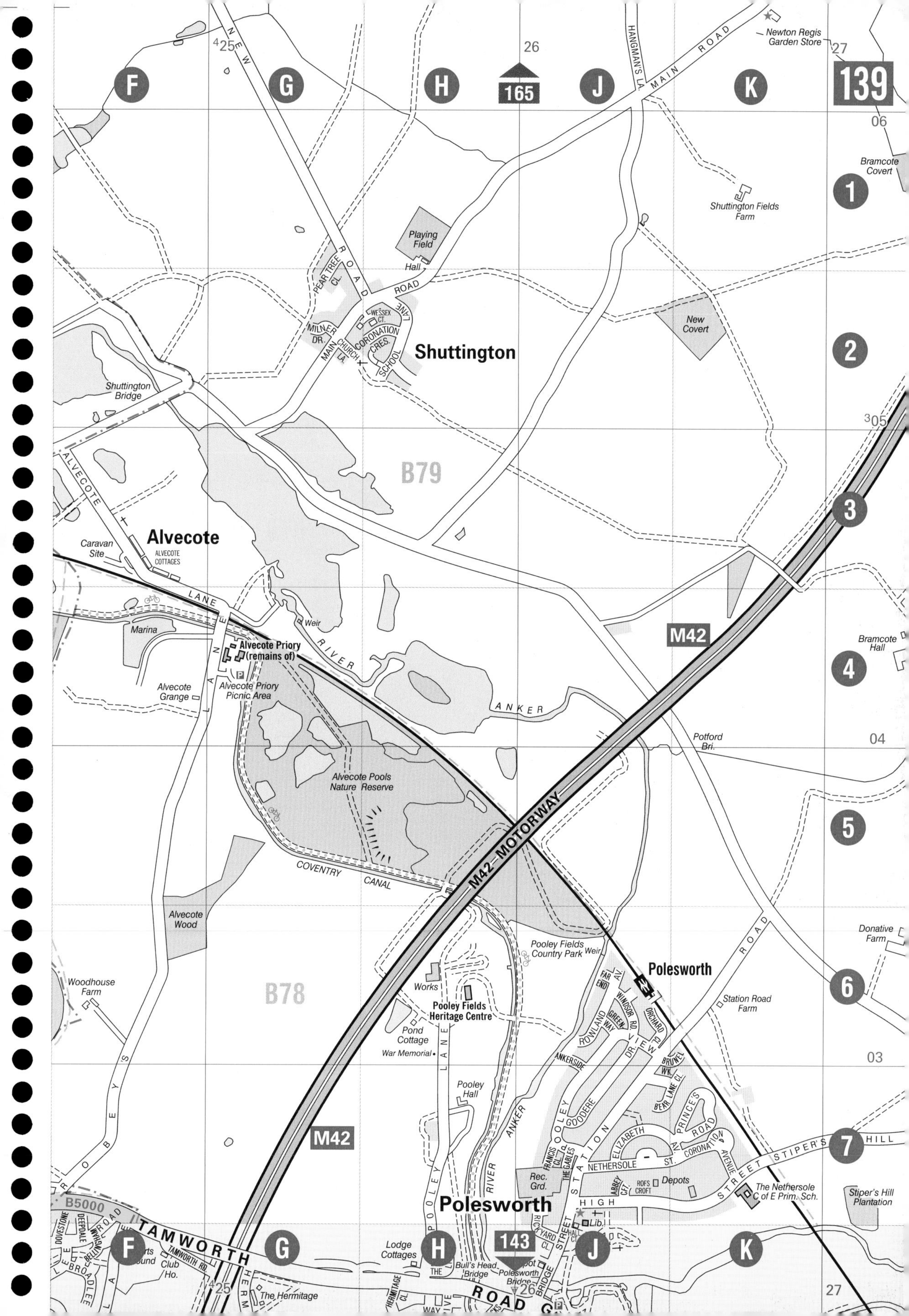

F
G
H
165
J
K
26
27
425
06
Newton Regis Garden Store
HANGMAN'S LA.
MAIN ROAD
NEW ROAD
Bramcote Covert
Shuttington Fields Farm
Playing Field
Hall
PEAR TREE CL.
WESSEX CT.
CORONATION CRES.
SCHOOL LANE
MILNER DR.
MAIN
CHURCH LA.
Shuttington
New Covert
Shuttington Bridge
305
B79
ALVECOTE
Alvecote
ALVECOTE COTTAGES
Caravan Site
LANE
Marina
Weir
RIVER
ANKER
Alvecote Priory (remains of)
Alvecote Priory Picnic Area
Alvecote Grange
M42
Bramcote Hall
Potford Bri.
04
Alvecote Pools Nature Reserve
M42 MOTORWAY
COVENTRY
CANAL
Alvecote Wood
Donative Farm
Pooley Fields Country Park
Weir
Polesworth
ROAD
Woodhouse Farm
B78
Works
Pooley Fields Heritage Centre
FAR END
AV.
WINDSOR RD.
ORCHARD CL.
GREEN WAY
ROWLAND
Station Road Farm
Pond Cottage
War Memorial
LANE
VIEW DR.
ANKERSIDE
BRUNEL WK.
03
BEAR LANE CL.
PRINCE'S ROAD
Pooley Hall
GOODERE
POOLEY
STATION
ELIZABETH AV.
CORONATION AVENUE
STIPER'S HILL
STREET
OBEYS
M42
ANKER
FRANCIS CL.
THE GABLES
NETHERSOLE ST.
Rec. Grd.
RIVER
ABBEY CFT.
ROFS CROFT
Depots
The Nethersole C of E Prim. Sch.
Stiper's Hill Plantation
B5000
DOVESTONE
DEEPDALE
ROAD
HIGH
Polesworth
RICKYARD CL.
Lib.
HALL CT.
TAMWORTH
F
G
H
143
J
K
Club Ho.
TAMWORTH RD.
Lodge Cottages
THE
Bull's Head Bridge
Polesworth Bridge
BRIDGE
425
HERM
The Hermitage
HERMITAGE CL.
ROAD
26
27
BROADLEE
1
2
3
4
5
6
7

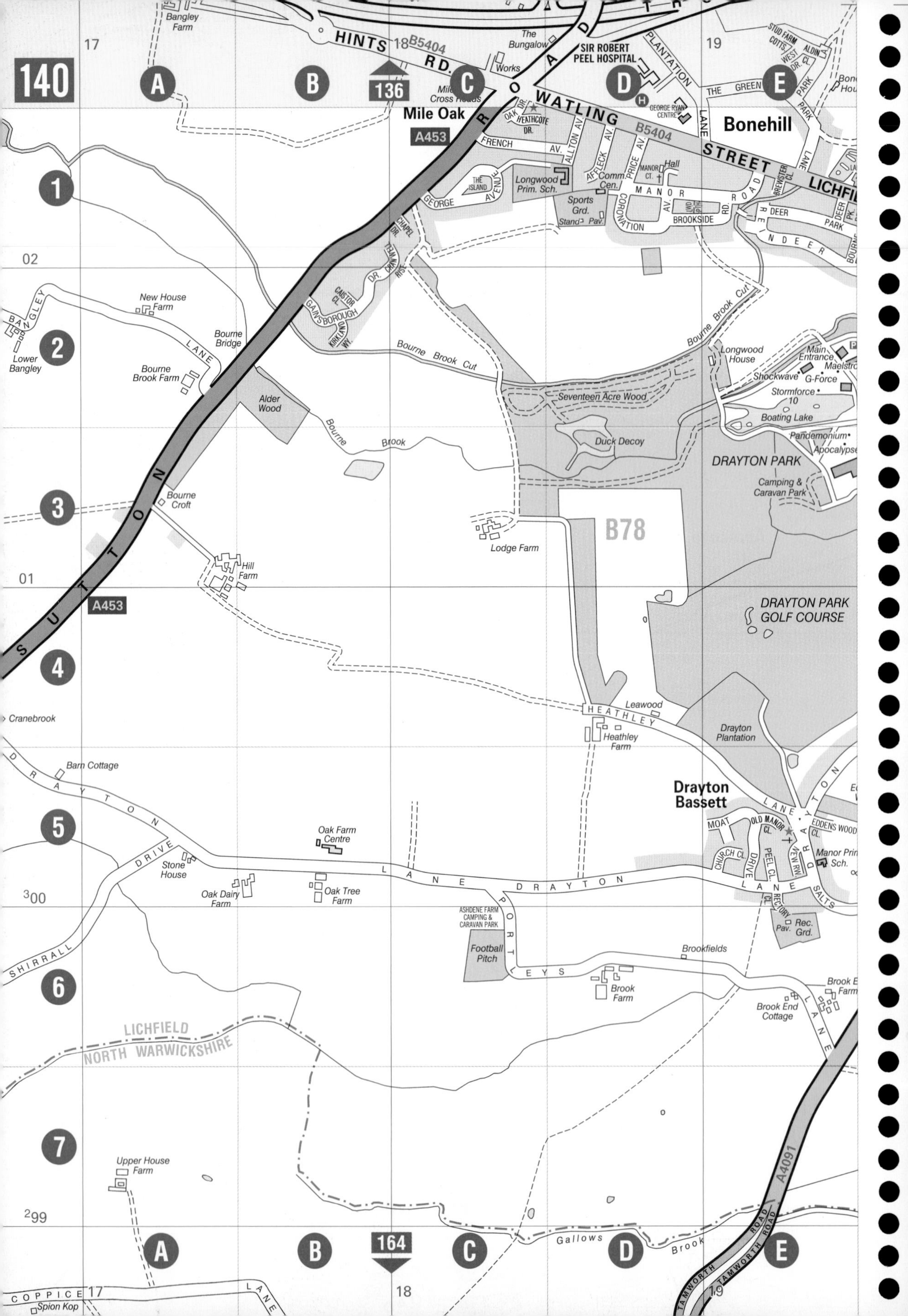

A   B   C   D   E

17

Bangley Farm

HINTS RD. 18 B5404

The Bungalow

Works

136

Mile Oak Cross Roads

Mile Oak

A453

WATLING

19

SIR ROBERT PEEL HOSPITAL

GEORGE RYAN CENTRE

STUD FARM COTTS WEST ALDIN CL

THE GREEN

Bone... House

PLANTATION

Oak Heathcote Dr.

FRENCH AV.

ALLTON AV.

AFFLECK AV.

PRICE AV.

MANOR CT.

Hall

Comm. Cen.

THE ISLAND

Longwood Prim. Sch.

Sports Grd.

Stand Pav.

CORONATION

MANOR

BROOKSIDE

RD.

STREET

LICHFI...

Bonehill

B5404

DEER PARK

RENDEER

DEER

BOURN...

CL

GEORGE AVENUE

CASTOR CL.

GAINSBOROUGH

KIRKLAND WY.

CHAPEL DR.

TRAMWAY RISE

1

02

New House Farm

BANGLEY LANE

Bourne Bridge

Bourne Brook Farm

Bourne Brook Cut

Bourne Brook Cut

Longwood House

Main Entrance

Maelstro...

Shockwave

G-Force

Stormforce 10

2

Lower Bangley

Alder Wood

Seventeen Acre Wood

Boating Lake

Pandemonium

Apocalypse...

Bourne

Brook

Duck Decoy

DRAYTON PARK

Camping & Caravan Park

3

Bourne Croft

Lodge Farm

B78

01

SUTTON

A453

Hill Farm

DRAYTON PARK GOLF COURSE

4

› Cranebrook

HEATHLEY

Leawood

Heathley Farm

Drayton Plantation

DRAYTON LANE

Barn Cottage

DRAYTON DRIVE

Drayton Bassett

MOAT

OLD MANOR CL

CHURCH CL

PEEL CL

KEW RD

RECTORY DRIVE

EDDENS WOOD

Manor Prim. Sch.

5

Stone House

Oak Farm Centre

LANE

DRAYTON

SALTS

Oak Dairy Farm

Oak Tree Farm

Ashdene Farm Camping & Caravan Park

PORTEYS

Rec. Grd.

Pav.

Brook E... Farm

3 00

SHIRRALL

Football Pitch

Brook Farm

Brookfields

Brook End Cottage

Brook E... Lane

6

LICHFIELD

NORTH WARWICKSHIRE

7

Upper House Farm

A4091

TAMWORTH ROAD

2 99

A   B   **164**   C   D   E

Gallows

Brook

COPPICE 17 LANE

Spion Kop

18

19

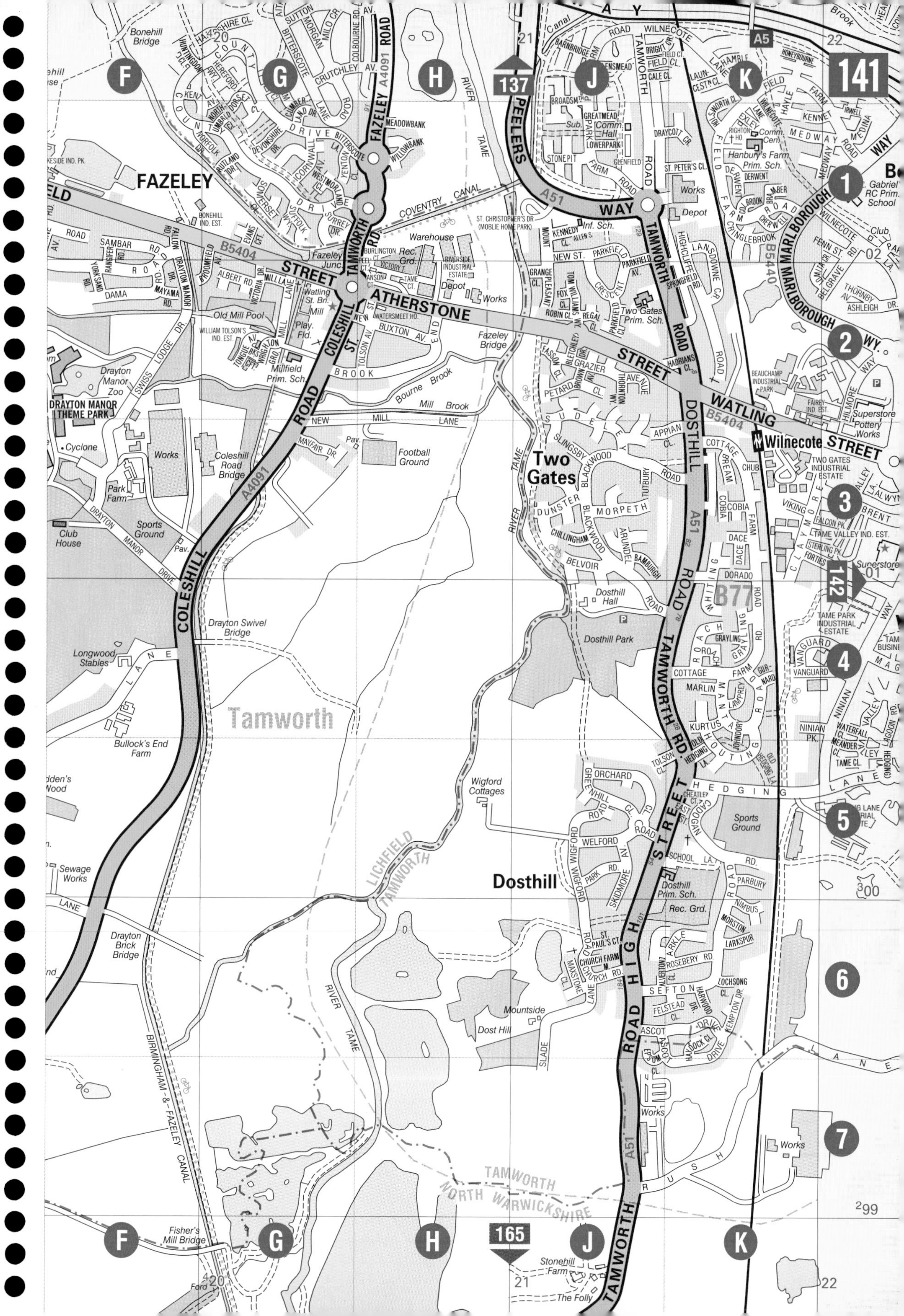

141
137
142
165
FAZELEY
Two Gates
Dosthill
Tamworth
Wilnecote
Drayton Manor Zoo
DRAYTON MANOR THEME PARK
Coleshill Road Bridge
Drayton Swivel Bridge
Longwood Stables
Bullock's End Farm
Sewage Works
Drayton Brick Bridge
Fisher's Mill Bridge
Fazeley Bridge
Fazeley Junc.
Old Mill Pool
Millfield Prim. Sch.
Two Gates Prim. Sch.
Hanbury's Farm Prim. Sch.
Dosthill Prim. Sch.
Dosthill Hall
Dosthill Park
Wigford Cottages
Mountside
Dost Hill
Stonehill Farm
The Folly
Football Ground
Sports Ground
Club House
Park Farm
Riverside Industrial Estate
Beauchamp Industrial Park
Two Gates Industrial Estate
Tame Valley Ind. Est.
Tame Park Industrial Estate
Superstore
Pottery Works
COLESHILL ROAD
WATLING STREET
ATHERSTONE STREET
PEELERS WAY
TAMWORTH ROAD
DOSTHILL ROAD
HIGH STREET
COVENTRY CANAL
BIRMINGHAM & FAZELEY CANAL
RIVER TAME
TAMWORTH
NORTH WARWICKSHIRE
LICHFIELD
A4091
A51
A5
B5404
B5440
B77

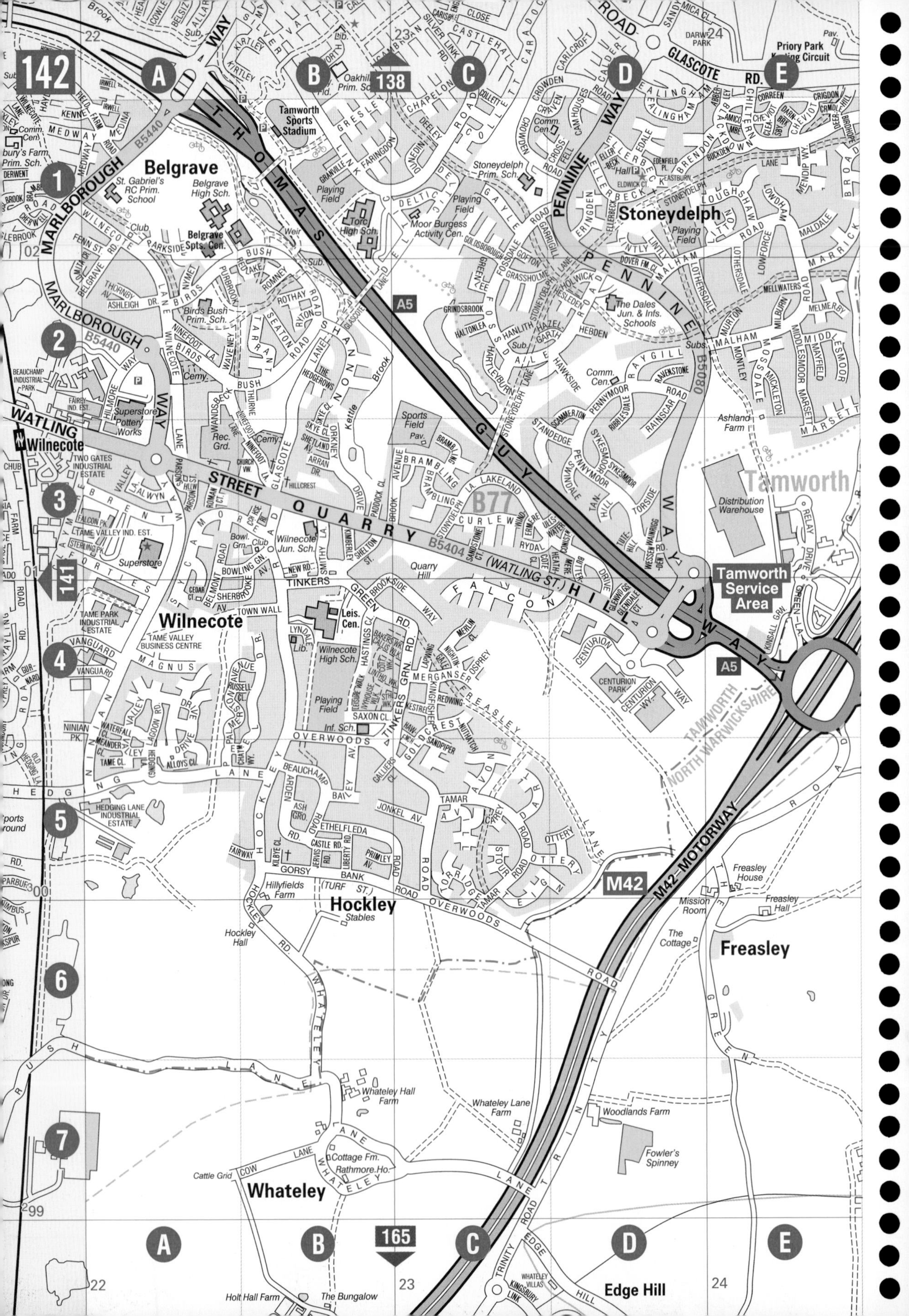
Belgrave
Stoneydelph
Wilnecote
Tamworth
Hockley
Freasley
Whateley
Edge Hill
Tamworth Service Area
Tamworth Sports Stadium
Belgrave High Sch.
St. Gabriel's RC Prim. School
Birds Bush Prim. Sch.
Torc High Sch.
Moor Burgess Activity Cen.
Stoneydelph Prim. Sch.
The Dales Jun. & Infs. Schools
Wilnecote Jun. Sch.
Wilnecote High Sch.
Distribution Warehouse
Priory Park Karting Circuit
Whateley Hall Farm
Whateley Lane Farm
Woodlands Farm
Fowler's Spinney
Freasley House
Freasley Hall
Mission Room
The Cottage
Hockley Hall
Hillyfields Farm
Holt Hall Farm
The Bungalow
Tame Valley Business Centre
Tame Park Industrial Estate
Two Gates Industrial Estate
Hedging Lane Industrial Estate
Centurion Park
Watling Street
Quarry Hill
Thomas Guy Way
Pennine Way
Marlborough Way
Glascote Rd.
M42 Motorway
A5
B5440
B5404
B5080
B77
138
141
165

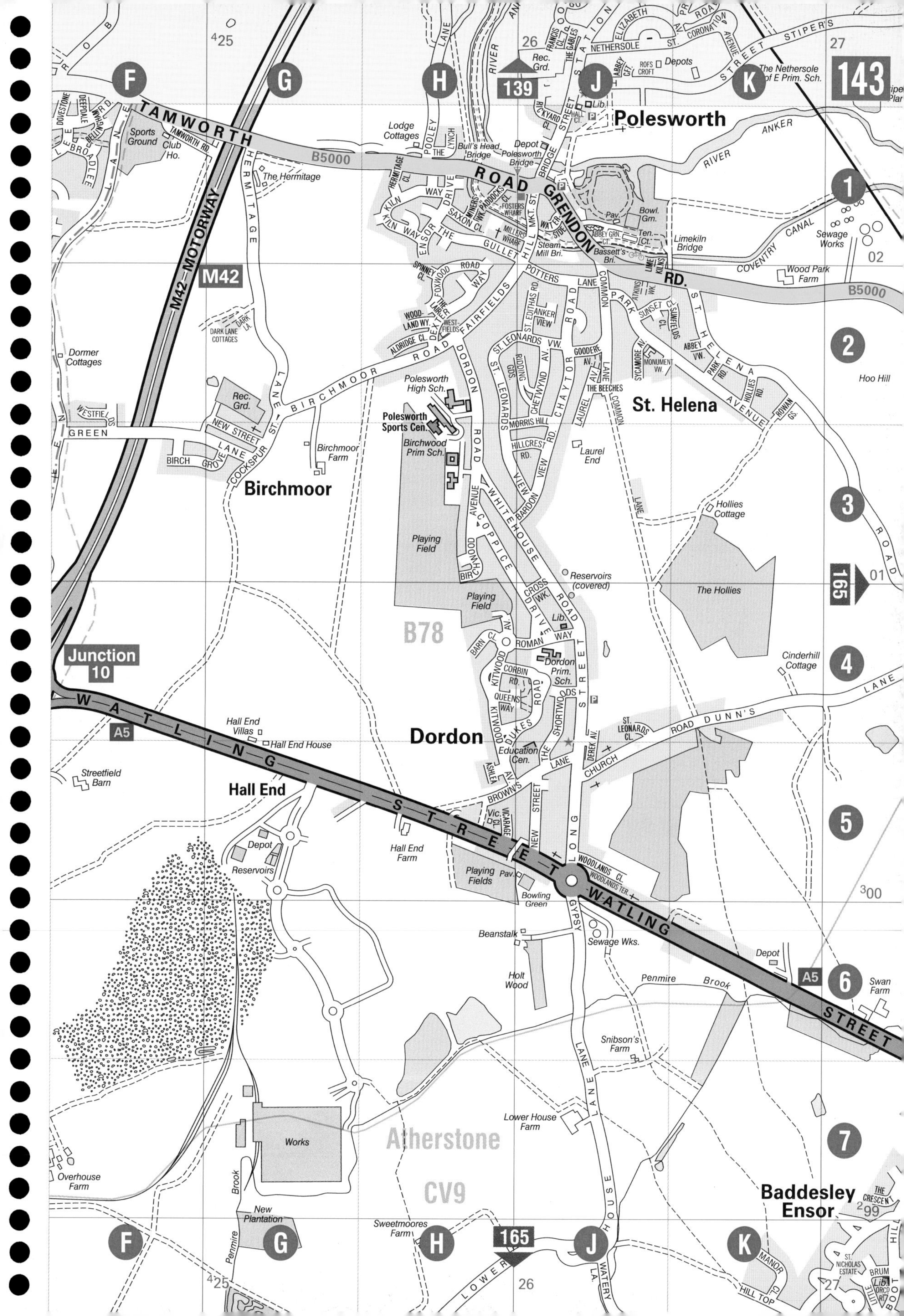
143
139
165
165
F
G
H
J
K
1
2
3
4
5
6
7
425
26
27
02
01
300
299
Polesworth
St. Helena
Birchmoor
Dordon
Hall End
Baddesley Ensor
Atherstone
CV9
B78
Junction 10
M42
M42 MOTORWAY
A5
B5000
TAMWORTH ROAD
GRENDON RD.
WATLING STREET
BIRCHMOOR ROAD
DORDON ROAD
LONG STREET
COMMON LANE
CHURCH ROAD
DUNN'S LANE
GYPSY LANE
HOUSE LANE
WATERY LA.
LOWER
RIVER ANKER
COVENTRY CANAL
ST. HELENA AVENUE
STIPER'S STREET
NETHERSOLE ST.
CORONATION AVENUE
HERMITAGE LANE
COCKSPUR ST.
NEW STREET
BIRCH GROVE LANE
GREEN
WHITEHOUSE ROAD
POTTERS LANE
FAIRFIELDS
THE GULLET
KILN WAY
ST. LEONARDS VW.
CHAYTOR ROAD
BARDON VIEW RD.
COPPICE DRIVE
ROMAN WAY
KITWOOD AV.
DUKES ROAD
SHORTWOODS
BROWN'S LANE
MANOR
HILL TOP
Sports Ground
Club Ho.
The Hermitage
Lodge Cottages
Bull's Head Bridge
Depot
Polesworth Bridge
Rec. Grd.
Lib.
Depots
The Nethersole of E Prim. Sch.
Pav.
Bowl. Grn.
Ten. Ct.
Steam Mill Bri.
Bassett's Bri.
Limekiln Bridge
Sewage Works
Wood Park Farm
Dormer Cottages
Dark Lane Cottages
Polesworth High Sch.
Polesworth Sports Cen.
Birchwood Prim Sch.
Birchmoor Farm
Playing Field
Laurel End
Hoo Hill
Hollies Cottage
The Hollies
Reservoirs (covered)
Dordon Prim. Sch.
Education Cen.
Cinderhill Cottage
Hall End Villas
Hall End House
Streetfield Barn
Hall End Farm
Reservoirs
Playing Fields
Bowling Green
Beanstalk
Sewage Wks.
Holt Wood
Penmire Brook
Swan Farm
Snibson's Farm
Lower House Farm
Works
Overhouse Farm
New Plantation
Sweetmoores Farm
Brook

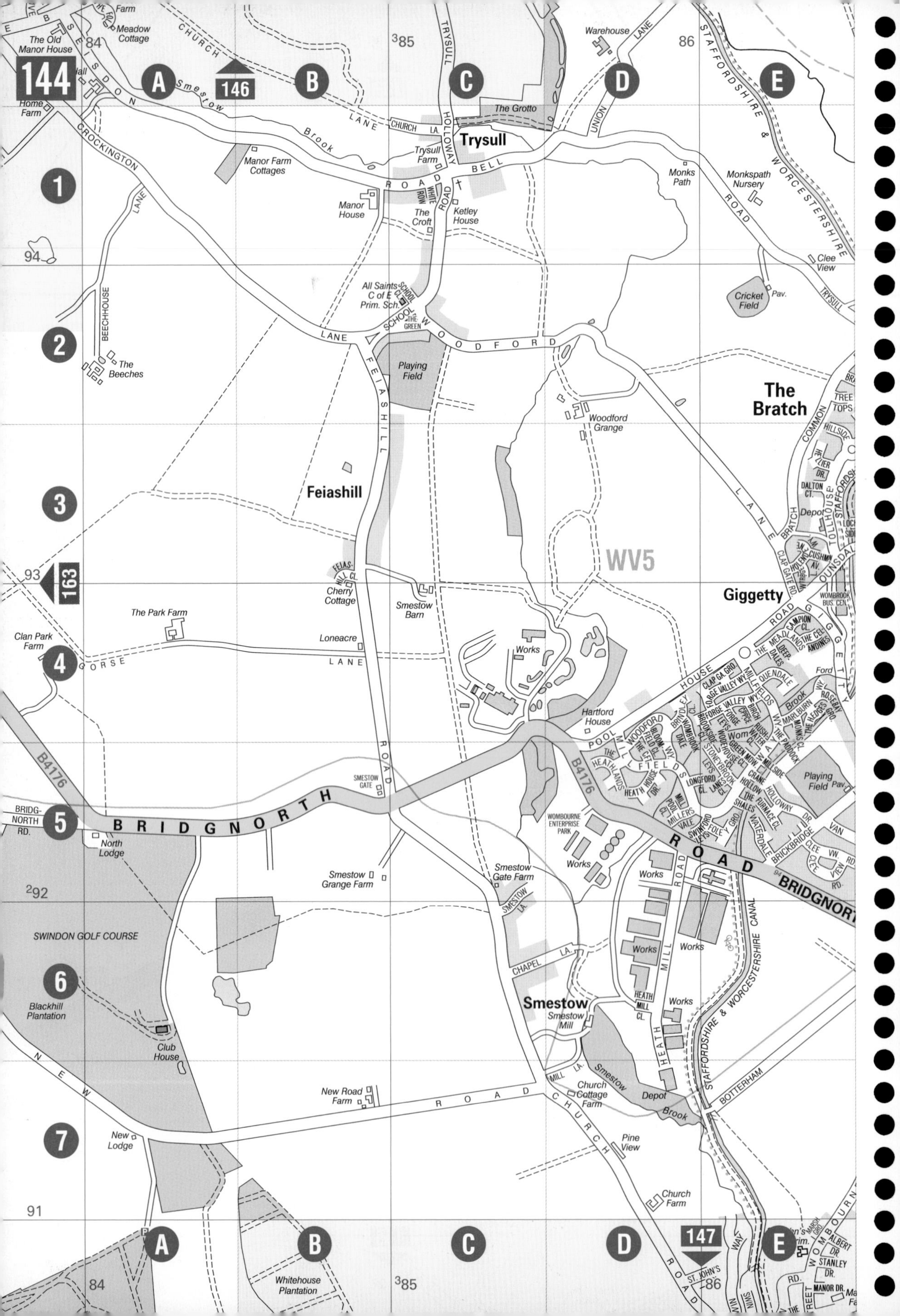
Trysull
Feiashill
The Bratch
Giggetty
Smestow
WV5
The Old Manor House
Meadow Cottage
Home Farm
Manor Farm Cottages
Trysull Farm
Manor House
The Croft
Ketley House
The Grotto
Warehouse
Monks Path
Monkspath Nursery
Clee View
Cricket Field
All Saints C of E Prim. Sch.
Playing Field
The Beeches
Woodford Grange
Cherry Cottage
Smestow Barn
The Park Farm
Clan Park Farm
Loneacre
Works
Hartford House
Wombourne Enterprise Park
Smestow Gate Farm
Smestow Grange Farm
North Lodge
Swindon Golf Course
Blackhill Plantation
Club House
New Road Farm
New Lodge
Smestow Mill
Church Cottage Farm
Depot
Pine View
Church Farm
Whitehouse Plantation
Bridgnorth Road
B4176
Smestow Brook
Staffordshire & Worcestershire Canal
Woodford Lane
School Lane
Bell Road
Church Lane
Crockington Lane
Gorse Lane
New Road
Church Road
Mill Lane
Chapel La.
Heath Mill Road
Pool House Road
Feiashill Road
Union Lane
Trysull Road
Bratch Lane
Botterham
146
147
163

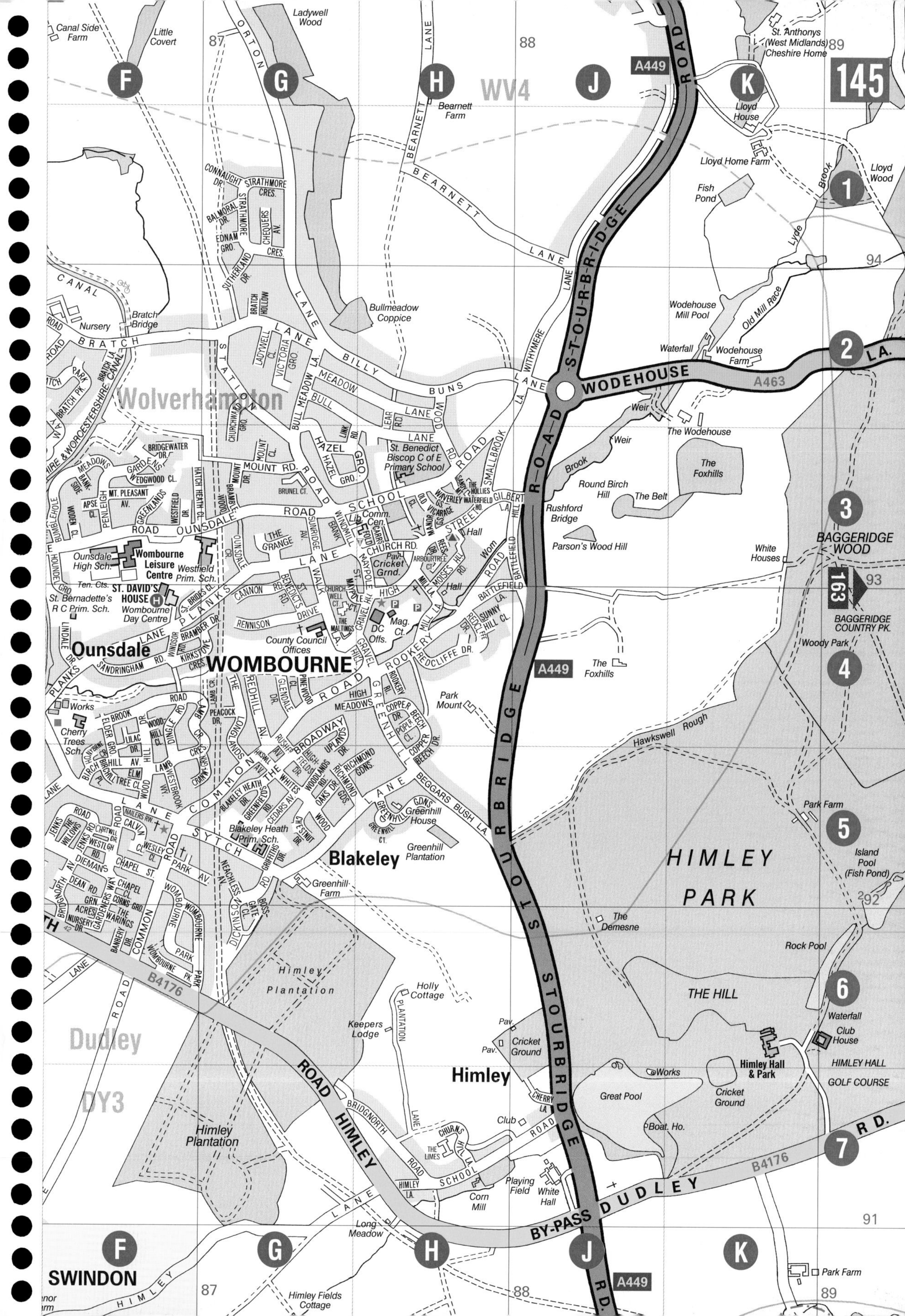
WOMBOURNE
Wolverhampton
Ounsdale
Blakeley
Himley
Dudley
SWINDON
WV4
DY3
HIMLEY PARK
BAGGERIDGE WOOD
BAGGERIDGE COUNTRY PK.
Baggeridge Country Pk.
Ladywell Wood
Little Covert
Canal Side Farm
Bearnett Farm
St. Anthonys (West Midlands) Cheshire Home
Lloyd House
Lloyd Home Farm
Lloyd Wood
Fish Pond
Bullmeadow Coppice
Wodehouse Mill Pool
Wodehouse Farm
Waterfall
Weir
The Wodehouse
The Foxhills
Round Birch Hill
The Belt
Rushford Bridge
Parson's Wood Hill
White Houses
Woody Park
Park Mount
Hawkswell Rough
Park Farm
Island Pool (Fish Pond)
Rock Pool
The Demesne
THE HILL
Club House
Himley Hall & Park
HIMLEY HALL GOLF COURSE
Great Pool
Cricket Ground
Boat. Ho.
Works
Himley Plantation
Holly Cottage
Keepers Lodge
Playing Field
White Hall
Corn Mill
Long Meadow
Himley Fields Cottage
Greenhill Farm
Greenhill House
Greenhill Plantation
Blakeley Heath Prim. Sch.
Wombourne Leisure Centre
Ounsdale High Sch.
Westfield Prim. Sch.
ST. DAVID'S HOUSE
Wombourne Day Centre
St. Bernadette's R C Prim. Sch.
Cherry Trees Sch.
St. Benedict Biscop C of E Primary School
County Council Offices
DC Offs.
Mag. Ct.
Cricket Grnd.
Comm. Cen.
Bratch Bridge
Nursery
A449
A463
B4176
STOURBRIDGE ROAD
WODEHOUSE LA.
DUDLEY BY-PASS
HIMLEY ROAD
163
F G H J K
1 2 3 4 5 6 7
87 88 89
91 92 93 94

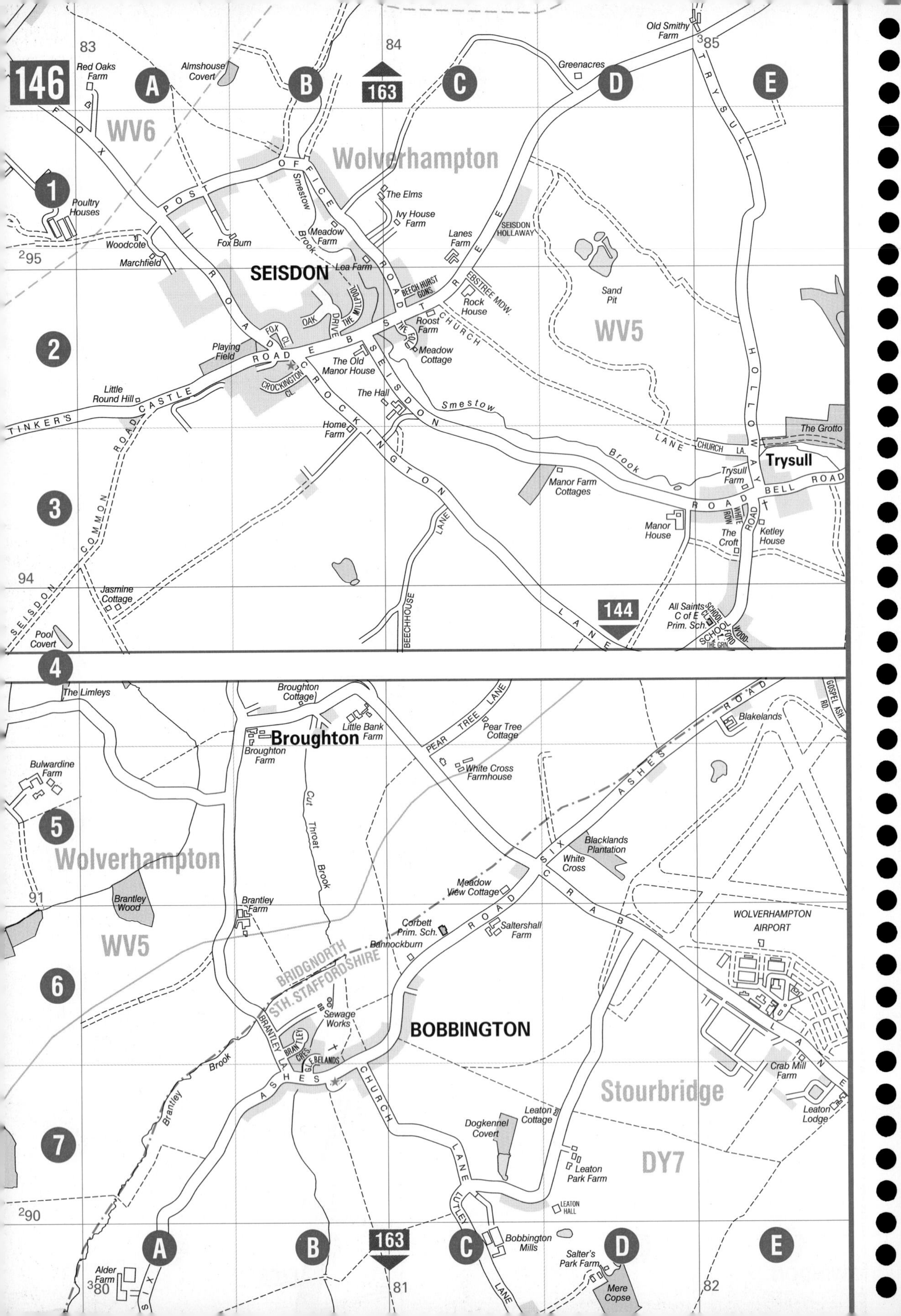
SEISDON
Wolverhampton
WV6
WV5
Trysull
Broughton
BOBBINGTON
Stourbridge
DY7
WOLVERHAMPTON AIRPORT
Red Oaks Farm
Almshouse Covert
Poultry Houses
Woodcote
Marchfield
Fox Burn
Meadow Farm
Lea Farm
The Elms
Ivy House Farm
Lanes Farm
SEISDON HOLLAWAY
Greenacres
Old Smithy Farm
Rock House
Roost Farm
Meadow Cottage
The Old Manor House
The Hall
Home Farm
Little Round Hill
Playing Field
Sand Pit
The Grotto
Trysull Farm
Manor Farm Cottages
Manor House
The Croft
Ketley House
All Saints C of E Prim. Sch.
Jasmine Cottage
Pool Covert
POST OFFICE ROAD
FOX ROAD
TRYSULL HOLLOWAY
TINKER'S CASTLE ROAD
SEISDON COMMON ROAD
CROCKINGTON LANE
SEISDON ROAD
CHURCH LANE
BELL ROAD
BEECHHOUSE LANE
Smestow Brook
The Limleys
Broughton Cottage
Little Bank Farm
Broughton Farm
Bulwardine Farm
Pear Tree Cottage
White Cross Farmhouse
Blakelands
Blacklands Plantation
White Cross
Brantley Wood
Brantley Farm
Meadow View Cottage
Corbett Prim. Sch.
Bannockburn
Saltershall Farm
Sewage Works
Cut Throat Brook
Brantley Brook
BRIDGNORTH
STH. STAFFORDSHIRE
PEAR TREE LANE
SIX ASHES ROAD
CRAB LANE
CHURCH LANE
LUTLEY LANE
GOSPEL ASH RD.
Crab Mill Farm
Leaton Lodge
Leaton Cottage
Dogkennel Covert
Leaton Park Farm
LEATON HALL
Bobbington Mills
Salter's Park Farm
Mere Copse
Alder Farm
163
144
83
84
385
295
94
91
290
380
81
82
A B C D E
1 2 3 4 5 6 7

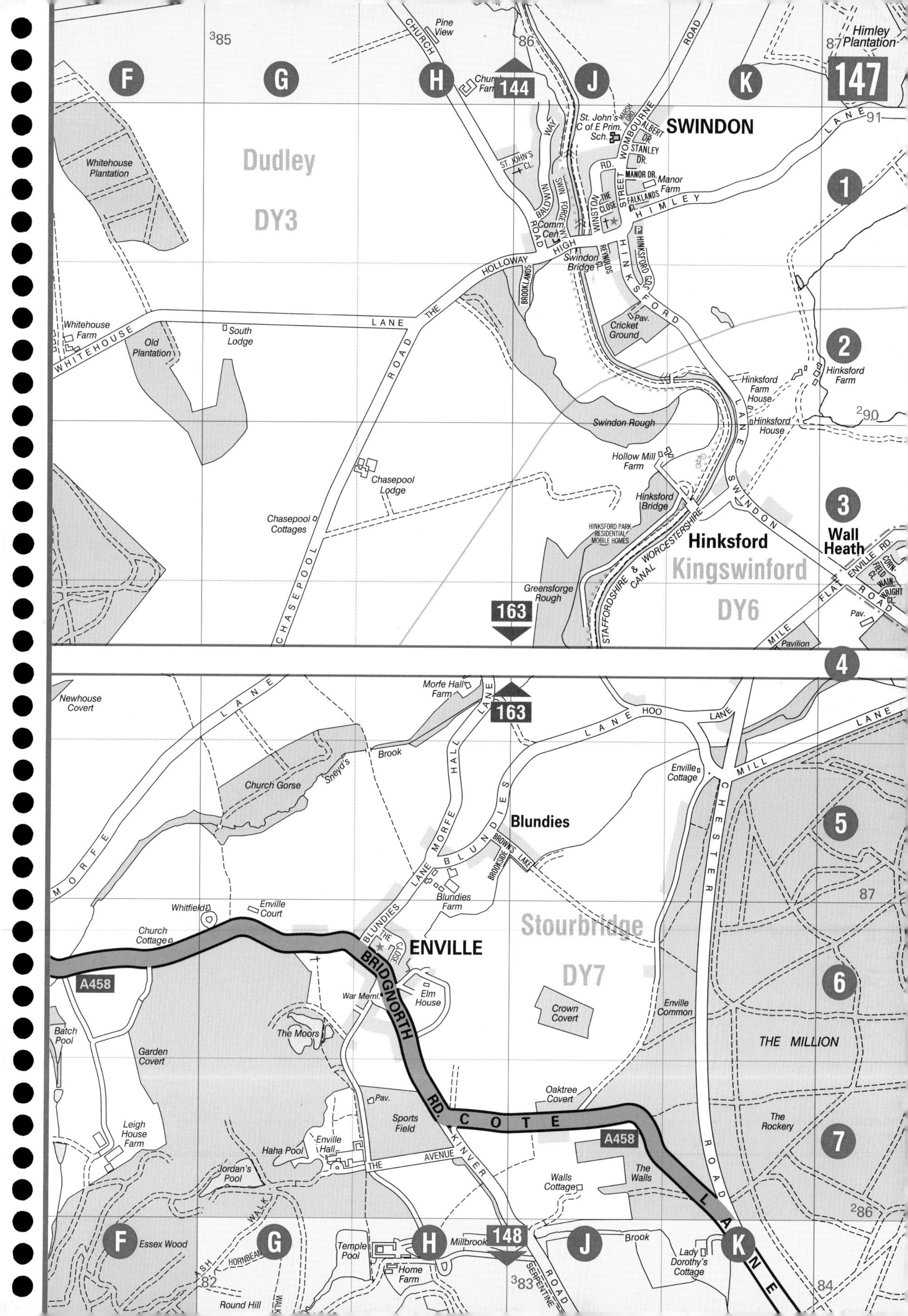

Dudley
DY3
SWINDON
Himley Plantation
Whitehouse Plantation
Whitehouse Farm
Old Plantation
South Lodge
WHITEHOUSE LANE
THE HOLLOWAY
CHASEPOOL ROAD
Chasepool Lodge
Chasepool Cottages
Pine View
CHURCH
Church Farm
144
St. John's C of E Prim. Sch.
ST. JOHN'S CL.
BALDWIN WAY
SWIN FORGE WY.
Comm. Cen.
HIGH
WOMBOURNE ROAD
STREET
MARSH GRO.
ALBERT DR.
STANLEY DR.
MANOR DR.
Manor Farm
WINSTON RD.
THE CLOSE
FALKLANDS CL.
HIMLEY LANE
BROOKLANDS
Swindon Bridge
REYNOLDS CL.
HINKSFORD GDS.
HINKSFORD LANE
Pav.
Cricket Ground
Swindon Rough
Hollow Mill Farm
Hinksford Bridge
Hinksford Farm House
Hinksford House
Hinksford Farm
HINKSFORD PARK RESIDENTIAL MOBILE HOMES
Hinksford
Kingswinford
DY6
SWINDON ROAD
STAFFORDSHIRE & WORCESTERSHIRE CANAL
Greensforge Rough
163
Wall Heath
ENVILLE RD.
CORNFIELD CL.
WAINWRIGHT CL.
FLAT ROAD
MILE
Pavilion
Newhouse Covert
MORFE LANE
Morfe Hall Farm
163
Church Gorse
Sneyd's Brook
MORFE HALL LANE
HOO LANE
LANE
MILL LANE
Enville Cottage
CHESTER ROAD
Blundies
BLUNDIES LANE
BROWN'S LAKE
BROOKSIDE
Blundies Farm
Whitfield
Enville Court
Church Cottage
ENVILLE
THE CLOSE
Stourbridge
DY7
A458
BRIDGNORTH RD.
Elm House
War Meml.
Crown Covert
Enville Common
THE MILLION
Batch Pool
The Moors
Garden Covert
Pav.
Sports Field
COTE LANE
Oaktree Covert
The Rockery
Leigh House Farm
Enville Hall
Haha Pool
THE AVENUE
KINVER
A458
The Walls
Jordan's Pool
Walls Cottage
Essex Wood
ASH WALK
HORNBEAM
Temple Pool
Millbrook
148
Brook
Lady Dorothy's Cottage
Home Farm
SERPENTINE ROAD
Round Hill
WALK
F
G
H
J
K
1
2
3
4
5
6
7
385
86
87
91
290
87
286
84
82
383

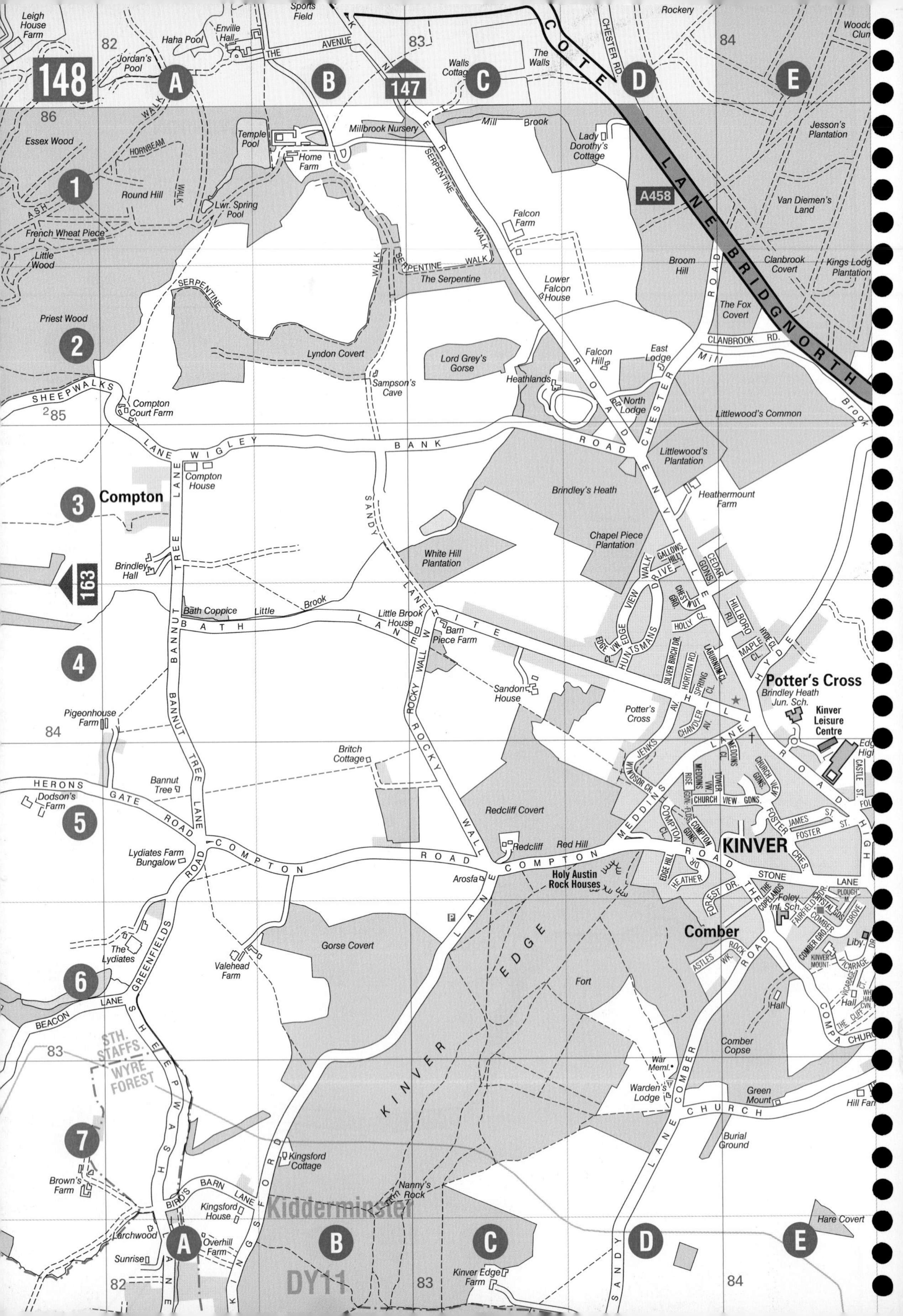
Leigh House Farm
Haha Pool
Enville Hall
Sports Field
Jordan's Pool
THE AVENUE
Walls Cottage
The Walls
Rockery
Essex Wood
HORNBEAM
Round Hill
Temple Pool
Home Farm
Millbrook Nursery
Mill Brook
Lady Dorothy's Cottage
Jesson's Plantation
A458
Van Diemen's Land
Lwr. Spring Pool
French Wheat Piece
Little Wood
Falcon Farm
SERPENTINE WALK
The Serpentine
Lower Falcon House
Broom Hill
Clanbrook Covert
Kings Lodge Plantation
The Fox Covert
Priest Wood
Lyndon Covert
Lord Grey's Gorse
Falcon Hill
East Lodge
CLANBROOK RD.
BRIDGNORTH LANE
COTE
CHESTER RD.
Heathlands
Sampson's Cave
North Lodge
Littlewood's Common
SHEEPWALKS
Compton Court Farm
WIGLEY BANK ROAD
Littlewood's Plantation
Compton House
Compton
Brindley's Heath
Heathermount Farm
Chapel Piece Plantation
White Hill Plantation
Brindley Hall
163
Bath Coppice
Little Brook
Little Brook House
BATH LANE
Barn Piece Farm
WHITE HILL
Potter's Cross
Brindley Heath Jun. Sch.
Kinver Leisure Centre
Sandon House
Pigeonhouse Farm
Britch Cottage
Bannut Tree
BANNUT TREE LANE
ROCKY WALL
HERONS GATE ROAD
Dodson's Farm
Redcliff Covert
Redcliff
Red Hill
COMPTON ROAD
KINVER
Lydiates Farm Bungalow
Arosfa
Holy Austin Rock Houses
STONE LANE
Comber
Foley Inf. Sch.
Gorse Covert
The Lydiates
Valehead Farm
KINVER EDGE
Fort
GREENFIELDS
BEACON LANE
STH. STAFFS.
WYRE FOREST
Comber Copse
War Meml.
Warden's Lodge
Green Mount
CHURCH
Hill Farm
Burial Ground
Kingsford Cottage
Brown's Farm
BIRD'S BARN LANE
Kingsford House
Nanny's Rock
Kidderminster
Larchwood
Overhill Farm
Sunrise
Kinver Edge Farm
Hare Covert
DY11
SANDY LANE
COMBER LANE
KINGSFORD LANE
HIGH STREET

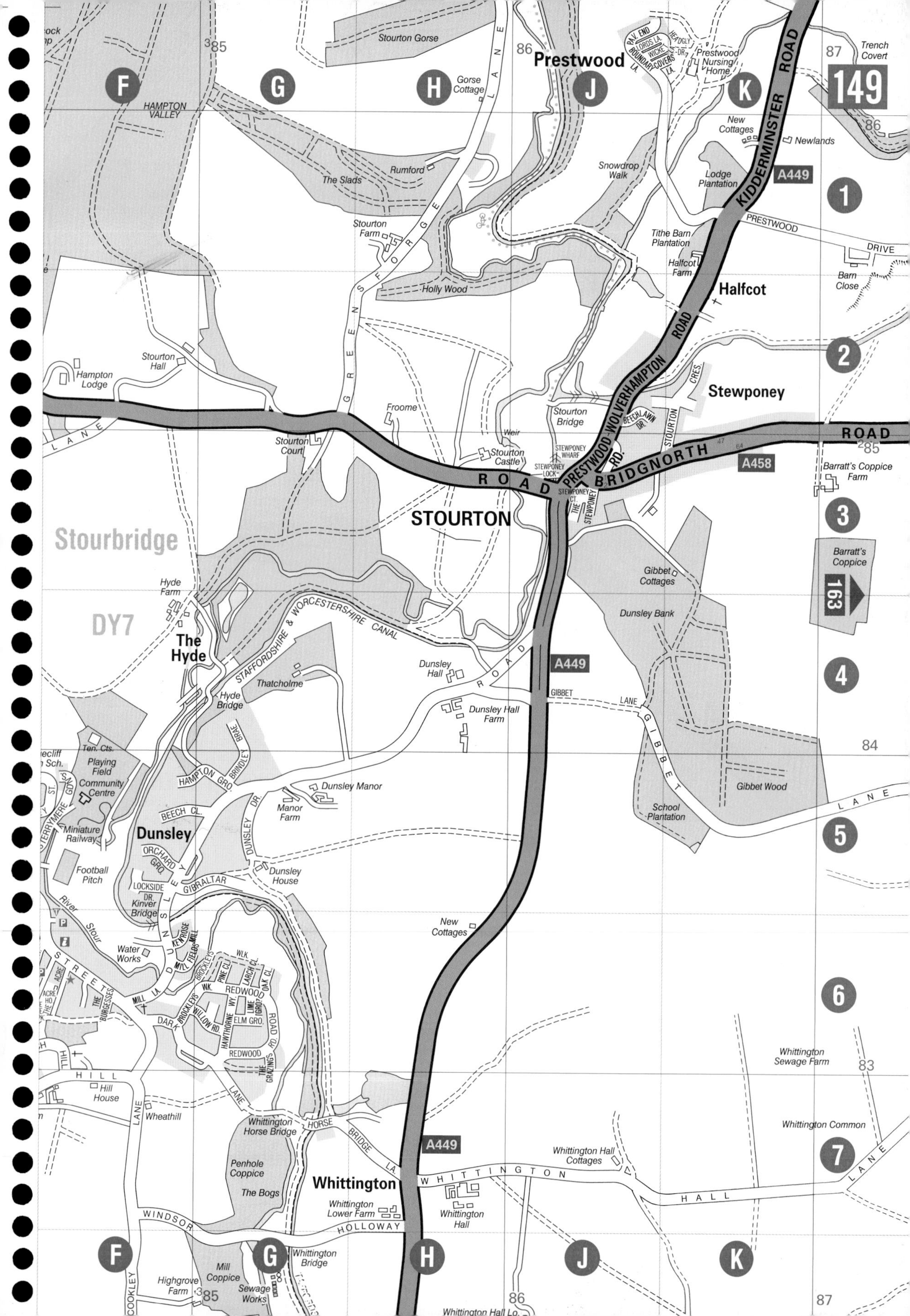

F **G** **H** **J** **K**

Stourton Gorse

Prestwood

PRV. END
CROS LA
NICKL
BOUNDARY COVERS
HEA
DGY
LA
Prestwood Nursing Home

New Cottages

Newlands

Trench Covert

87

86

Gorse Cottage

Snowdrop Walk

Lodge Plantation

KIDDERMINSTER ROAD

A449

PRESTWOOD

DRIVE

1

Rumford

The Slads

Tithe Barn Plantation

Halfcot Farm

Barn Close

Stourton Farm

Holly Wood

Halfcot

2

Hampton Lodge

Stourton Hall

HAMPTON VALLEY

385

GREENS FORGE LANE

Froome

Weir

Stourton Court

Stourton Castle

Stourton Bridge

STEWPONEY WHARF
STEWPONEY LOCK

THE STEWPONEY

PRESTWOOD-WOLVERHAMPTON ROAD

BEECHLAWN DR.

STOURTON RD.

CRES.

Stewponey

ROAD

A458

BRIDGNORTH

85

Barratt's Coppice Farm

3

STOURTON

Gibbet Cottages

Barratt's Coppice

163

Stourbridge

DY7

Hyde Farm

The Hyde

Hyde Bridge

Thatcholme

STAFFORDSHIRE & WORCESTERSHIRE CANAL

Dunsley Hall

Dunsley Hall Farm

GIBBET

ROAD

A449

GIBBET LANE

Dunsley Bank

School Plantation

Gibbet Wood

84

LANE

4

5

BRINDLEY GRO.

HAMPTON GRO.

Ten. Cts.

Playing Field Community Centre

Dunsley Manor

Manor Farm

Dunsley House

DUNSLEY DR.

New Cottages

Miniature Railway

Football Pitch

River Stour

Dunsley

ORCHARD GRO.

LOCKSIDE DR.

GIBRALTAR

BEECH CL.

Kinver Bridge

Water Works

KEY RISE

PINE CL.

ARCH CL.

OAK CL.

REDWOOD

HAWTHORNE WY.

LIME GRO.

ELM GRO.

WILLOW RD.

REDWOOD

THE GRKLINGS

A449

6

Whittington Sewage Farm

83

HILL

HILL LANE

Hill House

Wheathill

Whittington Horse Bridge

HORSE BRIDGE LA.

Penhole Coppice

Whittington

The Bogs

WINDSOR

Whittington Lower Farm

HOLLOWAY

Whittington Hall

A449

WHITTINGTON

Whittington Hall Cottages

Whittington Common

HALL LANE

7

Mill Coppice

Highgrove Farm

Sewage Works

Whittington Bridge

F **G** **H** **J** **K**

COOKLEY

385

86

87

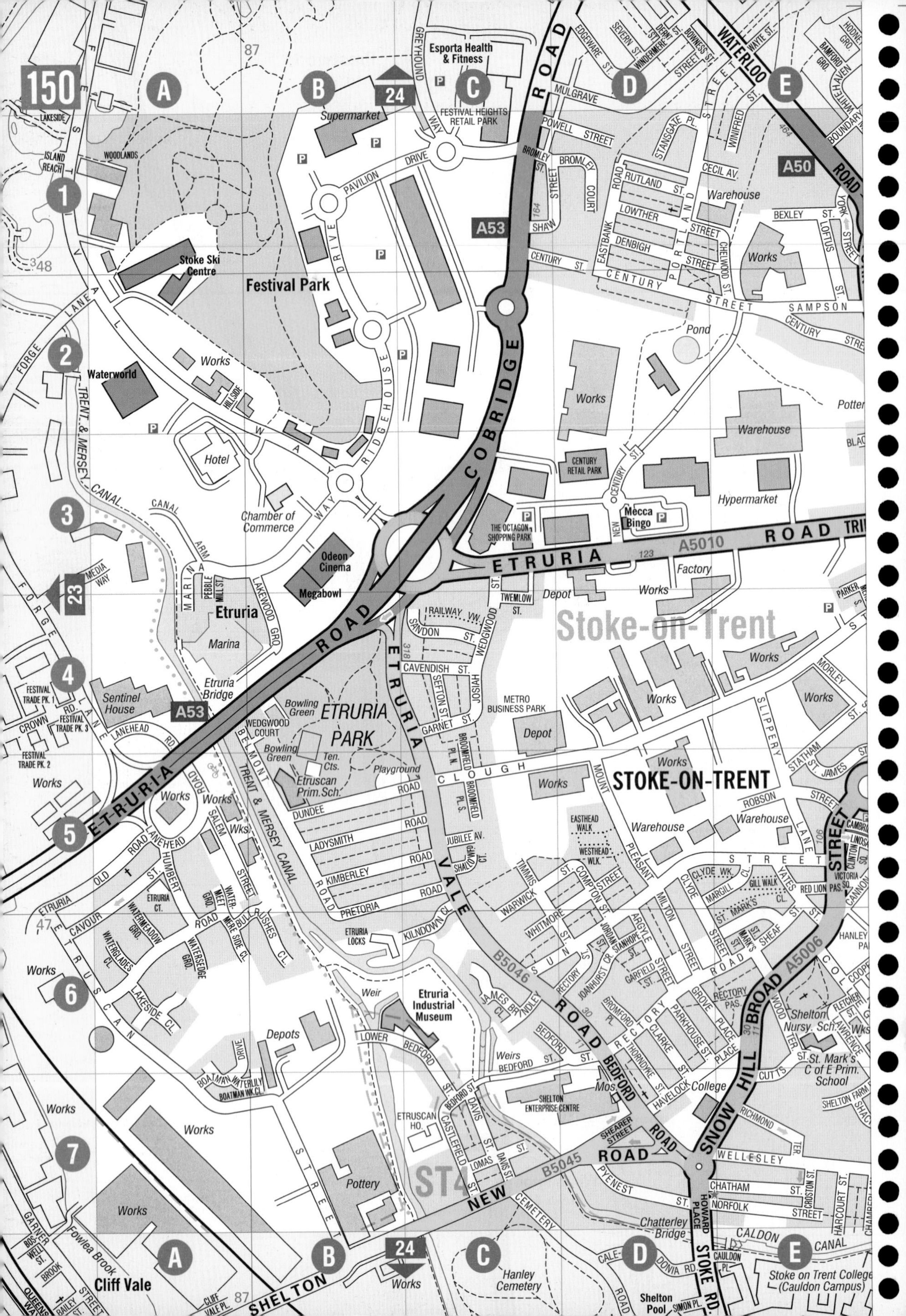
A
B
C
D
E
1
2
3
4
5
6
7
24
23
Esporta Health & Fitness
Festival Heights Retail Park
Supermarket
Festival Park
Stoke Ski Centre
Waterworld
Works
Hotel
Chamber of Commerce
Odeon Cinema
Megabowl
Etruria
Marina
Etruria Bridge
Sentinel House
Festival Trade Pk. 1
Festival Trade Pk. 2
Festival Trade Pk. 3
Etruria Park
Bowling Green
Ten. Cts.
Playground
Etruscan Prim.Sch.
Wedgwood Court
The Octagon Shopping Park
Century Retail Park
Mecca Bingo
Hypermarket
Warehouse
Factory
Depot
Pond
Stoke-on-Trent
STOKE-ON-TRENT
Metro Business Park
Etruria Locks
Weir
Etruria Industrial Museum
Depots
Weirs
Shelton Enterprise Centre
Etruscan Ho.
Pottery
ST4
College
Shelton Nursy. Sch.
St. Mark's C of E Prim. School
Chatterley Bridge
Caldon Canal
Hanley Cemetery
Stoke on Trent College (Cauldon Campus)
Shelton Pool
Cliff Vale
Fowlea Brook
Trent & Mersey Canal
A53
A50
A5010
A5006
B5046
B5045
Cobridge Road
Etruria Road
Etruria Vale Road
Waterloo Road
Snow Hill
Broad Street
Stoke Rd.
Shelton New Road
Bedford Road
Forge Lane
Festival Way
Ridgehouse Drive
Pavilion Drive
Century Street
Sampson Street
Clough Street
Mount Pleasant
Lakeside
Island Reach
Woodlands
Lakewood Gro.
Marina Way
Media Way
Lanehead Rd.
Crown

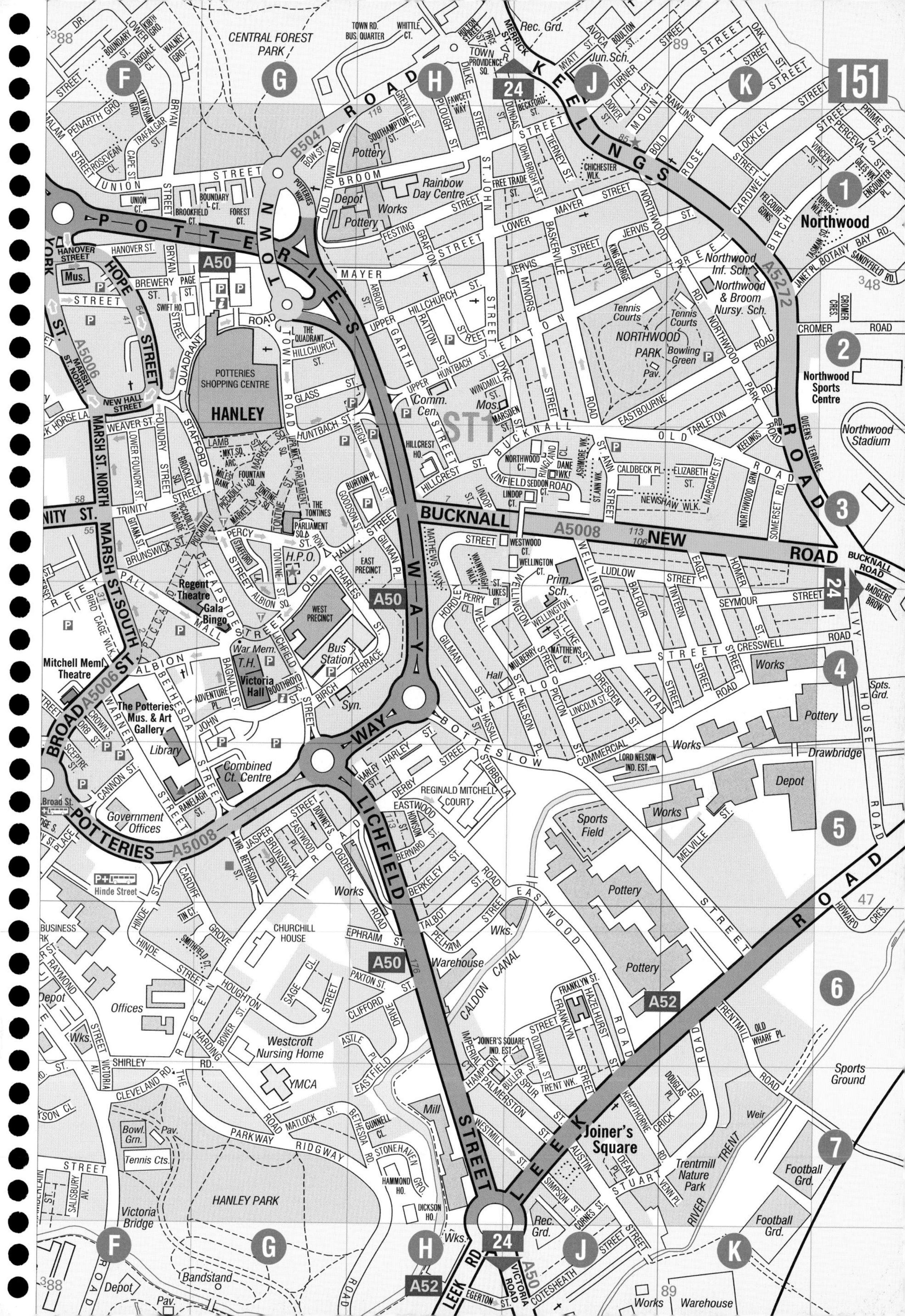

CENTRAL FOREST PARK
TOWN RD. BUS. QUARTER
Rec. Grd.
Jun. Sch.
Northwood
Northwood Inf. Sch.
Northwood & Broom Nursy. Sch.
NORTHWOOD PARK
Tennis Courts
Bowling Green
Pav.
Northwood Sports Centre
Northwood Stadium
Rainbow Day Centre
Depot
Pottery
Works
POTTERIES WAY
A50
A5272
A5008
A5006
A52
B5047
24
Mus.
POTTERIES SHOPPING CENTRE
HANLEY
ST1
Comm. Cen.
Mos.
Prim. Sch.
Hall
Regent Theatre
Gala Bingo
H.P.O.
EAST PRECINCT
WEST PRECINCT
Bus Station
Syn.
War Mem.
T.H.
Victoria Hall
Mitchell Meml. Theatre
The Potteries Mus. & Art Gallery
Library
Combined Ct. Centre
Government Offices
Hinde Street
Sports Field
Lord Nelson Ind. Est.
Drawbridge
Spts. Grd.
Warehouse
Wks.
Caldon Canal
Churchill House
Offices
Westcroft Nursing Home
YMCA
Mill
Joiner's Square
Joiner's Square Ind. Est.
Trentmill Nature Park
River Trent
Weir
Sports Ground
Football Grd.
Hanley Park
Bowl. Grn.
Tennis Cts.
Victoria Bridge
Bandstand
Hammond Ho.
Dickson Ho.
Rec. Grd.
BUCKNALL NEW ROAD
LICHFIELD STREET
LEEK ROAD
POTTERIES WAY
MARSH ST. NORTH
MARSH ST. SOUTH
BROAD ST.
QUEENS ROAD
KEELINGS ROAD
UNION STREET
TOWN ROAD
UPPER HUNTBACH ST.

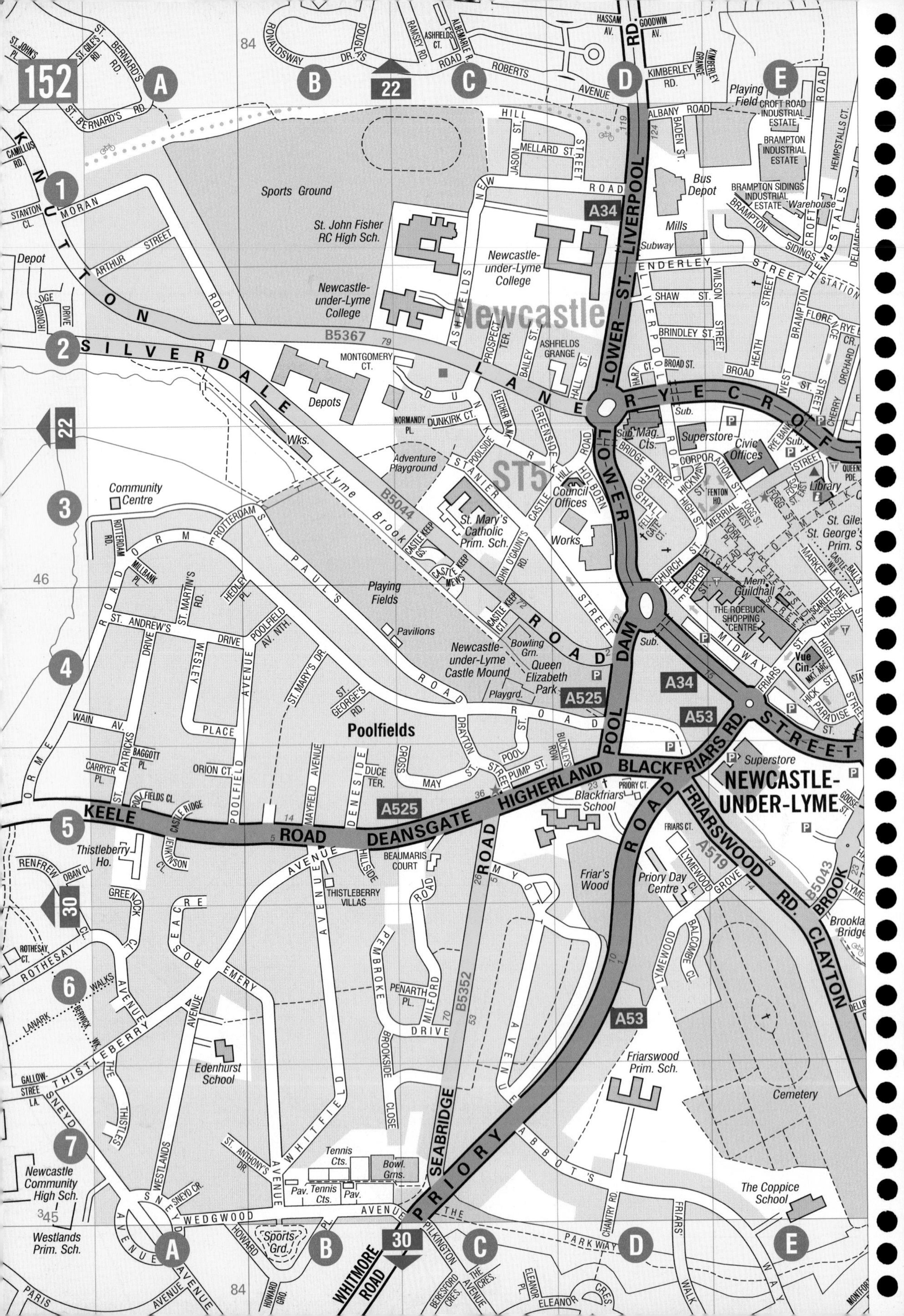

152
84
A
B
C
D
E
22
1
2
3
4
5
6
7
46
345
30
ST. JOHN'S PL.
ST. GILE'S RD.
ST. BERNARD'S RD.
RONALDSWAY
DOUGLAS DR.
RAMSEY RD.
ASHFIELDS CT.
ALBEMARLE ROAD
ROBERTS AVENUE
HASSAM AV.
GOODWIN AV.
KIMBERLEY RD.
KIMBERLEY GRANGE
Playing Field
CROFT ROAD INDUSTRIAL ESTATE
BRAMPTON INDUSTRIAL ESTATE
BRAMPTON SIDINGS INDUSTRIAL ESTATE
Warehouse
HEMPSTALLS CT.
ALBANY ROAD
BADEN ST.
Bus Depot
Mills
Subway
HILL STREET
JASON ST.
MELLARD ST.
CAMILLUS RD.
KNUTTON
MORAN
STANTON CL.
ARTHUR STREET
ROAD
Depot
IRONBRIDGE
DRIVE
Sports Ground
St. John Fisher RC High Sch.
Newcastle-under-Lyme College
Newcastle
NEW ROAD
ASHFIELDS
PROSPECT TER.
BAILEY ST.
ASHFIELDS GRANGE
HALL ST.
A34
LOWER ST. LIVERPOOL RD.
ENDERLEY STREET
SHAW ST.
WILSON STREET
BRINDLEY ST.
LIVERPOOL
HART CT.
BROAD ST.
STATION
HEATH STREET
FLORENCE
RYE BANK CR.
ORCHARD
BRAMPTON
CROFT
HEMPSTALLS
DELAMERE
SIDINGS
BROAD
WEST ST.
STREET
CHERRY
SILVERDALE
B5367
LANE
RYECROFT
MONTGOMERY CT.
Depots
DUNKIRK
NORMANDY PL.
DUNKIRK CT.
FLETCHER BANK
GREENSIDE
Wks.
Adventure Playground
POOLSIDE
STANIER
ST5
CASTLE HILL ROAD
HOLBORN
Council Offices
LOWER
Sub.
Mag. Cts.
BRIDGE STREET
Superstore
Civic Offices
RYE BANK
CORPORATION ST.
HICKMAN ST.
FENTON HO.
FOGG ST.
Library
QUEENS PDE.
IRON MARKET
Community Centre
Lyme Brook
B5044
St. Mary's Catholic Prim. Sch.
CASTLE KEEP GS.
CASTLE KEEP MEWS
JOHN O'GAUNT'S RD.
Works
FELL GATE CT.
FELL ST.
MERRIAL ST.
YORK PL.
LAD LANE
CHEAPSIDE
MARKET LANE
CASTLE WLK.
BALL'S YD.
St. Giles & St. George's Prim. S
ROTTERDAM RD.
ROTTERDAM
ORME
MILLBANK PL.
ST. PAUL'S
HEDLEY PL.
ST. MARTIN'S RD.
Playing Fields
CHURCH ST.
HIGH ST.
PEPPER ST.
Mem.
Guildhall
THE ROEBUCK SHOPPING CENTRE
SCARLETT ST.
HASSELL
ST. ANDREW'S DRIVE
POOLFIELD AV. NTH.
Pavilions
CASTLE KEEP CT.
ROAD
STREET
DAM
MIDWAY
WESLEY
AVENUE
Newcastle-under-Lyme Castle Mound
Bowling Grn.
Queen Elizabeth Park
Vue Cin.
MKT. ARC.
HICK ST.
HIGH STREET
FRIARS ST.
PARADISE ST.
ST. MARY'S DR.
ST. GEORGE'S RD.
Playgrd.
A525
A34
A53
WAIN AV.
PLACE
Poolfields
DRAYTON
POOL ST.
BUCKLEY'S ROW
POOL
BLACKFRIARS RD.
STREET
PATRICKS
BAGGOTT PL.
CARRYER PL.
ORION CT.
POOLFIELD
CROSS MAY ST.
MAYFIELD AVENUE
DENESIDE
DUCE TER.
PUMP ST.
PRIORY CT.
Blackfriars School
Superstore
NEWCASTLE-UNDER-LYME
GOOSE
POOL FIELDS CL.
CASTLE RIDGE
KEELE ROAD
DEANSGATE
HIGHERLAND
FRIARSWOOD RD.
FRIARS CT.
Thistleberry Ho.
JENKINSON CL.
AVENUE
BEAUMARIS COURT
HILLSIDE
THISTLEBERRY VILLAS
ROAD
MYOTT AVENUE
Friar's Wood
A519
Priory Day Centre
LYMEWOOD CL.
GROVE
B5043
BROOK
LYME
RENFREW
OBAN CL.
GREENOCK CL.
ROSEACRE
Brookla Bridge
CLAYTON
ROTHESAY CT.
ROTHESAY
EMERY
PEMBROKE
PENARTH PL.
MILFORD
DRIVE
B5352
LYMEWOOD
BALCOMBE CL.
LANARK
WALKS
BERWICK
WK.
A53
DELLA
THISTLEBERRY
THE THISTLES
Edenhurst School
BROOKSIDE CLOSE
Friarswood Prim. Sch.
Cemetery
GALLOW-STREE LA.
SNEYD
WESTLANDS
WHITFIELD
SEABRIDGE
PRIORY
ABBOT'S
Newcastle Community High Sch.
ST. ANTHONY'S DR.
Tennis Cts.
Bowl. Grns.
Pav.
The Coppice School
SNEYD CR.
WEDGWOOD
AVENUE
THE
CHANTRY RD.
FRIARS'
Westlands Prim. Sch.
HOWARD PL.
Sports Grd.
PILKINGTON
PARKWAY
WAY
PARIS
AVENUE
HOWARD GRO.
WHITMORE ROAD
BERESFORD CRES.
THE AVENUE
THE CRES.
ELEANOR PL.
ELEANOR CRES.
WALK
MONTFORD

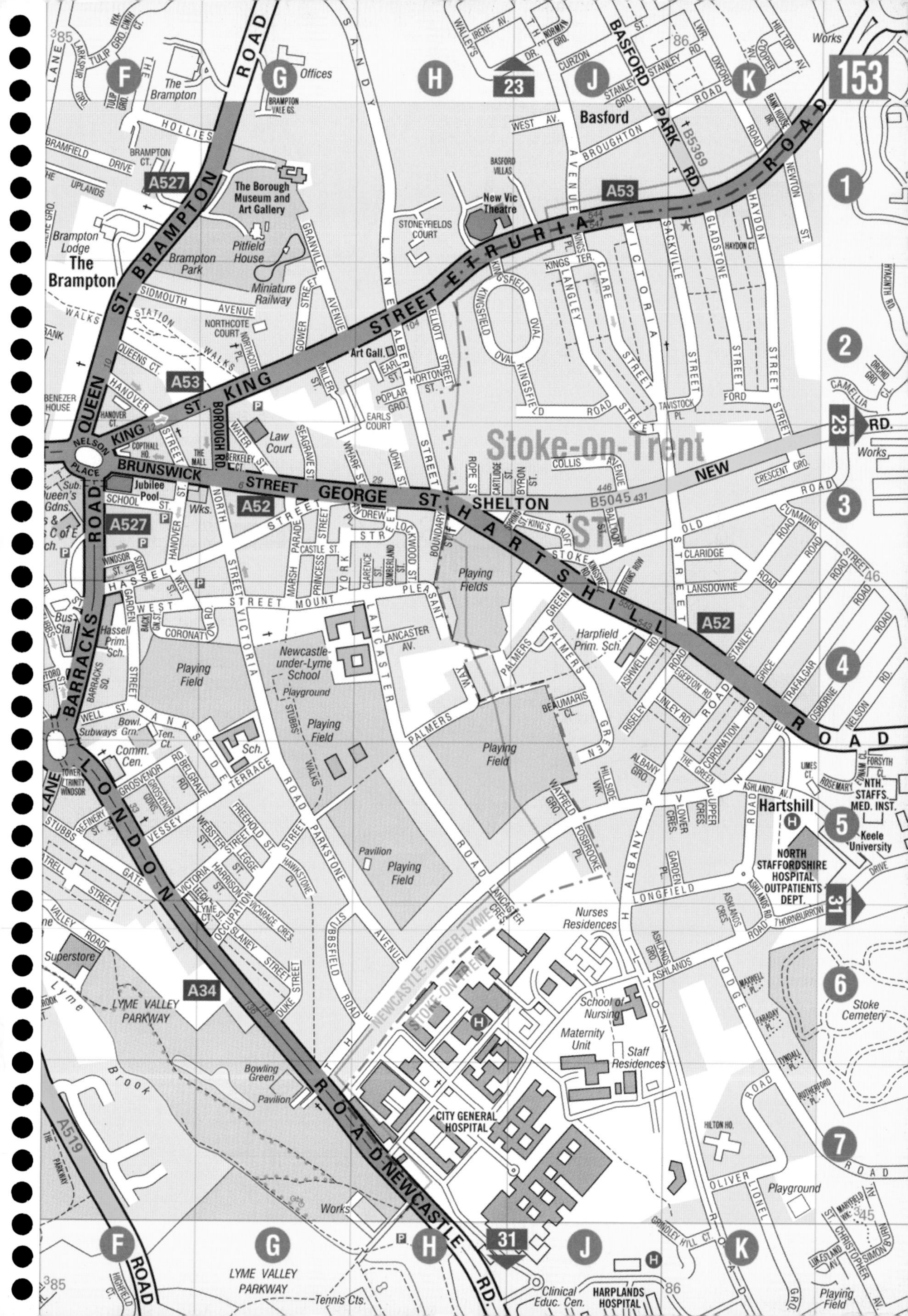
Stoke-on-Trent
Basford
Shelton
Hartshill
The Brampton
ST4
The Borough Museum and Art Gallery
Pitfield House
Brampton Park
Miniature Railway
New Vic Theatre
Art Gall.
Law Court
Jubilee Pool
Newcastle-under-Lyme School
Playing Fields
Playing Field
Harpfield Prim. Sch.
Hassell Prim. Sch.
Comm. Cen.
Bus Sta.
NORTH STAFFORDSHIRE HOSPITAL OUTPATIENTS DEPT.
NTH. STAFFS. MED. INST.
Keele University
Nurses Residences
School of Nursing
Maternity Unit
Staff Residences
CITY GENERAL HOSPITAL
HARPLANDS HOSPITAL
Clinical Educ. Cen.
Stoke Cemetery
LYME VALLEY PARKWAY
Superstore
Bowling Green
Pavilion
Works
Offices
Tennis Cts.
Playground
NEWCASTLE-UNDER-LYME
STOKE-ON-TRENT
ETRURIA ROAD
KING STREET
QUEEN ST.
BRAMPTON ROAD
BRUNSWICK ST.
GEORGE ST.
HARTSHILL ROAD
LONDON ROAD
NEWCASTLE RD.
BARRACKS ROAD
BASFORD PARK RD.
NEW ROAD
A527
A53
A52
A34
A519
B5045
B5369
23
31
F
G
H
J
K
1
2
3
4
5
6
7
385
86
345

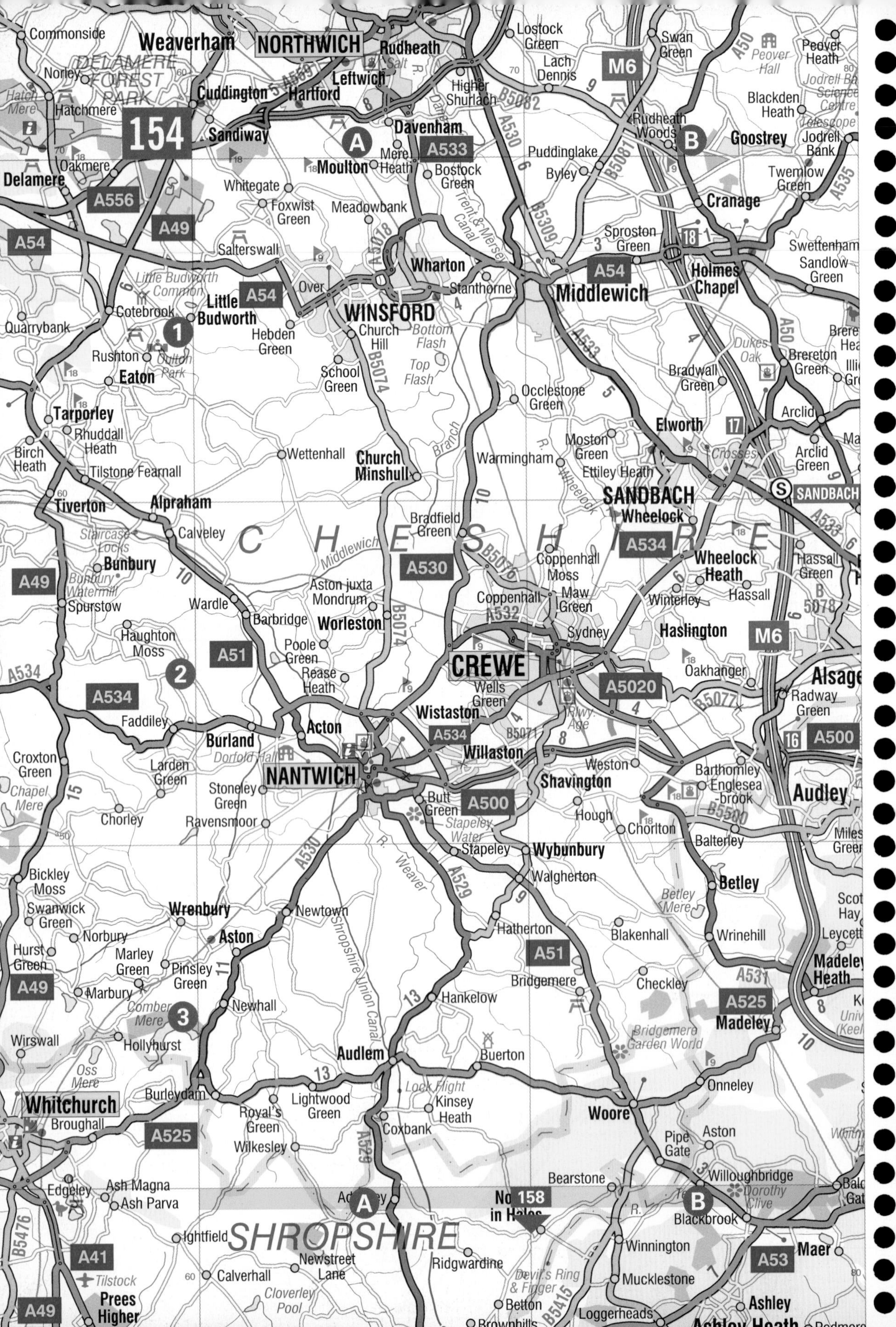

154
Commonside
Weaverham
NORTHWICH
Rudheath
Lostock Green
Swan Green
Peover Heath
Peover Hall
DELAMERE FOREST PARK
Norley
Leftwich
Lach Dennis
M6
Jodrell Bank Science Centre
Hatch Mere
Hatchmere
Cuddington
Hartford
Higher Shurlach
B5082
Blackden Heath
Sandiway
Davenham
Rudheath Woods
Goostrey
Jodrell Bank
Delamere
Oakmere
A
B
A533
Puddinglake
Moulton
Mere Heath
Bostock Green
Byley
Twemlow Green
A556
Whitegate
Foxwist Green
Meadowbank
Cranage
A49
A54
Trent & Mersey Canal
Sproston Green
Swettenham
Saltersweall
Wharton
Holmes Chapel
Sandlow Green
Little Budworth Common
Over
Stanthorne
Middlewich
Little Budworth
WINSFORD
Cotebrook
Church Hill
Quarrybank
Hebden Green
Bottom Flash
Rushton
Oulton Park
Top Flash
Dukes Oak
Brereton Green
Eaton
School Green
Bradwall Green
Occlestone Green
Tarporley
Arclid
Rhuddall Heath
Elworth
Birch Heath
Wettenhall
Church Minshull
Moston Green
Arclid Green
Warmingham
Tilstone Fearnall
Ettiley Heath
Crosses
SANDBACH
Tiverton
Alpraham
Wheelock
Bradfield Green
Staircase Locks
Calveley
C H E S H I R E
Bunbury
A534
Wheelock Heath
Hassall Green
Bunbury Watermill
Middlewich Branch
A530
Coppenhall Moss
Hassall
Spurstow
Aston juxta Mondrum
Coppenhall
Maw Green
Winterley
Wardle
Barbridge
Worleston
Haslington
Haughton Moss
Poole Green
Sydney
A51
CREWE
Oakhanger
Alsager
Rease Heath
Wells Green
A5020
Radway Green
Faddiley
Acton
Wistaston
Rlwy. Age
Croxton Green
Burland
Dorfold Hall
Willaston
A500
Larden Green
NANTWICH
Weston
Barthomley
Chapel Mere
Stoneley Green
Shavington
Englesea-brook
Audley
Chorley
Butt Green
Stapeley Water
Hough
Ravensmoor
Chorlton
Balterley
Miles Green
Stapeley
Wybunbury
Bickley Moss
Walgherton
Betley
Swanwick Green
Wrenbury
Newtown
Betley Mere
Scot Hay
Norbury
Hatherton
Blakenhall
Wrinehill
Leycett
Hurst Green
Aston
Shropshire Union Canal
Marley Green
Pinsley Green
Madeley Heath
Marbury
Bridgemere
Checkley
A525
Comber Mere
Newhall
Hankelow
Madeley
Wirswall
Hollyhurst
Bridgemere Garden World
Audlem
Buerton
Oss Mere
Lock Flight
Onneley
Whitchurch
Burleydam
Lightwood Green
Kinsey Heath
Woore
Broughall
Royal's Green
Coxbank
Pipe Gate
Aston
Wilkesley
Bearstone
Willoughbridge
Dorothy Clive
Edgeley
Ash Magna
Ash Parva
158
Blackbrook
SHROPSHIRE
Ightfield
Winnington
Newstreet Lane
Ridgwardine
Maer
A41
A53
Tilstock
Calverhall
Devil's Ring & Finger
Mucklestone
Cloverley Pool
Betton
Ashley
Prees Higher
Brownhills
Loggerheads
B5415
B5476
A529
B5074
B5070
A5018
B5309
B5081
A50
A535
B5071
B5077
B5078
B5500
A531
A532

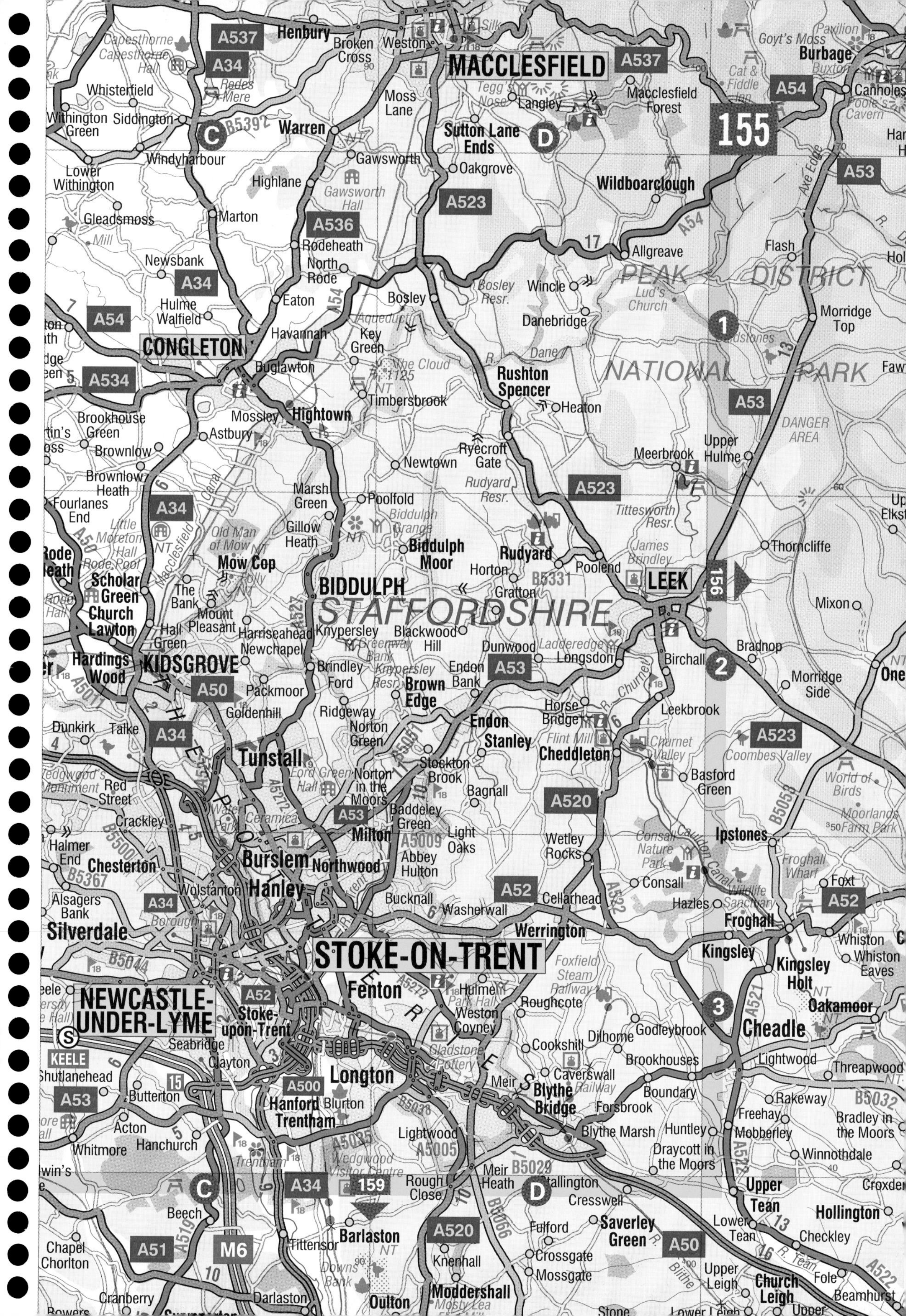
155
MACCLESFIELD
Henbury
Broken Cross
Weston
A537
A34
Capesthorne Hall
Redes Mere
Whisterfield
Withington Green
Siddington
B5392
C
Warren
Moss Lane
Sutton Lane Ends
D
Tegg's Nose
Langley
Macclesfield Forest
Cat & Fiddle Inn
A54
Goyt's Moss
Pavilion
Burbage
Buxton
Canholes
Poole's Cavern
Windyharbour
Lower Withington
Gawsworth
Gawsworth Hall
Highlane
Oakgrove
A523
Wildboarclough
A53
Axe Edge
Marton
Gleadsmoss
A536
Rodeheath
North Rode
Allgreave
Flash
PEAK DISTRICT
NATIONAL PARK
Newsbank
Eaton
Bosley
Bosley Resr.
Wincle
Lud's Church
Hulme Walfield
Danebridge
Morridge Top
1
CONGLETON
Havannah
Key Green
Aqueduct
A534
Buglawton
The Cloud
Timbersbrook
Rushton Spencer
Heaton
Mossley
Hightown
Brookhouse Green
Astbury
Brownlow
Brownlow Heath
Newtown
Ryecroft Gate
Meerbrook
Upper Hulme
DANGER AREA
Marsh Green
Poolfold
Rudyard Resr.
Tittesworth Resr.
Fourlanes End
Little Moreton Hall
Old Man of Mow
Macclesfield Canal
Gillow Heath
Biddulph Grange
Biddulph Moor
Rudyard
Horton
Poolend
James Brindley
LEEK
156
Thorncliffe
Rode Heath
Rode Pool
Scholar Green
Mow Cop
The Bank
Mount Pleasant
BIDDULPH
STAFFORDSHIRE
Gratton
B5331
Mixon
Church Lawton
Hall Green
Harriseahead
Newchapel
Knypersley
Blackwood Hill
Dunwood
Ladderedge
Longsdon
Birchall
Bradnop
2
Hardings Wood
KIDSGROVE
Brindley Ford
Knypersley Resr.
Endon Bank
Morridge Side
A50
Packmoor
Brown Edge
Horse Bridge
Leekbrook
Goldenhill
Ridgeway
Norton Green
Endon
Stanley
Flint Mill
Cheddleton
Churnet Valley
A523
Coombes Valley
Dunkirk
Talke
Tunstall
Stockton Brook
Basford Green
World of Birds
Red Street
Ford Green Hall
Norton in the Moors
Bagnall
A520
Moorlands Farm Park
Crackley
Baddeley Green
Light Oaks
Wetley Rocks
Ipstones
Halmer End
Chesterton
Burslem
Milton
Northwood
A5009
Abbey Hulton
Consall Nature Park
Caldon Canal
Froghall Wharf
B5367
Wolstanton
Hanley
Consall
Foxt
Alsagers Bank
A34
A52
Bucknall
Washerwall
Cellarhead
Hazles
Silverdale
Werrington
Froghall
Whiston
Kingsley
B5044
STOKE-ON-TRENT
Foxfield Steam Railway
Kingsley Holt
Whiston Eaves
NEWCASTLE-UNDER-LYME
Fenton
Hulme
Park Hall
Weston Coyney
Roughcote
Oakamoor
3
Cheadle
Stoke-upon-Trent
Seabridge
Clayton
Cookshill
Dilhorne
Godleybrook
KEELE
Gladstone Pottery
Caverswall
Brookhouses
Lightwood
Threapwood
Shutlanehead
Longton
Meir
Blythe Bridge
Boundary
Butterton
A500
Hanford
Blurton
Trentham
Forsbrook
Rakeway
B5032
A53
Acton
Lightwood
Blythe Marsh
Huntley
Freehay
Mobberley
Bradley in the Moors
Whitmore
Hanchurch
A5035
A5005
Draycott in the Moors
Winnothdale
Wedgwood Visitor Centre
Rough Close
Meir Heath
B5029
Stallington
Cresswell
Upper Tean
Croxden
C
A34
159
D
Beech
Saverley Green
Hollington
Lower Tean
Chapel Chorlton
A51
M6
Tittensor
Barlaston
A520
Fulford
A50
Checkley
B5066
Crossgate
Mossgate
Knenhall
Downs Bank
Upper Leigh
Church Leigh
Fole
Beamhurst
Cranberry
Darlaston
Oulton
Moddershall
A522

156
BUXTON
Fairfield
Burbage
Macclesfield
Wildboarclough
Allgreave
Flash
Hollinsclough
Earl Sterndale
Monyash
Glutton Bridge
Longnor
Crowdecote
Morridge Top
Fawfieldhead
Newtown
Pilsbury
Sheen
PEAK DISTRICT
NATIONAL PARK
STAFFORDSHIRE
Hartington
Upper Hulme
Meerbrook
Tittesworth Resr.
Upper Elkstone
Warslow
Hulme End
Thorncliffe
LEEK
Poolend
Longsdon
Mixon
Butterton
Wetton
Alstonefield
Onecote
Grindon
Bradnop
Morridge Side
Leekbrook
Cheddleton
Basford Green
Winkhill
Waterfall
Waterhouses
Ipstones
Cauldon
Cauldon Lowe
Calton
Ilam
Thorpe
Blore
Swinscoe
Mapleton
Froghall
Kingsley
Kingsley Holt
Oakamoor
Cheadle
Cotton
Whiston
Stanton
Mayfield
Ramshorn
Alton
Alton Towers
Ellastone
Denstone
Rocester
Stubwood
Great Gate
Hollington
Upper Tean
Checkley
Marston Montgomery
Church Leigh
Blythe Bridge
Tissington
Parwich
Newhaven
Friden
Biggin
Heathcote
Taddington
Chelmorton
Sheldon
Flagg
Little Longstone
Blackwell
Miller's Dale
Harpur Hill
Staden
King Sterndale
Sterndale Moor
Canholes
Clifton
Osmaston
Yeaveley
Cubley Common
Norbury
Roston
Mayfield
Church Mayfield
Wootton
Upper Ellastone
Longshaw
Farley
Threapwood
Rakeway
Boundary
Forsbrook
Cellarhead
Werrington
Consall
Hazles
A537 A54 A53 A515 A6 A523 A520 A52 A522 A521 A50 A515
155
160

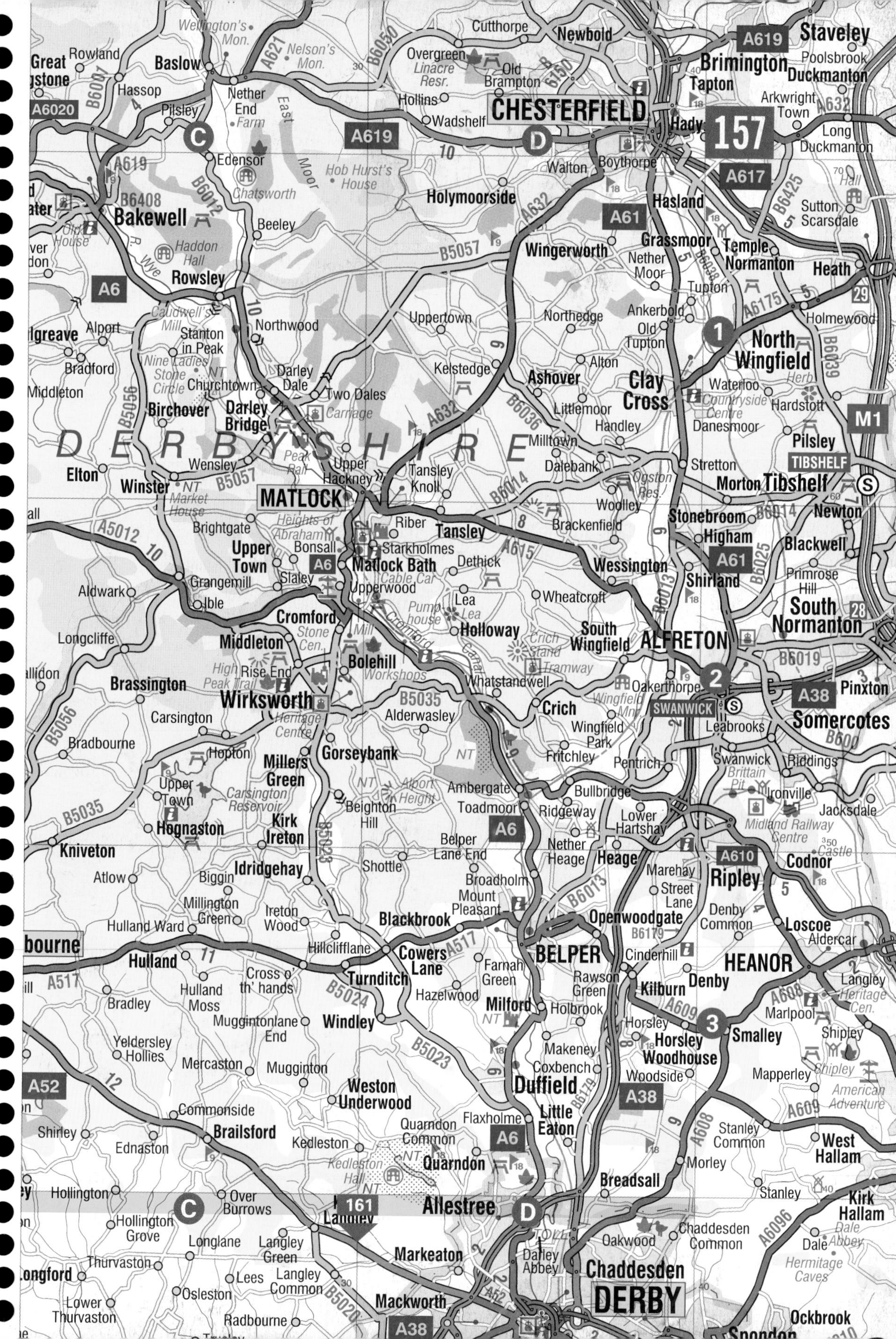
157
CHESTERFIELD
MATLOCK
DERBY
BELPER
HEANOR
ALFRETON
D E R B Y S H I R E
Staveley
Brimington
Tapton
Poolsbrook
Duckmanton
Arkwright Town
Long Duckmanton
Newbold
Cutthorpe
Overgreen
Linacre Resr.
Old Brampton
Hollins
Wadshelf
Hady
Boythorpe
Walton
Hasland
Sutton Scarsdale
Holymoorside
Hob Hurst's House
East Moor
Baslow
Rowland
Great
Hassop
Nether End
Farm
Pilsley
Edensor
Chatsworth
Bakewell
Beeley
Haddon Hall
Rowsley
Wellington's Mon.
Nelson's Mon.
Grassmoor
Nether Moor
Temple Normanton
Heath
Wingerworth
Tupton
Ankerbold
Old Tupton
Holmewood
North Wingfield
Clay Cross
Waterloo
Countryside Centre
Danesmoor
Hardstoft
Pilsley
Tibshelf
TIBSHELF
Morton
Stretton
Newton
Stonebroom
Higham
Blackwell
Shirland
Primrose Hill
South Normanton
Uppertown
Northedge
Kelstedge
Ashover
Alton
Littlemoor
Handley
Milltown
Dalebank
Ogston Res.
Woolley
Brackenfield
Wessington
Wheatcroft
South Wingfield
Crich
Crich Stand
Tramway
Whatstandwell
Oakerthorpe
SWANWICK
Leabrooks
Somercotes
Pinxton
Swanwick
Riddings
Wingfield Mnr
Wingfield Park
Fritchley
Pentrich
Brittain Pit
Ironville
Jacksdale
Midland Railway Centre
Castle
Codnor
Ripley
Marehay
Street Lane
Denby Common
Loscoe
Aldercar
Langley
Heritage Cen.
Northwood
Stanton in Peak
Nine Ladies Stone Circle
Caudwell's Mill
Alport
Bradford
Middleton
Birchover
Churchtown
Darley Dale
Two Dales
Darley Bridge
Carriage
Peak Rail
Wensley
Elton
Winster
Market House
Upper Hackney
Tansley Knoll
Tansley
Riber
Starkholmes
Matlock Bath
Cable Car
Heights of Abraham
Bonsall
Upper Town
Slaley
Brightgate
Grangemill
Ible
Aldwark
Upperwood
Lea
Dethick
Pump house
Holloway
Cromford
Cromford Canal
Stone Cen.
Mill
Middleton
High Peak Trail
Rise End
Bolehill
Workshops
Wirksworth
Heritage Centre
Longcliffe
Brassington
Carsington
Bradbourne
Hopton
Upper Town
Carsington Reservoir
Hognaston
Kniveton
Millers Green
Gorseybank
Alderwasley
Alport Height
Beighton Hill
Kirk Ireton
Ambergate
Toadmoor
Ridgeway
Bullbridge
Lower Hartshay
Nether Heage
Heage
Belper Lane End
Broadholm
Mount Pleasant
Shottle
Idridgehay
Biggin
Atlow
Millington Green
Ireton Wood
Blackbrook
Hulland Ward
Hillcliffelane
Openwoodgate
Cinderhill
Denby
Kilburn
Rawson Green
Holbrook
Cowers Lane
Farnah Green
Hazelwood
Milford
Turnditch
Hulland
Cross o' th' hands
Hulland Moss
Bradley
Windley
Muggintonlane End
Yeldersley Hollies
Mercaston
Mugginton
Horsley
Horsley Woodhouse
Smalley
Marlpool
Shipley
Makeney
Coxbench
Woodside
Duffield
Mapperley
American Adventure
Weston Underwood
Little Eaton
Flaxholme
Quarndon Common
Quarndon
Kedleston
Kedleston Hall
Commonside
Brailsford
Shirley
Ednaston
Stanley Common
West Hallam
Morley
Breadsall
Stanley
Kirk Hallam
Hollington
Over Burrows
Allestree
Hollington Grove
Longlane
Langley Green
Langley Common
Lees
Thurvaston
Longford
Osleston
Lower Thurvaston
Markeaton
Mackworth
Radbourne
Darley Abbey
Oakwood
Chaddesden
Chaddesden Common
Dale
Dale Abbey
Hermitage Caves
Ockbrook
Spondon
A6020
A619
B6001
B6408
B6012
A621
B6050
B6150
A632
A617
B6425
A61
B5057
B6038
A6175
B6039
M1
A6
B5056
A5012
B6036
B6014
A615
B6013
B6025
B600
B6019
A38
B5035
B5023
B6179
A610
A517
B5024
A609
A608
A52
A6096
161
C
D

158
Whitchurch
Audlem
Woore
Market Drayton
Ashley Heath
Shropshire
Hodnet
Prees
Moreton Say
Bletchley
Stoke Heath
Hinstock
Newport
Shawbury
High Ercall
Wellington
Hadley
Telford
Oakengates
Donnington
Shifnal
Dawley
Little Wenlock
Lilleshall
Edgmond
Tibberton
Waters Upton
Crudgington
Cheswardine
Adbaston
High Offley
Woodseaves
Norbury
Moreton
Sheriffhales
A41
A49
A53
A442
A518
A519
A525
A529
A5
M54
A51
A458
B5062
B5063
154
162

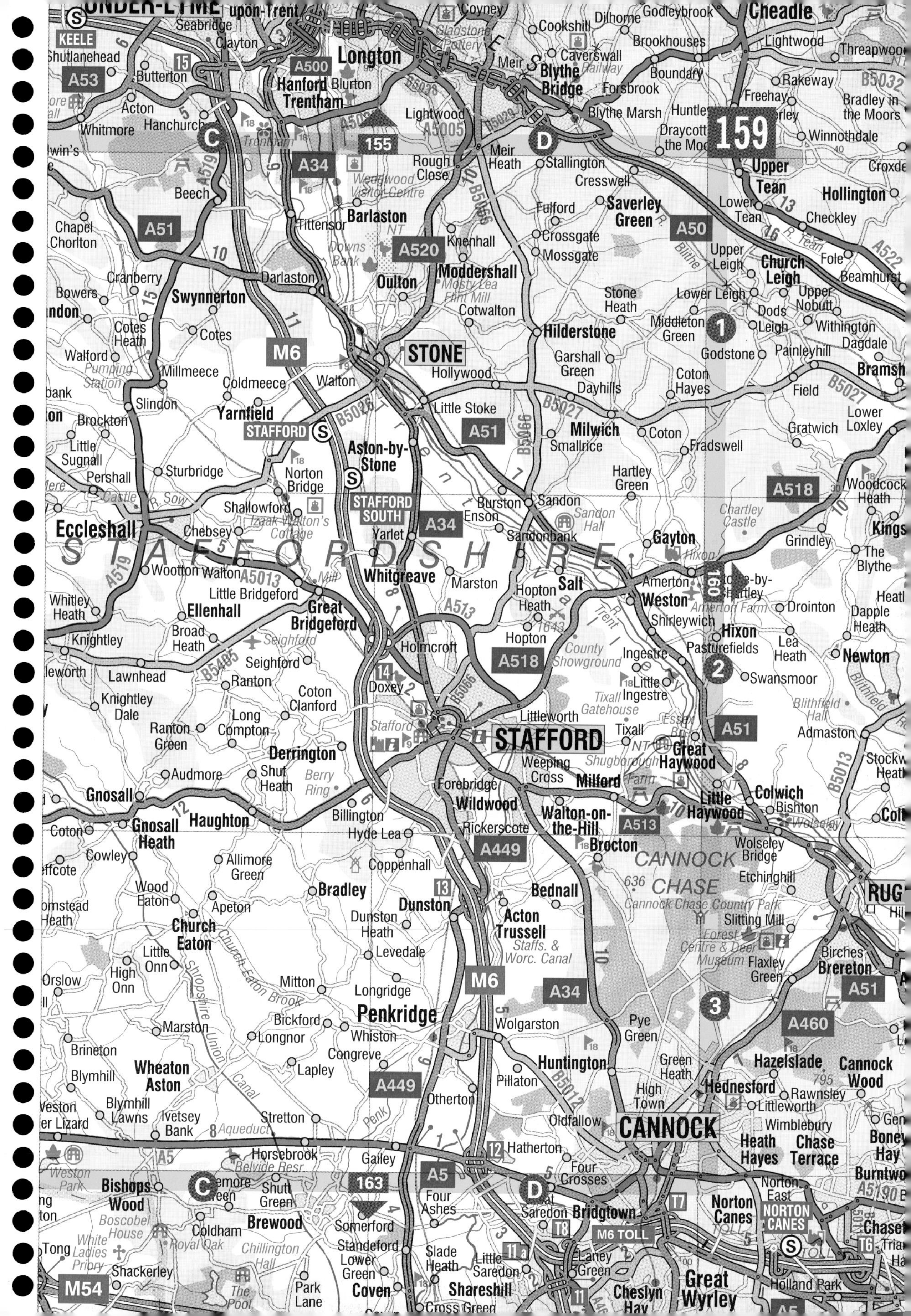
159
155
160
163
KEELE
Seabridge
Clayton
upon-Trent
Coyney
Gladstone Pottery
Cookshill
Dilhorne
Godleybrook
Cheadle
Lightwood
Threapwood
Shutlanehead
Butterton
A53
A500
Longton
Meir
Caverswall
Brookhouses
Blythe Bridge
Hanford
Blurton
Trentham
Boundary
Rakeway
B5032
Acton
Whitmore
Hanchurch
Trentham
Lightwood
A5005
Forsbrook
Blythe Marsh
Huntley
Freehay
Bradley in the Moors
Draycott in the Moors
Winnothdale
Meir Heath
Stallington
Upper Tean
Hollington
Croxden
Rough Close
A34
Wedgwood Visitor Centre
Beech
Cresswell
Lower Tean
Checkley
Chapel Chorlton
A51
Barlaston
Tittensor
Fulford
Saverley Green
A50
Crossgate
Mossgate
Downs Bank
A520
Knenhall
Moddershall
Mosty Lea Flint Mill
Upper Leigh
Church Leigh
Fole
Beamhurst
A522
Cranberry
Darlaston
Oulton
Bowers
Swynnerton
Stone Heath
Lower Leigh
Upper Nobutt
Cotwalton
Dods Leigh
Withington
Cotes Heath
Cotes
Hilderstone
Middleton Green
Dagdale
Walford
Pumping Station
M6
STONE
Godstone
Painleyhill
Bramshall
Millmeece
Coldmeece
Walton
Hollywood
Garshall Green
Coton Hayes
Field
Slindon
Dayhills
B5027
Yarnfield
Little Stoke
Lower Loxley
Brockton
STAFFORD
B5026
Milwich
Smallrice
Coton
Gratwich
Little Sugnall
Aston-by-Stone
A51
B5066
Fradswell
Pershall
Sturbridge
Norton Bridge
Hartley Green
A518
Woodcock Heath
Castle
Shallowford
Burston
Sandon
STAFFORD SOUTH
Izaak Walton's Cottage
Enson
Sandon Hall
Chartley Castle
Eccleshall
Chebsey
A34
Yarlet
Sandonbank
Gayton
Grindley
Kingston
STAFFORDSHIRE
Hixon
The Blythe
A519
Wootton
Walton
A5013
Whitgreave
Marston
Salt
Amerton
Stowe-by-Chartley
Little Bridgeford
Weston
Amerton Farm
Drointon
Heath
Whitley Heath
Ellenhall
Great Bridgeford
A513
Hopton Heath
Shirleywich
Dapple Heath
Broad Heath
Knightley
Seighford
Holmcroft
Hopton
Hixon
Lea Heath
Pasturefields
Newton
County Showground
Ingestre
Lawnhead
Seighford
B5405
A518
Swansmoor
Ranton
Doxey
Little Ingestre
Blithfield
Knightley Dale
Coton Clanford
Tixall Gatehouse
Blithfield Hall
Long Compton
Littleworth
Ranton Green
Stafford
STAFFORD
Tixall
Essex Br.
A51
Admaston
Great Haywood
Derrington
Shugborough Farm
Audmore
Shut Heath
Berry Ring
Weeping Cross
Milford
Stockwell Heath
Gnosall
Forebridge
Little Haywood
Colwich
B5013
Wildwood
Bishton
Billington
Walton-on-the-Hill
A513
Wolseley
Coton
Gnosall Heath
Haughton
Rickerscote
Brocton
Hyde Lea
A449
Wolseley Bridge
Cowley
CANNOCK CHASE
Allimore Green
Coppenhall
Etchinghill
Wood Eaton
Bradley
Bednall
Dunston
Cannock Chase Country Park
Apeton
Acton Trussell
Slitting Mill
Dunston Heath
Church Eaton
Staffs. & Worc. Canal
Forest Centre & Deer Museum
Little Onn
Levedale
Flaxley Green
Brereton
High Onn
Orslow
Mitton
M6
A34
A51
Longridge
Shropshire Union
Church Eaton Brook
Penkridge
Bickford
Wolgarston
A460
Marston
Longnor
Whiston
Pye Green
Brineton
Congreve
Huntington
Hazelslade
Cannock Wood
Wheaton Aston
Blymhill
Lapley
Green Heath
Pillaton
B5012
Hednesford
A449
Rawnsley
Blymhill Lawns
Ivetsey Bank
Canal
Otherton
High Town
Littleworth
Weston-under-Lizard
Aqueduct
Stretton
Penk
Oldfallow
CANNOCK
Wimblebury
Heath Hayes
Chase Terrace
Boney Hay
Horsebrook
A5
Belvide Resr.
Gailey
Hatherton
Four Crosses
Weston Park
A5
Burntwood
A5190
Bishops Wood
Shutt Green
Four Ashes
Norton East
Norton Canes
NORTON CANES
Brewood
Somerford
Saredon
Bridgtown
M6 TOLL
Boscobel House
Coldham
Royal Oak
Chasetown
Tong
White Ladies Priory
Chillington Hall
Standeford
Slade Heath
Little Saredon
Shackerley
Lower Green
Landywood
Great Wyrley
Holland Park
M54
The Pool
Park Lane
Coven
Shareshill
Cheslyn Hay
Cross Green

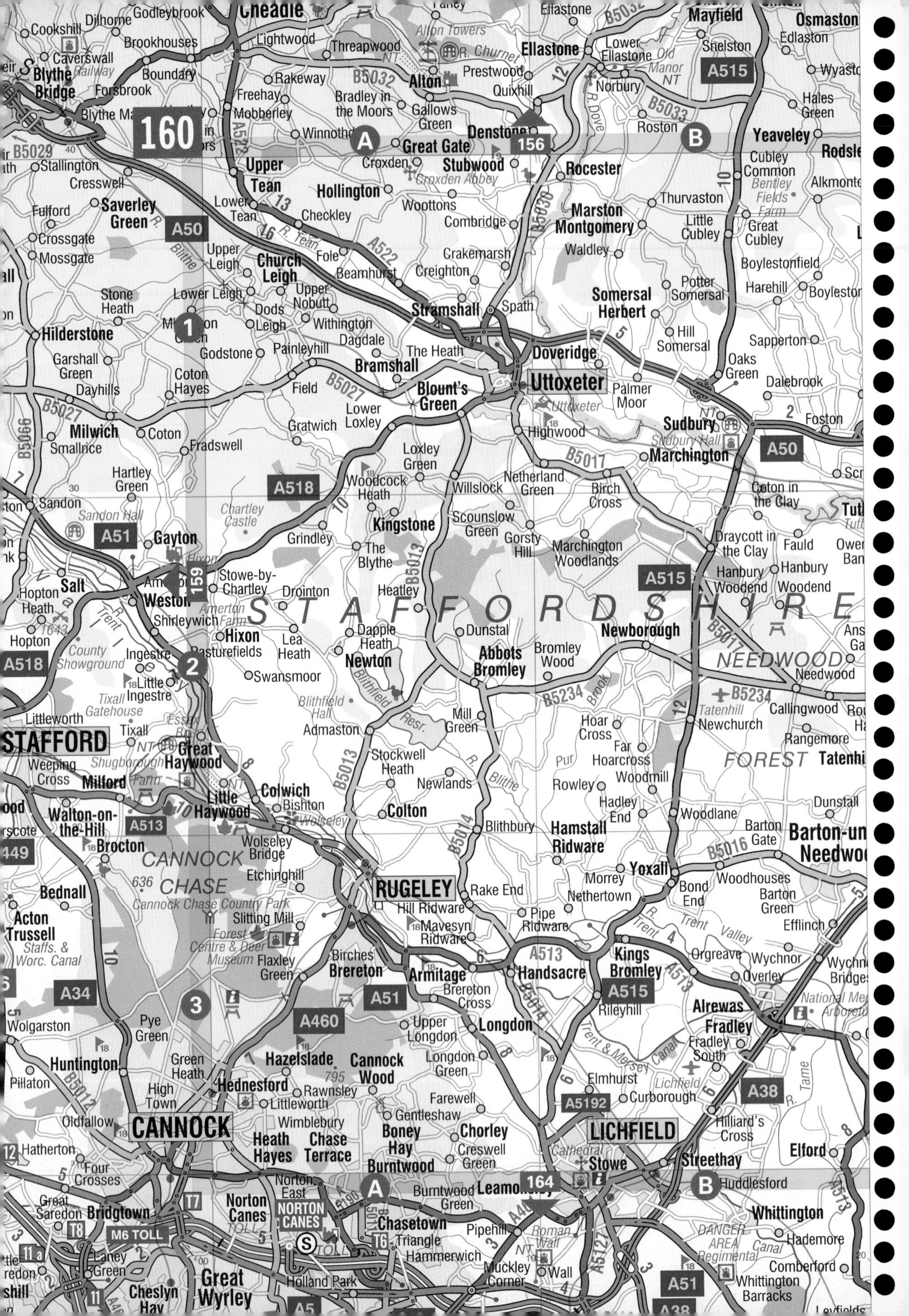

Cookshill
Dilhorne
Godleybrook
Cheadle
Ellastone
Mayfield
Osmaston
Edlaston
Brookhouses
Lightwood
Threapwood
Alton Towers
R. Churnet
Ellastone
Lower Ellastone
Snelston
Caverswall
Blythe Bridge
Caverswall Railway
Boundary
Rakeway
B5032
Alton
Prestwood
Quixhill
Norbury
Manor
NT
A515
Wyaston
Forsbrook
Freehay
Mobberley
Bradley in the Moors
Gallows Green
B5033
Roston
Hales Green
160
Winnothdale
A
Great Gate
Denstone
156
B
Yeaveley
Rodsley
B5029
Stallington
Upper Tean
Croxden
Stubwood
Croxden Abbey
Rocester
Cubley Common
Bentley Fields Farm
Alkmonton
Cresswell
Tean
Hollington
Thurvaston
Fulford
Saverley Green
Lower Tean
Checkley
Woottons
Marston Montgomery
Little Cubley
Great Cubley
A50
Crossgate
Combridge
Mossgate
Upper Leigh
Church Leigh
R. Tean
Fole
A522
Crakemarsh
Waldley
Beamhurst
Creighton
Boylestonfield
Stone Heath
Lower Leigh
Dods Leigh
Upper Nobutt
Withington
Stramshall
Spath
Somersal Herbert
Potter Somersal
Harehill
Boylestone
Hilderstone
Milwich Green
Godstone
Painleyhill
Dagdale
The Heath
Doveridge
Hill Somersal
Sapperton
Garshall Green
Coton Hayes
Bramshall
Uttoxeter
Oaks Green
Dalebrook
Dayhills
Field
B5027
Blount's Green
Palmer Moor
Lower Loxley
Uttoxeter
Milwich
Coton
Gratwich
Highwood
Sudbury
Sudbury Hall
Foston
B5066
Smallrice
Fradswell
Loxley Green
B5017
Marchington
A50
Hartley Green
A518
Woodcock Heath
Willslock
Netherland Green
Birch Cross
Scropton
Coton in the Clay
Sandon
Sandon Hall
Chartley Castle
Kingstone
Scounslow Green
Tutbury
A51
Gayton
Grindley
The Blythe
Gorsty Hill
Marchington Woodlands
Draycott in the Clay
Fauld
Owen's Bank
B5013
Hixon
Hanbury Woodend
Hanbury Woodend
A515
Hopton Heath
Salt
Amerton
159
Stowe-by-Chartley
Drointon
Heatley
Weston
Amerton Farm
STAFFORDSHIRE
Shirleywich
Trent
Hopton
1643
Hixon
Lea Heath
Dapple Heath
Dunstal
Newborough
Anslow Gate
County Showground
Ingestre
Pasturefields
Newton
Abbots Bromley
Bromley Wood
NEEDWOOD
A518
Little Ingestre
Swansmoor
Needwood
Tixall Gatehouse
Blithfield Hall
Blithfield Resr.
B5234
Brook
B5234
Littleworth
Essex Br.
Mill Green
Hoar Cross
Tatenhill
Newchurch
Callingwood
Rough Hayes
STAFFORD
Tixall
Great Haywood
Admaston
Far Hoarcross
Rangemore
Weeping Cross
Shugborough
Stockwell Heath
Pur
FOREST
Tatenhill
Milford
Farm
Little Haywood
Colwich
Newlands
R. Blithe
Rowley
Woodmill
Walton-on-the-Hill
Bishton
Wolseley
Colton
Hadley End
Woodlane
Dunstall
A513
Blithbury
Hamstall Ridware
Barton Gate
Barton-under-Needwood
Brocton
Wolseley Bridge
B5014
B5016
CANNOCK CHASE
Etchinghill
Yoxall
Woodhouses
636
Morrey
Bednall
Cannock Chase Country Park
RUGELEY
Rake End
Nethertown
Bond End
Barton Green
Hill Ridware
Acton Trussell
Slitting Mill
Pipe Ridware
Mavesyn Ridware
Efflinch
Trent
Trent Valley
Staffs. & Worc. Canal
Forest Centre & Deer Museum
Birches
Kings Bromley
Orgreave
Wychnor
Flaxley Green
A513
Wychnor Bridges
Brereton
Armitage
Handsacre
Overley
A34
Brereton Cross
A515
A51
National Memorial Arboretum
Alrewas
Wolgarston
Pye Green
A460
Upper Longdon
Rileyhill
Fradley
Longdon
Fradley South
Huntington
Green Heath
Hazelslade
Cannock Wood
Longdon Green
Trent & Mersey Canal
Tame
Pillaton
B5012
795
Elmhurst
Lichfield
High Town
Hednesford
Rawnsley
Farewell
Curborough
A38
Littleworth
Gentleshaw
A5192
Oldfallow
CANNOCK
Wimblebury
Boney Hay
Chorley
Creswell Green
LICHFIELD
Hilliard's Cross
Hatherton
Four Crosses
Heath Hayes
Chase Terrace
Burntwood
Cathedral
Stowe
Streethay
Elford
A
164
B
Huddlesford
Norton East
Burntwood Green
Leamonsley
Great Saredon
Bridgtown
Norton Canes
NORTON CANES
Chasetown
Whittington
M6 TOLL
TOLL
Triangle
Pipehill
Roman Wall
DANGER AREA
Canal
Hademore
Hammerwich
Regimental
Laney Green
Muckley Corner
Wall
A5127
Comberford
Great Wyrley
Holland Park
A51
Whittington Barracks
Cheslyn Hay
A5
A38
Levfields

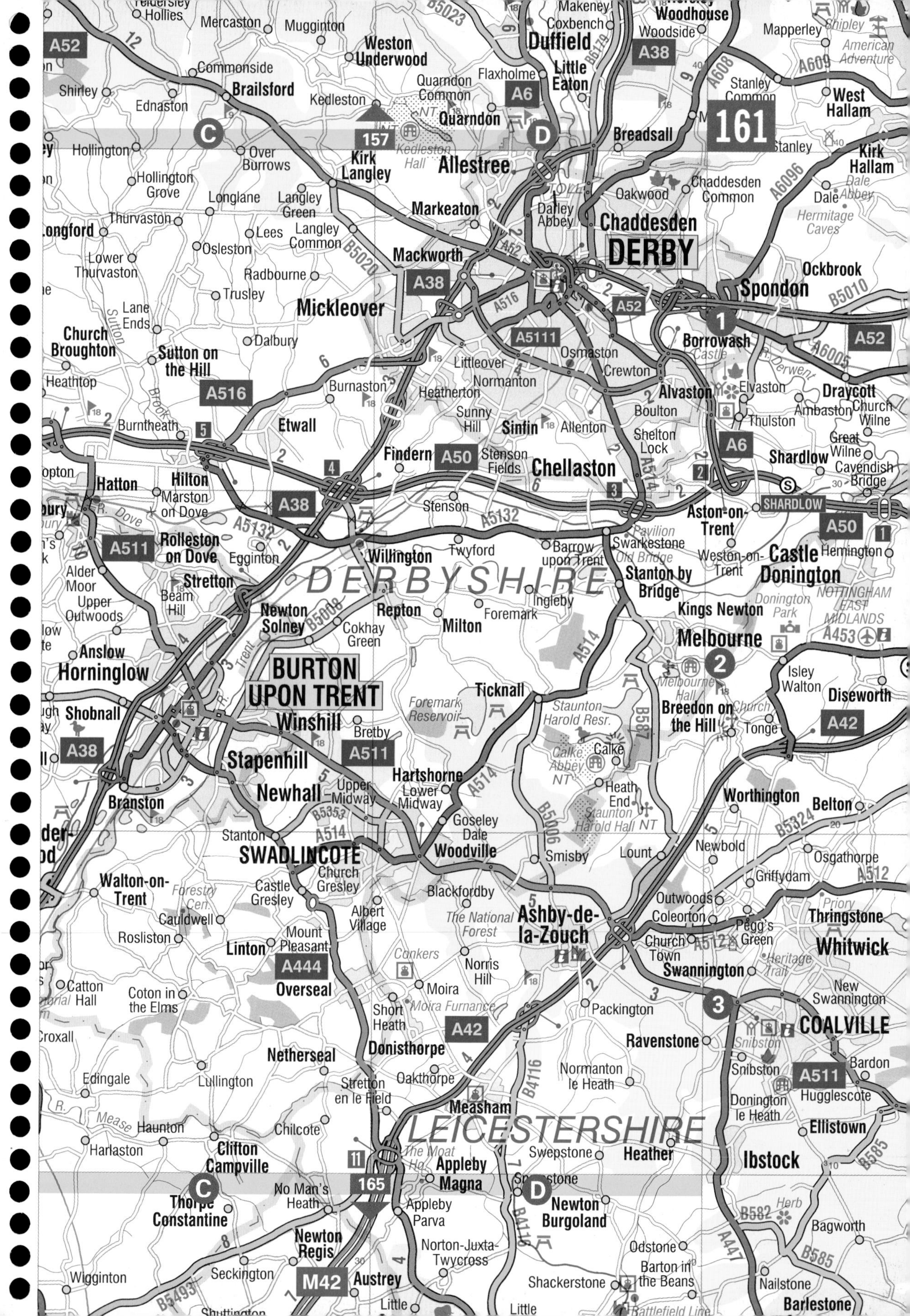
Hollies
Mercaston
Mugginton
B5023
Makeney
Coxbench
Woodhouse
Woodside
Mapperley
Shipley
American Adventure
A52
Weston Underwood
Duffield
A38
Commonside
Little Eaton
Flaxholme
Quarndon Common
A6
Stanley Common
A609
West Hallam
Shirley
Brailsford
Ednaston
Kedleston
Quarndon
Breadsall
161
Stanley
C
157
D
Kedleston Hall
Kirk Hallam
Hollington
Over Burrows
Kirk Langley
Allestree
Hollington Grove
Chaddesden Common
Oakwood
Dale
Dale Abbey
A6096
Longlane
Langley Green
Markeaton
Darley Abbey
Chaddesden
Hermitage Caves
Thurvaston
Longford
Lees
Langley Common
Osleston
DERBY
Lower Thurvaston
Radbourne
Mackworth
Ockbrook
B5020
A38
Spondon
B5010
Trusley
A516
A52
Mickleover
Lane Ends
Sutton
A5111
1
A52
Church Broughton
Dalbury
Borrowash
Castle
A6005
Sutton on the Hill
Littleover
Osmaston
R. Derwent
Normanton
Crewton
Heathtop
A516
Burnaston
Heatherton
Alvaston
Elvaston
Draycott
Ambaston
Church Wilne
Sunny Hill
Boulton
Thulston
Burntheath
5
Etwall
Sinfin
Allenton
Shelton Lock
A6
Great Wilne
Findern
A50
Stenson Fields
Chellaston
Shardlow
Cavendish Bridge
Hatton
Hilton
4
3
A514
2
Marston on Dove
A38
Stenson
SHARDLOW
R. Dove
A5132
Aston-on-Trent
A50
A511
Rolleston on Dove
Egginton
Willington
Twyford
Barrow upon Trent
Swarkestone
Pavilion
Old Bridge
Weston-on-Trent
Castle Donington
Hemington
Alder Moor
Stretton
DERBYSHIRE
Stanton by Bridge
NOTTINGHAM EAST MIDLANDS
Beam Hill
Upper Outwoods
Ingleby
Donington Park
Newton Solney
Repton
Milton
Foremark
Kings Newton
B5008
A453
Cokhay Green
A514
Melbourne
Anslow
Trent
2
Horninglow
BURTON UPON TRENT
Isley Walton
Melbourne Hall
Diseworth
Ticknall
Foremark Reservoir
Staunton Harold Resr.
Breedon on the Hill
Church
Shobnall
Winshill
Bretby
B587
Tonge
A42
A38
Calke
Calke Abbey NT
Stapenhill
A511
Hartshorne
Worthington
Belton
Branston
Newhall
Upper Midway
Lower Midway
Heath End
Staunton Harold Hall NT
B5353
A514
Goseley Dale
B5006
B5324
Stanton
Newbold
SWADLINCOTE
Woodville
Smisby
Lount
Osgathorpe
Church Gresley
Griffydam
A512
Walton-on-Trent
Forestry Cen.
Castle Gresley
Blackfordby
Outwoods
Albert Village
The National Forest
Ashby-de-la-Zouch
Coleorton
Priory
Thringstone
Cauldwell
Pegg's Green
Rosliston
Mount Pleasant
Church Town
A512
Whitwick
Linton
Conkers
Norris Hill
Heritage Trail
A444
Swannington
Catton Hall
Overseal
Moira
New Swannington
Coton in the Elms
3
Short Heath
Moira Furnance
Packington
COALVILLE
Croxall
A42
Ravenstone
Snibston
Netherseal
Donisthorpe
Bardon
Normanton le Heath
Snibston
Edingale
Lullington
Stretton en le Field
Oakthorpe
B4116
A511
Hugglescote
Measham
Donington le Heath
R. Mease
Haunton
Chilcote
LEICESTERSHIRE
Ellistown
Harlaston
Clifton Campville
The Moat Ho.
Appleby Magna
Swepstone
Heather
Ibstock
B585
11
165
C
D
Thorpe Constantine
No Man's Heath
Appleby Parva
Newton Burgoland
B4116
B582
Herb
Bagworth
Newton Regis
Norton-Juxta-Twycross
Odstone
A447
Barton in the Beans
B585
Wigginton
Seckington
Austrey
Shackerstone
Nailstone
M42
B5493
Little
Little
Battlefield Line
Barlestone

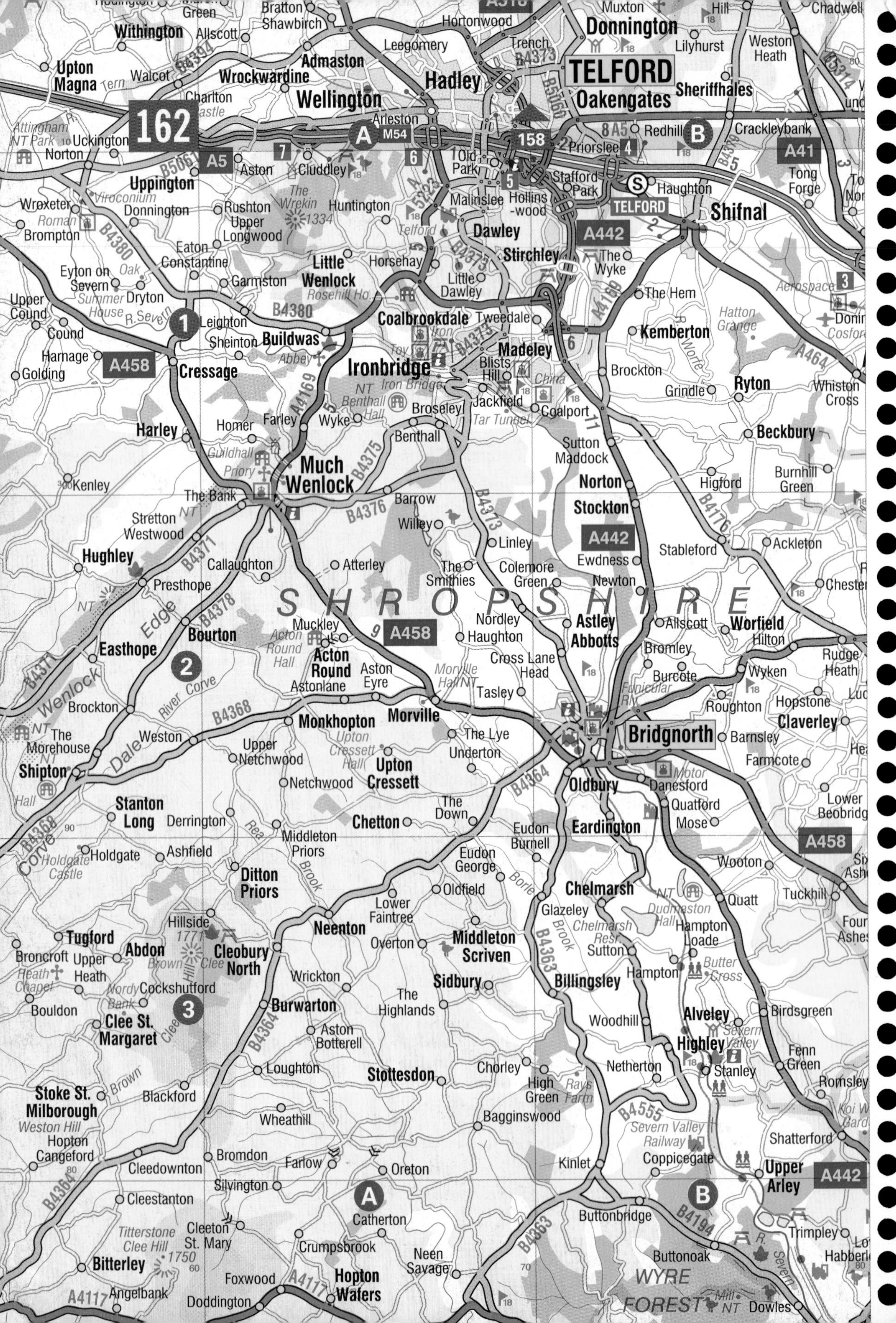
162
Withington
Allscott
Bratton
Shawbirch
Hortonwood
Muxton
Donnington
Hill
Chadwell
Upton
Magna
Walcot
Wrockwardine
Admaston
Leegomery
Trench
Lilyhurst
Weston
Heath
Hadley
TELFORD
Oakengates
Sheriffhales
Wellington
Charlton
Arleston
Attingham
NT Park
Uckington
Norton
M54
A5
Redhill
Crackleybank
A41
Aston
Cluddley
Old
Park
158
Priorslee
Stafford
Park
Haughton
Tong
Forge
Uppington
The
Wrekin
1334
Huntington
Malinslee
Hollins
-wood
TELFORD
Shifnal
Wroxeter
Viroconium
Roman
Brompton
Donnington
Rushton
Upper
Longwood
Telford
Dawley
A442
Eaton
Constantine
Little
Wenlock
Horsehay
Stirchley
The
Wyke
Eyton on
Severn
Garmston
Little
Dawley
Dryton
Summer
House
Rosehill Ho.
The Hem
Aerospace
Upper
Cound
R. Severn
Leighton
B4380
Coalbrookdale
Tweedale
Hatton
Grange
Cound
Buildwas
Kemberton
Sheinton
Abbey
Madeley
Harnage
A458
Ironbridge
Blists
Hill
Brockton
Cressage
Golding
NT
Iron Bridge
Benthall
Hall
Grindle
Ryton
Whiston
Cross
A464
Jackfield
Coalport
Broseley
Tar Tunnel
Harley
Homer
Farley
Wyke
Benthall
Sutton
Maddock
Beckbury
Guildhall
Priory
Much
Wenlock
B4375
Norton
Higford
Burnhill
Green
Kenley
The Bank
Barrow
Stockton
Stretton
Westwood
B4376
Willey
B4373
Linley
A442
Stableford
Ackleton
Hughley
B4371
Callaughton
Atterley
The
Smithies
Colemore
Green
Ewdness
Newton
Chester
Presthope
SHROPSHIRE
Edge
B4378
Muckley
Nordley
Haughton
Astley
Abbotts
Allscott
Worfield
Hilton
Bourton
Acton
Round
Hall
Acton
Round
A458
Bromley
Easthope
Cross Lane
Head
Rudge
Heath
Wenlock
Aston
Eyre
Morville
Hall NT
Burcote
Wyken
River Corve
Astonlane
Tasley
Funicular
Rly.
Roughton
Hopstone
Brockton
B4368
Monkhopton
Morville
Claverley
The
Morehouse
Weston
Upton
Cressett
Hall
The Lye
Bridgnorth
Barnsley
Dale
Upper
Netchwood
Underton
Farmcote
Shipton
Upton
Cressett
Motor
Hall
Netchwood
B4364
Oldbury
Danesford
Stanton
Long
Derrington
The
Down
Quatford
Lower
Beobridge
Rea
Chetton
Mose
Eardington
B4368
Middleton
Priors
Eudon
Burnell
A458
Holdgate
Ashfield
Eudon
George
Holdgate
Castle
Corve
Brook
Borle
Wooton
Ditton
Priors
Oldfield
Chelmarsh
NT
Dudmaston
Hall
Quatt
Tuckhill
Lower
Faintree
Glazeley
Hillside
1771
Neenton
Chelmarsh
Resr.
Hampton
Loade
Four
Ashes
Tugford
Abdon
Cleobury
North
Overton
Middleton
Scriven
B4363
Brook
Sutton
Butter
Cross
Broncroft
Upper
Heath
Brown
Clee
Hill
Heath
Chapel
Wrickton
Sidbury
Billingsley
Hampton
Nordy
Bank
Cockshutford
The
Highlands
Birdsgreen
Bouldon
Burwarton
Woodhill
Alveley
Clee St.
Margaret
B4364
Aston
Botterell
Severn
Valley
Highley
Netherton
Stanley
Fenn
Green
Loughton
Stottesdon
Chorley
High
Green
Rays
Farm
Romsley
Stoke St.
Milborough
Brown
Blackford
B4555
Weston Hill
Wheathill
Bagginswood
Severn Valley
Railway
Shatterford
Hopton
Cangeford
Bromdon
Farlow
Oreton
Kinlet
Coppicegate
Upper
Arley
A442
Cleedownton
Silvington
B4364
Cleestanton
Buttonbridge
B4194
Catherton
Cleeton
St. Mary
Titterstone
Clee Hill
1750
Trimpley
Crumpsbrook
Neen
Savage
B4363
Buttonoak
Habberley
Bitterley
R. Severn
WYRE
Foxwood
A4117
Hopton
Wafers
FOREST
Mill
NT
Dowles
A4117
Angelbank
Doddington

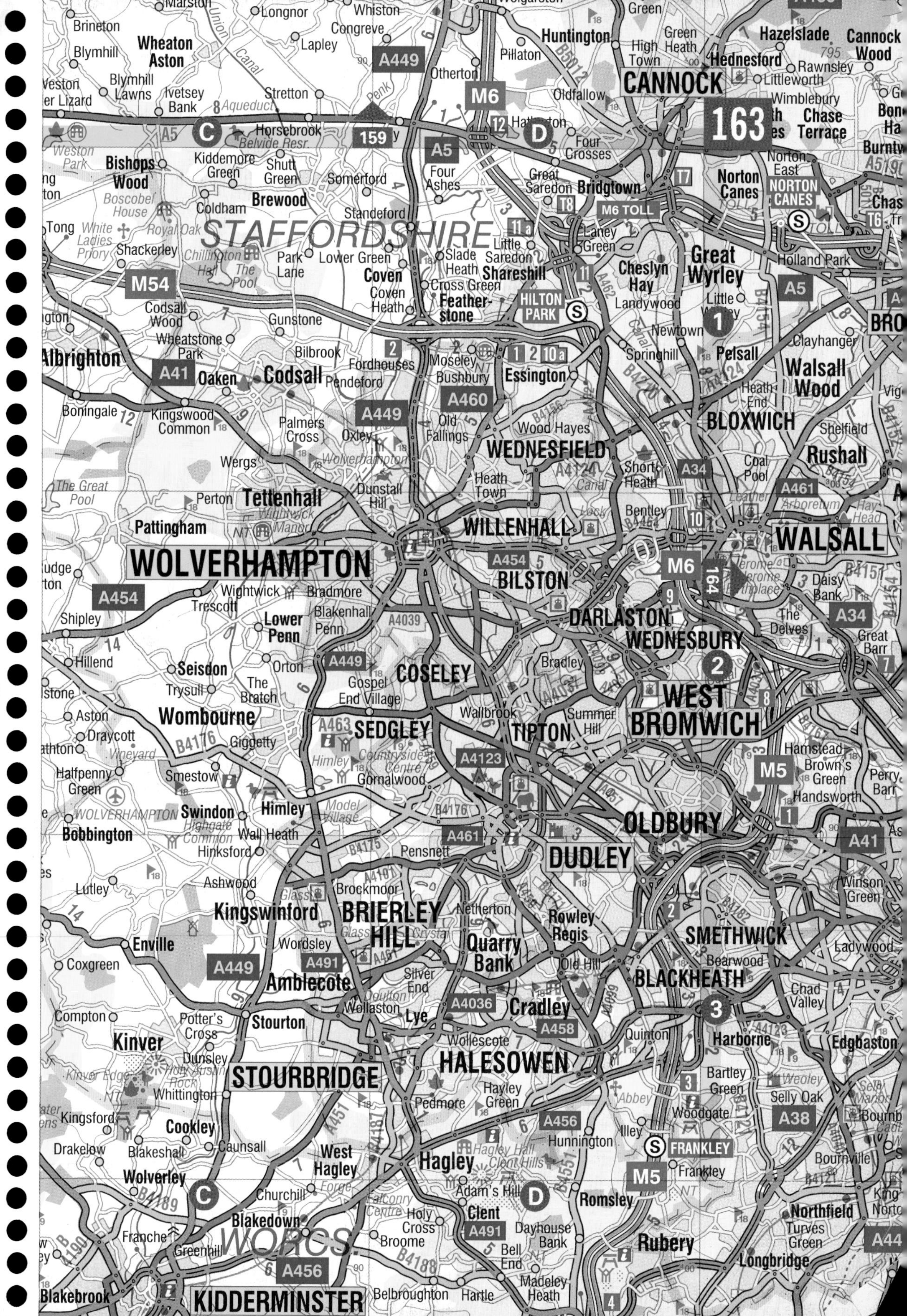
163
CANNOCK
WOLVERHAMPTON
WALSALL
WEST BROMWICH
DUDLEY
OLDBURY
STOURBRIDGE
KIDDERMINSTER
HALESOWEN
STAFFORDSHIRE
WORCS.
WEDNESFIELD
WILLENHALL
BILSTON
DARLASTON
WEDNESBURY
BLOXWICH
COSELEY
SEDGLEY
TIPTON
BRIERLEY HILL
SMETHWICK
BLACKHEATH
Tettenhall
Wombourne
Kingswinford
Amblecote
Codsall
Brewood
Great Wyrley
Cheslyn Hay
Walsall Wood
Pelsall
Rushall
Hednesford
Hazelslade
Cannock Wood
Chase Terrace
Norton Canes
Huntington
Shareshill
Featherstone
Essington
Albrighton
Pattingham
Himley
Swindon
Bobbington
Enville
Kinver
Cookley
Wolverley
Hagley
West Hagley
Clent
Romsley
Rubery
Northfield
Longbridge
Harborne
Edgbaston
Quarry Bank
Cradley
Lye
Rowley Regis
M6
M54
M5
A449
A5
A41
A454
A460
A34
A461
A4123
A463
A491
A4036
A458
A456
A38
159
164
M6 TOLL
HILTON PARK
NORTON CANES
FRANKLEY

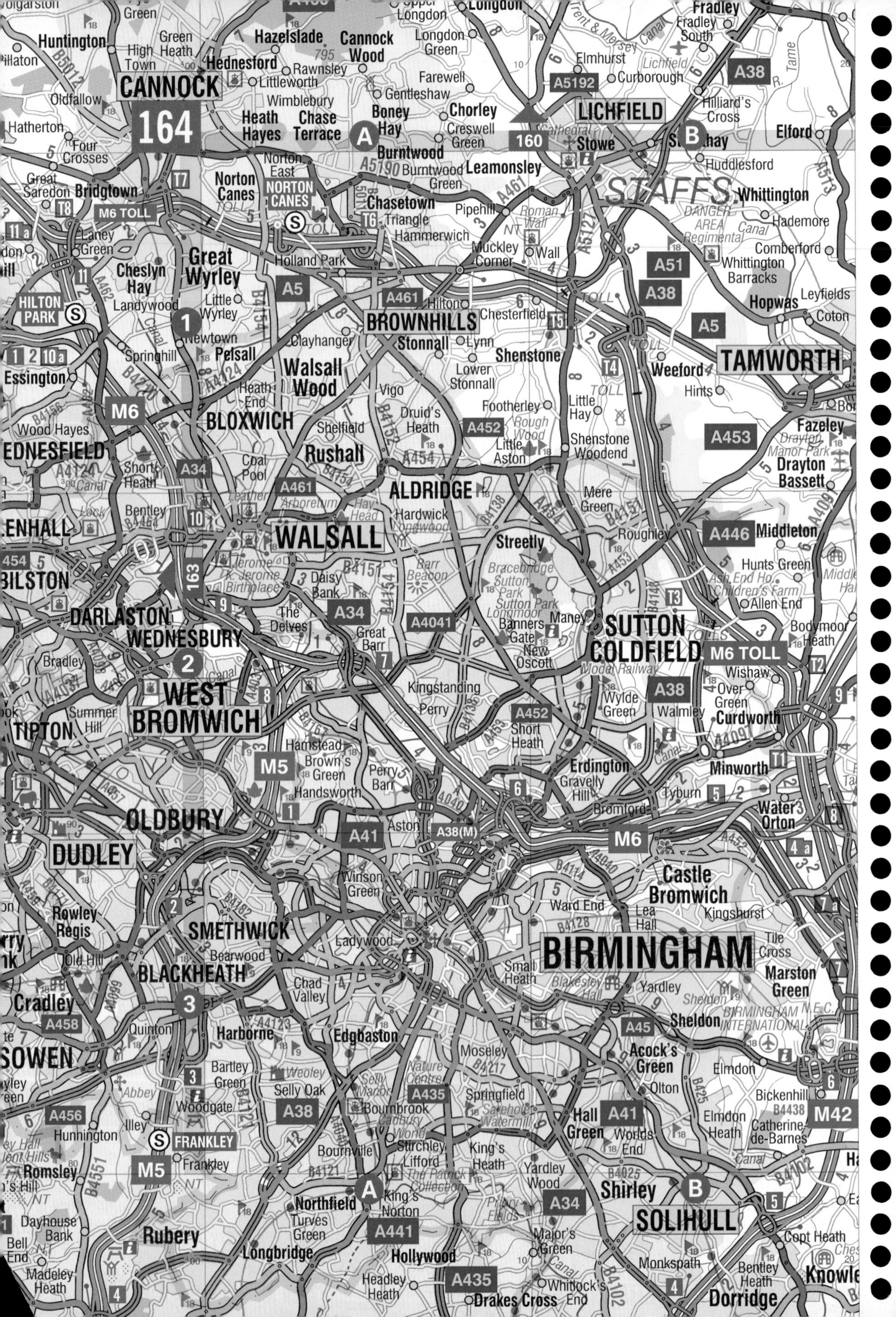

CANNOCK
164
Huntington
Pillaton
High Town
Green Heath
Hednesford
Hazelslade
Cannock Wood
Rawnsley
Littleworth
Longdon
Upper Longdon
Longdon Green
Farewell
Gentleshaw
Fradley
Fradley South
Elmhurst
Curborough
A5192
A38
Oldfallow
Hatherton
Four Crosses
Wimblebury
Heath Hayes
Chase Terrace
Boney Hay
Chorley
Creswell Green
Burntwood
Burntwood Green
LICHFIELD
160
Stowe
Hilliard's Cross
Streethay
Elford
Huddlesford
STAFFS.
Whittington
Hademore
Great Saredon
Bridgtown
Norton Canes
Norton East
NORTON CANES
Chasetown
Triangle
Hammerwich
Leamonsley
Pipehill
Roman Wall
Wall
Muckley Corner
A5190
A461
A5127
M6 TOLL
DANGER AREA
Regimental
Comberford
Whittington Barracks
A51
Laney Green
Holland Park
Cheslyn Hay
Great Wyrley
Landywood
Little Wyrley
HILTON PARK
A5
A461
Hilton
Chesterfield
BROWNHILLS
Clayhanger
Stonnall
Lynn
Shenstone
Hopwas
Leyfields
Coton
Newtown
Springhill
Pelsall
Essington
Walsall Wood
Lower Stonnall
Weeford
Hints
TAMWORTH
M6
Heath End
Vigo
Footherley
Little Hay
Wood Hayes
BLOXWICH
Shelfield
Druid's Heath
A452
Rough Wood
Little Aston
Shenstone Woodend
A453
Fazeley
Drayton Manor Park
Drayton Bassett
WEDNESFIELD
A34
Short Heath
Coal Pool
Rushall
A454
ALDRIDGE
Mere Green
A461
Arboretum
Hay Head
Hardwick
Longwood
Bentley
WALSALL
Streetly
Roughley
A446
Middleton
BILSTON
Jerome K. Jerome Birthplace
Daisy Bank
Barr Beacon
Bracebridge
Sutton Park
Hunts Green
Ash End Ho. Children's Farm
Allen End
DARLASTON
WEDNESBURY
The Delves
A34
Great Barr
A4041
Longmoor
Banners Gate
New Oscott
Maney
SUTTON COLDFIELD
Bodymoor Heath
M6 TOLL
Bradley
Model Railway
Wishaw
Over Green
A38
Kingstanding
Perry
A452
Short Heath
Wylde Green
Walmley
Curdworth
WEST BROMWICH
TIPTON
Summer Hill
Hamstead
Brown's Green
Handsworth
M5
Perry Barr
Erdington
Gravelly Hill
Minworth
Tyburn
Bromford
Water Orton
OLDBURY
A41
Aston
A38(M)
M6
DUDLEY
Winson Green
Castle Bromwich
Ward End
Lea Hall
Kingshurst
Rowley Regis
SMETHWICK
Ladywood
Bearwood
BIRMINGHAM
Tile Cross
Old Hill
BLACKHEATH
Small Heath
Blakesley Hall
Yardley
Marston Green
Cradley
Chad Valley
A458
Quinton
Harborne
Edgbaston
Sheldon
BIRMINGHAM INTERNATIONAL
A45
HALESOWEN
Moseley
Acock's Green
Elmdon
Bartley Green
Weoley
Selly Oak
Selly Manor
Nature Centre
Springfield
Olton
Bickenhill
Abbey
Woodgate
A38
Bournbrook
A435
Sarehole Watermill
Cadbury World
Hall Green
A41
Elmdon Heath
Catherine-de-Barnes
M42
A456
Illey
Hunnington
FRANKLEY
Frankley
Bournville
Stirchley
Lifford
The Patrick Collection
King's Heath
Worlds End
Romsley
M5
Yardley Wood
Shirley
SOLIHULL
Northfield
King's Norton
Turves Green
Priory Fields
A34
Dayhouse Bank
Rubery
A441
Major's Green
Copt Heath
Bell End
Longbridge
Hollywood
Monkspath
Bentley Heath
Madeley Heath
Headley Heath
A435
Drakes Cross
Whitlock's End
Dorridge
Knowle

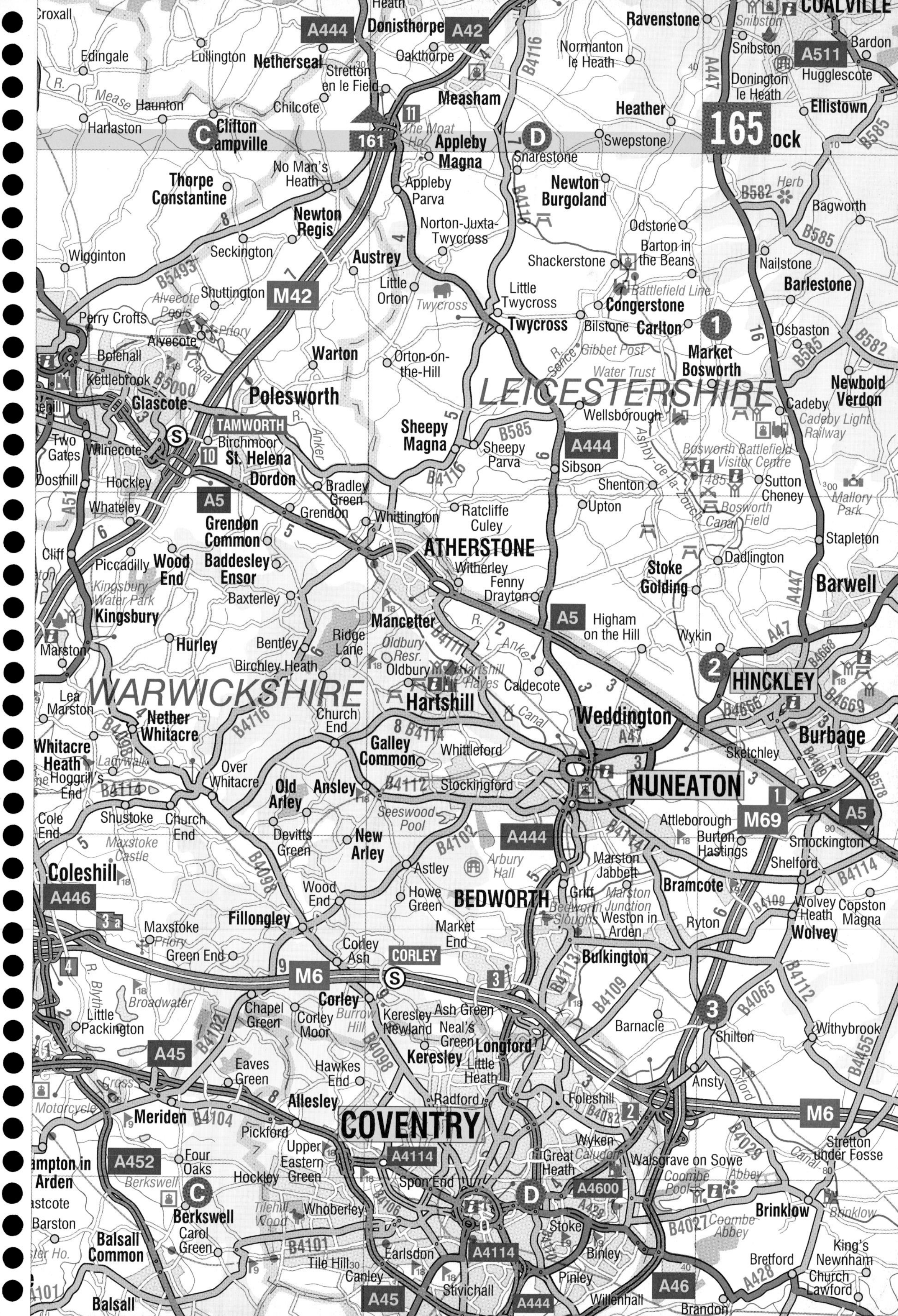
165
Croxall
Edingale
Lullington
Netherseal
A444
Donisthorpe
A42
Oakthorpe
Stretton en le Field
Measham
Normanton le Heath
Ravenstone
COALVILLE
Snibston
Bardon
A511
Hugglescote
Donington le Heath
Ellistown
Heather
Swepstone
Mease
Haunton
Chilcote
Harlaston
Clifton Campville
The Moat Ho.
161
Appleby Magna
Snarestone
Thorpe Constantine
No Man's Heath
Appleby Parva
Newton Burgoland
B582
Herb
Bagworth
Newton Regis
Norton-Juxta-Twycross
Odstone
B585
Seckington
Barton in the Beans
Wigginton
Austrey
Shackerstone
Nailstone
B5493
Little Orton
Twycross
Battlefield Line
Barlestone
Alvecote Pools
Shuttington
M42
Little Twycross
Congerstone
Perry Crofts
Priory
Twycross
Bilstone
Carlton
Osbaston
Alvecote
Canal
Warton
Orton-on-the-Hill
Gibbet Post
Market Bosworth
Bolehall
Kettlebrook
B5000
Water Trust
Newbold Verdon
Glascote
Polesworth
LEICESTERSHIRE
Cadeby
Wellsborough
Cadeby Light Railway
TAMWORTH
Sheepy Magna
Sheepy Parva
A444
Sibson
Bosworth Battlefield Visitor Centre
Two Gates
Wilnecote
Birchmoor
Anker
St. Helena
Dordon
B4116
1485
Sutton Cheney
Dosthill
Hockley
Bradley Green
Shenton
Mallory Park
Grendon
Whittington
Ratcliffe Culey
Upton
Bosworth Field
A5
A51
Whateley
Grendon Common
Ashby-de-la-Zouch Canal
ATHERSTONE
Stapleton
Cliff
Piccadilly
Wood End
Baddesley Ensor
Witherley
Stoke Golding
Dadlington
Kingsbury Water Park
Fenny Drayton
Barwell
Baxterley
A447
Kingsbury
Mancetter
A5
Higham on the Hill
Hurley
Ridge Lane
Oldbury Resr.
Wykin
Marston
Bentley
A47
Birchley Heath
Oldbury
Hartshill Hayes
Caldecote
HINCKLEY
B4668
WARWICKSHIRE
Hartshill
Lea Marston
Nether Whitacre
B4116
Church End
B4114
Weddington
B4666
B4669
Burbage
Galley Common
Whittleford
Sketchley
Whitacre Heath
Ladywalk
B4098
Over Whitacre
Hoggrill's End
B4114
Old Arley
Ansley
B4112
Stockingford
NUNEATON
Cole End
Shustoke
Church End
Seeswood Pool
Devitts Green
New Arley
Attleborough
M69
Burton Hastings
A5
Smockington
Maxstoke Castle
B4102
A444
Arbury Hall
Marston Jabbett
Shelford
Coleshill
Astley
B4114
A446
Wood End
Howe Green
BEDWORTH
Griff
Marston Junction
Bramcote
Wolvey Heath
Copston Magna
Bedworth Sloughs
Weston in Arden
B4109
Wolvey
Maxstoke Priory
Fillongley
Market End
Ryton
Corley Ash
Green End
CORLEY
Bulkington
B4065
B4112
M6
R. Blyth
Broadwater
Corley
B4113
B4109
Chapel Green
Corley Moor
Burrow Hill
Keresley Newland
Ash Green
Neal's Green
Barnacle
Withybrook
Little Packington
Shilton
B4455
A45
Longford
Keresley
Little Heath
Hawkes End
Eaves Green
Oxford
Ansty
Cross
Motorcycle
Allesley
Radford
Foleshill
B4082
M6
Meriden
B4104
COVENTRY
Pickford
Wyken
B4029
Stretton under Fosse
Upper Eastern Green
Great Heath
Caludon
Walsgrave on Sowe
Canal
Hampton in Arden
A452
Four Oaks
A4114
Hockley
Coombe Pool
Abbey
Berkswell
Spon End
A4600
Knowle
Barston
Berkswell
Tile Hill Wood
Whoberley
B4106
Brinklow
B4027
Coombe Abbey
Balsall Common
Carol Green
B4101
Stoke
Binley
King's Newnham
Earlsdon
A4114
Bretford
Tile Hill
Canley
A428
Church Lawford
A101
Balsall
A45
Stivichall
A444
Pinley
Willenhall
A46
Brandon

INDEX

Including Streets, Places & Areas, Industrial Estates,
Flats & Walkways, Stations and Places of Interest.

HOW TO USE THIS INDEX

1. Each street name is followed by its Postcode District and then by its Locality abbreviation(s) and then by its map reference; e.g. **Aarons Dr.** ST7: Big E . . . .5H **15** is in the ST7 Postcode District and the Bignell End Locality and is to be found in square 5H on page **15**. The page number is shown in bold type.

2. A strict alphabetical order is followed in which Av., Rd., St., etc. (though abbreviated) are read in full and as part of the street name; e.g. **Alders La.** appears after **Aldershaw Cl.** but before **Aldersleigh Dr.**

3. Streets and a selection of flats and walkways too small to be shown on street map pages **6-149**, appear in the index with the thoroughfare to which it is connected shown in brackets; e.g. **Aelfgar Cen.** WS15: Rug . . . .7G **95** (off Taylor's La.)

4. Addresses that are in more than one part are referred to as not continuous.

5. Places and areas are shown in the index in BLUE TYPE and the map reference is to the actual map square in which the town centre or area is located and not to the place name shown on the map. Map references for entries that appear on street map pages **6-149** are shown first, with references to road map pages **154-165** shown in brackets; e.g. ABBEY HULTON 2H **25** (3D **155**)

6. An example of a selected place of interest is Ancient High House & Yeomanry Mus. 3G **73**

7. An example of a station is **Barlaston Station (Rail)** . . . .2D **44**. Included are Rail **(Rail)** and Park & Ride **(Park & Ride)**

8. Junction names are shown in the index in BOLD CAPITAL TYPE; e.g. **BURNTWOOD JUNC.** 1H **121**

9. Map references for entries that appear on large scale pages **150-153** are shown first, with small scale map references shown in brackets; e.g. **Abbot's Way** ST5: N'tle 7C **152** (2F **31**)

GENERAL ABBREVIATIONS

All. : Alley	**Ct.** : Court	**Info.** : Information	**Ri.** : Rise
App. : Approach	**Cres.** : Crescent	**Junc.** : Junction	**Rd.** : Road
Arc. : Arcade	**Cft.** : Croft	**La.** : Lane	**Shop.** : Shopping
Av. : Avenue	**Dr.** : Drive	**Lit.** : Little	**Sth.** : South
Bk. : Back	**E.** : East	**Lwr.** : Lower	**Sq.** : Square
Blvd. : Boulevard	**Ent.** : Enterprise	**Mnr.** : Manor	**Sta.** : Station
Bri. : Bridge	**Est.** : Estate	**Mkt.** : Market	**St.** : Street
Bldgs. : Buildings	**Fld.** : Field	**Mdw.** : Meadow	**Ter.** : Terrace
Bus. : Business	**Flds.** : Fields	**Mdws.** : Meadows	**Trad.** : Trading
Cvn. : Caravan	**Gdn.** : Garden	**M.** : Mews	**Up.** : Upper
Cen. : Centre	**Gdns.** : Gardens	**Mt.** : Mount	**Va.** : Vale
Chu. : Church	**Ga.** : Gate	**Mus.** : Museum	**Vw.** : View
Cir. : Circus	**Gt.** : Great	**Nth.** : North	**Vs.** : Villas
Cl. : Close	**Grn.** : Green	**Pde.** : Parade	**Vis.** : Visitors
Coll. : College	**Gro.** : Grove	**Pk.** : Park	**Wlk.** : Walk
Comn. : Common	**Hgts.** : Heights	**Pas.** : Passage	**W.** : West
Cnr. : Corner	**Ho.** : House	**Pl.** : Place	**Yd.** : Yard
Cott. : Cottage	**Ho's.** : Houses	**Pct.** : Precinct	
Cotts. : Cottages	**Ind.** : Industrial	**Res.** : Residential	

LOCALITY ABBREVIATIONS

A Hul : Abbey Hulton	**B Woo** : Bowsey Wood	**Cong** : Congleton	**G Hea** : Gillow Heath
Abb B : Abbots Bromley	**Brad** : Bradley	**Copp** : Coppenhall	**Glas** : Glascote
Act : Acton	**B'nop** : Bradnop	**Cot H** : Cotes Heath	**Gno** : Gnosall
Act G : Acton Gate	**Brad** : Bradwell	**C Cla** : Coton-in-the-Clay	**Gold** : Goldenhill
Act T : Acton Trussell	**Bram** : Bramshall	**Cott** : Cotton	**Gt Bri** : Great Bridgeford
Alb : Albrighton	**B'ote** : Brancote	**Cove** : Coven	**Gt Hay** : Great Haywood
Ald : Aldridge	**B'ton** : Branston	**Cov H** : Coven Heath	**G Wyr** : Great Wyrley
Alre : Alrewas	**Bre** : Brereton	**C'ell** : Cresswell	**Gren** : Grendon
Als : Alsager	**Bret** : Bretby	**Cres** : Creswell	**Hal** : Hales
A Ban : Alsagers Bank	**Brew** : Brewood	**C Gre** : Cross Green	**H End** : Halmer End
Alt : Alton	**Brin F** : Brindley Ford	**Crow** : Crowdicote	**H Hea** : Hamley Heath
Alve : Alvecote	**Brin** : Brinsford	**Curb** : Curborough	**Hamm** : Hammerwich
Amin : Amington	**Broc** : Brocton	**Dens** : Denstone	**Ham R** : Hamstall Ridware
Ans : Anslow	**B Edg** : Brown Edge	**Derr** : Derrington	**H'ury** : Hanbury
Arm : Armitage	**Brow** : Brownhills	**Dilh** : Dilhorne	**Han** : Hanch
Ash : Ashbourne	**B Lee** : Brown Lees	**Dor** : Dordon	**H'rch** : Hanchurch
A'ley : Ashley	**Buck** : Bucknall	**Dost** : Dosthill	**Hand** : Handsacre
A Hea : Ashley Heath	**Burn** : Burntwood	**Drak** : Drakelow	**H'ord** : Hanford
Ast : Astbury	**B'lem** : Burslem	**Dray** : Draycott	**H'ley** : Hanley
Aston : Aston	**Burs** : Burston	**D Cla** : Draycott-in-the-Clay	**Harr** : Harriseahead
Aud : Audley	**B Tre** : Burton-on-Trent	**D Bas** : Drayton Bassett	**Hath** : Hatherton
B Ens : Baddesley Ensor	**Bush** : Bushbury	**Duns** : Dunston	**Hat** : Hatton
Bag : Bagnall	**Butt** : Butterton	**Duns H** : Dunston Heath	**Hau** : Haughton
B Gat : Baldwins Gate	**Calf H** : Calf Heath	**E Ster** : Earl Sterndale	**Haun** : Haunton
B Gre : Ball Green	**Cann** : Cannock	**Ecc** : Eccleshall	**Haz** : Hazelslade
Balt : Balterley	**Can W** : Cannock Wood	**Edin** : Edingale	**H Hay** : Heath Hayes
Barl : Barlaston	**Caul** : Cauldon	**Elf** : Elford	**Hed** : Hednesford
Bart : Barthomley	**Cave** : Caverswall	**Elm** : Elmhurst	**H Off** : High Offley
B Nee : Barton-under-Needwood	**C Ter** : Chase Terrace	**End** : Endon	**Hild** : Hilderstone
B Elm : Barwick in Elmet	**Chas** : Chasetown	**Ess** : Essington	**H Cho** : Hill Chorlton
Beam : Beamhurst	**Chea** : Cheadle	**Fare** : Farewell	**Hill R** : Hill Ridware
Bed : Bednall	**Chec** : Checkley	**Faze** : Fazeley	**Hilt** : Hilton
Bed H : Bednall Head	**Ched** : Cheddleton	**Fea** : Featherstone	**Him** : Himley
Bee : Beech	**Chel** : Chell	**Feg H** : Fegg Hayes	**Hin** : Hints
Bell : Bellamour	**C Hay** : Cheslyn Hay	**Fen** : Fenton	**Hixon** : Hixon
Bent : Bentilee	**C'eld** : Chesterfield	**Fish** : Fisherwick	**Hock** : Hockley
B Hil : Berry Hill	**C'ton** : Chesterton	**Foot** : Footherley	**Holl** : Hollington
Bet : Betley	**Chor** : Chorley	**Ford** : Fordhouses	**Holly** : Hollywood
Bidd : Biddulph	**C Eat** : Church Eaton	**Fors** : Forsbrook	**Hook** : Hookgate
Bid M : Biddulph Moor	**C Law** : Church Lawton	**F Ash** : Four Ashes	**Hopt** : Hopton
Big E : Bignall End	**Clav** : Claverley	**F Cro** : Four Crosses	**Hop** : Hopwas
Bilb : Bilbrook	**Clay** : Clayhanger	**F Oak** : Four Oaks	**Hort** : Horton
Bill : Billington	**Clif** : Cliff	**Fox** : Foxt	**Hun** : Huntington
Bir : Birchmoor	**C'ton** : Clifton	**Frad** : Fradley	**Hyde L** : Hyde Lea
Blac : Blackbrook	**C Camp** : Clifton Campville	**Fra P** : Fradley Park	**Ing** : Ingestre
B Moo : Blackshaw Moor	**Cods** : Codsall	**Frea** : Freasley	**Ips** : Ipstones
Blox : Bloxwich	**C Woo** : Codsall Wood	**Frog** : Froghall	**Keel** : Keele
Blur : Blurton	**Cold M** : Cold Meece	**Ful** : Fulford	**Kidd** : Kiddlestitch
B Bri : Blythe Bridge	**Col** : Colton	**Gay** : Gayton	**Kids** : Kidsgrove
Bob : Bobbington	**Colw** : Colwich	**Gen** : Gentleshaw	**K Bro** : King's Bromley

3 Spires Fitness —Aldbury Cl.

K'ley : **Kingsley**
K Hol : **Kingsley Holt**
King : **Kingswinford**
Kin : **Kinver**
Knen : **Knenhall**
Knig : **Knightley**
Knyp : **Knypersley**
Lap : **Lapley**
L Edg : **Lask Edge**
Lee : **Leek**
Lei : **Leigh**
Ley : **Leycett**
Lich : **Lichfield**
L Oak : **Light Oaks**
L'ood : **Lightwood**
L Ast : **Little Aston**
L Bri : **Little Bridgeford**
L Hay : **Little Haywood**
L Wyr : **Little Wyrley**
Logg : **Loggerheads**
L'don : **Longdon**
L'nor : **Longnor**
L'ton : **Longsdon**
Long : **Longton**
L Pen : **Lower Penn**
Lyn : **Lynn**
Mad : **Madeley**
Mad H : **Madeley Heath**
Mae : **Maer**
Mar : **Marchington**
Mars : **Marston**
Mav R : **Mavesyn Ridware**
May : **Mayfield**
Mea : **Meaford**
Mei : **Meir**
M Hea : **Meir Heath**
M May : **Middle Mayfield**
Midd : **Middleton**
M Oak : **Mile Oak**
Milf : **Milford**
Mil : **Milton**
Modd : **Moddershall**
More : **Moreton**
M Cop : **Mow Cop**
Muck : **Mucklestone**
M Cor : **Muckley Corner**
Nap : **Napley**
N Ast : **Newbold Astbury**
New : **Newborough**
N'tle : **Newcastle**
New : **Newchapel**
N Reg : **Newton Regis**
N Sol : **Newton Solney**
Nort : **Norton**
N Can : **Norton Canes**
O'moor : **Oakamoor**
Oak : **Oaken**
Oul : **Oulton**
Oul H : **Oulton Heath**
Oxl : **Oxley**
Pack : **Packmoor**
Patt : **Pattingham**
Pels : **Pelsall**
P'ord : **Pendeford**
P'ull : **Penkhull**
Penk : **Penkridge**
Pen : **Penn**
Per : **Perton**
Pic : **Piccadilly**
Pipe : **Pipehill**
P Rid : **Pipe Ridware**
Pole : **Polesworth**
Roce : **Rocester**
Roll D : **Rolleston-on-Dove**
Rook : **Rookery**
R Clo : **Rough Close**
Rudy : **Rudyard**
Rug : **Rugeley**
St G: **St George's**
Salt : **Salt**
Sand : **Sandon**
Sand B : **Sandon Bank**
Sandy : **Sandyford**
Sav G : **Saverley Green**
Sch G : **Scholar Green**
S Hay : **Scot Hay**
Seck : **Seckington**
Sed : **Sedgley**
Seigh : **Seighford**
Seis : **Seisdon**
Shar : **Shareshill**
S Har : **Shelton under Harley**
Shen : **Shenstone**
S Woo : **Shenstone Woodend**
Shir : **Shirleywich**
Shug : **Shugborough**
Shut : **Shuttington**
Sil : **Silverdale**
S Hea : **Slade Heath**
S Mil : **Slitting Mill**
Spa : **Spath**
Stab : **Stableford**
Staf : **Stafford**
S'ord : **Standeford**
S'ley : **Stanley**
Stan : **Stanton**
Stap : **Stapenhill**
S Broo : **Stockton Brook**
Stoc H : **Stockwell Heath**
S Tren : **Stoke-on-Trent**
Stone : **Stone**
Ston : **Stonnall**
Stou : **Stourton**
S Char : **Stowe-by-Chartley**
S'all : **Stramshall**
S'hay : **Streethay**
S'ly : **Streetly**
Stre : **Stretton**
Stub : **Stubwood**
Swin : **Swindon**
Swyn : **Swynnerton**
Talk : **Talke**
T Pit : **Talke Pits**
Tam : **Tamworth**
Tate : **Tatenhill**
Tea : **Tean**
Tett : **Tettenhall**
Thor : **Thorncliffe**
Titt : **Tittensor**
Tix : **Tixall**
Tren : **Trentham**
T Val : **Trent Vale**
Tres : **Trescott**
Trys : **Trysull**
Tuns : **Tunstall**
Tut : **Tutbury**
T Gat : **Two Gates**
U Lon : **Upper Longdon**
U May : **Upper Mayfield**
Utt : **Uttoxeter**
Wall : **Wall**
W Hea : **Wall Heath**
Wals : **Walsall**
W Woo : **Walsall Wood**
Walt : **Walton**
Wart : **Warton**
Wat : **Waterhouses**
Wed : **Wednesfield**
Werr : **Werrington**
West : **Weston**
W Ban : **Weston Bank**
W Coy : **Weston Coyney**
W Roc : **Wetley Rocks**
What : **Whateley**
Whe A : **Wheaton Aston**
Whis : **Whiston**
White : **Whitemore**
W'ave : **Whitgreave**
Whit : **Whitmore**
W'ton : **Whittington**
W Bar : **Whittington Barracks**
Wig : **Wigginton**
Wild : **Wildwood**
Will : **Willenhall**
Wiln : **Wilnecote**
Wimb : **Wimblebury**
Wink : **Winkhill**
Wins : **Winshill**
Wol B : **Wolseley Bridge**
W'ton : **Wolverhampton**
Wolv : **Wolverley**
Womb : **Wombourne**
Woo E : **Wood End**
W'ves : **Woodseaves**
Wrin : **Wrinehill**
W Par : **Wrottesley Park**
Yar : **Yarlet**
Yarn : **Yarnfield**
Yox : **Yoxall**

3 Spires Fitness 3B 114
2000 Fitness Cen. *2G 73*
(off St Patrick's St.)

A

Aarons Dr. ST7: Big E 5H **15**
Abberley B77: Wiln 7E **138**
Abberley Ho. ST5: N'tle 1G **23**
Abbey Arc. DE14: B Tre 2F **87**
Abbey Cl. ST14: Roce 5E **58**
ST17: Staf 6J **73**
ST19: Penk 4J **91**
Abbey Ct. ST2: A Hul 3H **25**
Abbey Cft. B78: Pole 7J **139**
Abbey Dr. ST18: L Hay 6J **81**
WS3: Pels 7C **120**
Abbeyfield Rd. WV10: Bush 1C **124**
Abbeyfields ST18: Gt Hay 4G **81**
Abbey Gdns. ST18: Gt Hay 4G **81**
Abbey Grn. Ct. B78: Pole 1J **143**
Abbey Grn. Rd. ST13: Lee 1E **48**
ABBEY HULTON 2H 25 (3D 155)
Abbey La. ST2: A Hul, Buck 4G **25**
Abbey Rd. B77: Glas 6K **137**
ST2: A Hul 2G **25**
ST9: W Roc 4J **27**
Abbey Rd. Ct. ST14: Roce 5D **58**
Abbey Sq. WS3: Blox 3E **126**
Abbey St. DE14: B Tre 3E **86**
ST2: Mil 2G **25**
ST5: Sil 7A **22**
ST15: Stone 4G **47**
WS12: Hed 3H **101**
Abbey Vw. B78: Pole 2K **143**
Abbeywood Cl. ST13: Lee 3E **48**
Abbot Cl. DE14: B Tre 1B **86**
ABBOTS BROMLEY 3C 88 (2A 160)
Abbotsfield WS11: Cann 5E **100**
Abbotsford Rd. WS14: Lich 4D **114**
Abbots Pl. ST2: A Hul 2H **25**
Abbots Rd. ST2: A Hul 1H **25**
Abbots Wlk. ST16: Staf 1G **73**
WS15: Bre 4K **97**
Abbot's Way ST5: N'tle 7C **152** (2F **31**)
Abbotts Ct. ST2: A Hul 1H **25**
Abbotts Dr. ST1: H'ley 7E **18**
Abbotts Pl. WS3: Blox 4K **127**
Abbott's Rd. ST13: Lee 3H **49**
Abbotts St. WS3: Blox 3K **127**
ABDON 3A 162
Abelia B77: Amin 6B **138**
Abercorn St. ST4: Fen 4F **33**
Aberford Gro. ST1: H'ley 3E **24**
Abingdon Rd. WS3: Blox 3F **127**
Abingdon Way ST4: Tren 3B **40**
WS3: Blox 3F **127**
Ablon Ct. ST19: Penk 5H **91**
Abnalls Cft. WS13: Lich 2K **113**
Abnalls La. WS13: Lich 3E **112**
(not continuous)
ABOVE CHURCH 1G 53
Acacia Av. ST5: N'tle 6C **22**
Acacia Cres. WV8: Bilb 1D **122**
Acacia Gdns. ST7: Kids 3G **11**
Acacia Gro. ST5: N'tle 6C **22**
WS12: Wimb 7B **102**
Academy, The 6D 32
Achilles Cl. WS6: G Wyr 3F **119**
(not continuous)
Achilles Way ST2: Buck 7F **25**
ACKERS CROSSING 3F 7
ACKLETON 2B 162
ACOCK'S GREEN 3B 164
Acorn Cl. TF9: Logg 4D **60**
WS6: G Wyr 3G **119**
WS7: C Ter 2J **111**
WS11: H Hay 1J **109**
Acorn Gro. WV8: Cods 3A **122**
Acorn Ri. ST3: L'ood 2K **41**
Acorn Rd. WV11: Wed 4A **126**
Acorn Starter Units WS7: C Ter 4F **111**
Acorn Way WS7: Burn 5A **112**
Acre, The DY7: Kin 6F **149**
Acre Ho. DY7: Kin 6F **149**
Acre Ri. WV12: Will 7B **126**
Acres, The ST5: Sil 7B **22**
WV3: W'ton 5K **129**
ACRES NOOK 7D 10
Acres Nook Rd. ST6: Tuns 7E **10**
Acreswood Rd. ST6: B'lem 5B **18**
ACTON
Nantwich 2A 154
Newcastle 3A 38 (3C 155)
Acton Ct. ST18: Act G 5H **77**
ACTON GATE 4H 77
Acton Hill Rd. ST17: Act T 5K **77**
Acton La. ST5: Act 2A **38**
ACTON ROUND 2A 162
Acton St. ST1: H'ley 2D **24**
ACTON TRUSSELL 6K 77 (3D 159)
Adam Ct. WS11: Cann 2D **108**
Adams Av. ST6: Sandy 2H **17**
Adams Gro. ST13: Lee 5C **48**
ADAM'S HILL 3D 163
Adamson Cl. WS11: Cann 2B **108**
Adams Rd. WS8: Brow 7J **121**
WV3: W'ton 7K **129**
Adams St. ST2: Mil 6H **19**
ST5: N'tle 4G **23**
Adamthwaite Cl. ST11: B Bri 3F **43**
Adamthwaite Dr. ST11: B Bri 2F **43**
Ada Wrighton Cl. WV12: Will 6C **126**
ADBASTON 2B 158
Addenbrooke St. WS3: Blox 6J **127**
ADDERLEY 1A 158
ADDERLEY GREEN 3K 33
Adderley Pl. ST12: Barl 7F **41**
Adderley Rd. ST6: Nort 4E **18**
Addie Rd. DE13: B Tre 5C **84**
Addington Way ST3: Long 4K **33**
Addison Cl. WS11: Cann 5E **100**
Addison Gro. WV11: Wed 4F **125**
Addison St. ST1: H'ley 2D **24**
Adelaide Cres. DE15: Wins 2K **87**
Adelaide Dr. WS12: Wimb 7B **102**
Adelaide St. ST6: B'lem 1A **24**
ADENEY .3B 158
Adey Rd. WV11: Wed 5K **125**
Adies All. ST15: Stone 4G **47**
Adkins St. ST6: B'lem 1C **24**
ADMASTON
Telford 3A 158
Rugeley 2A 160
Admiral Parker Dr. WS14: Shen 6C **134**
Adonis Cl. B79: Tam 2J **137**
Adrian St. ST4: Fen 3E **32**
Advanced Bus. Pk. WS11: H Hay . . .7H **101**
Adventure Pl. ST1: H'ley 4G **151** (5C **24**)
Adwalton Rd. WV6: Per 3G **129**
Aegean Cl. ST4: Tren 2C **40**
Aelfgar Cen. *WS15: Rug* *7G 95*
(off Taylor's La.)
Aelfgar Ho. *WS15: Rug* *7G 95*
(off Taylor's La.)
Affleck Av. B78: M Oak 1D **140**
AGGER HILL 7E 20
Agger Hill ST5: Ley 1D **28**
Aiden Ct. WS13: Lich 4C **114**
Aiden Ct. Rd. WS13: Lich 3C **114**
Ainsdale Cl. ST3: Long 1K **41**
Ainsley Cl. ST2: A Hul 2H **25**
Ainsworth Av. ST10: K'ley 6F **53**
Ainsworth Rd. WV10: Bush 7C **116**
Ainsworth St. ST4: Fen 4C **32**
Aintree Cl. DE14: B'ton 5A **86**
ST4: Tren 3B **40**
WS12: Haz 4B **102**
Aintree Rd. ST10: Tea 3G **55**
WV10: Ford 1B **124**
Airdale Gro. ST15: Stone 2H **47**
Airdale Rd. ST15: Stone 2H **47**
Airdale Spinney ST15: Stone 2H **47**
Aitken Cl. B78: Tam 7G **137**
Aitken St. ST6: B'lem 7J **17**
Ajax Cl. WS6: G Wyr 3F **119**
Ajax Way ST2: Buck 7F **25**
Akesmoor La. ST8: G Hea, M Cop 6K **7**
Alanbrooke Gro. ST3: L'ood 1A **42**
Alan Dale ST9: Werr 4D **26**
Alandale Av. WS15: Hand 5G **99**
Alanley Cl. ST6: B'lem 6D **18**
Alan Rd. ST2: Buck 5J **25**
Alastair Rd. ST4: T Val 5K **31**
Albany Dr. WS12: Wimb 7A **102**
WS15: Rug 5F **95**
Albany Gro. ST4: S Tren 5J **153** (1H **31**)
WV11: Ess 4C **126**
Albany Rd. ST4: S Tren 5J **153** (1H **31**)
ST5: N'tle 1D **152** (6F **23**)
Albany St. ST6: Gold 7G **11**
Albemarle Rd. ST5: N'tle . . .1C **152** (5E **22**)
Alberta St. ST3: Long 7J **33**
Albert Av. ST3: Long 6A **34**
Albert Clarke Dr. WV12: Will 6C **126**
Albert Cl. WV8: Cods 1A **122**
Albert Davie Dr. WS12: Hed 6A **102**
Albert Dr. DY3: Swin 1J **147**
Albert Pl. ST3: Long 1H **41**
Albert Rd. B78: Faze 2G **141**
B79: Tam 4H **137**
ST4: Tren 4B **40**
Albert Sq. ST4: Fen 3E **32**
Albert St. DE14: B Tre 7D **84**
ST3: Long 4J **33**
ST5: C'ton 1C **22**
ST5: N'tle 2H **153** (7H **23**)
ST5: Sil 6A **22**
ST7: Big E 4G **15**
ST8: Bidd 5D **8**
ST13: Lee 3F **49**
ST15: Stone 3G **47**
WS11: Cann 6E **100**
WS12: Hed 5K **101**
Albert Ter. ST5: N'tle 3G **23**
ST16: Staf 1G **73**
ALBERT VILLAGE 3D 161
Albion Mill ST13: Lee 4F **49**
Albion Pl. WS11: Cann 6E **100**
Albion Rd. WS8: Brow 4G **121**
Albion Sq. ST1: H'ley 4G **151** (5C **24**)
Albion St. B79: Tam 4J **137**
ST1: H'ley 4F **151** (5C **24**)
ST13: Lee 4F **49**
WS15: Rug 7G **95**
Albion Ter. *DE14: B Tre* *5F 85*
(off Derby Rd.)
Albion Way WS7: C Ter 2H **111**
ALBRIGHTON 1C 163
Albutts Rd. WS8: Brow 1D **120**
WS11: Brow 1D **120**
Alcester Cl. ST6: Chel 1B **18**
Alcove, The WS3: Blox 3K **127**
Aldbury Cl. ST16: Staf 4F **71**

Albury Pl.—Arthur Cotton Ct.

Aldbury Pl. ST3: Blur . . . 1E 40
Aldeburgh Cl. WS3: Blox . . . 2G 127
Aldeburgh Dr. ST5: N'tle . . . 7F 31
Alden Hurst WS7: C Ter . . . 3H 111
Alderbrook Cl. DE13: Roll D . . . 6H 83
ALDERCAR . . . 3D 157
Alder Cl. ST7: Kids . . . 6E 10
TF9: Logg . . . 4E 60
WS14: Lich . . . 4F 115
Alderflat Dr. ST4: Tren . . . 3D 40
Alderford Cl. WV8: P'ord . . . 5H 123
Aldergate B79: Tam . . . 4H 137
Alder Gro. DE15: Stap . . . 5G 87
ST5: C'ton . . . 7B 16
ST17: Staf . . . 7D 72
Alderhay La. ST7: Rook . . . 2G 11
Alderhithe Gro. B74: L Ast . . . 5G 135
Alderholme Dr. DE13: Stre . . . 2G 85
ALDER MOOR . . . 2C 161 & 1A 84
Alderney Cl. ST5: N'tle . . . 6C 30
Alderney Cres. ST3: Long . . . 6F 33
ALDERS, THE . . . 3E 136
Alders, The DE13: B Nee . . . 6F 89
Aldersea Cl. ST6: B'lem . . . 6J 17
Aldershaw Cl. ST16: Staf . . . 4E 70
Alders La. B79: Tam . . . 3E 136
Aldersleigh Dr. ST17: Wild . . . 2A 78
Aldersley Av. WV6: Tett . . . 6G 123
Aldersley Cl. WV6: Tett . . . 6H 123
Aldersley Leisure Village . . . 7H 123
Aldersley Rd. WV6: Tett . . . 7G 123
Aldersley Stadium . . . 7H 123
Alderson Dr. DE13: Stre . . . 2G 85
Alders Rd. ST8: Bid M . . . 4H 9
Alderton Gro. ST3: Mei . . . 4D 42
Alder Wlk. ST4: T Val . . . 5J 31
ALDERWASLEY . . . 2D 157
Alder Way WS12: Haz . . . 4C 102
Aldin Cl. B78: M Oak . . . 7E 136
ALDRIDGE . . . 1A 164
Aldridge Cl. B78: Bir . . . 2H 143
Aldridge Rd. B74: L Ast . . . 3F 135
WS9: Ald . . . 3F 135
Aldrin Cl. ST3: Mei . . . 3E 42
ST16: Staf . . . 1K 73
ALDWARK . . . 2C 157
Aldwyck Dr. WV3: W'ton . . . 6H 129
Alesmore Mdw. WS13: Lich . . . 5K 113
Alexander Cl. WS13: Frad . . . 4K 107
Alexander Rd. WV8: Bilb . . . 2E 122
Alexandra Ct. DE15: Wins . . . 1H 87
Alexandra Cres. ST14: Utt . . . 5G 63
Alexandra Dr. DE13: Yox . . . 1H 89
Alexandra Ho. WS13: Lich . . . 4A 114
Alexandra M. B79: Tam . . . 4J 137
Alexandra Rd. DE15: Wins . . . 1H 87
ST3: Long . . . 7A 34
ST5: N'tle . . . 3G 23
ST17: Staf . . . 5G 73
Alexandra St. ST15: Stone . . . 3F 47
Alford Dr. ST2: Bent . . . 5C 26
Alfred Lyons Cl. WS15: Abb B . . . 2B 88
Alfred St. B79: Tam . . . 4G 137
DE14: B Tre . . . 2D 86
ST4: Fen . . . 2E 32
WS3: Blox . . . 4H 127
ALFRETON . . . 2D 157
Alfreton Rd. ST4: Fen . . . 3G 33
Algar Rd. ST4: T Val . . . 3J 31
Alicia Way ST2: Mil . . . 4G 19
ALKMONTON . . . 1B 160
Allard B77: Glas . . . 7A 138
Aldersley High School Sports Cen. . . . 4F 123
Allen Birt Wlk. WS15: Rug . . . 5F 95
Allenby Sq. ST4: T Val . . . 5J 31
Allendale ST16: Staf . . . 5D 70
Allendale Wlk. ST3: Blur . . . 1E 40
ALLEN END . . . 2B 164
Allen's Cl. WV12: Will . . . 7B 126
Allens Cft. ST14: Mar . . . 2C 82
Allens La. ST14: Mar . . . 2C 82
Allensmead B77: Wiln . . . 7J 137
Allensmore Av. ST4: Fen . . . 4H 33
Allen St. B77: T Gat . . . 1J 141
ST4: S Tren . . . 1J 31
ST10: Chea . . . 5D 54
Allensway ST5: N'tle . . . 5C 30
ALLENTON . . . 1D 161
Allerdale Rd. WS8: Clay . . . 5G 121
Allerton Rd. ST4: Tren . . . 3K 39
ALLESLEY . . . 3C 165
Alleston Rd. WV10: Bush . . . 3B 124
Alleston Wlk. WV10: Bush . . . 3B 124
ALLESTREE . . . 1D 161
Alleynes Sports Cen. . . . 1H 47
Alley's La. ST20: C Eat . . . 2B 68
ALLGREAVE . . . 1D 155
Alliance St. ST16: Staf . . . 1E 72
ALLIMORE GREEN . . . 3C 159
Allington Av. WS13: Lich . . . 5K 113
Alliss Cl. ST16: Staf . . . 2K 73
Alloys Cl. B77: Wiln . . . 5A 142
Allport Rd. WS11: Cann . . . 2E 108
Allport St. WS11: Cann . . . 1E 108
All Saints Cft. DE14: B Tre . . . 4D 86
All Saints Rd. DE14: B Tre . . . 3C 86
ST4: S Tren . . . 4A 32
ALLSCOTT
Bridgnorth . . . 2B 162
Telford . . . 3A 158
Allthorpe Pl. ST5: N'tle . . . 6D 30
Allton Av. B78: M Oak . . . 1D 140
Allton Ct. B77: Glas . . . 6A 138
Almar Ct. WV8: P'ord . . . 4H 123
Almar Pl. ST6: Chel . . . 2A 18
Alma St. DE14: B Tre . . . 2D 86
ST4: Fen . . . 3D 32
ST13: Lee . . . 3E 48
ST15: Stone . . . 3F 47
ALMINGTON . . . 1B 158
Almond Cl. WS11: H Hay . . . 1J 109
Almond Ct. DE13: Stre . . . 2F 85
Almond Gro. ST3: Fen . . . 6E 32
Almond Pl. ST5: C'ton . . . 6B 16
Almond Rd. WS12: Hun . . . 2D 100
Almshouse Cft. ST18: Brad . . . 6B 68
Almshouses WS15: Rug . . . 7G 95
Alnwick Cl. WS12: H Hay . . . 1A 110
Alnwick Rd. WS3: Blox . . . 1H 127
Alpha Way WS6: G Wyr . . . 4G 119
Alpine Dr. WS12: Hed . . . 6K 101
Alpine Way WV3: W'ton . . . 4K 129
ALPORT . . . 1C 157
ALPRAHAM . . . 2A 154
ALREWAS . . . 5C 130 (3B 160)
ALREWAS HAYES . . . 1G 107
Alrewas Rd. DE13: K Bro . . . 2C 130
ALSAGER . . . 2B 154
Alsager Rd. ST7: Aud . . . 2F 15
ALSAGERS BANK . . . 2H 21 (3C 155)
Alsop Crest ST17: Act T . . . 6K 77
ALSOP EN LE DALE . . . 2B 156
Alsop St. ST13: Lee . . . 4F 49
Alston Cl. WS12: H Hay . . . 1A 110
Alstone Cl. ST16: Staf . . . 6D 70
ALSTONEFIELD . . . 2B 156
Alstone La. ST18: Hau . . . 7D 66
Alstonfield Av. ST2: A Hul . . . 2J 25
Althorp Way DE13: Stre . . . 3E 84
Althrop Gro. ST3: Long . . . 6K 33
ALTON
Chesterfield . . . 1D 157
Stoke-on-Trent . . . 5H 57 (3A 156)
Altona Cl. ST15: Stone . . . 4H 47
Alton Cl. ST5: Sil . . . 7K 21
WV10: Bush . . . 2C 124
Alton Gro. ST2: Bent . . . 2K 33
WS11: Cann . . . 2B 108
Alton Rd. ST14: Dens . . . 1B 58
Alton Towers . . . 2H 57
ALVASTON . . . 1D 161
Alvaston Cl. WS3: Blox . . . 2J 127
ALVECOTE . . . 3F 139 (1C 165)
Alvecote Cotts. B79: Alve . . . 3F 139
Alvecote La. B79: Alve . . . 3F 139
Alvecote Pools Nature Reserve . . . 5G 139
Alvecote Priory (remains of) . . . 4G 139
ALVELEY . . . 3B 162
Alverstoke Cl. WV9: P'ord . . . 3J 123
Alverton Cl. B77: Dost . . . 6J 141
Alvis Cl. B79: Tam . . . 2F 137
Alwyn B77: Wiln . . . 3A 142
Alwyn Cl. WS6: G Wyr . . . 1F 119
Alwyn Cres. ST6: B'lem . . . 7D 18
Alwyn Rd. DE13: Yox . . . 2H 89
AMBASTON . . . 1D 161
Amber Bus. Village B77: Amin . . . 6D 138
Amber Cl. B77: Amin . . . 6D 138
Amber Ct. B77: Amin . . . 6D 138
DE14: B Tre . . . 1D 86
(off Grants Yd.)
ST9: S Broo . . . 4A 50
Amberfield Cl. ST3: Long . . . 5A 34
AMBERGATE . . . 2D 157
Ambergate Cl. WS3: Blox . . . 2J 127
Amber Gro. WS11: H Hay . . . 7J 101
Amberlands DE13: Stre . . . 2G 85
AMBLECOTE . . . 3C 163
Amblecote Dr. ST3: Long . . . 5A 34
Amblefield Way ST16: Staf . . . 4E 70
Ambleside Cl. ST15: Stone . . . 4K 47
Ambleside Gro. WV12: Will . . . 4B 126
Ambleside Pl. ST6: B'lem . . . 4A 18
Ambrose Pl. ST6: Chel . . . 7K 11
Amelia Cl. ST2: Mil . . . 5G 19
America St. ST6: Tuns . . . 4H 17
AMERTON . . . 2D 159
Amerton La. ST18: Shir . . . 4E 80
Amerton Railway . . . 2D 159
Amerton Working Farm . . . 2D 159
AMF Bowling
Oxley . . . 7A 124
Amicable St. ST6: B'lem . . . 1K 23
Amicombe B77: Wiln . . . 1E 142
AMINGTON . . . 5C 138
Amington Ind. Est. B77: Amin . . . 6D 138
(not continuous)
Amington Pk. B77: Amin . . . 3C 138
B77: Tam . . . 4K 137
Amington Rd. B77: Tam, Amin . . . 5J 137
Amison St. ST3: Long . . . 5K 33
Amos Av. WV11: Wed . . . 6F 125
Amos La. WV11: Wed . . . 6G 125
Ampleforth Dr. ST17: Staf . . . 6K 73
Ampthill Pl. ST4: H'ord . . . 1K 39
Amsden Lodge ST13: Ched . . . 2G 51
Ancaster St. ST6: Gold . . . 7H 11
Anchor Cl. B77: Amin . . . 5A 138
Anchor Ind. Est. ST3: Long . . . 5J 33
Anchor Pl. ST3: Long . . . 5J 33
Anchor Rd. ST3: Long . . . 5J 33
Anchor Ter. ST3: Long . . . 5J 33
Anchor Way ST20: Gno . . . 3H 67
Ancient High House & Yeomanry Mus. . . . 3G 73
Anders B79: Tam . . . 3G 137
Anderson Pl. ST6: Nort . . . 4E 18
Anders Sq. WV6: Per . . . 2F 129
Anderstaff Ind. Est. DE14: B Tre . . . 6F 85
Anderton Vw. ST15: Stone . . . 1E 46
Andover Cl. ST3: Long . . . 3J 33
Andover Pl. WS11: Cann . . . 6G 101
Andrew Cl. WV12: Will . . . 7D 126
Andrew Dr. WV12: Will . . . 7D 126
Andrew Mulligan Cl. ST6: Tuns . . . 2G 17
Andrew Pl. ST5: N'tle . . . 3H 153 (7G 23)
Andrews Ho. WS13: Lich . . . 4A 114
Andrews Rd. WS9: W Woo . . . 7K 121
Andrew St. ST6: Gold . . . 7G 11
Aneurin Bevan Pl. WS15: Rug . . . 6F 95
ANGELBANK . . . 3A 162
Angel Cft. WS7: C Ter . . . 2G 111
Angelica B77: Amin . . . 5B 138
Anglesey Bus. Pk. DE14: B Tre . . . 2C 86
WS12: Hed . . . 6A 102
Anglesey Cl. WS7: Chas . . . 7G 111
Anglesey Ct. DE14: B Tre . . . 3C 86
Anglesey Cres. WS8: Brow . . . 2H 121
WS12: Hed . . . 5J 101
Anglesey Dr. ST3: Long . . . 6G 33
Anglesey Hollow WS12: Hed . . . 5H 101
Anglesey M. WS12: Hed . . . 5J 101
Anglesey Rd. DE14: B Tre . . . 3C 86
WS8: Brow . . . 2H 121
WS13: Lich . . . 1B 114
Anglesey St. DE14: B Tre . . . 1A 86
WS12: Hed . . . 5H 101
Angle St. ST13: Lee . . . 3E 48
Anglia Rd. WS11: Cann . . . 7D 100
Angorfa Cl. WS13: Lich . . . 4K 113
Angus Cl. ST2: Buck . . . 5J 25
ANKERBOLD . . . 1D 157
Anker Cl. WS7: Burn . . . 5B 112
Anker Dr. B77: Tam . . . 5H 137
B79: Tam . . . 5H 137
Ankermoor Ct. B77: Tam . . . 4A 138
Ankerside B78: Pole . . . 6J 139
Ankerside Shop. Cen. B79: Tam . . . 5H 137
Anker Vw. B77: Tam . . . 6J 137
B78: Pole . . . 2J 143
Annan Av. WV10: Bush . . . 6C 124
Anna Wlk. ST6: B'lem . . . 1K 23
Anne Ct. ST7: T Pit . . . 1B 16
Anne Cres. WS11: Cann . . . 4E 100
Anne St. ST6: Gold . . . 7G 11
Annette Rd. ST4: Fen . . . 3H 33
ANSLEY . . . 2C 165
ANSLOW . . . 2C 161
Anslow Gdns. WV11: Wed . . . 4K 125
ANSLOW GATE . . . 2B 160
Anslow Rd. DE13: B Tre, Roll D . . . 1B 84
DE13: H'ury . . . 7E 82
Ansmede Gro. ST3: Blur . . . 1F 41
Anson Av. WS13: Lich . . . 3A 114
Anson Cl. WS6: G Wyr . . . 3F 119
WS7: Burn . . . 4A 112
WV6: Per . . . 1F 129
Anson Ct. B78: Faze . . . 2H 141
DE14: B Tre . . . 1F 87
Anson Ct. Bus. Cen. ST18: Staf . . . 1B 74
Anson Dr. ST17: Walt . . . 1D 78
Anson M. WS15: Rug . . . 7H 95
Anson Rd. DE13: Alre . . . 6C 130
ST3: Mei . . . 2B 42
WS6: G Wyr . . . 3F 119
Anson Row ST18: L Hay . . . 6H 81
Anson St. WS15: Rug . . . 7G 95
(not continuous)
Anston Way WV11: Wed . . . 6H 125
Anstree Cl. WS6: C Hay . . . 3D 118
ANSTY . . . 3D 165
Ansty Dr. WS12: H Hay . . . 2K 109
Anthony Gro. ST3: M Hea . . . 6B 42
Anthony Pl. ST3: Long . . . 5K 33
Antler Dr. WS15: Rug . . . 6D 94
Antom Ct. ST16: Staf . . . 6H 71
APEDALE . . . 1J 21
Apedale Community Country Pk. . . . 3K 21
Apedale Heritage Cen. . . . 3A 22
Apedale Rd. ST5: C'ton . . . 2B 22
ST7: Big E . . . 7H 15
APETON . . . 1D 68 (3C 159)
Apex Bus. Pk. WS11: N Can . . . 6B 110
Apex Rd. WS8: Brow . . . 5E 120
Apley Pl. ST4: H'ord . . . 2K 39
Apollo B79: Tam . . . 3F 137
Apollo Cinema
Stafford . . . 4G 73
Apollo Cl. WS11: Cann . . . 5G 101
Apollo Wlk. ST6: B'lem . . . 6C 18
Appian Cl. B77: T Gat . . . 3J 141
Appleby Gdns. WV11: Ess . . . 3C 126
APPLEBY MAGNA . . . 1D 165
APPLEBY PARVA . . . 1D 165
Applecroft CW3: Mad . . . 2A 28
ST5: C'ton . . . 6C 16
Applecross B74: F Oak . . . 7K 135
Appledore Cl. ST17: Staf . . . 6C 74
WS6: G Wyr . . . 1G 119
WS12: Wimb . . . 7A 102
Appledore Ct. WS3: Blox . . . 5H 127
Appledore Gro. ST6: Chel . . . 6J 11
Appleford Pl. ST3: Blur . . . 1E 40
Applegarth Cl. ST4: Fen . . . 3H 33
Appleton Cl. DE15: Stap . . . 5F 87
ST8: Bidd . . . 7E 8
Appleton Dr. ST5: Whit . . . 5F 37
Apple Wlk. WS11: H Hay . . . 1J 109
Applewood Cl. ST14: Utt . . . 4F 63
Applewood Cres. ST3: Mei . . . 2E 42
Appleyard, The ST19: Brew . . . 2C 92
Appleyard Ct. ST16: Staf . . . 3G 73
Apse Cl. WV5: Womb . . . 3F 145
Aps Ind. Est. DE14: B Tre . . . 6F 85
Apsley Gro. ST12: Titt . . . 2A 44
Aqualate Ho. ST17: Staf . . . 1G 77
Aqueduct St. ST4: S Tren . . . 2B 32
Aquinas St. ST4: S Tren . . . 2A 32
Arbor Cl. B77: Tam . . . 6K 137
Arbour Cl. CW3: Mad . . . 2A 28
Arbourfield Dr. ST2: B Hil . . . 6G 25
Arbour M. WS11: N Can . . . 5B 110
Arbour St. ST1: H'ley . . . 2H 151 (4D 24)
ST7: T Pit . . . 2B 16
Arbourtree Ct. WV5: Womb . . . 3H 145
Arcadia Pk. WS15: Rug . . . 3K 97
Archer Rd. WS3: Blox . . . 7K 127
Arch St. WS15: Rug . . . 1H 97
ARCLID . . . 1B 154
ARCLID GREEN . . . 1B 154
Arclid Way ST2: B Hil . . . 6H 25
Arctic Pl. ST4: Tren . . . 2B 40
Arden Cl. B77: Amin . . . 4A 138
ST13: Lee . . . 4J 49
WS15: Rug . . . 6E 94
Arden Rd. B77: Hock . . . 5B 142
DE13: B Nee . . . 6G 89
Arden Wlk. WS15: Hand . . . 5G 99
(off Proctors Rd.)
Ardgay Dr. WS12: Hed . . . 3F 101
Ardingley Av. ST17: Staf . . . 5K 73
Argil Cl. WV11: Wed . . . 5H 125
Argles Rd. ST13: Lee . . . 2H 49
Argosy Cl. ST3: Mei . . . 3D 42
Argyle Av. B77: Tam . . . 5K 137
Argyle St. B77: Amin . . . 6A 138
ST1: H'ley . . . 6D 150 (6B 24)
Argyll Cl. ST11: B Bri . . . 4G 43
Argyll Rd. ST3: Long . . . 7K 33
Ariane B79: Tam . . . 2E 136
Aries Cl. ST6: Chel . . . 1K 17
Arion Cl. B77: Tam . . . 4K 137
Arkall Cl. B79: Tam . . . 2J 137
Arkle B77: Dost . . . 6K 141
Arkle Cl. ST14: Utt . . . 6J 63
Arkwright Gro. ST1: H'ley . . . 7F 19
Arkwright Rd. WS2: Wals . . . 7H 127
ARKWRIGHT TOWN . . . 1D 157
ARLESTON . . . 3A 158
Arlington Way ST3: Mei . . . 3C 42
Armishaw Pl. WS15: Bre . . . 4K 97
ARMITAGE . . . 4E 98 (3A 160)
Armitage Gdns. WS15: Rug . . . 3K 97
Armitage Ho. WS13: Lich . . . 2E 114
(off Hobs Rd.)
Armitage La. WS15: Bre . . . 4K 97
(not continuous)
WS15: Rug . . . 4A 98
Armitage Rd. WS15: Rug . . . 1H 97
ARMSHEAD . . . 4D 26
Armshead Rd. ST9: Werr . . . 3D 26
Armside Cl. WS3: Pels . . . 7D 120
Armstead Rd. WV9: P'ord . . . 2H 123
Armstrong B79: Tam . . . 3F 137
Armstrong Av. ST16: Staf . . . 1J 73
Armstrong Dr. WV6: W'ton . . . 7J 123
Armstrong Grn. ST6: B'lem . . . 1C 24
Arnhem Cl. WV11: Wed . . . 5F 125
Arnold Cl. B79: Tam . . . 3G 137
Arnold Gro. ST5: N'tle . . . 7F 17
Arnotdale Dr. WS12: Hed . . . 3F 101
Arnot Rd. DE14: B'ton . . . 4B 86
Arps Rd. WV8: Cods . . . 2B 122
Arran Cl. WS11: Cann . . . 7G 101
Arran Dr. B77: Wiln . . . 3B 142
ST7: Pack . . . 6K 11
Arrow Ind. Est. WV12: Will . . . 7C 126
Arrow Rd. WS3: Blox . . . 7K 127
Arthur Cotton Ct. ST6: B'lem . . . 6A 18

Arthur Evans Cl.—Badnall St.

Arthur Evans Cl. WS15: Bre 4J 97
Arthurs Ct. DE13: Stre 1F 85
Arthur St. DE14: B Tre 6D 84
ST5: N'tle 1A 152 (6D 22)
ST6: Tuns 4J 17
ST13: Lee 3G 49
ST15: Stone 2G 47
Arthur St. WS11: Cann 6F 101
WS12: Wimb 7A 102
Arthur Wood Pl. WS15: Rug 6F 95
Arundel B77: T Gat 3J 141
Arundel Dr. ST10: Chea 4E 54
Arundel Gro. WV6: Per 3G 129
Arundel Rd. WV10: Oxl 3K 123
WV12: Will 6C 126
Arundel Way ST3: Long 3J 33
Ascot Cl. DE15: Wins 1H 87
WS14: Lich 4D 114
Ascot Dr. B77: Dost 6J 141
WS11: Cann 3B 108
Ascot Rd. ST17: Staf 5A 74
ASH BANK 5B 26
Ash Bank Rd. ST2: Bent 5A 26
ST9: Werr 5A 26
ASHBOURNE 3B 156
Ashbourne Cl. WS11: Cann 6G 101
Ashbourne Dr. ST5: Sil 7J 21
Ashbourne Gro. ST1: H'ley 3C 24
Ashbourne Rd. DE6: May, M May . . . 6B 56
ST10: Chea 4D 54
ST13: B'nop, Lee 4G 49
ST14: Roce 4D 58
ST14: Spa, Utt 2G 63
WS3: Blox 2J 127
Ashbrook DE15: Stap 3H 87
Ashbrook Cl. ST14: Utt 7H 63
ST20: Gno 3H 67
Ashbrook La. WS15: Abb B 3C 88
Ashburton St. ST6: B'lem 1B 24
Ashby Cres. ST3: Blur 1F 41
ASHBY-DE-LA-ZOUCH 3D 161
Ashby Rd. B79: Amin 1J 137
B79: Tam 3H 137
DE15: Bret, Wins, B Tre 1G 87
Ash Cl. ST10: Chea 5E 54
ST14: Utt 5F 63
WV8: Bilb 2C 122
Ashcombe Grn. ST3: Blur 1F 41
Ashcombe Rd. ST13: Ched 6G 51
Ashcombe Way ST13: Lee 5G 49
Ashcott Wlk. ST2: Bent 7J 25
Ashcroft Av. ST4: T Val 6J 31
Ashcroft Cl. ST5: N'tle 2E 22
Ashcroft Gro. ST5: N'tle 2F 23
Ashcroft La.
WS14: C'eld, Wall, Shen 5B 134
Ashcroft Oval ST5: N'tle 2F 23
Ashcroft Pl. ST5: N'tle 2F 23
Ashcroft Rd. ST5: N'tle 2E 22
Ashdale Cl. DE15: Stap 4H 87
ST15: Stone 5G 47
WS12: Hun 3C 100
Ashdale Dr. ST16: Staf 5F 71
Ashdale Pk. ST15: Yarn 6D 64
Ashdale Ri. ST5: N'tle 6F 31
Ashdale Rd. B77: Tam 4K 137
ST4: Fen 4C 32
ST13: Lee 3J 49
Ashdene Farm Camping & Cvn. Pk.
B78: D Bas 6C 140
Ash Dr. ST18: Hau 7C 66
Ashendene Gro. ST4: H'ord 2K 39
Ashenden Ri. WV3: W'ton 5H 129
Ashenhurst Way ST13: Lee 5G 49
Ashenough Rd. ST7: T Pit 1B 16
ASHFIELD 3A 162
Ashfield Gro. WV10: Ford 2A 124
Ashfield Rd. WV3: W'ton 4K 129
WV10: Ford 2A 124
Ashfields Ct. ST5: N'tle 1C 152 (6E 22)
Ashfields Grange
ST5: N'tle 2D 152 (7F 23)
Ashfields New Rd.
ST5: N'tle 2C 152 (7E 22)
Ashfield Sq. ST2: B Hil 6G 25
ASHFLATS 4G 77
Ashflats La. ST17: Staf 4G 77
ST18: Staf 4G 77
Ashford Gro. ST15: Stone 5J 47
ASHFORD IN THE WATER 1B 156
Ashford Rd. DE13: B Tre 5B 84
Ashford St. ST4: S Tren 1B 32
ASH GREEN 3D 165
Ash Grn. Cl. ST4: Tren 3A 40
Ash Gro. B77: Hock 5B 142
ST2: Bent 5B 26
ST3: Blur 7E 32
ST5: Sil 6K 21
ST11: B Bri 2E 42
ST12: Barl 2D 44
ST19: Brew 2D 92
ST19: Whe A 2C 90
WS11: Cann 6F 101
WS13: Lich 3E 114
Ashgrove WS7: Chas 6H 111
Ashlands ST18: Hixon 5D 80
Ashlands Av. ST4: S Tren . . . 5K 153 (1J 31)
Ashlands Cl. B79: Tam 2J 137
Ashlands Cres.
ST4: S Tren 5K 153 (2J 31)
Ashlands Gro. ST4: S Tren. . . 6J 153 (2J 31)
Ashlands Rd. ST4: S Tren . . 6J 153 (2J 31)
Ash La. ST15: Yarn 7C 64
WS6: G Wyr 1G 119
Ashlar Cl. ST6: Feg H 6A 12
Ashlea B78: Dor 5H 143
Ashlea Dr. DE6: May 6C 56
Ashleigh Cres. ST19: Whe A 1C 90
Ashleigh Dr. B77: Wiln 2A 142
ST14: Utt 4E 62
Ashleigh Rd. ST10: Tea 3G 55
WS15: Rug 2G 97
ASHLEY 4J 61 (1B 158)
Ashley Cl. DE15: Wins 1H 87
ST16: Staf 2C 72
Ashley Ct. DE15: Wins 1H 87
Ashley Cft. ST20: C Eat 2B 68
ASHLEY DALE 4H 61
Ashley Gdns. WV8: Cods 1B 122
Ashley Gro. ST5: N'tle 4G 23
ASHLEY HEATH 5F 61 (1B 158)
Ashley Rd. WS3: Blox 4F 127
WS7: C Ter 2F 111
ASH MAGNA 1A 158
Ashmall WS7: Hamm 7B 112
Ashman St. ST6: B'lem 5C 18
Ashmead Rd. WS7: C Ter 3J 111
Ashmole Av. WS7: Burn 3C 112
Ashmole Cl. WS14: Lich 5E 114
Ashmore Av. WV11: Wed 5A 126
ASHMORE BROOK 1H 113
Ashmore Dr. ST20: Gno 3H 67
ASHMORE PARK 4K 125
Ashmore Wlk. ST1: H'ley 3J 151
ASHOVER 1D 157
Ashover Gro. ST6: Chel 6J 11
Ash Pk. Ind. Est. WS11: H Hay 7H 101
ASH PARVA 1A 158
Ashridge Av. ST5: N'tle 7F 31
Ashridge Gro. ST3: Long 4K 33
Ashridge Wlk. ST16: Staf 4F 71
Ash Ri. ST17: Staf 3G 77
Ash Rd. ST15: Stone 5H 47
Ash St. DE14: B Tre 3C 86
WS3: Blox 4K 127
Ashton Ct. ST5: N'tle 7G 31
ST9: Werr 5C 26
Ashtree Bank WS15: Bre 3J 97
Ashtree Cl. ST18: L Hay 6J 81
Ashtree Ct. WS11: Cann 6D 100
Ash Tree Hill ST10: Chea 5B 54
Ashtree La. WS13: S'hay 2G 115
Ash Tree Rd. DE13: B Nee 6F 89
Ashurst Gro. ST3: Mei 3D 42
Ash Vw. ST7: Kids 4F 11
WS12: Hun 2D 100
Ash Wlk. DY7: Stou 1A 148
Ash Way ST2: Bent 5B 26
ST5: N'tle 5D 30
Ashwell Rd. ST4: S Tren 4J 153 (1H 31)
Ashwells Gro. WV9: P'ord 3J 123
ASHWOOD 3C 163
Ashwood ST3: Long 4H 33
Ashwood Gro. ST11: B Bri 4J 43
Ashwood Ter. *ST3: Long 4J 33*
(off Ashwood)
Ashworth Av. DE15: Stap 2K 87
Ashworth Ho. WS11: Cann 6G 101
Ashworth St. ST4: Fen 3D 32
Askern Cl. ST3: L'ood 1A 42
Aspbury Cl. B77: Glas 6A 138
Aspen Cl. ST7: Harr 3J 11
WS13: Lich 3E 114
Aspen Ct. WS12: Haz 4C 102
Aspen Cft. ST17: Staf 6D 72
Aspen Gro. WS7: C Ter 3H 111
WV12: Will 6E 126
Aspen M. DE15: Stan 6G 87
Aspen Rd. DE13: B Nee 7G 89
Aspley Cl. WV10: F Ash 6H 93
Aspley La. WV10: S Hea 1B 116
Asquith Cl. ST8: Bidd 5D 8
Asquith Dr. WS11: H Hay 1J 109
ASTBURY 1C 155
Astbury Cl. ST7: Kids 3G 11
WS3: Blox 1G 127
Aster Cl. ST3: W Coy 3D 34
Aster Wlk. WV9: P'ord 2J 123
Astil St. DE15: Stap 3G 87
Astle Pl. ST1: H'ley 6H 151 (6D 24)
Astles Rock Wlk. DY7: Kin 6D 148
ASTLEY 3D 165
ASTLEY ABBOTTS 2B 162
ASTON
Birmingham 2A 164
Market Drayton 3B 154
Nantwich 3A 154
Stafford 2A 72
Telford 1A 162
Wolverhampton 2C 163
Aston Bank ST16: Aston 2A 72
ST18: Aston 2A 72
ASTON BOTTERELL 3A 162
ASTON-BY-STONE 2H 69 (1D 159)
Aston Chase ST15: Stone 4K 47
Aston Cl. ST18: L Hay 6J 81
ST19: Penk 5H 91
WS14: Shen 5C 134
Aston Ct. ST15: Stone 2E 46
ASTON EYRE 2A 162
Astonfields Ind. Est. ST16: Staf 7G 71
(not continuous)
Astonfields Rd. ST16: Staf 7G 71
Astonfields Rd. Bus. Pk.
ST16: Staf 7G 71
Aston Hill ST18: Aston 2A 72
ASTON JUXTA MONDRUM 2A 154
ASTONLANE 2A 162
Aston La. ST15: Aston 2H 69
Aston Lodge Parkway ST15: Stone . . . 6K 47
ASTON-ON-TRENT 2D 161
Aston Rd. ST5: C'ton 6A 16
Aston Ter. ST16: Staf 7G 71
Astoria Cl. WV12: Will 4D 126
Astoria Dr. ST17: Staf 1H 77
Astoria Gdns. WV12: Will 4D 126
Astor Rd. B74: S'ly 7F 135
Astro Gro. ST3: Long 5G 33
Athelstan Cl. ST19: Penk 4J 91
Athelstan Gro. WV6: Per 1G 129
Athelstan St. ST6: Tuns 4H 17
Athelstan Way B79: Tam 2F 137
Athena Rd. ST1: H'ley 3F 25
ATHERSTONE 2D 165
Atherstone Rd. ST4: Tren 3A 40
Atherstone St. B77: Faze, T Gat 2H 141
B78: Faze 2H 141
Athlestan Way DE13: Stre 1C 84
Athlone St. ST6: B'lem 5D 18
Atholl Rd. ST3: Long 1K 41
Atkins Wlk. B78: Pole 2J 143
Atkins Way ST14: Roce 5D 58
Atlam Cl. ST2: Buck 5G 25
Atlantic Gro. ST4: Tren 2B 40
Atlas Cft. WV10: Oxl 7A 124
Atlas St. ST4: Fen 4E 32
ATLOW 3C 157
ATTERLEY 2A 162
Attingham Dr. WS11: H Hay 1H 109
ATTLEBOROUGH 2D 165
Attlee Cres. ST17: Staf 7E 72
WS15: Rug 2H 97
Attlee Gro. WS11: H Hay 1J 109
Attlee Rd. ST10: Chea 5C 54
Attwood Ri. ST7: Kids 4E 10
Attwood Rd. WS7: C Ter 3E 110
Attwood St. ST7: Kids 4E 10
Aubrey St. ST6: Gold 7F 11
Auchinleck Dr. WS13: Lich 2C 114
Auckland St. ST6: B'lem 7A 18
Auden Ct. WV6: Per 2G 129
Auden Pl. ST3: Long 6K 33
Auden Way ST17: Staf 6E 72
AUDLEM 3A 154
AUDLEY 5F 15 (2B 154)
Audley Cl. DE13: Alre 5C 130
Audley Pl. ST5: N'tle 3F 31
Audley Rd. CW2: Bart 2A 14
ST5: C'ton 5A 16
ST7: Big E, T Pit 1J 15
Audley St. ST5: N'tle 5C 22
ST6: Tuns 4H 17
Audley Theatre 5F 15
AUDMORE 2J 67 (2C 159)
Audmore Rd. ST20: Gno 4H 67
Augustine Cl. ST15: Stone 5J 47
Augustines Wlk. WS13: Lich 7A 106
Austin Cl. ST10: Chea 5B 54
ST15: Stone 5G 47
Austin Cote La. WS14: Lich 4E 114
Austin Friars ST17: Staf 4G 73
Austin Ho. ST2: A Hul 4G 25
Austin St. ST1: H'ley 7J 151 (6D 24)
AUSTREY 1C 165
Austwick Gro. ST4: T Val 4J 31
Autumn Dr. WS13: Lich 1D 114
Avarne Pl. ST16: Staf 3G 73
Aveling Grn. ST1: H'ley 7F 19
Aveling Rd. ST1: H'ley 7F 19
Avenue, The DY7: Stou 7H 147
ST4: S Tren 7G 153 (2G 31)
ST5: N'tle 7G 153 (2G 31)
(London Rd.)
ST5: N'tle 1J 153 (6H 23)
(May Av.)
ST7: Kids 5D 10
ST9: End 2A 50
ST9: S Broo 5B 50
ST10: Chea 5C 54
ST11: B Bri 3J 43
ST13: Ched 6G 51
ST15: Stone 3G 47
WV3: W'ton 6J 129
WV10: Fea 5F 117
WV10: W'ton 7D 124
Avenue Rd. ST4: S Tren 7B 24
WS12: H Hay 1A 110
Averill Dr. WS15: Rug 6F 95
Averill Rd. ST17: Staf 6E 72
Avill B77: Hock 5C 142
Avion Cl. ST3: Mei 3E 42
Avoca St. ST1: H'ley 1J 151 (3D 24)
Avocet Cl. ST14: Utt 7H 63
Avon B77: Hock 5C 142
Avon Bus. Pk. WS11: Cann 4C 108
Avon Cl. ST5: N'tle 5F 31
ST7: Kids 4F 11
ST16: Staf 3K 73
WV6: Per 3G 129
Avondale St. ST6: B'lem 7H 17
Avon Gro. ST10: Chea 6D 54
ST15: Stone 6H 47
TF9: Logg 4E 60
Avon Hill ST16: Staf 3A 74
Avonlea Gdns. WS15: Rug 7E 94
Avon Ri. ST16: Staf 3K 73
Avon Rd. WS7: Chas 6H 111
WS11: Cann 4C 108
Avonside Av. ST6: Tuns 3K 17
Avon Way DE15: Stap 3H 87
Avonwick Gro. ST1: H'ley 2G 25
Awlmakers Gro. WS3: Blox 6J 127
Axbridge Wlk. *ST6: B'lem 6C 18*
(off Kinver St.)
Axon Cres. ST3: W Coy 6D 34
Aylesbury Rd. ST2: Bent 6H 25
Aylesford Dr. B74: F Oak 3K 135
Aynsley Av. ST5: N'tle 6F 31
Aynsley Cl. ST10: Chea 6C 54
Aynsley Rd. ST4: S Tren 7B 24
Aynsley's Dr. ST11: B Bri 3G 43
Ayreshire Gro. ST3: L'ood 1K 41
Ayr Rd. ST10: Chea 2D 54
Ayrton Cl. WV6: Per 2H 129
Ayshford St. ST3: Long 6H 33
Azalea Cl. WV8: Bilb 2D 122

B

Babbacombe Av. ST17: Staf 6C 74
Babbington Cl. DE13: Tut 3H 83
Babworth Cl. WV9: P'ord 3J 123
Bk. Brook St. ST8: B Lee 1A 12
Bk. Browning St. ST16: Staf 2F 73
Bk. Bunt's La. ST9: S Broo 3J 19
Backcester La. WS13: Lich 3B 114
Backcrofts WS11: Cann 2D 108
Bk. Ford Grn. Rd. ST6: B'lem 5D 18
Back Gdn. St. ST5: N'tle 4F 153 (1G 31)
Bk. Heathcote St. ST7: Kids 4E 10
Back La. CW2: Balt, Bet 1B 6
CW3: Bet 1B 6
DE13: Yox 1F 89
ST6: B Edg 7H 13
(Bank End, not continuous)
ST6: B Edg 5H 13
(Hill Top)
ST10: Alt 5J 57
ST13: Lee 3E 48
ST14: Utt 5H 63
ST18: Hau 6C 66
ST18: Hixon 5C 80
ST18: L Hay 6H 81
ST19: Whe A 3B 90
ST20: Gno 5G 67
ST20: W'ves 2D 66
TF9: A'ley 5G 61
WS14: W'ton 6K 115
Back Radfords ST15: Stone 4G 47
Back Vw. ST10: K'ley 6G 53
Bk. Westlands Rd. ST14: Utt 7G 63
BADDELEY EDGE 5K 19
BADDELEY GREEN 4H 19 (2D 155)
Baddeley Grn. La. ST2: Mil 5H 19
Baddeley Hall Rd. ST2: Mil 5J 19
Baddeley Rd. ST2: Mil 6H 19
Baddeley St. ST6: B'lem 6K 17
ST10: Chea 5D 54
BADDESLEY ENSOR 7K 143 (2C 165)
Baden Powell Cl. WS15: Can W 4H 103
Baden Rd. ST6: B'lem 6C 18
Baden St. ST5: N'tle 1D 152 (6F 23)
Bader Rd. WV6: Per 3F 129
Badger Brow Rd. TF9: Logg 4D 60
Badger Cl. WS12: Hun 4C 100
Badger Gro. ST3: Mei 3E 42
Badgers Brow ST1: H'ley . . . 4K 151 (5E 24)
Badgers Cl. WS3: Pels 7C 120
Badgers Cft. ST5: C'ton 6C 16
ST17: Wild 1A 78
ST21: Ecc 2J 65
Badger's End ST19: Whe A 2B 90
Badgers Hollow ST10: Chec 6K 55
Badgers Ri. ST13: Lee 3F 49
Badgers Sett ST13: Lee 3F 49
Badgers Way WS12: H Hay 1K 109
Badgery Cl. ST14: Utt 3F 63
Badnall Cl. ST13: Lee 3E 48
Badnall St. ST13: Lee 3E 48

A-Z Staffordshire Atlas 169

Beacon La.—Bewcastle Gro.

Beacon La. DY7: Kin 6A 148
Beacon Pk. 3K 113
Beacon Pk. ST19: B Elm 7C 90
Beacon Ri. ST15: Stone 6F 47
Beacon Rd. DE13: Roll D 1C 84
ST15: Stone 7G 47
WV12: Will 5C 126
Beaconsfield ST5: N'tle 1G 23
Beaconsfield Dr. ST3: Blur 1E 40
Beaconsfield Rd. DE13: B Tre 4B 84
BEACONSIDE 2K 73
Beaconside ST16: Staf 7J 71
ST18: Staf 4E 70
Beaconside Cl. ST16: Staf 1J 73
Beaconside Sports Cen. 2B 74
Beacon St. WS13: Lich 2K 113
Beacon Way WS12: Wimb 7B 102
Beadnell Gro. ST3: Long 1J 41
Bealeys Av. WV11: Wed 5G 125
Bealeys Cl. WS3: Blox 2G 127
Bealeys La. WS3: Blox 2G 127
Beam Cl. DE13: B Tre 3B 84
BEAM HILL 2C 84 (2C 161)
Beamhill Rd. DE13: Ans 3A 84
BEAMHURST 1B 62 (1A 160)
Beamish La. WV8: C Woo 7A 92
Beans Slade Dr. WS14: Lich 6A 114
Beard Gro. ST2: A Hul 1H 25
Bear La. Cl. B78: Pole 7J 139
Bearnett La. WV4: L Pen 1H 145
WV5: Womb 1H 145
BEARSTONE 1B 158
BEARWOOD 3A 164
Bearwood Hill Rd.
DE15: Wins 1G 87
BEASLEY 1D 22
Beasley Av. ST5: C'ton 2D 22
Beasley Pl. ST5: C'ton 1D 22
Beatrice Cl. ST4: H'ord 7A 32
Beatrice St. WS3: Blox 7J 127
Beatrice Wlk. ST8: Brin F 4B 12
Beattie Av. ST5: N'tle 5F 23
Beatty Rd. ST13: Lee 3H 49
Beauchamp Ind. Pk.
B77: Wiln 2K 141
Beauchamp Rd. B77: Hock 5B 142
Beau Ct. WS11: Cann 2E 108
Beaudesert WS7: C Ter 2J 111
Beaudesert Pk. WS15: Can W 4J 103
Beaudesert Vw. WS12: Haz 5C 102
Beaufighter Gro. ST6: Tuns 2G 17
Beaufort Av. ST9: Werr 5C 26
Beaufort Ct. *ST3: L'ood 1B 42*
(off Waterhead Rd.)
Beaufort Rd. DE15: Stap 3H 87
ST3: Long 7J 33
Beaulieu Cl. ST9: Werr 5D 26
Beaumaris Cl.
ST4: S Tren 4J 153 (1H 31)
Beaumaris Ct. ST5: N'tle 5B 152 (1E 30)
Beaumont Cl. ST8: Bidd 3D 8
WS6: G Wyr 2F 119
Beaumont Ct. *ST5: N'tle 6D 30*
(off The Bridle Path)
Beaumont Gdns. ST17: Staf 6D 72
Beaumont Ho. WV10: Brin 4B 116
Beaumont Ri. ST11: B Bri 7F 43
Beaumont Rd. ST6: Tuns 4J 17
WS6: G Wyr 2F 119
Beaumont Way WS11: N Can 7C 110
Beaver Cl. ST4: T Val 5J 31
WV11: Wed 7K 125
Beaver Dr. ST10: Chea 4A 54
(not continuous)
Bebington Cl. WV8: P'ord 5H 123
Beck, The B79: Elf 5H 131
BECKBURY 1B 162
Beckdale ST14: Utt 5F 63
Beckenham Cl. ST3: Mei 2E 42
Becket Cl. DE13: B Tre 5C 84
Beckett Av. ST3: Mei 1D 42
Becketts Ct. DE13: B Tre 4D 84
Beckfield Cl. ST8: Bid M 4H 9
Beckford St. ST1: H'ley 1J 151 (3D 24)
Beck Rd. CW3: Mad 2B 28
Beckton St. ST6: Tuns 4J 17
Bedale Pl. ST3: Blur 1E 40
Bedcroft ST12: Barl 1F 45
Beddows Rd. WS3: Wals 7K 127
Beddow Way ST6: Chel 1K 17
Bedford Av. ST16: Staf 3J 73
Bedford Cres. ST5: N'tle 5G 31
Bedford Pl. WS12: Hed 6H 101
Bedford Rd. DE15: Stap 5E 86
ST1: H'ley 6D 150 (6B 24)
ST7: Kids 3E 10
Bedford St. ST1: H'ley 7C 150 (6A 24)
(not continuous)
Bedford Way WS15: Rug 3F 97
Bedingstone Dr. ST19: Penk 6H 91
BEDNALL 7D 78 (3D 159)
Bednall Ct. ST17: Bed 7D 78
Bednall Rd. ST17: Act T 6K 77
BEDWORTH 3D 165
BEECH 1C 159
Beech Av. B77: Glas 6A 138
DE13: K Bro 2C 130
DE13: Stre 3G 85
ST13: Ched 6G 51
BEECHCLIFF 7H 39
Beechcliff La. ST4: Bee 7H 39
ST12: Titt 2A 44
Beech Cl. B79: Tam 1G 137
DY7: Kin 5F 149
ST8: Bid M 4H 9
ST10: Chea 5E 54
ST13: Lee 7D 48
ST14: Utt 5F 63
ST18: Hau 7C 66
ST19: Whe A 2C 90
WS15: Hand 5G 99
WV6: Patt 7B 128
WV10: Oxl 5K 123
Beech Ct. ST11: B Bri 3F 43
ST15: Stone 4H 47
WS6: G Wyr 7F 109
WS12: Hed 3H 101
Beech Cres. WS7: Chas 5H 111
Beech Cft. CW3: Mad 2A 28
WV6: Patt 7B 128
Beechcroft ST12: Barl 1F 45
Beechcroft Av. ST16: Staf 4E 72
Beechcroft Ct. WS11: Cann 1E 108
Beechcroft Grange ST16: Staf 5E 72
Beechcroft Pl. WV10: Oxl 6A 124
Beech Dr. DE13: Stre 3F 85
ST7: Kids 6C 10
Beechen Gro. WS7: C Ter 3H 111
Beeches, The B74: F Oak 4J 135
B78: Pole 2J 143
ST5: N'tle 1G 23
WS15: Rug 5E 94
Beeches Cft. WS13: Frad 3K 107
Beeches Pl. WS3: Blox 6K 127
Beeches Rd. WS3: Blox 7K 127
WS15: Rug 3J 97
Beeches Row ST6: Tuns 2H 17
Beechfield Dr. ST17: Staf 2B 78
Beechfield Ri. WS13: Lich 3D 114
Beechfield Rd. ST4: Tren 4B 40
Beechfields ST12: Barl 1F 45
Beech Gdns. WS14: Lich 5C 114
WV8: Cods 3B 122
Beech Ga. B74: L Ast 3G 135
Beech Gro. ST4: Fen 4C 32
ST5: N'tle 4G 23
ST13: Lee 3D 48
TF9: Logg 4E 60
WS12: Hun 2D 100
Beechhouse La. WV5: Seis 2A 144
Beech Hurst Gdns. WV5: Seis 2C 146
Beech La. DE13: Stre 2F 85
(not continuous)
ST4: Bee 7G 39
ST18: Copp 4E 76
Beechlawn Dr. DY7: Stou 2J 149
Beechmere Ri. WS15: Rug 6D 94
Beechmont Gro. ST1: H'ley 2F 25
Beechmount Ri. ST17: Wild 7A 74
Beech Pine Cl. WS12: Hed 2G 101
Beech Rd. B79: Tam 1G 137
DE13: B Nee 7G 89
ST3: Blur 1F 41
ST21: Ecc 3H 65
WV10: Oxl 5K 123
Beech St. DE14: B Tre 3C 86
ST3: Long 6J 33
Beech Tree Av. WV11: Wed 5G 125
Beech Tree La. WS11: Cann 3D 108
Beech Wlk. WS15: L'don 1E 104
Beechway ST16: Staf 7F 71
Beechwood WS14: W'ton 3G 131
Beechwood Av. WV11: Wed 5F 125
Beechwood Bus. Pk.
WS11: H Hay 7H 101
Beechwood Cl. ST5: N'tle 1G 39
ST11: B Bri 4H 43
WS3: Blox 2H 127
Beechwood Ct. WV6: Tett 3K 129
Beechwood Cres. B77: Amin 5B 138
Beechwood Cft. B74: L Ast 3J 135
Beechwood Dr. ST15: Stone 6G 47
WV6: Tett 4H 129
Beecroft Av. WS13: Lich 2B 114
Beecroft Rd. WS11: Cann 2E 108
Beekes Cft. B78: Faze 2G 141
Bee La. WV10: Ford 2B 124
BEELEY 1C 157
Bees La. WS15: Rug 7G 95
Beeston Ridge ST17: Staf 7D 72
Beeston St. ST3: Long 4J 33
Beeston Vw. ST7: Kids 7E 10
BEFFCOTE 3C 159
Beffcote Rd. ST20: Gno 6F 67
Beggars Bush La. WV5: Womb 5H 145
Beggars La. ST13: Lee 5D 48
BEIGHTON HILL 2C 157
BELBROUGHTON 3D 163
Belfast Cl. ST6: B'lem 5B 18
Belfield Av. ST5: N'tle 4G 23
Belford Pl. ST4: S Tren 7K 23
Belfort Way ST17: Staf 6J 73
Belfry, The DE13: Stre 2D 84
WV6: Per 2E 128
Belfry Cl. WS3: Blox 2G 127
Belgrade Rd. WV10: Oxl 4K 123
BELGRAVE 1K 141
Belgrave Av. ST3: Long 7H 33
Belgrave Cres. ST3: Long 1J 41
Belgrave Rd. B77: Wiln 2A 142
ST3: Long 1J 41
ST5: N'tle 5F 153 (1G 31)
Belgrave Sports Cen. 1A 142
Bellamour La. ST17: Wol B 2B 94
WS15: Bell 3F 95
WS15: Wol B 2B 94
Bellamour Way WS15: Col 3H 95
Bellamy La. WV11: Wed 6G 125
Bellasis St. ST16: Staf 7F 71
Bell Av. ST3: Long 7K 33
Bell Bri. La. WS13: Lich 5K 107
Bellbrook ST19: Penk 3G 91
Bell Cl. ST16: Staf 1H 73
WS13: Lich 2K 113
Bell Dr. WS12: Hed 3J 101
Bellefield Vw. *ST5: N'tle 5G 23*
Bellencroft Gdns. WV3: W'ton 7K 129
BELL END 3D 163
Bellerton La. ST6: Nort 5E 18
Belle Vue ST13: Lee 3E 48
Belle Vue Rd. ST13: Lee 3E 48
Bellflower Cl. WV10: Fea 5E 116
Bell Heather Rd. WS8: Clay 6F 121
Bell Ho. ST3: Blur 3F 41
Bellhurst La. ST19: Whe A 4A 90
Bellingham B77: Wiln 1F 143
Bellingham Gro. ST1: H'ley 2D 24
Bell La. DE13: B Nee 5G 89
ST12: Barl 6E 40
WS3: Blox 3G 127
Bell Orchard TF9: A'ley 4J 61
Bellow La. ST10: O'moor 1E 56
Bellringer Cl. ST8: Bidd 6C 8
Bellringer Rd. ST4: Tren 3D 40
Bell Rd. WV5: Trys 1C 144
Bell's Hollow ST5: C'ton 5C 16
Bellsize Cl. WS11: N Can 6B 110
Bells La. WS7: C Ter 2H 111
Bellwood Cl. ST3: Mei 5C 42
Belmont Av. WS11: Cann 1C 108
Belmont Cl. WS11: Cann 7G 109
Belmont Rd. B77: Wiln 4A 142
ST1: H'ley 4A 150 (5A 24)
ST10: Ips 2F 53
Belmot Rd. DE13: Tut 3G 83
BELPER 3D 157
BELPER LANE END 3D 157
Belper Rd. WS3: Blox 2J 127
Belsay Cl. ST3: Long 5J 33
Belsize B77: Glas 7A 138
BELTON 2D 161
Belton Av. WV11: Wed 4F 125
Belt Rd. WS12: Hed 4F 101
Belvedere Cl. B79: Tam 2J 137
ST17: Staf 6A 74
WS7: Chas 6H 111
Belvedere Gdns. WV6: Tett 6G 123
Belvedere Rd. DE13: B Tre 5B 84
ST4: H'ord 1A 40
Belvide Gdns. WV8: Cods 1B 122
Belvide Reservoir Bird Sanctuary
. . . . 3C 159
Belvoir B77: T Gat 3J 141
Belvoir Av. ST4: Tren 5C 40
Belvoir Cl. DE13: B Tre 6C 84
Belvoir Rd. DE13: B Tre 6B 84
Bembridge Cl. WV12: Will 5B 126
BEMERSLEY GREEN 5C 12
Bemersley Rd. ST6: B Gre, B Edg 6D 12
ST8: Brin F, Knyp 3C 12
Benches Cl. WS7: C Ter 5F 111
Bencroft WV8: Bilb 1D 122
Bend Oak Dr. DE15: Wins 7K 85
Benedict Pl. ST2: A Hul 3G 25
Benenden Cl. ST17: Staf 6K 73
Benfleet Pl. ST3: Long 6G 33
Bengal Gro. ST4: Tren 2C 40
Bengry Rd. ST3: Long 7A 34
Benion Rd. WS11: Cann 6F 101
Benjamins Way ST7: Big E 5H 15
Bennett Pl. ST5: N'tle 1F 23
Bennett Pct. *ST3: Long 6H 33*
(off The Strand)
Bennett Rd. B74: F Oak 5J 135
Bennetts La. ST14: Bram 6B 62
WV6: Patt, Tres 5A 128
Bennett St. ST6: B'lem 1J 23
Bennick Trad. Est. WS11: Cann 5E 108
Bennion Gro. ST14: Dens 3C 58
Bennion St. ST3: Long 6J 33
Benson Cl. WS13: Lich 2D 114
WV6: Per 1F 129
Benson St. ST6: Chel 2K 17
Benson Vw. B79: Tam 1J 137
BENTHALL 1A 162
BENTILEE 7J 25
Bentilee Temporary Retail Village
ST2: Bent 7K 25
Bent La.
ST5: Act, Stab, Whit, S Har 4J 37
ST5: S Har, Stab 6K 37
BENTLEY
Nuneaton 2C 165
Walsall 2D 163
Bentley Av. ST5: N'tle 4F 23
Bentley Brook La. WS12: Haz 4C 102
Bentley Cl. ST15: Stone 2E 46
Bentley Dr. WV8: Cods 1B 122
BENTLEY HEATH 3B 164
Bentley La. WS2: Wals 7E 126
WV12: Will 7D 126
Bentley Rd. ST6: Chel 2C 18
ST14: Utt 4E 62
WV10: Bush 3C 124
Bentley Way B79: Tam 2F 137
Benton Cres. WS3: Blox 3K 127
Bentons La. WS6: G Wyr 3G 119
Benty Grange La. ST13: Wink 5A 52
Benyon Cen., The WS2: Wals 6G 127
Beowulf Covert DE13: Stre 2C 84
Berdmore St. ST4: Fen 4G 33
Beresford Cres.
ST5: N'tle 7C 152 (3E 30)
Beresford Dale CW3: Mad 2A 28
Beresford St. ST4: S Tren 7B 24
Beresford Trad. Est. ST6: Tuns 2H 17
Bergamot Dr. ST3: Mei 4C 42
Berkeley Cl. ST20: Gno 3J 67
WV6: Per 3G 129
Berkeley Ct. ST5: N'tle 3G 153 (7G 23)
Berkeley St. ST1: H'ley 5H 151 (5D 24)
ST15: Stone 2F 47
Berkeley Way WS15: L'don 1E 104
Berkshire, The WS3: Blox 2G 127
Berkshire Gro. ST5: N'tle 4G 31
BERKSWELL 3C 165
Berkswell Cl. B74: F Oak 4K 135
Bernard Cheadle Cl. ST15: Swyn 2D 64
Bernard Gro. ST3: M Hea 6B 42
Bernard St. ST1: H'ley 5H 151 (5D 24)
Berne Av. ST5: N'tle 3C 30
Berryfield Gro. ST3: Long 5B 34
Berryfields WS9: Ston 5H 133
Berry Gdns. DE15: Wins 7K 85
Berry Hedge La. DE15: Wins 7K 85
BERRY HILL 7G 25
Berry Hill WS12: Hed 6J 101
Berryhill Fields 1H 33
Berry Hill Greenway ST2: B Hil 6H 25
Berryhill-Normacot Greenway
ST3: Long 3K 33
Berry Hill Rd. ST4: Fen 7D 24
(not continuous)
Berryhill Village ST2: B Hil 7G 25
Berry La. ST3: Long 6J 33
BERRY RING 7A 72
Berry Rd. ST16: Staf 6D 70
Berry St. ST4: S Tren 2B 32
Bertelin Rd. ST16: Staf 6H 71
Berwick Dr. WS11: Cann 3B 108
Berwick Rd. ST1: H'ley 7E 18
Berwick Wlk. ST5: N'tle 6A 152 (2D 30)
Berwyn Gro. WS6: C Hay 1F 119
Besom Way WS6: C Hay 2C 118
Best Av. DE15: Stap 3J 87
Best St. ST4: Fen 4F 33
Beswick Cl. ST10: Chea 6C 54
Beswick Rd. ST6: Chel 2K 17
Beta Rd. ST5: C'ton 6D 16
Bethell Rd. ST1: H'ley 1D 24
Bethesda Rd. ST1: H'ley 7H 151 (6D 24)
Bethesda St. ST1: H'ley 4F 151 (5C 24)
Betjeman Pl. WV10: Bush 4E 124
Betjeman Wlk. ST17: Staf 7E 72
BETLEY 2B 6 (3B 154)
BETLEY COMMON 2A 6
Betley Hall Gdns. CW3: Bet 1B 6
Betley Pl. ST5: N'tle 3G 31
Beton Way ST16: Staf 5F 71
Betony Rd. DE15: Stap 2K 87
Bettany Glade WV10: Bush 1C 124
Bettany Rd. ST6: B'lem 1A 24
BETTON 1A 158
Betty Hatch La. ST16: Staf 1E 72
Betty's La. WS11: N Can 7B 110
Bevan Av. ST7: T Pit 1B 16
Bevandean Cl. ST4: Tren 5C 40
Bevan Lee Rd. WS11: Cann 7D 100
Bevan Pl. CW3: Mad 2A 28
Beveridge Cl. ST3: Mei 7D 34
Beverley Cl. ST19: Penk 5H 91
Beverley Cres. ST11: Fors 2J 43
Beverley Dr. ST2: Bent, Buck 6H 25
ST16: Staf 5E 70
Beverley Hill WS12: Hed 3K 101
Beverley Rd. DE14: B'ton 5A 86
Beverston Rd. WV6: Per 2H 129
Beville St. ST4: Fen 3E 32
Bevin La. ST2: Buck 5G 25
Bewcastle Gro. ST3: Mei 3C 42

Bew St. ST6: B Gre . . . 2E 18
Bexhill Gro. ST1: H'ley . . . 2F 25
Bexley St. ST1: H'ley . . . 1E 150 (3B 24)
Bexmore Dr. WS13: S'hay . . . 2F 115
Beyer Cl. B77: Glas . . . 7C 138
Bhylls Cres. WV3: W'ton . . . 7K 129
Bhylls La. WV3: W'ton . . . 6J 129
Bibbey's Grn. WV10: Bush . . . 1D 124
BICKENHILL . . . 3B 164
BICKFORD . . . 3C 159
Bickford Rd. WV10: W'ton . . . 7D 124
Bickley Av. B74: F Oak . . . 3K 135
BICKLEY MOSS . . . 3A 154
BIDDULPH . . . 5C 8 (2C 155)
Biddulph Grange Country Pk. . . . 2F 9
Biddulph Grange Country Pk. Vis. Cen. . . . 2E 8
Biddulph Grange Gardens . . . 2E 8
Biddulph Mobile Home Pk.
WS7: C Ter . . . 2F 111
BIDDULPH MOOR . . . 5H 9 (2D 155)
BIDDULPH PARK . . . 1F 9
Biddulph Rd. ST6: Brin F, Feg H . . . 1A 18
ST7: Harr, M Cop . . . 7J 7
Biddulph Valley Leisure Cen. . . . 4D 8
Bideford Av. ST17: Staf . . . 6B 74
Bideford Way WS11: Cann . . . 3B 108
BIGGIN
Ashbourne . . . 3C 157
Buxton . . . 2B 156
Biggin Cl. WV6: Per . . . 1F 129
BIGNALL END . . . 5H 15
Bignall End Rd. ST7: Big E . . . 4J 15
BIGNALL HILL . . . 5J 15
Bignall Hill ST7: Big E . . . 5J 15
Bigsbury Wlk. *ST6: B'lem . . . 1A 24*
(off Leonora St.)
ST6: B'lem . . . 1A 24
(off Swainsley Clo.)
Bigwood La.
ST18: Bill, Copp, Hyde L, Brad . . . 4A 76
ST18: Bill, Hyde L . . . 3B 76
Bilberry Bank WS11: Cann . . . 4E 100
Bilberry Cl. WS15: Rug . . . 7E 94
Bilberry Cres. WS12: Hun . . . 5C 100
BILBROOK . . . 1D 122 (1C 163)
Bilbrook Ct. WV8: Bilb . . . 2D 122
Bilbrook Gro. WV8: Bilb . . . 2D 122
Bilbrook Ho. WV8: Bilb . . . 2D 122
Bilbrook Rd. WV8: Bilb, Cods . . . 1C 122
(not continuous)
Bilbrook Station (Rail) . . . 3D 122
Billinge St. ST6: B'lem . . . 7J 17
BILLINGSLEY . . . 3B 162
BILLINGTON . . . 1A 76 (2C 159)
Billington Av. ST18: L Hay . . . 5J 81
Billington La. ST18: Derr . . . 4A 72
Billy Buns La. WV5: Womb . . . 2G 145
BILSTON . . . 2D 163
BILSTONE . . . 1D 165
Bilton St. ST4: S Tren . . . 3A 32
BINGS HEATH . . . 3A 158
BINLEY . . . 3D 165
BIRCHALL . . . 6G 49 (2D 155)
Birchall Av. ST6: Tuns . . . 2G 17
Birchall Cl. ST13: Lee . . . 7G 49
Birchall La. ST13: Lee . . . 7G 49
Birchall Pk. Av. ST13: Lee . . . 6G 49
Bircham Wlk. ST5: N'tle . . . 7F 31
Birch Av. ST8: Knyp . . . 7A 8
WS7: Chas . . . 5H 111
WS8: Brow . . . 4G 121
WS11: Cann . . . 3C 108
Birchbrook Ind. Pk. WS14: Shen . . . 5B 134
Birchbrook La. WS14: Shen . . . 5B 134
Birch Bus. Pk. WS11: Cann . . . 5F 109
Birch Cl. DE14: B'ton . . . 4B 86
ST14: Dens . . . 2B 58
ST17: Walt . . . 1D 78
ST18: Gt Hay . . . 4H 81
Birch Coppice WV5: Womb . . . 4E 144
Birchcroft WV9: Cove . . . 3A 116
BIRCH CROSS . . . 3A 82 (1B 160)
Birch Dale CW3: Mad . . . 3A 28
Birchdown Av. ST6: B'lem . . . 4B 18
Birch Dr. B74: L Ast . . . 3J 135
Birchenwood Countryside Pk. . . . 4G 11
Birchenwood Rd. ST6: Chel . . . 6J 11
Birchenwood Way ST7: Kids . . . 5F 11
Birches, The *ST10: Chea . . . 4C 54*
(off Royal Wlk.)
ST10: Chea . . . 5C 54
(Lid La.)
ST17: Staf . . . 7H 73
Birches Av. WV8: Bilb . . . 4E 122
Birches Cl. DE13: Stre . . . 3E 84
Birches Farm M. CW3: Mad . . . 4B 28
BIRCHES HEAD . . . 3D 24
Birches Head Rd. ST1: H'ley . . . 2D 24
ST2: H'ley, Mil . . . 2D 24
Birches Pk. Rd. WV8: Cods . . . 3C 122
Birches Rd. WV8: Bilb . . . 3C 122
Birches Valley WS15: Rug . . . 3A 96
Birches Valley Forest Cen. . . . 2B 96
Birches Way ST7: Kids . . . 4F 11
Birchfield Av. WV6: Tett . . . 7D 122
Birchfield Rd. DE15: Stap . . . 6F 87
ST2: A Hul . . . 3J 25
Birchfields Cl. ST15: Stone . . . 6F 47
Birchfields Dr. WS12: H Hay . . . 2K 109
Birchgate ST2: Buck . . . 4J 25
Birchgate Gro. ST2: Buck . . . 4J 25
Birch Grn. Gro. ST1: H'ley . . . 1E 24
Birch Gro. B78: Bir . . . 3F 143
ST3: M Hea . . . 6C 42
ST11: Fors . . . 3J 43
WS13: Lich . . . 3D 114
BIRCH HEATH . . . 1A 154
Birch Hill Av. WV5: Womb . . . 5F 145
Birch Ho. Rd. ST5: C'ton . . . 7B 16
Birchill Pl. WV5: Womb . . . 5F 145
Birchlands Rd. ST1: H'ley . . . 2F 25
Birch La. WS9: Ald . . . 7H 133
WS15: Bre . . . 3H 97
BIRCHLEY HEATH . . . 2C 165
BIRCHMOOR . . . 3G 143 (1C 165)
Birchmoor Rd. B78: Bir . . . 2G 143
BIRCHOVER . . . 1C 157
Birchover Way ST6: Feg H . . . 6A 12
Birch Ri. TF9: A Hea . . . 6E 60
Birch Rd. ST7: Big E . . . 6H 15
ST15: Stone . . . 4H 47
WV11: Wed . . . 4K 125
Birch St. ST1: H'ley . . . 1K 151 (3E 24)
Birch Ter. ST1: H'ley . . . 4G 151 (5C 24)
WS7: C Ter . . . 2J 111
Birchtree Dr. ST13: Ched . . . 2G 51
Birchtree Hollow WV12: Will . . . 7D 126
Birch Tree La. ST5: Whit . . . 3E 36
ST7: Sch G . . . 6F 7
Birchtree La. WS15: Rug . . . 3G 97
Birch Valley Rd. ST7: Kids . . . 5G 11
Birch Wlk. ST3: Blur . . . 1G 41
Birchwood Av. B78: Dor . . . 3H 143
Birchwood Cl. WV11: Ess . . . 2A 126
Birchwood Ri. WS15: Abb B . . . 3D 88
Birchwood Rd. WS14: Lich . . . 4F 115
Bird Cage Wlk. ST1: H'ley . . . 4F 151 (5C 24)
Birdhope B77: Wiln . . . 1E 142
Bird Rd. ST3: Mei . . . 7D 34
Birds Barn La. DY11: Wolv . . . 7A 148
Birds Bush Rd. B77: Wiln . . . 2A 142
BIRDSGREEN . . . 3B 162
Birdsgrove La. DE6: May . . . 4C 56
Bird St. WS13: Lich . . . 3A 114
(not continuous)
Birkdale Av. DE14: B'ton . . . 6B 86
Birkdale Dr. ST7: Kids . . . 3G 11
ST16: Staf . . . 2A 74
Birkdale Rd. WS3: Blox . . . 2G 127
Birkholme Dr. ST3: M Hea . . . 5C 42
Birks Dr. TF9: A Hea . . . 4E 60
Birks St. ST4: S Tren . . . 4B 32
BIRMINGHAM . . . 3A 164
BIRMINGHAM INTERNATIONAL AIRPORT . . . 3B 164
Birmingham Rd. WS13: Lich . . . 5B 114
WS14: Lich, S Woo, Shen . . . 7D 134 & 7A 114
Birrell St. ST4: Fen . . . 4F 33
Biscay Gro. ST4: Tren . . . 2C 40
Bishop Cl. WS11: Cann . . . 1D 108
Bishop Ct. ST2: Buck . . . 3H 25
Bishop Rd. ST6: Chel . . . 2A 18
Bishop's Cl. ST7: Talk . . . 6B 10
Bishops Ct. ST21: Ecc . . . 2H 65
Bishops Dr. ST19: Brew . . . 1D 92
Bishops Grange WS15: Rug . . . 6H 95
BISHOP'S HILL . . . 6E 88
BISHOP'S OFFLEY . . . 2B 158
Bishop St. ST4: Fen . . . 4G 33
BISHOPS WOOD . . . 6B 90 (1C 163)
BISHTON . . . 2B 94 (2A 160)
Bishton La. ST17: Wol B . . . 2C 94
ST18: Wol B . . . 2C 94
Bitham Cl. ST19: Penk . . . 4H 91
Bitham Ct. DE13: Stre . . . 2D 84
Bitham La. DE13: Stre . . . 2D 84
Bittell Cl. WV10: Bush . . . 1C 124
BITTERLEY . . . 3A 162
Bitterne Pl. ST2: Bent . . . 1K 33
Bittern La. ST10: Chea . . . 4D 54
BITTERSCOTE . . . 7G 137
Bitterscote Dr. B78: Tam . . . 6G 137
Bitterscote La. B78: Tam . . . 7G 137
(not continuous)
BLACK BANK . . . 5J 21
Blackbank Rd.
ST5: A Ban, N'tle, C'ton . . . 4J 21
Blackberry La. B74: F Oak . . . 3K 135
ST16: Staf . . . 2E 72
(not continuous)
Blackberry Way ST20: W'ves . . . 2D 66
Blackbird Cl. ST14: Utt . . . 7H 63
Blackbird Way ST7: Pack . . . 6K 11
ST8: Bidd . . . 5E 8
BLACKBROOK
Belper . . . 3D 157
Stoke-on-Trent . . . 7A 36 (1B 158)
Blackbrook Av. ST5: C'ton . . . 7B 16
Blackbrook Way WV10: Bush . . . 1C 124
Blackbrook Zoological Pk. . . . 2A 156
Blackburn Av. WV6: Tett . . . 6G 123
BLACKDEN HEATH . . . 1B 154
Blackdown B77: Wiln . . . 1E 142
Black Dr. ST18: Ing . . . 1G 75
Blackeagle Ct. DE14: B Tre . . . 7D 84
Blackflats Rd. ST15: Cold M . . . 4B 64
BLACKFORD . . . 3A 162
BLACKFORDBY . . . 3D 161
BLACKFORDS . . . 1E 108
Blackfriars Cl. B79: Tam . . . 4E 136
Blackfriars Rd. ST5: N'tle . . . 5D 152 (1F 31)
Blackhalve La. WV11: Wed, Ess . . . 5F 125
Blackham Rd. WV11: Wed . . . 5K 125
BLACKHEATH . . . 3D 163
Blackheath Cl. ST3: Long . . . 6K 33
Blackheath La. ST18: Staf, Tix . . . 1C 74
Blackhole La. ST18: Derr . . . 4A 72
Black Horse La.
ST1: H'ley . . . 3E 150 (4B 24)
Blackies La. ST15: Stone . . . 6K 47
(not continuous)
Blacklake Dr. ST3: M Hea . . . 6C 42
Blackpool St. DE14: B Tre . . . 4D 86
Blackroot Cl. WS7: Hamm . . . 7B 112
Blacksmith La. WS14: W'ton . . . 2G 131
Blacksmiths Yd. DE13: Roll D . . . 6H 83
Blackthorn Cres. WS12: Haz . . . 4C 102
Blackthorne Av. WS7: Chas . . . 7H 111
Blackthorne Rd. WS14: Lich . . . 4D 114
Blackthorn Pl. ST5: C'ton . . . 7C 16
Blackthorn Rd. DE15: Stap . . . 6F 87
BLACKWELL
Alfreton . . . 2D 157
Buxton . . . 1B 156
Blackwell's Row ST6: B'lem . . . 2B 24
Blackwood Av. WV11: Wed . . . 5F 125
BLACKWOOD HILL . . . 2D 155
Blackwood Ho. Bank ST3: Hort . . . 6K 9
Blackwood Pl. ST3: W Coy . . . 5A 34
Blackwood Rd. B77: T Gat . . . 3J 141
Bladon Av. ST5: N'tle . . . 6F 31
Bladon Cl. ST6: Feg H . . . 6A 12
Bladon Ho's. DE15: N Sol . . . 5J 85
Bladon St. DE15: Wins . . . 7K 85
Bladon's Yd. DE13: Roll D . . . 6H 83
Bladon Vw. DE13: Stre . . . 1G 85
BLAKEBROOK . . . 3C 163
Blake Cl. WS11: Cann . . . 5G 101
BLAKEDOWN . . . 3C 163
BLAKELEY . . . 5G 145
Blakeley Av. WV6: Tett . . . 6H 123
Blakeley Cl. WS15: Rug . . . 6G 95
Blakeley Heath Dr. WV5: Womb . . . 5G 145
BLAKELEY LANE . . . 6K 27
Blakeley La. ST10: O'moor . . . 1B 56
Blakeley Ri. WV6: Tett . . . 6H 123
Blakelow Rd. ST2: A Hul . . . 3H 25
Blakeman Way WS13: Lich . . . 5K 113
Blakenall Cl. WS3: Blox . . . 5K 127
BLAKENALL HEATH . . . 5K 127
Blakenall Heath WS3: Blox . . . 5K 127
Blakenall La. WS3: Blox . . . 6J 127
Blakenall Row WS3: Blox . . . 5K 127
Blakeney Av. ST5: N'tle . . . 6F 31
Blakeney Way WS11: Cann . . . 5G 109
BLAKENHALL
Nantwich . . . 3B 154
Wolverhampton . . . 2C 163
BLAKESHALL . . . 3C 163
Blake St. B74: F Oak . . . 2K 135
ST6: B'lem . . . 7K 17
Blake Street Station (Rail) . . . 2K 135
Blakeways Cl. B79: Edin . . . 1B 132
Blakiston St. ST16: Staf . . . 2H 73
Blanchard Cl. ST3: Mei . . . 3E 42
Blandford Cl. ST3: Long . . . 5J 33
Blandford Gdns. WS7: Burn . . . 5A 112
Blanefield WV8: P'ord . . . 3G 123
Blantyre St. ST3: Long . . . 7J 33
Blantyre Wlk. ST3: Long . . . 7J 33
Blatchford Cl. ST3: Mei . . . 7D 34
Blaydon Rd. WV9: P'ord . . . 3J 123
Bleak Ho. Dr. WS7: C Ter . . . 3F 111
Bleak Pl. ST6: B'lem . . . 1A 24
Bleakridge Av. ST5: Brad . . . 7F 17
Bleak St. ST5: N'tle . . . 5H 23
Bleeding Wolf La. ST7: Sch G . . . 1C 10
Blencarn Gro. ST9: S Broo . . . 3J 19
Blenheim Cl. B77: Tam . . . 5J 137
DE15: Wins . . . 1K 87
ST18: Staf . . . 3B 74
Blenheim Rd. WS7: C Ter . . . 3J 111
WS11: N Can . . . 7D 110
WV12: Will . . . 7B 126
Blenheim St. ST4: Fen . . . 4D 32
Blenheim Way WS13: Fra P . . . 5H 107
Bleriot Cl. ST3: Mei . . . 3E 42
BLETCHLEY . . . 1A 158
Bletchley Dr. B77: T Gat . . . 2J 141
Blewitt St. WS12: Hed . . . 4H 101
BLISTS HILL . . . 1A 162
BLITHBURY . . . 2A 160
Blithbury La. WS15: Rug . . . 3K 95
Blithbury Rd. WS15: Rug . . . 5J 95
Blithe Vw. ST11: B Bri . . . 4H 43
Blithfield Cl. ST9: Werr . . . 6C 26
Blithfield Ho. ST17: Staf . . . 1H 77
Blithfield Pl. WS11: H Hay . . . 2H 109
Blithfield Reservoir Bird Sanctuary . . . 2A 160
Blithfield Rd. WS8: Brow . . . 2D 120
Bloomfield Cl. WV5: Womb . . . 4D 144
Bloomfield Cres. WS13: Lich . . . 1A 114
Bloomfield Dr. WV12: Will . . . 4D 126
Bloomfield Way B79: Tam . . . 2F 137
Bloomsbury Way WS14: Lich . . . 4E 114
BLORE
Ashbourne . . . 3B 156
Market Drayton . . . 7A 60
Blount Cl. ST19: Penk . . . 5H 91
Blount's Dr. ST14: Utt . . . 7F 63
BLOUNT'S GREEN . . . 7F 63 (1A 160)
BLOXWICH . . . 4H 127 (1A 164)
Bloxwich Bus. Pk. WS2: Wals . . . 6G 127
Bloxwich La. WS2: Wals . . . 7G 127
Bloxwich Library Theatre . . . 4H 127
Bloxwich North Station (Rail) . . . 2F 127
Bloxwich Rd. WS2: Wals . . . 6J 127
WS3: Blox . . . 6J 127
Bloxwich Rd. Nth. WV12: Will . . . 7D 126
Bloxwich Station (Rail) . . . 4G 127
Bloxwich Swimming Baths & Leisure Cen. . . . 5J 127
Bluebell Cl. ST8: Bidd . . . 6D 8
ST13: Lee . . . 2J 51
WS12: Hed . . . 4H 101
Bluebell Cres. WV11: Wed . . . 7H 125
Bluebell Dr. ST5: N'tle . . . 5E 30
Bluebell Hollow ST17: Staf . . . 7C 74
Bluebell La. WS6: G Wyr . . . 3G 119
Bluebird Cl. WS14: Lich . . . 3D 114
Bluebird Trad. Est. WV10: W'ton . . . 7C 124
Blue Cedars DE15: Bret . . . 2K 87
Bluestone Av. ST6: B'lem . . . 5B 18
Bluestone La. DE15: Stan . . . 5G 87
BLUNDIES . . . 5H 147
Blundies La. DY7: Stou . . . 6H 147
Blunt St. ST5: N'tle . . . 4G 23
BLURTON . . . 7F 33 (3C 155)
Blurton Priory ST3: Blur . . . 2F 41
Blurton Rd. ST3: Barl, Blur . . . 1G 45
ST4: Blur, Fen . . . 5E 32
ST12: Barl . . . 1G 45
Blurtons La. ST21: Ecc . . . 4K 65
BLYMHILL . . . 3C 159
BLYMHILL LAWNS . . . 3C 159
Blythe Av. ST3: M Hea . . . 5C 42
BLYTHE BRIDGE . . . 3J 43 (3D 155)
Blythe Bri. Rd. ST11: Cave . . . 7G 35
Blythe Bridge Station (Caverswall Rd.)
Foxfield Steam Railway . . . 1H 43
Blythe Bridge Station (Rail) . . . 3H 43
Blythe Cl. ST11: B Bri . . . 3F 43
WS7: Burn . . . 5B 112
Blythe Gdns. WV8: Cods . . . 1B 122
Blythe Lodge *ST11: B Bri . . . 3G 43*
(off Grindley La.)
BLYTHE MARSH . . . 3H 43 (3D 155)
Blythe Mt. Pk. ST11: B Bri . . . 3J 43
Blythe Rd. ST11: Fors . . . 3J 43
ST17: Staf . . . 1G 77
Blythe St. B77: Tam . . . 6J 137
BLYTHE, THE . . . 2A 160
Blythe Vw. ST11: Sav G . . . 1J 59
Blythfield DE14: B Tre . . . 7F 85
Boardman Cres. ST16: Staf . . . 4E 72
Boardmans Bank ST6: B Edg . . . 5G 13
Boathorse Rd. ST6: Tuns . . . 1E 16
ST7: Kids . . . 6D 10
Boat Ho. La. WS15: Arm . . . 4E 98
Boat La. ST18: West . . . 2B 80
WS14: M Cor . . . 1J 133
Boatman Dr. ST1: H'ley . . . 7A 150 (6K 23)
Boatman Wlk. ST1: H'ley . . . 7A 150
BOBBINGTON . . . 6B 146 (2C 163)
Bodiam Ct. WV6: Per . . . 3H 129
Bodington Cl. WS7: Burn . . . 4C 112
Bodmin Av. ST17: Staf . . . 6B 74
Bodmin Wlk. ST6: B'lem . . . 6D 18
BODNETTS, THE . . . 5B 136
BODYMOOR HEATH . . . 2B 164
Bognop Rd. WV11: Ess . . . 1G 125
Bogs La. ST11: B Bri . . . 4H 43
Bolberry Cl. ST3: L'ood . . . 1A 42
Bold St. ST1: H'ley . . . 1J 151 (3E 24)
Bolebridge M. B79: Tam . . . 4H 137
Bolebridge St. B79: Tam . . . 5H 137
BOLEHALL . . . 5J 137 (1C 165)
BOLEHILL . . . 2C 157
Boley Cl. WS14: Lich . . . 4C 114
Boley Cott. La. WS14: Lich . . . 4D 114
Boley La. WS14: Lich . . . 4C 114
Boleyn Cl. WS6: C Hay . . . 2D 118
BOLEY PARK . . . 4E 114
Boley Pk. Cen. WS14: Lich . . . 4E 114
Bolina Gro. ST3: Long . . . 3H 33
Bollin Gro. ST8: Bidd . . . 4E 8
Bolney Gro. ST1: H'ley . . . 3F 25

Bolsover Cl.—Brickhill La.

Bolsover Cl. ST6: Feg H 6A 12
Bolton Pl. ST3: L'ood 2B 42
Bolton Way WS3: Blox 2F 127
Boma Rd. ST4: Tren 2K 39
BOND END
DE13 . . . . .3H 89 (3B 160)
DE14 . . . . .3E 86
Bond End DE13: Yox 4F 89
Bondfield La. DE13: Yox 2F 89
Bondfield Way ST3: Mei 7D 34
Bond St. DE14: B Tre 3E 86
ST6: Tuns 3H 17
Bond Way WS12: Hed 2F 101
BONEHILL 7E 136 (1B 164)
Bonehill Ind. Est. B78: Faze 1G 141
Bonehill Rd. B78: M Oak, Tam 7D 136
(not continuous)
BONEY HAY 3H 111 (3A 160)
Boney Hay Rd. WS7: Burn 3K 111
Bonham Ho. ST16: Staf 3F 73
(off South St.)
BONINGALE 1C 163
Boningale Way ST17: Staf 6D 72
Bonington Cres. ST16: Staf 4D 72
Bonnard Cl. ST3: Mei 4E 42
Bonner Cl. ST4: T Val 5J 31
Bonney Dr. WS15: Rug 6G 95
Bonny Stile La. WV11: Wed 7F 125
BONSALL .2C 157
Bonville Gdns. WV10: Bush 1C 124
BOOLEY 2A 158
Boon Av. ST4: P'ull 3A 32
Boon Gro. ST17: Staf 1G 77
BOON HILL .6H 15
Boon Hill Rd. ST7: Big E 6H 15
Boons Ind. Est. ST18: Derr 5A 72
Booth Cl. WS3: Blox 5K 127
WS13: Lich 1A 114
BOOTHEN 4A 32
Boothen Grn. ST4: S Tren 4B 32
Boothen Old Rd. ST4: S Tren 4B 32
Boothen Pk. ST4: S Tren 3B 32
Boothen Rd. ST4: S Tren 3B 32
Boothenwood Ter. ST4: S Tren 4A 32
Boot Hill CV9: Gren 7K 143
Boothroyd St. ST1: H'ley 4G 151 (5C 24)
Boothstone Gdns. ST15: Yarn 6D 64
Boothstone Mobile Home Pk.
ST15: Yarn 6D 64
Booth St. ST4: S Tren 3B 32
ST5: C'ton 2D 22
ST7: Aud 6F 15
WS3: Blox 5J 127
WS12: Hed 4H 101
Bordeaux Rd. ST3: Mei 2C 42
Bordeaux Wlk. ST5: N'tle 6D 30
Borden Cl. ST19: Whe A 1C 90
WV8: P'ord 5H 123
Border Way ST17: Staf 1G 77
Bore St. WS13: Lich 4B 114
Borman B79: Tam 4F 137
Borough La. WS15: L'don 3B 104
Borough Mus. & Art Gallery, The
. . . . .1G 153 (6G 23)
BOROUGH PARK 1J 137
Borough Rd. B79: Tam 2H 137
DE14: B Tre 1D 86
ST5: N'tle 2G 153 (7G 23)
BORROWASH 1D 161
Borrowcop La. WS14: Lich 5C 114
Borrowdale Rd. ST6: Nort 4E 18
Boscobel Gro. ST19: Brew 1D 92
Boscobel House 1C 163
Boscobel La. ST19: B Elm 7C 90
Boscombe Gro. ST4: Tren 5C 40
BOSCOMOOR 5G 91
Boscomoor Cl. ST19: Penk 5G 91
Boscomoor Ct. ST19: Penk 5G 91
Boscomoor Ind. Est. ST19: Penk 5G 91
Boscomoor La. ST19: Penk 5G 91
Boscomoor Shop. Cen. ST19: Penk. . .5G 91
Bosinney Cl. ST3: Fen 4H 33
BOSLEY 1D 155
Bosley Brook CW12: White 1D 8
Bosley Gro. ST6: Gold 7G 11
Bossgate Cl. WV5: Womb 6G 145
Bostock Cl. ST15: Stone 7K 47
BOSTOCK GREEN 1A 154
Boston Cl. ST6: Tuns 3G 17
WS12: H Hay 2A 110
Boston Ind. Est. WS15: Rug 6H 95
Boswell Rd. WS11: Cann 6D 100
Boswell St. ST4: S Tren 7A 150 (6K 23)
Bosworth Dr. DE13: B Tre 5C 84
Botany Bay Rd. ST1: H'ley. . .1K 151 (3E 24)
Botesworth Gdns. ST6: B'lem 6H 17
Botham Dr. ST13: Ched 5H 51
Botterham La. DY3: Swin 7E 144
Botteslow St. ST1: H'ley 4H 151 (5D 24)
Bottom La. ST15: Swyn 1C 64
Boucher Ho. ST13: Ched 2G 51
Boucher Rd. ST13: Ched 6G 51
Boughey Rd. ST4: S Tren 1C 32
ST7: Big E 5H 15
Boughey St. ST4: S Tren 3A 32
BOULDON .3A 162
Boulevard, The ST6: Tuns 4J 17
(off High St.)
ST6: Tuns 4J 17
(Scotia Rd.)
BOULTON .1D 161
Boulton Cl. WS7: Burn 3A 112
Boulton St. ST1: H'ley 1J 151 (3D 24)
ST5: N'tle 2G 23
BOUNDARY 3D 155
Boundary Cl. ST13: Lee 6G 49
ST15: Stone 7F 47
Boundary Ct. ST1: H'ley 1G 151
Boundary Ind. Est. WV10: Ford 7A 116
Boundary La. DY7: Stou 1J 149
Boundary St. ST1: H'ley 1E 150 (3B 24)
(not continuous)
ST5: N'tle 3H 153 (7H 23)
Boundary Vw. ST10: Chea 5A 54
Boundary Way WV6: Tett 4G 129
BOURNBROOK 3A 164
Bourne Av. B78: Faze 1E 140
Bourne Cl. DE13: Tut 2G 83
WS12: H Hay 1K 109
Bourne Cotts. ST3: Long 7J 33
Bourne Ct. ST15: Hild 5H 59
Bourne Pl. ST13: Lee 3D 48
Bourne Rd. ST7: Kids 4D 10
Bournes Bank ST6: B'lem 7K 17
Bournes Bank Sth. ST6: B'lem 7K 17
Bourne St. ST4: Fen 5E 32
ST7: M Cop 6H 7
BOURNVILLE 3A 164
BOURTON .2A 162
Bouverie Pde. ST1: H'ley 1F 25
Bowden St. ST6: B'lem 6B 18
Bowen-Cooke Av. WV6: Per 7A 122
Bower Cl. WS13: Lich 1D 114
Bower End La. CW3: Mad 3A 28
Bower La. WS15: Rug 6D 94
BOWERS .1C 159
Bowers Ct. ST15: Stone 5K 47
Bowers La. ST15: Aston 2H 69
Bower St. ST1: H'ley 6G 151 (6C 24)
Bowes Dr. WS11: Cann 6F 101
Bowfell Gro. ST3: Long 2H 33
Bowhill La. CW3: Aud, Bet 2C 6
Bowland Av. ST5: N'tle 5C 22
Bowlers Cl. ST6: B'lem 2A 24
Bowling Grn. Av. B77: Wiln 3A 142
Bowman Gro. ST6: Feg H 7B 12
Bowman Ho. ST3: L'ood 2B 42
Bowmead Cl. ST4: Tren 4C 40
Bowmere Cl. ST8: Bidd 4C 8
Bowness Gro. WV12: Will 4B 126
Bowness St. ST1: H'ley 1D 150 (3B 24)
Bowood Dr. WV6: Tett 7F 123
BOWSEY WOOD 7E 6
Bowsey Wood Rd.
CW3: B Woo, Mad 7E 6
Bowstead St. ST4: S Tren 2B 32
Bow St. ST1: H'ley 1G 151 (3C 24)
WS15: Rug 7G 95
(not continuous)
Bowyer Av. ST6: B Gre 2E 18
Boxer Cl. WS15: Hand 6G 99
Box La. ST3: Mei 7B 34
Boxwood Pl. ST5: C'ton 7B 16
Boxwood Rd. ST10: Tea 3G 55
Boyden Cl. ST19: Penk 5J 91
Boydon Cl. WS11: Cann 2B 108
Boyles Hall Rd. ST7: Big E 5G 15
BOYLESTONE 1B 160
BOYLESTONFIELD 1B 160
BOYTHORPE 1D 157
Brabazon Cl. ST3: Mei 3E 42
Bracken Av. TF9: Logg 4E 60
Brackenberry ST5: N'tle 5F 23
Bracken Cl. ST3: R Clo 5B 42
ST12: Titt 2A 44
ST16: Staf 5D 70
WS7: Burn 4A 112
WS12: Hed 2K 101
WS14: Lich 5E 114
WV8: P'ord 4G 123
Brackendale ST13: Lee 5C 48
BRACKENFIELD 2D 157
Brackenfield Av. ST2: Bent 7J 25
Brackenfield Way ST16: Staf 5F 71
Brackenhill Rd. WS7: C Ter 3J 111
Bracken Rd. WS12: Hun 5C 100
Brackens, The ST5: N'tle 7F 31
Bracken St. ST4: Fen 5E 32
Bracken Vw. ST17: Broc 4G 79
Bracken Way WS15: Rug 6E 94
Brackenwood Rd. DE15: Stap 6F 87
Bracklesham Way B77: Amin 3C 138
Brackley Av. ST6: B'lem 6B 18
BRADBOURNE 2C 157
Bradburn Rd. WV11: Wed 5F 125
Bradbury Cl. ST6: Nort 4E 18
WS8: Brow 7H 121
Bradbury Ct. WS12: Hed 3H 101
Bradbury La. DE13: K Bro 2C 130
WS12: Hed 2G 101
Bradbury Ri. ST16: Staf 2C 72
BRADDOCKS HAY 5E 8
BRADELEY .4C 18
Bradeley Village ST6: B'lem 4B 18
BRADFIELD GREEN 2A 154
BRADFORD 1C 157
Bradford Rd. WS8: Brow 4G 121
Bradford St. B79: Tam 4F 137
WS11: Cann 5G 101
Bradford Ter. ST1: H'ley 2E 24
Bradgate Cl. WV12: Will 7C 126
Bradgate Dr. B74: F Oak 3K 135
BRADLEY
Ashbourne 3C 157
Bilston 2D 163
Stafford 6B 68 (3C 159)
BRADLEY GREEN 1C 165
BRADLEY IN THE MOORS
. . . . .7F 57 (3A 156)
Bradley Lakes WS15: L'don 7C 98
Bradley La.
ST18: Brad, Hau . . . . . .7D 66 & 4B 68
ST18: Hyde L 2D 76
Bradley St. DE15: Stap 5F 87
ST14: Utt 5H 63
BRADMORE 2C 163
Bradmore Rd. DE13: B Tre 6C 84
BRADNOP .2A 156
Bradshaw Way ST16: Staf 5F 71
BRADWALL GREEN 1B 154
BRADWELL .1E 22
Bradwell Grange ST5: N'tle 2F 23
Bradwell La. ST5: Brad, N'tle 7E 16
WS15: Can W 5H 103
Bradwell Lodge ST5: N'tle 2G 23
Bradwell St. ST6: B'lem 7H 17
Braeburn Cl. WS13: Lich 2D 114
Braemar Cl. ST2: Buck 5K 25
WV12: Will 7B 126
Braemar Gdns. WS12: Hed 3F 101
Braemar Rd. WS11: N Can 7C 110
WV6: Patt 7B 128
Braemore Rd. ST2: A Hul 2H 25
Braham B79: Tam 3D 136
BRAILSFORD 3C 157
Brailsford Cl. WV11: Wed 5J 125
Brain St. B77: Glas 7C 138
Braithwell Dr. ST2: Mil 5G 19
Brake, The ST7: Sch G 6F 7
Brakespeare St. ST6: Gold 7G 11
Brake Village ST7: Sch G 6F 7
Bramall Cl. ST16: Staf 7E 70
Bramall La. ST16: Staf 7E 70
Bramber B77: Wiln 1K 141
Bramber Dr. WV5: Womb 4F 145
Bramble Cl. WS8: Clay 7G 121
WV12: Will 6C 126
Bramble Ct. DE15: Stap 6F 87
Bramble Dr. WS12: Hed 3J 101
Bramble La. WS7: Burn 3K 111
Bramble Lea CW3: Mad 3A 28
Brambles, The ST5: N'tle 7G 31
WS11: N Can 6C 110
WS14: Lich 5D 114
WS15: Hand 4G 99
Brambles Ct. ST8: Bidd 6D 8
Brambleside ST17: Wild 7A 74
Bramble Way WS15: Rug 7E 94
Bramblewood WV5: Womb 3G 145
Brambling B77: Wiln 3C 142
Brambling Cl. ST14: Utt 7H 63
Bramblings, The ST17: Wild 1B 78
BRAMCOTE 3D 165
Bramdean Dr. ST19: Penk 3H 91
Bramdean Wlk. WV4: Pen 7K 129
Bramell Cl. DE14: B'ton 5A 86
Bramerton Cl. WV11: Wed 7E 124
Bramfield Dr. ST5: N'tle 1F 153 (6G 23)
Bramley Cl. ST10: Chea 5D 54
Bramley Pl. ST4: T Val 6J 31
Bramley Way WS14: W'ton 6K 115
Bramling Cross DE14: B Tre 5G 85
Brammall Dr. ST11: B Bri 3G 43
Brammer St. ST6: B'lem 4C 18
BRAMPTON, THE 1F 153 (6G 23)
Brampton Cl. ST9: End 1B 50
Brampton Ct. ST5: N'tle 1F 153 (6G 23)
Brampton Dr. WS12: H Hay 1A 110
Brampton Gdns. ST5: N'tle 5G 23
Brampton Ind. Est.
ST5: N'tle 1E 152 (6F 23)
Brampton Rd. ST5: N'tle . . .1F 153 (6G 23)
Brampton Sidings
ST5: N'tle 1E 152 (6F 23)
Brampton Sidings Ind. Est.
ST5: N'tle 1E 152 (6F 23)
Brampton Va. Gdns.
ST5: N'tle 1G 153 (6G 23)
Brampton Wlk. ST3: Long 1J 41
BRAMSHALL 6B 62 (1A 160)
Bramshall Rd.
ST14: Bram, Utt, Kidd 6C 62
Bramshaws Acre ST10: Chea 5D 54
Bramstead Av. WV6: Tett 4J 129
Bramwell Dr. WS6: C Hay 3D 118
Brancaster Cl. B77: Amin 3C 138
BRANDON 3D 165
Brandon Gro. ST4: H'ord 2K 39
Brandons, The ST17: Staf 2H 77
Brandon Wlk. ST15: Stone 5F 47
Bransdale Cl. WV6: W'ton 7J 123
Bransdale Rd. WS8: Clay 5G 121
Branson Av. ST3: Long 6A 34
BRANSTON 5A 86 (2C 161)
Branston Rd. DE14: B Tre 4D 86
DE14: B'ton, Tate 7A 86
Branston Water Pk. Vis. Cen. 7A 86
Bransty Gro. ST4: Tren 5C 40
Brant Av. ST5: N'tle 4E 22
Brantley Av. WV3: W'ton 5K 129
Brantley Cres. DY7: Bob 6B 146
Brantley La. DY7: Bob 6B 146
Brantwood Av. WS7: Chas 6J 111
BRASSINGTON 2C 157
Brassington St. CW3: Bet 2B 6
Brassington Way ST2: Bent 7J 25
BRATCH, THE 3E 144 (2C 163)
Bratch Comn. Rd. WV5: Womb 3E 144
Bratch Hollow WV5: Womb 2G 145
Bratch La. WV5: Womb 2F 145
Bratch Pk. WV5: Womb 2F 145
Brattice Pl. ST2: B Hil 2K 33
BRATTON .3A 158
Braunton Av. ST17: Staf 7C 74
Bray Ho. WV11: Wed 7G 125
Braystones Cl. ST6: Chel 6J 11
BRAZENHILL 5C 66
Brazenhill La. ST18: Hau 4B 66
Breach La. ST10: Tea 2F 55
Breach Rd. ST6: B Edg 7J 13
Breadmarket St. WS13: Lich 3B 114
BREADSALL 3D 157
Bream B77: T Gat 3K 141
Bream Way ST6: B'lem 5B 18
Brean Rd. ST17: Staf 7C 74
Brecon Way ST2: Bent 6J 25
Breech Cl. ST10: Wat 5B 52
Breedon Cl. ST5: N'tle 5D 22
BREEDON ON THE HILL 2D 161
Breeze Av. ST6: Tuns 3J 17
WS11: N Can 6D 110
Brempton Cft. ST15: Hild 5H 59
Brendale Cl. ST4: H'ord 1A 40
Brendon B77: Wiln 1D 142
Brendon Cl. ST17: Staf 6B 74
Brent B77: Wiln 3A 142
Brent Cl. ST17: Staf 6J 73
Brentmill Cl. WV10: Bush 1D 124
Brentnor Cl. ST3: Long 6B 34
Brentwood Ct. ST9: Werr 4D 26
Brentwood Dr. ST9: Werr 4D 26
Brentwood Gro. ST9: S Broo 4J 19
ST9: Werr 4D 26
BRERETON 4J 97 (3A 160)
BRERETON CROSS 6B 98 (3A 160)
BRERETON GREEN 1B 154
BRERETON HEATH 1C 155
BRERETONHILL 5K 97
Brereton Hill WS15: Bre 4K 97
Brereton Hill La. WS15: Rug 7A 98
Brereton Lodge WS15: Bre 3J 97
Brereton Mnr. Ct. WS15: Bre 4K 97
Brereton Pl. ST6: B'lem 6J 17
Brereton Rd. WS15: Rug 2H 97
WV12: Will 6C 126
BRETBY 2C 161
Bretby La. DE15: Bret 2K 87
BRETFORD 3D 165
Bretherton Pl. ST6: Chel 1A 18
Bretlands Way DE15: Stan 6H 87
Bretton Gdns. WV10: W'ton 7D 124
Brewery La. ST18: Gt Hay 4G 81
Brewery St. ST1: H'ley 2F 151 (4C 24)
WS15: Rug 1H 97
Brewester Rd. ST2: Buck 5F 25
Brewhouse Arts Cen. 2E 86
Brewhouse Ct. WS13: Lich 2K 113
(off Wheel La.)
BREWOOD 2C 92 (1C 163)
Brewood Rd. WV9: Cove 1H 93
WV10: C Gre 3A 116
Brewster Cl. B78: M Oak 1E 140
Brianson Av. ST6: B'lem 1C 24
Briar B77: Amin 6C 138
Briar Av. B74: S'ly 7F 135
Briarbank Cl. ST4: H'ord 1K 39
Briar Cl. ST17: Walt 1D 78
WS12: Hed 2G 101
WS15: Rug 7E 94
Briars, The ST5: N'tle 6F 23
Briarsleigh ST17: Wild 7A 74
Briars Way WS12: Haz 6F 103
Briarswood ST7: Kids 5F 11
ST8: Bidd .4C 8
Briar Way ST21: Cot H 4A 64
Briarwood Pl. ST3: Mei 1D 42
Brickbridge La. WV5: Womb 5E 144
Brickfield Cl. ST18: Hixon 5D 80
Brickfield Pl. ST3: Long 4J 33
Brickhill La. DE13: New 7D 88

Brickhouse La.—Brown Edge

Brickhouse La. B79: Elf 5G 131
Brick Ho. St. ST6: B'lem 7K 17
Brickiln St. WS8: Brow 5H 121
Brick Kiln La. ST4: S Tren 6J 23
ST5: C'ton 1C 22
ST17: Broc 4D 78
ST18: Hopt, W Ban 6G 69
(not continuous)
ST19: Whe A 3A 90
Brick Kiln Way WS15: Bre 4H 97
Brickworks Rd.
WS12: Hed, Wimb 7K 101
Bridestowe Cl. ST3: Mei 3C 42
Bridge, The ST10: Tea 1F 55
Bridge Av. WS6: C Hay 6E 108
Bridge Cl. ST7: Big E 5H 15
ST18: West 2B 80
WS8: Clay 6G 121
Bridge Ct. ST4: T Val 6J 31
ST14: Utt 6J 63
ST20: W'ves 3D 66
WS12: Hed 5H 101
Bridge Cres. ST15: Stone 5G 47
Bridge Cft. ST6: Chel 1B 18
Bri. Cross Rd. WS7: C Ter 4H 111
BRIDGE END 2E 48
Bridge Farm M. DE13: Stre 2F 85
Bridgefoot Wlk. WV8: P'ord 4H 123
Bridge Hill DE6: May 5C 56
Bridge Ind. Est. ST6: B'lem 1B 24
Bridgemary Cl. WV10: Bush 1D 124
BRIDGEMERE 3B 154
Bridge Rd. ST4: T Val 6J 31
ST14: Utt 6J 63
WS15: Hand 5G 99
Bridges Cres. WS11: N Can 6B 110
Bridgeside DE13: Stre 2F 85
Bridgeside Cl. WS8: Brow 6H 121
Bridgeside Trad. Est. B77: Tam 6J 137
Bridges Rd. WS11: N Can 6B 110
Bridge St. B77: Amin 4A 138
B78: Pole 1J 143
DE13: Stre 2F 85
DE13: Tut 1H 83
DE14: B Tre 1F 87
DE65: Tut 1H 83
ST5: N'tle 3D 152 (7F 23)
ST5: Sil 7A 22
ST8: Brin F 4B 12
ST14: Utt 6H 63
ST16: Staf 3G 73
WS8: Clay 6G 121
WS11: Cann 6E 108
Bridge St. Ind. Est. ST14: Utt 6H 63
Bridgett Cl. ST4: T Val 4J 31
Bridge Villa ST10: Tea 3F 55
Bridgewater Cl. ST19: Penk 4H 91
Bridgewater Dr. WV5: Womb 3F 145
Bridgewater Rd. WS15: Rug 1H 97
Bridgewater St. B77: Tam 4K 137
ST6: B'lem 7H 17
Bridge Way WS8: Clay 6G 121
Bridgewood St. ST3: Long 6J 33
Bridgford Av. DE14: B'ton 5A 86
BRIDGNORTH 2B 162
Bridgnorth Av. WV5: Womb 6F 145
Bridgnorth Gro. ST5: C'ton 5C 16
WV12: Will 7B 126
Bridgnorth Rd. DY3: Him 7H 145
DY3: Swin 5A 144
DY7: Stou 6H 147
(Enville)
DY7: Stou 2E 148
(Stourton, not continuous)
WV5: Womb 5E 144
WV6: Per, Tres, Tett 7D 128
BRIDGTOWN 5E 108 (1D 163)
Bridgtown Bus. Cen. WS11: Cann 5E 108
Bridgwood Rd. ST11: B Bri 3J 43
Bridle La. DE15: Stan 7H 87
(not continuous)
Bridle Path ST2: Bent 5C 26
ST3: Long 1J 41
(off Peel St.)
Bridle Path, The CW3: Mad 3A 28
ST5: N'tle 6D 30
Bridle Rd. ST17: Staf 1B 78
Bridle Wlk. WS15: Rug 6D 94
BRIERLEY HILL 3D 163
Brierley St. ST6: B'lem 6C 18
BRIERLY BROOK 4H 15
Briertey Hill La. WS15: Gen 6K 103
Brieryhurst Cl. ST2: A Hul 3J 25
Brieryhurst Rd. ST7: Kids 3F 11
Bright Cres. B77: Wiln 7J 137
BRIGHTGATE 2C 157
Brightgreen St. ST3: Long 3K 33
Brighton, The ST5: Sil 6K 21
Brighton St. ST4: P'ull 2A 32
Brights Av. ST7: Kids 4F 11
Brightstone Cl. WV10: Bush 1D 124
Bright St. ST3: Mei 1C 42
BRIMINGTON 1D 157
Brindiwell Gro. ST4: Tren 4C 40
Brindley Av. WV11: Wed 4A 126
Brindley Bank Rd. WS15: Rug 5G 95
Brindley Brae DY7: Kin 5G 149
Brindley Cl. ST7: Talk 6C 10
ST15: Stone 2E 46
ST16: Staf 5H 71
ST19: Penk 5J 91
WS2: Wals 7F 127
WV5: Womb 4D 144
Brindley Ct. ST5: C'ton 3D 22
Brindley Cres. ST13: Ched 6H 51
WS12: Hed 3J 101
Brindley Dr. B77: Amin 3B 138
BRINDLEY FORD 4B 12 (2C 155)
Brindley Heath Rd. WS12: Hed 3J 101
Brindley La. ST2: L Oak, S Broo 4J 19
ST9: S Broo 4J 19
Brindley Mill & James Brindley Mus.
.... 2E 48
Brindley Pl. ST6: Chel 1C 18
Brindley Rd. WS12: Hed 1F 101
Brindleys Bus. Pk. WS11: Hed 7H 101
Brindley St. ST5: N'tle 2D 152 (7F 23)
Brindleys Way ST7: Big E 5H 15
Brindon Cl. ST3: W Coy 6D 34
BRINETON 3C 159
Brinkburn Cl. WS15: Rug 7D 94
BRINKLOW 3D 165
Brinscall Grn. ST6: Feg H 7A 12
(off Charnock Pl.)
BRINSFORD 5B 116
Brinsford La. WV10: Brin 5B 116
Brinsford Rd. WV10: Ford 2A 124
Brinsley Av. ST4: Tren 4A 40
Brisbane Rd. ST16: Staf 6D 70
Brisbane Way WS12: Wimb 1A 110
Brisley Hill ST4: P'ull 3K 31
Bristol Cl. WS11: H Hay 2H 109
Bristol St. ST5: N'tle 3H 23
Britannia Dr. DE13: Stre 3E 84
Britannia Pk. Ind. Est. ST6: B'lem 1B 24
Britannia Stadium 6C 32
Britannia St. ST13: Lee 4E 48
Britannia Way WS14: Lich 3E 114
British Waterways Vis. Cen. 2F 107
Brittain Av. ST5: C'ton 1C 22
Brittain Rd. ST13: Ched 5H 51
Brittle Pl. ST6: B'lem 5D 18
Britton St. ST4: S Tren 7K 23
Brixham Cl. ST2: Buck 7F 25
Brizlincote La. DE15: Bret 3K 87
Brizlincote St. DE15: Stap 3G 87
Broadacres WV9: Cove 1K 93
Broadbent Cl. WS13: Lich 5K 113
BROADEYE 3F 73
Broad Eye ST16: Staf 3F 73
(not continuous)
Broadfield Rd. ST6: Gold, Tuns 7F 11
Broad Hayes Pk. Homes
ST10: Chea 1D 54
BROAD HEATH 2C 159
Broadholes La. ST19: Whe A 2A 90
BROADHOLM 3D 157
Broadhursr Cl. WS12: Hed 1F 101
Broadhurst Grn. WS12: Hed 1F 101
Broadhurst Grn. Rd. ST19: Penk 1C 100
Broadhurst St. ST6: B'lem 6B 18
Broadlands DE13: Stre 3E 84
WV10: Ford 7B 116
Broadlands Ri. WS14: Lich 4D 114
Broad La. ST6: B Edg 5J 13
ST20: C Eat 1A 68
WS3: Blox 6C 118
WS13: Lich, W'ton 3J 115
WS13: Pipe 7E 112
WS14: Lich 4D 114
WV11: Ess 6C 118
Broad La. Gdns. WS3: Blox 3G 127
Broad La. Nth. WV12: Will 7B 126
Broad La. Sth. WV11: Wed 7A 126
Broadlawns Dr. ST3: Long 3H 33
Broadlee B77: Wiln 1E 142
BROAD MEADOW 2C 22
Broadmeadow Ct. ST5: C'ton 2C 22
Broad Mdw. Cft. ST16: Staf 2C 72
Broadmeadow La. WS6: G Wyr 2G 119
Broadmeadows Cl. WV12: Will 5E 126
Broadmeadows Rd. WV12: Will 5E 126
Broadmine St. ST4: Fen 3E 32
Broad Oaks ST17: Staf 2G 77
Broadoaks Cl. WS11: N Can 5B 110
Broadoak Way ST3: Blur 1E 40
Broadsmeath B77: Wiln 7J 137
Broadstone Av. WS3: Blox 7K 127
Broad St. ST1: H'ley 6E 150 (6B 24)
ST5: N'tle 2D 152 (7F 23)
(not continuous)
ST13: Lee 4F 49
ST16: Staf 3F 73
WS11: Cann 5E 108
Broadway ST3: Mei 7B 34
WS12: Hed 4F 101
WV3: W'ton 5K 129
WV8: Cods 2A 122
WV10: Bush 3C 124
Broadway, The WV5: Womb 5G 145
Broadway Ct. ST3: Mei 1B 42
Broadway Gdns. WV10: Bush 3C 124
Broadway Pl. ST3: Mei 7B 34
Broadway St. DE14: B Tre 4D 86
Broadwell La. WV6: Patt 7A 128
Broc Cl. ST19: Penk 4J 91
Broches, The WS11: N Can 7D 110
Broc Hill Way ST17: Broc 2G 79
Brockbank Pl. ST6: Chel 2B 18
Brockeridge Cl. WV12: Will 4C 126
Brockhill TF9: Logg 4D 60
Brocklehurst Way ST1: H'ley 1E 24
Brockley Sq. ST1: H'ley 3F 151 (4C 24)
Brockleys Wlk. DY7: Kin 6F 149
BROCKMOOR 3C 163
Brocks Cft. Gdns. ST8: Bidd 4C 8
Brocksford St. ST4: Fen 4G 33
BROCKTON
Much Wenlock 2A 162
Newport 3B 158
Shifnal 1B 162
Stafford 1C 159
Brock Way ST5: N'tle 6B 22
BROCTON 4G 79 (3D 159)
Brocton Cl. WS3: Blox 5G 127
Brocton Cres. ST17: Broc 4D 78
Brocton Hgts. ST17: Broc 4G 79
Brocton La. ST17: Walt 1D 78
Brocton Nature Reserve 6G 79
Brocton Rd. ST17: Broc, Milf 2G 79
Brocton Wlk. ST3: Blur 1E 40
Brogan St. ST4: Fen 3F 33
BROKEN CROSS 1C 155
BROMDON 3A 162
Bromfield Ct. ST15: Stone 3G 47
WV6: Tett 4J 129
BROMFORD 2B 164
Bromford Pl. ST1: H'ley 6D 150 (6B 24)
BROMLEY 2B 162
Bromley Cl. WS12: Hed 3J 101
Bromley Ct. ST1: H'ley 1D 150 (3B 24)
Bromley Gdns. WV8: Cods 1C 122
Bromley Hough ST4: P'ull 4K 31
Bromley St. ST1: H'ley 1C 150 (3A 24)
BROMLEY WOOD 2B 160
BROMPTON 1A 162
Brompton Dr. ST2: Mil 4H 19
Brompton Lawns WV6: Tett 3H 129
Bromsberrow Way ST3: Mei 3C 42
Bromsgrove Pl. ST3: Long 6G 33
Bromstead Cres. ST16: Staf 7D 70
BROMSTEAD HEATH 3B 158
Bromwich Dr. WS13: Frad 2K 107
Bronant Wlk. ST6: B'lem 1A 24
(off Leonora St.)
BRONCROFT 3A 162
Bronte Cl. DE14: B Tre 4E 84
Bronte Ct. B79: Tam 3G 137
Bronte Dr. WS11: H Hay 1J 109
Bronte Gro. ST2: Mil 5G 19
Brook Av. B77: Wiln 3C 142
Brook Cl. ST9: End 1C 50
ST11: B Bri 3J 43
ST19: Penk 5G 91
WS13: Lich 2A 114
WV9: Cove 1K 93
Brook Cotts. ST9: End 1C 50
BROOK END 7E 98
Brook End B78: Faze 2G 141
ST18: Hau 6C 66
WS7: Chas 7J 111
WS15: L'don 1D 104
Brooke Rd. WS12: Hed 4F 101
Brookes Ct. ST4: Fen 3E 32
Brookfield TF9: Logg 4D 60
Brookfield Av. ST9: End 2A 50
Brookfield Ct. ST1: H'ley 1F 151
ST15: Stone 6J 47
ST18: Hau 7B 66
Brookfield Dr. WS11: Cann 4E 108
Brookfield Rd. ST2: Mil 4J 19
ST4: T Val 4J 31
WV8: Bilb 2D 122
Brookfields Rd. ST10: Ips 2H 53
Brook Gdns. ST8: Bidd 4D 8
Brookgate ST11: Fors 2K 43
Brookglen Rd. ST17: Staf 7G 73
Brook Gro. WV8: Bilb 2D 122
Brookhay La. WS13: Lich 6J 107
Brookhill Cl. WV12: Will 4C 126
Brookhill Way WV12: Will 4D 126
Brookhouse Cl. WV10: Fea 5F 117
Brookhouse Dr. ST12: Barl 1C 44
BROOKHOUSE GREEN 1C 155
Brook Ho. La. WV10: Fea 6C 116
Brookhouse La. ST2: Buck 5K 25
ST13: Ched 7F 51
Brookhouse Rd. ST3: Mei 7C 34
ST5: C'ton 6D 16
ST10: Chea 4A 54
ST20: Gno 4H 67
BROOKHOUSES 5A 54 (3D 155)
Brookhouses Ind. Est. ST10: Chea 5A 54
Brookhouse Way ST10: Chea 5A 54
ST20: Gno 4H 67
Brookland Av. ST3: Blur 1G 41
Brooklands DY3: Swin 2J 147
Brooklands, The ST17: Staf 4G 73
(off Friars' Wlk.)
Brooklands Av. WS6: G Wyr 7F 109
Brooklands Cl. ST14: Utt 7G 63
Brooklands Cotts. ST6: Gold 6J 11
Brooklands Rd. ST6: Chel 2K 17
WS11: Cann 6G 101
Brooklands Way ST13: Lee 2K 51
Brook La. ST5: N'tle 6E 152 (2F 31)
ST9: End 1B 50
ST17: Broc 3G 79
WS6: G Wyr 1G 119
Brooklime Gdns. ST16: Staf 1C 72
WV10: Fea 5F 117
Brooklyn Rd. WS7: Chas 7J 111
WS12: H Hay 2K 109
Brookmead Gro. ST3: Long 3H 33
Brookmead Ind. Est.
ST16: Staf 5H 71
Brook Mdw. ST6: Nort 6E 18
Brook Mdws. WV8: Bilb 1D 122
Brook Path ST15: Stone 4F 47
Brook Pl. ST4: S Tren 7A 150 (7K 23)
ST5: N'tle 4G 31
Brook Rd. ST4: Tren 3A 40
WS6: C Hay 6E 108
WV5: Womb 4F 145
Brookside DE13: Roll D 6H 83
DE15: Wins 6J 85
DY7: Stou 5H 147
ST6: B'lem 7H 17
ST10: Frog 5J 53
Brookside Bus. Pk. ST14: Utt 6J 63
Brookside Cl. ST5: N'tle 6B 152 (2E 30)
WV5: Womb 4E 144
Brookside Ct. ST10: Chea 4A 54
Brookside Dr. ST3: Blur 7E 32
ST9: End 1C 50
Brookside Gdns. ST19: B Elm 6B 90
Brookside Ind. Est. ST6: B'lem 7H 17
Brookside La. ST15: Stone 5E 46
Brookside Parks Cvn. Site
WV9: Cove 2K 93
Brookside Rd. B78: M Oak 1D 140
DE13: B Nee 6F 89
ST14: Utt 6J 63
Brookside Way B77: Wiln 4B 142
Brook Sq. WS15: Rug 7G 95
Brook St. DE14: B Tre 7E 84
ST4: S Tren 2B 32
ST5: Sil 6A 22
ST8: B Lee 1A 12
ST13: Lee 4F 49
Brook Va. WS11: Cann 3F 109
Brookview Dr. ST3: Long 6B 34
Brookweed B77: Amin 6C 138
Brookwillows ST17: Wild 7A 74
Brookwood Cl. ST5: N'tle 6E 30
Brookwood Dr. ST3: Mei 6C 34
BROOME 3D 163
Broome Cl. DE13: K Bro 2B 130
Broome Hill ST5: N'tle 1G 39
Broome Rd. WV10: Bush 6C 124
Broome Wlk. WS15: Hand 5G 99
(off Proctors Rd.)
Broomfield Av. B78: Faze 2G 141
Broomfield Cl. ST15: Stone 6H 47
Broomfield Pl. Nth.
ST1: H'ley 4C 150 (5A 24)
Broomfield Pl. Sth.
ST1: H'ley 5C 150 (5A 24)
Broomfield Rd. ST6: B Gre 2D 18
Broomfields ST8: Bid M 4H 9
Broomhall Av. WV11: Wed 7H 125
BROOMHILL 6E 100
Broomhill Bank WS11: Cann 7E 100
Broomhill Cl. WS11: Cann 6E 100
Broomhill St. ST6: Tuns 3G 17
Broom Hollow TF9: Logg 4E 60
Broom Lea TF9: Logg 5E 60
Brooms Pk. Cvn. Pk.
ST15: Stone 7H 47
Brooms Rd. ST15: Stone 7G 47
Broom St. ST1: H'ley 1G 151 (3D 24)
Broomyclose La. ST14: S'all 1F 63
BROOMYSHAW 7A 52
BROSELEY 1A 162
BROUGHALL 3A 154
Brough Cl. ST13: Lee 3F 49
Brough La. ST4: Tren 3B 40
Brough Pk. Leisure Cen. 3G 49
Brough Rd. DE15: Wins 1K 87
BROUGHTON
Stafford 1B 158
Wolverhampton 4B 146
Broughton Cl. ST16: Staf 6E 70
Broughton Ct. WV6: Per 3H 129
Broughton Cres. ST12: Barl 1E 44
Broughton Rd. ST2: Buck 5F 25
ST5: N'tle 1J 153 (6H 23)
WV3: W'ton 5K 129
Brown Av. B77: T Gat 2J 141
BROWN EDGE 6H 13 (2D 155)

Brown End Quarry—Cameron Cl.

Brown End Quarry (Geological Nature Reserve) .6D 52
Brownfield Rd. ST3: Mei .7C 34
Brownhill Rd. ST6: B Edg .7H 13
BROWNHILLS
Market Drayton .1A 158
Wolverhampton .5H 121 (1A 164)
Brown Hills Bus. Pk. ST6: Tuns .5H 17
Brownhills Bus. Pk. WS8: Brow .7H 121
BROWNHILLS COMMON .4G 121
Brownhills Rd. ST6: Tuns .6H 17
WS8: W Woo .7H 121
WS11: N Can .5C 110
BROWNHILLS WEST .2E 120
Brownhills West Station
Chasewater Railway .1E 120
Browning Cl. B79: Tam .1F 137
ST10: Chea .5B 54
WV12: Will .6E 126
Browning Cres. WV10: Ford .3A 124
Browning Gro. ST7: Talk .6A 10
WV6: Per .2F 129
Browning Rd. ST3: Blur .7F 33
WS7: Burn .4A 112
Browning St. ST16: Staf .2F 73
BROWN LEES .1A 12
Brown Lees Ind. Est. ST8: Knyp .2B 12
Brown Lees Rd. ST7: B Lee, Harr .2K 11
ST8: B Lee, Knyp .1B 12
Brownley Rd. ST6: B'lem .6D 18
BROWNLOW .1C 155
BROWNLOW HEATH .1C 155
Brownsea Pl. ST3: Fen .5E 32
Brownsfield Rd. WS13: Lich .2C 114
(not continuous)
BROWN'S GREEN .2A 164
Brownshore La. WV11: Ess .1A 126
Brown's Lake DY7: Stou .5H 147
Browns La. B78: Dor .5H 143
B79: Tam .1J 137
DE13: Yox .2H 89
Brown St. ST6: B'lem .7A 18
Browns Wlk. WS15: Rug .7F 95
Browsholme B79: Tam .3D 136
Broxwood Pk. WV6: Tett .3J 129
BRUND .1B 156
Brundall Oval ST2: Bent .6K 25
Brund La. ST13: Ched .7F 51
Brundle Av. ST16: Staf .3D 72
Brunel Cl. B79: Tam .3H 137
ST16: Staf .5H 71
WS7: Burn .3K 111
Brunel Ct. WV5: Womb .3G 145
WV10: F Ash .6G 93
Brunel Dr. DE13: Stre .3G 85
Brunel Gro. WV6: Per .7A 122
Brunel Wlk. B78: Pole .6J 139
ST3: Long .5J 33
Brunslow Cl. WV10: Oxl .4A 124
Brunswick Ind. Est. ST6: B'lem .7H 17
Brunswick Pl. ST1: H'ley .5G 151 (5C 24)
Brunswick Rd. WS11: Cann .1E 108
Brunswick St. ST1: H'ley .3F 151 (4C 24)
ST5: N'tle .3F 153 (7G 23)
ST13: Lee .3G 49
Brunswick Ter. ST16: Staf .4F 73
Brunt St. ST6: B'lem .1H 23
Brutus Rd. ST5: C'ton .3B 22
Bryans La. WS15: Rug .7H 95
Bryan St. ST1: H'ley .1F 151 (4C 24)
Bryans Way WS12: Hed .6B 102
Bryant Rd. ST2: Buck .3H 25
Brymbo Rd. ST5: N'tle .3D 22
Bryony DE14: B'ton .4C 86
Buccleuch Rd. ST3: Long .7K 33
Buckden B77: Wiln .1E 142
Buckingham Cl. DE13: Stre .3E 84
ST17: Staf .5A 74
Buckingham Ct. DE15: Wins .1K 87
Buckingham Cres. ST4: H'ord .1A 40
Buckingham Dr. WV12: Will .6B 126
Buckingham Gdns. WS14: Lich .5B 114
Buckingham Pl. WS12: H Hay .2J 109
Buckingham Rd. B79: Tam .3D 136
Buckland Cl. WS12: H Hay .2K 109
Buckland Gro. ST4: Tren .5C 40
Buckland Rd. ST16: Staf .4F 71
Buckley Cl. ST14: Bram .6B 62
Buckley Rd. ST6: Chel .1C 18
Buckleys Row ST5: N'tle .5D 152 (1F 31)
Buckmaster Av. ST5: N'tle .3G 31
BUCKNALL .5G 25 (3D 155)
Bucknall New Rd.
ST1: H'ley .3H 151 (4D 24)
Bucknall Old Rd.
ST1: H'ley .3H 151 (4D 24)
Bucknall Rd.
ST1: Buck, H'ley .3K 151 (4E 24)
WV11: Wed .4B 126
Buckthorn Cl. WS12: Hed .2F 101
BUDDILEIGH .1A 6
Bude Dr. ST17: Staf .5C 74
Buds Rd. WS15: Can W .5H 103
BUERTON .3A 154
BUGLAWTON .1C 155
BUILDWAS .1A 162
Buildwas Cl. WS3: Blox .3F 127
BULKINGTON .3D 165
BULLBRIDGE .2D 157
Bulldog La. WS13: Lich .2B 114
Buller St. ST1: H'ley .7J 151 (6D 24)
Bull Hill ST16: Staf .2G 73
Bull La. ST8: Brin F .4A 12
WV5: Womb .2G 145
Bull Mdw. La. WV5: Womb .2G 145
Bullmoor La. WS14: C'eld, Hilt .2K 133 & 2A 134
Bullocks Ho. Rd. ST7: Harr .3J 11
Bullows Rd. WS8: Brow .6E 120
Bull Ring, The ST18: West .2C 80
Bullrushes Cl. ST1: H'ley .6A 150 (6A 24)
Bulrush Cl. WS8: Brow .5G 121
Bulstrode St. ST6: B'lem .7J 17
Bumblehole Mdws. WV5: Womb .3F 145
BUNBURY .2A 154
Bungalows, The ST15: Stone .5H 47
Bungham La. ST19: Penk .4F 91
Bunny Hill ST5: N'tle .4G 31
Bunting, The ST9: W Roc .1K 27
ST10: K'ley .5F 53
Bunting Cl. ST14: Utt .7G 63
Bunt's La. ST9: S Broo .3J 19
Bunyan Pl. WS11: Cann .6E 100
BURBAGE
Burbage .1A 156
Hinckley .2D 165
Burbage Cl. WV10: W'ton .7D 124
Burcham Cl. ST16: Staf .6D 70
BURCOTE .2B 162
Burdock Cl. WS11: H Hay .7H 101
Burford Av. ST5: C'ton .6B 16
Burford Rd. ST17: Staf .5B 74
ST19: Whe A .2B 90
Burford Way ST2: Buck .7G 25
Burgage, The ST21: Ecc .2H 65
Burgesses, The DY7: Kin .6F 149
Burgess St. ST6: B'lem .1J 23
Burgis Cl. ST13: Ched .6H 51
Burgoyne St. WS11: Cann .5G 101
Burgundy Gro. ST3: Mei .2C 42
BURLAND .2A 154
Burland Av. WV6: Tett .6G 123
Burland Rd. ST5: C'ton .5A 16
Burleigh Cl. WS12: Hed .2G 101
WV12: Will .7B 126
Burleigh Cft. WS7: Chas .7J 111
Burleigh Gro. ST5: N'tle .5H 23
Burlidge Rd. ST6: Chel .1A 18
Burlington Av. ST5: N'tle .5H 23
Burlington Ct. B78: Faze .1H 141
Burlington Dr. ST17: Staf .6D 72
Burmarsh Wlk. ST6: B'lem .1K 23
WV8: P'ord .5H 123
Burnaby Rd. ST6: Tuns .1G 17
BURNASTON .1C 161
Burncross Way WV10: W'ton .7D 124
Burnet Gro. WV10: Fea .4F 117
Burnett Ct. ST16: Staf .1C 72
Burnett Pl. ST6: Nort .3D 18
Burnett Rd. B74: L Ast .6G 135
Burnfield Dr. WS15: Rug .7F 95
Burnham Av. ST17: Staf .1B 78
WV10: Oxl .5K 123
Burnham Grn. WS11: Cann .3B 108
Burnham St. ST4: Fen .4G 33
Burnhays Rd. ST6: B'lem .5K 17
BURNHILL GREEN .1B 162
BURNLEYDAM .3A 154
Burnley St. ST1: H'ley .2D 24
Burnsall Cl. WV9: P'ord .2J 123
Burns Av. ST17: Staf .6D 72
WV10: Ford .3B 124
Burns Cl. ST7: Kids .6E 10
WS14: Lich .5B 114
Burns Dr. WS7: Burn .4A 112
Burnside DE13: Roll D .7H 83
Burnside Cl. ST3: Mei .3C 42
Burns Rd. B79: Tam .3G 137
Burns Row ST3: Mei .7D 34
Burns St. WS11: Cann .6F 101
BURNTHEATH .1C 161
Burnthill La. WS15: Rug .2F 97
BURNTWOOD .5A 112 (1A 164)
BURNTWOOD GREEN .5C 112 (1A 164)
BURNTWOOD JUNC. .1H 121
Burntwood Leisure Cen. .5H 111
Burntwood Rd. WS7: Hamm .7B 112
WS11: N Can .5C 110
Burntwood Town Shop. Cen.
WS7: C Ter .3G 111
Burntwood Vw.
TF9: Logg .5E 60
Burnway Mdw. DE13: Alre .6C 130
Burnwood Ct. ST6: B'lem .5D 18
Burnwood Gro. ST7: Kids .4F 11
Burnwood Pl. ST6: Chel .2B 18
Burrington Dr. ST4: Tren .5B 40
BURSLEM .7K 17 (3C 155)
Burslem Cl. WS3: Blox .1G 127
Burslem Enterprise Cen.
ST6: B'lem .7A 18
Burslem Greenway ST6: B'lem .6K 17
Burslem Walkway ST6: B'lem .7A 18
Bursley Cl. ST17: Staf .1F 77
Bursley Rd. ST6: B'lem .1A 24
Bursley Way ST5: Brad .7E 16
Bursnips Rd. WV11: Ess .3B 126
BURSTON .1D 159
Burt Ct. ST18: Staf .1A 74
Burton Albion FC .4F 85
Burton Bank La. ST17: Staf .2F 77
(not continuous)
Burton Cl. B79: Tam .2J 137
Burton Ct. *ST17: Staf* .*7G 73*
(off Burton Sq.)
Burton Cres. ST1: H'ley .1E 24
ST10: K Hol .7H 53
Burton Enterprise Pk. DE14: B Tre .5F 85
BURTON HASTINGS .3D 165
Burton Ho. Gdns. ST17: Staf .2G 77
BURTON MANOR .7F 73
Burton Mnr. Rd. ST17: Staf .1F 77
ST18: Staf .1E 76
Burton M. ST14: Utt .4E 62
Burton Old Rd. WS13: S'hay .2F 115
WS14: Lich .3F 115
(not continuous)
Burton Old Rd. E. WS14: Lich .3E 114
Burton Old Rd. W. WS13: Lich .3C 114
Burton-on-Trent Station (Rail) .1D 86
Burton Pl. DE14: B Tre .2E 86
ST1: H'ley .3G 151 (4C 24)
Burton Rd. B79: Elf .6H 131
DE13: Alre .7C 130
DE13: Tut .1J 83
DE14: B'ton .5B 86
WS13: Fish, W'ton .1G 131
WS13: S'hay .2F 115
WS14: W'ton .2G 131
Burton Sq. ST17: Staf .7G 73
Burton St. DE13: Tut .2H 83
ST13: Lee .4E 48
Burton Ter. ST14: Utt .5H 63
BURTON UPON TRENT .2E 87 (2C 161)
Burt St. ST3: Mei .6D 34
BURWARTON .3A 162
Burwaye Cl. WS13: Lich .5A 114
BURYBANK .7C 44
Bury Ring ST18: Hau .1A 76
Bushberry Cl. ST15: Stone .6F 47
BUSHBURY .4C 124 (1D 163)
Bushbury Ct. WV10: Bush .3C 124
Bushbury Crematorium
WV10: Bush .2D 124
Bushbury La. WV10: Oxl, Bush .7A 124
Bushbury Rd. WV10: W'ton .7E 124
Bushbury Swimming Pool .4C 124
Bush Dr. WS15: Rug .7G 95
Bute Cl. WV12: Will .7B 126
Bute St. ST4: Fen .5G 33
Butler Ct. DE14: B Tre .1C 86
Butler St. ST4: S Tren .3B 32
Butterfield Cl. WV6: Per .3E 128
Butterfield Pl. ST6: Tuns .4J 17
BUTTERHILL .4A 76
Butterhill Bank ST15: Aston .7K 47
ST18: Aston, Burs .7K 47
Buttermere B77: Wiln .3D 142
Buttermere Cl. ST6: B'lem .7J 17
WS11: Cann .7G 101
WV6: Tett .5F 123
Buttermere Ct. WV6: Per .2G 129
Buttermere Dr. WV11: Ess .3A 126
Buttermere Gro. WV12: Will .4B 126
BUTTERS GREEN .5J 15
BUTTERTON
Leek .2A 156
Newcastle .7C 30 (3C 155)
Butterton La. ST5: Butt .6B 30
BUTT GREEN .2A 154
BUTT LANE .5A 10
BUTTONBRIDGE .3B 162
BUTTONOAK .3B 162
Butts, The CW3: Bet .3B 6
ST18: Gt Hay .5G 81
ST18: L Hay .6H 81
WS14: Wall .1A 134
Butts Cl. WS11: N Can .7A 110
Butts Cft. DE13: Alre .5B 130
Butts Grn. ST2: A Hul .2J 25
Butts La. ST10: Caul .7B 52
WS11: N Can .7A 110
Butts Way WS11: N Can .7A 110
BUXTON .1A 156
Buxton Av. B78: Faze .2H 141
ST5: Sil .6J 21
Buxton Cl. WS3: Blox .2J 127
Buxton Rd. SK17: L'nor .2C 52
ST13: B Moo, Lee .3G 49
WS3: Blox .2J 127
Buxton St. ST1: H'ley .1D 24
Byatt's Gro. ST3: Long .7G 33
Bycars Farm Cft. WS13: Frad .1K 107
Bycars La. ST6: B'lem .6K 17
Bycars Rd. ST6: B'lem .6K 17
Byeways WS3: Blox .2J 127
Byland B77: Glas .6K 137
Bylands Pl. ST5: N'tle .5E 30
Byland Way WS3: Blox .3F 127
BYLEY .1B 154
Byrds Cl. ST14: Utt .5E 62
Byrd's La. ST14: Utt .5E 62
Byrkley St. DE14: B Tre .7C 84
Byrom St. ST13: Lee .3E 48
Byron Av. DE15: Stap .5F 87
WS14: Lich .6B 114
Byron Cl. ST10: Chea .5A 54
ST16: Staf .1J 73
WS7: C Ter .2H 111
Byron Ct. ST7: Kids .6D 10
Byron Pl. WS11: Cann .5E 100
WS15: Rug .6E 94
Byron Rd. B79: Tam .2G 137
WV10: Bush .5E 124
WV12: Will .6E 126
Byron St. ST4: S Tren .3J 153 (7H 23)
Bywater Gro. ST3: Long .3K 33

C

Cabot Gro. WV6: Per .2F 129
CADEBY .1D 165
Cadeby Gro. ST2: Mil .5H 19
Cadle Rd. WV10: Bush .6C 124
Cadman Cres. ST6: Nort .4E 18
WV10: W'ton .7E 124
Cadman's La. WS3: Blox .6K 119
WS6: G Wyr .4J 119
Cadogan Rd. B77: Dost .5K 141
Caernarvon Av. ST15: Stone .7J 47
Caernarvon Cl. DE13: Stre .3E 84
WV12: Will .6C 126
Cairn Cl. ST2: Buck .5K 25
Cairns Cl. DE15: Wins .1K 87
Cairns Dr. ST16: Staf .1K 73
Caister B77: Amin .3C 138
Caistor Cl. B78: M Oak .2B 140
ST2: Mil .6G 19
Calais Rd. DE13: B Tre .5C 84
Calcot Dr. WV6: Tett .6G 123
Caldbeck Pl. ST1: H'ley .3J 151 (4D 24)
CALDECOTE .2D 165
Calder B77: Wiln .7D 138
Caldervale Dr. ST17: Wild .1B 78
Caldew Gro. ST4: Tren .5C 40
Caldon Way ST15: Stone .1E 46
Cale Cl. B77: Wiln .7J 137
Caledonian B77: Glas .7B 138
Caledonia Rd. ST4: S Tren. .7D 150 (7B 24)
CALF HEATH .5K 93
Calgary Cres. DE15: Wins .1K 87
Calibre Ind. Pk. WV10: F Ash .6G 93
California Bus. Pk. ST4: S Tren .4B 32
Californian Gro. WS7: C Ter .3H 111
California St. ST3: Long .6G 33
CALKE .2D 161
Callaghan Gro. WS11: H Hay .1J 109
CALLAUGHTON .2A 162
Callender Pl. ST6: B'lem .7A 18
CALLINGWOOD .2B 160
Callister Way DE14: B Tre .1A 86
Callis Wlk. B77: Wiln .4B 142
Calrofold Dr. ST5: C'ton .6B 16
CALTON .2B 156
Calvary Cres. ST2: Bent .1K 33
CALVELEY .2A 154
Calveley Cl. ST15: Yarn .6D 64
Calver Cres. WV11: Wed .7K 125
CALVERHALL .1A 158
Calverley St. ST3: Long .7K 33
Calver St. ST6: Tuns .4H 17
Calvert Gro. ST5: Brad .1F 23
Calvin Cl. WV5: Womb .5F 145
WV10: Ford .2B 124
Calving Hill WS11: Cann .1E 108
Camberwell Gro. ST4: Tren .4C 40
Camborne Cl. ST17: Staf .6C 74
Camborne Cres. ST5: N'tle .4D 30
Cambrian B77: Glas .7C 138
Cambrian La. WS15: Rug .5E 94
Cambrian Way ST2: Buck .4J 25
Cambria St. WS11: Cann .6D 100
Cambridge Cl. ST8: Bidd .4C 8
Cambridge Ct. ST5: N'tle .5H 31
Cambridge Dr. ST5: N'tle .4H 31
Cambridge St. DE14: B Tre .3C 86
ST1: H'ley .5E 150 (5B 24)
ST16: Staf .2J 73
Camden Dr. B77: Glas .6A 138
Camden St. ST4: Fen .5E 32
Camelford Cl. ST17: Staf .6C 74
Camellia Cl. ST4: S Tren .2K 153 (7J 23)
Camellia Gdns. WV9: P'ord .2H 123
Camelot Cl. DE13: Stre .1F 85
ST4: Tren .5C 40
WS11: Cann .6F 101
Cameo Way ST16: Staf .6D 70
Cameron Cl. DE15: Stap .3J 87

Cameron Wharf—Centre Way

Cameron Wharf ST15: Stone 3F 47
Camhouses B77: Wiln 1D 142
Camillus Rd. ST5: N'tle 1A 152 (6C 22)
Camoys Ct. ST6: B'lem 1A 24
Camoys Rd. ST6: B'lem 1A 24
Campbell Av. ST13: Lee 5E 48
Campbell Cl. B79: Tam 1F 137
WS15: Rug 6F 95
Campbell Pl. ST4: S Tren 2B 32
Campbell Rd. ST4: S Tren 5B 32
Campbell Ter. ST1: H'ley 2E 24
Camp Hill ST5: B Gat 4C 36
Campians Av. WS6: C Hay 2D 118
Campian Way ST6: Nort 5E 18
Campion Av. ST5: N'tle 5H 23
Campion Cl. ST21: Ecc 4G 65
WV5: Womb 4E 144
Campion Dr. B77: Tam 6J 137
WV10: Fea 5E 116
Camp Rd. ST6: B'lem 6C 18
ST17: Broc 5F 79
Camrose Gdns. WV9: P'ord 2J 123
Camsey La. WS7: Burn 3C 112
Canal Arm ST1: H'ley 3A 150
Canalarm ST1: H'ley 4K 23
Canal La. ST6: Tuns 5H 17
Canal M., The ST4: Tren 4C 40
Canal Side ST6: Nort 2F 19
ST12: Barl 2D 44
ST17: Act T 6J 77
Canalside Cl. ST19: Penk 5H 91
Canalside Rd. ST15: Stone 2E 46
Canal St. DE14: B Tre 2D 86
ST6: B'lem 7H 17
Canal Vw. Bus. Pk. WS15: Rug 3K 97
Canary Rd. ST2: B Hil 2K 33
Canaway Wlk. WS15: Rug 6E 94
Canberra Cres. ST3: Mei 3E 42
Canberra Dr. ST16: Staf 2K 73
Canford Cres. WV8: Cods 2A 122
Canford Pl. WS11: Cann 2F 109
CANHOLES 1A 156
CANLEY 3D 165
Cannel Rd. ST5: Sil 5J 21
WS7: C Ter 5F 111
Canning Rd. B77: Amin 5A 138
Canning St. ST4: Fen 4F 33
CANNOCK 2E 108 (3D 159)
Cannock Chase Camping & Caravanning Site
WS15: Rug 1F 103
Cannock Chase country Pk. 2A 96
Cannock Chase Country Pk. 2H 79
Cannock Chase Ent. Cen.
WS12: Hed 1K 101
Cannock Ind. Cen. WS11: Cann 6D 108
Cannock Motor Village WS11: Hed. . . 7H 101
Cannock Rd. ST17: Broc 3D 78
ST17: Staf 7B 74
ST19: Penk 3H 91
WS7: Burn 4K 111
WS7: C Ter 3E 110
WS7: H Hay 3B 110
WS11: Cann 1F 109
WS11: H Hay 3B 110
WS12: H Hay 3J 109
WS12: Hed 7F 101
WV10: Bush, Shar, Fea 7F 117
WV10: W'ton 7D 124
WV12: Will 6C 126
Cannock Shop. Cen. WS11: Cann . . . 2E 108
Cannock Sports Stadium 5F 101
Cannock Station (Rail) 3F 109
CANNOCK WOOD 5H 103 (3A 160)
Cannock Wood Ind. Est.
WS12: Haz 4E 102
Cannock Wood Rd. WS12: Haz 5D 102
Cannock Wood St. WS12: Haz 4C 102
Cannon Pl. ST1: H'ley 5E 150 (6B 24)
Cannon Rd. WV5: Womb 4G 145
Cannons Health Club 7H 101
Cannon St. ST1: H'ley 5F 151 (5C 24)
Canons Cl. ST15: Stone 6G 47
Canterbury Cl. B77: Tam 6K 137
WS3: Pels 7C 120
WS13: Lich 1C 114
Canterbury Dr. ST6: B'lem 3B 18
WS7: Burn 5B 112
WS15: Rug 3E 96
WV6: Per 2E 128
Canterbury Rd. DE15: Wins 1K 87
Canterbury Way WS12: H Hay 2H 109
Canvey Gro. ST3: Mei 3D 42
Cape Av. ST17: Staf 7D 72
Cape Cl. WS8: Brow 6J 121
Capercaillie Dr. WS11: H Hay 2G 109
Capesthorne Cl. ST9: Werr 5D 26
Cape St. ST1: H'ley 1F 151 (3C 24)
Capewell St. ST3: Long 5J 33
Capper Cl. ST7: Kids 4E 10
Capper's La. WS14: Lich 3E 114
Capper St. ST6: Tuns 4J 17
Capricorn Way ST6: Chel 1K 17
Capstone Av. WV10: Oxl 5K 123
Captain's Cl. WV3: W'ton 4K 129
Captain's La. DE13: B Nee 6F 89
Caradoc B77: Glas 7C 138
Caraway Dr. DE14: B'ton 4B 86
Caraway Pl. ST3: Mei 4C 42
Carberry Way ST3: W Coy 5B 34
Carder Av. ST16: Staf 6D 70
Carder Grn. SK17: L'nor 3C 52
Cardiff Gro. ST1: H'ley 5F 151 (5C 24)
Cardigan Av. WS15: Rug 3F 97
Cardigan Dr. WV12: Will 7B 126
Cardigan Gro. ST4: Tren 4C 40
Cardigan Ho. WS12: Hed 5J 101
Cardigan Pl. WS12: Hed 5J 101
Cardinal Way WS11: Cann 1D 108
Cardington Cl. ST5: N'tle 5E 30
Card St. ST6: B'lem 1K 23
Cardway, The ST5: N'tle 1F 23
Cardwell St. ST1: H'ley 1K 151 (3E 24)
Carey B77: Hock 5C 142
Careynon Ct. WS3: Blox 5H 127
Carfax WS11: Cann 3E 108
Carina Gdns. ST6: B'lem 6D 18
Carisbrooke B77: Glas 7C 138
Carisbrooke Dr. DE13: Stre 2F 85
ST17: Staf 7D 72
Carisbrooke Gdns. WV10: Bush 2C 124
Carisbrooke Rd. WV6: Per 3H 129
WV10: Bush 2C 124
Carisbrooke Way ST4: Tren 5C 40
Carlcroft B77: Wiln 7D 138
Carling Cl. ST16: Staf 4D 72
Carling Gro. ST4: Fen 4G 33
Carlisle Rd. WS11: Cann 4B 108
Carlisle St. ST3: Long 1H 41
Carlos Cl. ST10: Chea 4C 54
Carlos Pl. ST5: Brad 6F 17
Carl St. WS2: Wals 7K 127
CARLTON 1D 165
Carlton Av. B74: S'ly 6F 135
ST5: N'tle 6F 31
ST6: B Edg 1H 19
ST6: Chel 2A 18
WV11: Wed 6E 124
Carlton Cl. ST6: B Edg 1H 19
ST10: Chea 6C 54
WS12: H Hay 2K 109
Carlton Ct. *DE14: B Tre 1C 86*
(off Shobnall Rd.)
Carlton Cres. B79: Tam 1F 137
WS7: C Ter 3J 111
Carlton Cft. B74: S'ly 6F 135
Carlton Ho. Est. ST4: S Tren 1B 32
Carlton Rd. ST4: S Tren 1C 32
Carlton Sq. ST17: Staf 6D 72
Carlton St. DE13: B Tre 5C 84
Carlton Ter. ST13: Lee 3H 49
Carlyle Gro. WV10: Bush 5E 124
Carlyle Rd. WV10: Bush 5E 124
Carlyon Pl. ST1: H'ley 7D 18
Carmel Cl. WS12: Hed 5J 101
Carmichael Cl. WS14: Lich 4D 114
CARMOUNTHEAD 6K 19
Carmount Rd. ST2: A Hul 1H 25
CARMOUNTSIDE 1H 25
Carmountside Crematorium
ST2: Mil 7H 19
CARMOUTHEAD 6K 19
Carnation Cl. ST3: W Coy 3D 34
Carnforth Gro. ST6: Chel 6J 11
Carnoustie B77: Amin 4D 138
Carnoustie Cl. WS3: Blox 2G 127
Carol Cres. WV11: Wed 7J 125
CAROL GREEN 3C 165
Caroline Cl. ST9: Werr 4D 26
Caroline Ct. ST21: Ecc 3H 65
Caroline Cres. ST6: B Edg 1H 19
Caroline St. ST3: Long 5J 33
Carousels, The DE14: B Tre 6D 84
Carpenter Cl. DE15: Stap 2K 87
Carpenter Rd. ST3: Long 5G 33
CARR BANK 2B 56
Carr Bank ST10: O'moor 3B 56
Carriage Dr. ST8: Bidd 4E 8
Carrick Cl. WS3: Pels 7C 120
Carrick Pl. ST4: H'ord 1A 40
Carriers Fold WV5: Womb 3H 145
Carr La. ST7: Aud 6C 14
Carroll Dr. ST3: Long 5K 33
Carron St. ST4: Fen 4H 33
Carr St. ST7: Pack 5K 11
Carryer Pl. ST5: N'tle 5A 152 (1D 30)
CARSINGTON 2C 157
Carson Rd. ST6: B'lem 4K 17
Carson Way ST16: Staf 3E 72
Carter Av. WV8: Bilb 2D 122
Carter Rd. WV6: W'ton 7K 123
Carters Cft. ST10: Tea 4H 55
Cartersfield La. WS9: Ston 4G 133
Carter St. ST14: Utt 6H 63
Cartlich St. ST6: Sandy 2H 17
Cartlidge St. ST4: S Tren . . . 3H 153 (7H 23)
Cartmel Pl. ST6: B'lem 4B 18
Cartway, The WV6: Per 2E 128
Cartwright Dr. ST20: Gno 3H 67
Cartwright Ho. WS3: Blox 4H 127
Cartwright Ind. Est. ST3: Long 7H 33
Cartwright St. ST3: Long 7H 33
Carver Bus. Pk. ST16: Staf 7G 71
Carver Rd. DE13: B Tre 5C 84
ST16: Staf 7G 71
Casewell Rd. ST6: B'lem 1C 24
Casey La. DE14: B Tre 7C 84
Caspian Gro. ST4: Tren 3B 40
Caspian Way ST19: Whe A 2C 90
Castel Cl. ST5: N'tle 6C 30
Castle Acre ST17: Staf 7D 72
Castle Bank ST16: Staf 6C 72
ST17: Staf 6C 72
Castlebridge Gdns. WV11: Wed 6K 125
Castlebridge Rd. WV11: Wed 7K 125
CASTLE BROMWICH 3B 164
Castle Cl. B77: Amin 5A 138
WS8: Brow 2H 121
Castle Ct. DE13: Tut 1H 83
ST15: Stone 6J 47
CASTLECROFT 5H 129
Castlecroft WS11: N Can 6A 110
Castlecroft Av. WV3: W'ton 6H 129
Castlecroft Gdns. WV3: W'ton 6K 129
Castlecroft La. WV3: W'ton 6G 129
Castlecroft Rd. WV3: W'ton 6G 129
Castledene Dr. ST16: Staf 5E 72
Castledine Gro. ST3: Long 5K 33
CASTLE DONINGTON 2D 161
Castle Dr. WV12: Will 7B 126
Castle Dyke WS13: Lich 4B 114
Castlefields ST16: Staf 4F 73
Castlefield St. ST4: H'ley . . . 7C 150 (6A 24)
Castle Grange ST16: Staf 2B 72
CASTLE GRESLEY 3C 161
Castle Gro. ST2: Buck 3H 25
Castlehall B77: Glas 7C 138
Castle Hayes La. DE13: Tut 4F 83
Castle Hill ST16: Staf 3F 73
Castle Hill Rd. ST5: N'tle . . . 3C 152 (7E 22)
ST10: Alt 5H 57
Castlehill Rd. WS9: W Woo 7F 133
Castle Ho. Dr. ST17: Staf 5D 72
Castle Keep Ct. ST5: N'tle . . . 4C 152 (1E 30)
Castle Keep Gdns.
ST5: N'tle 3C 152 (7E 22)
Castle Keep M. ST5: N'tle . . . 3C 152 (1E 30)
Castle La. CW3: Mad 4A 28
Castle Mt. ST5: C'ton 2C 22
Castle Pk. Rd. DE13: B Tre 4C 84
Castle Pleasure Grounds 5H 137
Castle Ridge ST5: N'tle 5A 152 (1D 30)
Castle Rd. B77: Hock 5B 142
ST7: M Cop 6H 7
Castle St. DE13: Tut 1G 83
DY7: Kin 5E 148
ST5: C'ton 1C 22
ST5: N'tle 3G 153 (7G 23)
ST16: Staf 3F 73
ST21: Ecc 2H 65
WS8: Brow 2H 121
Castleton Rd. ST3: L'ood 3A 42
WS3: Blox 2J 127
CASTLETOWN 3E 72
Castletown Grange ST5: N'tle 6E 22
Castle Vw. B77: Tam 6J 137
ST8: Bidd 7C 8
ST16: Staf 3F 73
(Broadeye)
ST16: Staf 2B 72
(Doxey Fields)
ST18: Derr 5A 72
Castle Vw. Est. ST18: Derr 4A 72
Castleview Gro. ST6: Chel 7K 11
Castle Vw. Rd. ST7: Kids 3F 11
Castle Wlk. ST5: N'tle 3E 152 (7F 23)
Castle Way ST16: Staf 4E 72
Castrum ST14: Roce 5E 58
Catalan Cl. ST17: Staf 6J 73
Catalina Pl. ST3: Mei 4E 42
Cat & Kittens La. WV10: Fea 5C 116
Caterbanck Way WS13: Lich 5K 113
Caterham Pl. ST3: Mei 4D 42
Catharine Rd. ST6: Chel 1B 18
Cathedral Ri. WS13: Lich 3A 114
Cathedral Wlk. WS13: Lich 5K 113
CATHERINE-DE-BARNES 3B 164
Catherine St. ST5: N'tle 4H 23
CATHERTON 3A 162
Catisfield Cres. WV8: P'ord 4H 123
Catkin Wlk. WS15: Rug 6E 94
Catmeadow La. WS15: Rug 1B 104
Caton Cres. ST6: Mil 5F 19
CATSHILL 5J 121
Catshill Rd. WS8: Brow 5J 121
CATTON HALL 3C 161
Cauldmore La. ST19: Whe A 1A 90
CAULDON 7B 52 (3A 156)
Cauldon Av. ST5: Brad 1E 22
ST13: Ched 5H 51
Cauldon Cl. ST13: Lee 5G 49
CAULDON LOWE 3A 156
Cauldon Pl. ST4: S Tren 7E 150 (7B 24)
Cauldon Rd. ST4: S Tren 7B 24
CAULDWELL 3C 161
Caulton St. ST6: B'lem 6K 17
CAUNSALL 3C 163
Causeley Gdns. ST2: Buck 5H 25
Causeley Rd. ST2: Buck 5H 25
Cavalier Cir. WV10: Bush 1C 124
Cavans Cl. WS11: Cann 6E 100
Cavans Wood and The Pines Pk.
WS12: Hun 5D 100
Cavell Ct. ST11: B Bri 7F 43
Cavell Rd. WS7: Burn 3C 112
Cavendish B79: Tam 2E 136
CAVENDISH BRIDGE 1D 161
Cavendish Gro. ST5: N'tle 6F 31
Cavendish Rd. ST10: Tea 2G 55
Cavendish St.
ST1: H'ley 4C 150 (5A 24)
CAVERSWALL 7G 35 (3D 155)
CAVERSWALL COMMON 4F 35
Caverswall Comn. ST11: Cave 3E 34
Caverswall La. ST3: Mei 2E 42
Caverswall Old Rd. ST11: Fors 2H 43
Caverswall Rd. ST3: W Coy 5D 34
ST10: Dilh 6J 35
ST11: B Bri 3H 43
ST11: Cave, W Coy 5D 34
Cavour St. ST1: H'ley 6A 150 (6K 23)
Cawdry Bldgs. *ST13: Lee 3G 49*
(off Fountain St.)
Caxton Ct. DE14: B Tre 3E 86
WS11: Cann 3E 108
Caxton St. WS11: Cann 3E 108
Cayley Pl. ST3: Mei 4E 42
Cecil Av. ST1: H'ley 1E 150 (3B 24)
Cecilly St. ST10: Chea 3D 54
Cecilly Ter. *ST10: Chea 3D 54*
(off King Edward St.)
Cecil Payton Cl. WS15: Abb B 2B 88
Cecil Rd. ST8: G Hea 3C 8
Cecil St. WS11: Cann 6F 101
Cedar Av. ST7: Talk 5B 10
ST11: B Bri 4J 43
WS8: Brow 4J 121
Cedar Cl. ST10: Chea 5E 54
ST14: Utt 4E 62
WS7: Chas 5J 111
WS12: Hed 1G 101
WS14: Lich 4F 115
Cedar Ct. B77: Wiln 4A 142
Cedar Cres. ST7: Big E 6H 15
ST9: End 3A 50
WS15: Bre 4J 97
Cedar Dr. B79: Tam 1G 137
ST14: S'all 1F 63
Cedar Gdns. DY7: Kin 3D 148
Cedar Gro. ST3: Fen 6E 32
ST8: Bid M 4G 9
WS6: G Wyr 7H 109
WV8: Bilb 2D 122
Cedarhill ST10: Alt 5G 57
Cedarhill Dr. WS11: Cann 1F 109
Cedar Pk. ST15: Stone 4H 47
Cedar Pk. Rd. WV12: Will 4C 126
Cedar Rd. DE13: B Nee 6G 89
ST5: C'ton 6B 16
(not continuous)
WS7: Chas 4J 111
Cedars, The WV6: Tett 7F 123
Cedars Av. WV5: Womb 5G 145
Cedars Bus. Cen., The
WS11: Cann 4C 108
Cedars Dr. ST15: Stone 7H 47
Cedartree Gro. ST1: B'lem 6D 18
Cedar Way ST17: Walt 1D 78
WV11: Wed 6G 125
Cedarwood Cl. WV9: Cove 1K 93
Celandine B77: Tam 6J 137
Celandine Cl. DE15: Stap 2K 87
ST2: Mil 6H 19
Celandines, The WV5: Womb 4E 144
Celebration Ct. ST6: B'lem 4C 18
CELLARHEAD 4H 27 (3D 155)
Cellarhead Rd. ST9: Werr 4F 27
Celtic Av. ST7: Pack 6K 11
Celtic Rd. WS11: Cann 7E 100
Cemetery Av. ST3: Long 7H 33
Cemetery Rd.
ST4: S Tren 7C 150 (7B 24)
ST5: N'tle 5C 22
ST5: Sil 1H 30
WS11: Cann 6D 100
Cemetery St. WS6: C Hay 2C 118
Cemetery Vw. ST3: Long 7H 33
ST5: N'tle 5C 22
Cemetery Way WS3: Blox 4H 127
Cemlyn Av. ST3: Blur 6E 32
Central Av. ST2: Buck 4G 25
ST15: Cold M 4A 64
WS11: Cann 5F 101
Central Av. Sth. ST15: Cold M 5A 64
Central Cl. WS3: Blox 4G 127
Central Dr. ST3: Fen 6E 32
WS3: Blox 5F 127
Central Sq. ST10: Wat 6C 52
Central St. ST7: M Cop 7F 7
Central Way DE13: B Tre 4C 84

Centre 500—Chesterton

Centre 500 ST5: N'tle 2J 23
Centre Rd. ST15: Stone 2E 46
Centrum 100 DE14: B Tre 3A 86
Centrum E. Retail Pk. DE14: B Tre 6A 86
Centurion Pk. B77: Wiln 4D 142
Centurion Way B77: Wiln 4D 142
Century Retail Pk.
ST1: H'ley 3D 150 (4B 24)
Century Rd. ST5: C'ton 5D 16
Century St. ST1: H'ley 1C 150 (3A 24)
(not continuous)
Ceramica 7K 17
CHADDESDEN 1D 161
CHADDESDEN COMMON 1D 161
Chadsfield Rd. WS15: Rug 6G 95
CHADSMOOR 6F 101
Chadswell Hgts. WS13: Lich 1D 114
CHAD VALLEY 3A 164
CHADWELL 3B 158
Chadwell Gdns. WV8: Cods 1B 122
Chadwell Way ST2: Bent 7K 25
Chadwick Cl. WV4: Pen 7K 129
Chadwick Ct. WS15: Rug 1H 97
Chadwick Cres. WS15: Hill R 1E 98
Chadwick St. ST3: Long 6J 33
Chadwyn Dr. ST2: Mil 5H 19
Chaffinch Cl. WS12: Hed 6H 101
Chaffinch Dr. ST8: Bidd 5E 8
ST14: Utt 7H 63
Chain La. ST17: Staf 2G 77
Chain St. ST6: B'lem 5C 18
Chalcot Dr. WS12: Hed 3F 101
Chaldon Cl. WV9: P'ord 4J 123
Chalfield B79: Tam 3D 136
Chalfont Av. WS11: Cann 3C 108
Chalfont Ct. WS11: Cann 4C 108
Chalfont Grn. ST2: Bent 6H 25
Challenge Cl. *ST6: B'lem 4C 18*
(off Unwin St.)
Challenge Way WV10: W'ton 7C 124
Challinor Av. ST13: Lee 5F 49
Chamberlain Cl. DE13: K Bro 2D 130
Chamberlain Ct. CW3: Bet 2B 6
Chamberlain St.
ST1: H'ley 7E 150 (6C 24)
Chamberlain Way ST8: Bidd 5E 8
Chambley Grn. WV9: Cove 2K 93
Chancery Dr. WS12: Hed 3J 101
Chancery La. ST3: Long 6J 33
Chandler Av. DY7: Kin 4D 148
Chandlers Cl. WV9: P'ord 4J 123
Chandlers Dr. B77: Amin 4D 138
Chandlers Keep WS8: Brow 6H 121
Chandridge Ct. *ST15: Oul 7H 45*
(off Church La.)
Chantree Row ST7: M Cop 6H 7
Chantry Av. WS3: Blox 5J 127
Chantry Rd. ST5: N'tle 7D 152 (3F 31)
Chapel Av. WS8: Brow 2G 121
Chapel Bank ST7: M Cop 7H 7
ST19: Whe A 2C 90
(off Hawthorne Rd.)
CHAPEL CHORLTON 1C 159
Chapel Cl. ST7: M Cop 7F 7
WV5: Womb 5F 145
Chapel Cotts. ST6: B Edg 4H 13
Chapel Ct. ST5: Sil 6A 22
ST12: Barl 2C 44
ST20: Gno 4G 67
Chapel Dr. B78: M Oak 1C 140
WS8: Brow 2G 121
CHAPEL GREEN 3C 165
Chapel La. DE6: C'ton 7E 56
DE13: New 6C 88
DE13: Roll D 6H 83
DY3: Swin 6C 144
ST6: B Edg 5H 13
ST6: B'lem 7A 18
ST7: Aud 5F 15
ST7: Harr 2J 11
ST8: Bid M 5G 9
ST10: K Hol 7J 53
ST18: Brad 6B 68
TF9: A'ley 3H 61
TF9: Hook 6E 60
WS14: Lich 5B 114
WS14: W'ton 5K 115
WS15: Can W 5G 103
WS15: Gen 6J 103
WV8: Cods 2A 122
Chapel Mus., The 6H 7
Chapelon B77: Glas 1C 142
Chapel Rd. WS15: Arm 4D 98
Chapelside WS15: Rug 6F 95
Chapel Sq. WS6: C Hay 1D 118
Chapel St. SK17: L'nor 3C 52
ST2: Buck 4H 25
ST5: N'tle 5C 22
(Knutton)
ST5: N'tle 5G 23
(May Bank)
ST5: Sil 6A 22
ST7: Big E 4G 15
ST7: M Cop 7F 7
ST7: Talk 4B 10
Chapel St. ST10: Chea 4C 54
ST10: K'ley 5F 53
ST11: Fors 2J 43
ST16: Staf 3G 73
WS3: Blox 5K 127
WS7: C Ter 3G 111
WS8: Brow 2G 121
WS11: N Can 6A 110
WS12: H Hay 2A 110
WV5: Womb 5F 145
(not continuous)
Chapel Ter. ST16: Staf 2G 73
Chaplain Rd. WS12: H Hay 1A 110
Chaplin Rd. ST3: Long 2J 41
Chapter Wlk. ST2: A Hul 3G 25
Charlemonte Cl. WS12: Hed 7K 101
Charles Av. WV11: Ess 1K 125
Charles Cl. WS6: C Hay 3D 118
Charles Cotton Dr. CW3: Mad 3A 28
Charles Cotton St. ST16: Staf 7E 70
Charles Cres. WS3: Pels 7C 120
Charles St. ST1: H'ley 3G 151 (5D 24)
ST5: N'tle 5H 23
ST8: Bidd 6C 8
ST10: Chea 4C 54
Charlestown Gro. ST3: Mei 3C 42
Charlock Gro. WS11: H Hay 7J 101
Charlotte Cl. ST18: L Hay 6J 81
Charlotte Ct. DE14: B Tre 4D 86
ST14: Utt 5H 63
Charlotte St. ST6: Gold 7G 11
CHARLTON 3A 158
Charlton St. ST4: S Tren 1B 32
Charminster Rd. ST3: Mei 3C 42
Charmouth Cl. ST1: H'ley 2G 25
Charnesford La. TF9: A'ley 5H 61
Charnes Rd. TF9: A'ley 4J 61
Charnley Rd. ST16: Staf 7H 71
Charnock Pl. ST6: Feg H 7A 12
Charnwood ST7: Kids 5F 11
Charnwood Cl. ST13: Lee 5D 48
WS12: Hed 7J 101
WS13: Lich 2C 114
WS15: Rug 7E 94
Charnwood Ho. WS13: Lich 1B 114
Charnwood Rd. DE13: B Tre 4C 84
ST3: Mei 1B 42
Charolais Cres. ST3: L'ood 2K 41
Charsley Pl. ST3: Blur 1F 41
Charter Cl. WS11: N Can 7A 110
Charterfield Dr. WS12: H Hay 2J 109
Charterhouse Av. ST17: Staf 5K 73
Charter M. WS13: Lich 4A 114
Charter Rd. ST5: N'tle 5E 22
Charters, The WS13: Lich 2B 114
Charters Av. WV8: Bilb 4D 122
Chartley Cl. ST11: B Bri 4G 43
ST16: Staf 5E 70
WV6: Per 2G 129
Chartley Ct. ST14: Utt 6H 63
Chartley Ga. Cl. ST14: Utt 7F 63
Chartwell B79: Tam 2D 136
Chartwell Cl. ST9: Werr 5C 26
Chartwell Dr. B74: F Oak 4J 135
WV5: Womb 5F 145
WV10: Bush 4C 124
Chartwell Rd. ST17: Staf 6A 74
Chartwood TF9: Logg 4E 60
Chase, The WV6: W'ton 7K 123
Chase Av. WS6: C Hay 1F 119
Chase Cres. ST17: Broc 4E 78
Chaselands WS7: C Ter 4F 111
Chase La. ST12: Titt 4A 44
Chase Leisure Cen. 1D 108
Chaseley Av. WS11: Cann 1C 108
Chaseley Cl. WS15: Rug 7D 94
Chaseley Cft. WS11: Cann 1C 108
Chaseley Gdns. WS7: Burn 4A 112
WS15: Rug 7D 94
Chaseley Rd. WS15: Rug 7C 94
Chase Link, The WS8: Brow 3J 121
Chase Pk. Ind. Est. WS7: C Ter 4F 111
Chasepool Rd. DY3: Swin 4G 147
Chase Rd. ST17: Broc 4F 79
WS3: Blox 5G 127
WS7: Burn 6J 111
WS8: Brow 3J 121
Chase Sailing Club, The 7F 111
Chase Side Dr. WS15: Rug 7F 95
Chaseside Dr. WS11: Hed 7H 101
Chaseside Ind. Est. WS12: Hed 7H 101
CHASE TERRACE 3G 111 (1A 164)
CHASETOWN 5G 111 (1A 164)
Chasetown Ind. Est.
WS7: C Ter 4G 111
Chasetown Leisure Cen. 6G 111
Chasetown Station
Chasewater Railway 6F 111
Chase Va. WS7: Chas 5G 111
Chase Vw. WS15: Arm 5E 98
Chase Vw. La. ST18: Copp 3E 76
Chaseview Rd. DE13: Alre 6B 130
Chase Wlk. ST3: L'ood 3B 42
WS12: Hun 6C 100
Chasewater Country Pk. 6E 110
Chasewater Ct. Bus. Pk.
WS7: C Ter 4F 111
Chasewater Dr. ST6: Nort 5F 19
Chasewater Gro. ST10: Chea 3E 54
Chasewater Heaths Station
Chasewater Railway 5F 111
Chasewater Ind. Est. WS7: Chas 5G 111
Chasewater Outdoor Education Cen.
6F 111
Chasewater Railway 6D 110
Chasewater Railway Heritage Cen.
1F 121
Chasewater Sports Cen. 1E 120
Chasewater Way WS11: N Can 6B 110
Chasewood Pk. Bus. Cen.
WS12: H Hay 2A 110
CHATCULL 1B 158
Chatfield Cl. DE15: Stap 3K 87
Chatfield Pl. ST3: Long 7K 33
Chatham St. ST1: H'ley 7E 150 (6B 24)
Chatham Way B77: Wiln 5B 142
Chatsworth B79: Tam 2C 136
Chatsworth Dr. DE13: Tut 2H 83
ST6: Nort 3E 18
ST9: Werr 6C 26
WS11: Cann 6G 101
Chatsworth Gdns. WV6: Tett 6C 122
Chatsworth M *ST21: Ecc 2H 65*
(off High St.)
Chatsworth Pk. Av. ST4: H'ord 1A 40
Chatsworth Pl. ST3: Mei 1B 42
ST5: C'ton 1D 22
Chatteris Cl. ST3: Mei 4D 42
CHATTERLEY 4E 16
Chatterley Cl. ST5: Brad 7F 17
Chatterley Dr. ST7: Kids 7E 10
Chatterley Rd. ST6: Tuns 3F 17
Chatterley St. ST6: B'lem 6J 17
CHATTERLEY WHITFIELD 7C 12
Chatterton Av. WS13: Lich 5J 113
Chatterton Pl. ST3: Long 6K 33
Chaucer Av. WV12: Will 5E 126
Chaucer Cl. B79: Tam 3G 137
DE14: B Tre 5E 84
WS14: Lich 5B 114
Chaucer Courts ST3: Long 1H 41
Chaucer Dr. WS7: C Ter 2J 111
Chaucer Rd. ST17: Staf 6E 72
WS3: Blox 5K 127
Chaulden Rd. ST16: Staf 4F 71
Chawner Cl. WS7: C Ter 2G 111
Chaytor Rd. B78: Pole 2J 143
CHEADLE 4C 54 (3A 156)
Cheadle Cl. ST19: Penk 5H 91
Cheadle Rd. ST9: W Roc 1K 27
ST10: Alt 5H 57
ST10: K'ley 6F 53
ST10: Tea 2F 55
ST11: B Bri, Fors 3J 43
ST13: Ched 7F 51
ST13: Lee 2J 51
ST14: Utt 4G 63
Cheadle Shop. Cen. ST10: Chea 4C 54
Cheam Gdns. WV6: Tett 5G 123
Cheapside ST1: H'ley 3G 151 (4C 24)
ST5: N'tle 3E 152 (1F 31)
Cheatle Ct. B77: Dost 5K 141
CHEBSEY 2C 159
Chebsey Cl. ST2: Buck 4J 25
Chebsey Dr. ST16: Staf 7C 70
CHECKLEY
Nantwich 3B 154
Stoke-on-Trent 7K 55 (1A 160)
Checkley Dr. ST8: Bidd 4D 8
Checkley Gro. ST3: Long 3K 33
Checkley La. CW3: Wrin 7A 6
TF2: St G 7A 6
Checkley Rd. ST5: C'ton 6A 16
Cheddar Dr. ST5: Sil 6H 21
CHEDDLETON 6H 51 (2D 155)
Cheddleton Flint Mill 4G 51
CHEDDLETON HEATH 3J 51
Cheddleton Heath Rd. ST13: Lee 3H 51
Cheddleton Pk. Av. ST13: Ched 5H 51
Cheddleton Rd. ST13: Lee 5F 49
Cheddleton Station
Churnet Valley Railway 5J 51
Cheedale Cl. DE15: Wins 6H 85
Chelford Cl. ST19: Penk 3J 91
CHELLASTON 1D 161
Chell Cl. ST19: Penk 5H 91
Chell Grn. Av. ST6: Chel 1A 18
Chell Grn. Ct. ST6: Chel 1A 18
Chell Gro. ST5: Brad 1E 22
CHELL HEATH 2B 18
Chell Heath Rd. ST6: B'lem, Chel 1B 18
(not continuous)
Chell Rd. ST16: Staf 3F 73
Chell St. ST1: H'ley 3D 24
CHELMARSH 3B 162
Chelmarsh Av. WV3: W'ton 5H 129
CHELMORTON 1B 156
Chelmorton Dr. ST3: Long 1A 42
Chelmsford Dr. ST2: Bent 6J 25
Chelmsford Rd. ST5: N'tle 3F 23
Chelsea Cl. ST8: Bidd 4C 8
Chelsea Way ST16: Staf 4E 72
Chelson St. ST3: Long 6J 33
Cheltenham Av. ST10: Chea 2D 54
Cheltenham Cl. WV6: W'ton 7K 123
Cheltenham Dr. ST17: Wild 7K 73
Cheltenham Gro. ST1: H'ley 3F 25
ST5: Sil 6H 21
Chelwood St. ST1: H'ley 1E 150 (3B 24)
Chemical La. ST6: B'lem 5F 17
Chemical La. Ind. Est. ST6: B'lem 6G 17
Chenet Way WS11: Cann 1E 108
Cheniston Rd. WV12: Will 7C 126
Chepstow Cl. ST8: Bidd 4C 8
WV6: Per 2G 129
Chepstow Dr. ST17: Wild 7A 74
Chepstow Pl. ST3: Long 3J 33
Chepstow Rd. WS3: Blox 4F 127
WV10: Ford 7B 116
Chepstow Way WS3: Blox 4F 127
Chequers, The WS13: Lich 3C 114
Chequers Av. WV5: Womb 1G 145
Chequers Ct. WS11: N Can 6C 110
Cherished Chimneys Mus. 7H 17
Cheriton Grn. ST2: Bent 7K 25
Cheriton Gro. WV6: Per 3F 129
CHERRINGTON 2A 158
Cherrington Dr. WS6: G Wyr 7F 109
Cherrington Gdns. WV6: Tett 4J 129
Cherry Bank WS12: Hed 4J 101
Cherrybrook Dr. ST19: Penk 3J 91
Cherry Cl. ST5: C'ton 6B 16
ST11: Ful 3G 59
WS7: Chas 5H 111
Cherry Ct. DE14: B'ton 4B 86
Cherry Gro. ST3: Fen 6E 32
WV11: Wed 6G 125
Cherry Hill CW3: Mad 3A 28
Cherry Hill Av. ST3: Mei 7C 34
Cherry Hill La. ST5: N'tle 6C 22
(not continuous)
Cherry La. DY3: Him 7J 145
ST18: Gt Bri 5H 65
Cherry Leys DE15: Wins 7K 85
Cherry Orchard ST5: N'tle 2E 152 (7F 23)
ST15: Stone 5J 47
WS14: Lich 4C 114
Cherry St. B79: Tam 4H 137
Cherry Tree Cl. ST4: Tren 4A 40
ST15: Stone 7F 47
ST21: Ecc 2H 65
Cherrytree Cres. ST18: Gt Bri 6G 65
Cherry Tree Gdns. WV8: Bilb 2D 122
Cherry Tree Ho. WS15: Rug 3H 97
Cherry Tree La. ST8: Bid M 5G 9
WV8: Bilb 2D 122
Cherry Tree Rd. DE15: Stap 6G 87
ST5: C'ton 6C 16
ST7: Big E 6H 15
WS11: N Can 7D 110
WS12: Hun 2D 100
WS15: Rug 3H 97
Cherry Tree Wlk. B79: Tam 1G 137
Cherrywood Cl. ST17: Wild 1A 78
Cherrywood Gro. ST3: L'ood 4B 42
Cherrywood Way B74: L Ast 3J 135
Chertsey Pl. ST1: H'ley 7D 18
Chervil Cl. ST3: Mei 4C 42
Cherwell B77: Wiln 1K 141
Cherwell Dr. WS8: Brow 2E 120
Chesham Gro. ST3: Mei 4C 42
Chesham Rd. ST16: Staf 7H 71
Cheshire Cl. WS7: Burn 3D 112
Cheshire Dr. ST19: Brew 2D 92
Cheshire Gro. WV6: Per 2F 129
Cheslyn Dr. WS6: C Hay 1D 118
CHESLYN HAY 2D 118 (1D 163)
Cheslyn Hay Leisure Cen. 1C 118
Chessington Cres.
ST4: Tren 3C 40
CHESTALL 4J 103
Chestall Rd. WS15: Can W 5H 103
Chestbut M. DE15: Stap 6G 87
Chester Av. WV6: Tett 6H 123
Chester Cl. ST7: Talk 7C 10
WS11: H Hay 2H 109
WS13: Lich 1C 114
Chester Cres. ST5: N'tle 4E 30
CHESTERFIELD
Chesterfield 1D 157
Lichfield 3B 134 (1B 164)
Chesterfield Rd. WS13: Lich 5A 114
WS14: Lich 6A 114
Chester Rd. DY7: Kin 3D 148
DY7: Stou 5K 147
ST7: Aud 5F 15
ST7: Talk 7B 10
ST21: Ecc 1F 65
WS8: Brow, W Woo 6J 121
WS9: W Woo 6J 121
WS15: Rug 3E 96
Chester Rd. Nth. WS8: Brow 3F 121
CHESTERTON
Bridgnorth 2B 162
Newcastle 1C 22 (3C 155)

Clayhanger St.—Conway Cres.

Clayhanger St. ST6: B'lem 7K 17
Clay Hills ST6: Tuns 4G 17
Clay Lake ST9: End 7K 13
CLAY MILLS 1G 85
Claymills Pumping Station 3H 85
Claymills Rd. DE13: Stre 1G 85
Claymore B77: Wiln 3K 141
Claypit La.
WS14: Lich, Wall 1B 134 & 7J 113
Clay's La. DE14: B'ton 5A 86
Clay St. DE15: Stap 3G 87
ST19: Penk 3G 91
Clay St. E. DE15: Stap 3H 87
CLAYTON 4G 31 (3C 155)
Clayton La. ST4: T Val 5G 31
ST5: N'tle 5G 31
Clayton Rd. ST5: N'tle 6E 152 (2F 31)
Clayton Sports Cen. 4H 31
Clayton St. ST3: Long 6H 33
Claytonwood Rd. ST4: T Val 6J 31
Cleadon Pl. ST2: A Hul 2H 25
Cleasby B77: Wiln 1E 142
Cleaveland M. WS13: Lich 2K 113
Cleave Rd. DE14: B'ton 4B 86
CLEEDOWNTON 3A 162
Clee Hill Dr. WV3: W'ton 5H 129
CLEE ST MARGARET 3A 162
CLEESTANTON 3A 162
CLEETON ST MARY 3A 162
Cleeton St. WS12: H Hay 2K 109
Cleeve B77: Glas 6K 137
Cleeve Dr. B74: F Oak 2K 135
Cleeve Rd. WS3: Blox 2F 127
Cleeve Way WS3: Blox 3F 127
Clee Vw. Rd. WV5: Womb 5E 144
Clegg Rd. WS7: Burn 4C 112
Clematis B77: Amin 6B 138
Clematis Av. ST11: B Bri 4H 43
Clematis Cl. ST18: Gt Bri 6G 65
Clematis Cres. DE15: Stap 4H 87
Clematis Dr. WV9: P'ord 2H 123
Clement Cl. ST16: Staf 1H 73
Clement Pl. ST6: Nort 4E 18
Clement Rd. ST6: Chel 2A 18
Clements La. B79: Elf 5H 131
CLENT 3D 163
CLEOBURY NORTH 3A 162
Clerk Bank ST13: Lee 3F 49
CLERKS BANK 1G 53
Clermont Av. ST4: H'ord 7A 32
Clevedon Av. ST17: Staf 7B 74
Cleveland Cl. WV11: Wed 4K 125
Cleveland Dr. WS11: Cann 6H 101
Cleveland Rd. ST1: H'ley 7F 151 (6C 24)
ST5: N'tle 5C 22
Cleveland St. ST6: B'lem 7K 17
Cleveland Wlk. ST17: Staf 6D 72
Cleves Cres. WS6: C Hay 3D 118
Clewley Dr. WV9: P'ord 2J 123
Clewley Rd. DE14: B'ton 4A 86
Clewlow Pl. ST3: Long 4K 33
Clewlows Bank ST9: Bag, S Broo 5B 50
Clews St. ST6: B'lem 1J 23
Clews Wlk. ST5: N'tle 3G 23
Cley Gro. ST5: N'tle 7F 31
Cley Rd. WS11: Cann 6H 109
CLIFF 2C 165
Cliff, The DY7: Kin 6E 148
Cliffe Pl. ST6: B'lem 4A 18
Clifford Av. ST6: Nort 2F 19
Clifford Cl. B77: Glas 6B 138
Clifford St. B77: Glas 6A 138
ST1: H'ley 6H 151 (6D 24)
CLIFFORD'S WOOD 1A 64
Cliff Rd. ST18: Gt Hay 4H 81
Cliff St. ST6: B'lem 6C 18
CLIFF VALE 7A 150 (6A 24)
Cliff Va. Pl. ST4: S Tren 7A 150 (7K 23)
Clift Cl. WV12: Will 7C 126
CLIFTON 6E 56 (3B 156)
Clifton Av. B79: Tam 2F 137
WS8: Brow 5F 121
WS11: Cann 4C 108
CLIFTON CAMPVILLE 6D 132 (3C 161)
Clifton Cl. ST4: Fen 4E 32
ST16: Staf 3K 73
Clifton Dr. ST16: Staf 3K 73
Clifton Gdns. WV8: Bilb 2E 122
Clifton Rd. DE6: C'ton 7E 56
(not continuous)
WV6: Tett 7F 123
Clifton St. ST4: Fen 4E 32
ST5: N'tle 4H 23
Clifton Way DE15: Stap 2J 87
Clinton Cres. WS7: C Ter 3K 111
Clinton Gdns. ST15: Stone 5G 47
Clinton Sq. ST1: H'ley 5E 150 (5C 24)
Clive Av. ST2: Mil 4H 19
Cliveden Pl. ST3: Long 7J 33
Cliveden Rd. ST2: Buck 3H 25
Clive Ho. DE15: Wins 1K 87
Clive Rd. ST5: N'tle 2H 23
WS7: C Ter 4J 111
WV6: Patt 6B 128
Clive St. ST6: Tuns 3J 17
Cloister Rd. ST4: S Tren 4A 32
Cloisters, The DE15: Stap 3G 87
ST20: Gno 3J 67
Cloister Wlk. ST2: A Hul 3G 25
WS14: W'ton 3G 131
Close, The CW3: Mad 2A 28
DE13: Tut 2G 83
DY3: Swin 1J 147
DY7: Stou 6H 147
ST3: W Coy 4D 34
ST9: End 2B 50
ST16: Staf 5E 72
ST17: Staf 2G 77
WS13: Lich 3A 114
Close Bank DE13: Tut 2H 83
Close Banks Wlk. DE13: Tut 2H 83
Close La. ST7: M Cop 6H 7
CLOUGH HALL 6D 10
Clough Hall Dr. ST7: Talk 7C 10
Clough Hall Rd. ST7: Kids 6D 10
Clough La. ST9: Werr 5C 26
Clough St. ST1: H'ley 5C 150 (5A 24)
Cloughwood Way ST6: B'lem 6H 17
Clovelly Wlk. ST6: B'lem 1J 23
Clover Ct. DE14: B'ton 7A 86
Cloverdale ST17: Wild 7A 74
WV6: Per 2E 128
Cloverdale Pl. ST3: Long 6B 34
Cloverdale Rd. ST5: N'tle 5F 23
Clover Mdws. WS12: H Hay 2J 109
Clover Ridge WS6: C Hay 1C 118
Clover Rd. ST5: N'tle 2H 23
Clowes Rd. ST2: Buck 5G 25
Club La. WV10: Cov H 6A 116
Club St. ST4: S Tren 3B 32
CLUDDLEY 1A 162
Clumber Av. ST5: N'tle 3G 31
Clumber Gro. ST5: N'tle 4G 31
Cluny Pl. ST2: A Hul 3G 25
Clyde Av. ST8: Bidd 4E 8
Clyde Pl. ST5: N'tle 5E 30
Clyde Rd. ST6: B'lem 1A 24
Clydesdale Rd. WS8: Clay 6G 121
Clyde St. ST1: H'ley 5D 150 (5B 24)
Clyde Wlk. ST1: H'ley 5D 150 (5B 24)
Clynes Way ST3: Mei 6D 34
Coach Gdns. ST19: Whe A 2C 90
Coach Ho. La. WS15: Rug 7G 95
Coach Ho. Ri. B77: Wiln 3B 142
Coachmans Cl. ST16: Staf 5E 70
COALBROOKDALE 1A 162
Coaldale Rd. ST5: C'ton 4C 22
Coal Haulage La. WS11: Cann 5F 109
Coal Haulage Rd.
WS12: H Hay 3B 110
Coalmeadow Cl. WS3: Blox 2F 127
COALPIT HILL 6A 10
Coalpit Hill ST7: Talk 7B 10
Coalpit La. WS15: Bre 4J 97
COAL POOL 1A 164
COALPORT 1B 162
Coalport Cl. ST10: Chea 6B 54
Coalport Dr. ST15: Stone 6E 46
COALVILLE 3D 161
Coalville Pl. ST3: W Coy 4D 34
Coalway Rd. WS3: Blox 5G 127
WS15: Bre 3K 97
WV3: Pen 7K 129
Coates Pl. ST6: Feg H 6B 12
Coatsgate Wlk. WV8: P'ord 4H 123
Cobbett Rd. WS7: C Ter 4E 110
Cobbles, The ST19: Whe A 2C 90
Cobden Cl. WS12: Hed 3J 101
Cobden St. ST3: Long 1H 41
ST5: N'tle 2H 23
Cobham Cl. ST15: Yarn 6D 64
Cobham Pl. ST3: Mei 2C 42
Cobia B77: T Gat 3K 141
Cobmoor Rd. ST7: Kids 2E 10
COBRIDGE 2B 24
Cobridge Ind. Est. ST6: B'lem 1B 24
Cobridge Rd. ST1: H'ley 3C 150 (4A 24)
Cock All. WS13: Lich 4B 114
Cocketts Nook WS15: Rug 5E 94
Cock Hill DE6: C'ton 7E 56
Cock La. ST17: Bed 7C 78
Cocklesall La. ST11: Ful, Hild 3G 59
COCKNAGE 5J 41
Cocknage Rd. ST3: Long 1H 41
COCKSHUTFORD 3A 162
Cockshut La. DE13: K Bro 2D 130
Cocks La. ST9: S Broo 4J 19
Cocksparrow La. WS12: Hun 6A 100
Cockspur St. B78: Bir 3G 143
Cockster Brook La. ST3: Blur 6F 33
Cockster Rd. ST3: Long 6F 33
Cockstubbles Rd. ST14: Utt 5G 63
Cocton Cl. WV6: Per 1F 129
CODNOR 3D 157
CODSALL 1B 122 (1C 163)
Codsall Gdns. WV8: Cods 1A 122
Codsall Ho. WV8: Cods 1A 122
Codsall Leisure Cen. 1C 122
Codsall Rd. WV6: Tett 4E 122
WV8: Tett 4E 122
Codsall Station (Rail) 2A 122
CODSALL WOOD 5B 92 (1C 163)
Codsall Wood Rd.
WV8: Cods, C Woo 5B 92
Coghlan Dr. ST17: Staf 6E 72
COKHAY GREEN 2C 161
Colbourne Rd. B78: Tam 7G 137
Colbrook B77: Wiln 1K 141
Colclough Av. ST5: N'tle 7E 16
Colclough La. ST6: Gold 7H 11
Colclough Rd. ST3: Mei 1D 42
COLDHAM 1C 163
COLD HATTON 2A 158
COLD HATTON HEATH 2A 158
COLDMEECE 6B 64 (1C 159)
Cold Meece Est. ST15: Cold M 6A 64
COLD NORTON 7B 46
Coldridge Cl. WV8: P'ord 4H 123
COLDWELL 6K 103
Cole Dr. ST16: Staf 4E 72
COLE END 3C 165
Colehill B79: Tam 4H 137
COLEMORE GREEN 2B 162
Colenso Way ST5: Brad 7F 17
COLEORTON 3D 161
Coleridge Cl. B79: Tam 3G 137
WS3: Pels 7C 120
WV12: Will 6E 126
Coleridge Ct. *DE14: B Tre 5D 84*
(off Horninglow Rd.)
Coleridge Dr. ST10: Chea 5B 54
ST17: Staf 6E 72
WV6: Per 2F 129
Coleridge Rd. ST3: Blur 7F 33
COLESHILL 3C 165
Coleshill Rd. B78: Faze 4F 141
Coleshill St. B78: Faze 2G 141
Cole St. ST8: Bidd 6C 8
COLEY 4K 81
Coley Gro. ST18: L Hay 6J 81
Coley La. ST18: L Hay 6J 81
Colin Cres. ST3: W Coy 5D 34
Colindene Gro. ST4: P'ull 3K 31
Colinwood Cl. WS6: G Wyr 3F 119
Collard Av. ST5: N'tle 5F 23
College Cl. CW3: Mad 1A 28
College Ct. WV6: Tett 2K 129
College Farm Cl. WV6: Patt 6B 128
College Flds. ST15: Yarn 6D 64
College La. B79: Tam 4H 137
College Rd. ST1: H'ley 6E 150 (6B 24)
ST4: S Tren 6E 150 (1B 32)
ST14: Dens 2A 58
College Vw. WV6: Tett 3K 129
Collett B77: Glas 1C 142
Collett Rd. WV6: Per 1F 129
Colley Av. WV10: Bush 5D 124
Colley Rd. ST6: Chel 1K 17
Collier Cl. WS6: C Hay 2D 118
WS8: Brow 5E 120
Collier's Cl. WV12: Will 7B 126
Colliery Dr. WS3: Blox 2F 127
Colliery Rd. WS15: Bre 7G 97
Collinbourne Cl. ST4: Tren 4B 40
Colling Dr. WS13: Lich 5K 113
Collingwood Ct. *ST15: Stone 4H 47*
(off Lichfield St.)
Collingwood Gro. ST4: S Tren 1J 31
Collingwood Rd. WV10: Bush 3C 124
Collin Rd. ST4: T Val 5J 31
Collins Hill WS13: Lich 1A 114
Collinson Rd. DE13: B Nee 6G 89
ST6: Gold 7H 11
Collins Rd. WS8: Brow 7J 121
Collin St. ST14: Utt 6G 63
Collis Av. ST4: S Tren 3J 153 (7H 23)
Colman Av. WV11: Wed 7K 125
Colne Mt. ST14: Utt 6G 63
Colonnade, The *ST16: Staf 3G 73*
(off Eastgate St.)
Coltham Rd. WV12: Will 7C 126
Coltman Cl. WS14: Lich 4D 114
COLTON 2J 95 (2A 160)
Colton Rd. WS15: Bell, Rug, Col 2G 95
Coltsfoot Vw. WS6: C Hay 2E 118
COLTSTONE 1F 53
Columbian Cres. WS7: C Ter 3H 111
Columbian Dr. WS11: Cann 7F 101
Columbian Way WS11: Cann 7F 101
Columbine Wlk. *ST6: Tuns 4H 17*
(off Ladywell Rd.)
Colville St. ST4: Fen 3F 33
COLWICH 7K 81 (2A 160)
Colwich Cres. ST16: Staf 3A 74
Colwyn Dr. ST8: Knyp 1D 12
Combe Dr. ST3: M Hea 5C 42
COMBER 5E 148
COMBERFORD 1B 164
Comberford Rd. B79: Tam 1G 137
Comber Gro. DY7: Kin 6E 148
Comber Rd. DY7: Kin 7D 148
COMBRIDGE 7A 58 (1A 160)
Comfrey Cl. ST3: Mei 4C 42
Commerce Dr. ST19: Penk 5G 91
Commerce St. ST3: Long 6J 33
Commercial Rd. ST1: H'ley 5J 151 (5D 24)
WS2: Wals 6G 127
Commercial St. ST6: B'lem 1A 24
Common La. B78: Dor, Pole 2J 143
B79: Tam 5H 137
CW3: Bet 2A 6
ST3: R Clo 6A 42
ST5: Whit 4F 37
ST15: Stone 6E 46
ST17: Bed 7D 78
WS11: Cann 7G 101
WS13: Frad 3J 107
WS14: W'ton, W Bar
7K 115 & 4F 131
Common Rd. ST16: Staf 4G 71
WV5: Womb 6F 145
Common Rd. Ind. Est. ST16: Staf 5G 71
(not continuous)
COMMONSIDE
Ashbourne 3C 157
Northwich 1A 154
COMMON SIDE 2C 120
Common Side WS15: Gen 5J 103
Commonside WS8: Brow 6J 121
WS15: Gen 6J 103
Commonside Cl. ST16: Staf 7F 71
Common Vw. WS7: C Ter 2J 111
WS12: Hed 3H 101
Common Wlk. ST16: Staf 7F 71
WS12: Hun 5C 100
Community Dr. ST6: B'lem 6D 18
Como Pl. ST5: N'tle 3C 30
Compa, The DY7: Kin 5E 148
COMPTON
Stourbridge 3A 148 (3C 163)
Wolverhampton 4K 129
Compton ST13: Lee 4F 49
Compton Cl. DY7: Kin 5D 148
ST17: Staf 4H 73
Compton Ct. B74: F Oak 5K 135
Compton Gdns. DY7: Kin 5D 148
Compton Hill Dr. WV3: W'ton 4K 129
Compton M. ST13: Lee 4G 49
Compton Rd. B79: Tam 2F 137
DY7: Kin 5A 148
ST17: Staf 5B 74
Compton Rd. W. WV3: W'ton 4K 129
Compton St. ST1: H'ley 5D 150 (5B 24)
Comwall Cl. WS3: Blox 7J 127
(not continuous)
Condlyffe Rd. ST13: Lee 5F 49
Condor Gro. WS12: H Hay 2J 109
Conduit Rd. WS11: N Can 7C 110
Conduit St. WS13: Lich 3B 114
Conewood Pl. ST3: Blur 1E 40
Coneybere Gdns. ST19: Brew 1D 92
Coneygreave Cl. ST10: Chea 6C 54
Coneygreave La. ST5: Whit 5F 37
Conford Cl. ST2: Buck 6F 25
CONGERSTONE 1D 165
CONGLETON 1C 155
CONGLETON EDGE 1A 8
Congleton Edge Rd. CW12: Cong 1B 8
Congleton Rd. CW12: White 1D 8
ST7: M Cop 5J 7
ST7: Talk 6B 10
ST8: Bidd 5C 8
Congleton Rd. Nth.
ST7: C Law, Sch G 3B 10
Congleton Rd. Sth. ST7: C Law 3B 10
CONGREVE 3D 159
Congreve Cl. ST17: Walt 7D 74
Congreve Rd. ST3: Blur 7F 33
Conifer Cl. WS12: Hed 2G 101
Conifer Gro. ST3: Blur 7F 33
ST17: Staf 7D 72
Coniston B77: Wiln 3D 142
Coniston Cl. ST15: Stone 5K 47
Coniston Dr. ST10: Chea 3E 54
Coniston Gro. ST5: N'tle 5F 31
Coniston Ho. ST16: Staf 3H 73
Coniston Pl. ST4: Tren 3K 39
Coniston Rd. WV6: Tett 5F 123
Coniston Way WS11: Cann 2E 108
Connaught Dr. WV5: Womb 1G 145
Connaught St. ST6: Tuns 5H 17
Conrad Cl. ST3: Long 6K 33
CONSALL 3D 155
Consall Gro. ST4: Tren 4C 40
Consall La. ST9: W Roc 4K 27 & 2K 27
Consall Nature Pk. Vis. Cen. 3D 155
Consett Rd. ST3: Blur 2F 41
Consort Pl. B79: Tam 4J 137
Consort St. ST4: S Tren 2B 32
Constable Av. ST5: C'ton 2C 22
Constable Cl. ST3: Mei 3D 42
Constance Av. ST4: Tren 2B 40
Convent Cl. DE15: Stap 4G 87
ST4: S Tren 1A 32
ST18: L Hay 7J 81
WS11: Cann 3D 108
Convent Ct. ST4: S Tren 1A 32
Convent La. ST15: Oul 7H 45
Conway Cl. DE13: Stre 3E 84
Conway Cres. WV12: Will 6C 126

Dartford Rd. WS3: Blox 4F 127
Dart Gro. ST10: Chea 6D 54
Dartmouth Av. ST5: N'tle 3E 30
WS3: Wals 7K 127
WS11: Cann 3C 108
WV6: Patt 7A 128
Dartmouth Cl. WS3: Wals 7K 127
Dartmouth Pl. ST3: L'ood 2B 42
Dartmouth Rd. WS11: Cann 2D 108
Dartmouth St. ST6: B'lem 6B 18
ST16: Staf 3J 73
Dart Pl. ST5: N'tle 5E 30
Darwell Pk. B77: Amin 7D 138
Darwin Cl. DE15: Stap 3K 87
ST15: Stone 2E 46
ST16: Staf 2A 74
WS7: Burn 4K 111
WS12: H Hay 1A 110
WS13: Lich 3A 114
Darwin Ct. WV6: Per 2F 129
Darwin Pl. WS2: Wals 7H 127
Darwin Rd. WS2: Wals 7H 127
Dash Gro. ST6: B'lem 6C 18
Datteln Rd. WS11: Cann 6G 101
Daurada Dr. ST17: Staf 6J 73
DAVENHAM 1A 154
Davenport Cl. ST13: Lee 5C 48
Davenport Ct. ST13: Lee 3F 49
Davenport Rd. WV6: Tett 1J 129
WV11: Wed 7J 125
Davenport St. ST6: B'lem 7H 17
Davenport Way ST5: N'tle 6D 30
Daventry Cl. ST2: Buck 6F 25
David Garrick Gdns. WS13: Lich 1B 114
David Rd. ST3: L'ood 1B 42
Davidson Rd. WS14: Lich 4B 114
Davies Cl. ST16: Staf 2J 73
Davies Dr. ST14: Utt 4E 62
Davies Ho. WS3: Blox 3H 127
Davison St. ST6: B'lem 1A 24
Davis Rd. B77: Amin 5B 138
WV12: Will 5D 126
Davis St. ST4: H'ley 7C 150 (6A 24)
Davy Cl. ST2: Buck 5G 25
WS7: Chas 7H 111
Davy Pl. WS15: Rug 3F 97
Dawes Cl. WS15: Arm 5D 98
Dawes La. WS8: Brow 3J 121
DAWLEY 1A 162
Dawlish Av. ST17: Staf 7B 74
Dawlish Dr. ST2: Bent 6H 25
Dawn Av. ST6: Chel 3A 18
Dawn Vw. ST3: W Coy 6D 34
Dawson St. WS3: Blox 5K 127
Day Av. WV11: Wed 6J 125
DAYHILLS 1D 159
DAYHOUSE BANK 3D 163
Dayson Pl. ST5: Brad 1E 22
Dayton Dr. WS15: Rug 6E 94
Daywell Ri. WS15: Rug 5E 94
Deacons Way WS15: Rug 6H 95
Deakin Av. WS8: Brow 3H 121
Deakin Gro. ST5: N'tle 4G 31
Deakin Rd. ST6: Chel 2B 18
Deal Av. WS7: C Ter 3J 111
Dean Ct. WV6: Per 7A 122
DEANERY, THE 4F 91
Deanery Cl. WS15: Rug 6G 95
WV10: Shar 2G 117
Dean Hollow ST7: Aud 5F 15
Dean Pl. ST1: H'ley 7J 151 (6D 24)
Dean Rd. WV5: Womb 5F 145
Deansberry Cl. ST4: Tren 2A 40
Deans Cft. WS13: Lich 3C 114
Deanscroft Way ST3: Long 5A 34
Deansfield Cl. ST19: Brew 2D 92
Deansfield Ho. ST19: Brew 1D 92
Deansfield Rd. ST19: Brew 2C 92
Deansgate ST5: N'tle 5B 152 (1E 30)
ST13: Lee 3G 49
Deanshill Cl. ST16: Staf 4E 72
Deans La. ST5: C'ton 5A 16
Dean St. ST2: Buck 4J 25
ST19: Brew 2C 92
Deans Way ST4: Tren 4B 40
Dean Vw. ST7: Aud 6F 15
Dearnsdale Cl. ST16: Staf 6D 70
Deavall Way WS11: H Hay 1H 109
Deaville Rd. ST2: Buck 5J 25
Debenham Cres. ST2: Buck 6F 25
Decade Cl. ST5: C'ton 5D 16
Deebank Av. ST13: Lee 3J 49
Dee Cl. ST7: Talk 7C 10
ST8: Bidd 4E 8
Dee Gro. WS11: Cann 4D 108
Dee La. ST5: N'tle 5F 31
Deeley B77: Glas 1C 142
Deeley Pl. WS3: Blox 5H 127
Deeley St. WS3: Blox 5H 127
Deepdale B77: Wiln 7F 139
Deepdale Cl. DE15: Wins 6J 85
ST6: Mil 5F 19
Deepdales ST17: Wild 1A 78
WV5: Womb 4E 144
Deep Hayes Country Pk. 2D 155
Deepmore Cl. DE13: Alre 6C 130
WV10: F Ash 6G 93
Deer Cl. WS3: Blox 4J 127
WS11: N Can 4C 110
WS12: Hun 4C 100
Deerfold Cres. WS7: Burn 4K 111
Deer Hill ST17: Broc 3G 79
Deerhill B77: Wiln 1E 142
Deerhurst Ri. WS12: Haz 4B 102
Deerleap Way WS15: Rug 7E 94
Dee Rd. WS3: Blox 4K 127
Deer Pk. ST20: Gno 3J 67
Deer Pk. Rd. B78: Faze 1E 140
Deers Leap WV6: Patt 1A 128
Deer Wlk. WV8: P'ord 3H 123
De Ferrers Cft. DE13: Stre 3D 84
Defoe Dr. ST3: W Coy 5A 34
De Havilland Dr. ST15: Yarn 6D 64
Delafield Way WS15: Rug 6E 94
DELAMERE 1A 154
Delamere Gro. ST4: Tren 3A 40
ST5: N'tle 1E 152 (6G 23)
Delamere La. ST17: Staf 6C 72
Delamere Rd. WV12: Will 6C 126
Delaney Dr. ST3: W Coy 5B 34
Delhi Cl. DE15: Wins 1K 87
Delius Gro. ST1: H'ley 3F 25
Dell, The B79: Tam 3H 137
ST5: Sil 7A 22
WS12: Hed 6B 102
WS13: Lich 4K 113
Dellbrook Ct. ST5: N'tle 6E 152 (2F 31)
Dell Cl. ST16: Staf 5D 70
Dellwood Gro. ST3: Long 3K 33
Delphouse Rd. ST10: Chea 5A 54
Delph Side ST7: Big E 5H 15
Delph Wlk. ST4: Fen 3F 33
Delta Way WS11: Cann 5D 108
Delta Way Bus. Cen. WS11: Cann 5D 108
Deltic B77: Glas 1C 142
Delves Pl. ST5: N'tle 4F 31
DELVES, THE 2A 164
Demontfort Way ST14: Utt 7H 63
Denbigh Cl. DE13: Stre 4E 84
ST5: N'tle 5H 31
ST8: Knyp 7C 8
Denbigh St. ST1: H'ley 1D 150 (3B 24)
Denbury Cl. WS12: H Hay 2K 109
DENBY 3D 157
Denby Av. ST3: Long 4J 33
DENBY COMMON 3D 157
Denby Turn DE14: B Tre 6E 84
Dency Gro. ST6: B'lem 4A 18
Dene Cl. ST19: Penk 4H 91
Dene Cft. WS3: Blox 4G 127
Denefield ST19: Penk 4H 91
Denehurst Cl. ST3: Mei 7C 34
Deneside ST5: N'tle 5B 152 (1E 30)
Denewood Pl. ST3: Mei 1D 42
Denham Gdns. WV3: W'ton 6J 129
Denham Sq. ST3: Blur 1E 40
Den La. CW3: Wrin 4A 6
Denmark Ho. ST4: Fen 4F 33
Denmark Ri. WS12: Hed 3K 101
Denmead Dr. WV11: Wed 5K 125
Dennfield Dr. WS6: C Hay 1C 118
Dennington Cres. ST3: Blur 1E 40
Dennis B77: Glas 7A 138
Dennis St. ST4: Fen 4F 33
Dennis Violet Av. ST4: Tren 6C 32
Dennis Viollet Av. ST4: Tren 6C 32
Denry Cres. ST5: N'tle 1E 22
DENSTONE 2B 58 (3B 156)
Denstone Av. ST17: Staf 5K 73
Denstone Cres. ST3: Blur 7F 33
Denstone Gdns. WV10: Bush 2C 124
Denstone La. ST10: Alt 6H 57
ST14: Dens 1A 58
(not continuous)
Dentdale Cl. ST3: Mei 3C 42
Denton Cl. ST5: N'tle 6F 31
Denton Gro. ST3: Long 6A 34
Denton Ri. DE13: B Tre 4B 84
Denton Rd. DE13: B Tre 5B 84
Dent St. B79: Tam 4J 137
Denver Fold ST17: Staf 6C 72
Denyer Ct. WS13: Frad 4J 107
Denzil Grn. ST17: Staf 6C 72
DERBY 1D 161
Derby Av. WV6: Tett 6G 123
Derby M. ST14: Utt 4E 62
Derby Pl. ST5: N'tle 5G 31
Derby Rd. DE13: B Tre, Stre 4F 85
DE14: B Tre 6E 84
DE65: Stre 1H 85
ST7: Talk 7B 10
ST14: Utt 5J 63
Derby St. DE14: B Tre 1D 86
ST1: H'ley 5H 151 (5D 24)
ST13: Lee 4F 49
ST16: Staf 3F 73
Derby St. E. DE14: B Tre 7D 84
Dereham Way ST2: Bent 7K 25
Derek Av. B78: Dor 5J 143
Derek Dr. ST1: H'ley 2E 24
DERRINGTON
Bridgnorth 2A 162
Stafford 4A 72 (2C 159)
Derrington La. ST18: Bill, Derr 5A 72
Derry St. ST4: Fen 5E 32
Derwent B77: Wiln 1K 141
Derwent Av. ST15: Stone 5K 47
Derwent Cl. DE14: B Tre 1F 87
Derwent Cres. ST7: Kids 4G 11
Derwent Dr. ST8: Bidd 4E 8
ST10: Chea 6D 54
TF9: Logg 4E 60
Derwent Gro. WS7: Burn 5B 112
WS11: Cann 3D 108
Derwent Ho. ST17: Staf 7G 73
Derwent Pk. DE14: B Tre 6E 84
Derwent Pl. ST5: N'tle 5E 22
Derwent Rd. DE15: Stap 3H 87
WV6: Tett 5F 123
Derwent St. ST1: H'ley 1D 150 (3B 24)
Derwick Ind. Est. ST17: Broc 4D 78
DETHICK 2D 157
Devall Cl. WS15: Rug 2G 97
Devana Wlk. ST3: Mei 7E 34
Devereux Ho. B79: Tam 5G 137
Deveron Cl. DE13: Stre 2D 84
Devil's Elbow La. WV11: Wed 6J 125
Devil's La. ST9: L'ton 5A 48
DEVITTS GREEN 2C 165
Devon Cl. DE15: Stap 6F 87
ST5: N'tle 5G 31
Devon Ct. WS11: Cann 3E 108
Devon Grn. WS11: Cann 3F 109
Devon Gro. ST8: Bidd 4C 8
Devon Rd. WS11: Cann 3F 109
Devonshire Dr. B78: Tam 1G 141
WS15: Rug 3F 97
Devonshire Sq. ST2: Bent 7J 25
Devon Way ST3: L'ood 1K 41
ST17: Staf 1F 77
De-Wint Rd. ST15: Stone 5H 47
Dewsbury Dr. WS7: Burn 5A 112
Dewsbury Rd. ST4: Fen 2E 32
Dexter Way B78: Bir 2H 143
Dexton Ri. ST17: Staf 6C 72
Deykin Rd. WS13: Lich 5A 114
Deyncourt Rd. WV10: W'ton 6E 124
Diamond Av. ST7: Kids 4F 11
Diamond Cl. ST3: M Hea 6C 42
ST8: Bidd 5C 8
ST12: Barl 3C 44
Diamond Cres. ST2: Mil 5F 19
Diamond Gro. WS11: H Hay 7J 101
Diamond Ridge ST12: Barl 2C 44
Diamond Way ST15: Stone 7H 47
Diana Rd. ST1: H'ley 2F 25
Diarmid Rd. ST4: H'ord 1K 39
Dibble Rd. DE14: B'ton 5B 86
Dibden Ct. ST4: S Tren 2A 32
Dickens Cl. DE14: B Tre 5E 84
Dickenson Rd. E. ST6: B'lem 1C 24
Dickenson Rd. W. ST6: B'lem 1C 24
Dickens Rd. WV10: Bush 5E 124
Dickens St. ST2: Buck 4J 25
Dickinson Av. WV10: Bush 5C 124
Dickinson Rd. WV5: Womb 6G 145
Dickson Ho. ST1: H'ley 7H 151 (7D 24)
Dickson Rd. ST16: Staf 1J 73
Dicky's La. ST20: W'ves 3E 66
DIGLAKE 4J 15
Diglake Cl. ST7: T Pit 1A 16
Diglake St. ST7: Big E 4H 15
DILHORNE 3D 155
Dilhorne Gro. ST3: Long 1J 41
Dilhorne La. ST11: Cave 6G 35
Dilhorne Park Station
Foxfield Steam Railway 3K 35
Dilhorne Rd. ST10: Chea 4A 54
ST10: Dilh, Fors 2K 43
ST11: Fors 2K 43
Dilke St. ST1: H'ley 1H 151 (3D 24)
Dill Gro. ST3: Mei 4D 42
Dimble La. ST10: Alt 6H 57
Dimbles, The WS13: Lich 7A 106
Dimbles Hill WS13: Lich 2B 114
Dimbles La. WS13: Lich 7A 106
Dimensions 5K 17
Dimmelow St. ST3: W Coy 4D 34
DIMSDALE 3F 23
Dimsdale Pde. E. ST5: N'tle 3F 23
Dimsdale Pde. W. ST5: N'tle 2E 22
Dimsdale St. ST6: B'lem 1J 23
Dimsdale Vw. ST5: C'ton 2D 22
Dimsdale Vw. E. ST5: N'tle 2F 23
Dimsdale Vw. W. ST5: N'tle 2F 23
Dingle, The DE15: Stap 4F 87
ST6: B Edg 7H 13
WV3: W'ton 5K 129
Dingle La. ST8: Bidd 1K 9
ST15: Hild 5G 59
Dingle Rd. WS8: Clay 6G 121
WV5: Womb 4F 145
Dippons Dr. WV6: Tett 3H 129
Dippons La. WV6: Per 7A 122
WV6: Tett 7B 122
Dippons Mill Cl. WV6: Tett 3H 129
Dirty La. ST19: Brew 2C 92
DISEWORTH 2D 161
DITTON PRIORS 3A 162
Dividy Rd. ST2: B Hil, Buck 5F 25
ST3: B Hil 1J 33
Dixon Cl. ST15: Stone 2E 46
Dobbinhorse La. *DE6: C'ton 7E 56*
(off Clifton Rd.)
Dobell Gro. ST3: Long 5K 33
Dobree Cl. ST17: Colw 7K 81
Doctor's Bank TF9: A'ley 4J 61
Doctors Cl. ST8: Bidd 5C 8
Doctors La. WS14: Shen 5D 134
DODDINGTON 3A 162
Doddington Pl. ST5: N'tle 3F 31
Doddlespool Barns CW3: Bet 1A 6
Dodds La. WS13: Chor 7A 104
DODS LEIGH 1A 160
Dodslow Av. DE13: Roll D 7H 83
Dodson St. ST6: B'lem 1C 24
Dogcroft Rd. ST6: Chel 2C 18
DOGINGTREE ESTATE 2D 100
Dog La. B77: Amin 3D 138
ST5: Stab 7K 37
ST13: Lee 3F 49
Dogshead La. DE13: B Nee 7F 89
Dolefoot La. DE13: New 7E 88
Doles La. DE6: C'ton 6E 56
Dolespring Cl. ST11: Fors 2J 43
DOLEY 2B 158
Doley Cl. ST20: Gno 3H 67
DOLEYGATE 3F 67
Dollymakers Hill WS15: Gen 5K 103
Dolly's La. ST6: B'lem 5A 18
Dolphin Cl. ST17: Staf 5A 74
Dolphin Ct. *WV12: Will 6D 126*
(off Huntington Rd.)
Dominic Ct. *ST15: Stone 3G 47*
(off Dominic St.)
Dominic St. ST4: S Tren 1A 32
ST15: Stone 3G 47
Donald Bates Ho. ST4: P'ull 3K 31
Donald Rd. ST1: H'ley 2E 24
Doncaster La. ST4: P'ull 2K 31
Don Gro. WS11: Cann 4D 108
DONINGTON 1C 163
DONINGTON LE HEATH 3D 161
DONISTHORPE 3D 161
Donithorne Cl. DE13: B Tre 4D 84
Donkey La. ST10: Chea 2D 54
DONNINGTON
Telford 3B 158
Shrewsbury 1A 162
Dorado B77: T Gat 3K 141
Dorcas Dr. ST3: Fen 5F 33
Dorchester Cl. ST7: Kids 3E 10
WV12: Will 5C 126
Dorchester Rd. WS11: Cann 2B 108
WV12: Will 5C 126
Dorchester Wlk. ST2: Buck 6J 25
DORDON 5J 143 (1C 165)
Dordon Rd. B78: Dor 2H 143
Dorian Way ST9: End 2B 50
Doris Robinson Ct. ST3: Mei 3B 42
Dorking Cl. ST2: Buck 6F 25
Dorlan Cl. ST9: S Broo 4J 19
Dormer Av. B77: Tam 4K 137
Dorothy Clive Garden 1B 158
DORRIDGE 3B 164
Dorridge Gro. ST5: N'tle 4J 23
Dorrington Cl. ST2: Mil 5G 19
Dorrington Dr. ST16: Staf 7G 71
Dorrington Gro. ST5: N'tle 2G 23
Dorrington Ind. Pk.
ST16: Staf 7F 71
Dorset Cl. B78: Tam 1G 141
DE15: Stap 6F 87
ST2: Buck 5J 25
Dorset Dr. ST8: Bidd 5B 8
Dorset Pl. ST5: N'tle 5H 31
ST7: Kids 3E 10
Dorset Rd. WS12: H Hay 2A 110
Dorsett Pl. WS3: Blox 6J 127
DOSTHILL 6J 141
Dosthill Rd. B77: T Gat 3K 141
Douglas Av. ST4: S Tren 4K 31
ST8: Bidd 6C 8
Douglas Pl. ST1: H'ley 7K 151 (6E 24)
WV10: Oxl 7A 124
Douglas Rd. ST5: N'tle 1B 152 (5E 22)
ST16: Staf 1J 73
Douglas Rd. W. ST16: Staf 1J 73
Douglas St. ST1: H'ley 2B 24
Doulton Cl. ST10: Chea 6C 54
ST15: Stone 6E 46
Doulton Dr. ST5: N'tle 1F 23
Doulton Gro. ST2: Mil 4H 19
Doulton Rd. ST18: Hopt 5K 71
Doulton St. ST6: B'lem 7A 18
Doval Gdns. ST10: Tea 3G 55
DOVE BANK 4E 10
Dove Bank ST14: Utt 5H 63
Dovebank Gro. ST3: Mei 4C 42
Dovecliff Cres. DE13: Stre 1G 85

Edgefield Rd.—Ezekiel La.

Edgefield Rd. ST3: Long 4J 33
EDGE HILL 7C 142
Edge Hill CV9: Woo E 7C 142
DY7: Kin 5D 148
Edge Hill Av. WV10: Bush 3E 124
Edge Hill Dr. WV6: Per 3F 129
Edge Hill Rd. B74: F Oak 4J 135
Edgehill Rd. ST13: Lee 4D 48
Edge La. ST9: End 7K 13
EDGELEY 3A 154
Edgeley Rd. ST8: Bidd 6D 8
Edgemoor Mdw.
WS12: H Hay 2J 109
Edge St. ST6: B'lem 5K 17
Edge Vw. Cl. DY7: Kin 4D 148
Edgeview Cl. ST2: Mil 5J 19
Edge Vw. Ct. ST8: Bidd 6C 8
Edge Vw. Rd. ST2: Mil 4J 19
Edge Vw. Wlk. DY7: Kin 4D 148
Edgeware St. ST1: H'ley 1D 150 (3B 24)
Edgeworth Ho. WS13: Lich 1A 114
EDGMOND 3B 158
EDGMOND MARSH 2B 158
EDIAL 5D 112
Edinburgh Dr. WV12: Will 7B 126
Edinburgh Way DE13: Stre 3E 84
EDINGALE 1B 132 (3C 161)
Edison Cl. WS12: Hed 3J 101
Edison Ct. *WV12: Will 6D 126*
(off Huntington Rd.)
Edison Rd. ST16: Staf 1H 73
WS2: Wals 7G 127
Edison St. ST4: Fen 3D 32
EDLASTON 3B 156
Edmonton Cl. WS11: H Hay 1H 109
Edmonton Gro. ST2: Mil 6F 19
Edmonton Pl. DE15: Wins 1K 87
Edmoor Cl. WV12: Will 7C 126
Edmund Av. ST17: Staf 5D 72
Ednam Gro. WV5: Womb 1G 145
Ednam Pl. ST3: Mei 1C 42
EDNASTON 3C 157
Edwal Rd. ST3: W Coy 5C 34
Edward Av. ST4: Tren 3B 40
ST5: N'tle 3F 31
Edward Ct. B77: Amin 5A 138
Edward Davies Rd. ST6: B'lem 5C 18
Edward Rd. WV6: Per 1F 129
Edwards Cl. WS15: Rug 7G 95
Edwards Dr. ST16: Staf 3E 72
Edwards Farm Rd. WS13: Frad 1K 107
Edward's Rd. WS7: Chas 6H 111
Edward St. B79: Tam 4G 137
DE14: B Tre 7C 84
ST4: Fen 2E 32
ST5: N'tle 4H 23
ST7: Big E 4H 15
ST15: Stone 3F 47
WS11: Cann 6E 100
Edwin Cl. ST17: Staf 6D 72
ST19: Penk 4H 91
EFFLINCH 7H 89 (3B 160)
Efflinch La. DE13: B Nee 6G 89
Egelwin Cl. WV6: Per 1F 129
Egerton Cl. ST11: B Bri 4J 43
Egerton Rd. ST4: S Tren . . . 4K 153 (1J 31)
WV10: Bush 2C 124
Egerton St. ST1: H'ley 7H 151 (7D 24)
EGGINGTON 2C 161
Eggington Dr. ST19: Penk 5H 91
Egg La. ST18: Hixon 6C 80
Egmont Gdns. WV11: Wed 7K 125
Eighth Av. DE14: B Tre 4A 86
Eights Cft. WS7: C Ter 3F 111
Elaine Av. ST6: B'lem 6B 18
Elburton Rd. ST4: Fen 3G 33
Elder Cl. ST14: Utt 7G 63
WS11: H Hay 1J 109
Elder Gro. WV5: Womb 4F 145
Elder La. WS7: Burn 4A 112
Elder Pl. ST6: B'lem 2B 24
Elder Rd. ST6: B'lem 1B 24
Elderside Cl. WS8: Brow 4H 121
Elder Tree La. TF9: A'ley 3J 61
Eldon St. DE15: Wins 1J 87
ST1: H'ley 2D 24
Eldridge Cl. WV9: P'ord 3H 123
Eldwick Ct. B77: Wiln 1D 142
Eleanor Cres. ST5: N'tle . . . 7C 152 (3E 30)
Eleanor Pl. ST5: N'tle 7C 152 (3E 30)
Eleanor Vw. ST5: N'tle 3F 31
Electric St. DE14: B Tre 6F 85
Electric St. Ind. Est. DE14: B Tre 6F 85
Elenora St. ST4: S Tren 2B 32
Elers Gro. ST6: B'lem 1J 23
ELFORD 6G 131 (3B 160)
Elford Cl. B74: S'ly 6F 135
ST16: Staf 5E 70
ELFORD HEATH 2F 65
Elgar Cl. WS11: Cann 5E 100
WS13: Lich 1B 114
Elgar Cres. ST1: H'ley 3G 25
Elgin Ct. WV6: Per 2F 129
Elgin Rd. WS3: Blox 1G 127
Elgin St. ST4: S Tren 7B 24
Elgood La. ST6: Gold 7G 11
Elias Cl. WS14: Lich 5E 114
Eliases La. ST8: Bidd 3G 9
Eliot Cl. B79: Tam 2G 137
WS15: Arm 5F 99
Eliot Way ST17: Staf 5E 72
Elizabethan Way WS15: Rug 2F 97
Elizabeth Av. B78: Pole 7J 139
DE13: Roll D 7H 83
Elizabeth Ct. DE15: Wins 1K 87
ST4: S Tren 1K 31
ST7: T Pit 2B 16
Elizabeth Dr. B79: Tam 3G 137
ST5: C'ton 1C 22
Elizabeth Rd. WS11: Cann 4E 100
Elizabeth St. ST1: H'ley 3K 151 (4E 24)
Elkes Gro. ST14: Utt 3E 62
Elkington Ri. CW3: Mad 2B 28
Elkstone Cl. ST6: Tuns 3J 17
Ellam's Pl. ST5: N'tle 7C 22
Ellards Dr. WV11: Wed 7K 125
ELLASTONE 3B 156
Ellastone Gro. ST4: P'ull 3K 31
Elldawn Av. ST6: Mil 5F 19
ELLENHALL 2C 159
Ellerbeck B77: Wiln 1D 142
(not continuous)
Ellerby Rd. ST3: Blur 2E 40
ELLERDINE 2A 158
ELLERDINE HEATH 2A 158
ELLERTON 2B 158
Ellesmere Rd. WS11: Cann 3B 108
Ellgreave St. ST6: B'lem 7J 17
Ellington Av. ST16: Staf 2K 73
Ellington Cl. ST2: Buck 6G 25
Elliot Dr. ST9: Werr 4D 26
Elliot Rd. ST4: Fen 3F 33
Elliott Cl. WS11: Cann 5F 101
Elliotts La. WV8: Cods 2C 122
Elliott St. ST5: N'tle 2H 153 (7H 23)
Ellison St. ST5: N'tle 3H 23
Ellis St. ST6: B'lem 1C 24
ELLISTOWN 3D 161
Ellis Wlk. WS11: Cann 3F 109
Elm Av. ST17: Walt 1D 78
WV11: Wed 5F 125
Elmbrook Cl. ST3: L'ood 2B 42
Elm Cl. DE14: B'ton 4A 86
ST7: Kids 6F 11
ST13: Lee 4D 48
ST18: Gt Hay 4G 81
Elm Ct. ST18: Hyde L 2E 76
Elm Cres. ST18: Hixon 6B 80
Elmcroft Ct. WS11: Cann 2E 108
Elmcroft Gdns. WV10: Bush 2C 124
Elmcroft Rd. ST2: A Hul 2H 25
ELMDON 3B 164
Elmdon Cl. ST19: Penk 4J 91
WV10: Oxl 4J 123
ELMDON HEATH 3B 164
Elmdon Pl. ST3: Mei 3D 42
Elmdon Rd. WV10: Oxl 4J 123
Elm Dr. ST10: Chea 5E 54
ST18: Brad 6C 68
Elm Gdns. WS14: Lich 4C 114
Elm Gro. DY7: Kin 6G 149
WS12: Hun 2D 100
WV8: Bilb 2C 122
ELMHURST 5A 106 (3B 160)
Elmhurst ST5: N'tle 5D 30
Elmhurst Cl. ST2: Buck 6F 25
ST16: Staf 5E 70
WV9: Cove 1K 93
Elmhurst Dr. B78: Tam 6G 137
WS7: Chas 7J 111
Elmley Gro. WV6: Per 3G 129
Elmore Ct. *WS15: Rug 1G 97*
(off Elmore La.)
Elmore Grn. Cl. WS3: Blox 5H 127
Elmore Grn. Rd. WS3: Blox 4G 127
Elmore Ho. WS15: Rug 7G 95
Elmore La. WS15: Rug 1G 97
Elmore Row WS3: Blox 4H 127
Elm Pl. ST3: Blur 1F 41
Elm Rd. ST15: Stone 4H 47
WS3: Blox 7K 127
WS11: N Can 6D 110
Elms, The ST5: N'tle 1G 23
Elms Cl. WV10: Shar 3G 117
Elmsdale WV6: Tett 4H 129
Elms Dr. WS11: Cann 2C 108
Elms La. WV10: Shar 3G 117
Elmsmere Av. ST3: Blur 1G 41
Elmsmere Rd. ST2: A Hul 2H 25
Elms Paddock, The
WV6: Patt 7B 128
Elms Rd. DE15: Stap 2G 87
Elmstead Cl. ST4: H'ord 1K 39
Elmstone Cl. ST17: Staf 2C 78
Elm St. ST5: N'tle 6H 23
ST6: B'lem 1A 24
Elms Way ST3: Mei 7C 34
Elm Tree Cl. WV5: Womb 5F 145
Elm Tree Dr. ST7: Big E 6H 15
Elm Tree Wlk. B79: Tam 2F 137
Elm Vw. ST14: Dens 2C 58
Elm Wlk. ST19: Penk 4F 91
Elmwood Av. WV11: Ess 2A 126
Elmwood Cl. ST11: B Bri 4J 43
ST20: Gno 2H 67
WS11: Cann 7G 101
Elmwood Dr. ST11: B Bri 4J 43
Elmwood Gro. ST14: Utt 3E 62
Elphinstone Rd. ST4: T Val 6K 31
Elsby Pl. ST6: Feg H 1A 18
Elsdon Rd. ST17: Staf 1E 76
Elsing St. ST4: Fen 3D 32
Elsmore Mdw. WS13: Lich 5A 114
Elston Hall La. WV10: Bush 4B 124
Elstree Cl. ST3: Mei 7B 34
Elstree Gro. ST1: H'ley 2G 25
Elswick Rd. ST4: Fen 1E 32
Eltham Gdns. ST5: N'tle 5H 23
ELTON 1C 157
Elton Cl. DE13: New 5C 88
WV10: Bush 1C 124
Elton La. DE13: New 5C 88
Elton Ter. ST6: Gold 7H 11
Elton Way ST20: Gno 3H 67
Elunda Gro. WS7: Chas 5G 111
ELVASTON 1D 161
Elviron Dr. WV6: Tett 1J 129
ELWORTH 1B 154
Elworthy Cl. ST16: Staf 1J 73
Elwyn Cl. DE13: Stre 2E 84
Ely Cl. WS11: H Hay 2H 109
Ely Wlk. ST3: Long 5J 33
Embers Way ST9: End 1C 50
Emberton St. ST5: C'ton 1C 22
ST5: N'tle 3G 23
Emberton Way B77: Amin 4B 138
Embleton Wlk. ST6: B'lem 1J 23
Embry Av. ST16: Staf 1J 73
Emerald Ct. ST2: Mil 5F 19
Emerald Way ST2: Mil 5F 19
ST15: Stone 1G 69
Emerson Gro. WV10: Bush 5D 124
Emerson Rd. ST6: B'lem 2A 24
WV10: Bush 4D 124
Emery Av. ST1: H'ley 7E 18
ST5: N'tle 6A 152 (2D 30)
Emery St. ST6: B'lem 2B 24
Emmanuel Rd. WS7: Burn 4K 111
Empire Pas. ST4: S Tren 3A 32
Empire Rd. DE15: Wins 1K 87
Empire St. ST4: S Tren 3A 32
Emsworth Cres. WV9: P'ord 3J 123
Emsworth Rd. ST3: Blur 2E 40
Encounter Pl. ST1: H'ley . . . 1K 151 (3E 24)
Enderby Ri. DE13: B Tre 4B 84
Enderley Cl. WS3: Blox 2H 127
Enderley Dr. WS3: Blox 2H 127
Enderley St. ST5: N'tle 2D 152 (6F 23)
End Hall Rd. WV6: Tett 3H 129
ENDON 1A 50 (2D 155)
ENDON BANK 1B 50 (2D 155)
Endon Dr. ST8: B Lee 1B 12
ENDON EDGE 3A 50
Endon Rd. ST6: Nort 3E 18
Endwood Dr. B74: L Ast 4H 135
Engine La. B77: Glas 7C 138
WS8: Brow 4D 120
Englesea Av. ST3: W Coy 4C 34
ENGLESEABROOK 2B 154
Engleton La. ST19: Brew 1D 92
Engleton Mill La. ST19: Brew 1E 92
Ennerdale Cl. ST6: B'lem 7J 17
WS8: Clay 5G 121
Ennerdale Dr. WV6: Per 2G 129
Ennerdale Rd. WV6: Tett 5F 123
Enoch St. ST6: B'lem 1K 23
Ensford Cl. B74: F Oak 3K 135
ENSON 2D 159
Enson La. ST15: Aston 4H 69
Ensor Dr. B78: Pole 1H 143
Enstone Cl. ST3: Blur 2F 41
Enstone Ct. ST5: N'tle 6F 31
Enterprise Dr. WV10: F Ash 6G 93
Enterprise Gro. WS3: Pels 7D 120
Enterprise Ind. Pk.
WS14: Lich 3F 115
ENVILLE 6H 147 (3C 163)
Enville Cl. WS3: Blox 2G 127
Enville Rd. DY6: W Hea 3K 147
DY7: Kin 3D 148
Ephraim St. ST1: H'ley 6H 151 (6D 24)
Epping Rd. ST4: T Val 6J 31
Epsom Cl. B77: Dost 6J 141
DE14: B'ton 5A 86
ST10: Chea 2D 54
ST17: Wild 7A 74
WS14: Lich 4D 114
WV6: Per 2G 129
Epworth Ho. DE15: Wins 1K 87
Epworth St. ST4: S Tren 2A 32
Erasmus Darwin House 3A 114
Erasmus Way WS13: Lich 3A 114
ERDINGTON 2B 164
Eremon Cl. WS15: Rug 3H 97
Eringden B77: Wiln 1D 142
Ernald Gdns. ST15: Stone 5G 47
Ernest Egerton Cl. ST6: Tuns 2G 17
Ernest Pl. ST4: Fen 2E 32
Eros Cres. ST1: H'ley 2E 24
Errill Cl. ST4: Fen 3C 32
Erskine St. ST3: Long 1J 41
Eshton Way *B77: Wiln 1D 142*
(off Ellerbeck)
Eskdale Pl. ST4: Tren 3K 39
ST5: N'tle 4F 31
Eskrett St. WS12: Hed 5H 101
Esk Way ST5: N'tle 5F 31
Esperanto Way ST6: B'lem 7C 18
Espley's Yd. ST16: Staf 4G 73
Esporta Health & Fitness
Broadlands 7B 116
Shenstone 2D 134
Stafford 1F 73
Stoke-on-Trent 1C 150 (3A 24)
Esselie Av. TF9: A'ley 4J 61
Essex Dr. ST7: Kids 4D 10
ST8: G Hea 3D 8
ST15: Stone 7F 47
ST18: Gt Hay 3G 81
WS12: Hed 6H 101
WS15: Rug 3F 97
Essex Packhorse Bridge 4G 81
Essex Pl. ST5: N'tle 3E 30
Essex Rd. DE15: Stap 6E 86
ESSINGTON 2A 126 (1D 163)
Essington Cl. DE13: Alre 5C 130
WS14: Lich 6A 114
WS14: Shen 5C 134
Essington Ind. Est. WV11: Ess 1K 125
Essington Rd. WV12: Will 3B 126
Estridge La. WS6: G Wyr 2G 119
Etchell Rd. B78: Tam 6F 137
ETCHINGHILL 6F 95 (3A 160)
Etching Hill Rd. WS15: Rug 7C 94
Ethelfleda Rd. B77: Hock 5B 142
Etna Works ST4: Fen 4F 33
Eton Av. ST5: N'tle 5D 30
Eton Cl. DE14: B Tre 5F 85
ST17: Staf 5K 73
Eton Ct. WS14: Lich 5B 114
Eton Pk. DE14: B Tre 5F 85
Eton Rd. DE14: B Tre 5E 84
ETRURIA 4B 150 (4K 23)
Etruria Ct. ST1: H'ley 5A 150
Etruria Industrial Mus. 6C 150 (6A 24)
Etruria Locks ST1: H'ley 6B 150 (6A 24)
Etruria Old Rd. ST1: H'ley . . 5A 150 (5K 23)
Etruria Rd.
ST5: N'tle . . . 2H 153 & 5A 150 (6H 23)
Etruria Trad. Est. ST4: S Tren 5J 23
Etruria Va. Rd. ST1: H'ley . . 4B 150 (5A 24)
Etruria Way ST4: S Tren 5J 23
Etruscan Ho. ST4: H'ley . . . 7C 150 (6A 24)
Etruscan St. ST1: H'ley 6A 150 (6K 23)
Etruscan Wlk. ST12: Barl 6F 41
ETTILEY HEATH 1B 154
Eturia Rd. ST4: S Tren 6H 23
ETWALL 1C 161
EUDON BURNELL 3B 162
EUDON GEORGE 3A 162
Europa Way WS14: Lich 3F 115
Eva Gro. ST5: N'tle 2H 39
Evans Cft. B78: Faze 1G 141
Evans St. ST6: B'lem 6K 17
Evelyn St. ST4: Fen 4E 32
Everest Rd. ST7: Kids 3F 11
Evergreen Hgts. WS12: Hed 2G 101
Evergreens, The DE13: Stre 3G 85
Evershed Way DE14: B Tre 2D 86
Eversley Av. ST13: Lee 4F 49
Eversley Gro. WV11: Wed 7G 125
Eversley Rd. ST3: Long 7A 34
Evesham Cres. WS3: Blox 2F 127
Evesham Way ST3: Long 6A 34
EWDNESS 2B 162
Exbury Cl. WV9: P'ord 3H 123
Excelsior Gro. WS3: Pels 7D 120
Exchange, The WS3: Blox 4H 127
Exchange Ho. *ST16: Staf 3G 73*
(off Eastgate St.)
Exchange Ind. Est.
WS11: Cann 5E 108
Exchange Rd. DE13: Alre 5C 130
Exeter Dr. B79: Tam 3E 136
Exeter Grn. ST2: Bent 6J 25
Exeter Rd. WS11: Cann 3B 108
Exeter St. ST17: Staf 6H 73
Exley B77: Wiln 1K 141
Exmoor Grn. WV11: Wed 6G 125
Exmouth Gro. ST6: B'lem 1A 24
Exonbury Wlk.
WS11: Cann 1F 109
Exton Cl. WV11: Wed 5K 125
Eyam Cl. DE15: Stap 2J 87
Eyre St. ST6: B'lem 1J 23
Eyrie, The DE15: Wins 1K 87
EYTON ON SEVERN 1A 162
EYTON UPON THE WEALD MOORS
. . . . 3A 158
Ezekiel La. WV12: Will 7C 126

Faceby Gro.—Fishley Cl.

F

Faceby Gro. ST3: Mei 3E 42
FADDILEY 2A 154
Faifield Rd. ST14: Utt 5G 63
Fairbank Av. ST4: S Tren 4K 31
Fairbanks Wlk.
ST15: Swyn 3C 64
Fairburn Cres. WS3: Pels 7D 120
Fairclough Pl. ST6: B'lem 4A 18
Fairey Ind. Est. B77: Wiln 2K 141
Fairfax Cl. ST8: Bidd 4C 8
Fairfax Rd. WV10: Bush 3B 124
Fairfax St. ST1: H'ley 2D 24
FAIRFIELD 1A 156
Fairfield Av. DE13: Roll D 6K 83
ST3: Long 2J 41
ST5: N'tle 4G 23
ST6: B Edg 7H 13
Fairfield Cl. WS12: H Hay 2K 109
Fairfield Ct. ST16: Staf 7H 71
Fairfield Dr. DY7: Kin 6E 148
ST19: Penk 6G 91
WS3: Pels 7D 120
WV8: Cods 1A 122
Fairfields ST7: Big E 5H 15
Fairfields Hill B78: Pole 2H 143
Fairfields Rd. ST8: Bid M 4H 9
Fairford Gdns. WS7: Burn 5A 112
Fair-Green Rd. ST5: B Gat 5F 37
Fairgreen Way B74: S'ly 7F 135
Fairham Rd. DE13: Stre 2G 85
Fairhaven Gro. ST1: H'ley 2E 24
Fair Lady Dr. WS7: C Ter 2F 111
Fairlawn Cl. ST3: L'ood 2A 42
WV12: Will 4C 126
Fairlawns ST5: N'tle 6F 23
Fairlawn Way WV12: Will 4C 126
Fairlight Gro. ST3: Mei 3C 42
Fairmead Cl. ST17: Wild 1A 78
Fairmount Dr. WS11: Cann 3E 108
Fairmount Way WS15: Rug 7E 94
FAIROAK 1B 158
Fairoak ST5: N'tle 5D 30
Fairoak Av. ST16: Staf 5E 70
Fairoak Dr. WV6: Tett 3J 129
Fair Oak Rd. ST5: C'ton 6B 16
Fair Oaks WS15: S Mil 3D 96
Fair Oaks Dr. WS6: G Wyr 4G 119
Fair Vw. WS15: Hand 5G 99
Fairview Cl. B77: Amin 4B 138
WS6: C Hay 2D 118
WV11: Wed 7F 125
Fairview Ct. ST19: Whe A 3C 90
Fairview Cres. WV11: Wed 6F 125
Fairview Gro. WV11: Wed 6F 125
Fair Vw. Rd. ST13: Lee 4H 49
Fairview Rd. WV11: Wed 6F 125
Fairview Vs. ST5: B Gat 5F 37
Fairview Way ST17: Staf 6A 74
Fairway B77: Hock 5A 142
DE14: B'ton 6C 86
ST4: Tren 2J 39
ST16: Staf 3J 73
ST17: Staf 3J 73
WS11: Cann 5D 108
Fairway Ct. B77: Amin 6E 138
Fairway Rd. ST6: B'lem 4A 18
Fairways, The DE6: C'ton 7E 56
Falcon B77: Wiln 4C 142
Falcon Cl. DE14: B Tre 6F 85
WS6: C Hay 2C 118
WS11: Cann 1C 108
Falcondale Rd. WV12: Will 4C 126
Falcon Dr. WS14: W'ton 3G 131
Falcon Pk. B77: Wiln 3A 142
Falcon Rd. ST3: Mei 4C 42
Faldo Cl. DE14: B'ton 6C 86
Falkirk Grange ST5: N'tle 2D 30
Falklands Cl. DY3: Swin 1J 147
FALLINGS PARK 7D 124
Fallings Pk. Ind. Est.
WV10: W'ton 7D 124
Fallow Fld. B74: L Ast 5G 135
WS13: Lich 7C 106
Fallowfield ST3: Blur 2F 41
ST17: Wild 1A 78
WS11: Cann 7E 100
WV6: Per 2E 128
WV8: P'ord 3G 123
Fallowfield Cl. ST15: Stone 6J 47
ST19: Penk 4G 91
Fallowfield Dr. DE13: B Nee 5F 89
Fallow Rd. B78: Faze 1F 141
Falmouth Av. ST17: Staf 6C 74
Falmouth Cl. ST17: Staf 6C 74
Falmouth Dr. B77: Amin 4B 138
Falna Cres. B79: Tam 2F 137
Fancy Wlk. ST16: Staf 1F 73
Fane Rd. WV11: Wed 4A 126
Fanlizard La. ST20: Gno 7G 67
Faraday Av. DE13: Stre 3E 84
Faraday Ct. DE14: B Tre 7A 86
Faraday Pl. ST4: S Tren 6K 153 (2J 31)
Faraday Rd. ST16: Staf 1H 73
WS2: Wals 7H 127
Farbrook Way WV12: Will 7B 126
Farcroft Av. ST5: C'ton 2D 22
Fareham Cres. WV4: Pen 7K 129
Fareham Gro. ST3: L'ood 3A 42
FAREWELL 6E 104 (3A 160)
Farewell Hall M. WS13: Fare 6E 104
Farewell La. WS7: Burn 5C 112
Far Grn. Ind. Est. ST1: H'ley 3D 24
FAR HOARCROSS 2B 160
Faringdon B77: Glas 1B 142
Farington Pl. ST6: Feg H 1A 18
Farland Gro. ST6: Feg H 1A 18
Far La. ST10: Ips 3H 53
Far La. Ind. Est. ST10: Ips 3H 53
Farleigh Dr. WV3: W'ton 6H 129
Farleigh Gro. ST2: Bent 7J 25
Farleigh Rd. WV6: Per 3H 129
FARLEY
Much Wedlock 1A 162
Stoke-on-Trent 1H 57 (3A 156)
Farley Cnr. ST18: Gt Hay 1H 81
Farley La. ST10: Alt 3G 57
ST18: Gt Hay 1H 81
Farley Rd. ST10: O'moor 3C 56
FARLOW 3A 162
Farmadine ST4: Tren 3B 40
Farman Cl. ST3: Mei 3E 42
Farmbrook Av. WV10: Ford 2B 124
Farm Cl. B79: Tam 2J 137
DE13: B Tre 4C 84
WS12: Hed 7J 101
WS15: Rug 6E 94
WV8: Bilb 3D 122
FARMCOTE 2B 162
Farm Ct. Flats *DE13: B Tre 4D 84*
(off Farm Rd.)
Farmdown Rd. ST17: Staf 5A 74
Farmers Bank ST5: Sil 7A 22
Farmer St. ST3: Long 7J 33
Farm Hollow ST7: Big E 5J 15
Farmhouse Rd. WV12: Will 7D 126
Farmhouse Way WV12: Will 7E 126
Farm Lea ST6: B Gre 1E 18
ST15: Hild 5H 59
Farmoor Way WV10: Bush 1C 124
Farm Rd. DE13: B Tre 4D 84
WV3: W'ton 6K 129
Farmside Grn. WV9: P'ord 3H 123
Farmside La. ST8: Bid M 4H 9
Farm Vw. ST15: Hild 5H 59
Farmwood Cl. ST3: Mei 1D 42
FARNAH GREEN 3D 157
Farnborough Dr. ST3: Mei 3E 42
Farncote Dr. B74: F Oak 5K 135
Farndale Av. WV6: W'ton 7H 123
Farndale St. ST6: Tuns 4H 17
Farne Gro. ST3: Long 6G 33
Farnham Dr. ST8: B Lee 1B 12
Farnworth Cl. ST8: Knyp 7B 8
Farnworth Rd. ST3: Long 5A 34
Far Ridding ST20: Gno 5G 67
Farrier Cl. ST15: Stone 5K 47
Farrington Cl. ST6: Nort 4E 18
Farway Gdns. WV8: Cods 3B 122
Far Winter's Wlk. *ST18: Sand 1A 80*
(off London Rd.)
Fasson Cl. B77: T Gat 2J 141
FAULD 2B 160
Fauld La. DE13: C Cla 5E 82
DE13: Tut 2F 83
Faulkner Pl. ST3: W Coy 5B 34
FAULS 1A 158
Faversham Cl. WV8: P'ord 5G 123
Faversham Rd. DE13: B Tre 5B 84
Fawcett Way ST1: H'ley 1H 151
Fawfield Dr. ST6: Gold 1G 17
FAWFIELDHEAD 1A 156
Fawn Cl. ST3: Mei 2C 42
WS12: Hun 4C 100
FAZELEY 2G 141 (1B 164)
Fazeley Rd. B78: Tam 5G 137
(not continuous)
Fearns Av. ST5: Brad 6E 16
Fearon Grn. ST6: Nort 4E 18
Featherbed La. ST18: Hixon 6C 80
WS13: Lich 7J 105
FEATHERSTONE 5F 117 (1D 163)
Featherstone Gro. ST4: P'ull 2A 32
Featherstone La.
WV10: Fea, Shar 4F 117
Featherston Rd. B74: S'ly 6F 135
Fecknam Way WS13: Lich 1C 114
Federation Rd. ST6: B'lem 6J 17
Federation Trad. Est. ST6: B'lem 6K 17
FEGG HAYES 1B 18
Fegg Hayes Rd. ST6: Feg H 1A 18
FEIASHILL 3B 144
Feiashill Cl. WV5: Trys 3B 144
Feiashill Rd. WV5: Trys 2B 144
Felcourt Gdns. ST1: H'ley 1K 151 (3E 24)
Felden Cl. ST16: Staf 4F 71
Fellbrook Ct. ST2: Buck 4G 25
Fellbrook La. ST2: Buck 4G 25
Fellfield Way ST16: Staf 5F 71
Fellgate Ct. ST5: N'tle 3D 152 (7F 23)
Fell St. ST6: B'lem 6C 18
Felspar Rd. B77: Amin 6C 138
Felstead Cl. B77: Dost 6J 141
Felstead St. ST2: Mil 4H 19
Femwork Ind. Est. DE14: B Tre 6F 85
Fence La. CW12: More, N Ast 2G 7
Fenlow Av. ST2: Buck 6F 25
Fennel Cl. ST14: Utt 7G 63
WS6: C Hay 1D 118
Fennel Dr. ST17: Staf 2H 77
Fennel Gro. ST3: Mei 4D 42
Fenners Gro. ST4: Tren 2D 40
FENN GREEN 3B 162
Fenn Ri. WV12: Will 7B 126
Fenn St. B77: Wiln 1A 142
FENNY BENTLEY 2B 156
FENNY DRAYTON 2D 165
Fen Pk. Ind. Est. ST4: Fen 4G 33
Fenpark Rd. ST4: Fen 3F 33
FENTON 3E 32 (3C 155)
Fenton Cft. ST19: Whe A 2C 90
Fenton Grn. DE13: Stre 2F 85
Fenton Ho. ST5: N'tle 3E 152
Fenton Ho. La. ST19: Whe A 2B 90
Fenton Ind. Est. ST4: Fen 1E 32
(Elswick Rd.)
ST4: Fen 1E 32
(Spedding Rd)
FENTON LOW 3E 32
Fenton Manor Sports Complex 2D 32
Fenton Pk. ST4: Fen 2G 33
Fenton Rd. ST2: Buck 7F 25
Ferguson St. WV11: Wed 4A 126
Fermain Cl. ST5: N'tle 6D 30
Ferncombe Dr. WS15: Rug 6E 94
Fern Cft. WS13: Lich 2K 113
Ferncroft Cl. ST4: Tren 3B 40
Ferndale Cl. ST9: Werr 4C 26
ST11: B Bri 4H 43
WS7: Burn 5K 111
WS13: Lich 2K 113
Ferndale Gdns. ST7: Harr 3J 11
Ferndale Rd. WS13: Lich 1K 113
WV11: Ess 2B 126
Ferndell Cl. WS11: Cann 1C 108
Fern Dene CW3: Mad 2A 28
Ferndown Cl. ST3: Long 1K 41
WS3: Blox 1H 127
Ferndown Dr. ST5: N'tle 7G 31
Ferndown Dr. Sth. ST5: N'tle 1H 39
Fern Dr. ST16: Staf 2C 72
WS6: G Wyr 7G 109
Ferney Pl. ST6: Tuns 1G 17
Fernhurst Cl. ST15: Stone 5J 47
Fernhurst Gro. ST3: L'ood 2A 42
Fernie Cl. ST15: Stone 6J 47
Fernlea Cres. ST9: End 1B 50
Fernlea Gro. ST3: M Hea 6C 42
ST3: W Coy 4D 34
Fernleigh Av. WS7: C Ter 3J 111
Fernleigh Gdns. ST16: Staf 1B 72
Fern Leys WV3: W'ton 5K 129
Fern Pl. ST3: Long 7J 33
Fern Rd. WS12: Hun 5D 100
Fernwood ST16: Staf 6F 71
Fernwood Cen., The WS15: Rug 6F 95
Fernwood Cft. ST13: Lee 5D 48
Fernwood Dr. ST13: Lee 5D 48
WS15: Rug 6F 95
Fernwood Grn. ST4: Tren 3C 40
Ferrand Cl. ST4: H'ord 7A 32
Ferranti Cl. ST18: Staf 1A 74
Ferrers Av. DE13: Tut 3G 83
Ferrers Rd. B77: Tam 5K 137
DE13: Yox 2G 89
ST18: West 3C 80
Ferrie Gro. WS8: Brow 5G 121
Ferry Farm Dr. ST17: Staf 6J 73
Ferry St. DE15: Stap 5F 87
Ferry Va. Cl. DE15: Stap 4F 87
Festing St. ST1: H'ley 1H 151 (3D 24)
Festival Cl. ST6: B'lem 3A 24
Festival Ct. WS11: Cann 5E 100
Festival Hgts. Retail Pk.
ST1: H'ley 1C 150 (3A 24)
Festival M. WS12: Cann 4F 101
FESTIVAL PARK 2B 150 (3K 23)
Festival Rd. DE14: B'ton 7A 86
Festival Trade Pk. 1
ST1: H'ley 4A 150 (5K 23)
Festival Trade Pk. 2
ST1: H'ley 4A 150 (5K 23)
Festival Trade Pk. 3
ST1: H'ley 4A 150 (5K 23)
Festival Way ST1: H'ley 1A 150 (3K 23)
WV6: W'ton 7K 123
Fiddlers Bank ST6: B Edg 6H 13
Fiddler's La. DE13: Tut 6F 83
FIELD 1A 160
Field Av. ST2: Mil 5H 19
Field Cl. B77: Wiln 7J 137
DE13: B Tre 4B 84
ST5: B Gat 5E 36
Field Cl. ST11: B Bri 4G 43
WS3: Blox 5J 127
Field Ct. B77: Wiln 7J 137
Field Cres. ST18: Derr 4A 72
Field Dr. DE13: Roll D 6H 83
Fielden Cl. ST6: Mil 5F 19
Field End Cl. ST4: Tren 3B 40
Fieldfare WS7: Hamm 6B 112
Fld. Farm Dr. B79: Edin 1B 132
Fld. Farm Rd. B77: Wiln 7K 137
Fld. Head Pl. WV6: Tett 2J 129
Field Ho. Ct. ST15: Stone 2F 47
Fieldhouse Rd. WS7: C Ter 4J 111
WS12: Hed 3F 101
Fielding St. ST4: S Tren 4B 32
Field La. DE13: B Tre 4A 84
WS6: G Wyr 1F 119
Field Pl. ST3: Long 4J 33
ST16: Staf 7G 71
WS15: S Mil 2D 96
Field Ri. DE13: B Tre 4B 84
Field Rd. WS3: Blox 5J 127
WS13: Lich 7B 106
Field Rd. Ind. Est. WS3: Blox 5J 127
Fields, The WV8: Bilb 1D 122
Fieldside ST15: Yarn 5C 64
ST17: Wild 2B 78
Field St. ST13: Lee 4F 49
WS11: Cann 7F 101
Fieldsway ST15: Stone 4E 46
Field Ter. ST15: Stone 3G 47
Field Vw. ST3: W Coy 5D 34
ST8: Bidd 4D 8
Fieldway ST2: Bent 5B 26
ST3: Fen 6E 32
ST4: Tren 3J 39
ST11: B Bri 3F 43
Fife St. ST4: Fen 5G 33
Fifth Av. DE14: B Tre 2B 86
ST7: Kids 5C 10
WV10: Bush 6B 124
Filance Cl. ST19: Penk 5H 91
Filance La. ST19: Penk 5H 91
Filey B77: Amin 3B 138
Filey Cl. ST2: Bent 6K 25
WS11: Cann 3C 108
Filey Rd. WV10: Oxl 3K 123
FILLONGLEY 3C 165
Fillybrooks, The ST15: Stone 3E 46
Fillybrooks Cl. ST15: Stone 4F 47
Film Theatre 1B 32
Filton Av. WS7: C Ter 3J 111
Fincham Cl. WV9: P'ord 2J 123
Finchdean Cl. ST3: Mei 3C 42
Finches Hill WS15: Rug 6E 94
Finchfield Hill WV3: W'ton 4K 129
(not continuous)
Finchfield La. WV3: W'ton 6K 129
Finchfield Rd. W. WV3: W'ton 5K 129
Finch Pl. ST8: Brin F 4B 12
Finchsmith Pl. ST3: Long 7H 33
Finch St. ST8: Brin F 5C 12
Finch Way WS13: Frad 1K 107
FINDERN 1D 161
Fine La. WS13: Lich 4K 107
Fingerpost Dr. WS3: Pels 7C 120
FINNEY GREEN 7F 21
Finney Grn. ST2: Buck 4G 25
Finstock Av. ST3: Blur 2E 40
Firbank Pl. ST3: W Coy 5B 34
Firbeck Gdns. ST17: Wild 7A 74
Fir Cl. WS12: Hun 2D 100
Fircroft Cl. WS11: Cann 7G 101
Firecrest Cl. WS11: H Hay 1J 109
Firs, The WS11: Cann 1G 109
WS15: Can W 5H 103
Firs Cl., The ST17: Staf 7B 74
Firs Mobile Home Pk., The
WS11: Cann 1G 109
First Av. DE14: B Tre 7A 86
ST2: Buck 4K 25
ST5: N'tle 1G 23
ST7: Kids 5C 10
ST16: Staf 5E 70
WS8: Brow 4J 121
WV10: Bush 7C 124
Firsvale Rd. WV11: Wed 7K 125
Firsway WV6: Tett 4H 129
Firsway, The ST19: B Elm 6B 90
Firtree Cl. B79: Tam 2E 136
ST18: Copp 4E 76
Fir Tree Pl. ST5: C'ton 7C 16
Fir Tree Rd. ST3: L'ood 2A 42
Firwood Rd. ST8: Bidd 4F 9
Fisher Rd. WS3: Blox 3F 127
Fisher St. ST8: Brin F 2B 12
WS12: Hed 2F 101
FISHERWICK 3K 131
Fisherwick Cl.
WS14: W'ton 2G 131
Fisherwick Rd. B79: Fish 7G 131
WS13: Fish 3J 131 & 7G 131
WS14: Fish, W'ton 3G 131
FISHLEY 2J 127
Fishley Cl. WS3: Blox 1J 127

Fullerton Cl.—Goods Sta. La.

Fullerton Cl. WV8: P'ord 4G 123
Fullmore Cl. ST19: Penk 5H 91
Fullwood Wlk. ST2: Bent 7J 25
Fulmar Pl. ST3: Mei 3D 42
Furlong, The ST15: Yarn 6D 64
Furlong Av. ST10: Tea 4G 55
Furlong Cl. DE13: Alre 6C 130
ST10: Tea 4G 55
ST18: West 3B 80
Furlong Dr. ST10: Tea 4G 55
Furlong Ind. Est. ST6: B'lem 1J 23
Furlong La. DE13: Alre 6C 130
ST6: B'lem 1J 23
ST18: Brad 4A 76
Furlong Pde. ST6: B'lem 7K 17
Furlong Pas. ST6: B'lem 7K 17
Furlong Rd. ST6: Tuns 3J 17
Furlongs, The WV11: Wed 7F 125
Furmston Pl. ST13: Lee 2H 49
Furnace Cl. WV5: Womb 5E 144
Furnace La. CW3: Mad 2A 28
Furnace Rd. ST3: Long 7K 33
Furness B77: Glas 6K 137
Furness Cl. WS3: Blox 2F 127
Furness Gro. ST17: Staf 7D 72
Furnivall Cres. WS13: Lich 2D 114
Furnival St. ST6: B'lem 2B 24
Furrows Dr. DE13: B Tre 3B 84
Furst St. WS8: Brow 4J 121
Future Fitness 3F 49
Fyfield Rd. DE15: Stap 6F 87
Fynney Flds. ST13: Lee 2K 51
Fynney St. ST13: Lee 4G 49

G

Gable Cft. WS14: Lich 5E 114
Gables, The B78: Pole 7J 139
Gable St. ST4: S Tren 3B 32
Gadsby Av. WV11: Wed 6A 126
Gaelic Rd. WS11: Cann 6D 100
Gagarin B79: Tam 4F 137
Gaiafields Rd. WS13: Lich 2B 114
Gaialands Cres. WS13: Lich 2B 114
Gaia La. WS13: Lich 3A 114
Gaiastowe WS13: Lich 2B 114
GAILEY 3D 159
Gainford Cl. WV8: P'ord 4H 123
Gainsborough Dr. B78: M Oak 2B 140
WV6: Per 2G 129
Gainsborough Rd. ST3: Blur 2E 40
ST5: C'ton 2C 22
Gainsborough Way DE15: Wins 1J 87
Gainsbrook Cres. WS11: N Can 6B 110
Gains La. WS3: L Wyr 2J 119
WS11: L Wyr 2J 119
Gairloch Rd. WV12: Will 4B 126
Gala Bingo
Bushbury 5B 124
Fenton 4G 151 (1D 32)
Stafford 6J 73
Stoke-on-Trent 5C 24
Tamworth 4H 137
Wednesfield 6K 125
Galahad Dr. DE13: Stre 1F 85
Galena Cl. B77: Amin 7D 138
GALLEY COMMON 2D 165
Galleys Bank ST7: Kids 3F 11
Galliers Cl. B77: Hock 5B 142
Gallimore Cl. ST6: B'lem 6J 17
Galloway Rd. ST2: Bent 1A 34
GALLOWS GREEN 6H 57 (3A 156)
Gallows Hill DY7: Kin 3D 148
Gallowstree La. DE6: U May 4B 56
ST5: N'tle 7A 152 (2C 30)
Galsworthy Rd. ST3: Fen 3H 33
Galton Cft. ST11: B Bri 7F 43
Galveston Gro. ST4: Fen 4F 33
Galway Rd. WS7: C Ter 4J 111
Gandy Rd. WV12: Will 7A 126
Ganton Rd. WS3: Blox 1G 127
Ganton Wlk. WV8: P'ord 5H 123
Gaol Butts ST21: Ecc 3G 65
Gaolgate St. ST16: Staf 3G 73
Gaol M. ST16: Staf 2G 73
Gaol Rd. ST16: Staf 2G 73
Gaol Sq. ST16: Staf 2G 73
Garage Cl. B77: Tam 4K 137
Garbett St. ST6: Gold 7G 11
Garden Dr. WS15: Rug 2H 97
Gardeners Cl. ST8: B Lee 1B 12
Gardeners Way WV5: Womb 6F 145
Garden Flds. DY7: Kin 5D 148
Gardenholm Cl. ST3: L'ood 2B 42
Garden Pl. ST4: S Tren 5K 153 (1J 31)
ST17: Staf 4H 73
Garden Rd. ST13: Lee 3E 48
Gardens, The B79: Elf 5G 131
ST7: C Law 2A 10
ST10: K'ley 6F 53
Garden St. ST4: P'ull 3K 31
ST5: N'tle 4F 153 (1G 31)
ST17: Staf 4G 73
Garden Vw. WS15: Rug 7F 95
Garden Village ST10: Tea 3F 55
Gardiner Dr. ST3: Long 7G 33
Gardner Rd. ST14: Utt 4F 63
Garfield Av. ST4: H'ord 1K 39
Garfield Ct. ST4: H'ord 1K 39
Garfield Cres. ST4: H'ord 1K 39
Garfield St. ST1: H'ley 6D 150 (6B 24)
Garlands, The WV11: Wed 6G 125
Garlick St. ST6: B'lem 6B 18
GARMELOW 2B 158
GARMSTON 1A 162
Garner St. ST4: S Tren 7A 150 (5J 23)
Garner's Wlk. CW3: Mad 2A 28
Garnet Cl. WS9: Ston 6H 133
Garnet St. ST1: H'ley 4C 150 (5A 24)
Garnett Rd. E. ST5: N'tle 3F 23
Garnett Rd. W. ST5: N'tle 2F 23
Garrett Sq. DE13: Roll D 6J 83
Garrick Cl. WS13: Lich 1K 113
Garrick Ct. WS13: Lich 1K 113
Garrick Ri. WS7: Burn 4K 111
WS15: Bre 3K 97
Garrick Rd. WS11: Cann 6D 100
WS13: Lich 1K 113
Garrigill B77: Wiln 1C 142
Garrod Sq. ST16: Staf 1K 73
Garsdale Cres. ST3: Blur 2F 41
GARSHALL GREEN 1D 159
Gartan Rd. DE14: B'ton 4B 86
Garth, The WS13: Lich 1B 114
Garth Cl. ST17: Staf 2G 77
Garth Rd. ST17: Staf 2H 77
Garth St. ST1: H'ley 2H 151 (4D 24)
Gaskell Rd. ST2: Buck 5K 25
Gas St. ST14: Utt 5H 63
Gas Works Ind. Est. ST7: Kids 4C 10
Gatcombe Cl. DE13: Stre 2E 84
WV10: Bush 1D 124
Gatcombe Pl. B79: Tam 2H 137
Gatehouse Theatre 3G 73
Gatehouse Trad. Est. WS8: Brow 3K 121
Gates Ct. ST18: Staf 1A 74
Gate Sq. WS15: Arm 5E 98
Gate St. ST3: W Coy 4D 34
Gate Way ST5: C'ton 5B 16
Gateway Av. ST5: B Gat 5E 36
Gatley Gro. ST3: Mei 4D 42
Gauledge La. SK17: L'nor 3C 52
Gaunt St. ST13: Lee 3E 48
Gawain Gro. DE13: Stre 1F 85
GAWSWORTH 1C 155
Gawsworth B79: Tam 2D 136
Gawsworth Cl. ST3: Long 3J 33
Gaydon Cl. WV6: Per 1F 129
Gayle B77: Wiln 1C 142
GAYTON 2D 159
Gayton Av. ST2: Mil 5H 19
Gedney Gro. ST5: N'tle 7F 31
Geen St. ST4: S Tren 2B 32
Gemini Dr. WS11: Cann 5F 109
Gemini Gro. ST6: Chel 1J 17
Geneshall Cl. ST20: Gno 3H 67
Geneva Dr. ST1: H'ley 1F 25
ST5: N'tle 3C 30
Genista Cl. DE15: Stap 4H 87
GENTLESHAW 6J 103 (3A 160)
Geoffrey Av. ST13: Lee 4E 48
Geoffrey Gro. ST3: W Coy 5C 34
George Av. B78: M Oak 1C 140
ST3: Mei 1D 42
George Bailey Ct. ST17: Staf 5H 73
George Brealey Cl. WS15: Rug 2H 97
George Ct. ST3: Long 6H 33
George Eardley Cl. ST6: Tuns 2G 17
George Eastham Av. ST4: Tren 6D 32
George Elliott Cl. ST14: Utt 7H 63
George La. ST15: Stone 5K 47
WS13: Lich 3C 114
George Ryan Cen. B78: M Oak 1D 140
George St. B79: Tam 5H 137
DE14: B Tre 1E 86
ST4: Fen 2E 32
ST5: C'ton 1C 22
ST5: N'tle 2G 23
(Boulton St.)
ST5: N'tle 3G 153 (7G 23)
(Brunswick St.)
ST5: Sil 7K 21
ST7: Aud 6F 15
ST16: Staf 1F 73
WS12: Hed 6J 101
Georges Way ST7: Big E 5H 15
George Walker Ct. DE14: B Tre 6D 84
Georgian Crystal 2H 83
Georgian Pl. WS11: Cann 1E 108
Gerard B79: Tam 2E 136
Gerards Way TF9: A'ley 4J 61
GERRARD'S BROMLEY 1B 158
Gerrard St. ST4: S Tren 1A 32
Getliffe Yd. *ST13: Lee 3G 49*
(off Derby St.)
Gettings Cl. WS7: Burn 4C 112
Gibbet La. DY7: Kin 4J 149
Gibbins St. ST1: H'ley 3D 24
Gibraltar DY7: Kin 5F 149
Gibson Cl. ST16: Staf 1H 73
Gibson Gro. ST5: C'ton 7B 16
Gibson Pl. ST3: Mei 7C 34
Gibson Rd. WV6: Per 3F 129
Gibson St. ST6: Tuns 5J 17
Giddywell La. WS15: L'don 1D 104
Giffard Cl. ST19: Brew 2D 92
Giffard Rd. WV10: Bush 2C 124
Gifford Pl. ST4: P'ull 3K 31
Giffords Cft. WS13: Lich 2A 114
GIGGETTY 4E 144 (2C 163)
Giggetty La. WV5: Womb 4E 144
Gilbern Dr. ST8: Knyp 1B 12
Gilbert Cl. ST7: Kids 4E 10
WV11: Wed 6A 126
Gilbert La. WV5: Womb 3H 145
Gilbert Rd. WS13: Lich 1C 114
Gilbert St. ST6: Gold 7G 11
Gilbert Wlk. *WS13: Lich 1C 114*
(off Gilbert Rd.)
Gilchrist Ct. *ST6: B'lem 2B 24*
(off Grange St.)
Giles Cl. ST10: Chea 4C 54
Giles Ho. ST13: Ched 2G 51
Giles Rd. WS13: Lich 7A 106
Giles Wlk. ST1: H'ley 1K 151 (3E 24)
Gill Bank Rd. ST6: Gold 7F 11
ST7: Kids 6F 11
Gillespie Cl. WS13: Frad 4K 107
Gillette Cl. ST18: Staf 1A 74
Gilliards Cft. DE13: K Bro 2C 130
Gilliat Wlk. ST2: Bent 7J 25
Gillingham Cres. ST16: Staf 4D 72
GILLOW HEATH 3C 8 (2C 155)
Gill Wlk. ST1: H'ley 5E 150
GILLWAY 2H 137
Gillway La. B79: Tam 1G 137
Gillyflower Cl. ST6: Nort 5E 18
Gilman Av. ST2: Mil 5H 19
Gilman Pl. ST1: H'ley 3H 151 (4D 24)
Gilman St. ST1: H'ley 4H 151 (5D 24)
Gilmour La. DE13: B Nee 6H 89
Gilpin Cres. WS3: Pels 7C 120
Gilpins Cft. WS6: C Hay 3D 118
Gilwell Rd. WS15: Can W 4H 103
Gimson St. ST4: Fen 3E 32
Ginger Hill ST20: Gno 5H 67
Girsby Cl. ST4: Tren 5C 40
Girton Rd. WS11: Cann 3E 108
Gisborne Cl. DE13: Yox 1H 89
Gitana St. ST1: H'ley 3F 151 (4C 24)
Glade, The ST5: N'tle 7E 30
ST17: Staf 6K 73
WS11: Cann 1C 108
WV8: P'ord 4G 123
Glades, The ST1: H'ley 3K 23
Gladstone Gro. ST8: Bidd 5D 8
Gladstone Pl. ST4: S Tren 4K 31
Gladstone Pottery Mus. 6J 33
Gladstone Rd. WS12: H Hay 2K 109
Gladstone St. ST4: S Tren 1K 153 (6J 23)
ST13: Lee 4F 49
Gladstone Ter. ST10: Alt 6H 57
Gladstone Way ST16: Staf 2K 73
Gladwyn St. ST2: Buck 4J 25
Glaisher Dr. ST3: Mei 3E 42
WV10: W'ton 7A 124
Glamis Cl. DE13: Stre 3E 84
Glamis Dr. ST15: Stone 7J 47
Glamis Rd. WV12: Will 6B 126
Glandore Rd. ST3: W Coy 5B 34
GLASCOTE 7B 138 (1C 165)
Glascote Ct. B77: Amin 5A 138
Glascote La. B77: Wiln 3B 142
(not continuous)
Glascote Rd.
B77: Glas, Wiln, Tam 5J 137
Glasscroft Cotts. WS7: Burn 4D 112
Glassford Dr. WV6: Tett 7G 123
Glass St. ST1: H'ley 2G 151 (4C 24)
Glastonbury Cl. ST9: S Broo 4K 19
ST17: Staf 1B 78
Glastonbury Cres. WS3: Blox 3E 126
Glastonbury Way WS3: Blox 4E 126
GLAZELEY 3B 162
GLEADSMOSS 1C 155
Glebe Av. ST16: Staf 7F 71
Glebe Cl. DE13: Roll D 6G 83
ST11: B Bri 4J 43
Glebe Ct. ST4: S Tren 2C 32
ST10: Chea 5A 54
Glebedale Ct. ST4: Fen 4E 32
Glebedale Rd. ST4: Fen 3E 32
Glebefields ST20: W'ves 3D 66
Glebe Gdns. ST10: Chea 5B 54
Glebelands DY7: Bob 6B 146
ST17: Staf 1H 77
Glebelands Ct. ST17: Staf 2H 77
Glebe La. ST20: Gno 3J 67
Glebe Rd. ST10: Chea 5A 54
ST10: K'ley 6G 53
WS15: Hand 4G 99
Glebe St. ST4: S Tren 2B 32
ST7: Talk 4B 10
Glebeville ST13: Lee 5F 49
Gledhill Pk. WS14: Lich 6C 114
Glen, The ST15: Stone 5G 47
Glencastle Way ST4: Tren 5C 40
Glen Cl. WS11: Cann 5E 100
Glencoe Dr. WS11: Cann 6G 101
Glencoe St. ST3: Long 7H 33
Glencote Cvn. Pk. ST13: Ched 5J 51
Glen Ct. WV8: Cods 1C 122
Glencroft Cl. DE14: B'ton 5C 86
Glendale Cl. WV3: W'ton 6K 129
Glendale Ct. B77: Wiln 4D 142
ST5: N'tle 7G 31
Glendale Dr. WV5: Womb 4G 145
Glendale Gdns. WS11: Cann 6F 101
Glendale St. ST6: B'lem 1A 24
Glendawn Cl. WS11: Cann 7G 101
Glendene Rd. WS12: Hed 4K 101
Glendower Cl. ST20: Gno 4G 67
Glen Dr. ST10: Alt 6H 57
Glendue Gro. ST4: Tren 4C 40
Gleneagles B77: Amin 4D 138
Gleneagles Cres. ST1: H'ley 2E 24
Gleneagles Dr. DE13: Stre 2D 84
ST16: Staf 3A 74
Gleneagles Rd. WS3: Blox 2F 127
WV6: Per 1E 128
Glenfield B77: Wiln 1J 141
WV8: P'ord 3G 123
Glenfield Ri. DE13: B Tre 4B 84
Glenfield Way ST2: Bent 1A 34
Glenhaven WS15: Rug 6E 94
Glenmore Av. WS7: Burn 5J 111
Glen Ri. DE13: B Tre 4B 84
Glenroyd Av. ST2: Buck 7G 25
Glenroyd Wlk. ST2: Bent 7J 25
Glensyl Way DE14: B Tre 7F 85
Glenthorne Cl. ST17: Wild 2B 78
Glenthorne Dr. WS6: C Hay 1E 118
Glentworth Gdns. WV6: W'ton 7K 123
Glenwood Cl. ST3: Long 5H 33
ST5: Sil 7A 22
Glenwood Gdns. B77: Wiln 4D 142
Glenwood Ri. WS9: Ston 7G 133
Globe Av. ST17: Staf 1H 77
Globe Ct. *ST15: Stone 4G 47*
(off Newcastle St.)
Globe Island WS15: Rug 1G 97
Globe St. ST6: B'lem 7J 17
Gloucester Cl. WS13: Lich 7B 106
Gloucester Grange ST5: N'tle 4G 31
Gloucester Rd. ST7: Kids 4D 10
Gloucester Way DE15: Stap 3J 87
WS11: H Hay 2H 109
Glovers Cl. WS12: Haz 5C 102
Glover St. ST1: H'ley 3D 24
ST16: Staf 2F 73
WS12: Wimb 7B 102
GLUTTON BRIDGE 1A 156
Glyme Dr. WV6: Tett 7G 123
Glyndebourne B79: Tam 2D 136
Glyn Pl. ST6: B'lem 4K 17
GNOSALL 4H 67 (2C 159)
GNOSALL HEATH 5G 67 (2C 159)
Gnosall Rd. ST20: Gno 1G 67
Goblin's La. WS15: Abb B 1C 88
Goddard St. ST3: Long 5J 33
Godfrey Dr. WS13: Frad 4J 107
Godfrey Rd. ST2: Buck 5H 25
GODLEYBROOK 3D 155
Godolphin B79: Tam 3D 136
GODSTONE 1A 160
Godwin Way ST4: T Val 4J 31
Gofton B77: Wiln 1C 142
Golborn Av. ST3: M Hea 6C 42
Golborn Cl. ST3: M Hea 6C 42
Goldcrest B77: Wiln 5C 142
Goldcrest Way ST8: Bidd 5E 8
Golden Cl. WS15: Rug 2F 97
GOLDENHILL 7G 11 (2C 155)
Goldenhill Rd. ST4: Fen 5H 33
Goldfinch Rd. ST7: Pack 5K 11
Goldfinch Vw. TF9: Logg 6C 60
Goldhurst ST10: Holl 4K 55
Goldhurst Dr. ST10: Tea 5H 55
GOLDING 1A 162
Golding Cres. DE14: B Tre 5G 85
Goldsborough B77: Wiln 1C 142
Goldsmith Pl. B79: Tam 2G 137
ST3: Long 5K 33
GOLDSTONE 2B 158
Gold St. ST3: Long 6H 33
Goldthorne Av. WS11: Cann 1F 109
Golf La. ST5: N'tle 3D 30
Golf Links Cl. ST6: Gold 7G 11
Goms Mill Rd. ST3: Blur 1G 41
ST3: Long 7H 33
Goodere Av. B78: Pole 2J 143
Goodere Dr. B78: Pole 7J 139
Goodfellow St. ST6: Tuns 3H 17
(not continuous)
Goodill Cl. ST15: Stone 7F 47
Goodman St. DE14: B Tre 6E 84
Goodrich Av. WV6: Per 3H 129
Goodson St. ST1: H'ley 3G 151 (4C 24)
Goods Sta. La. ST19: Penk 2G 91

Goodwick Cl.—Greenwood Av.

Goodwick Cl. ST4: Tren .5C 40
Goodwin Av. ST5: N'tle .1D 152 (6F 23)
Goodwin Rd. ST3: Mei .7D 34
Goodwood Av. ST10: Chea .3E 54
Goodwood Cl. DE13: Stre .2D 84
WS12: Haz .4C 102
WS14: Lich .4D 114
Goodwood Pl. ST4: Tren .3A 40
Goodyear Av. WV10: Bush .5C 124
Goose La. WS15: Abb B .2B 88
GOOSEMOOR GREEN .6A 104
Goosemoor Gro. ST3: Mei .3D 42
Goose St. ST5: N'tle .5E 152 (1F 31)
GOOSTREY .1B 154
Goostry Cl. B77: Tam .5K 137
Goostry Rd. B77: Tam .4K 137
Gordon Av. ST6: B'lem .1C 24
ST10: Chea .4A 54
ST16: Staf .6E 70
Gordon Banks Dr. ST4: Tren .6D 32
Gordon Cl. ST13: Lee .5D 48
Gordon Ct. ST5: N'tle .5C 22
Gordon Cres. ST1: H'ley .1E 24
Gordon Rd. ST6: Tuns .1G 17
Gordon St. DE14: B Tre .7D 84
ST5: N'tle .5C 22
ST6: B'lem .6B 18
Gorey Cl. WV12: Will .5B 126
GORNALWOOD .2D 163
Gorsebrook Leys ST16: Staf .1C 72
Gorsebrook Rd. WV6: W'ton .7K 123
WV10: W'ton .7K 123
Gorseburn Way WS15: Rug .6E 94
Gorse Cres. TF9: Logg .4E 60
Gorse Dr. WS12: Hun .5D 100
Gorse La. CW12: Ast .1H 7
WS13: Frad .4F 107
WS14: Lich .5D 114
WS15: Rug .3H 97
WV5: Trys .4A 144
Gorsemoor Rd. WS12: H Hay .2J 109
Gorsemoor Way WV11: Ess .2B 126
Gorse Rd. WS15: Rug .3H 97
WV11: Wed .5A 126
Gorse St. ST4: Fen .5E 32
Gorse Way WS12: Hed .2J 101
Gorseway WS7: Burn .6K 111
GORSEYBANK .2C 157
Gorsey Bank ST6: B Gre .1E 18
Gorsey La. WS3: L Wyr .2K 119
WS6: G Wyr .3F 119
WS11: Cann .2B 108
Gorsley Dale ST17: Wild .1A 78
Gorstey Lea WS7: Burn .4A 112
GORSTEY LEY .3A 112
GORSTY BANK .5A 22
Gorsty Bank WS14: Lich .3E 114
GORSTYBIRCH .5G 43
Gorsty Hayes WV8: Cods .2B 122
GORSTY HILL .2A 160
GORSTYHILL .2H 55
Gorsty Hill Rd. ST10: Tea .3F 55
Gorsy Bank Rd. B77: Hock .5B 142
Gorsy La. ST21: Cot H .1A 64
Gort Rd. ST5: N'tle .4D 22
Goscote La. WS3: Blox, Wals .4K 127
GOSELEY DALE .2D 161
Gosforth Gro. ST3: Mei .3E 42
Gospel Ash Rd. DY7: Bob .4E 146
GOSPEL END VILLAGE .2C 163
Gough Av. WV11: Wed .5F 125
Gough Cl. ST16: Staf .5E 70
Gough Ho. ST13: Ched .3G 51
Gough Side DE14: B Tre .2E 86
Govan Rd. ST4: Fen .1E 32
Gowan Av. ST6: Chel .3A 18
Gower Rd. ST15: Stone .5H 47
Gower St. ST3: Long .6J 33
ST5: N'tle .2G 153 (7G 23)
Gowland Dr. WS11: Cann .2B 108
Goya Cl. WS11: H Hay .1J 109
Grace Moore Ct. WS11: Cann .6F 101
Grace Rd. ST4: Tren .3C 40
Grace St. ST13: Lee .3D 48
Graffam Gro. ST10: Chea .3E 54
Grafton Av. ST6: B'lem .6B 18
Grafton Rd. DE15: Stap .3H 87
ST3: Long .5J 33
Grafton St. ST1: H'ley .1H 151 (3D 24)
Graham Cl. DE14: B'ton .5D 86
Graham St. ST2: Buck .5G 25
Grainger Ct. WS11: Cann .1D 108
Grain Warehouse Yd. DE14: B Tre .1D 86
Graiseley La. WV11: Wed .7F 125
Granary Cl. WS12: Hed .5H 101
Granary Rd. WV8: P'ord .4G 123
Granby Wlk. ST4: P'ull .3K 31
Granchester Cl. ST3: Mei .4D 42
Grange, The DE13: K Bro .2C 130
DE14: B Tre .1C 86
ST3: Mei .7C 34
ST11: Fors .2J 43
ST18: Hyde L .2E 76
WS15: U Lon .7A 98
WV5: Womb .3G 145
Grange Av. ST19: Penk .4G 91
WS7: Burn .5K 111
Grange Cl. B77: T Gat .2J 141
DE14: B Tre .7C 84
(not continuous)
Grange Ct. ST5: N'tle .3H 23
ST8: Bidd .3D 8
ST18: Hixon .6C 80
Grange Cres. ST19: Penk .5F 91
Grange Dr. WS11: Cann .1F 109
Grangefield Cl. ST13: Ched .6H 51
WV8: P'ord .4H 123
Grangefields ST8: Bidd .1E 8
Grange Gdns. ST13: Lee .5E 48
Grange Hill WS15: U Lon .7A 98
Grange La. ST5: N'tle .4H 23
(not continuous)
WS13: Lich .7J 105
WS13: Lich, Pipe .4G 113
WS14: Shen .3D 134
GRANGEMILL .2C 157
Grange Pk. Dr. ST8: Bidd .2E 8
Grange Rd. ST3: Mei .4B 42
ST8: Bidd .2E 8
ST13: Ched .6G 51
ST14: Utt .4F 63
ST15: Stone .5J 47
ST19: Penk .5G 91
WS7: Burn .6J 111
WS11: N Can .5D 110
WV6: Tett .1K 129
Grange St. DE14: B Tre .1C 86
ST6: B'lem .2B 24
Grangewood Av. ST3: Mei .4B 42
Grangewood Rd. ST3: Mei .2C 42
Granstone Cl. ST6: Feg H .7A 12
Grantham Pl. ST2: Mil .2G 25
Grantley Cl. ST3: Blur .1G 41
Grantown Gro. WS3: Blox .1G 127
Grant St. ST4: S Tren .2C 32
WS3: Blox .5H 127
Grants Yd. DE14: B Tre .1D 86
Grants Yd. Bldgs. *DE14: B Tre .1D 86*
(off Grants Yd.)
Granville B77: Glas .1B 142
Granville Av. ST1: H'ley .1D 24
ST5: N'tle .1G 153 (6G 23)
Granville Ct. ST15: Stone .3G 47
Granville Rd. ST2: Buck .4H 25
Granville Sq. ST15: Stone .3G 47
Granville Ter. ST15: Stone .3G 47
Grasmere Av. B74: L Ast .6F 135
ST5: N'tle .5F 31
WV6: Per .3G 129
Grasmere Cl. DE15: Stap .3J 87
WV6: Tett .5G 123
WV11: Wed .6G 125
Grasmere Pl. WS11: Cann .5E 100
Grasmere Ter. ST6: B'lem .4A 18
Grassholme B77: Wiln .2C 142
Grassmere Ct. WS6: C Hay .1D 118
Grassmere Hollow ST16: Staf .1B 72
GRASSMOOR .1D 157
Grass Rd. ST6: Nort .2G 19
Grassy Grn. La. ST7: Aud .6F 15
Grassy La. ST18: Hau .6C 66
WV10: Wed .4F 125
Gratley Cft. WS12: Hun .6C 100
GRATTON .2D 155
Gratton La. ST9: End .1C 50
Gratton Rd. ST2: Buck .5K 25
GRATWICH .1A 160
Gravel Hill WV5: Womb .4H 145
Gravel La. ST17: Staf .3H 77
WS12: Hun .4B 100
(not continuous)
Gravelly Bank ST3: L'ood .3B 42
GRAVELLY HILL .2B 164
Gravelly Hill TF9: A'ley .4F 61
Gravelly La. WS9: Ston .7H 133
Graycar Bus. Pk. DE13: B Nee .6K 89
Grayling B77: Dost .4K 141
Grayling Gro. ST6: B'lem .4B 18
Grayling Willows CW3: Mad .3A 28
Gray Rd. WS12: Hed .4F 101
Gray's Cl. ST7: Sch G .6F 7
Grayshott Rd. ST6: Tuns .2J 17
Grayston Av. B77: Amin .5A 138
Gray Wlk. ST17: Staf .7E 72
Grazewood Cl. WV12: Will .5B 126
Grazier Av. B77: T Gat .2J 141
Grazings, The DY7: Kin .7G 149
Greadier St. WV12: Will .7C 126
Greasley Rd. ST2: A Hul, Buck .2H 25
GREAT BARR .2A 164
Greatbatch Av. ST4: P'ull .2K 31
GREAT BOLAS .2A 158
GREAT BRIDGEFORD .6H 65 (2C 159)
Gt. Charles St. WS8: Brow .4H 121
GREAT CHATWELL .3B 158
GREAT CHELL .1A 18
GREAT CUBLEY .1B 160
GREAT EAVES .3J 25
Gt. Fenton Bus. Pk. ST4: Fen .5D 32
Gt. Furlong DE13: Alre .6C 130
GREAT GATE .3A 156
GREAT HAYWOOD .4G 81 (2D 159)
GREAT HEATH .3D 165
GREAT LONGSTONE .1C 157
Greatmead B77: Wiln .1J 141
GREAT MOOR .5A 128
Gt. Moor Rd. WV6: Patt .4A 128
Greatoak Rd. ST7: Big E .3H 15
GREAT SAREDON .1D 163
GREAT WILNE .1D 161
Gt. Wood Rd. ST10: Tea .3G 55
GREAT WYRLEY .1E 118 (1D 163)
GREAT WYTHEFORD .3A 158
Greaves Cres. WV12: Will .5C 126
Greaves La. DE6: D Cla .6B 82
DE13: D Cla, H'ury .6B 82
GREEN, THE .4G 73
Green, The B77: Amin .3D 138
B78: Frea .5E 142
B78: M Oak .7E 136
B79: Elf .5H 131
DE13: B Nee .6F 89
DE13: Stre .2F 85
ST4: S Tren .5K 153 (1J 31)
ST5: N'tle .6G 31
ST6: B Edg .7H 13
ST9: Bag .7B 50
ST9: S Broo .3H 19
ST10: Chea .5A 54
ST10: K'ley .6F 53
ST11: Cave .6F 35
ST15: Yarn .6D 64
ST17: Broc .4F 79
ST17: Milf .7G 75
ST18: West .3C 80
ST20: W'ves .2C 66
WS3: Blox .4H 127
(not continuous)
WS11: Cann .1G 109
(Hawks Grn. La.)
WS11: Cann .2D 108
(Newhall St.)
WS14: W'ton .3G 131
WS15: Hand .4G 99
WS15: Rug .3J 97
(not continuous)
WV5: Trys .2C 144
Greenacre ST18: Hixon .5D 80
Greenacre, The DE6: C'ton .6E 56
Greenacre Cl. B77: Amin .4D 138
Greenacre Dr. WV8: Bilb .3D 122
Green Acres WV5: Womb .5F 145
WV9: Cove .1K 93
Greenacres WS15: Rug .2F 97
WV6: Tett .1J 129
Greenacres Av. ST11: B Bri .2E 42
WV10: Bush .3F 125
Greenacres Dr. ST14: Utt .3F 63
Greenaway Ct. *WV10: Fea .5G 117*
(off The Avenue)
Greenbank Rd. ST5: N'tle .5G 23
ST6: Tuns .4K 17
Grn. Barn Ct. ST18: West .3C 80
Greenbirches Ind. Est.
ST6: Tuns .3H 17
Greenbrook Ct. ST5: N'tle .5F 23
Green Cl. ST11: B Bri .3F 43
ST12: Barl .2D 44
ST15: Stone .5F 47
WV6: Patt .7B 128
Green Ct. WS13: Lich .4B 114
Green Cft. ST15: Yarn .6D 64
Greencroft WS13: Lich .1A 114
Greendale Dr. ST5: C'ton .6B 16
Greendock St. ST3: Long .6H 33
Green Dr. WV10: Oxl .6A 124
GREEN END .3C 165
Greenfield ST8: Bidd .7D 8
Greenfield Av. ST6: B Edg .7J 13
WS15: Arm .5E 98
Greenfield Cl. ST6: B Edg .7J 13
Greenfield Cres. ST10: Chea .3D 54
Greenfield Dr. ST14: Utt .5F 63
Greenfield La. WV10: Bush, Ford .7B 116
Greenfield Pl. ST6: B Edg .7J 13
Greenfield Rd. ST6: Tuns .2J 17
ST9: End .1A 50
ST17: Staf .1B 78
Greenfields ST14: Dens .2B 58
ST20: Gno .3H 67
WS11: Cann .1E 108
Greenfields Dr. WS15: Rug .7F 95
Greenfields Rd. DY7: Kin .6A 148
ST18: Hixon .5C 80
WV5: Womb .5G 145
Greenfinch Cl. ST14: Utt .7H 63
Greengates St. ST6: Tuns .3J 17
Greengate St. ST16: Staf .3G 73
(not continuous)
Grn. Gore La. ST17: Walt .7D 74
Greenhead St. ST6: B'lem .7K 17
Greenheart B77: Amin .5C 138
GREEN HEATH .3F 101 (3D 159)
Green Heath Rd. WS12: Hed .3G 101
GREENHILL .3C 163
Greenhill WS13: Lich .3C 114
WV5: Womb .4H 145
Greenhill Cl. B77: Dost .5J 141
Greenhill Ct. WV5: Womb .5H 145
Greenhill Gdns. WV5: Womb .5H 145
Greenhill La. ST19: Whe A .2C 90
Greenhill M. WS13: Lich .3C 114
Greenhill Rd. ST6: B Gre .1E 18
Greenhough Rd. WS13: Lich .3A 114
Greenhouse Gardening & Environmental Cen., The .2G 87
Greenlands WV5: Womb .3F 145
GREEN LANE .2A 158
Green La. B77: Wiln .3E 142
(not continuous)
B78: Bir .3F 143
DE6: Ash .5D 56
DE13: B Nee .7F 89
DE13: B Tre .4C 84
DE13: Tut .3H 83
(not continuous)
SK17: Crow, E Ster .1D 52
ST11: B Bri .4J 43
ST13: Rudy .1A 48
ST14: Mar .1D 82
ST18: Hyde L .3E 76
ST18: W'ave .1C 70
ST21: Ecc .3H 65
TF9: A'ley .4J 61
WS2: Wals .7J 127
WS3: Blox .6J 127
WS3: Pels .7C 120
WS7: Burn .2B 112
WS8: Hamm .2J 121
WS11: Cann .5E 108
WS13: Chor .7A 104
WS14: Wall .7H 113
(not continuous)
WS15: Gen .6K 103
WS15: Rug .6E 94
WV6: Tett .6G 123
Greenlea Cl. ST4: Tren .5C 40
Greenlee B77: Wiln .2C 142
Greenline Bus. Pk. DE14: B Tre .1C 86
Green Mdw. WV11: Wed .7J 125
Green Mdw. Cl. WV5: Womb .5E 144
Greenmeadow Gro. ST9: End .3A 50
Green Mdw. Rd. WV12: Will .6B 126
Green Mdws. WS12: H Hay .2J 109
Greenmeadows Rd. CW3: Mad .2A 28
Greenmoor Av. ST6: Feg H .6A 12
Grn. Oak Rd. WV8: Bilb .3D 122
Greenock Cl. ST5: N'tle .5A 152 (1D 30)
Green Pk. ST11: Ful .2G 59
ST21: Ecc .3H 65
Green Rd. ST4: T Val .6J 31
ST18: West .3B 80
Grn. Rock La. WS3: Blox .4K 127
Greens, The *WV6: Per .3F 129*
(off Edge Hill Dr.)
Greensforge La. DY7: Stou .2G 149
Greens Health & Fitness .6D 32
Greenside ST5: N'tle .2C 152 (7E 22)
ST15: Yarn .6D 64
Greenside Av. ST9: S Broo .4J 19
Greenside Cl. ST7: Kids .7E 10
Greens Ind. Est. WS12: Hed .3J 101
Greenslade Gro. WS12: Hed .3J 101
Green's La. ST2: Bent .5A 26
Greensmith Cl. DE15: Wins .1K 87
Greensome Cl. ST16: Staf .1C 72
Greensome Ct. ST16: Staf .2C 72
Greensome Cres. ST16: Staf .1C 72
Greensome La. ST16: Staf .1C 72
Green St. DE14: B Tre .3E 86
Greensway WV11: Wed .5F 125
Greenvale Cl. DE15: Stap .4G 87
Grn. Valley Dr. DE13: B Tre .3B 84
Green Way ST14: Utt .5G 63
Greenway B78: Pole .6J 139
DE15: Wins .7H 85
ST3: Fen .6E 32
ST4: Tren .3J 39
ST16: Staf .3J 73
ST21: Ecc .3H 65
Greenway, The ST5: N'tle .5G 23
WV6: Patt .7B 128
Greenway Av. ST6: B'lem .5B 18
ST15: Stone .6G 47
Greenway Bank ST2: L Oak .5J 19
ST8: Brin F .4C 12
Greenway Bank Country Pk. .2F 13
Greenway Gdns. WV6: Patt .7B 128
Greenway Hall Rd. ST2: L Oak .5K 19
ST9: S Broo .4J 19
Greenway Pl. ST2: A Hul .1H 25
Greenway Rd. ST8: Bidd .3E 8
Greenways ST7: Big E .5H 15
ST10: Chea .5A 54
ST18: Hyde L .2E 76
ST19: Penk .4J 91
WS13: Chor .7C 104
Greenways, The ST2: Mil .4J 19
Greenways Dr. ST10: Chea .3C 54
Greenwood Av. ST4: T Val .7J 31

Greenwood Dr. WS14: Lich 5B **114**
Greenwood Gro. ST17: Staf 7E **72**
Greenwood Pk. WS12: Hed 2H **101**
Greenwood Rd. DE15: Stap 4F **87**
ST11: Fors 2J **43**
WV10: Oxl 6K **123**
Greeting St. ST6: B'lem 1A **24**
Gregory Rd. WS7: Burn 4C **112**
Gregorys Grn. WV9: Cove 1K **93**
Gregory St. ST3: Long 6H **33**
Gregson Cl. ST3: Long 6G **33**
Greig Ct. WS11: H Hay 1J **109**
Grenadier Cl. ST4: Tren 6C **40**
GRENDON 2C 165
GRENDON COMMON 2C 165
Grendon Grn. ST2: Bent 6J **25**
Grendon Rd. B78: Pole 1J **143**
Grenfell Rd. WS3: Blox 2K **127**
Grenville Cl. ST14: Utt 4E **62**
Gresham Rd. WS11: Cann 7F **101**
Gresley B77: Glas 1B **142**
Gresley Row WS13: Lich 4B **114**
(not continuous)
Gresley Way ST7: Big E 5H **15**
Gresty St. ST4: P'ull 2A **32**
Gretton Av. DE13: Stre 2F **85**
Greville Cl. ST19: Penk 4H **91**
Greville St. ST1: H'ley 1H **151** (3D **24**)
Grey Friars ST16: Staf 1F **73**
Greyfriars Bus. Pk. ST16: Staf 2F **73**
Greyfriars Ct. *ST16: Staf 1F 73*
(off Marsh St.)
Greyfriars Dr. B79: Tam 3E **136**
Grey Friars Pl. ST16: Staf 1F **73**
Greyfriars Rd. ST2: A Hul 3G **25**
Grey Friars Way ST16: Staf 2F **73**
Greyhound Cnr. *CW3: Mad 2A 28*
(off Newcastle Rd.)
Greyhound Ct. CW3: Mad 3A **28**
Greyhound Way
ST1: H'ley 1C **150** (3A **24**)
ST6: B'lem 3A **24**
Greylarch La. ST17: Wild 1A **78**
Greysan Av. ST7: Pack 6K **11**
Greysbrook WS14: Shen 6D **134**
Greyswood Rd. ST4: T Val 6J **31**
Grice Rd. ST4: S Tren 4K **153** (1J **31**)
GRIFF 3D 165
Griffin Cl. WS7: C Ter 3G **111**
Griffin St. ST3: Long 5H **33**
Griffiths Dr. WV5: Womb 5G **145**
WV11: Wed 5K **125**
Griffiths Rd. WV12: Will 5D **126**
Griffiths Way ST15: Stone 6K **47**
GRIFFYDAM 3D 161
Grimley Way WS11: Cann 6F **101**
Grindcobbe Gro. WS15: Rug 5F **95**
GRINDLE 1B 162
GRINDLEY 2A 160
Grindley Hill Ct.
ST4: S Tren 7K **153** (2H **31**)
Grindley La. ST3: Mei, M Hea 5C **42**
ST11: B Bri 3G **43**
ST11: Mei 5C **42**
Grindley Pl. ST4: P'ull 3K **31**
GRINDON 2A 156
Grindsbrook B77: Wiln 2C **142**
Grisedale Cl. ST3: Mei 3C **42**
Grissom Cl. ST16: Staf 1J **73**
Gristhorpe Way ST2: Bent 7K **25**
Gritton St. ST6: Tuns 5H **17**
Grizedale Cl. DE15: Stap 3J **87**
Grocott Cl. ST19: Penk 2G **91**
G Rose Bus. Cen. ST17: Staf 4H **77**
Grosvenor Av. ST4: T Val 5K **31**
Grosvenor Cl. ST9: End 1B **50**
ST19: Penk 3H **91**
WS14: Lich 5D **114**
WV10: Bush 3B **124**
Grosvenor Ct. WS15: Rug 3K **97**
WV11: Wed 7H **125**
Grosvenor Cres. WV10: Bush 3B **124**
Grosvenor Gdns.
ST5: N'tle 5F **153** (1G **31**)
Grosvenor Pl. ST5: N'tle 3G **23**
ST6: Tuns 3H **17**
Grosvenor Rd. ST3: L'ood 1B **42**
ST5: N'tle 5F **153** (1G **31**)
WV10: Bush 3B **124**
Grosvenor St. ST3: Long 6H **33**
ST13: Lee 4G **49**
Grosvenor Way ST17: Walt 1C **78**
Grotto La. WV6: Tett 7G **123**
Grouse Way WS11: H Hay 2G **109**
Grove, The B74: L Ast 3G **135**
ST5: N'tle 3F **31**
ST6: B'lem 5B **18**
ST11: B Bri 4G **43**
ST15: Aston 2H **69**
WS7: C Ter 3F **111**
WV11: Wed 7F **125**
Grove Av. ST4: Fen 5E **32**
ST7: Kids 5C **10**
Grovebank Rd. ST4: T Val 6J **31**
Grove Cl. WS11: N Can 6B **110**
Grove Cotts. WS3: Blox 5H **127**
Grovelands Cres. WV10: Ford 2B **124**
Grove La. WS3: L Wyr 3A **120**
WV6: Tett 4J **129**
Grove Pl. ST1: H'ley 6D **150** (6B **24**)
Grove Rd. ST4: Fen 5D **32**
ST15: Stone 4E **46**
Grove Rd. Ind. Est. ST4: Fen 5D **32**
Groveside Way WS3: Pels 7C **120**
Grove St. ST5: N'tle 5C **22**
ST6: B'lem 2A **24**
ST13: Lee 3E **48**
Grove Ter. *ST13: Lee 3E 48*
(off Westwood Gro.)
GRUB STREET 3A 66 (2B 158)
Grub St. ST20: H Off 4A **66**
Grunmore Dr. DE13: Stre 1F **85**
Guardian Ho. WS13: Lich 4C **114**
Guernsey Dr. ST5: N'tle 5C **30**
Guernsey Wlk. *ST3: Long 6G 33*
(off Anglesey Dr.)
Guest Av. WV11: Wed 5G **125**
Guild Av. WS3: Blox 6K **127**
Guildford St. ST4: S Tren 1C **32**
Guildhall Shop. Cen. ST16: Staf 3G **73**
Guild St. DE14: B Tre 1E **86**
Guinevere Av. DE13: Stre 1F **85**
Gullet, The B78: Pole 1H **143**
Gullick Way WS7: C Ter 3F **111**
Gun Battery La. ST8: Bid M 5G **9**
Gunnell Cl. ST1: H'ley 7H **151** (6D **24**)
ST16: Staf 4E **72**
Gunn St. ST8: Bidd 5C **8**
GUNSTONE 1C 163
Gunstone La. WV8: Cods, C Woo 1B **122**
(not continuous)
Gurnard B77: Dost 4K **141**
Gurnard Cl. WV12: Will 4B **126**
Gurney Pl. WS2: Wals 7G **127**
Gurney Rd. WS2: Wals 7G **127**
Guthrum Cl. WV6: Per 1G **129**
Guy Av. WV10: Bush 7B **124**
Guy's Almshouses B79: Tam 4H **137**
Guys Cl. B79: Tam 2F **137**
Guys Motors Ind. Pk.
WV10: W'ton 7D **124**
Guy St. ST2: Buck 4H **25**
Gwenys Cres. ST3: Fen 5E **32**
Gwyn Av. ST8: Knyp 1D **12**
Gypsum Way DE6: D Cla 5B **82**
Gypsy La. B78: Dor 6J **143**
CV9: B Ens 6J **143**

H

Hackett Cl. ST3: Long 5K **33**
Hackwood Cl. ST12: Barl 6F **41**
Hadden Cl. ST9: Werr 6D **26**
Haddon Cres. WV12: Will 6C **126**
Haddon Gro. ST5: C'ton 2D **22**
Haddon Pl. ST2: Buck 3J **25**
ST15: Stone 5K **47**
HADEMORE 3J 131 (1B 164)
Haden Cres. WV11: Wed 7A **126**
Hadfield Grn. ST6: B'lem 5D **18**
Hadleigh Cl. ST5: N'tle 7F **31**
Hadleigh Rd. ST2: A Hul 2H **25**
HADLEY 3A 158
HADLEY END 2B 160
Hadley End DE13: Yox 2K **89**
Hadley Rd. WS2: Wals 7F **127**
Hadley St. DE13: Yox 1G **89**
Hadley Way WS2: Wals 7F **127**
Hadrians Cl. B77: T Gat 2K **141**
Hadrian Way ST5: C'ton 3B **22**
HADY 1D 157
HAGLEY 3D 163
Hagley Dr. WS15: Rug 7F **95**
Hagley Pk. Gdns. WS15: Rug 2F **97**
Hagley Rd. WS15: Rug 7F **95**
Haig Cl. WS11: Cann 5G **101**
Haigh Cl. ST13: Ched 5H **51**
Haig Rd. ST13: Lee 2H **49**
Haig St. ST3: Long 7K **33**
Hailsham Cl. ST6: Tuns 2K **17**
Hainer Cl. ST17: Staf 6J **73**
Halcyon Ct. DE14: B Tre 7C **84**
Halcyon Way DE14: B Tre 7C **84**
Halecroft Av. WV11: Wed 7H **125**
HALES 1B 158
HALES GREEN 3B 156
Hales Hall Pool (Nature Reserve) 3E 54
Hales Hall Rd. ST10: Chea 3E **54**
HALESOWEN 3D 163
Hales Pl. ST3: Long 1J **41**
Halesworth Cres. ST5: N'tle 7G **31**
Halesworth Rd. WV9: P'ord 4H **123**
Haley St. WV12: Will 7C **126**
HALFCOT 2K 149
Halford La. B79: Tam 4G **137**
Halford St. B79: Tam 4G **137**
HALFPENNY GREEN 2C 163
Halfpenny Green Vineyard 2C 163
Halfway Pl. ST5: N'tle 7C **22**
Halifax Cl. ST3: Mei 3E **42**
Haliford Av. ST1: H'ley 1D **24**
Haling Cl. ST19: Penk 4H **91**
Haling Rd. ST19: Penk 3H **91**
Hallahan Cl. ST15: Stone 6J **47**
Hallahan Gro. ST4: S Tren 1A **32**
Hallam Cres. WV10: W'ton 7C **124**
Hallam Rd. ST14: Utt 4E **62**
Hallams Row DE14: B Tre 7D **84**
Hallam St. ST4: Fen 3D **32**
Hall Av. ST13: Lee 2H **49**
Hall Cl. ST17: Staf 7J **73**
WV6: Patt 7B **128**
Hall Ct. B78: Pole 1J **143**
Hallcourt Cl. WS11: Cann 3E **108**
Hallcourt Cres. WS11: Cann 3E **108**
Hallcourt La. WS11: Cann 3E **108**
Halldearn Av. ST11: Cave 6F **35**
Hall Dr. DE13: H'ury 7E **82**
ST3: W Coy 5D **34**
HALL END 5H 143
Hall End Cl. WV6: Patt 7B **128**
Hall End La. WV6: Patt 7B **128**
Hall Farm Cl. ST18: Hixon 5C **80**
Hallfarm Cl. ST19: Brew 2D **92**
Hall Farm Rd. ST19: Brew 2D **92**
Hallfield Gro. ST6: Tuns 2J **17**
Hallfields Rd. DE15: Stan 7K **87**
Hall Gdns. ST14: Mar 2C **82**
HALL GREEN
B13 3B 164
ST7 1C 10 (2C 155)
ST10 5G 55
Hall Green Av. DE13: Stre 1F **85**
Hall Grounds DE13: Roll D 6G **83**
Hall Hill Dr. ST2: B Hil 1K **33**
Hallhill La. WS15: Abb B 3C **88**
(not continuous)
Hall La. ST15: Hild 5J **59**
ST15: Swyn 3D **64**
WS6: G Wyr 7F **109**
WS7: Hamm 7B **112**
(not continuous)
WS14: M Cor 1J **133**
Hall Mdw. ST10: Tea 4G **55**
WS11: Cann 5B **108**
Hall Orchard ST10: Chea 4C **54**
ST14: Bram 6B **62**
Hall Pl. ST5: N'tle 3H **23**
Hall Rd. DE13: Roll D 6F **83**
ST14: Mar 1C **82**
ST14: Utt 5F **63**
WS15: Hand 4G **99**
Halls Rd. ST7: M Cop 6G **7**
ST8: Bidd 4C **8**
Hall St. ST5: N'tle 2D **152** (7F **23**)
ST6: B'lem 7J **17**
ST7: Aud 5F **15**
Hallwater ST9: End 1B **50**
Hall Yd. ST10: Tea 3G **55**
HALMER END 1F 21 (3C 155)
Halston Rd. WS7: C Ter 3K **111**
Halton Grn. ST3: Blur 2E **40**
Haltonlea B77: Wiln 2C **142**
Hamble B77: Wiln 7K **137**
Hambledon Cl. WV9: P'ord 3J **123**
Hamble Gro. WV6: Per 3F **129**
Hamble Rd. WV4: Pen 7K **129**
Hambleton Pl. ST8: Knyp 1B **12**
Hamble Way ST2: Bent 7K **25**
Hambridge Cl. ST17: Staf 7F **73**
Hambro Pl. ST6: Feg H 7B **12**
Hamelin St. WS11: Cann 7E **100**
Hamil Dr. ST13: Lee 3E **48**
Hamil Rd. ST6: B'lem 6A **18**
Hamilton Cl. WS12: Hed 6B **102**
Hamilton Ct. ST5: N'tle 7G **31**
Hamilton Flds. DE15: B Tre 2H **87**
Hamilton Gdns. WV10: Bush 2C **124**
Hamilton Ho. WS3: Blox 4J **127**
Hamilton Ind. Cen. ST4: Fen 4E **32**
Hamilton Lea WS11: N Can 5C **110**
Hamilton Ri. ST2: Mil 5H **19**
Hamilton Rd. DE15: B Tre 2H **87**
ST3: Long 7K **33**
Hamilton St. ST4: Fen 4C **32**
WS3: Blox 4J **127**
Hamlet, The WS11: N Can 6A **110**
Hamlett Pl. ST6: Nort 4E **18**
Hammersley Hayes Rd.
ST10: Chea 1D **54**
Hammersley St. ST1: H'ley 2E **24**
Hammerton Av. ST2: Buck 6F **25**
HAMMERWICH 7B 112 (1A 164)
Hammerwich Rd. WS7: Burn 5B **112**
Hammond Av. ST6: B Edg 7H **13**
WV10: Bush 5C **124**
Hammond Ho. ST1: H'ley 7H **151** (6D **24**)
Hammond Rd. ST5: C'ton 7C **16**
Hammonds Cft. ST18: Hixon 6C **80**
Hammoon Gro. ST2: Buck 6H **25**
Hamner Grn. ST2: Bent 1K **33**
Hamps Cl. WS7: Burn 4B **112**
Hampshire Cl. B78: Tam 7G **137**
ST9: End 2B **50**
Hampshire Cres. ST3: L'ood 2J **41**
Hampshire Gdns. ST7: Kids 4D **10**
Hampson Ct. *ST15: Stone 4H 47*
(off Church St.)
Hampstead Gro. ST4: Tren 3C **40**
Hamps Valley Rd. ST10: Wat 5B **52**
HAMPTON 3B 162
Hampton Cl. B79: Tam 2J **137**
Hampton Ct. ST13: Lee 4E **48**
WS15: Rug 5F **95**
WV10: Bush 3F **125**
Hampton Gdns. ST18: Staf 3B **74**
Hampton Grn. WS11: Cann 4E **108**
Hampton Gro. DY7: Kin 5F **149**
WS3: Pels 7C **120**
HAMPTON IN ARDEN 3C 165
HAMPTON LOADE 3B 162
Hampton Rd. WV10: Oxl 4K **123**
Hampton St. ST1: H'ley 7H **151** (6D **24**)
WS11: Cann 4D **108**
Hams Cl. ST8: Bidd 6C **8**
HAMSTALL RIDWARE 3B 160
HAMSTEAD 2A 164
Hamstead Cl. WV11: Wed 7H **125**
Hanbridge Av. ST5: Brad 2E **22**
HANBURY 7E 82 (2B 160)
Hanbury La. DE13: C Cla, H'ury 7E **82**
Hanbury Rd. B77: Amin 5B **138**
WS8: Brow 2G **121**
WS11: N Can 6B **110**
HANBURY WOODEND 2B 160
HANCH 1J 105
HANCHURCH 3F 39 (3C 155)
Hanchurch Cl. DE15: Wins 7H **85**
Hanchurch Flds. ST4: H'rch 4D **38**
Hanchurch La. ST4: H'rch 3F **39**
Hancock St. ST4: S Tren 2C **32**
Handel Ct. WS11: H Hay 1J **109**
Handel Gro. ST1: H'ley 2G **25**
Handel Wlk. WS13: Lich 1C **114**
HANDLEY 1D 157
Handley Banks ST11: Cave 6G **35**
Handley Dr. ST8: Brin F 4B **12**
Handley Rd. DE14: B Tre 1A **86**
Handley St. ST7: Pack 4A **12**
HANDSACRE 5G 99 (3A 160)
Handsacre Cres. WS15: Hand 6G **99**
Handsacre Rd. ST3: Long 4K **33**
Hand St. ST6: Tuns 5J **17**
HANDSWORTH 2A 164
HANFORD 1K 39 (3C 155)
HANGINGBRIDGE 5D 56
Hangman's La. B79: Seck 1J **139**
HANKELOW 3A 154
HANLEY 3G 151 (4C 24)
Hanley Bus. Pk.
ST1: H'ley 6E **150** (6C **24**)
Hanley Mall *ST1: H'ley 2G 151*
(off Stafford St.)
Hanley Rd. ST1: H'ley 6C **18**
ST6: B'lem 6C **18**
Hanlith B77: Wiln 2C **142**
Hannaford Way WS11: Cann 1F **109**
Hanney Hay Rd.
WS7: Chas, Hamm 7J **111**
WS8: Hamm 2K **121**
Hanover Ct. B79: Tam 2E **136**
ST5: N'tle 2F **153**
WV6: Tett 2K **129**
Hanover Pl. WS11: Cann 1E **108**
Hanover St. ST1: H'ley 1F **151** (4C **24**)
ST5: N'tle 2F **153** (7G **23**)
(not continuous)
HANYARDS, THE 1F 75
Hanyards La. ST18: Ing, Tix 3C **74**
Hapden Ho. DE15: Stap 6F **87**
Harald Cl. WV6: Per 1F **129**
Harber St. ST3: Long 6J **33**
HARBORNE 3A 164
Harborne Cotts. ST10: Chea 3D **54**
Harborne Cres. ST10: Chea 3D **54**
Harborne Rd. ST10: Chea 3C **54**
Harbury St. DE13: B Tre 5B **84**
Harcourt Av. ST3: Mei 1B **42**
Harcourt Dr. B74: F Oak 4K **135**
Harcourt Ho. B79: Tam 5G **137**
Harcourt Rd. DE14: B'ton 6A **86**
Harcourt St. ST1: H'ley 7E **150** (6B **24**)
Harcourt Way ST16: Staf 6D **70**
HARDEN 6K 127
Harden Gro. WS3: Blox 6K **127**
Harden Rd. WS3: Blox, Wals 6K **127**
Hardewick Cl. ST9: Werr 5D **26**
Hardie Av. WS15: Rug 2G **97**
Hardie Grn. WS11: Cann 7F **101**
Hardinge St. ST4: Fen 3D **32**
Harding Rd. ST1: H'ley 6G **151** (6C **24**)
Hardings Mdw. ST7: Kids 4C **10**
Hardings Row ST7: M Cop 6H **7**
HARDINGS WOOD 4B 10 (2C 155)
Hardingswood ST7: Kids 4C **10**
Hardingswood Ind. Est. ST7: Kids 4C **10**
Hardingswood Rd. ST7: Kids 4C **10**
Harding Ter. ST4: S Tren 3A **32**
Hardman St. ST2: Mil 6G **19**

Holyrood Cl.—Izaak Walton St.

Holyrood Cl. ST15: Stone 6J **47**
ST18: Staf 3A **74**
Holywell Cl. ST8: Knyp 7E **8**
Holywell Ri. WS14: Lich 5D **114**
Homage Pl. WV9: Cove 2K **93**
Home Farm Mobile Home Pk.
DE13: Roll D 6G **83**
Homefield Rd. WV8: Bilb 2D **122**
Homelands Pk. WV10: Cov H 6A **116**
Homelodge Ho. *WS13: Lich* *4B 114*
(off Castle Dyke)
HOMER .1A **162**
Homer Pl. ST6: Chel 2B **18**
Homer St. ST1: H'ley 3K **151** (4E **24**)
Homestead, The ST2: Mil 4J **19**
ST5: N'tle 6H **23**
Homestead Ct. ST16: Staf 6G **71**
Homestead St. ST2: Bent 1K **33**
Honesty Cl. WS8: Clay 6F **121**
Honeybourne B77: Wiln 7K **137**
Honeybourne Cres. WV5: Womb 5F **145**
Honeysuckle Av. ST11: B Bri 4H **43**
Honeysuckle Cl. ST10: Tea 4H **55**
Honeysuckle Dr. WV10: Fea 5G **117**
Honeysuckle Ri. ST17: Staf 7D **74**
Honeysuckle Vw. DE15: Stap 4H **87**
Honeysuckle Way WS6: G Wyr 7H **109**
Honeywall ST4: P'ull, S Tren 2A **32**
Honeywall Ho. ST4: P'ull 2A **32**
Honeywall La. CW3: Mad H 1D **28**
Honeywood ST5: N'tle 6F **23**
Honiton Cl. ST17: Staf 6C **74**
Honiton Wlk. ST3: Long 6K **33**
HONNINGTON 3B **158**
Hood & Broomfield Fine Art Gallery
. . . . .2H **153** (7H **23**)
Hood La. WS15: Arm, L'don 5E **98**
Hook Dr. B74: F Oak 4K **135**
Hooke La. WS14: Foot 7A **134**
HOOKGATE 6F **61** (1B **158**)
Hoo La. DY7: Stou 4J **147**
Hoomill La. ST18: Gt Hay 2F **81**
Hoon Av. ST5: N'tle 4F **23**
HOON HAY .1K **83**
Hoover St. ST6: Tuns 4H **17**
HOPE 2B **156**
HOPEDALE .2B **156**
Hopedale Cl. ST4: Fen 2H **33**
ST5: N'tle .6F **31**
Hope Dr. WS11: N Can 6D **110**
Hope St. ST1: H'ley 2F **151** (4C **24**)
ST7: Big E 4H **15**
Hopley's Cl. B77: Amin 5A **138**
Hopmeadow Way DE15: Stap 3H **87**
HOPSTONE 2B **162**
HOPTON
Matlock 2C **157**
Shrewsbury 2A **158**
Stafford 6F **69** (2D **159**)
Hopton Bank ST18: Hopt 6F **69**
HOPTON CANGEFORD 3A **162**
Hopton Cl. WV6: Per 3G **129**
Hopton Ct. ST16: Staf 1F **73**
Hopton Cres. WV11: Wed 7J **125**
Hoptonhall La. ST18: Hopt 6F **69**
HOPTON HEATH 6H **69** (2D **159**)
Hopton La. ST18: Hopt 4K **71**
Hopton Mdw. WS12: H Hay 2J **109**
Hopton St. ST16: Staf 7H **71**
HOPTON WAFERS 3A **162**
Hopton Way ST6: Feg H 6A **12**
HOPWAS 2B **136** (1B **164**)
Hopwas Hays La. WS14: W Bar 7K **115**
Hopwas Hill B78: Hop 3A **136**
Hopwood La. DE14: B Tre 5G **85**
Hopwood Pl. ST2: Buck 5H **25**
Horatius Rd. ST5: C'ton 2B **22**
Hordern Cl. WV6: W'ton 7H **123**
Hordern Pk. WV10: Cov H 6A **116**
Hordern Rd. WV6: W'ton 7H **123**
Hordley St. ST1: H'ley 4H **151** (4D **24**)
Hornbeam B77: Amin 5C **138**
Hornbeam Cres. WS12: Haz 4C **102**
Hornbeams, The ST14: Utt 4F **63**
Hornbeam Wlk. DY7: Stou 1A **148**
Hornbrook Cl. DE13: B Tre 3C **84**
Hornbrook Rd. DE13: B Tre 4C **84**
Hornby Row ST4: S Tren 2A **32**
Horner Av. WS13: Frad 4J **107**
HORNINGLOW 4C **84** (2C **161**)
Horninglow Cft. DE13: B Tre 5D **84**
Horninglow Rd. DE14: B Tre 5D **84**
Horninglow Rd. Nth. DE13: B Tre 4C **84**
Horninglow St. DE14: B Tre 7E **84**
Hornscroft WS15: S Mil 2D **96**
Hornton Cl. B74: L Ast 3J **135**
Hornton Rd. DE13: B Tre 4C **84**
HORSE BRIDGE 2D **155**
Horse Bri. La. DY7: Kin 7G **149**
HORSEBROOK 1C **92** (3C **159**)
Horsebrook La. ST19: Brew 1C **92**
Horsecroft Cres. ST13: Lee 1H **49**
Horsecroft Gro. ST13: Lee 2H **49**
Horse Fair ST21: Ecc 2H **65**
WS15: Rug 1G **97**
HORSEHAY 1A **162**
Horse Rd. ST10: Alt 5H **57**
Horseshoe Dr. WS12: Wimb 6B **102**
WS15: Rug 6D **94**
Horsey La. WS15: L'don, U Lon 2A **104**
HORSLEY .3D **157**
Horsley Gro. ST3: Blur 2E **40**
Horsley La. WS14: C'eld 3A **134**
Horsley Rd. B74: L Ast 6G **135**
ST15: Cold M 4A **64**
Horsley Way ST15: Cold M 5A **64**
HORSLEY WOODHOUSE 3D **157**
HORTON .2D **155**
Horton Av. DE13: Stre 4G **85**
Horton Cl. WS11: Cann 6F **101**
Horton Dr. ST3: W Coy 5C **34**
Horton Rd. DY7: Kin 4D **148**
Horton St. ST5: N'tle 2H **153** (7H **23**)
ST13: Lee 3G **49**
HORTONWOOD 3A **158**
Horwood ST5: Keel 3C **30**
Horwood Gdns. ST6: B'lem 6C **18**
Horwood Hall ST5: Keel 2A **30**
Hose St. ST6: Tuns 4H **17**
Hoskings Ct. ST15: Stone 5J **47**
Hoskins Rd. ST6: Tuns 2J **17**
Hospital La. WS6: C Hay 1B **118**
Hospital Rd. WS7: Burn 7J **111**
Hospital St. B79: Tam 4H **137**
Hot La. ST6: B'lem 1B **24**
ST8: Bid M 4H **9**
Hot La. Ind. Est. ST6: B'lem 7B **18**
HOUGH 2B **154**
Hougher Wall Rd. ST7: Aud 6F **15**
Hough Hill ST6: B Edg 5H **13**
Houghton St. ST1: H'ley 6G **151** (6C **24**)
HOUGHWOOD 4K **19**
Houghwood La. ST9: S Broo 3K **19**
Houlbrooke Ho. WS13: Lich 3C **114**
Houldsworth Dr. ST6: Feg H 7B **12**
Houndel Gro. WV5: Womb 3F **145**
HOUNDHILL 3D **82**
Housefield Rd. ST2: Bent 1K **33**
Houseman Dr. ST3: W Coy 4B **34**
Houston Av. ST9: End 1A **50**
Houting B77: Dost 5K **141**
Hoveringham Dr. ST2: Buck 7F **25**
Howard Cl. ST9: Werr 4D **26**
ST13: Lee 5D **48**
Howard Cres. ST1: H'ley 6K **151** (6E **24**)
WS12: Hed 3J **101**
Howard Gro. ST5: N'tle 7B **152** (3E **30**)
Howard Pl. ST1: H'ley 7D **150** (6B **24**)
ST5: N'tle 7A **152** (3E **30**)
Howard Rd. ST17: Staf 7G **73**
WV11: Wed 5K **125**
Howard St. ST3: Long 7J **33**
Howard Wlk. ST3: Long 7J **33**
Howdle's La. WS8: Brow 2H **121**
Howe Cres. WV12: Will 7C **126**
HOWE GREEN 3D **165**
Howe Gro. ST5: N'tle 6C **22**
Howitt Cres. ST14: Utt 4G **63**
Howland Cl. WV9: P'ord 3H **123**
HOWLE 2A **158**
Howson St. ST1: H'ley 5H **151** (5D **24**)
Hoylake B77: Amin 5D **138**
Hoylake Cl. WS3: Blox 2H **127**
Hoylake Rd. WV6: Per 1E **128**
HUDDLESFORD 3J **115** (1B **164**)
Huddlesford La. WS13: W'ton 3J **115**
WS14: W'ton 3J **115**
Huddlestone Cl. WV10: Fea 6F **117**
Huddocks Vw. WS3: Pels 7B **120**
Hudson Cl. ST20: Gno 2J **67**
WS11: H Hay 1H **109**
Hudson Dr. WS7: Burn 5A **112**
Hudson Gro. WV6: Per 1F **129**
Hudson Wlk. *ST3: Long* *5J 33*
(off Caroline St.)
HUGGLESCOTE 3D **161**
Hugh Bourne Pl. ST8: Brin F 4B **12**
Hughes Av. ST5: N'tle 6F **23**
Hughes St. ST6: B'lem 1A **24**
HUGHLEY .2A **162**
Hugh Porter Way WV6: Tett 6H **123**
Hughson Gro. ST6: Nort 4E **18**
Hugo St. ST13: Lee 4F **49**
Hugo Way TF9: Logg 5E **60**
HULLAND .3C **157**
Hulland Cl. ST5: Sil 7K **21**
HULLAND MOSS 3C **157**
HULLAND WARD 3C **157**
Hullock's Pool Rd. ST7: Aud 2F **15**
HULME 1C **34** (3D **155**)
Hulme Cl. ST5: Sil 7K **21**
HULME END 2B **156**
Hulme La. ST3: W Coy 6C **26**
ST9: Werr 6C **26**
Hulme Rd. ST3: W Coy 4B **34**
Hulme St. ST4: S Tren 1J **31**
HULME WALFIELD 1C **155**
Hulse St. ST4: Fen 3H **33**
Hulton Rd. ST2: A Hul 2H **25**
Hulton St. ST1: H'ley 1H **151** (3D **24**)
Humber Dr. ST8: Bidd 5E **8**
Humbert Rd. ST1: H'ley 5A **150** (5K **23**)
Humber Way ST5: N'tle 6F **31**
Humphrey's Rd. WV10: Bush 6B **124**
Humphries Ho. WS8: Brow 5H **121**
Hungerford La. CW3: Mad 4B **28**
HUNGRYHATTON 2A **158**
HUNNINGTON 3D **163**
Hunslet Rd. WS7: Burn 3K **111**
Huntbach St. ST1: H'ley 3G **151** (4C **24**)
Hunter Av. WS7: Burn 4K **111**
Hunter Cl. WS14: Lich 5D **114**
Hunter Rd. WS11: Cann 3E **108**
Hunters Cl. ST8: Bidd 5C **8**
ST18: Gt Hay 3G **81**
Hunters Dr. ST4: P'ull 3K **31**
Hunters Point TF9: Logg 4D **60**
Hunters Ride ST17: Staf 3G **77**
Hunters Row ST16: Staf 3G **73**
Hunter St. DE14: B Tre 6D **84**
Hunters Way ST4: P'ull 4K **31**
ST7: Talk 6B **10**
Huntilee Rd. ST6: Tuns 4J **17**
Huntingdon Cl. B78: Tam 7F **137**
Huntingdon Pl. ST1: H'ley 2F **25**
Huntingdon Rd. DE15: Stap 5E **86**
HUNTINGTON
Cannock 3C **100** (3D **159**)
Telford 1A **162**
Huntington Belt WS11: Hun 4D **100**
Huntington Rd. WV12: Will 6D **126**
Huntington Ter. Rd. WS11: Cann 6F **101**
HUNTLEY 7B **54** (3A **156**)
Huntley Av. ST4: P'ull 3A **32**
Huntley Cl. ST10: Chea 7C **54**
Huntley La. ST10: Chea . . . . .7A **54** & 1F **55**
Huntsbank Dr. ST5: C'ton 6B **16**
HUNTS GREEN 2B **164**
Hunt's La. WV12: Will 7D **126**
Huntsmans Dr. DY7: Kin 4D **148**
Huntsmans Ga. WS7: Burn 3K **111**
Huntsman's Hill WS15: U Lon 7A **98**
Huntsmans Ri. WS12: Hun 2C **100**
Huntsmans Wlk. DY7: Kin 3D **148**
WS15: Rug 7E **94**
Hunt St. ST6: Tuns 4J **17**
HURLEY 2C **165**
Hurlingham Rd. ST16: Staf 6D **70**
Huron Cl. WS11: H Hay 1H **109**
Huron Gro. ST4: Tren 2A **40**
Hurricane Cl. ST16: Staf 4D **70**
Hurricane Gro. ST6: Tuns 3G **17**
Hurstbourne Cl. *WS15: Rug* *6E 94*
(off Lansdowne Way)
Hurst Cl. ST7: T Pit 1B **16**
Hurst Dr. DE13: Stre 2F **85**
HURST GREEN 3A **154**
Hurstmead Dr. ST17: Wild 2A **78**
Hurstons La. ST10: Alt 5H **57**
Hurst Rd. ST8: Bidd 1F **9**
Hurst St. ST3: Long 6G **33**
Husphins La. WV8: Cods, C Woo 7A **92**
Hussey Cl. ST19: Penk 5H **91**
Hussey Rd. WS8: Brow 4G **121**
WS11: N Can 6B **110**
Hutchinson Cl. WS15: Rug 6D **94**
Hutchinson Wlk. ST3: Long 6G **33**
Hut Hill La. WS6: G Wyr 7G **109**
Hutton Way ST2: Bent 6K **25**
Huxley Cl. WV9: P'ord 2J **123**
Huxley Pl. ST3: Long 5K **33**
Hyacinth Ct. ST5: N'tle 1F **153** (6G **23**)
Hyacinth Rd ST4: S Tren 2K **153** (7J **23**)
HYDE, THE 4F **149**
Hyde Cl. DY7: Kin 4E **148**
Hyde Ct. ST17: Staf 7F **73**
Hyde La. DY7: Kin 4E **148**
HYDE LEA 2E **76** (2D **159**)
Hyde Lea Bank ST18: Hyde L 2E **76**
Hyde Mill Cft. ST19: Brew 3C **92**
Hyde Mill La. ST19: Brew 3B **92**
Hyde Pk. Ind. Est. ST4: S Tren 3C **32**
Hyde Rd. WV11: Wed 7H **125**
Hydrant Way ST18: Staf 2A **74**
Hylstone Cres. WV11: Wed 7H **125**
Hylton Cl. DE14: B'ton 5B **86**
Hyndley Cl. ST2: Buck 5G **25**
Hyssop Cl. WS11: H Hay 1H **109**
Hyssop Pl. ST6: Nort 5D **18**

I

Ian Rd. ST7: New 4H **11**
IBLE 2C **157**
Ibsen Rd. ST3: W Coy 5C **34**
IBSTOCK .3D **161**
Ibstock St. DE13: B Tre 5C **84**
Icknield Cl. B74: S'ly 7F **135**
Idonia Rd. WV6: Per 1F **129**
IDRIDGEHAY 3C **157**
IGHTFIELD 1A **158**
Ikins Dr. ST7: Big E 5H **15**
ILAM 2B **156**
Ilam Cl. ST5: Sil 7K **21**
Ilam Pk. 2B **156**
Ilam Pk. Info. Cen. 2B **156**
Ilford Side ST3: Blur 2E **40**
Ilkley Pl. ST5: Sil 6K **21**
ILLEY 3D **163**
ILLIDGE GREEN 1B **154**
Illshaw WV9: P'ord 2K **123**
Image Bus. Pk. WS12: Hed 7H **101**
Imandra Cl. ST4: Tren 3A **40**
Imex Bus. Pk. DE14: B Tre 1C **86**
ST4: Tren 3D **40**
I-Mex Bus. Pk. ST4: Fen 4F **33**
Imogen Cl. ST4: Fen 3H **33**
Imperial Ct. ST1: H'ley 6H **151** (6D **24**)
Impstones ST20: Gno 5G **67**
Inchlaggan Rd. WV10: W'ton 7D **124**
Inge Dr. DE13: Alre 6C **130**
Ingelow Cl. ST3: Blur 7G **33**
INGESTRE 1J **75** (2D **159**)
Ingestre Cl. WS3: Blox 2F **127**
WS11: H Hay 2H **109**
Ingestre Rd. ST17: Staf 5G **73**
WV10: Oxl 4A **124**
Ingestre Sq. ST3: Blur 2E **40**
Ingleborough Pl. ST2: L Oak 6K **19**
INGLEBY 2D **161**
Ingleby Gdns. WV6: W'ton 7J **123**
Ingleby Rd. ST3: Blur 2E **40**
Inglefield Av. ST6: B'lem 6B **18**
Inglemere Dr. ST17: Wild 1A **78**
Ingleside WS15: Rug 7E **94**
Ingleton Gro. ST3: Mei 3C **42**
Inglewood ST17: Staf 5F **73**
Inglewood Dr. ST5: N'tle 2G **23**
Inglewood Gro. ST5: N'tle 2G **23**
Inglis St. ST4: S Tren 1C **32**
Ingot Cl. WS2: Wals 7H **127**
Ingram Pit La. B77: Amin 4C **138**
Ingram Pl. WS3: Blox 4K **127**
Ingram Rd. WS3: Blox 4J **127**
Inkerman Ter. ST13: Lee 2E **48**
Instow Cl. WV12: Will 5B **126**
Intake La. ST20: C Eat 2A **68**
Intake Rd. ST6: Nort 3D **18**
Inworth WV9: P'ord 2K **123**
Iona Pl. ST3: Long 6F **33**
IPSTONES 2H **53** (3A **156**)
Ipswich Wlk. ST2: Bent 6H **25**
Irene Av. ST5: N'tle 1H **153** (6H **23**)
ST6: Tuns 4K **17**
Ireton Rd. WV10: Bush 2C **124**
IRETON WOOD 3C **157**
Iris Cl. B79: Tam 3J **137**
ST3: W Coy 4E **34**
IRONBRIDGE 1A **162**
Ironbridge Dr. ST5: N'tle 2A **152** (7D **22**)
Ironmarket ST5: N'tle 3E **152** (7F **23**)
Ironstone La. WS13: Lich 5K **107**
Ironstone Rd. WS7: C Ter 2F **111**
WS12: Haz 7E **102**
IRONVILLE .2D **157**
Ironwalls La. DE13: Tut 3H **83**
Irvine Cl. WS3: Blox 6H **127**
Irvine Rd. ST9: Werr 4E **26**
WS3: Blox 5H **127**
Irving Cl. WS13: Lich 1J **113**
Irwell B77: Wiln 1A **142**
Isabel Cl. ST17: Staf 6D **72**
Isherwood Pl. ST3: Long 5K **33**
Island, The B78: M Oak 1C **140**
ST10: Tea 3F **55**
Island Grn. ST17: Staf 1B **78**
Island Reach ST1: H'ley 1A **150** (3K **23**)
Islay Wlk. ST3: Long 6G **33**
ISLEY WALTON 2D **161**
ISLINGTON 2B **158**
Itchen Gro. WV6: Per 3F **129**
Ivanhoe Rd. WS14: Lich 5B **114**
Ivatt B77: Glas 7B **138**
IVETSEY BANK 4D **90** (3C **159**)
Ivetsey Bank Rd. ST19: B Elm 6C **90**
Ivetsey Cl. ST19: Whe A 3B **90**
Ivetsey Rd. ST19: Whe A 4A **90**
Ivy Cl. ST11: B Bri 4H **43**
ST14: Utt .5F **63**
ST17: Act T 6K **77**
WS11: Cann 3D **108**
Ivy Cott. Mobile Home Pk.
ST18: Hopt 5G **69**
Ivy Ct. ST17: Act T 6J **77**
ST18: Hixon 6B **80**
Ivy Cft. WV9: P'ord 2H **123**
Ivy Gdns. WS11: N Can 6C **110**
Ivy Gro. DE13: B Tre 4D **84**
ST4: Tren 2K **39**
WS8: W Woo 7J **121**
Ivyhouse Dr. ST12: Barl 6E **40**
Ivy Ho. Rd. ST1: H'ley 3K **151** (5E **24**)
ST8: G Hea 3C **8**
Ivyhouse Wlk. B77: Wiln 4B **142**
Ivy La. WS15: Can W 5H **103**
Ivy Lodge Cl. DE15: Stap 5F **87**
Izaak Walton Cl. ST16: Staf 7F **71**
Izaak Walton Cottage Mus. 2C **159**
Izaak Walton St. ST16: Staf 1F **73**

Izaak Walton Wlk.—Kiddemore Green

Izaak Walton Wlk. ST16: Staf 4F 73
Izaak Walton Way CW3: Mad 4A 28

J

Jack Ashley Ct. ST4: Fen 3D 32
JACKFIELD 1A 162
Jackfield St. ST6: B'lem 6B 18
Jack Haye La. ST2: L Oak ...6K 19 & 1B 26
Jacklin Cl. DE14: B'ton 6B 86
Jackman Cl. WS13: Frad 4K 107
Jackman Rd. WS13: Frad 4K 107
JACKSDALE 2D 157
Jacks La. ST14: Mar 3C 82
Jackson Av. DE13: Stre 4G 85
Jackson Cl. WS11: N Can 7A 110
WV10: Fea 6E 116
Jackson Rd. WS13: Lich 7B 106
Jackson St. ST6: B'lem 7A 18
Jacobean Ct. DE15: Wins 7K 85
Jacobs Cft. ST16: Staf 6E 70
Jacob's Hall La. WS6: G Wyr 3G 119
Jacqueline St. ST6: Tuns 3G 17
Jade Ct. ST3: Long 5K 33
Jade Gro. WS11: H Hay 1J 109
Jaguar B77: Glas 7A 138
Jamage Ind. Est. ST7: T Pit 1A 16
Jamage Rd. ST7: T Pit 1B 16
(not continuous)
James Brindley Cl.
ST1: H'ley 6C 150 (6A 24)
James Brindley Way DE13: Stre 2G 85
James Ct. DE14: B Tre 2E 86
(off James St.)
James Cres. ST9: Werr 4E 26
James Greenway WS13: Lich 1A 114
James St. DE14: B Tre 2D 86
DY7: Kin 5E 148
ST4: S Tren 4K 31
ST5: N'tle 3G 23
ST13: Lee 4E 48
ST14: Utt 5G 63
WS11: Cann 5F 101
James Warner Cl. WS15: Rug 7F 95
James Way ST8: Knyp 7A 8
Janet Pl. ST1: H'ley........2K 151 (4E 24)
Janine Av. WV11: Wed 6J 125
Janson St. ST4: H'ord 1K 39
Jardines La. ST14: Stub 4B 58
Jasmine Cl. DE15: Stap 4H 87
ST11: B Bri 3H 43
WV9: P'ord 2H 123
Jasmine Cres. ST7: New 4H 11
Jasmine Gro. WV8: Bilb 2D 122
Jasmine Rd. B77: Amin 5C 138
ST18: Gt Bri 6G 65
Jasmin Way ST7: Pack 5K 11
Jason Cl. B77: Tam 4K 137
Jason St. ST5: N'tle 1C 152 (6E 22)
Jasper Cl. ST5: N'tle 1F 23
ST12: Barl 6F 41
Jasper St. ST1: H'ley 5G 151 (5C 24)
Jasper Way ST15: Stone 1F 69
Java Cres. ST4: Tren 3B 40
Jaycean Av. ST6: Tuns 3J 17
Jayne Cl. WV11: Wed 6H 125
Jean Cl. ST6: B'lem 5A 18
Jedburgh Av. WV6: Per 2F 129
Jefferson St. ST6: Tuns 3H 17
Jeffery Cl. WS15: Rug 5F 95
Jenkinson Cl. ST5: N'tle 5A 152 (1D 30)
Jenkins St. ST6: B'lem 7K 17
Jenkinstown Rd. WS12: Haz 4C 102
Jenks Av. DY7: Kin 5D 148
WV10: Bush 5C 124
Jenks Rd. WV5: Womb 5F 145
Jenner Cl. WS2: Wals 7G 127
Jenner Ho. WS2: Wals 7F 127
Jenner Rd. WS2: Wals 7F 127
Jennings Way DE14: B Tre 1B 86
Jenny Walkers La. WV6: Per 6E 128
Jensen B77: Glas 7A 138
Jephson Cl. DE14: B'ton 5C 86
Jerbourg Cl. ST5: N'tle 5C 30
Jeremy Cl. ST4: P'ull 3K 31
Jerningham St. ST16: Staf 3F 73
Jerome Cl. WS11: N Can 6C 110
Jerome Dr. WS11: N Can 6C 110
Jerome Rd. WS11: N Can 6B 110
Jerome Way WS7: Burn 4K 111
Jerram's La. DE15: Stap 4F 87
Jersey Cl. ST5: N'tle 5C 30
Jersey Cres. ST3: L'ood 1J 41
Jervis Cres. B74: F Oak 5J 135
Jervis La. ST15: Mea 1B 46
Jervison St. ST3: Long 3K 33
Jervis Pk. B74: L Ast 4H 135
Jervis Rd. B77: Hock 5B 142
ST15: Stone 5H 47
Jervis St. ST1: H'ley 2J 151 (3D 24)
(not continuous)
Jesmond Cl. WS12: Haz 4C 102
Jesmond Gro. ST3: Blur 2E 40
Jessica Gro. ST2: Buck 5K 25
Jessop Dr. B77: Tam 4K 137
Jinny Cl. DE65: Hat 1H 83
Joanhurst Cres.
ST1: H'ley 6D 150 (6B 24)
JODRELL BANK 1B 154
Jodrell Vw. ST7: Kids 6F 11
Joey's La. WV8: Bilb 1E 122
John Amery Dr. ST17: Staf 1F 77
John Ball Cl. WS15: Rug 5F 95
John Bright St. ST1: H'ley ...1J 151 (3D 24)
John Donne St. ST16: Staf 7F 71
Johndory B77: Dost 5K 141
John Offley Rd. CW3: Mad 3A 28
John O'Gaunt's Rd.
ST5: N'tle 3C 152 (7E 22)
John Pershall Ct. ST21: Ecc 2G 65
(off High St.)
John Rhodes Way ST6: Tuns 2G 17
John Riley Dr. WV12: Will 5C 126
Johns Av. WS15: Hand 5G 99
Johnsgate ST19: Brew 1D 92
Johns La. WS6: G Wyr 1F 119
Johnson Av. ST5: N'tle 4E 22
WV11: Wed 6K 125
Johnson Cl. WS13: Lich 2C 114
WS15: Rug 6F 95
Johnson Cres. ST10: K'ley 6F 53
Johnson Gro. ST15: Stone 5K 47
Johnson Pl. ST6: Feg H 1B 18
Johnson Rd. ST14: Utt 4G 63
WS7: C Ter 3H 111
WS11: Cann 6D 100
WV12: Will 6D 126
Johnstone Av. ST9: Werr 4E 26
John St. B77: Amin 6A 138
ST1: H'ley 4G 151 (5C 24)
ST5: C'ton 7C 16
ST5: N'tle 6C 22
(Knutton)
ST5: N'tle 3H 153 (7H 23)
(Newcastle-under-Lyme)
ST8: Bidd 6C 8
ST13: Lee 4F 49
ST14: Utt 5G 63
ST16: Staf 2J 73
WS11: Cann 5F 101
WS12: Wimb 6B 102
John Till Cl. WS15: Rug 7G 95
JOINER'S SQUARE 7J 151 (6D 24)
Joiner's Sq. Ind. Est. ST1: H'ley 6H 151
Jolley St. ST6: B'lem 6C 18
Jolliffe St. ST13: Lee 4F 49
(off Cornhill St.)
Jolly Sailor Island B78: Tam 5G 137
Jolly Sailor Retail Pk. B78: Tam 6F 137
Jolt La. ST18: Hau 7B 66
Jolyon Cl. ST4: Fen 3H 33
Jonathan Rd. ST4: Tren 6C 40
Jones Cl. ST17: Staf 7F 73
WS13: Frad 1K 107
Jones La. WS7: Burn 4D 112
WS15: S Mil 1E 96
Jones Rd. WV10: Oxl 7A 124
WV12: Will 4D 126
Jones's La. WS6: G Wyr 3G 119
Jonkel Av. B77: Hock 5B 142
Jordan Av. DE13: Stre 1G 85
Jordan Cl. WS13: Frad 4K 107
WS13: Lich 3A 114
Jordan Cft. WS13: Frad 3K 107
Jordan St. ST1: H'ley 6D 150 (6B 24)
Jordan Way ST15: Stone 5H 47
Joseph Dewsbury Cl. WS7: C Ter ...3H 111
Joseph Dix Dr. WS15: Rug 6F 95
Joseph St. ST6: B'lem 7J 17
Josiah Wedgwood St.
ST1: H'ley 4C 150 (5A 24)
Joules Dr. ST15: Stone 1E 46
Joules Pas. ST15: Stone 4G 47
(off Market Pl.)
Jowett B77: Glas 7K 137
Joyce Av. ST6: B'lem 5B 18
Joyce's La. ST17: Bed H 7E 78
Jubilee Av. ST1: H'ley 5C 150 (5A 24)
Jubilee Cl. ST8: Bidd 6D 8
WS6: G Wyr 2F 119
Jubilee Ct. ST14: Utt 6G 63
ST16: Staf 1H 73
Jubilee Pool 3F 153 (7G 23)
Jubilee Ri. DE15: Wins 1K 87
(off Canterbury Rd.)
Jubilee Rd. ST4: Tren 2K 39
ST5: N'tle 5H 23
Jubilee Sq. DE6: May 6C 56
Jubilee St. WS15: Rug 7F 95
Jubilee Ter. ST13: Lee 3E 48
Jude Wlk. WS13: Lich 1K 113
Judgefield La. ST6: B Edg 4F 13
Judith Gro. ST4: Fen 4C 32
JUGBANK 5G 61
Jug Bank ST6: B'lem 2B 24
TF9: A'ley 5H 61
Julian Cl. WS6: G Wyr 1G 119
Junction Rd. ST13: Lee 5E 48
June Cres. B77: Amin 4A 138
June Rd. ST4: Fen 3H 33
Juniper B77: Amin 5C 138
Juniper Cl. ST3: Mei 4C 42
ST5: C'ton 6C 16
WS12: Haz 4C 102
Jupiter Bus. Pk. ST18: S Char 4C 80
Jupiter St. ST6: B'lem 6C 18
Jupiter Way ST17: Staf 6J 73
Justin Cl. ST5: N'tle 2H 23

K

Kamienna Cl. ST17: Staf 6H 73
Kara Pl. ST4: Tren 2B 40
Kaydor Cl. ST9: Werr 4D 26
Kean Cl. WS13: Lich 1J 113
Kearsley Way ST3: Blur 2E 40
Keary St. ST4: S Tren 3B 32
Keates St. ST6: B'lem 7K 17
Keats Av. ST17: Staf 7E 72
WS11: Cann 5E 100
Keats Cl. B79: Tam 1F 137
Keats Gdns. ST7: Kids 6E 10
Keats Gro. WV10: Bush 5E 124
Keats Rd. WV10: Bush 3E 124
WV12: Will 6E 126
Keble Cl. DE15: Stap 2K 87
WS7: Burn 4A 112
WS11: Cann 3E 108
Keble Wlk. B79: Tam 3G 137
(not continuous)
Keble Way ST3: Blur 7F 33
KEDLESTON 3D 157
Kedleston Cl. DE13: Stre 2D 84
WS3: Blox 2G 127
Kedleston Rd. ST6: B'lem 5A 18
KEELE 2H 29 (3C 155)
Keele By-Pass ST5: Keel 1G 29
Keele Observatory 2A 30
Keele Rd. CW3: Mad H 5A 152 (1D 28)
ST5: Keel, Mad H 1D 28
ST5: Keel, N'tle 2J 29
Keele St. ST6: Tuns 3H 17
Keele University 2K 29
Keele University Art Gallery 2K 29
Keele University Leisure Cen. 2K 29
Keeling Dr. WS11: Cann 2B 108
Keeling Rd. ST10: Chea 4D 54
Keelings Dr. ST4: T Val 5J 31
Keelings Rd. ST1: H'ley 1J 151 (3D 24)
Keeling St. ST5: N'tle 2G 23
Keene Cl. ST6: Nort 4E 18
Keep, The ST17: Staf 6E 72
Keepers Cl. ST11: B Bri 4J 43
WS7: Burn 5J 111
WS14: Lich 4E 114
Keepers La. WV6: Tett 4C 122
WV8: Cods 3C 122
Keepers Rd. B74: L Ast 3H 135
Keld Av. ST17: Staf 6C 72
Kelly Av. WS15: Rug 3H 97
Kelly Grn. ST6: Feg H 1B 18
Kelman Rd. ST4: Fen 3G 33
Kelmore Cl. ST3: Long 5H 33
Kelsall St. ST6: B'lem 6B 18
Kelsall Way ST7: Aud 6F 15
Kelso Gdns. WV6: Per 2E 128
KELSTEDGE 1D 157
Kelvedon Way WS15: Rug 7E 94
Kelverstone Ho.
WS11: Cann 2D 108
Kelvin Av. ST1: H'ley 2D 24
Kelvin Dr. WS11: Cann 7G 101
Kelvin Pl. WS2: Wals 7H 127
Kelvin Rd. WS2: Wals 7G 127
Kelvin St. ST5: N'tle 4H 23
Kemball Av. ST4: Fen 5C 32
KEMBERTON 1B 162
Kemberton Cl. WV3: W'ton 5K 129
Kemberton Rd. WV3: W'ton 5K 129
Kemnay Av. ST6: Feg H 6B 12
Kempson Rd. ST19: Penk 3H 91
Kempthorne Av. WV10: Bush 4C 124
Kempthorne Gdns. WS3: Blox 3G 127
Kempthorne Rd.
ST1: H'ley 7J 151 (6D 24)
Kempton Cl. WS12: Haz 4C 102
Kempton Dr. B77: Dost 6K 141
WS6: G Wyr 2F 119
Kempton Gro. ST10: Chea 2D 54
Kempton Rd. DE15: Wins 1H 87
Kendal Cl. ST17: Staf 7D 72
WV6: Tett 7H 123
Kendal Ct. WS11: Cann 3B 108
Kendal Gro. ST2: Buck 6K 25
Kendal Pl. ST5: N'tle 3F 31
Kendal Ri. WV6: Tett 7H 123
Kenderdine Cl. ST17: Bed 7D 78
Kendrick Rd. WV10: Bush 7C 124
Kendrick St. ST3: Long 6J 33
Kenelyn Cres. ST3: Fen 5E 32
Kenilworth Av. DE13: Stre 4E 84
Kenilworth Cl. ST19: Penk 4J 91
Kenilworth Ct. WS11: Cann 2E 108
Kenilworth Dr. WS11: Cann 6D 100
Kenilworth Gro. ST3: Mei 1B 42
ST5: N'tle 5J 23
Kenilworth Ho. WS3: Blox 7J 127
(off Providence La.)
Kenilworth Rd. B77: Amin 5A 138
WS14: Lich 5B 114
WV6: Per 2G 129
Kenilworth Wlk. ST10: Chea 5A 54
KENLEY 1A 162
Kenley Av. ST9: End 1B 50
Kenmore Av. WS12: Hed 3F 101
Kennedy Cl. B77: T Gat 1J 141
Kennedy Pl. ST21: Ecc 3G 65
Kennedy Rd. ST4: Tren 3B 40
Kennedy Wlk. ST9: Werr 4D 26
Kennedy Way ST16: Staf 5D 70
Kennermont Rd. ST2: A Hul 3J 25
Kennet B77: Wiln 1K 141
Kennet Cl. ST5: N'tle 6F 31
WS8: Brow 2E 120
Kennington Oval ST4: Tren 3C 40
Kennington Rd. WV10: W'ton 7D 124
(off Eastcote Rd.)
Kenrose Mill DY7: Kin 6F 149
Kensington Cl. ST15: Stone 7J 47
Kensington Ct. ST4: T Val 6J 31
ST6: Tuns 3J 17
Kensington Dr. B74: F Oak 3K 135
B79: Tam 2H 137
ST18: Staf 2A 74
Kensington Gdns. WS11: Cann 1C 108
Kensington Pl. WS12: H Hay 2J 109
Kensington Rd. DE15: Wins 1H 87
ST4: T Val 5K 31
WV12: Will 6B 126
KENSTONE 2A 158
Kensworth Cl. ST5: N'tle 6E 30
Kent Av. B78: Tam 7F 137
Kent Dr. ST9: End 3A 50
Kent Gro. ST5: C'ton 7B 16
ST15: Stone 2F 47
Kentish Cl. ST17: Staf 6C 72
Kentmere Cl. ST4: Fen 4H 33
ST17: Staf 6D 72
ST19: Penk 3J 91
Kentmere Pl. ST5: N'tle 4F 31
Kent Pl. ST4: Fen 3E 32
WS12: H Hay 2A 110
Kent Rd. DE15: Stap 6F 87
Kents La. ST5: Sil 5H 21
Kents Row ST12: Barl 1E 44
Kent St. WS2: Wals 7K 127
Kent Way ST17: Staf 6K 73
Kentwell B79: Tam 2D 136
Kenworthy Rd. ST16: Staf 7G 71
Kenworthy St. ST6: Tuns 3J 17
Kepler B79: Tam 2E 136
KERESLEY 3D 165
KERESLEY NEWLAND 3D 165
Kerria Cen. B77: Amin 5C 138
Kerria Rd. B77: Amin 5D 138
Kerridge Cl. WV9: P'ord 3J 123
KERRY HILL 1A 26
Kerry La. ST21: Ecc 3F 65
Kersbrook Cl. ST4: Tren 4C 40
Kersley Gdns. WV11: Wed 7K 125
Kervis Gro. ST3: Mei 4D 42
Kesterton Rd. B74: F Oak 3K 135
Kesteven Wlk. ST2: Buck 5H 25
Kestral Ct. WS7: Burn 3D 112
Kestrel B77: Wiln 4C 142
Kestrel Av. ST3: Mei 3E 42
Kestrel Cl. ST8: Knyp 7B 8
ST14: Utt 7G 63
ST17: Staf 5A 74
Kestrel Dr. TF9: Logg 5D 60
Kestrel Gro. WS12: H Hay 2J 109
WV12: Will 5C 126
Kestrel La. ST10: Chea 4D 54
Kestrel Ri. WV6: Tett 6H 123
Kestrel Way DE15: Wins 1K 87
WS6: C Hay 2C 118
Keswick Gro. ST17: Staf 6C 72
Keswick Pl. ST5: N'tle 3F 31
Kettering Dr. ST2: Buck 6F 25
KETTLEBROOK 6J 137 (1C 165)
Kettlebrook Rd. B77: Tam 5J 137
Ketton Cl. ST6: Feg H 6B 12
Kewstoke Cl. WV12: Will 4B 126
Kewstoke Rd. WV12: Will 4B 126
Key Cl. WS12: Hed 7J 101
KEY GREEN 1C 155
Keynsham Wlk. ST6: B'lem 5D 18
Keys Pk. 7K 101
Keys Pk. Rd.
WS12: Hed, Wimb 7K 101
Keystone La. WS15: Rug 1H 97
Keystone M. WS15: Rug 1H 97
Keystone Rd. WS15: Rug 1H 97
Keyworth Wlk. ST2: Buck 6G 25
Kibblestone Rd. ST15: Oul 7H 45
Kibworth Gro. ST1: H'ley 1F 151 (3C 24)
Kidbrooke Pl. ST3: Blur 2D 40
KIDDEMORE GREEN 7E 90 (1C 163)

Kiddemore Grn. Rd.—Landywood

Kiddemore Grn. Rd.
ST19: B Elm, Brew 7D **90**
ST19: Brew 2A **92**
KIDDERMINSTER 3C **163**
Kidderminster Rd. DY7: Stou 1K **149**
KIDSGROVE 5E **10** (2C **155**)
Kidsgrove Bank ST7: Kids 6F **11**
Kidsgrove Rd. ST6: Gold 6G **11**
Kidsgrove Ski Cen. 7D **10**
Kidsgrove Sports Cen. 5D **10**
Kidsgrove Station (Rail) 5D **10**
Kielder Cl. WS12: H Hay 1A **110**
KILBURN 3D **157**
Kilburn Pl. ST2: Buck 6F **25**
Kilbye Cl. B77: Hock 5B **142**
Kildare St. ST3: Long 7J **33**
(not continuous)
Kilmorie Rd. WS11: Cann 1C **108**
Kiln Cft. ST10: Tea 3F **55**
Kilndown Cl. ST1: H'ley . . . 6C **150** (6A **24**)
Kiln La. ST13: Lee 3D **48**
Kiln Way B78: Pole 1H **143**
Kilsby Gro. ST2: Mil 5H **19**
Kimberley B77: Wiln 3B **142**
Kimberley Bus. Pk. WS15: Bre 4H **97**
Kimberley Cl. B74: S'ly 5F **135**
Kimberley Dr. DE15: Wins 1K **87**
ST14: Utt 4E **62**
Kimberley Grange
ST5: N'tle 1E **152** (6F **23**)
Kimberley Rd. ST1: H'ley . . 5B **150** (5A **24**)
ST5: N'tle 1D **152** (6F **23**)
Kimberley St. ST3: Long 7H **33**
Kimberley Way ST17: Staf 6C **72**
WS15: Bre 4H **97**
Kinder Pl. ST5: Sil 7K **21**
Kinfare Dr. WV6: Tett 2J **129**
King Charles Cl. ST3: Mei 3C **42**
Kingcross St. ST3: Long 6J **33**
Kingcup Rd. ST17: Staf 2G **77**
King Edward VI Leisure Cen. 5C **114**
King Edward Pl. DE14: B Tre 1C **86**
King Edward St. ST10: Chea 3D **54**
Kingfisher B77: Wiln 4C **142**
Kingfisher Cl. CW3: Mad 2B **28**
WS8: Brow 5G **121**
Kingfisher Ct. WS7: Burn 3D **112**
Kingfisher Cres. ST10: Chea 4E **54**
ST11: Ful 3G **59**
Kingfisher Dr. ST18: Colw 6K **81**
WS12: Hed 6J **101**
Kingfisher Gro. ST6: B'lem 4C **18**
WV12: Will 5B **126**
Kingfisher Holiday Pk.
DE13: Alre 1F **107**
Kingfisher Wlk. ST19: Penk 4H **91**
Kingfisher Way ST14: Utt 7G **63**
King George St.
ST1: H'ley 1J **151** (3D **24**)
King Georges Way ST7: Kids 5G **11**
Kings Av. ST5: N'tle 3G **23**
ST15: Stone 3F **47**
WS12: Hed 6J **101**
Kings Bri. WV9: Cove 1J **93**
Kingsbridge Av. ST5: N'tle 4F **31**
KING'S BROMLEY 2C **130** (3B **160**)
King's Bromley La. DE13: K Bro 3G **99**
WS15: Hand, K Bro 3G **99**
King's Bromley Rd. DE13: Alre 6A **130**
KINGSBURY 2C **165**
Kingsbury Cl. DE15: Wins 7H **85**
Kingsbury Gro. ST1: H'ley 2F **25**
Kingsbury Link B78: Pic 7C **142**
Kingsclere Gro. ST1: H'ley 1E **24**
Kingsclere Wlk. WV4: Pen 7K **129**
King's Cft. ST4: S Tren 3J **153** (7H **23**)
Kingscroft ST18: L Hay 5J **81**
WS12: Wimb 6A **102**
Kingsdale Cl. ST3: Mei 3C **42**
Kingsdale Cft. DE13: Stre 3E **84**
Kingsdown M. ST5: N'tle 5G **31**
Kingsdown Rd. WS7: C Ter 2F **111**
Kings Dr. ST18: Hopt 7G **69**
Kingsfield Cres. ST8: Bidd 5D **8**
Kingsfield Oval
ST4: S Tren 2H **153** (7H **23**)
Kingsfield Rd.
ST4: S Tren 2J **153** (7H **23**)
ST8: Bidd 5D **8**
KINGSFORD 3C **163**
Kingsford La. DY7: Wolv 7B **148**
DY11: Wolv 7A **148**
Kingsford Pl. ST3: Mei 2C **42**
KING'S HEATH 3A **164**
King's Hill Rd. WS14: Lich 5C **114**
KINGSHURST 3B **164**
Kingside Gro. ST4: Tren 5C **40**
Kingsland Av. ST4: S Tren 5K **31**
Kingsland Cl. ST15: Stone 5J **47**
Kingsland Ct. *ST15: Stone 5J 47*
(off Kingsland Rd.)
Kingsland Rd. ST15: Stone 5J **47**
KINGSLEY 5F **53** (3A **156**)
Kingsley & Froghall Station
Churnet Valley Railway 5K **53**
Kingsley Av. WS12: Hed 3J **101**
WV6: Tett 2J **129**
KINGSLEY BANKS 5J **53**
Kingsley Cl. B79: Tam 3G **137**
ST7: T Pit 1B **16**
ST17: Staf 6G **73**
Kingsley Gdns. WV8: Cods 2A **122**
KINGSLEY HOLT 7J **53** (3A **156**)
Kingsley Rd. DE14: B Tre 4E **84**
ST7: T Pit 1B **16**
ST9: Werr 4H **27**
ST10: Dilh 4H **27**
ST10: K'ley 5F **53**
ST17: Staf 6G **73**
Kingsley St. ST3: Mei 1C **42**
Kingsley Vw. ST13: Ched 5H **51**
Kingsley Wood Rd. WS15: Rug 2A **96**
Kingsmead DE13: Stre 3F **85**
Kingsmead Marsh Nature Reserve
. . . . 3H **73**
Kingsmead Rd. ST3: L'ood 3B **42**
KING'S NEWNHAM 3D **165**
KINGS NEWTON 2D **161**
Kingsnorth Pl. ST3: Mei 4D **42**
KING'S NORTON 3A **164**
Kings Pl. ST4: S Tren 1J **153** (6H **23**)
Kings Rd. ST4: H'ord 1A **40**
WV10: Calf H 5K **93**
KINGSTANDING 2A **164**
KING STERNDALE 1A **156**
Kings Ter. ST4: S Tren 2J **153** (7H **23**)
Kingston Av. ST1: H'ley 1E **24**
ST16: Staf 2K **73**
Kingston Cen., The ST16: Staf 3J **73**
Kingston Cl. B79: Tam 2J **137**
Kingston Ct. WS11: Cann 2E **108**
Kingston Dr. ST15: Stone 6H **47**
KINGSTONE 2A **160**
KINGSTON HILL 3B **74**
Kingston Hill Ct. ST16: Staf 3A **74**
Kingston Pl. ST6: Nort 4E **18**
ST8: Bidd 3E **8**
Kingston Rd. DE15: Wins 2K **87**
Kingston Row ST16: Staf 3J **73**
King St. B79: Tam 4H **137**
DE13: Yox 1H **89**
DE14: B Tre 4D **86**
ST3: Long 3E **32**
ST4: Fen 3E **32**
ST5: C'ton 1C **22**
ST5: N'tle 5E **22**
(Cross Heath)
ST5: N'tle 3F **153** (7G **23**)
(Newcastle-under-Lyme)
ST7: Aud 6F **15**
ST7: Kids 4E **10**
ST7: T Pit 2B **16**
(not continuous)
ST8: Bidd 5C **8**
ST13: Lee 4F **49**
WS7: Chas 6H **111**
WS15: Rug 1H **97**
Kings Wlk. DE13: K Bro 2B **130**
Kingsway DE14: B'ton 4C **86**
ST4: S Tren 2B **32**
ST16: Staf 4E **72**
WS11: Cann 6G **101**
WV10: W'ton 7E **124**
WV11: Ess 1A **126**
Kingsway E. ST5: N'tle 3F **31**
Kingsway Rd. WV10: W'ton 7E **124**
Kingsway W. ST5: N'tle 3E **30**
Kingswear Av. WV6: Per 3G **129**
Kingswell Rd.
ST4: S Tren 3J **153** (7H **23**)
KINGSWINFORD 3C **163**
Kingswinford Pl. ST6: B'lem 1D **24**
Kingswood ST7: Kids 5F **11**
Kingswood Av. WS11: Cann 4C **108**
KINGSWOOD COMMON 1C **163**
Kingswood Dr. WS6: G Wyr 7G **109**
WS11: N Can 6B **110**
Kington Cl. WV12: Will 5B **126**
King William St. ST6: Tuns 4J **17**
KINLET 3B **162**
Kinlet Cl. WV3: W'ton 6H **129**
Kinnersley Av. ST7: Kids 6D **10**
Kinnersley St. ST7: Kids 4E **10**
Kinross Av. WS12: Hed 3F **101**
Kinsall Grn. B77: Wiln 4E **142**
KINSEY HEATH 3A **154**
Kinsey St. ST5: Sil 7K **21**
KINVER 4E **148** (3C **163**)
Kinver Cl. DE6: May 5B **56**
Kinver Edge 7B **148**
Kinver Leisure Cen. 4E **148**
Kinver Mt. DY7: Kin 6E **148**
Kinver Rd. DE15: Wins 7H **85**
DY7: Kin, Stou 7H **147**
Kinver St. ST6: B'lem 6C **18**
Kipling Av. WS7: C Ter 2J **111**
Kipling Ri. B79: Tam 1F **137**
Kipling Rd. WV10: Ford 3B **124**
WV12: Will 6E **126**
Kipling Way ST2: Bent 7K **25**
Kirby St. ST6: B'lem 2A **24**
Kirkbride Cl. ST3: Long 5K **33**
KIRK HALLAM 3D **157**
Kirkham Lodge ST13: Ched 3G **51**
Kirkham St. ST4: S Tren 3A **32**
KIRK IRETON 2C **157**
Kirkland La. ST4: P'ull 2A **32**
Kirkland Way B78: M Oak 2B **140**
KIRK LANGLEY 1C **161**
Kirkside Gro. WS8: Brow 5H **121**
Kirkside M. WS8: Brow 5H **121**
Kirkstall Av. ST17: Staf 7D **72**
Kirkstall Cl. WS3: Blox 3F **127**
Kirkstall Cres. WS3: Blox 3F **127**
Kirkstall Pl. ST5: N'tle 5F **31**
Kirkstone Cres. WV5: Womb 4F **145**
Kirk St. ST6: B'lem 5C **18**
Kirkup Wlk. ST3: Long 6G **33**
Kirkwall Gro. ST2: Mil 5H **19**
Kirmond Wlk. WV6: W'ton 7K **123**
Kirstead Gdns. WV6: Tett 3J **129**
Kirtley B77: Glas 7B **138**
Kirton Gro. WV6: Tett 1K **129**
Kitchen La. WV11: Wed 4J **125**
Kite Gro. ST3: Mei 3C **42**
ST7: Kids 3H **11**
Kitling Greaves La. DE13: B Tre 3B **84**
Kitlings La. ST17: Walt 7D **74**
Kitwood Av. B78: Dor 4H **143**
Knarsdale Cl. ST3: Long 4K **33**
Knaves Castle Av. WS8: Brow 2H **121**
KNENHALL 3K **45** (1D **159**)
Knenhall ST15: Knen 2K **45**
Knight Av. ST16: Staf 2J **73**
Knight La. ST10: Alt 5H **57**
KNIGHTLEY 2C **159**
Knightley CW3: Mad 4B **28**
Knightley Cl. ST20: Gno 3H **67**
KNIGHTLEY DALE 2C **159**
Knightley Rd. ST20: Gno 1G **67**
Knightley Way ST20: Gno 3H **67**
KNIGHTON 2B **158**
Knighton Dr. B74: F Oak 5K **135**
Knighton Rd. B74: F Oak 3J **135**
WS12: Wimb 7A **102**
Knight Rd. WS7: C Ter 2G **111**
Knights Av. WV6: Tett 7F **123**
Knightsbridge Cl. B74: F Oak 4K **135**
Knightsbridge La. WV12: Will 7C **126**
Knightsbridge Way DE13: Stre 4E **84**
ST6: Tuns 4H 17
(off Madeira Pl.)
Knights Cl. ST19: Penk 5H **91**
Knights Ct. DE13: Stre 2F **85**
WS11: N Can 7C **110**
Knights Cres. WV6: Tett 6G **123**
Knights Cft. ST5: Keel 2H **29**
Knight St. ST6: Tuns 3H **17**
Kniveden La. ST13: Lee 4H **49**
KNIVETON 2C **157**
Knoll Cl. WS7: Chas 6J **111**
KNOWL BANK 1B **20**
Knowlbank Rd. CW3: Aud 3A **20**
ST7: Aud 3A **20**
KNOWLE 3B **164**
Knowle La. WS14: Lich 1D **134**
Knowle Rd. ST8: Bidd 6C **8**
ST17: Staf 1B **78**
Knowles Hill DE13: Roll D 7H **83**
Knowle St. ST4: S Tren 1A **32**
KNOWLE STYLE 6C **8**
Knowle Wood Vw. ST3: Blur 6F **33**
KNOWL WALL 7G **39**
Knowsley La. ST7: C Law 2C **10**
Knox's Grave La. B78: Hop 2A **136**
KNUTTON 5C **22**
Knutton La. ST5: N'tle 1A **152** (6D **22**)
Knutton Recreation Cen. 6C **22**
Knutton Rd. ST5: N'tle 3G **23**
Knype Cl. ST5: Brad 1E **22**
KNYPERSLEY 1B **12** (2C **155**)
Knypersley Gdns. ST8: Knyp 1D **12**
Knypersley Rd. ST6: Nort 2E **18**
Knype Way ST5: Brad 1E **22**
ST8: Knyp 7B **8**
Kurtus B77: Dost 4K **141**
Kyffin Rd. ST2: A Hul 2H **25**
Kyle Cl. WV10: Oxl 4K **123**
Kynaston Cres. WV8: Cods 3D **122**
KYNNERSLEY 3A **158**
Kynnersley Cft. ST14: Utt 4G **63**

L

Laburnum Av. B79: Tam 1H **137**
WS11: Cann 4D **108**
Laburnum Cl. DY7: Kin 4D **148**
ST7: Kids 6C **10**
ST11: B Bri 4J **43**
ST18: Gt Bri 6G **65**
WS11: Cann 4E **108**
Laburnum Ct. WS14: Lich 6C **114**
Laburnum Gro. ST3: Fen 6E **32**
WS7: Chas 5H **111**
Laburnum Pl. ST3: L'ood 2B **42**
ST5: C'ton 6B **16**
Laburnum Rd. DE15: Stap 6G **87**
LACH DENNIS 1B **154**
LACHES, THE 1D **116**
Laches Cl. WV10: F Ash 6G **93**
Laches La. WV10: Cove 2C **116**
Ladderedge ST13: Lee, L'ton 7B **48**
Ladderedge Country Pk. 6E **48**
Lad La. ST5: N'tle 3E **152** (7F **23**)
Lady Bank B79: Tam 5H **137**
Ladybank Gro. ST3: Blur 2E **40**
Lady Bennett Ct. *ST3: Long 6G 33*
(off Grosvenor St)
Ladydale Cl. ST13: Lee 5G **49**
Ladygates CW3: Bet 2B **6**
Lady Hill Ter. WS15: S Mil 2D **96**
Lady Meadow Cl. B78: Tam 6G **137**
Ladymeadow Cl. ST14: Dens 3C **58**
LADYMOOR GATE 2H **13**
Ladymoor La. ST6: B Edg 2H **13**
Ladysmith Rd. ST1: H'ley . . 5B **150** (5A **24**)
Ladysmith St. ST3: Long 7H **33**
Ladywell Cl. DE13: Stre 2F **85**
WV5: Womb 2G **145**
Ladywell Rd. ST6: Tuns 4H **17**
(not continuous)
LADYWOOD 3A **164**
Lagonda B77: Glas 6A **138**
Lagonda Cl. ST8: Knyp 1B **12**
Lagoon Rd. B77: Wiln 4A **142**
Lagrange B79: Tam 3E **136**
Lair, The B78: Bir 2H **143**
Lakefield Rd. WV11: Wed 7J **125**
Lakeland Dr. B77: Wiln 3C **142**
Lakenheath B79: Tam 2J **137**
Lakesedge ST15: Stone 7B **46**
Lakeside B74: L Ast 3G **135**
CW3: Bet 2B **6**
ST1: H'ley 1A **150** (3K **23**)
Lakeside Cl. ST1: H'ley 6A **150** (6K **23**)
ST5: B Gat 6E **36**
Lakeside Dr. WS11: N Can 5C **110**
Lakeside Ind. Pk. B78: Faze 1F **141**
Lakeside Plaza WS11: Cann 6D **108**
Lakeside Vw. WS15: Arm 5F **99**
WS15: Rug 1H **97**
Lake Vw. ST6: B'lem 6H **17**
Lakeview Av. B78: Tam 7G **137**
Lakewood Dr. ST12: Barl 6E **40**
Lakewood Gro. ST1: H'ley . . 3B **150** (5A **24**)
Lally Pl. ST8: Brin F 4B **12**
Lamb Cres. WV5: Womb 4F **145**
Lambert Dr. WS7: C Ter 4J **111**
Lambert Rd. ST14: Utt 5E **62**
WV10: W'ton 7D **124**
Lambert St. ST6: Tuns 4J **17**
Lamb Ground, The 6J **137**
Lamb La. ST15: Stone 6F **47**
Lambourn Cl. WS3: Blox 3J **127**
Lambourne Cl. WS6: G Wyr 1F **119**
WS14: Lich 3E **114**
Lambourne Dr. ST2: L Oak 6J **19**
Lambourne Way WS11: N Can 6C **110**
Lambourn Pl. ST3: Blur 2D **40**
Lamb St. ST1: H'ley 3G **151** (4C **24**)
ST7: Kids 4E **10**
Lamerton Gro. ST3: Long 7B **34**
Lammascote Rd. ST16: Staf 3H **73**
Lamorna Cl. WV3: W'ton 6J **129**
Lamotte Cl. ST4: Fen 4H **33**
Lamprey B77: Dost 4K **141**
Lanark Walks ST5: N'tle 6A **152** (2D **30**)
Lancaster Av. ST5: N'tle 4H **153** (1H **31**)
ST11: Ful 2G **59**
ST13: Lee 2G **49**
Lancaster Bldgs. *ST5: N'tle 3E 152*
(off Ironmarket)
Lancaster Ct. ST18: Staf 1A **74**
Lancaster Cres.
ST4: S Tren 5H **153** (1H **31**)
Lancaster Dr. DE13: Tut 3G **83**
ST6: Nort 3F **19**
Lancaster Ho. WS12: H Hay 2K **109**
WS13: Fra P 6H **107**
Lancaster Pl. WS3: Blox 3J **127**
Lancaster Rd. ST5: N'tle . . . 4H **153** (1H **31**)
ST17: Staf 6J **73**
WS13: Fra P 5J **107**
Lance Dr. WS7: C Ter 2G **111**
Lancelot Dr. DE13: Stre 2F **85**
Lanchester Cl. B79: Tam 2E **136**
ST8: Knyp 7B **8**
Lancia Cl. ST8: Knyp 1B **12**
Lancing Av. ST17: Staf 6K **73**
Lander Cl. ST15: Stone 5K **47**
Lander Pl. ST6: Chel 1C **18**
Landon St. ST3: Long 6J **33**
Landor Cres. WS15: Rug 3G **97**
Landor Way ST17: Staf 6D **72**
Landrake Gro. ST6: Chel 7K **11**
Landsberg B79: Tam 3E **136**
Landseer Pl. ST5: C'ton 2C **22**
Landstone Rd. ST17: Staf 6J **73**
LANDYWOOD 2G **119** (1D **163**)

Landywood Ent. Pk.—Lichfield Health & Fitness Club

Landywood Ent. Pk. WS6: G Wyr ... 4F 119
Landywood Grn. WS6: C Hay ... 2E 118
Landywood La.
WS6: C Hay, G Wyr ... 2D 118
Landywood Station (Rail) ... 2F 119
Lane, The ST18: Copp ... 4D 76
LANE ENDS
Mickleover ... 1C 161
Stoke-on-Trent ... 4K 11
Lane Farm Gro. ST1: H'ley ... 1E 24
LANE GREEN ... 2D 122
Lane Grn. Av. WV8: Bilb ... 4E 122
Lane Grn. Ct. WV8: Bilb ... 2D 122
Lane Grn. Rd. WV8: Bilb ... 2D 122
Lane Grn. Shop. Pde. WV8: Bilb ... 2D 122
LANE HEAD ... 7C 126
Lane Head SK17: L'nor ... 2C 52
Lanehead Rd. ST1: H'ley ... 5A 150 (5K 23)
Lanehead Wlk. WS15: Rug ... 6E 94
Lanes Cl. DE13: K Bro ... 2C 130
WV5: Womb ... 5E 144
LANEY GREEN ... 2A 118 (1D 163)
Langdale Cl. WS8: Clay ... 6G 121
Langdale Ct. B77: Amin ... 3C 138
Langdale Cres. ST1: H'ley ... 1D 24
Langdale Dr. WS11: Cann ... 4B 108
Langdale Grn. WS11: Cann ... 4C 108
Langdale Rd. ST5: N'tle ... 4F 31
Langer Cl. DE14: B'ton ... 6B 86
Langford Rd. ST2: Buck ... 5J 25
ST5: N'tle ... 5E 30
Langford St. ST13: Lee ... 4E 48
Langham Rd. ST2: Mil ... 6G 19
Langholm Dr. WS12: H Hay ... 1K 109
Langland Dr. ST3: Blur ... 7F 33
LANGLEY
Heanor ... 3D 157
Macclesfield ... 1D 155
Langley Cl. ST5: C'ton ... 5B 16
LANGLEY COMMON ... 1C 161
Langley Ct. WV4: Pen ... 7K 129
LANGLEY GREEN ... 1C 161
Langley Rd. WV4: L Pen ... 7G 129
Langley St. ST4: S Tren ... 2J 153 (7H 23)
Langton Ct. ST9: Werr ... 4C 26
WS13: Lich ... 2A 114
Langton Cres. WS14: W'ton ... 2G 131
Langtree Cl. WS12: H Hay ... 2K 109
Lanrick Gdns. WS15: Rug ... 6G 95
Lansbury Cl. ST17: Staf ... 6G 73
Lansbury Dr. WS11: Cann ... 6E 100
Lansbury Gro. ST3: Mei ... 6D 34
Lansbury Rd. WS15: Rug ... 3G 97
Lansdell Av. ST5: N'tle ... 2E 22
Lansdowne Av. WV8: Cods ... 3A 122
Lansdowne Cl. ST13: Lee ... 4C 48
ST15: Stone ... 7F 47
Lansdowne Cres. B77: T Gat ... 1K 141
ST9: Werr ... 4D 26
Lansdowne Rd. DE14: B'ton ... 5A 86
ST4: S Tren ... 4K 153 (1J 31)
Lansdowne St. ST3: Long ... 1H 41
Lansdowne Ter. DE14: B Tre ... 6E 84
Lansdowne Way ST17: Wild ... 1A 78
WS15: Rug ... 6E 94
Lant Cl. DE13: K Bro ... 2D 130
Lanthorn Cl. WS13: Lich ... 4A 114
LAPLEY ... 3C 159
Lapley Av. ST16: Staf ... 6C 70
Lapley Dr. DE13: Stre ... 3F 85
Lapley Rd. ST19: Whe A ... 1D 90
Lapwing B77: Wiln ... 4C 142
Lapwing Cl. ST7: Pack ... 5J 11
WS6: C Hay ... 3C 118
WS8: Brow ... 5G 121
Lapwing Rd. ST7: Kids ... 3H 11
Lara Cl. ST16: Staf ... 3D 72
Larch Cl. DY7: Kin ... 6G 149
ST7: Kids ... 6E 10
WS14: Lich ... 4E 114
Larch Ct. *ST6: B'lem ... 1A 24*
(off Commercial St.)
Larchfields ST15: Stone ... 6H 47
Larch Gro. ST3: Blur ... 7E 32
Larchmere Dr. WV11: Ess ... 2B 126
Larchmount Cl. ST4: Tren ... 3B 40
Larch Pl. ST5: C'ton ... 7C 16
Larch Rd. WS15: Rug ... 3H 97
Larchwood ST5: Keel ... 3J 29
ST17: Wild ... 2A 78
Larchwood Dr. WS11: Cann ... 6G 101
LARDEN GREEN ... 2A 154
Lark Av. ST7: Kids ... 3H 11
Larkfield ST7: Kids ... 5F 11
Larkhill La. TF9: A'ley ... 5G 61
Larkholme Cl. WS15: Rug ... 7C 94
Larkin Av. ST3: Long ... 5K 33
Larkin Cl. ST17: Staf ... 7E 72
WV10: Bush ... 4E 124
Lark Ri. ST14: Utt ... 7G 63
Larksfield Rd. ST6: B'lem ... 6D 18
Larksmeadow Va. ST17: Wild ... 1A 78
Larkspur B77: Dost ... 6K 141
Larkspur Av. WS7: Burn ... 6J 111
Larkspur Dr. WV10: Fea ... 5F 117
Larkspur Gro. ST5: N'tle ... 1F 153 (6G 23)
Larkspur Way WS8: Clay ... 6F 121
Lascelles St. ST6: Tuns ... 4H 17
LASK EDGE ... 6K 9
Lask Edge Rd. ST13: L Edg ... 5J 9
Laski Cres. ST3: Mei ... 7D 34
LATEBROOK ... 1F 17
Latebrook Cl. ST6: Gold ... 7G 11
Latham Cl. DE15: Stap ... 2K 87
Latham Gro. ST6: Feg H ... 7B 12
LATHERFORD ... 6K 93
Latherford Cl. WV10: F Ash ... 6H 93
Latherford La.
WV10: Calf H ... 6K 93 & 1F 117
Latimer Way ST2: Bent ... 6J 25
Lauderdale Cl. WS8: Clay ... 6G 121
Lauderdale Gdns. WV10: Bush ... 2C 124
Lauder Gro. ST18: Hixon ... 6C 80
Lauder Pl. Nth. ST2: Bent ... 1A 34
Lauder Pl. Sth. ST2: Bent ... 1A 34
Launceston Cl. B77: Wiln ... 7K 137
Laurel Av. B78: Pole ... 2J 143
Laurel Bank B79: Tam ... 3H 137
Laurel Cl. WS13: Lich ... 3D 114
Laurel Cres. ST9: Werr ... 5C 26
Laurel Dr. ST7: Harr ... 3J 11
WS7: Burn ... 4A 112
WS12: Hed ... 6A 102
Laurel Gro. DE15: Stap ... 7F 87
ST3: Blur ... 7D 32
ST17: Staf ... 7H 73
Laurels, The WS15: Rug ... 2H 97
Laurence Gro. WV6: Tett ... 6G 123
Lauren Cl. ST4: Fen ... 3E 32
Lavender Av. ST11: B Bri ... 4H 43
Lavender Cl. DE14: B'ton ... 4B 86
ST3: W Coy ... 4E 34
ST18: Gt Bri ... 6H 65
WV9: P'ord ... 2H 123
Lavender Gro. WS3: Wals ... 7K 127
Lavender Lodge *ST17: Colw ... 7K 81*
(off Main Rd.)
Lavender Rd. B77: Amin ... 5B 138
Laverock Gro. CW3: Mad ... 3A 28
Lawford Av. WS14: Lich ... 4E 114
Lawley St. ST3: Long ... 6K 33
Lawn, The ST17: Staf ... 1G 77
Lawn Farm Cres. ST2: B Hil ... 2K 33
LAWNHEAD ... 2C 159
Lawn La. WV9: Cove ... 1H 123 & 4K 93
Lawnoaks Cl. WS8: Brow ... 2F 121
Lawn Rd. ST17: Staf ... 5F 73
Lawns, The DE13: Roll D ... 6G 83
ST14: Utt ... 3F 63
Lawnsfield Wlk. ST16: Staf ... 4E 70
Lawnswood Av. WS7: Chas ... 6H 111
WV6: Tett ... 5G 123
Lawnswood Cl. WS12: H Hay ... 2K 109
Lawnswood Ri. WV6: Tett ... 5H 123
Lawrence Av. WV11: Wed ... 7K 125
Lawrence Ct. B79: Tam ... 3G 137
Lawrence Dr. ST15: Swyn ... 3C 64
Lawrence St. ST1: H'ley ... 6E 150 (6B 24)
ST17: Staf ... 5G 73
Lawrence Way WS13: Lich ... 6K 113
Lawson Ter. ST5: N'tle ... 2F 23
(Dimsdale Vw. E.)
ST5: N'tle ... 6C 22
(John St.)
Lawton Av. ST7: C Law ... 3B 10
Lawton Coppice ST7: C Law ... 2C 10
Lawton Cres. ST8: Bidd ... 5D 8
Lawton Hall Dr. ST7: C Law ... 2A 10
Lawton St. ST6: B'lem ... 5A 18
ST7: Rook ... 2G 11
ST8: Bidd ... 5D 8
Laxey Rd. ST5: N'tle ... 6E 22
Laxton Gro. ST4: Tren ... 6C 40
Lazar La. ST17: Broc, Milf ... 1F 79
Lazy Hill WS9: Ald ... 7G 133
WS9: Ston ... 7G 133
Lazy Hill Rd. WS9: Ald ... 7F 133
LEA ... 2D 157
Lea, The ST4: Tren ... 3B 40
Lea Bank WV3: W'ton ... 4K 129
LEABROOKS ... 2D 157
Lea Cl. ST5: B Gat ... 5F 37
Leacote Dr. WV6: Tett ... 2K 129
Lea Cres. ST17: Staf ... 7F 73
LEACROFT ... 5E 108
Lea Cft. WS15: Col ... 1J 95
Leacroft ST15: Stone ... 5K 47
WV12: Will ... 6C 126
Leacroft Av. WV10: Bush ... 5C 124
Leacroft La. WS11: Cann ... 3G 109
(Lichfield Rd.)
WS11: Cann ... 6F 109
(Walsall Rd.)
Leacroft Rd. ST3: Mei ... 2C 42
ST19: Penk ... 2H 91
Leadbeater Av. ST4: S Tren ... 4K 31
Leadbeater Ho. *WS3: Blox ... 5H 127*
(off Somerfield Rd.)
LEADENDALE ... 7B 42
Leadendale La. ST3: R Clo ... 7A 42
Leadendale M. ST3: L'ood ... 2B 42
Leafdown Cl. WS12: Hed ... 6K 101
Leafenden Av. WS7: Burn ... 5J 111
Leaford Wlk. ST2: Buck ... 6F 25
Leafy Glade B74: S'ly ... 5F 135
Lea Grn. ST16: Staf ... 5E 70
LEA HALL ... 3B 164
Lea Hall Dr. WS7: C Ter ... 2F 111
Lea Hall Ent. Pk. WS15: Rug ... 3K 97
Leahall La. WS15: Bre ... 4K 97
Lea Hall Way WS15: Rug ... 1J 97
LEA HEATH ... 2A 160
Leahurst Cl. ST17: Wild ... 1A 78
Leaks All. ST3: Long ... 7H 33
Lea La. WS6: G Wyr ... 1G 119
LEA MARSTON ... 2C 165
Leam Dr. WS7: Burn ... 4B 112
Leamington Cl. WS11: Cann ... 3C 108
Leamington Gdns. ST5: N'tle ... 5J 23
Leamington Rd. DE14: B'ton ... 7A 86
LEAMONSLEY ... 5K 113 (1B 164)
LEAMORE ... 7H 127
Leamore Cl. WS2: Wals ... 6G 127
Leamore Ent. Pk. WS2: Wals ... 7G 127
(Fryer's Rd.)
WS2: Wals ... 6G 127
(Willenhall La., not continuous)
Leamore Ind. Est. WS2: Wals ... 7H 127
Leamore La. WS2: Wals ... 6G 127
WS3: Blox ... 7H 127
Leander Cl. WS6: G Wyr ... 3F 119
WS7: C Ter ... 2F 111
Leander Ri. DE15: Stap ... 4G 87
Lea Pl. ST3: Mei ... 7D 34
Lea Rd. ST15: Stone ... 6F 47
ST18: Hixon ... 5D 80
Lear Rd. WV5: Womb ... 2H 145
Leas, The WV10: Fea ... 5G 117
Leaside Av. WS15: Hand ... 4G 99
Leaside Rd. ST4: T Val ... 4J 31
Leason La. WV10: Bush ... 5E 124
Leason Rd. ST3: Mei ... 7C 34
Leason St. ST4: S Tren ... 2B 32
Leasowe, The WS13: Lich ... 2A 114
Leasowe Cl. ST18: Gt Hay ... 4H 81
Leasowe Dr. WV6: Per ... 2E 128
Leasowe Rd. WS15: Bre ... 4J 97
Leasowes Dr. WV4: Pen ... 7K 129
Leaswood Cl. ST5: N'tle ... 7G 31
Leaswood Pl. ST5: N'tle ... 7G 31
Leathermill La. WS15: Rug ... 7H 95
Leaton Hall DY7: Bob ... 7D 146
Leawood Rd. ST4: T Val ... 6J 31
Lebanon Gro. WS7: C Ter ... 3H 111
Ledbury Cres. ST1: H'ley ... 3F 25
Ledstone Way ST3: Long ... 5A 34
LEE BROCKHURST ... 2A 158
Leech Av. ST5: C'ton ... 2D 22
Leech St. ST5: N'tle ... 5G 153 (1G 31)
Leedham Av. B77: Tam ... 4K 137
Leeds St. ST4: Fen ... 4F 33
LEEGOMERY ... 3A 158
Lee Gro. ST5: N'tle ... 5F 31
LEEK ... 4G 49 (2D 155)
LEEKBROOK ... 2K 51 (2D 155)
Leekbrook Way ST13: Lee ... 2J 51
Leek Edge Holiday Cotts.
ST13: Lee ... 2J 49
Leek La. ST8: Bid M, L Edg ... 5H 9
ST13: L Edg ... 5J 9
Leek New Rd. ST1: H'ley ... 2B 24
ST2: Mil, S Broo ... 5G 19
ST6: B'lem ... 2B 24
ST9: S Broo ... 5G 19
Leek Rd. SK17: L'nor ... 3C 52
ST1: A Hul, H'ley ... 7J 151 (6D 24)
ST2: A Hul, Mil ... 3G 25
ST3: W Coy ... 3D 34
ST4: H'ley, S Tren ... 7H 151 (1C 32)
ST6: B Edg ... 7J 13
ST9: End, S Broo ... 2K 19
ST9: W Roc ... 4K 27
ST9: Werr ... 1F 35
ST9: Werr, W Roc ... 4H 27
ST10: Chea ... 1A 54
ST10: Wat ... 6C 52
ST13: Ched, Lee ... 4G 51
ST13: Wat, Wink ... 5A 52
Leek Town FC ... 3D 48
LEES ... 1C 161
Lees Cl. WS15: Bre ... 4K 97
Leese La. ST17: Act T ... 6K 77
Leese St. ST4: S Tren ... 2B 32
Leet Cl. WS15: Hand ... 5F 99
Lee Wlk. WS11: Cann ... 6H 101
LEFTWICH ... 1A 154
Legge La. ST18: Hixon ... 5C 80
Legge St. ST5: N'tle ... 5G 153 (1G 31)
Legion Cl. WS11: N Can ... 5C 110
Legs La. WV10: Bush ... 1C 124
Leicester Cl. ST5: N'tle ... 4G 31
Leicester Ct. ST14: Utt ... 4E 62
Leicester Pl. ST2: Bent ... 6J 25
Leicester St. DE14: B Tre ... 4D 86
Leigh Av. WS7: Burn ... 4K 111
Leigh Bank ST10: Lei ... 7H 55
Leigh Cl. ST17: Staf ... 2H 77
Leigh La. ST6: B'lem ... 6G 17
ST10: Lei ... 7H 55
ST10: Tea ... 6H 55
ST14: Bram ... 5A 62
Leigh Rd. ST14: Bram ... 2A 62
Leigh St. ST6: B'lem ... 5A 18
Leighswood ST17: Wild ... 7A 74
Leighswood Cl. WS11: N Can ... 6B 110
LEIGHTON ... 1A 162
Leighton Cl. ST9: S Broo ... 3J 19
ST14: Utt ... 7H 63
Leighton Rd. ST14: Utt ... 7H 63
Leisure Wlk. B77: Wiln ... 4B 142
Lema Way ST16: Staf ... 3K 73
Len Davis Rd. WV12: Will ... 6B 126
Lennox Rd. ST3: Long ... 7K 33
Leofric Cl. DE13: K Bro ... 2C 130
Leomansley Cl. WS13: Lich ... 4K 113
Leomansley Ct. WS13: Lich ... 4J 113
Leomansley Rd. WS13: Lich ... 4K 113
Leomansley Vw. WS13: Lich ... 4J 113
Leonard Av. ST2: Mil ... 4H 19
Leonard Dr. ST6: B Edg ... 7H 13
Leonard St. ST6: B'lem ... 5B 18
ST13: Lee ... 4G 49
Leonora St. ST6: B'lem ... 1K 23
Leons Way ST16: Staf ... 5H 71
Leopold St. ST4: Fen ... 3E 32
Leslie Rd. B74: L Ast ... 6G 135
Lesscroft Cl. WV9: P'ord ... 2J 123
Lessways Cl. ST5: Brad ... 7E 16
Lessways Wlk. ST6: B'lem ... 1K 23
Letchmere Cl. WV6: Patt ... 6B 128
Letchmere La. WV6: Patt ... 7B 128
Lethbridge Gdns. ST17: Staf ... 6C 72
LEVEDALE ... 3C 159
Levedale Cl. ST16: Staf ... 6C 70
Levedale Rd. ST18: Brad ... 6C 68
ST18: Penk ... 1F 91
ST19: Penk ... 1F 91
Levels, The WS15: Bre ... 4H 97
Levels Ind. Est., The WS15: Bre ... 4H 97
Leven Dr. WV12: Will ... 4B 126
Leverton Ri. WV10: Oxl ... 7A 124
Leveson Av. WS6: C Hay ... 2E 118
Leveson Rd. ST4: H'ord ... 1K 39
WV11: Wed ... 5K 125
Leveson St. ST3: Long ... 7J 33
Levett Rd. B77: Amin ... 4D 138
Levetts Flds. WS13: Lich ... 4C 114
Levetts Hollow WS12: Hed ... 7K 101
Levett's Sq. WS13: Lich ... 4B 114
Levington Cl. WV6: Per ... 2G 129
Levita Rd. ST4: T Val ... 5K 31
Lewis Cl. WS14: Lich ... 4E 114
Lewis Dr. DE13: B Tre ... 4C 84
Lewis Gro. WV11: Wed ... 7H 125
Lewisham Dr. ST6: Gold ... 7G 11
Lewisham Rd. WV10: Oxl ... 3K 123
Lewis's La. DE13: K Bro ... 2B 130
Lewis St. ST4: S Tren ... 1B 32
Lexham Pl. ST3: Long ... 7A 34
Lexington Grn. ST17: Staf ... 6C 72
Leybourne Cres. WV9: P'ord ... 3H 123
LEYCETT ... 6E 20 (3B 154)
Leycett La. CW3: Mad H ... 1D 28
ST5: Ley, Mad H ... 1D 28
Leycett Rd. ST5: S Hay ... 4F 21
Leyfield Rd. ST4: Tren ... 4B 40
LEYFIELDS ... 2F 137 (1C 165)
Leyfields WS13: Lich ... 1B 114
Ley Gdns. ST3: Long ... 7G 33
Leyland Cft. WS3: Pels ... 7B 120
Leyland Dr. WS15: Rug ... 6G 95
Leyland Grn. *ST6: Feg H ... 7A 12*
(off Coppull Pl.)
Leyland Rd. B77: Glas ... 6A 138
LEYS, THE ... 4G 137
Leys Dr. ST5: N'tle ... 5C 30
Leys La. ST2: L Oak ... 5J 19
Liberty Ct. WS6: C Hay ... 1D 118
Liberty La. *ST6: B'lem ... 4C 18*
(off Bradeley Village)
Liberty Pk. ST17: Staf ... 6C 72
Liberty Rd. B77: Hock ... 5B 142
Libra Cl. B79: Tam ... 2F 137
Libra Pl. ST6: Chel ... 1K 17
Lich Av. WV11: Wed ... 6J 125
Lichen Cl. WS12: Hun ... 4C 100
LICHFIELD ... 3B 114 (1B 164)
Lichfield Bus. Cen.
WS13: Lich ... 2D 114
Lichfield Cathedral ... 3B 114
Lichfield City Station (Rail) ... 4B 114
Lichfield Cl. ST5: Sil ... 6B 22
WS6: G Wyr ... 3G 119
Lichfield Ct. ST17: Staf ... 4H 73
Lichfield Cres. B78: Hop ... 2B 136
Lichfield Dr. ST18: Gt Hay ... 5G 81
Lichfield Friary Lawn Tennis Club ... 6F 115
Lichfield Garrick Theatre ... 4B 114
Lichfield Health & Fitness Club ... 3C 114

Lichfield Heritage Cen.—Long Furrow

Lichfield Heritage Cen. 3B 114
Lichfield Rd. B78: Hop 2B 136
B79: Tam 2C 136
DE13: B Nee 7J 89
DE13: K Bro 3B 130
DE14: B Nee, B'ton 7A 86
ST7: Talk 7B 10
ST15: Stone 4H 47
ST17: Staf 4G 73
(not continuous)
ST18: Sand, West 1A 80
WS3: Blox 3H 127
WS3: Pels 7C 120
WS7: Burn, Pipe 5B 112
WS8: Brow 4H 121
WS9: W Woo, Brow 7J 121
WS11: Cann 2E 108
WS13: Han 6G 99
WS13: Pipe 5B 112
WS15: Abb B 3C 88
WS15: Arm, Hand 5G 99
WV11: Wed 7H 125
WV12: Will 5D 126
Lichfield Rd. Ind. Est. B79: Tam . . . 4F 137
(Bradford St.)
B79: Tam 3E 136
(Gerard)
B79: Tam 2E 136
(Kepler)
B79: Tam 3F 137
(Lovell)
Lichfield St. B78: Faze 1E 140
B79: Tam 4G 137
DE14: B Tre 3E 86
ST1: H'ley 4G 151 (5C 24)
ST15: Stone 4G 47
WS15: Rug 1H 97
Lichfield Trent Valley Station (Rail)
. . . . 3F 115
Lichwood Rd. WV11: Wed 6K 125
Liddle St. ST4: S Tren 3A 32
Lidgate Gro. ST3: Blur 7F 33
Lidgate Wlk. ST5: N'tle 7G 31
Lid La. ST10: Chea 4B 54
(not continuous)
LIFFORD 3A 164
Light Ash WV9: Cove 1A 116
Light Ash Cl. WV9: Cove 1K 93
Light Ash La. WV9: Cove 1K 93
Lightfoot Rd. ST14: Utt 4E 62
LIGHT OAKS 6K 19 (2D 155)
LIGHTOAKS 4A 56
Light Oaks Av. ST2: L Oak 6K 19
Lightwater Gro. ST2: Mil 6F 19
LIGHTWOOD
ST3 . . . . 3B 42 (3D 155)
ST10 . . . . 5E 54 (3A 156)
Lightwood Cl. WS13: Lich 5K 113
Lightwood Driving Range 3K 41
LIGHTWOOD GREEN 3A 154
Lightwood Rd. DE13: Yox 3G 89
ST3: L'ood, R Clo, Long 7J 33
ST5: C'ton 6B 16
Lilac Av. WS11: Cann 4D 108
Lilac Cl. ST3: W Coy 4E 34
ST5: C'ton 6B 16
ST14: Utt 7G 63
ST18: Gt Bri 6H 65
Lilac Dr. WV5: Womb 4F 145
Lilac Gro. DE15: Stap 6G 87
ST3: Fen 6E 32
ST17: Staf 7H 73
WS7: Chas 4H 111
Lilac La. WS6: G Wyr 4F 119
Lilac Rd. B79: Tam 1G 137
WV12: Will 6E 126
LILLESHALL 3B 158
Lilleshall Rd. ST5: N'tle 4H 31
Lilleshall St. ST3: Long 7J 33
Lilleshall Way ST17: Staf 7D 72
Lillington Cl. WS13: Lich 3A 114
Lillydale Rd. ST2: Buck 5H 25
Lily Ct. ST6: Nort 6E 18
Lily Dr. ST6: Nort 6E 18
LILYHURST 3B 158
Lily St. ST5: N'tle 3G 23
Limbrick Rd. ST7: Aud 6C 14
Lime Cl. ST3: W Coy 4E 34
WS6: G Wyr 7F 109
Lime Ct. DE15: Stap 5F 87
Limedale Ct. ST15: Stone 3F 47
Lime Gro. DE15: Stap 6F 87
DY7: Kin 6G 149
ST10: Wat 4B 52
ST12: Barl 6F 41
WS7: Burn 5A 112
WS13: Lich 3D 114
Limeheath Pl. ST6: Tuns 2J 17
Limehurst Av. WV3: W'ton 6K 129
Lime Kiln La. ST7: C Law 4C 10
ST10: Alt 5H 57
Lime Kilns B78: Pole 2J 143
Lime La. WS3: L Wyr 2B 120
Limepit La. WS12: Hun, Cann 4C 100
Lime Rd. WS12: Hun 2D 100
Limes, The DE15: Wins 2K 87
DY3: Him 7H 145
ST5: N'tle 1G 23
ST14: Utt 4G 63
Limes Ct. ST4: S Tren 5K 153 (1J 31)
Limes Rd. WV6: Tett 2K 129
Lime St. ST4: S Tren 4B 32
Lime Tree Av. ST16: Staf 1F 73
WV6: Tett 3H 129
Lime Tree Gdns. WV8: Bilb 2D 122
Lime Tree Rd. WV8: Bilb 2D 122
Lime Wlk. ST19: Penk 4G 91
Limewood Cl. ST11: B Bri 4J 43
Linacre Rd. ST21: Ecc 3H 65
Linacre Way ST3: W Coy 4A 34
Lincoln Av. B79: Tam 3E 136
ST5: N'tle 4G 31
Lincoln Cl. WS13: Lich 7C 106
Lincoln Ct. ST14: Utt 4E 62
Lincoln Cft. WS14: Shen 5C 134
Lincoln Dr. WS11: Cann 3F 109
Lincoln Grn. WV10: Bush 3B 124
Lincoln Gro. ST5: N'tle 4G 31
Lincoln Ho. WS13: Fra P 6H 107
Lincoln Mdw. ST17: Staf 6C 72
Lincoln Rd. DE15: Stap 5E 86
ST6: B'lem 1A 24
ST7: Kids 4D 10
Lincoln St. ST1: H'ley 4J 151 (5D 24)
Lindale Dr. WV5: Womb 4F 145
Lindale Gro. ST3: Mei 3D 42
Linda Rd. ST6: Tuns 2J 17
Linden Av. WS7: C Ter 3J 111
Lindenbrook Va. ST17: Wild 7A 74
Linden Cl. B77: Amin 5B 138
ST5: N'tle 5F 23
ST17: Staf 6D 72
Linden Dr. ST8: G Hea 4C 8
Linden Gro. ST5: N'tle 5F 23
ST8: G Hea 3C 8
Linden La. WV12: Will 6E 126
Linden Pl. ST3: Blur 1F 41
Linden Rd. DE13: B Nee 6G 89
Lindens, The ST15: Stone 7H 47
Linden Vw. WS12: Hed 6H 101
Lindera B77: Amin 5C 138
Lindisfarne B77: Glas 6K 137
Lindley Pl. ST3: M Hea 6C 42
Lindley St. ST6: B'lem 1B 24
Lindon Cl. WS8: Brow 6J 121
Lindon Dr. WS8: Brow 5H 121
Lindon Rd. WS8: Brow 7H 121
Lindon Vw. WS8: Brow 7J 121
Lindop Ct. ST1: H'ley 3H 151
Lindops La. CW3: Mad 2B 28
Lindop St. ST1: H'ley 3H 151 (4D 24)
Lindrick Cl. WS3: Blox 2F 127
Lindsay Hall ST5: Keel 3K 29
Lindsay St. ST1: H'ley 5E 150 (5B 24)
Linhum Av. ST4: Tren 3C 40
LINE HOUSES 1F 17
Lineker Cl. ST16: Staf 3D 72
Linfield Rd. ST1: H'ley 3H 151 (4D 24)
Linford Cl. WS15: Hand 5G 99
Lingard St. ST6: B'lem 7A 18
Lingfield Av. ST6: B Edg 6G 13
WV10: Ford 7B 116
Lingfield Cl. WS6: G Wyr 2F 119
Lingfield Dr. WS6: G Wyr 2F 119
Lingfield Grange B74: S'ly 7F 135
Lingfield Gro. WV6: Per 2G 129
Lingfield Rd. DE14: B'ton 5A 86
WS11: N Can 6C 110
Ling Rd. WS12: Hun 5C 100
Linhope Gro. ST3: Mei 3D 42
Linkend Cl. ST1: H'ley 3F 25
Link Rd. WV5: Womb 3G 145
Links Av. ST5: N'tle 4F 23
WV6: Tett 6F 123
Linksfield Gro. ST16: Staf 5F 71
Links Vw. B74: S'ly 7G 135
Linkway Retail Pk. WS11: Cann 5B 108
LINLEY 2A 162
Linley Dr. WV10: Bush 4C 124
Linley Rd. ST4: S Tren 4J 153 (1J 31)
ST7: Talk 6A 10
Linley Trad. Est. ST7: Talk 5A 10
Linnburn Rd. ST3: Long 5K 33
Linnet Cl. WS12: Hun 3D 100
Linnet Gro. WV12: Will 5B 126
Linnett Gro. ST7: Pack 5J 11
Linnet Way ST8: Bidd 5E 8
Lintake Dr. WS15: Abb B 2B 88
Linthouse La. WV11: Wed 5H 125
Linthouse Wlk. B77: Wiln 4B 142
Lintly B77: Wiln 1D 142
LINTON 3C 161
Linwood Dr. WS12: Hed 3F 101
Linwood Way ST6: Tuns 2J 17
Lionel Gro. ST4: S Tren 7K 153 (2J 31)
Lion Gro. ST5: C'ton 7C 16
Lion's Den WS7: Hamm 1H 133
Lion St. ST4: P'ull 2A 32
WS15: Rug 7G 95
Lion Way ST17: Staf 6J 73
LIPLEY 1B 158
Lisbon Pl. ST5: N'tle 2C 30
Liskeard Cl. ST2: Buck 7G 25
Lister Gro. ST11: B Bri 7F 43
Lister Rd. ST16: Staf 1H 73
Litley Dr. ST10: Chea 7C 54
LITTLE ASTON 3H 135 (1A 164)
Little Aston Golf Course 4H 135
Lit. Aston Hall Dr. B74: L Ast 3F 135
Lit. Aston La. B74: L Ast 2H 135
Lit. Aston Pk. Rd. B74: L Ast 5F 135
Lit. Barrow Wlk. WS13: Lich 2A 114
LITTLE BLOXWICH 2K 127
LITTLE BOLAS 2A 158
LITTLE BRIDGEFORD 5G 65 (2C 159)
Little Brum CV9: Gren 7K 143
LITTLE BUDWORTH 1A 154
LITTLE BURTON 6D 84
Lit. Burton E. DE14: B Tre 6E 84
Lit. Burton W. DE14: B Tre 7E 84
LITTLE CHELL 2K 17
Lit. Chell La. ST6: Tuns 2K 17
Lit. Church La. B79: Tam 4H 137
Lit. Cliffe Rd. ST3: Fen 5E 32
Little Comn. WS3: Pels 7C 120
Littlecote B79: Tam 2D 136
LITTLE CUBLEY 1B 160
LITTLE DAWLEY 1A 162
LITTLE DRAYTON 1A 158
LITTLE EATON 3D 157
Lit. Eaves La. ST2: Buck 2J 25
Littlefield ST4: T Val 5J 31
Little Grange WS13: Lich 2K 113
LITTLE HAY 1B 164
LITTLE HAYWOOD 6J 81 (2A 160)
LITTLE HEATH
Coventry 3D 165
Stafford 7B 76
LITTLE INGESTRE 1K 75 (2D 159)
Little La. ST3: R Clo 6A 42
WV12: Will 6D 126
Lit. Lawns Cl. WS8: W Woo 7J 121
LITTLE LONGSTONE 1B 156
LITTLE MADELEY 2C 28
Lit. Marsh Gro. ST19: Penk 3H 91
Lit. Marsh Pk. ST19: Penk 3H 91
LITTLEMOOR 1D 157
LITTLE-MOSS 1D 10
Lit. Moss Cl. ST7: Sch G 1C 10
Lit. Moss La. ST7: Sch G 1C 10
LITTLE ONN 3C 159
Lit. Onn Rd. ST20: C Eat 4B 68
Lit. Orchard WS15: Rug 6G 95
LITTLE ORTON 1D 165
LITTLEOVER 1D 161
LITTLE PACKINGTON 3C 165
Lit. Pipe La. WS13: Lich 2D 112
Little Row ST4: Fen 1F 33
ST7: Kids 4F 11
(off Brights Av.)
LITTLE SAREDON 1H 117 (1D 163)
LITTLE SOUDLEY 2B 158
LITTLE STOKE 6J 47 (1D 159)
LITTLE SUGNALL 1C 159
LITTLE TIXALL 4H 81
Lit. Tixall La. ST18: Gt Hay 4G 81
Littleton Bus. Pk. WS12: Hun 3C 100
Littleton Cl. ST16: Staf 2J 73
Littleton Cres. ST19: Penk 3H 91
Littleton Dr. WS12: Hun 3C 100
Littleton M. ST19: Penk 3G 91
Littleton Rd. WV12: Will 6C 126
Littleton Way WS7: C Ter 2F 111
LITTLE TWYCROSS 1D 165
LITTLE WENLOCK 1A 162
LITTLEWOOD 7E 108
Littlewood La. WS6: C Hay 7E 108
(not continuous)
Littlewood Rd. WS6: C Hay 7E 108
LITTLEWORTH
ST16 . . . . 3J 73 (2D 159)
ST20 . . . . 3D 66 (2B 158)
WS12 . . . . 6A 102 (3A 160)
Littleworth Hill WS12: Hed 6K 101
Littleworth Rd. WS12: Hed, Haz 6J 101
LITTLE WYRLEY 4A 120 (1A 164)
Litton B77: Wiln 1E 142
Littywood La. ST18: Brad 5C 68
Live & Let Live Mobile Home Pk.
WV10: Fea 5G 117
Liverpool Rd. ST4: S Tren 2B 32
ST5: C'ton 4B 16
ST5: N'tle 1D 152 (3E 22)
(not continuous)
ST7: Kids 4D 10
Liverpool Rd. E. ST7: C Law 3B 10
Liverpool Rd. W. ST7: C Law 2A 10
Livingstone Av. WV6: Per 1F 129
Livingstone Rd. WS3: Blox 3K 127
Livingstone St. ST6: B'lem 5C 18
ST13: Lee 4G 49
Livingwell Health Club
Burton on Trent 6A 86
Tamworth 5F 137
Lloyd George Gro. WS11: H Hay . . . 1J 109
Lloyd Rd. WV6: Tett 7F 123
Lloyd St. ST3: Long 7J 33
ST16: Staf 2G 73
WS11: Cann 2D 108
Lochalsh Gro. WV12: Will 4B 126
Lochsong Cl. B77: Dost 6K 141
Lockerbie Cl. ST13: Lee 4J 49
Locketts Ct. WS11: Cann 5F 101
Locketts La. ST3: Long 7J 33
(Lightwood Rd.)
ST3: Long 7K 33
(Normacot Rd.)
Lockett St. ST1: H'ley 2D 24
Locke Way ST16: Staf 3K 73
Lockington Av. ST2: Bent 6K 25
Lock Keepers Cl. WS11: N Can 7B 110
Lockley St. ST1: H'ley 1K 151 (3E 24)
LOCKLEYWOOD 2A 158
Lock Rd. ST19: Penk 4H 91
Lockside WV5: Womb 3E 144
Lockside Dr. DY7: Kin 5F 149
Lockside Vw. WS15: Rug 1H 97
Lockwood Cl. ST10: K Hol 7J 53
Lockwood Rd. ST10: Chea, K Hol . . . 7J 53
Lockwood St. ST2: Mil 4H 19
ST5: N'tle 3H 153 (7H 23)
Lodge Barn Rd. ST8: Knyp 7F 9
Lodgefield Pk. ST17: Staf 4B 74
Lodge Gro. ST5: N'tle 2G 23
Lodge La. ST20: W'ves 4D 66
WS11: Cann 6C 108
WS13: Chor 7B 104
Lodge Ri. WS7: C Ter 2H 111
Lodge Rd. ST4: S Tren 6K 153 (2J 31)
ST7: T Pit 1B 16
WS15: Bre 3J 97
WV10: Oxl 5K 123
Lodge St. WV12: Will 7C 126
Lodge Vw. WS6: C Hay 1C 118
Loftus Ct. WS7: Chas 6J 111
Loftus St. ST1: H'ley 1E 150 (3B 24)
Loganbeck Gro. ST3: Long 4K 33
Logan Cl. WV10: Oxl 7A 124
LOGGERHEADS 4E 60 (1B 158)
Lohengrin Ct. DE13: Stre 1F 85
Lomas St. ST4: H'ley 7C 150 (6A 24)
Lomax Cl. WS13: Lich 2A 114
Lomax Rd. WS12: Hed 3H 101
Lombard St. WS13: Lich 3B 114
Lombardy Gdns. WV12: Will 6E 126
Lombardy Gro. ST3: Mei 7C 34
WS7: C Ter 3H 111
Lomita Cres. B77: Wiln 2K 141
Lomond Cl. B79: Tam 1F 137
Lomond Gro. ST10: Chea 3D 54
Lomond Wlk. ST3: Blur 3F 41
London Rd. ST4: S Tren, T Val 6J 31
ST5: C'ton 7C 16
ST5: N'tle 5F 153 (1G 31)
ST18: West 2C 80
WS14: Lich 6C 114
London St. ST13: Lee 4G 49
Long Acre WV8: Cods 3B 122
Longacres B74: L Ast 4H 135
WS12: Hed 5B 102
Longbow Cl. DE13: Stre 2C 84
Longbow Gro. DE13: Stre 2D 84
LONGBRIDGE 3A 164
Longbridge Hayes Rd. ST6: B'lem . . 7G 17
Long Bri. Rd. WS14: Lich 6C 114
Longbrook Av. ST3: Blur 7F 33
LONGCLIFFE 2C 157
Longclough Rd. ST5: C'ton 5B 16
LONG COMPTON 2C 159
Long Cft. WS12: Hun 6C 100
Longcroft La. DE13: Yox 1H 89
Longdoles Av. ST3: Long 6A 34
LONGDON 1D 104 (3A 160)
Longdon Dr. B74: F Oak 4K 135
LONGDON GREEN 2F 105 (3A 160)
LONGDON ON TERN 3A 158
LONG DUCKMANTON 1D 157
Longfellow Cl. DE14: B Tre 4E 84
Longfellow Pl. WS11: Cann 6E 100
Longfellow Rd. WS7: C Ter 2H 111
Longfellow Wlk. B79: Tam 1F 137
Longfield Av. ST15: Stone 5F 47
Longfield Cl. B77: Amin 5A 138
Longfield Cres. B77: Amin 5A 138
Longfield Dr. B74: L Ast 4J 135
Longfield Rd. ST4: S Tren . . . 5J 153 (1H 31)
LONGFORD
Ashbourne 1C 161
Cannock 4B 108
Coventry 3D 165
Market Drayton 1A 158
Newport 3B 158
Longford Cl. DE15: Stap 2J 87
WV5: Womb 5D 144
Longford Ct. WS11: Cann 3B 108
Longford Grn. WS11: Cann 4C 108
Longford Ind. Est. WS11: Cann 5D 108
Longford Rd. WS11: Cann 2B 108
Longford Wlk. ST2: Buck 6G 25
Long Furrow WV8: P'ord 4G 123

Longhedge La. DE13: Ans, B Tre 3A 84
Longhope Dr. ST15: Stone 5F 47
Longhurst Dr. ST16: Staf 2K 73
Long Knowle La. WV11: Wed 5F 125
Longlake Av. WV6: Tett 3H 129
Longlands, The WV5: Womb 4G 145
Longlands Dr. B77: Amin 5B 138
Longlands Pl. WS15: Abb B 2B 88
LONGLANE 1C 161
LONG LANE 3A 158
Long La. ST7: Harr 2J 11
ST11: Ful 3G 59
ST15: Ful, Hild 3G 59
WS6: G Wyr 7D 118
WS11: N Can 3A 110
WS13: Frad 1K 107
WV11: Ess 7D 118
Longleat B79: Tam 2D 136
Longley La. WS15: Col 2K 95
Longley Rd. ST3: Long 4J 33
Long Mdw. ST5: N'tle 6G 31
ST17: Staf 3G 77
Longmead Rd. DE13: B Tre 5D 84
Long Mill Av. WV11: Wed 6F 125
Long Mill Nth. WV11: Wed 6F 125
Long Mill Sth. WV11: Wed 6F 125
Long Mynd Cl. WV12: Will 4B 126
LONGNOR
Buxton 2C 52 (1A 156)
Stafford 3C 159
Longnor Craft Cen. 2C 52
Longnor Pl. ST2: Buck 6G 25
Longnor Wood Cvn. & Camping Pk.
SK17: L'nor 3C 52
LONGPORT 7H 17
Longport Rd. ST6: B'lem 1H 23
Longport Station (Rail) 1H 23
LONGRIDGE 3D 159
Long Row ST7: Kids 5E 10
ST11: Cave 6F 35
LONGSDON 7A 48 (2D 155)
Longsdon Cl. ST5: C'ton 6A 16
Longsdon Gro. ST3: Long 5A 34
LONGSHAW 3A 156
Longshaw Av. ST5: Brad 1F 23
Longshaw La. ST10: O'moor 1H 57
(not continuous)
Longshaw St. ST6: B'lem 7H 17
Longshore Cl. ST17: Staf 1E 76
LONGSLOW 1A 158
Longstaff Av. WS12: Haz 6E 102
Longstaff Cft. WS13: Lich 1K 113
Long St. B78: Dor 5J 143
DE15: Stap 5F 87
ST19: Whe A 2C 90
(not continuous)
LONGTON 6H 33 (3D 155)
Longton Exchange ST3: Long 6H 33
(off The Strand)
Longton Hall Rd. ST3: Blur, Long 7F 33
Longton Pool 7B 34
Longton Rd. ST4: Tren 4A 40
ST12: Barl 2E 44
ST15: Knen 4K 45
ST15: Knen, Stone 3G 47
Longton Station (Rail) 5H 33
Longus Ind. Est. ST6: Tuns 3H 17
Long Valley Rd. ST8: G Hea 3C 8
Longview Cl. ST3: Long 4K 33
Longwood Path B78: M Oak 1D 140
Lonpark Ind. Est. ST3: Long 6J 33
Lonsdale Cl. WV12: Will 7B 126
Lonsdale Ct. ST21: Ecc 2G 65
(off High St.)
Lonsdale Rd. DE14: B'ton 4C 86
Lonsdale St. ST4: S Tren 3B 32
Loomer Rd. ST5: C'ton 3B 22
Loomer Rd. Ind. Est. ST5: C'ton 3C 22
Loop Rd. ST15: Cold M 5A 64
Lord Cromwell Ct. WS11: Cann 5G 101
Lord Nelson Ind. Est.
ST1: H'ley 5J 151 (5D 24)
Lords Cl. ST4: Tren 3D 40
Lordship La. ST4: S Tren 2C 32
Lordshire Pl. ST7: Pack 5K 11
Lords La. DY7: Stou 1J 149
LORDSLEY .1F 61
Lordsley La. TF9: A'ley 1G 61
Lord St. ST6: B'lem 6C 18
ST8: Bidd 6D 8
Lordswell Rd.
DE14: B Tre 7A 84
Lordswood Rd. ST4: Tren 3D 40
Lorien Cl. ST13: Lee 5D 48
Loring Rd. ST5: N'tle 2F 23
Loring Ter. Sth. ST5: N'tle 2G 23
Lorna Bailey Vis. Cen. 7H 17
Lorne St. ST6: B'lem 6A 18
WS7: C Ter 3G 111
Lorraine St. ST7: Pack 5K 11
Lorton B79: Tam 2D 136
LOSCOE .3D 157
LOSTOCK GREEN 1A 154
Lothersdale B77: Wiln 2D 142
(not continuous)
Lothians Rd. WS3: Pels 7C 120
WV6: Tett 7G 123
Lotus B77: Glas 6A 138
Lotus Av. ST8: Knyp 7B 8
Lotus Ct. ST15: Stone 2G 47
Lotus Dr. WS11: Cann 5E 100
Lotus Way ST16: Staf 1H 73
Loughborough Wlk.
ST3: Long 5J 33
Loughshaw B77: Wiln 1E 142
LOUGHTON 3A 162
Louise Dr. ST3: Fen 6F 33
Louise St. ST6: B'lem 6A 18
LOUNT 3D 161
Louvain Av. ST1: H'ley 1D 24
Lovatt Av. ST5: N'tle 4E 22
Lovatt Cl. DE13: Stre 1G 85
Lovatt Pl. WS11: Cann 5E 100
Lovatt St. ST4: S Tren 2B 32
ST16: Staf 1F 73
Loveage Dr. ST2: Buck 5H 25
Lovelace Cl. ST17: Staf 6E 72
Love La. ST18: Seigh 7H 65
WS6: G Wyr 1G 119
WS15: Rug 7H 95
WV6: Tett 7F 123
Lovell B79: Tam 3F 137
Lovell Dr. ST16: Staf 1K 73
Lovell Rd. DE13: Yox 3G 89
Loveridge Cl. WV8: Cods 2B 122
Lovers La. TF9: Hook 5F 61
Lovers Wlk. B78: Tam 5G 137
Loveston Gro. ST3: Long 5K 33
Lovett Ct. WS15: Rug 6F 95
Lowcroft Gdns. WV10: Bush 5C 124
Lowdham B77: Wiln 1E 142
LOWE HILL 6J 49
Lowell Dr. ST3: W Coy 5A 34
Lwr. Ash Rd. ST7: Kids 6C 10
Lower Av. ST19: Cove 1G 93
WV9: Cove 1G 93
Lwr. Bedford St.
ST4: H'ley 6B 150 (6A 24)
LOWER BEOBRIDGE 2B 162
Lwr. Bethesda St.
ST1: H'ley 5G 151 (5C 24)
Lwr. Birches Way WS15: Rug 3F 97
Lwr. Brook St. WS15: Rug 7G 95
Lwr. Bryan St. ST1: H'ley . . .1F 151 (3C 24)
Lower Cres. ST4: S Tren 5K 153 (1J 31)
Lowercroft Way B74: F Oak 3K 135
Lwr. Cross St. ST3: Long 5J 33
LOWER DRAYTON 1H 91
LOWER ELLASTONE 3B 156
LOWER FAINTREE 3A 162
Lwr. Foundry St.
ST1: H'ley 3F 151 (4C 24)
LOWER GREEN 1K 93 (1D 163)
Lwr. Gungate B79: Tam 4H 137
Lwr. Hadderidge ST6: B'lem 7K 17
LOWER HARTSHAY 2D 157
Lwr. High St. DE13: Tut 1H 83
ST7: M Cop 6H 7
Lower Ho. La. CV9: B Ens 7H 143
Lwr. Keys Bus. Pk. WS12: Hed 7K 101
Lower La. ST18: Hopt 7G 69
WS13: Chor 1A 112
LOWER LEIGH 1A 160
Lwr. Lodge Mobile Ho. Pk.
WS15: Arm 4C 98
LOWER LOXLEY 1A 160
Lwr. Mayer St. ST1: H'ley . . .1H 151 (3D 24)
Lwr. Milehouse La. ST5: N'tle 6D 22
LOWER MODDERSHALL 5K 45
LOWER OUTWOODS 5A 84
Lwr. Outwoods Rd. DE13: B Tre 6A 84
Lwr. Oxford Rd.
ST5: N'tle 1K 153 (6J 23)
Lowerpark B77: Wiln 1J 141
Lwr. Penkridge Rd. ST17: Act T 6K 77
LOWER PENN 2C 163
Lwr. Prestwood Rd. WV11: Wed 6G 125
Lower Rd. TF9: A'ley, Hook 6F 61
WS12: Hed 7H 101
Lwr. Rookery Rd. ST15: Cold M 5A 64
Lwr. Sandford St. WS13: Lich 4A 114
Lwr. Spring Rd. ST3: Long 7K 33
(not continuous)
LOWER STONNALL 6K 133 (1A 164)
Lower St. ST5: N'tle 2D 152 (7F 23)
ST6: B'lem 1A 24
WV6: Tett 7G 123
LOWER TEAN 5H 55 (1A 160)
LOWER THURVASTON 1C 161
Lower Way WS15: U Lon 1K 103
LOWER WITHINGTON 1C 155
Lowe's Pas. ST3: Long 7K 33
Lowe St. ST4: S Tren 2B 32
Lowfield Dr. ST5: N'tle 3J 23
Lowfield La. ST20: Gno 4J 67
Low Force B77: Wiln 2E 142
LOW HABBERLEY 3C 163
LOW HILL 6C 124
Low Hill Cres. WV10: Bush 5C 124
Lowhurst Dr. ST6: Feg H 7K 11
Lowland Rd. WS12: Hun 5C 100
(not continuous)
Lowlands Av. WV6: Tett 7G 123
Lowlands Ct. WV6: Tett 7G 123
Lowlands Rd. ST6: Tuns 3E 16
Lowndes Cl. ST4: P'ull 3K 31
Lowry Cl. WV6: Per 2G 129
Low St. WS6: C Hay 1D 118
Lowther Pl. ST13: Lee 4H 49
Lowther St. ST1: H'ley 1D 150 (3B 24)
Lowthorpe Way ST2: Bent 7A 26
LOWTOP 1H 53
LOXLEY GREEN 1A 160
Loxley La. ST14: Utt 7B 62
Loxley Pl. ST3: Mei 3B 42
Loxton Cl. B74: L Ast 3J 135
Loynton Cl. ST16: Staf 6D 70
Lucas St. ST6: B'lem 1J 23
Lucepool La. DE13: Yox 1K 89
Lucerne Pl. ST5: N'tle 2C 30
Luce Rd. WV10: Bush 7C 124
Lucknow Rd. WV12: Will 7B 126
Ludbrook Rd. ST4: Fen 4H 33
Ludford Cl. ST5: C'ton 5B 16
Ludgate B79: Tam 4G 137
Ludgate St. DE13: Tut 2H 83
Ludgrove Way ST17: Staf 6K 73
Lud La. B79: Tam 4G 137
Ludlow Cl. WS11: H Hay 1J 109
WV12: Will 7B 126
Ludlow Ho. WS3: Blox 7J 127
(off Providence La.)
Ludlow St. ST1: H'ley 3J 151 (4D 24)
Lud's Church 1D 155
LUDSTONE 2C 163
Ludwall Rd. ST3: Long 1A 42
Lugano Cl. ST5: N'tle 3D 30
Lukesland Av.
ST4: S Tren 7K 153 (3J 31)
Luke St. ST6: B'lem 1J 23
Lukes Wlk. WS13: Lich 1A 114
LULLINGTON 3C 161
Lullington Rd. B79: C Camp 5D 132
B79: Edin 1C 132
Lulworth Gro. ST6: Chel 1K 17
Lulworth Rd. WS7: C Ter 4J 111
Lulworth Wlk. WV4: Pen 7K 129
Lundy Rd. ST3: Long 6F 33
Lunn's Cft. WS13: Lich 3C 114
LUTLEY 3C 163
Lutley La. DY7: Bob 7C 146
LUZLOW 1C 26
Lychgate Cl. ST4: S Tren 4A 32
Lydford Pl. ST3: Long 6B 34
Lydford Rd. WS3: Blox 3H 127
Lydia Cft. B74: F Oak 2K 135
Lydia Dr. ST1: H'ley 2F 25
LYE 3D 163
LYE, THE .2A 162
Lymebrook Pl. ST4: T Val 6J 31
Lyme Ct. ST5: N'tle 6G 153
Lymedale Bus. Pk. ST5: C'ton 3C 22
Lymedale Ct. Ent. Cen. ST5: C'ton . . .3D 22
Lyme Dr. ST4: T Val 3H 31
Lyme Gro. ST5: N'tle 5G 23
Lyme Rd. ST3: Mei 1D 42
Lymer Rd. WV10: Oxl 4A 124
LYMES, THE 6B 30
Lymes Rd. ST5: Butt, Keel 3H 29
Lymevale Rd. ST4: T Val 5J 31
Lyme Valley Rd.
ST5: N'tle 5E 152 (2F 31)
Lymewood Cl. ST5: N'tle 5D 152 (1F 31)
Lymewood Gro.
ST5: N'tle 6D 152 (2F 31)
Lymington Rd. ST16: Staf 2A 74
WS7: C Ter 2H 111
Lyminster Gro. ST2: Mil 6H 19
Lynam St. ST4: P'ull 2A 32
Lynam Way CW3: Mad 2A 28
Lyn Av. WS13: Lich 2K 113
Lynch, The B78: Pole 1H 143
Lyndale B77: Wiln 4B 142
Lyndale Dr. WV11: Wed 7J 125
Lyndham Av. DE15: Stap 3G 87
Lyndhurst Dr. ST8: B Lee 7A 8
Lyndhurst Gro. ST15: Stone 6K 47
Lyndhurst Rd. WS12: H Hay 2K 109
Lyndhurst St. ST6: B'lem 7J 17
Lyne Ct. DE14: B Tre 1B 86
Lyneham Cl. B79: Tam 1H 137
LYNE HILL .6H 91
Lyne Hill Ind. Est. ST19: Penk 5G 91
Lyne Hill La. ST19: Penk 6F 91
Lyneside Rd. ST8: B Lee, Knyp 7B 8
Lynfield Rd. WS13: Lich 2K 113
Lynmouth Cl. ST8: Bidd 7C 8
Lynmouth Gro. ST6: Chel 7K 11
LYNN
Newport 3B 158
Lichfield 5J 133 (1A 164)
Lynn Av. ST7: Talk 6A 10
Lynn La.
WS14: Lyn, Shen . . . .5J 133 & 5A 134
Lynn St. ST3: W Coy 4D 34
Lynsey Cl. ST7: H End 1G 21
Lynton Av. ST17: Staf 7B 74
WV6: Tett 6G 123
Lynton Gro. ST3: L'ood 2B 42
Lynton Rd. ST5: N'tle 4D 30
Lynwood Cl. DE14: B'ton 5A 86
WV12: Will 5E 126
Lynwood Rd. DE14: B'ton 7A 86
Lyric Cl. ST17: Staf 1H 77
Lysander Rd. ST3: Mei 3C 42
Lysander Way WS11: Cann 7E 100
Lysways La.
WS13: Han, L'don 2F 105
WS15: L'don 2F 105
Lytham B77: Amin 4E 138
Lytham Dr. ST16: Staf 3A 74
Lytham Gro. WS3: Blox 1G 127
Lytham Rd. WV6: Per 2E 128
Lytton St. ST4: S Tren 2C 32

M

Macadam Cl. WS7: Burn 3K 111
McAdam Cl. DE15: Stap 2J 87
MACCLESFIELD 1D 155
MACCLESFIELD FOREST 1D 155
Macclesfield Rd. ST13: Lee, Rudy . . .1C 48
Macclesfield St. ST6: B'lem 6B 18
Macdonald Cres. ST3: Mei 6C 34
Mace St. ST4: T Val 5K 31
McGeough Wlk. WS11: Cann 5H 101
McGhie St. WS12: Hed 4H 101
McGough St. ST6: Tuns 4H 17
Macgregor Cres. B77: Amin 5B 138
Macgregor Tithe B79: Tam 4H 137
Machin Cres. ST5: N'tle 1E 22
Machin St. ST6: Tuns 3J 17
Macintyre St. ST6: B'lem 1A 24
Mackay Rd. WS3: Blox 3K 127
McKellin Cl. ST7: Big E 5G 15
Mackenzie Cres. ST10: Chea 6D 54
McKie Way WS15: Rug 3H 97
McKinley St. ST6: Tuns 4H 17
(not continuous)
MACKWORTH 1D 161
Maclagan St. ST4: S Tren 3B 32
McLean Rd. WV10: Oxl 3A 124
Macrome Rd. WV6: Tett 5G 123
Madden Cl. WS15: Rug 3H 97
Maddock St. ST6: B'lem 1J 23
ST7: Aud 6F 15
Madeira Av. WV8: Cods 3C 122
Madeira Pl. ST6: Tuns 4H 17
MADELEY
Crewe 3A 28 (3B 154)
Telford 1A 162
MADELEY HEATH
Crewe 1C 28 (3B 154)
Stourbridge 3D 163
MADELEY PARK WOOD 3C 36
Madeley St. ST5: Sil 7K 21
ST6: Tuns 3H 17
Madeley St. Nth. ST5: Sil 6K 21
Madford Retail Pk. ST16: Staf 2F 73
Madison Ct. ST6: Tuns 3H 17
Madison St. ST6: Tuns 3H 17
Madocke Wlk. WS13: Lich 5K 113
Madox Cl. B79: Tam 2E 136
Madras Rd. DE15: Wins 1K 87
Madrona B77: Amin 5D 138
MAER 1B 158
Mafeking St. ST3: Long 7H 33
Magazine La. ST19: Whe A 1C 90
Magdalen Rd. ST3: Blur 2E 40
Magdalen Wlk. ST3: Blur 3E 40
Magenta Dr. ST5: N'tle 6C 22
Magna Cl. WS6: C Hay 1E 118
Magness Cres. WV12: Will 7C 126
Magnolia B77: Amin 5C 138
Magnolia Cl. ST18: Gt Bri 6G 65
Magnolia Dr. ST6: Mil 5F 19
Magnolia Gro. WV8: Bilb 2C 122
Magnus B77: Wiln 4A 142
Magnus St. ST6: B'lem 1K 23
Magpie Cres. ST7: Kids 4F 11
Mahogany Dr. ST16: Staf 2E 72
Maidstone Dr. WS7: Burn 5B 112
Maidstone Gro. ST2: Bent 6J 25
Main Line Ind. Est. DE14: B Tre 5F 85
Main Rd. B79: Edin 1C 132
B79: N Reg, Shut 2G 139
B79: Tam, Wig 1H 137
CW3: Bet, Mad, Wrin, B Woo 1A 6
DE6: D Cla 5B 82
DE6: May 5C 56
ST9: W Roc 1J 27
ST14: Dens 2C 58
ST15: Cold M 4A 64
ST17: Colw 7J 81
ST17: Milf, Shug 7E 74
ST18: Gt Hay, L Hay 4G 81
ST18: Shug 7G 81
WS15: Bre, Rug 3J 97
WS15: Rug 5K 97

Main St.—Mathews Wlk.

Main St. B79: C Camp 6D 132
DE13: Alre 5B 130
DE13: B Nee 5F 89
DE13: Stre 2F 85
DE13: Yox 2H 89
DE14: B'ton 7A 86
DE15: Stap 4F 87
ST3: W Coy 4D 34
WS9: Ston 7G 133
WS14: Shen 5C 134
WS14: W'ton 3G 131
Maitland B77: Glas 7B 138
Maitland Gro. ST4: Tren 4B 40
MAJORS BARN 5B 54
Majors Barn ST10: Chea 5B 54
(not continuous)
MAJOR'S GREEN 3B 164
MAKENEY 3D 157
Malam St. ST1: H'ley 1F 151 (3C 24)
Malcolm Cl. ST2: Mil 5H 19
Malcolm Ct. ST2: Buck 3J 25
Malcolm Dr. ST2: Buck 3J 25
Malcolm Rd. ST17: Staf 1F 77
Maldale B77: Wiln 1E 142
Malham Rd. B77: Wiln 2D 142
ST5: N'tle 5C 22
MALINSLEE 1A 162
Malkin Way ST6: B'lem 2J 23
Mall, The ST5: N'tle 3F 153
Mallard Av. ST17: Staf 7J 73
Mallard Cl. ST14: Utt 7H 63
ST19: Penk 6H 91
WS3: Pels 6C 120
Mallard Cft. WS13: Lich 3C 114
Mallard Way ST6: B'lem 4C 18
Mallens Cft. ST14: Bram 6B 62
Mallicot Cl. WS13: Lich 2D 114
Mallorie Rd. ST6: Nort 3D 18
Mallory Cl. ST15: Stone 6H 47
Mallory Cres. WS3: Blox 3K 127
Mallory Rd. WV6: Per 3F 129
Mallory Way ST10: Chea 4E 54
Mallow Cl. ST21: Ecc 4H 65
Mallowdale Cl. ST4: Tren 4C 40
Malpass Gdns. WV8: Cods 7E 92
Malpas Wlk. ST6: Gold 7G 11
Malstone Av. ST2: Mil 5J 19
Malthouse La. ST3: W Coy 1D 34
ST12: Barl 1E 44
ST18: Brad 5C 68
ST19: Whe A 2B 90
ST20: C Eat 2B 68
WV6: Tett 7G 123
Malt Ho. Rd. WS15: Gen 5J 103
Malthouse Rd. ST2: Buck 5H 25
ST10: Alt 5H 57
Malthouses WS15: Gen 5K 103
Maltings, The *DE14: B Tre 1D 86*
(off Grants Yd.)
DE14: B Tre 7F 85
(Wharf Rd.)
DE15: Stap 3H 87
ST14: Utt 5H 63
WS14: Lich 6A 114
WV5: Womb 4G 145
Maltings Ind. Est. DE14: B Tre 5F 85
Malt La. ST3: Long 7K 33
Malt Mill La. ST16: Staf 3G 73
Malton Gro. ST6: Tuns 2H 17
Malvern Av. DE15: Stap 3G 87
ST5: Sil 6H 21
Malvern Cl. ST4: Tren 3A 40
ST17: Staf 5K 73
Malvern Ct. WV10: Bush 5B 124
Malvern Dr. WS15: Rug 6E 94
Malvern St. DE15: Stap 3G 87
Mammouth Dr. WV10: W'ton 7B 124
MANCETTER 2D 165
Mancroft Gdns. WV6: Tett 1K 129
Mancroft Rd. WV6: Tett 1K 129
Mandale Rd. WV10: W'ton 7D 124
Mandela Way ST3: Long 7K 33
Mandeville Cl. ST6: B'lem 4C 18
MANEY 2B 164
Manifold Cl. ST5: Sil 7K 21
ST10: Wat 5B 52
WS7: Burn 5B 112
Manifold Dr. ST10: Chea 7D 54
Manifold Rd. ST11: Fors 2H 43
Manifold Wlk. ST2: B Hil 7J 25
Manley Rd. WS13: Lich 2D 114
Mannin Cl. ST3: W Coy 5C 34
Mann St. ST3: Mei 7E 34
Manor Av. WS6: G Wyr 7G 109
WS11: Cann 2D 108
Manor Cl. CV9: B Ens 7K 143
DE15: Stan 6H 87
ST14: Utt 5H 63
ST18: Gt Hay 4G 81
ST18: West 3C 80
WV8: Bilb 1D 122
Manor Ct. B78: M Oak 1D 140
DE13: B Nee 5G 89
ST15: Stone 6F 47
Manor Ct. Dr. WS15: Hand 5F 99
Manor Ct. St. ST4: P'ull 3K 31
Manor Cres. DE15: Stan 6H 87
Manor Cft. DE14: B Tre 2F 87
Manorcroft Rd. ST14: Utt 5H 63
Manor Dr. DE14: B Tre 2F 87
DY3: Swin 1J 147
WV10: Shar 2H 117
Mnr. Farm Cres. ST17: Staf 2G 77
Mnr. Farm Dr. WV12: Will 7D 126
Mnr. Farm Rd. ST18: L Hay 6J 81
Manorfield Cl. ST19: Penk 4G 91
Manor Flds. DE13: Alre 5B 130
Manor Gdns. WV5: Womb 3H 145
Manor Glade ST5: B Gat 3C 36
Manor Grn. ST17: Staf 7F 73
Manor Ho. Pk. WV8: Bilb 1D 122
Manor Pk. DE13: K Bro 2A 130
Manor Pk. Sailing Club 2A 130
Manor Ri. ST15: Stone 5F 47
WS7: Burn 6J 111
WS14: Lich 5C 114
Manor Rd. B74: S'ly 7F 135
B77: Tam 5J 137
B78: M Oak 1D 140
CW3: Mad 4A 28
DE13: K Bro 2B 130
DE15: Stan 6H 87
ST5: B Gat 3C 36
ST7: M Cop 6H 7
ST14: Utt 5G 63
ST20: Gno 3J 67
WV10: Oxl 6A 124
Manor Sq. ST17: Staf 7F 73
Manor St. ST4: Fen 3E 32
WV6: Tett 1K 129
Manor Trad. Est. DE14: B Tre 6E 84
Manor Wlk. DE13: K Bro 2B 130
Manor Way WS15: Col 2J 95
Mansard Cl. WV10: Bush 5F 125
Manse Cl. ST3: Long 5J 33
Mansell Cl. ST16: Staf 4E 72
Mansfield Cl. B79: Tam 3E 136
ST5: N'tle 7G 31
Mansfield Dr. ST8: B Lee 1A 12
Mansion Cl. ST10: Chea 5D 54
Mansion Ct. *WV5: Womb 5D 144*
(off Heath Ho. Dr.)
Mansion Dr. WS7: Hamm 7B 112
Manston Dr. WV6: Per 1F 129
Manston Hill ST19: Penk 5G 91
Manston Vw. B79: Tam 1J 137
MANSTY 4A 100
Mansty La. ST19: Penk 1A 100
Manta Rd. B77: Dost 4K 141
Manton Cl. DE13: Stre 2G 85
Maple Av. ST5: C'ton 6C 16
ST7: Talk 6B 10
Maple Cl. DY7: Kin 4E 148
ST6: Nort 2G 19
ST10: Chea 5E 54
ST15: Yarn 7D 64
WS7: Chas 4H 111
Maple Ct. WS14: Lich 6C 114
Maple Cres. ST11: B Bri 4J 43
WS11: Cann 2C 108
Mapledene Cl. ST17: Wild 2B 78
Maple Dr. TF9: Logg 4D 60
WS12: Hun 2D 100
Maple Gdns. ST15: Stone 6G 47
Maple Gro. DE15: Stap 7F 87
ST13: Ched 3G 51
ST17: Staf 7G 73
WS14: Lich 4F 115
WV3: W'ton 4K 129
Maplehurst Cl. ST6: B'lem 7B 18
Maple Pl. ST3: Mei 7D 34
Maple Ri. B77: Amin 5C 138
Maple St. WS3: Blox 3K 127
MAPLETON 3B 156
Maple Way DE14: B'ton 4A 86
Maple Wood ST17: Wild 2A 78
MAPPERLEY 3D 157
MARBURY 3A 154
Marcel Cl. ST4: H'ord 7A 32
MARCHAMLEY 2A 158
March Banks WS15: Rug 7F 95
March Cl. WS6: C Hay 3D 118
MARCH END 7J 125
MARCHINGTON 2C 82 (1B 160)
Marchington Ind. Est. ST14: Mar 3C 82
MARCHINGTON WOODLANDS 2B 160
March La. ST9: Werr 5J 27
ST18: Gt Bri, W'ave 5J 65
March Rd. ST3: Long 5H 33
Marchwood Ct. ST4: P'ull 3J 31
Marconi Ga. ST18: Staf 1A 74
Marconi Pl. WS12: Hed 3J 101
Marcus Ind. Est. ST1: H'ley 5F 25
Maree Gro. WV12: Will 4B 126
MAREHAY 3D 157
Margam Cres. WS3: Blox 3F 127
Margam Ter. WS3: Blox 3F 127
Margam Way WS3: Blox 3F 127
Margaret Av. ST4: Tren 2K 39
Margaret Dr. WS11: Cann 4E 100
Margaret's Rd. TF9: Logg 4D 60
Margaret St. ST1: H'ley 3K 151 (4E 24)
ST15: Stone 3F 47
Margill Cl. ST1: H'ley 5E 150 (5B 24)
Marholm Cl. WV9: P'ord 3H 123
Maries Way ST5: Sil 7B 22
Marigold Cl. WS11: H Hay 7J 101
Marina Cres. WS12: Hed 5G 101
Marina Dr. ST5: N'tle 4G 23
Marina Rd. ST4: T Val 6K 31
Marina Way ST1: H'ley 4A 150 (4K 23)
Mariner B79: Tam 2E 136
MARKEATON 1D 161
Market Arc. ST5: N'tle 4E 152
MARKET BOSWORTH 1D 165
MARKET DRAYTON 1A 158
Market Drayton Rd. TF9: Logg 5C 60
MARKET END 3D 165
Marketfields ST21: Ecc 2H 65
Mkt. Hall Pct. WS11: Cann 2E 108
Mkt. Hall St. WS11: Cann 2E 108
Market La. ST1: H'ley 3G 151 (4C 24)
ST5: N'tle 3E 152 (7F 23)
WS14: Wall 1A 134
Market Pas. ST6: B'lem 7K 17
Market Pl. DE14: B Tre 2F 87
SK17: L'nor 3C 52
ST6: B'lem 7K 17
ST10: Chea 4C 54
ST13: Lee 3F 49
(off Church St.)
ST14: Utt 6H 63
ST19: Brew 2C 92
ST19: Penk 3G 91
WS3: Blox 4H 127
WS11: Cann 2D 108
(not continuous)
WS15: Abb B 2C 88
Market Sq. ST1: H'ley 3G 151 (4C 24)
ST15: Stone 4G 47
ST16: Staf 3G 73
WS15: Rug 7G 95
Market Sq. Arc. ST1: H'ley 3G 151
Market St. B78: Pole 1J 143
B79: Tam 5H 137
ST3: Long 5J 33
ST7: Kids 5E 10
ST13: Lee 3G 49
ST14: Utt 6H 63
ST16: Staf 3G 73
ST19: Penk 3G 91
WS12: Hed 4H 101
WS13: Lich 4B 114
(not continuous)
WS15: Rug 7H 95
Markham Cft. WV9: P'ord 3J 123
Marklew Cl. WS8: Brow 7J 121
Marklin Av. WV10: Oxl 4B 124
Marks Wlk. WS13: Lich 1A 114
Marlborough Av. ST16: Staf 2A 74
Marlborough Cl. B74: F Oak 2K 135
ST18: Gt Hay 4H 81
Marlborough Ct. WS13: Lich 4B 114
Marlborough Cres. DE15: Stap 4G 87
ST9: End 1A 50
Marlborough Rd. ST3: Long 5J 33
ST15: Stone 7F 47
Marlborough St. ST4: Fen 4D 32
WS3: Blox 4H 127
Marlborough Way B77: Wiln 1K 141
ST6: Tuns 2G 17
ST14: Utt 4E 62
Marlbrook La. WV6: Patt 7A 128
Marlburn Way WV5: Womb 4E 144
Marldon Pl. ST6: Tuns 1G 17
MARLEY GREEN 3A 154
Marlin B77: Dost 4K 141
Marlow Cl. ST3: Long 4K 33
Marlow Dr. DE14: B'ton 4B 86
Marlowe Dr. WV12: Will 6A 126
Marlowe Rd. ST17: Staf 6D 72
Marlow Rd. B77: Tam 4K 137
ST3: Long 4K 33
Marlpit La. ST14: Dens 2A 58
MARLPITS 2G 97
MARLPOOL 3D 157
Marmion Pk. B79: Tam 3H 137
Marmion St. B79: Tam 4H 137
Marney Wlk. ST6: B'lem 5B 18
Marquis's Dr. ST17: Wol B 2K 79
WS12: Hed 6A 96
WS15: Hed, Rug 6C 96
Marrick B77: Wiln 2E 142
Marriott St. ST4: Fen 4G 33
Marsden St. ST1: H'ley 2H 151 (4D 24)
Marsett B77: Wiln 3E 142
MARSH, THE 3H 91
Marshall Av. ST6: B Edg 7H 13
Marshall St. B77: Tam 4A 138
ST6: B'lem 6K 17
Marsh Av. ST5: N'tle 3G 23
ST6: B'lem 5B 18
ST7: New 4J 11
Marsh Cl. ST9: Werr 4C 26
Marsh Ct. ST16: Staf 1F 73
Marshfield La. ST8: G Hea 3C 8
MARSH GREEN
Stoke-on-Trent 2D 8 (2C 155)
Telford 3A 158
Marsh Grn. Cl. ST8: Bidd 3D 8
Marsh Grn. Rd. ST8: Bidd 2D 8
Marsh Gro. DY3: Swin 1J 147
ST8: G Hea 2C 8
Marshland Gro. ST6: Feg H 6A 12
Marsh La. ST19: Penk 3H 91
WS14: Lich 6B 114
WS14: W'ton 6G 115
WV10: Ford 2K 123
Marsh La. Pde. WV10: Oxl 3A 124
Marshmeadow La. ST20: C Eat 4A 68
Marsh Pde. ST5: N'tle 4G 153 (7G 23)
Marsh St. ST16: Staf 1F 73
Marsh St. Nth. ST1: H'ley 2F 151 (4C 24)
Marsh St. Sth. ST1: H'ley 3F 151 (4C 24)
MARSH, THE
Market Drayton 2A 158
Stafford 3H 91
Marsh Vw. ST3: M Hea 5C 42
Marsh Way ST5: N'tle 3G 23
Marshwood Cl. WS11: Cann 1G 109
Marsland Cl. ST16: Staf 2C 72
Marsland Rd. ST16: Staf 2C 72
Mars St. ST6: B'lem 6C 18
MARSTON
Shifnal 3C 159
Stafford 1G 71 (2D 159)
Sutton Coldfield 2C 165
Marston Cl. ST19: Whe A 2C 90
Marston Ct. ST16: Staf 7G 71
Marston Cft. ST19: Whe A 2C 90
Marston Dr. ST16: Staf 1G 73
MARSTON GREEN 3B 164
Marston Gro. ST1: H'ley 7D 18
ST16: Staf 1G 73
Marston Ho. ST16: Staf 1G 73
MARSTON JABBETT 3D 165
Marston La. DE13: Roll D 6G 83
DE65: Hat 1J 83
(not continuous)
ST18: Mars 4F 71
MARSTON MONTGOMERY 1B 160
Marston Old La. DE65: Hat 1J 83
MARSTON ON DOVE 2C 161
Marston Pk. B78: Tam 5F 137
Marston Ri. DE15: Stap 4G 87
Marston Rd. ST16: Staf 1G 73
ST19: Whe A 1A 90
WS12: Hed 4F 101
Marston Road Stadium 7G 71
Marston Rd. Trad. Pk. ST16: Staf 7G 71
Marston's Vis. Cen. 1B 86
Marsworth Way ST16: Staf 4F 71
Martham Dr. WV6: Tett 4J 129
Martin Cft. WS13: Lich 2A 114
Martin Dale TF9: Logg 4D 60
Martindale ST17: Wild 1B 78
WS11: Cann 1G 109
Martindale Cl. ST3: L'ood 2B 42
Martindale Trad. Est. WS11: Cann 1G 109
Martin Dr. ST16: Staf 3E 72
WV12: Will 7C 126
Martin Gro. WS6: G Wyr 1G 119
Martin Ho. ST13: Ched 2G 51
Martin's La. DE13: H'ury 7E 82
MARTIN'S MOSS 1C 155
Martin St. ST6: B'lem 1B 24
ST16: Staf 3G 73
Martins Way ST18: Hixon 6C 80
Martlin La. WS15: Col 3J 95
MARTON 1C 155
Marton Av. WS7: C Ter 3J 111
Marwood Cft. B74: S'ly 6F 135
Marychurch Rd. ST2: Buck 5H 25
Maryfield Wlk.
ST4: S Tren 7K 153 (2J 31)
Maryhill Cl. ST7: Kids 3E 10
Mary Rand Cl. ST17: Staf 6F 73
Mary Rose Cl. ST2: Buck 5H 25
WS6: C Hay 3D 118
Marysgate ST19: Brew 1D 92
Mary St. WS12: Hed 3H 101
Maryvale Ct. WS14: Lich 4D 114
Masefield Cl. ST10: Chea 2C 54
WS7: C Ter 2J 111
WS14: Lich 5B 114
Masefield Cres. DE14: B Tre 5E 84
Masefield Dr. B79: Tam 2G 137
ST17: Staf 6E 72
Masefield Gro. WS11: Cann 6E 100
Masefield M. WV10: Bush 4E 124
Masefield Rd. ST3: Blur 7G 33
WS3: Blox 6K 127
WV10: Bush 4E 124
Mason Dr. ST8: Bidd 5B 8
Masons Lawn ST20: Gno 5G 67
Mason St. ST4: Fen 4F 33
Massbrook Gro. WV10: W'ton 7D 124
Massbrook Rd. WV10: W'ton 7D 124
Masterson St. ST4: Fen 3D 32
Mathews Wlk. ST1: H'ley 3H 151

Matlock—Middleport

MATLOCK . . . 1C 157
MATLOCK BATH . . . 2C 157
Matlock Cl. WS3: Blox . . . 2J 127
Matlock Dr. WS11: Cann . . . 6G 101
Matlock Pl. ST5: Sil . . . 6J 21
Matlock Rd. WS3: Blox . . . 2J 127
Matlock St. ST1: H'ley . . . 7G 151 (6C 24)
Matrix Health & Leisure Club . . . 6H 17
Matthews Ct. ST1: H'ley . . . 4J 151
Matthews Rd. ST17: Staf . . . 7E 72
Matthews Wlk. ST1: H'ley . . . 4D 24
WS13: Lich . . . 1A 114
Mattox Rd. WV11: Wed . . . 7H 125
Maud St. ST4: Fen . . . 2E 32
Maunders Rd. ST2: Mil . . . 6G 19
Maureen Av. ST6: Gold . . . 1H 17
Maureen Gro. ST5: N'tle . . . 5G 23
Maurice Gro. WV10: W'ton . . . 7E 124
Mavesyn Cl. WS15: Hill R . . . 1E 98
MAVESYN RIDWARE . . . 3E 98 (3A 160)
Mavis Rd. WS12: Hed . . . 3H 101
Mavor Av. WS7: C Ter . . . 2F 111
Mawdesley St. ST6: B'lem . . . 2B 24
Mawgan Dr. WS14: Lich . . . 5D 114
MAW GREEN . . . 2B 154
Mawson Gro. ST4: S Tren . . . 7D 24
MAXSTOKE . . . 3C 165
Maxstoke Cl. B77: Dost . . . 6J 141
WS3: Blox . . . 2G 127
Maxtock Av. WS13: Lich . . . 5A 114
Maxton Way ST3: Mei . . . 7D 34
Maxwell Cl. WS13: Lich . . . 4C 114
Maxwell Pl. ST4: S Tren . . . 6K 153 (2J 31)
Mayama Rd. B78: Faze . . . 2F 141
May Av. ST5: N'tle . . . 5H 23
ST6: Tuns . . . 4J 17
MAY BANK . . . 5H 23
May Bank ST5: N'tle . . . 5H 23
Maybank WS15: Rug . . . 1G 97
(off Horse Fair)
Maybank Cl. WS14: Lich . . . 3E 114
Maybrook Ind. Est. WS8: Brow . . . 7H 121
(not continuous)
Maybrook Rd. WS8: Brow . . . 7H 121
Maybury Cl. WV8: Cods . . . 1A 122
Maybury Way ST2: Mil . . . 6G 19
Maybush Gdns. WV10: Oxl . . . 4A 124
May Cl. WS7: C Ter . . . 2H 111
Maycroft Cl. WS12: Hed . . . 3F 101
Mayer Av. ST5: N'tle . . . 6F 23
Mayer Bank ST6: B'lem . . . 7A 18
Mayers Ct. ST13: Lee . . . 4E 48
Mayer St. ST1: H'ley . . . 2G 151 (4D 24)
Mayfair Av. ST10: Ips . . . 2H 53
Mayfair Dr. B78: Faze . . . 3G 141
Mayfair Gdns. ST6: Tuns . . . 4H 17
(off Wesley St.)
Mayfair Gro. ST9: End . . . 1A 50
MAYFIELD . . . 6C 56 (3B 156)
Mayfield B77: Wiln . . . 2E 142
Mayfield Av. DE6: May . . . 6C 56
ST1: H'ley . . . 3E 24
ST5: N'tle . . . 5B 152 (1E 30)
ST19: Penk . . . 4G 91
Mayfield Cl. ST13: Lee . . . 4C 48
Mayfield Cres. ST1: H'ley . . . 3E 24
Mayfield Dr. DE15: Stap . . . 4H 87
ST11: B Bri . . . 2F 43
Mayfield Pl. ST5: N'tle . . . 4G 23
Mayfield Pl. E. ST4: T Val . . . 4J 31
Mayfield Pl. W. ST4: T Val . . . 4J 31
Mayfield Rd. DE6: Ash, May . . . 5C 56
DE15: Wins . . . 1H 87
ST8: Bidd . . . 7D 8
ST17: Staf . . . 5A 74
Mayfields Dr. WS8: Brow . . . 2D 120
Mayfield Ter. DE6: May . . . 7C 56
Mayflower Dr. WS15: Rug . . . 7E 94
Maylea Cres. ST6: B'lem . . . 1C 24
Mayneford Pl. ST4: H'ord . . . 1K 39
Mayne St. ST4: H'ord . . . 7K 31
Mayock Cres. ST16: Staf . . . 4D 72
May Pl. ST4: Fen . . . 4H 33
ST5: N'tle . . . 5G 23
Maypole Ct. WV5: Womb . . . 4G 145
Maypole St. WV5: Womb . . . 3H 145
May St. ST5: Sil . . . 7A 22
ST6: B'lem . . . 6B 18
WS3: Blox . . . 7J 127
Mays Wlk. DE13: Alre . . . 5B 130
Mayswood Dr. WV6: Tett . . . 5G 129
Maythorne Rd. ST3: Blur . . . 1G 41
Maythorn Gdns. WV6: Tett . . . 3K 129
WV8: Bilb . . . 1C 122
Mead, The ST4: Tren . . . 3B 40
Mead Cres. DE15: Stan . . . 6H 87
Meadlands, The WV5: Womb . . . 4E 144
Meadow Av. ST3: Long . . . 2J 41
ST5: N'tle . . . 4E 22
ST9: W Roc . . . 1K 27
MEADOWBANK . . . 1A 154
Meadowbank B78: Tam . . . 1H 141
Meadowbank Av. ST18: West . . . 3B 80
Meadowbank Grange
WS6: G Wyr . . . 7E 108
Meadowbank Rd. WS13: Lich . . . 7B 106
Meadowbank Wlk. ST16: Staf . . . 5E 70
Meadowbrook Ct. ST15: Stone . . . 6J 47
Meadowbrook Gdns. WV8: Bilb . . . 1D 122
Meadowbrook Rd. WS13: Lich . . . 7B 106
Meadow Cl. ST11: B Bri . . . 4G 43
ST11: Fors . . . 2K 43
ST13: Lee . . . 4H 49
ST19: Penk . . . 5H 91
ST19: Whe A . . . 2B 90
ST20: Gno . . . 3J 67
ST21: Ecc . . . 2H 65
WV12: Will . . . 5C 126
Meadow Ct. DE14: B Tre . . . 1G 87
(off Meadow Rd.)
ST7: New . . . 4J 11
ST12: Barl . . . 1C 44
ST17: Staf . . . 6J 73
Meadow Cft. WS12: Hun . . . 6C 100
WS13: S'hay . . . 2F 115
WV6: Per . . . 3E 128
Meadowcroft Av. ST3: Mei . . . 2E 42
Meadowcroft Gdns. ST19: Whe A . . . 2C 90
Meadow Dr. ST3: Blur . . . 2G 41
ST10: Chea . . . 4C 54
ST18: Hau . . . 6B 66
Meadow Glade ST18: Hixon . . . 6C 80
Mdw. Grange Dr. WV12: Will . . . 6C 126
Meadow Gro. WS6: G Wyr . . . 2G 119
Mdw. Hill Dr. WS11: Cann . . . 1G 109
Meadow La. DE13: Stre . . . 3H 85
DE13: Yox . . . 4K 89 & 3G 89
(not continuous)
ST4: Tren . . . 3C 40
ST5: N'tle . . . 5E 22
ST11: Ful . . . 3G 59
ST17: Act T . . . 7K 77
ST17: Staf . . . 7H 73
ST18: Derr . . . 4A 72
ST18: L Hay . . . 7H 81
WV5: Womb . . . 2G 145
WV10: Cov H . . . 6A 116
WV12: Will . . . 7A 126
Mdw. Lark Cl. WS12: Hed . . . 6H 101
Meadow Pk. B79: Tam . . . 4F 137
Meadow Pl. ST3: Mei . . . 1D 42
Meadow Ridge ST17: Staf . . . 6A 74
Meadow Ri. DE13: B Nee . . . 6H 89
Meadow Rd. B78: Tam . . . 6E 136
DE14: B Tre . . . 1G 87
ST6: B Edg . . . 1H 19
ST6: Chel . . . 2C 18
ST12: Barl . . . 1D 44
ST17: Staf . . . 6H 73
WV3: W'ton . . . 6K 129
Meadows, The CW3: Wrin . . . 5B 6
ST2: B Hil . . . 7H 25
ST7: Kids . . . 5D 10
ST9: End . . . 2B 50
ST14: Utt . . . 3F 63
ST15: Hild . . . 5H 59
ST19: Brew . . . 2D 92
WS11: Cann . . . 6B 108
WS15: Bre . . . 3K 97
Meadows Gro. WV8: Bilb . . . 1C 122
Meadow Side ST8: Knyp . . . 7B 8
Meadowside DE6: May . . . 7C 56
ST4: Tren . . . 3B 40
ST11: Sav G . . . 1K 59
TF9: Logg . . . 4E 60
Meadowside Av. ST7: Aud . . . 6E 14
Meadowside Dr. DE14: B Tre . . . 1F 87
Meadowside La. ST7: Sch G . . . 6F 7
Meadowside Leisure Cen. . . . 1F 87
Meadows Rd. ST7: Kids . . . 5D 10
Meadow St. B77: Tam . . . 6J 137
ST2: Mil . . . 6H 19
ST5: C'ton . . . 2D 22
Mdw. Style Pk. ST8: M Cop . . . 7A 8
Meadows Way ST8: Bidd . . . 6C 8
Meadowsweet Cl. ST6: Nort . . . 5E 18
Mdw. Sweet Dr. ST17: Staf . . . 7D 74
Meadowsweet Way WS12: Hed . . . 6A 102
Meadow Va. WV8: Bilb . . . 3D 122
Meadow Vw. DE13: Roll D . . . 6J 83
WS7: Burn . . . 5B 112
Meadowview ST6: Nort . . . 4E 18
ST15: Yarn . . . 6C 64
Meadow Vw. Mobile Home Pk.
WV10: Cov H . . . 6A 116
Meadow Way ST5: B Gat . . . 5E 36
ST10: Tea . . . 4F 55
ST15: Stone . . . 6F 47
WS12: H Hay . . . 2J 109
WS15: Arm . . . 5F 99
WV8: Cods . . . 3A 122
Meadowwyrthe B79: Tam . . . 2H 137
Mead Wlk. DE15: Stan . . . 6H 87
Meadway, The WV6: Tett . . . 1H 129
Meadway Cl. WS12: Hed . . . 7J 101
Meadway Dr. ST17: Wild . . . 2A 78
Meadway St. WS7: Chas . . . 6J 111
MEAFORD . . . 7D 44
Meaford Av. ST15: Stone . . . 2F 47
Meaford Dr. ST3: Blur, Fen . . . 7E 32
Meaford Rd. ST12: Barl, Mea . . . 2D 44
ST15: Mea . . . 1D 46
Meakin Av. ST5: N'tle . . . 6F 31
Meakin Cl. ST10: Chea . . . 6B 54
ST15: Stone . . . 6J 47
Meakin Gro. ST16: Staf . . . 7D 70
Meakin Ho. ST15: Stone . . . 3F 47
Meakins Row ST4: Fen . . . 4F 33
Meander Cl. B77: Wiln . . . 5A 142
Mear Greaves La. DE15: Wins . . . 7J 85
Mease Av. WS7: Burn . . . 5B 112
Mease La. B79: Haun . . . 5A 132
MEASHAM . . . 3D 161
Measham Way WV11: Wed . . . 6J 125
Mecca Bingo
Burton . . . 1E 86
Stoke-on-Trent . . . 3D 150 (4B 24)
Meddins Cl. DY7: Kin . . . 5E 148
Meddins La. DY7: Kin . . . 5D 148
Meddins Ri. DY7: Kin . . . 5D 148
Media Way ST1: H'ley . . . 4A 150 (4K 23)
Medina B77: Wiln . . . 1A 142
Medina Cl. WV10: Bush . . . 1D 124
Medina Way ST7: Kids . . . 4F 11
Medway B77: Wiln . . . 1K 141
Medway Dr. ST8: Bidd . . . 4D 8
Medway Pl. ST5: N'tle . . . 5F 31
Medway Rd. WS8: Brow . . . 2E 120
Medway Wlk. ST6: Chel . . . 3A 18
WS8: Brow . . . 2E 120
Meece Av. ST15: Cold M . . . 6A 64
Meece Rd. ST15: Cold M . . . 6B 64
ST15: Yarn . . . 6C 64
Meerash La.
WS7: Hamm . . . 7A 112 & 1K 121
MEERBROOK . . . 1D 155
Meerbrook Cl. ST4: Tren . . . 5B 40
Meere Cl. ST6: Nort . . . 4E 18
MEESON . . . 2A 158
Megabowl
Stafford . . . 2F 73
Stoke-on-Trent . . . 4B 150 (5A 24)
MEGACRE . . . 5J 15
Megacre ST7: Big E . . . 5J 15
Meg La. WS7: Burn . . . 2J 111
Meigh Rd. ST2: Bent . . . 5C 26
ST9: Werr . . . 5C 26
Meigh St. ST1: H'ley . . . 3H 151 (4C 24)
Meiklejohn Pl. ST6: Feg H . . . 1A 18
MEIR . . . 1C 42 (3D 155)
MEIR HAY . . . 5K 33
Meir Hay Rd. ST3: Long . . . 7K 33
MEIR HEATH . . . 5C 42 (3D 155)
Meir Leisure Cen. . . . 1C 42
Meir Rd. ST3: Long . . . 1A 42
Meir St. ST6: Tuns . . . 3H 17
Meir Vw. ST3: Mei . . . 7C 34
MELBOURNE . . . 2D 161
Melbourne Av. DE15: Wins . . . 1K 87
Melbourne Cres. ST16: Staf . . . 1K 73
WS12: H Hay . . . 1B 110
Melbourne Rd. WS12: H Hay . . . 1A 110
Melbourne St. ST3: Long . . . 4K 33
Melbury Way WS11: Cann . . . 1F 109
Melchester Gro. ST3: L'ood . . . 1A 42
Melchester Wlk. WS11: Cann . . . 1F 109
Melfont St. ST6: Tuns . . . 4J 17
Melford B79: Tam . . . 3E 136
Melford Grange WS7: C Ter . . . 2G 111
Melford Ri. WS7: C Ter . . . 2H 111
Meliden Way ST4: P'ull . . . 3K 31
Mellard St. ST5: N'tle . . . 1C 152 (6E 22)
ST7: Aud . . . 6F 15
Mellor Dr. B74: F Oak . . . 5K 135
DE13: Alre . . . 6B 130
ST14: Utt . . . 4G 63
Mellor Rd. DE14: B'ton . . . 5B 86
Mellors Bank ST7: M Cop . . . 7H 7
Mellor St. ST7: Pack . . . 5K 11
Mellwaters B77: Wiln . . . 2E 142
Melmerby B77: Wiln . . . 2E 142
Melrose Av. ST1: H'ley . . . 1D 24
ST3: M Hea . . . 6C 42
ST5: N'tle . . . 4E 30
ST15: Stone . . . 7J 47
ST17: Staf . . . 7D 72
Melrose Cotts. WS14: M Cor . . . 1J 133
Melrose Dr. WS12: Hed . . . 3F 101
WV6: Per . . . 2E 128
Melrose Pl. ST13: Lee . . . 4C 48
Melstone Av. ST6: Tuns . . . 4K 17
Melverton Av. WV10: Bush . . . 5B 124
Melville Ct. ST5: N'tle . . . 1G 39
Melville Rd. ST3: Long . . . 7A 34
Melville St. ST1: H'ley . . . 5K 151 (5E 24)
Melvyn Cres. ST5: N'tle . . . 1G 23
Memory La. WV11: Wed . . . 7F 125
Menai Cl. WV12: Will . . . 7C 126
Menai Dr. ST8: Knyp . . . 7D 8
Menai Gro. ST3: Long . . . 4J 33
Mendip Av. ST17: Staf . . . 1C 78
Mendip Grn. ST2: Mil . . . 6G 19
Mendip Pl. ST5: N'tle . . . 5C 22
Mendip Rd. WS12: Hed . . . 1G 101
Mendip Way B77: Wiln . . . 1E 142
Menzies Ho. ST3: L'ood . . . 2B 42
ST13: Ched . . . 3G 51
Meon Gro. WV6: Per . . . 2G 129
Meon Way WV11: Wed . . . 6K 125
Meranti Cl. WV12: Will . . . 5C 126
MERCASTON . . . 3C 157
Mercer Av. ST15: Stone . . . 5J 47
Mercer Gro. WV11: Wed . . . 6J 125
Mercer St. ST3: Long . . . 1H 41
Merchant Cl. WV6: Patt . . . 6B 128
Mercia Cl. B79: Tam . . . 2E 136
Mercia Cres. ST6: B'lem . . . 2A 24
Mercia Dr. WV6: Per . . . 1F 129
Mercian Ct. WS13: Lich . . . 4C 114
Mercian Pk. B77: Amin . . . 6C 138
Mercian Way B77: Amin . . . 4C 138
Mercury Ct. B77: Amin . . . 6E 138
Mercury Pl. ST6: B'lem . . . 6D 18
Mercury Rd. WS11: Cann . . . 5G 101
Mere Cl. WV12: Will . . . 7A 126
Mere Cft. WS11: N Can . . . 6B 110
Meredith Cl. DE14: B Tre . . . 5E 84
Meredith Rd. WV11: Wed . . . 5G 125
MERE GREEN . . . 2B 164
MERE HEATH . . . 1A 154
Merelake Rd. ST7: Als, T Pit . . . 6A 10
Mere La. ST19: Penk . . . 6F 91
Meremore Dr. ST5: C'ton . . . 5B 16
Mere Oak Rd. WV6: Per . . . 1F 129
Mere Side Cl. ST1: H'ley . . . 6A 150 (6K 23)
MERETOWN . . . 2B 158
Merevale Av. ST2: Buck . . . 6G 25
Merganser B77: Wiln . . . 4C 142
MERIDEN . . . 3C 165
Meriden Cl. WS11: Cann . . . 3B 108
Meriden Rd. ST5: N'tle . . . 7G 31
WV10: Oxl . . . 5J 123
Merino Cl. ST3: L'ood . . . 2J 41
Merlin Cl. B77: Wiln . . . 4C 142
ST6: Feg H . . . 6A 12
ST14: Utt . . . 7H 63
WS11: Cann . . . 1C 108
Merlin Ct. WS7: Burn . . . 3D 112
Merlin Cres. DE14: B'ton . . . 4A 86
Merlin Grn. CW3: Mad . . . 3A 28
Merlin Way ST7: Kids . . . 3H 11
WS14: W'ton . . . 3H 131
Merrey Rd. ST17: Staf . . . 7G 73
Merrial St. ST5: N'tle . . . 3E 152 (7F 23)
Merrick Rd. WV11: Wed . . . 7A 126
Merrick St. ST1: H'ley . . . 1H 151 (3D 24)
Merrill Cl. WS6: C Hay . . . 2E 118
Merrion Dr. ST6: B'lem . . . 5B 18
Merrivale Rd. ST17: Staf . . . 7G 73
Merrydale Rd. DE15: Stap . . . 4H 87
MERRY HILL . . . 7K 129
Merryhills Ent. Pk. WV10: W'ton . . . 7D 124
Mersey Cl. WS15: Rug . . . 5G 95
Mersey Pl. WS3: Blox . . . 4K 127
Mersey Rd. ST5: N'tle . . . 6E 30
WS3: Blox . . . 4K 127
Mersey St. ST1: H'ley . . . 4E 150 (4B 24)
Merthyr Gro. ST8: Knyp . . . 7E 8
Merton St. ST3: Long . . . 5J 33
Mervyn Rd. DE15: Wins . . . 1H 87
Mesnes Grn. WS14: Lich . . . 4C 114
Metcalf Cl. WS7: Burn . . . 3A 112
Metcalfe Cl. WS12: Hed . . . 4J 101
Metcalfe Rd. ST6: B'lem . . . 4A 18
Metfield Cl. B79: Tam . . . 1J 137
Metro Bus. Pk. ST1: H'ley . . . 4C 150 (5A 24)
Mews, The DE14: B Tre . . . 5D 86
ST5: N'tle . . . 4H 23
Mews Cl. ST2: Buck . . . 6G 25
Meynell Cl. DE15: Stap . . . 3J 87
Meynellfield TF9: Logg . . . 5E 60
Meyrick Rd. ST17: Staf . . . 5G 73
Mica Cl. B77: Amin . . . 7D 138
Michael Cl. ST3: W Coy . . . 6D 34
Michaels Cl. ST5: N'tle . . . 1G 23
Michigan Cl. WS11: H Hay . . . 1H 109
Michigan Gro. ST4: Tren . . . 2B 40
Micklea La. ST9: L'ton . . . 7A 48
Mickleby Way ST3: Mei . . . 3E 42
Micklegate ST19: Brew . . . 1D 92
Micklehome Dr. DE13: Alre . . . 5D 130
Micklemore La. ST19: Whe A . . . 1A 90
MICKLEOVER . . . 1D 161
Mickleton B77: Wiln . . . 2E 142
Micklewood Cl. ST19: Penk . . . 5H 91
Micklewood La. ST19: Penk . . . 7J 91
Mickley Av. WV10: W'ton . . . 7C 124
Middle Cross St. ST3: Long . . . 5J 33
Middle Entry B79: Tam . . . 4H 137
Middlefield ST20: Gno . . . 3J 67
WV8: P'ord . . . 3G 123
Middlefield Rd. ST2: Bent . . . 1K 33
Middle Friars ST17: Staf . . . 4G 73
MIDDLE HILL . . . 7B 108
MIDDLE HILL JUNC. . . . 7A 108
Middle La. WV8: Oak . . . 3A 122
WV9: Cove . . . 1H 123
MIDDLE MADELEY . . . 2B 28
MIDDLE MAYFIELD . . . 6A 56 (3B 156)
MIDDLEPORT . . . 1J 23

Middlesmoor—Moorview Gdns.

Middlesmoor B77: Wiln 2E 142
MIDDLETON
Bakewell 1B 156
Matlock 2C 157
Tamworth 2B 164
Middleton Cl. ST6: Nort 4E 18
MIDDLETON GREEN 1D 159
MIDDLETON PRIORS 2A 162
Middleton Rd. B74: S'ly 7F 135
WS8: Brow 3J 121
WS14: W'ton 2G 131
MIDDLETON SCRIVEN 3A 162
Middleway WS12: Haz 4C 102
Middleway Pk. DE14: B Tre 1F 87
MIDDLEWICH 1B 154
Midfield Cl. ST8: G Hea 3C 8
Midhurst Cl. ST7: Pack 6K 11
Midhurst Dr. WS12: Hed 3J 101
Midhurst Gro. WV6: Tett 1K 129
Midland Grain Warehouse
DE14: B Tre 1D 86
(off Derby St.)
Midland Karting 4F 107
Midland Rd. WS12: Hun 5C 100
MIDWAY 2D 161
Midway, The ST5: N'tle 4D 152 (1F 31)
Midway Dr. ST11: B Bri 4G 43
Midwinter Ct. ST6: B'lem 2J 23
Miflins Valley WS15: Rug 5D 96
Milan Dr. ST5: N'tle 3C 30
Milan Gro. ST3: Long 5A 34
Milborne Dr. ST5: N'tle 4G 31
Milburn B77: Wiln 2E 142
Milburn Rd. ST6: B'lem 1B 24
Mildenhall B79: Tam 1J 137
Mile Flat DY6: King 4K 147
Milehouse La. ST5: N'tle 4F 23
MILE OAK 1C 140
Miles Bank ST1: H'ley 3G 151
MILES GREEN 7G 15 (2C 155)
Miles Grn. Rd. ST7: Big E 7G 15
Miles Mdw. Cl. WV12: Will 5C 126
Milestone Ct. WV6: Tett 3H 129
Milestone Way WS7: Chas 5G 111
WV12: Will 5B 126
MILFORD
Belper 3D 157
Stafford 7G 75 (2D 159)
Milford Av. ST9: Werr 4D 26
Milford Common Vis. Cen. 7G 75
Milford Dr. DE13: Stre 3G 85
Milford Rd. ST5: N'tle 6C 152 (2E 30)
ST17: Walt 7C 74
Milford St. ST4: Fen 4F 33
Milgreen Av. ST1: H'ley 1D 24
Milk St. ST13: Lee 2G 49
Mill Bank ST16: Staf 3G 73
Mill Bank Dr. ST14: Roce 5E 58
Millbank Pl. ST5: N'tle 3A 152 (7D 22)
Millbank St. ST3: Long 6J 33
WV11: Wed 4K 125
Millbridge Cl. ST3: Mei 4D 42
Millbrook Cl. WS11: Cann 1F 109
Millbrook Dr. WS14: Shen 5C 134
Millbrook Gdns. ST11: B Bri 3H 43
Millbrook Gro. ST2: Mil 6G 19
Millbrook Way ST10: Chea 5D 54
Mill Cl. ST11: Cave 6E 34
Mill Ct. ST4: Tren 3J 39
ST16: Staf 3G 73
(off Mill St.)
ST18: Gt Hay 3G 81
WS14: Shen 5D 134
Mill Cres. DE13: B Nee 7H 89
WS11: H Hay 1H 109
Millcroft Way WS15: Hand 5F 99
MILLDALE 2B 156
Milldale Cres. WV10: Ford 1B 124
Milldale Packhorse Bridge 2B 156
Milldale Rd. WV10: Ford 1B 124
MILLEND 2E 14
Mill End La. DE13: Alre 5B 130
ST7: Aud 2E 14
Millennium Chapel, The 6E 130
(off Croxhall Rd.)
Millennium Way ST5: C'ton 5D 16
ST15: Stone 2E 46
WV8: Bilb 1D 122
MILLER'S DALE 1B 156
Millersdale Cl. DE15: Wins 6J 85
Millers Ga. ST15: Stone 4G 47
(off Christchurch Way)
MILLERS GREEN 2C 157
Millers La. DE14: B Tre 1D 86
ST2: Mil 6G 19
Miller St. ST5: N'tle 2G 153 (7G 23)
Millers Va. WS12: H Hay 2K 109
WV5: Womb 5D 144
Millers Vw. ST7: Kids 5E 10
ST10: Chea 5E 54
Millers Wharf B78: Pole 1H 143
Millett Rd. ST2: Buck 5G 25
Millfield Av. WS3: Blox 3K 127
Millfield Cres. ST2: Mil 6G 19
Millfield Rd. WS8: Brow 5J 121
Mill Flds. DY7: Kin 6F 149
Millfields Way WV5: Womb 4E 144
MILL GREEN
Cannock 3F 109
Market Drayton 2A 158
Rugeley 2A 160
Walsall 1F 135
Mill Grn. WV10: Ford 1B 124
Mill Green Nature Pk. 2G 109
Mill Gro. ST7: Talk 5B 10
ST10: Chea 5D 54
WV8: Bilb 2E 122
Mill Hayes Rd. ST6: B'lem 6J 17
ST8: Knyp 3C 12
Mill Hill Cres. ST6: Chel 3A 18
Mill Hill Dr. DE15: Wins 7J 85
Mill Hill La. DE15: Wins 7H 85
Mill Ho. Dr. ST10: Chea 6D 54
Millhouse Gdns. ST19: Penk 3H 91
Millicent Cl. WS12: Hed 4H 101
Millicent St. ST4: Fen 3E 32
MILLINGTON GREEN 3C 157
Millington Rd. WV10: Bush 7C 124
Millington St. WS15: Rug 6H 95
Mill La. B78: Faze 2G 141
B79: Edin 2C 132
B79: Tam 4J 137
CW3: Mad 2B 28
CW3: Wrin 7B 6
DE13: B Nee 7H 89
DY7: Kin 6F 149
DY7: Stou 5K 147
ST9: W Roc 2G 27
ST10: Tea 5G 55
ST15: Modd 5K 45
ST17: Act G 4H 77
ST18: Gt Hay 3G 81
ST19: Whe A 3C 90
ST20: Gno 5G 67
WS7: Hamm 7B 112
WS9: Ald 1F 135
WS9: Ston 5K 133
WS14: Shen 5D 134
WS15: Rug 7H 95
WV5: Swin 7D 144
WV5: Womb 3H 145
WV6: Tett 3H 129
WV8: Cods 1B 122 & 6E 92
WV11: Wed 6E 124
WV12: Will 7C 126
MILLMEECE 1C 159
Mill Meece Pumping Station 1C 159
Millmoor Av. WS15: Arm 5E 98
Mill Pk. WS11: Cann 1G 109
Mill Pk. Ind. Est.
WS11: Cann 1G 109
Millpond, The WS13: Lich 1C 114
Millpool, The WV5: Seis 2B 146
Mill Pool Cl. WV5: Womb 5D 144
Millpool Rd. WS12: Hed 4H 101
Mill Ri. ST7: Kids 5E 10
Millrise Rd. ST2: Mil 6G 19
Mill Rd. ST10: Chea 5D 54
ST10: O'moor 3B 56
WS8: Brow 5J 121
Mills Cl. WV11: Wed 5F 125
Millside WS15: S Mil 2D 96
WV5: Womb 5E 144
Millstone Av. ST7: Talk 5C 10
Millstone Ct. ST15: Stone 3G 47
Mill Stream Cl. WV8: Bilb 1D 122
Millstream Cl. ST10: Chea 5D 54
Mill Stream La. DE13: Stre 2H 85
Mill St. ST5: Sil 7B 22
ST13: Lee 3E 48
ST14: Roce 5D 58
ST15: Stone 4G 47
ST16: Staf 3G 73
ST19: Penk 3G 91
WS11: Cann 2E 108
Mill St. Chambers WS11: Cann 2E 108
(off Mill St.)
MILLTOWN 1D 157
Milltown Way ST13: Lee 5H 49
Mill Vw. ST6: B Gre 1D 18
Millwalk Av. ST15: Stone 5J 47
Millwalk Dr. WV9: P'ord 2J 123
Millward Rd. ST2: Buck 5J 25
Millwaters ST10: Chea 5D 54
Millway, The ST15: Swyn 2C 64
Milne Av. WS13: Frad 4K 107
Milner Dr. B79: Shut 2G 139
Milner Ter. ST13: Lee 2H 49
Milnes Cl. ST3: Blur 7G 33
Milo Cres. B78: Tam 7G 137
MILTON
Buton upon Trent 2D 161
Stoke-on-Trent 6H 19 (2D 155)
Milton Av. B79: Tam 2G 137
Milton Cl. WV12: Will 6E 126
Milton Ct. WV6: Per 2F 129
Milton Cres. ST7: Talk 6A 10
Milton Gro. ST17: Staf 7D 72
Milton Ho. DE14: B Tre 1D 86
(off Cross St.)
Milton Rd. ST1: H'ley 1D 24
WS11: Cann 6E 100
WV10: W'ton 7E 124
Milton St. DE14: B Tre 2D 86
ST1: H'ley 5D 150 (5B 24)
Milvale St. ST6: B'lem 1J 23
Milverton Dr. ST14: Utt 4E 62
Milverton Pl. ST3: Long 6G 33
Milward Gro. ST3: L'ood 4B 42
MILWICH 1D 159
Minard Gro. ST3: W Coy 5C 34
Minden Gro. ST6: B'lem 7D 18
Minehead Rd. WV10: Oxl 3K 123
Mineral Rd. ST2: B Hil 2K 33
Miners Wlk. B78: Pole 1H 143
Miners Way WS7: C Ter, Chas 4E 110
Minerva Cl. B77: Tam 4K 137
ST8: Knyp 1B 12
Minerva Rd. ST4: Fen 3F 33
Minewood Cl. WS3: Blox 2F 127
Minfield Cl. ST7: Kids 6E 10
Minnie Cl. ST7: H End 1G 21
Minors Hill WS14: Lich 5D 114
Minshall Ct. ST4: Fen 4C 32
(off Minshall St.)
Minshall St. ST4: Fen 4C 32
Minsterpool Wlk. WS13: Lich 3B 114
Minster St. ST6: B'lem 6B 18
Minstrel Ct. ST8: Bidd 6D 8
Minton Cl. ST10: Chea 6C 54
Minton Pl. ST5: N'tle 3H 23
Minton St. ST4: S Tren 1J 31
ST5: N'tle 3H 23
MINWORTH 2B 164
Miranda Gro. ST6: B'lem 6D 18
Miras Bus. Est. WS12: Hed 7K 101
Mires Brook La. WS15: Abb B 2B 88
Mirfield Cl. WV9: P'ord 2J 123
Miss Pickerings Fld.
ST17: Act T 6K 77
Mistley Wlk. ST6: Gold 7G 11
Mitcham Cl. WS12: Hed 3F 101
Mitchell Av. ST7: Talk 5B 10
Mitchell Cl. WS13: Frad 4J 107
Mitchell Dr. ST7: Talk 5B 10
Mitchell Memorial Theatre
4F 151 (5C 24)
Mitchell Ri. ST15: Yarn 6D 64
Mitchells Ct. B79: Tam 4H 137
(off Lwr. Gungate)
Mitchell St. ST6: B'lem 6K 17
Mitchell Way ST6: Tuns 2G 17
Mitre Cl. WV11: Ess 2A 126
WV12: Will 6D 126
Mitre Rd. WS6: C Hay 2C 118
MITTON 3C 159
Mitton Rd. ST18: Brad 2G 69
MIXON 2A 156
Moat, The ST3: W Coy 5C 34
MOAT BANK 1K 133
Moat Bank DE15: Bret 2K 87
Moatbrook Av. WV8: Cods 7E 92
Moatbrook La. WV8: Cods 7C 92
Moat Dr. B78: D Bas 5E 140
Moat Farm Way WS3: Pels 7C 120
Moat Grn. Av. WV11: Wed 6J 125
MOAT HILL 7C 88
Moathouse Cl. ST17: Act T 7K 77
Moat Ho. Dr. ST18: Hau 6B 66
Moat Ho. La. E. WV11: Wed 6H 125
Moat Ho. La. W. WV11: Wed 6H 125
Moat La. DE13: New 7B 88
ST7: Aud 5C 14
WS6: G Wyr 2G 119
Moatside Cl. WS3: Pels 7C 120
Moat Way WS15: Hand 5F 99
MOBBERLEY 7C 54 (3A 156)
Mobberley Rd. ST6: Gold 6G 11
Moccasin Way ST16: Staf 7H 71
MODDERSHALL 1D 159
Modular Ct. WV10: F Ash 6G 93
Moffat Gro. ST2: Bent 2A 34
Moffatt Way ST5: Sil 6H 21
MOIRA 3D 161
Moises Hall Rd. WV5: Womb 3H 145
Moisty La. ST14: Mar 1A 82
Mollatts Cl. ST13: Lee 7C 48
Mollatts Wood Rd. ST13: Lee 7C 48
Mollison Rd. ST3: Mei 2C 42
Monachy Cl. WS15: Rug 2F 97
Monaco Pl. ST5: N'tle 2C 30
Monarch Cl. DE13: Stre 3F 85
Mona Rd. DE13: B Tre 6C 84
Moncreiff Dr. DE13: Stre 2H 85
MONEYSTONE 1B 56
Monkey Forest 7K 39
MONKHOPTON 2A 162
MONKHOUSE 3C 54
Monkhouse ST10: Chea 4C 54
Monkleigh Cl. ST4: Tren 5B 40
Monks Cl. ST5: N'tle 3G 31
WV5: Womb 4E 144
MONKSPATH 3B 164
Monk St. DE13: Tut 2H 83
Monks Wlk. ST20: Gno 6G 67
Monks Way B77: Amin 4B 138
ST15: Swyn 2C 64
Monkton Cl. ST3: Blur 1G 41
Monmouth Pl. ST5: N'tle 5H 31
Monsaldale Cl. DE15: Wins 7J 85
WS8: Clay 6F 121
Monsal Gro. ST1: H'ley 3F 25
Montfort Pl. ST5: N'tle 7E 152 (3F 31)
Montgomery Ct. ST5: N'tle 2B 152 (7E 22)
Montgomery Ho. WV10: Brin 4A 116
Montgomery Pl. ST3: Mei 7D 34
Montley B77: Wiln 2E 142
Montpelier Cl. DE14: B'ton 5B 86
Montrose Cl. WS11: Cann 5F 101
Montrose St. ST4: Fen 4F 33
Montville Dr. ST17: Staf 6D 72
Monty Pl. ST4: Fen 4H 33
Monument Cl. ST12: Titt 1A 44
Monument Dr. WV10: Fea 4G 117
Monument La. ST12: Titt 1A 44
Monument Rd. ST7: T Pit 1B 16
Monument Vw. B78: Pole 2J 143
CW3: Mad H 1C 28
ST7: Big E 5H 15
MONYASH 1B 156
Monyash Cl. ST3: Mei 3E 42
Monyash Dr. ST13: Lee 4H 49
Moons La. WS6: C Hay 2D 118
Moor, The WS13: Frad 2K 107
Moor Cl. ST8: Bidd 4E 8
ST17: Act T 5K 77
WS7: Burn 4K 111
Moor Cft. WS15: Col 2J 95
Moorcroft Av. ST5: N'tle 6F 31
Moorcroft Cl. ST10: Chea 6B 54
Moorcroft Mus. 1B 24
Moore Cl. B74: F Oak 2K 135
ST15: Stone 6J 47
WV6: Per 2G 129
Moore Rd. WV12: Will 5D 126
Moores Cl. DE13: B Tre 5C 84
Moores Cft. B79: Edin 1B 132
Moore St. ST6: B'lem 1A 24
WS12: Hed 3J 101
Moorfield Av. ST8: Bidd 5C 8
Moorfield Cl. ST21: Cot H 3A 64
Moorfields ST13: Lee 4G 49
ST16: Staf 6F 71
Moorfields Ind. Est. ST21: Cot H 2A 64
Moor Furlong DE13: Stre 2G 85
Moorgate B79: Tam 4G 137
MOOR GREEN 2J 43
Moor Gro. ST14: Utt 5F 63
Moor Hall La. ST19: Penk 5J 91
Moorhead Dr. ST9: S Broo 5B 50
Moorhen Cl. WS8: Brow 5G 121
Moorhen Way ST7: Pack 6J 11
Moorhouse Ct. ST15: Yarn 6A 46
Moorhouse St. ST13: Lee 4G 49
Moorings, The DE13: Alre 5B 130
ST15: Stone 4G 47
ST17: Colw 7K 81
WV9: P'ord 3H 123
Moorland Arts & Antique Cen. 4G 49
(off Ashbourne Rd.)
Moorland Av. ST9: Werr 4D 26
WV10: Oxl 7A 124
Moorland Cl. ST9: Werr 4D 26
WS15: Rug 7E 94
Moorland Rd. ST6: B'lem 7A 18
ST7: M Cop 6H 7
ST8: Bidd 5D 8
ST13: Ched 5G 51
ST13: Lee 4J 49
WS3: Blox 5G 127
WS11: Cann 5E 100
Moorlands, The B74: F Oak 7K 135
Moorlands Ct. ST8: Bidd 5D 8
Moorlands Dr. DE6: May 6B 56
Moorlands Farm Pk. of British Rare Breeds
2A 156
Moorlands Hgts. ST8: Bidd 5D 8
Moorland Vw. ST6: B'lem 4C 18
Moorland Wlk. ST10: Chea 4C 54
(off High St.)
Moor La. B77: Amin 3C 138
B77: Amin, Tam 4K 137
ST10: Chea 3E 54
ST18: Seigh 6A 70
WS15: H Hea, Stoc H 1H 95
WV6: Patt 7B 128 & 5A 128
Moor Pk. WS3: Blox 2H 127
WV6: Per 1E 128
Moors Dr. WV9: Cove 2K 93
MOORS GORSE 6D 96
Moors Gorse WS15: Rug 6C 96
Moorside Rd. ST9: Werr 4F 27
Moor St. B79: Tam 4G 137
DE14: B Tre 2D 86
(not continuous)
Moorsyde Rd. ST4: T Val 4J 31
Moorthorne Cres. ST5: Brad 2E 22
MOORTOWN 3A 158
Moor Vw. WS15: Gen 1K 111
Moorview Gdns. ST7: Harr 1J 11

Newchapel Rd.—Oak Av.

Newchapel Rd. ST7: Kids 3F 11
NEWCHURCH 2B 160
New Cl. Av. ST11: Fors 2K 43
Newcomen Cl. WS7: Burn 3A 112
Newcomen Gro. ST2: B Hil 2K 33
Newcott Cl. WV9: P'ord 3H 123
Newcroft Ct. ST5: N'tle 3G 23
Newcrofts Wlk. ST6: B Gre 1D 18
NEW CROSS 7F 125
Newey Rd. WV11: Wed 5A 126
NEWFIELD 3G 17
Newfield Cl. WS2: Wals 7J 127
Newfield Rd. DE15: Wins 7J 85
Newfield St. ST6: Tuns 3H 17
Newfield Trad. Est. ST6: Sandy 2H 17
Newfold Cres. ST6: B Edg 6H 13
Newford Cres. ST2: Mil 6F 19
New Gdn. St. ST17: Staf 4G 73
Newgate WV6: Patt 6B 128
Newgate St. WS7: Chas 6J 111
New Haden Rd. ST10: Chea 5A 54
NEWHALL
Nantwich 3A 154
Swadlincote 2C 161
Newhall Cres. WS11: H Hay 7H 101
Newhall Gdns. WS11: Cann 1F 109
New Hall Rd. ST3: Long 7K 33
New Hall St. ST1: H'ley 2F 151 (4C 24)
Newhall St. ST10: K'ley 5F 53
WS11: Cann 3D 108
NEWHAVEN 1B 156
Newhaven Gro. ST4: Tren 5B 40
Newhay DE13: Stre 2G 85
New Hayes Rd. ST6: Tuns 3J 17
WS12: Haz 6E 102
New Homage Gdns. WV9: Cove 2K 93
New Horse Rd. WS6: C Hay 1E 118
Newhouse Ct. ST2: Buck 3H 25
Newhouse Rd. ST2: Buck 3H 25
Newick Av. B74: L Ast 5G 135
Newington Gro. ST4: Tren 5C 40
New Inn La. ST4: H'ord, Tren 1K 39
New Inn Row ST17: Broc 4D 78
NEW INVENTION 6D 126
New King St. ST7: Aud 6E 14
New Kingsway ST3: W Coy 5C 34
Newland Av. ST16: Staf 6F 71
NEWLANDS 2A 160
Newlands Cl. ST5: N'tle 4F 31
ST15: Stone 6F 47
ST19: Penk 5H 91
Newlands Ct. WS12: H Hay 3A 110
Newlands La. WS12: H Hay 3H 109
(not continuous)
WS15: Col, Stoc H 1K 95
Newlands St. ST4: S Tren 7B 24
New Landywood La.
WV11: Ess 6E 118
New La. ST6: B Edg 5H 13
Newleigh St. ST2: Mil 6H 19
Newlyn Cl. WS14: Lich 4D 114
Newman Cl. ST15: Stone 5J 47
Newman Dr. DE14: B'ton 4C 86
Newman Gro. WS15: Rug 2H 97
Newman Rd. WV10: Bush 4E 124
Newmarket Cl. WV6: W'ton 7J 123
Newmarket Rd.
WS11: N Can 7C 110
Newmarket Way ST10: Chea 2D 54
New Mill La. B78: Faze 3G 141
Newmill St. ST2: Mil 6G 19
Newmount Rd. ST4: Fen 4H 33
NEW OSCOTT 2B 164
New Pk. Gdns. ST4: Tren 5C 40
New Penkridge Rd.
WS11: Cann, Hath 6A 100
Newplant La. WS7: C Ter 4E 110
NEWPOOL 7B 8
Newpool Cotts. ST8: B Lee 1B 12
Newpool Rd. ST8: Knyp 7A 8
Newpool Ter. ST8: B Lee 1B 12
NEWPORT 3B 158
Newport B77: Amin 4B 138
Newport Cl. DE14: B Tre 4E 84
Newport Cft. ST19: Brew 2C 92
Newport Gro. ST5: C'ton 5C 16
Newport La. ST6: B'lem 7J 17
Newport Rd. ST16: Staf 5D 72
ST18: Gt Bri 6H 65
ST18: Hau 6A 66
ST20: Gno 5F 67
ST20: W'ves 4D 66
ST21: Ecc 4H 65
Newport St. ST6: B'lem 7J 17
ST19: Brew 2C 92
Newquay Av. ST17: Staf 6B 74
New Rd. B77: Wiln 3B 142
B79: Shut 1G 139
CW3: Mad 2A 28
CW12: More 1F 7
DY3: Swin 7A 144
ST2: Bent 5B 26
ST7: Big E 5F 15
ST10: Alt 5H 57
ST10: Chec 7K 55
New Rd. ST10: Dilh 6K 35
ST10: Tea 3F 55
ST14: Utt 3F 63
ST18: Hixon 6A 80
ST19: Penk 3G 91
WS7: Burn 5K 111
WS8: Brow 5H 121
WS14: Shen 5C 134
WS15: Arm, Hand 4E 98
WV10: Bush 5F 125
WV10: C Gre, S Hea, Fea 3B 116
New Rd. Est. ST18: Hixon 5B 80
New Row B78: D Bas 5E 140
CW3: Mad H 1C 28
DE6: D Cla 6B 82
ST18: Hyde L 2E 76
NEWSBANK 1C 155
Newshaw Wlk. ST1: H'ley 3J 151 (4D 24)
NEWSTEAD 3F 41
Newstead B79: Tam 3D 136
Newstead Rd. ST2: A Hul 3H 25
Newstead Trad. Est. ST4: Tren 3D 40
New St. B77: Amin 5A 138
B77: T Gat 1J 141
B78: Bir 3G 143
B78: Dor 5J 143
B78: Faze 2H 141
B79: Tam 5G 137
DE14: B Tre 2E 86
ST5: N'tle 3H 23
ST6: B'lem 7K 17
ST8: Bid M 7F 9
ST13: Lee 3G 49
ST14: Utt 5G 63
ST16: Staf 1F 73
WS3: Blox 4H 127
WS6: G Wyr 2G 119
WS7: C Ter 2H 111
WS7: Chas 6G 111
WS11: Cann 3E 108
(Mill St.)
WS11: Cann 5D 108
(Watling St.)
WS12: Hed 6J 101
WV3: W'ton 7K 129
WV11: Ess 2A 126
NEWSTREET LANE 1A 158
NEW SWANNINGTON 3D 161
NEWTON
Alfreton 2D 157
Bridgnorth 2B 162
Rugeley 2A 160
NEWTON BURGOLAND 1D 165
Newton Ct. ST9: Werr 4C 26
WV9: P'ord 2H 123
Newton Leys DE15: Wins 7K 85
Newton M. DE15: Wins 1G 87
Newton Pl. WS2: Wals 7H 127
NEWTON REGIS 1C 165
Newton Rd. DE15: B Tre 1G 87
ST5: N'tle 3F 23
ST16: Staf 1H 73
WS2: Wals 7H 127
WS13: Lich 1K 113
Newtons Coll. WS13: Lich 3A 114
NEWTON SOLNEY 3K 85 (2C 161)
Newton St. ST4: S Tren 1K 153 (6J 23)
NEWTOWN
Biddulph 1D 155
Buxton 1A 156
Nantwich 3A 154
NEW TOWN 3K 121
NEWTOWN 4D 78
Great Wyrley 7G 119 (1D 163)
Newtown ST7: New 4J 11
New Vic Theatre 1H 153 (6H 23)
New Villas WV11: Wed 7E 124
Niall Rd. ST4: H'ord 1K 39
Nicholas Gro. ST13: Lee 5C 48
Nicholas St. ST6: B'lem 7K 17
Nicholl's La. ST15: Oul 2H 47
Nicholls St. ST4: S Tren 4B 32
Nicholls Way
WS12: H Hay 2B 110
Nicholson Institute Art Gallery, The
....3F 49
Nicholson Way ST13: Lee 3E 48
Nicklaus Cl. DE14: B'ton 5B 86
Nicolson Way DE14: B Tre 3B 86
Nightingale B77: Wiln 4C 142
Nightingale Cl. ST10: Tea 6H 55
WS12: Hun 3C 100
Nightingale Ct. WS7: Burn 3D 112
Nightingale Cres.
WV12: Will 5B 126
Nightingale Wlk. ST11: B Bri 7F 43
WS7: Burn 4C 112
Nile St. ST6: B'lem 7A 18
Nimbus B77: Dost 6K 141
Ninefoot La. B77: Wiln 2A 142
(not continuous)
Ninian Pk. B77: Wiln 4K 141
Ninian Way B77: Wiln 5A 142
Nirvana Cl. WS11: Cann 1C 108
Noblett Rd. ST1: H'ley 1E 24
Nocke Rd. WV11: Wed 4K 125
Noddington Av. WS14: W'ton 2G 131
Noddington La. WS14: W'ton 2G 131
NO MAN'S HEATH 1C 165
No Name Rd. WS7: C Ter 4G 111
Nook, The WS6: C Hay 3C 118
Noon Cft. DE13: Alre 6B 130
NOONSUN COMMON 2F 53
NORBURY
Ashbourne 3B 156
Newport 2B 158
Whitchurch 3A 154
Norbury Av. ST2: Mil 6H 19
Norbury Cl. ST20: Gno 4H 67
Norbury Ct. ST15: Stone 4G 47
Norbury Rd. ST20: Gno 4F 67
WV10: W'ton 7D 124
NORDLEY 2A 162
Nordley Rd. WV11: Wed 7G 125
Nordley Wlk. WV11: Wed 7G 125
Norfolk Cl. ST5: N'tle 7F 31
Norfolk Dr. B78: Tam 1G 141
Norfolk Gro. ST8: Bidd 4C 8
WS6: G Wyr 3F 119
Norfolk Rd. DE15: Stap 6E 86
ST7: Kids 4D 10
Norfolk St. ST1: H'ley 7E 150 (6B 24)
Norfolk Way ST17: Staf 7E 72
Norington La. WS14: W'ton 2G 131
NORLEY 1A 154
NORMACOT 7K 33
Normacot Grange Rd. ST3: Mei 3B 42
Normacot Rd. ST3: Long 6J 33
(Millbank St.)
ST3: Long 7K 33
(Queensberry Rd.)
Norman Av. ST6: Tuns 4K 17
Norman Cl. B79: Tam 2E 136
Normandy Gro. ST2: Mil 5G 19
Normandy Pl. ST5: N'tle 2C 152 (7E 22)
Norman Gro. ST5: N'tle 1J 153 (6H 23)
Norman Keep DE13: Tut 2H 83
Norman Rd. DE13: Tut 2H 83
ST19: Penk 4H 91
NORMANTON 1D 161
Normanton Gro. ST3: Long 3K 33
NORMANTON LE HEATH 3D 161
Norris Cl. TF9: A'ley 4J 61
NORRIS HILL 3D 161
Norris Rd. ST6: B'lem 4K 17
Northam Rd. ST1: H'ley 2D 24
North Av. ST13: Lee 4E 48
ST16: Staf 6F 71
WV11: Wed 7G 125
Nth. Castle St. ST16: Staf 3F 73
Northcliffe *ST13: Lee 3E 48*
(off Belle Vue Rd.)
Northcote Av. ST4: S Tren 1A 32
Northcote Cl. ST18: L Hay 6K 81
Northcote Ct. ST5: N'tle 2G 153 (7G 23)
Northcote Pl. ST5: N'tle 2G 153 (7G 23)
Northcote St. ST4: S Tren 7B 24
North Cres. WV10: Fea 5F 117
Northdale WV6: Tett 2J 129
North Dr. ST20: Gno 4G 67
NORTHEDGE 1D 157
Northesk Pl. ST5: N'tle 4E 30
Northesk St. ST15: Stone 3F 47
NORTHFIELD 3A 164
Northfield Av. ST14: Roce 4D 58
Northfield Cl. ST14: Utt 3F 63
Northfield Dr. ST8: Bidd 3E 8
Northfield Gro. WV3: W'ton 7K 129
Northfield Rd. DE13: B Tre 4D 84
Northfields Way WS8: Clay 6F 121
Northfleet St. ST2: Buck 5G 25
Northgate Cl. ST4: H'ord 1K 39
Northicote Recreation & Community Cen.
....2C 124
Northover Cl. WV9: P'ord 3J 123
North Pl. ST2: A Hul 2H 25
ST16: Staf 1F 73
North Rd. ST6: B'lem 1B 24
ST15: Cold M 6B 64
NORTH RODE 1C 155
Northside Bus. Pk. DE14: B Tre 5F 85
North St. DE15: Wins 1J 87
ST4: S Tren 7K 23
ST5: N'tle 3G 153 (7G 23)
ST7: M Cop 7F 7
ST13: Lee 3D 48
WS7: C Ter 2H 111
WS11: Cann 5E 108
North Ter. ST5: N'tle 3F 23
Northumberland Cl. B78: Tam 1G 141
Northumberland Rd. DE15: Stap 5E 86
North Wlk. ST3: Mei 1D 42
North Walls ST16: Staf 3G 73
Nth. West Ter. ST6: B'lem 6C 18
NORTHWICH 1A 154
NORTH WINGFIELD 1D 157
NORTHWOOD
Matlock 1C 157
Newcastle 1G 39
Stoke-on-Trent 1J 151 (3C 155)
Northwood Cl. ST5: N'tle 7H 31
Northwood Ct. ST1: H'ley 3J 151
Northwood Grn.
ST1: H'ley 3K 151 (4E 24)
Northwood La. ST5: N'tle 7G 31
Northwood Pk. Cl. WV10: Bush 2B 124
Northwood Pk. Rd.
ST1: H'ley 1J 151 (3D 24)
(not continuous)
WV10: Bush 2C 124
Northwood Sports Cen. 2K 151 (4E 24)
Northycote Farm 2E 124
Northycote Farm Country Pk. 2E 124
Northycote La. WV10: Bush 1D 124
NORTON
Shifnal 1B 162
Shrewsbury 1A 162
Norton Av. ST6: B'lem 4A 18
NORTON BRIDGE 1C 159
NORTON CANES 6D 110 (1A 164)
Norton Cl. B79: Tam 2J 137
Norton Cres. ST6: B'lem 7D 18
Norton Dr. ST6: B'lem 6D 18
NORTON EAST
Burntwood 4E 110 (1A 164)
Cannock 5C 110
Norton E. Rd. WS11: N Can 6C 110
Norton Grange WS11: N Can 7B 110
Norton Grange Cres. WS11: N Can 7B 110
NORTON GREEN
Stoke-on-Trent 2G 19 (2D 155)
Walsall 1B 120
Norton Grn. La. WS11: N Can 7A 110
Norton Hall Cl. ST6: Nort 4E 18
Norton Hall La. WS11: N Can 7K 109
Norton Ind. Est. ST6: Nort 5E 18
NORTON IN HALES 1B 158
NORTON IN THE MOORS
....3F 19 (2C 155)
NORTON-JUXTA-TWYCROSS 1D 165
Norton Lakeside Station
Chasewater Railway 5E 110
Norton Lakeside Wildfowl Reserve
....5D 110
Norton La. ST6: Mil, Nort 3E 18
WS6: G Wyr 7G 109
WS7: Burn 6A 112
WS11: Cann, N Can 4J 109
Norton Rd. DE13: B Tre 5B 84
WS3: Pels 6C 120
WS12: H Hay 3B 110
Norton Springs WS11: N Can 6B 110
Norton St. ST2: Mil 6H 19
Norton Ter. WS11: N Can 5B 110
Norwich Cl. WS13: Lich 7C 106
Norwich Pl. ST5: N'tle 4G 31
Norwich Rd. ST2: Buck 6K 25
Nottingham Dr. WV12: Will 6C 126
NOTTINGHAM EAST MIDLANDS AIRPORT
....2D 161
Novi La. ST13: Lee 2H 49
NUNEATON 2D 165
Nunn's Cl. ST3: W Coy 4E 34
Nunn St. ST13: Lee 3E 48
Nurseries, The WV9: Cove 2K 93
Nursery Av. ST9: S Broo 4J 19
Nursery Cl. *ST6: B Edg 7H 13*
(off High La.)
ST7: Talk 5B 10
ST10: Chea 4B 54
ST18: Brad 6B 68
Nursery Cft. WS13: Lich 2K 113
Nursery Dr. ST8: G Hea 3C 8
ST19: Penk 2G 91
WV5: Womb 6F 145
Nursery Gdns. ST9: S Broo 3K 19
WV8: Cods 1B 122
Nursery La. B78: Hop 3B 136
ST9: S Broo 4J 19
ST16: Staf 1F 73
Nursery Rd. ST7: Sch G 1C 10
WS3: Blox 5H 127
Nursery St. ST4: S Tren 4A 32
Nursery Wlk. WV6: Tett 2K 129
Nursery Way ST18: Gt Hay 3G 81
Nursey Rd. WS15: Bre 4J 97
NURTON 3B 128
Nurton Bank WV6: Patt 3B 128
Nutbrook Av. ST4: Fen 4C 32
Nuthurst Dr. WS11: Cann 7F 109
Nyewood Av. ST3: Long 4K 33
Nymet B77: Wiln 2A 142

O

Oadby Ri. DE13: B Tre 5B 84
OAKAMOOR 3B 56 (3A 156)
Oakamoor Rd. ST10: Chea 3E 54
ST10: O'moor 4A 56
Oakapple Cl. ST19: B Elm 6B 90
Oak Av. ST13: Ched 6G 51
ST17: Walt 1D 78
WS6: G Wyr 3G 119
WS12: Hun 2D 100

Oak Cl.—Osprey

Oak Cl. DY7: Kin 6G 149
ST14: Utt 4E 62
ST18: Gt Hay 5H 81
ST20: C Eat 3C 68
WS15: Rug 5F 95
Oak Ct. ST19: Brew 2D 92
Oak Cres. WS3: Blox 7K 127
Oakdale ST5: N'tle 6G 31
Oakden Cl. ST14: Bram 6B 62
Oakdene Av. ST5: N'tle 2E 22
Oakdene Cl. ST5: N'tle 2E 22
ST11: B Bri 4K 43
WS6: C Hay 2D 118
Oakdene Gro. ST5: N'tle 2E 22
Oakdene Rd. WS7: Chas 5J 111
Oakdene Way ST8: Bidd 6D 8
Oak Dr. B78: M Oak 1C 140
ST19: Whe A 2C 90
WV5: Seis 2B 146
OAKEN 3A 122 (1C 163)
Oaken Covert WV8: Cods 3A 122
Oaken Dr. WV8: Cods, Oak 3A 122
WV12: Will 6E 126
Oakenfield WS13: Lich 1A 114
Oaken Gdns. WS7: C Ter 3J 111
OAKENGATES 3B 158
Oaken Grange WS6: G Wyr 3F 119
Oaken Gro. WV8: Cods 3A 122
Oakenhayes Cres.
WS8: Brow 3H 121
Oakenhayes Dr. WS8: Brow 3H 121
Oaken Lanes WV8: Cods 2A 122
Oaken Pk. WV8: Cods 3C 122
OAKERTHORPE 2D 157
Oak Farm Cen. 5B 140
Oakfield Cl. WS15: Rug 6D 94
Oakfield Dr. WS3: Pels 7D 120
Oakfield Gro. ST8: Bidd 6E 8
Oakfield Rd. DE13: Alre 6B 130
WV8: Bilb 3D 122
Oakfields DE13: H'ury 7E 82
Oak Gdns. ST18: Hau 6C 66
Oak Grn. WV6: Tett 3J 129
OAKGROVE 1D 155
Oak Gro. WV11: Wed 6F 125
Oakham Way ST2: Bent 6J 25
OAKHANGER 2B 154
OAK HILL 5K 31
Oak Hill WV3: W'ton 6K 129
Oakhill Av. ST4: S Tren 5K 31
Oakhill Cl. ST10: Tea 3F 55
Oakhill Hall ST4: S Tren 5K 31
Oakhill Rd. WS11: Cann 1F 109
Oak Ho. WS6: G Wyr 3G 119
Oakhurst WS14: Lich 4C 114
Oakhurst Cres. ST3: Mei 4C 42
Oakhurst Pk. WS15: Bre 4H 97
Oakland Rd. WS3: Blox 6K 127
Oaklands, The ST15: Cold M 6B 64
ST20: C Eat 3B 68
WS15: Rug 7E 94
Oaklands Av. ST5: N'tle 2G 23
Oaklands Bus. Pk.
WS12: Hed 7H 101
Oaklands Cl. ST9: W Roc 2J 27
WS12: Hun 4C 100
WS13: Frad 4K 107
WS15: Hill R 1E 98
Oaklands Ct. B79: Tam 4G 137
Oaklands Dr. ST17: Staf 5F 73
Oak La. CW12: Ast, N Ast 1F 7
ST18: Brad 7C 68
WS7: C Ter 2H 111
Oak Lea ST13: Lee 5C 48
Oaklea Ct. ST7: Big E 2J 15
Oakleigh Ct. ST15: Stone 6K 47
Oakleigh Dr. WS15: Bre 3K 97
WV8: Bilb 2C 122
Oakley Cl. ST19: Penk 3J 91
WS13: Lich 1B 114
Oakley Copse WS15: S Mil 2D 96
Oakley Pl. ST6: Feg H 6A 12
Oak Leys WV3: W'ton 5K 129
Oakleys ST19: Brew 2D 92
OAKMERE 1A 154
Oak Mt. Rd ST9: Werr 4E 26
Oakover Cl. ST14: Utt 7H 63
Oakover Grange ST17: Walt 1D 78
Oak Pk. Ct. B74: F Oak 5K 135
(off Walsall Rd.)
Oak Pk. Leisure Cen. 7H 121
Oak Pl. ST3: Mei 7B 34
Oakridge Cl. ST17: Staf 2C 78
Oakridge Dr. WS6: C Hay 2F 119
Oakridge Way ST17: Staf 2C 78
Oak Rd. DE13: B Nee 6G 89
ST5: N'tle 5B 22
ST14: Dens 3B 58
ST15: Stone 4H 47
ST19: Brew 2D 92
ST21: Ecc 3G 65
WS3: Pels 7B 120
Oaks, The ST5: Keel 3J 29
ST17: Walt 7D 74
WS3: Blox 4G 127
Oaks Dr. WS11: Cann 2C 108
WV5: Womb 5G 145
WV10: Brin 3D 116
OAKS GREEN 1B 160
Oakshaw Cl. WV9: Cove 1K 93
Oakshaw Gro. ST4: Tren 2B 40
Oaks Moor Cl. ST19: Whe A 2C 90
Oak St. DE14: B Tre 3C 86
ST1: H'ley 1K 151 (2E 24)
ST5: N'tle 5H 23
ST10: Chea 4C 54
OAKTHORPE 3D 161
Oak Tree Cl. ST17: Staf 7D 72
Oaktree Dr. TF9: Logg 4E 60
Oaktree La. ST7: Talk, T Pit 2B 16
Oak Tree Pk. WV10: Fea 3D 116
Oaktree Ri. WV8: Cods 7E 92
Oaktree Rd. ST4: Tren 4B 40
WS15: Rug 3H 97
Oak Tree Wlk. B79: Tam 2F 137
Oakville Av. ST6: B'lem 5B 18
Oakwell Ct. ST3: Long 1J 41
Oakwell Gro. ST3: Long 1J 41
OAKWOOD 1D 161
Oakwood WS15: Rug 7D 94
Oakwood Cl. WS14: Shen 5D 134
WV11: Ess 2B 126
Oakwood Pl. ST5: C'ton 7C 16
Oakwood Rd. ST3: Blur 1E 40
ST13: Lee 3D 48
Oakwoods WS11: Cann 3D 108
Oatfield Cl. WS7: Chas 7J 111
Oatlands Way WV6: Per 3E 128
Oban Cl. ST5: N'tle 5A 152 (1D 30)
Oberon Cl. ST6: B'lem 6D 18
OCCLESTONE GREEN 1A 154
Occupation Rd. WS8: W Woo 7J 121
Occupation St. ST5: N'tle 6G 153 (2G 31)
OCKBROOK 1D 161
Octagon Cen., The DE14: B Tre 2E 86
Octagon Shop. Pk., The
ST1: H'ley 3C 150 (4A 24)
Oddfellows ST15: Stone 4G 47
(off Adies All.)
Odell Cres. WS3: Blox 6J 127
Odell Gro. ST6: B'lem 6J 17
Odell Rd. WS3: Blox 6H 127
Odell Way WS3: Blox 6H 127
Odeon Cinema
Stoke-on-Trent 3B 150 (4A 24)
Odger Cl. ST3: Mei 7D 34
Odiham Cl. B79: Tam 1J 137
Odin Cl. WS11: Cann 5G 101
ODSTONE 1D 165
Offadrive B79: Tam 4H 137
Offa's Dr. WV6: Per 1F 129
Offa St. B79: Tam 4H 137
OFFLEYHAY 2C 159
OFFLEYMARSH 2B 158
Offoxey Rd. ST19: B Elm 7A 90
Ogden Rd. ST1: H'ley 5G 151 (5C 24)
Ogley Cres. WS8: Brow 5J 121
Ogley Hay Rd. WS7: C Ter 1J 111
WS7: Chas 7K 111
WS8: Brow 2J 121
WS8: Chas 2J 121
Ogley Rd. WS8: Brow 5J 121
Ogley Va. WS7: Burn 3K 111
Ogmore Gro. ST3: Mei 2C 42
O'Hare Pl. ST13: Lee 2H 49
Ohio Gro. ST6: B'lem 7B 18
Oldacre La. ST17: Broc 4F 79
Oldacres Rd. ST4: Tren 5B 40
OLD ARLEY 2C 165
Old Bank DE6: May, U May 5C 56
Old Barn Cl. ST20: Gno 2J 67
OLD BRAMPTON 1D 157
OLDBURY
Bridgnorth 2B 162
Nuneaton 2D 165
Oldbury 3D 163
Oldbury Ct. B79: Tam 3H 137
Old Butt La. ST7: Talk 4A 10
Old Cannock Rd. WV10: Shar 3H 117
Oldcastle Av. ST5: Brad 2E 22
Old Castle Gro. WS8: Brow 2H 121
Old Chancel Rd. WS15: Rug 6G 95
Old Chapel Cl. ST5: Keel 1G 29
Old Coach La. ST17: Broc 3F 79
Old Coach Rd. ST19: B Elm 7C 90
Old Coton La. B79: Tam 3F 137
Oldcott Cres. ST7: Kids 6G 11
Oldcott Dr. ST7: Kids 6G 11
Oldcourt St. ST6: Tuns 4H 17
Old Cft. Rd. ST17: Staf, Walt 2C 78
Old Eaton Rd. WS15: Rug 5G 95
Olde Hall Ct. WV10: Fea 5G 117
Olde Hall La. WS6: G Wyr 7F 109
Olde Hall Rd. WV10: Fea 5G 117
Oldershaws La. ST20: H Off 3A 66
OLD FALLINGS 5C 124 (1D 163)
Old Fallings Cres. WV10: Bush 6C 124
Old Fallings La. WV10: Bush 4D 124
OLDFALLOW 7D 100 (3D 159)
Old Fallow Av. WS11: Cann 7E 100
Old Fallow Rd. WS11: Cann 7E 100
Old Falls Cl. WS6: C Hay 1D 118
Old Farm Dr. WV8: Bilb 1C 122
Old Farm Mdw. WV3: W'ton 6K 129
OLDFIELD 3A 162
Oldfield Av. ST6: B Gre 2D 18
Oldfield Bus. Pk. ST4: Fen 5F 33
Oldfield Dr. ST15: Stone 6J 47
Oldfields Cres. ST18: Gt Hay 4H 81
Oldfields La. ST18: Gt Hay 3H 81
Oldfield Sports Ground 5G 63
Oldfields Rd. ST14: Utt 6G 63
Oldfield St. ST4: Fen 4G 33
Old Granary, The DE14: B Tre 6F 85
Old Hall Dr. B79: Elf 5F 131
ST5: Brad 7D 16
Old Hall Ind. Est. WS3: Blox 5J 127
Old Hall La. WS11: Cann 4H 109
WS12: Cann 4H 109
WS13: Frad 2K 107
Old Hall St. ST1: H'ley 4G 151 (4C 24)
Old Hampton La. WV10: Bush 3F 125
Oldham St. ST1: H'ley 6J 151 (6D 24)
Old Hedging La. B77: Dost 5K 141
Old Hednesford Rd.
WS11: Cann, Hed 1F 109
WS12: Hed 1F 109
OLD HILL 3D 163
Oldhill Cl. ST7: T Pit 2C 16
Oldhill La. ST18: Tix 5H 75
Old Knotty Way ST14: Utt 7G 63
Old Landywood La. WV11: Ess 6C 118
Old La. ST6: B Edg 5G 13
WS3: Blox 6J 127
WV6: Tett 4G 129
WV10: Fea 5G 117
Old Man of Mow, The 5H 7
Old Mnr. Cl. B78: D Bas 5E 140
Old Mill La. ST9: Bag 7C 50
(not continuous)
Oldmill St. ST4: S Tren 2C 32
OLD PARK 1A 162
Old Pk. Rd. WS12: Haz 5C 102
Old Penkridge M. WS11: Cann 2D 108
Old Penkridge Rd. WS11: Cann 1C 108
Old Pl. WS3: Blox 5J 127
Old Rectory Rd. ST15: Stone 4H 47
Old Rickerscote La. ST17: Staf 2H 77
Old Rd. CW3: Wrin 5B 6
DE14: B'ton 7A 86
ST7: Big E 4G 15
ST10: Tea 3F 55
ST12: Barl 7C 40
ST15: Oul H, Stone 3G 47
ST18: West 3C 80
WS15: Arm, Hand 4E 98
Old Rd. Cl. ST15: Stone 2G 47
Old Saddler's Yd. ST14: Utt 6H 63
Old School Cl. ST7: Kids 5E 10
ST18: West 2C 80
Old School Ct. ST19: Whe A 3C 90
Old School Dr. ST16: Staf 5E 70
Old School Row B78: D Bas 5E 140
(off Drayton La.)
Old School Wlk. B79: Tam 3H 137
Old Smithy Cl. WV6: Patt 6B 128
Old Stafford Rd.
WV10: C Gre, S Hea 4A 116
Old Stoneyard, The WS13: Lich 3B 114
Old Tamworth Rd. B77: Amin 3C 138
Old Town Rd. ST1: H'ley 1G 151 (3C 24)
Old Tramway ST4: Fen 4F 33
OLD TUPTON 1D 157
Old Vicarage Cl. WV5: Womb 3H 145
Old Warstone La. WV11: Ess 4B 118
Oldway Pl. ST3: Long 4J 33
Old Weston Rd. ST19: B Elm 6C 90
Old Wharf Pl. ST1: H'ley 6K 151 (6E 24)
Old Whieldon Rd. ST4: S Tren 3C 32
Olinthus Av. WV11: Wed 6J 125
Olive Gro. ST5: C'ton 6B 16
Oliver Ho. ST15: Stone 5E 46
Oliver Lodge Ho. ST4: S Tren 2A 32
(off Epworth St.)
Oliver Rd. ST4: S Tren 7K 153 (2J 31)
OLLERTON 2A 158
Olof Palme Gro. ST3: Long 7J 33
OLTON 3B 164
Omega Way ST4: Tren 2A 40
ONECOTE 2A 156
Onecote Rd. ST10: Ips 1H 53
One Oak Ri. ST17: Staf 2H 77
On-Line Bus. Pk. WS11: Cann 5D 108
ONNELEY 3B 154
Onsetter Rd. ST2: B Hil 2K 33
Onslow Dr. ST5: Brad 7F 17
Ontario Cl. ST4: Tren 2A 40
Onyx Gro. ST2: Mil 5G 19
Opal Rd. ST4: Fen 4E 32
Opal Way ST15: Stone 7F 47
Opel Bus. Cen. ST15: Stone 7G 47
OPENWOODGATE 3D 157
Oram's La. ST19: Brew 1C 92
Orbital Retail Cen. WS11: Cann 5F 109
Orbital Way WS11: Cann 5F 109
Orb St. ST1: H'ley 4F 151 (5C 24)
Orchard, The ST6: B Edg 6G 13
ST14: S'all 1F 63
ST15: Swyn 2C 64
ST18: Hopt 5F 69
ST18: L Hay 6H 81
ST19: Brew 2C 92
WS3: Blox 3K 127
WS7: Chas 4G 111
WV6: Tett 7G 123
Orchard Av. WS11: Cann 1C 108
Orchard Cvn. Site ST18: Hopt 5F 69
Orchard Cl. B77: Dost 5J 141
B78: Pole 6J 139
ST14: Utt 4G 63
ST15: Oul 7J 45
ST15: Stone 5F 47
ST19: Penk 3H 91
TF9: A'ley 4J 61
WS6: C Hay 1E 118
WS13: Lich 2K 113
WS15: Rug 5G 95
WV3: W'ton 7J 129
WV6: Patt 6B 128
WV9: Cove 2K 93
Orchard Cres. ST7: Talk 5B 10
ST19: Penk 3H 91
WV3: W'ton 7J 129
Orchard Farm Activity Cen. 7C 52
Orchard Gdns. ST13: Lee 3D 48
WS12: Cann 4F 101
Orchard Gro. DY7: Kin 5F 149
Orchard La. ST17: Wol B 3D 94
ST18: Hyde L 2E 76
WV8: Bilb 2D 122
WV10: Shar 1F 117
Orchard Pk. DE14: B Tre 2E 86
Orchard Pl. ST12: Barl 2D 44
Orchard Ri. CV9: Gren 7K 143
ST11: B Bri 3G 43
Orchard Rd. WV11: Wed 6G 125
Orchards, The ST3: Fen 5E 32
WS15: Hand 5G 99
Orchard St. B77: Tam 6J 137
B79: Tam 4H 137
DE14: B Tre 3E 86
ST5: N'tle 3G 23
ST17: Staf 4G 73
Orchid Cl. DE15: Stap 4H 87
Orchid Gro. ST4: S Tren 2K 153 (7J 23)
Ordish Ct. DE14: B Tre 2E 86
(not continuous)
Ordish St. DE14: B Tre 2D 86
Oregon Dr. WV12: Will 6E 126
Oregon Gdns. WS7: C Ter 3H 111
ORETON 3A 162
Orford Rd. ST9: End 2B 50
Orford St. ST5: N'tle 1H 23
Orford Way ST3: Blur 2E 40
ORGREAVE 3B 160
Orgreaves Cl. ST5: Brad 7E 16
Orgreave St. ST6: B'lem 1A 24
Oriel Cl. WS11: Cann 3E 108
Oriel Dr. WV10: Ford 2B 124
Oriel St. ST4: P'ull 2A 32
Oriole Cl. ST14: Utt 7H 63
Orion Cl. WS6: G Wyr 3F 119
Orion Ct. ST5: N'tle 5A 152 (1D 30)
Orion St. ST6: B'lem 6C 18
Orion Way WS11: Cann 5F 101
Orkney Av. ST7: Pack 6K 11
Orkney Dr. B77: Wiln 3B 142
Orlestone Pl. ST6: Feg H 7A 12
Orme Rd. ST5: N'tle 5A 152 (1D 30)
ST8: Knyp 1D 12
Ormes La. WV6: Tett 3K 129
Orme St. ST6: B'lem 7J 17
Ormonde St. ST4: Fen 4F 33
Ormonds Cl. WS13: Lich 5J 113
Orpheus Gro. ST1: H'ley 2F 25
ORSLOW 3C 159
ORTON 2C 163
Orton La. WV4: L Pen 1G 145
WV5: Womb 1G 145
ORTON-ON-THE-HILL 1D 165
Orton Rd. ST5: N'tle 6E 22
Orwell Dr. ST3: W Coy 4B 34
ST17: Staf 6D 72
Orwell Pl. ST5: N'tle 5F 31
OSBASTON 1D 165
Osborne B79: Tam 2D 136
Osborne Ct. DE13: B Tre 5C 84
Osborne Cres. ST17: Staf 6A 74
Osborne Rd. ST4: S Tren 4K 153 (1J 31)
Osborne St. DE15: Wins 1H 87
ST13: Lee 3H 49
Osbourne Gdns. DE15: Wins 1H 87
(off Osborne St.)
OSGATHORPE 3D 161
OSLESTON 1C 161
Oslo Gro. ST1: H'ley 2E 24
OSMASTON
Ashbourne 3C 157
Derby 1D 161
Osprey B77: Wiln 4C 142

Pasturefields Ind. Est.—Pits Hill

Pasturefields Ind. Est.
ST18: Hixon 7B 80
Pasturefields La. ST18: Hixon 7B 80
(not continuous)
Pasture Ga. WS11: Cann 1C 108
Pastures, The WV6: Per 2E 128
Pasture Way ST5: B Gat 5F 37
Patch Cl. DE13: B Tre 5C 84
Patch Mdw. Rd. ST10: Chea 4A 54
Paterson Pl. WS8: Brow 7K 121
Patrick Gregory Rd. WV11: Wed 6K 125
Patrick M. WS13: Lich 2K 113
Patrick Pl. ST8: Brin F 4B 12
Patshull Av. WV10: Ford 2K 123
Patshull Gro. WV10: Ford 2K 123
Patshull Rd. WV6: Patt 6A 128
Patterdale Rd. WS11: Cann 6G 101
Patterdale St. ST6: B'lem 4A 18
PATTINGHAM 6B 128 (2C 163)
Pattingham Rd. WV6: Per, Tett 3B 128
Pauls Coppice WS8: Brow 7H 121
Pauls Wlk. WS13: Lich 7A 106
PAVE LANE 3B 158
Pavement, The ST19: Brew 3D 92
Pavilion, The B77: Amin 6D 138
Pavilion Ct. WS13: Lich 2K 113
Pavilion Dr. ST1: H'ley 1B 150 (3A 24)
Pavilion End DY7: Stou 1J 149
Pavior's Rd. WS7: Chas 7G 111
Paxton Av. WV6: Per 3F 129
Paxton St. ST1: H'ley 6H 151 (6D 24)
Paynter St. ST4: Fen 4F 33
Peace Cl. WS6: C Hay 1E 118
Peacehaven Gro. ST4: Tren 5C 40
Peach Av. ST17: Staf 1H 77
Peach Rd. WV12: Will 7A 126
Peacock Av. WV11: Wed 5A 126
Peacock Cft. WS6: G Wyr 2G 119
PEACOCK HAY 3D 16
Peacock Hay Rd. ST7: Talk, Tuns . . . 3C 16
Peacock Ho. ST4: Tren 3K 39
Peacock La. ST4: H'rch 2E 38
ST5: Butt, H'rch 2E 38
Peacock Rd. ST5: C'ton 3D 22
Peacock Vw. ST4: Fen 7F 25
Peak Cl. WS15: Arm 5E 98
Peak Dale Av. ST6: Gold 7F 11
Peake Cres. WS8: Brow 7H 121
Peake Rd. WS8: Brow 7J 121
Peakes Rd. WS15: Rug 7D 94
Peake St. ST5: N'tle 5C 22
Peaks Leisure Cen. 6H 137
Peak Vw. ST13: Lee 4H 49
Pearis Dr. ST10: Alt 6H 57
Pearl Gro. ST3: Mei 2C 42
Pear Pl. ST2: B Hil 2K 33
Pearson Dr. ST15: Stone 4J 47
Pear Tree Cl. B79: Shut 2G 139
ST12: Barl 2D 44
ST20: Gno 4J 67
WS12: Hun 3C 100
Pear Tree Ct. WS15: Rug 2F 97
Pear Tree Dr. CW3: Mad 2A 28
Pear Tree La. ST5: C'ton 7B 16
WS8: Brow 2E 120
WV5: Clav 4C 146
WV11: Wed 4F 125
Pear Tree Rd. ST7: Big E 6H 15
Peascroft Rd. ST6: Nort 3D 18
Pebble Cl. B77: Amin 6D 138
Pebble Mill Cl. WS11: Cann 1F 109
Pebble Mill Dr. WS11: Cann 1F 109
Pebble Mill St.
ST1: H'ley 3A 150 (5K 23)
Pebworth Ho. ST13: Ched 2G 51
Peckforton Vw. ST7: Kids 7E 10
Peck Mill La. ST8: Brin F 5C 12
Pedley Ct. ST3: Blur 2F 41
Pedley Gro. ST6: B'lem 6D 18
PEDMORE 3D 163
Peebles Grn. ST2: Bent 6J 25
Peebles Rd. ST5: Sil 6H 21
Peel Cl. B78: D Bas 5E 140
Peel Ct. B78: Faze 2H 141
ST7: Kids 4E 10
(off Attwood St.)
Peel Dr. B77: Wiln 5A 142
WS12: Hed 2G 101
Peelers Way B77: Tam 6J 137
Peel Hollow ST7: Aud 6C 14
Peel Ho. B79: Tam 5G 137
Peel St. DE14: B Tre 3D 86
ST3: Long 1J 41
ST5: N'tle 3G 23
ST6: B'lem 7G 17
ST16: Staf 3F 73
Peel Ter. ST16: Staf 1G 73
Pegasus Gro. ST6: B'lem 6D 18
Pegasus Wlk. B79: Tam 2F 137
PEGG'S GREEN 3D 161
Peggs La. ST20: H Off 2A 66
Peggs Row WS7: Burn 4C 112
Peggy's Bank ST7: Big E 7H 15
Pegroy Gro. ST6: B'lem 6D 18
Pelham St. ST1: H'ley 6H 151 (6D 24)
Pellfield Ct. ST18: West 3C 80
PELSALL 7D 120 (1A 164)
Pelsall La. WS3: Blox 2K 127
(not continuous)
Pelsall Rd. WS8: Brow 6E 120
PELSALL WOOD 7B 120
Pemberton Dr. ST3: M Hea 5C 42
Pembridge Rd. ST3: Blur 3E 40
Pembroke Cl. B79: Tam 3E 136
WV12: Will 7C 126
Pembroke Dr. ST5: N'tle 6B 152 (2E 30)
ST15: Stone 5J 47
Pembroke Ho. *WS3: Blox 7J 127*
(off Cornwall Clo.)
Pembroke Rd. ST2: Mil 6G 19
Penarth Gro. ST1: H'ley 1F 151 (3C 24)
Penarth Pl. ST5: N'tle 6C 152 (2E 30)
Penda Gro. WV6: Per 1G 129
PENDEFORD 2J 123 (1D 163)
Pendeford Av. WV6: Tett 5G 123
Pendeford Bus. Pk. WV9: P'ord . . . 2H 123
Pendeford Cl. WV6: Tett 5G 123
Pendeford Hall La.
WV9: Cove, P'ord 1G 123
Pendeford Hall Mobile Home Pk.
WV9: P'ord 1G 123
Pendeford La. WV9: P'ord 1J 123
Pendeford Mill La. WV8: Bilb 2D 122
Penderell Cl. WV10: Fea 6E 116
Penderel St. WS3: Blox 5J 127
Pendinas Dr. WV8: Bilb 2D 122
Pendine Gro. ST4: Fen 3H 33
Pendle Hill WS12: Hed 6J 101
Pendrel Cl. WS6: G Wyr 4F 119
Pendrell Cl. WV8: Cods 2C 122
Pendrell Ct. WV8: Cods 2C 122
Pendrill Rd. WV10: Bush 2C 124
Pendryl Cl. ST19: Brew 1C 92
Penfleet Av. ST3: Mei 1C 42
Pengrove Cl. ST6: Chel 6J 11
Penk Dr. WS7: Burn 5B 112
Penk Dr. Nth. WS15: Rug 6D 94
Penk Dr. Sth. WS15: Rug 7D 94
PENKHULL 2A 32
Penkhull Ct. ST4: S Tren 2A 32
Penkhull New Rd.
ST4: P'ull, S Tren 3K 31
Penkhull Ter. ST4: P'ull 2A 32
PENKRIDGE 3G 91 (3D 159)
Penkridge Bank Rd.
WS15: Rug, S Mil 3A 96
Penkridge Ind. Est. ST19: Penk 5G 91
Penkridge Leisure Cen. 4K 91
Penkridge Rd. ST17: Act T 6K 77
Penkridge Station (Rail) 4G 91
Penkridge Wharf ST19: Penk 4H 91
Penk Ri. WV6: Tett 2H 129
Penk Rd. ST11: Fors 3J 43
Penkside WV9: Cove 1K 93
Penkvale M. ST17: Staf 1H 77
Penkvale Rd. ST17: Staf 1H 77
Penkville St. ST4: S Tren 4A 32
Penleigh Gdns. WV5: Womb 3F 145
Penmark Gro. ST3: L'ood 2A 42
Penmere Dr. ST5: N'tle 1G 39
ST9: Werr 5C 26
PENN 2C 163
Penn Cl. WS3: Blox 5J 127
Penn Cft. ST18: L Hay 6J 81
Pennell St. ST2: Buck 4H 25
Pennine Dr. WS11: Cann 1E 108
Pennine Way B77: Wiln 1D 142
ST5: N'tle 5C 22
ST8: Bidd 3E 8
Pennington Cl. ST3: Mei 7E 34
Pennwood Ct. WV4: Pen 7K 129
Penny Bank Ct. *WS15: Rug 7G 95*
(off Market Sq.)
Penny Ct. B79: Tam 4H 137
WS6: G Wyr 4F 119
Pennycress Gdns. WV10: Fea 5G 117
Pennycress Grn. WS11: N Can 7B 110
Pennycroft La. ST14: Utt 4H 63
Pennycroft Rd. ST14: Utt 4F 63
Pennycrofts ST16: Staf 3H 73
Pennycrofts Ct. ST16: Staf 3H 73
Pennyfields Av. ST6: B'lem 6H 17
Pennyfields Rd. ST7: New 4H 11
Pennyghael Way ST7: Harr 3J 11
Penny La. Shop. Mall ST10: Chea . . . 4C 54
Pennymoor Rd. B77: Wiln 2D 142
Pennymore Cl. ST4: Tren 2B 40
Pennys Cft. WS13: Lich 2E 114
Penport Gro. ST3: Blur 7G 33
Penrhyn Av. ST6: B'lem 6B 18
Penrith Cl. ST4: Tren 5C 40
Penrith Ct. ST5: N'tle 3F 31
Pensford Gro. ST1: H'ley 3F 25
Pensgreave Rd. DE13: B Tre 5C 84
Penshaw Cl. WV9: P'ord 2J 123
PENSNETT 3D 163
Pentire Rd. WS14: Lich 4D 114
Pentland Gro. ST5: N'tle 5C 22
Penton Pl. ST3: Blur 3E 40
Penton Wlk. ST3: Blur 3E 40
PENTRICH 2D 157
Pen y Bont Wlk. ST8: Knyp 7E 8
Penzance Way ST17: Staf 5C 74
PEOVER HEATH 1B 154
PEPLOW 2A 158
Pepper St. ST5: Keel, Sil 1G 29
ST5: N'tle 4D 152 (7F 23)
Perceval St. ST1: H'ley 1K 151 (3E 24)
Percival Dr. ST9: S Broo 4J 19
Percy St. ST1: H'ley 3G 151 (4C 24)
Peregrine Cl. DE15: Wins 1K 87
WS14: W'ton 3H 131
Peregrine Gro. ST3: Mei 3C 42
Perivale Cl. ST1: H'ley 2G 25
Periwinkle Cl. WS8: Clay 6F 121
Perkins St. ST6: Gold 7G 11
Perks Rd. WV11: Wed 4A 126
Perle Brook ST21: Ecc 2G 65
Perrin Cl. ST17: Staf 1H 77
PERRY 2A 164
Perry Av. WV10: Bush 5D 124
PERRY BARR 2A 164
Perry Cl. B79: Tam 3H 137
ST1: H'ley 4H 151 (5D 24)
PERRY CROFTS 2J 137 (1C 165)
Perrycrofts Cres. B79: Tam 2J 137
Perry Hall Dr. WV12: Will 7B 126
Perry Hall Rd. WV11: Wed 7K 125
Perrymount Ct. ST4: P'ull 3K 31
PERSHALL 1C 159
Pershore Cl. WS3: Blox 3F 127
Pershore Dr. DE14: B'ton 4B 86
Pershore Rd. WS3: Blox 3F 127
Pershore Way WS3: Blox 3F 127
Persia Wlk. ST6: Tuns 4H 17
Perth Cl. DE15: Wins 2K 87
Perth Rd. WV12: Will 7B 126
Perth St. ST4: Fen 4G 33
Perthy Gro. ST4: Tren 3K 39
PERTON 2F 129 (2C 163)
Perton Brook Va. WV6: Tett 4G 129
Perton Gro. WV6: Tett 4G 129
Perton Rd. WV6: Tett 4F 129
Perton Wood Vw. ST3: Blur 6F 33
Pessall La. B79: Edin 1B 132
Petard Cl. B77: T Gat 2J 141
Peterborough Dr. WS12: H Hay 2J 109
Peterhead B77: Amin 4B 138
Peter James Ct. ST16: Staf 1G 73
Petersfield WS11: Cann 6F 101
Petersfield Rd. ST6: Feg H 7A 12
Peter's La. WS7: Burn 6E 112
Peterson Ho. ST3: L'ood 2B 42
Peters Wlk. WS13: Lich 1A 114
Petrel Gro. ST3: Mei 3D 42
Pettiford Cl. WS13: Frad 4K 107
Pevensey Gro. ST3: Long 3J 33
Peverill Rd. WV6: Per 2G 129
Pheasant Wlk. TF9: Logg 6D 60
Pheasant Way WS11: H Hay 2G 109
Philip Gro. WS11: Cann 4E 100
Philip La. ST9: Werr 4D 26
Philip St. ST4: Fen 3E 32
Phillips Av. WV11: Wed 4K 125
Phillips Cl. ST15: Stone 5K 47
Phillipson Way ST6: B'lem 7D 18
Phoenix Cen. WS11: Cann 5E 108
Phoenix Cl. ST7: Kids 4G 11
WS15: Rug 7H 95
Phoenix Rd. WS11: Cann 1G 109
Phoenix St. ST6: Tuns 4H 17
Picasso Cl. WS11: H Hay 1K 109
Picasso Ri. ST3: Mei 4D 42
PICCADILLY 2C 165
Piccadilly ST1: H'ley 4F 151 (5C 24)
Piccadilly Arc. ST1: H'ley . . . 3F 151 (4C 24)
Piccadilly La. DE6: U May 4B 56
Piccadilly St. ST6: Tuns 4H 17
Pickering Cl. ST3: Blur 1G 41
Pickering Rd. WV11: Wed 7H 125
PICKFORD 3C 165
Pickford Pl. ST3: Mei 1B 42
Pickmere Cl. ST2: Mil 4H 19
Picknal La. ST14: Utt 6F 63
Picknalls ST14: Utt 6G 63
PICKSTOCK 2B 158
Pickwick Pl. ST7: Talk 4B 10
Pickwood Av. ST13: Lee 4H 49
Pickwood Cl. ST13: Lee 4H 49
Pickwood Rd. ST13: Lee 4F 49
Picton St. ST1: H'ley 4J 151 (5D 24)
ST13: Lee 3E 48
Picture House, The 2E 108
Piddocks Rd. DE15: Stan 7J 87
(not continuous)
Pidduck St. ST6: B'lem 1J 23
Pierce St. ST6: Tuns 4H 17
Pier St. WS8: Brow 5H 121
Pigeonhay La.
ST14: Beam, Utt, Bram 4A 62
Piggott Gro. ST2: Buck 5G 25
Pike Cl. ST16: Staf 1J 73
PIKEHALL 2B 156
Pike La. WS15: Arm 5E 98
Pilgrim Pl. ST16: Staf 4G 73
Pilgrim St. ST16: Staf 4G 73
Pilkington Av. ST5: N'tle . . . 7C 152 (3E 30)
Pillar Cl. ST2: B Hil 2K 33
PILLATON 5K 91 (3D 159)
Pillaton Cl. ST19: Penk 5H 91
Pillaton Dr. WS12: Hun 4C 100
PILSBURY 1B 156
Pilsbury St. ST5: N'tle 2H 23
Pilsden Pl. ST3: Mei 3E 42
PILSLEY
Bakewell 1C 157
Chesterfield 1D 157
Pimbury Rd. WV12: Will 6D 126
Pine Cl. B79: Tam 1H 137
DE14: B'ton 4B 86
DY7: Kin 6G 149
ST7: Talk 7B 10
WS6: G Wyr 7F 109
Pine Ct. ST11: B Bri 3F 43
TF9: Logg 5D 60
Pine Cres. ST17: Walt 1D 78
Pinefold St. ST14: Utt 6H 63
Pine Gro. WS7: Chas 6H 111
Pinehurst Cl. ST5: N'tle 6F 31
Pine Rd. ST4: Fen 5C 32
Pines, The WS14: Lich 4F 115
WV3: W'ton 5K 129
Pineside Av. WS15: Can W 4H 103
Pine St. WS3: Blox 3K 127
Pine Tree Cl. WS12: Hed 1G 101
Pine Tree Dr. ST11: B Bri 3F 43
Pinetrees WS15: Bre 5H 97
Pinetrees La. TF9: A Hea 4F 61
Pine Vw. WS15: Rug 5E 94
Pine Wlk. ST14: Utt 5E 62
WV8: Cods 3B 122
Pineways B74: F Oak 5H 135
Pinewood Av. WS11: Cann 6D 100
Pinewood Cl. WS8: Brow 2G 121
WV3: W'ton 6H 129
WV5: Womb 4G 145
WV12: Will 7D 126
Pinewood Cres. ST3: Mei 7D 34
Pinewood Dr. ST18: L Hay 6J 81
TF9: A Hea 5E 60
Pinewood Gro. ST5: C'ton 6C 16
ST11: B Bri 4J 43
Pine Wood Rd.
TF9: A Hea, Hook 6F 61
Pinewood Rd. DE15: Stap 6G 87
TF9: A'ley 3F 61
Pinfold, The WS3: Blox 5J 127
Pinfold Av. ST6: Nort 3D 18
Pinfold Cl. DE13: Tut 3H 83
ST19: Whe A 2B 90
Pinfold Dr. WS15: Hand 4F 99
Pinfold Gdns. WV11: Wed 7H 125
Pinfold Gro. WV4: Pen 7K 129
Pinfold Hill WS14: Shen 5C 134
Pinfold Ind. Est. WS3: Blox 5J 127
Pinfold La. ST19: Penk 4F 91
ST19: Whe A 2B 90
WS6: C Hay 2C 118
WS11: N Can 7A 110
Pinfold Rd. WS13: Lich 2K 113
Pinfold Ter. ST18: L Hay 6H 81
Pingle, The WS15: S Mil 2D 96
Pingle La. ST15: Stone 5H 47
ST17: Bed 6D 78
WS7: Hamm 6B 112
Pinhoe Pl. ST3: Long 6A 34
PINLEY 3D 165
Pinnox St. ST6: Tuns 5J 17
PINSLEY GREEN 3A 154
Pintail Cl. ST17: Staf 7J 73
PINXTON 2D 157
Pioli Pl. WS2: Wals 7K 127
Pioneer Pl. *ST6: B'lem 4C 18*
(off Brammer St.)
Pioneer Way ST17: Staf 7J 73
PIPE GATE 3B 154
Pipehay La. DE6: D Cla 6B 82
PIPEHILL 6G 113 (1A 164)
Pipe La. WS15: P Rid 1E 98
Piper Cl. WV6: Per 2G 129
PIPE RIDWARE 1H 99 (3A 160)
Piper Rd. WV3: W'ton 6K 129
Pipers Cft. WS13: Lich 1A 114
Pipe Wood La.
WS15: P Rid 1G 99
Pippins, The ST5: N'tle 6G 31
ST17: Staf 2G 77
Pireford Pl. ST5: Brad 6E 16
PIREHILL 3G 69
Pirehill La. ST15: Stone 7F 47
Pirehill Rd. ST5: Brad 6F 17
Pirelli Stadium 4F 85
Pitcairn St. ST6: Tuns 4J 17
Pitcher La. ST13: Lee 4J 49
Pitfield Av. ST5: N'tle 5H 23
Pitgreen La. ST5: N'tle 2G 23
Pit La. ST7: T Pit 1A 16
Pitlea Pl. ST3: Long 3J 33
Pitsford St. ST3: Long 7K 33
PITS HILL 2J 17

Pitstone Cl.—Queens Ct.

Pitstone Cl. ST16: Staf 4F 71
Pitts Hill Bank ST6: Chel 2K 17
Pitt St. ST16: Staf 7E 70
Pitt St. E. ST6: B'lem 7A 18
Pitt St. W. ST6: B'lem 1A 24
Plainfield Gro. ST2: Bent 1K 33
Plaisaunce, The ST5: N'tle 3F 31
Plane Gro. ST5: C'ton 6C 16
Planks La. WV5: Womb 4F 145
Plantation La. B78: Hop, M Oak 3A 136
(not continuous)
DY3: Him 6H 145
Plantation Pk. ST5: Keel 3A 30
Plantation Rd. ST4: Tren 4D 40
WS12: Hed 1G 101
Plant Cres. ST17: Staf 7H 73
Plant La. WS7: C Ter 4F 111
Plants Cl. WS6: G Wyr 4G 119
Plant St. ST3: Long 5J 33
ST10: Chea 4D 54
Plant Way WS3: Pels 7B 120
PLARDIWICK 4F 67
Plardiwick Rd. ST20: Gno 4F 67
Platts Av. ST9: End 3A 50
Platt St. WS11: Cann 5G 101
Pleasant St. ST6: B'lem 1K 23
Plex St. ST6: Tuns 4H 17
Pleydell St. ST1: H'ley 1F 25
Plough Bank ST9: W Roc 1K 27
Ploughmans Wlk.
WS13: Lich 7C 106
WV8: P'ord 4G 123
Plough M. DY7: Kin 5E 148
Plough St. ST1: H'ley 1H 151 (3D 24)
Plover Cl. ST3: Mei 3C 42
WV10: Fea 5F 117
Plover Dr. ST8: Bidd 5E 8
Plover Fld. CW3: Mad 3A 28
Plovers Ri. WS15: Rug 7F 95
Plumtree Gro. ST1: H'ley 2F 25
Plymouth Gro. ST5: C'ton 1D 22
Pochard Cl. ST6: B'lem 5D 18
PODMORE 1B 158
Podmore Av. ST7: A Ban 2H 21
Podmore La. ST7: H End 2F 21
(not continuous)
Podmore St. ST6: B'lem 1A 24
Podmore Ter. ST7: H End 2F 21
Pointon Gro. ST6: Nort 2G 19
POLESWORTH 7J 139 (1C 165)
Polesworth Sports Cen. 2H 143
Polesworth Station (Rail) 6J 139
Polperro Way ST3: Mei 3C 42
Pomona Ri. ST1: B'lem 7D 18
Ponesfield Rd. WS13: Lich 1B 114
Ponesgreen WS13: Lich 1B 114
Pool Av. WS11: N Can 6D 110
Pool Cl. WV10: Shar 3H 117
Pool Cotts. WS7: Chas 7G 111
Pool Dam ST5: N'tle 4D 152 (1F 31)
Poole Av. ST2: Mil 5H 19
Poole Cres. WS8: Brow 2E 120
POOLE GREEN 2A 154
POOLEND 1C 48 (2D 155)
Pooles La. WV12: Will 5E 126
Pooles Rd. ST8: Bid M 5H 9
Poole's Way WS7: Burn 4A 112
Pooley Fields Country Pk. 6J 139
Pooley Fields Heritage Cen. 6H 139
Pooley La. B78: Pole 1H 143
Pooley Vw. B78: Pole 7J 139
Poolfield Av. ST5: N'tle 5A 152 (1D 30)
Poolfield Av. Nth.
ST5: N'tle 4B 152 (1E 30)
Poolfield Rd. WS13: Lich 5J 113
POOLFIELDS 5C 152 (1E 30)
Poolfields Cl. ST5: N'tle 5A 152 (1D 30)
Poolfields Ct. ST6: B Edg 7J 13
POOLFOLD 1E 8 (2C 155)
Pool Hall Cres. WV3: W'ton 6G 129
Pool Hall Rd. WV3: W'ton 6G 129
Pool Hayes La. WV12: Will 7A 126
Poolhill Cl. ST3: Blur 7G 33
Pool Ho. Rd. WV5: Womb 4D 144
Pool La. ST17: Broc 4F 79
Pool Mdw. WS6: C Hay 3D 118
Pool Mdw. Cl. WS15: Rug 1F 97
Pool Rd. WS7: Chas 7G 111
(not continuous)
WS8: Brow 2G 121
WV11: Wed 7A 126
POOLSBROOK 1D 157
Poolside CW3: Mad 3A 28
ST3: Blur 2F 41
ST5: N'tle 3C 152 (7E 22)
Pool St. ST4: Fen 3H 33
ST5: N'tle 5C 152 (1E 30)
Pool Vw. WS6: G Wyr 7G 109
Pope Gdns. ST17: Staf 7E 72
Pope Gro. WS12: Hed 4F 101
Pope Rd. WV10: Bush 5E 124
Popes La. WV6: Tett 7C 122
Poplar Av. ST5: N'tle 5E 22
WS7: Chas 5H 111
WS8: Brow 4J 121
Poplar Av. WS11: Cann 6F 101
WV11: Wed 6F 125
Poplar Cl. ST5: N'tle 5E 22
ST11: B Bri 4J 43
ST14: Utt 4E 62
ST15: Stone 5F 47
ST18: Hau 6B 66
ST21: Ecc 3H 65
WV5: Womb 4H 145
Poplar Ct. ST5: N'tle 5E 22
Poplar Dr. ST3: Blur 7E 32
ST7: Kids 5E 10
Poplar Gro. ST3: Blur 1G 41
ST5: N'tle 2H 153 (7H 23)
Poplar La. WS11: Hath, Cann 3A 108
Poplar Ri. B74: L Ast 3J 135
Poplar Rd. WS6: G Wyr 3F 119
WS8: Brow 4J 121
Poplars, The WS11: Cann 6E 100
Poplars Dr. WV8: Cods 3B 122
Poplars Farm Way WV9: Cove 2K 93
Poplars Rd. DE13: B Tre 4D 84
WS15: Hand 5G 99
Poplar St. WS11: N Can 5C 110
Poplar Way ST17: Staf 1G 77
Poppit's La. ST14: S'all 1E 62
Poppy Gdns. DE13: Alre 6C 130
Porlock Av. ST17: Staf 6B 74
Porlock Gro. ST4: Tren 4B 40
Portal Rd. ST16: Staf 1K 73
Portchester Dr. WV11: Wed 7H 125
PORTHILL 1G 23
Porthill Bank ST5: N'tle 2G 23
Porthill Grange ST5: N'tle 2G 23
Porthill Grn. ST5: N'tle 2G 23
Porthill Rd. ST6: B'lem 1H 23
Portland Av. B79: Tam 1F 137
DE14: B'ton 5B 86
Portland Cl. ST11: B Bri 3F 43
Portland Dr. ST7: Sch G 1C 10
ST8: Bidd 3D 8
ST11: Fors 2K 43
Portland Gro. ST5: N'tle 6F 31
Portland M. ST5: N'tle 2F 23
Portland Pl. ST10: Wat 5B 52
ST12: Barl 6F 41
WS11: Cann 4C 108
Portland Rd. ST3: Long 5H 33
Portland St. ST1: H'ley 1D 150 (3B 24)
ST13: Lee 3G 49
Portland St. Nth. ST13: Lee 3G 49
Portland St. Sth. ST13: Lee 3G 49
Port La. ST19: Cove 4C 92
WS15: Abb B 4A 88
Portleven Cl. ST17: Staf 7C 74
Portleys La. B78: D Bas 6C 140
Portobello WS15: Rug 6G 95
Portrush Rd. WV6: Per 2E 128
Portsdown Cl. WV10: Bush 6D 124
Portsea St. WS3: Blox 7J 127
Port St. ST6: B'lem 1J 23
Portswood Cl. WV9: P'ord 4H 123
Port Va. Ct. ST6: B'lem 6A 18
Port Vale FC 6A 18
Port Va. St. ST6: B'lem 1J 23
Portway Dr. DE13: Tut 3H 83
Post La. ST9: End 2B 50
Post Office La. WS15: S Mil 2D 96
Post Office Rd. DE13: Alre 5C 130
WV5: Seis 1A 146
Post Office Sq. CW3: Mad 4A 28
Post Office Ter. ST11: Ful 3G 59
POT BANK 2A 8
Pottal Pool Rd. ST19: Penk 1A 100
Potteries Mus. & Art Gallery, The
4F 151 (5C 24)
Potteries Shop. Cen.
ST1: H'ley 2G 151 (4C 24)
Potteries Way ST1: H'ley 1F 151 (3C 24)
(not continuous)
Potters Av. ST15: Yarn 6D 64
Potters Cft. B79: C Camp 5D 132
POTTER'S CROSS 4E 148 (3C 163)
Potters End ST8: Bidd 4B 8
Potters La. B78: Pole 2J 143
POTTER SOMERSAL 1B 160
Potters Way DE13: B Nee 6H 89
Pouk La. WS14: Hilt 2H 133
Poulson St. ST4: S Tren 2B 32
Pound Gdns. ST6: Nort 3D 18
Poundsgate Gro. ST4: Tren 2B 40
Povey Pl. ST5: Brad 6F 17
Powderham Cl. ST6: Chel 6J 11
Powell St. ST1: H'ley 1D 150 (3B 24)
Power Gro. ST3: Long 5G 33
Power Sta. Rd. WS15: Rug 6H 95
Power Sta. Rd. Ind. Est.
WS15: Rug 7H 95
Power Wash Trad. Est. ST8: Knyp 1B 12
Powy Dr. ST7: Kids 4F 11
Poynings, The WV6: Tett 1K 129
POYNTON 3A 158
POYNTON GREEN 3A 158
Precinct, The B79: Tam 4H 137
Preedys Cl. WS15: Abb B 3B 88
PREES 1A 158
PREES GREEN 1A 158
PREES HIGHER HEATH 1A 158
Premier Gdns. ST7: Kids 4D 10
Prescott Av. ST16: Staf 2J 73
Prescott Dr. ST19: Penk 3J 91
Prestbury Av. ST5: N'tle 1F 39
PRESTHOPE 2A 162
Preston St. ST6: B'lem 7C 18
PRESTON UPON THE WEALD MOORS
3A 158
Preston Va. La. ST19: Penk 3F 91
PRESTWOOD
Ashbourne 3A 156
Stourbridge 1J 149
Prestwood Av. WV11: Wed 6H 125
Prestwood Ct. ST17: Staf 5G 73
Prestwood Dr. DY7: Stou 1K 149
Prestwood Rd. DY7: Stou 3J 149
WV11: Wed 7E 124
Prestwood Rd. W. WV11: Wed 7E 124
Pretoria Rd. ST1: H'ley 6B 150 (5A 24)
Priam Cl. ST5: Brad 6F 17
Priam Gro. WS3: Pels 6D 120
Price Av. B78: M Oak 1D 140
Price Cl. TF9: Logg 5D 60
Price Ct. DE14: B Tre 7A 84
(not continuous)
Price St. ST6: B'lem 6K 17
WS11: Cann 2E 108
PRIESTCLIFFE 1B 156
Priestley Dr. ST3: Long 5K 33
Priestley Rd. WS2: Wals 7G 127
Priestly Ct. ST18: Staf 1A 74
Prime St. ST1: H'ley 1K 151 (3E 24)
Primitive St. ST7: M Cop 6G 7
Primley Av. B77: Hock 5B 142
Primrose Av. WV10: Ford, Bush 2B 124
Primrose Cl. ST19: Whe A 1C 90
WS3: Pels 7C 120
Primrose Dell CW3: Mad 3A 28
Primrose Dr. DE14: B'ton 4B 86
Primrose Gdns. WV8: Cods 2C 122
WV10: Fea 5F 117
Primrose Gro. ST5: N'tle 6G 23
PRIMROSE HILL 2D 157
Primrose Hill ST4: H'ord 7A 32
Primrose La. WV10: Bush 1C 124
(Cromwell Rd.)
WV10: Bush 5D 124
(Old Fallings La.)
Primrose Mdw. WS11: H Hay 1J 109
Primrose Way ST14: Utt 5G 63
Prince Av. ST18: Hau 7C 66
Prince Charles Av. ST13: Lee 2J 49
PRINCEFIELD 4H 91
Princefield Av. ST19: Penk 4H 91
Prince George St. ST10: Chea 4C 54
Prince of Wales Cen.
WS11: Cann 2E 108
Prince Rupert M. WS13: Lich 3A 114
Prince Rupert's Way WS13: Lich 3A 114
Princes Dr. WV8: Cods 2C 122
Princes Gdns. WV8: Cods 2B 122
Prince's Rd. B78: Pole 7K 139
ST4: P'ull, S Tren 1K 31
Princess Av. ST7: Aud 6F 15
ST13: Lee 1J 49
Princess Cl. WS7: C Ter 4G 111
Princess Ct. ST7: T Pit 2B 16
WV10: W'ton 7E 124
Princess Dr. ST3: W Coy 6C 34
Princess Pl. ST16: Staf 1G 73
Princes Sq. ST6: B'lem 7H 17
Princess Rd. ST14: Utt 4F 63
Princess St. DE14: B Tre 7D 84
ST5: N'tle 4G 153 (1G 31)
ST7: T Pit 2B 16
(not continuous)
ST8: Bidd 6D 8
WS7: C Ter 3G 111
WS11: Cann 5E 100
Princes St. ST15: Stone 2G 47
ST16: Staf 3G 73
Princess Way DE13: Stre 3F 85
Princes Ter. DE6: May 5C 56
Prince St. ST13: Lee 2G 49
WS11: Cann 4E 100
Princeton Gdns. WV9: P'ord 3H 123
Princetown Cl. ST3: Mei 3C 42
Priorfield Cl. ST3: Long 5H 33
PRIORSLEE 3B 158
Priory, The ST9: End 1C 50
Priory Av. ST13: Lee 1H 49
Priory Cl. B79: Tam 2F 137
DE13: Tut 3G 83
Priory Ct. ST2: Buck 3J 25
ST5: N'tle 5D 152
Priory Dr. ST18: L Hay 6J 81
Priory Lands DE13: Stre 1F 85
Priory Pk. Karting Circuit 7E 138
Priory Pl. ST7: Kids 3F 11
Priory Rd. ST2: A Hul 2H 25
ST5: N'tle 7C 152 (2E 30)
ST15: Stone 4H 47
Priory Rd. WS12: Hed 6K 101
WS15: Bre 4K 97
Priory Wlk. ST15: Stone 5H 47
Pritchard Av. WV11: Wed 7J 125
Probert Rd. WV10: Oxl 5J 123
Probyn Ct. ST3: Long 7J 33
Proctors Rd. WS15: Hand 5G 99
Proffitt Cl. WS8: Brow 7J 121
Progress Dr. WS11: Cann 4E 108
Progress Ind. Cen. WS11: Cann 5E 108
Prospect Dr. WS14: Lich 3F 115
Prospect Mnr. Ct. WS12: Hed 7J 101
Prospect Pk. WS11: Cann 4D 108
Prospect Pl. ST13: Lee 4F 49
ST17: Staf 1J 77
Prospect Rd. ST13: Lee 4H 49
ST16: Staf 2H 73
WS7: Burn 5K 111
Prospect St. B79: Tam 4G 137
ST6: B'lem 2J 23
Prospect Ter. ST5: N'tle 2C 152 (7E 22)
PROSPECT VILLAGE 6E 102
Prospect Way ST8: Knyp 3B 12
Providence Cl. WS3: Blox 6J 127
(not continuous)
Providence La. WS3: Blox 7J 127
Providence Sq. ST1: H'ley 1H 151
Providence St. ST1: H'ley 1H 151 (3D 24)
Provost Pl. ST13: Lee 2H 49
PUDDINGLAKE 1B 154
Puddle Bank La. CW12: N Ast 1K 7
Puddle Hill ST18: Hixon 5D 80
Puddy La. ST9: S'ley 4B 50
Pugin Cl. WV6: Per 3E 128
PULESTON 2B 158
Pullman Cl. B77: Glas 7C 138
Pullman Ct. ST10: Chea 5B 54
Pulteney Dr. ST16: Staf 7D 70
Pump Bank ST5: Keel 2H 29
Pump Ct. ST7: Big E 5G 15
Pump La. WS15: Rug 5E 94
Pump St. ST4: S Tren 2A 32
ST5: N'tle 5C 152 (1E 30)
ST13: Lee 2G 49
Pump Way WS15: Rug 6E 94
Purbeck St. ST6: B'lem 1B 24
Purbrook B77: Wiln 2A 142
Purcell Av. WS13: Lich 1B 114
Purcel Rd. WV10: Bush 5B 124
Purser Cres. ST5: N'tle 3F 23
PYE GREEN 2G 101 (3D 159)
Pye Grn. Rd. WS11: Cann 1D 108
WS12: Hed 4E 100
Pyenest St. ST1: H'ley 7D 150 (6B 24)
Pyrus Gro. WS15: Rug 3F 97

Q

Quabbs La. ST11: Fors 2K 43
Quadrangle, The ST9: End 2B 50
Quadrant, The ST1: H'ley 2G 151
Quadrant Rd. ST1: H'ley 2F 151 (4C 24)
Quadrille Lawns WV9: P'ord 3H 123
Quail Grn. WV6: Tett 4G 129
Quail Gro. ST3: Mei 3C 42
Quantico Cl. ST17: Staf 6H 73
Quantock Cl. WS8: W Woo 7J 121
QUARNDON 3D 157
QUARNDON COMMON 3D 157
QUARRY, THE 5E 14
Quarry Av. ST4: S Tren 1K 31
QUARRYBANK 1A 154
QUARRY BANK
Brierley Hill 3D 163
Newcastle 7H 21
Quarry Bank Rd. ST5: Keel 7H 21
Quarry Cl. ST9: S Broo 4J 19
ST9: Werr 4C 26
WS6: C Hay 1E 118
WS15: S Mil 1D 96
QUARRY HEATH 3K 91
Quarry Hill B77: Wiln 3B 142
Quarry Hills La. WS14: Lich 6D 114
Quarry La. ST20: Gno 5G 67
Quarry Rd. ST4: S Tren 1K 31
Quarry Ter. ST7: Kids 5E 10
QUATFORD 2B 162
QUATT 3B 162
Quay Point B77: Tam 6K 137
Queen Anne St. ST4: S Tren 1B 32
Queen Elizabeth II Ct.
ST4: Fen 3D 32
Queen Mary Rd. ST4: H'ord 1A 40
Queen Mary's Dr. ST12: Barl 6E 40
Queens Av. ST6: Tuns 4J 17
Queensberry Rd. ST3: Long 7K 33
Queens Cl. ST12: Barl 1F 45
Queens Ct. DE14: B'ton 4C 86
ST3: Long 1H 41
(off Queen's Pk. Av.)
ST4: S Tren 1K 31
ST5: N'tle 2F 153 (7G 23)
ST11: Cave 6F 35
WV10: W'ton 7E 124

Queens Dr.—Ricardo St.

Queens Dr. ST8: Bidd 7D 8
ST13: Lee 1J 49
WS7: Chas 6H 111
Queens Gdns. ST7: T Pit 1B 16
WV8: Cods 2B 122
Queensland Cres. DE15: Wins 2K 87
Queensmead Rd. ST3: L'ood 3B 42
Queens Pde. ST5: N'tle 3E 152
WS3: Blox 4H 127
Queen's Pk. Av. ST3: Long 1H 41
Queens Ri. DE13: Tut 2H 83
Queens Rd. ST4: P'ull, S Tren 1K 31
WV10: Calf H 5K 93
Queens Row ST12: Barl 1F 45
Queens Sq. ST15: Stone 2G 47
(not continuous)
WS11: Cann 2E 108
Queens Ter. ST1: H'ley 2K 151 (4E 24)
Queens Theatre 7K 17
Queen St. DE14: B Tre 3D 86
SK17: L'nor 3C 52
ST5: C'ton 1C 22
ST5: N'tle 2F 23
(Heaton Ter.)
ST5: N'tle 2F 153 (7G 23)
(Nelson Pl.)
ST6: B'lem 7K 17
ST7: Aud 6E 14
ST7: Kids 4E 10
ST10: Chea 4D 54
ST13: Lee 3G 49
ST14: Utt 6H 63
WS6: C Hay 1D 118
WS7: Chas 6H 111
WS11: Cann 5G 101
(Bradford St.)
WS11: Cann 2D 108
(Newhall St.)
WS13: Lich 4A 114
WS15: Rug 1H 97
Queen St. Ind. Est. WS7: Chas 6H 111
QUEENSVILLE 6K 73
Queensville ST17: Staf 5J 73
(not continuous)
Queensville Av. ST17: Staf 5J 73
Queensville Bri. ST17: Staf 5J 73
Queensville Retail Pk. ST17: Staf 5J 73
Queens Wlk. ST3: W Coy 5D 34
Queens Way B78: Dor 4H 143
ST5: N'tle 3F 31
Queensway B79: Tam 1G 137
ST4: S Tren 7A 150 (6K 23)
ST16: Staf 2G 73
WS15: Rug 2G 97
Queensway Ct. *ST3: Mei 1C 42*
(off Broadway)
Queensway Ind. Est. ST6: B'lem 7G 17
Quendale WV5: Womb 4E 144
Quince B77: Amin 6D 138
QUINTON 3D 163
Quinton Av. WS6: G Wyr 1F 119
Quinton Gro. ST5: N'tle 4F 23
Quinton Pl. WS11: N Can 7C 110
QUIXHILL 1C 58 (3B 156)
Quixhill Dr. ST10: Alt 3J 57
Quixhill La. ST14: Dens 1C 58
Quonton Wlk. ST6: B'lem 5C 18
Quonian's La. WS13: Lich 3B 114
Quorn Cl. DE15: Stap 3H 87

R

Rabbit La. WV10: Fea 5E 116
Racecourse ST5: Sil 7A 22
Racecourse Rd. ST4: T Val 5A 32
WV6: W'ton 7J 123
Racecourse Rd. Ind. Est.
WV6: W'ton 7J 123
Rachel Gro. ST4: Fen 3H 33
RADBOURNE 1C 161
Raddle La. B79: Edin 1C 132
RADFORD 3D 165
Radford Bank ST17: Staf 6K 73
Radford Cl. ST15: Stone 3G 47
Radford La. WV3: W'ton 7G 129
WV4: L Pen 7G 129
Radford Ri. ST17: Staf 6A 74
Radford Rd. ST4: S Tren 7K 23
Radford St. ST15: Stone 3G 47
Radhurst Ri. DE13: B Nee 5F 89
Radley Way ST9: Werr 5D 26
Radmore Cl. WS7: C Ter 3F 111
Radmore La. WS15: Abb B 3C 88
RADMORE WOOD 1E 88
Radnor Ri. WS12: Hed 6H 101
Radstock Cl. ST17: Staf 1B 78
Radstock Rd. WV12: Will 4C 126
Radstone Ri. ST5: N'tle 6F 31
RADWAY GREEN 2B 154
Radway Grn. Rd. CW2: Bart 1A 14
RADWOOD 4B 36
Raglan Av. WV6: Per 3G 129
Raglan Cl. DE13: Stre 3E 84
Raglan St. ST4: Fen 3D 32
Raglan Wlk. *ST4: Fen 3D 32*
(off Raglan St.)
Ragley Cl. WS3: Blox 4G 127
Raikes La. WS14: C'eld, Shen 4A 134
Railton Av. ST3: Blur 1G 41
Railway Cotts. ST4: Tren 6C 32
ST8: B Lee 2B 12
ST17: Colw 7J 81
ST18: Gt Bri 6H 65
WS15: Bre 4J 97
Railway Ct. ST9: End 2B 50
Railway Enterprise Cen.
ST4: S Tren 7A 24
Railway La. WS7: C Ter 2G 111
Railway Pas. ST3: Long 5J 33
Railway St. ST6: Tuns 5J 17
ST16: Staf 3F 73
WS11: Cann 3E 108
WS11: N Can 6C 110
Railway Ter. ST3: Long 6J 33
ST10: Frog 5J 53
ST11: B Bri 3G 43
ST17: Milf 7G 75
Railway Vw. ST1: H'ley 4C 150
WS12: Hed 5H 101
(off Cannock Rd.)
Railway Wlk. WS11: Cann 3F 109
WS11: N Can 7C 110
Rainford Cl. ST7: Pack 5K 11
Rainham Gro. ST6: Feg H 6A 12
Rainscar B77: Wiln 3D 142
RAKE END 1D 98 (3A 160)
Rake Hill WS7: Burn 3K 111
RAKESDALE 4F 57
RAKEWAY 6E 54 (3A 156)
Rakeway Rd. ST10: Chea, Tea 6D 54
Ralph Ct. ST17: Staf 6D 72
Ralph Dr. ST1: H'ley 7E 18
Ralston Cl. WS3: Blox 1G 127
Ramage Gro. ST3: Long 1K 41
Rambleford Way ST16: Staf 5F 71
Ramillies Cres. WS6: G Wyr 3F 119
Ramsay Cl. ST12: Barl 6E 40
Ramsey Rd. ST5: N'tle 1C 152 (6E 22)
WS2: Wals 7G 127
Ramsey St. ST4: Fen 4C 32
Ramshaw Gro. ST3: Long 3K 33
Ramshaw Vw. ST13: Lee 1H 49
RAMSHORN 3A 156
Ramshorn Rd. ST10: O'moor 1E 56
Randel La. ST6: Gold 6F 11
Randles La. ST9: W Roc 3J 27
Ranelagh St. ST1: H'ley 5F 151 (5C 24)
Rangeley Vw. ST15: Stone 2E 46
RANGEMORE 2B 160
Rangemore St. DE14: B Tre 1C 86
Rangemore Ter. ST5: N'tle 5H 23
Ranger's Wlk. WS15: Rug 7D 94
Rangifer Rd. B78: Faze 2F 141
Rank, The ST20: Gno 5G 67
Ransome Pl. ST3: W Coy 5A 34
RANTON 2C 159
Ranton Bus. Pk. WS11: Cann 1G 109
RANTON GREEN 2C 159
Ranworth Cl. ST5: N'tle 7F 31
Ratcliffe Av. DE14: B'ton 4C 86
RATCLIFFE CULEY 2D 165
Ratcliffe Rd. WV11: Wed 7A 126
Rathbone Av. ST5: N'tle 5H 23
Rathbone St. ST6: Tuns 4J 17
Rathlin Cl. WV9: P'ord 2J 123
Rathwell Cl. WV9: P'ord 3J 123
Rattigan Dr. ST3: W Coy 5B 34
Ratton St. ST1: H'ley 2H 151 (4D 24)
Raven Cl. WS6: C Hay 2D 118
WS12: Hed 6A 102
WS12: Hun 3C 100
(Foxfields Way)
WS12: Hun 6C 100
(Highland Rd.)
Raven Cres. WV11: Wed 5K 125
Ravenhill Cl. WS15: Rug 2H 97
Ravenhill Dr. WV8: Cods 2C 122
Ravenhill Ter. WS15: Rug 2H 97
Ravenna Way ST3: Long 5A 34
Raven Rd. DE13: Yox 2H 89
Ravensbank Pk. ST18: Hopt 5G 69
RAVENSCLIFFE 2D 16
Ravenscliffe Rd. ST7: Kids 6E 10
Ravens Cl. ST7: Big E 4G 15
Ravens Ct. WS8: Brow 5H 121
RAVENSDALE 5G 17
RAVENSHALL 3B 6
Ravensholme WV6: Tett 4G 129
Ravenside Retail Pk.
ST4: S Tren 1D 32
Raven's La. ST7: Big E 4H 15
Ravenslea Rd. WS15: Rug 3H 97
RAVENSMOOR 2A 154
RAVENSTONE 3D 161
Ravenstone B77: Wiln 2D 142
Ravens Way DE14: B Tre 7C 84
Ravenswood Cl. ST5: N'tle 6E 30
Ravenswood Crest ST17: Wild 7A 74
Rawle Cl. ST10: Chea 4B 54
Rawlett Community Leisure Cen.
1G 137
Rawlins St. ST1: H'ley 1K 151 (3E 24)
RAWNSLEY 5C 102 (3A 160)
Rawnsley Rd. WS12: Hed, Haz 3K 101
RAWSON GREEN 3D 157
Raygill B77: Wiln 2D 142
Rayleigh Way ST2: Bent 7K 25
Raymond Av. ST1: H'ley 1D 24
Raymond Cl. WS2: Wals 7K 127
Raymond Gdns. WV11: Wed 7J 125
Raymond St. ST1: H'ley 6F 151 (6C 24)
Raynor Rd. WV10: W'ton 7D 124
Read Av. ST16: Staf 1H 73
Reading Room Dr. WS15: Col 3J 95
Reading Way ST2: Buck 6K 25
Reads Rd. ST4: Fen 1F 33
Reapers Cl. WV12: Will 7D 126
Reapers Wlk. WV8: P'ord 4H 123
REASE HEATH 2A 154
Reason Rd. ST17: Staf 2G 77
Reaymer Cl. WS2: Wals 7H 127
Rebecca St. ST4: S Tren 1B 32
Recorder Gro. ST6: Chel 1B 18
Recreation Rd. ST3: Long 7A 34
Rectory Cl. B78: D Bas 5E 140
Rectory Ct. ST17: Staf 4F 73
Rectory Gdns. ST7: T Pit 1B 16
ST15: Swyn 2D 64
WS15: Arm 5E 98
Rectory La. ST18: Hau 7C 66
WS15: Arm 5D 98
Rectory Pas. ST1: H'ley 6E 150 (6B 24)
Rectory Rd. ST1: H'ley 6D 150 (6B 24)
Rectory St. ST1: H'ley 6D 150 (6B 24)
Rectory Vw. ST7: T Pit 1B 16
Redacres WV6: Tett 7G 123
Red Bank ST3: Long 1J 41
Redbourn Rd. WS3: Blox 1G 127
Redbridge Cl. ST4: H'ord 1K 39
Redbrook Cl. WS12: H Hay 1K 109
Redbrook La. WS15: Bre 4H 97
Redbrook La. Ind. Est. WS15: Bre 4H 97
RED BULL 3B 10
Redcar Rd. ST4: Tren 3A 40
WV10: Ford 1B 124
Redcliff B77: Amin 4B 138
Redcliffe Dr. WV5: Womb 4H 145
Redcott's Cl. WV10: Bush 5E 124
Redfern Dr. WS7: Burn 6K 111
Redfern Rd. ST14: Utt 4F 63
ST15: Stone 7F 47
Redgrave Dr. ST16: Staf 3D 72
Red Hall La. ST7: H End 4D 20
Redheath Cl. ST5: Sil 6J 21
Redheath Cotts. ST5: Sil 6H 21
REDHILL 3B 158
RED HILL 1A 104
REDHILL 3J 65
Redhill ST16: Staf 5E 70
Redhill Av. WV5: Womb 4G 145
Redhill Cl. B79: Tam 2G 137
Redhill Dr. ST10: Tea 2G 55
Redhill Gdns. ST15: Stone 4H 47
Redhill Gorse ST16: Staf 5E 70
Redhill La. DE13: Tut 3G 83
Red Hill Rd. ST15: Stone 4H 47
Redhill Rd. WS11: Cann 6E 100
Redhills ST21: Ecc 3J 65
Redhills Rd. ST2: Mil 7F 19
Red Ho. Cres. ST3: Long 6G 33
Redhouse Rd. WV6: Tett 1H 129
Redhurst Dr. WV10: Ford 2K 123
Redlake B77: Wiln 2B 142
Redland Dr. ST2: Buck 5K 25
Redlands, The ST15: Stone 5J 47
Redlands Way B74: S'ly 7F 135
Red La. CW3: Mad 5A 28
ST2: L Oak 5J 19
WV11: Ess 4C 126
Red Lion Av. WS11: N Can 7C 110
Red Lion Cl. ST7: Talk 7B 10
Red Lion Cres. WS11: N Can 7C 110
Red Lion La. WS11: N Can 7C 110
Red Lion Pas. ST1: H'ley 5E 150 (5B 24)
Red Lion Sq. ST5: C'ton 1C 22
Red Lion St. ST16: Staf 2G 73
Redlock Fld. WS14: Lich 6A 114
Redman Gro. ST6: B'lem 1C 24
Redmine Cl. ST5: N'tle 4E 22
Redmond Cl. WS15: Rug 6E 94
Redmoor Cl. DE15: Wins 1J 87
Redmoor Rd. WS15: Gen 7H 103
Red Rd. ST10: Alt 2F 57
Redrock Cres. ST7: Kids 5G 11
Red Rock Dr. WV8: Cods 3B 122
Red Rose Theatre 7G 95
Redruth Dr. ST17: Staf 5B 74
Redstone Dr. WV11: Wed 7K 125
RED STREET 4B 16 (2C 155)
Redwell Cl. B77: Tam 4K 137
Redwing B77: Wiln 4C 142
Redwing Cl. WS7: Hamm 6B 112
Redwing Dr. ST8: Bidd 5E 8
WS12: Hun 3C 100
Redwing Gro. ST7: Pack 5J 11
Redwood Av. ST15: Stone 6H 47
Redwood Dr. DE15: Stap 4H 87
WS7: C Ter 3H 111
WS11: Cann 7G 101
Redwood Pl. ST3: Mei 1B 42
Redwood Rd. DY7: Kin 6G 149
Redwood Way WV12: Will 5B 126
Reedbed Gro. ST6: B'lem 4C 18
Reedham Way ST2: Bent 6K 25
Reedly Rd. WV12: Will 4C 126
Reedmace B77: Tam 7J 137
Rees Dr. WV5: Womb 3H 145
Reeve Cl. WS15: Hand 5F 99
Reeve End DE13: Yox 1H 89
Reeve La. WS13: Lich 3B 114
Reeves Av. ST5: N'tle 4F 23
ST6: B'lem 4A 18
Reeves Gdns. WV8: Cods 1C 122
Reeves St. WS3: Blox 5H 127
Refinery St. ST5: N'tle 5F 153 (1G 31)
Regal Cl. B77: T Gat 2J 141
Regency Cl. ST7: T Pit 2B 16
Regency Ct. WS15: Rug 3K 97
Regency Dr. ST9: S Broo 3H 19
Regency Wlk. B74: F Oak 3J 135
Regency Way DE13: Stre 3E 84
Regent Av. ST6: Tuns 4K 17
Regent Ct. ST5: N'tle 2F 23
ST10: Ips 2H 53
Regent Ho. *ST8: Brin F 4B 12*
(off Outclough Rd)
Regent Rd. ST1: H'ley 6F 151 (6C 24)
Regents Pk. Rd. DE14: B'ton 5B 86
Regent St. ST4: S Tren 4K 31
ST13: Lee 3G 49
ST15: Stone 3F 47
Regent Theatre 4F 151 (5C 24)
Regina Cres. WV6: Tett 2J 129
Reginald Mitchell Ct.
ST1: H'ley 5H 151 (5D 24)
Reginald Mitchell Way ST6: Tuns 3G 17
Reginald St. ST6: B'lem 7A 18
Regina St. ST6: B'lem 5D 18
Regis Beeches WV6: Tett 1K 129
Regis Rd. WV6: Tett 1J 129
Registry St. ST4: S Tren 1B 32
Reid Av. WV12: Will 7D 126
Reid Cl. WS7: Burn 4D 112
Reid St. ST6: B'lem 7J 17
Reindeer Rd. B78: Faze 1E 140
Relay Dr. B77: Wiln 3E 142
Rembrandt Cl. WS11: H Hay 1K 109
Rembrandt Way ST3: Mei 4D 42
Remer St. ST6: B'lem 2B 24
Remington Dr. WS11: Cann 3F 109
Remington Pl. WS2: Wals 7J 127
Remington Rd. WS2: Wals 7H 127
Renard Way ST3: Mei 3D 42
Rendel Gro. ST15: Stone 2E 46
Rendermore Cl. ST19: Penk 4G 91
Rene Rd. B77: Tam 4A 138
Renfrew Cl. ST5: N'tle 5A 152 (1D 30)
Renfrew Pl. ST4: H'ord 1A 40
Rennie Cres. ST13: Ched 6H 51
Rennison Dr. WV5: Womb 4G 145
Renown Cl. ST2: Buck 7F 25
Renton Gro. WV10: Oxl 4J 123
Renton Rd. WV10: Oxl 4J 123
Renwick La. ST10: Chea 1J 55
Repington Rd. ST1: H'ley 7F 19
Repington Rd. Nth. B77: Amin 4C 138
Repington Rd. Sth. B77: Amin 4C 138
REPTON 2D 161
Repton Av. WV6: Per 3F 129
Repton Cl. ST17: Staf 5K 73
WS11: Cann 3B 108
Repton Dr. ST5: N'tle 4D 30
Reservoir Rd. DE14: B Tre 7A 84
ST3: Long 7A 34
WS12: Hed 6K 101
Retreat Gdns., The WV6: Patt 6B 128
Reva Rd. ST17: Staf 6G 73
Revival St. WS3: Blox 4H 127
Reynards Ri. TF9: Logg 4D 60
Reynolds Av. ST5: C'ton 2C 22
Reynolds Cl. DY3: Swin 1J 147
WS13: Lich 1B 114
Reynolds Gro. WV6: Per 1G 129
Reynolds Rd. ST6: B'lem 4A 18
Reynolds Wlk. WV11: Wed 5B 126
Rhein Way ST17: Staf 6J 73
Rhodes Ct. ST5: N'tle 1G 23
Rhodes Ho. DE15: Wins 1K 87
Rhodes St. ST1: H'ley 2D 24
Rhondda Av. ST6: B'lem 1C 24
RHUDDALL HEATH 1A 154
Rialto Pl. ST6: Tuns 4H 17
Ribbesford Av. WV10: Oxl 5K 123
Ribble Cl. ST5: N'tle 5F 31
Ribble Dr. ST8: Bidd 4E 8
Ribble Ind. Est. ST6: B'lem 1J 23
Ribblesdale B77: Wiln 3D 142
RIBER 2D 157
Ricardo St. ST3: Long 1H 41

Ricardson Way—Roundway

Ricardson Way WS15: Rug 5F **95**
Riceyman Rd. ST5: Brad 6F **17**
Richard Cooper Rd. WS14: Shen . . .6C **134**
Richards Av. ST6: Tuns 4K **17**
ST16: Staf 2J **73**
Richards Ct. ST17: Bed 7D **78**
WS11: N Can 5B **110**
Richardson Pl. ST6: Chel 1B **18**
Richfield La. ST17: Bed 7D **78**
Richmere Ct. WV6: Tett 3J **129**
Richmond Av. ST1: H'ley 1D **24**
Richmond Cl. B79: Tam 4G **137**
ST17: Staf 7G **73**
WS11: Cann 5G **101**
Richmond Dr. WS14: Lich 4D **114**
WV6: Per 2G **129**
Richmond Gdns. WV5: Womb 5G **145**
Richmond Gro. ST5: N'tle 5H **23**
ST15: Stone 5G **47**
Richmond Pk. WS15: Bre 4H **97**
Richmond Rd. ST4: H'ord 1K **39**
Richmond St. DE14: B Tre 7D **84**
ST4: P'ull 1A **32**
Richmond Ter. ST1: H'ley . . .7E **150** (6B **24**)
RICHMOORHILL 6K 27
RICKERSCOTE 1H 77 (2D 159)
Rickerscote Av. ST17: Staf 1J **77**
Rickerscote Hall La. ST17: Staf 2J **77**
Rickerscote Rd. ST17: Staf 1G **77**
Ricknild St. DE14: B'ton 4A **86**
Rickyard Cl. B78: Pole 7J **139**
Ridding Bank ST4: H'rch 3F **39**
Ridding Gdns. B78: Pole 2J **143**
RIDDINGS
Alfreton 2D 157
Uttoxeter 4A 58
Riddings, The B77: Amin 4A **138**
WV10: Bush 6E **124**
Riddings Cres. WS3: Pels 7B **120**
Riddings La. DE6: C Cla, D Cla 6B **82**
Rider's Way WS15: Rug 7D **94**
Ridge Cl. ST12: Barl 3C **44**
Ridge Cres. ST3: L'ood 4B **42**
Ridge Cft. ST15: Stone 5J **47**
RIDGEFIELD 4H 9
Ridgefields ST8: Bid M 4H **9**
Ridgehill Dr. CW3: Mad H 2D **28**
Ridgehouse Dr.
ST1: H'ley 3B **150** (4A **24**)
RIDGE LANE 2C 165
Ridge La. WV11: Wed 6H **125**
Ridgemont Ct. ST15: Stone 5J **47**
Ridge Rd. ST6: Sandy 1H **17**
Ridget La. DE13: Alre 7C **130**
WS13: Alre 7C **130**
Ridge Wlk. ST3: L'ood 3B **42**
RIDGEWAY
Belper .2D 157
Stoke-on-Trent 6E 12 (2C 155)
Ridgeway ST6: B Edg 6D **12**
ST18: Hixon 6D **80**
Ridgeway, The ST16: Staf 1C **72**
WS7: Burn 6J **111**
Ridgeway Cl. ST18: Hopt 5K **71**
ST18: Hyde L 2E **76**
Ridgeway Rd. DE15: Stap 6F **87**
Ridgewood Ri. B77: Amin 4C **138**
Ridgmont Rd. ST5: N'tle 5D **30**
RIDGWARDINE 1A 158
Ridgway Dr. ST11: B Bri 3F **43**
Ridgway Pl. ST5: N'tle 2H **23**
Ridgway Rd. ST1: H'ley 7G **151** (7C **24**)
ST4: S Tren 7C **24**
Ridings, The ST19: Brew 1C **92**
WS11: Cann 3F **109**
Ridings Brook Dr. WS11: Cann 1G **109**
Ridings Pk. WS11: Cann 7G **101**
Riding Way WV12: Will 7D **126**
Ridley St. ST4: Fen 4C **32**
Ridley Wlk. ST4: Fen 4C **32**
Ridware Ho. *WS13: Lich* *2E* ***114***
(off Hobs Rd.)
Ridware Rd.
WS15: Hand, Mav R, Hill R 1F **99**
Ridware Theatre 1H 99
Rigby Dr. WS11: Cann 6E **100**
Rigby Rd. ST7: Kids 3F **11**
Righton Ho. B77: Wiln 1K **141**
Riley B77: Glas 6A **138**
Riley Av. ST6: B'lem 5B **18**
RILEYHILL 3B 160
Riley La. ST20: Knig, W'ves 3E **66**
Riley St. Nth. ST6: B'lem 7J **17**
Riley St. Sth. ST6: B'lem 7K **17**
Rileys Way ST7: Big E 5H **15**
Rill St. ST4: Fen 5H **33**
Rimbach Dr. ST18: L Hay 6J **81**
Rimini Cl. ST3: Long 4A **34**
Rindle, The ST10: Chea 4A **54**
Ring, The ST18: L Hay 5H **81**
Ringhills Rd. WV8: Bilb 3D **122**
Ringland Cl. ST1: H'ley 3J **151** (4D **24**)
Ring Rd. WS7: C Ter 4F **111**
Ringway WS11: Cann 2E **108**
Ringway Ind. Est. WS13: Lich 7C **106**
Ringwood Rd. WV10: Bush 4B **124**
RIPLEY 3D 157
Ripon Av. ST5: C'ton 1C **22**
Ripon Dr. ST17: Wild 7A **74**
Ripon Rd. ST3: Blur 2F **41**
WV10: Oxl 6A **124**
Rise, The ST17: Walt 7C **74**
WS13: Lich 4K **113**
WS15: Rug 3H **97**
RISE END 2C 157
Riseley Rd. ST4: S Tren 4J **153** (1H **31**)
Rishworth Av. WS15: Rug 6G **95**
RISING BROOK 1F 77
Rising Brook ST17: Staf 7G **73**
WV6: Tett 2J **129**
Rists Ind. Est. ST5: N'tle 4D **22**
Rists Rd. ST5: N'tle 4D **22**
Rivendell Gdns. WV6: Tett 1J **129**
Rivendell La. ST13: Lee 7G **49**
Rivercroft Cl. ST14: Roce 5E **58**
(not continuous)
Riverdale Cl. DE15: Wins 6J **85**
Riverdale Dr. ST6: Chel 6J **11**
River Dr. B77: Tam 6G **137**
B78: Tam 6G **137**
Riverfield Gro. B77: Tam 4K **137**
Riverhead Cl. ST6: Nort 2F **19**
River Lea M. CW3: Mad 3A **28**
Riversfield Dr. ST14: Roce 5D **58**
Riverside ST10: O'moor 2B **56**
ST16: Staf 3G **73**
WS15: Rug 6H **95**
Riverside Cen., The DE14: B Tre 1F **87**
Riverside Ct. ST1: H'ley 4F **25**
Riverside Dr. DE14: B'ton 5A **86**
Riverside Gdns. DE14: B Tre 6G **85**
WV8: Bilb 1D **122**
Riverside Gro. ST15: Stone 3F **47**
Riverside Ind. Est. B78: Faze 2H **141**
Riverside Pk. DE14: B Tre 5G **85**
Riverside Recreation Cen. 3G 73
Riverside Rd. ST4: T Val 6J **31**
ST10: Tea 3F **55**
Riverside Way WV9: Cove 2K **93**
Riversmead ST5: N'tle 5F **31**
Riversmeade Way ST16: Staf 1C **72**
River Way ST15: Stone 5G **47**
Riverway ST16: Staf 4H **73**
Rivington Cres. ST6: Feg H 1A **18**
Rixdale Cl. ST1: H'ley 1F **151** (3C **24**)
Roach B77: Dost 4K **141**
Roach Cres. WV11: Wed 5K **125**
Robert Cl. B79: Tam 2F **137**
Robert Heath St. ST6: B'lem 5C **18**
Roberts Av. ST5: N'tle 1C **152** (6E **22**)
Roberts Cl. ST7: A Ban 2H **21**
Robertson Dr. ST5: N'tle 5D **22**
Robertson Sq. ST4: T Val 5J **31**
Robert St. ST6: Tuns 3H **17**
Robertville Rd. ST2: Buck 5H **25**
Robey's La. B78: Alve, Bir 7F **139**
Robina Dr. ST10: Chea 4D **54**
Robin Cl. B77: T Gat 2J **141**
ST7: Pack 6K **11**
ST14: Utt 7G **63**
WS12: Hun 3C **100**
Robin Cft. ST6: B'lem 7K **17**
Robin Gro. WV11: Wed 6G **125**
ROBIN HILL 6G 9
Robin Hill ST8: Bid M 6G **9**
Robin Hill Gro. ST4: Fen 4H **33**
Robinia B77: Amin 5C **138**
Robins, The TF9: Logg 5D **60**
Robins Cl. WS6: C Hay 3D **118**
Robins Cft. WS11: H Hay 2H **109**
Robinson Av. ST6: B'lem 7D **18**
Robinson Cl. B79: Tam 2E **136**
Robinson Ct. ST3: Blur 2F **41**
Robinson Rd. ST4: Tren 2K **39**
WS7: C Ter 2H **111**
Robins Rd. WS7: C Ter 5F **111**
Robinswood ST17: Wild 1A **78**
Robottom Cl. WS2: Wals 7H **127**
Robson Cl. WS8: Brow 7J **121**
Robson St. ST1: H'ley 5E **150** (5B **24**)
ROCESTER 5D 58 (1B 160)
Rocester Av. WV11: Wed 6J **125**
Rocester La. ST10: Wat 4C **52**
Roche, The ST13: Ched 6G **51**
WS13: Lich 2D **112**
Roche Av. ST13: Lee 1H **49**
Roche Rd. WS3: Blox 4F **127**
Rochester Av. WS7: C Ter 4J **111**
Rochester Rd. ST3: Long 4H **33**
Rochester Way WS12: H Hay 2J **109**
Roche Way WS3: Blox 4F **127**
Rochford Cl. ST13: Lee 4D **48**
Rochford Way ST2: Bent 7K **25**
Rock Cres. ST15: Oul 7J **45**
ROCK END .7F 9
Rockeries, The ST17: Staf 1J **77**
Rock Farm Rd.
WS14: W'ton 2G **131**
Rockfield Av. ST2: L Oak 6K **19**
Rock Ho. Dr. ST12: Barl 2D **44**
Rockhouse Dr. ST18: Gt Hay 5G **81**
Rockhouse La. ST7: Talk 6A **10**
(not continuous)
Rockingham Cl. WS3: Blox 4H **127**
Rockingham Dr. ST10: Chea 4E **54**
WV6: Per 3F **129**
Rocklands ST5: N'tle 1G **23**
Rocklands Cres. WS13: Lich 2D **114**
Rock La. TF9: A'ley 2J **61**
TF9: Muck 2B **60**
Rockrose Gdns. WV10: Fea 5E **116**
Rocks, The ST6: B Edg 6H **13**
Rockside ST7: M Cop 7G **7**
Rock Wlk. ST10: Alt 3J **57**
Rocky Wall DY7: Kin 4C **148**
RODBASTON 7G 91
Rodbaston Dr. ST19: Penk 7F **91**
(not continuous)
RODEHEATH 1C 155
RODE HEATH 2C 155
RODEN 3A 158
Roderick Dr. WV11: Wed 6H **125**
Rodger Av. CW3: Bet 2B **6**
Rodgers Ct. *ST6: Gold* *7G* ***11***
(off Rodgers St.)
Rodgers St. ST6: Gold 6G **11**
RODINGTON 3A 158
RODINGTON HEATH 3A 158
RODSLEY 3C 157
RODWAY .3A 158
Roebuck Ct. ST15: Hild 5H **59**
Roebuck Pl. WS3: Blox 7K **127**
Roebuck Rd. WS3: Blox 7K **127**
Roebuck Shop. Cen., The
ST5: N'tle 4E **152** (1F **31**)
Roebuck St. ST4: S Tren 1C **32**
Roedean Av. ST17: Staf 6K **73**
Roe La. ST5: N'tle 5E **30**
Roe Pk ST7: M Cop 4J **7**
Rofs Cft. B78: Pole 7J **139**
Rogate Cl. ST4: Fen 3H **33**
Rogers Av. ST5: N'tle 5D **22**
Rogers Cl. WV11: Wed 4A **126**
Rogerson Rd. WS13: Frad 4K **107**
Rogerstone Av. ST4: S Tren 3J **31**
Rokholt Cres. WS11: Cann 2C **108**
Rolfe Cl. ST4: H'ord 7A **32**
Rolleston La. DE13: Tut 3J **83**
ROLLESTON ON DOVE 7H 83 (2C 161)
Rolleston Rd. DE13: B Tre 2C **84**
Rolleston Trad. Est. DE14: B Tre 7E **84**
Rolling Mill Rd. WS11: N Can 7C **110**
Rolt Cl. ST15: Stone 1E **46**
Roma Cl. ST3: L'ood 2K **41**
Roman Cl. WS8: Brow 2G **121**
Roman Ct. B77: Wiln 3A **142**
WS11: Cann 6E **108**
Roman Dr. ST5: C'ton 3B **22**
Roman La. B74: L Ast 4G **135**
Roman Pk. B74: L Ast 4G **135**
Roman Pl. B74: L Ast 6G **135**
Roman Rd. B74: L Ast 3H **135**
Roman Vw. WS11: Cann 6F **109**
Roman Wlk. WS14: Wall 1A **134**
Roman Way B78: Dor 4J **143**
B79: Tam 2E **136**
WS14: Lich 4D **114**
Romer Side ST2: Bent 1J **33**
Romesco Way ST17: Staf 6J **73**
Romford Mdw. ST21: Ecc 3G **65**
Romford Pl. ST3: Mei 3D **42**
Romford Rd. ST16: Staf 7G **71**
Romilly Cl. WS14: Lich 4E **114**
Romney B77: Wiln 2B **142**
Romney Av. ST5: C'ton 2C **22**
Romney Dr. ST16: Staf 2D **72**
Romney Gro. ST3: L'ood 2J **41**
Romsey Cl. ST2: Bent 1K **33**
Romsey Gro. WV10: Ford 2A **124**
Romsey Rd. WV10: Ford 2A **124**
Romsey Way WS3: Blox 2F **127**
ROMSLEY
Halesowen 3D 163
Bridgnorth 3B 162
Ronald St. ST3: Long 7J **33**
(not continuous)
Ronaldsway Dr.
ST5: N'tle 1B **152** (6E **22**)
Ronald Wlk. ST3: Long 7J **33**
Ronson Av. ST4: T Val 5J **31**
ROOKERY, THE 3G 11
Rookery, The ST5: Sil 7A **22**
Rookery Av. ST3: Blur 1G **41**
Rookery Cl. DE13: Yox 2H **89**
WS15: Hand 4G **99**
Rookery Ct. ST4: T Val 6J **31**
WS13: Lich 4J **113**
Rookery La. ST4: T Val 6K **31**
Rookery Ri. WV5: Womb 4H **145**
Rookery Rd. ST7: Kids 3G **11**
ST15: Cold M 5A **64**
WV5: Womb 4H **145**
Rookswood Copse ST17: Wild 1A **78**
Rookwood Dr. WV6: Tett 4G **129**
Roost Hill DE13: New 7A **88**
Rope St. ST4: S Tren 3H **153** (7H **23**)
Rope Wlk., The DE14: B Tre 3D **86**
Rosalind Gro. WV11: Wed 7A **126**
Roseacre ST5: N'tle 6A **152** (2D **30**)
Roseacre Gro. ST3: L'ood 4B **42**
Roseacre La. ST11: B Bri 4H **43**
Rose Av. DE13: Stre 1H **85**
Rose Bank B74: L Ast 3J **135**
Rose Bank St. ST13: Lee 3G **49**
Rosebank Ter. ST10: O'moor 3C **56**
ST13: Lee 3G **49**
Rosebay Gro. WV5: Womb 4E **144**
Rosebay Mdw. WS11: H Hay 1J **109**
Roseberry Dr. CW3: Mad 2A **28**
Roseberry St. ST6: Chel 2K **17**
Rosebery Cl. ST8: Bidd 5E **8**
Rosebery Rd. B77: Dost 6K **141**
Rose Cott. Cl. DE14: B Tre 3D **86**
Rose Cott. Gdns. DE14: B Tre 3E **86**
Rose Cotts. ST9: End 1C **50**
Rose Dr. WS8: Clay 6G **121**
Roseford La. ST17: Act T 4J **77**
ROSEHILL 1A 158
Rose Hill ST16: Staf 3E **72**
Rosehill WS12: Hed 2F **101**
Rosehill Cl. ST2: Mil 6H **19**
Rose Hill Shop. Cen. WS12: Hed . . .2F **101**
Roseland Cres. ST2: Mil 6H **19**
Rose La. WS7: Burn 4A **112**
Rosemary Av. ST17: Staf 2H **77**
WS6: C Hay 1D **118**
Rosemary Cl. WS8: Clay 6F **121**
Rosemary Ct. WV11: Wed 6K **125**
Rosemary Dr. B74: L Ast 5H **135**
ST14: Utt 7G **63**
Rosemary Ednam Cl.
ST4: S Tren 5K **153** (1J **31**)
Rosemary Hill Rd. B74: F Oak 5H **135**
Rosemary Nook B74: L Ast 3J **135**
Rosemary Pl. ST1: H'ley 1E **24**
Rosemary Rd. B77: Amin 5B **138**
WS6: C Hay 7D **108**
(not continuous)
Rosemary St. ST5: Sil 7C **22**
Rosemill TF9: Logg 4E **60**
Rosemount Rd. DE15: B Tre 2G **87**
Rosendale Av. ST5: C'ton 2D **22**
Roseneath Pl. ST2: Mil 6H **19**
Rose St. ST1: H'ley 1K **151** (3E **24**)
Rose Tree Av. ST4: T Val 7J **31**
Rosevale Bus. Pk. ST5: C'ton 7D **16**
Rosevale Ct. ST5: C'ton 7C **16**
Rosevale La. ST5: C'ton 7C **16**
Rosevale Rd. ST5: C'ton 7C **16**
Rosevale St. ST2: Mil 6H **19**
Rosevean Cl. ST1: H'ley 1F **151** (3C **24**)
Roseville Gdns. WV8: Cods 1C **122**
Roseway WS15: Rug 6E **94**
Rosewood Av. ST9: S Broo 3J **19**
Rosewood Cl. B74: L Ast 3J **135**
B77: Tam 5K **137**
Rosewood Ct. B77: Tam 5K **137**
Rosewood Dr. WV12: Will 5B **126**
Rosewood Gdns. ST16: Staf 3E **72**
WV11: Ess 2B **126**
Rosewood Pk. WS6: C Hay 2D **118**
Rosewood Rd. DE15: Stap 6G **87**
ROSLISTON 3C 161
Rosliston Rd. DE15: Stap 6F **87**
Rosliston Rd. Sth. DE15: Stap 7F **87**
Rossall Av. ST5: N'tle 4D **30**
Ross Cl. ST3: W Coy 5C **34**
Rossett Gro. ST6: Chel 6K **11**
Ross La. ST10: Whis 7K **53**
Rosslyn Rd. ST3: Long 7J **33**
ROSTON .3B 156
Rosy Bank ST9: S Broo 4J **19**
Rosy Cross B79: Tam 4J **137**
Rothay B77: Wiln 2B **142**
Rothbury Grn. WS12: H Hay 1A **110**
Rother Wlk. ST6: Chel 3A **18**
Rotherwood Dr. ST17: Staf 5E **72**
Rothesay Av. ST5: N'tle 6A **152** (2D **30**)
Rothesay Ct. ST3: Long 7K **33**
ST5: N'tle 6A **152** (2D **30**)
Rothesay Rd. ST3: Long 7K **33**
Rothesay Way WV12: Will 7B **126**
Rothley Grn. ST3: Blur 2F **41**
Rothsay Av. ST1: H'ley 7D **18**
Rothwell St. ST4: P'ull 3K **31**
Rotten Row WS13: Lich 4C **114**
Rotterdam ST5: N'tle 3A **152** (7D **22**)
Rotterdam Rd. ST5: N'tle . . .3A **152** (7D **22**)
ROUGH CLOSE 7A 42 (1D 159)
ROUGH CLOSE COMMON 6K 41
ROUGHCOTE 3E 34 (3D 155)
Roughcote La. ST11: Cave 3E **34**
ROUGH HAY 2C 161
ROUGHLEY 2B 164
ROUGHTON 2B 162
Rough Wood Country Pk. 7E 126
Roundfields ST9: S Broo 4J **19**
Roundhill Way WS8: Brow 2H **121**
Roundlea Cl. WV12: Will 5B **126**
Roundway ST3: Blur 7E **32**

Roundway Down—St Joseph's Ct.

Roundway Down WV6: Per 3F 129
Roundwell St. ST6: Tuns 4H 17
Rounton Cl. B74: F Oak 4J 135
Rouse Cl. ST16: Staf 4D 72
Rowanall Vw. ST13: Lee 5D 48
Rowanburn Cl. ST3: Long 4K 33
Rowan Cl. ST7: Kids 6E 10
ST8: Bid M 5H 9
ST15: Stone 6H 47
WS13: Lich 3D 114
Rowan Ct. ST14: Roce 4D 58
WS11: Cann 2E 108
Rowan Dr. WS15: Hand 6G 99
WV11: Ess 2B 126
Rowan Gdns. B78: Pole 2K 143
Rowan Glade ST17: Wild 1A 78
Rowan Grange B74: L Ast 3H 135
Rowan Gro. ST3: Fen 6D 32
ST19: Brew 2D 92
WS7: Chas 4H 111
Rowan La. TF9: A Hea 4F 61
Rowan Pl. ST5: C'ton 7C 16
Rowan Rd. WS11: Cann 1B 108
Rowbury Dr. DE15: B Tre 2J 87
Rowhurst Cl. ST5: C'ton 1A 22
Rowhurst Cl. Ind. Est.
ST5: C'ton 1A 22
Rowhurst Pl. ST6: Chel 2C 18
ROWLAND 1C 157
Rowland Av. B78: Pole 6J 139
Rowland St. ST3: Long 1H 41
ROWLEY 2B 160
Rowley Av. ST5: C'ton 1D 22
ST17: Staf 5F 73
Rowley Bank ST17: Staf 6G 73
Rowley Bank Gdns. ST17: Staf 6G 73
Rowley Bank Ho. *ST17: Staf 6G 73*
(off Rowley Bank)
Rowley Cl. B79: Edin 1B 132
WS12: Hed 2H 101
WS15: Bre 3J 97
Rowley Gro. ST17: Staf 5G 73
Rowley Hall Cl. ST17: Staf 6F 73
Rowley Hall Dr. ST17: Staf 6E 72
ROWLEY PARK 5F 73
Rowley Pk. Sports Stadium 6F 73
ROWLEY REGIS 3D 163
Rowley St. ST16: Staf 1F 73
Row Moor Way ST6: Nort 5E 18
Rownall Pl. ST3: Mei 7C 34
Rownall Rd. ST3: Mei 7C 34
ST9: Werr, W Roc 4F 27
Rowney Cl. TF9: Logg 5D 60
ROWSLEY 1C 157
ROWTON 3A 158
Rowton Av. WV6: Per 3F 129
Rowton St. DE13: B Tre 4C 84
Roxburghe Av. ST3: Long 7K 33
Roxby Gdns. WV6: W'ton 7J 123
Royal Cl. ST2: Mil 4G 19
WS15: Rug 2F 97
Royal Doulton Vis. Cen. 7A 18
Royal Oak 1C 163
Royal Oak Dr. ST19: B Elm 6B 90
ROYAL'S GREEN 3A 154
Royal St. ST4: Fen 4G 33
Royal Wlk. ST10: Chea 4C 54
Royal Way ST2: Mil 4H 19
Royce Av. ST8: Knyp 1B 12
Roycroft Cl. ST5: Brad 7F 17
Royden Av. ST1: H'ley 4F 25
Royds Cl. ST18: Hau 6B 66
Roylance St. ST6: Tuns 4H 17
Royston Chase B74: L Ast 5G 135
Royston Wlk. ST3: Long 6J 33
Royville Pl. ST6: B'lem 7D 18
Ruabon Cl. ST8: Knyp 7E 8
Rubens Way ST3: Mei 3D 42
RUBERY 3D 163
Rubian St. ST4: Fen 3F 33
Ruby Cl. ST2: Mil 5F 19
RUDGE 2C 163
Rudge Dale Rd. TF9: A'ley 5G 61
RUDGE HEATH 2B 162
Rudge Rd. WV6: Patt 7A 128
RUDHEATH 1A 154
RUDHEATH WOODS 1B 154
RUDYARD 1A 48 (2D 155)
Rudyard Cl. ST15: Stone 2E 46
WV10: Bush 1C 124
Rudyard Gro. ST5: N'tle 4G 23
Rudyard Ho. ST17: Staf 1G 77
Rudyard Lake Steam Railway 1A 48
Rudyard Lake Vis. Cen. 2D 155
Rudyard Rd. ST8: Bid M 4H 9
ST13: Rudy 1A 48
Rudyard Way ST10: Chea 3E 54
Ruelow Mdw. ST10: Ips 3H 53
Ruffin Ct. ST15: Stone 5J 47
Rufford B79: Tam 3E 136
Rugby Cl. DE14: B Tre 4D 86
ST5: N'tle 4D 30
Rugby Dr. ST3: Long 1H 41
RUGELEY 7G 95 (3A 160)
Rugeley Av. WV12: Will 5D 126
Rugeley Eastern By-Pass
WS15: Wol B 4F 95
Rugeley Leisure Cen. 1F 97
Rugeley Rd. DE13: K Bro 3K 99
WS7: Burn 1A 112
WS7: C Ter 4H 111
WS12: Haz 4B 102
WS12: Hed 5J 101
WS15: Arm, Rug 3A 98
WS15: C Ter 4H 111
WS15: Can W, Rug 4B 102
Rugeley Squash & Fitness Cen. *7G 95*
(off Taylor's La.)
Rugeley Town Station (Rail) 2G 97
Rugeley Trent Valley Station (Rail)
5H 95
Rumbold Av. WS13: Frad 4K 107
RUMER HILL 3E 108
Rumer Hill Bus. Est. WS11: Cann 4E 108
Rumer Hill Ind. Est. WS11: Cann 4F 109
Rumer Hill Rd. WS11: Cann 3E 108
Running Hills WS15: Arm 5D 98
Runnymede ST15: Stone 6G 47
Runnymede Cl. ST2: Buck 5H 25
Rupert St. ST8: Bidd 5C 8
RUSHALL 1A 164
Rushall Rd. WV10: Bush 3C 124
Rushbrook Cl. WS8: Clay 6G 121
Rushcliffe Dr. ST3: Mei 3C 42
Rushford Av. WV5: Womb 4G 145
Rush La. B77: Dost 7K 141
Rushmoor Gro. ST3: Mei 3D 42
RUSHTON
Tarporley 1A 154
Telford 1A 162
Rushton ST5: N'tle 5D 30
Rushton Av. ST10: K'ley 6F 53
Rushton Cl. DE13: Tut 2H 83
ST6: B Edg 7H 13
Rushton Gro. ST6: B'lem 1A 24
Rushton M. WS12: Haz 6E 102
Rushton Rd. ST6: B'lem 1A 24
RUSHTON SPENCER 1D 155
Rushton Way ST11: Fors 2J 43
Rushwater Cl. WV5: Womb 4E 144
Ruskin Cl. ST3: Long 5K 33
Ruskin Dr. ST18: Derr 4A 72
Ruskin Pl. DE14: B Tre 5E 84
Ruskin Rd. WV10: Bush 5D 124
Rusper Cl. ST1: H'ley 2F 25
Russell Bank Rd. B74: F Oak 4K 135
Russell Cl. B77: Wiln 4B 142
ST14: Utt 5J 63
WV11: Wed 4K 125
Russell Ct. B74: F Oak 5J 135
Russell Gro. ST9: Werr 4D 26
Russell Ho. WV8: Cods 7E 92
Russell Pl. ST6: Sandy 1H 17
Russell Rd. ST6: Sandy 1H 17
Russell St. DE14: B Tre 2E 86
ST3: Long 1H 41
ST5: N'tle 3G 23
ST13: Lee 4F 49
Russel St. ST16: Staf 3F 73
Russet Cl. ST3: Mei 3C 42
Russett Cl. WS7: Burn 5J 111
Russetts, The ST17: Staf 1H 77
Russet Wlk. WV8: P'ord 4G 123
Rustington Av. ST3: Long 6A 34
Ruston Av. ST6: Chel 1B 18
Rutherford Av. ST5: N'tle 6F 31
Rutherford Ct. ST18: Staf 1A 74
Rutherford Pl.
ST4: S Tren 7K 153 (2J 31)
Rutherford Rd. WS2: Wals 7G 127
Rutherglen Cl. WS15: Rug 7E 94
Ruthin Gro. ST8: Knyp 7E 8
Ruthin Rd. ST2: Buck 6J 25
Rutland Av. WS15: Rug 3F 97
Rutland Cl. DE15: Stap 6E 86
Rutland Dr. B78: Tam 1G 141
Rutland Pl. ST5: N'tle 5G 31
Rutland Rd. ST3: Long 5J 33
ST7: Kids 4E 10
WS12: H Hay 2A 110
Rutland St. ST1: H'ley 1D 150 (3B 24)
Ruxley Ct. ST2: Buck 5G 25
Ruxley Rd. ST2: Buck 5G 25
Ryan Av. WV11: Wed 5A 126
Rydal B77: Wiln 3C 142
Rydal Cl. WS12: Hed 2G 101
WV11: Wed 6G 125
Rydal Dr. WV6: Per 2G 129
Rydal Est. WS15: Rug 4H 95
Rydall Ho. ST16: Staf 3H 73
Rydal Way ST5: N'tle 5F 31
Ryder Rd. ST3: Mei 2C 42
Ryders Hayes La. WS3: Pels 7C 120
Rye Bank ST5: N'tle 3E 152 (7F 23)
Rye Bank Cres. ST5: N'tle 2E 152 (7G 23)
Ryebrook Gro. ST6: Chel 1K 17
Rye Ct. ST16: Staf 1C 72
Ryecroft ST5: N'tle 2D 152 (7F 23)
Ryecroft Cl. ST10: Tea 4H 55
Ryecroft Dr. WS7: C Ter 3J 111
RYECROFT GATE 1D 155
Ryecroft Rd. ST6: Nort 4E 18
Ryecroft Shop. Cen. WS7: C Ter 3J 111
Ryefield WV8: P'ord 3G 123
RYE HILLS 6G 15
Rye Hills ST7: Big E 6G 15
Ryeland Cl. ST3: L'ood 2J 41
Ryhope Wlk. WV9: P'ord 2J 123
(not continuous)
Rykneld St. WS13: Lich, S'hay 1H 115
Ryknild Cl. B74: F Oak 2K 135
Ryknild St. DE13: Alre 7C 130
WS14: Lich 5E 114
Ryknild Trad. Est. DE14: B Tre 5F 85
Rylestone Cl. ST3: Mei 3D 42
Ryle St. WS3: Blox 3K 127
RYTON
Bedworth 3D 165
Shifnal 1B 162
Ryton B77: Wiln 2B 142

S

Sabine St. ST17: Staf 5H 73
Sabrina Rd. WV6: Tett 5F 129
Sackville St. ST4: S Tren 1J 153 (6J 23)
Saddler Av. ST15: Stone 5J 47
Saddlers Cl. WS14: Lich 3E 114
Saddlers Ct. Ind. Est. WS2: Wals 6G 127
SADDLESALL 1B 130
Saddleworth Rd. WS3: Blox 1G 127
Sadler Rd. WS8: Brow 5J 121
Sadlers Mill WS8: Brow 5J 121
Saffron B77: Amin 5D 138
Saffron Cl. DE13: B Nee 6F 89
ST3: Mei 4C 42
Sage Cl. ST1: H'ley 6G 151 (6C 24)
St Aidan's Cl. DE13: B Tre 4D 84
St Aidan's Rd. WS11: Cann 6E 100
St Aidan's St. ST6: Tuns 3H 17
St Albans Cl. WV11: Wed 5A 126
St Albans Ct. DE13: B Tre 4D 84
St Albans Rd. ST16: Staf 6G 71
St Albans Rd. Ind. Est. ST16: Staf 6G 71
St Andrew Cl. WS12: Haz 5C 102
St Andrews B77: Amin 5D 138
St Andrew's Av. WS3: Pels 7C 120
St Andrew's Cl. B79: C Camp 6E 132
St Andrews Cres. ST1: H'ley 1D 24
St Andrews Dr. DE13: B Tre 3D 84
ST5: N'tle 4A 152 (1D 30)
ST7: Kids 3G 11
WV6: Per 1E 128
St Andrews Rd. ST17: Staf 7E 72
St Andrews Sq. ST4: S Tren 2A 32
St Anne's Cl. WS7: Chas 7G 111
St Annes Rd. WS13: Lich 7B 106
WV10: Oxl 3A 124
St Anne's Va. ST6: B Edg 5H 13
St Ann St. ST1: H'ley 3J 151 (4D 24)
St Ann Wlk. ST1: H'ley 3J 151
St Anthonys Cl. WS15: Rug 1H 97
St Anthony's Ct. ST4: S Tren 4B 32
St Anthony's Dr.
ST5: N'tle 7A 152 (2D 30)
WS3: Pels 7D 120
St Augustine's Rd. WS15: Rug 3G 97
St Austell Cl. B79: Tam 3G 137
ST17: Staf 6B 74
St Barbara Ho. WS15: Rug 6G 95
St Barbara's Rd. WS15: Hand 4G 99
St Bartholomews Cl. ST6: Nort 3E 18
St Benedicts Dr. ST18: L Hay 6J 81
St Benedicts Rd. WS7: Burn 5K 111
WV5: Womb 4G 145
St Bernard Pl. ST2: A Hul 3G 25
St Bernards Cl. WS12: Haz 6E 102
St Bernard's Rd.
ST5: N'tle 1A 152 (6D 22)
St Bertellin Ct. *ST16: Staf 7E 70*
(off Holmcroft Rd.)
St Brides Cl. WV5: Womb 4F 145
St Catherines Cl. ST14: Utt 5J 63
St Catherines Rd. WS13: Lich 7B 106
St Chad Ct. B77: Glas 7B 138
St Chads Cl. DE13: B Tre 3D 84
ST14: Dens 2B 58
ST15: Stone 5J 47
ST18: L Hay 7J 81
ST19: Brew 2C 92
WS11: Cann 6G 101
WS13: Lich 2B 114
WV6: Patt 7B 128
St Chads Ct. WS13: Lich 3B 114
St Chad's Pl. ST16: Staf 3G 73
St Chads Rd. DE13: B Tre 4D 84
ST6: Tuns 4J 17
ST21: Ecc 3G 65
WS13: Lich 2B 114
WV10: Bush 5D 124
St Chad's Ter. ST5: C'ton 5B 16
St Christopher Av.
ST4: S Tren 7K 153 (2J 31)
St Christopher Cl. WS12: Haz 5C 102
St Christopher's Dr. (Mobile Home Pk.)
B77: Tam 1J 141
St Clair St. ST3: Long 7J 33
St Clements Av. WS3: Blox 6K 127
St David Cl. WS12: Haz 4C 102
St David's Cl. WS3: Pels 7D 120
St David's Dr. DE13: B Tre 3D 84
St Davids Pl. WS3: Blox 3K 127
St Davids Rd. B79: C Camp 6E 132
ST17: Staf 7F 73
St Davids Way ST8: Knyp 7E 8
St Dominic's Ct. ST4: S Tren 1A 32
St Editha's Cl. B79: Tam 4H 137
St Editha's Ct. *B79: Tam 2H 137*
(off Kensington Dr.)
ST20: C Eat 2C 68
St Edithas Rd. B78: Pole 2J 143
St Edmund's Av. ST5: N'tle 1H 23
St Edwards Grn. WS15: Rug 2G 97
St Edward's Hall ST13: Ched 2G 51
St Edwards Rd. ST13: Ched 6G 51
St Edward St. ST13: Lee 4F 49
Sainte Foy Av. WS13: Lich 6K 113
St Francis Cl. DE13: B Tre 3E 84
WS3: Pels 7D 120
WS12: Haz 5C 102
St George Dr. WS12: Haz 5C 102
St George Hill Ct. *ST16: Staf 1F 73*
(off Fancy Wlk.)
St Georges Av. ST6: Chel 3A 18
ST9: End 3A 50
St Georges Av. Nth. ST5: N'tle 3F 23
St George's Av. Sth. ST5: N'tle 3F 23
St George's Av. W. ST5: N'tle 3F 23
St Georges Ct. B74: F Oak 3K 135
St Georges Cres. ST4: H'ord 1A 40
St Georges Rd. DE13: B Tre 6A 84
ST5: N'tle 4B 152 (1E 30)
ST15: Stone 4H 47
ST17: Staf 4J 73
St George's St. ST13: Lee 3F 49
St George's Way B77: Amin 5A 138
St Giles Gro. ST18: Hau 6C 66
St Giles Rd. ST5: N'tle 1A 152 (6D 22)
WS7: Burn 5K 111
St Gregorys Rd. ST3: Long 6G 33
ST HELENA 2J 143 (1C 165)
St Helena Rd. B78: Pole 2K 143
St Helens Rd. WS13: Lich 7B 106
St Helier Cl. ST5: N'tle 6D 30
St Hilda's Av. ST13: Ched 6G 51
St Ives Cl. B79: Tam 3H 137
ST17: Staf 6B 74
St James Cl. WS3: Pels 7D 120
WS15: L'don 1E 104
St James Ct. DE13: B Nee 5G 89
ST7: Aud 5F 15
ST8: Bidd 2E 8
St James Cres. ST17: Act T 7K 77
St James Gdns. WS8: Brow 5H 121
St James Grn. ST21: Cot H 3A 64
St James Pk. WV10: Fea 3D 116
St James Pl. ST4: H'ord 1A 40
St James Rd. DE13: B Nee 6G 89
WS11: Cann 2C 108
WS11: N Can 6D 110
St James St. ST1: H'ley 5E 150 (5B 24)
St James Wlk. *WS8: Brow 5H 121*
(off Short St.)
St John's Av. ST4: T Val 5J 31
ST5: N'tle 4G 23
ST15: Oul 1J 47
St Johns Cl. DY3: Swin 1H 147
WS7: C Ter 2G 111
WS11: Cann 3D 108
WS13: Lich 5B 114
WS15: S Mil 1E 96
St Johns Ct. DE13: B Tre 4D 84
ST13: Ched 2G 51
WS3: Blox 4H 127
WS12: H Hay 2A 110
St Johns Dr. WS14: Shen 6C 134
St Johns Hill WS14: Shen 6C 134
St Johns Pl. ST5: N'tle 1A 152 (6D 22)
ST8: Bidd 6D 8
St Johns Rd. DE13: B Tre 4D 84
ST8: Bidd 7C 8
ST17: Staf 6F 73
TF9: A'ley 4J 61
WS3: Pels 7D 120
WS8: Brow 7J 121
WS11: Cann 3D 108
WV11: Ess 2A 126
St John's Sq. ST6: B'lem 7K 17
ST14: Utt 4E 62
St Johns St. B79: Tam 4H 137
St John St. ST1: H'ley 1H 151 (3D 24)
WS13: Lich 4B 114
St John's Wlk. *ST16: Staf 3J 73*
(off Tithe Barn Rd., not continuous)
St John's Way TF9: A'ley 4J 61
St Johns Wood ST7: Kids 5D 10
WS14: Shen 6D 134
St Josephs Cl. WS3: Pels 7C 120
St Joseph's Ct. WV4: Pen 7K 129

St Joseph St.—School La.

St Joseph St. ST6: Gold 7G 11
St Jude's Way DE13: B Tre 3D 84
St Lawrence Dr. WS11: H Hay 1H 109
St Lawrence Way ST20: Gno 3H 67
St Leonard's Av. ST10: Ips 2H 53
ST17: Staf 5J 73
St Leonards Cl. B78: Dor 4J 143
St Leonards Vw.
B78: Dor, Pole 2H 143
St Lucy's Dr. ST5: N'tle 1G 23
St Luke's Cl. ST5: Sil 6K 21
WS11: Cann 3C 108
St Luke's Ct. ST1: H'ley 4H 151
St Luke's Rd. DE13: B Nee 6G 89
DE13: B Tre 3D 84
WS7: Burn 5A 112
St Luke St. ST1: H'ley 4J 151 (5D 24)
St Luke's Wlk. *WS15: Hand 5G 99*
(off Proctors Rd.)
St Margarets B74: F Oak 5H 135
DE13: B Tre 6A 84
St Margarets Ct. CW3: Bet 2C 6
ST5: N'tle 3H 23
St Margaret's Dr. ST1: H'ley 7E 18
St Margarets Gro. ST3: Fen 6E 32
St Margarets Rd. B79: Tam 2H 137
WS13: Lich 1B 114
St Marks Cl. ST1: H'ley 6E 150 (6B 24)
WS6: G Wyr 7F 109
St Marks Rd. DE13: B Tre 3D 84
WS3: Pels 7C 120
WS7: Burn 5A 112
WS8: Brow 7J 121
St Mark's St. ST1: H'ley 6E 150 (6B 24)
St Martin's Cl. DE13: B Tre 3C 84
St Martin's La. ST3: Long 6J 33
St Martin's Pl. ST16: Staf 3G 73
St Martin's Rd. ST5: N'tle . . .4A 152 (1D 30)
ST7: T Pit 1C 16
St Mary's Abbey *7J 81*
St Marys Cl. ST10: Chec 7K 55
ST18: Brad 5C 68
WV10: Shar 2G 117
St Mary's Cres. ST14: Utt 4G 63
St Mary's Dr. DE13: Stre 3D 84
(Horninglow)
DE13: Stre 1G 85
(Stretton)
ST5: N'tle 4B 152 (1E 30)
St Mary's Ga. ST16: Staf 3G 73
St Mary's Gro. ST16: Staf 3G 73
St Mary's M. *ST16: Staf 3G 73*
(off St Mary's Pl.)
St Mary's Pl. ST16: Staf 3G 73
St Marys Rd. ST3: Long 4K 33
ST5: N'tle 3H 23
ST18: L Hay 7J 81
TF9: Logg 4D 60
WS13: Lich 7B 106
St Mary's Way B77: Amin 5A 138
St Matthew Cl. WS12: Haz 5C 102
St Matthew's Av. WS7: Burn 4D 112
St Matthew's Cl. WS3: Pels 7D 120
St Matthews Ct. ST4: Fen 4F 33
St Matthews Dr. ST18: Derr 4A 72
St Matthew's Rd. WS7: Burn 4C 112
St Matthew's St. DE14: B Tre 5D 86
St Matthew St. ST4: Fen 3F 33
St Mawes Cl. ST17: Staf 6B 74
St Mawes Rd. WV6: Per 3G 129
St Michael Rd. WS13: Lich 2C 114
St Michaels Cl. ST15: Stone 4G 47
ST17: Staf 6C 74
ST19: Penk 4G 91
St Michael's Ct. *ST15: Stone 4G 47*
(off Church St.)
St Michaels Dr. WS12: Haz 5C 102
WS15: Bre 4J 97
St Michael's Ho. ST6: Chel 1K 17
St Michael's Mt. ST15: Stone 6J 47
St Michaels Rd. DE13: B Tre 3E 84
ST5: N'tle 5F 23
ST6: Chel 2K 17
ST14: S'all 1E 62
ST19: Penk 3G 91
WS15: Bre 4J 97
St Michael's Sq. ST19: Penk 3G 91
St Modwena Way ST19: Penk 5H 91
St Modwen's Cl. DE13: B Tre 4D 84
St Modwen's Wlk.
DE14: B Tre 2E 86
St Nicholas Av. ST6: Nort 4E 18
St Nicholas Cl. WS3: Pels 7C 120
St Nicholas Est. CV9: Gren 7K 143
St Nicholas Way
WS15: Abb B 2B 88
St Patrick Cl. WS12: Haz 5C 102
St Patricks Dr.
ST5: N'tle 5A 152 (1D 30)
St Patrick's Pl. *ST16: Staf 2G 73*
(off St Patrick's St.)
St Patricks Rd. DE13: B Tre 3D 84
St Patrick's St. ST16: Staf 2F 73
St Paul's Cl. WS11: H Hay 2H 109
WV9: Cove 2A 116
St Pauls Ct. B77: Dost 6J 141
DE14: B Tre 1C 86
ST3: Blur 7F 33
ST6: B'lem 7J 17
(off St Pauls St.)
St Paul's Cres. WS3: Pels 7D 120
St Paul's M. WS15: Rug 1H 97
St Pauls Rd. ST5: N'tle 3B 152 (7E 22)
WS7: Burn 5A 112
WS12: Wimb 7A 102
WS15: Rug 1H 97
St Paul's Sq. DE14: B Tre 7C 84
St Pauls St. ST6: B'lem 7J 17
St Paul's St. W. DE14: B Tre 7C 84
St Peter's Bri. DE14: B Tre 3E 86
DE15: B Tre 3E 86
St Peters Cl. B77: Wiln 1K 141
ST4: S Tren 2B 32
ST17: Staf 1H 77
WS9: Ston 6H 133
St Peters Ct. DE15: Stap 3G 87
WS3: Blox 4H 127
St Peter's Dr. WS3: Pels 7C 120
St Peter's Gdns. ST17: Staf 2H 77
St Peters La. ST11: B Bri 3J 43
St Peters Retail Pk.
DE14: B Tre 3E 86
St Peter's Rd. WS7: Burn 5A 112
St Peters' Rd. WS12: Hed 6K 101
St Peter's St. DE15: Stap 3G 87
St Peter's Wlk. ST6: B'lem 2A 24
St Saviours St. ST7: Talk 5B 10
St Stephens Ct. DE13: B Tre 4D 84
ST8: Bidd .4D 8
(off Thames Dr.)
ST18: Gt Hay 4G 81
WS12: Hed 6J 101
St Stephen's Rd. WS7: Burn 5A 112
St Thomas Dr. WS12: Haz 5C 102
St Thomas La. ST18: Staf 3B 74
St Thomas Pl. ST6: P'ull 3K 31
St Thomas's Rd. ST10: Tea 3G 55
St Thomas St. ST7: M Cop 6H 7
ST16: Staf 3J 73
St Vincent M. ST15: Mea 7D 44
St Vincent Pl. ST5: N'tle 6C 22
St Vincent Rd. ST15: Stone 4E 46
Salcombe Av. ST17: Staf 6B 74
Salcombe Cl. WS11: Cann 4C 108
Salcombe Pl. ST1: H'ley 1D 24
Sale La. DE13: Alre 2H 107
WS13: Alre 2H 107
Salem St. ST1: H'ley 5A 150 (5K 23)
Sales La. DE15: Wins 1K 87
Salisbury Av. DE15: Wins 1K 87
ST1: H'ley 7F 151 (6C 24)
Salisbury Cl. CW3: Mad 2B 28
WS13: Lich 7C 106
WS15: Rug 3E 96
Salisbury Dr. ST16: Staf 2K 73
WS12: H Hay 2H 109
Salisbury Rd. ST16: Staf 2K 73
Salisbury St. ST6: Tuns 4J 17
ST13: Lee 3F 49
Salkeld Pl. ST6: Chel 2B 18
Sallow Gro. WS8: Brow 3H 121
Salmond Av. ST16: Staf 2K 73
Salop Dr. WS11: Cann 3F 109
Salop Gro. ST5: N'tle 5G 31
Salop Pl. ST7: Kids 3E 10
SALT 2D 159
Salt Av. ST17: Staf 5G 73
Saltdean Cl. ST3: Long 7A 34
Salters Cl. ST9: Werr 5D 26
Saltersford La. ST10: Alt 6H 57
Saltersford Ri. ST15: Stone 1E 46
Salters Grange WS15: Abb B 2B 88
Salters Grn. Way DE13: Alre 5D 130
Salters La. B79: Tam 3H 137
ST3: W Coy 5D 26
ST9: Werr, W Coy 5D 26
Salter St. ST16: Staf 3G 73
SALTERSWALL 1A 154
SALT HEATH 4H 69
Saltheath La. ST18: Salt 4H 69
Saltings, The ST18: Staf 4B 74
Salt Rd. ST17: Staf 5G 73
Salts La. B78: D Bas 5E 140
Salt Works La. ST18: West 3C 80
Sam Barber Ct. WS12: H Hay 2A 110
Sambar Rd. B78: Faze 1F 141
SAMBROOK 2B 158
Sambrook Rd. WV10: W'ton 7E 124
Sampson St. ST1: H'ley 2E 150 (4B 24)
Samuel Cl. WS13: Lich 1C 114
Samuel Johnson Birthplace Mus.
. . . . *3B 114*
Samuel St. ST7: Pack 5K 11
WS3: Blox 4H 127
Sancton Grn. ST6: B'lem 7J 17
Sandalwood Cl. WV12: Will 5B 126
Sandalwood Dr. ST16: Staf 1H 73
Sandalwood Rd. DE15: Stap 6F 87
SANDBACH 1B 154
Sandbach Rd. ST6: B'lem 1B 24
Sandbank WS3: Blox 4G 127
Sandcrest Pl. ST3: L'ood 1B 42
Sandcrest Wlk. ST3: L'ood 1B 42
Sanderling Cl. WV10: Fea 5F 117
Sanderling Ri. WS7: Burn 3K 111
Sandfield Farm Home Pk.
WS8: Brow 3K 121
Sandfield Mdw. WS13: Lich 5A 114
SANDFIELDS 6A 114
SANDFORD 1A 158
Sandford Cl. WS15: Hill R 1E 98
SANDFORD HILL 5J 33
Sandford Ho. WS13: Lich 4A 114
Sandford Ri. WV6: Tett 7G 123
Sandford St. ST3: Long 4J 33
ST5: C'ton 7C 16
WS13: Lich 4B 114
Sandgate St. ST3: Long 6K 33
Sandhill St. WS3: Blox 4G 127
Sandhurst Av. ST3: Mei 1B 42
Sandhurst Cl. ST5: N'tle 3G 23
Sandhurst Pl. ST3: L'ood 2B 42
Sandhurst Rd. B74: F Oak 3K 135
SANDIWAY 1A 154
Sandiway DE13: B Nee 7H 89
Sandiway Pl. ST1: H'ley 2E 24
Sandland Rd. WV12: Will 5D 126
SANDLOW GREEN 1B 154
Sand Martin Ct. *ST14: Utt 7H 63*
(off Kingfisher Way)
Sandmere Ri. WV10: Bush 4C 124
SANDON .2D 159
Sandon Av. ST5: N'tle 4E 30
SANDONBANK 2D 159
Sandon Ct. ST3: Mei 3B 42
Sandon M. ST16: Staf 7H 71
Sandon Old Rd. ST3: Mei 3B 42
Sandon Rd. ST3: Mei 3B 42
ST11: C'ell, Sav G 1K 59
ST15: Hild 7H 59
ST16: Staf 1G 73
ST18: Hopt, Sand B 5H 71
WV10: Ford 3K 123
Sandon St. ST1: H'ley 4C 150 (5A 24)
ST13: Lee 5F 49
Sandown B77: Amin 4B 138
Sandown Av. WS6: C Hay 1E 118
Sandown Cl. DE14: B'ton 5B 86
ST10: Chea 2D 54
WS7: C Ter 2H 111
WS12: Haz 4C 102
Sandown Cft. ST17: Staf 4F 73
Sandown Dr. WV6: Per 2G 129
Sandown Pl. ST2: Mil 5J 19
Sandpiper B77: Wiln 5C 142
Sandpiper Cl. WS12: Hed 3J 101
Sandpiper Ct. ST7: Kids 4G 11
Sandpiper Dr. ST14: Utt 7G 63
Sandpits La. DE13: Yox 1F 89
Sandra Cl. ST6: B'lem 5A 18
Sandringham Av. DE15: Stap 3H 87
WV12: Will 6B 126
Sandringham Cl. ST17: Staf 6A 74
WS7: C Ter 2G 111
Sandringham Ct. *B79: Tam 2H 137*
(off Wigginton Rd.)
Sandringham Cres. ST4: H'ord 1A 40
Sandringham Rd. ST17: Staf 6A 74
WV5: Womb 4F 145
Sandsdown Cl. ST8: Bidd 4C 8
Sands La. ST6: B Edg 3G 13
Sands Rd. ST7: Harr 7J 7
Sandstone Ct. B77: Wiln 3C 142
Sandwell Pl. ST3: L'ood 2A 42
WV12: Will 6D 126
Sandwell Rd. WV10: Oxl 4K 123
Sandwick Cres. ST1: H'ley 2F 25
Sandwood Cres. ST3: Long 4J 33
Sandy Brook Cl. ST13: Lee 6G 49
Sandybrook La. ST13: Lee 7G 49
Sandy Cres. WV11: Wed 5A 126
Sandyfield Ct. ST8: Bidd 4C 8
Sandyfield Rd. ST1: H'ley . . .1K 151 (3E 24)
Sandyfields ST5: B Gat 5E 36
SANDYFORD 1H 17
Sandyford Ct. ST16: Staf 1G 73
Sandyford St. ST16: Staf 1G 73
Sandy Gro. WS8: Brow 3H 121
Sandy Hill ST9: Werr 4E 26
Sandy Hollow WV6: Tett 4K 129
Sandy La. DY7: Kin 3B 148
DY7: Wolv 7D 148
DY11: Wolv 7D 148
ST2: Mil .5J 19
ST5: B Gat, H Cho 6E 36
ST5: N'tle 1G 153 (6G 23)
ST6: B Edg 6H 13
ST18: West 2A 80
ST19: Brew 2C 92
TF9: A'ley 2H 61
WS11: Cann 2A 108
WS11: Cann, Hath 2A 108
WS14: Lich 7J 115
WS15: Rug 2G 97
WV6: Tett 7G 123
Sandy La. WV8: Cods 1B 122
WV10: Bush 4C 124
Sandy Mt. WV5: Womb 3H 145
Sandy Rd. ST6: Sandy 7H 11
ST8: G Hea 3C 8
Sandy Way B77: Amin 6C 138
Sangster La. ST6: B'lem 5D 18
Sankey Cres. WS15: Rug 2G 97
Sankey Rd. WS11: Cann 7F 101
Sanstone Cl. WS3: Blox 2J 127
Sanstone Rd. WS3: Blox 2H 127
Sant St. ST6: B'lem 7J 17
Sapling Ri. ST10: Tea 4G 55
Saplings, The ST5: N'tle 6G 31
ST17: Staf 5J 73
ST19: Penk 3H 91
Saplings Cl. ST19: Penk 3H 91
SAPPERTON 1B 160
Sapphire Dr. ST2: Mil 5F 19
WS11: H Hay 1J 109
Saracen Way ST3: Mei 1C 42
Sarah Challinor Cl. WS15: Rug 1G 97
Sarah Siddons Ho. *WS13: Lich 4B 114*
(off Wade St.)
Saredon Rd. WS6: C Hay 7B 108
WV10: Shar . . . . . . .2H 117 & 7A 108
Sargeant Av. ST6: Chel 1A 18
Sark Cl. ST5: N'tle 5C 30
Sark Pl. ST3: Long 3K 33
Sarraine Ind. Pk. ST10: Chea 5A 54
Sash St. ST16: Staf 2F 73
Saturn Rd. ST6: B'lem 6C 18
WS11: Cann 5F 101
Saunders Cl. WS12: Haz 4B 102
Saunders Rd. ST5: N'tle 4F 23
Saunton Rd. WS3: Blox 2G 127
SAVERLEY GREEN 7K 43 (1D 159)
Saverley Grn. Rd.
ST11: Ful, Sav G 3H 59
Savey La. DE13: Yox 2G 89
Savoureuse Dr. ST17: Staf 6J 73
Sawpit La. ST17: Broc 4E 78
Sawpit Yd. CW3: Mad 2B 28
Sawyer Dr. ST8: Bidd 4C 8
Saxifrage Dr. ST15: Stone 6J 47
Saxon Cl. B77: Wiln 4B 142
B78: Pole 1H 143
DE15: Stap 5G 87
WS6: G Wyr 2G 119
Saxon Ct. WS13: Lich 4J 113
WV6: Tett 1K 129
Saxon Dr. B79: Tam 5J 137
Saxonfields WV6: Tett 1K 129
Saxon Mill La. B79: Tam 4J 137
Saxon Rd. ST19: Penk 4H 91
Saxon St. DE15: Stap 5G 87
Saxon Wlk. WS13: Lich 4J 113
Sayers Rd. ST16: Staf 6E 70
Scalpcliffe Cl. DE15: B Tre 2G 87
Scalpcliffe Rd. DE15: B Tre 1G 87
Scammerton B77: Wiln 3D 142
Scampton Cl. WV6: Per 1F 129
Scampton Way B79: Tam 1J 137
Scarlett St. ST5: N'tle 4E 152 (1F 31)
Scarratt Cl. ST11: Fors 2K 43
Scarratt Dr. ST11: Fors 3K 43
Sceptre St. ST1: H'ley 5F 151 (5C 24)
Schofield La. B79: Edin 1C 132
SCHOLAR GREEN 1C 10 (2C 155)
Scholars Ga. WS7: Burn 5B 112
WS15: Bre 4J 97
School Av. WS3: Blox 5J 127
WS8: Brow 4H 121
School Cl. ST7: Big E 6J 15
ST13: Lee 5D 48
WS7: C Ter 3F 111
WS11: N Can 5C 110
WV3: W'ton 7J 129
WV5: Trys 2C 144
WV8: Cods 1C 122
School Ct. WS12: Hed 4J 101
School Cres. WS11: N Can 5C 110
School Dr. ST10: O'moor 2B 56
Schoolfields Rd. WS14: Shen 6D 134
SCHOOL GREEN 1A 154
School Grn. DE13: Yox 1G 89
ST10: Ips 2H 53
School Ho. La. WS15: Abb B 2C 88
School La. B77: Dost 5K 141
B78: Hop 2B 136
B79: Edin 2B 132
B79: Shut 2H 139
DE13: Roll D 6H 83
ST3: Blur 2F 41
ST8: Bid M 3H 9
ST9: L'ton 6A 48
ST11: Cave 6F 35
ST17: Staf 2G 77
ST17: Walt 1D 78
ST18: Duns 7F 77
ST18: Gt Hay 4G 81
TF9: A'ley 3H 61
WS3: L Wyr 2A 120
WS7: C Ter 3F 111
WS11: L Wyr 2A 120

Sparch Av.—Station Rd.

Sparch Av. ST5: N'tle .4G 23
Sparch Gro. ST5: N'tle .4G 23
Sparch Hollow ST5: N'tle .4G 23
Spark St. ST4: S Tren .2A 32
Spark Ter. ST4: S Tren .2A 32
Sparrow Butts Gro. ST7: Kids .4G 11
Sparrow Cl. ST18: L Hay .6J 81
Sparrows End La. ST19: Brew .2D 92
Sparrow St. ST6: B'lem .5D 18
Sparrow Ter. ST5: N'tle .2F 23
Spa St. ST6: B'lem .1C 24
SPATH .2G 63 (1A 160)
Speakman St. ST3: Long .7K 33
Spearhill WS14: Lich .4E 114
Spedding Rd. ST4: Fen .1E 32
Spedding Way ST8: Bidd .5E 8
Speechly Dr. WS15: Rug .6F 95
Speedwall St. ST3: Long .4J 33
Speedwell Gdns. WV10: Fea .4F 117
Speedwell Ri. ST16: Staf .1C 72
Speedwell Rd. ST5: C'ton .6D 16
Speedy Cl. WS11: Cann .5E 100
Spelter Works WS3: Blox .6G 127
Spencer Av. ST9: End .3A 50
ST13: Lee .4F 49
Spencer Cl. DE13: Stre .2E 84
ST14: Utt .7H 63
ST18: West .3B 80
Spencer Dr. WS7: C Ter .3G 111
Spencer Pl. ST5: C'ton .2C 22
Spencer Rd. ST4: S Tren .1C 32
WS14: Lich .5B 114
Spencroft Rd. ST5: C'ton .3D 22
Spenser Av. WV6: Per .2G 129
Spenser Cl. B79: Tam .3G 137
ST17: Staf .6E 72
Spens St. ST6: B'lem .7K 17
Sperry Cl. ST3: Mei .3D 42
Spey Dr. ST7: Kids .4G 11
Spiceal M. ST14: Utt .6H 63
Spicerstone Est. ST13: Lee .2J 51
Spindlewood Cl. WS12: H Hay .2K 109
Spinney, The B74: L Ast .3G 135
CW3: Mad H .1C 28
ST5: N'tle .7G 31
ST7: C Law .2C 10
WV3: W'ton .5K 129
Spinney Cl. B78: Bir .2H 143
ST9: End .1A 50
WS7: C Ter .2J 111
WS11: N Can .6B 110
Spinney Farm Rd. WS11: Cann .4B 108
Spinneyfields ST17: Wild .2B 78
Spinney La. WS7: C Ter .2H 111
Spinney Rd. DE14: B'ton .4A 86
Spinning School La. B79: Tam .4H 137
Spiral Ct. WV11: Wed .6H 125
Spire Cl. ST6: Nort .4E 18
Spires, The WS14: Lich .5E 114
Spirescroft WV10: Shar .3H 117
SPITALHILL .3B 156
Spitfire Cl. ST16: Staf .4D 70
Spitfire Way ST6: Tuns .3G 17
Splash La. WS12: Hed .7J 101
Spode Av. ST18: Staf .5K 71
(not continuous)
Spode Cl. ST10: Chea .5B 54
ST15: Stone .7E 46
Spode Gro. ST5: N'tle .6F 31
Spode Mus. & Vis. Cen. .2B 32
Spode Pl. WS11: H Hay .1H 109
Spode St. ST4: S Tren .4B 32
SPONDON .1D 161
Spondon Rd. WV11: Wed .5J 125
SPON END .3D 165
Spot La. WS8: Clay .6H 121
Spoutfield Rd. ST4: S Tren .7K 23
Spout Hollow ST7: T Pit .1B 16
Spout La. ST2: L Oak .6J 19
Spragg Ho. La. ST6: Nort .4E 18
Spratslade Dr. ST3: Long .7H 33
Spreadoaks Dr. ST17: Wild .2B 78
Sprengers Cl. ST19: Penk .3J 91
Springbank Av. ST9: End .3A 50
Spring Banks Flats ST16: Staf .7F 71
Spring Cl. DY7: Kin .4D 148
Spring Cres. ST6: B Edg .7J 13
Springcroft ST11: B Bri .4H 43
Spring Dr. WS6: G Wyr .2G 119
Spring Farm Rd. DE15: Stap .3H 87
SPRINGFIELD .3A 164
Springfield TF9: Logg .4E 60
Springfield Av. WS15: Rug .2H 97
Springfield Cl. ST5: C'ton .2D 22
ST13: Lee .4H 49
Springfield Ct. ST13: Lee .3H 49
ST17: Staf .2G 77
(off Springfield Dr.)
Springfield Cres. ST3: Long .7H 33
Springfield Dr. ST7: Kids .6B 10
ST11: Fors .2J 43
ST13: Lee .3H 49
ST17: Staf .2G 77
ST19: Whe A .1C 90
Springfield Gro. ST8: Bidd .6D 8
Springfield La. WV10: Ford .1B 124
Springfield Ri. WS12: Hed .4J 101
Springfield Rd. B77: T Gat .2K 141
ST8: Bidd .6D 8
ST13: Lee .4H 49
ST14: Utt .5G 63
SPRINGFIELDS .4J 31
Springfields ST11: B Bri .4G 43
Springfields Est. WS15: Rug .5F 95
Springfields Pk. ST4: T Val .4J 31
Springfields Rd. ST4: T Val .3J 31
WS15: Rug .5F 95
Springfield Vs. DE15: Stap .3H 87
Spring Gdn. Rd. ST3: Long .7H 33
Spring Gdns. ST11: Fors .2K 43
ST13: Lee .4E 48
ST15: Stone .7G 47
Springhead Cl. ST7: T Pit .1B 16
SPRINGHILL
Essington .7D 118 (1D 163)
Lynn .3H 133
Springhill Cl. WV12: Will .6D 126
Springhill Rd. WS7: Burn .5J 111
WS8: Brow .5J 121
WV11: Wed .5J 125
Springhill Ter. WS15: Rug .3H 97
Spring Hollow ST21: Ecc .3H 65
Spring La. ST19: B Elm .5B 90
WS14: W'ton .3G 131
Springle Styche La. WS7: Burn .2A 112
Spring Mdw. WS6: C Hay .3D 118
Spring Mdws. Cl. WV8: Bilb .1D 122
Springpool ST5: Keel .3A 30
Spring Rd. ST3: Long .7A 34
WS13: Lich .1D 114
Springs, The CW3: Mad .3A 28
Springs Bank ST9: Bag .7B 50
Springside Pl. ST3: Blur .3E 40
Spring St. ST4: S Tren .3H 153 (7H 23)
WS11: Cann .3E 108
Spring Ter. WS7: Chas .6G 111
Spring Ter. Rd. DE15: Stap .3G 87
Springvale Ri. ST16: Staf .5F 71
Spring Vw. ST6: B Edg .7J 13
Spring Vs. *ST3: Long .7H 33*
(off Cemetery Vw.)
SPRINGWOOD .6A 16
Springwood Dr. ST15: Stone .5K 47
Springwood Rd. ST5: C'ton .7A 16
Sprinkbank Rd. ST6: Chel .2A 18
Sprink La. ST10: K'ley .5H 53
Sprinkswood La DE6: C'ton .7D 56
Sprinkwood Gro. ST3: W Coy .6C 34
SPROSTON GREEN .1B 154
Sproston Rd. ST6: Chel .2K 17
Spruce B77: Amin .5D 138
Spruce Rd. WS12: Hed .1F 101
Spruce Wlk. WS15: Rug .5E 94
Spruce Way ST16: Staf .3E 72
WV3: W'ton .5K 129
Spur Lea ST18: Brad .5C 68
SPURSTOW .2A 154
Spur St. ST1: H'ley .7J 151 (6D 24)
Spur Tree Av. WV3: W'ton .5H 129
Square, The B79: Elf .5G 131
ST3: Mei .7D 34
ST5: N'tle .3E 30
(not continuous)
ST8: Bidd .5C 8
(off Cross St.)
ST10: O'moor .3B 56
ST11: Cave .7G 35
ST14: Mar .2C 82
ST18: Derr .4A 72
ST18: Gt Hay .4G 81
WV6: Patt .7B 128
WV8: Cods .1B 122
WV12: Will .5D 126
Squires Ga. WS7: Burn .3A 112
Squires Vw. ST4: S Tren .2C 32
Squirrel Cl. WS12: H Hay .1K 109
WS12: Hun .4C 100
Squirrel Hayes Av. ST8: Knyp .7E 8
Squirrels, The ST5: N'tle .6G 31
WS14: Lich .4C 114
Squirrels Corner DE13: New .6C 88
Squirrels Hollow WS7: C Ter .1J 111
Squirrel Wlk. B74: L Ast .3H 135
ST17: Staf .3G 77
STABLEFORD
Bridgnorth .2B 162
Newcastle .7K 37
Stable La. WV10: Calf H .4K 93
Stables, The ST18: Gt Hay .4G 81
Stacey Gdns. ST20: Gno .4H 67
Staddlestones, The WV6: Per .2E 128
STADEN .1A 156
Stadium Ct. ST6: B'lem .2A 24
STADMORSLOW .2K 11
Stadmorslow La. ST7: Harr .2K 11
STAFFORD .3G 73 (2D 159)
Stafford Av. ST5: N'tle .4G 31
Stafford Brook Rd. WS15: Rug .2B 96
Stafford Bus. Village ST18: Staf .1B 74
Stafford Castle .5C 72
Stafford Castle Vis. Cen. .5C 72
Stafford Cl. ST15: Stone .5G 47
WS3: Blox .3H 127
Stafford Coastal Cruising Club .1K 77
Stafford Ct. ST18: Staf .2B 74
WV10: Ford .7A 116
Stafford Crematorium ST18: Staf .2B 74
Stafford Cres. ST5: N'tle .5G 31
Stafford La. ST1: H'ley .3G 151 (4C 24)
WS12: Hed .5H 101
WV8: Cods .4A 122
STAFFORD PARK .1B 162
Stafford Rangers FC .7G 71
Stafford Rd. ST14: Utt .7E 62
ST15: Aston, Yar, Stone .5G 47
ST18: West .2A 80
ST19: Penk .2G 91
ST20: Gno .4H 67
ST20: W'ves .3D 66
ST21: Ecc .3H 65
WS3: Blox .6G 119
WS6: G Wyr .6G 119
WS11: Cann .5C 100
WS12: Hun .1C 100
WS13: Lich, L'don .7J 105
(not continuous)
WV9: Cove .7F 93
WV10: Cov H .3A 116
WV10: Ford, W'ton, Oxl .5A 124
WV10: S'ord .4F 93
Staffordshire County Showground .7J 69
Staffordshire Regiment Mus. .1B 164
Staffordshire Technology Pk.
ST18: Staf .1B 74
Staffordshire University .1C 32
(Stafford Campus)
Beaconside .1A 74
Blackheath La. .2C 74
Stafford Sports Arena .6J 73
Stafford Station (Rail) .4F 73
Stafford St. DE14: B Tre .6E 84
ST1: H'ley .3F 151 (4C 24)
ST5: N'tle .4E 152 (1F 31)
ST15: Stone .4G 47
ST16: Staf .3G 73
ST19: Brew .2C 92
ST21: Ecc .2H 65
WS12: H Hay .2A 110
Stafford University Lichfield Cen. .4B 114
Staffs Moor Ind. Est. B79: Tam .4F 137
Stagborough Way WS12: Hed .6H 101
Stag Cl. WS15: Rug .7D 94
Stag Cres. WS11: N Can .5C 110
Stag Dr. WS12: Hun .4C 100
Stag Hill Rd. WS3: Blox .6K 127
Staines Ct. ST15: Stone .5J 47
Staley Cft. WS12: Hun .6C 100
STALLINGTON .7F 43 (1D 159)
Stallington Cl. ST11: B Bri .6F 43
Stallington Gdns. ST11: B Bri .4H 43
Stallington Rd. ST3: B Bri .7D 42
ST11: B Bri .6F 43
Stamer St. ST4: S Tren .3B 32
Stamford Cres. WS7: C Ter .3J 111
Stamps Cl. DE15: Wins .1K 87
Standard St. ST4: Fen .3D 32
Standedge B77: Wiln .3C 142
STANDEFORD .7F 93 (1D 163)
Standersfoot Pl. ST6: Chel .1B 18
STANDFORD BRIDGE .2B 158
STANDON .1C 159
Standon Av. ST5: C'ton .5A 16
STANFIELD .4K 17
Stanfield Cres. ST10: Chea .6C 54
Stanfield Rd. ST6: B'lem .6A 18
Stanfield St. ST3: Long .3K 33
Stanford Cl. ST19: Penk .3G 91
Stanhope Ho. B79: Tam .5G 137
Stanhope St. DE15: Wins .1J 87
ST1: H'ley .6D 150 (6B 24)
Stanier St. ST4: Fen .3E 32
ST5: N'tle .3C 152 (7E 22)
STANLEY
Bridgnorth .3B 162
Ilkeston .3D 157
Stoke-on-Trent .4C 50 (2D 155)
Stanley Bank ST9: S'ley .4C 50
Stanley Cl. WV11: Wed .5K 125
STANLEY COMMON .3D 157
Stanley Ct. WV6: Per .2F 129
Stanley Cres. ST14: Utt .3F 63
Stanley Dr. DY3: Swin .1J 147
ST5: C'ton .6A 16
Stanley Grn. ST2: Mil .5G 19
Stanley Gro. ST2: Mil .5H 19
ST5: N'tle .1J 153 (6H 23)
Stanley Matthews Way ST4: Tren .6C 32
STANLEY MOOR .5B 50
STANLEY MOSS .3B 50
Stanley Moss La. ST9: S Broo .4A 50
Stanley Moss Rd. ST9: S Broo .4A 50
Stanley Rd. ST4: S Tren .4K 153 (1J 31)
ST5: N'tle .1J 153 (6J 23)
ST8: G Hea .3C 8
Stanley Rd. ST9: S Broo .3K 19
WS12: Hed .5G 101
(not continuous)
WV10: Bush .4B 124
Stanley St. DE14: B Tre .2D 86
ST6: Tuns .3J 17
ST8: Bidd .5C 8
ST13: Lee .4F 49
WS3: Blox .5J 127
Stansgate Pl. ST1: H'ley .1D 150 (3B 24)
STANSHOPE .2B 156
Stansmore Rd. ST3: Mei .7D 34
STANTHORNE .1A 154
STANTON
Ashbourne .3B 156
Burton upon Trent .7J 87 (3C 161)
STANTON BY BRIDGE .2D 161
Stanton Cl. ST5: N'tle .1A 152 (6D 22)
STANTON IN PEAK .1C 157
STANTON LONG .2A 162
Stanton Rd. DE15: Stan, Stap .4G 87
ST3: Mei .1C 42
STANTON UPON HINE HEATH .2A 158
Stanway Av. ST6: B'lem .1C 24
Stanway Cl. ST14: Utt .7F 63
Stanway Ct. ST16: Staf .1H 73
Stanway La. ST8: Bid M .3H 9
STAPELEY .3A 154
STAPENHILL .4G 87 (2C 161)
Stapenhill Rd. DE15: B Tre, Stap .3G 87
Stapleford Gdns. WS7: Burn .5B 112
STAPLETON .2D 165
Stapleton Cres. ST3: Blur .1G 41
Star & Garter Rd. ST3: L'ood, Long .1A 42
Star Bank ST10: O'moor .3C 56
Star Cvn. & Camping Pk.
ST10: O'moor .1E 56
Starkey's La. ST19: Whe A .1D 90
STARKHOLMES .2D 157
Starling Cl. ST7: Kids .3H 11
Star Mobile Home Pk., The
WV9: Cove .3K 93
Startley La.
WS15: Can W, U Lon, Rug .7G 97
Starwood Rd. ST3: L'ood .2A 42
Starwood Ter. ST10: O'moor .2B 56
Statfold La. DE13: Alre .4B 130
WS13: Frad .2K 107
Statham St. ST1: H'ley .5E 150 (5B 24)
Station App. B74: F Oak .2K 135
ST15: Stone .3F 47
WS7: Chas .5F 111
WS13: Lich .3E 114
Station Bri. Rd. ST4: Fen .4E 32
Station Cl. WS3: Blox .5H 127
WV8: Cods .2B 122
Station Cotts. ST5: B Gat .5F 37
Station Ct. WS11: Cann .3F 109
Station Cres. ST6: B'lem .5D 18
Station Dr. ST5: Keel .1F 29
WS15: Hand .5F 99
WV10: F Ash .6F 93
Stationfields Pk. Homes
B79: Tam .4J 137
Station Gro. ST2: Mil .6G 19
Station Pl. WS3: Blox .5H 127
Station Rd. B78: Pole .7J 139
B79: Pole .6K 139
CW3: Mad .4A 28
CW12: More .3F 7
DE13: B Nee .6G 89
DE13: Roll D .6H 83
DE65: Hat .1H 83
ST4: S Tren .1B 32
ST5: Keel .1E 28
ST5: Sil .6K 21
ST7: Big E, H End .1F 21
ST7: Kids .5D 10
ST7: M Cop .5F 7
ST7: New .4J 11
ST8: Bidd .4C 8
(not continuous)
ST9: End .2B 50
ST10: Alt .5H 57
ST10: Chea .5C 54
ST12: Barl .2D 44
ST13: Ched .4G 51
ST14: Mar .1C 82
ST14: Utt .6J 63
ST15: Cold M .6A 64
ST15: Stone .3F 47
ST16: Staf .4F 73
ST17: Colw .7J 81
ST18: Hau .5B 66
ST19: Penk .3G 91
ST20: Gno .5H 67
ST21: Cot H .3A 64
WS6: G Wyr .7F 109
WS12: Hed .4H 101
WS13: Lich .4B 114
WS14: Shen .5C 134
WS15: Rug .7G 95
WV5: Womb .2G 145
WV8: Cods .2A 122
WV10: F Ash .6G 93

214 A-Z Staffordshire Atlas

Station St.—Swainsley Cl.

Station St. DE14: B Tre ... 1D 86
(not continuous)
ST6: B'lem ... 1H 23
ST13: Lee ... 4E 48
WS3: Blox ... 5H 127
WS6: C Hay ... 1E 118
Station Vw. ST3: Mei ... 1C 42
Station Wlk. DE13: Stre ... 2F 85
Station Walks ST5: N'tle ... 2E 152 (7F 23)
(not continuous)
ST7: H End ... 1F 21
Station Yd. DE13: Alre ... 6D 130
STAVELEY ... 1D 157
Staveley Cl. ST2: Buck ... 5G 25
Staveley Pl. ST5: Sil ... 7J 21
Stead Cl. WS2: Wals ... 7J 127
Steadman Cres. ST17: Staf ... 1G 77
Stedman St. ST1: H'ley ... 3D 24
Steel Dr. WV10: Bush ... 5B 124
Steele Av. ST6: B'lem ... 5B 18
Steele Cl. ST13: Ched ... 5J 51
Steel St. ST4: S Tren ... 1J 31
Steeplechase, The ST14: Utt ... 5H 63
Steeple Way ST4: S Tren ... 4A 32
Steere Av. B79: Tam ... 2J 137
Stellar St. ST6: B'lem ... 6C 18
Stenbury Cl. WV10: Bush ... 1D 124
STENSON ... 2D 161
STENSON FIELDS ... 1D 161
Stephanie Gro. B77: Amin ... 3C 138
Stephen Av. ST10: K'ley ... 6F 53
Stephens Cl. WV11: Wed ... 5K 125
Stephenson Av. WS2: Wals ... 7G 127
Stephenson Cl. B77: Glas ... 7C 138
Stephenson Dr. WV6: Per ... 7A 122
Stephenson Sq. WS2: Wals ... 7H 127
Stephenson Way WS12: Hed ... 5H 101
Stephens Rd. DE14: B'ton ... 4C 86
Stephens Wlk. WS13: Lich ... 1A 114
Stephens Way ST7: Big E ... 5H 15
Stepping Stone La. ST19: Brew ... 2B 92
Step Row *ST13: Lee* ... *4F 49*
(off Cornhill St.)
Steps Gdns. ST18: Hau ... 6B 66
Sterling Pk. B77: Wiln ... 3K 141
Sterndale Dr. ST4: Fen ... 3H 33
ST5: N'tle ... 6F 31
STERNDALE MOOR ... 1B 156
Sterrymere Gdns. DY7: Kin ... 5F 149
Stevens Dr. WS12: Hed ... 4K 101
Stevenson Dr. ST17: Staf ... 7E 72
Stevenson Rd. B79: Tam ... 3G 137
ST2: Buck ... 4G 25
Stevenson Wlk. WS14: Lich ... 5B 114
Steventon Pl. ST6: B'lem ... 7K 17
Stewart Cl. DE14: B'ton ... 6B 86
Stewart St. ST4: Fen ... 3D 32
STEWPONEY ... 3J 149
Stewponey, The DY7: Stou ... 3J 149
Stewponey Ct. DY7: Stou ... 3J 149
Stewponey Lock DY7: Stou ... 3J 149
Stewponey Wharf DY7: Stou ... 3J 149
Stile Cl. ST8: B Lee ... 1B 12
WS15: Rug ... 3H 97
Stile Cop Rd. WS15: Rug ... 4F 97
Stiper's Hill B79: Wart ... 7K 139
STIRCHLEY
Birmingham ... 3A 164
Telford ... 1B 162
Stirling Cl. ST2: Bent ... 2A 34
Stirling Cres. WV12: Will ... 7B 126
Stirling Ho. *ST6: B'lem* ... *1A 24*
(off Bleak Pl.)
Stirling Pl. WS11: Cann ... 3B 108
Stirling Ri. DE13: Stre ... 3E 84
Stirling St. ST6: B'lem ... 7A 18
STIVICHALL ... 3D 165
Stockbridge Cl. WV6: Tett ... 4G 129
Stockfield Rd. ST3: Mei ... 3B 42
Stockhay La. WS7: Hamm ... 6B 112
Stockholm Gro. ST1: H'ley ... 1F 25
STOCKINGFORD ... 2D 165
Stockings La. ST19: Whe A ... 3D 90
WS14: Lich ... 2D 134
WS15: Rug ... 7A 98
Stockland Ct. B74: S'ly ... 7F 135
Stock La. ST14: Mar ... 4A 82
Stocks La. ST14: Bram ... 6B 62
STOCKTON
Newport ... 3B 158
Shifnal ... 2B 162
STOCKTON BROOK ... 2K 19 (2D 155)
Stockton La. ST17: Staf ... 7C 74
STOCKWELL END ... 7F 123
Stockwell End WV6: Tett ... 7F 123
Stockwell Gro. ST3: Long ... 6K 33
STOCKWELL HEATH ... 1K 95 (2A 160)
Stockwell Rd. WV6: Tett ... 7F 123
Stockwell St. ST13: Lee ... 3F 49
Stockwell Vs. ST13: Lee ... 3F 49
Stockwood Rd. ST5: N'tle ... 5D 30
STOKE ... 3D 165
Stoke Bus. Pk. ST4: S Tren ... 2B 32
Stoke City ... 6D 32
Stoke City FC ... 6C 32
STOKE GOLDING ... 2D 165
Stoke Gymnastics Cen. ... 7J 17
STOKE HEATH ... 2A 158
Stoke Old Rd.
ST4: S Tren ... 3J 153 (7H 23)
STOKE ON TERN ... 2A 158
STOKE-ON-TRENT ... 5D 150 (3C 155)
Stoke-on-Trent College
Cauldon Campus ... 7E 150 (7B 24)
Stoke-on-Trent Repertory Theatre ... 7D 24
Stoke-on-Trent Station (Rail) ... 1B 32
Stoke Recreation Cen. ... 3B 32
Stoke Rd. ST4: S Tren ... 7D 150 (7B 24)
STOKE ST MILBOROUGH ... 3A 162
Stokesay Av. WV6: Per ... 3G 129
Stokesay Dr. ST10: Chea ... 4E 54
Stokesay Gro. ST6: B'lem ... 1A 24
Stoke Ski Cen. ... 1A 150 (3K 23)
Stokes La. WS11: N Can ... 5A 110
Stoke Speedway ... 3B 22
Stokes St. WS3: Blox ... 5H 127
STOKE-UPON-TRENT ... 2B 32 (3C 155)
STONE ... 4G 47 (1D 159)
Stoneacre Cl. WV3: W'ton ... 5H 129
Stone Bank Rd. ST7: Kids ... 6E 10
Stonebridge Rd. ST19: Brew ... 2D 92
STONEBROOM ... 2D 157
Stone Bus. Pk. ST15: Stone ... 7H 47
Stonecrop Cl. WS8: Clay ... 6F 121
Stone Cross ST19: Penk ... 3G 91
Stone Enterprise Cen. ST15: Stone ... 1G 69
STONEFIELD ... 2F 47
Stonefield Ct. *ST15: Stone* ... *2F 47*
(off Mount Rd.)
Stonefield M. ST15: Stone ... 3F 47
Stonefield Pk. ... *3G 47*
(off Albert St.)
Stonefield Sq. ST15: Stone ... 3G 47
Stonehaven B77: Amin ... 4B 138
Stonehaven Gro.
ST1: H'ley ... 7H 151 (6D 24)
STONE HEATH ... 1D 159
Stonehill Wlk. B77: Wiln ... 4B 142
Stonehouse Cres. ST9: Werr ... 5D 26
Stonehouse Dr. B74: L Ast ... 4H 135
Stonehouse La. ST6: B Edg ... 5G 13
Stone Ho. Rd. ST9: Werr ... 5D 26
Stonehouse Rd. WS15: Rug ... 1C 96
STONEHOUSES ... 4K 43
Stone La. DY7: Kin ... 5E 148
Stoneleigh Ct. ST18: Hyde L ... 2E 76
Stoneleigh Gdns. WV8: Cods ... 1B 122
Stoneleigh Rd. ST6: Chel ... 2A 18
STONELEY GREEN ... 2A 154
Stone Pine Cl. WS12: Hed ... 2F 101
Stonepine Cl. ST17: Wild ... 1A 78
Stonepit B77: Wiln ... 1J 141
Stone Rd. ST3: R Clo ... 7A 42
ST4: H'ord, Tren, T Val ... 6J 31
ST5: H Cho, Mae ... 7E 36
ST12: Titt ... 1A 44
ST14: Utt ... 5F 63
ST16: Staf ... 5E 70
(not continuous)
ST18: Yar ... 1D 70
ST21: Ecc ... 2H 65
Stone Station (Rail) ... 2F 47
Stone St. ST4: P'ull ... 2A 32
(not continuous)
Stonewall Ind. Est. ST5: Sil ... 6B 22
Stonewall Pl. ST5: Sil ... 6B 22
Stonewood Cl. ST4: T Val ... 6J 31
Stoneybrook Cl. ST18: Hixon ... 5D 80
Stoneybrook Leys WV5: Womb ... 5E 144
Stoney Cft. WS11: Cann ... 2F 109
Stoneycroft ST2: Mil ... 5H 19
STONEYDELPH ... 1D 142
Stoneydelph La. B77: Wiln ... 3C 142
Stoneyfields ST8: Bid M ... 5H 9
Stoneyfields Av. ST2: Mil ... 5H 19
Stoneyfields Cl. WS11: Cann ... 1G 109
Stoneyfields Ct.
ST5: N'tle ... 1H 153 (6H 23)
Stoney La. ST9: End ... 2A 50
WS3: Blox ... 2H 127
(not continuous)
STONEY LEA ... 1F 109
Stoney Lea Rd. WS11: Cann ... 1F 109
STONNALL ... 6H 133 (1A 164)
Stonor St. ST6: B'lem ... 2A 24
Stonydelph La. B77: Wiln ... 3C 142
STONY LOW ... 5E 28
STONYWELL ... 5D 104
Stonywell La. WS15: L'don ... 4B 104
Stormont Cl. ST6: B'lem ... 5C 18
STOTTESDON ... 3A 162
Stour B77: Hock ... 5C 142
STOURBRIDGE ... 3C 163
Stourbridge Rd. DY3: Him ... 6J 145
WV4: Pen, Womb ... 2J 145
WV5: Him, Womb ... 5J 145
Stour Cl. WS7: Burn ... 5B 112
Stourmore Cl. WV12: Will ... 7D 126
STOURTON ... 3H 149 (3C 163)
Stourton Cres. DY7: Stou ... 3K 149
STOWE ... 2C 114 (3B 160)
STOWE-BY-CHARTLEY ... 2A 160
Stowecroft WS13: Lich ... 1C 114
Stowe Hill Gdns. WS13: Lich ... 2C 114
Stowe La. ST18: Hixon, S Char ... 5C 80
Stowe Rd. WS13: Lich ... 3B 114
Stowe St. WS3: Blox ... 6J 127
WS13: Lich ... 3C 114
(not continuous)
Stowford Gro. ST4: Tren ... 2B 40
Stradbroke Dr. ST3: Blur ... 1G 41
Straight Mile WV10: Calf H, F Ash ... 5H 93
Straight Rd. WV12: Will ... 7D 126
STRAMSHALL ... 1F 63 (1A 160)
Strand, The ST3: Long ... 6H 33
Strand Cl. ST2: Buck ... 6G 25
Strand Pas. *ST3: Long* ... *5H 33*
(off The Strand)
Stranger's La. DE13: Yox ... 2K 89
Strangman St. ST13: Lee ... 4F 49
Stranraer Cl. ST3: W Coy ... 5D 34
Stratford Av. ST5: N'tle ... 5H 23
Stratford Cl. ST6: Mil ... 6F 19
ST11: Fors ... 2J 43
Stratford Way WS11: Cann ... 5F 101
Stratheden Rd. ST6: B'lem ... 5B 18
Strathfield Wlk. WV4: Pen ... 7K 129
Strathmore Cres. WV5: Womb ... 1G 145
Strathmore Pl. WS11: Cann ... 1F 109
Strawberry La. WS6: G Wyr ... 4E 118
Strawmoor La. WV8: Oak, Cods ... 7C 92
Streamside Cl. ST19: Penk ... 4H 91
STREETHAY ... 2G 115 (3B 160)
STREET LANE ... 3D 157
STREETLY ... 7F 135 (2A 164)
Streetly Cres. B74: F Oak ... 5J 135
Streetly Dr. B74: F Oak ... 5J 135
Streetly La. B74: F Oak ... 6H 135
Streetly Wood B74: S'ly ... 6F 135
Streets La. WS6: G Wyr ... 4E 118
Streetway Rd. WS14: Shen ... 4E 134
STRETTON
Alfreton ... 1D 157
Burton upon Trent ... 2F 85 (2C 161)
Stafford ... 3C 159
Stretton Aqueduct ... 3C 159
Stretton Av. ST16: Staf ... 7D 70
STRETTON EN LE FIELD ... 3D 161
Stretton Gdns. WV8: Cods ... 1B 122
Stretton Rd. ST5: Sil ... 6H 21
WV12: Will ... 5C 126
Stretton St. B77: Glas ... 6A 138
STRETTON UNDER FOSSE ... 3D 165
STRETTON WESTWOOD ... 2A 162
Stringer Ct. ST6: Tuns ... 4H 17
Stringers Hill WS12: Hed ... 3K 101
Stringer St. ST8: Bidd ... 5C 8
Strode Ho. B79: Tam ... 5G 137
Stroma Cl. ST6: B'lem ... 1K 23
Stross Av. ST6: Chel ... 2K 17
Stroud Cl. ST3: Mei ... 3D 42
Stuart Av. ST4: Tren ... 3A 40
ST11: Dray ... 4K 43
Stuart Cl. ST15: Stone ... 7F 47
Stuart Cl. Nth. ST15: Stone ... 6F 47
Stuart Gro. ST5: N'tle ... 4G 23
Stuart Rd. ST1: H'ley ... 7J 151 (6D 24)
Stuart St. WS3: Blox ... 5H 127
Stubbs Dr. ST15: Stone ... 5K 47
Stubbsfield Rd.
ST5: N'tle ... 6G 153 (2G 31)
Stubbs Ga. ST5: N'tle ... 5F 153 (1G 31)
Stubbs La. ST1: H'ley ... 5H 151 (5D 24)
Stubbs St. ST5: N'tle ... 4F 153 (1F 31)
ST6: B'lem ... 7J 17
Stubbs' Walks ST5: N'tle ... 4G 153 (1G 31)
Stubby La. DE6: D Cla ... 5A 82
ST14: Mar ... 3C 82
WV11: Wed ... 7K 125
Stubley Dr. WV10: W'ton ... 7C 124
STUBWOOD ... 3B 58 (1A 160)
Stubwood La. ST14: Dens, Stub ... 5B 58
Stud Farm Cotts. B78: M Oak ... 7E 136
Studley Rd. WV3: W'ton ... 6K 129
STURBRIDGE ... 1C 159
Sturgeon's Hill WS14: Lich ... 4C 114
Sturgess St. ST4: S Tren ... 3A 32
Stychbrook Gdns. WS13: Lich ... 1B 114
Stychfields ST17: Staf ... 5H 73
Suckling Grn. La. WV8: Cods ... 3B 122
Sudbourne Cl. ST6: Chel ... 6J 11
SUDBURY ... 1B 160
Sudbury Cl. WV11: Wed ... 5J 125
Sudbury Pl. ST5: N'tle ... 7F 31
Sudbury Rd. DE13: Yox ... 1H 89
Sudeley B77: T Gat ... 3J 141
Sudgrove Pl. ST3: Mei ... 3D 42
Sudlow St. ST6: B'lem ... 1B 24
Suffolk Cl. ST5: N'tle ... 5H 31
WV11: Wed ... 6G 125
Suffolk Rd. DE15: Stap ... 6E 86
ST3: L'ood ... 2J 41
Suffolk Way B78: Tam ... 1G 141
SUGNALL ... 1B 158
Sullivan Wlk. WS13: Lich ... 1C 114
Sullivan Way WS13: Lich ... 1C 114
Summerbank Rd. ST6: Tuns ... 3H 17
Summerfield ST7: Kids ... 5F 11
Summerfield Cl. B77: Tam ... 5K 137
Summerfield Dr. ST14: Utt ... 5F 63
Summerfield Rd. B77: Tam ... 5K 137
WS7: Chas ... 6J 111
Summerfields ST15: Yarn ... 5C 64
Summer Gro. WS13: Lich ... 1D 114
SUMMER HILL ... 2D 163
SUMMERHILL ... 2H 133
Summerhill Dr. ST5: C'ton ... 6B 16
Summerhill La. ST18: W'ave ... 1A 70
Summerhouse La.
WS13: Chor ... 7B 104
Summer Row ST3: Long ... 7H 33
Summerside Av. WS12: Haz ... 6E 102
Summer St. ST4: S Tren ... 4A 32
Summerville Rd. ST4: T Val ... 6J 31
Sunbeam B77: Glas ... 6A 138
Sunbeam Dr. WS6: G Wyr ... 1F 119
Sunbury Av. WS14: Lich ... 4E 114
Sunbury Cl. ST4: Tren ... 4C 40
Sundorne Pl. ST2: Bent ... 6H 25
Sundour Cres. WV11: Wed ... 4F 125
Sundown Dr. ST17: Staf ... 6C 72
Sunfield Rd. WS11: Cann ... 2A 108
Sunfields Cl. B78: Pole ... 2K 143
Sunley Dr. WS12: Hed ... 3K 101
Sunningdale B77: Amin ... 4E 138
ST15: Stone ... 5G 47
Sunningdale Av. WV6: Per ... 1E 128
Sunningdale Cl. DE13: Stre ... 2D 84
ST6: B'lem ... 4B 18
Sunningdale Dr. ST16: Staf ... 3A 74
Sunningdale Gro. ST5: C'ton ... 7B 16
Sunningdale Vw. ST3: R Clo ... 7A 42
Sunningdale Way WS3: Blox ... 2G 127
Sunny Bank DE6: May ... 6B 56
ST6: B'lem ... 2J 23
Sunnybank Cvn. Pk. ST19: Lap ... 1E 90
Sunnybank Ct. ST6: B'lem ... 4A 18
Sunnycroft Av. ST3: Blur ... 1G 41
Sunnyfield Oval ST2: Mil ... 6J 19
SUNNY HILL ... 1D 161
Sunny Hill Cl. WV5: Womb ... 4H 145
Sunnyhills Rd. ST13: Lee ... 6E 48
Sunny Hollow ST5: N'tle ... 5G 23
Sunnymead Rd. WS7: C Ter ... 2H 111
Sunny Side ST10: K'ley ... 5F 53
Sunnyside Av. ST6: Tuns ... 4K 17
Sunnyside Rd. ST14: Utt ... 4G 63
Sunridge Av. WV5: Womb ... 3G 145
Sunridge Cl. ST2: Mil ... 5H 19
Sunrise Hill WS12: Hed ... 4H 101
Sunset Cl. B78: Pole ... 2J 143
B79: Tam ... 4G 137
WS6: G Wyr ... 1F 119
WV9: Cove ... 1K 93
Sun St. ST1: H'ley ... 6C 150 (6A 24)
ST10: Chea ... 4D 54
Sunwell Gdns. ST10: Chea ... 4D 54
Superbowl 2000 ... 1F 87
Surrey Cl. WS11: Cann ... 3F 109
WS15: Rug ... 3F 97
Surrey Dr. B78: Tam ... 1G 141
Surrey Rd. ST7: Kids ... 4E 10
ST17: Staf ... 6E 72
Surtees Gro. ST4: Fen ... 4H 33
Sussex Dr. ST7: Kids ... 4D 10
WS12: Hed ... 5H 101
Sussex Pl. ST3: L'ood ... 1K 41
Sussex Rd. DE15: Stap ... 6E 86
Sutherland Av. ST3: Long ... 1H 41
Sutherland Cres. ST11: B Bri ... 3G 43
Sutherland Dr. ST5: N'tle ... 4D 30
WV5: Womb ... 2G 145
Sutherland Gro. WV6: Per ... 2G 129
Sutherland Rd. ST3: Long ... 6J 33
ST9: L'ton ... 7B 48
ST12: Titt ... 1A 44
ST15: Stone ... 5H 47
WS6: C Hay ... 1E 118
Sutherland St. ST4: Fen ... 3C 32
SUTTON
Bridgnorth ... 3B 162
Market Drayton ... 1A 158
Newport ... 2B 158
Sutton Av. B78: Tam ... 7G 137
SUTTON CHENEY ... 1D 165
Sutton Cl. WS15: Rug ... 3H 97
SUTTON COLDFIELD ... 2B 164
Sutton Dr. ST4: T Val ... 5K 31
ST16: Staf ... 2C 72
SUTTON LANE ENDS ... 1D 155
SUTTON MADDOCK ... 1B 162
SUTTON ON THE HILL ... 1C 161
Sutton Pl. ST6: Chel ... 2B 18
Sutton Rd. B78: D Bas, M Oak ... 4A 140
SUTTON SCARSDALE ... 1D 157
Sutton St. ST5: C'ton ... 2C 22
SWADLINCOTE ... 3C 161
Swaffham Way ST2: Bent ... 6K 25
Swainsfield Rd. DE13: Yox ... 2H 89
Swainsley Cl. ST6: B'lem ... 1A 24

Trubshawe St.—Victoria Mdw.

Trubshawe St. ST6: B'lem 7H 17
Trubshaw Pl. ST7: Kids 3F 11
Truro Cl. WS13: Lich 7B 106
WS15: Rug 3F 97
Truro Pl. ST2: Bent 6H 25
WS12: H Hay 2J 109
Truro Way ST17: Staf 5B 74
TRUSLEY 1C 161
Trusley Cl. DE14: B'ton 5C 86
Trussell Cl. ST17: Act T 6J 77
TRYSULL 1C 144 (2C 163)
Trysull Gdns. WV3: W'ton 7K 129
Trysull Holloway WV5: Trys 1E 146
Trysull Rd. WV3: W'ton 7K 129
WV5: Womb 2E 144
TUCKHILL 3B 162
Tudor Cl. ST4: S Tren 3A 32
ST15: Stone 6F 47
WS6: C Hay 1E 118
WS7: Burn 5K 111
WS14: Lich 5F 115
Tudor Ct. ST5: N'tle 2F 23
ST11: Ful 2G 59
WV11: Ess 2K 125
Tudor Cres. B77: Amin 5B 138
(not continuous)
Tudor Gro. ST5: N'tle 4G 23
Tudor Hollow DE13: Stre 3E 84
ST11: Ful 2G 59
Tudor Pk. Ct. B74: F Oak 5K 135
Tudor Pk. Gdns. WS7: Burn 5K 111
Tudor Ri. B79: C Camp 6D 132
ST16: Staf 5E 70
Tudor Rd. WS7: Burn 5A 112
WS12: Hed 2F 101
Tudor Rose Ct. ST6: Nort 5E 18
Tudor Rose Way ST6: Nort 5D 18
Tudor Row *WS13: Lich 4B 114*
(off Wade St.)
Tudors, The ST6: Tuns 3J 17
Tudor Way ST17: Staf 5D 72
WS6: C Hay 3D 118
TUGFORD 3A 162
Tuke Pl. WS13: Lich 2K 113
Tulip Gro. ST5: N'tle 1F 153 (6G 23)
Tulip Way ST13: Lee 2J 51
Tulley Pl. ST2: Buck 5G 25
Tullis Cl. ST16: Staf 4E 72
Tulsa Cl. ST2: Buck 7G 25
Tunbridge Dr. ST5: Sil 6H 21
Tunley St. ST15: Stone 3F 47
Tunnel Ter. ST6: Tuns 2F 17
Tunnicliffe Cl. ST3: Long 6A 34
Tunnicliffe Dr. WS15: Rug 7F 95
Tunnicliffe Way ST14: Utt 3D 62
TUNSTALL
Stafford 2B 158
Stoke-on-Trent 4J 17 (2C 155)
Tunstall Greenway ST6: Tuns 2J 17
(not continuous)
Tunstall La. ST20: H Off 1A 66
Tunstall Pool 4J 17
Tunstall Rd. ST8: Bidd, Knyp 1C 12
Tunstall Rd. Ind. Est. ST8: B Lee 2B 12
Tunstall Western By-Pass ST6: Tuns 5F 17
TUPPENHURST 5H 99
Tuppenhurst La. WS13: Hand 6J 99
WS15: Hand 5G 99
TUPTON 1D 157
Turf Cl. WS11: N Can 7C 110
Turin Dr. ST5: N'tle 3C 30
Turnberry B77: Amin 4E 138
Turnberry Cl. WV6: Per 1E 128
Turnberry Dr. ST4: Tren 2K 39
Turnberry Rd. WS3: Blox 2F 127
Turnbull Rd. WS13: Frad 4J 107
Turnbury Cl. DE14: B'ton 5B 86
TURNDITCH 3C 157
Turner Av. ST7: Big E 6J 15
Turner Cl. WS11: H Hay 1K 109
Turner Cres. ST5: C'ton 2C 22
Turner Gro. WV6: Per 2H 129
Turner St. ST1: H'ley 1J 151 (3D 24)
Turney Gro. ST17: Staf 6E 72
Turnham Grn. WV6: Per 3F 129
Turnhill Cl. ST17: Staf 1E 76
Turnhill Gro. ST5: Brad 1F 23
TURNHURST 6J 11
Turnhurst Rd. ST7: Pack 5K 11
Turnlea Cl. ST8: Knyp 7B 8
Turnock St. ST2: Buck 4J 25
Turnpike Way WV9: Cove 3A 116
Turnstone Dr. WV10: Fea 5F 117
Turquoise Gro. WS11: H Hay 7J 101
Turton Cl. DE13: Alre 6C 130
WS3: Blox 1G 127
TURVES GREEN 3A 164
Tuscan Cl. ST10: Chea 6B 54
Tuscan Ho. ST3: Long 7H 33
Tuscan St. ST3: Long 5J 33
Tuscan Way ST5: C'ton 2B 22
TUTBURY 2H 83 (2C 161)
Tutbury B77: T Gat 3J 141
Tutbury & Hatton Station (Rail) 1J 83
Tutbury Av. WV6: Per 3G 129
Tutbury Castle (remains) 1G 83
Tutbury Cl. WS11: H Hay 7J 101
Tutbury Crystal 2H 83
Tutbury Gro. ST3: Long 5K 33
Tutbury Mus. 2H 83
Tutbury Rd. DE13: B Tre, Tut 1A 84
Tutehill B77: Wiln 3D 142
Twayblade DE14: B'ton 4C 86
TWEEDALE 1B 162
Tweed Gro. ST5: N'tle 5E 30
Tweed St. ST4: Fen 5E 32
TWEMLOW GREEN 1B 154
Twemlow St. ST1: H'ley 4C 150 (5A 24)
Twentylands DE13: Roll D 6K 83
Twigg St. ST2: Buck 6H 25
Twizles La. B79: Haun 6A 132
TWO DALES 1C 157
TWO GATES 2J 141 (1C 165)
Two Gates Ind. Est. B77: Wiln 3K 141
Two Oaks Av. WS7: C Ter 3E 110
Two Trees Cl. B78: Hop 3C 136
TWYCROSS 1D 165
TWYFORD 2D 161
Twyford Gro. WV11: Wed 6K 125
Twyning Grn. ST3: Blur 3F 41
TYBURN 2B 164
Tylecote Cres. ST18: Gt Hay 4G 81
Tyler Gro. ST6: B'lem 7J 17
ST15: Stone 5E 46
Tyndall Pl. ST4: S Tren 6K 153 (2J 31)
Tyne Cl. WS8: Brow 2E 120
Tyneham Gro. ST2: Mil 5G 19
Tyne Way ST5: N'tle 5E 30
Tyning Cl. WV9: P'ord 3J 123
Tyninghame Av. WV6: Tett 7F 123
Tynwald Grange ST5: N'tle 6E 22
Tyrell Gro. ST1: H'ley 7F 19
Tyria Way ST17: Staf 6J 73
Tyrley Cl. WV6: Tett 4J 129
Tyson Grn. ST2: Bent 1K 33
Tythe Barn ST10: Alt 6H 57
Tythe Barn Rd. ST10: Alt 6G 57

U

UBBERLEY 7J 25
Ubberley Grn. ST2: Bent 6J 25
Ubberley Rd. ST2: Bent 6H 25
UCI Cinema
Tamworth 5J 137
UCKINGTON 3A 158
Uffington Pde. ST2: B Hil 7J 25
Ufton Cl. ST3: Blur 4F 41
Ullswater B77: Wiln 3C 142
Ullswater Av. ST6: B'lem 7J 17
Ullswater Dr. ST10: Chea 3D 54
ST15: Stone 5K 47
Ullswater Ho. *ST17: Staf 1G 77*
(off Merrivale Rd.)
Ullswater Pl. WS11: Cann 2E 108
Ullswater Rd. WV12: Will 4B 126
Ulster Cl. WS11: Cann 7G 101
Ulster Ter. ST4: S Tren 4A 32
Ulverston Rd. ST3: Blur 3F 41
Umberleigh Rd. ST3: Blur 3E 40
Underhill La. WV10: Bush 2D 124
Underhill Wlk. DE14: B Tre 2E 86
Under the Hill ST8: Bid M 4G 9
UNDERTON 2A 162
Underwood Cl. ST16: Staf 5E 70
Underwood Rd. ST5: Sil 7H 21
Unicorn Ind. Est. ST6: B'lem 7H 17
Unicorn Pl. ST6: Chel 2K 17
Union Cl. B77: Tam 6J 137
Union Ct. ST1: H'ley 1F 151 (3C 24)
Union La. WV5: Trys 1D 144
Union St. DE14: B Tre 2E 86
ST1: H'ley 1F 151 (3C 24)
ST13: Lee 3G 49
WS7: Chas 6G 111
WS11: Cann 5E 108
Unity Av. ST1: H'ley 1D 24
Unity Way ST7: Talk 6B 10
University Ct. ST18: Staf 1A 74
Unwin St. ST6: B'lem 4B 18
(not continuous)
Upfields WS7: Burn 4C 112
Upfields Cotts. WS7: Burn 4C 112
Upfield Way WS15: Rug 6E 94
Uplands, The ST5: N'tle 1F 153 (6G 23)
ST8: Bidd 3E 8
ST18: Gt Hay 4G 81
Uplands Av. ST6: Chel 1K 17
ST9: Werr 5C 26
Uplands Cl. ST19: Penk 2G 91
WS15: Can W 5H 103
Uplands Cft. ST9: Werr 4C 26
Uplands Dr. ST9: Werr 5C 26
WV5: Womb 4G 145
Uplands Grn. WS15: Rug 3F 97
Uplands Rd. ST2: A Hul 1H 25
ST17: Staf 1F 77
Upmeadows Dr. ST16: Staf 5D 72
UPPER ARLEY 3B 162
Up. Belgrave Rd. ST3: Long 1K 41
Up. Brook St. WS15: Rug 1G 97
UPPER COUND 1A 162
Upper Cres. ST4: S Tren 5K 153 (1J 31)
Up. Cross Rd. WS15: Rug 2G 97
Up. Cross St. ST3: Long 5J 33
UPPER EASTERN GREEN 3C 165
UPPER ELKSTONE 2A 156
UPPER ELLASTONE 3B 156
Up. Furlong St. ST4: Fen 3D 32
Upper Grn. WV6: Tett 1K 129
Up. Gungate B79: Tam 4H 137
UPPER HACKNEY 1C 157
UPPER HEATH 3A 162
Up. Hillchurch St.
ST1: H'ley 2H 151 (4D 24)
UPPER HULME 1A 156
Up. Huntbach St.
ST1: H'ley 2H 151 (4D 24)
Up. Keys Bus. Pk. WS12: Hed 7K 101
UPPER LANDYWOOD 4E 118
Up. Landywood La.
WS6: C Hay, G Wyr 3D 118
UPPER LEIGH 1A 160
Up. Lodge Rd. WS15: Arm 5D 98
UPPER LONGDON 7A 98 (3A 160)
UPPER LONGWOOD 1A 162
Upper Mkt. Sq. ST1: H'ley 3G 151 (4C 24)
Upper Marsh ST5: N'tle 5H 23
UPPER MAYFIELD 4B 56
UPPER MIDWAY 2C 161
UPPER NETCHWOOD 2A 162
UPPER NOBUT 1A 160
Up. Normacot Rd. ST3: Long 7K 33
(not continuous)
UPPER OUTWOODS 3A 84 (2C 161)
Up. St John St. WS14: Lich 4B 114
Up. Sneyd Rd. WV11: Ess 3B 126
UPPER TEAN 3G 55 (1A 160)
UPPERTOWN 1D 157
UPPER TOWN
Ashbourne 2C 157
Matlock 2C 157
Upper Way WS15: U Lon 1K 103
UPPERWOOD 2C 157
UPPINGTON 1A 162
UPTON 2D 165
UPTON CRESSETT 2A 162
UPTON MAGNA 3A 158
Upton Pl. WS15: Rug 6F 95
Urmston Pl. ST3: Blur 3F 41
USAM Trad. Est. WV10: Ford 3B 124
Usk Cl. WS3: Blox 5K 127
Usulwall Cl. ST21: Ecc 3G 65
Utterby Side ST2: B Hil 1J 33
UTTOXETER 5H 63 (1A 160)
Uttoxeter Cl. WV6: W'ton 7K 123
Uttoxeter Heritage Cen. 6H 63
Uttoxeter Leisure Cen. 6G 63
Uttoxeter Racecourse 7K 63
Uttoxeter Racecourse Cvn. Club Site
ST14: Utt 6J 63
Uttoxeter Rd. ST3: Long, Mei 6J 33
ST10: Alt 6H 57
ST10: Chec, Tea 4G 55
ST11: B Bri 2E 42
ST11: B Bri, Dray 4K 43
ST15: Holly, Stone 6K 47
WS15: Abb B 1A 88
WS15: Hand 5G 99
WS15: Hill R 1D 98
Uttoxeter Station (Rail) 6J 63
Uxbridge Ct. WS7: Chas 6G 111
WS12: Hed 5J 101
Uxbridge St. DE14: B Tre 3D 86
WS12: Hed 6J 101

V

Vale Cl. WS13: Lich 2B 114
Vale Gdns. ST19: Penk 5G 91
Vale Head Dr. WV6: Tett 4H 129
Valentine Rd. ST7: Kids 5E 10
Vale Pk. 6A 18
Vale Pleasant ST5: Sil 6A 22
Valerian Way ST3: Mei 4C 42
Vale Ri. ST19: Penk 4G 91
Vale St. ST4: S Tren 2B 32
ST5: C'ton 7C 16
ST5: Sil 6K 21
Vale Vw. ST5: N'tle 1H 23
ST13: Ched 5H 51
Valley, The WS7: C Ter 3F 111
Valley Dr. B77: Wiln 4A 142
ST13: Lee 4C 48
Valley Grn. WS6: C Hay 2E 118
Valley La. B77: Wiln 3A 142
WS13: Lich 3D 114
Valley Pk. Way ST3: Blur 6F 33
Valley Rd. ST3: W Coy 6D 34
ST15: Stone 5G 47
WS3: Blox 5J 127
WS12: Haz 4C 102
WS12: Hed 4J 101
Valley Vw. DE6: May 6B 56
WS8: Brow 5J 121
Valleyview Wlk. ST14: Roce 5E 58
Vanbrugh Ct. WV6: Per 3F 129
Vancouver Dr. DE15: Wins 1K 87
Van Diemans Rd. WV5: Womb 5E 144
Van Gogh Cl. WS11: H Hay 1K 109
Vanguard B77: Wiln 4K 141
Vanity Cl. ST15: Oul 7J 45
Vanity La. ST15: Oul, Stone 7J 45
Varden Ct. WS15: Rug 7G 95
Vardon Cl. ST16: Staf 3A 74
Vauban Dr. ST17: Staf 6H 73
Vaughan Gdns. WV8: Cods 1B 122
Vaughan Way ST17: Staf 5D 72
Venice Ct. ST5: N'tle 2C 30
Venn Pl. ST1: H'ley 7K 151 (6E 24)
Ventnor Gro. ST3: Blur 4F 41
Venton Cl. ST6: Nort 3E 18
Ventura Pk. Rd. B78: Tam 5E 136
Ventura Retail Pk. B78: Tam 6G 137
Venture Ct. WV10: Ford 7B 116
Venture Way *ST6: B'lem 4C 18*
(off Bradeley Village)
Vercourt B74: L Ast 5G 135
Verdi Ct. WS13: Lich 1C 114
Verdon Cl. ST19: Penk 5J 91
Vermont Grn. WS11: Cann 7G 101
Verney Cl. ST14: Bram 6B 62
Verney Way ST3: Blur 3F 41
Vernon Av. ST7: Aud 5E 14
WS8: Brow 4J 121
Vernon Cl. B74: F Oak 3K 135
ST7: Aud 5F 15
WV11: Ess 1K 125
Vernon Ho. ST14: Utt 6H 63
Vernon Rd. ST4: S Tren 1B 32
Vernons Pl. WV10: Shar 3H 117
Vernon Ter. DE14: B Tre 7D 84
Vernon Way WS3: Blox 4D 126
Verona Gro. ST3: Long 4A 34
Verulam Ct. ST16: Staf 6G 71
Verulam Rd. ST16: Staf 6G 71
Verwood Cl. ST16: Staf 2A 74
Vesey Cl. B74: F Oak 6K 135
Vessey Ter. ST5: N'tle 5F 153 (1G 31)
Viaduct Dr. WV6: W'ton 7K 123
Vicarage Cl. B78: Dor 5H 143
DE15: Wins 7J 85
ST21: Ecc 2G 65
WS8: Brow 5J 121
(not continuous)
Vicarage Ct. DY7: Kin 6E 148
Vicarage Cres. ST5: N'tle 6G 153 (2G 31)
ST10: Tea 4G 55
ST11: Cave 6F 35
ST12: Titt 2A 44
Vicarage Cft. DE13: K Bro 2D 130
Vicarage Dr. DY7: Kin 6E 148
ST14: S'all 1E 62
Vicarage Fld. *DE15: Stap 3G 87*
(off Stapenhill Rd.)
Vicarage La. CW3: Mad 4A 28
DE13: K Bro 2D 130
ST4: T Val 5J 31
ST12: Barl 1E 44
ST17: Bed 7D 78
WS14: W'ton 3G 131
Vicarage Rd. ST4: S Tren 1K 31
ST10: Tea 4G 55
ST13: Lee 3G 49
ST19: Brew 2D 92
WS8: Brow 5H 121
WV10: F Ash 5H 93
WV11: Wed 7F 125
Vicarage Way ST17: Staf 5F 73
ST18: Hixon 5C 80
Vicar's Cl. ST15: Oul 7J 45
WS13: Lich 3A 114
Vicars Cft. WS15: Rug 6H 95
Vichy Cl. ST5: N'tle 2C 30
Vickers Rd. ST6: Chel 2A 18
Victoria Arc. B79: Tam 4H 137
Victoria Av. ST1: H'ley 7F 151 (6C 24)
ST7: Big E 1G 21
ST7: Kids 4D 10
WS3: Blox 4H 127
Victoria Cl. ST5: Sil 6A 22
Victoria Cotts. ST3: Long 7A 34
Victoria Ct. *ST4: Fen 3E 32*
(off Frederick St.)
ST5: N'tle 5G 23
ST7: Kids 4E 10
(off Attwood St.)
ST13: Lee 4E 48
WS11: N Can 6D 110
Victoria Cres. DE14: B Tre 6D 84
Victoria Dr. B78: Faze 2G 141
Victoria Gdns. WS13: Lich 5K 113
Victoria Gro. WV5: Womb 2G 145
Victoria Hall 4G 151 (5C 24)
Victoria Ho. WS3: Blox 5K 127
Victoria Ind. Complex
ST4: Fen 4G 33
Victoria Mdw. DE13: K Bro 2D 130

Victoria Pk.—Watson Cl.

Victoria Pk. *ST16: Staf* . . . *3F 73*
(off Tenterbanks)
Victoria Pk. Rd. ST6: Tuns . . . 4J 17
Victoria Pl. ST4: Fen . . . 3E 32
(not continuous)
ST5: C'ton . . . 1C 22
ST5: N'tle . . . 3H 23
Victoria Pl. Link ST4: Fen . . . 4F 33
Victoria Rd. B79: Tam . . . 4H 137
DE14: B Tre . . . 7D 84
ST1: H'ley . . . 7J 151 (7D 24)
ST4: Fen . . . 7D 24
ST5: N'tle . . . 4G 153 (1G 31)
ST16: Staf . . . 3F 73
WV6: Tett . . . 7G 123
WV10: W'ton . . . 7D 124
WV11: Wed . . . 7F 125
Victoria Row ST8: Knyp . . . 2C 12
Victoria Sq. ST1: H'ley . . . 5E 150 (5B 24)
ST16: Staf . . . 3F 73
WS13: Lich . . . 5B 114
Victoria St. DE13: Yox . . . 1H 89
DE14: B Tre . . . 7D 84
ST4: S Tren . . . 1J 153 (6H 23)
ST5: C'ton . . . 1C 22
ST5: N'tle . . . 5F 153 (1G 31)
ST5: Sil . . . 6A 22
ST10: Chea . . . 4D 54
ST13: Lee . . . 3H 49
ST15: Stone . . . 3G 47
ST16: Staf . . . 2G 73
WS11: Cann . . . 6E 100
(Cemetery Rd.)
WS11: Cann . . . 3D 108
(Newhall St.)
WS12: Hed . . . 4J 101
Victoria Ter. ST16: Staf . . . 1G 73
Victoria Way ST17: Staf . . . 2C 78
Victor St. ST15: Stone . . . 3F 47
Victory Av. WS7: C Ter . . . 4H 111
Victory Cl. ST10: Chea . . . 3D 54
WS12: Hed . . . 6A 102
Victory Ter. B78: Faze . . . 2H 141
Vienna Pl. ST5: N'tle . . . 3D 30
Vienna Way ST3: Long . . . 4A 34
Viewfield Av. WS12: Hed . . . 3F 101
Viewlands Dr. WV6: Tett . . . 4H 129
Views, The ST7: New . . . 4J 11
View St. WS12: Hed . . . 4F 101
Viggars Pl. ST5: N'tle . . . 6D 22
VIGO . . . 1A 164
Viking B77: Wiln . . . 3K 141
Villa Cl. ST8: Bidd . . . 6C 8
WV10: Shar . . . 3H 117
VILLAGE, THE . . . 1C 50
Village, The ST5: Keel . . . 2H 29
ST17: Walt . . . 7D 74
(not continuous)
Village Gdns. ST17: Walt . . . 7D 74
Village M., The WV6: Tett . . . 1K 129
Villa Rd. ST13: Ched . . . 2G 51
Villas, The ST4: S Tren . . . 4A 32
Villa St. ST4: S Tren . . . 4A 32
Villiers St. ST3: Long . . . 1H 41
Vincent St. ST1: H'ley . . . 1K 151 (3E 24)
Vine Bank Rd. ST7: Kids . . . 4E 10
Vinebank St. ST4: S Tren . . . 3A 32
Vine Cl. ST18: Hixon . . . 6B 80
Vine La. WS11: Cann . . . 6D 108
Vine Row ST4: S Tren . . . 3A 32
Violet La. DE15: Stap . . . 4G 87
Violet Way DE15: Stap . . . 4G 87
Virage Pk. WS11: Cann . . . 5F 109
Virginia Av. ST17: Staf . . . 6J 73
Viscount Rd. WS7: C Ter . . . 2G 111
Viscount Wlk. ST3: Mei . . . 3C 42
Vivian Rd. ST4: Fen . . . 3F 33
Vowchurch Way ST2: B Hil . . . 7J 25
Voyager Dr. WS11: Cann . . . 5F 109
Vue Cinema . . . 4E 152 (1F 31)
Vulcan Ind. Est. WS2: Wals . . . 7J 127
Vulcan Rd. WS13: Lich . . . 2E 114

W

Wadden La. ST18: Gay . . . 1D 80
Wade Av. ST5: N'tle . . . 2H 23
Wadebridge Rd. ST2: B Hil . . . 7H 25
Wade Cl. ST10: Chea . . . 6C 54
WS15: Hill R . . . 1D 98
Wade La. WS15: Hill R . . . 1D 98
Wadesmill Lawns WV10: Bush . . . 1C 124
Wade St. ST6: B'lem . . . 6B 18
WS13: Lich . . . 4B 114
Wadham St. ST4: P'ull . . . 2A 32
WADSHELF . . . 1D 157
Wain Av. ST5: N'tle . . . 4A 152 (1D 30)
ST6: B Gre . . . 2E 18
Wain Dr. ST4: T Val . . . 3J 31
(not continuous)
Waine Ho. WS8: Brow . . . 6J 121
WAIN LEA . . . 2K 11
Wainrigg B77: Wiln . . . 3D 142
Wain St. ST6: B'lem . . . 6K 17
Wainwood Ri. ST4: T Val . . . 4K 31
Wainwright Cl. DY6: W Hea . . . 4K 147
Wainwright Wlk. ST1: H'ley . . . 3H 151
Wakefield Av. DE13: Tut . . . 2G 83
Wakefield Rd. ST4: T Val . . . 5K 31
Wakeman Ct. WV11: Ess . . . 2K 125
WALCOT . . . 3A 158
Walcot Gro. ST2: Buck . . . 7G 25
Waldale Cl. WV11: Ess . . . 4C 126
Walden Av. ST16: Staf . . . 7F 71
WALDLEY . . . 1B 160
Wales La. DE13: B Nee . . . 6G 89
WALFORD . . . 1C 159
Walford Rd. DE13: Roll D . . . 6K 83
WALGHERTON . . . 3A 154
Walhouse Dr. ST19: Penk . . . 5H 91
Walhouse St. WS11: Cann . . . 3E 108
Walker Av. WV10: Bush . . . 5C 124
Walker Pl. WS3: Blox . . . 5K 127
Walker Rd. ST6: Chel . . . 3K 17
WS3: Blox . . . 5K 127
Walkers Cft. WS13: Lich . . . 1C 114
Walkers Fold WV12: Will . . . 7D 126
Walkersgreen Rd. ST5: C'ton . . . 5B 16
Walkers Ri. WS12: Hed . . . 2K 101
Walker St. DE14: B Tre . . . 3C 86
ST6: Tuns . . . 5H 17
Walkfield Rd. DE13: Alre . . . 6B 130
Walk La. WV5: Womb . . . 3G 145
Walklate Av. ST5: N'tle . . . 5H 23
WALKMILL BRIDGE . . . 6C 108
Walkmill Bus. Pk. WS11: Cann . . . 6D 108
Walkmill La. WS11: Cann . . . 6D 108
Walkmill Way WS11: Cann . . . 6D 108
Walks, The ST13: Lee . . . 4E 48
WALL . . . 1A 134 (1B 164)
Wallace Cl. WS11: N Can . . . 6B 110
Wallace Ct. WS6: C Hay . . . 3D 118
Wallace Rd. WS8: Brow . . . 4G 121
Wallace Sports & Education Cen. . . . 1H 25
Walland Gro. ST16: Staf . . . 2D 72
Wallash DE6: May . . . 6B 56
Wallbridge Cl. ST13: Lee . . . 5D 48
Wallbridge Dr. ST13: Lee . . . 4D 48
WALLBRIDGE PARK . . . 5C 48
Wallbridge Pct. ST13: Lee . . . 5D 48
WALLBROOK . . . 2D 163
Walled Garden, The ST8: Bidd . . . 2E 8
Wall End Cl. WS2: Wals . . . 6G 127
Walley Dr. ST6: Sandy . . . 1H 17
Walley Pl. ST6: B'lem . . . 1A 24
Walley's Dr. ST5: N'tle . . . 1H 153 (6H 23)
Walley St. ST6: B'lem . . . 1A 24
ST8: Bidd . . . 5C 8
Wallfield Cl. ST10: Tea . . . 3F 55
WALL HEATH . . . 3K 147 (3C 163)
Wallheath Cres. WS9: Ston . . . 5H 133
Wall Heath La. WS9: Ston . . . 5J 133
Wall Hill Ct. *ST13: Lee* . . . *5F 49*
(off Junction Rd.)
Wallington Cl. WS3: Blox . . . 3H 127
WALLINGTON HEATH . . . 3G 127
Wallington Heath WS3: Blox . . . 3H 127
Wallis Pl. ST2: Buck . . . 3J 25
Wallis St. ST4: Fen . . . 3F 33
Wallis Way ST2: Mil . . . 5G 19
Wall La. WS14: Wall . . . 7H 113 & 1B 134
Wall La. Ter. ST13: Ched . . . 3G 51
Wallmires La. ST9: Werr . . . 7F 27
Wall Rd. DE14: B'ton . . . 4B 86
Wall Roman Site (Mus.) . . . 1A 134
Walls Wood ST5: B Gat . . . 3D 36
Walmer Pl. ST3: Long . . . 4H 33
WALMLEY . . . 2B 164
Walney Gro. ST1: H'ley . . . 1F 151 (3C 24)
Walnut Av. WV8: Bilb . . . 2C 122
Walnut Cl. WS11: Cann . . . 7F 101
Walnut Ct. WS15: Bre . . . 4J 97
Walnut Crest ST18: Hixon . . . 6C 80
Walnut Dr. WS11: Cann . . . 1F 109
WV3: W'ton . . . 5K 129
Walnut Gro. ST5: C'ton . . . 7B 16
WS14: Lich . . . 4F 115
Walnut Wlk. WS13: Lich . . . 5J 113
Walpole St. ST3: Long . . . 4K 33
WALSALL . . . 2A 164
Walsall Rd. B74: F Oak . . . 4J 135
B74: L Ast . . . 2H 135
WS6: G Wyr . . . 6F 109
WS11: Cann . . . 3E 108
WS11: N Can . . . 1B 120
WS13: Lich, Pipe . . . 7F 113
WS14: Hilt, M Cor, Pipe, Wall, Lyn . . . 3G 133
WALSALL WOOD . . . 7H 121 (1A 164)
WALSGRAVE ON SOWE . . . 3D 165
Walsingham Gdns. ST5: N'tle . . . 7F 31
WALTON
Chesterfield . . . 1D 157
Stafford . . . 2C 159
Stone . . . 5F 47 (1C 159)
Telford . . . 3A 158
Waltonbury Cl. ST17: Walt . . . 1D 78
Walton Cres. ST4: Fen . . . 4C 32
Walton Cross ST15: Stone . . . 5G 47
Walton Gdns. WV8: Cods . . . 1B 122
Walton Grange ST15: Stone . . . 5G 47
Walton Gro. ST7: Talk . . . 6A 10
Walton Heath WS3: Blox . . . 2F 127
Walton Ind. Est. ST15: Stone . . . 6G 47
(Beacon Dr.)
ST15: Stone . . . 7F 47
(Beacon Rd.)
Walton La. DE13: B Nee . . . 6K 89
ST17: Broc . . . 2E 78
Walton Lodge ST17: Walt . . . 1D 78
Walton Mead Cl. ST17: Staf . . . 7D 74
WALTON-ON-THE-HILL . . . 1D 78 (2D 159)
WALTON-ON-TRENT . . . 3C 161
Walton Pl. ST5: C'ton . . . 2D 22
Walton Rd. DE15: Drak . . . 7D 86
ST4: T Val . . . 6K 31
Walton Way ST7: Talk . . . 6A 10
ST15: Stone . . . 5F 47
Wandsbeck B77: Wiln . . . 2A 142
Warburton Ct. *ST6: B'lem* . . . *1A 24*
(off Warburton St.)
Warburton St. ST6: B'lem . . . 1A 24
Ward Cl. WS13: Frad . . . 4K 107
WARD END . . . 3B 164
WARDLE . . . 2A 154
Wardle Cres. ST13: Lee . . . 5F 49
Wardle Gdns. ST13: Lee . . . 2J 51
Wardle La. ST2: L Oak . . . 6J 19
Wardle Pl. WS11: Cann . . . 5E 100
Wardles La. WS6: G Wyr . . . 2F 119
Wardle St. B79: Tam . . . 4G 137
ST6: Tuns . . . 4J 17
Ward Pl. ST6: Chel . . . 2B 18
Ward Rd. WV8: Cods . . . 2B 122
Ward St. WS12: Hed . . . 4F 101
Warings, The WV5: Womb . . . 6F 145
Warmadine La. ST5: Blac . . . 7B 36
Warm Cft. ST15: Stone . . . 5J 47
WARMINGHAM . . . 1B 154
Warminster Pl. ST3: Long . . . 6G 33
Warmson Cl. ST3: Long . . . 3J 33
Warner Rd. WV8: Cods . . . 2B 122
Warner St. ST1: H'ley . . . 4F 151 (5C 24)
Warnford Wlk. WV4: Pen . . . 7K 129
WARREN . . . 1C 155
Warren Av. WV10: W'ton . . . 7D 124
Warren Cl. DE13: Stre . . . 2F 85
WS12: Haz . . . 5C 102
WS14: Lich . . . 4E 114
Warren Cft. WS15: Hand . . . 6G 99
Warren La. DE14: B'ton . . . 5A 86
Warren Pl. ST3: Long . . . 7K 33
WS8: Brow . . . 5J 121
Warren Rd. ST6: Chel . . . 1B 18
WS7: Burn . . . 6J 111
Warrens La. ST16: Staf . . . 7D 70
Warren St. ST3: Long . . . 7K 33
Warrilow Cl. ST3: Mei . . . 3C 42
Warrilow Heath Rd. ST5: C'ton . . . 6A 16
Warrington Dr. ST13: Lee . . . 4D 48
Warrington Rd. ST1: H'ley . . . 7D 24
Warrington St. ST4: Fen . . . 3F 33
Warsill Gro. ST3: Long . . . 5K 33
WARSLOW . . . 2A 156
WARSTONE . . . 5B 118
Warstone Hill Rd. WV6: Patt . . . 2A 128
Warstone Rd. WV10: Shar . . . 2A 118
WV11: Ess . . . 2A 118
Warstones Gdns. WV4: Pen . . . 7K 129
Warstones Ho. WV4: Pen . . . 7K 129
WARTON . . . 1C 165
Warwick Av. ST3: Mei . . . 1B 42
ST5: N'tle . . . 5G 31
ST10: Chea . . . 5B 54
WV6: Per . . . 3G 129
Warwick Cl. DE14: B'ton . . . 4A 86
ST7: Kids . . . 4E 10
WS11: Cann . . . 3F 109
Warwick Dr. WV8: Cods . . . 1A 122
Warwick Gro. ST5: N'tle . . . 5J 23
Warwick Rd. B77: Amin . . . 5A 138
ST17: Staf . . . 6K 73
Warwick St. DE13: B Tre . . . 5D 84
ST1: H'ley . . . 5C 150 (5A 24)
ST5: C'ton . . . 1C 22
ST8: Bidd . . . 6C 8
Wasdale Rd. WS8: Clay . . . 6F 121
Washbrook La. WS11: N Can . . . 7J 109
Wash Dale La. ST15: Mea, Oul H . . . 6F 45
WASHERWALL . . . 4C 26 (3D 155)
Washerwall La. ST9: Werr . . . 3C 26
Washerwall St. ST2: Bent . . . 1K 33
Washington Cl. ST8: G Hea . . . 3C 8
Washington Dr. ST17: Staf . . . 6J 73
Washington St. ST6: Tuns . . . 4J 17
Wastwater Ct. WV6: Per . . . 2G 129
Watchfield Cl. ST3: Mei . . . 1B 42
Waterbeck Gro. ST4: Tren . . . 5C 40
Waterbridge La. WV5: Womb . . . 3E 144
Waterbrook Cl. ST19: Penk . . . 5G 91
Waterbrook Way WS11: Cann . . . 5E 108
Waterdale WV5: Womb . . . 5E 144
Waterdale Gro. ST3: Long . . . 6A 34
WATERFALL . . . 2A 156
Waterfall Cl. B77: Wiln . . . 4A 142
Waterfall Cotts. ST9: End . . . 1K 19
Waterfall La. ST10: Wat . . . 4B 52
Waterfield Ho. WV5: Womb . . . 3H 145
Waterford Ct. *ST16: Staf* . . . *1J 73*
(off Elworthy Clo.)
Watergate St. ST6: Tuns . . . 5G 17
(not continuous)
Waterglades Cl. ST1: H'ley. . . 6A 150 (6K 23)
WATERHAYS VILLAGE . . . 5A 16
Waterhead Cl. WV10: Bush . . . 3E 124
Waterhead Dr. WV10: Bush . . . 3E 124
Waterhead Rd. ST3: Mei . . . 1B 42
WATERHOUSES . . . 5B 52 (2A 156)
Watering Cl. ST5: B Gat . . . 6E 36
Watering Trough Bank CW3: Mad H . . . 1D 28
Waterlily Cl. ST1: H'ley . . . 7A 150 (6A 24)
WS12: Hed . . . 7A 102
Water Lily Gro. WS8: Brow . . . 5G 121
WATERLOO . . . 1D 157
Waterloo Blvd. WS12: Hed . . . 6A 102
Waterloo Ct. ST13: Lee . . . 4E 48
Waterloo Gro. ST7: Kids . . . 4E 10
Waterloo M. ST13: Lee . . . 4E 48
Waterloo Pk. ST14: Beam . . . 2C 62
Waterloo Rd. ST1: H'ley . . . 7A 18
ST6: B'lem . . . 1E 150 (7A 18)
Waterloo St. DE14: B Tre . . . 7D 84
ST1: H'ley . . . 4H 151 (5D 24)
ST13: Lee . . . 4E 48
Watermead Grange WS8: Brow . . . 5G 121
Watermeadow Gro.
ST1: H'ley . . . 6A 150 (6K 23)
Watermeet Gro. ST1: H'ley. . . 5A 150 (5K 23)
Watermill Cl. WV10: Ford . . . 2B 124
Watermills Cl. ST6: Nort . . . 5F 19
Watermills Rd. ST5: C'ton . . . 1A 22
Watermint Cl. WS12: Wimb . . . 6A 102
WATER ORTON . . . 2B 164
Waters Dr. B74: F Oak . . . 5J 135
Waters Edge ST1: H'ley . . . 2D 24
WS15: Hand . . . 4G 99
Watersedge Gro.
ST1: H'ley . . . 6A 150 (6K 23)
Waterside B78: Pole . . . 1J 143
DE15: Stap . . . 4F 87
WS15: Rug . . . 3H 97
Waterside Bus. Pk. WS15: Rug . . . 2J 97
Waterside Cl. CW3: Mad . . . 3A 28
WV10: Cove . . . 2C 116
Waterside Ct. B77: Amin . . . 4B 138
DE14: B Tre . . . 3A 86
ST20: Gno . . . 5G 67
Waterside Dr. ST3: Blur . . . 3E 40
Waterside Rd. DE15: Stap . . . 6D 86
Waterside Way WS8: Brow . . . 2E 120
WV9: P'ord . . . 2J 123
Watersmead Cl.
WS12: Wimb . . . 6A 102
Watersmeet Ct. ST15: Stone . . . 6J 47
Watersmeet Ho. B78: Faze . . . 2H 141
Water St. ST4: S Tren . . . 4A 32
ST5: C'ton . . . 5B 16
ST5: N'tle . . . 3G 153 (7G 23)
ST16: Staf . . . 3G 73
WS7: C Ter . . . 4G 111
WATERS UPTON . . . 3A 158
Waters Vw. WS3: Pels . . . 7D 120
Waterton Cl. DE13: Stre . . . 2H 85
Waterworld . . . 2A 150 (4K 23)
Watery La. CV9: B Ens . . . 7J 143
CW12: Ast . . . 1G 7
DE6: Ash . . . 4E 56
(not continuous)
DE6: Ash, C'ton . . . 5D 56
(not continuous)
ST3: Long . . . 1K 41
ST14: Beam . . . 1B 62
ST18: Hau . . . 7C 66
WS13: Chor, Gen . . . 6K 103
WS13: Curb, Lich . . . 6C 106
WV8: Cods . . . 1C 122
Watford St. ST4: S Tren . . . 1C 32
Watkins Rd. WV12: Will . . . 7C 126
Watkin St. ST4: Fen . . . 4D 32
Watkiss Dr. WS15: Rug . . . 7F 95
Watlands Av. ST5: N'tle . . . 3G 23
Watlands Rd. ST7: Big E . . . 5G 15
Watlands Vw. ST5: N'tle . . . 3F 23
Watling St. B77: T Gat, Wiln . . . 2K 141
B78: Dor . . . 4F 143
B78: Hin . . . 6A 136
CV9: Gren . . . 5J 143
WS7: M Cor . . . 1G 133
WS8: Brow . . . 2B 120
WS8: M Cor . . . 2K 121
WS11: Brow . . . 2B 120
WS11: Cann . . . 6F 109
(not continuous)
WS11: Cann, N Can, F Cro . . . 4A 108
(not continuous)
WS14: M Cor, Wall . . . 1K 133 & 1A 134
Watling St. Bus. Pk. WS11: Brow . . . 2C 120
Watson Cl. WS13: Frad . . . 1K 107
WS15: Rug . . . 5F 95

Watson Rd.—Wharfedale Wlk.

Watson Rd. ST4: T Val 5K 31
WV10: Ford 3K 123
Watson St. DE14: B Tre 3E 86
ST4: S Tren 1K 31
Wattfield WS15: Bre 5J 97
Wattles La. ST17: Act T 5K 77
Watt Pl. ST10: Chea 4C 54
Watts Cl. ST17: Staf 6D 72
Wat Tyler Cl. WS15: Rug 5F 95
Waveney B77: Wiln 2A 142
Waveney Av. WV6: Per 2F 129
Waveney Ct. ST5: N'tle 5F 31
Waveney Gro. ST5: N'tle 5F 31
WS11: Cann 2B 108
Waveney Wlk. Nth. ST6: Chel 3A 18
Waveney Wlk. Sth. ST6: Chel 3A 18
Wavenham Cl. B74: F Oak 3K 135
Waverley Gdns. WS15: Rug 6D 94
WV5: Womb 3H 145
Waverley La. DE14: B Tre 1C 86
Waverley Pl. ST5: N'tle 5E 30
Waverley Rd. WS3: Blox 3F 127
Waverley Wlk. WS14: Lich 5B 114
Waverton Rd. ST2: Bent 2A 34
Wayfield Dr. ST16: Staf 5F 71
Wayfield Gro. ST4: S Tren 5J 153 (1H 31)
Wayside WV8: P'ord 3G 123
Wayside Acres WV8: Cods 3B 122
Wayside Av. ST5: N'tle 4G 23
Wayside Dr. B74: L Ast 5H 135
Wayte St. ST1: H'ley 1E 150 (3B 24)
Wealden Hatch WV10: Bush 1C 124
Weatheroaks WS9: W Woo 7K 121
Weaver Cl. ST8: Bidd 4D 8
ST10: Chea 2D 54
Weaver Dr. ST17: Staf 6D 72
WEAVERHAM 1A 154
Weaverlake Dr. DE13: Yox 1G 89
Weaver Pl. ST5: N'tle 5F 31
Weaver Rd. ST14: Utt 3G 63
Weavers, The ST14: Dens 2B 58
WEAVERSLAKE 1H 89
Weavers La. ST15: Stone 6H 47
Weaver St. ST1: H'ley 3F 151 (4C 24)
Weavers Wlk. ST15: Swyn 2D 64
Weaving Gdns. WS11: Cann 2E 108
Webb Av. WV6: Per 1F 129
Webb Cl. WS13: Frad 4J 107
Webberley La. ST3: Long 6J 33
Webb St. ST3: Mei 6D 34
Webley Ri. WV10: Bush 1D 124
Webster Av. ST3: W Coy 4A 34
Webster St. ST5: N'tle 5G 153 (1G 31)
Webster Wlk. WS11: Cann 6G 101
WEDDINGTON 2D 165
Wedgewood Cl. DE15: Stap 3J 87
WS7: Burn 4A 112
WV5: Womb 3F 145
WEDGWOOD 6E 40
Wedgwood Av. ST5: N'tle 7A 152 (2D 30)
ST7: Big E 6H 15
ST15: Stone 6E 46
Wedgwood Ct. ST1: H'ley 4B 150 (5A 24)
Wedgwood Dr. ST12: Barl 7C 40
Wedgwood La. ST8: G Hea 3C 8
(not continuous)
ST12: Barl 6E 40
Wedgwood Pl. ST6: B'lem 7K 17
Wedgwood Rd. ST4: Fen 3F 33
ST7: T Pit 7B 10
ST10: Chea 6B 54
ST18: Hopt 5K 71
Wedgwoods Monument 4A 16
(Deans La.)
1B 32
(off Station Rd.)
Wedgwood Station (Rail) 7D 40
Wedgwood St. ST5: N'tle 3H 23
ST6: B'lem 4C 150 (7K 17)
Wedgwood Vis. Cen., The 6D 40
WEDNESBURY 2D 163
WEDNESFIELD 7H 125 (1D 163)
Wednesfield High Sports Cen. 7J 125
WEEFORD 1B 164
WEEPING CROSS 6C 74 (2D 159)
Weeping Cross ST17: Staf 7B 74
Weetman Cl. ST6: Gold 7G 11
Weighton Gro. ST2: Bent 7A 26
Weir Bank DE15: Stap 6F 87
Weir Gro. ST7: Kids 4F 11
Weirside DE6: May 6C 56
Welbeck Av. WV10: Bush 6B 124
Welbeck Pl. ST2: Buck 3J 25
Welbury Gdns. WV6: W'ton 7H 123
Welby St. ST4: Fen 4D 32
Welch St. ST4: S Tren 2B 32
Weldon Av. ST3: W Coy 5D 34
Welford Ri. DE13: B Tre 4B 84
Welford Rd. B77: Dost 5J 141
Welland Cl. DE15: Wins 6H 85
Welland Gro. ST5: N'tle 6E 30
Wellbury Cl. ST4: Tren 5C 40
Weller Cl. ST11: B Bri 7F 43
Weller St. ST4: S Tren 1K 31
Wellesbourne B79: Tam 1J 137
Wellesbourne Cl. WV3: W'ton 6J 129
Wellesley St. ST1: H'ley 7E 150 (6B 24)
Wellfield Cl. WS11: Cann 4B 108
Wellfield Rd. DE13: Alre 6C 130
ST2: Bent 6H 25
WELLINGTON 3A 158
Wellington Cl. ST16: Staf 1G 73
Wellington Ct. ST1: H'ley 3J 151 (4D 24)
ST13: Lee 4F 49
Wellington Cres. WS13: Fra P 6H 107
Wellington Dr. WS11: Cann 2B 108
WS15: Rug 1H 97
Wellington Pk. DE14: B'ton 3B 86
Wellington Rd. DE14: B Tre 7A 86
ST1: H'ley 3J 151 (4D 24)
ST7: Kids 4E 10
Wellington St. DE14: B Tre 1C 86
ST1: H'ley 4J 151 (5D 24)
ST5: N'tle 3G 23
ST13: Lee 3F 49
Wellington St. E. DE14: B Tre 1C 86
Wellington St. W. DE14: B Tre 1C 86
Wellington Ter. ST1: H'ley 4J 151 (5D 24)
Well La. ST8: G Hea 3C 8
WS3: Blox 6K 127
WS6: G Wyr 3G 119
Well Pl. WS3: Blox 5K 127
WELLSBOROUGH 1D 165
Wells Cl. ST8: Bidd 5D 8
WS11: Cann 5E 100
WS15: Rug 3E 96
WV6: Per 2E 128
Wells Dr. ST17: Staf 7C 74
WELLS GREEN 2A 154
Wells La. ST18: Brad 6C 68
Well St. ST1: H'ley 4H 151 (5D 24)
ST5: N'tle 4F 153 (1G 31)
ST7: M Cop 6H 7
ST8: Bidd 5C 8
ST10: Chea 4D 54
ST11: Fors 2J 43
ST13: Lee 4G 49
Wellyards Cl. ST18: West 3C 80
Welney Gdns. WV9: P'ord 2J 123
Welsh Cl. ST3: L'ood 1K 41
Welsh Row ST7: M Cop 6J 7
Wembley La. WS7: C Ter 3F 111
Wembury B77: Amin 4A 138
Wem Gdns. WV11: Wed 7H 125
Wem Gro. ST5: C'ton 5C 16
Wendell Crest WV10: Bush 1D 124
Wendling Cl. ST2: Bent 7K 25
Wendover Gro. ST2: B Hil 7H 25
Wendy Cl. ST2: B Hil 7H 25
Wenger Cres. ST4: Tren 3K 39
Wenham Dr. ST3: Mei 3D 42
Wenlock B77: Glas 6K 137
Wenlock Cl. ST5: C'ton 5C 16
ST6: Feg H 6B 12
WENSLEY 1C 157
Wensleydale Cl. ST1: H'ley 1D 24
Wentlows Av. ST10: Tea 2F 55
Wentlows Rd. ST10: Tea 2F 55
Wentworth Cl. WS7: Burn 4A 112
Wentworth Dr. DE13: Stre 2E 84
ST7: Kids 3G 11
ST16: Staf 3A 74
WS14: Lich 6D 114
Wentworth Gro. ST1: H'ley 1F 25
WV6: Per 1E 128
Wentworth Rd. WS3: Blox 1F 127
WV10: Bush 3C 124
Werburgh Dr. ST4: Tren 3K 39
WERETON 6F 15
Wereton Rd. ST7: Aud 6F 15
WERGS 7B 122 (1C 163)
Wergs Dr. WV6: Tett 6C 122
Wergs Hall Rd. WV6: Tett 4B 122
WV8: Cods 4B 122
Wergs Rd. WV6: Tett 7C 122
Werneth Gro. WS3: Blox 1G 127
WERRINGTON 5D 26 (3D 155)
Werrington Rd. ST2: Buck 5G 25
Wesker Pl. ST3: W Coy 5B 34
Wesleyan Rd. TF9: A'ley 3G 61
Wesley Av. WS6: C Hay 1D 118
WV8: Bilb 3D 122
Wesley Cl. WS7: C Ter 2H 111
WV5: Womb 5F 145
Wesley Ct. CW3: Bet 3B 6
WS11: Cann 2E 108
Wesley Dr. ST15: Stone 6J 47
Wesley Gdns. ST7: Kids 4E 10
Wesley Pl. ST5: N'tle 4A 152 (1D 30)
ST7: H End 1F 21
WS12: Hed 3J 101
Wesley Rd. WV8: Bilb 3D 122
WV12: Will 7C 126
Wesley St. ST6: Tuns 4H 17
ST7: Big E 6J 15
ST11: B Bri 3J 43
Wesley Way B77: Amin 5A 138
Wessenden B77: Wiln 3D 142
Wessex Cl. WS8: Brow 5H 121
Wessex Ct. B79: Shut 2H 139
Wessex Dr. ST4: Tren 2A 40
WS11: Cann 1F 109
WESSINGTON 2D 157
Westacre ST1: Buck 5F 25
Westacre Cres. WV3: W'ton 6J 129
West Av. ST4: S Tren 1K 31
ST5: N'tle 1J 153 (6H 23)
ST7: Talk 6A 10
WV11: Wed 7G 125
West Bank ST4: S Tren 3A 32
West Beeches WV9: Cove 2K 93
Westbeech Rd. WV6: Patt 6B 128
Westbourne Av. WS6: C Hay 7E 108
WS11: Cann 1D 108
Westbourne Cl. ST13: Lee 3D 48
Westbourne Cres. WS7: Burn 4K 111
Westbourne Dr. ST6: Tuns 2J 17
W. Brampton ST5: N'tle 2E 152 (7F 23)
Westbridge Pk. Sports Cen. 4G 47
WEST BROMWICH 2D 163
Westbrook Way WV5: Womb 5F 145
Westbury Cen., The ST5: N'tle 7F 31
Westbury Cl. ST1: H'ley 3F 25
Westbury Hayes ST17: Staf 6C 72
WESTBURY PARK 6F 31
Westbury Rd. ST5: N'tle 6F 31
W. Butts Rd. WS15: Rug 7D 94
W. Cannock Way WS12: Hed 1K 101
WEST CHADSMOOR 4C 100
WESTCLIFFE 1K 17
Westcliffe *ST13: Lee* *3E 48*
(off Alma St.)
Westcliffe Av. ST5: N'tle 6E 30
West Cl. ST15: Stone 5F 47
ST16: Staf 3J 73
W. Coppice Rd. WS8: Brow 4E 120
West Cres. ST1: H'ley 7E 18
WESTCROFT 4E 124
Westcroft Av. WV10: Bush 4E 124
Westcroft Rd. WV6: Tett 7B 122
West Dr. B78: M Oak 7E 136
ST13: Ched 3G 51
West End Av. ST13: Lee 4E 48
Westerby Dr. ST9: Werr 5C 26
Westerham Cl. ST4: Tren 3K 39
Westering Parkway WV10: Bush 1C 124
Western By-Pass WS13: Lich 2J 113
WESTERN DOWNS 6E 72
Western Rd. WS12: Hed 4H 101
Western Springs Rd.
WS15: Rug 6F 95
Western Vw. *WS15: Rug* *6F 95*
(off Frank Rogers Wlk.)
Westfield Av. ST7: Aud 6E 14
Westfield Dr. WV5: Womb 3F 145
Westfield Gro. WV3: W'ton 6K 129
Westfield Rd. DE13: B Tre 4C 84
ST2: Buck 5H 25
ST7: M Cop 6G 7
Westfields B78: Bir 2H 143
(Dexter Way)
B78: Bir 2F 143
(Green La.)
ST13: Lee 4G 49
Westfields Rd. WS15: Arm 5D 98
Westgate ST19: Brew 1D 92
WS12: Haz 4B 102
Westgate Cl. ST14: Roce 5E 58
WEST HAGLEY 3C 163
WEST HALLAM 3D 157
Westhall Cl. ST19: Brew 2D 92
Westhall Ga. WS3: Blox 3H 127
Westhead Av. ST16: Staf 2J 73
Westhead Wlk.
ST1: H'ley 5D 150 (5B 24)
WEST HILL 4H 101
West Hill ST14: Utt 7H 63
Westhill WV3: W'ton 4K 129
W. Hill Av. WS12: Hed 5H 101
Westhorpe ST17: Staf 5F 73
WESTLANDS 4E 30
Westlands ST7: Big E 5H 15
Westlands, The ST14: Dens 2B 58
Westlands Av. ST5: N'tle 7A 152 (2D 30)
Westlands Rd. ST14: Utt 7F 63
Westland St. ST4: P'ull 2A 32
Westleigh Rd. WV5: Womb 5F 145
Westmarsh Gro. ST6: Chel 3A 18
Westmead Rd. DE13: B Nee 6F 89
Westmill St. ST1: H'ley 7H 151 (6D 24)
Westminster Cl. ST17: Staf 6A 74
Westminster Dr. DE13: Stre 3E 84
Westminster Pl. ST4: H'ord 1A 40
Westminster Rd. ST13: Lee 2H 49
WS11: Cann 4E 100
Westmorland Av. ST7: Kids 7D 10
Westmorland Cl. B78: Tam 1G 141
ST6: Feg H 6A 12
WESTON
Macclesfield 1D 155
Crewe 2B 154
Much Wedlock 2A 162
Shrewsbury 2A 158
Stafford 2C 80 (2D 159)
Weston Bank ST18: Hopt, W Ban 7J 69
Weston Cl. ST2: Bent 5C 26
ST5: N'tle 5D 22
ST19: B Elm 6B 90
WS11: H Hay 2J 109
Weston Ct. ST3: W Coy 5C 34
WESTON COYNEY 5C 34 (3D 155)
Weston Coyney Rd.
ST3: Long, W Coy 6K 33
Weston Dr. ST3: W Coy 5C 34
WS6: G Wyr 4E 118
Westonfields Dr. ST3: Long 6A 34
WESTON HEATH 3B 158
WESTON IN ARDEN 3D 165
WESTON JONES 2B 158
WESTON-ON-TRENT 2D 161
Weston Pk. 3C 159
Weston Pk. Av. DE14: B Tre 4E 84
Weston Rd. ST3: Mei, W Coy 1C 42
ST16: Staf 3J 73
ST18: Staf 3J 73
WS13: Lich 2A 114
Weston St. ST3: Long 4K 33
ST13: Lee 3H 49
WESTON UNDER LIZARD 3C 159
WESTON UNDERWOOD 3C 157
Westonview Av. ST3: Long 3K 33
Westover Dr. ST15: Stone 5J 47
West Pde. ST4: Fen 4C 32
Westport Cres. WV11: Wed 7K 125
Westport Greenway ST6: Tuns 5J 17
(not continuous)
Westport Lake Pk. 6H 17
Westport Lake Rd. ST6: B'lem 6H 17
Westport Rd. ST6: B'lem 6J 17
West Pct. ST1: H'ley 4G 151 (5C 24)
Westsprink Cres. ST3: Long 7A 34
West St. B77: Tam 6J 137
B79: Tam 4J 137
DE15: Wins 1J 87
ST3: W Coy 4D 34
ST5: N'tle 4F 153 (1G 31)
(Newcastle-under-Lyme)
ST5: N'tle 1H 23
(Porthill)
ST5: Sil 7K 21
ST7: M Cop 7F 7
ST8: Bidd 6C 8
ST13: Lee 3F 49
WS3: Blox 6J 127
WS11: Cann 5E 108
West Ter. ST6: Feg H 1B 18
ST7: Kids 5E 10
West Vw. DE6: May 7C 56
ST3: R Clo 6B 42
ST5: N'tle 3F 23
ST14: Roce 5E 58
Westview Cl. ST13: Lee 3D 48
Westward Cl. ST14: Utt 4G 63
West Way ST14: Utt 4E 62
ST17: Staf 5E 72
W. Way Grn. ST17: Staf 6E 72
Westwick Cl. WS9: Ston 6H 133
West Winds WV10: Fea 5G 117
Westwood Cl. ST13: Ched 6G 51
Westwood Ct. ST1: H'ley 3J 151 (4D 24)
Westwood Dr. ST19: Penk 4H 91
Westwood Gro. ST13: Lee 3E 48
Westwood Heath Rd. ST13: Lee 4D 48
Westwood Pk. Av. ST13: Lee 4C 48
Westwood Pk. Dr. ST13: Lee 4C 48
Westwood Rd. ST3: Mei 7C 34
ST5: N'tle 2H 23
ST13: Lee 4D 48
Westwoods Hollow WS7: Burn 3K 111
Westwood Ter. *ST13: Lee* *3E 48*
(off Wellington St.)
Westwood Vw. ST13: Lee 4E 48
Wetenhall Dr. ST13: Lee 4C 48
Wetherall Cl. WS15: Rug 6F 95
Wetherby Cl. ST5: C'ton 1C 22
ST10: Chea 2D 54
WV10: Ford 1B 124
Wetherby Ct. DE14: B'ton 5A 86
Wetherby Rd. ST4: Tren 3B 40
WS3: Blox 1G 127
Wetherel Rd. DE15: Stap 2K 87
Wetley Av. ST9: Werr 4H 27
WETLEY MOOR 2B 26
WETLEY ROCKS 1K 27 (3D 155)
WETMORE 5G 85
Wetmore La. DE14: B Tre 5G 85
Wetmore Rd. DE14: B Tre 5F 85
(not continuous)
WETTENHALL 1A 154
WETTON 2B 156
WETWOOD 1B 158
Weybourne Av. ST2: Mil 4H 19
Weyhill Cl. WV9: P'ord 3H 123
Weymouth Dr. B74: F Oak 4K 135
Weymouth Ho. B79: Tam 5G 137
Whalley Av. ST4: S Tren 2J 31
WHARF, THE 4H 63
Wharf Cl. WS14: Lich 4C 114
Wharfe Cl. ST14: Utt 5H 63
Wharfedale Wlk. ST3: Long 6G 33

Wharf Ho.—Windmill Bank

Wharf Ho. *WS15: Rug* *7H 95*
(off Bryans La.)
Wharf La. CW12: More 1F 7
ST19: Brew 1B 92
WS7: Chas 1J 121
Wharf Pl. ST4: S Tren 2C 32
Wharf Rd. DE14: B Tre 6F 85
ST8: Bidd 5B 8
(not continuous)
ST20: Gno 5G 67
WS15: Rug 2G 97
Wharf Rd. Ind. Est. DE14: B Tre 6F 85
Wharf St. ST5: N'tle 3G 153 (7H 23)
Wharf Ter. CW3: Mad H 1D 28
Wharmadine La. TF9: A'ley 3J 61
WHARTON 1A 154
Wharwell La. WS6: G Wyr 3G 119
WHATELEY 7B 142 (2C 165)
Whateley La. B78: Hock 6B 142
B78: What 7B 142
Whateley Vs. B78: Pic 7C 142
Whatmore St. ST6: B'lem 6C 18
WHATSTANDWELL 2D 157
Wheat Breach Cl. DE13: B Tre 5C 84
WHEATCROFT 2D 157
Wheatcroft Cl. ST19: Penk 4G 91
WS7: Burn 6J 111
Wheatfields ST6: B'lem 4C 18
WHEATHILL 3A 162
Wheatlands, The WV6: Per 3E 128
Wheatlands Cl. WS12: H Hay 2J 109
Wheatlands Rd. DE15: Stap 5F 87
Wheatley Bank Cotts. ST2: Buck 5G 25
Wheatley Gro. WS6: G Wyr 2G 119
Wheatley La. DE15: Wins 7J 85
Wheatly Av. ST4: T Val 3J 31
WHEATON ASTON 2C 90 (3C 159)
Wheaton Cl. WV10: Oxl 6A 124
Wheatsheaf Rd. WV8: P'ord 4G 123
WHEATSTONE PARK 6D 92 (1C 163)
Wheel Av. WV8: Cods 2B 122
Wheel Ct., The WV8: Cods 2B 122
Wheeler Cl. WV8: Cods 7E 92
Wheeler Rd. WV11: Wed 5G 125
Wheelfield WV8: Cods 2B 122
Wheelhouse Rd. WS15: Rug 2J 97
Wheel La. ST10: Alt 5J 57
WS13: Lich 2K 113
WHEELOCK 2B 154
WHEELOCK HEATH 2B 154
Wheelock Way ST7: Kids 4F 11
Whernside Dr. WV6: W'ton 7J 123
Whetstone Grn. WV10: Bush 4B 124
Whetstone Gro. WV10: Bush 5B 124
Whetstone Rd. ST8: G Hea 3C 8
WV10: Bush 5B 124
Whieldon Cres. ST4: Fen 4D 32
Whieldon Ind. Est. ST4: Fen 3C 32
Whieldon Rd. ST4: Fen, S Tren 3C 32
Whilmot Cl. WV10: Fea 6F 117
Whimple Side ST2: B Hil 7H 25
Whimster Sq. ST17: Staf 6C 72
Whinyates Ri. WS11: Cann 3F 109
WHISTERFIELD 1C 155
Whistler Gro. WV10: Bush 5E 124
WHISTON
Penkridge 3C 159
Stoke-on-Trent 3A 156
Whiston Av. WV11: Wed 6A 126
Whiston Bank ST10: Frog 5K 53
WHISTON CROSS 1B 162
WHISTON EAVES 3A 156
WHITACRE HEATH 2C 165
Whitacre La. WS14: Lyn 3H 133
Whitaker Rd. ST3: Fen 6E 32
Whitbread Dr. ST8: Bidd 5E 8
Whitburn Cl. WV9: P'ord 3J 123
Whitby Cl. ST17: Staf 7E 72
WS3: Blox 2F 127
Whitby Way WS11: Cann 3C 108
WHITCHURCH 3A 154
Whitchurch Gro. ST5: C'ton 5C 16
Whitcliffe Pl. ST3: Fen 6F 33
Whitcombe Rd. ST3: Mei 7C 34
White Bark Cl. WS12: Hed 2G 101
Whitebeam Cl. ST5: C'ton 6B 16
WS8: Clay 6G 121
Whitebridge La. ST15: Stone 2E 46
Whitebridge La. Ind. Est.
ST15: Stone 2E 46
Whitebridge Way ST15: Stone 2E 46
White Farm Rd. B74: F Oak 3K 135
Whitefield Cl. WV8: Bilb 3D 122
Whitefields La. ST10: Wat 4C 52
WHITEGATE 1A 154
Whitegates CW12: White 1D 8
Whitehall WS13: Lich 3A 114
Whitehall Av. ST7: Kids 4D 10
Whitehall Rd. ST7: Kids 4D 10
White Harte Cvn. Pk. DY7: Kin 6E 148
Whitehaven Dr. ST1: H'ley . . . 1E 150 (3B 24)
Whitehead Rd. ST6: Chel 2B 18
WHITEHILL 3F 11
White Hill DY7: Kin 4C 148
Whitehill Rd. ST7: Kids 4E 10
Whitehill Ter. ST7: Kids 4F 11
White Hollies WS3: Pels 7B 120
White Horse Rd. WS8: Brow 2G 121
Whitehouse Av. WV3: W'ton 6K 129
WV11: Wed 6K 125
Whitehouse Ct. WS11: Cann 5E 108
Whitehouse Cres. WS7: Burn 4K 111
WV11: Wed 4K 125
Whitehouse Dr. WS13: Lich 5K 113
Whitehouse La. DY3: Stou, Swin 2F 147
ST15: Holly 7F 59
WV8: Cods, C Woo 5B 92
Whitehouse Rd. B78: Dor 3H 143
ST2: A Hul 3G 25
ST5: N'tle 5F 23
Whitehouse Rd. Nth. ST5: N'tle 4F 23
White Ho's. La. WV10: Fea 6E 116
(not continuous)
White Lion St. ST17: Staf 4G 73
Whitemill La. ST15: Stone 5F 47
White Oak Dr. WV3: W'ton 6K 129
White Oaks ST17: Wild 2A 78
Whiteoaks Dr. ST19: B Elm 6B 90
Whiteridge Rd. ST7: Kids 4E 10
White Row WV5: Trys 1C 144
Whitesands Cl. B77: Amin 4A 138
Whitesands Gro. ST3: Mei 4D 42
Whitestone Rd. ST3: Mei 4D 42
Whites Wood WV5: Womb 5G 145
Whitesytch La.
ST15: Hild, Stone 7F 59
Whitethorn Av. ST12: Barl 2D 44
Whitethorn Cl. WS12: Hed 2G 101
Whitethorn Way ST5: C'ton 6C 16
WHITFIELD 1D 18
Whitfield Av. ST5: N'tle 7B 152 (1E 30)
Whitfield Greenway ST6: Chel 2K 17
(not continuous)
ST6: Tuns 4K 17
Whitfield Rd. ST6: B Gre 7D 12
ST7: Kids 4F 11
WS12: Hed 3J 101
Whitfield St. ST13: Lee 5F 49
Whitfield Vs. ST6: B Gre 1D 18
WHITGREAVE 1B 70 (2C 159)
Whitgreave Av. WV10: Bush 5C 124
WV10: Fea 5F 117
Whitgreave Ct. ST16: Staf 1F 73
WV10: Fea 6F 117
Whitgreave La. ST18: Gt Bri 5H 65
ST18: W'ave 1C 70
WS15: Rug 3G 97
Whiting B77: T Gat 4K 141
Whitley Av. B77: Amin 4A 138
Whitley Cl. WV6: Tett 4J 129
WHITLEY HEATH 2C 159
Whitley Rd. ST6: B Gre 1D 18
WHITLOCK'S END 3B 164
WHITMORE 3J 37 (3C 155)
Whitmore Av. ST9: Werr 4D 26
Whitmore Hall 3J 37
Whitmore Rd. ST4: N'tle, Tren 2G 39
ST5: Butt, N'tle 2F 39
ST5: Butt, Whit, N'tle . . . 7B 152 (3J 37)
Whitmore St. ST1: H'ley 6C 150 (6A 24)
Whitridge Gro. ST2: Bent 1K 33
Whittamore La. ST18: Penk 1F 91
Whittingham Dr. ST17: Staf 6D 72
Whittingham Gro. WV11: Wed 7K 125
WHITTINGTON
Atherstone 2C 165
Lichfield 2G 131 (1B 164)
Stourbridge 7H 149 (3C 163)
WHITTINGTON BARRACKS
. . . . 7K 115 (1B 164)
Whittington Comn. Rd.
WS14: W'ton 6G 115
Whittington Hall La. DY7: Kin 7H 149
Whittington Ho. *WS13: Lich* *2E 114*
(off Hobs Rd.)
Whittle Ct. ST1: H'ley 1H 151 (3D 24)
WHITTLEFORD 2D 165
Whittle Ri. ST18: Staf 1A 74
Whittle Rd. ST3: Mei 2D 42
WHITWICK 3D 161
Whitworth La. WS15: Rug 6D 94
WHOBERLEY 3C 165
Whygate Gro. ST1: H'ley 2F 25
Whytmore, The WS13: Lich 6K 113
Wickenstones Ct. ST8: Bidd 6D 8
Wicket La. DY7: Stou 1J 149
Wickets, The DE15: Stap 4G 87
Wickham Gdns. WV11: Wed 7F 125
Wickstead Row CW3: Bet 2B 6
Widecombe Av. ST17: Staf 7C 74
Widecombe Rd. ST1: H'ley 2F 25
Widgeon Gro. WV10: Fea 5F 117
Wigford Rd. B77: Dost 5J 141
Wiggin Ho. WS3: Blox 2J 127
WIGGINTON 1C 165 (1H 137)
Wigginton Rd. B79: Tam 2H 137
Wightman Cl. WS14: Lich 5E 114
WIGHTWICK 5J 129 (2C 163)
Wightwick Bank WV6: Tett 5H 129
Wightwick Cl. WS3: Blox 4H 127
Wightwick Ct. WV6: Tett 4H 129
Wightwick Gro. WV6: Tett 4H 129
Wightwick Hall Rd. WV6: Tett 5F 129
Wightwick Leys WV6: Tett 4G 129
Wightwick Manor 5G 129
Wigley Bank Rd. DY7: Kin 3A 148
Wigmore Pl. ST3: Long 3J 33
Wignall Rd. ST6: Sandy 1H 17
Wilbraham's Wlk. ST7: Aud 5F 15
Wilcox Av. WS12: Hed 3H 101
WILDBOARCLOUGH 1D 155
Wildfowl Wlk. ST5: B Gat 6E 36
Wild Goose Av. ST7: Kids 3H 11
Wilding Rd. ST6: B Gre 1D 18
Wildlife Foundation Trust 3A 156
Wildside Activity Cen. 7H 123
Wildtree Av. WV10: Bush 3E 124
WILDWOOD 7A 74 (2D 159)
Wildwood Dr. ST17: Wild 7A 74
Wildwood Ga. ST17: Wild 1B 78
Wildwood Lawns ST17: Wild 7A 74
Wildwood Shop. Cen. *ST17: Wild 1B 78*
(off Wildwood Ga.)
Wileman Pl. ST4: Fen 3E 32
Wileman St. ST4: Fen 3E 32
Wilfred Pl. ST4: S Tren 1J 31
WILKESLEY 3A 154
Wilkes Rd. WV8: Cods 1B 122
Wilke's Wood ST18: Staf 5B 70
Wilkin, The WS8: Brow 2E 120
Wilkin Rd. WS8: Brow 2E 120
Wilkins Cft. DE13: Alre 6B 130
Wilkins Ho. ST13: Ched 2G 51
WS3: Blox 4G 127
(off Sandbank)
Wilkinson Cl. WS7: Burn 3K 111
Wilkinson St. ST6: Tuns 5H 17
Wilks St. ST6: Tuns 3J 17
WILLASTON 2A 154
Willatt Pl. ST2: Mil 6G 19
Willcock Rd. DE14: B'ton 5B 86
Willdale Gro. ST1: H'ley 3F 25
WILLENHALL
Coventry 3D 165
Willenhall 2D 163
Willenhall La. WS2: Wals 6F 127
WS3: Blox 6F 127
Willenhall La. Ind. Est.
WS3: Blox 5G 127
Willerby Fold WV10: Bush 1D 124
Willeton St. ST2: Buck 5G 25
Willett Av. WS7: Chas 6G 111
WILLEY 2A 162
Willey La. ST20: Gno 4G 67
Willfield La. ST6: B Edg 7H 13
ST9: S Broo 7H 13
William Av. ST3: Mei 2E 42
ST8: Bidd 6D 8
William Bentley Ct.
WV11: Wed 7G 125
William Birch Ct. ST2: Buck 7G 25
William Birch Rd. ST2: Buck 7G 25
William Cl. ST11: Fors 3K 43
William Clowes St. ST6: B'lem 7K 17
William Coltman Way ST6: Tuns 2G 17
William Fiske Ct. ST4: T Val 5J 31
William Morris Ct. WS15: Rug 5F 95
William Morris Gro.
WS11: Cann 6E 100
William Rd. DE13: Alre 5C 130
ST7: Kids 4E 10
William Ruston Rd. ST6: B'lem 5D 18
Williams Av. WS13: Frad 4J 107
Williams Cl. ST16: Staf 3D 72
WV12: Will 7C 126
Williams Ct. ST16: Staf 6H 71
Williamson Av. ST6: B Gre 1D 18
WS12: Haz 6E 102
Williamson St. ST6: Tuns 5J 17
William St. DE14: B Tre 6D 84
ST4: Fen 3E 32
Williams Wlk. ST15: Swyn 2D 64
William Ter. ST6: Feg H 1B 18
William Tolson's Ind. Est.
B78: Faze 2G 141
William Wiggin Av. WS3: Blox 3H 127
WILLINGTON 2C 161
Willington Rd. B79: Tam 2H 137
Willisford Av. ST14: Utt 6J 63
Willmer Cres. ST7: M Cop 7F 7
Willotts Hill Rd. ST5: C'ton 6B 16
WILLOUGHBRIDGE 3B 154
Willoughby Cl. ST19: Penk 5H 91
Willoughby Ct. ST14: Bram 6B 62
Willoughby Rd. B79: Tam 2E 136
Willoughby St. ST6: Gold 7H 11
Willow Av. WS7: Burn 5A 112
WV11: Wed 5E 124
Willow Bank WV3: W'ton 5K 129
Willowbank B78: Tam 1H 141
Willow Bottom La. B79: Elf 7J 131
Willowbrook ST18: Derr 4A 72
Willowbrook Dr. ST6: Nort 6E 18
Willowbrook Farm (Camping & Cvn. Site)
DE13: Alre 4E 130
Willowbrook Wlk. ST6: Nort 6F 19
Willow Cl. ST5: C'ton 6B 16
ST7: Kids 7E 10
ST10: Tea 2F 55
ST17: Walt 1D 78
ST19: Penk 5H 91
WS13: Frad 1K 107
WV9: Cove 2K 93
Willow Ct. WS14: Lich 6C 114
Willowcroft ST20: W'ves 3E 66
Willowcroft Ri. ST11: B Bri 2E 42
Willowcroft Way ST7: Harr 2J 11
Willow Dale ST15: Aston 2H 69
Willowdale Av. ST4: Fen 4C 32
Willowdale Grange WV6: Tett 7G 123
Willow Dr. ST13: Ched 2G 51
WV8: Bilb 2D 122
Willowfield Ct. ST4: Tren 3C 40
Willowfield Dr. ST4: Tren 3C 40
Willow Gro. ST3: Blur 7E 32
WV11: Ess 2B 126
Willowherb Cl. WS11: H Hay 1J 109
Willow La. ST3: M Hea 7C 42
Willowmoor ST17: Staf 2G 77
Willowood Gro. ST3: Mei 1E 42
Willow Pl. DE15: Stap 5F 87
ST8: Bid M 4H 9
Willow Rd. DE13: B Nee 6G 89
DY7: Kin 6G 149
ST15: Stone 5H 47
Willow Row ST3: Long 6H 33
Willows, The CW3: Wrin 5B 6
DE14: B Tre 2E 86
(off Orchard Pk.)
ST13: Lee 4D 48
ST15: Stone 6H 47
ST15: Yarn 6C 64
WS11: Cann 2C 108
WS15: Bre 4J 97
WV5: Womb 5F 145
Willows Dr. ST3: M Hea 6C 42
Willowsmere Dr. WS14: Lich 4F 115
Willow Tree Cl. WS13: Lich 1B 114
Willow Tree Gro. ST4: Fen 4E 32
Willow Wlk. ST15: Stone 5H 47
WS12: Hun 2D 100
Willow Way ST11: Fors 2J 43
WILLSLOCK 1A 160
Wilmore Ct. ST18: Hopt 6G 69
Wilmore Hill La. ST18: Hopt 6F 69
Wilmot Cl. ST5: N'tle 5D 22
Wilmot Dr. ST5: N'tle 5D 22
Wilmot Gro. ST3: Fen 3J 33
Wilmott Cl. WS13: Lich 4K 113
WILNECOTE 3A 142 (1C 165)
Wilnecote La. B77: Wiln 7J 137
(not continuous)
Wilnecote Leisure Cen. 4B 142
Wilnecote Station (Rail) 3K 141
Wilner's Vw. WS3: Pels 7B 120
Wilson Gro. WS11: H Hay 1J 109
Wilson Keys Ct. WS15: Rug 6G 95
Wilson Rd. ST4: H'ord 1K 39
Wilson St. ST5: N'tle 2E 152 (7F 23)
ST6: B'lem 5B 18
Wilson Way ST6: Gold 7G 11
Wiltell Rd. WS14: Lich 5B 114
Wiltell Rd. Ind. Est. *WS14: Lich 5B 114*
(off Wiltell Rd.)
Wilton Av. ST9: Werr 4H 27
Wilton St. ST5: N'tle 6E 22
Wiltshire Gro. ST5: N'tle 5G 31
Wimberry Dr. ST5: C'ton 6B 16
WIMBLEBURY 7B 102 (3A 160)
Wimblebury Rd.
WS12: H Hay, Wimb 2B 110
WS12: Hed, Wimb 6B 102
Wimborne Av. ST3: Blur 3F 41
Wimborne Rd. WV10: W'ton 7E 124
Wimhurst Mdw. WV10: Bush 1D 124
Winceby Rd. WV6: Per 3G 129
Winchcombe Dr. DE15: Stap 3J 87
Winchester Av. ST2: Bent 6J 25
Winchester Cl. WS13: Lich 7C 106
WS15: Hand 5F 99
Winchester Ct. ST17: Wild 1A 78
Winchester Dr. DE14: B Tre 4D 86
ST5: N'tle 5D 30
Winchester Rd. B78: Tam 6F 137
WS11: Cann 7G 101
WV10: Ford 2A 124
WINCLE 1D 155
Wincote Dr. WV6: Tett 2K 129
Windermere B77: Wiln 3C 142
Windermere Ho. ST16: Staf 3H 73
Windermere Pl. WS11: Cann 2E 108
Windermere Rd. ST5: N'tle 5F 31
WV6: Tett 5F 123
Windermere St. ST1: H'ley 3B 24
Windermere Way ST10: Chea 3E 54
Windings, The WS13: Lich 2A 114
WINDLEY 3D 157
Windmill Av. ST7: Kids 6E 10
Windmill Bank WS15: Gen 5J 103
WV5: Womb 3G 145

Windmill Cl.—Wood St.

Windmill Cl. B79: Tam 1G 137
ST3: R Clo 6B 42
ST14: Utt 4G 63
WS13: Lich 1K 113
Windmill Cres. WV3: W'ton 5H 129
Windmill Dr. ST14: Mar 1C 82
Windmill Hill ST3: R Clo 6B 42
Windmill La. WS13: Lich 1A 114
WS14: W'ton 3G 131
WS15: Gen 6J 103
WV3: W'ton 5H 129
Windmill St. ST1: H'ley 2H 151 (4D 24)
Windmill Vw. ST9: Werr 4E 26
Windrow, The WV6: Per 2E 128
Windrush Cl. ST4: Tren 5C 40
Windrush Rd. WS11: Cann 4E 100
Windsmoor St. ST4: S Tren 4B 32
Windsor ST5: N'tle 5F 153
Windsor Av. ST3: Long 7K 33
WS12: Hed 4H 101
Windsor Cl. B79: Tam 2J 137
ST15: Stone 7F 47
WS7: C Ter 2G 111
WS15: Rug 2F 97
Windsor Ct. WS12: Hed 4H 101
WS14: Lich 5B 114
Windsor Cres. DY7: Kin 5D 148
Windsor Dr. DE15: Stap 3G 87
ST13: Lee 2J 49
Windsor Gdns. WV3: W'ton 7H 129
WV8: Cods 2B 122
Windsor Holloway DY7: Kin 7F 149
Windsor Ind. Est. DE14: B Tre 6F 85
Windsor Rd. B78: Pole 6J 139
ST4: H'ord 1A 40
ST14: Utt 4F 63
ST17: Staf 7K 73
WS6: C Hay 7E 108
WV5: Womb 4F 145
WV6: Patt 7B 128
Windsor St. ST5: N'tle 3F 153 (7G 23)
Windy Arbour ST10: Chea 3D 54
Windy Arbour La. WV10 1J 117
Windycote La. ST10: Dilh 6J 27
WINDYHARBOUR 1C 155
Windyridge SK17: L'nor 3C 52
Wingate Ct. B74: F Oak 4K 135
Wingate Wlk. ST3: Blur 3F 41
WINGERWORTH 1D 157
WINGFIELD PARK 2D 157
Wingfoot Av. WV10: Bush 5C 124
Winghay Cl. ST6: B'lem 7G 17
Winghay Pl. ST6: Chel 2B 18
Winghay Rd. ST7: Kids 4F 11
Winghouse La.
ST12: Sandy, Titt 2A 44
Wingrove Av. ST3: Long 1K 41
Winifred Gdns. ST3: Blur 2E 40
Winifred St. ST1: H'ley 1E 150 (3B 24)
WINKHILL 2A 156
WINNINGTON 1B 60 (1B 158)
Winnipeg Cl. ST4: Tren 2B 40
WINNOTHDALE 1K 55 (3A 156)
Winpenny Rd. ST5: C'ton 7D 16
WINSFORD 1A 154
Winsford Av. ST3: Long 7A 34
Winsford Cres. ST17: Staf 1C 78
WINSHILL 1J 87 (2C 161)
Winslow Grn. ST2: Bent 7J 25
WINSON GREEN 3A 164
Winstanley Cl. WS15: Rug 6F 95
Winstanley Pl. WS15: Rug 6F 95
WINSTER 1C 157
Winston Pl. ST2: Buck 5G 25
Winston Rd. DY3: Swin 1J 147
Winston Ter. ST5: N'tle 2G 23
Winterbourne Gro. ST3: Long 6A 34
Winter Cl. WS13: Lich 1D 114
Winterfield La. ST3: W Coy 1D 34
WINTERLEY 2B 154
Winterside Cl. ST5: C'ton 6B 16
Wintonfield St. ST4: S Tren 2C 32
Winton Sq. ST4: S Tren 1B 32
WIRKSWORTH 2C 157
WIRSWALL 3A 154
Wiscombe Av.
ST19: Penk 3H 91
Wise St. ST3: Long 1J 41
WISHAW 2B 164
Wissage Ct. WS13: Lich 3D 114
Wissage Cft. WS13: Lich 2C 114
Wissage La. WS13: Lich 3D 114
Wissage Rd. WS13: Lich 2C 114
WISTANSWICK 2A 158
WISTASTON 2A 154
Wisteria Dr. WS8: Brow 2E 120
Wistwood Hayes WV10: Bush 1D 124
Witchford Cres. ST3: Blur 3F 41
Witham Way ST8: Bidd 4E 8
WITHERLEY 2D 165
Withers Rd. WV8: Bilb 2D 122
Withies Rd. ST4: T Val 5J 31
WITHINGTON
Shrewsbury 3A 158
Uttoxeter 1A 160
WITHINGTON GREEN 1C 155
Withington Rd. ST6: Feg H 7A 12
Within La. ST18: Hopt 5F 69
Withnell Grn. ST6: Feg H 7A 12
WITHYBROOK 3D 165
Withymere La.
WV5: Womb 2J 145
WITHYSAKES 4F 27
Withystakes Rd. ST9: Werr 4F 27
Withywood Cl. WV12: Will 4C 126
Witley Dr. WS13: Lich 3E 114
Witney Cl. B79: Tam 2F 137
Witney Gro. WV10: Ford 2K 123
Witney Rd. ST17: Staf 5B 74
Witney Wlk. ST3: Blur 3F 41
WIXHILL 2A 158
Wobaston Rd. WV9: P'ord 2F 123
WV10: Ford 1H 123
Woburn B77: Glas 6K 137
Woburn Av. WV12: Will 7B 126
Woburn Cl. ST4: Tren 5C 40
Wodehouse Cl. WV5: Womb 4E 144
Wodehouse La. DY3: Sed 2J 145
WV5: Womb 2J 145
Woden Av. WV11: Wed 7G 125
Woden Cl. WV5: Womb 3F 145
Woden Cres. WV11: Wed 7G 125
Woden Way WV11: Wed 7G 125
Wogan St. ST16: Staf 1G 73
Wolfe St. ST4: S Tren 3B 32
WOLGARSTON 3K 91 (3D 159)
Wolgarston Way ST19: Penk 5H 91
WOLLASTON 3C 163
Wollaston Cres. WV11: Wed 7H 125
WOLLERTON 1A 158
WOLLESCOTE 3D 163
Wolmer Rd. WV11: Wed 3K 125
Wolseley B77: Glas 7B 138
Wolseley Bank WV10: Bush 6D 124
WOLSELEY BRIDGE 3D 94 (2A 160)
Wolseley Cen., The 3C 94
Wolseley Cl. ST17: Colw 7K 81
WV10: Bush 6D 124
Wolseley Ct. Bus. Cen.
ST18: Staf 1B 74
Wolseley Ga. WV10: Bush 6D 124
Wolseley Rd. ST4: T Val 5K 31
ST5: N'tle 3F 23
ST16: Staf 3A 74
WS15: Rug 7A 94
(Stafford Brook Rd.)
WS15: Rug 5F 95
(Western Spring Rd.)
Wolsey Rd. WS13: Lich 1K 113
WOLSTANTON 3H 23 (3C 155)
Wolstanton Retail Pk. ST5: N'tle 3H 23
Wolstanton Rd. ST5: C'ton 2D 22
Wolstern Rd. ST3: Long 4K 33
WOLVERHAMPTON 2D 163
WOLVERHAMPTON AIRPORT 6E 146
Wolverhampton Cricket Ground 7E 122
Wolverhampton Race Course 7J 123
Wolverhampton Rd. ST17: Staf 5G 73
ST19: Penk 6F 91
WS3: Blox 4H 127
WS3: Pels 7B 120
WS6: C Hay 3B 118
WS11: Cann 6B 108
(not continuous)
WV6: Patt 6B 128 & 3A 128
WV8: Cods 1B 122
(not continuous)
WV10: Shar 2K 117
(Saredon Rd., not continuous)
WV10: Shar 3B 118
(Warstone Rd.)
WV11: Ess 2K 125
Wolverhampton Science Pk.
WV10: W'ton 7A 124
Wolverhampton Sports Arena 7J 123
Wolverhamton Rd. DY7: Stou 2J 149
WOLVERLEY 3C 163
WOLVEY 3D 165
WOLVEY HEATH 3D 165
WOMBOURNE 5F 145 (2C 163)
Wombourne Ent. Pk.
WV5: Womb 5D 144
Wombourne Leisure Cen. 3F 145
Wombourne Pk. WV5: Womb 5F 145
Wombourne Rd. DY3: Swin 1J 147
Wombrook Bus. Cen.
WV5: Womb 4E 144
Wombrook Dale WV5: Womb 4D 144
Wood, The ST3: Mei 7D 34
Woodall St. ST1: H'ley 3B 24
WS3: Blox 4J 127
(not continuous)
Wood Av. ST10: K'ley 6F 53
WV9: Cove 1K 93
WV11: Wed 7H 125
WOOD BANK 2J 91
Woodbank La. ST19: Penk 2J 91
Wood Bank Rd. WV3: W'ton 6H 129
Woodbank St. ST6: B'lem 7K 17
Woodberry Av. ST4: T Val 4J 31
Woodberry Cl. *ST4: T Val 4K 31*
(off Woodberry Av.)
ST17: Staf 3H 77
Woodbine Cl. DE14: B'ton 7A 86
Woodbridge Cl. WS3: Blox 2G 127
Woodbridge Rd. ST5: N'tle 7F 31
Woodburn Rd. ST6: Nort 5E 18
Woodcock Gdns.
WV10: Fea 5F 117
WOODCOCK HEATH 2A 160
Woodcock La. ST7: M Cop 7G 7
Woodcock Rd. WS15: Rug 7E 94
Wood Comn. Grange
WS3: Pels 7B 120
WOODCOTE 3B 158
Woodcote, The ST17: Wild 7A 74
Woodcote Rd. WV6: Tett 2K 129
Wood Cotts. ST9: End 2A 50
Wood Ct. DE14: B Tre 3D 86
Wood Cres. ST15: Stone 7F 47
ST16: Staf 7D 70
WOODCROFT 5D 48
Woodcroft ST7: Big E 6J 15
Woodcroft Av. B79: Tam 3H 137
ST13: Lee 5E 48
Woodcroft Rd. ST13: Lee 5E 48
WOOD EATON 2B 68 (3C 159)
Wood Eaton Rd. ST20: C Eat 3B 68
WOODEND 2B 160
WOOD END
Atherstone 2C 165
Coventry 3C 165
Wolverhampton 7G 125
Wood End La.
WS13: Curb, Frad, Fra P, Elm 2K 105
Woodend Pl. WV6: Tett 2J 129
Wood End Rd. WV11: Wed 5G 125
Woodend St. ST4: Fen 3F 33
Woodfield Cl. WS11: N Can 4B 110
Woodfield Ct. ST13: Lee 3H 49
Woodfield Dr. WS11: N Can 4B 110
Woodfields Dr. WS14: Lich 5E 114
Woodford Cl. WV9: P'ord 3H 123
Woodford Cres. WS7: Burn 4K 111
Woodford End WS11: Cann 6F 101
Woodford La.
WV5: Trys, Womb 2C 144
Woodford Way WS12: H Hay 2J 109
WV5: Womb 4D 144
WOODGATE 3D 163
WOOD GATE 6A 82
WOODGATE 7K 63
Woodgate St. ST3: Mei 1C 42
Wood Grn. WS6: C Hay 6E 108
Woodhall Ho. *WS3: Blox 5J 127*
(off Woodhall St.)
Woodhall Pl. ST5: Sil 6H 21
Woodhall Rd. ST7: Kids 3G 11
Woodhaven ST20: W'ves 3E 66
WS11: Cann 6B 108
WOOD HAYES 5G 125 (1D 163)
Wood Hayes Cft. WV10: Bush 3G 125
Wood Hayes Rd. WV10: Bush 3F 125
WV11: Wed 3F 125
Woodhead Rd. ST2: A Hul 1H 25
Woodhead Yd. ST10: Chea 2D 54
Woodheyes Lawns WS15: Rug 7E 94
WOODHILL 3B 162
Woodhill Cl. WV5: Womb 4F 145
Wood Hill Dr. WV5: Womb 5F 145
WOODHOUSE FIELDS 6A 58
Woodhouse La. B77: Amin 4C 138
ST6: B Gre, B Edg 1E 18
ST8: Bidd 3D 8
ST18: Hau 5A 66
ST20: Gno 7H 67
Woodhouse Rd. WV6: Tett 2J 129
Woodhouse Rd. Nth. WV6: Tett 2J 129
WOODHOUSES
Buton upon Trent 2K 89 (3B 160)
Burntwood 4E 112
Woodhouses La. WS7: Burn 5C 112
Woodhouse Sports Cen. 5B 138
Woodhouses Rd. WS7: Burn 4E 112
Woodhouse St. ST4: S Tren 3B 32
Woodhurst Cl. B77: Amin 4B 138
Woodingdean Av. ST3: Long 4K 33
Woodings Yd. *ST17: Staf 4G 73*
(off Bailey St.)
Woodkirk Cl. ST6: Feg H 6A 12
Woodland Av. ST5: N'tle 3G 23
ST6: Nort 3F 19
WV6: Tett 3J 129
Woodland Cl. ST13: Lee 7G 49
WS12: Hed 2H 101
WV12: Will 7D 126
Woodland Ct. WS12: Hun 6C 100
Woodland Dr. ST14: Roce 5D 58
WS6: C Hay 7E 108
Woodland Gro. ST6: B'lem 5B 18
Woodland Hills CW3: Mad 7A 20
Woodland Rd. B77: Amin 6C 138
DE15: Stan 6H 87
WV3: W'ton 7K 129
Woodlands ST1: H'ley 1A 150 (3K 23)
Woodlands, The ST4: T Val 5J 31
ST15: Cold M 6A 64
WS13: Lich 3D 114
WV8: Cods 3C 122
Woodlands Av. ST7: Talk 4B 10
ST15: Stone 4E 46
Woodlands Cen., The WV12: Will 6E 126
Woodlands Cl. B78: Dor 5J 143
ST15: Stone 4E 46
ST16: Staf 6E 70
Woodlands Cres. WS3: Pels 7B 120
Woodlands Dr. ST15: Aston 2H 69
WV9: Cove 1K 93
Woodlands Gro. ST3: M Hea 6C 42
Woodlands La. ST11: B Bri 5K 43
Woodlands Rd. ST4: T Val 5J 31
ST16: Staf 6D 70
WV5: Womb 5G 145
Woodlands Ter. B78: Dor 5J 143
Woodland St. ST6: Tuns 4J 17
ST8: Bidd 6D 8
Woodlands Views ST14: Mar 2C 82
Woodlands Way WS15: Hand 5G 99
Woodland Way B78: Bir 2H 143
WS7: Burn 5J 111
WOODLANE
Burton upon Trent 2B 160
Market Drayton 2A 158
WOOD LANE 6J 15
Wood La. DE6: D Cla 7A 82
DE13: H'ury 7D 82
ST5: Blac 7A 36
ST14: Utt 7J 63
ST15: Stone 7F 47
WS3: Pels 7B 120
WS11: Cann 5A 108
WS12: Hed 6J 101
WV10: Ford 4B 124
WV12: Will 6E 126
Wood La. Cl. WV12: Will 6E 126
Woodleighton Gro. ST14: Utt 7H 63
Woodleyes Cres. ST17: Wild 1B 78
Woodman La. WS6: C Hay 7E 108
Woodman St. ST2: Mil 6H 19
WOODMILL 2B 160
Woodmill La. WS15: Abb B 1C 88
Woodpark La. ST3: L'ood 4J 41
Woodpecker Dr. ST7: Pack 6J 11
Woodpecker Vw. TF9: Logg 6C 60
Woodpecker Way WS11: H Hay 7J 101
Woodpigeon Dr. WS11: H Hay 2G 109
Wood Pl. ST3: Mei 7D 34
Wood Ridings WS13: Lich 2A 114
Wood Rd. WV5: Womb 2H 145
WV6: Tett 3J 129
WV8: Cods 7D 92
Woodrow Way ST5: C'ton 6C 16
TF9: A'ley 4J 61
Woodruff Cl. ST7: Pack 5K 11
Woods Ct. B77: Tam 6J 137
Woods Cft. WS13: Lich 2A 114
WOODSEAT 6B 58
Woodseat Gro. ST14: Roce 4E 58
WOODSEAVES
Market Drayton 1A 158
Stafford 3D 66 (2B 158)
Woodseaves Cutting 2B 158
Woodshoot Av.
WS15: Hand 5G 99
WOODSHUTTS 5C 10
Woodshutts St. ST7: Talk 5B 10
WOODSIDE 3D 157
Wood Side WV11: Wed 5A 126
Woodside B74: F Oak 6K 135
CW3: Mad 2A 28
ST5: B Gat 6E 36
ST7: C Law 2C 10
ST13: Lee 6G 49
Woodside Av. ST6: B Edg 1H 19
ST7: Kids 5E 10
Woodside Cl. ST18: L Hay 6J 81
Woodside Cotts.
ST10: O'moor 2A 56
Woodside Cres. ST5: N'tle 7G 31
Woodside Dr. B74: L Ast 3H 135
ST3: M Hea 6C 42
Woodside Gro. WV8: Bilb 2D 122
Woodside La. ST13: Lee 7D 48
Woodside Pl. ST2: Mil 6H 19
WS11: Cann 5E 100
Woodside Vs. ST3: Long 5K 33
Woodside Way WV12: Will 6E 126
Woods La. DE15: Stap 4G 87
(not continuous)
WOODSTOCK 7E 10
Woodstock Cl. ST5: N'tle 5G 23
Woodstock Dr. B74: F Oak 4J 135
WS12: Hun 3C 100
Woodstock Rd. ST6: Tuns 7E 10
ST17: Staf 5B 74
Woodstock St. ST6: Gold 6F 11
Woodstone Av. ST9: End 3A 50
Wood St. DE14: B Tre 3D 86
ST3: Long 5J 33
ST7: Big E 4G 15

HOSPITALS and HOSPICES
covered by this atlas.

N.B. Where Hospitals and Hospices are not named on the map, the reference given is for the road in which they are situated.

BARTON COTTAGE HOSPITAL 6G **89**
Short Lane
Barton Under Needwood
BURTON-ON-TRENT
DE13 8LB
Tel: 01283 712323

BLOXWICH HOSPITAL 5H **127**
Reeves Sreet
WALSALL
WS3 2JJ
Tel: 01922 858600

BRADWELL HOSPITAL 1E **22**
Talke Road
Chesterton
NEWCASTLE
ST5 7NJ
Tel: 01782 425400

BUCKNALL HOSPITAL 3H **25**
Eaves Lane
STOKE-ON-TRENT
ST2 8LD
Tel: 01782 273510

CANNOCK CHASE HOSPITAL 1D **108**
Brunswick Road
CANNOCK
WS11 5XY
Tel: 01543 572757

CHEADLE HOSPITAL 5C **54**
Royal Walk
Cheadle
STOKE-ON-TRENT
ST10 1NS
Tel: 01538 487500

CITY GENERAL HOSPITAL (STOKE) 7H 153 (2H **31**)
Newcastle Road
STOKE-ON-TRENT
ST4 6QG
Tel: 01782 715444

COMPTON HOSPICE 4K **129**
Compton Road West
WOLVERHAMPTON
WV3 9DH
Tel: 01902 758151

DONNA LOUISE TRUST HOSPICE 3C **40**
Grace Road
STOKE-ON-TRENT
ST4 8FN
Tel: 01782 654440

DOUGLAS MACMILLAN HOSPICE 3G **41**
Barlaston Road
STOKE-ON-TRENT
ST3 3NZ
Tel: 01782 344300

HAMMERWICH HOSPITAL 6K **111**
Hospital Road
BURNTWOOD
WS7 0EH
Tel: 01543 686224

HARPLANDS (PSYCHIATRIC) HOSPITAL 3H **31**
Hilton Road
Harpfields
STOKE-ON-TRENT
ST4 6TH
Tel: 01782 441600

HAYWOOD HOSPITAL 4A **18**
High Lane
Burslem
STOKE-ON-TRENT
ST6 7AG
Tel: 01782 715444

KATHARINE HOUSE HOSPICE 2K **73**
Weston Road
STAFFORD
ST16 3SB
Tel: 01785 254645

LEEK MOORLANDS HOSPITAL 4H **49**
Ashbourne Road
LEEK
ST13 5BQ
Tel: 01538 487100

LITTLE ASTON BUPA HOSPITAL 3G **135**
Little Aston Hall Drive
SUTTON COLDFIELD
B74 3UP
Tel: 0121 3532444

LITTLE BLOXWICH DAY HOSPICE 2K **127**
Stoney Lane
WALSALL
WS3 3DW
Tel: 01922 858735

LONGTON COTTAGE HOSPITAL 1K **41**
Upper Belgrave Road
STOKE-ON-TRENT
ST3 4QX
Tel: 01782 425600

MOSSLEY DAY UNIT 4G **127**
Sneyd Lane
WALSALL
WS3 2LW
Tel: 01922 858680

NHS WALK-IN CENTRE STOKE (HAYWOOD) 4A **18**
Haywood Hospital
High Lane
STOKE-ON-TRENT
ST6 7AG
Tel: 01782 581112

NORTH STAFFORDSHIRE HOSPITAL
CENTRAL OUTPATIENTS DEPT. 5K 153 (1J **31**)
Hartshill Road
STOKE-ON-TRENT
ST4 7PA
Tel: 01782 715444

NORTH STAFFORDSHIRE NUFFIELD HOSPITAL 6G **31**
Clayton Road
NEWCASTLE
ST5 4DB
Tel: 01782 625431

NORTH STAFFORDSHIRE ROYAL INFIRMARY 2K **31**
Princes Road
STOKE-ON-TRENT
ST4 7LN
Tel: 01782 715444

QUEENS HOSPITAL 5B **84**
Belverdere Road
BURTON-ON-TRENT
DE13 0RB
Tel: 01283 566333

ROWLEY HALL CAPIO HOSPITAL 6F **73**
Rowley Avenue
STAFFORD
ST17 9AQ
Tel: 01785 223203

SIR ROBERT PEEL HOSPITAL 7D **136**
Plantation Lane
TAMWORTH
B78 3NG
Tel: 01827 263800

ST DAVID'S HOUSE (DAY HOSPITAL) 4F **145**
Planks Lane
Wombourne
WOLVERHAMPTON
WV5 8DU
Tel: 01902 326001

ST GEORGE'S HOSPITAL (STAFFORD) 2H **73**
Corporation Street
STAFFORD
ST16 3AG
Tel: 01785 257888

ST GILES HOSPICE 3G **131**
Fisherwick Road
LICHFIELD
WS14 9LH
Tel: 01543 432031

ST MICHAEL'S HOSPITAL (LICHFIELD) 3D **114**
Trent Valley Road
LICHFIELD
WS13 6EF
Tel: 01543 414555

STAFFORDSHIRE GENERAL HOSPITAL 2J **73**
Weston Road
STAFFORD
ST16 3SA
Tel: 01785 257731

VICTORIA HOSPITAL 5A **114**
Friary Road
LICHFIELD
WS13 6QM
Tel: 01543 442000

WESTCLIFFE HOSPITAL 7K **11**
Turnhurst Road
STOKE-ON-TRENT
ST6 6LA
Tel: 01782 425860

WOLVERHAMPTON NUFFIELD HOSPITAL 2K **129**
Wood Road
WOLVERHAMPTON
WV6 8LE
Tel: 01902 754177